Among the Dayaks

Among the Dayaks

Lim Poh Chiang

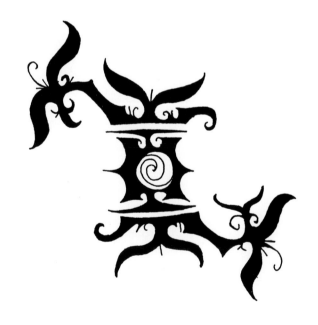

Graham Brash
Singapore

© text and photographs, Lim Poh Chiang, 1989
© poetry translations, Carol Rubenstein, 1975

First published in 1989 by
Graham Brash (Pte) Ltd
227 Rangoon Road
Singapore 0821

ISBN 9971-49-110-9, paperback edition
ISBN 9971-49-123-0, hardcover edition

Cover design by Eric C H Yeo
Typeset by Superskill Graphics Pte Ltd
Printed in Singapore by General Printing Services Pte Ltd

Acknowledgements

I wish to thank Carol Rubenstein for her kind permission to print, as part of this book, the Dayak poems which she has spent so much effort collecting. Complete poems can be found in **The Nightbird Sings** (Graham Brash Pte. Ltd., Singapore, 1989); **The Honey Tree Song: Poems and Chants of Sarawak Dayaks** (Ohio University Press, USA, 1985); and **Poems of Indigenous Peoples of Sarawak: Some of the Songs and Chants** (Special Monograph No. 2, Sarawak Museum Journal, Vol.21, No.42, Parts 1 and 2, Museum, Kuching, Sarawak, 1975).

I thank the publishers, Graham Brash, and especially my editor, Lisa Reinhardt, whose interest and enthusiasm for this project gave me so much encouragement.

I thank my wife, Leh Hua, for her patience and support through all these years and for bearing with my frequent absences from home on photographic trips.

Also heart-felt thanks to my daughters, Ling Mei and Bea Fung for their help in the preparation of the manuscript.

Most of all, I wish to thank all my Dayak friends whose way of life forms the very substance of this book. I thank them for their friendship and company during my journeys. It is my hope that this book will help preserve for our future generations a record of the Dayak way of life.

Lim Poh Chiang
Sibu, Sarawak, 1988.

For what reason, my dear, have you come?
Probably you have heard with your own ears of our fame,
have heard news of the groups who live along this Mara river.
Daringly, you have jumped in among us.
Boldly, you, my son, have come forward.
I think you are bold, my son,
to come to meet us of this river,
to come to meet us of this river, this night beneath the moon.
For what reason have you come so far?
You have come up this river,
come to our plateau, this place of tigers —
and this is the way our life is,
this which you have come to see, our home, our longhouse.
This is what our lives look like.

— from Kenyah "Entertainment Song While Offering Drink"

Contents

Introduction

When I bought my first camera in 1952 and began the hobby of photographing the indigenous peoples of Sarawak, I had little idea that this hobby would turn into a major preoccupation of my life. Nor could I have foreseen how the simple joy of expressing on film the fascination and interest I felt for these people would, in time, help to preserve a pictorial record of their cultures.

As is happening throughout the world, primitive cultures are awakening to 20th century modernity. Changes have swept Sarawak, rapidly transforming the way of life which my photographs depict. The modern traveller to Sarawak is more likely to see these same tribes fully dressed in Western clothing, living in sturdy wooden buildings with modern plumbing, possessing televisions and stereo equipment. Many are being drawn to the towns and cities where they are taking their place alongside Chinese and Malay urban-dwellers.

But then cultures do not stand still and changes have been taking place among these indigenous peoples ever since the Brookes came to Sarawak in the 19th century and the Dayaks were gradually persuaded to give up piracy and head-hunting. The life that my photographs recorded had already been touched by Western influence. But in the 1950s and '60s, the pace of change was relatively slow and the external influences on the indigenous peoples were superficial. On the whole, the main rhythm and shape of their cultural world then was still unfragmented. They were poised at that fragile, tranquil prelude on the threshold of change.

The tribes of Sarawak have been photographed and studied by anthropologists from as early as the last century. During the period when most of the photographs in this collection were taken, there were capable ethnologists like Tom Harrisson and Hedda Morrison who had combined their studies with skill in photography. It is therefore not my purpose to present a systematic pictorial documentation of the indigenous peoples of Sarawak. My interest has perhaps a more personal and neighbourly beginning.

Like most of the Chinese immigrants of Sarawak, my parents came from the southern province of Fukien, and left China to escape the hardship, famine and political instability of the late 19th and early 20th centuries. They were welcomed to Sarawak by the Brooke administration, who saw the Chinese as a needed source of labour for the general economic development of the country. Most of the Chinese concentrated their efforts on developing commerce and building urban settlements; but in those days, these activities were still in their pioneering stages. I was born in Sibu on the delta of the Rejang River and my childhood memories were of little riverside towns, bazaars and *kampung* which were never far from the life of the rainforests surrounding them.

My mother came from Song, at the junction of the Rejang and Katibas Rivers. In the 1930's, Song's bazaar was little more than a row of wooden Chinese shophouses, raised high on stilts like Dayak longhouses. The bazaar served Dayaks living along the Katibas who came down to Song in their boats to procure the little conveniences of modern life: canned food, enamel cups and plates, cotton *sarung* and cigarettes.

Bazaar days were also occasions when Dayaks from different longhouses met to gossip, drink wine and arrange cockfights. As a young boy in Song, I had Iban playmates with whom I spent delightful times fishing with homemade hooks, and catching mud crabs and water snakes. Young Chinese boys like myself delighted in the excitement of cockfights and kept track of the fortunes of prize-fighters. On special festival days, the Dayaks descended on the bazaar splendidly attired in colorful *sirats*, hats of hornbill feathers, necklaces and bracelets of beads and shells, displaying striking tattoos upon their bare backs and thighs. I remember a man who wore round his shoulder a string of little Chinese medicine bottles of different coloured glass in which were kept poisons of varying strengths to be smeared on the sharp spikes tied to the claws of fighting cocks.

Sometimes drunken brawls broke out and threatened to become increasingly violent. Alarm would spread quickly throughout the bazaar and cries of the unlikely "They're coming for our heads!" were echoed by wails from women and children. Shop-windows and doors slammed shut, ladders were swiftly withdrawn and the community waited breathlessly for the commotion to pass. In that sometimes precarious existence in Song, there was plenty to stir the imagination and to fulfil my boyish sense of adventure and wonder.

My interest in photography came later as an extension of a general love for art. In my mid-twenties, I attended for several years a Seventh-Day Adventist college in Singapore. While there, I had the good fortune to make friends with a very genial Balinese schoolmate who used to bring back from his vacations photographs of Balinese folk art and village life. Later he presented me with two volumes on photography of Bali. I was very attracted to these photos which evoked memories of the life and people I had known in Song. I came to admire greatly the photographic medium as an art form with a special capacity to capture the particular sensibilities of a society, and I was inspired to think that what it did for Balinese culture could equally well be done for the Dayak tribes of Sarawak.

When I returned to Sibu with my first camera, a Rolleiflex, I found other men who were just as enthusiastic about photography. For the Chinese in Sarawak at that time, the camera was still a relative novelty and its mimetic capability was a new and wonderful way to examine and express life around us. A photographic society was formed in 1952 and trips were arranged to photograph longhouses and native life. In this way, my interest in the Dayaks and the art of photography finally came together.

The photographs I took tend to fall into two main categories — those in which Dayaks posed for my camera, and candid shots taken of their daily activities. On the whole, the Dayaks are very natural subjects for the camera.

The Ibans or Sea Dayaks, the largest native group, have had the greatest contact with modernity due to their mobility. They are the most frequently photographed, and in fact, pose easily for the camera. Relaxed and smiling, they project the image of a genial and warm race. Often they would ask for copies of their photographs and I was glad to comply. After the photographs were developed, I sometimes sent them back to the longhouses by way of those Dayaks who came to town or through itinerant Chinese traders.

All the Dayak tribes are open and hospitable, happy to show the curious visitor how they go about their various crafts and daily work. Their communal life is relatively unburdened by strict religious rituals, taboos or tight social and segregative rules. Their rituals are mainly those of propitiation and augury and are not secretive, so the stranger has no problems of access to their customs and ceremonies.

I took advantage of those public celebrations when the Dayaks put on their festive best. On occasions such as the regattas, tribes from all over a region would gather in one town to compete in boat-racing, to display and sell their crafts and to swap stories. These occasions were a feast for the photographer: the multitude of bright costumes, the striking designs of shields and swords, the delicate beaded whorls of hats and bags, and the Kayan women with patterns tattooed so finely on their hands and feet, they seemed to have on fine-meshed black gloves and stockings.

Eventually, I went into the interior to photograph the Penans. These shy, nomadic jungle tribes offered no resistance to the camera — an enigmatic box which flashed like lightning when it clicked at them. They learnt to shield their eyes from the dazzling light, but did not run or hide from the photographer. Isolated from much of the modern world at that time, some Penans had no comprehension of the function of the camera and it was a testimony to their gentle and trusting nature that they let themselves be photographed.

On my photographic journeys, I was concerned with capturing the natural rhythm of the daily life in the longhouses, the special and attractive qualities of the indigenous people and the tenor of their cultural world. Most of the time, I let the circumstances and the activities going on at the time guide the photographs I took, but I also enjoyed taking portraits. On seeing my camera, the Dayaks frequently asked me to take their pictures and they were eager to pose for me. I believe that the personal qualities of grace, beauty, strength and dignity in these people come out best in portraits — portraits of young men and maidens, of old warrior chiefs and headmen, of hunters, mothers and children. Group portraits have a way of bringing out the distinctive cultural features of the different tribal groups. Seen in a group, physical features, costumes and ornamentation are repeated and the aggregate effect emphasises their cultural style, their conception of beauty and social identity, and their image of themselves.

Whether posing or going about their daily lives, the indigenous people were not touched by affectation and projected their cultural world with a natural and gentle pride which is their gift to the photographer. In turn, it is my hope that these photographs pay tribute to the magnanimity and grace of the indigenous peoples of Sarawak.

The Penans of the Rainforest

Of all the tribal peoples, the Penans are the most elusive. As jungle wanderers, they seldom venture beyond the headwaters of the Rejang and Baram rivers and so they are the least accessible native group to the photographer. The journey I made to photograph them, though by far the most strenuous, was also the most memorable. My curiosity had begun in my youth when I heard rumours and tall tales of cannibalism among the Penan tribes. Even the other native groups considered the Penans to be more primitive and elemental than themselves. The exaggerated false image of the Penans existed because they were so remote from urban settlements and frequently their only contact with the world outside of the primary jungle was through bartering with the Kayans and Kenyahs.

In 1962, a Kayan friend named Tama Bulan visited me in Sibu. When I learned he was on his way up the Rejang to trade with the Penans of the Linau and Kajang tributaries, I leaped at the chance to accompany him. So on October 14th, with my two Leicas and the Rolleiflex, we left Sibu for the Upper Rejang.

The journey to Tama Bulan's longhouse on the Linau involved negotiating two sets of rapids — the Pelagus, where I had had an earlier misadventure, and the Bakun rapids, 23 miles upriver from Belaga. Since it was the monsoon season, our journey was interrupted by several unplanned stops to wait out some particularly severe downpours which made river travel virtually impossible. Provisions ran low, and we made do with plain rice and salt or with whatever game could be hunted in the brief interludes between the rains. Once it was a three-foot-long snake which was smoked over the fire and served up, skin and all. My Kayan companions found it good eating, "*bagus makan*", they said, but despite my hunger, I couldn't relish the meal. More often our source of meat was wild boar, served either roasted or boiled. However, one kill was made to last several days in the tropical heat, which meant that the leftovers always tasted half-spoiled.

Tama Bulan's longhouse at the junction of the Linau and Balui rivers was the last stop before we entered Penan territory. The pace of the journey was now determined by my Kayan friend, for here I was on his ground and the natural rhythm of his life in the interior took over. In the interior, activities are regulated not only by the cycles of nature and the temper of the weather, but also by the disposition of the spirit world, made known to men through omens and augury. The sighting of some particular bird might be taken as a portent of danger, and travelling would be put off for that day. I waited for Tama Bulan to indicate a good day for departure. Finally on the fifth day, he began preparing provisions and goods.

Early the next morning, seven bamboo poles were stuck into the ground. Each pole was frayed and split at the top where it held aloft a boiled egg. Tama Bulan stood before the poles, and waving his *parang*, chanted aloud, calling on guardian spirits from the other world to protect and assist us on the journey. Then we were ready to depart.

Our first stop was the tribe of Penan Lusong whose territory was on the northern bank of the Linau. The journey took four days of boat travel and jungle trekking. We slept out at night beside the constant roar of the river. When darkness fell, the jungle vibrated with the sounds of its nocturnal orchestra: the whirling, twittering and croaking of frogs, cicadas, and insects, the calls of nightbirds, the barking of deer, and as Tama Bulan once pointed out to me, the call of the rare clouded leopard. The dense canopy of the tall forest tops broke the impact of the falling rain so that it came through only as a muffled and distant patter. The interior of these rainforests is a world in itself.

Where the Jakah tributary meets the Linau was as far up the river as we could proceed in our motor-powered boats; from that point on, the Linau was too shallow for our engines. So we began our trek through the primary forest, which confronted us with a variety of challenging terrain. It involved ascending near vertical slopes by pulling on creepers and heaving ourselves up over the rocks. Then there were swift, waist-deep mountain streams to cross.

Crossing one stream, my energy was soon drained due to fighting the powerful currents, encumbered as I was by my photographic equipment. I lagged behind the Kayans, and overcome by fatigue, lost my footing. The swift waters would have swept me away if my companions had not managed to pull me out. Hoping to remedy the situation, I abandoned the plimsolls I was wearing and walked barefooted like the Kayans. But things did not get any easier as my feet, unaccustomed to the rocky terrain, became sore and raw.

It was a great relief to reach Penan Lusong territory on the fourth day. Here Tama Bulan had built a permanent camp: a thatched hut in which bins of rice could be stored. He had also planted the surrounding area with tobacco plants. The Kayans brought along their usual items for barter with the Penans — fish hooks and nets, cotton cloth, salt, tobacco, enamel cups and plates in exchange for rattan, beeswax, baskets, resin, camphor and the *bezoar* stones of monkeys and porcupines.

Two hours after our arrival, a group of Penans came from their settlement a few hundred yards away on the other side of the river. The headman who led the group immediately broke into a continuous torrent of speech which I did not understand. His tone was loud and harsh, as though he were angry about something. But Tama Bulan later told me the headman was only recounting to them what they had been doing since the Kayans last visited them. The Penans are paler than the Kayans and the Ibans since they spend most of their time in the shaded gloom of the jungle and dislike the sunlight. But they have heavily-muscled torsos and are a healthy-looking group of people.

I followed the Penans back to their camp — a group of huddled shelters made from simple frameworks of branches and twigs, covered with broad leaves. Each family had its own hut. I took photographs of the camp as well as of several men who were making a blowpipe.

The Kayans decided to move on to a Penan Apoh camp the next day and this time the Penan Lusong took us in their *perahu*. When we were again stalled by heavy rains and high flood waters, the Penans spent the day fishing; the catch was good and they smoked the fish over the campfire. After a steady diet of wild boar meat, the fish was incomparably delicious. The Penans stuck a fish on top of a pole to mark the spot where fish were plentiful.

The following day, a trek of five hours through the rainforest brought us to the main Penan Apoh settlement. We arrived to find most of the group of 70-odd Penans in that tribe had gone off on a hunting expedition and the camp was reduced to 20 people. These were mainly women and I was able to photograph them making mats and baskets.

The Kayans' last destination was the territory of the Penan Busang up the Kajang River near the Indonesian border. This stretch of the journey was the most difficult as the gradient of slopes and valleys was even steeper than before. At one point along the trek, we heard a sound like a long, drawn-out roar and looked in the direction of the sound to see an avalanche of logs dislodged by the rain rolling down a slope and taking along all the trees in its path.

As we walked on, we came across wooden sticks stuck into the ground with curls of bark shavings hanging down their sides. These are Penan signposts indicating the way to their settlement. In addition, the track that we followed was littered with the thorns of wild sago palm, which is the Penans' staple source of starch.

We met three Penans before we arrived at their camp. The first two were a couple carrying baskets on their backs. They were immediately friendly, accepting Tama Bulan's offer of tobacco with alacrity. Later, as the Kayans had decided to start building their camp, I headed on towards the settlement alone. The third Penan, a woman, walked up behind me with hardly a sound. She was on her way back to the camp after gathering a whole basketful of edible roots and shoots. As I watched her, a large hornbill flew down on to her basket and began to peck at the contents. I had my camera ready and quickly took a shot. At the settlement, I discovered that they have many hornbill 'pets'. These birds are essentially wild and free to fly, but have learned to come to the camp where the Penans feed them.

The Penan Busang had been in that settlement for two months and they willingly admitted us into their midst. They shared their food with us and I accompanied them on a hunting expedition. All the game and food collected was shared equally among the families, although this did not apply to jungle produce which was collected to sell.

As a people, the Penans live more simply than the other tribes. Occasions such as marriage and divorce, birth and death, are treated casually, pragmatically, and with a minimum of ritual fuss or ceremony. A couple will decide to live together, and if a child comes along, they are considered married. The man gives a dowry to his in-laws in the form of dogs, spears, cooking pots or other items important to Penan survival. The Penans are monogamous and in the event of a divorce, family property is shared between the two parties. After the divorce, a Penan man may still help his former wife with chores such as hut-building, though he no longer lives with her.

Their religious beliefs, mostly vague and undefined, are generally animistic and are the most rudimentary of all the tribes of Sarawak. Some Penans do not believe in life after death, but others believe that there is a special place where the spirits of the dead go, so they may place *parang*, blowpipes and household implements near the dead for use in the after-life. It may well be that a life so taken up with finding the bare necessities does not allow the Penans to develop more complex social and religious ideas. Yet this elemental quality about the Penans is also attractive. They are straightforward and direct, sometimes to the point of bluntness; they lack the calculated cunning and the questionable sophistication one encounters in townsfolk.

At night, the Penan community gathered around the campfire and brought out their wooden guitars and bamboo lyres. The simple and repetitious tunes of these instruments set up a rhythm for their dances. When the men and women got up to dance, their slow movements simulated the flight of birds. No swords or shields were used, as in the Iban dances, only graceful turns of hands and body to the rhythm of the music. A woman squatting by the fire began to sing, and though I did not understand the lyrics, I was moved. Her voice completed the mood of the evening and her song seemed to express the heart and spirit of the primary forest looming above the flickering light of the campfire and the circle of Penans around it.

On the third morning, Tama Bulan said they had a surprise. The headman of the Penan Busang had arranged a special ceremony for me to photograph. I was pleased and flattered. When they were all assembled, I was struck by the splendour of their costumes which displayed an abundance of beads, shells, ivory and hornbill feathers. The men brought out their blowpipes, *parang*, and bamboo dart containers.

In a clearing in the forest, I took first their formal group portraits, and then the men and women separately. It seemed to be a solemn matter for these Penans and they faced the camera with serious and intent faces. Then afterwards the women performed some dances while the men played their guitars. It was a most satisfactory conclusion to an arduous journey. I wanted to stay longer with the Penan Busang, but my Kayan companions were ready to leave.

The next morning, the Penans came to say goodbye. There was a young Penan man who was coming with us down to

Belaga, and his elderly mother wept at the parting since it would be many months before he would return. The world of towns seems so terribly remote to these people who find the rainforest to be a hospitable and protective home. Bidding the Penans a sad farewell, I decided that I would try to return to them at the earliest opportunity.

In 1963, the following year, I bought a 16 mm cine-camera with the intention of returning to film the Penan Busang. My plan, however, coincided with the beginning of the Indonesian confrontation with Malaysia. I got only as far as Tama Bulan's longhouse before turning back and returning to Sibu. That trip in 1962 remains my first and only visit to the Penan Busang of the upper Linau and Kajang Rivers.

The rich rainforests of Sarawak, home of the Penans, offer a profusion of
wildlife. The Rhinocerous Hornbill is commonly seen, its characteristic series of
raucous calls descending from the forest tops. The casque of the less common
species, the Helmeted Hornbill, is solid as ivory and was collected by the
Chinese as far back as the Ming dynasty. Taken back to the courts of China,
such hornbill 'ivory' was carved into objects of great beauty.

The Penan Busang of the Linau River share the same tropical home as the hornbills. Like them, the Penans are jungle survivors, dependent on the bounty of the rainforest. Their co-existence is further cemented by the fact that in Penan camps, hornbills are fed and kept as pets.

16

The Penans who search the rainforest for food live in temporary camps with make-shift huts such as this one. Each family of the Penan Busang builds its own hut, which consists of a large sloping roof and two walls of leaves and bark. This is just sufficient to keep out the rain but is otherwise open and airy. In the past few decades, the Penan tribes have been encouraged to develop a more settled lifestyle based on agriculture. In 1962 when I travelled to photograph the Penans, already some tribes had settled in more permanent villages, but the Penan Apoh and the Penan Busang of the Linau River valley were still people of the jungle.

The origin of the Penan people has been a subject of much theory and speculation among anthropologists, as their oral traditions reveal little about their past. Perhaps the best guess is that they are the earliest indigenous race in Sarawak who persisted in a nomadic lifestyle, wandering through the primary jungle in search of wild game, edible plants and fruit. This Penan Busang couple pose just outside their hut.

When I stayed for several days at this Penan Busang camp, the headman called on the whole camp to dress up and pose for my camera. Fully assembled, they formed an impressive group. Their finery included headgear with hornbill feathers, heavy brass rings worn in stretched earlobes, and plenty of beads, shells, bangles and wild boar tusks. Though rather formidable-looking, the Penans are a gentle people whose blowpipes and *parang* are used only for hunting wild animals.

The Penans hunt with blowpipes, each about eight feet long with a spearhead attached to the upper end. This weapon is made from a single length of straight-grain hardwood and the hole is bored through the wood manually — a laborious process requiring much patience. Darts for the pipe, carried in a bamboo container tied at the waist, are tipped with poison from the sap of the Ipoh tree.

Monkeys, though hunted for food, are especially sought-after for their *bezoar* stones. These intestinal growths look like smooth, round rocks or egg-shaped pebbles, and are highly prized for use in Chinese medicine. The Penans trade them with the Kayans, who in turn sell them in town to the Chinese.

Where is my blowpipe,
my quiver for holding darts?
O Bale Salabet, spirit of speed,
send good omen on my right.
Let it be simple to fulfil my wish
that I get bezoar stones from inside the leaf monkey,
let it be simple to fulfil my wish
that I also get rhinoceros,
that I also get deer and get wild boar.
Bale Salabet, spirit of speed,
send good omen on my right.
Let it be simple to fulfil my wish:
Give me what I want so that I hold it in my hand.
There is where I am going, that way.
I want to meet there wild boar,
leaf monkey with bezoar stones,
porcupine with bezoar stones.

— Penan "Prayer for Hunting with Blowpipe"

The poison from the darts can paralyse and kill a deer within an hour. Usually the stricken animal is hounded by hunting dogs, and when it is cornered, is speared to death.

But hunting for monkeys, deer and wild boar is not the only reason for the Penans' nomadic lifestyle. Besides game, the Penans move in search of the wild sago plant. The pith of the sago palm, mixed with water and then seived, is rolled into balls for baking, or cooked into a gluey paste which is eaten with wooden tongs. It is the staple food of the forest Penans.

There is much communal sharing among the Penans who make few social
distinctions between themselves. Food is shared among all in the camp and
both the young and the old are well taken care of. The open huts of the camp
give the photographer access to a whole range of activities, from this group of
children helping to rid each other of lice to the skinning of a monkey.

28

29

Penan women are skilled in weaving rattan mats and baskets. Rattan vines are split and heated to make them supple before they are woven by hand. Mats are used for bedding and flooring, and Penan baskets are much sought-after by other tribes as they are strong, well-made and beautifully designed. Though they rely principally on the rainforest for food, the Penans do trade with the neighbouring Kayans and Kenyahs, for things like cloth, tobacco, salt, enamel basins and so on.

After the day's work is done, the Penans gather round for music and dance. A Penan Busang man and his eager students play a guitar-like instrument of two or three strings called a *sapeh*, which was adopted from the Kayans. They favour a repetitive and rather melancholy rhythm to which the women dance with slow, swaying steps and fluid hand movements.

Penan men wear their hair cropped straight in front, and both men and women
pluck their eyebrows completely.

34

Penan families tend not to be large, as the infant mortality rate is high and they are continually on the move. Perhaps because of their nomadic lifestyle, little ceremony marks the passage from birth to death. Although there appear to be few differences in social rank, there is a division of tasks between the sexes, with men going out to do the hunting and women staying behind to work around the camp and look after the children.

Because of the frigid water, mountain-fed rivulets and streams of the Linau River can be used by the Penans for storing surplus meat. Submerged on the riverbed, it keeps in this natural form of refrigeration.

Meanwhile, the upper reaches of the Rejang abound in fish and and it is easy for the Penans to catch more than the whole camp can consume. But despite the abundance of fish, the Penans do not like to stay in one place for long. The spirit of the nomadic life beckons and the time always comes for the camp to move on.

As we part, we give all we can give,
using our mouths, using our eyes.
We are not like other people.
All we have is the roof overhead
and the ground of our house —
even the walls we sleep between are made of nothing.
Even if we go to our house
there is nothing from there we can give to you.
All we can do is gaze at you two with our eyes,
and let the words they form speak for me.

— Penan "Song to Please Someone"

The Ibans of the Rivers

Since most of the indigenous tribes live in longhouses along the major river systems, river transport is the chief means of reaching them. In Sarawak's dense tropical jungles, rivers are the major highways linking the sea with the interior, the coastal and delta towns with the native settlements in the *ulu*. Most of my photographic trips were taken up the Rejang and the Baram — two giant, winding rivers whose topography can easily become a favourite theme for any photographer.

From the large flat delta plain on which Sibu town is situated, the Rejang River winds east through undulating hill country until Kapit, a small town 70 miles from Sibu. Here the river forks into the Batang Baleh, which leads southeast to the Indonesian border, and the Batang Rejang, which continues on in a northeasterly direction and branches out into a vast network of tributaries above Belaga town. This region is the home of the *Orang Ulu*, or people of the interior. The Batang Baleh, on the other hand, is Iban territory.

Sometimes my journeys up the Rejang and the Baram were undertaken with Dayak friends and their boats, sometimes with hired guides and motor launches. Occasionally, I accompanied Chinese itinerant boatshops trading in the region. Travel between Sibu and Kapit is easy, as boats are frequent and the river is placid and broad. Above Kapit, one enters the turbulence of the Pelagus and Bakun rapids and swift rushing streams strewn with giant boulders.

The river changes its moods through different phases of tropical weather. In October and November, the northeast monsoon brings heavy rains which swell the river and the strength of currents, whirlpools and cataracts. The rain comes in bursts. After a rainstorm, the sky clears into a bright adamantine blue until gradually clouds gather again, piling up in immense grey masses and the rain returns, falling hard and full as a mighty waterfall. And in response, the river rises and falls as precipitously. A night of torrential downpour can raise the level of the river by ten feet, but it subsides quickly to its normal level only a few hours after the rain has stopped. River travel along the upper reaches of the Rejang is thus a hazardous venture during the rainy season. On more than one occasion, our boats were stranded on hillslopes or caught in thickets as the waters swiftly receded.

The jungle terrain and the rivers with their treacherous rapids, complete with their attendant problems and headaches, offer a special sense of challenge and excitement for the adventurous photographer. Though I kept my cameras and films in tins to protect them from water, such measures proved of little consequence in the event of a boat capsizing — something one must always be prepared for on the upper Rejang and Baram.

On one of the return journeys from a particularly fruitful photographic trip to Belaga, we had to negotiate again the difficult Pelagus rapids. On such occasions we split into two parties to lighten the load of the boat — one party proceeding on land beside the river, while the other remained with the boat to steer it through the rough waters. Several Kayan companions and I set out on foot, and my fellow Chinese traveller, an itinerant dentist, remained with two Kayans in the boat. The currents proved too strong, however, and the boat capsized. As it was dragged down by the undercurrents, all of our luggage went overboard. The dentist clung to the boat and his tin of gold dental fillings — the chief profit of his craft came from crowning the teeth of the native women for whom flashing gold teeth is a feature of beauty. But the boat, so dashed and beaten by the currents, was quickly breaking up; to save his own life and swim for shore, the dentist had to let go of his precious tin. I saw also my camera tins with the hard-earned fruits of my labour being borne down the river and was desperate enough to consider plunging into the water to rescue them. But my Kayan companions, being wiser, quickly dissuaded me. All the men overboard made it safely back to land and we watched as the boat and our belongings disappeared down the river.

However, there is a postscript to this disappointing trip. Some months later, back in Sibu, I was approached by a Kayan *penghulu* who informed me that a tin had been picked up by some Kenyahs further down the river. It was found to contain a camera and some rolls of film. Hearing about this, the *penghulu* made some investigations and concluded that the tin was very likely mine. He had come down to Sibu to offer to retrieve the tin for a sum, but he could tell me nothing about the condition of its contents. Nonetheless, it was an offer I couldn't refuse. So when the tin finally did come back to me, it was only to discover that the camera was rusted and useless. As for the films, the Kenyahs, knowing that film rolls contain photographs, had pulled the films out from the cartridges expecting to see the pictures. The whole lot of negatives were exposed and ruined. How I chided myself for not having the foresight to carry those tins overland!

In these tumultuous stretches, the rivers challenge and battle the wits, courage, and strength of those tribes who seek to breach their isolation in the interior. Yet the river which claims lives is also a bountiful supplier of food and produce for the natives. Ellipeanut trees growing beside the rivers shed their fruit which is borne upon the water and carried downstream where it is harvested by Dayaks with baskets.

In its gentle, placid stretches, the river is the Dayaks' main thoroughfare, a playground for children who are seldom out of the water and an indispensable part of the daily routine of the longhouse. Clad in *sarung*, the women first make their way to the river through the early morning mist with the sun barely breaking through the trees. They return frequently during the day to wash, bathe and fetch water, and glimpses of families splashing about in the river show just how important a role the river plays in these people's lives.

The Ibans, formerly known as the Sea Dayaks, comprise the largest group of native people in Sarawak. They are a sociable and gregarious people, and the longhouse — their communal home — reflects this quality in its inhabitants.

The longhouse is essentially a small, compact village built into one architectural structure. Often the entire tribe of 40 to 60 families live in one longhouse. Thus, it is necessary that the house serve both communal and private functions. An internal verandah or *ruai* runs the entire length of the longhouse and serves as the communal place for work, social gatherings, and family entertainment. Each family also has its own private rooms arranged alongside each other which open onto the hall or *ruai*.

During festivals, the *ruai* is used as a large party hall for music, dancing and drinking rice wine. But on most evenings after the work is done, the men gather among flickering oil lamps to chat casually and to swap stories. Serious matters pertaining to the whole community are also discussed and debated here. This is where young leaders develop their debating skills and make their first impressions on their elders. Each longhouse has a *tuai rumah*, or headman, who oversees the community's welfare and is the judge in matters of spiritual practice and social justice. The *tuai rumah* himself is answerable to the *penghulu*, the local district leader of the Dayaks who acts as chief of several long-houses in his region.

Each tribe has its own unique crafts and designs; but at the same time, there is some borrowing of ideas among tribes, so that despite the wide variety of handicrafts, certain basic similarities of design and motif result.

The Dayaks produce a great many of the items they need for their daily life. Hunting equipment (like blowpipes and spears), fishing nets, boats and paddles, winnowing baskets and rice trestles are all made manually from local raw materials.

Beyond these necessities, their rich religious practices and social customs call for the making of special costumes and ornamental accessories, such as decorative wall-hangings and ceremonial swords. The Ibans, with their history of having been the most fearsome warriors, make beautiful knives called *parang* and large handsome shields. Kayan and Kenyah women from along the Baram River make large beaded hats and beautiful baskets, while the men are skilled wood carvers, and make elaborate totem poles. Penan women are known for their basket and mat weaving, and Iban women specialise in a type of tie-dye weaving called *ikat*. This cloth, with its intricate patterns of head-hunters, jungle plants, and omen birds and beasts, is imbued with religious significance and used to decorate the longhouse during religious festivals.

The large expanse of rainforest in Sarawak's interior is criss-crossed by many winding rivers. In their upper courses, these rivers are rushing streams with turbulent rapids. To travel from the interior to visit the other tribes who inhabit the lower plains, it is necessary to negotiate these rapids — a journey made even more anxious by the Dayaks' belief that rapids are the work of demons in the riverbeds.

The Pelagus Rapids are the largest rapids in Sarawak and pose a major challenge to river traffic between the towns of Kapit and Belaga. Frequent accidents led to the macabre saying that a jugful of human eyes could be collected from the riverbed. During the colonial days, the British used explosives to clear the rivers of larger boulders. Nonetheless, during the dry season when the water level is low, bare rocks protrude from the riverbed and boats must be carried over-land.

Travelling along the Rejang River, one sees groups of Dayaks paddling their longboats downstream on their way to sell their handiwork and live game at market, or going upriver from the ricefields to their longhouses. The river is the chief means of transport and a vital part of the lives of the Dayaks who live throughout the region.

The Dayaks of Sarawak live in longhouses, usually built on stilts beside rivers. These longhouses, one belonging to the Ibans along the Katibas River near Song, and a Kenyah settlement beside Long Jawi in Ulu Belaga, are situated close to hilly ground where hill *padi* can be grown.

On the *ruai*, the communal hallway of the longhouse, one sees groups of women or men, like these Kayans, chatting and gossiping during the idle periods of the day. Others do household work at a leisurely pace. The absence of an established work schedule allows work, play and rest to run easily into each other.

The outer verandah of an Iban longhouse is constructed of roughly-hewn ironwood tied with rope to crossbeams, without using any nails. Despite its flimsy appearance, this verandah is actually quite sturdy.

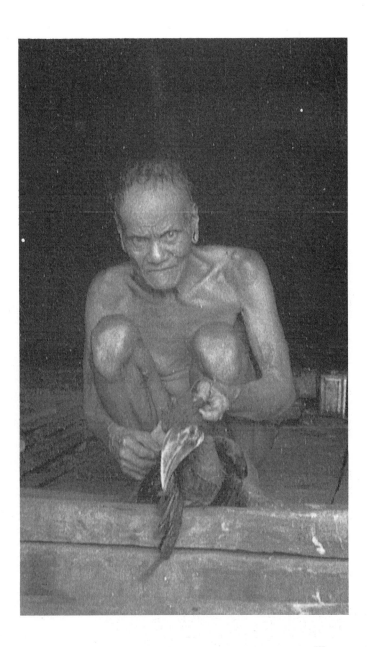

While the longhouse provides the security of communal living, each family has its own private room (or *bilik*) where they can cook over their fireplace, keep their treasured possessions, and enjoy time away from the others.

The Dayaks move easily between the open spaces of nature and the interior of the longhouse, so that as much living takes place outdoors as indoors.

The river is an integral part of routine daily life. Preparing traps and nets and going fishing are frequent activities.

The sun, the shade of the trees, a cool frolic in the river in the noonday heat —
these simple delights mix with the work of washing, bathing, and fetching
water.

Beyond Survival:
Beauty and Craftsmanship

The major portion of my photo collection was taken between 1953 and 1964, when I made over 13 trips to the Katibas and Baleh, the Oya, the Baram and the Upper Rejang rivers. Not all these journeys involved braving rapids and danger. There are many longhouses which one can easily reach by motor launches or small outboard motor boats, and a friendly welcome by the Dayaks awaits at the end of the journey.

From the riverside landing, notched logs lead up to the longhouse. Sometimes they are slippery with wet mud and the wary visitor may have to get down on all fours. The Ibans, however, ascend these logs without difficulty — the women carrying water gourds and babies on their backs.

If he is in, the *tuai rumah*, or headman, comes out to greet the visitors. The longhouse, which is home to as many as 70 families, has a common corridor running its entire length. Here the longhouse community gathers to talk, to work at pounding rice, weaving *pua* or baskets, woodcarving, or to watch over the children or entertain. Each family also has their separate private rooms for cooking and sleeping; these units or *bilik* run parallel to the corridor and open onto it. The headman's *bilik* is situated at the centre and the visitor is usually invited to sit just outside while the headman brings the *tuak* or rice wine.

A visit to a longhouse frequently involves having a meal with the *tuai rumah* and friendly talk and wine with the other families. The women may bring out their handicrafts to show.

65

Some of the most admirable aspects of Dayak culture are their skilled craftsmanship and love of beauty and the arts. In the midst of meeting the needs of daily survival, the Dayak tribes find pleasure in producing articles of ornamental and spiritual value to grace the bare necessities with which nature has endowed them.

Making use of repeating geometric patterns in light and dark, the art motifs of the Dayaks recall those of the Northern Vietnamese Dongson culture (750 B.C.), causing anthropologists to speculate whether the Borneo Dayaks could have originated there.

The motifs, passed down through generations, have their roots in tribal memory but are also influenced and inspired by the wide variety of flora and fauna to be found in the rainforest. The jungle surrounding the Dayaks thus provides not only raw material, but is the source of new ideas for their art. Motifs of monkeys, lizards, crocodiles, birds, trees and ferns occur frequently.

Each tribe has its own unique crafts and designs; but at the same time, there is some borrowing of ideas among tribes, so that despite the wide variety of handicrafts, certain basic similarities of design and motif result.

The Dayaks produce a great many of the items they need for their daily life. Hunting equipment (like blowpipes and spears), fishing nets, boats and paddles, winnowing baskets and rice trestles are all made manually from local raw materials.

Beyond these necessities, their rich religious practices and social customs call for the making of special costumes and ornamental accessories, such as decorative wall-hangings and ceremonial swords. The Ibans, with their history of having been the most fearsome warriors, make beautiful knives called *parangs* and large handsome shields. Kayan and Kenyah women from along the Baram River make large beaded hats and beautiful baskets, while the men are skilled wood carvers, and make elaborate totem poles. Penan women are known for their basket and mat weaving, and Iban women specialise in a type of tie-dye weaving called *ikat*. This cloth, with its intricate patterns of head-hunters, jungle plants, and omen birds and beasts, is imbued with religious significance and used to decorate the longhouse during religious festivals.

There she comes, my lttle sister, waving and tripping,
comes with body and soul, comes swinging.
Come my little sister, come tripping.
Her feet are like the feet of a brass tray
covered by the coloured woven cloth worn for a skirt,
her waist is wrapped in red-coloured rattan,
her wrists are covered with coloured beads.
The sides of her body are graceful in shape
like a sliced band of timaran bark.
Her teeth are sharp and shiny,
her face is bright.
The neck of my little sister is long,
from her ears hang earrings with many loops,
on her finger is a ring like the red eye of a prawn,
her hair is like blue dye.
She is the perfect creation of a master carpenter.

— from Bidayuh "Bibajo Songs"

Anyone who has travelled among the Dayak tribes could not fail to be struck by the natural beauty and grace of these people. They themselves have their own notions of what is attractive, differing slightly from group to group. For example, tattooing is practised widely among Iban and Penan men, and among both men and women of the Kayan and Kenyah tribes.

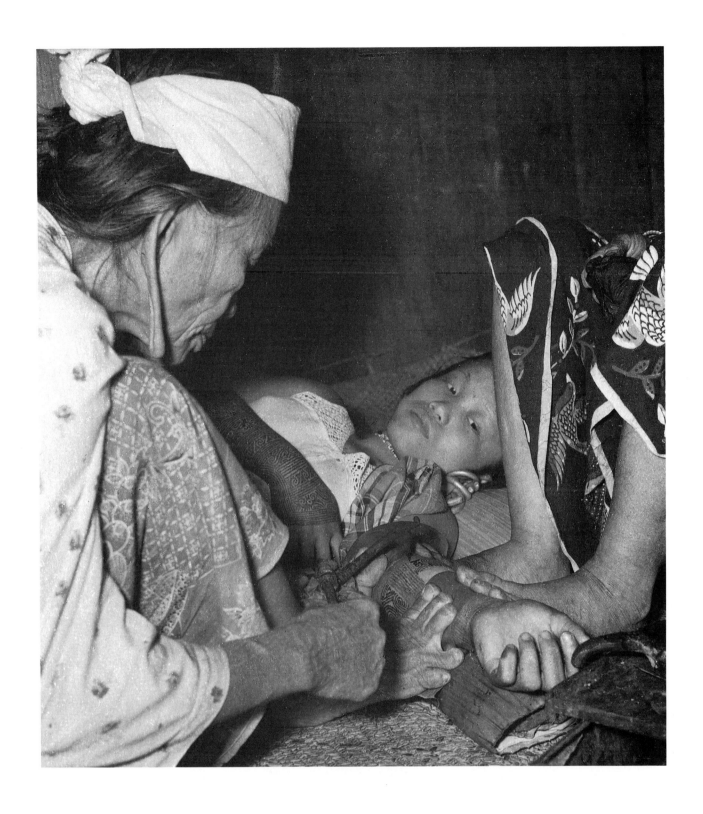

The patterns are primitive motifs painted in soot and animal fat, and then
tattooed into the skin with a sharp needle. The tattoos of Kayan women, done
mostly on the lower arms, hands and legs, use fine, intricate patterns.

A distinguishing feature between Iban women and Kayan women is that Kayans stretch their earlobes with heavy brass rings, while the Ibans do not. This process begins in infancy, and is common among Penans and Kenyahs as well, who see the result as a sign of beauty.

The men's tattoos use bold designs, and cover the legs, arms and back. Sometimes tattoos are also done on the front of the throat.

This Kayan is making a *parang*, while the man behind him keeps the fire
burning by using bellows fashioned from hollowed-out tree trunks.

Although each tribe has its own distinctive crafts and designs, the Kayans and Kenyahs are considered the best craftsmen. They, along with all the other tribes of Sarawak, express their artistic skills in the production of both household items and ornamental goods. These Kayan craftsmen from Long Jegan on the Baram River are making large serving platters and ornamental bottle stoppers to sell.

This fanciful mask is the creation of Ding Bepat, a Kenyah of the Upper Rejang. Masks like these are striking not only because of their basic design, but also for the fine, ornate painting on the faces, done in bright contrasting colours.

Masks are frequently used in ceremonial dances as the Dayaks believe they possess the power to repel evil spirits.

Elaborately carved tombs can be found near some Kayan and Kenyah longhouses. Called *silong*, these structures contain the bones of chiefs as well as valuable old beads, tobacco, rice and other provisions for the journey that the soul takes into the next world. *Parang* and shields, offered to the sky, hang from the pole which supports the house-like tomb on top. In the old days when slaves were kept, a male and female slave would be buried in the hole before the post was put in so that they could look after the spirit of the chief.

Relatively self-sufficient, the Dayaks use wood, rattan, bamboo and other raw materials which they gather from the jungle, to fashion items such as boats, paddles, and fishing equipment which they need for their daily lives.

Rattan — one of the most versatile materials of the rainforest — is split and ready to use for weaving, making fish-traps, and one hundred and one other purposes.

Mats, used as work surfaces or as flooring, and utilitarian baskets are woven from rattan vines by the women. Most of this work is done on the *ruai* of the longhouse during the day.

In Sarawak, the weaving of *ikat* cloth, called *pua*, is done only by Iban women. Cotton for the yarn is grown in a small patch near the longhouse. The colour patterns are created by tying up bundles of yarn in a particular way before immersing them in a reddish dye produced from seeds, bark and roots. After colouring, the yarn is ready to be woven on hand-built looms.

Pua weaving takes place during the day, between the field work and cooking, and often must be put aside when more pressing matters arise.

These Dayak girls pose proudly with the splendid crafts of their tribe. *Pua*, woven with sacred motifs, are vested with the protective powers of the gods. In the old days, heads taken from a head-hunting raid were often wrapped in *pua*. Nowadays, *pua* are more often used as wall-hangings during religious ceremonies. They may also be made into *sarung* and loin-cloths, which led anthropologists Haddon and Start to say that "these attractive people are literally clothed with prayers".

The Spirits of the Rice and Land

The cultivation of hill *padi* governs to a large extent the general rhythm of life in a Dayak community. Rice is the staple food of the Dayaks and also a source of income when a good harvest results in a surplus. Due to the poor soil, Dayak farmers practise shifting cultivation, moving their fields from one area to another from year to year. They may return to their old farms only after a period of some 15 years, during which time the area becomes overgrown and the soil recovers its fertility.

In the growing of rice, the farmer relies on powers greater than himself. As only the spirits' cooperation can ensure a good harvest, they are called upon for help and protection in special rites and rituals at every stage of the cultivation.

Furthermore, for the Ibans, permission to farm the land must first be obtained from a spirit called Pulang Gana who dwells in the earth. Sacrificial offerings are made to him. The Ibans' belief that the souls of human beings dissolve in dew and are absorbed into the *padi* grains emphasises in a spiritual way the crucial dependence of the Dayaks on rice for survival.

For women, childcare and field work are sometimes inseparable. This Kayan
woman, from Long Jawi on the Balui River, is going to the fields with a baby on
her back. The delicate beadwork design of the baby carrier is believed to help
ward off evil spirits.

The Dayaks cultivate hill *padi*. The agricultural cycle begins with the clearing of
slopes. Rites to propitiate the spirits of earth and *padi* are performed before work
begins. Then the men cut down the trees while the women clear the
undergrowth. The fields are burned to clear the land of fallen timber and to
provide ash to fertilise the soil. Prayers and sacrifices may also be offered to
ensure dry weather for the period of planting.

Before the seeds can be sown, further religious ceremonies must take place.
Incantations are recited to ward off insects, worms and other pests. Only after
appeasing the gods does the sowing begin. The men walk at the head of
processions, making holes in the ground with wooden sticks, while the women
follow behind, dropping a few seeds into each hole. This tedious work under the
blazing sun is eased by fellow farmers who take turns bringing water and doing
the cooking for the day.

After a hard day's work in the hot sun, this woman is grateful to be offered a cigarette. Tobacco is one of the Dayaks' greatest loves (and vices) from the outside world.

Sprouting rice shoots reward the farmers of Sungei Ngemah, a tributary along the middle Rejang. Most of the rice is consumed by the longhouse, but in times of good harvest, or cash shortage, surplus rice is sold to the Chinese who live in the towns.

Because of the practice of shifting cultivation, some seasons the *padi* fields are several hours away from the longhouse and so the Dayaks may stay near-by in temporary shelters. But if the field is not far, the Dayaks return to the longhouse each evening after caring for the *padi*.

92

One of the main tasks in the longhouse involves the processing of rice, the staple food of the Dayaks. *Padi* is dried on the verandah, while inside the *ruai*, the winnowing, grinding and pounding take place. This part of the work is usually done by the women, though both men and women take part in the planting and harvesting of rice.

The Kayan woman carrying water in bamboo containers passes the special rice storage buildings, constructed away from the longhouse to protect the precious grain in case of fire.

Tuak or rice beer is an essential item for the religious rituals and festivities that always follow the harvest. As a focal point of both the welcoming ceremony and the propitiation of the spirits, no festival would be complete without *tuak*.

To make the potent brew, glutinous rice is washed in the river and scooped into long bamboo tubes, which are then placed over a low fire to cook. Afterwards, the cooked rice is laid out on rattan mats, mixed with yeast and placed in large jars to ferment.

The Warrior Past

Before the arrival of the British, Dayak culture was ruled by the warrior's heroic code. The status and prestige of a tribe was determined by its capacity to make war, which was measured by the number of heads captured in conflicts between tribal groups and during adventures of piracy on the high seas. This practice of head-hunting earned Sarawak her reputation as the 'land of the head-hunters'. Manhood in Dayak society was largely defined by courage in head-hunting. Warriors who returned with heads after a successful raid were fêted. The women danced with the trophies up and down the longhouse and there was much feasting and drinking. After feeding the skulls with choice morsels of food and giving them tobacco or betel nuts, the souls of the vanquished victims were petitioned to be loyal and to assist in harvesting more heads in the future. Later, the skulls were smoked or left to dry in the sun, then plaited with rattan and hung up proudly in the longhouse.

Head-hunting also became part of many social customs in the Dayak community. When someone in the longhouse died, the period of mourning could be ended only by the taking of a fresh head. Since the Dayaks believe that a severed skull retains the soul of the victim, the taking of a fresh head was seen as a means of infusing new energy and life into the community.

James Brooke, the British sea-adventurer who founded a dynasty of three generations in Sarawak, sought to end the practice of head-hunting. He built forts and garrisons along the rivers, so that Dayak expeditions out to sea could be watched and landings prevented. He and his successors also organised large peace-making ceremonies to draw up truces between the warring tribes. These measures, together with the moral persuasion of missionaries, finally succeeded in bringing an end to the warrior lifestyle. The aggressive and adventurous spirit of the Dayaks was redirected to more peaceable agricultural pursuits.

"Udub-udub ..." comes the victory cry
from high in the mountains above the house.
Have you all come back, young men, our dear sons and cousins?
You come bringing many heads,
many bleached heads to place on the earth, the earth of Bario,
to place them near our house.
Di-ah!

"Udub-udub ..." comes the victory cry
from the mountains, from the distant waves of the mountains.
Have you all come back, young men, our dear sons and cousins?
You come bringing many bleached heads to place on the earth,
the cleared earth around our house in Bario.
Di-ah!

— Kelabit "Victory Song"

These totem poles seem to point to the past — when men were head-hunters and their chief was the bravest warrior in the tribe. The death of mighty men was commemorated by such giant monoliths which bear within them old beads and other valuable items intended to accompany the departed spirits of the dead.

Although head-hunting belongs to the past, reminders of the old days can still be seen in the longhouses. Skulls hang from the rafters and a few old warriors remain who remember what the head-hunting days were like.

Originally, there were various reasons for taking skulls — to mark the end of mourning, as evidence of the transition from boyhood to manhood and as trophies in tribal clashes. Today, they are objects of ritual importance and feature prominently in the celebrations in which the Dayaks re-enact the heroic code of the past.

The Ibans, formerly the most mobile and aggressive Dayak group, were pirates
in the South China Sea until the White Rajahs put an end to piracy.
Something of the pride and confidence of the warriors of the past can still be
seen in the young Iban men.

The traditional costumes of Dayak men evoke the concept of manhood from their warrior past. Dressed in goatskin cloaks, hornbill feathers and swords, this Dayak man looks ready for any challenge. Some swords, passed down for several generations, are still adorned with the hair of their human victims.

The fierce appearance of this Iban man seems to have struck fear into the hearts of even his own sons!

The Penans, once rumoured to be the most savage of the jungle peoples, were really the least war-like of all the Dayak tribes. Even so, the power and determination of this Penan elder is daunting.

This old Kayan warrior, wearing a bearskin cloak and his faithful sword, is the *tua rumah* or headman of a Kayan longhouse in Long Kahai in Upper Belaga. He has seen much change in the Kayan lifestyle during his lifetime, just as the young Iban man of the Oya River, dressed in his regalia, is likely to see great changes in the years to come.

This Iban warrior, judging from his acquisition of a watch and beret, has recently made a less traditional conquest. The source of his modern trophies, Mr Malcolm MacDonald, then Commissioner General, South-East Asia, remains in the background.

Festivals

In the evenings, after the day's work, the Dayaks relax on the *ruai* and when the mood takes them, they like to put on special costumes and dance to the sounds of a gong ensemble. The dances vary from tribe to tribe, but in general the men's dances portray scenes from hunting life or re-enact head-hunting raids. The Ibans are an energetic people and the men dance at a quicker and more vigorous pace than men from the other tribes. To the beat of the gong, the dancer dramatises how, when strolling through the forest, turning this way and that to listen to the sounds of birds and animals, he suddenly sights a man who is an enemy. Picking up sword and shield, he creeps close, and with a sudden war-cry pounces. They thrust and parry. Sometimes the dancer succeeds in carrying off his enemy's head triumphantly, sometimes he is killed and drops to the floor where he convulses and dies with affected rigor mortis. These dances may be done in the spirit of fun and laughter or with soberness and intensity.

To enjoy the very grandest of celebrations, it is necessary to time one's journey to fall during major festivals or *gawai*. For most of the year, however, life in the longhouse is tranquil as the men and women spend their days out in the fields looking after the *padi*. But, when the grains ripen and are gathered in, the longhouse awakens for the celebration of the harvest. Though there are several different types of *gawai* at different times of the year, they are always religious in nature. These occasions are for recounting stories of the gods and propitiating them by offering sacrifices and prayers. They are also times for great feasting and ostentatious display.

When the dates for the *gawai* have been fixed at a community meeting in the longhouse, it is time to start preparing the *tuak*. The making of *tuak* from rice, yeast and water is accompanied by rituals which involve processions of women beating gongs, food offerings, and men waving chickens and praying for a successful brew.

Invitations are sent out to neighbouring longhouses and the host longhouse is decorated with palm fronds and bunting. Guests arrive at the *gawai* to the sounds of drums and gongs. The women have on their best party dress — glittering silver tiaras, collars of beads and red cotton tassles, and skirts of *ikat* material fastened with heavy silver belts. The men are proud in their finest *sirat* and head-hunting swords.

In the welcoming ceremony, small brass cannon are fired to herald important guests, and the women line up along the stairways and entrances, bearing glasses of *tuak*. Pigs may be killed and the blood smeared on the wrists and foreheads of guests. Once the welcoming ceremony is over, there is little formality to the celebrations; the men go off to watch cock-fights, the women exchange gossip in the *bilik*, a continual feast is kept up throughout the day and pigs are slaughtered as food runs low. Dancing and drinking go on into the small hours until sleep overcomes everyone.

Amidst all the merry-making, the religious side of the *gawai* is conducted by a group of bards called *lemambang* who chant re-ligious verses as they proceed up and down the length of the longhouse. They wear long cloaks of *ikat* material to protect them on their spiritual journey and carry in their hands long staffs of ornately carved bamboo with which they beat a rhythm as they walk.

The verses of the bards tell of a journey to the spirit world to invite Singalang Burong, the god of war and the ancestor of the Ibans, to attend the *gawai*. They recount the difficulties encountered along the journey and the preparations of the god to attend the festivities. Singalang, the eldest of seven sibling gods, is wise and knows all the correct Iban customs and ritual procedures necessary to ensure a good harvest and general prosperity. It was Singalang Burong who taught the Ibans the art of augury. The chants end with the arrival of the spirit guest and his retinue. Thus at the *gawai*, men and gods meet and there is harmony between the two.

The *gawai*, which usually lasts several days, closes with the performance of the *bedara*, a ceremony to invoke the blessings of the gods for a good rice harvest, and the ceremonial killing of pigs in order to examine their livers to make prophecies.

In these festivals, the religious and oral traditions of the past assume their full significance. As the Dayaks are now exchanging their traditional life in the longhouse for more urban lifestyles and goals, such festivals remain the only occasions when their ethnic traditions can be fully relived. Those who have already left the longhouse return for reunions, and during these few days of togetherness, the Dayak communities re-affirm their ethnic identities and age-old beliefs.

One of the joys of the festivals is dressing up. The women welcome these opportunities to put on their best and show off their beauty. Amidst the hustle and bustle of the longhouse, these women help each other to oil and comb their hair and to put on their *bidang*, or *sarung* made of *ikat* cloth.

These maidens are taking part in a beauty contest organised in Dalat on the Oya River. Sometimes such contests seem more a show of fashion than of beauty as the women vie with each other to put on the most finery. They may wear several silver belts, layers of threaded silver coins and enormous silver tiaras on their heads. The weight of the jewellery is so great, that it is dangerous for these fully costumed ladies to travel in boats.

Flowers in her hair and bells on her toes, this little Iban girl in Song does not
have to wait till she grows up to dress like her older sisters.

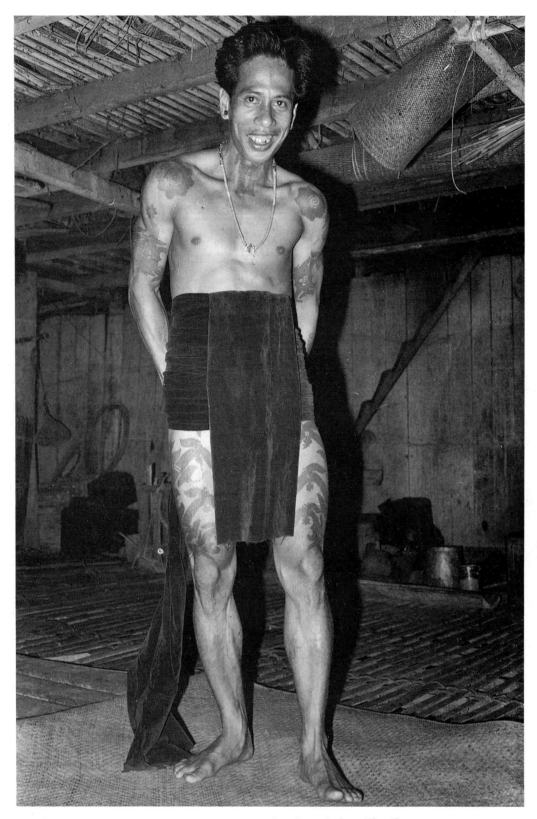

The men as well take this opportunity to put on their best clothes. This Iban man looks slightly abashed as he ties on his new loin-cloth.

As preparations are made for the coming festival, this curious display appears —
cigarettes pre-rolled for the pleasure of the guests.

The procession of warriors ascending the notched log from the riverside is greeted warmly by maidens bearing never-ending glasses of *tuak*.

Cockfighting is a favourite sport of Dayak men. Sharp spikes are tied to the claws of the cocks who sometimes duel to the death. When the men of neighbouring longhouses come together for festivals, cockfighting is the most popular activity.

124

This white cock seems to have brought his owner some success, as the boy sports a watch and fancy town clothes.

Absorbed in watching the cockfight, this man pauses while rolling his cigarette.

125

The main theme of the men's dancing is head-hunting. The dances follow an age-old pattern, but there is room for improvisation and the audience loves acrobatic stunts, such as when a dancer, gripping the sword in his teeth or between his toes, stands on his head.

The beating of drum and gongs is a favourite way of welcoming guests to the longhouse festivities. This old man, wearing a headdress of hornbill feathers and beating out a vigorous tattoo on his drum, is happy to see his guests.

Essential to the *gawai*, the rite of augury requires the sacrifice
of a pig in order to examine its liver for signs for the coming
year. The colour, shape and size of the liver's lobes are
interpreted, as the Dayaks seek reassurance for the success of
the next year's harvest.

Chickens are included in many Dayak rites, as waving them over brewing *tuak*
or offerings of rice is part of the ritual for invoking the blessings of the gods.

A high point of the Dayak *gawai* is the *bedara*, a ceremony to bring blessings to the longhouse and the next year's harvest. A cock, usually white in colour to signify purity, is waved over saucers filled with an array of Dayak delicacies: puffed rice, red beans, fish, tobacco, sticky cakes. This is followed by the sacrifice of the cock, whose blood is sprinkled over the food offerings as the spirits of the forefathers are called upon to protect and bless the longhouse.

We offer you this water of life,
this juice of the padi, this pure rainwater.
Let us all pleasantly and slowly drink.
You have come, my son, to visit us,
come happily with wholehearted feeling in your body.
Whatever evil spirit may come later to try to make trouble,
spirit of sickness, spirit of fever, spirit of ill health —
may this drink make them disappear, finished forever.
My son, slowly drink my juice;
let your troubles go away
as if you opened the shirt on your body,
as if you took off your shirt,
throwing them off forever, as I say this,
after you have slowly taken this juice.
That is the end of my voice and of my song.

— from Kenyah "Entertainment Song While Offering Drink"

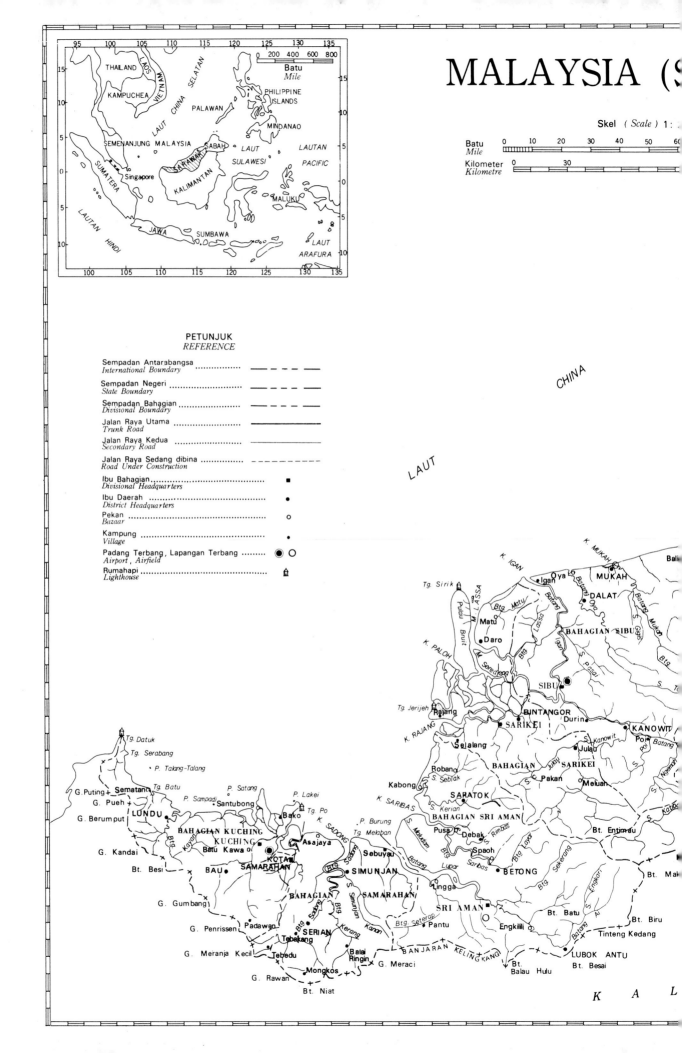

MALAYSIA (S

Inset map

THAILAND
LAOS
VIETNAM
KAMPUCHEA
LAUT CHINA SELATAN
PHILIPPINE ISLANDS
PALAWAN
MINDANAO
SEMENANJUNG MALAYSIA
SABAH
SARAWAK
LAUT SULAWESI
LAUTAN PACIFIC
SUMATERA
Singapore
KALIMANTAN
MALUKU
LAUTAN HINDI
JAWA
SUMBAWA
LAUT ARAFURA

Batu
Mile
200 400 600 800

Skel (Scale) 1:

Batu
Mile
0 10 20 30 40 50 60

Kilometer
Kilometre
0 30

PETUNJUK
REFERENCE

Sempadan Antarabangsa
International Boundary ....

Sempadan Negeri ....
State Boundary

Sempadan Bahagian ....
Divisional Boundary

Jalan Raya Utama ....
Trunk Road

Jalan Raya Kedua ....
Secondary Road

Jalan Raya Sedang dibina ....
Road Under Construction

Ibu Bahagian................................. ■
Divisional Headquarters

Ibu Daerah .... •
District Headquarters

Pekan .... o
Bazaar

Kampung .... ·
Village

Padang Terbang, Lapangan Terbang .... ◉ ○
Airport , Airfield

Rumahapi .... ⌂
Lighthouse

CHINA

LAUT

K. IGAN
K. MUKAH
Bali
Tg. Sirik
Oya
Igan
MUKAH
DALAT
Matu
Daro
BAHAGIAN SIBU
K. PALOH
SIBU
Tg. Jerijeh
Rajang
BINTANGOR
Durin
SARIKEI
KANOWIT
K. RAJANG
Selalang
Julau
Poi
Robang
BAHAGIAN SARIKEI
Kabong
Pakan
Meluan
SARATOK
K. SARIBAS
BAHAGIAN SRI AMAN
Pusa
Debak
Bt. Entimau
Tg. Datuk
Tg. Serabang
P. Talang-Talang
G. Puting
Sematan
Tg. Batu
G. Pueh
P. Satang
Santubong
P. Sampadi
P. Lakei
Bako
Tg. Po
LUNDU
BAHAGIAN KUCHING
KUCHING
Asajaya
Spaoh
G. Berumput
Batu Kawa
KOTA SAMARAHAN
Sebuyau
BETONG
G. Kandai
BAU
Lingga
Bt. Mak
Bt. Besi
SIMUNJAN
SRI AMAN
Bt. Batu
BAHAGIAN
SAMARAHAN
G. Gumbang
Pantu
Engkilili
Bt. Biru
G. Penrissen
Padawan
SERIAN
Tinteng Kedang
Tebakang
Balai Ringin
G. Meraci
BANJARAN KELINGKANG
LUBOK ANTU
G. Meranja Kecil
Tebedu
Mongkos
Bt. Balau Hulu
Bt. Besai
G. Rawan
Bt. Niat

K A L

The history of Van Buren County, Iowa, containing a history of the county, its cities, towns, &c, a biographical directory of citizens, war record of its volunteers in the late rebellion, general and local statistics ... history of the Northwest, history

Western Historical Co

THE

HISTORY

OF

VAN BUREN COUNTY,

IOWA,

CONTAINING

A History of the County, its Cities, Towns, &c.,

A Biographical Directory of Citizens, War Record of its Volunteers in the late Rebellion, General and Local Statistics,
Portraits of Early Settlers and Prominent Men, History of the Northwest, History of Iowa, Map
of Van Buren County, Constitution of the
United States, Miscellaneous
Matters, &c.

ILLUSTRATED.

CHICAGO:
WESTERN HISTORICAL COMPANY.
1878.

Entered, according to Act of Congress, in the year 1878, by

THE WESTERN HISTORICAL COMPANY

In the Office of the Librarian of Congress, at Washington, D C

PREFACE.

.•.

THE history of Van Buren County differs from that of almost every other county in Iowa, in one essential respect viz., the records of its towns No one locality, outside of the county seat, calls for special elaboration, but many sections present about equal opportunities for comment It is a cause of sincere regret to us, and will no doubt, be to our readers, that the official papers and books of the several towns are no longer in existence The pages here offered were prepared under serious difficulties, and are the product of much hard labor If inaccuracies appear in them, the fault is not with the compiler, for every effort was put forth to secure correct data

The Western Historical Company extends its thanks to those who have so generously aided in the work of securing reliable information.

The importance of the task here undertaken will be more fully realized and admitted in years to come, when time shall have added to the obstacles in the way of determining proper historic truth

THE PUBLISHERS

December, 1878

CONTENTS.

HISTORY NORTHWEST AND STATE OF IOWA

HISTORY VAN BUREN COUNTY.

ILLUSTRATIONS

CONTENTS.

VAN BUREN COUNTY VOLUNTEERS.

BIOGRAPHICAL TOWNSHIP DIRECTORY.

LITHOGRAPHIC PORTRAITS.

ABSTRACT OF IOWA STATE LAWS.

MISCELLANEOUS.

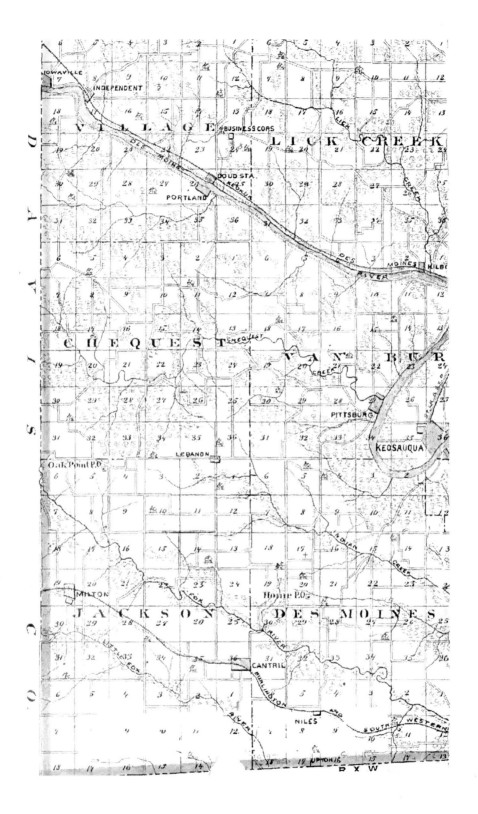

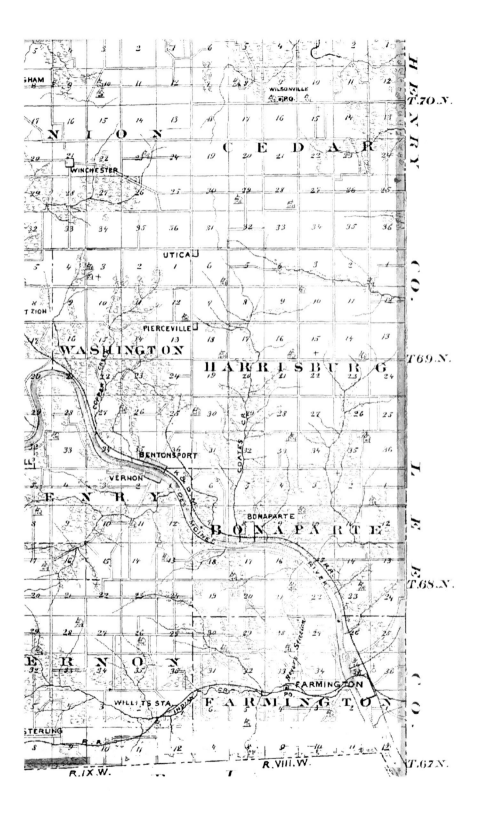

THE NORTHWEST TERRITORY.

GEOGRAPHICAL POSITION.

When the Northwestern Territory was ceded to the United States by Virginia in 1784, it embraced only the territory lying between the Ohio and the Mississippi Rivers, and north to the northern limits of the United States. It coincided with the area now embraced in the States of Ohio, Indiana, Michigan, Illinois, Wisconsin, and that portion of Minnesota lying on the east side of the Mississippi River. The United States itself at that period extended no farther west than the Mississippi River, but by the purchase of Louisiana in 1803, the western boundary of the United States was extended to the Rocky Mountains and the Northern Pacific Ocean. The new territory thus added to the National domain, and subsequently opened to settlement, has been called the " New Northwest," in contradistinction from the old " Northwestern Territory."

In comparison with the old Northwest this is a territory of vast magnitude. It includes an area of 1,887,850 square miles; being greater in extent than the united areas of all the Middle and Southern States, including Texas. Out of this magnificent territory have been erected eleven sovereign States and eight Territories, with an aggregate population, at the present time, of 13,000,000 inhabitants, or nearly one third of the entire population of the United States

Its lakes are fresh-water seas, and the larger rivers of the continent flow for a thousand miles through its rich alluvial valleys and far-stretching prairies, more acres of which are arable and productive of the highest percentage of the cereals than of any other area of like extent on the globe

For the last twenty years the increase of population in the North-west has been about as three to one in any other portion of the United States.

EARLY EXPLORATIONS.

In the year 1541, DeSoto first saw the Great West in the New World. He, however, penetrated no farther north than the 35th parallel of latitude. The expedition resulted in his death and that of more than half his army, the remainder of whom found their way to Cuba, thence to Spain, in a famished and demoralized condition. DeSoto founded no settlements, produced no results, and left no traces, unless it were that he awakened the hostility of the red man against the white man, and disheartened such as might desire to follow up the career of discovery for better purposes. The French nation were eager and ready to seize upon any news from this extensive domain, and were the first to profit by DeSoto's defeat. Yet it was more than a century before any adventurer took advantage of these discoveries.

In 1616, four years before the pilgrims "moored their bark on the wild New England shore," Le Caron, a French Franciscan, had penetrated through the Iroquois and Wyandots (Hurons) to the streams which run into Lake Huron ; and in 1634, two Jesuit missionaries founded the first mission among the lake tribes. It was just one hundred years from the discovery of the Mississippi by DeSoto (1541) until the Canadian envoys met the savage nations of the Northwest at the Falls of St. Mary, below the outlet of Lake Superior. This visit led to no permanent result ; yet it was not until 1659 that any of the adventurous fur traders attempted to spend a Winter in the frozen wilds about the great lakes, nor was it until 1660 that a station was established upon their borders by Mesnard, who perished in the woods a few months after. In 1665, Claude Allouez built the earliest lasting habitation of the white man among the Indians of the Northwest. In 1668, Claude Dablon and James Marquette founded the mission of Sault Ste. Marie at the Falls of St. Mary, and two years afterward, Nicholas Perrot, as agent for M. Talon, Governor General of Canada, explored Lake Illinois (Michigan) as far south as the present City of Chicago, and invited the Indian nations to meet him at a grand council at Sault Ste. Marie the following Spring, where they were taken under the protection of the king, and formal possession was taken of the Northwest. This same year Marquette established a mission at Point St. Ignatius, where was founded the old town of Michillimackinac.

During M. Talon's explorations and Marquette's residence at St. Ignatius, they learned of a great river away to the west, and fancied —as all others did then—that upon its fertile banks whole tribes of God's children resided, to whom the sound of the Gospel had never come. Filled with a wish to go and preach to them, and in compliance with a

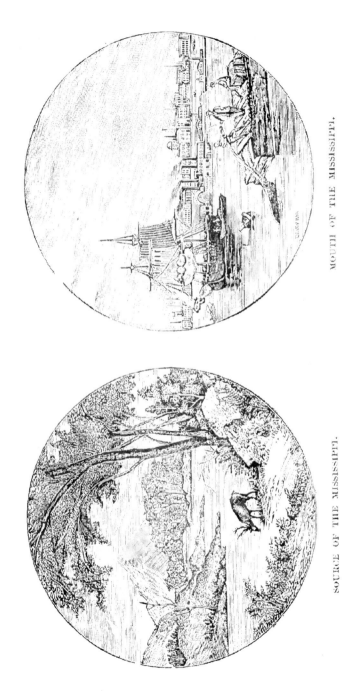

MOUTH OF THE MISSISSIPPI.

SOURCE OF THE MISSISSIPPI.

request of M Talon, who earnestly desired to extend the domain of his king, and to ascertain whether the river flowed into the Gulf of Mexico or the Pacific Ocean, Marquette with Joliet, as commander of the expedition, prepared for the undertaking.

On the 13th of May, 1673, the explorers, accompanied by five assistant French Canadians, set out from Mackinaw on their daring voyage of discovery   The Indians, who gathered to witness their departure, were astonished at the boldness of the undertaking, and endeavored to dissuade them from their purpose by representing the tribes on the Mississippi as exceedingly savage and cruel, and the river itself as full of all sorts of frightful monsters ready to swallow them and their canoes together. But, nothing daunted by these terrific descriptions, Marquette told them he was willing not only to encounter all the perils of the unknown region they were about to explore, but to lay down his life in a cause in which the salvation of souls was involved ; and having prayed together they separated.   Coasting along the northern shore of Lake Michigan, the adventurers entered Green Bay, and passed thence up the Fox River and Lake Winnebago to a village of the Miamis and Kickapoos.   Here Marquette was delighted to find a beautiful cross planted in the middle of the town ornamented with white skins, red girdles and bows and arrows, which these good people had offered to the Great Maniton, or God, to thank him for the pity he had bestowed on them during the Winter in giving them an abundant " chase."   This was the farthest outpost to which Dablon and Allouez had extended their missionary labors the year previous   Here Marquette drank mineral waters and was instructed in the secret of a root which cures the bite of the venomous rattlesnake He assembled the chiefs and old men of the village, and, pointing to Joliet, said   " My friend is an envoy of France, to discover new countries, and I am an ambassador from God to enlighten them with the truths of the Gospel "   Two Miami guides were here furnished to conduct them to the Wisconsin River, and they set out from the Indian village on the 10th of June, amidst a great crowd of natives who had assembled to witness their departure into a region where no white man had ever yet ventured.   The guides, having conducted them across the portage, returned   The explorers launched their canoes upon the Wisconsin, which they descended to the Mississippi and proceeded down its unknown waters   What emotions must have swelled their breasts as they struck out into the broadening current and became conscious that they were now upon the bosom of the Father of Waters   The mystery was about to be lifted from the long-sought river.   The scenery in that locality is beautiful and on that delightful seventeenth of June must have been clad in all its primeval loveliness as it had been adorned by the hand of

Nature. Drifting rapidly, it is said that the bold bluffs on either hand "reminded them of the castled shores of their own beautiful rivers of France." By-and-by, as they drifted along, great herds of buffalo appeared on the banks. On going to the heads of the valley they could see a country of the greatest beauty and fertility, apparently destitute of inhabitants yet presenting the appearance of extensive manors, under the fastidious cultivation of lordly proprietors.

THE WILD PRAIRIE.

On June 25, they went ashore and found some fresh traces of men upon the sand, and a path which led to the prairie. The men remained in the boat, and Marquette and Joliet followed the path till they discovered a village on the banks of a river, and two other villages on a hill, within a half league of the first, inhabited by Indians. They were received most hospitably by these natives, who had never before seen a white person. After remaining a few days they re-embarked and descended the river to about latitude 33°, where they found a village of the Arkansas, and being satisfied that the river flowed into the Gulf of Mexico, turned their course up the river, and ascending the stream to the mouth of the Illinois, rowed up that stream to its source, and procured guides from that point to the lakes. "Nowhere on this journey,' says Marquette, "did we see such grounds, meadows, woods, stags. buffaloes, deer, wildcats, bustards, swans ducks, parroquets and even beavers. as on the Illinois River ' The party without loss or injury. reached Green Bay in September, and reported their discovery—one of the most important of the age, but of which no record was preserved save Marquette's. Joliet losing his by the upsetting of his canoe on his way to Quebec. Afterward Marquette returned to the Illinois Indians by their request, and ministered to them until 1675. On the 18th of May, in that year, as he was passing the mouth of a stream—going with his boatmen up Lake Michigan—he asked to land at its mouth and celebrate Mass. Leaving his men with the canoe, he retired a short distance and began his devotions. As much time passed and he did not return, his men went in search of him, and found him upon his knees, dead. He had peacefully passed away while at prayer. He was buried at this spot. Charlevoix, who visited the place fifty years after found the waters had retreated from the grave, leaving the beloved missionary to repose in peace. The river has since been called Marquette.

While Marquette and his companions were pursuing their labors in the West two men, differing widely from him and each other were preparing to follow in his footsteps and perfect the discoveries so well begun by him. These were Robert de La Salle and Louis Hennepin.

After LaSalle's return from the discovery of the Ohio River (see the narrative elsewhere), he established himself again among the French trading posts in Canada. Here he mused long upon the pet project of those ages—a short way to China and the East and was busily planning an expedition up the great lakes, and so across the continent to the Pacific, when Marquette returned from the Mississippi. At once the vigorous mind of LaSalle received from his and his companions' stories the idea that by following the Great River northward, or by turning up some of the numerous western tributaries the object could easily be gained. He applied to Frontenac, Governor General of Canada, and laid before him the plan, dim but gigantic. Frontenac entered warmly into his plans and saw that LaSalle's idea to connect the great lakes by a chain of forts with the Gulf of Mexico would bind the country so wonderfully together, give unmeasured power to France, and glory to himself, under whose administration he earnestly hoped all would be realized.

LaSalle now repaired to France, laid his plans before the King, who warmly   '   ll   received
from all   ' he Chev

alier returned to Canada, and busily entered upon his work. He at once rebuilt Fort Frontenac and constructed the first ship to sail on these fresh-water seas. On the 7th of August, 1679, having been joined by Hennepin, he began his voyage in the Griffin up Lake Erie. He passed over this lake, through the straits beyond, up Lake St. Clair and into Huron. In this lake they encountered heavy storms. They were some time at Michillimackinac, where LaSalle founded a fort, and passed on to Green Bay, the "Baie des Puans" of the French, where he found a large quantity of furs collected for him. He loaded the Griffin with these, and placing her under the care of a pilot and fourteen sailors,

LA SALLE LANDING ON THE SHORE OF GREEN BAY.

started her on her return voyage. The vessel was never afterward heard of. He remained about these parts until early in the Winter, when, hearing nothing from the Griffin, he collected all the men—thirty working men and three monks—and started again upon his great undertaking.

By a short portage they passed to the Illinois or Kankakee, called by the Indians, "Theakeke," *wolf*, because of the tribes of Indians called by that name, commonly known as the Mahingans, dwelling there. The French pronounced it *Kiakiki*, which became corrupted to Kankakee. "Falling down the said river by easy journeys, the better to observe the country," about the last of December they reached a village of the Illinois India- moment no inhabitants. The Seur de LaSalle being in want of some breadstuffs, took advantage of the absence of the Indians to help himself to a suffi- ciency of maize, large quantities of which he found concealed in holes under the wigwams. This village was situated near the present village of Utica in LaSalle County, Illinois. The corn being securely stored, the voyagers again betook themselves to the stream, and toward evening, on the 4th day of January, 1680, they came into a lake which must have been the lake of Peoria. This was called by the Indians *Pim-i-te-wi*, that is, *a place where there are many fat beasts.* Here the natives were met with in large numbers, but they were gentle and kind, and having spent some time with them, LaSalle determined to erect another fort in that place, for he had heard rumors that some of the adjoining tribes were trying to disturb the good feeling which existed, and some of his men were disposed to complain, owing to the hardships and perils of the travel He called this fort " *Crevecœur* ' (broken-heart), a name expressive of the very natural sorrow and anxiety which the pretty certain loss of his ship, Griffin, and his consequent impoverishment, the danger of hostility on the part of the Indians, and of mutiny among his own men, might well cause him. His fears were not entirely groundless At one time poison was placed in his food, but fortunately was discovered.

While building this fort, the Winter wore away, the prairies began to look green, and LaSalle, despairing of any reinforcements, concluded to return to Canada, raise new means and new men, and embark anew in the enterprise For this purpose he made Hennepin the leader of a party to explore the head waters of the Mississippi, and he set out on his jour- ney. This journey was accomplished with the aid of a few persons, and was successfully made, though over an almost unknown route, and in a bad season of the year. He safely reached Canada, and set out again for the object of his search.

Hennepin and his party left Fort Crevecœur on the last of February, 1680 When LaSalle reached this place on his return expedition, he found the fort entirely deserted, and he was obliged to return again to Canada. He embarked the third time, and succeeded. Seven days after leaving the fort. Hennepin reached the Mississippi, and paddling up the icy stream as best he could, reached no higher than the Wisconsin River by the 11th of April. Here he and his followers were taken prisoners by a band of Northern Indians, who treated them with great kindness. Hen- nepin's comrades were Anthony Auguel and Michael Ako. On this voy- age they found several beautiful lakes, and "saw some charming prairies.' Their captors were the Isaute or Sauteurs Chippewas, a tribe of the Sioux nation, who took them up the river until about the first of May, when they reached some falls, which Hennepin christened Falls of St. Anthony

in honor of his patron saint. Here they took the land, and traveling
nearly two hundred miles to the northwest, brought them to their villages.
Here they were kept about three months, were treated kindly by their
captors, and at the end of that time, were met by a band of Frenchmen,

BUFFALO HUNT.

headed by one Seur de Luth, who, in pursuit of trade and game, had penetrated thus far by the route of Lake Superior; and with these fellow-
countrymen Hennepin and his companions were allowed to return to the
borders of civilized life in November, 1680, just after LaSalle had
returned to the wilderness on his second trip. Hennepin soon after went
to France, where he published an account of his adventures.

The Mississippi was first discovered by De Soto in April, 1541, in his vain endeavor to find gold and precious gems. In the following Spring, De Soto, weary with hope long deferred, and worn out with his wanderings, he fell a victim to disease, and on the 21st of May died. His followers reduced by fatigue and disease to less than three hundred men, wandered about the country nearly a year, in the vain endeavor to rescue themselves by land, and finally constructed seven small vessels, called brigantines, in which they embarked, and descending the river, supposing it would lead them to the sea, in July they came to the sea (Gulf of Mexico), and by September reached the Island of Cuba.

They were the first to see the great outlet of the Mississippi; but, being so weary and discouraged, made no attempt to claim the country, and hardly had an intelligent idea of what they had passed through.

To La Salle, the intrepid explorer, belongs the honor of giving the first account of the mouths of the river. His great desire was to possess this entire country for his king, and in January, 1682, he and his band of explorers left the shores of Lake Michigan on their third attempt, crossed the portage, passed down the Illinois River, and on the 6th of February, reached the banks of the Mississippi.

On the 13th they commenced their downward course, which they pursued with but one interruption, until upon the 6th of March they discovered the three great passages by which the river discharges its waters into the gulf. La Salle thus narrates the event:

"We landed on the bank of the most western channel, about three leagues (nine miles) from its mouth. On the seventh, M. de LaSalle went to reconnoitre the shores of the neighboring sea, and M. de Tonti meanwhile examined the great middle channel. They found the main outlets beautiful, large and deep. On the 8th we reascended the river, a little above its confluence with the sea, to find a dry place beyond the reach of inundations. The elevation of the North Pole was here about twenty-seven degrees. Here we prepared a column and a cross and to the column were affixed the arms of France with this inscription:

Louis Le Grand, Roi De France et de Navarre, regne, Le neuvieme Avril, 1682.

The whole party, under arms chanted the *Te Deum*, and then, after a salute and cries of "*Vive le Roi,*" the column was erected by M. de La Salle, who, standing near it, proclaimed in a loud voice the authority of the King of France. LaSalle returned and laid the foundations of the Mississippi settlements in Illinois, thence he proceeded to France, where another expedition was fitted out, of which he was commander, and in two succeeding voyages failed to find the mouth of the river by sailing along the shore of the gulf. On his third voyage he was killed through the treachery of his followers, and the object of his expeditions was not accomplished until 1699, when D'Iberville, under the authority of the crown, discovered, on the second of March, by way of the sea, the mouth of the "Hidden River." This majestic stream was called by the natives "*Malbouchia*," and by the Spaniards, "*la Palissade*," from the great

TRAPPING.

number of trees about its mouth. After traversing the several outlets, and satisfying himself as to its certainty, he erected a fort near its western outlet, and returned to France.

An avenue of trade was now opened out which was fully improved. In 1718, New Orleans was laid out and settled by some European colonists. In 1762, the colony was made over to Spain, to be regained by France under the consulate of Napoleon. In 1803, it was purchased by the United States for the sum of fifteen million dollars, and the territory of Louisiana and commerce of the Mississippi River came under the charge of the United States. Although LaSalle's labors ended in defeat and death, he had not worked and suffered in vain. He had thrown open to France and the world an immense and most valuable country: had established several ports, and laid the foundations of more than one settlement there. " Peoria, Kaskaskia and Cahokia, are to this day monuments of LaSalle's labors: for, though he had founded neither of them (unless Peoria, which was built nearly upon the site of Fort Crevecœur,) it was by those whom he led into the West that these places were peopled and civilized. He was, if not the discoverer, the first settler of the Mississippi Valley, and as such deserves to be known and honored."

The French early improved the opening made for them. Before the year 1698, the Rev. Father Gravier began a mission among the Illinois, and founded Kaskaskia. For some time this was merely a missionary station, where none but natives resided, it being one of three such villages, the other two being Cahokia and Peoria. What is known of these missions is learned from a letter written by Father Gabriel Marest, dated "Aux Cascaskias, autrement dit de l Immaculate Conception de la Sainte Vierge, le 9 Novembre, 1712." Soon after the founding of Kaskaskia, the missionary Pinet, gathered a flock at Cahokia, while Peoria arose near the ruins of Fort Crevecœur. This must have been about the year 1700. The post at Vincennes on the Oubache river, (pronounced Wă-bă, meaning *summer cloud moving swiftly*) was established in 1702, according to the best authorities.* It is altogether probable that on LaSalle's last trip he established the stations at Kaskaskia and Cahokia. In July, 1701, the foundations of Fort Ponchartrain were laid by De la Motte Cadillac on the Detroit River. These stations, with those established further north, were the earliest attempts to occupy the Northwest Territory. At the same time efforts were being made to occupy the Southwest, which finally culminated in the settlement and founding of the City of New Orleans by a colony from England in 1718. This was mainly accomplished through the efforts of the famous Mississippi Company, established by the notorious John Law, who so quickly arose into prominence in France, and who with his scheme so quickly and so ignominiously passed away.

From the time of the founding of these stations for fifty years the French nation were engrossed with the settlement of the lower Mississippi, and the war with the Chicasaws, who had, in revenge for repeated

* There is considerable dispute about this date some asserting it was founded as late as 1742. When the new court house . . . . 1702 fixed upon . . . . house

injuries, cut off the entire colony at Natchez. Although the company did little for Louisiana, as the entire West was then called, yet it opened the trade through the Mississippi River, and started the raising of grains indigenous to that climate   Until the year 1750, but little is known of the settlements in the Northwest, as it was not until this time that the attention of the English was called to the occupation of this portion of the New World, which they then supposed they owned   Vivier, a missionary among the Illinois, writing from " Aux Illinois " six leagues from Fort Chartres, June 8, 1750, says: ' We have here whites, negroes and Indians, to say nothing of cross-breeds.   There are five French villages, and three villages of the natives, within a space of twenty-one leagues situated between the Mississippi and another river called the Kaskadaid (Kaskaskias)   In the five French villages are, perhaps, eleven hundred whites, three hundred blacks and some sixty red slaves or savages.   The three Illinois towns do not contain more than eight hundred souls all told   Most of the French till the soil, they raise wheat, cattle, pigs and horses, and live like princes.   Three times as much is produced as can be consumed ; and great quantities of grain and flour are sent to New Orleans "   This city was now the seaport town of the Northwest, and save in the extreme northern part, where only furs and copper ore were found, almost all the products of the country found their way to France by the mouth of the Father of Waters   In another letter, dated November 7, 1750, this same priest says: ' For fifteen leagues above the mouth of the Mississippi one sees no dwellings, the ground being too low to be habitable.   Thence to New Orleans, the lands are only partially occupied   New Orleans contains black, white and red, not more, I think, than twelve hundred persons.   To this point come all lumber, bricks, salt-beef, tallow, tar, skins and bear s grease, and above all pork and flour from the Illinois   These things create some commerce, as forty vessels and more have come hither this year   Above New Orleans, plantations are again met with, the most considerable is a colony of Germans, some ten leagues up the river.   At Point Coupee, thirty-five leagues above the German settlement, is a fort   Along here, within five or six leagues, are not less than sixty habitations   Fifty leagues farther up is the Natchez post, where we have a garrison, who are kept prisoners through fear of the Chickasaws   Here and at Point Coupee, they raise excellent tobacco   Another hundred leagues brings us to the Arkansas, where we have also a fort and a garrison for the benefit of the river traders. * * *   From the Arkansas to the Illinois, nearly five hundred leagues, there is not a settlement   There should be, however, a fort at the Oubache (Ohio), the only path by which the English can reach the Mississippi.   In the Illinois country are numberless mines, but no one to work them as they deserve." Father Marest, writing from the post at Vincennes in 1812, makes the same observation. Vivier also says: "Some individuals dig lead near the surface and supply the Indians and Canada. Two Spaniards now here, who claim to be adepts, say that our mines are like those of Mexico, and that if we would dig deeper, we should find silver under the lead; and at any rate the lead is excellent. There is also in this country, beyond doubt, copper ore, as from time to time large pieces are found in the streams."

HUNTING.

At the close of the year 1750, the French occupied, in addition to the lower Mississippi posts and those in Illinois, one at Du Quesne, one at the Maumee in the country of the Miamis, and one at Sandusky in what may be termed the Ohio Valley. In the northern part of the Northwest they had stations at St. Joseph's on the St. Joseph's of Lake Michigan, at Fort Ponchartrain (Detroit), at Michillimackanac or Massillimacanac, Fox River of Green Bay, and at Sault Ste. Marie. The fondest dreams of LaSalle were now fully realized. The French alone were possessors of this vast realm, basing their claim on discovery and settlement. Another nation, however, was now turning its attention to this extensive country, and hearing of its wealth, began to lay plans for occupying it and for securing the great profits arising therefrom.

The French, however, had another claim to this country, namely, the

DISCOVERY OF THE OHIO.

This " Beautiful " river was discovered by Robert Cavalier de LaSalle in 1669, four years before the discovery of the Mississippi by Joliet and Marquette.

While LaSalle was at his trading post on the St Lawrence, he found leisure to study nine Indian dialects, the chief of which was the Iroquois. He not only desired to facilitate his intercourse in trade, but he longed to travel and explore the unknown regions of the West. An incident soon occurred which decided him to fit out an exploring expedition.

While conversing with some Senecas, he learned of a river called the Ohio, which rose in their country and flowed to the sea, but at such a distance that it required eight months to reach its mouth In this statement the Mississippi and its tributaries were considered as one stream. LaSalle believing, as most of the French at that period did, that the great rivers flowing west emptied into the Sea of California, was anxious to embark in the enterprise of discovering a route across the continent to the commerce of China and Japan

He repaired at once to Quebec to obtain the approval of the Governor. His eloquent appeal prevailed. The Governor and the Intendant, Talon, issued letters patent authorizing the enterprise, but made no provision to defray the expenses. At this juncture the seminary of St. Sulpice decided to send out missionaries in connection with the expedition, and LaSalle offering to sell his improvements at LaChine to raise money, the offer was accepted by the Superior. and two thousand eight hundred dollars were raised, with which LaSalle purchased four canoes and the necessary supplies for the outfit

On the 6th of July, 1669, the party, numbering twenty-four persons, embarked in seven canoes on the St Lawrence; two additional canoes carried the Indian guides. In three days they were gliding over the bosom of Lake Ontario Their guides conducted them directly to the Seneca village on the bank of the Genesee, in the vicinity of the present City of Rochester, New York Here they expected to procure guides to conduct them to the Ohio, but in this they were disappointed

The Indians seemed unfriendly to the enterprise., LaSalle suspected that the Jesuits had prejudiced their minds against his plans After waiting a month in the hope of gaining their object, they met an Indian from the Iroquois colony at the head of Lake Ontario, who assured them that they could there find guides, and offered to conduct them thence.

On their way they passed the mouth of the Niagara River, when they heard for the first time the distant thunder of the cataract. Arriving

IROQUOIS CHIEF.

among the Iroquois, they met with a friendly reception, and learned from a Shawanee prisoner that they could reach the Ohio in six weeks. Delighted with the unexpected good fortune, they made ready to resume their journey; but just as they were about to start they heard of the arrival of two Frenchmen in a neighboring village. One of them proved to be Louis Joliet, afterward famous as an explorer in the West. He had been sent by the Canadian Government to explore the copper mines on Lake Superior, but had failed, and was on his way back to Quebec. He gave the missionaries a map of the country he had explored in the lake region, together with an account of the condition of the Indians in that quarter. This induced the priests to determine on leaving the expedition and going to Lake Superior. LaSalle warned them that the Jesuits were probably occupying that field, and that they would meet with a cold reception. Nevertheless they persisted in their purpose, and after worship on the lake shore, parted from LaSalle. On arriving at Lake Superior, they found, as LaSalle had predicted, the Jesuit Fathers, Marquette and Dablon, occupying the field.

These zealous disciples of Loyola informed them that they wanted no assistance from St Sulpice, nor from those who made him their patron saint, and thus repulsed, they returned to Montreal the following June without having made a single discovery or converted a single Indian

After parting with the priests. LaSalle went to the chief Iroquois village at Onondaga, where he obtained guides. and passing thence to a tributary of the Ohio south of Lake Erie, he descended the latter as far as the falls at Louisville. Thus was the Ohio discovered by LaSalle, the persevering and successful French explorer of the West, in 1669.

The account of the latter part of his journey is found in an anonymous paper, which purports to have been taken from the lips of LaSalle himself during a subsequent visit to Paris. In a letter written to Count Frontenac in 1667, shortly after the discovery, he himself says that he discovered the Ohio and descended it to the falls. This was regarded as an indisputable fact by the French authorities, who claimed the Ohio Valley upon another ground When Washington was sent by the colony of Virginia in 1753, to demand of Gordeur de St. Pierre why the French had built a fort on the Monongahela, the haughty commandant at Quebec replied. "We claim the country on the Ohio by virtue of the discoveries of LaSalle, and will not give it up to the English. Our orders are to make prisoners of every Englishman found trading in the Ohio Valley."

ENGLISH EXPLORATIONS AND SETTLEMENTS

When the new year of 1750 broke in upon the Father of Waters and the Great Northwest, all was still wild save at the French posts already described In 1749, when the English first began to think seriously about sending men into the West, the greater portion of the States of Indiana, Ohio, Illinois, Michigan, Wisconsin, and Minnesota were yet under the dominion of the red men The English knew, however, pretty conclusively of the nature of the wealth of these wilds. As early as 1710, Governor Spotswood, of Virginia, had commenced movements to secure the country west of the Alleghenies to the English crown In Pennsylvania, Governor Keith and James Logan, secretary of the province, from 1719 to 1731, represented to the powers of England the necessity of securing the Western lands Nothing was done, however, by that power save to take some diplomatic steps to secure the claims of Britain to this unexplored wilderness.

England had from the outset claimed from the Atlantic to the Pacific, on the ground that the discovery of the seacoast and its possession was a discovery and possession of the country, and, as is well known, her grants to the colonies extended " from sea to sea." This was not all her claim She had purchased from the Indian tribes large tracts of land This latter was also a strong argument. As early as 1684, Lord Howard. Governor of Virginia, held a treaty, with the six nations. These were the great Northern Confederacy, and comprised at first the Mohawks, Oneidas, Onondagas, Cayugas, and Senecas Afterward the Tuscaroras were taken into the confederacy, and it became known as the SIX NATIONS. They came under the protection of the mother country, and again in 1701, they repeated the agreement, and in September, 1726 a formal deed was drawn up and signed by the chiefs The validity of this claim has often been disputed, but never successfully. In 1744, a purchase was made at Lancaster, Pennsylvania, of certain lands within the " Colony of Virginia," for which the Indians received £200 in gold and a like sum in goods, with a promise that, as settlements increased, more should be paid. The Commissioners from Virginia were Colonel Thomas Lee and Colonel William Beverly. As settlements extended, the promise of more pay was called to mind, and Mr Conrad Weiser was sent across the mountains with presents to appease the savages Col Lee, and some Virginians accompanied him with the intention of sounding the Indians upon their feelings regarding the English. They were not satisfied with their treatment, and plainly told the Commissioners why The English did not desire the cultivation of the country, but the monopoly of the Indian trade In 1748, the Ohio Company was formed, and petitioned the king for a grant of land beyond the Alleghenies. This was granted, and the government of Virginia was ordered to grant to them a half million acres, two hundred thousand of which were to be located at once. Upon the 12th of June, 1749, 800,000 acres from the line of Canada north and west was made to the Loyal Company, and on the 29th of October, 1751, 100,000 acres were given to the Greenbriar Company All this time the French were not idle. They saw that should the British gain a foothold in the West, especially upon the Ohio they might not only prevent the French settling upon it, but in time would come to the lower posts and so gain possession of the whole country. Upon the 10th of May, 1774, Vaudreuil, Governor of Canada and the French possessions, well knowing the consequences that must arise from allowing the English to build trading posts in the Northwest, seized some of their frontier posts, and to further secure the claim of the French to the West, he, in 1749, sent Louis Celeron with a party of soldiers to plant along the Ohio River, in the mounds and at the mouths of its principal tributaries, plates of lead, on which were inscribed the claims of France These were heard of in 1752, and within the memory of residents now living along the "Oyo," as the beautiful river was called by the French. One of these plates was found with the inscription partly defaced. It bears date August 16, 1749, and a copy of the inscription with particular account of the discovery of the plate, was sent by DeWitt Clinton to the American Antiquarian Society, among whose journals it may now be found.* These measures did not, however, deter the English from going on with their explorations, and though neither party resorted to arms, yet the conflict was gathering, and it was only a question of time when the storm would burst upon the frontier settlements. In 1750, Christopher Gist was sent by the Ohio Company to examine its lands. He went to a village of the Twigtwees, on the Miami, about one hundred and fifty miles above its mouth He afterward spoke of it as very populous. From there he went down the Ohio River nearly to the falls at the present City of Louisville, and in November he commenced a survey of the Company's lands. During the Winter, General Andrew Lewis performed a similar work for the Greenbriar Company. Meanwhile the French were busy in preparing their forts for defense, and in opening roads, and also sent a small party of soldiers to keep the Ohio clear. This party, having heard of the English post on the Miami River, early in 1652, assisted by the Ottawas and Chippewas, attacked it, and, after a severe battle, in which fourteen of the natives were killed and others wounded, captured the garrison (They were probably garrisoned in a block house). The traders were carried away to Canada, and one account says several were burned. This fort or post was called by the English Pickawillany. A memorial of the king's ministers refers to it as "Pickawillanes, in the center of the territory between the Ohio and the Wabash. The name is probably some variation of Pickaway or Piequa in 1773, written by Rev David Jones Pickaweke."

* The following is a translation of the inscription on the plate "In the year 1749 reign of Louis XV King of France, we, Celeron, commandant of a detachment by Monsieur the Marquis of Gallisoniere, commander-in-chief of ... within ... to ... public ... Indians ... antons have buried this pl ... the ... of th ... of twen ... niati ... io, otherwise Beautiful Ri ... its mouth ... of ... on whi ... te ... er, and all its tributaries, ... which is th ... still ... h ... and ... have caj ... d th ... ... their arms and treaties, espe ... by thos ... La ... ick ... and ... La Chapelle."

This was the first blood shed between the French and English, and occurred near the present City of Piqua, Ohio, or at least at a point about forty-seven miles north of Dayton.   Each nation became now more interested in the progress of events in the Northwest   The English determined to purchase from the Indians a title to the lands they wished to occupy, and Messrs. Fry (afterward Commander-in-chief over Washington at the commencement of the French War of 1775–1763), Lomax and Patton were sent in the Spring of 1752 to hold a conference with the natives at Logstown to learn what they objected to in the treaty of Lancaster already noticed, and to settle all difficulties.   On the 9th of June, these Commissioners met the red men at Logstown, a little village on the north bank of the Ohio, about seventeen miles below the site of Pittsburgh.   Here had been a trading point for many years, but it was abandoned by the Indians in 1750.   At first the Indians declined to recognize the treaty of Lancaster, but, the Commissioners taking aside Montour, the interpreter, who was a son of the famous Catharine Montour, and a chief among the six nations, induced him to use his influence in their favor   This he did, and upon the 13th of June they all united in signing a deed, confirming the Lancaster treaty in its full extent, consenting to a settlement of the southeast of the Ohio, and guaranteeing that it should not be disturbed by them.   These were the means used to obtain the first treaty with the Indians in the Ohio Valley.

Meanwhile the powers beyond the sea were trying to out-manœuvre each other, and were professing to be at peace.   The English generally outwitted the Indians, and failed in many instances to fulfill their contracts.   They thereby gained the ill-will of the red men, and further increased the feeling by failing to provide them with arms and ammunition   Said an old chief, at Easton, in 1758: " The Indians on the Ohio left you because of your own fault   When we heard the French were coming, we asked you for help and arms, but we did not get them   The French came, they treated us kindly, and gained our affections   The Governor of Virginia settled on our lands for his own benefit, and, when we wanted help, forsook us."

At the beginning of 1653, the English thought they had secured by title the lands in the West, but the French had quietly gathered cannon and military stores to be in readiness for the expected blow.   The English made other attempts to ratify these existing treaties, but not until the Summer could the Indians be gathered together to discuss the plans of the French   They had sent messages to the French, warning them away ; but they replied that they intended to complete the chain of forts already begun and would not abandon the field.

Soon after this, no satisfaction being obtained from the Ohio regarding the positions and purposes of the French, Governor Dinwiddie of Virginia determined to send to them another messenger and learn from them, if possible, their intentions For this purpose he selected a young man, a surveyor, who, at the early age of nineteen, had received the rank of major, and who was thoroughly posted regarding frontier life. This personage was no other than the illustrious George Washington, who then held considerable interest in Western lands. He was at this time just twenty-two years of age. Taking Gist as his guide, the two, accompanied by four servitors, set out on their perilous march. They left Will's Creek on the 10th of November, 1753, and on the 22d reached the Monongahela, about ten miles above the fork. From there they went to Logstown, where Washington had a long conference with the chiefs of the Six Nations. From them he learned the condition of the French, and also heard of their determination not to come down the river till the following Spring The Indians were non-committal, as they were afraid to turn either way, and, as far as they could, desired to remain neutral. Washington, finding nothing could be done with them, went on to Venango, an old Indian town at the mouth of French Creek Here the French had a fort, called Fort Machault. Through the rum and flattery of the French, he nearly lost all his Indian followers. Finding nothing of importance here, he pursued his way amid great privations, and on the 11th of December reached the fort at the head of French Creek Here he delivered Governor Dinwiddie's letter, received his answer, took his observations, and on the 16th set out upon his return journey with no one but Gist, his guide, and a few Indians who still remained true to him, notwithstanding the endeavors of the French to retain them Their homeward journey was one of great peril and suffering from the cold, yet they reached home in safety on the 6th of January, 1754

From the letter of St. Pierre, commander of the French fort, sent by Washington to Governor Dinwiddie, it was learned that the French would not give up without a struggle. Active preparations were at once made in all the English colonies for the coming conflict, while the French finished the fort at Venango and strengthened their lines of fortifications, and gathered their forces to be in readiness

The Old Dominion was all alive. Virginia was the center of great activities, volunteers were called for, and from all the neighboring colonies men rallied to the conflict and everywhere along the Potomac men were enlisting under the Governor's proclamation—which promised two hundred thousand acres on the Ohio. Along this river they were gathering as far as Will's Creek, and far beyond this point, whither Trent had come for assistance for his little band of forty-one men, who were working away in hunger and want, to fortify that point at the fork of the Ohio, to which both parties were looking with deep interest.

"The first birds of Spring filled the air with their song; the swift river rolled by the Allegheny hillsides, swollen by the melting snows of Spring and the April showers. The leaves were appearing; a few Indian scouts were seen, but no enemy seemed near at hand; and all was so quiet, that Frazier, an old Indian scout and trader, who had been left by Trent in command ventured to his home at the mouth of Turtle Creek, ten miles up the Monongahela. But, though all was so quiet in that wilderness keen eyes had seen the low intrenchment rising at the fork, and swift feet had borne the news of it up the river; and upon the morning of the 17th of April, Ensign Ward, who then had charge of it, saw upon the Allegheny a sight that made his heart sink—sixty batteaux and three hundred canoes filled with men and laden deep with cannon and stores. * * * That evening he supped with his captor, Contrecœur, and the next day he was bowed off by the Frenchman, and with his men and tools, marched up the Monongahela.'

The French and Indian war had begun. The treaty of Aix la Chapelle, in 1748, had left the boundaries between the French and English possessions unsettled, and the events already narrated show the French were determined to hold the country watered by the Mississippi and its tributaries, while the English laid claims to the country by virtue of the discoveries of the Cabots, and claimed all the country from Newfoundland to Florida, extending from the Atlantic to the Pacific. The first decisive blow had now been struck, and the first attempt of the English, through the Ohio Company, to occupy these lands, had resulted disastrously to them. The French and Indians immediately completed the fortifications begun at the Fork, which they had so easily captured, and when completed gave to the fort the name of DuQuesne. Washington was at Will's Creek when the news of the capture of the fort arrived. He at once departed to recapture it. On his way he entrenched himself at a place called the "Meadows," where he erected a fort called by him Fort Necessity. From there he surprised and captured a force of French and Indians marching against him, but was soon after attacked in his fort by a much superior force, and was obliged to yield on the morning of July 4th. He was allowed to return to Virginia.

The English Government immediately planned four campaigns; one against Fort DuQuesne, one against Nova Scotia; one against Fort Niagara, and one against Crown Point. These occurred during 1755-6, and were not successful in driving the French from their possessions. The expedition against Fort DuQuesne was led by the famous General Braddock, who, refusing to listen to the advice of Washington and those acquainted with Indian warfare, suffered such an inglorious defeat. This occurred on the morning of July 9th, and is generally known as the battle of Monongahela, or "Braddock's Defeat." The war continued with various vicissitudes through the years 1756–7; when, at the commencement of 1758, in accordance with the plans of William Pitt, then Secretary of State, afterwards Lord Chatham, active preparations were made to carry on the war. Three expeditions were planned for this year: one, under General Amherst, against Louisburg; another, under Abercrombie, against Fort Ticonderoga; and a third, under General Forbes, against Fort DuQuesne. On the 26th of July, Louisburg surrendered after a desperate resistance of more than forty days, and the eastern part of the Canadian possessions fell into the hands of the British. Abercrombie captured Fort Frontenac, and when the expedition against Fort DuQuesne, of which Washington had the active command, arrived there, it was found in flames and deserted. The English at once took possession, rebuilt the fort, and in honor of their illustrious statesman, changed the name to Fort Pitt.

The great object of the campaign of 1759, was the reduction of Canada. General Wolfe was to lay siege to Quebec; Amherst was to reduce Ticonderoga and Crown Point, and General Prideaux was to capture Niagara. This latter place was taken in July, but the gallant Prideaux lost his life in the attempt. Amherst captured Ticonderoga and Crown Point without a blow, and Wolfe, after making the memorable ascent to the Plains of Abraham, on September 13th, defeated Montcalm, and on the 18th, the city capitulated. In this engagement Montcolm and Wolfe both lost their lives. De Levi, Montcalm's successor, marched to Sillery, three miles above the city, with the purpose of defeating the English, and there, on the 28th of the following April, was fought one of the bloodiest battles of the French and Indian War. It resulted in the defeat of the French, and the fall of the City of Montreal. The Governor signed a capitulation by which the whole of Canada was surrendered to the English. This practically concluded the war, but it was not until 1763 that the treaties of peace between France and England were signed. This was done on the 10th of February of that year, and under its provisions all the country east of the Mississippi and north of the Iberville River, in Louisiana, were ceded to England. At the same time Spain ceded Florida to Great Britain.

On the 13th of September, 1760, Major Robert Rogers was sent from Montreal to take charge of Detroit, the only remaining French post in the territory. He arrived there on the 19th of November, and summoned the place to surrender. At first the commander of the post, Beletre, refused, but on the 29th, hearing of the continued defeat of the

French arms, surrendered. Rogers remained there until December 23d under the personal protection of the celebrated chief, Pontiac, to whom, no doubt, he owed his safety. Pontiac had come here to inquire the purposes of the English in taking possession of the country. He was assured that they came simply to trade with the natives, and did not desire their country. This answer conciliated the savages, and did much to insure the safety of Rogers and his party during their stay, and while on their journey home.

Rogers set out for Fort Pitt on December 23, and was just one month on the way. His route was from Detroit to Maumee, thence across the present State of Ohio directly to the fort. This was the common trail of the Indians in their journeys from Sandusky to the fork of the Ohio. It went from Fort Sandusky, where Sandusky City now is, crossed the Huron river, then called Bald Eagle Creek, to "Mohickon John's Town" on Mohickon Creek, the northern branch of White Woman's River, and thence crossed to Beaver's Town, a Delaware town on what is now Sandy Creek. At Beaver's Town were probably one hundred and fifty warriors, and not less than three thousand acres of cleared land. From there the track went up Sandy Creek to and across Big Beaver, and up the Ohio to Logstown, thence on to the fork.

The Northwest Territory was now entirely under the English rule. New settlements began to be rapidly made, and the promise of a large trade was speedily manifested. Had the British carried out their promises with the natives none of those savage butcheries would have been perpetrated, and the country would have been spared their recital.

The renowned chief, Pontiac, was one of the leading spirits in these atrocities. We will now pause in our narrative, and notice the leading events in his life. The earliest authentic information regarding this noted Indian chief is learned from an account of an Indian trader named Alexander Henry, who, in the Spring of 1761, penetrated his domains as far as Missillimacnac. Pontiac was then a great friend of the French, but a bitter foe of the English, whom he considered as encroaching on his hunting grounds. Henry was obliged to disguise himself as a Canadian to insure safety, but was discovered by Pontiac, who bitterly reproached him and the English for their attempted subjugation of the West. He declared that no treaty had been made with them, no presents sent them, and that he would resent any possession of the West by that nation. He was at the time about fifty years of age, tall and dignified, and was civil and military ruler of the Ottawas, Ojibwas and Pottawatamies.

The Indians, from Lake Michigan to the borders of North Carolina, were united in this feeling, and at the time of the treaty of Paris, ratified February 10, 1763, a general conspiracy was formed to fall suddenly

PONTIAC, THE OTTAWA CHIEFTAIN.

upon the frontier British posts, and with one blow strike every man dead. Pontiac was the marked leader in all this, and was the commander of the Chippewas, Ottawas, Wyandots, Miamis, Shawanese, Delawares and Mingoes, who had, for the time, laid aside their local quarrels to unite in this enterprise.

The blow came, as near as can now be ascertained, on May 7, 1763. Nine British posts fell and the Indians drank, "scooped up in the hollow of joined hands," the blood of many a Briton

Pontiac's immediate field of action was the garrison at Detroit. Here, however, the plans were frustrated by an Indian woman disclosing the plot the evening previous to his arrival. Everything was carried out, however, according to Pontiac's plans until the moment of action, when Major Gladwyn, the commander of the post, stepping to one of the Indian chiefs, suddenly drew aside his blanket and disclosed the concealed musket Pontiac, though a brave man, turned pale and trembled He saw his plan was known, and that the garrison were prepared. He endeavored to exculpate himself from any such intentions, but the guilt was evident, and he and his followers were dismissed with a severe reprimand, and warned never to again enter the walls of the post.

Pontiac at once laid siege to the fort, and until the treaty of peace between the British and the Western Indians, concluded in August, 1764, continued to harass and besiege the fortress He organized a regular commissariat department, issued bills of credit written out on bark, which, to his credit, it may be stated, were punctually redeemed. At the conclusion of the treaty, in which it seems he took no part, he went further south, living many years among the Illinois.

He had given up all hope of saving his country and race. After a time he endeavored to unite the Illinois tribe and those about St Louis in a war with the whites. His efforts were fruitless, and only ended in a quarrel between himself and some Kaskaskia Indians, one of whom soon afterwards killed him His death was, however, avenged by the northern Indians, who nearly exterminated the Illinois in the wars which followed.

Had it not been for the treachery of a few of his followers, his plan for the extermination of the whites, a masterly one, would undoubtedly have been carried out

It was in the Spring of the year following Rogers' visit that Alexander Henry went to Missillimacnac, and everywhere found the strongest feelings against the English, who had not carried out their promises, and were doing nothing to conciliate the natives Here he met the chief, Pontiac, who, after conveying to him in a speech the idea that their French father would awake soon and utterly destroy his enemies, said: "Englishman, although you have conquered the French, you have not yet conquered us! We are not your slaves! These lakes, these woods, these mountains, were left us by our ancestors. They are our inheritance, and we will part with them to none. Your nation supposes that we, like the white people, can not live without bread and pork and beef. But you ought to know that He, the Great Spirit and Master of Life, has provided food for us upon these broad lakes and in these mountains. '

He then spoke of the fact that no treaty had been made with them, no presents sent them, and that he and his people were yet for war. Such were the feelings of the Northwestern Indians immediately after the English took possession of their country. These feelings were no doubt encouraged by the Canadians and French, who hoped that yet the French arms might prevail. The treaty of Paris, however, gave to the English the right to this vast domain, and active preparations were going on to occupy it and enjoy its trade and emoluments.

In 1762, France, by a secret treaty, ceded Louisiana to Spain, to prevent it falling into the hands of the English, who were becoming masters of the entire West. The next year the treaty of Paris, signed at Fontainbleau, gave to the English the domain of the country in question. Twenty years after, by the treaty of peace between the United States and England, that part of Canada lying south and west of the Great Lakes, comprehending a large territory which is the subject of these sketches, was acknowledged to be a portion of the United States, and twenty years still later, in 1803, Louisiana was ceded by Spain back to France, and by France sold to the United States.

In the half century, from the building of the Fort of Crevecœur by LaSalle, in 1680, up to the erection of Fort Chartres, many French settlements had been made in that quarter. These have already been noticed, being those at St Vincent (Vincennes), Kohokia or Cahokia, Kaskaskia and Prairie du Rocher, on the American Bottom, a large tract of rich alluvial soil in Illinois, on the Mississippi, opposite the site of St. Louis.

By the treaty of Paris, the regions east of the Mississippi, including all these and other towns of the Northwest, were given over to England; but they do not appear to have been taken possession of until 1765, when Captain Stirling, in the name of the Majesty of England, established himself at Fort Chartres bearing with him the proclamation of General Gage, dated December 30, 1764, which promised religious freedom to all Catholics who worshiped here, and a right to leave the country with their effects if they wished, or to remain with the privileges of Englishmen. It was shortly after the occupancy of the West by the British that the war with Pontiac opened. It is already noticed in the sketch of that chieftain. By it many a Briton lost his life, and many a frontier settle-

ment in its infancy ceased to exist.   This was not ended until the year
1764, when, failing to capture Detroit, Niagara and Fort Pitt, his confederacy became disheartened, and, receiving no aid from the French, Pontiac abandoned the enterprise and departed to the Illinois, among whom
he afterward lost his life

As soon as these difficulties were definitely settled, settlers began
rapidly to survey the country and prepare for occupation.   During the
year 1770, a number of persons from Virginia and other British provinces
explored and marked out nearly all the valuable lands on the Monongahela and along the banks of the Ohio as far as the Little Kanawha.   This
was followed by another exploring expedition, in which George Washington was a party.   The latter, accompanied by Dr Craik, Capt. Crawford
and others, on the 20th of October, 1770, descended the Ohio from Pittsburgh to the mouth of the Kanawha; ascended that stream about fourteen
miles, marked out several large tracts of land, shot several buffalo, which
were then abundant in the Ohio Valley, and returned to the fort

Pittsburgh was at this time a trading post, about which was clustered a village of some twenty houses, inhabited by Indian traders   This
same year, Capt. Pittman visited Kaskaskia and its neighboring villages.
He found there about sixty-five resident families, and at Cahokia only
forty-five dwellings   At Fort Chartres was another small settlement, and
at Detroit the garrison were quite prosperous and strong.   For a year
or two settlers continued to locate near some of these posts, generally
Fort Pitt or Detroit, owing to the fears of the Indians, who still maintained some feelings of hatred to the English   The trade from the posts
was quite good, and from those in Illinois large quantities of pork and
flour found their way to the New Orleans market   At this time the
policy of the British Government was strongly opposed to the extension
of the colonies west   In 1763, the King of England forbade, by royal
proclamation, his colonial subjects from making a settlement beyond the
sources of the rivers which fall into the Atlantic Ocean.   At the instance
of the Board of Trade, measures were taken to prevent the settlement
without the limits prescribed, and to retain the commerce within easy
reach of Great Britain

The commander-in-chief of the king's forces wrote in 1769 ·   "In the
course of a few years necessity will compel the colonists, should they
extend their settlements west, to provide manufactures of some kind for
themselves, and when all connection upheld by commerce with the mother
country ceases, an *independency* in their government will soon follow "

In accordance with this policy, Gov. Gage issued a proclamation
in 1772 commanding the inhabitants of Vincennes to abandon their settlements and join some of the Eastern English colonies.   To this they

strenuously objected, giving good reasons therefor, and were allowed to remain. The strong opposition to this policy of Great Britain led to its change, and to such a course as to gain the attachment of the French population. In December, 1773, influential citizens of Quebec petitioned the king for an extension of the boundary lines of that province, which was granted, and Parliament passed an act on June 2, 1774, extending the boundary so as to include the territory lying within the present States of Ohio, Indiana, Illinois and Michigan

In consequence of the liberal policy pursued by the British Government toward the French settlers in the West, they were disposed to favor that nation in the war which soon followed with the colonies; but the early alliance between France and America soon brought them to the side of the war for independence.

In 1774, Gov. Dunmore, of Virginia, began to encourage emigration to the Western lands. He appointed magistrates at Fort Pitt under the pretense that the fort was under the government of that commonwealth. One of these justices, John Connelly, who possessed a tract of land in the Ohio Valley, gathered a force of men and garrisoned the fort, calling it Fort Dunmore. This and other parties were formed to select sites for settlements, and often came in conflict with the Indians, who yet claimed portions of the valley, and several battles followed. These ended in the famous battle of Kanawha in July, where the Indians were defeated and driven across the Ohio.

During the years 1775 and 1776, by the operations of land companies and the perseverance of individuals, several settlements were firmly established between the Alleghanies and the Ohio River, and western land speculators were busy in Illinois and on the Wabash. At a council held in Kaskaskia on July 5, 1773, an association of English traders, calling themselves the "Illinois Land Company," obtained from ten chiefs of the Kaskaskia, Cahokia and Peoria tribes two large tracts of land lying on the east side of the Mississippi River south of the Illinois In 1775, a merchant from the Illinois Country, named Viviat, came to Post Vincennes as the agent of the association called the "Wabash Land Company." On the 8th of October he obtained from eleven Piankeshaw chiefs, a deed for 37,497,600 acres of land This deed was signed by the grantors, attested by a number of the inhabitants of Vincennes, and afterward recorded in the office of a notary public at Kaskaskia. This and other land companies had extensive schemes for the colonization of the West; but all were frustrated by the breaking out of the Revolution. On the 20th of April, 1780, the two companies named consolidated under the name of the "United Illinois and Wabash Land Company." They afterward made strenuous efforts to have these grants sanctioned by Congress, but all signally failed

When the War of the Revolution commenced, Kentucky was an unorganized country, though there were several settlements within her borders.

In Hutchins' Topography of Virginia, it is stated that at that time "Kaskaskia contained 80 houses, and nearly 1,000 white and black inhabitants — the whites being a little the more numerous. Cahokia contains 50 houses and 300 white inhabitants, and 80 negroes. There were east of the Mississippi River, about the year 1771"—when these observations were made — "300 white men capable of bearing arms, and 230 negroes."

From 1775 until the expedition of Clark, nothing is recorded and nothing known of these settlements, save what is contained in a report made by a committee to Congress in June, 1778. From it the following extract is made

"Near the mouth of the River Kaskaskia, there is a village which appears to have contained nearly eighty families from the beginning of the late revolution. There are twelve families in a small village at la Prairie du Rochers, and near fifty families at the Kahokia Village. There are also four or five families at Fort Chartres and St. Philips, which is five miles further up the river"

St. Louis had been settled in February, 1764, and at this time contained, including its neighboring towns, over six hundred whites and one hundred and fifty negroes. It must be remembered that all the country west of the Mississippi was now under French rule, and remained so until ceded again to Spain, its original owner, who afterwards sold it and the country including New Orleans to the United States. At Detroit there were, according to Capt. Carver, who was in the Northwest from 1766 to 1768, more than one hundred houses, and the river was settled for more than twenty miles, although poorly cultivated—the people being engaged in the Indian trade. This old town has a history, which we will here relate

It is the oldest town in the Northwest, having been founded by Antoine de Lamotte Cadillac, in 1701. It was laid out in the form of an oblong square, of two acres in length, and an acre and a half in width. As described by A. D. Frazer, who first visited it and became a permanent resident of the place, in 1778, it comprised within its limits that space between Mr. Palmer's store (Conant Block) and Capt. Perkins' house (near the Arsenal building), and extended back as far as the public barn, and was bordered in front by the Detroit River. It was surrounded by oak an̲ in the ground, and had four ga   —   ̲ ̲ Over the first three of these gates were block houses provided with four guns apiece, each a six-pounder Two six-gun batteries were planted fronting the river and in a parallel direction with the block houses. There were four streets running east and west, the main street being twenty feet wide and the rest fifteen feet, while the four streets crossing these at right angles were from ten to fifteen feet in width

At the date spoken of by Mr. Frazer, there was no fort within the enclosure, but a citadel on the ground corresponding to the present northwest corner of Jefferson Avenue and Wayne Street. The citadel was inclosed by pickets, and within it were erected barracks of wood, two stories high, sufficient to contain ten officers, and also barracks sufficient to contain four hundred men, and a provision store built of brick The citadel also contained a hospital and guard-house. The old town of Detroit, in 1778, contained about sixty houses, most of them one story, with a few a story and a half in height. They were all of logs, some hewn and some round. There was one building of splendid appearance, called the "King's Palace," two stories high, which stood near the east gate. It was built for Governor Hamilton, the first governor commissioned by the British. There were two guard-houses, one near the west gate and the other near the Government House. Each of the guards consisted of twenty-four men and a subaltern, who mounted regularly every morning between nine and ten o'clock, Each furnished four sentinels, who were relieved every two hours. There was also an officer of the day, who performed strict duty. Each of the gates was shut regularly at sunset; even wicket gates were shut at nine o'clock, and all the keys were delivered into the hands of the commanding officer They were opened in the morning at sunrise No Indian or squaw was permitted to enter town with any weapon, such as a tomahawk or a knife It was a standing order that the Indians should deliver their arms and instruments of every kind before they were permitted to pass the sentinel, and they were restored to them on their return. No more than twenty-five Indians were allowed to enter the town at any one time, and they were admitted only at the east and west gates. At sundown the drums beat, and all the Indians were required to leave town instantly There was a council house near the water side for the purpose of holding council with the Indians. The population of the town was about sixty families, in all about two hundred males and one hundred females This town was destroyed by fire, all except one dwelling, in 1805. After which the present "new" town was laid out.

On the breaking out of the Revolution, the British held every post of importance in the West. Kentucky was formed as a component part of Virginia, and the sturdy pioneers of the West, alive to their interests, and recognizing the great benefits of obtaining the control of the trade in this part of the New World, held steadily to their purposes, and those within the commonwealth of Kentucky proceeded to exercise their civil privileges, by electing John Todd and Richard Gallaway, burgesses to represent them in the Assembly of the parent state Early in September of that year (1777) the first court was held in Harrodsburg, and Col. Bowman, afterwards major, who had arrived in August, was made the commander of a militia organization which had been commenced the March previous. Thus the tree of loyalty was growing. The chief spirit in this far-out colony, who had represented her the year previous east of the mountains, was now meditating a move unequaled in its boldness. He had been watching the movements of the British throughout the Northwest, and understood their whole plan. He saw it was through their possession of the posts at Detroit, Vincennes, Kaskaskia, and other places, which would give them constant and easy access to the various Indian tribes in the Northwest, that the British intended to penetrate the country from the north and south, and annihilate the frontier fortresses. This moving, energetic man was Colonel, afterwards General, George Rogers Clark. He knew the Indians were not unanimously in accord with the English, and he was convinced that, could the British be defeated and expelled from the Northwest, the natives might be easily awed into neutrality, and by spies sent for the purpose, he satisfied himself that the enterprise against the Illinois settlements might easily succeed. Having convinced himself of the certainty of the project, he repaired to the Capital of Virginia, which place he reached on November 5th. While he was on his way, fortunately, on October 17th. Burgoyne had been defeated, and the spirits of the colonists greatly encouraged thereby. Patrick Henry was Governor of Virginia, and at once entered heartily into Clark's plans. The same plan had before been agitated in the Colonial Assemblies, but there was no one until Clark came who was sufficiently acquainted with the condition of affairs at the scene of action to be able to guide them.

Clark, having satisfied the Virginia leaders of the feasibility of his plan, received, on the 2d of January, two sets of instructions—one secret, the other open—the latter authorized him to proceed to enlist seven companies to go to Kentucky, subject to his orders, and to serve three months from their arrival in the West. The secret order authorized him to arm these troops, to procure his powder and lead of General Hand at Pittsburgh, and to proceed at once to subjugate the country.

With these instructions Clark repaired to Pittsburgh, choosing rather to raise his men west of the mountains, as he well knew all were needed in the colonies in the [...] there. He sent Col. W. B. Smith to Holston for the same purpose, but neither succeeded in raising the required number of men. The settlers in these parts were afraid to leave their own firesides exposed to a vigilant foe, and but few could be induced to join the proposed expedition. With three companies and several private volunteers, Clark at length commenced his descent of the Ohio, which he navigated as far as the Falls, where he took possession of and fortified Corn Island, a small island between the present Cities of Louisville, Kentucky, and New Albany, Indiana. Remains of this fortification may yet be found. At this place he appointed Col. Bowman to meet him with such recruits as had 'reached Kentucky by the southern route, and as many as could be spared from the station. Here he announced to the men their real destination. Having completed his arrangements, and chosen his party, he left a small garrison upon the island, and on the 24th of June, during a total eclipse of the sun, which to them augured no good, and which fixes beyond dispute the date of starting, he with his chosen band, fell down the river. His plan was to go by water as far as Fort Massac or Massacie, and thence march direct to Kaskaskia. Here he intended to surprise the garrison, and after its capture go to Cahokia, then to Vincennes, and lastly to Detroit. Should he fail, he intended to march directly to the Mississippi River and cross it into the Spanish country. Before his start he received two good items of information : one that the alliance had been formed between France and the United States : and the other that the Indians throughout the Illinois country and the inhabitants, at the various frontier posts, had been led to believe by the British that the " Long Knives ' or Virginians, were the most fierce, bloodthirsty and cruel savages that ever scalped a foe. With this impression on their minds, Clark saw that proper management would cause them to submit at once from fear, if surprised, and then from gratitude would become friendly if treated with unexpected lemency.

The march to Kaskaskia was accomplished through a hot July sun, and the town reached on the evening of July 4. He captured the fort near the village, and soon after the village itself by surprise, and without the loss of a single man or by killing any of the enemy. After sufficiently working upon the fears of the natives, Clark told them they were at perfect liberty to worship as they pleased, and to take whichever side of the great conflict they would, also he would protect them from any barbarity from British or Indian foe. This had the desired effect, and the inhabitants, so unexpectedly and so gratefully surprised by the unlooked for turn of affairs, at once swore allegiance to the American arms, and when Clark desired to go to Cahokia on the 6th of July, they accompanied him, and through their influence the inhabitants of the place surrendered, and gladly placed themselves under his protection. Thus the two important posts in Illinois passed from the hands of the English into the possession of Virginia

In the person of the priest at Kaskaskia, M Gibault, Clark found a powerful ally and generous friend. Clark saw that, to retain possession of the Northwest and treat successfully with the Indians within its boundaries, he must establish a government for the colonies he had taken. St Vincent. the next important post to Detroit, remained yet to be taken before the Mississippi Valley was conquered. M Gibault told him that he would alone, by persuasion, lead Vincennes to throw off its connection with England Clark gladly accepted his offer, and on the 14th of July, in company with a fellow-townsman, M Gibault started on his mission of peace, and on the 1st of August returned with the cheerful intelligence that the post on the "Oubache" had taken the oath of allegiance to the Old Dominion. During this interval, Clark established his courts, placed garrisons at Kaskaskia and Cahokia, successfully re-enlisted his men, sent word to have a fort, which proved the germ of Louisville, erected at the Falls of the Ohio, and dispatched Mr Rocheblave, who had been commander at Kaskaskia, as a prisoner of war to Richmond. In October the County of Illinois was established by the Legislature of Virginia, John Todd appointed Lieutenant Colonel and Civil Governor, and in November General Clark and his men received the thanks of the Old Dominion through their Legislature.

In a speech a few days afterward, Clark made known fully to the natives his plans, and at its close all came forward and swore allegiance to the Long Knives. While he was doing this Governor Hamilton, having made his various arrangements, had left Detroit and moved down the Wabash to Vincennes intending to operate from that point in reducing the Illinois posts and then proceed on down to Kentucky and drive the rebels from the West Gen. Clark had, on the return of M. Gibault, dispatched Captain Helm, of Fauquier County, Virginia, with an attendant named Henry. across the Illinois prairies to command the fort. Hamilton knew nothing of the capitulation of the post. and was greatly surprised on his arrival to be confronted by Capt Helm, who, standing at the entrance of the fort by a loaded cannon ready to fire upon his assailants, demanded upon what terms Hamilton demanded possession of the fort Being granted the rights of a prisoner of war, he surrendered to the British General who could scarcely believe his eyes when he saw the force in the garrison

Hamilton, not realizing the character of the men with whom he was contending, gave up his intended campaign for the Winter, sent his four hundred Indian warriors to prevent troops from coming down the Ohio.

and to annoy the Americans in all ways, and sat quietly down to pass the Winter. Information of all these proceedings having reached Clark, he saw that immediate and decisive action was necessary, and that unless he captured Hamilton, Hamilton would capture him. Clark received the news on the 29th of January, 1779, and on February 4th, having sufficiently garrisoned Kaskaskia and Cahokia, he sent down the Mississippi a " battoe," as Major Bowman writes it, in order to ascend the Ohio and Wabash, and operate with the land forces gathering for the fray

On the next day, Clark, with his little force of one hundred and twenty men, set out for the post, and after incredible hard marching through much mud, the ground being thawed by the incessant spring rains, on the 22d reached the fort, and being joined by his " battoe," at once commenced the attack on the post. The aim of the American backwoodsman was unerring, and on the 24th the garrison surrendered to the intrepid boldness of Clark. The French were treated with great kindness, and gladly renewed their allegiance to Virginia Hamilton was sent as a prisoner to Virginia, where he was kept in close confinement. During his command of the British frontier posts, he had offered prizes to the Indians for all the scalps of Americans they would bring to him, and had earned in consequence thereof the title " Hair-buyer General,' by which he was ever afterward known

Detroit was now without doubt within easy reach of the enterprising Virginian, could he but raise the necessary force. Governor Henry being apprised of this, promised him the needed reinforcement, and Clark concluded to wait until he could capture and sufficiently garrison the posts. Had Clark failed in this bold undertaking, and Hamilton succeeded in uniting the western Indians for the next Spring's campaign, the West would indeed have been swept from the Mississippi to the Allegheny Mountains, and the great blow struck, which had been contemplated from the commencement by the British

" But for this small army of dripping, but fearless Virginians, the union of all the tribes from Georgia to Maine against the colonies might have been effected, and the whole current of our history changed "

At this time some fears were entertained by the Colonial Governments that the Indians in the North and Northwest were inclining to the British, and under the instructions of Washington, now Commander-in-Chief of the Colonial army, and so bravely fighting for American independence, armed forces were sent against the Six Nations, and upon the Ohio frontier, Col Bowman, acting under the same general's orders, marched against Indians within the present limits of that State These expeditions were in the main successful, and the Indians were compelled to sue for peace.

During this same year (1779) the famous "Land Laws" of Virginia were passed   The passage of these laws was of more consequence to the pioneers of Kentucky and the Northwest than the gaining of a few Indian conflicts   These laws confirmed in main all grants made, and guaranteed to all actual settlers their rights and privileges.   After providing for the settlers, the laws provided for selling the balance of the public lands at forty cents per acre.   To carry the Land Laws into effect, the Legislature sent four Virginians westward to attend to the various claims, over many of which great confusion prevailed concerning their validity.   These gentlemen opened their court on October 13, 1779, at St Asaphs, and continued until April 26, 1780, when they adjourned, having decided three thousand claims.   They were succeeded by the surveyor, who came in the person of Mr. George May, and assumed his duties on the 10th day of the month whose name he bore   With the opening of the next year (1780) the troubles concerning the navigation of the Mississippi commenced.   The Spanish Government exacted such measures in relation to its trade as to cause the overtures made to the United States to be rejected.   The American Government considered they had a right to navigate its channel   To enforce their claims, a fort was erected below the mouth of the Ohio on the Kentucky side of the river   The settlements in Kentucky were being rapidly filled by emigrants   It was during this year that the first seminary of learning was established in the West in this young and enterprising Commonwealth.

The settlers here did not look upon the building of this fort in a friendly manner, as it aroused the hostility of the Indians.   Spain had been friendly to the Colonies during their struggle for independence, and though for a while this friendship appeared in danger from the refusal of the free navigation of the river, yet it was finally settled to the satisfaction of both nations.

The Winter of 1779–80 was one of the most unusually severe ones ever experienced in the West   The Indians always referred to it as the " Great Cold "   Numbers of wild animals perished, and not a few pioneers lost their lives   The following Summer a party of Canadians and Indians attacked St. Louis, and attempted to take possession of it in consequence of the friendly disposition of Spain to the revolting colonies   They met with such a determined resistance on the part of the inhabitants, even the women taking part in the battle, that they were compelled to abandon the contest   They also made an attack on the settlements in Kentucky, but, becoming alarmed in some unaccountable manner, they fled the country in great haste.

About this time arose the question in the Colonial Congress concerning the western . . . . Virginia, New York, Massachusetts and Connecticut. The agitation concerning this subject finally led New York, on the 19th of February, 1780, to pass a law giving to the delegates of that State in Congress the power to cede her western lands for the benefit of the United States. This law was laid before Congress during the next month, but no steps were taken concerning it until September 6th, when a resolution passed that body calling upon the States claiming western lands to release their claims in favor of the whole body. This basis formed the union, and was the first after all of those legislative measures which resulted in the creation of the States of Ohio, Indiana, Illinois, Michigan, Wisconsin and Minnesota. In December of the same year, the plan of conquering Detroit again arose. The conquest might have easily been effected by Clark had the necessary aid been furnished him. Nothing decisive was done, yet the heads of the Government knew that the safety of the Northwest from British invasion lay in the capture and retention of that important post, the only unconquered one in the territory.

Before the close of the year, Kentucky was divided into the Counties of Lincoln, Fayette and Jefferson, and the act establishing the Town of Louisville was passed This same year is also noted in the annals of American history as the year in which occurred Arnold's treason to the United States

Virginia, in accordance with the resolution of Congress, on the 2d day of January, 1781, agreed to yield her western lands to the United States upon certain conditions, which Congress would not accede to, and the Act of Cession, on the part of the Old Dominion, failed, nor was anything farther done until 1783. During all that time the Colonies were busily engaged in the struggle with the mother country, and in consequence thereof but little heed was given to the western settlements. Upon the 16th of April, 1781, the first birth north of the Ohio River of American parentage occurred. being that of Mary Heckewelder, daughter of the widely known Moravian missionary, whose band of Christian Indians suffered in after years a horrible massacre by the hands of the frontier settlers, who had been exasperated by the murder of several of their neighbors, and in their rage committed, without regard to humanity, a deed which forever afterwards cast a shade of shame upon their lives. For this and kindred outrages on the part of the whites, the Indians committed many deeds of cruelty which darken the years of 1771 and 1772 in the history of the Northwest.

During the year 1782 a number of battles among the Indians and frontiersmen occurred, and between the Moravian Indians and the Wyandots. In these, horrible acts of cruelty were practised on the captives, many of such dark deeds transpiring under the leadership of the notorious frontier outlaw, Simon Girty, whose name, as well as those of his brothers, was a terror to women and children. These occurred chiefly in the Ohio valleys. Cotemporary with them were several engagements in Kentucky, in which the famous Daniel Boone engaged, and who, often by his skill and knowledge of Indian warfare, saved the outposts from cruel destruc-

INDIANS ATTACKING FRONTIERSMEN.

tion. By the close of the year victory had perched upon the American banner, and on the 30th of November, provisional articles of peace had been arranged between the Commissioners of England and her uncon- querable colonies. Cornwallis had been defeated on the 19th of October preceding, and the liberty of America was assured. On the 19th of April following, the anniversary of the battle of Lexington, peace was proclaimed to the army of the United States, and on the 3d of the next September, the definite treaty which ended our revolutionary struggle was concluded. By the terms of that treaty, the boundaries of the West were as follows: On the north the line was to extend along the center of the Great Lakes; from the western point of Lake Superior to Long Lake, thence to the Lake of the Woods, thence to the head of the Mississippi River; down its center to the 31st parallel of latitude, then on that line east to the head of the Appalachicola River, down its center to its junction with the Flint; thence straight to the head of St. Mary's River, and thence down along its center to the Atlantic Ocean.

Following the cessation of hostilities with England, several posts were still occupied by the British in the North and West. Among these was Detroit, still in the hands of the enemy. Numerous engagements with the Indians throughout Ohio and Indiana occurred, upon whose lands adventurous whites would settle ere the title had been acquired by the proper treaty.

To remedy this latter evil, Congress appointed commissioners to treat with the natives and purchase their lands, and prohibited the settlement of the territory until this could be done. Before the close of the year another attempt was made to capture Detroit, which was, however, not pushed, and Virginia, no longer feeling the interest in the Northwest she had formerly done, withdrew her troops, having on the 20th of December preceding authorized the whole of her possessions to be deeded to the United States. This was done on the 1st of March following, and the Northwest Territory passed from the control of the Old Dominion. To Gen. Clark and his soldiers, however, she gave a tract of one hundred and fifty thousand acres of land, to be situated any where north of the Ohio wherever they chose to locate them. They selected the region opposite the falls of the Ohio, where is now the dilapidated village of Clarksville, about midway between the Cities of New Albany and Jeffersonville, Indiana.

While the frontier remained thus, and Gen. Haldimand at Detroit refused to evacuate alleging that he had no orders from his King to do so, settlers were rapidly gathering about the inland forts. In the Spring of 1784, Pittsburgh was regularly laid out, and from the journal of Arthur Lee, who passed through the town soon after on his way to the Indian council at Fort McIntosh, we suppose it was not very prepossessing in appearance. He says:

"Pittsburgh is inhabited almost entirely by Scots and Irish, who live in paltry log houses, and are as dirty as if in the north of Ireland or even Scotland. There is a great deal of trade carried on, the goods being bought at the vast expense of forty-five shillings per pound from Philadelphia and Baltimore. They take in the shops flour, wheat, skins and money There are in the town four attorneys, two doctors, and not a priest of any persuasion, nor church nor chapel "

Kentucky at this time contained thirty thousand inhabitants, and was beginning to discuss measures for a separation from Virginia. A land office was opened at Louisville, and measures were adopted to take defensive precaution against the Indians who were yet, in some instances, incited to deeds of violence by the British Before the close of this year, 1784, the military claimants of land began to occupy them, although no entries were recorded until 1787.

The Indian title to the Northwest was not yet extinguished. They held large tracts of lands, and in order to prevent bloodshed Congress adopted means for treaties with the original owners and provided for the surveys of the lands gained thereby, as well as for those north of the Ohio, now in its possession On January 31, 1786, a treaty was made with the Wabash Indians. The treaty of Fort Stanwix had been made in 1784. That at Fort McIntosh in 1785, and through these much land was gained The Wabash Indians, however, afterward refused to comply with the provisions of the treaty made with them, and in order to compel their adherence to its provisions, force was used. During the year 1786, the free navigation of the Mississippi came up in Congress, and caused various discussions, which resulted in no definite action, only serving to excite speculation in regard to the western lands. Congress had promised bounties of land to the soldiers of the Revolution, but owing to the unsettled condition of affairs along the Mississippi respecting its navigation, and the trade of the Northwest, that body had, in 1783, declared its inability to fulfill these promises until a treaty could be concluded between the two Governments. Before the close of the year 1786, however, it was able, through the treaties with the Indians, to allow some grants and the settlement thereon, and on the 14th of September Connecticut ceded to the General Government the tract of land known as the " Connecticut Reserve," and before the close of the following year a large tract of land north of the Ohio was sold to a company, who at once took measures to settle it. By the provisions of this grant, the company were to pay the United States one dollar per acre, subject to a deduction of one-third for bad lands and other contingencies They received 750,000 acres, bounded on the south by the Ohio, on the east by the seventh range of townships, on the west by the sixteenth range, and on the north by a line so drawn as to make the grant complete without the reservations. In addition to this, Congress afterward granted 100,000 acres to actual settlers, and 214,285 acres as army bounties under the resolutions of 1789 and 1790

While Dr. Cutler, one of the agents of the company, was pressing its claims before Congress, that body was bringing into form an ordinance for the political and social organization of this Territory. When the cession was made by Virginia, in 1784, a plan was offered, but rejected. A motion had been made to strike from the proposed plan the prohibition of slavery, which prevailed. The plan was then discussed and altered, and finally passed unanimously, with the exception of South Carolina. By this proposition, the Territory was to have been divided into states

A PRAIRIE STORM.

by parallels and meridian lines. This, it was thought, would make ten states, which were to have been named as follows — beginning at the northwest corner and going southwardly: Sylvania, Michigania, Chersonesus, Assenisipia, Metropotamia, Illenoia, Saratoga, Washington, Polypotamia and Pelisipia.

There was a more serious objection to this plan than its category of names,— the boundaries. The root of the difficulty was in the resolution of Congress passed in October, 1780, which fixed the boundaries of the ceded lands to be from one hundred to one hundred and fifty miles square. These resolutions being presented to the Legislatures of Virginia and Massachusetts, they desired a change, and in July, 1786, the subject was taken up in Congress, and changed to favor a division into not more than five states, and not less than three. This was approved by the State Legislature of Virginia. The subject of the Government was again taken up by Congress in 1786, and discussed throughout that year and until July, 1787, when the famous "Compact of 1787" was passed, and the foundation of the government of the Northwest laid. This compact is fully discussed and explained in the history of Illinois in this book, and to it the reader is referred.

The passage of this act and the grant to the New England Company was soon followed by an application to the Government by John Cleves Symmes, of New Jersey, for a grant of the land between the Miamis. This gentleman had visited these lands soon after the treaty of 1786, and, being greatly pleased with them, offered similar terms to those given to the New England Company. The petition was referred to the Treasury Board with power to act, and a contract was concluded the following year. During the Autumn the directors of the New England Company were preparing to occupy their grant the following Spring, and upon the 23d of November made arrangements for a party of forty-seven men, under the superintendency of Gen. Rufus Putnam, to set forward. Six boat-builders were to leave at once, and on the first of January the surveyors and their assistants, twenty-six in number, were to meet at Hartford and proceed on their journey westward; the remainder to follow as soon as possible. Congress, in the meantime, upon the 3d of October, had ordered seven hundred troops for defense of the western settlers, and to prevent unauthorized intrusions; and two days later appointed Arthur St. Clair Governor of the Territory of the Northwest.

AMERICAN SETTLEMENTS.

The civil organization of the Northwest Territory was now complete, and notwithstanding the uncertainty of Indian affairs, settlers from the East began to come into the country rapidly. The New England Company sent their men during the Winter of 1787–8 pressing on over the Alleghenies by the old Indian path which had been opened into Braddock's road, and which has since been made a national turnpike from Cumberland westward. Through the weary winter days they toiled on, and by April were all gathered on the Yohogany, where boats had been built, and at once started for the Muskingum. Here they arrived on the 7th of that month, and unless the Moravian missionaries be regarded as the pioneers of Ohio, these first men can justly claim that honor.

Gen. St. Clair, the appointed Governor of the Northwest, not having yet arrived, a set of laws were passed, written out, and published by being nailed to a tree in the embryo town, and Jonathan Meigs appointed to administer them.

Washington in writing of this, the first American settlement in the Northwest, said: "No colony in America was ever settled under such favorable auspices as that which has just commenced at Muskingum. Information, property and strength will be its characteristics. I know many of its settlers personally, and there never were men better calculated to promote the welfare of such a community."

A PIONEER DWELLING.

On the 2d of July a meeting of the directors and agents was held on the banks of the Muskingum, "for the purpose of naming the new-born city and its squares." As yet the settlement was known as the "Muskingum," but that was now changed to the name Marietta, in honor of Marie Antoinette. The square upon which the block-houses stood was called "*Campus Martius;*" square number 19, "*Capitolium;*" square number 61, "*Cecilia;*" and the great road through the covert way, "*Sacra Via.*" Two days after, an oration was delivered by James M. Varnum, who with S. H. Parsons and John Armstrong had been appointed to the judicial bench of the territory on the 16th of October, 1787. On July 9, Gov. St. Clair arrived, and the colony began to assume form. The act of 1787 provided two district grades of government for the Northwest, under the first of which the whole power was invested in the hands of a governor and three district judges. This was immediately formed upon the Governor's arrival, and the first laws of the colony passed on the 25th of July. These provided for the organization of the militia, and on the next day appeared the Governor's proclamation, erecting all that country that had been ceded by the Indians east of the Scioto River into the County of Washington. From that time forward, notwithstanding the doubts yet existing as to the Indians, all Marietta prospered, and on the 2d of September the first court of the territory was held with imposing ceremonies.

The emigration westward at this time was very great. The commander at Fort Harmer, at the mouth of the Muskingum, reported four thousand five hundred persons as having passed that post between February and June, 1788 — many of whom would have purchased of the "Associates," as the New England Company was called, had they been ready to receive them.

On the 26th of November, 1787, Symmes issued a pamphlet stating the terms of his contract and the plan of sale he intended to adopt. In January, 1788, Matthias Denman, of New Jersey, took an active interest in Symmes' purchase, and located among other tracts the sections upon which Cincinnati has been built. Retaining one-third of this locality, he sold the other two-thirds to Robert Patterson and John Filson, and the three, about August, commenced to lay out a town on the spot, which was designated as being opposite Licking River, to the mouth of which they proposed to have a road cut from Lexington. The naming of the town is thus narrated in the "Western Annals".—" Mr. Filson, who had been a schoolmaster, was appointed to name the town, and, in respect to its situation, and as if with a prophetic perception of the mixed race that were to inhabit it in after days. he named it Losantiville, which, being interpreted, means . *ville*. the town , *anti*, against or opposite to , *os*. the mouth . *L*. of Licking "

Meanwhile, in July, Symmes got thirty persons and eight four-horse teams under way for the West. These reached Limestone (now Maysville) in September, where were several persons from Redstone. Here Mr. Symmes tried to found a settlement, but the great freshet of 1789 caused the " Point, as it was and is yet called. to be fifteen feet under water and the settlement to be abandoned. The little band of settlers removed to the mouth of the Miami. Before Symmes and his colony left the " Point," two settlements had been made on his purchase. The first was by Mr. Stites, the original projector of the whole plan, who, with a colony of Redstone people had located at the mouth of the Miami, whither Symmes Maysville colony Here a clearing had been made by the Indians owing to the great fertility of the soil. Mr. Stiltes with his colony came to this place on the 18th of November, 1788, with twenty-six persons, and, building a block-house, prepared to remain through the Winter. They named the settlement Columbia. Here they were kindly treated by the Indians, but suffered greatly from the flood of 1789.

On the 4th of March, 1789, the Constitution of the United States went into operation, and on April 30, George Washington was inaugurated President of the American people, and during the next Summer, an Indian war was commenced by the tribes north of the Ohio. The President at first used pacific means; but these failing, he sent General Harmer against the hostile tribes. He destroyed several villages, but

BREAKING PRAIRIE.

was defeated in two battles, near the present City of Fort Wayne, Indiana. From this time till the close of 1795, the principal events were the wars with the various Indian tribes. In 1796, General St. Clair was appointed in command, and marched against the Indians; but while he was encamped on a stream, the St. Mary, a branch of the Maumee, he was attacked and defeated with the loss of six hundred men.

General Wayne was now sent against the savages. In August, 1794, he met them near the rapids of the Maumee, and gained a complete victory. This success, followed by vigorous measures, compelled the Indians to sue for peace, and on the 30th of July, the following year, the treaty of Greenville was signed by the principal chiefs, by which a large tract of country was ceded to the United States.

Before proceeding in our narrative, we will pause to notice Fort Washington, erected in the early part of this war on the site of Cincinnati. Nearly all of the great cities of the Northwest, and indeed of the whole country, have had their *nuclei* in those rude pioneer structures, known as forts or stockades.   Thus Forts Dearborn, Washington, Pontchartrain, mark the original sites of the now proud Cities of Chicago, Cincinnati and Detroit.   So of most of the flourishing cities east and west of the Mississippi.   Fort Washington, erected by Doughty in 1790, was a rude but highly interesting structure   It was composed of a number of strongly-built hewed log cabins.   Those designed for soldiers' barracks were a story and a half high, while those composing the officers quarters were more imposing and more conveniently arranged and furnished. The whole were so placed as to form a hollow square, enclosing about an acre of ground, with a block house at each of the four angles.

The logs for the construction of this fort were cut from the ground upon which it was erected.   It stood between Third and Fourth Streets of the present city (Cincinnati) extending east of Eastern Row, now Broadway, which was then a narrow alley, and the eastern boundary of of the town as it was originally laid out   On the bank of the river, immediately in front of the fort, was an appendage of the fort, called the Artificer's Yard   It contained about two acres of ground, enclosed by small contiguous buildings, occupied by workshops and quarters of laborers.   Within this enclosure there was a large two-story frame house, familiarly called the " Yellow House," built for the accommodation of the Quartermaster General.   For many years this was the best finished and most commodious edifice in the Queen City   Fort Washington was for some time the headquarters of both the civil and military governments of the Northwestern Territory.

Following the consummation of the treaty various gigantic land speculations were entered into by different persons, who hoped to obtain from the Indians in Michigan and northern Indiana, large tracts of lands. These were generally discovered in time to prevent the outrageous schemes from being carried out, and from involving the settlers in war. On October 27, 1795, the treaty between the United States and Spain was signed, whereby the free navigation of the Mississippi was secured.

No sooner had the treaty of 1795 been ratified than settlements began to pour rapidly into the West.   The great event of the year 1796 was the occupation of that part of the Northwest including Michigan, which was this year, under the provisions of the treaty, evacuated by the British forces.   The United States, owing to certain conditions, did not feel justified in addressing the authorities in Canada in relation to Detroit and other frontier posts.   When at last the British authorities were called to give them up, they at once complied, and General Wayne who had de   '   f   and who, before the   y   transferred his headquarters to the neighborhood of the lakes, where a county named after him was formed, which included the northwest of Ohio, all of Michigan, and the northeast of Indiana. During this same year settlements were formed at the present City of Chillicothe, along the Miami from Middletown to Piqua, while in the more distant West, settlers and speculators began to appear in great numbers. In September, the City of Cleveland was laid out, and during the Summer and Autumn, Samuel Jackson and Jonathan Sharpless erected the first manufactory of paper—the "Redstone Paper Mill"—in the West. St. Louis contained some seventy houses, and Detroit over three hundred, and along the river, contiguous to it, were more than three thousand inhabitants, mostly French Canadians, Indians and half-breeds, scarcely any Americans venturing yet into that part of the Northwest.

The election of representatives for the territory had taken place, and on the 4th of February, 1799, they convened at Losantiville — now known as Cincinnati, having been named so by Gov. St. Clair, and considered the capital of the Territory—to nominate persons from whom the members of the Legislature were to be chosen in accordance with a previous ordinance. This nomination being made, the Assembly adjourned until the 16th of the following September. From those named the President selected as members of the council, Henry Vandenburg, of Vincennes, Robert Oliver, of Marietta, James Findlay and Jacob Burnett, of Cincinnati, and David Vance, of Vanceville. On the 16th of September the Territorial Legislature met, and on the 24th the two houses were duly organized, Henry Vandenburg being elected President of the Council.

The message of Gov. St. Clair was addressed to the Legislature September 20th, and on October 13th that body elected as a delegate to Congress Gen. Wm. Henry Harrison, who received eleven of the votes cast, being a majority of one over his opponent, Arthur St. Clair, son of Gen. St. Clair.

The whole number of acts passed at this session, and approved by the Governor, were thirty-seven — eleven others were passed, but received his veto. The most important of those passed related to the militia, to the administration, and to taxation. On the 19th of December this protracted session of the first Legislature in the West was closed, and on the 30th of December the President nominated Charles Willing Byrd to the office of Secretary of the Territory *vice* Wm. Henry Harrison, elected to Congress. The Senate confirmed his nomination the next day.

DIVISION OF THE NORTHWEST TERRITORY.

The increased emigration to the Northwest, the extent of the domain, and the inconvenient modes of travel, made it very difficult to conduct the ordinary operations of government, and rendered the efficient action of courts almost impossible. To remedy this, it was deemed advisable to divide the territory for civil purposes. Congress, in 1800, appointed a committee to examine the question and report some means for its solution. This committee, on the 3d of March, reported that:

"In the three western counties there has been but one court having cognizance of crimes, in five years, and the immunity which offenders experience attracts, as to an asylum, the most vile and abandoned criminals, and at the same time deters useful citizens from making settlements in such society. The extreme necessity of judiciary attention and assistance is experienced in civil as well as in criminal cases * * * * To minister a remedy to these and other evils, it occurs to this committee that it is expedient that a division of said territory into two distinct and separate governments should be made, and that such division be made by a line beginning at the mouth of the Great Miami River, running directly north until it intersects the boundary between the United States and Canada."

The report was accepted by Congress, and, in accordance with its suggestions, that body passed an Act extinguishing the Northwest Territory, which Act was approved May 7. Among its provisions were these:

"That from and after July 4 next, all that part of the Territory of the United States northwest of the Ohio River, which lies to the westward of a line beginning at a point on the Ohio, opposite to the mouth of the Kentucky River, and running thence to Fort Recovery, and thence north until it shall intersect the territorial line between the United States and Canada, shall, for the purpose of temporary government, constitute a separate territory, and be called the Indiana Territory."

After providing for the exercise of the civil and criminal powers of the territories, and other provisions, the Act further provides:

"That until it shall otherwise be ordered by the Legislatures of the said Territories, respectively, Chillicothe on the Scioto River shall be the seat of government of the Territory of the United States northwest of the Ohio River, and that St. Vincennes on the Wabash River shall be the seat of government for the Indiana Territory."

Gen. Wm. Henry Harrison was appointed Governor of the Indiana Territory and entered upon his duties about a year later. Connecticut also ab   in March a law was passed accepting this cession Settlements had been made upon thirty-five of the townships in the reserve, mills had been built, and seven hundred miles of road cut in various directions. On the 3d of November the General Assembly met at Chillicothe Near the close of the year, the first missionary of the Connecticut Reserve came, who found no township containing more than eleven families. It was upon the first of October that the secret treaty had been made between Napoleon and the King of Spain, whereby the latter agreed to cede to France the province of Louisiana.

In January, 1802, the Assembly of the Northwestern Territory chartered the college at Athens From the earliest dawn of the western colonies, education was promptly provided for, and as early as 1787, newspapers were issued from Pittsburgh and Kentucky, and largely read throughout the frontier settlements. Before the close of this year, the Congress of the United States granted to the citizens of the Northwestern territory the formation of a State government. One of the provisions of the " compact of 1787 " provided that whenever the number of inhabitants within prescribed limits exceeded 45.000. they should be entitled to a separate government. The prescribed limits of Ohio contained, from a census taken to ascertain the legality of the act, more than that number, and on the 30th of April, 1802, Congress passed the act defining its limits, and on the 29th of November the Constitution of the new State of Ohio. so named from the beautiful river forming its southern boundary, came into existence The exact limits of Lake Michigan were not then known, but the territory now included within the State of Michigan was wholly within the territory of Indiana.

Gen Harrison, while residing at Vincennes, made several treaties with the Indians, thereby gaining large tracts of lands The next year is memorable in the history of the West for the purchase of Louisiana from France by the United States for $15,000,000 Thus by a peaceful mode, the domain of the United States was extended over a large tract of country west of the Mississippi, and was for a time under the jurisdiction of the Northwest government, and, as has been mentioned in the early part of this narrative, was called the "New Northwest' The limits of this history will not allow a description of its territory. The same year large grants of land were obtained from the Indians, and the House of Representatives of the new State of Ohio signed a bill respecting the College Township in the district of Cincinnati.

Before the close of the year, Gen. Harrison obtained additional grants of lands from the various Indian nations in Indiana and the present limits of Illinois, and on the 18th of August, 1804, completed a treaty at St. Louis, whereby over 51,000,000 acres of lands were obtained from the aborigines.   Measures were also taken to learn the condition of affairs in and about Detroit.

C. Jouett, the Indian agent in Michigan, still a part of Indiana Territory, reported as follows upon the condition of matters at that post.

"The Town of Detroit.—The charter, which is for fifteen miles square, was granted in the time of Louis XIV. of France, and is now, from the best information I have been able to get, at Quebec   Of those two hundred and twenty-five acres, only four are occupied by the town and Fort Lenault.   The remainder is a common, except twenty-four acres, which were added twenty years ago to a farm belonging to Wm. Macomb.   *   *   *   A stockade incloses the town, fort and citadel.   The pickets, as well as the public houses, are in a state of gradual decay.   The streets are narrow, straight and regular, and intersect each other at right angles.   The houses are, for the most part, low and inelegant."

During this year, Congress granted a township of land for the support of a college, and began to offer inducements for settlers in these wilds, and the country now comprising the State of Michigan began to fill rapidly with settlers along its southern borders.   This same year, also, a law was passed organizing the Southwest Territory, dividing it into two portions, the Territory of New Orleans, which city was made the seat of government, and the District of Louisiana, which was annexed to the domain of Gen Harrison.

On the 11th of January, 1805, the Territory of Michigan was formed, Wm Hull was appointed governor, with headquarters at Detroit, the change to take effect on June 30.   On the 11th of that month, a fire occurred at Detroit, which destroyed almost every building in the place   When the officers of the new territory reached the post, they found it in ruins, and the inhabitants scattered throughout the country   Rebuilding, however, soon commenced, and ere long the town contained more houses than before the fire, and many of them much better built.

While this was being done, Indiana had passed to the second grade of government, and through her General Assembly had obtained large tracts of land from the Indian tribes   To all this the celebrated Indian, Tecumthe or Tecumseh, vigorously protested, and it was the main cause of his attempts to unite the various Indian tribes in a conflict with the settlers.   To obtain a full account of these attempts, the workings of the British, and the signal failure, culminating in the death of Tecumseh at the battle of the Thames, and the close of the war of 1812 in the Northwest, we will step aside in our story, and relate the principal events of his life, and his connection with this conflict.

TECUMSEH, THE SHAWANOE CHIEFTAIN.

TECUMSEH, AND THE WAR OF 1812.

This famous Indian chief was born about the year 1768, not far from the site of the present City of Piqua, Ohio His father, Puckeshinwa, was a member of the Kisopok tribe of the Swanoese nation, and his mother, Methontaske, was a member of the Turtle tribe of the same people They removed from Florida about the middle of the last century to the birthplace of Tecumseh. In 1774, his father, who had risen to be chief, was slain at the battle of Point Pleasant, and not long after Tecumseh, by his bravery, became the leader of his tribe In 1795 he was declared chief and then lived at Deer Creek, near the site of the present City of Urbana He remained here about one year, when he returned to Piqua, and in 1798, he went to White River, Indiana. In 1805, he and his brother, Laulewasikan (Open Door), who had announced himself as a prophet, went to a tract of land on the Wabash River, given them by the Pottawatomies and Kickapoos From this date the chief comes into prominence He was now about thirty-seven years of age, was five feet and ten inches in height, was stoutly built, and possessed of enormous powers of endurance His countenance was naturally pleasing, and he was, in general, devoid of those savage attributes possessed by most Indians It is stated he could read and write, and had a confidential secretary and adviser, named Billy Caldwell, a half-breed, who afterward became chief of the Pottawatomies. He occupied the first house built on the site of Chicago At this time, Tecumseh entered upon the great work of his life. He had long objected to the grants of land made by the Indians to the whites, and determined to unite all the Indian tribes into a league, in order that no treaties or grants of land could be made save by the consent of this confederation

He traveled constantly, going from north to south; from the south to the north, everywhere urging the Indians to this step He was a matchless orator, and his burning words had their effect

Gen. Harrison, then Governor of Indiana, by watching the movements of the Indians, became convinced that a grand conspiracy was forming, and made preparations to defend the settlements. Tecumseh's plan was similar to Pontiac's, elsewhere described, and to the cunning artifice of that chieftain was added his own sagacity.

During the year 1809, Tecumseh and the prophet were actively preparing for the work. In that year, Gen. Harrison entered into a treaty with the Delawares, Kickapoos, Pottawatomies, Miamis, Eel River Indians and We _____ _____ _____ the whites certain lands upon the Wal _____ _____ _____ entered bitter protest, averring as one principal reason that he did not want the Indians to give up any lands north and west of the Ohio River

Tecumseh, in August, 1810, visited the General at Vincennes and held a council relating to the grievances of the Indians. Becoming unduly angry at this conference he was dismissed from the village, and soon after departed to incite the southern Indian tribes to the conflict.

Gen. Harrison determined to move upon the chief's headquarters at Tippecanoe, and for this purpose went about sixty-five miles up the Wabash, where he built Fort Harrison. From this place he went to the prophet's town, where he informed the Indians he had no hostile intentions, provided they were true to the existing treaties. He encamped near the village early in October, and on the morning of November 7, he was attacked by a large force of the Indians, and the famous battle of Tippecanoe occurred. The Indians were routed and their town broken up. Tecumseh returning not long after, was greatly exasperated at his brother, the prophet, even threatening to kill him for rashly precipitating the war, and foiling his (Tecumseh's) plans.

Tecumseh sent word to Gen. Harrison that he was now returned from the South, and was ready to visit the President as had at one time previously been proposed. Gen. Harrison informed him he could not go as a chief, which method Tecumseh desired, and the visit was never made.

In June of the following year, he visited the Indian agent at Fort Wayne. Here he disavowed any intention to make a war against the United States, and reproached Gen. Harrison for marching against his people. The agent replied to this; Tecumseh listened with a cold indifference, and after making a few general remarks, with a haughty air drew his blanket about him, left the council house, and departed for Fort Malden, in Upper Canada, where he joined the British standard.

He remained under this Government, doing effective work for the Crown while engaged in the war of 1812 which now opened. He was, however, always humane in his treatment of the prisoners, never allowing his warriors to ruthlessly mutilate the bodies of those slain, or wantonly murder the captive.

In the Summer of 1813, Perry's victory on Lake Erie occurred, and shortly after active preparations were made to capture Malden. On the 27th of September, the American army, under Gen. Harrison, set sail for the shores of Canada, and in a few hours stood around the ruins of Malden, from which the British army, under Proctor, had retreated to Sandwich, intending to make its way to the heart of Canada by the Valley of the Thames. On the 29th Gen. Harrison was at Sandwich, and Gen. McArthur took possession of Detroit and the territory of Michigan.

On the 2d of October, the Americans began their pursuit of Proctor, whom they overtook on the 5th, and the battle of the Thames followed. Early in the engagement, Tecumseh who was at the head of the column of Indians was slain, and they, no longer hearing the voice of their chieftain, fled. The victory was decisive, and practically closed the war in the Northwest.

INDIANS ATTACKING A STOCKADE.

Just who killed the great chief has been a matter of much dispute; but the weight of opinion awards the act to Col. Richard M. Johnson, who fired at him with a pistol, the shot proving fatal.

In 1805 occurred Burr's Insurrection. He took possession of a beautiful island in the Ohio, after the killing of Hamilton, and is charged by many with attempting to set up an independent government. His plans w   his property confiscated and he   safety.

In January, 1807, Governor Hull, of Michigan Territory, made a treaty with the Indians, whereby all that peninsula was ceded to the United States. Before the close of the year, a stockade was built about Detroit. It was also during this year that Indiana and Illinois endeavored to obtain the repeal of that section of the compact of 1787, whereby slavery was excluded from the Northwest Territory. These attempts, however, all signally failed.

In 1809 it was deemed advisable to divide the Indiana Territory. This was done, and the Territory of Illinois was formed from the western part, the seat of government being fixed at Kaskaskia. The next year, the intentions of Tecumseh manifested themselves in open hostilities, and then began the events already narrated.

While this war was in progress, emigration to the West went on with surprising rapidity. In 1811, under Mr. Roosevelt of New York, the first steamboat trip was made on the Ohio, much to the astonishment of the natives, many of whom fled in terror at the appearance of the "monster." It arrived at Louisville on the 10th day of October. At the close of the first week of January, 1812, it arrived at Natchez after being nearly overwhelmed in the great earthquake which occurred while on its downward trip.

The battle of the Thames was fought on October 6, 1813. It effectually closed hostilities in the Northwest, although peace was not fully restored until July 22, 1814, when a treaty was formed at Greenville, under the direction of General Harrison, between the United States and the Indian tribes, in which it was stipulated that the Indians should cease hostilities against the Americans if the war were continued. Such, happily, was not the case, and on the 24th of December the treaty of Ghent was signed by the representatives of England and the United States. This treaty was followed the next year by treaties with various Indian tribes throughout the West and Northwest, and quiet was again restored in this part of the new world.

On the 18th of March, 1816, Pittsburgh was incorporated as a city. It then had a population of 8,000 people, and was already noted for its manufacturing interests. On April 19, Indiana Territory was allowed to form a state government. At that time there were thirteen counties organized, containing about sixty-three thousand inhabitants. The first election of state officers was held in August, when Jonathan Jennings was chosen Governor. The officers were sworn in on November 7, and on December 11, the State was formally admitted into the Union. For some time the seat of government was at Corydon, but a more central location being desirable, the present capital, Indianapolis (City of Indiana), was laid out January 1, 1825.

On the 28th of December the Bank of Illinois, at Shawneetown, was chartered, with a capital of $300,000. At this period all banks were under the control of the States, and were allowed to establish branches at different convenient points.

Until this time Chillicothe and Cincinnati had in turn enjoyed the privileges of being the capital of Ohio. But the rapid settlement of the northern and eastern portions of the State demanded, as in Indiana, a more central location, and before the close of the year, the site of Columbus was selected and surveyed as the future capital of the State. Banking had begun in Ohio as early as 1808, when the first bank was chartered at Marietta, but here as elsewhere it did not bring to the state the hoped-for assistance. It and other banks were subsequently unable to redeem their currency, and were obliged to suspend.

In 1818, Illinois was made a state, and all the territory north of her northern limits was erected into a separate territory and joined to Michigan for judicial purposes. By the following year, navigation of the lakes was increasing with great rapidity and affording an immense source of revenue to the dwellers in the Northwest, but it was not until 1826 that the trade was extended to Lake Michigan, or that steamships began to navigate the bosom of that inland sea.

Until the year 1832, the commencement of the Black Hawk War, but few hostilities were experienced with the Indians. Roads were opened, canals were dug, cities were built, common schools were established, universities were founded, many of which, especially the Michigan University, have achieved a world wide-reputation. The people were becoming wealthy. The domains of the United States had been extended, and had the sons of the forest been treated with honesty and justice, the record of many years would have been that of peace and continuous prosperity.

BLACK HAWK AND THE BLACK HAWK WAR

This conflict, though confined to Illinois, is an important epoch in the Northwestern history, being the last war with the Indians in this part of the United States.

Ma-ka-tai-me-she-kia-kiah, or Black Hawk, was born in the principal Sac village, about three miles from the junction of Rock River with the Mississippi, in the year 1767. His father's name was Py-e-sa or Pahaes; his grandfather's, Na-na-ma-kee, or the Thunderer. Black Hawk early distinguished himself as a warrior, and at the age of fifteen was permitted to part _ _ _ _ _ _. About the year 1783, he went _ _ _ _ _ _ _ _ _ _ his nation, the Osages, one

BLACK HAWK, THE SAC CHIEFTAIN.

of whom he killed and scalped, and for this deed of Indian bravery he was permitted to join in the scalp dance. Three or four years after he, at the head of two hundred braves, went on another expedition against the Osages, to avenge the murder of some women and children belonging to his own tribe. Meeting an equal number of Osage warriors, a fierce battle ensued, in which the latter tribe lost one-half their number. The Sacs lost only about nineteen warriors. He next attacked the Cherokees for a similar cause. In a severe battle with them, near the present City of St. Louis, his father was slain, and Black Hawk, taking possession of the "Medicine Bag," at once announced himself chief of the Sac nation. He had now conquered the Cherokees, and about the year 1800, at the head of five hundred Sacs and Foxes, and a hundred Iowas, he waged war against the Osage nation and subdued it. For two years he battled successfully with other Indian tribes, all of whom he conquered.

Black Hawk does not at any time seem to have been friendly to the Americans. When on a visit to St. Louis to see his "Spanish Father," he declined to see any of the Americans, alleging, as a reason, he did not want *two* fathers.

The treaty at St. Louis was consummated in 1804. The next year the United States Government erected a fort near the head of the Des Moines Rapids, called Fort Edwards. This seemed to enrage Black Hawk, who at once determined to capture Fort Madison, standing on the west side of the Mississippi above the mouth of the Des Moines River. The fort was garrisoned by about fifty men. Here he was defeated. The difficulties with the British Government arose about this time, and the War of 1812 followed. That government, extending aid to the Western Indians, by giving them arms and ammunition, induced them to remain hostile to the Americans. In August, 1812, Black Hawk, at the head of about five hundred braves, started to join the British forces at Detroit, passing on his way the site of Chicago, where the famous Fort Dearborn Massacre ' 'a few days before occurred. Of his connection with the British _ernment but little is known. In 1813 he with his little band descended the Mississippi, and attacking some United States troops at Fort Howard was defeated.

In the early part of 1815, the Indian tribes west of the Mississippi were notified that peace had been declared between the United States and England, and nearly all hostilities had ceased. Black Hawk did not sign any treaty, however, until May of the following year. He then recognized the validity of the treaty at St. Louis in 1804. From the time of signing this treaty in 1816, until the breaking out of the war in 1832, he and his band passed their time in the common pursuits of Indian life.

Ten   ... ...ment of this war, the Sac and Fox

Indians were urged to join the Iowas on the west bank of the Father of Waters. All were agreed, save the band known as the British Band, of which Black Hawk was leader. He strenuously objected to the removal, and was induced to comply only after being threatened with the power of the Government. This and various actions on the part of the white settlers provoked Black Hawk and his band to attempt the capture of his native village now occupied by the whites. The war followed. He and his actions were undoubtedly misunderstood, and had his wishes been acquiesced in at the beginning of the struggle, much bloodshed would have been prevented.

Black Hawk was chief now of the Sac and Fox nations, and a noted warrior. He and his tribe inhabited a village on Rock River, nearly three miles above its confluence with the Mississippi, where the tribe had lived many generations. When that portion of Illinois was reserved to them, they remained in peaceable possession of their reservation, spending their time in the enjoyment of Indian life. The fine situation of their village and the quality of their lands incited the more lawless white settlers, who from time to time began to encroach upon the red men's domain. From one pretext to another, and from one step to another, the crafty white men gained a foothold, until through whisky and artifice they obtained deeds from many of the Indians for their possessions. The Indians were finally induced to cross over the Father of Waters and locate among the Iowas. Black Hawk was strenuously opposed to all this, but as the authorities of Illinois and the United States thought this the best move, he was forced to comply. Moreover other tribes joined the whites and urged the removal. Black Hawk would not agree to the terms of the treaty made with his nation for their lands, and as soon as the military, called to enforce his removal, had retired, he returned to the Illinois side of the river. A large force was at once raised and marched against him. On the evening of May 14, 1832, the first engagement occurred between a band from this army and Black Hawk's band, in which the former were defeated.

This attack and its result aroused the whites. A large force of men was raised, and Gen. Scott hastened from the seaboard, by way of the lakes, with United States troops and artillery to aid in the subjugation of the Indians. On the 24th of June Black Hawk, with 200 warriors, was repulsed by Major Demont between Rock River and Galena. The American army continued to move up Rock River toward the main body of the Indians, and on the 21st of July came upon Black Hawk and his band, and defeated them near the Blue Mounds.

Before this action, Gen. Henry, in command, sent word to the main army by whom he was immediately rejoined, and the whole crossed the

NOTE—The above is the generally accepted version of the cause of the Black Hawk War, but in our History of Jo Daviess County Ill., we have occasion to get at the bottom of this matter, and have, we think, found the actual cause of the war, which will be found in p. 7

Wisconsin in pursuit of Black Hawk and his band who were fleeing to the Mississippi. They were overtaken on the 2d of August, and in the battle which followed the power of the Indian chief was completely broken. He fled, but was seized by the Winnebagoes and delivered to the whites.

On the 21st of September, 1832, Gen. Scott and Gov. Reynolds concluded a treaty with the Winnebagoes, Sacs and Foxes by which they ceded to the United States a vast tract of country, and agreed to remain peaceable with the whites. For the faithful performance of the provisions of this treaty on the part of the Indians, it was stipulated that Black Hawk, his two sons, the prophet Wabokieshiek, and six other chiefs of the hostile bands should be retained as hostages during the pleasure of the President. They were confined at Fort Barracks and put in irons.

The next Spring, by order of the Secretary of War, they were taken to Washington. From there they were removed to Fortress Monroe, "there to remain until the conduct of their nation was such as to justify their being set at liberty." They were retained here until the 4th of June, when the authorities directed them to be taken to the principal cities so that they might see the folly of contending against the white people. Everywhere they were observed by thousands, the name of the old chief being extensively known. By the middle of August they reached Fort Armstrong on Rock Island, where Black Hawk was soon after released to go to his countrymen. As he passed the site of his birthplace, now the home of the white man, he was deeply moved. His village where he was born, where he had so happily lived, and where he had hoped to die, was now another's dwelling place, and he was a wanderer.

On the next day after his release, he went at once to his tribe and his lodge. His wife was yet living, and with her he passed the remainder of his days. To his credit it may be said that Black Hawk always remained true to his wife, and served her with a devotion uncommon among the Indians, living with her upward of forty years.

Black Hawk now passed his time hunting and fishing. A deep melancholy had settled over him from which he could not be freed. At all times when he visited the whites he was received with marked attention. He was an honored guest at the old settlers' reunion in Lee County, Illinois, at some of their meetings, and received many tokens of esteem. In September, 1838, while on his way to Rock Island to receive his annuity from the Government, he contracted a severe cold which resulted in a fatal attack of bilious fever which terminated his life on October 3. His faithful wife, who was devotedly attached to him, mourned deeply during his sickness. After his death he was dressed in the uniform presented to him by the President while at Washington. He was buried in a grave   a beautiful eminence. "The body was placed in the middle of the grave, in a sitting posture, upon a seat constructed for the purpose   On his left side, the cane, given him by Henry Clay, was placed upright, with his right hand resting upon it. Many of the old warrior's trophies were placed in the grave, and some Indian garments, together with his favorite weapons "

No sooner was the Black Hawk war concluded than settlers began rapidly to pour into the northern parts of Illinois, and into Wisconsin, now free from Indian depredations   Chicago from a trading post, had grown to a commercial center, and was rapidly coming into prominence. In 1835, the formation of a State Government in Michigan was discussed, but did not take active form until 'two years later, when the State became a part of the Federal Union

The main attraction to that portion of the Northwest lying west of Lake Michigan, now included in the State of Wisconsin, was its alluvial wealth.   Copper ore was found about Lake Superior.   For some time this region was attached to Michigan for judiciary purposes, but in 1836 was made a territory, then including Minnesota and Iowa   The latter State was detached two years later   In 1848, Wisconsin was admitted as a State, Madison being made the capital   We have now traced the various divisions of the Northwest Territory (save a little in Minnesota) from the time it was a unit comprising this vast territory, until circumstances compelled its present division

OTHER INDIAN TROUBLES.

Before leaving this part of the narrative, we will narrate briefly the Indian troubles in Minnesota and elsewhere by the Sioux Indians

In August, 1862, the Sioux Indians living on the western borders of Minnesota fell upon the unsuspecting settlers, and in a few hours massacred ten or twelve hundred persons   A distressful panic was the immediate result, fully thirty thousand persons fleeing from their homes to districts supposed to be better protected.   The military authorities at once took active measures to punish the savages, and a large number were killed and captured   About a year after, Little Crow, the chief, was killed by a Mr. Lampson near Scattered Lake.   Of those captured, thirty were hung at Mankato, and the remainder, through fears of mob violence, were removed to Camp McClellan, on the outskirts of the City of Davenport.   It was here that Big Eagle came into prominence and secured his release by the following order:

BIG EAGLE.

"Special Order, No. 430.   "WAR DEPARTMENT,
      "ADJUTANT GENERAL'S OFFICE, WASHINGTON, Dec 3, 1864

"Big Eagle, an Indian now in confinement at Davenport, Iowa, will, upon the receipt of this order, be immediately released from confinement and set at liberty.

"By order of the President of the United States
"Official   "E. D. TOWNSEND, Ass't Adj't Gen.
      "CAPT JAMES VANDERVENTER, Com y Sub Vols.
      "Through Com g Gen'l, Washington, D C "

Another Indian who figures more prominently than Big Eagle, and who was more cowardly in his nature, with his band of Modoc Indians, is noted in the annals of the New Northwest we refer to Captain Jack. This distinguished Indian, noted for his cowardly murder of Gen. Canby, was a chief of a Modoc tribe of Indians inhabiting the border lands between California and Oregon. This region of country comprises what is known as the "Lava Beds," a tract of land described as utterly impenetrable, save by those savages who had made it their home.

The Modocs are known as an exceedingly fierce and treacherous race. They had, according to their own traditions, resided here for many generations, and at one time were exceedingly numerous and powerful. A famine carried off nearly half their numbers, and disease, indolence and the vices of the white man have reduced them to a poor, weak and insignificant tribe.

Soon after the settlement of California and Oregon, complaints began to be heard of massacres of emigrant trains passing through the Modoc country. In 1847, an emigrant train, comprising eighteen souls, was entirely destroyed at a place since known as "Bloody Point." These occurrences caused the United States Government to appoint a peace commission, who, after repeated attempts, in 1864 made a treaty with the Modocs, Snakes and Klamaths, in which it was agreed on their part to remove to a reservation set apart for them in the southern part of Oregon

With the exception of Captain Jack and a band of his followers, who remained at Clear Lake, about six miles from Klamath, all the Indians complied The Modocs who went to the reservation were under chief Schonchin. Captain Jack remained at the lake without disturbance until 1869, when he was also induced to remove to the reservation. The Modocs and the Klamaths soon became involved in a quarrel, and Captain Jack and his band returned to the Lava Beds.

Several attempts were made by the Indian Commissioners to induce them to return to the reservation and finally becoming involved in a difficulty with the commissioner and his military escort, a fight ensued, in which the chief and his band were routed. They were greatly enraged, and on their retreat, before the day closed, killed eleven inoffensive whites.

The nation was aroused and immediate action demanded. A commission was at once appointed by the Government to see what could be done. It comprised the following persons: Gen. E. R. S. Canby. Rev. Dr. E. Thomas, a leading Methodist divine of California; Mr. A. B. Meacham. Judge Rosborough, of California, and a Mr. Dyer, of Oregon. After several interviews, in which the savages were always aggressive, often appearing with scalps in their belts, Bogus Charley came to the commission on the evening of April 10, 1873, and informed them that Capt. Jack and his band would have a "talk" to-morrow at a place near Clear Lake, about three miles distant. Here the Commissioners, accompanied by Charley, Riddle, the interpreter, and Boston Charley repaired. After the usual greeting the council proceedings commenced. On behalf of the Indians there were present. Capt. Jack, Black Jim, Schnac Nasty Jim, Ellen's Man, and Hooker Jim. They had no guns, but carried pistols. After short speeches by Mr. Meacham, Gen. Canby and Dr. Thomas, Chief Schonchin arose to speak. He had scarcely proceeded when, as if by a preconcerted arrangement, Capt. Jack drew his pistol and shot Gen. Canby dead. In less than a minute a dozen shots were fired by the savages, and the massacre completed. Mr. Meacham was shot by Schonchin, and Dr. Thomas by Boston Charley. Mr. Dyer barely escaped, being fired at twice. Riddle, the interpreter, and his squaw escaped. The troops rushed to the spot where they found Gen. Canby and Dr. Thomas dead, and Mr. Meacham badly wounded. The savages had escaped to their impenetrable fastnesses and could not be pursued.

The whole country was aroused by this brutal massacre; but it was not until the following May that the murderers were brought to justice. At that time Boston Charley gave himself up, and offered to guide the troops to Capt. Jack's stronghold. This led to the capture of his entire gang, a number of whom were murdered by Oregon volunteers while on their way to trial. The remaining Indians were held as prisoners until July when their trial occurred, which led to the conviction of Capt. Jack, Schonchin, Boston Charley, Hooker Jim, Broncho, *alias* One-Eyed Jim, and Slotuck, who were sentenced to be hanged. These sentences were approved by the President, save in the case of Slotuck and Broncho whose sentences were commuted to imprisonment for life. The others were executed at Fort Klamath, October 3, 1873.

These closed the Indian troubles for a time in the Northwest, and for several years the borders of civilization remained in peace. They were again involved in trouble with the savages about the country of the

CAPTAIN JACK, THE MODOC CHIEFTAIN.

Black Hills, in which war the gallant Gen. Custer lost his life. Just now the borders of Oregon and California are again in fear of hostilities ; but as the Government has learned how to deal with the Indians, they will be of short duration   The red man is fast passing away before the march of the white man, and a few more generations will read of the Indians as one of the nations of the past.

The Northwest abounds in memorable places   We have generally noticed them in the narrative, but our space forbids their description in detail, save of the most important places   Detroit, Cincinnati, Vincennes, Kaskaskia and their kindred towns have all been described.   But ere we leave the narrative we will present our readers with an account of the Kinzie house, the old landmark of Chicago, and the discovery of the source of the Mississippi River, each of which may well find a place in the annals of the Northwest.

Mr. John Kinzie, of the Kinzie house, represented in the illustration established a trading house at Fort Dearborn in 1804.   The stockade had been erected the year previous, and named Fort Dearborn in honor of the Secretary of War.   It had a block house at each of the two angles, on the southern side a sallyport, a covered way on the north side, that led down to the river, for the double purpose of providing means of escape, and of procuring water in the event of a siege.

Fort Dearborn stood on the south bank of the Chicago River, about half a mile from its mouth.   When Major Whistler built it, his soldiers hauled all the timber, for he had no oxen, and so economically did he work that the fort cost the Government only fifty dollars   For a while the garrison could get no grain, and Whistler and his men subsisted on acorns   Now Chicago is the greatest grain center in the world

Mr Kinzie bought the hut of the first settler, Jean Baptiste Point au Sable, on the site of which he erected his mansion.   Within an inclosure in front he planted some Lombardy poplars, seen in the engraving, and in the rear he soon had a fine garden and growing orchard.

In 1812 the Kinzie house and its surroundings became the theater of stirring events   The garrison of Fort Dearborn consisted of fifty-four men, under the charge of Capt Nathan Heald, assisted by Lieutenant Lenai T Helm (son-in-law to Mrs Kinzie), and Ensign Ronan.   The surgeon was Dr Voorhees   The only residents at the post at that time were the wives of Capt. Heald and Lieutenant Helm and a few of the soldiers, Mr Kinzie and his family, and a few Canadian voyagers with their wives and children.   The soldiers and Mr Kinzie were on the most friendly terms with the Pottawatomies and the Winnebagoes, the principal tribes ... ... with them from their attachment to ... ...

After the battle of Tippecanoe it was observed that some of the leading chiefs became sullen, for some of their people had perished in that conflict with American troops.

One evening in April, 1812, Mr. Kinzie sat playing his violin and his children were dancing to the music, when Mrs. Kinzie came rushing into the house pale with terror, and exclaiming, "The Indians! the Indians!" "What? Where?" eagerly inquired Mr. Kinzie. "Up at Lee's, killing and scalping," answered the frightened mother, who, when the alarm was given, was attending Mrs. Burns, a newly-made mother, living not far off.

KINZIE HOUSE.

Mr. Kinzie and his family crossed the river in boats, and took refuge in the fort, to which place Mrs. Burns and her infant, not a day old, were conveyed in safety to the shelter of the guns of Fort Dearborn, and the rest of the white inhabitants fled. The Indians were a scalping party of Winnebagoes, who hovered around the fort some days, when they disappeared, and for several weeks the inhabitants were not disturbed by alarms.

Chicago was then so deep in the wilderness, that the news of the declaration of war against Great Britain, made on the 19th of June, 1812, did not reach the commander of the garrison at Fort Dearborn till the 7th of August. Now the fast mail train will carry a man from New York to Chicago in twenty-seven hours, and such a declaration might be sent, every word, by the telegraph in less than the same number of minutes.

PRESENT CONDITION OF THE NORTHWEST.

Preceding chapters have brought us to the close of the Black Hawk war, and we now turn to the contemplation of the growth and prosperity of the Northwest under the smile of peace and the blessings of our civilization. The pioneers of this region date events back to the deep snow

A REPRESENTATIVE PIONEER.

of 1831, no one arriving here since that date taking first honors. The inciting cause of the immigration which overflowed the prairies early in the '30s was the reports of the marvelous beauty and fertility of the region distributed through the East by those who had participated in the Black Hawk campaign with Gen. Scott. Chicago and Milwaukee then had a few hundred inhabitants, and Gurdon S. Hubbard's trail from the former to Kaskaskia led through a wilderness. Vegetables and clothing were transported through the regions adjoining the lakes by steamers from the Ohio towns. There are men now living in Illinois who came to the state when barely an acre was in cultivation, and a man now prominent in the business circles of Chicago looked over the swampy, cheerless site of that metropolis in 1818 and went south ward into civilization. Emigrants from Pennsylvania in 1830 left behind

LINCOLN MONUMENT, SPRINGFIELD, ILLINOIS.

them but one small railway in the coal regions, thirty miles in length, and made their way to the Northwest mostly with ox teams, finding in Northern Illinois petty settlements scores of miles apart, although the southern portion of the state was fairly dotted with farms. The water courses of the lakes and rivers furnished transportation to the second great army of immigrants, and about 1850 railroads were pushed to that extent that the crisis of 1837 was precipitated upon us,

from the effects of which the Western country had not fully recovered
at the outbreak of the war. Hostilities found the colonists of the prairies
fully alive to the demands of the occasion, and the honor of recruiting

A PIONEER SCHOOL HOUSE.

the vast armies of the Union fell largely to the Governors of the Western
States. The struggle, on the whole, had a marked effect for the better on the
new Northwest, giving it an impetus which twenty years of peace would not have
produced. The loss in men and treasure was an inflated one, and, with
the rest of the nation, was compelled to atone therefor by four

years of depression of values, of scarcity of employment, and loss of fortune. To a less degree, however, than the manufacturing or mining regions has the West suffered during the prolonged panic now so near its end. Agriculture, still the leading feature in our industries, has been quite prosperous through all these dark years, and the farmers have cleared away many incumbrances resting over them from the period of fictitious values. The population has steadily increased, the arts and sciences are gaining a stronger foothold, the trade area of the region is becoming daily more extended, and we have been largely exempt from the financial calamities which have nearly wrecked communities on the seaboard dependent wholly on foreign commerce or domestic manufacture.

At the present period there are no great schemes broached for the Northwest, no propositions for government subsidies or national works of improvement, but the capital of the world is attracted hither for the purchase of our products or the expansion of our capacity for serving the nation at large. A new era is dawning as to transportation, and we bid fair to deal almost exclusively with the increasing and expanding lines of steel rail running through every few miles of territory on the prairies. The lake marine will no doubt continue to be useful in the warmer season, and to serve as a regulator of freight rates; but experienced navigators forecast the decay of the system in moving to the seaboard the enormous crops of the West. Within the past five years it has become quite common to see direct shipments to Europe and the West Indies going through from the second-class towns along the Mississippi and Missouri.

As to popular education, the standard has of late risen very greatly, and our schools would be creditable to any section of the Union

More and more as the events of the war pass into obscurity will the fate of the Northwest be linked with that of the Southwest, and the next Congressional apportionment will give the valley of the Mississippi absolute control of the legislation of the nation, and do much toward securing the removal of the Federal capitol to some more central location.

Our public men continue to wield the full share of influence pertaining to their rank in the national autonomy, and seem not to forget that for the past sixteen years they and their constituents have dictated the principles which should govern the country

In a work like this, destined to lie on the shelves of the library for generations, and not doomed to daily destruction like a newspaper, one can not indulge in the same glowing predictions, the sanguine statements of actualities that fill the columns of ephemeral publications. Time may bring grief to the pet projects of a writer, and explode castles erected on a pedestal of facts. Yet there are unmistakable indications before us of the same radical change in our great Northwest which characterizes its history for the past thirty years. Our domain has a sort of natural geographical border, save where it melts away to the southward in the cattle raising districts of the southwest.

Our prime interest will for some years doubtless be the growth of the food of the world, in which branch it has already outstripped all competitors, and our great rival in this duty will naturally be the fertile plains of Kansas, Nebraska and Colorado, to say nothing of the new empire so rapidly growing up in Texas. Over these regions there is a continued progress in agriculture and in railway building, and we must look to our laurels. Intelligent observers of events are fully aware of the strides made in the way of shipments of fresh meats to Europe, many of these ocean cargoes being actually slaughtered in the West and transported on ice to the wharves of the seaboard cities. That this new enterprise will continue there is no reason to doubt. There are in Chicago several factories for the canning of prepared meats for European consumption, and the orders for this class of goods are already immense. English capital is becoming daily more and more dissatisfied with railway loans and investments, and is gradually seeking mammoth outlays in lands and live stock. The stock yards in Chicago, Indianapolis and East St. Louis are yearly increasing their facilities, and their plant steadily grows more valuable. Importations of blooded animals from the progressive countries of Europe are destined to greatly improve the quality of our beef and mutton. Nowhere is there to be seen a more enticing display in this line than at our state and county fairs, and the interest in the matter is on the increase.

To attempt to give statistics of our grain production for 1877 would be useless, so far have we surpassed ourselves in the quantity and quality of our product. We are too liable to forget that we are giving the world its first article of necessity — its food supply. An opportunity to learn this fact so it never can be forgotten was afforded at Chicago at the outbreak of the great panic of 1873, when Canadian purchasers, fearing the prostration of business might bring about an anarchical condition of affairs, went to that city with coin in bulk and foreign drafts to secure their supplies in their own currency at first hands. It may be justly claimed by the agricultural community that their combined efforts gave the nation its first impetus toward a restoration of its crippled industries, and their labor brought the gold premium to a lower depth than the government was able to reach by its most intense efforts of legislation and compulsion. The hundreds of millions about to be disbursed for farm products have already, by the anticipation common to all commercial nations, set the wheels in motion, and will relieve us from the perils so long shadowing our efforts to return to a healthy tone.

Manufacturing has attained in the chief cities a foothold which bids fair to render the Northwest independent of the outside world. Nearly

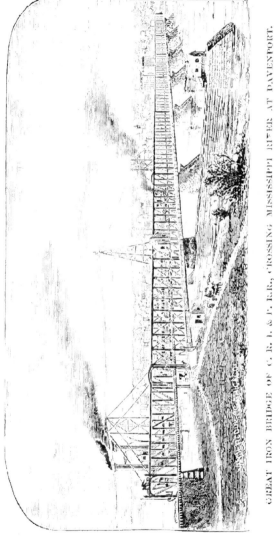

GREAT IRON BRIDGE OF C. R. I. & P. R.R., CROSSING MISSISSIPPI RIVER AT DAVENPORT.

our whole region has a distribution of coal measures which will in time support the manufactures necessary to our comfort and prosperity. As to transportation, the chief factor in the production of all articles except food, no section is so magnificently endowed, and our facilities are yearly increasing beyond those of any other region.

The period from a central point of the war to the outbreak of the panic was marked by a tremendous growth in our railway lines, but the depression of the times caused almost a total suspension of operations. Now that prosperity is returning to our stricken country we witness its anticipation by the railroad interest in a series of projects, extensions, and leases which bid fair to largely increase our transportation facilities. The process of foreclosure and sale of incumbered lines is another matter to be considered. In the case of the Illinois Central road, which formerly transferred to other lines at Cairo the vast burden of freight destined for the Gulf region, we now see the incorporation of the tracks connecting through to New Orleans, every mile co-operating in turning toward the northwestern metropolis the weight of the inter-state commerce of a thousand miles or more of fertile plantations. Three competing routes to Texas have established in Chicago their general freight and passenger agencies. Four or five lines compete for all Pacific freights to a point as as far as the interior of Nebraska. Half a dozen or more splendid bridge structures have been thrown across the Missouri and Mississippi Rivers by the railways. The Chicago and Northwestern line has become an aggregation of over two thousand miles of rail, and the Chicago, Milwaukee and St. Paul is its close rival in extent and importance. The three lines running to Cairo via Vincennes form a through route for all traffic with the states to the southward. The chief projects now under discussion are the Chicago and Atlantic, which is to unite with lines now built to Charleston, and the Chicago and Canada Southern, which line will connect with all the various branches of that Canadian enterprise. Our latest new road is the Chicago and Lake Huron, formed of three lines, and entering the city from Valparaiso on the Pittsburgh, Fort Wayne and Chicago track. The trunk lines being mainly in operation, the progress made in the way of shortening tracks, making air-line branches, and running extensions does not show to the advantage it deserves, as this process is constantly adding new facilities to the established order of things. The panic reduced the price of steel to a point where the railways could hardly afford to use iron rails, and all our northwestern lines report large relays of Bessemer track. The immense crops now being moved have given a great rise to the value of railway stocks, and their transportation must result in heavy pecuniary advantages.

Few are aware of the importance of the wholesale and jobbing trade of Chicago. One leading firm has since the panic sold $24,000,000 of dry goods in one year, and they now expect most confidently to add seventy per cent to the figures of their last year's business. In boots and shoes and in clothing, twenty or more great firms from the east have placed . . . . in their stores, and in groceries

Chicago supplies the entire Northwest at rates presenting advantages over New York.

Chicago has stepped in between New York and the rural banks as a financial center, and scarcely a banking institution in the grain or cattle regions but keeps its reserve funds in the vaults of our commercial institutions. Accumulating here throughout the spring and summer months, they are summoned home at pleasure to move the products of the prairies. This process greatly strengthens the northwest in its financial operations, leaving home capital to supplement local operations on behalf of home interests.

It is impossible to forecast the destiny of this grand and growing section of the Union. Figures and predictions made at this date might seem ten years hence so ludicrously small as to excite only derision.

PIONEERS' FIRST WINTER.

CHICAGO.

It is impossible in our brief space to give more than a meager sketch of such a city as Chicago, which is in itself the greatest marvel of the Prairie State. This mysterious, majestic, mighty city, born first of water, and next of fire; sown in weakness, and raised in power; planted among the willows of the marsh, and crowned with the glory of the mountains; sleeping on the bosom of the prairie, and rocked on the bosom of the sea,

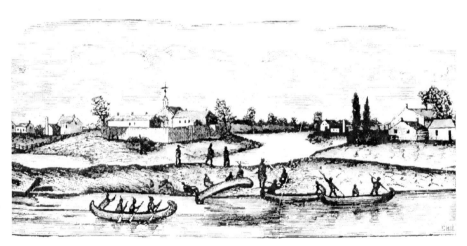

CHICAGO IN 1833.

the youngest city of the world, and still the eye of the prairie, as Damascus, the oldest city of the world, is the eye of the desert. With a commerce far exceeding that of Corinth on her isthmus, in the highway to the East; with the defenses of a continent piled around her by the thousand miles, making her far safer than Rome on the banks of the Tiber;

with schools eclipsing Alexandria and Athens; with liberties more conspicuous than those of the old republics; with a heroism equal to the first
Carthage, and with a sanctity scarcely second to that of Jerusalem—set
your thoughts on all this, lifted into the eyes of all men by the miracle of
its growth, illuminated by the flame of its fall, and transfigured by the
divinity of its resurrection, and you will feel, as I do, the utter impossibility of compassing this subject as it deserves. Some impression of her
importance is received from the shock her burning gave to the civilized
world.

When the doubt of her calamity was removed, and the horrid fact
was accepted, there went a shudder over all cities, and a quiver over all
lands. There was scarcely a town in the civilized world that did not
shake on the brink of this opening chasm The flames of our homes red-
dened all skies The city was set upon a hill, and could not be hid. All
eyes were turned upon it. To have struggled and suffered amid the
scenes of its fall is as distinguishing as to have fought at Thermopylæ, or
Salamis, or Hastings, or Waterloo, or Bunker Hill.

Its calamity amazed the world, because it was felt to be the common
property of mankind.

The early history of the city is full of interest, just as the early history of such a man as Washington or Lincoln becomes public property,
and is cherished by every patriot

Starting with 560 acres in 1833, it embraced and occupied 23,000
acres in 1869, and, having now a population of more than 500,000, it com-
mands general attention.

The first settler—Jean Baptiste Pointe au Sable, a mulatto from the
West Indies—came and began trade with the Indians in 1796. John
Kinzie became his successor in 1804, in which year Fort Dearborn was
erected.

A mere trading-post was kept here from that time till about the time
of the Blackhawk war, in 1832. It was not the city. It was merely a
cock crowing at midnight. The morning was not yet. In 1833 the settlement about the fort was incorporated as a town. The voters were
divided on the propriety of such corporation, twelve voting for it and one
against it. Four years later it was incorporated as a city, and embraced
560 acres

The produce handled in this city is an indication of its power. Grain
and flour were imported from the East till as late as 1837. The first
exportation by way of experiment was in 1839. Exports exceeded imports
first in 1842 The Board of Trade was organized in 1848, but it was so
weak that it needed nursing till 1855. Grain was purchased by the
wagon-load in the street

I remember sitting with my father on a load of wheat, in the long line of wagons along Lake street, while the buyers came and untied the bags, and examined the grain, and made their bids. That manner of business had to cease with the day of small things. Now our elevators will hold 15,000,000 bushels of grain. The cash value of the produce handled in a year is $215,000,000, and the produce weighs 7.000,000 tons or 700,000 car loads. This handles thirteen and a half ton each minute, all the year round. One tenth of all the wheat in the United States is handled in Chicago. Even as long ago as 1853 the receipts of grain in Chicago exceeded those of the goodly city of St. Louis, and in 1854 the exports of grain from Chicago exceeded those of New York and doubled those of St. Petersburg, Archangel, or Odessa, the largest grain markets in Europe.

The manufacturing interests of the city are not contemptible. In 1873 manufactories employed 45,000 operatives; in 1876, 60,000. The manufactured product in 1875 was worth $177,000,000.

No estimate of the size and power of Chicago would be adequate that did not put large emphasis on the railroads. Before they came thundering along our streets canals were the hope of our country. But who ever thinks now of traveling by canal packets? In June, 1852, there were only forty miles of railroad connected with the city. The old Galena division of the Northwestern ran out to Elgin. But now, who can count the trains and measure the roads that seek a terminus or connection in this city? The lake stretches away to the north, gathering in to this center all the harvests that might otherwise pass to the north of us. If you will take a map and look at the adjustment of railroads, you will see, first, that Chicago is the great railroad center of the world, as New York is the commercial city of this continent; and, second, that the railroad lines form the iron spokes of a great wheel whose hub is this city. The lake furnishes the only break in the spokes, and this seems simply to have pushed a few spokes together on each shore. See the eighteen trunk lines, exclusive of eastern connections

Pass round the circle, and view their numbers and extent. There is the great Northwestern, with all its branches, one branch creeping along the lake shore, and so reaching to the north, into the Lake Superior regions, away to the right, and on to the Northern Pacific on the left, swinging around Green Bay for iron and copper and silver, twelve months in the year, and reaching out for the wealth of the great agricultural belt and isothermal line traversed by the Northern Pacific. Another branch, not so far north, feeling for the heart of the Badger State. Another pushing lower down the Mississippi—all these make many connections, and tapping all the vast wheat regions of Minnesota, Wisconsin, Iowa, and all the regions this side of sunset. There is that elegant road, the Chicago, Burlington & Quincy, running out a goodly number of

OLD FORT DEARBORN, 1830.

PRESENT SITE OF LAKE STREET BRIDGE, CHICAGO, IN 1833.

branches, and reaping the great fields this side of the Missouri River. I can only mention the Chicago, Alton & St. Louis, *our* Illinois Central, described elsewhere, and the Chicago & Rock Island. Further around we come to the lines connecting us with all the eastern cities. The Chicago, Indianapolis & St. Louis, the Pittsburgh, Fort Wayne & Chicago, the Lake Shore & Michigan Southern, and the Michigan Central and Great Western, give us many highways to the seaboard. Thus we reach the Mississippi at five points, from St. Paul to Cairo and the Gulf itself by two routes. We also reach Cincinnati and Baltimore, and Pittsburgh and Philadelphia, and New York. North and south run the water courses of the lakes and the rivers, broken just enough at this point to make a pass. Through this, from east to west, run the long lines that stretch from ocean to ocean.

This is the neck of the glass, and the golden sands of commerce must pass into our hands. Altogether we have more than 10,000 miles of railroad, directly tributary to this city, seeking to unload their wealth in our coffers. All these roads have come themselves by the infallible instinct of capital. Not a dollar was ever given by the city to secure one of them, and only a small per cent. of stock taken originally by her citizens, and that taken simply as an investment. Coming in the natural order of events, they will not be easily diverted,

There is still another showing to all this. The connection between New York and San Francisco is by the middle route. This passes inevitably through Chicago. St. Louis wants the Southern Pacific or Kansas Pacific, and pushes it out through Denver, and so on up to Cheyenne. But before the road is fairly under way, the Chicago roads shove out to Kansas City, making even the Kansas Pacific a feeder, and actually leaving St. Louis out in the cold. It is not too much to expect that Dakota, Montana, and Washington Territory will find their great market in Chicago.

But these are not all. Perhaps I had better notice here the ten or fifteen new roads that have just entered, or are just entering, our city. Their names are all that is necessary to give. Chicago & St. Paul, looking up the Red River country to the British possessions; the Chicago, Atlantic & Pacific; the Chicago. Decatur & State Line; the Baltimore & Ohio; the Chicago, Danville & Vincennes; the Chicago & LaSalle Railroad; the Chicago, Pittsburgh & Cincinnati. the Chicago and Canada Southern; the Chicago and Illinois River Railroad. These, with their connections, and with the new connections of the old roads, already in process of erection, give to Chicago not less than 10,000 miles of new tributaries from the richest land on the continent. Thus there will be added to the reserve power, to the capital within reach of this city, not less than $1,000,000,000.

Add to all this transporting power the ships that sail one every nine minutes of the business hours of the season of navigation; add, also, the canal boats that leave one every five minutes during the same time—and you will see something of the business of the city.

THE COMMERCE OF THIS CITY

has been leaping along to keep pace with the growth of the country around us. In 1852, our commerce reached the hopeful sum of $20,000,000. In 1870 it reached $400,000,000. In 1871 it was pushed up above $450 000,000. And in 1875 it touched nearly double that.

One-half of our imported goods come directly to Chicago. Grain enough is exported directly from our docks to the old world to employ a semi-weekly line of steamers of 3,000 tons capacity. This branch is not likely to be greatly developed. Even after the great Welland Canal is completed we shall have only fourteen feet of water. The great ocean vessels will continue to control the trade.

The banking capital of Chicago is $24,431,000. Total exchange in 1875, $650.000,000. Her wholesale business in 1875 was $294,000,000. The rate of taxes is less than in any other great city.

The schools of Chicago are unsurpassed in America. Out of a population of 300,000 there were only 186 persons between the ages of six and twenty-one unable to read. This is the best known record.

In 1831 the mail system was condensed into a half-breed, who went on foot to Niles, Mich., once in two weeks, and brought back what papers and news he could find. As late as 1846 there was often only one mail a week. A post-office was established in Chicago in 1833, and the postmaster nailed up old boot-legs on one side of his shop to serve as boxes for the nabobs and literary men.

It is an interesting fact in the growth of the young city that in the active life of the business men of that day the mail matter has grown to a daily average of over 6,500 pounds. It speaks equally well for the intelligence of the people and the commercial importance of the place, that the mail matter distributed to the territory immediately tributary to Chicago is seven times greater than that distributed to the territory immediately tributary to St Louis

The improvements that have characterized the city are as startling as the city itself. In 1831, Mark Beaubien established a ferry over the river, and put himself under bonds to carry all the citizens free for the privilege of charging strangers. Now there are twenty-four large bridges and two tunnels.

In 1833 the government expended $30,000 on the harbor. Then commenced that series of improvements with the river that has made it one of the world's curiosities. It used to wind around in the lower end of the town, and make its way rippling over the sand into the lake at the foot of Madison street. They took it up and put it down where it now is. It was a narrow stream, so narrow that even moderately small crafts had to go up through the willows and cat's tails to the point near Lake street bridge, and back up one of the branches to get room enough in which to turn around.

In 1844 the quagmires in the streets were first pontooned by plank roads, which acted in wet weather as public squirt-guns. Keeping you out of the mud, they compromised by squirting the mud over you. The wooden-block pavements came to Chicago in 1857. In 1840 water was delivered by peddlers in carts or by hand. Then a twenty-five horse-power engine pushed it through hollow or bored logs along the streets till 1854, when it was introduced into the houses by new works. The first fire-engine was used in 1835, and the first steam fire-engine in 1859. Gas was utilized for lighting the city in 1850. The Young Men's Christian Association was organized in 1858, and horse railroads carried them to their work in 1859. The museum was opened in 1863. The alarm telegraph adopted in 1864. The opera-house built in 1865. The city grew from 560 acres in 1833 to 23,000 in 1869. In 1834, the taxes amounted to $48.90, and the trustees of the town borrowed $60 more for opening and improving streets. In 1835, the legislature authorized a loan of $2,000, and the treasurer and street commissioners resigned rather than plunge the town into such a gulf.

Now the city embraces 36 square miles of territory, and has 30 miles of water front, besides the outside harbor of refuge, of 400 acres, inclosed by a crib sea-wall. One-third of the city has been raised up an average of eight feet, giving good pitch to the 263 miles of sewerage. The water of the city is above all competition. It is received through two tunnels extending to a crib in the lake two miles from shore. The closest analysis fails to detect any impurities, and, received 35 feet below the surface, it is always clear and cold. The first tunnel is five feet two inches in diameter and two miles long, and can deliver 50,000,000 of gallons per day. The second tunnel is seven feet in diameter and six miles long, running four miles under the city, and can deliver 100,000,000 of gallons per day. This water is distributed through 410 miles of water-mains.

The three grand engineering exploits of the city are: First, lifting the city up on jack-screws, whole squares at a time, without interrupting the business, thus giving us good drainage; second, running the tunnels under the lake, giving us the best water in the world; and third, the turning the current of the river in its own channel, delivering us from the old abominations, and making decency possible. They redound about equally to the credit of the engineering, to the energy of the people, and to the health of the city.

That which really constitutes the city, its indescribable spirit, its soul, the way it lights up in every feature in the hour of action, has not been touched. In meeting strangers, one is often surprised how some homely women marry so well. Their forms are bad, their gait uneven and awkward, their complexion is dull, their features are misshapen and mismatched, and when we see them there is no beauty that we should desire them. But when once they are aroused on some subject, they put on new proportions. They light up into great power. The real person comes out from its unseemly ambush, and captures us at will. They have power. They have ability to cause things to come to pass. We no longer wonder why they are in such high demand. So it is with our city.

There is no grand scenery except the two seas, one of water, the other of prairie. Nevertheless, there is a spirit about it, a push, a breadth, a power, that soon makes it a place never to be forsaken. One soon ceases to believe in impossibilities. Balaams are the only prophets that are disappointed. The bottom that has been on the point of falling out has been there so long that it has grown fast. It can not fall out. It has all the capital of the world itching to get inside the corporation.

The two great laws that govern the growth and size of cities are, first, the amount of territory for which they are the distributing and receiving points; second, the number of medium or moderate dealers that do this distributing. Monopolists build up themselves, not the cities. They neither eat, wear, nor live in proportion to their business. Both these laws help Chicago.

The tide of trade is eastward—not up or down the map, but across the map. The lake runs up a wingdam for 500 miles to gather in the business. Commerce can not ferry up there for seven months in the year, and the facilities for seven months can do the work for twelve. Then the great region west of us is nearly all good, productive land. Dropping south into the trail of St. Louis, you fall into vast deserts and rocky districts, useful in holding the world together. St. Louis and Cincinnati, instead of rivaling and hurting Chicago, are her greatest sureties of dominion. They are far enough away to give sea-room,—farther off than Paris is from London,—and yet they are near enough to prevent the springing up of any other great city between them.

St. Louis will be helped by the opening of the Mississippi, but also hurt. That will put New Orleans on her feet, and with a railroad running over into Texas and so West, she will tap the streams that now crawl up the Texas and Missouri road. The current is East, not North, and a seaport at .... with help St. Louis.

Chi...... .. .. the ..... almost alone, to handle the wealth of one-fourth of the territory of this great republic. This strip of seacoast divides its margins between Portland, Boston, New York, Philadelphia, Baltimore and Savannah, or some other great port to be created for the South in the next decade But Chicago has a dozen empires casting their treasures into her lap On a bed of coal that can run all the machinery of the world for 500 centuries: in a garden that can feed the race by the thousand years, at the head of the lakes that give her a temperature as a summer resort equaled by no great city in the land ; with a climate that insures the health of her citizens ; surrounded by all the great deposits of natural wealth in mines and forests and herds, Chicago is the wonder of to-day, and will be *the city of the future.*

MASSACRE AT FORT DEARBORN.

During the war of 1812, Fort Dearborn became the theater of stirring events The garrison consisted of fifty-four men under command of Captain Nathan Heald, assisted by Lieutenant Helm (son-in-law of Mrs Kinzie) and Ensign Ronan. Dr. Voorhees was surgeon The only residents at the post at that time were the wives of Captain Heald and Lieutenant Helm, and a few of the soldiers, Mr. Kinzie and his family, and a few Canadian *voyageurs*, with their wives and children The soldiers and Mr. Kinzie were on most friendly terms with the Pottawattamies and Winnebagos, the principal tribes around them, but they could not win them from their attachment to the British.

One evening in April, 1812, Mr. Kinzie sat playing on his violin and his children were dancing to the music, when Mrs. Kinzie came rushing into the house, pale with terror, and exclaiming: " The Indians! the Indians!" " What? Where?" eagerly inquired Mr. Kinzie. " Up at Lee's, killing and scalping," answered the frightened mother, who, when the alarm was given, was attending Mrs. Barnes (just confined) living not far off. Mr. Kinzie and his family crossed the river and took refuge in the fort, to which place Mrs. Barnes and her infant not a day old were safely conveyed. The rest of the inhabitants took shelter in the fort. This alarm was caused by a scalping party of Winnebagos, who hovered about the fort several days, when they disappeared, and for several weeks the inhabitants were undisturbed.

On the 7th of August, 1812, General Hull, at Detroit, sent orders to Captain Heald to evacuate Fort Dearborn, and to distribute all the United States property to the Indians in the neighborhood—a most insane order The Pottawattamie chief, who brought the dispatch, had more wisdom than the commanding general. He advised Captain Heald not to make the distribution. Said he : " Leave the fort and stores as they are, and let the Indians make distribution for themselves, and while they are engaged in the business, the white people may escape to Fort Wayne."

RUINS OF CHICAGO.

Captain Heald held a council with the Indians on the afternoon of the 12th, in which his officers refused to join, for they had been informed that treachery was designed—that the Indians intended to murder the white people in the council, and then destroy those in the fort. Captain Heald, however, took the precaution to open a port-hole displaying a cannon pointing directly upon the council, and by that means saved his life

Mr Kinzie, who knew the Indians well, begged Captain Heald not to confide in their promises, nor distribute the arms and munitions among them, for it would only put power into their hands to destroy the whites. Acting upon this advice, Heald resolved to withhold the munitions of war ; and on the night of the 13th, after the distribution of the other property had been made, the powder, ball and liquors were thrown into the river, the muskets broken up and destroyed.

Black Partridge, a friendly chief, came to Captain Heald, and said: " Linden birds have been singing in my ears to-day: be careful on the march you are going to take." On that dark night vigilant Indians had crept near the fort and discovered the destruction of their promised booty going on within. The next morning the powder was seen floating on the surface of the river. The savages were exasperated and made loud complaints and threats.

On the following day when preparations were making to leave the fort, and all the inmates were deeply impressed with a sense of impending danger, Capt. Wells, an uncle of Mrs. Heald, was discovered upon the Indian trail among the sand-hills on the borders of the lake, not far distant, with a band of mounted Miamis, of whose tribe he was chief, having been adopted by the famous Miami warrior, Little Turtle. When news of Hull's surrender reached Fort Wayne, he had started with this force to assist Heald in defending Fort Dearborn. He was too late. Every means for its defense had been destroyed the night before, and arrangements were made for leaving the fort on the morning of the 15th.

It was a warm bright morning in the middle of August. Indications were positive that the savages intended to murder the white people; and when they moved out of the southern gate of the fort, the march was like a funeral procession. The band, feeling the solemnity of the occasion, struck up the Dead March in Saul.

Capt Wells, who had blackened his face with gun-powder in token of his fate, took the lead with his band of Miamis, followed by Capt. Heald, with his wife by his side on horseback. Mr. Kinzie hoped by his personal influence to avert the impending blow, and therefore accompanied them, leaving his family in a boat in charge of a friendly Indian, to be taken to his trading station at the site of Niles, Michigan, in the event of his death.

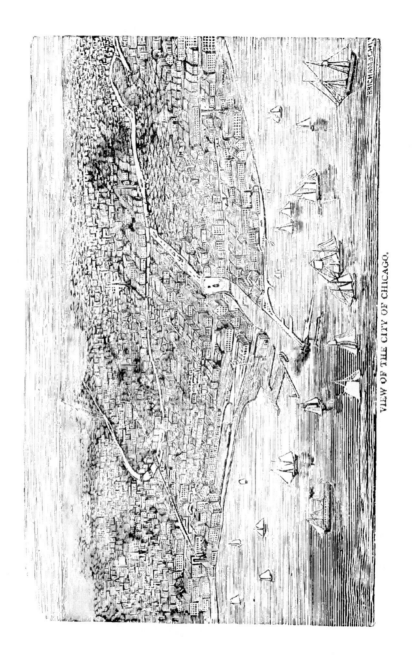

VIEW OF THE CITY OF CHICAGO.

The procession moved slowly along the lake shore till they reached the sand-hills between the prairie and the beach, when the Pottawattamie escort, under the leadership of Blackbird, filed to the right, placing those hills between them and the white people Wells, with his Miamis, had kept in the advance. They suddenly came rushing back, Wells exclaiming, " They are about to attack us ; form instantly." These words were quickly followed by a storm of bullets, which came whistling over the little hills which the treacherous savages had made the covert for their murderous attack. The white troops charged upon the Indians, drove them back to the prairie, and then the battle was waged between fifty-four soldiers, twelve civilians and three or four women (the cowardly Miamis having fled at the outset) against five hundred Indian warriors. The white people, hopeless, resolved to sell their lives as dearly as possible. Ensign Ronan wielded his weapon vigorously, even after falling upon his knees weak from the loss of blood. Capt Wells, who was by the side of his niece, Mrs. Heald, when the conflict began, behaved with the greatest coolness and courage. He said to her, " We have not the slightest chance for life. We must part to meet no more in this world. God bless you. ' And then he dashed forward Seeing a young warrior, painted like a demon, climb into a wagon in which were twelve children, and tomahawk them all, he cried out, unmindful of his personal danger, " If that is your game, butchering women and children, I will kill too. ' He spurred his horse towards the Indian camp, where they had left their squaws and papooses, hotly pursued by swift-footed young warriors, who sent bullets whistling after him. One of these killed his horse and wounded him severely in the leg With a yell the young braves rushed to make him their prisoner and reserve him for torture. He resolved not to be made a captive, and by the use of the most provoking epithets tried to induce them to kill him instantly. He called a fiery young chief a *squaw*, when the enraged warrior killed Wells instantly with his tomahawk, jumped upon his body, cut out his heart, and ate a portion of the warm morsel with savage delight !

In this fearful combat women bore a conspicuous part. Mrs. Heald was an excellent equestrian and an expert in the use of the rifle. She fought the savages bravely, receiving several severe wounds. Though faint from the loss of blood, she managed to keep her saddle A savage raised his tomahawk to kill her, when she looked him full in the face, and with a sweet smile and in a gentle voice said, in his own language, " Surely you will not kill a squaw ! " The arm of the savage fell, and the life of the heroic woman was saved.

Mrs. Helm, the step-daughter of Mr Kinzie, had an encounter with a stout Indian, who attempted to tomahawk her. Springing to one side, she received the glancing blow on her shoulder, and at the same instant seized the savage round the neck with her arms and endeavored to get hold of his scalping knife, which hung in a sheath at his breast. While she was thus struggling she was dragged from her antagonist by another powerful Indian, who bore her, in spite of her struggles, to the margin of the lake and plunged her in. To her astonishment she was held by him so that she would not drown, and she soon perceived that she was in the hands of the friendly Black Partridge, who had saved her life.

The wife of Sergeant Holt, a large and powerful woman, behaved as bravely as an Amazon. She rode a fine, high-spirited horse, which the Indians coveted, and several of them attacked her with the butts of their guns, for the purpose of dismounting her. but she used the sword which she had snatched from her disabled husband so skillfully that she foiled them, and, suddenly wheeling her horse, she dashed over the prairie, followed by the savages shouting, " The brave woman ! the brave woman ! Don't hurt her !' They finally overtook her, and while she was fighting them in front, a powerful savage came up behind her, seized her by the neck and dragged her to the ground. Horse and woman were made captives. Mrs. Holt was a long time a captive among the Indians, but was afterwards ransomed.

In this sharp conflict two-thirds of the white people were slain and wounded, and all their horses, baggage and provision were lost. Only twenty-eight straggling men now remained to fight five hundred Indians rendered furious by the sight of blood. They succeeded in breaking through the ranks of the murderers and gaining a slight eminence on the prairie near the Oak Woods. The Indians did not pursue, but gathered on their flanks, while the chiefs held a consultation on the sand-hills, and showed signs of willingness to parley. It would have been madness on the part of the whites to renew the fight, and so Capt. Heald went forward and met Blackbird on the open prairie, where terms of surrender were soon agreed upon. It was arranged that the white people should give up their arms to Blackbird, and that the survivors should become prisoners of war, to be exchanged for ransoms as soon as practicable. With this understanding captives and captors started for the Indian camp near the fort, to which Mrs. Helm had been taken bleeding and suffering by Black Partridge, and had met her step-father and learned that her husband was safe.

A new scene of horror was now opened at the Indian camp. The wounded, not being included in the terms of surrender, as it was interpreted by the Indians, and the British general, Proctor, having offered a liberal bounty for American scalps, delivered at Malden, nearly all the wounded men were killed and scalped, and the price of the trophies was afterw   ␣   ␣   ␣   ␣   ment.

THE STATE OF IOWA.

GEOGRAPHICAL SITUATION.

The State of Iowa has an outline figure nearly approaching that of a rectangular parallelogram, the northern and southern boundaries being nearly due east and west lines, and its eastern and western boundaries determined by southerly flowing rivers—the Mississippi on the east, and the Missouri, together with its tributary, the Big Sioux, on the west   The northern boundary is upon the parallel of forty-three degrees thirty minutes, and the southern is approximately upon that of forty degrees and thirty-six minutes   The distance from the northern to the southern boundary, excluding the small prominent angle at the southeast corner, is a little more than two hundred miles   Owing to the irregularity of the river boundaries, however, the number of square miles does not reach that of the multiple of these numbers, but according to a report of the Secretary of the Treasury to the United States Senate, March 12, 1863, the State of Iowa contains 35,228,200 acres, or 55,044 square miles.   When it is understood that all this vast extent of surface, except that which is occupied by our rivers, lakes and peat beds of the northern counties, is susceptible of the highest cultivation, some idea may be formed of the immense agricultural resources of the State   Iowa is nearly as large as England, and twice as large as Scotland . but when we consider the relative area of surface which may be made to yield to the wants of man, those countries of the Old World will bear no comparison with Iowa.

TOPOGRAPHY

No complete topographical survey of the State of Iowa has yet been made   Therefore all the knowledge we have yet upon the subject has been obtained from incidental observations of geological corps, from barometrical observations by authority of the General Government, and levelings done by railroad engineer corps within the State.

Taking into view the facts that the highest point in the State is but a little more than twelve hundred feet above the lowest point that these two points are nearly three hundred miles apart and that the whole State is traversed by gently flowing rivers, it will be seen that in reality the State of Iowa rests wholly within, and comprises a part of, a vast plain, with no mountain or hill ranges within its borders

A clearer idea of the great uniformity of the surface of the State may be obtained from a statement of the general slopes in feet per mile, from point to point, in straight lines across it:

From the N E corner to the S E corner of the State	1 foot 1 inch per mile
From the N E corner to Spirit Lake	5 feet 5 inches per mile
From the N W corner to Spirit Lake . .	5 feet 0 inches per mile.
From the N W corner to the S W corner of the State	.2 feet 0 inches per mile
From the S W corner to the highest ridge between the two great rivers (in Ringgold County)..	4 feet 1 inch per mile
From the dividing ridge in the S E corner of the State	5 feet 7 inches per mile.
From the highest point in the State (near Spirit Lake) to the lowest point in the State (at the mouth of Des Moines River)	4 feet 0 inches per mile

It will be seen, therefore, that there is a good degree of propriety in regarding the whole State as a part of a great plain, the lowest point of which within its borders, the southeast corner of the State, is only 444 feet above the level of the sea. The average height of the whole State above the level of the sea is not far from eight hundred feet, although it is more than a thousand miles inland from the nearest sea coast These remarks are, of course, to be understood as applying to the surface of the State as a whole When we come to consider its surface feature in detail, we find a great diversity of surface by the formation of valleys out of the general level, which have been evolved by the action of streams during the unnumbered years of the terrace epoch

It is in the northeastern part of the State that the river valleys are deepest; consequently the country there has the greatest diversity of surface, and its physical features are most strongly marked

DRAINAGE SYSTEM.

The Mississippi and Missouri Rivers form the eastern and western boundaries of the State, and receive the eastern and western drainage of it.

The eastern drainage system comprises not far from two-thirds of the entire surface of the State The great watershed which divides these two systems is formed by the highest land between those rivers along the whole length of a line running southward from a point on the northern boundary line of the State near Spirit Lake, in Dickinson County, to a nearly central point in the northern part of Adair County.

From the last named point, this highest ridge of land, between the two great rivers, continues southward, without change of character, through Ringgold County into the State of Missouri; but southward from that point, in Adair County, it is no longer the great watershed From that point, another and lower ridge bears off more nearly southeastward, through the counties of Madison, Clarke, Lucas and Appanoose and becomes itself the great watershed.

RIVERS.

All streams that rise in Iowa rise upon the incoherent surface deposits, occupying at first only slight depressions in the surface, and scarcely perceptible These successively coalesce to form the streams.

The drift and bluff deposits are both so thick in Iowa that its streams not only rise upon their surface, but they also reach considerable depth into these deposits alone, in some cases to a depth of nearly two hundred feet from the general prairie level

The majority of streams that constitute the western system of Iowa drainage run, either along the whole or a part of their course, upon that peculiar deposit known as bluff deposit Their banks are often, even of the small streams, from five to ten feet in height, quite perpendicular, so that they make the streams almost everywhere unfordable, and a great impediment to travel across the open country where there are no bridges

The material of this deposit is of a slightly yellowish ash color, except where darkened by decaying vegetation, very fine and silicious, but not sandy, not very cohesive, and not at all plastic. It forms excellent soil, and does not bake or crack in drying, except limy concretions, which are generally distributed throughout the mass, in shape and size resembling pebbles, not a stone or pebble can be found in the whole deposit It was called "silicious marl" by Dr. Owen, in his geological report to the General Government, and its origin referred to an accumulation of sediment in an ancient lake, which was afterward drained, when its sediment became dry land Prof Swallow gives it the name of "bluff," which is here adopted; the term Lacustral would have been better. The peculiar properties of this deposit are that it will stand securely with a precipitous front two hundred feet high, and yet is easily excavated with a spade Wells dug in it require only to be walled to a point just above the water line. Yet, compact as it is, it is very porous, so that water which falls on its surface does not remain, but percolates through it; neither does it accumulate within its mass, as it does upon the surface of and within the drift and the stratified formations.

The bluff deposit is known to occupy a region through which the Missouri runs almost centrally, and measures, as far as is known, more than two hundred miles in length and nearly one hundred miles in width. The thickest part yet known in Iowa is in Fremont County, where it reaches two hundred feet The boundaries of this deposit in Iowa are nearly as follows. Commencing at the southeast corner of Fremont County, follow up the watershed between the East Nishnabotany and the West Tarkio Rivers to the southern boundary of Cass County; thence to the center of Audubon County; thence to Tip Top Station, on the Chicago & Northwestern Railway; thence by a broad curve westward to the northwest corner of Plymouth County

This deposit is composed of fine sedimentary particles, similar to that which the Missouri River now deposits from its waters, and is the same which

that river did deposit in a broad depression in the surface of the drift that
formed a lake-like expansion of that river in the earliest period of the history
of its valley.   That lake, as shown by its deposit, which now remains, was
about one hundred miles wide and more than twice as long.   The water of the
river was muddy then, as now, and the broad lake became filled with the sediment which the river brought down, before its valley had enough in the lower
portion of its course to drain it.   After the lake became filled with the sediment, the valley below became deepened by the constant erosive action of the
waters, to a depth of more than sufficient to have drained the lake of its first
waters; but the only effect then was to cause it to cut its valley out of the deposits its own muddy waters had formed.   Thus along the valley of that river,
so far as it forms the western boundary of Iowa, the bluffs which border it are
composed of that sediment known as bluff deposit, forming a distinct border
along the broad, level flood plain, the width of which varies from five to fifteen
miles, while the original sedimentary deposit stretches far inland.

All the rivers of the western system of drainage, except the Missouri itself,
are quite incomplete as rivers, in consequence of their being really only
branches of other larger tributaries of that great river, or, if they empty into
the Missouri direct, they have yet all the usual characteristics of Iowa rivers,
from their sources to their mouths

Chariton and Grand Rivers both rise and run for the first twenty-five miles
of their courses upon the drift deposit alone.   The first strata that are exposed
by the deepening valleys of both these streams belong to the upper coal measures, and they both continue upon the same formation until they make their
exit from the State (the former in Appanoose County, the latter in Ringgold
County), near the boundary of which they have passed nearly or quite through
the whole of that formation to the middle coal measures.   Their valleys gradually deepen from their upper portions downward, so that within fifteen or twenty
miles they have reached a depth of near a hundred and fifty feet below the general level of the adjacent high land.   When the rivers have cut their valleys
down through the series of limestone strata, they reach those of a clayey composition   Upon these they widen their valleys and make broad flood plains
(commonly termed "bottoms"), the soil of which is stiff and clayey, except
where modified by sandy washings

A considerable breadth of woodland occupies the bottoms and valley sides
along a great part of their length, but their upper branches and tributaries are
mostly prairie streams

Platte River.—This river belongs mainly to Missouri   Its upper branches
pass through Ringgold County, and, with the west fork of the Grand River,
drain a large region of country.

Here the drift deposit reaches its maximum thickness on an east and west
line across the State, and the valleys are eroded in some instances to a depth of
two hundred feet apparently through this deposit alone.

The term "drift deposit" applies to the soil and sub-soil of the greater part of the State, and in it alone many of our wells are dug and our forests take root. It rests upon the stratified rocks. It is composed of clay, sand, gravel and boulders, promiscuously intermixed, without stratification, varying in character in different parts of the State.

The proportion of lime in the drift of Iowa is so great that the water of all our wells and springs is too "hard" for washing purposes, and the same substance is so prevalent in the drift clays that they are always found to have sufficient flux when used for the manufacture of brick

One Hundred and Two River is represented in Taylor County, the valleys of which have the same general character of those just described. The country around and between the east and west forks of this stream is almost entirely prairie.

Nodaway River.—This stream is represented by east, middle and west branches. The two former rise in Adair County, the latter in Cass County These rivers and valleys are fine examples of the small rivers and valleys of Southern Iowa They have the general character of drift valleys, and with beautiful undulating and sloping sides. The Nodaways drain one of the finest agricultural regions in the State, the soil of which is tillable almost to their very banks The banks and the adjacent narrow flood plains are almost everywhere composed of a rich, deep, dark loam.

Nishnabotany River—This river is represented by east and west branches, the former having its source in Anderson County, the latter in Shelby County. Both these branches, from their source to their confluence—and also the main stream, from thence to the point where it enters the great flood plain of the Missouri—run through a region the surface of which is occupied by the bluff deposit. The West Nishnabotany is probably without any valuable mill sites. In the western part of Cass County, the East Nishnabotany loses its identity by becoming abruptly divided up into five or six different creeks. A few good mill sites occur here on this stream. None, however, that are thought reliable exist on either of these rivers, or on the main stream below the confluence, except, perhaps, one or two in Montgomery County. The valleys of the two branches, and the intervening upland, possess remarkable fertility.

Boyer River.—Until it enters the flood plain of the Missouri, the Boyer runs almost, if not quite, its entire course through the region occupied by the bluff deposit, and has cut its valley entirely through it along most of its passage. The only rocks exposed are the upper coal measures, near Reed's mill, in Harrison County. The exposures are slight, and are the most northerly now known in Iowa. The valley of this river has usually gently sloping sides, and an indistinctly defined flood plain. Along the lower half of its course the adjacent upland presents a surface of the billowy character, peculiar to the bluff deposit. The source of this river is in Sac County.

Soldier River.—The east and middle branches of this stream have their source in Crawford County, and the west branch in Ida County. The whole course of this river is through the bluff deposit. It has no exposure of strata along its course

Little Sioux River—Under this head are included both the main and west branches of that stream, together with the Maple, which is one of its branches. The west branch and the Maple are so similar to the Soldier River that they need no separate description. The main stream has its boundary near the northern boundary of the State, and runs most of its course upon drift deposit alone, entering the region of the bluff deposit in the southern part of Cherokee County. The two principal upper branches, near their source in Dickinson and Osceola Counties, are small prairie creeks, with indistinct valleys. On entering Clay County, the valley deepens, and at their confluence has a depth of one hundred feet, which still further increases until along the boundary line between Clay and Buena Vista Counties, it reaches a depth of two hundred feet. Just as the valley enters Cherokee County, it turns to the southward and becomes much widened, with its sides gently sloping to the uplands. When the valley enters the region of the bluff deposit, it assumes the billowy appearance. No exposures of strata of any kind have been found in the valley of the Little Sioux or any of its branches.

Floyd River.—This river rises upon the drift in O Brien County, and flowing southward enters the region of the bluff deposit a little north of the center of Plymouth County. Almost from its source to its mouth it is a prairie stream, with slightly sloping valley sides, which blend gradually with the uplands. A single slight exposure of sandstone of cretaceous age occurs in the valley near Sioux City, and which is the only known exposure of rock of any kind along its whole length. Near this exposure is a mill site, but farther up the stream it is not valuable for such purposes

Rock River.—This stream passes through Lyon and Sioux Counties. It was evidently so named from the fact that considerable exposures of the red Sioux quartzite occur along the main branches of the stream in Minnesota, a few miles north of our State boundary. Within this State the main stream and its branches are drift streams, and strata are exposed. The beds and banks of the streams are usually sandy and gravelly, with occasional boulders intermixed.

Big Sioux River—The valley of this river, from the northwest corner of the State to its mouth, possesses much the same character as all the streams of the surface deposits. At Sioux Falls, a few miles above the northwest corner of the State, the stream meets with remarkable obstructions from the presence of Sioux quartzite, which outcrops directly across the stream, and causes a fall of about sixty feet within a distance of half a mile, producing a series of cascades. For the first twenty-five miles above its mouth, the valley is very broad, with a broad, flat flood plain with gentle slopes occasionally showing indistinctly defin........... I........ ...valley bottoms constitute some of the finest agricultural land of the region   On the Iowa side of the valley the upland presents abrupt bluffs, steep as the materials of which they are composed will stand, and from one hundred to nearly two hundred feet high above the stream. At rare intervals, about fifteen miles from its mouth, the cretaceous strata are found exposed in the face of the bluffs of the Iowa side.   No other strata are exposed along that part of the valley which borders our State, with the single exception of Sioux quartzite at its extreme northwestern corner   Some good mill sites may be secured along that portion of this river which borders Lyon County, but below this the fall will probably be found insufficient and the location for dams insecure

Missouri River —This is one of the muddiest streams on the globe, and its waters are known to be very turbid far toward its source.   The chief peculiarity of this river is its broad flood plains, and its adjacent bluff deposits. Much the greater part of the flood plain of this river is upon the Iowa side and continuous from the south boundary line of the State to Sioux City, a distance of more than one hundred miles in length, varying from three to five miles in width   This alluvial plain is estimated to contain more than half a million acres of land within the State, upward of four hundred thousand of which are now tillable

The rivers of the eastern system of drainage have quite a different character from those of the western system.   They are larger, longer and have their valleys modified to a much greater extent by the underlying strata   For the latter reason, water-power is much more abundant upon them than upon the streams of the western system.

Des Moines River.—This river has its source in Minnesota, but it enters Iowa before it has attained any size, and flows almost centrally through it from northwest to southeast, emptying into the Mississippi at the extreme southeastern corner of the State   It drains a greater area than any river within the State.   The upper portion of it is divided into two branches known as the east and west forks.   These unite in Humboldt County   The valleys of these branches above their confluence are drift-valleys, except a few small exposures of subcarboniferous limestone about five miles above their confluence   These exposures produce several small mill-sites   The valleys vary from a few hundred yards to half a mile in width, and are the finest agricultural lands.   In the northern part of Webster County, the character of the main valley is modified by the presence of ledges and low cliffs of the subcarboniferous limestone and gypsum.   From a point a little below Fort Dodge to near Amsterdam, in Marion County, the river runs all the way through and upon the lower coal-measure strata   Along this part of its course the flood-plain varies from an eighth to half a mile or more in width   From Amsterdam to Ottumwa the subcarboniferous limestone appears at intervals in the valley sides.   Near Ottumwa, the subcarboniferous rocks pass beneath the river again, bringing down the coal-measure strata into its bed; but they rise again from it in the extreme northwestern part of Van Buren County, and subcarboniferous strata resume and keep their place along the valley to the north of the river. From Fort Dodge to the northern part of Lee County, the strata of the lower coal measures are present in the valley. Its flood plain is frequently sandy, from the debris of the sandstone and sandy shales of the coal measures produced by their removal in the process of the formation of the valley.

The principal tributaries of the Des Moines are upon the western side. These are the Raccoon and the three rivers, viz. South, Middle and North Rivers. The three latter have their source in the region occupied by the upper coal-measure limestone formation, flow eastward over the middle coal measures, and enter the valley of the Des Moines upon the lower coal measures. These streams, especially South and Middle Rivers, are frequently bordered by high, rocky cliffs. Raccoon River has its source upon the heavy surface deposits of the middle region of Western Iowa, and along the greater part of its course it has excavated its valley out those deposits and the middle coal measures alone. The valley of the Des Moines and its branches are destined to become the seat of extensive manufactures in consequence of the numerous mill sites of immense power, and the fact that the main valley traverses the entire length of the Iowa coal fields.

Skunk River —This river has its source in Hamilton County, and runs almost its entire course upon the border of the outcrop of the lower coal measures, or, more properly speaking, upon the subcarboniferous limestone, just where it begins to pass beneath the coal measures by its southerly and westerly dip. Its general course is southeast. From the western part of Henry County, up as far as Story County, the broad, flat flood plain is covered with a rich deep clay soil, which, in time of long-continued rains and overflows of the river has made the valley of Skunk River a terror to travelers from the earliest settlement of the country. There are some excellent mill sites on the lower half of this river, but they are not so numerous or valuable as on other rivers of the eastern system.

Iowa River —This river rises in Hancock County, in the midst of a broad, slightly undulating drift region. The first rock exposure is that of subcarboniferous limestone, in the southwestern corner of Franklin County. It enters the region of the Devonian strata near the southwestern corner of Benton County, and in this it continues to its confluence with the Cedar in Louisa County. Below the junction with the Cedar, and for some miles above that point, its valley is broad, and especially on the northern side, with a well marked flood plain. Its borders gradually blend with the uplands as they slope away in the distance from the river. The Iowa furnishes numerous and valuable mill sites.

Cedar River —This stream is usually understood to be a branch of the Iowa, but it ought, really, to be regarded as the main stream. It rises by numerous branches in the north part of the State and flows the entire length of the State, through the region occupied by the Devonian strata and along the trend occupied by that formation.

The valley of this river, in the upper part of its course, is narrow, and the sides slope so gently as to scarcely show where the lowlands end and the uplands begin Below the confluence with the Shell Rock, the flood plain is more distinctly marked and the valley broad and shallow. The valley of the Cedar is one of the finest regions in the State, and both the main stream and its branches afford abundant and reliable mill sites

Wapsipinnicon River —This river has its source near the source of the Cedar, and runs parallel and near it almost its entire course, the upper half upon the same formation—the Devonian. In the northeastern part of Linn County, it enters the region of the Niagara limestone, upon which it continues to the Mississippi. It is one hundred miles long, and yet the area of its drainage is only from twelve to twenty miles in width Hence, its numerous mill sites are unusually secure

Turkey River —This river and the Upper Iowa are, in many respects, unlike other Iowa rivers The difference is due to the great depth they have eroded their valleys and the different character of the material through which they have eroded. Turkey River rises in Howard County, and in Winneshiek County, a few miles from its source, its valley has attained a depth of more than two hundred feet, and in Fayette and Clayton Counties its depth is increased to three and four hundred feet The summit of the uplands, bordering nearly the whole length of the valley, is capped by the Maquoketa shales. These shales are underlaid by the Galena limestone, between two and three hundred feet thick. The valley has been eroded through these, and runs upon the Trenton limestone. Thus, all the formations along and within this valley are Lower Silurian. The valley is usually narrow, and without a well-marked flood plain. Water power is abundant, but in most places inaccessible

Upper Iowa River —This river rises in Minnesota, just beyond the northern boundary line, and enters our State in Howard County before it has attained any considerable size Its course is nearly eastward until it reaches the Mississippi It rises in the region of the Devonian rocks, and flows across the outcrops, respectively, of the Niagara, Galena and Trenton limestone, the lower magnesian limestone and Potsdam sandstone, into and through all of which, except the last, it has cut its valley, which is the deepest of any in Iowa The valley sides are, almost everywhere, high and steep, and cliffs of lower magnesian and Trenton limestone give them a wild and rugged aspect . In the lower part of the valley, the flood plain reaches a width sufficient for the location of small farms, but usually it is too narrow for such purposes On the higher surface however, as soon as you leave the valley you come immediately upon a cultivated country This stream has the greatest slope per mile of any in Iowa consequently it furnishes immense water power. In some places, where creeks come into it, the valley widens and affords good locations for farms The town of Decorah, in Winneshiek County, is located in one of these spots, which makes it a lovely location, and the power of the river and the small spring streams around it offer fine facilities for manufacturing. This river and its tributaries are the only trout streams in Iowa.

Mississippi River.—This river may be described, in general terms, as a broad canal cut out of the general level of the country through which the river flows. It is bordered by abrupt hills or bluffs. The bottom of the valley ranges from one to eight miles in width. The whole space between the bluffs is occupied by the river and its bottom, or flood plain only, if we except the occasional terraces or remains of ancient flood plains, which are not now reached by the highest floods of the river. The river itself is from half a mile to nearly a mile in width. There are but four points along the whole length of the State where the bluffs approach the stream on both sides. The Lower Silurian formations compose the bluffs in the northern part of the State, but they gradually disappear by a southerly dip, and the bluffs are continued successively by the Upper Silurian, Devonian, and subcarboniferous rocks, which are reached near the southeastern corner of the State.

Considered in their relation to the present general surface of the state, the relative ages of the river valley of Iowa date back only to the close of the glacial epoch; but that the Mississippi, and all the rivers of Northeastern Iowa, if no others, had at least a large part of the rocky portions of their valleys eroded by pre-glacial, or perhaps even by palæozoic rivers, can scarcely be doubted.

LAKES

The lakes of Iowa may be properly divided into two distinct classes. The first may be called *drift lakes*, having had their origin in the depressions left in the surface of the drift at the close of the glacial epoch and have rested upon the undisturbed surface of the drift deposit ever since the glaciers disappeared. The others may be properly termed *fluvatile* or *alluvial lakes*, because they have had their origin by the action of rivers while cutting their own valleys out from the surface of the drift as it existed at the close of the glacial epoch, and are now found resting upon the alluvium, as the others rest upon the drift. By the term alluvium is meant the deposit which has accumulated in the valleys of rivers by the action of their own currents. It is largely composed of sand and other coarse material and upon that deposit are some of the best and most productive soils in the State. It is this deposit which form the flood plains and deltas of our rivers, as well as the terraces of their valleys.

The regions to which the drift lakes are principally confined are near the head waters of the principal streams of the State. We consequently find them in those regions which lie between the Cedar and Des Moines Rivers, and the Des Moines and Little Sioux. No drift lakes are found in Southern Iowa. The largest of the lakes to be found in the State are Spirit and Okoboji, in

Dickinson County, Clear Lake, in Cerro Gordo County, and Storm Lake, in Buena Vista County.

Spirit Lake.—The width and length of this lake are about equal, and it contains about twelve square miles of surface, its northern border resting directly on the boundary of the State. It lies almost directly upon the great watershed. Its shores are mostly gravelly, and the country about it fertile

Okoboji Lake.—This body of water lies directly south of Spirit Lake, and has somewhat the shape of a horse-shoe, with its eastern projection within a few rods of Spirit Lake, where it receives the outlet of the latter Okoboji Lake extends about five miles southward from Spirit Lake, thence about the same distance westward, and then bends northward about as far as the eastern projection The eastern portion is narrow, but the western is larger, and in some places a hundred feet deep. The surroundings of this and Spirit Lake are very pleasant. Fish are abundant in them, and they are the resort of myriads of water fowl

Clear Lake.—This lake is situated in Cerro Gordo County, upon the watershed between the Iowa and Cedar Rivers It is about five miles long, and two or three miles wide, and has a maximum depth of only fifteen feet. Its shores and the country around it are like that of Spirit Lake.

Storm Lake.—This body of water rests upon the great water shed in Buena Vista County. It is a clear, beautiful sheet of water, containing a surface area of between four and five square miles

The outlets of all these drift-lakes are dry during a portion of the year except Okoboji.

Walled Lakes—Along the water sheds of Northern Iowa great numbers of small lakes exist, varying from half a mile to a mile in diameter. One of the lakes in Wright County, and another in Sac, have each received the name of ' Walled Lake," on account of the existence of embankments on their borders, which are supposed to be the work of ancient inhabitants. These embankments are from two to ten feet in height, and from five to thirty feet across They are the result of natural causes alone, being referable to the periodic action of ice, aided, to some extent, by the force of the waves These lakes are very shallow, and in winter freeze to the bottom, so that but little unfrozen water remains in the middle The ice freezes fast to everything upon the bottom, and the expansive power of the water in freezing acts in all directions from the center to the circumference, and whatever was on the bottom of the lake has been thus carried to the shore, and this has been going on from year to year, from century to century, forming the embankments which have caused so much wonder.

SPRINGS

Springs issue from all formations, and from the sides of almost every valley, but they are more numerous and assume proportions which give rise to the name of sink holes, along the upland borders of the Upper Iowa River, owing to the peculiar fissured and laminated character and great thickness of the strata of the age of the Trenton limestone which underlies the whole region of the valley of that stream

No mineral springs, properly so called, have yet been discovered in Iowa, though the water of several artesian wells is frequently found charged with soluble mineral substances

ORIGIN OF THE PRAIRIES

It is estimated that seven-eighths of the surface of the State was prairie when first settled. They are not confined to level surfaces, nor to any particular variety of soil, for within the State they rest upon all formations, from those of the Azoic to those of the Cretaceous age, inclusive. Whatever may have been their *origin*, their present existence in Iowa is not due to the influence of climate, nor the soil, nor any of the underlying formations. The real cause is the prevalence of the annual fires. If these had been prevented fifty years ago, Iowa would now be a timbered country. The encroachment of forest trees upon prairie farms as soon as the bordering woodland is protected from the annual prairie fires, is well known to farmers throughout the State

The soil of Iowa is justly famous for its fertility, and there is probably no equal area of the earth's surface that contains so little untillable land, or whose soil has so high an average of fertility. Ninety-five per cent. of its surface is tillable land

GEOLOGY.

The soil of Iowa may be separated into three general divisions, which not only possess different physical characters, but also differ in the mode of their origin. These are drift, bluff and alluvial, and belong respectively to the deposits bearing the same names. The drift occupies a much larger part of the surface of the State than both the others. The bluff has the next greatest area of surface, and the alluvial least

All soil is disintegrated rock. The drift deposit of Iowa was derived, to a considerable extent, from the rocks of Minnesota, but the greater part of Iowa drift was derived from its own rocks much of which has been transported but a short distance. In general terms the *constant* component element of the drift soil is that portion which was transported from the north, while the *inconstant* elements are those portions which were derived from the adjacent or underlying strata. For example in Western Iowa, wherever that cretaceous formation known as the Nishnabotany sandstone exists, the soil contains more sand than elsewhere. The same may be said of the soil of some parts of the State occupied by the lower coal measures the sand-tones and sandy shales of that formation furnishing the sand

In Northern and Northwestern Iowa the drift contains more sand and gravel [illegible] ved from the cretaceous rocks that now do, or formerly did, exist there, and also in part from the conglomerate and pudding-stone beds of the Sioux quartzite.

In Southern Iowa, the soil is frequently stiff and clayey This preponderating clay is doubtless derived from the clayey and shaly beds which alternate with the limestones of that region

The bluff soil is that which rests upon, and constitutes a part of, the bluff deposit. It is found only in the western part of the State, and adjacent to the Missouri River Although it contains less than one per cent of clay in its composition it is in no respect inferior to the best drift soil

The alluvial soil is that of the flood plains of the river valleys, or bottom lands. That which is periodically flooded by the rivers is of little value for agricultural purposes, but a large part of it is entirely above the reach of the highest floods, and is very productive

The stratified rocks of Iowa range from the Azoic to the Mesozoic, inclusive; but the greater portion of the surface of the State is occupied by those of the Palæozoic age The table below will show each of these formations in their order.

SYSTEMS	GROUPS	FORMATIONS	THICKNESS
AGES	PERIODS	EPOCHS	IN FEET
Cretaceous	Post Tertiary	Drift	10 to 200
	Lower Cretaceous	Inoceramous bed.	50
		Woodbury Sandstone and Shales	130
		Nishnabotany Sandstone	100
Carboniferous	Coal Measures	Upper Coal Measures	200
		Middle Coal Measures	200
		Lower Coal Measures	200
	Subcarboniferous	St. Louis Limestone	75
		Keokuk Limestone	90
		Burlington Limestone	196
		Kinderhook beds	175
Devonian	Hamilton	Hamilton Limestone and Shales	200
Upper Silurian	Niagara	Niagara Limestone	350
	Cincinnati	Maquoketa Shales	80
	Trenton	Galena Limestone	250
		Trenton Limestone	200
Lower Silurian		St Peter's Sandstone	80
	Primordial	Lower Magnesian Limestone	250
		Potsdam Sandstone	300
Azoic	Huronian	Sioux Quartzite.	50

THE AZOIC SYSTEM

The Sioux quartzite is found exposed in natural ledges only upon a few acres in the extreme northwest corner of the State, upon the banks of the Big Sioux River, for which reason the specific name of Sioux Quartzite has been given them. It is an intensely hard rock, breaks in splintery fracture. and a color varying, in different localities from a light to deep red The process of metamorphism has been so complete throughout the whole formation that the rock is almost everywhere of uniform texture The dip is four or five degrees to the northward and the trend of the outcrop is eastward and westward This rock may be quarried in a few rare cases, but usually it cannot be secured in dry forms except that into which it naturally cracks, and the tendency is to angular pieces. It is absolutely indestructible.

LOWER SILURIAN SYSTEM.
PRIMORDIAL GROUP

Potsdam Sandstone —This formation is exposed only in a small portion of the northeastern portion of the State. It is only to be seen in the bases of the bluffs and steep valley sides which border the river there. It may be seen underlying the lower magnesian limestone, St Peter's sandstone and Trenton limestone, in their regular order, along the bluffs of the Mississippi from the northern boundary of the State as far south as Guttenburg, along the Upper Iowa for a distance of about twenty miles from its mouth, and along a few of the streams which empty into the Mississippi in Allamakee County

It is nearly valueless for economic purposes

No fossils have been discovered in this formation in Iowa

Lower Magnesian Limestone —This formation has but little greater geographical extent in Iowa than the Potsdam sandstone. It lacks a uniformity of texture and stratification, owing to which it is not generally valuable for building purposes

The only fossils found in this formation in Iowa are a few traces of crinoids, near McGregor

St. Peter's Sandstone.—This formation is remarkably uniform in thickness throughout its known geographical extent; and it is evident it occupies a large portion of the northern half of Allamakee County, immediately beneath the drift.

TRENTON GROUP

Trenton Limestone —With the exception of this, all the limestones of both Upper and Lower Silurian age in Iowa are magnesian limestones—nearly pure dolomites. This formation occupies large portions of Winneshiek and Allamakee Counties and a portion of Clayton. The greater part of it is useless for economic purposes, yet there are in some places compact and evenly bedded layers, which afford fine material for window caps and sills

In this formation, fossils are abundant, so much so that, in some places, the rock is made up of a mass of shells, corals and fragments of tribolites, cemented by calcareous material into a solid rock. Some of these fossils are new to science and peculiar to Iowa.

The Galena Limestone —This is the upper formation of the Trenton group. It seldom exceeds twelve miles in width, although it is fully one hundred and fifty miles long. The outcrop traverses portions of the counties of Howard, Winneshiek, Allamakee, Fayette, Clayton, Dubuque and Jackson. It exhibits its greatest development in Dubuque County. It is nearly a pure dolomite, with a . . . . It is usually unfit for dressing, though sometimes near the top of the bed good blocks for dressing are found. This formation is the source of the lead ore of the Dubuque lead mines. The lead region proper is confined to an area of about fifteen miles square in the vicinity of Dubuque. The ore occurs in vertical fissures, which traverse the rock at regular intervals from east to west; some is found in those which have a north and south direction. The ore is mostly that known as Galena, or sulphuret of lead, very small quantities only of the carbonate being found with it.

CINCINNATI GROUP

Maquoketa Shales.—The surface occupied by this formation is singularly long and narrow, seldom reaching more than a mile or two in width, but more than a hundred miles in length. Its most southerly exposure is in the bluffs of the Mississippi near Bellevue, in Jackson County, and the most northerly yet recognized is in the western part of Winneshiek County. The whole formation is largely composed of bluish and brownish shales, sometimes slightly arenaceous, sometimes calcareous, which weather into a tenacious clay upon the surface, and the soil derived from it is usually stiff and clayey. Its economic value is very slight.

Several species of fossils which characterize the Cincinnati group are found in the Maquoketa shales, but they contain a larger number that have been found anywhere else than in these shales in Iowa, and their distinct faunal characteristics seem to warrant the separation of the Maquoketa shales as a distinct formation from any others of the group.

UPPER SILURIAN SYSTEM.
NIAGARA GROUP

Niagara Limestone.—The area occupied by the Niagara limestone is nearly one hundred and sixty miles long from north to south, and forty and fifty miles wide.

This formation is entirely a magnesian limestone, with in some places a considerable proportion of silicious matter in the form of chert or coarse flint. A large part of it is evenly bedded, and probably affords the best and greatest amount of quarry rock in the State. The quarries at Anamosa, LeClaire and Farley are all opened in this formation.

DEVONIAN SYSTEM.
HAMILTON GROUP

Hamilton Limestone.—The area of surface occupied by the Hamilton limestone and shales is fully as great as those by all the formations of both Upper and Lower Silurian age in the State. It is nearly two hundred miles long and from forty to fifty miles broad. The general trend is northwestward and southeastward.

Although a large part of the eastern [part?] of this formation is practically quite worthless, y   [illegible]   [illegible] having a large geographical extent in the State, is one of the most important formations, in a practical point of view. At Waverly, Bremer County, its value for the production of hydraulic lime has been practically demonstrated. The heavier and more uniform magnesian beds furnish material for bridge piers and other material requiring strength and durability.

All the Devonian strata of Iowa evidently belong to a single epoch, and referable to the Hamilton as recognized by New York geologists.

The most conspicuous and characteristic fossils of this formation are brachiopod mollusks and corals. The coral Acervularia Davidsoni occurs near Iowa City and is known as "Iowa City Marble," and "bird's-eye marble."

CARBONIFEROUS SYSTEM

Of the three groups of formations that constitute the carboniferous system, viz.: the subcarboniferous, coal measures and permian, only the first two are found in Iowa.

SUBCARBONIFEROUS GROUP

The area of the surface occupied by this group is very large. Its eastern border passes from the northeastern part of Winnebago County, with considerable directness in a southeasterly direction to the northern part of Washington County. Here it makes a broad and direct bend nearly eastward, striking the Mississippi River at Muscatine. The southern and western boundary is to a considerable extent the same as that which separates it from the coal field. From the southern part of Pocahontas County it passes southeast to Fort Dodge, thence to Webster City thence to a point three or four miles northeast of Eldora, in Hardin County thence southward to the middle of the north line of Jasper County thence southeastward to Sigourney in Keokuk County, thence to the northeastern corner of Jefferson County, thence sweeping a few miles eastward to the southeast corner of Van Buren County. Its area is nearly two hundred and fifty miles long, and from twenty to fifty miles wide.

The Kinderhook Beds.—The most southerly exposure of these beds is near the mouth of Skunk River in Des Moines County. The most northerly now known is in the eastern part of Pocahontas County, more than two hundred miles distant. The principal exposures of this formation are along the bluffs which border the Mississippi and Skunk Rivers, where they form the eastern and northern boundary of Des Moines County, along English River, in Washington County, along the Iowa River, in Tama, Marshall, Hamlin and Franklin Counties, and along the Des Moines River, in Humboldt County.

The economic value of this formation is very considerable, particularly in the northern portion of the region it occupies. In Pocahontas and Humboldt Counties it is almost invaluable, as no other stone except a few boulders are found here. At Iowa Falls the lower division is very good for building purposes. In Marshall County all the limestone to be obtained comes from this formation   At this point some of the layers are finely veined with peroxide of iron and are wrought into ornamental and useful objects

In Tama County, the oolitic member is well exposed, where it is manufactured into lime   It is not valuable for building, as upon exposure to atmosphere and frost, it crumbles to pieces

The remains of fishes are the only fossils yet discovered in this formation that can be referred to the sub-kingdom VERTEBRATA; and so far as yet recognized, they all belong to the order selachians

Of ARTICULATES, only two species have been recognized both of which belong to the genus *phillipsia*

The sub-kingdom MOLLUSCA is largely represented

The RADIATA are represented by a few crinoids, usually found in a very imperfect condition.   The sub-kingdom is also represented by corals.

The prominent feature in the life of this epoch was mollu-can; so much so in fact as to overshadow all other branches of the animal kingdom.   The prevailing classes are: *lamellibranchiates*, in the more arenaceous portions, and brachiopods, in the more calcareous portions.

No remains of vegetation have been detected in any of the strata of this formation

The Burlington Limestone —This formation consists of two distinct calcareous divisions, which are separated by a series of silicious beds   Both divisions are eminently crinoidal.

The southerly dip of the Iowa rocks carries the Burlington limestone down, so that it is seen for the last time in this State in the valley of Skunk River, near the southern boundary of Des Moines County   The most northerly point at which it has been recognized is in the northern part of Washington County It probably exists as far north as Marshall County

This formation affords much valuable material for economic purposes.   The upper division furnishes excellent common quarry rock

The great abundance and variety of its fossils—*crinoids*—now known to be more than three hundred, have justly attracted the attention of geologists in all parts of the world

The only remains of vertebrates discovered in this formation are those of fishes, and consist of teeth and spines, bone of bony fishes, like those most common at the present day, are found in these rocks.   On Buffington Creek in Louisa County, is a stratum in an exposure so fully charged with these remains that it might with propriety be called bone breccia

Remains of articulates are rare in this formation.   So far as yet discovered, they are confined to two species of trilobites of the genus *phillipsia*

Fossil shells are very common.

The two lowest classes of the sub-kingdom radiata are represented in the genera *zaphrentis* amplexus and syringopora while the highest class—echinoderms—are found in the most extensive profusion

The Keokuk Limestone—It is only in the four counties of Lee, Van Buren, Henry and Des Moines that this formation is to be seen

In some localities the upper silicious portion of this formation is known as the Geode bed. It is not recognizable in the northern portion of the formation, nor in connection with it where it is exposed, about eighty miles below Keokuk.

The geodes of the Geode bed are more or less spherical masses of silex, usually hollow and lined with crystals of quartz. The outer crust is rough and unsightly, but the crystals which stud the interior are often very beautiful. They vary in size from the size of a walnut to a foot in diameter.

The economic value of this formation is very great. Large quantities of its stone have been used in the finest structures in the State, among which are the post offices at Dubuque and Des Moines. The principal quarries are along the banks of the Mississippi, from Keokuk to Nauvoo

The only vertebrate fossils found in the formation are fishes, all belonging to the order selachians, some of which indicate that their owners reached a length of twenty-five or thirty feet.

Of the articulates, only two species of the genus *phillipsia* have been found in this formation.

Of the mollusks, no cephalopods have yet been recognized in this formation in this State; gasteropods are rare, brachiopods and polyzoans are quite abundant.

Of radiates, corals of genera zaphrentes, amplexus and aulopera are found, but crinoids are most abundant.

Of the low forms of animal life, the protozoans, a small fossil related to the sponges, is found in this formation in small numbers.

The St Louis Limestone—This is the uppermost of the subcarboniferous group in Iowa. The superficial area it occupies is comparatively small, because it consists of long, narrow strips, yet its extent is very great. It is first seen resting on the geode division of the Keokuk limestone, near Keokuk. Proceeding northward, it forms a narrow border along the edge of the coal fields in Lee, Des Moines, Henry, Jefferson, Washington, Keokuk and Mahaska Counties. It is then lost sight of until it appears again in the banks of Boone River, where it again passes out of view under the coal measures until it is next seen in the banks of the Des Moines, near Fort Dodge. As it exists in Iowa, it consists of three tolerably distinct subdivisions—the magnesian, arenaceous and calcareous

The upper division furnishes excellent material for quicklime, and when quarries are well opened, as in the northwestern part of Van Buren County, large blocks are obtained. The sandstone, or middle division, is of little economic value. The lower or magnesian division furnishes a valuable and durable stone, exposures of which are found on Lick Creek, in Van Buren County, and on Long Creek, seven miles west of Burlington

Of the fossils of this formation, the vertebrates are represented only by the remai............................... two orders, selachians and ganoids. The articulates are represented by one species of the trilobite, genus *phillipsia*, and two ostracoid genera, *cythre* and *beyricia* The mollusks distinguish this formation more than any other branch of the animal kingdom Radiates are exceedingly rare, showing a marked contrast between this formation and the two preceding it

The rocks of the subcarboniferous period have in other countries, and in other parts of our own country, furnished valuable minerals, and even coal, but in Iowa the economic value is confined to its stone alone

The Lower Silurian, Upper Silurian and Devonian rocks of Iowa are largely composed of limestone Magnesia also enters largely into the subcarboniferous group With the completion of the St. Louis limestone, the production of the magnesian limestone seems to have ceased among the rocks of Iowa

Although the Devonian age has been called the age of fishes, yet so far as Iowa is concerned, the rocks of no period can compare with the subcarboniferous in the abundance and variety of the fish remains, and for this reason, the Burlington and Keokuk limestones will in the future become more famous among geologists, perhaps, than any other formations in North America

It will be seen that the Chester limestone is omitted from the subcarboniferous group, and which completes the full geological series It is probable the whole surface of Iowa was above the sea during the time of the formation of the Chester limestone to the southward about one hundred miles.

At the close of the epoch of the Chester limestone the shallow seas in which the lower coal measures were formed again occupied the land, extending almost as far north as that sea had done in which the Kinderhook beds were formed and to the northeastward its deposits extended beyond the subcarboniferous groups, outlines of which are found upon the next, or Devonian rock

THE COAL-MEASURE GROUP.

The coal-measure group of Iowa is properly divided into three formations. viz , the lower, middle and upper coal measures, each having a vertical thickness of about two hundred feet

A line drawn upon the map of Iowa as follows, will represent the eastern and northern boundaries of the coal fields of the State: Commencing at the southeast corner of Van Buren County, carry the line to the northeast corner of Jefferson County by a slight easterly curve through the western portions of Lee and Henry Counties. Produce this line until it reaches a point six or eight miles northward from the one last named, and then carry it northwestward, keeping it at about the same distance to the northward of Skunk River and its north branch that it had at first, until it reaches the southern boundary of Marshall County, a little west of its center Then carry it to a point three or four miles northeast from Eldora, in Hardin County, thence westward to a point a little north of Webster City in Hamilton County; and thence further westward to a point a little north of Fort Dodge, in Webster County

Lower Coal Measures —In consequence of the recedence to the southward of the borders of the middle and upper coal measures. the lower coal measures alone exist to the eastward and northward of Des Moines River. They also occupy a large area westward and southward of that river, but their southerly dip passes them below the middle coal measures at no great distance from the river

No other formation in the whole State possesses the economic value of the lower coal measures   The clay that underlies almost every bed of coal furnishes a large amount of material for potters' use   The sandstone of these measures is usually soft and unfit, but in some places, as near Red Rock, in Marion County, blocks of large dimensions are obtained which make good building material, samples of which can be seen in the State Arsenal, at Des Moines. On the whole, that portion of the State occupied by the lower coal measures, is not well supplied with stone.

But few fossils have been found in any of the strata of the lower coal measures, but such animal remains as have been found are without exception of marine origin.

Of fossil plants found in these measures, all probably belong to the class *acrogens*   Specimens of *calamites*, and several species of ferns, are found in all of the coal measures, but the genus *lepidodendron* seems not to have existed later than the epoch of the middle coal measures.

Middle Coal Measures —This formation within the State of Iowa occupies a narrow belt of territory in the southern central portion of the State, embracing a superficial area of about fourteen hundred square miles   The counties more or less underlaid by this formation are Guthrie, Dallas, Polk, Madison. Warren, Clarke, Lucas, Monroe, Wayne and Appanoose.

This formation is composed of alternating beds of clay sandstone and limestone, the clays or shales constituting the bulk of the formation, the limestone occurring in their bands, the lithological peculiarities of which offer many contrasts to the limestones of the upper and lower coal measures   The formation is also characterized by regular wave-like undulations, with a parallelism which indicates a widespread disturbance, though no dislocation of the strata have been discovered

Generally speaking, few species of fossils occur in these beds   Some of the shales and sandstone have afforded a few imperfectly preserved land plants— three or four species of ferns, belonging to the genera   Some of the carboniferous shales afford beautiful specimens of what appear to have been sea-weeds   Radiates are represented by coral.   The mollusks are most numerously represented   ... ...   are the only remains known of articulates.

Vertebrates are only known by the remains of *salachians*, or sharks, and ganoids.

Upper Coal Measures —The area occupied by this formation in Iowa is very great, comprising thirteen whole counties, in the southwestern part of the State. It adjoins by its northern and eastern boundaries the area occupied by the middle coal measures.

The prominent lithological features of this formation are its limestones, yet it contains a considerable proportion of shales and sandstones. Although it is known by the name of upper coal measures, it contains but a single bed of coal, and that only about twenty inches in maximum thickness.

The limestone exposed in this formation furnishes good material for building as in Madison and Fremont Counties. The sandstones are quite worthless. No beds of clay for potter's use are found in the whole formation.

The fossils in this formation are much more numerous than in either the middle or lower coal measures. The vertebrates are represented by the fishes of the orders selachians and ganoids. The articulates are represented by the trilobites and ostracoids. Mollusks are represented by the classes *cephalapoda, gasteropoda, lamelli, branchiata, brachiapoda* and *polyzou.* Radiates are more numerous than in the lower and middle coal measures. Protogoans are represented in the greatest abundance, some layers of limestone being almost entirely composed of their small fusiform shells.

CRETACIOUS SYSTEM

There being no rocks, in Iowa, of permian, triassic or jurassic age, the next strata in the geological series are of the cretaceous age. They are found in the western half of the State, and do not dip, as do all the other formations upon which they rest, to the southward and westward, but have a general dip of their own to the north of westward, which, however, is very slight. Although the actual exposures of cretaceous rocks are few in Iowa, there is reason to believe that nearly all the western half of the State was originally occupied by them, but being very friable, they have been removed by denudation, which has taken place at two separate periods. The first period was during its elevation from the cretaceous sea, and during the long tertiary age that passed between the time of that elevation and the commencement of the glacial epoch. The second period was during the glacial epoch, when the ice produced their entire removal over considerable areas.

It is difficult to indicate the exact boundaries of these rocks: the following will approximate the outlines of the area:

From the northeast corner to the southwest corner of Kossuth County; thence to the southeast corner of Guthrie County, thence to the southeast corner of Cass County, thence to the middle of the south boundary of Montgomery County, thence to the middle of the north boundary of Pottawattamie County; thence to the middle of the south boundary of Woodbury County;

thence to Sergeant's bluffs: up the Missouri and Big Sioux Rivers to the northwest corner of the State, eastward along the State line to the place of beginning

All the cretaceous rocks in Iowa are a part of the same deposits farther up the Missouri River, and in reality form their eastern boundary

Nishnabotany Sandstone.—This rock has the most easterly and southerly extent of the cretaceous deposits of Iowa, reaching the southeastern part of Guthrie County and the southern part of Montgomery County   To the northward, it passes beneath the Woodbury sandstones and shales, the latter passing beneath the inoceramus, or chalky, beds   This sandstone is, with few exceptions almost valueless for economic purposes.

The only fossils found in this formation are a few fragments of angiospermous leaves.

Woodbury Sandstones and Shales—These strata rest upon the Nishnabotany sandstone, and have not been observed outside of Woodbury County, hence their name.   Their principal exposure is at Sergeant's Bluffs, seven miles below Sioux City

This rock has no value except for purposes of common masonry

Fossil remains are rare   Detached scales of a lepidogmoid species have been detected, but no other vertebrate remains   Of remains of vegetation, leaves of *salix meekii* and sassafras cretaceum have been occasionally found.

Inoceramus Beds—These beds rest upon the Woodbury sandstones and shales.   They have not been observed in Iowa, except in the bluffs which border the Big Sioux River in Woodbury and Plymouth Counties   They are composed almost entirely of calcareous material, the upper portion of which is extensively used for lime   No building material is to be obtained from these beds; and the only value they possess, except lime, are the marls, which at some time may be useful on the soil of the adjacent region

The only vertebrate remains found in the cretaceous rocks are the fishes Those in the inoceramus beds of Iowa are two species of squoloid selachians, or cestratront and three genera of teliosts   Molluscan remains are rare

PEAT

Extensive beds of peat exist in Northern Middle Iowa, which, it is estimated contain the following areas.

Counties	Acres
Cerro Gordo	1,500
Worth	2,000
Winnebago	2,000
Hancock	1,500
Wright	500
Kossuth	700
Dickinson	80

Several ... peat beds, but the character of the peat is inferior ... of the State   The character of the peat named is equal to that of Ireland The beds are of an average depth of four feet. It is estimated that each acre of these beds will furnish two hundred and fifty tons of dry fuel for each foot in depth. At present, owing to the sparseness of the population, this peat is not utilized ; but, owing to its great distance from the coal fields and the absence of timber, the time is coming when their value will be realized, and the fact demonstrated that Nature has abundantly compensated the deficiency of other fuel.

GYPSUM

The only deposits of the sulphates of the alkaline earths of any economic value in Iowa are those of gypsum at and in the vicinity of Fort Dodge, in Webster County All others are small and unimportant The deposit occupies a nearly central position in Webster County, the Des Moines River running nearly centrally through it, along the valley sides of which the gypsum is seen in the form of ordinary rock cliff and ledges, and also occurring abundantly in similar positions along both sides of the valleys of the smaller streams and of the numerous ravines coming into the river valley.

The most northerly known limit of the deposit is at a point near the mouth of Lizard Creek, a tributary of the Des Moines River, and almost adjoining the town of Fort Dodge. The most southerly point at which it has been found exposed is about six miles, by way of the river, from this northerly point before mentioned. Our knowledge of the width of the area occupied by it is limited by the exposures seen in the valleys of the small streams and in the ravines which come into the valley within the distance mentioned. As one goes up these ravines and minor valleys, the gypsum becomes lost beneath the overlying drift There can be no doubt that the different parts of this deposit, now disconnected by the valleys and ravines having been cut through it, were originally connected as a continuous deposit and there seems to be as little reason to doubt that the gypsum still extends to considerable distance on each side of the valley of the river beneath the drift which covers the region to a depth of from twenty to sixty feet.

The country round about this region has the prairie surface approximating a general level which is so characteristic of the greater part of the State, and which exists irrespective of the character or geological age of the strata beneath, mainly because the drift is so deep and uniformly distributed that it frequently almost alone gives character to the surface The valley sides of the Des Moines River, in the vicinity of Fort Dodge, are somewhat abrupt, having a depth there from the general level of the upland of about one hundred and seventy feet, and consequently presents somewhat bold and interesting features in the landscape.

As one walks up and down the creeks and ravines which come into the valley of the Des Moines River there, he sees the gypsum exposed on either side of them, jutting out from beneath the drift in the form of ledges and bold quarry fronts, having almost the exact appearance of ordinary limestone exposures, so horizontal and regular are its lines of stratification, and so similar in color is it to some varieties of that rock   The principal quarries now opened are on Two Mile Creek, a couple of miles below Fort Dodge.

The reader will please bear in mind that the gypsum of this remarkable deposit does not occur in "heaps" or "nests," as it does in most deposits of gypsum in the States farther eastward, but that it exists here in the form of a regularly stratified, continuous formation, as uniform in texture, color and quality throughout the whole region, and from top to bottom of the deposit as the granite of the Quincy quarries is   Its color is a uniform gray, resulting from alternating fine horizontal lines of nearly white, with similar lines of darker shade   The gypsum of the white lines is almost entirely pure, the darker lines containing the impurity.   This is at intervals barely sufficient in amount to cause the separation of the mass upon those lines into beds or layers, thus facilitating the quarrying of it into desired shapes.   These bedding surfaces have occasionally a clayey feeling to the touch, but there is nowhere any intercalation of clay or other foreign substance in a separate form   The deposit is known to reach a thickness of thirty feet at the quarries referred to, but although it will probably be found to exceed this thickness at some other points, at the natural exposures, it is seldom seen to be more than from ten to twenty feet thick

Since the drift is usually seen to rest directly upon the gypsum, with nothing intervening, except at a few points where traces appear of an overlying bed of clayey material without doubt of the same age as the gypsum the latter probably lost something of its thickness by mechanical erosion during the glacial epoch; and it has, doubtless, also suffered some diminution of thickness since then by solution in the waters which constantly percolate through the drift from the surface   The drift of this region being somewhat clayey, particularly in its lower part, it has doubtless served in some degree as a protection against the diminution of the gypsum by solution in consequence of its partial imperviousness to water   If the gypsum had been covered by a deposit of sand instead of the drift clays, it would have no doubt long since disappeared by being dissolved in the water that would have constantly reached it from the surface   Water merely resting upon it would not dissolve it away to any extent, but it rapidly disappears under the action of running water   Where little rills of water at the time of every rain run over the face of an unused quarry, from the surface above it deep grooves are thereby cut into it, giving it somewhat the appearance of melting ice around a waterfall   The fact that gypsum is now suffering a constant, but, of course, very slight, diminution, is apparent in the fact the springs of the region contain more or less of it in solution in their waters.   An analysis of water from one of these springs will be found in Prof. Emery's

Besides the clayey beds that are sometimes seen to rest upon the gypsum, there are occasionally others seen beneath them that are also of the same age, and not of the age of the coal-measure strata upon which they rest

Age of the Gypsum Deposit —In neither the gypsum nor the associated clays has any trace of any fossil remains been found, nor has any other indication of its geological age been observed, except that which is afforded by its stratigraphical relations; and the most that can be said with certainty is that it is newer than the coal measures, and older than the drift   The indications afforded by the stratigraphical relations of the gypsum deposit of Fort Dodge are, however, of considerable value

As already shown, it rests in that region directly and unconformably upon the lower coal measures; but going southward from there, the whole series of coal-measure strata from the top of the subcarboniferous group to the upper coal measures, inclusive, can be traced without break or unconformability. The strata of the latter also may be traced in the same manner up into the Permian rocks of Kansas, and through this long series, there is no place or horizon which suggests that the gypsum deposit might belong there

Again, no Tertiary deposits are known to exist within or near the borders of Iowa to suggest that the gypsum might be of that age; nor are any of the palaeozoic strata newer than the subcarboniferous unconformable upon each other as the other gypsum is unconformable upon the strata beneath it.   It therefore seems, in a measure, conclusive, that the gypsum is of Mesozoic age, perhaps older than the Cretaceous

Lithological Origin —As little can be said with certainty concerning the lithological origin of this deposit as can be said concerning its geological age, for it seems to present itself in this relation, as in the former one, as an isolated fact.   None of the associated strata show any traces of a double decomposition of pre-existing materials, such as some have supposed all deposits of gypsum to have resulted from.   No considerable quantities of oxide of iron nor any trace of native sulphur have been found in connection with it; nor has any salt been found in the waters of the region   These substances are common in association with other gypsum deposits, and are regarded by some persons as indicative of the method of or resulting from their origin as such.   Throughout the whole region, the Fort Dodge gypsum has the exact appearance of a sedimentary deposit   It is arranged in layers like the regular layers of limestone, and the whole mass, from top to bottom, is traced with fine horizontal laminæ of alternating white and gray gypsum, parallel with the bedding surfaces of the layers, but the whole so intimately blended as to form a solid mass.   The darker lines contain almost all the impurity there is in the gypsum, and that impurity is evidently sedimentary in its character   From these facts, and also from the further one that no trace of fossil remains has been detected in the gypsum, it seems not unreasonable to entertain the opinion that the gypsum of Fort Dodge originated as a chemical precipitate in comparatively still water which were saturated with sulphate of lime and destitute of life, its stratification and impurities being deposited at the same time as clayey impurities which had been held suspended in the same waters

Physical Properties.—Much has already been said of the physical properties or character of this gypsum, but as it is so different in some respects from that of other deposits, there are yet other matters worthy of mention in connection with those   According to the results of a complete and exhaustive analysis by Prof. Emery, the ordinary gray gypsum contains only about eight per cent of impurity; and it is possible that the average impurity for the whole deposit will not exceed that proportion, so uniform in quality is it from to top to bottom and from one end of the region to the other

When it is remembered that plaster for agricultural purposes is sometimes prepared from gypsum that contains as much as thirty per cent. of impurity, it will be seen that ours is a very superior article for such purposes   The impurities are also of such a character that they do not in any way interfere with its value for use in the arts.   Although the gypsum rock has a gray color, it becomes quite white by grinding, and still whiter by the calcining process necessary in the preparation of plaster of Paris   These tests have all been practically made in the rooms of the Geological Survey, and the quality of the plaster of Paris still further tested by actual use and experiment.   No hesitation, therefore, is felt in stating that the Fort Dodge gypsum is of as good a quality as any in the country, even for the finest uses.

In view of the bounteousness of the primitive fertility of our Iowa soils, many persons forget that a time may come when Nature will refuse to respond so generously to our demand as she does now, without an adequate return   Such are apt to say that this vast deposit of gypsum is valueless to our commonwealth, except to the small extent that it may be used in the arts.   This is undoubtedly a short-sighted view of the subject, for the time is even now rapidly passing away when a man may purchase a new farm for less money than he can re-fertilize and restore the partially wasted primitive fertility of the one he now occupies   There are farms even now in a large part of the older settled portions of the State that would be greatly benefited by the proper application of plaster, and such areas will continue to increase until it will be difficult to estimate the value of the deposit of gypsum at Fort Dodge.   It should be remembered, also, that the inhabitants of an extent of country adjoining our State more than three times as great as its own area will find it more convenient to obtain their supplies from Fort Dodge than from any other source

For want of direct railroad communication between this region and other parts of the State, the only use yet made of the gypsum by the inhabitants is for the purposes of ordinary building stone   It is so compact that it is found to be comparatively unaffected by the frost, and its ordinary situation in walls of houses is such that it is protected from the dissolving action of water, which can at most reach it only from occasional rains, and the effect of these is too slight to be perceived after the lapse of several years.

One of the citizens of Fort Dodge, Hon John F. Duncombe, built a large, fine residence of it in 1861, the walls of which appear as unaffected by exposure and as beautiful as they were when first erected It has been so long and successfully used for building stone by the inhabitants that they now prefer it to the limestone of good quality, which also exists in the immediate vicinity. This preference is due to the cheapness of the gypsum, as compared with the stone. The cheapness of the former is largely due to the facility with which it is quarried and wrought Several other houses have been constructed of it in Fort Dodge, including the depot building of the Dubuque & Sioux City Railroad. The company have also constructed a large culvert of the same material to span a creek near the town, limestone only being used for the lower courses, which come in contact with the water. It is a fine arch, each stone of gypsum being nicely hewn, and it will doubtless prove a very durable one. Many of the sidewalks in the town are made of the slabs or flags of gypsum which occur in some of the quarries in the form of thin layers They are more durable than their softness would lead one to suppose They also possess an advantage over stone in not becoming slippery when worn.

The method adopted in quarrying and dressing the blocks of gypsum is peculiar, and quite unlike that adopted in similar treatment of ordinary stone. Taking a stout auger-bit of an ordinary brace, such as is used by carpenters, and filing the cutting parts of it into a peculiar form, the quarryman bores his holes into the gypsum quarry for blasting, in the same manner and with as great facility as a carpenter would bore hard wood The pieces being loosened by blasting, they are broken up with sledges into convenient sizes, or hewn into the desired shapes by means of hatchets or ordinary chopping axes, or cut by means of ordinary wood-saws. So little grit does the gypsum contain that these tools, made for working wood, are found to be better adapted for working the former substance than those tools are which are universally used for working stone.

MINOR DEPOSITS OF SULPHATE OF LIME.

Besides the great gypsum deposit of Fort Dodge, sulphate of lime in the various forms of fibrous gypsum, selenite, and small, amorphous masses, has also been discovered in various formations in different parts of the State, including the coal measure shales near Fort Dodge, where it exists in small quantities, quite independently of the great gypsum deposit there. The quantity of gypsum in these minor deposits is always too small to be of any practical value, and frequently minute They usually occur in shales and shaly clays, associated with strata that contain more or less sulphuret of iron (iron pyrites). Gypsum has thus been detected in the coal measures, the St Louis limestone, the cretaceous strata, and also in the lead caves of Dubuque In most of these cases it is evidently the result of double decomposition of iron pyrites and carbonate of lime, previously existing there, in which cases the gypsum is of course not an original deposit as the great one at Fort Dodge is supposed to be.

The existence of these comparatively minute quantities of gypsum in the shales of the coal measures and the subcarboniferous limestone which are exposed within the region of and occupy a stratigraphical position beneath the great gypsum deposits, suggests the possibility that the former may have originated as a precipitate from percolating waters, holding gypsum in solution which they had derived from that deposit in passing over or through it. Since, however, the same substance is found in similar small quantities and under similar conditions in regions where they could have had no possible connection with that deposit, it is believed that none of those mentioned have necessarily originated from it, not even those that are found in close proximity to it.

The gypsum found in the lead caves is usually in the form of efflorescent fibers, and is always in small quantity. In the lower coal-measure shale near Fort Dodge, a small mass was found in the form of an intercalated layer, which had a distinct fibrous structure, the fibers being perpendicular to the plane of the layer. The same mass had also distinct, horizontal planes of cleavage at right angles with the perpendicular fibers. Thus, being more or less transparent, the mass combined the characters of both fibrous gypsum and selenite. No anhydrous sulphate of lime (*anhydrite*) has been found in connection with the great gypsum deposit, nor elsewhere in Iowa, so far as yet known.

SULPHATE OF STRONTIA.

(*Celestine*)

The only locality at which this interesting mineral has yet been found in Iowa, or, so far as is known, in the great valley of the Mississippi, is at Fort Dodge. It occurs there in very small quantity in both the shales of the lower coal measures and in the clays that overlie the gypsum deposit, and which are regarded as of the same age with it. The first is just below the city, near Rees' coal bank, and occurs as a layer intercalated among the coal measure shales, amounting in quantity to only a few hundred pounds weight. The mineral is fibrous and crystalline, the fibers being perpendicular to the plane of the layer. Breaking also with more or less distinct horizontal planes of cleavage, it resembles, in physical character, the layer of fibro-crystalline gypsum before mentioned. Its color is light blue, is transparent and shows crystalline facets upon both the upper and under surfaces of the layer, those of the upper surface being smallest and most numerous. It breaks up readily into small masses along the lines of the perpendicular fibers or columns. The layer is probably not more than a rod in extent in any direction and about three inches in maximum thickness. Apparent lines of stratification occur in it, corresponding with those of the shales which imbed it.

The other deposit was still smaller in amount and occurred as a mass of crystals imbedded in the clay that overlie the gypsum at Cummins' quarry in the valley of Soldier Creek, upon the north side of the town The mineral is in this case nearly colorless, and but for the form of the separate crystals would closely resemble masses of impure salt. The crystals are so closely aggregated that they enclose but little impurity in the mass, but in almost all cases their fundamental forms are obscured This mineral has almost no real practical value, and its occurrence, as described, is interesting only as a mineralogical fact

SULPHATE OF BARYTA
(Barytes, Heavy Spar)

This mineral has been found only in minute quantities in Iowa It has been detected in the coal-measure shales of Decatur, Madison and Marion Counties, the Devonian limestone of Johnson and Bremer Counties and in the lead caves of Dubuque. In all these cases. it is in the form of crystals or small crystalline masses.

SULPHATE OF MAGNESIA
(Epsomite)

Epsomite, or native epsom salts, having been discovered near Burlington, we have thus recognized in Iowa all the sulphates of the alkaline earths of natural origin ; all of them, except the sulphate of lime being in very small quantity. Even if the sulphate of magnesia were produced in nature, in large quantities, it is so very soluble that it can accumulate only in such positions as afford it complete shelter from the rains or running water The epsomite mentioned was found beneath the overhanging cliff of Burlington limestone, near Starr's mill, which are represented in the sketch upon another page, illustrating the subcarboniferous rocks It occurs in the form of efflorescent encrustations upon the surface of stones and in similar small fragile masses among the fine debris that has fallen down beneath the overhanging cliff. The projection of the cliff over the perpendicular face of the strata beneath amounts to near twenty feet at the point where epsomite was found Consequently the rains never reach far beneath it from any quarter The rock upon which the epsomite accumulates is an impure limestone, containing also some carbonate of magnesia, together with a small proportion of iron pyrites in a finely divided condition. It is doubtless by double decomposition of these that the epsomite results By experiments with this native salt in the office of the Survey, a fine article of epsom salts was produced. but the quantity that might be annually obtained there would amount to only a few pounds, and of course is of no practical value whatever, on account of its cheapness in the market.

CLIMATOLOGY.

No extended record of the climatology of Iowa has been made, yet much of great value may be learned from observations made at a single point Prof T. S. Parvin, of the State University. has recorded observations made from 1839 to the present time. Previous to 1860, these observations were made at Muscatine. Since that date, they were made in Iowa City. The result is that the atmospheric conditions of the climate of Iowa are in the highest degree favorable to health.

The highest temperature here occurs in August, while July is the hottest month in the year by two degrees, and January the coldest by three degrees.

The mean temperature of April and October most nearly corresponds to the mean temperature of the year, as well as their seasons of Spring and Fall, while that of Summer and Winter is best represented in that of August and December.

The period of greatest heat ranges from June 22d to August 31st; the next mean time being July 27th. The lowest temperature extends from December 16th to February 15th, the average being January 20th—the range in each case being two full months.

The climate of Iowa embraces the range of that of New York, Pennsylvania, Ohio, Indiana and Illinois. The seasons are not characterized by the frequent and sudden changes so common in the latitudes further south. The temperature of the Winters is somewhat lower than States eastward, but of other seasons it is higher. The atmosphere is dry and invigorating. The surface of the State being free at all seasons of the year from stagnant water, with good breezes at nearly all seasons. the miasmatic and pulmonary diseases are unknown. Mortuary statistics show this to be one of the most healthful States in the Union, being one death to every ninety-four persons. The Spring, Summer and Fall months are delightful; indeed, the glory of Iowa is her Autumn, and nothing can transcend the splendor of her Indian Summer, which lasts for weeks, and finally blends, almost imperceptibly, into Winter.

HISTORY OF THE STATE OF IOWA.

DISCOVERY AND OCCUPATION

Iowa, in the symbolical and expressive language of the aboriginal inhabitants, is said to signify "The Beautiful Land," and was applied to this magnificent and fruitful region by its ancient owners, to express their appreciation of its superiority of climate, soil and location. Prior to 1803, the Mississippi River was the extreme western boundary of the United States. All the great empire lying west of the "Father of Waters," from the Gulf of Mexico on the south to British America on the north, and westward to the Pacific Ocean was a Spanish province. A brief historical sketch of the discovery and occupation of this grand empire by the Spanish and French governments will be a fitting introduction to the history of the young and thriving State of Iowa, which, until the commencement of the present century, was a part of the Spanish possessions in America.

Early in the Spring of 1542, fifty years after Columbus discovered the New World, and one hundred and thirty years before the French missionaries discovered its upper waters, Ferdinand De Soto discovered the mouth of the Mississippi River at the mouth of the Washita. After the sudden death of De Soto, in May of the same year his followers built a small vessel, and in July, 1543, descended the great river to the Gulf of Mexico.

In accordance with the usage of nations under which title to the soil was claimed by right of discovery, Spain, having conquered Florida and discovered the Mississippi, claimed all the territory bordering on that river and the Gulf of Mexico. But it was also held by the European nations that, while discovery gave title, that title must be perfected by actual possession and occupation. Although Spain claimed the territory by right of first discovery, she made no effort to occupy it; by no permanent settlement had she perfected and held her title, and therefore had forfeited it when, at a later period, the Lower Mississippi Valley was re-discovered and occupied by France.

The unparalleled labors of the zealous French Jesuits of Canada in penetrating the unknown region of the West, commencing in 1611, form a history of no ordinary interest, but have no particular connection with the scope of the present work, until in the Fall of 1665 Pierre Claude Allouez, who had entered Lake Superior in September, and sailed along the southern coast in search of copper, had arrived at the great village of the Chippewas at Chegoincegon. Here a grand council of some ten or twelve of the principal Indian nations was held. The Pottawatomies of Lake Michigan, the Sacs and Foxes of the West, the Hurons from the North, the Illinois from the South, and the Sioux from the land of the prairie and wild rice were all assembled there. The Illinois told

1

the story of their ancient glory and about the noble river on the banks of which they dwelt   The Sioux also told their white brother of the same great river, and Allouez promised to the assembled tribes the protection of the French nation against all their enemies, native or foreign

The purpose of discovering the great river about which the Indian nations had given such glowing accounts appears to have originated with Marquette in 1669   In the year previous, he and Claude Dablon had established the Mission of St Mary's, the oldest white settlement within the present limits of the State of Michigan   Marquette was delayed in the execution of his great undertaking, and spent the interval in studying the language and habits of the Illinois Indians, among whom he expected to travel.

About this time, the French Government had determined to extend the dominion of France to the extreme western borders of Canada.   Nicholas Perrot was sent as the agent of the government, to propose a grand council of the Indian nations, at St Mary's

When Perrot reached Green Bay, he extended the invitation far and near, and, escorted by Pottawatomies, repaired on a mission of peace and friendship to the Miamis, who occupied the region about the present location of Chicago

In May, 1671, a great council of Indians gathered at the Falls of St Mary, from all parts of the Northwest, from the head waters of the St. Lawrence, from the valley of the Mississippi and from the Red River of the North Perrot met with them, and after grave consultation formally announced to the assembled nations that their good French Father felt an abiding interest in their welfare, and had placed them all under the powerful protection of the French Government

Marquette, during that same year, had gathered at Point St Ignace the remnants of one branch of the Hurons   This station, for a long series of years, was considered the key to the unknown West

The time was now auspicious for the consummation of Marquette's grand project   The successful termination of Perrot's mission, and the general friendliness of the native tribes, rendered the contemplated expedition much less perilous   But it was not until 1673 that the intrepid and enthusiastic priest was finally ready to depart on his daring and perilous journey to lands never trod by white men.

The Indians, who had gathered in large numbers to witness his departure, were astounded at the boldness of the proposed undertaking, and tried to discourage him, representing that the Indians of the Mississippi Valley were cruel and bloodthirsty, and would resent the intrusion of strangers upon their domain The great river itself, they said, was the abode of terrible monsters, who could swallow both canoes and men

But Marquette was not to be diverted from his purpose by these fearful reports.   He assured his dusky friends that he was ready to make any sacrifice, even to lay down his life for the sacred cause in which he was engaged   He prayed with them; and having implored the blessing of God upon his undertaking, on the 13th day of May, 1673, with Joliet and five Canadian-French voyageurs, or boatmen, he left the mission on his daring journey.   Ascending Green Bay and Fox River, these bold and enthusiastic pioneers of religion and discovery proceeded until they reached a Miami and Kickapoo village, where Marquette was delighted to see a beautiful cross planted in the middle of the town, ornamented with white skins and belts and bows and arrows, which these good people had offered to the Great Manitou or God, to thank Him for the pity He had bestowed on them during the Winter, in having given them abundant chase."

This was the extreme point beyond which the explorations of the French missionaries had not then extended. Here Marquette was instructed by his Indian hosts in the secret of a root that cures the bite of the venomous rattle-snake, drank mineral water with them and was entertained with generous hospitality. He called together the principal men of the village, and informed them that his companion, Joliet, had been sent by the French Governor of Canada to discover new countries, to be added to the dominion of France, but that he himself, had been sent by the Most High God, to carry the glorious religion of the Cross, and assured his wondering hearers that on this mission he had no fear of death, to which he knew he would be exposed on his perilous journeys

Obtaining the services of two Miami guides, to conduct his little band to the Wisconsin River he left the hospitable Indians on the 10th of June. Conducting them across the portage, their Indian guides returned to their village, and the little party descended the Wisconsin, to the great river which had so long been so anxiously looked for, and boldly floated down its unknown waters

On the 25th of June, the explorers discovered indications of Indians on the west bank of the river and landed a little above the mouth of the river now known as Des Moines, and for the first time Europeans trod the soil of Iowa Leaving the Canadians to guard the canoes, Marquette and Joliet boldly followed the trail into the interior for fourteen miles (some authorities say six), to an Indian village situate on the banks of a river, and discovered two other villages, on the rising ground about half a league distant Their visit, while it created much astonishment, did not seem to be entirely unexpected, for there was a tradition or prophecy among the Indians that white visitors were to come to them. They were, therefore, received with great respect and hospitality, and were cordially tendered the calumet or pipe of peace They were informed that this band was a part of the Illini nation and that their village was called Mon-in gou-ma or Moingona which was the name of the river on which it stood. This, from its similarity of sound, Marquette corrupted into Des Moines (Monk's River), its present name

Here the voyagers remained six days, learning much of the manners and customs of their new friends. The new religion they boldly preached and the authority of the King of France they proclaimed were received without hostility or remonstrance by their savage entertainers On their departure, they were accompanied to their canoes by the chiefs and hundreds of warriors Marquette received from them the sacred calumet the emblem of peace and safeguard among the nations, and re-embarked for the rest of his journey.

It is needless to follow him further, as his explorations beyond his discovery of Iowa more properly belong to the history of another State

In 1682, La Salle descended the Mississippi to the Gulf of Mexico, and in the name of the King of France, took formal possession of all the immense region watered by the great river and its tributaries from its source to its mouth, and named it Louisiana, in honor of his master, Louis XIV The river he called "Colbert" after the French Minister, and at its mouth erected a column and a cross bearing the inscription, in the French language,

"LOUIS THE GREAT, KING OF FRANCE AND NAVARRE,
REIGNING APRIL 9TH, 1682'

At the close of the seventeenth century France claimed by right of discovery and occupancy the whole valley of the Mississippi and its tributaries, including Texas as far as the Rio del Norte.

The province of Louisiana stretched from the Gulf of Mexico to the sources of the Tennessee, the Kanawha, the Allegheny and the Monongahela on the east, and the Missouri and the other great tributaries of the Father of Waters on the west   Says Bancroft, "France had obtained, under Providence, the guardianship of this immense district of country, not, as it proved, for her own benefit, but rather as a trustee for the infant nation by which it was one day to be inherited "

By the treaty of Utrecht, France ceded to England her possessions in Hudson's Bay, Newfoundland and Nova Scotia. France still retained Louisiana; but the province had so far failed to meet the expectations of the crown and the people that a change in the government and policy of the country was deemed indispensable   Accordingly, in 1711, the province was placed in the hands of a Governor General, with headquarters at Mobile.   This government was of brief duration, and in 1712 a charter was granted to Anthony Crozat, a wealthy merchant of Paris, giving him the entire control and monopoly of all the trade and resources of Louisiana.   But this scheme also failed   Crozat met with no success in his commercial operations , every Spanish harbor on the Gulf was closed against his vessels , the occupation of Louisiana was deemed an encroachment on Spanish territory ; Spain was jealous of the ambition of France.

Failing in his efforts to open the ports of the district, Crozat "sought to develop the internal resources of Louisiana, by causing trading posts to be opened, and explorations to be made to its remotest borders   But he actually accomplished nothing for the advancement of the colony.   The only prosperity which it ever possessed grew out of the enterprise of humble individuals, who had succeeded in instituting a little barter between themselves and the natives, and a petty trade with neighboring European settlements. After a persevering effort of nearly five years, he surrendered his charter in August, 1717 "

Immediately following the surrender of his charter by Crozat, another and more magnificent scheme was inaugurated.   The national government of France was deeply involved in debt; the colonies were nearly bankrupt, and John Law appeared on the scene with his famous Mississippi Company, as the Louisiana branch of the Bank of France   The charter granted to this company gave it a legal existence of twenty-five years, and conferred upon it more extensive powers and privileges than had been granted to Crozat   It invested the new company with the exclusive privilege of the entire commerce of Louisiana, and of New France, and with authority to enforce their rights.   The Company was authorized to monopolize all the trade in the country; to make treaties with the Indians; to declare and prosecute war, to grant lands, erect forts, open mines of precious metals, levy taxes, nominate civil officers, commission those of the army, and to appoint and remove judges, to cast cannon, and build and equip ships of war   All this was to be done with the paper currency of John Law's Bank of France   He had succeeded in getting His Majesty the French King to adopt and sanction his scheme of financial operations both in France and in the colonies, and probably there never was such a huge financial bubble ever blown by a visionary theorist   Still, such was the condition of France that it was accepted as a national deliverance, and Law became the most powerful man in France.   He became a Catholic, and was appointed Comptroller General of Finance

Among the first operations of the Company was to send eight hundred emigrants to Louisiana who arrived at Dauphine Island in 1718

In 1719, Philipe Francis Renault arrived in Illinois with two hundred miners and artisans. The war between France and Spain at this time rendered it extremely probable that the Mississippi Valley might become the theater of Spanish hostilities against the French settlements; to prevent this as well as to extend French claims, a chain of forts was begun, to keep open the connection between the mouth and the sources of the Mississippi. Fort Orleans, high up the Mississippi River, was erected as an outpost in 1720.

The Mississippi scheme was at the zenith of its power and glory in January, 1720, but the gigantic bubble collapsed more suddenly than it had been inflated, and the Company was declared hopelessly bankrupt in May following. France was impoverished by it, both private and public credit were overthrown, capitalists suddenly found themselves paupers, and labor was left without employment. The effect on the colony of Louisiana was disastrous.

While this was going on in Lower Louisiana, the region about the lakes was the theater of Indian hostilities, rendering the passage from Canada to Louisiana extremely dangerous for many years. The English had not only extended their Indian trade into the vicinity of the French settlements, but through their friends, the Iroquois, had gained a marked ascendancy over the Foxes, a fierce and powerful tribe, of Iroquois descent, whom they incited to hostilities against the French. The Foxes began their hostilities with the siege of Detroit in 1712, a siege which they continued for nineteen consecutive days, and although the expedition resulted in diminishing their numbers and humbling their pride, yet it was not until after several successive campaigns, embodying the best military resources of New France, had been directed against them that were finally defeated at the great battles of Butte des Morts, and on the Wisconsin River, and driven west in 1746.

The Company, having found that the cost of defending Louisiana exceeded the returns from its commerce, solicited leave to surrender the Mississippi wilderness to the home government. Accordingly, on the 10th of April, 1732, the jurisdiction and control over the commerce reverted to the crown of France. The Company had held possession of Louisiana fourteen years. In 1735, Bienville returned to assume command for the King.

A glance at a few of the old French settlements will show the progress made in portions of Louisiana during the early part of the eighteenth century. As early as 1705, traders and hunters had penetrated the fertile regions of the Wabash, and from this region, at that early date, fifteen thousand hides and skins had been collected and sent to Mobile for the European market.

In the year 1716, the French population on the Wabash kept up a lucrative commerce with Mobile by means of traders and voyageurs. The Ohio River was comparatively unknown.

In 1746, agriculture on the Wabash had attained to greater prosperity than in any of the French settlements besides, and in that year six hundred barrels of flour were manufactured and shipped to New Orleans, together with considerable quantities of hides, peltry, tallow and beeswax.

In the Illinois country, also, considerable settlements had been made, so that, in 1730, they embraced one hundred and forty French families, about six hundred "converted Indians," and many traders and voyageurs.

In 1753, the first actual conflict arose between Louisiana and the Atlantic colonies. From the earliest advent of the Jesuit fathers, up to the period of which we speak, the great ambition of the French had been, not alone to preserve their possessions in the West, but by every possible means to prevent the slightest attempt of the English west of the mountains, to extend their settlements toward the Mississippi. France was resolved on retaining possession of the great territory which her missionaries had discovered and revealed to the world. French commandants had avowed their purpose of seizing every Englishman within the Ohio Valley.

The colonies of Pennsylvania, New York and Virginia were most affected by the encroachments of France in the extension of her dominion, and particularly in the great scheme of uniting Canada with Louisiana. To carry out this purpose, the French had taken possession of a tract of country claimed by Virginia, and had commenced a line of forts extending from the lakes to the Ohio River. Virginia was not only alive to her own interests, but attentive to the vast importance of an immediate and effectual resistance on the part of all the English colonies to the actual and contemplated encroachments of the French.

In 1753, Governor Dinwiddie, of Virginia, sent George Washington, then a young man just twenty-one, to demand of the French commandant " a reason for invading British dominions while a solid peace subsisted." Washington met the French commandant, Gardeur de St. Pierre, on the head waters of the Alleghany, and having communicated to him the object of his journey, received the insolent answer that the French would not discuss the matter of right, but would make prisoners of every Englishman found trading on the Ohio and its waters. The country, he said, belonged to the French, by virtue of the discoveries of La Salle, and they would not withdraw from it.

In January, 1754, Washington returned to Virginia, and made his report to the Governor and Council. Forces were at once raised, and Washington, as Lieutenant Colonel, was dispatched at the head of a hundred and fifty men, to the forks of the Ohio, with orders to "finish the fort already begun there by the Ohio Company, and to make prisoners, kill or destroy all who interrupted the English settlements."

On his march through the forests of Western Pennsylvania, Washington, through the aid of friendly Indians, discovered the French concealed among the rocks, and as they ran to seize their arms, ordered his men to fire upon them, at the same time, with his own musket, setting the example. An action lasting about a quarter of an hour ensued; ten of the Frenchmen were killed, among them Jumonville, the commander of the party, and twenty-one were made prisoners. The dead were scalped by the Indians, and the chief, bearing a tomahawk and a scalp, visited all the tribes of the Miamis, urging them to join the Six Nations and the English against the French. The French, however, were soon re-enforced, and Col. Washington was compelled to return to Fort Necessity. Here, on the 3d day of July, De Villiers invested the fort with 600 French troops and 100 Indians. On the 4th, Washington accepted terms of capitulation, and the English garrison withdrew from the valley of the Ohio.

This attack of Washington upon Jumonville aroused the indignation of France, and war was formally declared in May, 1756, and the " French and Indian War" devastated the colonies for several years. Montreal, Detroit and all Canada were surrendered to the English, and on the 10th of February, 1763, by the treaty of Paris—which had been signed, though not formally ratified by the respective governments, on the 3d of November, 1762—France relinquished to Great Britain all that portion of the province of Louisiana lying on the east side of ? M   l   l   l   l   ol w   f N   O   ns. On the same c   l   treaty, ceded to Sp   including the

whole country to the head waters of the Great River, and west to the Rocky
Mountains, and the jurisdiction of France in America, which had lasted nearly
a century, was ended.

At the close of the Revolutionary war, by the treaty of peace between Great
Britain and the United States, the English Government ceded to the latter
all the territory on the east side of the Mississippi River and north of the thirty-
first parallel of north latitude   At the same time, Great Britain ceded to
Spain all the Floridas, comprising all the territory east of the Mississippi and
south of the southern limits of the United States.

At this time, therefore, the present State of Iowa was a part of the Spanish
possessions in North America, as all the territory west of the Mississippi River
was under the dominion of Spain.   That government also possessed all the
territory of the Floridas east of the great river and south of the thirty-first
parallel of north latitude.   The Mississippi, therefore, so essential to the prosperity of the western portion of the United States, for the last three hundred
miles of its course flowed wholly within the Spanish dominions, and that government claimed the exclusive right to use and control it below the southern boundary of the United States

The free navigation of the Mississippi was a very important question during
all the time that Louisiana remained a dependency of the Spanish Crown, and
as the final settlement intimately affected the status of the then future State
of Iowa, it will be interesting to trace its progress

The people of the United States occupied and exercised jurisdiction over
the entire eastern valley of the Mississippi, embracing all the country drained
by its eastern tributaries; they had a natural right, according to the accepted international law, to follow these rivers to the sea, and to the use of the Mississippi River accordingly, as the great natural channel of commerce.   The river
was not only necessary but absolutely indispensable to the prosperity and growth
of the western settlements then rapidly rising into commercial and political
importance   They were situated in the heart of the great valley, and with
wonderfully expansive energies and accumulating resources, it was very evident
that no power on earth could deprive them of the free use of the river below
them, only while their numbers were insufficient to enable them to maintain
their right by force   Inevitably, therefore, immediately after the ratification of
the treaty of 1783, the Western people began to demand the free navigation
of the Mississippi—not as a favor, but as a right   In 1786, both banks of
the river, below the mouth of the Ohio, were occupied by Spain, and military
posts on the east bank enforced her power to exact heavy duties on all imports by way of the river for the Ohio region   Every boat descending the
river was forced to land and submit to the arbitrary revenue exactions of the
Spanish authorities.   Under the administration of Governor Miro, these rigorous exactions were somewhat relaxed from 1787 to 1790; but Spain held it as
her right to make them   Taking advantage of the claim of the American people
that the Mississippi should be opened to them, in 1791, the Spanish Government concocted a scheme for the dismemberment of the Union   The plan was
to induce the Western people to separate from the Eastern States by liberal land
grants and extraordinary commercial privileges

Spanish emissaries, among the people of Ohio and Kentucky, informed them
that the Spanish Government would grant them favorable commercial privileges,
provided they would secede from the Federal Government east of the mountains
The Spanish Minister to the United States plainly declared to his confidential
correspondent that, unless the Western people would declare their independence

and refuse to remain in the Union, Spain was determined never to grant the free navigation of the Mississippi

By the treaty of Madrid, October 20, 1795 however, Spain formally stipulated that the Mississippi River, from its source to the Gulf, for its entire width, should be free to American trade and commerce, and that the people of the United States should be permitted, for three years, to use the port of New Orleans as a port of deposit for their merchandise and produce, duty free

In November, 1801, the United States Government received, through Rufus King its Minister at the Court of St James, a copy of the treaty between Spain and France, signed at Madrid March 21, 1801, by which the cession of Louisiana to France, made the previous Autumn, was confirmed

The change offered a favorable opportunity to secure the just rights of the United States, in relation to the free navigation of the Mississippi, and ended the attempt to dismember the Union by an effort to secure an independent government west of the Alleghany Mountains.   On the 7th of January, 1803, the American House of Representatives adopted a resolution declaring their "unalterable determination to maintain the boundaries and the rights of navigation and commerce through the River Mississippi, as established by existing treaties"

In the same month, President Jefferson nominated and the Senate confirmed Robert R. Livingston and James Monroe as Envoys Plenipotentiary to the Court of France, and Charles Pinckney and James Monroe to the Court of Spain, with plenary powers to negotiate treaties to effect the object enunciated by the popular branch of the National Legislature   These envoys were instructed to secure, if possible, the cession of Florida and New Orleans, but it does not appear that Mr Jefferson and his Cabinet had any idea of purchasing that part of Louisiana lying on the *west* side of the Mississippi   In fact, on the 2d of March following, the instructions were sent to our Ministers, containing a plan which expressly left to France "all her territory on the west side of the Mississippi"   Had these instructions been followed, it might have been that there would not have been any State of Iowa or any other member of the glorious Union of States west of the "Father of Waters"

In obedience to his instructions, however, Mr. Livingston broached this plan to M. Talleyrand, Napoleon's Prime Minister, when that courtly diplomatist quietly suggested to the American Minister that France *might* be willing to cede the *whole French domain* in North America to the United States, and asked how much the Federal Government would be willing to give for it   Livingston intimated that twenty millions of francs might be a fair price   Talleyrand thought that not enough, but asked the Americans to "think of it"   A few days later, Napoleon, in an interview with Mr. Livingston, in effect informed the American Envoy that he had secured Louisiana in a contract with Spain for the purpose of turning it over to the United States for a mere nominal sum   He had been compelled to provide for the safety of that province by the treaty, and he was "anxious to give the United States a magnificent bargain for a mere trifle"   The price proposed was one hundred and twenty-five million francs.   This was subsequently modified to fifteen million dollars, and on this basis a treaty was negotiated, and was signed on the 30th day of April, 1803.

This treaty was ratified by the Federal Government, and by act of Congress, approved October 31, 1803, the President of the United States was authorized to take possession of the territory and provide for it a temporary government   Accordingly, on the 20th day of December following, on behalf of the President, Gen Claiborne and Gen Wilkinson took possession of the Louisiana purchase, and raised the American flag over the newly acquired domain, at New Orleans. Spain, although it had by treaty ceded the province to France in 1801, still held *quasi* possession, and at first objected to the transfer, but withdrew her opposition early in 1804.

By this treaty, thus successfully consummated, and the peaceable withdrawal of Spain, the then infant nation of the New World extended its dominion west of the Mississippi to the Pacific Ocean, and north from the Gulf of Mexico to British America

If the original design of Jefferson's administration had been accomplished, the United States would have acquired only that portion of the French territory lying east of the Mississippi River, and while the American people would thus have acquired the free navigation of that great river, all of the vast and fertile empire on the west, so rich in its agricultural and inexhaustible mineral resources, would have remained under the dominion of a foreign power. To Napoleon's desire to sell the whole of his North American possessions, and Livingston's act transcending his instructions, which was acquiesced in after it was done, does Iowa owe her position as a part of the United States by the Louisiana purchase

By authority of an act of Congress, approved March 26, 1804, the newly acquired territory was, on the 1st day of October following, divided: that part lying south of the 33d parallel of north latitude was called the Territory of Orleans, and all north of that parallel the District of Louisiana, which was placed under the authority of the officers of Indiana Territory, until July 4, 1805, when it was organized, with territorial government of its own, and so remained until 1812, when the Territory of Orleans became the State of Louisiana, and the name of the Territory of Louisiana was changed to Missouri. On the 4th of July, 1814, that part of Missouri Territory comprising the present State of Arkansas, and the country to the westward, was organized into the Arkansas Territory.

On the 2d of March, 1821, the State of Missouri, being a part of the Territory of that name, was admitted to the Union. June 28, 1834, the territory west of the Mississippi River and north of Missouri was made a part of the Territory of Michigan, but two years later, on the 4th of July, 1836, Wisconsin Territory was erected, embracing within its limits the present States of Iowa, Wisconsin and Minnesota

By act of Congress, approved June 12, 1838, the

TERRITORY OF IOWA

was erected, comprising, in addition to the present State, much the larger part of Minnesota, and extending north to the boundary of the British Possessions.

THE ORIGINAL OWNERS.

Having traced the early history of the great empire lying west of the Mississippi, of which the State of Iowa constitutes a part, from the earliest discovery to the organization of the Territory of Iowa, it becomes necessary to give some history of

THE INDIANS OF IOWA.

According to the policy of the European nations, possession perfected title to any territory. We have seen that the country west of the Mississippi was first discovered by the Spaniards, but afterward, was visited and occupied by the French. It was ceded by France to Spain, and by Spain back to France again,

and then was purchased and occupied by the United States   During all that
time, it does not appear to have entered into the heads or hearts of the high
contracting parties that the country they bought, sold and gave away was in
the possession of a race of men who, although savage, owned the vast domain
before Columbus first crossed the Atlantic.   Having purchased the territory,
the United States found it still in the possession of its original owners, who had
never been dispossessed; and it became necessary to purchase again what had
already been bought before, or forcibly eject the occupants; therefore, the history of the Indian nations who occupied Iowa prior to and during its early settlement by the whites, becomes an important chapter in the history of the State,
that cannot be omitted

For more than one hundred years after Marquette and Joliet trod the virgin
soil of Iowa, not a single settlement had been made or attempted.   not even a
trading post had been established   The whole country remained in the undisputed possession of the native tribes, who roamed at will over her beautiful and
fertile prairies hunted in her woods, fished in her streams, and often poured out
their life-blood in obstinately contested contests for supremacy   That this State
so aptly styled "The Beautiful Land," had been the theater of numerous,
fierce and bloody struggles between rival nations, for possession of the favored
region, long before its settlement by civilized man, there is no room for doubt
In these savage wars, the weaker party, whether aggressive or defensive, was
either exterminated or driven from their ancient hunting grounds

In 1673, when Marquette discovered Iowa, the Illini were a very powerful
people, occupying a large portion of the State, but when the country was again
visited by the whites, not a remnant of that once powerful tribe remained on
the west side of the Mississippi, and Iowa was principally in the possession of
the Sacs and Foxes, a warlike tribe which, originally two distinct nations,
residing in New York and on the waters of the St Lawrence, had gradually
fought their way westward, and united, probably, after the Foxes had been driven
out of the Fox River country, in 1846, and crossed the Mississippi   The death
of Pontiac, a famous Sac chieftain, was made the pretext for war against the
Illini, and a fierce and bloody struggle ensued, which continued until the Illinois
were nearly destroyed and their hunting grounds possessed by their victorious
foes   The Iowas also occupied a portion of the State for a time, in common
with the Sacs, but they, too, were nearly destroyed by the Sacs and Foxes, and,
in "The Beautiful Land" these natives met their equally warlike foes the
Northern Sioux with whom they maintained a constant warfare for the possession of the country for many years

When the United States came in possession of the great valley of the Mississippi, by the Louisiana purchase, the Sacs and Foxes and Iowas possessed
the entire territory now comprising the State of Iowa   The Sacs and Foxes,
also, occupied the most of the State of Illinois

The Sacs had four principal villages, where most of them resided, viz :
Their largest and most important town—if an Indian village may be called
such—and from which emanated most of the obstacles and difficulties encountered by the Government in the extinguishment of Indian titles to land in this
region, was on Rock River, near Rock Island, another was on the east bank of
the Mississippi, near the mouth of Henderson River; the third was at the
head of the Des Moines Rapids, near the present site of Montrose, and the fourth
was n   l   f   ' ' p I w

T   l   a t   ,   d llag   t   One n the west side of the
Missi   r   n l   d   e r pid   Rock River   another about twelve

miles from the river, in the rear of the Dubuque lead mines, and the third on Turkey River.

The Iowas, at one time identified with the Sacs, of Rock River, had withdrawn from them and become a separate tribe. Their principal village was on the Des Moines River, in Van Buren County, on the site where Iowaville now stands. Here the last great battle between the Sacs and Foxes and the Iowas was fought, in which Black Hawk, then a young man, commanded one division of the attacking forces. The following account of the battle has been given:

' Contrary to long established custom of Indian attack, this battle was commenced in the day time, the attending circumstances justifying this departure from the well settled usages of Indian warfare. The battle field was a level river bottom, about four miles in length, and two miles wide near the middle, narrowing to a point at either end. The main area of this bottom rises perhaps twenty feet above the river, leaving a narrow strip of low bottom along the shore, covered with trees that belted the prairie on the river side with a thick forest, and the immediate bank of the river was fringed with a dense growth of willows. Near the lower end of this prairie, near the river bank, was situated the Iowa village. About two miles above it and near the middle of the prairie is a mound, covered at the time with a tuft of small trees and underbrush growing on its summit. In the rear of this little elevation or mound lay a belt of wet prairie, covered, at that time with a dense growth of rank, coarse grass. Bordering this wet prairie on the north, the country rises abruptly into elevated broken river bluffs, covered with a heavy forest for many miles in extent, and in places thickly clustered with undergrowth, affording a convenient shelter for the stealthy approach of the foe.

"Through this forest the Sac and Fox war party made their way in the night and secreted themselves in the tall grass spoken of above, intending to remain in ambush during the day and make such observations as this near proximity to their intended victim might afford, to aid them in their contemplated attack on the town during the following night. From this situation their spies could take a full survey of the village, and watch every movement of the inhabitants, by which means they were soon convinced that the Iowas had no suspicion of their presence.

"At the foot of the mound above mentioned, the Iowas had their race course, where they diverted themselves with the excitement of horse racing, and schooled their young warriors in cavalry evolutions. In these exercises mock battles were fought, and the Indian tactics of attack and defense carefully inculcated, by which means a skill in horsemanship was acquired rarely excelled. Unfortunately for them this day was selected for their equestrian sports, and wholly unconscious of the proximity of their foes, the warriors repaired to the race ground, leaving most of their arms in the village and their old men and women and children unprotected.

"Pash-a-po-po, who was chief in command of the Sacs and Foxes, perceived at once the advantage this state of things afforded for a complete surprise of his now doomed victims, and ordered Black Hawk to file off with his young warriors through the tall grass in [ ] gain the cover of the timber along the river bank, and with the utmost speed reach the village and commence the battle, while he remained with his division in the ambush to make a simultaneous assault on the unarmed men whose attention was engrossed with the excitement of the races. The plan was skillfully laid and most dexterously executed. Black Hawk with his forces reached the village undiscovered, and made a furious onslaught upon the defenseless inhabitants, by firing one general volley into their midst, and completing the slaughter with the tomahawk and scalping knife, aided by the devouring flames with which they enveloped the village as soon as the fire brand could be spread from lodge to lodge.

"On the instant of the report of fire arms at the village the forces under Pash-a-po po leaped from their couchant position in the grass and sprang tiger-like upon the astonished and unarmed Iowas in the midst of their racing sports. The first impulse of the latter naturally led them to make the utmost speed toward their arms in the village, and protect if possible their wives and children from the attack of their merciless assailants. The distance from the place of attack on the prairie was two miles, and a great number fell in their flight by the bullets and tomahawks of their enemies, who pressed them closely with a running fire the whole way, and the survivors only reached their town in time to witness the horrors of its destruction. Their whole village was in flames, and the dearest objects of their lives lay in slaughtered heaps amidst the devouring element, and the agonizing groans of the dying, mingled with the exulting shouts of the victorious foe, filled their hearts with maddening despair. Their wives and children who had been spared the general massacre were prisoners, and together with their arms were in the hands of the victors, and all that could now be done was to draw off their shattered and defenseless forces, and save as many lives as possible by a retreat across the Des Moines River, which they effected in the best possible manner, and took a position among the Soap Creek Hills."

The Sacs and Foxes [ ] [ ] destruction of their village [ ] Rock River, had a fierce conflict with the Winnebagoes [ ] [ ] [ ] [ ] session

of their lands. Their village on Rock River, at one time, contained upward of
sixty lodges, and was among the largest Indian villages on the continent. In
1825, the Secretary of War estimated the entire number of the Sacs and Foxes
at 4,600 souls. Their village was situated in the immediate vicinity of the
upper rapids of the Mississippi, where the beautiful and flourishing towns of
Rock Island and Davenport are now situated. The beautiful scenery of the
island, the extensive prairies, dotted over with groves; the picturesque bluffs
along the river banks, the rich and fertile soil, producing large crops of corn,
squash and other vegetables, with little labor, the abundance of wild fruit,
game, fish, and almost everything calculated to make it a delightful spot for an
Indian village, which was found there, had made this place a favorite home of
the Sacs and secured for it the strong attachment and veneration of the whole
nation

North of the hunting grounds of the Sacs and Foxes, were those of the
Sioux a fierce and warlike nation, who often disputed possession with their
rivals in savage and bloody warfare. The possessions of these tribes were
mostly located in Minnesota but extended over a portion of Northern and
Western Iowa to the Missouri River. Their descent from the north upon the
hunting grounds of Iowa frequently brought them into collision with the Sacs
and Foxes, and after many a conflict and bloody struggle, a boundary line was
established between them by the Government of the United States, in a treaty
held at Prairie du Chien, in 1825. But this, instead of settling the difficulties,
caused them to quarrel all the more, in consequence of alleged trespasses upon
each other's side of the line. These contests were kept up and became so unre-
lenting that, in 1830, Government bought of the respective tribes of the Sacs
and Foxes, and the Sioux, a strip of land twenty miles in width, on both sides
of the line and thus throwing them forty miles apart by creating between them
a "neutral ground," commanded them to cease their hostilities. Both the
Sacs and Foxes and the Sioux, however, were allowed to fish and hunt on this
ground unmolested, provided they did not interfere with each other on United
States territory. The Sacs and Foxes and the Sioux were deadly enemies, and
neither let an opportunity to punish the other pass unimproved.

In April, 1852, a fight occurred between the Musquaka band of Sacs and
Foxes and a band of Sioux, about six miles above Algona, in Kossuth County,
on the west side of the Des Moines River. The Sacs and Foxes were under
the leadership of Ko-ko-wah, a subordinate chief, and had gone up from their
home in Tama County, by way of Clear Lake, to what was then the "neutral
ground." At Clear Lake, Ko-ko-wah was informed that a party of Sioux were
encamped on the west side of the East Fork of the Des Moines, and he determined to attack them. With sixty of his warriors, he started and arrived at a
point on the east side of the river, about a mile above the Sioux encampment,
in the night, and concealed themselves in a grove, where they were able to discover the position and strength of their hereditary foes. The next morning,
after many of the Sioux braves had left their camp on hunting tours the vin-
dictive Sacs and Foxes crossed the river and suddenly attacked the camp. The
conflict was desperate for a short time, but the advantage was with the assailants, and the Sioux were routed. Sixteen of them, including some of their
women and children, were killed, and a boy 14 years old was captured. One
of the Musquakas was shot in the breast by a squaw as they were rushing into
the Sioux's camp. He started to run away, when the same brave squaw shot
him through the head at a distance of twenty rods, and he fell dead. Three
other Sac braves were killed. But few of the Sioux escaped. The victorious

party hurriedly buried their own dead, leaving the dead Sioux above ground, and made their way home, with their captive, with all possible expedition.

PIKE'S EXPEDITION.

Very soon after the acquisition of Louisiana, the United States Government adopted measures for the exploration of the new territory, having in view the conciliation of the numerous tribes of Indians by whom it was possessed, and, also, the selection of proper sites for the establishment of military posts and trading stations The Army of the West, Gen James Wilkinson commanding had its headquarters at St. Louis From this post, Captains Lewis and Clark with a sufficient force, were detailed to explore the unknown sources of the Missouri, and Lieut Zebulon M. Pike to ascend to the head waters of the Mississippi Lieut Pike, with one Sergeant, two Corporals and seventeen privates, left the military camp, near St. Louis, in a keel-boat, with four months' rations on the 9th day of August, 1805 On the 20th of the same month, the expedition arrived within the present limits of Iowa at the foot of the Des Moines Rapids, where Pike met William Ewing who had just been appointed Indian Agent at this point, a French interpreter and four chiefs and fifteen Sac and Fox warriors

At the head of the Rapids, where Montrose is now situated, Pike held a council with the Indians, in which he addressed them substantially as follows · "Your great Father, the President of the United States, wished to be more intimately acquainted with the situation and wants of the different nations of red people in our newly acquired territory of Louisiana, and has ordered the General to send a number of his warriors in different directions to take them by the hand and make such inquiries as might afford the satisfaction required" At the close of the council he presented the red men with some knives, whisky and tobacco.

Pursuing his way up the river, he arrived, on the 23d of August, at what is supposed, from his description, to be the site of the present city of Burlington, which he selected as the location of a military post.   He describes the place as being " on a hill, about forty miles above the River de Moyne Rapids, on the west side of the river, in latitude about 41° 21' north The channel of the river runs on that shore, the hill in front is about sixty feet perpendicular, nearly level on top, four hundred yards in the rear is a small prairie fit for gardening, and immediately under the hill is a limestone spring, sufficient for the consumption of a whole regiment" In addition to this description, which corresponds to Burlington, the spot is laid down on his map at a bend in the river, a short distance below the mouth of the Henderson, which pours its waters into the Mississippi from Illinois. The fort was built at Fort Madison, but from the distance, latitude, description and map furnished by Pike it could not have been the place selected by him, while all the circumstances corroborate the opinion that the place he selected was the spot where Burlington is now located, called by the early voyagers on the Mississippi, " Flint Hills '

On the 24th, with one of his men he went on shore on a hunting expedition, and following a stream which they supposed to be a part of the Mississippi, they were led away from their course Owing to the intense heat and tall grass, his two favorite dogs, which he had taken with him, became exhausted and he left them on the prairie, supposing that they would follow him as soon as they should get rested, and went on to overtake his boat. Reaching the river, he waited some time for his canine friends but they did not come and as he deemed it inexpedient to detain the boat longer, two of his men volunteered to go in pursuit of them, and he continued on his way up the river, expecting that the two men would soon overtake him.   They lost their way, however, and for six days were without food, except a few morsels gathered from the stream, and might have perished, had they not accidentally met a trader from St Louis who induced two Indians to take them up the river, and they overtook the boat at Dubuque

At Dubuque, Pike was cordially received by Julien Dubuque, a Frenchman, who held a mining claim under a grant from Spain   Dubuque had an old field piece and fired a salute in honor of the advent of the first Americans who had visited that part of the Territory   Dubuque, however, was not disposed to publish the wealth of his mines, and the young and evidently inquisitive officer obtained but little information from him

After leaving this place, Pike pursued his way up the river, but as he passed beyond the limits of the present State of Iowa, a detailed history of his explorations on the upper waters of the Mississippi more properly belongs to the history of another State

It is sufficient to say that on the site of Fort Snelling, Minnesota at the mouth of the Minnesota River, Pike held a council with the Sioux, September 23 and obtained from them a grant of one hundred thousand acres of land On the 8th of January, 1806, Pike arrived at a trading post belonging to the Northwest Company, on Lake De Sable, in latitude 47°   At this time the then powerful Northwest Company carried on their immense operations from Hudson's Bay to the St Lawrence, up that river on both sides, along the great lakes to the head of Lake Superior, thence to the sources of the Red River of the north and west, to the Rocky Mountains   embracing within the scope of their operations the entire Territory of Iowa   After successfully accomplishing his mission, and performing a valuable service to Iowa and the whole Northwest, Pike returned to St Louis, arriving there on the 30th of April, 1806.

INDIAN WARS

The Territory of Iowa, although it had been purchased by the United States, and was ostensibly in the possession of the Government, was still occupied by the Indians, who claimed title to the soil by right of ownership and possession. Before it could be open to settlement by the whites it was indispensable that the Indian title should be extinguished and the original owners removed   The accomplishment of this purpose required the expenditure of large sums of money and blood   and for a long series of years the frontier was disturbed by Indian wars, terminated repeatedly by treaty, only to be renewed by some act of oppression on the part of the whites or some violation of treaty stipulation.

As previously shown   at the time when the United States assumed the control of the country by virtue of the Louisiana purchase, nearly the whole State was in possession of the Sacs and Foxes, a powerful and warlike nation, who were not disposed to submit without a struggle to what they considered the encroachments of the pale faces

Among the most noted chiefs, and one whose restlessness and hatred of the Americans occasioned more trouble to the Government than any other of his tribe, was Black Hawk, who was born at the Sac village, on Rock River, in 1767   He was simply the chief of his own band of Sac warriors, but by his energy and ambition he became the leading spirit of the united nation of Sacs and F... ... ... in the history of the country from 1804 ... ... he attained ... distinction as a fighting ... ... campaigns against the Osages and other neighboring tribes   About the beginning of the present century he began to appear prominent in affairs on the Mississippi   Some historians have added to the statement that "it does not appear that he was ever a great general, or possessed any of the qualifications of a successful leader"   If this was so, his life was a marvel   How any man who had none of the qualifications of a leader became so prominent as such, as he did, indicates either that he had some ability, or that his cotemporaries, both Indian and Anglo-Saxon, had less than he   He is said to have been the "victim of a narrow prejudice and bitter ill-will against the Americans," but the impartial historian must admit that if he was the enemy of the Americans, it was certainly not without some reason.

It will be remembered that Spain did not give up possession of the country to France on its cession to the latter power, in 1801, but retained possession of it, and, by the authority of France, transferred it to the United States, in 1804. Black Hawk and his band were in St Louis at the time, and were invited to be present and witness the ceremonies of the transfer, but he refused the invitation, and it is but just to say that this refusal was caused probably more from regret that the Indians were to be transferred from the jurisdiction of the Spanish authorities than from any special hatred toward the Americans   In his life he says: "I found many sad and gloomy faces because the United States were about to take possession of the town and country.   Soon after the Americans came, I took my band and went to take leave of our Spanish father. The Americans came to see him also   Seeing them approach, we passed out of one door as they entered another, and immediately started in our canoes for our village, on Rock River. not liking the change any more than our friends appeared to at St Louis   On arriving at our village, we gave the news that strange people had arrived at St Louis, and that we should never see our Spanish father again   The information made all our people sorry"

On the 3d day of November, 1804, a treaty was concluded between William Henry Harrison, then Governor of Indiana Territory, on behalf of the United States, and five chiefs of the Sac and Fox nation, by which the latter, in consideration of two thousand two hundred and thirty-four dollars' worth of goods then delivered, and a yearly annuity of one thousand dollars to be paid in goods at just cost, ceded to the United States all that land on the east side of the Mississippi, extending from a point opposite the Jefferson, in Missouri, to the Wisconsin River, embracing an area of over fifty-one millions of acres.

To this treaty Black Hawk always objected and always refused to consider it binding upon his people   He asserted that the chiefs or braves who made it had no authority to relinquish the title of the nation to any of the lands they held or occupied · and, moreover, that they had been sent to St Louis on quite a different errand, namely, to get one of their people released, who had been imprisoned at St Louis for killing a white man

The year following this treaty (1805), Lieutenant Zebulon M Pike came up the river for the purpose of holding friendly councils with the Indians and selecting sites for forts within the territory recently acquired from France by the United States   Lieutenant Pike seems to have been the first American whom Black Hawk ever met or had a personal interview with, and he was very much prepossessed in Pike's favor   He gives the following account of his visit to Rock Island:

"A boat came up the river with a young American chief and a small party of soldiers.   We heard of them soon after they passed Salt River.   Some of our young braves watched them every day to see what sort of people he had on board   The boat at length arrived at Rock River, and the young .   me on

shore with his interpreter. and made a speech and gave us some presents   We
in turn presented them with meat and such other provisions as we had to spare
We were well pleased with the young chief · He gave us good advice, and said
our American father would treat us well."

The events which soon followed Pike's expedition were the erection of Fort
Edwards, at what is now Warsaw, Illinois, and Fort Madison, on the site of the
present town of that name, the latter being the first fort erected in Iowa   These
movements occasioned great uneasiness among the Indians   When work was
commenced on Fort Edwards, a delegation from their nation, headed by some of
their chiefs, went down to see what the Americans were doing, and had an interview with the commander ; after which they returned home apparently satisfied   In like manner, when Fort Madison was being erected, they sent down
another delegation from a council of the nation held at Rock River   According to Black Hawk's account, the American chief told them that he was building a house for a trader who was coming to sell them goods cheap, and that the
soldiers were coming to keep him company—a statement which Black Hawk
says they distrusted at the time, believing that the fort was an encroachment
upon their rights, and designed to aid in getting their lands away from them

It has been held by good American authorities, that the erection of Fort
Madison at the point where it was located *was a violation of the treaty of 1804*
By the eleventh article of that treaty, the United States had a right to build a
fort near the mouth of the Wisconsin River ; by article six they had bound
themselves "that if any citizen of the United States or any other white persons
should form a settlement upon their lands, such intruders should forthwith be
removed"   Probably the authorities of the United States did not regard the
establishment of military posts as coming properly within the meaning of the
term "settlement," as used in the treaty   At all events, they erected Fort
Madison within the territory reserved to the Indians, who became very indignant.   Not long after the fort was built, a party led by Black Hawk attempted
its destruction   They sent spies to watch the movements of the garrison, who
ascertained that the soldiers were in the habit of marching out of the fort every
morning and evening for parade and the plan of the party was to conceal themselves near the fort, and attack and surprise them when they were outside.   On
the morning of the proposed day of attack, five soldiers came out and were fired
upon by the Indians, two of them being killed.   The Indians were too hasty in
their movement, for the regular drill had not yet commenced.   However, they
kept up the attack for several days attempting the old Fox strategy of setting
fire to the fort with blazing arrows, but finding their efforts unavailing, they
soon gave up and returned to Rock River

When war was declared between the United States and Great Britain, in
1812. Black Hawk and his band allied themselves with the British, partly
because he was dazzled by their specious promises, and more probably because
they had been deceived by the Americans.   Black Hawk himself declared that
they were 'forced into the war by being deceived"   He narrates the circumstances as follows : "Several of the chiefs and head men of the Sacs and
Foxes were called upon to go to Washington to see their Great Father.   On
their return, they related what had been said and done   They said the Great
Father wished them in the event of a war taking place with England, not to
interfere on either side, but to remain neutral   He did not want our help, but
wished us to hunt and support our families and live in peace   He said that
British ···· would ···· ········ to come ··· the Mississippi to furnish us
with go·· ·· ···· ·· ···· ·· ·· supply us with ·· American trader.   Our

chiefs then told him that the British traders always gave them credit in the Fall for guns, powder and goods, to enable us to hunt and clothe our families He repeated that the traders at Fort Madison would have plenty of goods, that we should go there in the Fall and he would supply us on credit, as the British traders had done '

Black Hawk seems to have accepted of this proposition, and he and his people were very much pleased. Acting in good faith, they fitted out for their Winter's hunt, and went to Fort Madison in high spirits to receive from the trader their outfit of supplies. But, after waiting some time, they were told by the trader that he would not trust them It was in vain that they pleaded the promise of their great father at Washington The trader was inexorable, and, disappointed and crestfallen, they turned sadly toward their own village. 'Few of us," says Black Hawk, "slept that night; all was gloom and discontent In the morning, a canoe was seen ascending the river; it soon arrived, bearing an express, who brought intelligence that a British trader had landed at Rock Island with two boats loaded with goods, and requested us to come up immediately, because he had good news for us, and a variety of presents The express presented us with tobacco, pipes and wampum The news ran through our camp like fire on a prairie Our lodges were soon taken down, and all started for Rock Island Here ended all hopes of our remaining at peace, having been forced into the war by being deceived "

He joined the British, who flattered him, styled him " Gen Black Hawk," decked him with medals, excited his jealousies against the Americans, and armed his band, but he met with defeat and disappointment, and soon abandoned the service and came home

With all his skill and courage, Black Hawk was unable to lead all the Sacs and Foxes into hostilities to the United States. A portion of them, at the head of whom was Keokuk ("the Watchful Fox"), were disposed to abide by the treaty of 1804, and to cultivate friendly relations with the American people Therefore, when Black Hawk and his band joined the fortunes of Great Britain, the rest of the nation remained neutral, and, for protection, organized, with Keokuk for their chief. This divided the nation into the " War and the Peace party "

Black Hawk says he was informed, after he had gone to the war, that the nation, which had been reduced to so small a body of fighting men, were unable to defend themselves in case the Americans should attack them, and having all the old men and women and children belonging to the warriors who had joined the British on their hands to provide for, a council was held, and it was agreed that Quash-qua-me (the Lance) and other chiefs, together with the old men, women and children, and such others as chose to accompany them, should go to St Louis and place themselves under the American chief stationed there They accordingly went down, and were received as the "friendly band" of the Sacs and Foxes, and were provided for and sent up the Missouri River On Black Hawk's return from the British army, he says Keokuk was introduced to him as the war chief of the braves then in the village. He inquired how he had become chief, and was informed that their spies had seen a large armed force going toward Peoria, and fears were entertained of an attack upon the village; whereupon a council was held, which concluded to leave the village and cross over to the west side of the Mississippi Keokuk had been standing at the door of the lodge where the council was held, not being allowed to enter on account of his not having killed an enemy, wherefore a man named Wa-co-me came out. Keokuk asked permission to speak in the council, which Wa-co-me obtained for him. Keokuk then addressed the chiefs , he remonstrated against the desertion of their village, their own homes and the graves of their fathers, and offered to defend the village The council consented that he should be their war chief He marshaled his braves, sent out spies, and advanced on the trail leading to Peoria, but returned without seeing the enemy The Americans did not disturb the village, and all were satisfied with the appointment of Keokuk

Keokuk, like Black Hawk, was a descendant of the Sac branch of the nation, and was born on Rock River, in 1780 He was of a pacific disposition, but possessed the elements of true courage, and could fight, when occasion required, with a cool judgment and heroic energy In his first battle, he encountered and killed a Sioux, which placed him in the rank of warriors, and he was honored with a public feast by his tribe in commemoration of the event

Keokuk has been described as an orator, entitled to rank with the most gifted of his race. In person, he was tall and of portly bearing ; in his public speeches, he displayed a commanding attitude and graceful gestures, he spoke rapidly, but his enunciation was clear, distinct and forcible, he culled his figures from the stores of nature and based his arguments on skillful logic Unfortunately for the reputation of Keokuk, as an orator among white people, he was never able to obtain an interpreter who could claim even a slight acquaintance with philosophy With one exception only, his interpreters were unacquainted with the elements of their mother-tongue. Of this serious hindrance to his fame, Keokuk was well aware, and retained Frank Labershure, who had received a rudimental education in the French and English languages, until the latter broke down by dissipation and died. But during the meridian of his career among the white people, he was compelled to submit his speeches for translation to uneducated men, whose range of thought fell below the flights of a gifted mind, and the fine imagery drawn from nature was beyond their power of reproduction He had sufficient knowledge of the English language to make him sensible of this bad rendering of his thoughts, and often a feeling of mortification at the bungling efforts was depicted on his countenance while speaking. The proper place to form a correct estimate of his ability as an orator was in the Indian council, where he addressed himself exclusively to those who understood his language, and witness the electrical effect of his eloquence upon his audience

Keokuk seems to have possessed a more sober judgment, and to have had a more intelligent view of the great strength and resources of the United States, than his noted and restless cotemporary, Black Hawk He knew from the first that the reckless war which Black Hawk and his band had determined to carry on could result in nothing but defeat and disaster, and used every argument against it The large number of warriors whom he had dissuaded from following Black Hawk became, however, greatly excited with the war spirit after Stillman's defeat, and but for the signal tact displayed by Keokuk on that occasion, would have forced him to submit to their wishes in joining the rest of the warriors in the field. A war-dance was held, and Keokuk took part in it, seeming to be moved with the current of the rising storm When the dance was over, he called the council to prepare for war. He made a speech in which he admitted the justice of their complaints against the Americans To seek redress was a noble aspiration of their nature The blood of their brethren had been shed by the white man and the spirits of their braves slain in battle called loudly for vengeance I am your chief and it is my duty to lead you to battle, if, after fully considering the matter, you are determined to go But before-you decide on taking this important step, it is wise to inquire into the chances of success." He then portrayed to them the great power of the United States, against whom they would have to contend, that their chance of success was utterly hopeless. "But," said he, "if you do determine to go upon the war-path, I will agree to lead you, on one condition, viz. that before we go, we will kill all our old men and our wives and children, to save them from a lingering death of starvation, and that every one of us determine to leave our homes on the other side of the Mississippi."

This was a strong but truthful picture of the prospect before them, and was presented in such a forcible light as to cool their ardor, and cause them to abandon the rash undertaking.

But during the war of 1832, it is now considered certain that small bands of Indians, from the west side of the Mississippi, made incursions into the white settlements, in the lead mining region, and committed some murders and depredations.

When peace was declared between the United States and England, Black Hawk was required to make peace with the former and entered into a treaty at Portage des Sioux, September 14, 1815, but did not "touch the goose-quill to it until May 13, 1816, when he smoked the pipe of peace with the great white chief," at St. Louis. This treaty was a renewal of the treaty of 1804, but Black Hawk declared he had been deceived, that he did not know that by signing the treaty he was giving away his village. This weighed upon his mind, already soured by previous disappointment and the irresistible encroachments of the whites, and when, a few years later, he and his people were driven from their possessions by the military, he determined to return to the home of his fathers.

It is also to be remarked that, in 1816, by treaty with various tribes, the United States relinquished to the Indians all the lands lying north of a line drawn from the southernmost point of Lake Michigan west to the Mississippi, except a reservation five leagues square, on the Mississippi River, supposed then to be sufficient to include all the mineral lands on and adjacent to Fever River, and one league square at the mouth of the Wisconsin River.

THE BLACK HAWK WAR

The immediate cause of the Indian outbreak in 1830 was the occupation of Black Hawk's village, on the Rock River, by the whites, during the absence of the chief and his braves on a hunting expedition, on the west side of the Mississippi. When they returned, they found their wigwams occupied by white families, and their own women and children were shelterless on the banks of the river. The Indians were indignant, and determined to repossess their village at all hazards, and early in the Spring of 1831 recrossed the Mississippi and menacingly took possession of their own cornfields and cabins. It may be well to remark here that it was expressly stipulated in the treaty of 1804, to which they attributed all their troubles, that the Indians should not be obliged to leave their lands until they were sold by the United States, and it does not appear that they occupied any lands other than those owned by the Government. If this was true, the Indians had good cause for indignation and complaint. But the whites, driven out in turn by the returning Indians, became so clamorous against what they termed the encroachments of the natives, that Gov. Reynolds, of Illinois, ordered Gen. Gaines to Rock Island with a military force to drive the Indians again from their homes to the west side of the Mississippi. Black Hawk says he did not intend to be provoked into war by anything less than the blood of some of his own people, in other words, that there would be no war unless it should be commenced by the pale faces. But it was said and probably thought by the military commanders along the frontier that the Indians intended to unite in a general war against the whites, from Rock River to the Mexican borders. But it does not appear that the hardy frontiersmen themselves had any fears, for their experience had been that, when well treated, their Indian neighbors were not dangerous. Black Hawk and his band had done no more than to attempt to repossess the the old homes of which they had been deprived in their absence. No blood had been shed. Black Hawk and his chiefs sent a flag of truce, and a new treaty was made, by which Black Hawk and his band agreed to remain forever on the Iowa side and never recross the river without the permission of the President or the Governor of Illinois. Whether the Indians clearly understood the terms of this treaty is uncertain. As was usual, the Indian traders had dictated terms on their behalf, and they had received a large amount of provisions, etc., from the Government but it may well be doubted whether the Indians comprehended that they could never revisit the graves of their fathers without violating their treaty. They undoubtedly thought that they had agreed never to recross the Mississippi with hostile intent. However this may be, on the 6th day of April, 1832, Black Hawk and his entire band, with their women and children, again recrossed the Mississippi in plain view of the garrison of Fort Armstrong, and went up Rock River. Although this act was construed into an act of hostility by the military authorities, who declared that Black Hawk intended to recover his village, or the site where it stood, by force; but it does not appear that he made any such attempt, nor did his apearance create any special alarm among the settlers. They knew that the Indians never went on the war path encumbered with the old men, their women and their children.

The *Galenian*, printed in Galena, of May 2, 1832, says that Black Hawk was invited by the Prophet and had taken possession of a tract about forty miles up Rock River; but that he did not remain there long, but commenced his march up Rock River. Capt. W. B. Green, who served in Capt Stephenson's company of mounted rangers, says that "Black Hawk and h's band crossed the river with no hostile intent, but that his band had had bad luck in hunting during the previous Winter, were actually in a starving condition, and had come over to spend the Summer with a friendly tribe on the head waters of the Rock and Illinois Rivers, by invitation from their chief. Other old settlers, who all agree that Black Hawk had no idea of fighting, say that he came back to the west side expecting to negotiate another treaty, and get a new supply of provisions. The most reasonable explanation of this movement, which resulted so disastrously to Black Hawk and his starving people, is that, during the Fall and Winter of 1831-2, his people became deeply indebted to their favorite trader at Fort Armstrong (Rock Island). They had not been fortunate in hunting, and he was likely to lose heavily, as an Indian debt was outlawed in one year. If, therefore, the Indians could be induced to come over, and the fears of the military could be sufficiently aroused to pursue them, another treaty could be negotiated, and from the payments from the Government the shrewd trader could get his pay. Just a week after Black Hawk crossed the river on the 13th of April, 1832, George Davenport wrote to Gen Atkinson: "I am informed that the British band of Sac Indians are determined to make war on the frontier settlements * * * From every information that I have received I am of the opinion that the intention of the British band of Sac Indians commit depredations on the inhabitants of the frontier." And yet, from the 6th day of April until after Stillman's men commenced war by firing on a flag of truce from Black Hawk, no murders nor depredations were committed by the British band of Sac Indians

It is not the purpose of this sketch to detail the incidents of the Black Hawk war of 1832, as it pertains rather to the history of the State of Illinois It is sufficient to say that, after the disgraceful affair at Stillman's Run, Black Hawk, concluding that the whites, refusing to treat with him, were determined to exterminate his people, determined to return to the Iowa side of the Mississippi. He could not return by the way he came, for the army was behind him, an army, too, that would sternly refuse to recognize the white flag of peace His only course was to make his way northward and reach the Mississippi, if possible, before the troops could overtake him, and this he did but, before he could get his women and children across the Wisconsin, he was overtaken, and a battle ensued Here, again, he sued for peace, and, through his trusty Lieutenant, "the Prophet," the whites were plainly informed that the starving Indians did not wish to fight, but would return to the west side of the Mississippi, peaceably, if they could be permitted to do so No attention was paid to this second effort to negotiate peace, and, as soon as supplies could be obtained, the pursuit was resumed, the flying Indians were overtaken again eight miles before they reached the mouth of the Bad Axe, and the slaughter (it should not be dignified by the name of battle) commenced Here, overcome by starvation and the victorious whites, his band was scattered, on the 2d day of August, 1832. Black Hawk escaped, but was brought into camp at Prairie du Chien by three Winnebagoes He was confined in Jefferson Barracks until the Spring of 1833, when he was sent to Washington, arriving there April 22 On the 26th of April, they were taken to Fortress Monroe, where they remained till the 4th of June, 1833, when orders were given for them to be liberated and returned to their own country By order of the President, he was brought back to Iowa through the principal Eastern cities. Crowds flocked to see him all along his route, and he was very much flattered by the attentions he received He lived among his people on the Iowa River till that reservation was sold, in 1836, when, with the rest of the Sacs and Foxes, he removed to the Des Moines Reservation, where he remained till his death, which occurred on the 3d of October, 1838.

INDIAN PURCHASES, RESERVES AND TREATIES

At the close of the Black Hawk War, in 1832, a treaty was made at a council held on the west bank of the Mississippi, where now stands the thriving city of Davenport, on grounds now occupied by the Chicago, Rock Island & Pacific Railroad Company, on the 21st day of September, 1832 At this council, the United States were represented by Gen Winfield Scott and Gov. Reynolds, of Illinois Keokuk, Pash-a-pa-ho and some thirty other chiefs and warriors of the Sac and Fox nation were present. By this treaty, the Sacs and Foxes ceded to the United States a strip of land on the eastern border of Iowa fifty miles wide, from the northern boundary of Missouri to the mouth of the Upper Iowa River, containing about six million acres The western line of the purchase was parallel with the Mississippi. In consideration of this cession, the United States Government stipulated to pay annually to the confederated tribes, for thirty consecutive years, twenty thousand dollars in specie, and to pay the debts of the Indians at Rock Island which had been accumulating for

seventeen years and amounted to fifty thousand dollars, due to Davenport &
Farnham, Indian traders. The Government also generously donated to the
Sac and Fox women and children whose husbands and fathers had fallen in the
Black Hawk war, thirty-five beef cattle, twelve bushels of salt, thirty barrels of
pork, fifty barrels of flour and six thousand bushels of corn.

This territory is known as the "Black Hawk Purchase" Although it was
not the first portion of Iowa ceded to the United States by the Sacs and Foxes,
it was the first opened to actual settlement by the tide of emigration that flowed
across the Mississippi as soon as the Indian title was extinguished. The treaty
was ratified February 13, 1833, and took effect on the 1st of June following,
when the Indians quietly removed from the ceded territory, and this fertile and
beautiful region was opened to white settlers

By the terms of the treaty, out of the Black Hawk Purchase was reserved for
the Sacs and Foxes 400 square miles of land situated on the Iowa River, and including within its limits Keokuk's village on the right bank of that river. This
tract was known as 'Keokuk's Reserve,' and was occupied by the Indians until
1836, when, by a treaty made in September between them and Gov. Dodge, of
Wisconsin Territory, it was ceded to the United States. The council was held
on the banks of the Mississippi, above Davenport, and was the largest assem-
blage of the kind ever held by the Sacs and Foxes to treat for the sale of lands.
About one thousand of their chiefs and braves were present, and Keokuk was
their leading spirit and principal speaker on the occasion. By the terms of the
treaty the Sacs and Foxes were removed to another reservation on the Des
Moines River, where an agency was established for them at what is now the
town of Agency City.

Besides the Keokuk Reserve, the Government gave out of the Black Hawk
Purchase to Antoine Le Claire, interpreter, in fee simple one section of land
opposite Rock Island, and another at the head of the first rapids above the
island, on the Iowa side. This was the first land title granted by the United
States to an individual in Iowa.

Soon after the removal of the Sacs and Foxes to their new reservation
on the Des Moines River, Gen. Joseph M. Street was transferred from the
agency of the Winnebagoes, at Prairie du Chien, to establish an agency
among them. A farm was selected, on which the necessary buildings were
erected, including a comfortable farm house for the agent and his family, at
the expense of the Indian Fund. A salaried agent was employed to superintend the farm and dispose of the crops. Two mills were erected, one on Soap
Creek and the other on Sugar Creek. The latter was soon swept away by a
flood, but the former remained and did good service for many years. Connected
with the agency were Joseph Smart and John Goodell, interpreters. The
latter was interpreter for Hard Fish's band. Three of the Indian chiefs Keokuk, Wapello and Appanoose, had each a large field improved, the two former
on the right bank of the Des Moines, back from the river, in what is now
'Keokuk's Prairie," and the latter on the present site of the city of Ottumwa
Among the traders connected with the agency were the Messrs. Ewing, from
Ohio, and Phelps & Co., from Illinois, and also Mr. J. P. Eddy, who established his post at what is now the site of Eddyville

The Indians at this agency became idle and listless in the absence of their
natural and wonted excitements, and many of them plunged into dissipation
Keokuk himself became dissipated in the latter years of his life, and it has
been   at the   his removal with his
tribe

In May, 1843, most of the Indians were removed up the Des Moines River, above the temporary line of Red Rock, having ceded the remnant of their lands in Iowa to the United States on the 21st of September, 1837, and on the 11th of October, 1842   By the terms of the latter treaty, they held possession of the ' New Purchase" till the Autumn of 1845, when the most of them were removed to their reservation in Kansas, the balance being removed in the Spring of 1846

1   *Treaty with the Sioux*—Made July 19, 1815   ratified December 16, 1815   This treaty was made at Portage des Sioux, between the Sioux of Minnesota and Upper Iowa and the United States, by William Clark and Ninian Edwards, Commissioners, and was merely a treaty of peace and friendship on the part of those Indians toward the United States at the close of the war of 1812

2   *Treaty with the Sacs*—A similar treaty of peace was made at Portage des Sioux, between the United States and the Sacs, by William Clark, Ninian Edwards and Auguste Choteau, on the 13th of September, 1815, and ratified at the same date as the above   In this, the treaty of 1804 was re-affirmed, and the Sacs here represented promised for themselves and their bands to keep entirely separate from the Sacs of Rock River, who, under Black Hawk, had joined the British in the war just then closed

3   *Treaty with the Foxes*—A separate treaty of peace was made with the Foxes at Portage des Sioux, by the same Commissioners on the 14th of September, 1815, and ratified the same as the above, wherein the Foxes re-affirmed the treaty of St Louis, of November 3, 1804, and agreed to deliver up all their prisoners to the officer in command at Fort Clark, now Peoria, Illinois

4   *Treaty with the Iowas*—A treaty of peace and mutual good will was made between the United States and the Iowa tribe of Indians, at Portage des Sioux, by the same Commissioners as above on the 16th of September, 1815, at the close of the war with Great Britain, and ratified at the same date as the others

5   *Treaty with the Sacs of Rock River*—Made at St Louis on the 13th of May, 1816, between the United States and the Sacs of Rock River, by the Commissioners, William Clark, Ninian Edwards and Auguste Choteau, and ratified December 30, 1816   In this treaty, that of 1804 was re-established and confirmed by twenty-two chiefs and head men of the Sacs of Rock River, and Black Hawk himself attached to it his signature, or, as he said, ' touched the goose quill '

6.   *Treaty of 1824*—On the 4th of August, 1824 a treaty was made between the United States and the Sacs and Foxes in the city of Washington, by William Clark, Commissioner, wherein the Sac and Fox nation relinquished their title to all lands in Missouri and that portion of the southeast corner of Iowa known as the ' Half-Breed Tract" was set off and reserved for the use of the half-breeds of the Sacs and Foxes, they holding title in the same manner as Indians   Ratified January 18, 1825

7   *Treaty of August 19, 1825*—At this date a treaty was made by William Clark and Lewis Cass, at Prairie du Chien, between the United States and the Chippewas, Sacs and Foxes, Menomonees, Winnebagoes and a portion of the Ottawas and Pottawatomies   In this treaty, in order to make peace between the contending tribes as to the limits of their respective hunting grounds in Iowa, it was agreed that the United States Government should run a boundary line between the Sioux, on the north, and the Sacs and Foxes, on the south, as follows.

Commencing at the mouth of the Upper Iowa River, on the west bank of the Mississippi, and ascending said Iowa River to its west fork, thence up the fork to its source, thence crossing the fork of Red Cedar River in a direct line to the second or upper fork of the Des Moines River, thence in a direct line to the lower fork of the Calumet River, and down that river to its junction with the Missouri River

8   *Treaty of 1830*—On the 15th of July, 1830 the confederate tribes of the Sacs and Foxes ceded to the United States a strip of country lying south of the above line, twenty miles in width, and extending along the line aforesaid from the Mississippi to the Des Moines River   The Sioux also. whose possessions were north of the line, ceded to the Government, in the same treaty, a like strip on the north side of the boundary   Thus the United States, at the ratification of this treaty, February 24 1831, came into possession of a portion of Iowa forty miles wide, extending along the Clark and Cass line of 1825, from the Mississippi to the Des Moines River   This territory was known as the "Neutral Ground," and the tribes on either side of the line were allowed to fish and hunt on it unmolested till it was made a Winnebago reservation, and the Winnebagoes were removed to it in 1841

9   *Treaty with the Sacs and Foxes and other Tribes*—At the same time of the above treaty respecting the "Neutral Ground" (July 15, 1830), the Sacs and Foxes, Western Sioux, Omahas, Iowas and Miss ..... be boundaries of which ..... River, and passing the ..... creek that falls into the B ..... Calumet

River to the Missouri River; thence down said Missouri River to the Missouri State line above the Kansas, thence along said line to the northwest corner of said State, thence to the high lands between the waters falling into the Missouri and Des Moines, passing to said high lands along the dividing ridge between the forks of the Grand River; thence along said high lands or ridge separating the waters of the Missouri from those of the Des Moines, to a point opposite the source of the Boyer River, and thence in a direct line to the upper fork of the Des Moines, the place of beginning

It was understood that the lands ceded and relinquished by this treaty were to be assigned and allotted, under the direction of the President of the United States, to the tribes then living thereon, or to such other tribes as the President might locate thereon for hunting and other purposes   In consideration of three tracts of land ceded in this treaty, the United States agreed to pay to the Sacs three thousand dollars, to the Foxes, three thousand dollars, to the Sioux, two thousand dollars, to the Yankton and Santie bands of Sioux, three thousand dollars; to the Omahas, two thousand five hundred dollars, and to the Ottoes and Missouris, two thousand five hundred dollars—to be paid annually for ten successive years   In addition to these annuities, the Government agreed to furnish some of the tribes with blacksmiths and agricultural implements to the amount of two hundred dollars, at the expense of the United States, and to set apart three thousand dollars annually for the education of the children of these tribes. It does not appear that any fort was erected in this territory prior to the erection of Fort Atkinson on the Neutral Ground, in 1840-41

This treaty was made by William Clark, Superintendent of Indian affairs, and Col Willoughby Morgan, of the United States First Infantry, and came into effect by proclamation, February 24, 1831

10 *Treaty with the Winnebagoes* —Made at Fort Armstrong, Rock Island, September 15, 1832, by Gen Winfield Scott and Hon John Reynolds, Governor of Illinois   In this treaty the Winnebagoes ceded to the United States all their land lying on the east side of the Mississippi, and in part consideration therefor the United States granted to the Winnebagoes, to be held as other Indian lands are held, that portion of Iowa known as the Neutral Ground   The exchange of the two tracts of country was to take place on or before the 1st day of June, 1833   In addition to the Neutral Ground, it was stipulated that the United States should give the Winnebagoes, beginning in September, 1833 and continuing for twenty-seven successive years, ten thousand dollars in specie, and establish a school among them, with a farm and garden, and provide other facilities for the education of their children, not to exceed in cost three thousand dollars a year, and to continue the same for twenty-seven successive years   Six agriculturists, twelve yoke of oxen and plows and other farming tools were to be supplied by the Government

11 *Treaty of 1832 with the Sacs and Foxes* —Already mentioned as the Black Hawk purchase

12 *Treaty of 1836*, with the Sacs and Foxes, ceding Keokuk's Reserve to the United States, for which the Government stipulated to pay thirty thousand dollars, and an annuity of ten thousand dollars for ten successive years, together with other sums and debts of the Indians to various parties

13 *Treaty of 1837* — On the 21st of October 1837, a treaty was made at the city of Washington, between Carey A Harris, Commissioner of Indian Affairs, and the confederate tribes of Sacs and Foxes, ratified February 21, 1838, wherein another slice of the soil of Iowa was obtained, described in the treaty as follows: "A tract of country containing 1,250,000 acres, lying west and adjoining the tract conveyed by them to the United States in the treaty of September 21, 1832   It is understood that the points of termination for the present cession shall be the northern and southern points of said tract as fixed by the survey made under the authority of the United States, and that a line shall be drawn between them so as to intersect a line extended westwardly from the angle of said tract nearly opposite to Rock Island, as laid down in the above survey, so far as may be necessary to include the number of acres hereby ceded, which last mentioned line, it is estimated, will be about twenty-five miles"

This piece of land was twenty-five miles wide in the middle, and ran off to a point at both ends, lying directly back of the Black Hawk Purchase, and of the same length

14 *Treaty of Relinquishment* —At the same date as the above treaty, in the city of Washington, Carey A Harris, Commissioner, the Sacs and Foxes ceded to the United States all their right and interest in the country lying south of the boundary line between the Sacs and Foxes and Sioux, as described in the treaty of August 19, 1825, and between the Mississippi and Missouri Rivers, the United States paying for the same one hundred and sixty thousand dollars   The Indians also gave up all claims and interests under the treaties previously made with them, for the satisfaction of which no appropriations had been made

15 *Treaty of 1842* —The last treaty was made with the Sacs and Foxes October 11, 1842 ratified March 23, 1843   It was made at the Sac and Fox agency (Agency City), by John Chambers, Commissioner on behalf of the United States   In this treaty the Sac and Fox Indians "ceded to the United States all their lands west of the Mississippi to which they had any claim or title"   By the terms of this treaty they were to be removed from the country at the expiration of three years, and all who remained after that were to move at their own expense   Part of them were removed to Kansas in the fall of 1845 and the rest the spring following

SPANISH GRANTS

While the territory now embraced in the State of Iowa was under Spanish rule as a part of its province of Louisiana, certain claims to and grants of land were made by the Spanish authorities, with which, in addition to the extinguishment of Indian titles, the United States had to deal   It is proper that these should be briefly reviewed.

Dubuque —On the 22d day of September, 1788, Julien Dubuque, a Frenchman, from Prairie du Chien, obtained from the Foxes a cession or lease of lands on the Mississippi River for mining purposes, on the site of the present city of Dubuque.   Lead had been discovered here eight years before, in 1780, by the wife of Peosta Fox, a warrior, and Dubuque's claim embraced nearly all the lead bearing lands in that vicinity   He immediately took possession of his claim and commenced mining, at the same time making a settlement.   The place became known as the "Spanish Miners," or, more commonly, "Dubuque's Lead Mines"

In 1796, Dubuque filed a petition with Baron de Carondelet, the Spanish Governor of Louisiana, asking that the tract ceded to him by the Indians might be granted to him by patent from the Spanish Government.   In this petition, Dubuque rather indefinitely set forth the boundaries of this claim as "about seven leagues along the Mississippi River, and three leagues in width from the river," intending to include, as is supposed, the river front between the Little Maquoketa and the Tete des Mertz Rivers, embracing more than twenty thousand acres   Carondelet granted the prayer of the petition, and the grant was subsequently confirmed by the Board of Land Commissioners of Louisiana.

In October, 1804, Dubuque transferred the larger part of his claim to Auguste Choteau, of St Louis, and on the 17th of May, 1805, he and Choteau jointly filed their claims with the Board of Commissioners   On the 20th of September, 1806, the Board decided in their favor, pronouncing the claim to be a regular Spanish grant, made and completed prior to the 1st day of October, 1800, only one member, J B C Lucas, dissenting.

Dubuque died March 24, 1810   The Indians, understanding that the claim of Dubuque under their former act of cession was only a permit to occupy the tract and work the mines during his life, and that at his death they reverted to them, took possession and continued mining operations, and were sustained by the military authority of the United States, notwithstanding the decision of the Commissioners   When the Black Hawk purchase was consummated, the Dubuque claim thus held by the Indians was absorbed by the United States, as the Sacs and Foxes made no reservation of it in the treaty of 1832.

The heirs of Choteau, however, were not disposed to relinquish their claim without a struggle   Late in 1832, they employed an agent to look after their interests, and authorized him to lease the right to dig lead on the lands   The miners who commenced work under this agent were compelled by the military to abandon their operations, and one of the claimants went to Galena to institute legal proceedings, but found no court of competent jurisdiction, although he did bring an action for the recovery of a quantity of lead dug at Dubuque, for the purpose of testing the title.   Being unable to identify the lead, however, he was non-suited

By act of Congress, approved July 2 1836, the town of Dubuque was surveyed and platted   After lots had been sold and occupied by the purchasers, Henry Choteau brought an action of ejectment against Patrick Malony, who held land in Dubuque under a patent from the United States, for the recovery of seven undivided eighth parts of the Dubuque claim, as purchased by Auguste Choteau in 1804   The case was tried in the District Court of the United States for the District of Iowa, and was decided adversely to the plaintiff.   The case was carried to the Supreme Court of the United States on a writ of error, when it was heard at the December term, 1853, and the decision of the lower court was affirmed, the court holding that the permit from Carondolet was merely a lease or permit to work the mines, that Dubuque asked, and the Governor of Louisiana granted, nothing more than the "peaceable possession" of certain lands obtained from the Indians, that Carondelet had no legal authority to make such a grant as claimed, and that, even if he had, this was but an "inchoate and imperfect title"

Giard —In 1795, the Lieutenant Governor of Upper Louisiana granted to Basil Giard five thousand eight hundred and sixty acres of land, in what is now Clayton County, known as the "Giard Tract"   He occupied the land during the time that Iowa passed from Spain to France, and from France to the United States, in consideration of which the Federal Government granted a patent of the same to Giard in his own right   His heirs sold the whole tract to James H Lockwood and Thomas P Burnett, of Prairie du Chien, for three hundred dollars

Honori —March 30, 1799, Zenon Trudeau, Acting Lieutenant Governor of Upper Louisiana, granted to Louis Honori a tract of land on the site of the present town of Montrose, as follows: " It is permitted to Mr. Louis (Fresson) Henori, or Louis Honore Fesson, to establish himself at the head of the rapids of the River Des Moines, and his establishment once formed, notice of it shall be given to the Governor General, in order to obtain for him a commission of a space sufficient to give value to such establishment, and at the same time to render it useful to the commerce of the peltries of this country, to watch the Indians and keep them in the fidelity which they owe to His Majesty "

Honori took immediate possession of his claim, which he retained until 1805. While trading with the natives, he became indebted to Joseph Robedoux, who obtained an execution on which the property was sold May 13, 1803, and was purchased by the creditor.   In these proceedings the property was described as being "about six leagues above the River Des Moines"   Robedoux died soon after he purchased the property   Auguste Choteau, his executor, disposed of the Honori tract to Thomas F Reddeck, in April, 1805, up to which time Honori continued to occupy it.   The grant, as made by the Spanish government, was a league square, but only one mile square was confirmed by the United States.   After the half-breeds sold their lands, in which the Honori grant was included, various claimants resorted to litigation in attempts to invalidate the title of the Reddeck heirs, but it was finally confirmed by a decision of the Supreme Court of the United States in 1839, and is the oldest legal title to any land in the State of Iowa.

THE HALF-BREED TRACT

Before any permanent settlement had been made in the Territory of Iowa, white adventurers, trappers and traders, many of whom were scattered along the Mississippi and its tributaries, as agents and employes of the American Fur Company, intermarried with the females of the Sac and Fox Indians, producing a race of half-breed who number was never definitely ascertained.   There were some respectable and intelligent people among their children of men of some reputation and education for that distance: Dr Muir, a gentleman educated at Edinburgh, Scotland, a surgeon in the United States Army, stationed at a military post located on the present site of Warsaw, married an Indian woman, and reared his family of three daughters in the city of Keokuk. Other examples might be cited, but they are probably exceptions to the general rule, and the race is now nearly or quite extinct in Iowa.

A treaty was made at Washington, August 4, 1824, between the Sacs and Foxes and the United States, by which that portion of Lee County was reserved to the half-breeds of those tribes, and which was afterward known as "The Half-Breed Tract." This reservation is the triangular piece of land, containing about 119,000 acres, lying between the Mississippi and Des Moines Rivers. It is bounded on the north by the prolongation of the northern line of Missouri. This line was intended to be a straight one, running due east, which would have caused it to strike the Mississippi River at or below Montrose, but the surveyor who run it took no notice of the change in the variation of the needle as he proceeded eastward, and, in consequence, the line he run was bent, deviating more and more to the northward of a direct line as he approached the Mississippi, so that it struck that river at the lower edge of the town of Fort Madison. "This erroneous line," says Judge Mason, "has been acquiesced in as well in fixing the northern limit of the Half-Breed Tract as in determining the northern boundary line of the State of Missouri." The line thus run included in the reservation a portion of the lower part of the city of Fort Madison, and all of the present townships of Van Buren, Charleston, Jefferson, Des Moines, Montrose and Jackson.

Under the treaty of 1824, the half-breeds had the right to occupy the soil, but could not convey it, the reversion being reserved to the United States. But on the 30th day of January, 1834, by act of Congress, this reversionary right was relinquished, and the half-breeds acquired the lands in fee simple. This was no sooner done, than a horde of speculators rushed in to buy land of the half-breed owners, and, in many instances, a gun, a blanket, a pony or a few quarts of whisky was sufficient for the purchase of large estates. There was a deal of sharp practice on both sides; Indians would often claim ownership of land by virtue of being half-breeds, and had no difficulty in proving their mixed blood by the Indians, and they would then cheat the speculators by selling land to which they had no rightful title. On the other hand, speculators often claimed land in which they had no ownership. It was diamond cut diamond until at last things became badly mixed. There were no authorized surveys, and no boundary lines to claims, and, as a natural result, numerous conflicts and quarrels ensued.

To settle these difficulties, to decide the validity of claims or sell them for the benefit of the real owners, by act of the Legislature of Wisconsin Territory, approved January 16, 1838, Edward Johnstone, Thomas S. Wilson and David Brigham were appointed Commissioners, and clothed with power to effect these objects. The act provided that these Commissioners should be paid six dollars a day each. The commission entered upon its duties and continued until the next session of the Legislature, when the act creating it was repealed, invalidating all that had been done and depriving the Commissioners of their pay. The repealing act, however, authorized the Commissioners to commence action against the owners of the Half-Breed Tract, to receive pay for their services, in the District Court of Lee County. Two judgments were obtained, and on execution the whole of the tract was sold to Hugh T. Reid, the Sheriff executing the deed. Mr. Reid sold portions to various parties, but his title was questioned and he became involved in litigation. Decisions in favor of Reid and those holding under him were made by both District and Supreme Courts, but in December, 1850, these decisions were finally reversed by the Supreme Court of the United States in the case of Joseph Webster, plaintiff in error, vs. Hugh T Reid, and the judgment titles failed   About nine years before the "judgment titles" were finally abrogated as above, another class of titles were brought into competition with them, and in the conflict between the two the final decision was obtained   These were the titles based on the "decree of partition" issued by the United States District Court for the Territory of Iowa, on the 8th of May, 1841, and certified to by the Clerk on the 2d day of June of that year   Edward Johnstone and Hugh T Reid then law partners at Fort Madison, filed the petition for the decree in behalf of the St. Louis claimants of half-breed lands.   Francis S Key, author of the Star Spangled Banner, who was then attorney for the New York Land Company, which held heavy interests in these lands, took a leading part in the measure, and drew up the document in which it was presented to the court   Judge Charles Mason, of Burlington, presided.   The plan of partition divided the tract into one hundred and one shares and arranged that each claimant should draw his proportion by lot, and should abide the result, whatever it might be.   The arrangement was entered into, the lots drawn, and the plat of the same filed in the Recorder's office, October 6, 1841.   Upon this basis the titles to land in the Half-Breed Tract are now held

EARLY SETTLEMENTS.

The first permanent settlement by the whites within the limits of Iowa was made by Julien Dubuque, in 1788, when, with a small party of miners, he settled on the site of the city that now bears his name, where he lived until his death in 1810   Louis Honori settled on the site of the present town of Montrose, probably in 1799, and resided there until 1805, when his property passed into other hands.   Of the Giard settlement, opposite Prairie du Chien, little is known, except that it was occupied by some parties prior to the commencement of the present century, and contained three cabins in 1805   Indian traders, although not strictly to be considered settlers, had established themselves at various points at an early date.   A Mr Johnson, agent of the American Fur Company, had a trading post below Burlington, where he carried on traffic with the Indians some time before the United States possessed the country.   In 1820, Le Moliese, a French trader, had a station at what is now Sandusky, six miles above Keokuk, in Lee County   In 1829, Dr Isaac Gallaud made a settlement on the Lower Rapids, at what is now Nashville

The first settlement in Lee County was made in 1820, by Dr. Samuel C Muir, a surgeon in the United States army, who had been stationed at Fort Edwards, now Warsaw, Ill , and who built a cabin where the city of Keokuk now stands   Dr Muir was a man of strict integrity and irreproachable character   While stationed at a military post on the Upper Mississippi, he had married an Indian woman of the Fox nation   Of his marriage, the following romantic account is given

The post at which he was stationed was visited by a beautiful Indian maiden—whose native name, unfortunately, has not been preserved—who, in her dreams, had seen a white brave unmoor his canoe, paddle it across the river and come directly to her lodge   She felt assured, according to the superstitious belief of her race, that, in her dreams, she had seen her future husband, and had come to the fort to find him   Meeting Dr Muir she instantly recognized him as [illegible] with childlike innocence and simplicity she related to him [illegible] with Sophia [illegible] innocence and devotion, the [illegible] but after a while the sneers and gibes of his brother officers—less honorable than he, perhaps—made him feel ashamed of his dark-skinned wife, and when his regiment was ordered down the river, to Bellefontaine, it is said he embraced the opportunity to rid himself of her, and left her, never expecting to see her again, and little dreaming that she would have the courage to follow him. But, with her infant child, this intrepid wife and mother started alone in her canoe, and, after many days of weary labor and a lonely journey of nine hundred miles, she, at last, reached him. She afterward remarked, when speaking of this toilsome journey down the river in search of her husband, "When I got there I was all perished away—so thin!" The doctor, touched by such unexampled devotion, took her to his heart, and ever after, until his death, treated her with marked respect. She always presided at his table with grace and dignity, but never abandoned her native style of dress. In 1819–20, he was stationed at Fort Edward, but the senseless ridicule of some of his brother officers on account of his Indian wife induced him to resign his commission.

After building his cabin, as above stated, he leased his claim for a term of years to Otis Reynolds and John Culver, of St. Louis, and went to La Pointe, afterward Galena, where he practiced his profession for ten years when he returned to Keokuk. His Indian wife bore to him four children—Louise (married at Keokuk, since dead), James, (drowned at Keokuk), Mary and Sophia. Dr. Muir died suddenly of cholera, in 1832, but left his property in such condition that it was soon wasted in vexatious litigation, and his brave and faithful wife, left friendless and penniless, became discouraged, and, with her children, disappeared, and, it is said, returned to her people on the Upper Missouri.

Messrs. Reynolds & Culver, who had leased Dr. Muir's claim at Keokuk, subsequently employed as their agent Mr. Moses Stillwell, who arrived with his family in 1828, and took possession of Muir's cabin. His brothers-in-law Amos and Valencourt Van Ausdal, came with him and settled near.

His daughter, Margaret Stillwell (afterward Mrs. Ford) was born in 1831, at the foot of the rapids, called by the Indians Puch-a-she-tuck, where Keokuk now stands. She was probably the first white American child born in Iowa.

In 1831, Mr. Johnson, Agent of the American Fur Company, who had a station at the foot of the rapids, removed to another location, and, Dr. Muir having returned from Galena, he and Isaac R. Campbell took the place and buildings vacated by the Company and carried on trade with the Indians and half-breeds. Campbell, who had first visited and traveled through the southern part of Iowa, in 1821, was an enterprising settler, and besides trading with the natives carried on a farm and kept a tavern.

Dr. Muir died of cholera in 1832.

In 1830, James L. and Lucius H. Langworthy, brothers and natives of Vermont, visited the Territory for the purpose of working the lead mines at Dubuque. They had been engaged in lead mining at Galena, Illinois, the former from as early as 1824. The lead mines in the Dubuque region were an object of great interest to the miners about Galena, for they were known to be rich in lead ore. To explore these mines and to obtain permission to work them was therefore eminently desirable.

In 1829, James L. Langworthy resolved to visit the Dubuque mines. Crossing the Mississippi at a point now known as Dunleith, in a canoe, and swimming his horse by his side, he landed on the spot now known as Jones Street Levee. Before him spread out a beautiful prairie, on which the city of Dubuque now stands. Two miles south, at the mouth of Catfish Creek, was a village of Sacs and Foxes. Thither Mr. Langworthy proceeded, and was well received by the natives. He endeavored to obtain permission from them to mine in their hills, but this they refused. He, however, succeeded in gaining the confidence of the chief to such an extent as to be allowed to travel in the interior for three weeks and explore the country. He employed two young Indians as guides, and traversed in different directions the whole region lying between the Maquoketa and Turkey Rivers. He returned to the village secured the good will of the Indians, and, returning to Galena, formed plans for future operations, to be executed as soon as circumstances would permit.

In 1830, with his brother Lucius H , and others having obtained the consent of the Indians, Mr Langworthy crossed the Mississippi and commenced mining in the vicinity around Dubuque

At this time the lands were not in the actual possession of the United States Although they had been purchased from France, the Indian title had not been extinguished, and these adventurous persons were beyond the limits of any State or Territorial government The first settlers were therefore obliged to be their own law-makers, and to agree to such regulations as the exigencies of the case demanded The first act resembling civil legislation within the limits of the present State of Iowa was done by the miners at this point, in June, 1830 They met on the bank of the river by the side of an old cottonwood drift log, at what is now the Jones Street Levee, Dubuque, and elected a Committee, consisting of J L Langworthy, H. F Lander, James McPheters, Samuel Scales, and E M Wien This may be called the first Legislature in Iowa the members of which gathered around that old cottonwood log, and agreed to and reported the following, written by Mr Langworthy, on a half sheet of coarse, unruled paper, the old log being the writing desk .

We, a Committee having been chosen to draft certain rules and regulations (laws) by which we as miners will be governed, and having duly considered the subject, do unanimously agree that we will be governed by the regulations on the east side of the Mississippi River,* with the following exceptions, to wit

ARTICLE I That each and every man shall hold 200 yards square of ground by working said ground one day in six

ARTICLE II We further agree that there shall be chosen, by the majority of the miners present, a person who shall hold this article, and who shall grant letters of arbitration on application having been made, and that said letters of arbitration shall be obligatory on the parties so applying

The report was accepted by the miners present, who elected Dr Jarote, in accordance with Article 2 Here, then, we have, in 1830, a primitive Legislature elected by the people, the law drafted by it being submitted to the people for approval, and under it Dr. Jarote was elected first Governor within the limits of the present State of Iowa And it is to be said that the laws thus enacted were as promptly obeyed, and the acts of the executive officer thus elected as duly respected, as any have been since

The miners who had thus erected an independent government of their own on the west side of the Mississippi River continued to work successfully for a long time and the new settlement attracted considerable attention. But the west side of the Mississippi belonged to the Sac and Fox Indians, and the Government, in order to preserve peace on the frontier, as well as to protect the Indians in their rights under the treaty, ordered the settlers not only to stop mining, but to remove from the Indian territory They were simply intruders. The execution of this order was entrusted to Col Zachary Taylor, then in command of the military post at Prairie du Chien, who, early in July, sent an officer to the miners with orders to forbid settlement, and to command the miners to remove within ten days to the east side of the Mississippi, or they would be driven off by armed force The miners, however were reluctant about leaving the rich " leads " they had already discovered and opened, and were not disposed to obey the order to remove with any considerable degree of alacrity. In due time, Col Taylor dispatched a detachment of troops to enforce his order The miners, anticipating their arrival, had, excepting three, recrossed the river, and from the east bank saw the troops land on the western shore The three who had h   t   t   t   then escape unmolested. From this time, a military force was stationed at Dubuque to prevent the settlers from returning, until June, 1832. The Indians returned, and were encouraged to operate the rich mines opened by the late white occupants.

In June, 1832, the troops were ordered to the east side to assist in the annihilation of the very Indians whose rights they had been protecting on the west side. Immediately after the close of the Black Hawk war, and the negotiations of the treaty in September, 1832, by which the Sacs and Foxes ceded to the United States the tract known as the "Black Hawk Purchase," the settlers, supposing that now they had a right to re-enter the territory, returned and took possession of their claims, built cabins, erected furnaces and prepared large quantities of lead for market. Dubuque was becoming a noted place on the river, but the prospects of the hardy and enterprising settlers and miners were again ruthlessly interfered with by the Government, on the ground that the treaty with the Indians would not go into force until June 1, 1833, although they had withdrawn from the vicinity of the settlement. Col. Taylor was again ordered by the War Department to remove the miners, and in January 1833, troops were again sent from Prairie du Chien to Dubuque for that purpose. This was a serious and perhaps unnecessary hardship imposed upon the settlers. They were compelled to abandon their cabins and homes in mid-winter. It must now be said, simply, that "red tape" should be respected. The purchase had been made, the treaty ratified, or was sure to be; the Indians had retired, and, after the lapse of nearly fifty years, no very satisfactory reason for this rigorous action of the Government can be given.

But the orders had been given, and there was no alternative but to obey. Many of the settlers recrossed the river, and did not return; a few however, removed to an island near the east bank of the river, built rude cabins of poles, in which to store their lead until Spring, when they could float the fruits of their labor to St. Louis for sale, and where they could remain until the treaty went into force, when they could return. Among these were James L. Langworthy, and his brother Lucius, who had on hand about three hundred thousand pounds of lead.

Lieut. Covington, who had been placed in command at Dubuque by Col. Taylor, ordered some of the cabins of the settlers to be torn down, and wagons and other property to be destroyed. This wanton and inexcusable action on the part of a subordinate clothed with a little brief authority was sternly rebuked by Col. Taylor, and Covington was superseded by Lieut. George Wilson, who pursued a just and friendly course with the pioneers, who were only waiting for the time when they could repossess their claims.

June 1, 1833, the treaty formally went into effect; the troops were withdrawn, and the Langworthy brothers and a few others at once returned and resumed possession of their home claims and mineral prospects, and from this time the first permanent settlement of this portion of Iowa must date. Mr. John P. Sheldon was appointed Superintendent of the mines by the Government, and a system of permits to miners and licenses to smelters was adopted, similar to that which had been in operation at Galena, since 1825, under Lieut. Martin Thomas and Capt. Thomas C. Legate. Substantially the primitive law enacted by the miners assembled around that old cottonwood drift log in 1830 was adopted and enforced by the United States Government, except that miners were required to sell their mineral to licensed smelters, and the smelter was required to give bonds for the payment of six per cent of all lead manufactured to the Government. This was the same rule adopted in the United States mines on Fever River in

Illinois, except that, until 1830, the Illinois miners were compelled to pay 10 per cent tax. This tax upon the miners created much dissatisfaction among the miners on the west side as it had on the east side of the Mississippi. They thought they had suffered hardships and privations enough in opening the way for civilization, without being subjected to the imposition of an odious Government tax upon their means of subsistence, when the Federal Government could better afford to aid than to extort from them. The measure soon became unpopular. It was difficult to collect the taxes, and the whole system was abolished in about ten years.

During 1833, after the Indian title was fully extinguished, about five hundred people arrived at the mining district, about one hundred and fifty of them from Galena.

In the same year, Mr. Langworthy assisted in building the first school house in Iowa, and thus was formed the nucleus of the now populous and thriving City of Dubuque. Mr. Langworthy lived to see the naked prairie on which he first landed become the site of a city of fifteen thousand inhabitants, the small school house which he aided in constructing replaced by three substantial edifices, wherein two thousand children were being trained, churches erected in every part of the city, and railroads connecting the wilderness which he first explored with all the eastern world. He died suddenly on the 13th of March, 1865, while on a trip over the Dubuque & Southwestern Railroad, at Monticello, and the evening train brought the news of his death and his remains.

Lucius H. Langworthy, his brother, was one of the most worthy, gifted and influential of the old settlers of this section of Iowa. He died, greatly lamented by many friends, in June, 1865.

The name Dubuque was given to the settlement by the miners at a meeting held in 1834.

In 1832, Captain James White made a claim on the present site of Montrose. In 1834, a military post was established at this point, and a garrison of cavalry was stationed here, under the command of Col. Stephen W. Kearney. The soldiers were removed from this post to Fort Leavenworth, Kansas, in 1837.

During the same year, 1832, soon after the close of the Black Hawk War, Zachariah Hawkins, Benjamin Jennings, Aaron White, Augustine Horton, Samuel Gooch, Daniel Thompson and Peter Williams made claims at Fort Madison. In 1833, these claims were purchased by John and Nathaniel Knapp, upon which, in 1835, they laid out the town. The next Summer, lots were sold. The town was subsequently re-surveyed and platted by the United States Government.

At the close of the Black Hawk War, parties who had been impatiently looking across upon "Flint Hills," now Burlington, came over from Illinois and made claims. The first was Samuel S. White, in the Fall of 1832, who erected a cabin on the site of the city of Burlington. About the same time, David Tothero made a claim on the prairie about three miles back from the river, at a place since known as the farm of Judge Morgan. In the Winter of that year, they were driven off by the military from Rock Island, as intruders upon the rights of the Indians, and White's cabin was burnt by the soldiers. He retired to Illinois, where he spent the Winter, and in the Summer, as soon as the Indian title was extinguished, returned and rebuilt his cabin. White was joined by his brother-in-law, Doolittle, and they laid out the original town of Burlington in 1834.

All along the river borders of the Black Hawk Purchase settlers were flocking into Iowa. Immediately after the treaty with the Sacs and Foxes, in September, 1832, Col. George Davenport made the first claim on the spot where the thriving city of Davenport now stands. As early as 1827, Col. Davenport had established a flatboat ferry, which ran between the island and the main shore of Iowa, by which he carried on a trade with the Indians west of the Mississippi. In 1833, Capt. Benjamin W. Clark moved across from Illinois, and laid the foundation of the town of Buffalo, in Scott County, which was the first actual settlement within the limits of that county. Among other early settlers in this part of the Territory were Adrian H. Davenport, Col. John Sullivan, Mulligan and Franklin Easly, Capt. John Coleman, J. M. Camp, William White, H. W. Higgins, Cornelius Harrold, Richard Harrison, E. H. Shepherd and Dr. E. S. Barrows.

The first settlers of Davenport were Antoine LeClaire, Col. George Davenport, Major Thomas Smith, Major William Gordon, Philip Hambough, Alexander W. McGregor, Levi S. Colton, Capt. James May and others. Of Antoine LeClaire, as the representative of the two races of men who at this time occupied Iowa, Hon. C. C. Nourse, in his admirable Centennial Address, says: "Antoine LeClaire was born at St. Joseph, Michigan, in 1797. His father was French, his mother a granddaughter of a Pottowatomie chief. In 1818, he acted as official interpreter to Col. Davenport, at Fort Armstrong (now Rock Island). He was well acquainted with a dozen Indian dialects, and was a man of strict integrity and great energy. In 1820, he married the granddaughter of a Sac chief. The Sac and Fox Indians reserved for him and his wife two sections of land in the treaty of 1833, one at the town of LeClaire and one at Davenport. The Pottawatomies, in the treaty at Prairie du Chien, also reserved for him two sections of land, at the present site of Moline, Ill. He received the appointment of Postmaster and Justice of the Peace in the Black Hawk Purchase, at an early day. In 1833, he bought for $100 a claim on the land upon which the original town of Davenport was surveyed and platted in 1836. In 1836, LeClaire built the hotel, known since, with its valuable addition, as the LeClaire House. He died September 25, 1861."

In Clayton County, the first settlement was made in the Spring of 1832, on Turkey River, by Robert Hatfield and William W. Wayman. No further settlement was made in this part of the State till the beginning of 1836.

In that portion now known as Muscatine County, settlements were made in 1834, by Benjamin Nye, John Vanater and G. W. Kasey, who were the first settlers. E. E. Fay, William St. John, N. Fullington, H. Reece, Jona. Pettibone, R. P. Lowe, Stephen Whicher, Abijah Whiting, J. E. Fletcher, W. D. Abernethy and Alexis Smith were early settlers of Muscatine.

During the Summer of 1835, William Bennett and his family, from Galena, built the first cabin within the present limits of Delaware County, in some timber since known as Eads' Grove.

The first post office in Iowa was established at Dubuque in 1833. Milo H. Prentice was appointed Postmaster.

The first Justice of the Peace was Antoine Le Claire, appointed in 1833, as "a very suitable person to adjust the difficulties between the white settlers and the Indians still remaining there."

The first Methodist Society in the Territory was formed at Dubuque on the 18th of May, 1834, and the first class meeting was held June 1st of that year.

The first church bell brought into Iowa was in March, 1834.

The first mass of the Roman Catholic Church in the Territory was celebrated at Dubuque, in the house of Patrick Quigley, in the Fall of 1833.

The first school house in the Territory was erected by the Dubuque miners in 1833.

The first Sabbath school was organized at Dubuque early in the Summer of 1834.

The first woman who came to this part of the Territory with a view to permanent residence was Mrs Noble F Dean, in the Fall of 1832

The first family that lived in this part of Iowa was that of Hosea T Camp, in 1832

The first meeting house was built by the Methodist Episcopal Church, at Dubuque, in 1834

The first newspaper in Iowa was the Dubuque *Visitor*, issued May 11th, 1836 John King, afterward Judge King, was editor, and William C Jones, printer

The pioneers of Iowa, as a class, were brave, hardy, intelligent and enterprising people.

As early as 1824, a French trader named Hart had established a trading post, and built a cabin on the bluffs above the large spring now known as ' Mynster Spring," within the limits of the present city of Council Bluffs, and had probably been there some time, as the post was known to the employes of the American Fur Company as *Lacote de Hart*, or " Hart's Bluff ' In 1827, an agent of the American Fur Company, Francis Guittar, with others, encamped in the timber at the foot of the bluffs, about on the present location of Broadway and afterward settled there In 1839, a block house was built on the bluff in the east part of the city. The Pottawatomie Indians occupied this part of the State until 1846–7, when they relinquished the territory and removed to Kansas. Billy Caldwell was then principal chief There were no white settlers in that part of the State except Indian traders, until the arrival of the Mormons under the lead of Brigham Young. These people on their way westward halted for the Winter of 1846–7 on the west bank of the Missouri River, about five miles above Omaha, at a place now called Florence Some of them had reached the eastern bank of the river the Spring before, in season to plant a crop. In the Spring of 1847, Young and a portion of the colony pursued their journey to Salt Lake, but a large portion of them returned to the Iowa side and settled mainly within the limits of Pottawattamie County The principal settlement of this strange community was at a place first called " Miller s Hollow," on Indian Creek and afterward named Kanesville, in honor of Col Kane, of Pennsylvania, who visited them soon afterward The Mormon settlement extended over the county and into neighboring counties, wherever timber and water furnished desirable locations. Orson Hyde, priest, lawyer and editor, was installed as President of the Quorum of Twelve, and all that part of the State remained under Mormon control for several years In 1846, they raised a battalion, numbering some five hundred men, for the Mexican war In 1848, Hyde started a paper called the *Frontier Guardian*, at Kanesville In 1849, after many of the faithful had left to join Brigham Young at Salt Lake, the Mormons in this section of Iowa numbered 6,552 and in 1850, 7,828, but they were not all within the limits of Pottawattamie County This county was organized in 1848, all the first officials being Mormons In 1852, the order was promulgated that all the true believers should gather together at Salt Lake Gentiles flocked in, and in a few years nearly all the first settlers were gone

May 9, 1846, Captain James Allen, with a small detachment of troops on board .... at the present site of the capital of the State, Des M ....   The troops .... in the Summer to ascend the Des Moines River to this ....   The troops and stores were landed on what is now the foot of

Court avenue. Des Moines, and Capt Allen returned in the steamer to Fort Sanford to arrange for bringing up more soldiers and supplies In due time they, too, arrived, and a fort was built near the mouth of Raccoon Fork, at its confluence with the Des Moines, and named Fort Des Moines. Soon after the arrival of the troops, a trading post was established on the east side of the river, by two noted Indian traders named Ewing, from Ohio.

Among the first settlers in this part of Iowa were Benjamin Bryant, J B Scott, James Drake (gunsmith), John Sturtevant, Robert Kinzie, Alexander Turner, Peter Newcomer, and others.

The Western States have been settled by many of the best and most enterprising men of the older States, and a large immigration of the best blood of the Old World, who, removing to an arena of larger opportunities, in a more fertile soil and congenial climate, have developed a spirit and an energy peculiarly Western. In no country on the globe have enterprises of all kinds been pushed forward with such rapidity, or has there been such independence and freedom of competition. Among those who have pioneered the civilization of the West, and been the founders of great States, none have ranked higher in the scale of intelligence and moral worth than the pioneers of Iowa, who came to the territory when it was an Indian country, and through hardship, privation and suffering, laid the foundations of the populous and prosperous commonwealth which to-day dispenses its blessings to a million and a quarter of people. From her first settlement and from her first organization as a territory to the present day, Iowa has had able men to manage her affairs, wise statesmen to shape her destiny and frame her laws, and intelligent and impartial jurists to administer justice to her citizens ; her bar, pulpit and press have been able and widely influential, and in all the professions, arts, enterprises and industries which go to make up a great and prosperous commonwealth, she has taken and holds a front rank among her sister States of the West

TERRITORIAL HISTORY

By act of Congress, approved October 31, 1803, the President of the United States was authorized to take possession of the territory included in the Louisiana purchase, and provide for a temporary government. By another act of the same session, approved March 26, 1804, the newly acquired country was divided, October 1, 1804 into the Territory of Orleans, south of the thirty-third parallel of north latitude, and the district of Louisiana, which latter was placed under the authority of the officers of Indiana Territory

In 1805, the District of Louisiana was organized as a Territory with a government of its own In 1807, Iowa was included in the Territory of Illinois and in 1812 in the Territory of Missouri When Missouri was admitted as a State, March 2, 1821, " Iowa," says Hon C C Nourse, "was left a political orphan," until by act of Congress, approved June 28, 1834, the Black Hawk purchase having been made, all the territory west of the Mississippi and north of the northern boundary of Missouri was made a part of Michigan Territory Up to this time there had been no county or other organization in what is now the State of Iowa, although one or two Justices of the Peace had been appointed and a post office was established at Dubuque in 1833. In September, 1834, however, the Territorial Legislature of Michigan created two counties on the west side of the Mississippi River, viz.: Dubuque and Des Moines, separated by a line drawn westward from the foot of Rock Island. These counties were partially organized   John King was appointed Chief Justice of Dubuque County, and Isaac Leffler, of Burlington of Des Moines County   Two Associate Justices, in each county, were appointed by the Governor.

On the first Monday in October, 1835, Gen. George W Jones, now a citizen of Dubuque was elected a Delegate to Congress from this part of Michigan Territory.   On the 20th of April, 1836, through the efforts of Gen Jones, Congress passed a bill creating the Territory of Wisconsin, which went into operation, July 4, 1836, and Iowa was then included in

THE TERRITORY OF WISCONSIN,

of which Gen. Henry Dodge was appointed Governor, John S. Horner, Secretary of the Territory; Charles Dunn, Chief Justice, David Irwin and William C Frazer, Associate Justices.

September 9, 1836, Governor Dodge ordered the census of the new Territory to be taken   This census resulted in showing a population of 10,531 in the counties of Dubuque and Des Moines   Under the apportionment these two counties were entitled to six members of the Council and thirteen of the House of Representatives.   The Governor issued his proclamation for an election to be held on the first Monday of October, 1836, on which day the following members of the First Territorial Legislature of Wisconsin were elected from the two counties in the Black Hawk purchase:

Dubuque County.—Council. John Fally, Thomas McKnight, Thomas McCraney   *House ·* Loring Wheeler, Hardin Nowlan, Peter Hill Engle, Patrick Quigley, Hosea T. Camp

Des Moines County —Council: Jeremiah Smith, Jr, Joseph B Teas, Arthur B Ingram   *House :* Isaac Leffler, Thomas Blair, Warren L Jenkins, John Box, George W Teas, Eli Reynolds, David R Chance.

The first Legislature assembled at Belmont, in the present State of Wisconsin, on the 25th day of October, 1836, and was organized by electing Henry T. Baird President of the Council, and Peter Hill Engle, of Dubuque, Speaker of the House   It adjourned December 9, 1836

The second Legislature assembled at Burlington, November 10, 1837. Adjourned January 20 1838   The third session was at Burlington; commenced June 1st, and adjourned June 12 1838

During the first session of the Wisconsin Territorial Legislature, in 1836, the county of Des Moines was divided into Des Moines, Lee, Van Buren, Henry, Muscatine and Cook (the latter being subsequently changed to Scott) and defined their boundaries.   During the second session, out of the territory embraced in Dubuque County, were created the counties of Dubuque, Clayton, Fayette, Delaware, Buchanan, Jackson, Jones, Linn, Clinton and Cedar, and their boundaries defined, but the most of them were not organized until several years afterward, under the authority of the Territorial Legislature of Iowa

The question of a separate territorial organization for Iowa, which was then a part of Wisconsin Territory, began to be agitated early in the Autumn of 1837   The wishes of the people found expression in a convention held at Burlington on the 1st of November, which memorialized Congress to organize a Territory west of the Mississippi, and to settle the boundary line between Wisconsin Territory and Missouri   The Territorial Legislature of Wisconsin, then in session at Burlington, joined in the petition   Gen George W Jones, of Dubuque, then residing at Sin-sin-awa Mound in what is now Wisconsin, was Delegate to Congress from Wisconsin Territory, and labored so earnestly and successfully, that " An act to divide the Territory of Wisconsin, and to establish the Territorial Government of Iowa," was approved June 12, 1838, to take effect and be in force on and after July 3, 1838. The new Territory embraced "all that part of the present Territory of Wisconsin which lies west of the Mississippi River, and west of a line drawn due north from the head water or sources of the Mississippi to the territorial line" The organic act provided for a Governor, whose term of office should be three years, and for a Secretary, Chief Justice, two Associate Justices, and Attorney and Marshal, who should serve four years, to be appointed by the President, by and with the advice and consent of the Senate. The act also provided for the election, by the white male inhabitants, citizens of the United States, over twenty-one years of age, of a House of Representatives, consisting of twenty-six members, and a Council, to consist of thirteen members. It also appropriated $5,000 for a public library, and $20,000 for the erection of public buildings

President Van Buren appointed Ex-Governor Robert Lucas, of Ohio, to be the first Governor of the new Territory William B Conway, of Pittsburgh, was appointed Secretary of the Territory; Charles Mason, of Burlington, Chief Justice, and Thomas S Wilson, of Dubuque, and Joseph Williams, of Pennsylvania, Associate Judges of the Supreme and District Courts; Mr Van. Allen, of New York, Attorney; Francis Gehon, of Dubuque, Marshal; Augustus C. Dodge, Register of the Land Office at Burlington, and Thomas Mc Knight, Receiver of the Land Office at Dubuque. Mr Van Allen, the District Attorney, died at Rockingham, soon after his appointment and Col Charles Weston was appointed to fill his vacancy Mr. Conway, the Secretary, also died at Burlington, during the second session of the Legislature, and James Clarke, editor of the *Gazette*, was appointed to succeed him.

Immediately after his arrival, Governor Lucas issued a proclamation for the election of members of the first Territorial Legislature, to be held on the 10th of September, dividing the Territory into election districts for that purpose, and appointing the 12th day of November for meeting of the Legislature to be elected, at Burlington

The first Territorial Legislature was elected in September and assembled at Burlington on the 12th of November, and consisted of the following members:

Council.—Jesse B Brown, J. Keith, E A. M Swazey, Arthur Ingram, Robert Ralston, George Hepner, Jesse J Payne, D. B. Hughes, James M Clark, Charles Whittlesey, Jonathan W. Parker, Warner Lewis, Stephen Hempstead.

House.—William Patterson, Hawkins Taylor, Calvin J. Price, James Brierly, James Hall, Gideon S. Bailey, Samuel Parker, James W. Grimes, George Temple, Van B Delashmutt, Thomas Blair, George H. Beeler,* William G Coop, William H Wallace, Asbury B. Porter, John Frierson, William L Toole Levi Thornton, S. C. Hastings, Robert G. Roberts, Laurel Summers,† Jabez A Burchard, Jr., Chauncey Swan, Andrew Bankson, Thomas Cox and Hardin Nowlin

Notwithstanding a large majority of the members of both branches of the Legislature were Democrats, yet Gen. Jesse B. Browne (Whig), of Lee County, was elected President of the Council, and Hon William H. Wallace (Whig), of Henry County, Speaker of the House of Representatives—the former unanimously and the latter with but little opposition At that time, national politics

*Cyrus S Jacobs, who was elected for Des Moines County, was killed in an unfortunate encounter at Burlington before the meeting of the Legislature, and Mr Beeler was elected to fill the vacancy

†Samuel R Murray was returned as elected from Clinton County, but his seat was successfully contested by Burchard

were little heeded by the people of the new Territory, but in 1840, during the Presidential campaign, party lines were strongly drawn.

At the election in September, 1838, for members of the Legislature, a Congressional Delegate was also elected. There were four candidates, viz : William W. Chapman and David Rohrer, of Des Moines County; B. F. Wallace, of Henry County, and P. H. Engle, of Dubuque County. Chapman was elected, receiving a majority of thirty-six over Engle.

The first session of the Iowa Territorial Legislature was a stormy and exciting one. By the organic law, the Governor was clothed with almost unlimited veto power. Governor Lucas seemed disposed to make free use of it, and the independent Hawkeyes could not quietly submit to arbitrary and absolute rule, and the result was an unpleasant controversy between the Executive and Legislative departments. Congress, however, by act approved March 3, 1839, amended the organic law by restricting the veto power of the Governor to the two-thirds rule, and took from him the power to appoint Sheriffs and Magistrates.

Among the first important matters demanding attention was the location of the seat of government and provision for the erection of public buildings, for which Congress had appropriated $20,000. Governor Lucas, in his message, had recommended the appointment of Commissioners, with a view to making a central location. The extent of the future State of Iowa was not known or thought of. Only on a strip of land fifty miles wide, bordering on the Mississippi River, was the Indian title extinguished, and a central location meant some central point in the Black Hawk Purchase. The friends of a central location supported the Governor's suggestion. The southern members were divided between Burlington and Mount Pleasant, but finally united on the latter as the proper location for the seat of government. The central and southern parties were very nearly equal, and, in consequence, much excitement prevailed. The central party at last triumphed, and on the 21st day of January, 1839, an act was passed, appointing Chauncey Swan, of Dubuque County; John Ronalds, of Louisa County, and Robert Ralston, of Des Moines County, Commissioners, to select a site for a permanent seat of Government within the limits of Johnson County.

Johnson County had been created by act of the Territorial Legislature of Wisconsin, approved December 21, 1837, and organized by act passed at the special session at Burlington in June, 1838, the organization to date from July 4th, following. Napoleon, on the Iowa River, a few miles below the future Iowa City, was designated as the county seat, temporarily.

Then there existed good reason for locating the capital in the county. The Territory of Iowa was bounded on the north by the British Possessions; east, by the Mississippi River to its source; thence by a line drawn due north to the northern boundary of the United States; south, by the State of Missouri, and west, by the Missouri and White Earth Rivers. But this immense territory was in undisputed possession of the Indians, except a strip on the Mississippi, known as the Black Hawk Purchase. Johnson County was, from north to south, in the geographical center of this purchase, and as near the east and west geographical center of the future State of Iowa as could then be made, as the boundary line between the lands of the United States and the Indians, established by the treaty of October 21, 1837, was immediately west of the county limits.

The Commissioners, after selecting the site, were directed to lay out 640 acres in ___ and to ___ ___ lots and erect public buildings the ___ ___ having ___ a section of land to be selected by the Territory for the purpose. The Commissioners met at Napoleon, Johnson County, May 1, 1839, selected for a site Section 10, in Township 79 North of Range 6 West of the Fifth Principal Meridian, and immediately surveyed it and laid off the town. The first sale of lots took place August 16, 1839. The site selected for the public buildings was a little west of the geographical center of the section, where a square of ten acres on the elevated grounds overlooking the river was reserved for the purpose. The capitol is located in the center of this square. The second Territorial Legislature, which assembled in November, 1839, passed an act requiring the Commissioners to adopt such plan for the building that the aggregate cost when complete should not exceed $51,000, and if they had already adopted a plan involving a greater expenditure they were directed to abandon it. Plans for the building were designed and drawn by Mr. John F Rague, of Springfield, Ill., and on the 4th day of July, 1840, the corner stone of the edifice was laid with appropriate ceremonies. Samuel C. Trowbridge was Marshal of the day, and Gov Lucas delivered the address on that occasion

When the Legislature assembled at Burlington in special session, July 13, 1840, Gov. Lucas announced that on the 4th of that month he had visited Iowa City, and found the basement of the capitol nearly completed. A bill authorizing a loan of $20,000 for the building was passed, January 15, 1841, the unsold lots of Iowa City being the security offered, but only $5,500 was obtained under the act

THE BOUNDARY QUESTION.

The boundary line between the Territory of Iowa and the State of Missouri was a difficult question to settle in 1838, in consequence of claims arising from taxes and titles, and at one time civil war was imminent. In defining the boundaries of the counties bordering on Missouri, the Iowa authorities had fixed a line that has since been established as the boundary between Iowa and Missouri. The Constitution of Missouri defined her northern boundary to be the parallel of latitude which passes through the rapids of the Des Moines River. The lower rapids of the Mississippi immediately above the mouth of the Des Moines River had always been known as the Des Moines Rapids, or "the rapids of the Des Moines River." The Missourians (evidently not well versed in history or geography) insisted on running the northern boundary line from the rapids in the Des Moines River, just below Keosauqua, thus taking from Iowa a strip of territory eight or ten miles wide. Assuming this as her northern boundary line, Missouri attempted to exercise jurisdiction over the disputed territory by assessing taxes, and sending her Sheriffs to collect them by distraining the personal property of the settlers. The Iowans, however, were not disposed to submit, and the Missouri officials were arrested by the Sheriffs of Davis and Van Buren Counties and confined in jail. Gov. Boggs, of Missouri, called out his militia to enforce the claim and sustain the officers of Missouri. Gov. Lucas called out the militia of Iowa, and both parties made active preparations for war. In Iowa, about 1,200 men were enlisted, and 500 were actually armed and encamped in Van Buren County, ready to defend the integrity of the Territory. Subsequently, Gen. A. C. Dodge, of Burlington, Gen Churchman, of Dubuque, and Dr. Clark, of Fort Madison were sent to Missouri as envoys plenipotentiary, to effect, if possible, a peaceable adjustment of the difficulty. Upon their arrival they found that the Commissioners of Clarke County, Missouri had rescinded their order for the collection of the taxes, and that Gov Boggs had despatched messengers to the Governor of Iowa proposing to submit an agreed case to the Supreme Court of the United States for the final settlement of the boundary question This proposition was declined, but afterward Congress authorized a suit to settle the controversy, which was instituted, and which resulted in a judgment for Iowa Under this decision, William G Miner, of Missouri, and Henry B. Hendershott were appointed Commissioners to survey and establish the boundary Mr Nourse remarks that " the expenses of the war on the part of Iowa were never paid, either by the United States or the Territorial Government The patriots who furnished supplies to the troops had to bear the cost and charges of the struggle "

The first legislative assembly laid the broad foundation of civil equality, on which has been constructed one of the most liberal governments in the Union Its first act was to recognize the equality of woman with man before the law by providing that " no action commenced by a single woman, who intermarries during the pendency thereof, shall abate on account of such marriage " This principle has been adopted by all subsequent legislation in Iowa, and to-day woman has full and equal civil rights with man, except only the right of the ballot.

Religious toleration was also secured to all, personal liberty strictly guarded, the rights and privileges of citizenship extended to all white persons, and the purity of elections secured by heavy penalties against bribery and corruption The judiciary power was vested in a Supreme Court, District Court, Probate Court, and Justices of the Peace Real estate was made divisible by will, and intestate property divided equitably among heirs. Murder was made punishable by death, and proportionate penalties fixed for lesser crimes A system of free schools, open for every class of white citizens, was established Provision was made for a system of roads and highways. Thus under the territorial organization, the country began to emerge from a savage wilderness, and take on the forms of civil government

By act of Congress of June 12, 1838, the lands which had been purchased of the Indians were brought into market, and land offices opened in Dubuque and Burlington. Congress provided for military roads and bridges, which greatly aided the settlers, who were now coming in by thousands, to make their homes on the fertile prairies of Iowa—" the Beautiful Land " The fame of the country had spread far and wide; even before the Indian title was extinguished, many were crowding the borders, impatient to cross over and stake out their claims on the choicest spots they could find in the new Territory As soon as the country was open for settlement, the borders, the Black Hawk Purchase, all along the Mississippi, and up the principal rivers and streams, and out over the broad and rolling prairies, began to be thronged with eager land hunters and immigrants, seeking homes in Iowa It was a sight to delight the eyes of all comers from every land—its noble streams, beautiful and picturesque hills and valleys, broad and fertile prairies extending as far as the eye could reach, with a soil surpassing in richness anything which they had ever seen It is not to be wondered at that immigration into Iowa was rapid, and that within less than a decade from the organization of the Territory, it contained a hundred and fifty thousand people

As rapidly as the Indian titles were extinguished and the original owners removed, the resistless tide of emigration flowed westward The following extract from Judge Nourse's Centennial Address shows how the immigrants gathered on the Indian boundary, ready for the removal of the barrier ·

In of the ce   t i   t is ve spirit the Government of the United States made ai ie   th   l   Indians, on the 11th day of August 1842, for the remaini   portion the tr ni oo I se The treaty provided that the Indians should retain possession of all the lands thus ceded until May 1, 1843, and should occupy that portion of the ceded territory west of a line running north and south through Redrock, until October 11, 1845. These tribes, at this time, had their principal village at Ot-tum-wa-no, now called Ottumwa. As soon as it became known that the treaty had been concluded, there was a rush of immigration to Iowa, and a great number of temporary settlements were made near the Indian boundary, waiting for the 1st day of May. As the day approached, hundreds of families encamped along the line, and their tents and wagons gave the scene the appearance of a military expedition. The country beyond had been thoroughly explored, but the United States military authorities had prevented any settlement or even the making out of claims by any monuments whatever.

To aid them in making out their claims when the hour should arrive, the settlers had placed piles of dry wood on the rising ground, at convenient distances, and a short time before twelve o'clock of the night of the 30th of April, these were lighted, and when the midnight hour arrived, it was announced by the discharge of firearms. The night was dark, but this army of occupation pressed forward, torch in hand, with axe and hatchet, blazing lines with all manner of curves and angles. When daylight came and revealed the confusion of these wonderful surveys, numerous disputes arose, settled generally by compromise, but sometimes by violence. Between midnight of the 30th of April and sundown of the 1st of May, over one thousand families had settled on their new purchase.

While this scene was transpiring, the retreating Indians were enacting one more impressive and melancholy. The Winter of 1842-43 was one of unusual severity, and the Indian prophet, who had disapproved of the treaty, attributed the severity of the Winter to the anger of the Great Spirit, because they had sold their country. Many religious rites were performed to atone for the crime. When the time for leaving Ot-tum-wa-no arrived, a solemn silence pervaded the Indian camp, and the faces of their stoutest men were bathed in tears, and when their cavalcade was put in motion, toward the setting sun, there was a spontaneous outburst of frantic grief from the entire procession.

The Indians remained the appointed time beyond the line running north and south through Redrock. The government established a trading post and military encampment at the Raccoon Fork of the Des Moines River, then and for many years known as Fort Des Moines. Here the red man lingered until the 11th of October, 1845, when the same scene that we have before described was re-enacted, and the wave of immigration swept over the remainder of the "New Purchase." The lands thus occupied and claimed by the settlers still belonged in fee to the General Government. The surveys were not completed until some time after the Indian title was extinguished. After their survey, the lands were publicly proclaimed or advertised for sale at public auction. Under the laws of the United States, a pre-emption or exclusive right to purchase public lands could not be acquired until after the lands had thus been publicly offered and not sold for want of bidders. Then, and not until then, an occupant making improvements in good faith might acquire a right over others to enter the land at the minimum price of $1 25 per acre. The "claim laws" were unknown to the United States statutes. They originated in the "eternal fitness of things," and were enforced, probably, as belonging to that class of natural rights not enumerated in the constitution, and not impaired or disparaged by its enumeration.

The settlers organized in every settlement prior to the public land sales, appointed officers, and adopted their own rules and regulations. Each man's claim was duly ascertained and recorded by the Secretary. It was the duty of *all* to attend the sales. The Secretary bid off the lands of each settler at $1 25 per acre. The others were *there*, to see, first, that he did his duty and bid in the land, and, secondly, to see that *no one else bid*. This, of course, sometimes led to trouble, but it saved the excitement of competition, and gave a formality and degree of order and regularity to the proceedings they would not otherwise have attained. As far as practicable, the Territorial Legislature recognized the validity of these "claims" upon the public lands, and in 1839 passed an act legalizing their sale and making their transfer a valid consideration to support a promise to pay for the same. (Acts of 1843, p 456). The Supreme Territorial Court held this law to be valid. (See Hill v Smith, 1st Morris Rep 70). The opinion not only contains a decision of the question involved, but also contains much valuable erudition upon that "spirit of Anglo-Saxon liberty" which the Iowa settlers unquestionably inherited in a direct line of descent from the said "Anglo-Saxons." But the early settler was not always able to pay even this dollar and twenty-five cents per acre for his land.

Many of the settlers had nothing to begin with, save their hands, health and courage and their family jewels, "the pledges of love," and the "consumers of bread." It was not so easy to accumulate money in the early days of the State, and the "beautiful prairies," the "noble streams," and all that sort of poetic imagery, did not prevent the early settlers from becoming discouraged.

An old settler, in speaking of the privations and trials of those early days, says:

Well do the "old settlers" of Iowa remember the days from the first settlement to 1840. Those were days of sadness and distress. The endearments of home in another land had been broken up, and all that was hallowed on earth, the home of childhood and the scenes of youth, we severed, and we sat down by the gentle waters of our noble river, and often "hung our harps on the willows"

Another, from another part of the State, testifies

There was no such thing as getting money for any kind of labor   I laid brick at $3 00 per thousand, and took my pay in anything I could eat or wear   I built the first Methodist Church at Keokuk, 42x60 feet, of brick, for $600, and took my pay in a subscription paper, part of which I never collected, and upon which I only received $50 00 in money   Wheat was hauled 100 miles from the interior, and sold for 37½ cents per bushel

Another old settler, speaking of a later period, 1843, says:

Land and everything had gone down in value to almost nominal prices   Corn and oats could be bought for six or ten cents a bushel, pork, $1 00 per hundred, and the best horse a man could raise sold for $50 00   Nearly all were in debt, and the Sheriff and Constable, with legal processes, were common visitors at almost every man's door   These were indeed "the times that tried men's souls"

"A few," says Mr. Nourse, "who were not equal to the trial, returned to their old homes, but such as had the courage and faith to be the worthy founders of a great State remained, to more than realize the fruition of their hopes, and the reward of their self-denial."

On Monday, December 6, 1841, the fourth Legislative Assembly met, at the new capital, Iowa City, but the capitol building could not be used, and the Legislature occupied a temporary frame house, that had been erected for that purpose, during the session of 1841-2. At this session, the Superintendent of Public Buildings (who, with the Territorial Agent, had superseded the Commissioners first appointed), estimated the expense of completing the building at $33,330, and that rooms for the use of the Legislature could be completed for $15,600.

During 1842, the Superintendent commenced obtaining stone from a new quarry, about ten miles northeast of the city. This is now known as the "Old Capitol Quarry," and contains, it is thought, an immense quantity of excellent building stone   Here all the stone for completing the building was obtained, and it was so far completed, that on the 5th day of December, 1842, the Legislature assembled in the new capitol. At this session, the Superintendent estimated that it would cost $39,143 to finish the building. This was nearly $6,000 higher than the estimate of the previous year, notwithstanding a large sum had been expended in the meantime. This rather discouraging discrepancy was accounted for by the fact that the officers in charge of the work were constantly short of funds   Except the congressional appropriation of $20,000 and the loan of $5,500, obtained from the Miners' Bank, of Dubuque, all the funds for the prosecution of the work were derived from the sale of the city lots (which did not sell very rapidly), from certificates of indebtedness, and from scrip based upon unsold lots, which was to be received in payment for such lots when they were sold   At one time, the Superintendent made a requisition for bills of iron and glass, which could not be obtained nearer than St Louis   To meet this, the Agent sold some lots for a draft, payable at Pittsburgh, Pa, for which he was compelled to pay twenty-five per cent exchange. This draft, amounting to $507, that officer reported to be more than one-half the cash actually handled by him during the entire season, when the disbursements amounted to very nearly $24,000

With such uncertainty, it could not be expected that estimates could be very accurate   With all these disadvantages, however, the work appears to have been prudently prosecuted, and as rapidly as circumstances would permit

Iowa remained a Territory from 1838 to 1846, during which the office of Governor was held by Robert Lucas, John Chambers and James Clarke

STATE ORGANIZATION.

By an act of the Territorial Legislature of Iowa, approved February 12, 1844, the question of the formation of a State Constitution and providing for the election of Delegates to a convention to be convened for that purpose was submitted to the people, to be voted upon at their township elections in April following. The vote was largely in favor of the measure, and the Delegates elected assembled in convention at Iowa City, on the 7th of October, 1844. On the first day of November following, the convention completed its work and adopted the first State Constitution.

The President of the convention, Hon Shepherd Leffler, was instructed to transmit a certified copy of this Constitution to the Delegate in Congress, to be by him submitted to that body at the earliest practicable day It was also provided that it should be submitted, together with any conditions or changes that might be made by Congress, to the people of the Territory, for their approval or rejection, at the township election in April, 1845.

The boundaries of the State, as defined by this Constitution, were as follows.

Beginning in the middle of the channel of the Mississippi River, opposite mouth of the Des Moines River, thence up the said river Des Moines, in the middle of the main channel thereof, to a point where it is intersected by the Old Indian Boundary line, or line run by John C Sullivan, in the year 1816, thence westwardly along said line to the "old" northwest corner of Missouri, thence due west to the middle of the main channel of the Missouri River, thence up in the middle of the main channel of the river last mentioned to the mouth of the Sioux or Calumet River; thence in a direct line to the middle of the main channel of the St. Peters River, where the Watonwan River—according to Nicollet's map—enters the same, thence down the middle of the main channel of said river to the middle of the main channel of the Mississippi River, thence down the middle of the main channel of said river to the place of beginning

These boundaries were rejected by Congress. but by act approved March 3, 1845, a State called Iowa was admitted into the Union, provided the people accepted the act, bounded as follows

Beginning at the mouth of the Des Moines River, at the middle of the Mississippi, thence by the middle of the channel of that river to a parallel of latitude passing through the mouth of the Mankato or Blue Earth River, thence west, along said parallel of latitude, to a point where it is intersected by a meridian line seventeen degrees and thirty minutes west of the meridian of Washington City, thence due south, to the northern boundary line of the State of Missouri, thence eastwardly, following that boundary to the point at which the same intersects the Des Moines River, thence by the middle of the channel of that river to the place of beginning

These boundaries, had they been accepted, would have placed the northern boundary of the State about thirty miles north of its present location, and would have deprived it of the Missouri slope and the boundary of that river. The western boundary would have been near the west line of what is now Kossuth County. But it was not so to be In consequence of this radical and unwelcome change in the boundaries, the people refused to accept the act of Congress and rejected the Constitution at the election, held August 4, 1845, by a vote of 7,656 to 7,235

A second Constitutional Convention assembled at Iowa City on the 4th day of May, 1846, and on the 18th of the same month another Constitution for the new State with the present boundaries was adopted and submitted to the people for ratification on the 3d day of August following when it was accepted; 9,492 votes were cast "for the Constitution" and 9,036 "against the Constitution"

The Constitution was approved by Congress, and by act of Congress approved December 28, 1846, Iowa was admitted as a sovereign State in the American Union

Prior to this action of Congress, however, the people of the new State held an election under the new Constitution on the 26th day of October, and elected Onesel Briggs, Governor; Elisha Cutler, Jr., Secretary of State; Joseph T. Fales, Auditor, Morgan Reno, Treasurer, and members of the Senate and House of Representatives

At this time there were twenty-seven organized counties in the State, with a population of nearly 100,000, and the frontier settlements were rapidly pushing toward the Missouri River. The Mormons had already reached there.

The first General Assembly of the State of Iowa was composed of nineteen Senators and forty Representatives It assembled at Iowa City, November 30, 1846, about a month *before* the State was admitted into the Union

At the first session of the State Legislature, the Treasurer of State reported that the capitol building was in a very exposed condition liable to injury from storms, and expressed the hope that some provision would be made to complete it, at least sufficiently to protect it from the weather The General Assembly responded by appropriating $2,500 for the completion of the public buildings At the first session also arose the question of the re-location of the capital The western boundary of the State, as now determined, left Iowa City too far toward the eastern and southern boundary of the State, this was conceded Congress had appropriated five sections of land for the erection of public buildings, and toward the close of the session a bill was introduced providing for the re-location of the seat of government, involving to some extent the location of the State University, which had already been discussed This bill gave rise to a deal of discussion and parliamentary manenvering, almost purely sectional in its character It provided for the appointment of three Commissioners, who were authorized to make a location as near the geographical center of the State as a healthy and eligible site could be obtained; to select the five sections of land donated by Congress, to survey and plat into town lots not exceeding one section of the land so selected; to sell lots at public sale, not to exceed two in each block Having done this, they were then required to suspend further operations, and make a report of their proceedings to the Governor The bill passed both Houses by decisive votes, received the signature of the Governor, and became a law Soon after, by "An act to locate and establish a State University," approved February 25, 1847, the unfinished public buildings at Iowa City, together with the ten acres of land on which they were situated, were granted for the use of the University, reserving their use, however, by the General Assembly and the State officers, until other provisions were made by law.

The Commissioners forthwith entered upon their duties, and selected four sections and two half sections in Jasper County. Two of these sections are in what is now Des Moines Township, and the others in Fairview Township, in the southern part of that county. These lands are situated between Prairie City and Monroe, on the Keokuk & Des Moines Railroad, which runs diagonally through them Here a town was platted, called Monroe City, and a sale of lots took place. Four hundred and fifteen lots were sold, at prices that were not considered remarkably remunerative. The cash payments (one-fourth) amounted to $1,797 43, while the expenses of the sale and the claims of the Commissioners for services amounted to $2 206.57. The Commissioners made a report of their proceedings to the Governor as required by law, but the location was generally condemned

When the report of the Commissioners, showing this brilliant financial operation, had been read in the House of Representatives, at the next session, and while it was under consideration, an indignant member, afterward known as the eccentric Judge McFarland, moved to refer the report to a select Committee of Five, with instructions to report "how much of said city of Monroe was under water and how much was burned" The report was referred, without the instructions, however, but Monroe City never became the seat of government. By an act approved January 15, 1849, the law by which the location had been made was repealed and the new town was vacated, the money paid by purchasers of lots being refunded to them. This, of course, retained the seat of government at Iowa City, and precluded, for the time, the occupation of the building and grounds by the University

At the same session, $3,000 more were appropriated for completing the State building at Iowa City In 1852, the further sum of $5,000, and in 1854 $4,000 more were appropriated for the same purpose, making the whole cost $123,000, paid partly by the General Government and partly by the State, but principally from the proceeds of the sale of lots in Iowa City.

But the question of the permanent location of the seat of government was not settled, and in 1851 bills were introduced for the removal of the capital to Pella and to Fort Des Moines The latter appeared to have the support of the majority, but was finally lost in the House on the question of ordering it to its third reading

At the next session, in 1853, a bill was introduced in the Senate for the removal of the seat of government to Fort Des Moines, and, on final vote, was just barely defeated. At the next session, however, the effort was more successful, and on the 15th day of January, 1855, a bill re-locating the capital within two miles of the Raccoon Fork of the Des Moines, and for the appointment of Commissioners, was approved by Gov. Grimes. The site was selected in 1856, in accordance with the provisions of this act, the land being donated to the State by citizens and property-holders of Des Moines. An association of citizens erected a building for a temporary capitol, and leased it to the State at a nominal rent

The third Constitutional Convention to revise the Constitution of the State assembled at Iowa City, January 19, 1857. The new Constitution framed by this convention was submitted to the people at an election held August 3, 1857, when it was approved and adopted by a vote of 40,311 "for" to 38,681 "against," and on the 3d day of September following was declared by a proclamation of the Governor to be the supreme law of the State of Iowa.

Advised of the completion of the temporary State House at Des Moines, on the 19th of October following, Governor Grimes issued another proclamation, declaring the City of Des Moines to be the capital of the State of Iowa

The removal of the archives and offices was commenced at once and continued through the Fall It was an undertaking of no small magnitude; there was not a mile of railroad to facilitate the work and the season was unusually disagreeable. Rain, snow and other accompaniments increased the difficulties; and it was not until December, that the last of the effects—the safe of the State Treasurer, loaded on two large "bob-sleds"—drawn by ten yoke of oxen was deposited in the new capital It is not imprudent now to remark that, during this passage over hills and prairies, across rivers, through bottom lands and timber, the safes belonging to the several departments contained large sums of money, mostly individual funds, however. Thus, Iowa City ceased to be the capital of the State, after four Territorial Legislatures six State Legislatures and three

Constitutional Conventions had held their sessions there   By the exchange, the old capitol at Iowa City became the seat of the University, and, except the rooms occupied by the United States District Court, passed under the immediate and direct control of the Trustees of that institution.

Des Moines was now the permanent seat of government, made so by the fundamental law of the State, and on the 11th day of January, 1858, the seventh General Assembly convened at the new capital   The building used for governmental purposes was purchased in 1864   It soon became inadequate for the purposes for which it was designed, and it became apparent that a new, large and permanent State House must be erected.   In 1870, the General Assembly made an appropriation and provided for the appointment of a Board of Commissioners to commence the work   The board consisted of Gov Samuel Merrill, ex officio, President, Grenville M Dodge, Council Bluffs James F Wilson, Fairfield; James Dawson, Washington; Simon G Stein, Muscatine, James O. Crosby, Gainsville, Charles Dudley Agency City; John N. Dewey, Des Moines, William L Joy, Sioux City ; Alexander R Fulton, Des Moines, Secretary

The act of 1870 provided that the building should be constructed of the best material and should be fire proof; to be heated and ventilated in the most approved manner, should contain suitable legislative halls, rooms for State officers, the judiciary, library, committees. archives and the collections of the State Agricultural Society, and for all purposes of State Government, and should be erected on grounds held by the State for that purpose The sum first appropriated was $150,000, and the law provided that no contract should be made. either for constructing or furnishing the building, which should bind the State for larger sums than those at the time appropriated A design was drawn and plans and specifications furnished by Cochrane & Piquenard, architects, which were accepted by the board, and on the 23d of November, 1871, the corner stone was laid with appropriate ceremonies The estimated cost and present value of the capitol is fixed at $2,000,000

From 1858 to 1860, the Sioux became troublesome in the northwestern part of the State.   These warlike Indians made frequent plundering raids upon the settlers, and murdered several families In 1861, several companies of militia were ordered to that portion of the State to hunt down and punish the murderous thieves No battles were fought. however, for the Indians fled when they ascertained that systematic and adequate measures had been adopted to protect the settlers

"The year 1856 marked a new era in the history of Iowa.   In 1854, the Chicago & Rock Island Railroad had been completed to the east bank of the Mississippi River, opposite Davenport   In 1854, the corner stone of a railroad bridge, that was to be the first to span the "Father of Waters," was laid with appropriate ceremonies at this point.   St. Louis had resolved that the enterprise was unconstitutional, and by writs of injunction made an unsuccessful effort to prevent its completion   Twenty years later in her history, St Louis repented her folly, and made atonement for her sin by imitating our example On the 1st day of January, 1856, this railroad was completed to Iowa City In the meantime, two other railroads had reached the east bank of the Mississippi—one opposite Burlington, and one opposite Dubuque—and these were being extended into the interior of the State.   Indeed, four lines of railroad had been   the Missouri, having east   the Congress of the United   in the construction of railroads, the public lands in alternate sections, six miles on either side of the proposed lines.   An extra session of the General Assembly was called in July of this year, that disposed of the grant to the several companies that proposed to complete these enterprises.   The population of our State at this time had increased to 500,000.   Public attention had been called to the necessity of a railroad across the continent.   The position of Iowa, in the very heart and center of the Republic, on the route of this great highway across the continent, began to attract attention   Cities and towns sprang up through the State as if by magic.   Capital began to pour into the State, and had it been employed in developing our vast coal measures and establishing manufactories among us, or if it had been expended in improving our lands, and building houses and barns it would have been well   But all were in haste to get rich, and the spirit of speculation ruled the hour.

" In the meantime, every effort was made to help the speedy completion of the railroads.   Nearly every county and city on the Mississippi, and many in the interior, voted large corporate subscriptions to the stock of the railroad companies. and issued their negotiable bonds for the amount."   Thus enormous county and city debts were incurred, the payment of which these municipalities tried to avoid upon the plea that they had exceeded the constitutional limit-ation of their powers.   The Supreme Court of the United States held these bonds to be valid , and the courts by mandamus compelled the city and county authorities to levy taxes to pay the judgments.   These debts are not all paid even yet, but the worst is over and ultimately the burden will be entirely removed

The first railroad across the State was completed to Council Bluffs in Jan-uary, 1871   The others were completed soon after   In 1854. there was not a mile of railroad in the State.   In 1874, twenty years after, there were 3,765 miles in successful operation

GROWTH AND PROGRESS

When Wisconsin Territory was organized, in 1836, the entire population of that portion of the Territory now embraced in the State of Iowa was 10 531. The Territory then embraced two counties, Dubuque and Des Moines, erected by the Territory of Michigan, in 1834.   From 1836 to 1838, the Territorial Legislature of Wisconsin increased the number of counties to sixteen, and the population had increased to 22,859   Since then, the counties have increased to ninety-nine, and the population, in 1875, was 1,366,000   The following table will show the population at different periods since the erection of Iowa Territory:

Year	Population	Year.	Population	Year	Population
1838	22,589	1852	230,713	1869	1,010,819
1840	43,115	1854	326,013	1870	1,191,727
1841.	75,152	1856	519 055	1873	1,251,333
1846	97,588	1859	638,775	1875	1,366,000
1847	116,651	1860	674,913	1876	
1849	152,988	1863	701,732	1877	
1850	191,982	1865	754,699		
1851	204,774	1867	902,040		

The most populous county in the State is Dubuque   Not only in popula-tion, but in everything contributing to the growth and greatness of a State has Iowa made rapid progress.   In a little more than thirty years. its wild but beautiful prairies have advanced upon the home of the savage to a highly civ-ilized commonwealth embracing all the elements of progress which characterize the older States

Thriving cities and towns dot its fair surface; an iron net-work of thousands of miles of railroads is woven over its broad acres; ten thousand school houses, in which more than five hundred thousand children are being taught the rudiments of education, testify to the culture and liberality of the people; high schools, colleges and universities are generously endowed by the State; manufactories spring up on all her water courses, and in most of her cities and towns

Whether measured from the date of her first settlement, her organization as a Territory or admission as a State, Iowa has thus far shown a growth unsurpassed, in a similar period, by any commonwealth on the face of the earth; and, with her vast extent of fertile soil, with her inexhaustible treasures of mineral wealth, with a healthful, invigorating climate, an intelligent, liberty-loving people; with equal just and liberal laws, and her free schools, the future of Iowa may be expected to surpass the most hopeful anticipations of her present citizens

Looking upon Iowa as she is to-day—populous, prosperous and happy—it is hard to realize the wonderful changes that have occurred since the first white settlements were made within her borders When the number of States was only twenty-six, and their total population about twenty millions, our republican form of government was hardly more than an experiment, just fairly put upon trial The development of our agricultural resources and inexhaustible mineral wealth had hardly commenced. Westward the "Star of Empire" had scarcely started on its way. West of the great Mississippi was a mighty empire, but almost unknown, and marked on the maps of the period as "The Great American Desert."

Now, thirty-eight stars glitter on our national escutcheon, and forty-five millions of people, who know their rights and dare maintain them, tread American soil, and the grand sisterhood of States extends from the Gulf of Mexico to the Canadian border, and from the rocky coast of the Atlantic to the golden shores of the Pacific.

THE AGRICULTURAL COLLEGE AND FARM

Ames, Story County

The Iowa State Agricultural College and Farm were established by an act of the General Assembly, approved March 22, 1858 A Board of Trustees was appointed, consisting of Governor R. P. Lowe, John D Wright, William Duane Wilson, M W Robinson, Timothy Day, Richard Gaines, John Pattee, G W F. Sherwin, Suel Foster, S. W. Henderson Clement Coffin and E G. Day; the Governors of the State and President of the College being ex officio members. Subsequently the number of Trustees was reduced to five The Board met in June, 1859, and received propositions for the location of the College and Farm from Hardin, Polk, Story and Boone, Marshall, Jefferson and Tama Counties. In July, the proposition of Story County and some of its citizens and by the citizens of Boone County was accepted, and the farm and the site for the buildings were located In 1860–61, the farm-house and barn were erected In 1862, Congress granted to the State 240,000 acres of land for the endowment of schools of agriculture and the mechanical arts, and 195,000 acres were located by Peter Melendy, Commissioner, in 1862–3. George W. Bassett was appointed Land Agent for the institution In 1864 the General Assembly appropriated $20,000 for the erection of the college building.

In June of that year, the Building Committee, consisting of Suel Foster, Peter Melendy and A J. Bronson, proceeded to let the contract.   John Browne, of Des Moines, was employed as architect, and furnished the plans of the building, but was superseded in its construction by C A Dunham   The $20,000 appropriated by the General Assembly were expended in putting in the foundations and making the brick for the structure.   An additional appropriation of $91,000 was made in 1866, and the building was completed in 1868

Tuition in this college is made by law forever free to pupils from the State over sixteen years of age, who have been resident of the State six months previous to their admission.   Each county in the State has a prior right of tuition for three scholars from each county ; the remainder, equal to the capacity of the college, are by the Trustees distributed among the counties in proportion to the population, and subject to the above rule.   All sale of ardent spirits, wine or beer are prohibited by law within a distance of three miles from the college, except for sacramental, mechanical or medical purposes.

The course of instruction in the Agricultural College embraces the following branches. Natural Philosophy. Chemistry, Botany, Horticulture, Fruit Growing, Forestry, Animal and Vegetable Anatomy, Geology, Mineralogy, Meteorology, Entomology, Zoology, the Veterinary Art, Plane Mensuration, Leveling, Surveying, Bookkeeping, and such Mechanical Arts as are directly connected with agriculture ; also such other studies as the Trustees may from time to time prescribe, not inconsistent with the purposes of the institution.

The funds arising from the lease and sale of lands and interest on investments are sufficient for the support of the institution.   Several College Societies are maintained among the students, who publish a monthly paper.   There is also an " out-law " called the " ΑΖΑ, Chapter Omega "

The Board of Trustees in 1877 was composed of C. W. Warden, Ottumwa, Chairman ; Hon. Samuel J Kirkwood, Iowa City ; William B Treadway, Sioux City ; Buel Sherman, Fredericksburg, and Laurel Summers, Le Claire. E. W Starten, Secretary ; William D. Lucas, Treasurer

Board of Instruction —A. S. Welch, LL D., President and Professor of Psychology and Philosophy of Science ; Gen. J L Geddes, Professor of Military Tactics and Engineering ; W. H Wynn, A M , Ph. D., Professor of English Literature ; C. E Bessey, M. S , Professor of Botany, Zoology, Entomology ; A Thompson, C E., Mechanical Engineering and Superintendent of Workshops, F E L Beal, B S , Civil Engineering, T E Pope, A M , Chemistry ; M. Stalker, Agricultural and Veterinary Science ; J. L. Budd, Horticulture ; J K. Macomber, Physics, E W. Stanton, Mathematics and Political Economy ; Mrs. Margaret P. Stanton, Preceptress, Instructor in French and Mathematics.

THE STATE UNIVERSITY.

Iowa City, Johnson County.

In the famous Ordinance of 1787, enacted by Congress before the Territory of the United States extended beyond the Mississippi River, it was declared that in all the territory northwest of the Ohio River, " Schools and the means of education shall forever be encouraged " By act of Congress, approved July 20, 1840, the Secretary of the Treasury was authorized " to set apart and reserve from sale, out of any of the public lands within the Territory of Iowa, to which the Indian title has been or may be extinguished, and not otherwise appropriated, a quantity of land, not exceeding the entire townships, for the use

and support of a university within said Territorry when it becomes a State, and
for no other use or purpose whatever, to be located in tracts of not less than an
entire section, corresponding with any of the large divisions into which the public land are authorized to be surveyed."

William W. Dodge, of Scott County, was appointed by the Secretary of the
Treasury to make the selections. He selected Section 5 in Township 78, north
of Range 3, east of the Fifth Principal Meridian, and then removed from the
Territory No more lands were selected until 1846, when, at the request of the
Assembly, John M. Whitaker of Van Buren County, was appointed, who selected
the remainder of the grant except about 122 acres

In the first Constitution, under which Iowa was admitted to the Union, the
people directed the disposition of the proceeds of this munificent grant in accordance with its terms, and instructed the General Assembly to provide, as soon
as may be, effectual means for the improvement and permanent security of the
funds of the university derived from the lands

The first General Assembly, by act approved February 25, 1847, established
the "State University of Iowa" at Iowa City, then the capital of the State,
"with such other branches as public convenience may hereafter require "
The " public buildings at Iowa City, together with the ten acres of land in which
they are situated," were granted for the use of said university, *provided*, however, that the sessions of the Legislature and State offices should be held in the
capitol until otherwise provided by law   The control and management of the
University were committed to a board of fifteen Trustees, to be appointed by the
Legislature, five of whom were to be chosen biennially. The Superintendent
of Public Instruction was made President of this Board   Provisions were made
for the disposal of the two townships of land, and for the investment of the funds
arising therefrom. The act further provides that the University shall never be
under the exclusive control of any religious denomination whatever," and as
soon as the revenue for the grant and donations amounts to $2,000 a year, the
University should commence and continue the instruction, free of charge, of fifty
students annually. The General Assembly retained full supervision over the
University, its officers and the grants and donations made and to be made to it
by the State

Section 5 of the act appointed James P Carleton, H D Downey, Thomas
Snyder, Samuel McCrory, Curtis Bates, Silas Foster, E C Lyon James H
Gower, George G Vincent, Wm G Woodward, Theodore S Parvin, George
Atchinson, S G Matson, H W. Starr and Ansel Briggs, the first Board of
Trustees

The organization of the University at Iowa City was impracticable, however, so long as the seat of government was retained there.

In January, 1849, two branches of the University and three Normal
Schools were established   The branches were located—one at Fairfield, and
the other at Dubuque, and were placed upon an equal footing, in respect to
funds and all other matters, with the University established at Iowa City
"This act," says Col Benton, "created *three* State Universities, with equal
rights and powers, instead of a 'University with such branches as public convenience *may hereafter demand*,' as provided by the Constitution "

The Board of Directors of the Fairfield Branch consisted of Barnet Ris-
tine, Christian W Slagle, Daniel Rider, Horace Gaylord, Bernhart Henn and
Samuel S. Bayard. At the first meeting of the Board, Mr Henn was elected
Preside, Mr Slagle Secretary, and Mr. Gaylord Treasurer. Twenty acres
of land were purchased and a building erected thereon, costing $2,500

This building was nearly destroyed by a hurricane, in 1850, but was rebuilt more substantially, all by contributions of the citizens of Fairfield. This branch never received any aid from the State or from the University Fund, and by act approved January 24, 1853, at the request of the Board, the General Assembly terminated its relation to the State.

The branch at Dubuque was placed under the control of the Superintendent of Public Instruction, and John King, Caleb H. Booth, James M Emerson, Michael J. Sullivan, Richard Benson and the Governor of the State as Trustees   The Trustees never organized, and its existence was only nominal

The Normal Schools were located at Andrew, Oskaloosa and Mount Pleasant, respectively.   Each was to be governed by a board of seven Trustees, to be appointed by the Trustees of the University   Each was to receive $500 annually from the income of the University Fund, upon condition that they should educate eight common school teachers, free of charge for tuition, and that the citizens should contribute an equal sum for the erection of the requisite buildings. The several Boards of Trustees were appointed   At Andrew, the school was organized Nov 21, 1849; Samuel Ray, Principal, Miss J S Dorr, Assistant.   A building was commenced and over $1,000 expended on it, but it was never completed.   At Oskaloosa, the Trustees organized in April, 1852.   This school was opened in the Court House, September 13, 1852, under the charge of Prof. G. M Drake and wife.   A two story brick building was completed in 1853, costing $2,473   The school at Mount Pleasant was never organized. Neither of these schools received any aid from the University Fund, but in 1857 the Legislature appropriated $1,000 each for those at Oskaloosa and Andrew, and repealed the law authorizing the payment of money to them from the University Fund.   From that time they made no further effort to continue in operation

At a special meeting of the Board of Trustees, held February 21, 1850, the " College of Physicians and Surgeons of the Upper Mississippi," established at Davenport, was recognized as the " College of Physicians and Surgeons of the State University of Iowa," expressly stipulating, however, that such recognition should not render the University liable for any pecuniary aid, nor was the Board to have any control over the property or management of the Medical Association   Soon after, this College was removed to Keokuk, its second session being opened there in November, 1850.   In 1851, the General Assembly confirmed the action of the Board, and by act approved January 22, 1855, placed the Medical College under the supervision of the Board of Trustees of the University, and it continued in operation until this arrangement was terminated by the new Constitution, September 3, 1857

From 1847 to 1855, the Board of Trustees was kept full by regular elections by the Legislature, and the Trustees held frequent meetings, but there was no effectual organization of the University.   In March, 1855, it was partially opened for a term of sixteen weeks   July 16, 1855, Amos Dean, of Albany, N. Y., was elected President, but he never entered fully upon its duties   The University was again opened in September, 1855, and continued in operation until June, 1856, under Professors Johnson, Welton, Van Valkenburg and Guffin

In the Spring of 1856, the capital of the State was located at Des Moines; but there were no buildings there, and the capitol at Iowa City was not vacated by the State until December, 1857

In June, 1856, the faculty was re-organized, with some changes, and the University was again opened on the third Wednesday of September, 1856.

There were one hundred and twenty-four students—eighty-three males and forty-one females—in attendance during the year 1856–7, and the first regular catalogue was published.

At a special meeting of the Board, September 22, 1857, the honorary degree of Bachelor of Arts was conferred on D Franklin Wells   This was the first degree conferred by the Board.

Article IX, Section 11, of the new State Constitution, which went into force September 3, 1857, provided as follows :

The State University shall be established at one place, without branches at any other place , and the University fund shall be applied to that institution, and no other

Article XI, Section 8, provided that

The seat of Government is hereby permanently established, as now fixed by law, at the city of Des Moines, in the county of Polk , and the State University at Iowa City, in the county of Johnson

The new Constitution created the Board of Education, consisting of the Lieutenant Governor, who was ex officio President, and one member to be elected from each judicial district in the State.   This Board was endowed with " full power and authority to legislate and make all needful rules and regulations in relation to common schools and other educational institutions," subject to alteration, amendment or repeal by the General Assembly, which was vested with authority to abolish or re-organize the Board at any time after 1863

In December, 1857, the old capitol building, now known as Central Hall of the University, except the rooms occupied by the United States District Court, and the property, with that exception, passed under the control of the Trustees, and became the seat of the University.   The old building had had hard usage, and its arrangement was illy adapted for University purposes Extensive repairs and changes were necessary, but the Board was without funds for these purposes

The last meeting of the Board, under the old law, was held in January. 1858.   At this meeting, a resolution was introduced, and seriously considered, to exclude females from the University; but it finally failed.

March 12, 1858, the first Legislature under the new Constitution enacted a new law in relation to the University, but it was not materially different from the former.   March 11, 1858, the Legislature appropriated $3,000 for the repair and modification of the old capitol building, and $10,000 for the erection of a boarding house, now known as South Hall

The Board of Trustees created by the new law met and duly organized April 27, 1858, and determined to close the University until the income from its fund should be adequate to meet the current expenses, and the buildings should be ready for occupation   Until this term, the building known as the "Mechanics' Academy' had been used for the school.   The Faculty, except the Chancellor (Dean), was dismissed, and all further instruction suspended, from the close of the term then in progress until September, 1859.   At this meeting, a resolution was adopted excluding females from the University after the close of the existing term , but this was afterward, in August, modified, so as to admit them to the Normal Department

At the meeting of the Board, August 4, 1858, the degree of Bachelor of Science was conferred upon Dexter Edson Smith, being the first degree conferred upon a student of the University.   Diplomas were awarded to the members of the first graduating class of the Normal Department as follows : Levi P. Aylworth, Cellina H Aylworth, Elizabeth L Humphrey, Annie A. Pinney and Sylvia M. Thompson

An "Act for the Government and Regulation of the State University of Iowa" approved December 25, 1858, was mainly a re-enactment of the law of March 12, 1858, except that changes were made in the Board of Trustees, and manner of their appointment This law provided that both sexes were to be admitted on equal terms to all departments of the institution, leaving the Board no discretion in the matter

The new Board met and organized, February 2, 1859, and decided to continue the Normal Department only to the end of the current term, and that it was unwise to re-open the University at that time; but at the annual meeting of the Board, in June of the same year, it was resolved to continue the Normal Department in operation; and at a special meeting October 25, 1859, it was decided to re-open the University in September, 1860. Mr. Dean had resigned as Chancellor prior to this meeting, and Silas Totten, D D , LL. D , was elected President, at a salary of $2,000, and his term commenced June, 1860.

At the annual meeting, June 28, 1860, a full Faculty was appointed, and the University re-opened, under this new organization, September 19, 1860 (third Wednesday), and at this date the actual existence of the University may be said to commence

August 19, 1862, Dr Totten having resigned, Prof. Oliver M Spencer was elected President and the honorary degree of Doctor of Laws was conferred upon Judge Samuel F. Miller, of Keokuk.

At the commencement, in June, 1863, was the first class of graduates in the Collegiate Department

The Board of Education was abolished March 19, 1864, and the office of Superintendent of Public Instruction was restored: the General Assembly resumed control of the subject of education, and on March 21, an act was approved for the government of the University It was substantially the same as the former law, but provided that the Governor should be ex officio President of the Board of Trustees. Until 1858, the Superintendent of Public Instruction had been ex officio President. During the period of the Board of Education, the University Trustees were elected by it, and elected their own President

President Spencer was granted leave of absence from April 10, 1866, for fifteen months, to visit Europe, and Prof Nathan R. Leonard was elected President pro tem

The North Hall was completed late in 1866

At the annual meeting in June, 1867, the resignation of President Spencer (absent in Europe) was accepted, and Prof. Leonard continued as President pro tem., until March 4, 1868, when James Black, D. D., Vice President of Washington and Jefferson College, Penn., was elected President. Dr. Black entered upon his duties in September, 1868.

The Law Department was established in June, 1868, and, in September following, an arrangement was perfected with the Iowa Law School, at Des Moines, which had been in successful operation for three years, under the management of Messrs. George G. Wright, Chester C Cole and William G Hammond, by which that institution was transferred to Iowa City and merged in the Law Department of the University. The Faculty of this department consisted of the President of the University, Hon Wm G Hammond, Resident Professor and Principal of the Department, and Professors G G. Wright and C C. Cole.

Nine students entered at the commencement of the first term, and during the year ending June, 1877, there were 103 students in this department.

At a special meeting of the Board, on the 17th of September 1868, a Committee was appointed to consider the expediency of establishing a Medical Department. This Committee reported at once in favor of the proposition, the Faculty to consist of the President of the University and seven Professors, and recommended that, if practicable, the new department should be opened at the commencement of the University year, in 1869–70   At this meeting, Hon. Ezekiel Clark was elected Treasurer of the University

By an act of the General Assembly, approved April 11, 1870, the "Board of Regents" was instituted as the governing power of the University, and since that time it has been the fundamental law of the institution. The Board of Regents held its first meeting June 28, 1870. Wm J. Haddock was elected Secretary, and Mr Clark, Treasurer

Dr. Black tendered his resignation as President, at a special meeting of the Board, held August 18, 1870, to take effect on the 1st of December following His resignation was accepted

The South Hall having been fitted up for the purpose, the first term of the Medical Department was opened October 24, 1870, and continued until March, 1871, at which time there were three graduates and thirty-nine students

March 1, 1871, Rev George Thacher was elected President of the University. Mr Thacher accepted, entered upon his duties April 1st, and was formally inaugurated at the annual meeting in June, 1861

In June, 1874, the "Chair of Military Instruction" was established, and the President of the United States was requested to detail an officer to perform its duties   In compliance with this request, Lieut A. D. Schenck, Second Artillery, U. S. A, was detailed as "Professor of Military Science and Tactics," at Iowa State University, by order of the War Department, August 26, 1874, who reported for duty on the 10th of September following   Lieut. Schenck was relieved by Lieut James Chester, Third Artillery, January 1, 1877

Treasurer Clark resigned November 3, 1875, and John N Coldren elected in his stead.

At the annual meeting, in 1876, a Department of Homœopathy was established

In March, 1877, a resolution was adopted affiliating the High Schools of the State with the University.

In June, 1877, Dr Thacher's connection with the University was terminated, and C W. Slagle, a member of the Board of Regents, was elected President

In 1872, the ex officio membership of the Superintendent of Public Instruction was abolished; but it was restored in 1876. Following is a catalogue of the officers of this important institution, from 1847 to 1878:

TRUSTEES OR REGENTS.

PRESIDENTS

	FROM	TO
James Harlan, Superintendent Public Instruction, ex officio	1847	1848
Thomas H Benton, Jr, Superintendent Public Instruction, ex officio	1849	1854
James D Eads, Superintendent Public Instruction, ex officio	1854	1857
Maturin L Fisher, Superintendent Public Instruction, ex officio	1857	1858
Amos Dean, Chancellor, ex officio	1858	1859
Thomas H Benton, Jr	1859	1863
Francis Springer	1863	1864
William M Stone, Governor, ex officio	1864	1868
Samuel Merrill, Governor, ex officio	1868	1872
Cyrus C Carpenter, Governor, ex officio	1872	1876
Samuel J Kirkwood, Governor, ex officio	1876	1877
John H Newbold, Governor, ex officio	1877	1878
John H Gear	1878	...

VICE PRESIDENTS	FROM	TO
Silas Foster	1847	1851
Robert Lucas	1851	1853
Edward Connelly	1854	1855
Moses J Morsman	1855	1858

SECRETARIES		
Hugh D Downey	1847	1851
Anson Hart	1851	1857
Elijah Sells	1857	1858
Anson Hart	1858	1864
William J Haddock	1864	

TREASURERS		
Morgan Reno, State Treasurer, ex officio	1847	1850
Israel Kister, State Treasurer ex officio	1850	1852
Martin L Morris, State Treasurer, ex officio	1852	1855
Henry W Lathrop	1855	1862
William Crum	1862	1868
Ezekiel Clark	1868	1876
John N Coldren	1876	

PRESIDENTS OF THE UNIVERSITY		
Amos Dean, LL D	1855	1858
Silas Totten, D D , LL D	1860	1862
Oliver M Spencer, D D *	1862	1867
James Black, D D	1868	1870
George Thacher, D D	1871	1877
C W Slagle	1877	

The present educational corps of the University consists of the President, nine Professors in the Collegiate Department, one Professor and six Instructors in Military Science ; Chancellor, three Professors and four Lecturers in the Law Department, eight Professor Demonstrators of Anatomy; Prosector of Surgery and two Lecturers in the Medical Department, and two Professors in the Homœopathic Medical Department.

STATE HISTORICAL SOCIETY.

By act of the General Assembly, approved January 28, 1857, a State Historical Society was provided for in connection with the University. At the commencement, an appropriation of $250 was made, to be expended in collecting, embodying, and preserving in an authentic form a library of books, pamphlets, charts, maps, manuscripts, papers, paintings, statuary, and other materials illustrative of the history of Iowa, and with the further object to rescue from oblivion the memory of the early pioneers, to obtain and preserve various accounts of their exploits, perils and hardy adventures; to secure facts and statements relative to the history and genius, and progress and decay of the Indian tribes of Iowa, to exhibit faithfully the antiquities and past and present resources of the State, to aid in the publication of such collections of the Society as shall from time to time be deemed of value and interest; to aid in binding its books, pamphlets, manuscripts and papers, and in defraying other necessary incidental expenses of the Society

There was appropriated by law to this institution, till the General Assembly shall otherwise direct, the sum of $500 per annum. The Society is under the management of a Board of Curators, consisting of eighteen persons, nine of whom are appointed by the Governor, and nine elected by the members of the Society. The Curators receive no compensation for their services. The annual meeting is provided for by law, to be held at Iowa City on Monday preceding the last Wednesday in June of each year.

The State Historical Society has published a series of very valuable collections, including history, biography, sketches, reminiscences, etc., with quite a large number of finely engraved portraits of prominent and early settlers, under the title of "Annals of Iowa."

THE PENITENTIARY
Located at Fort Madison, Lee County.

The first act of the Territorial Legislature, relating to a Penitentiary in Iowa, was approved January 25, 1839, the fifth section of which authorized the Governor to draw the sum of $20,000 appropriated by an act of Congress approved July 7, 1838, for public buildings in the Territory of Iowa. It provided for a Board of Directors of three persons elected by the Legislature, who should direct the building of the Penitentiary, which should be located within one mile of the public square, in the town of Fort Madison, Lee County, provided Fort Madison should deed to the directors a tract of land suitable for a site, and assign them, by contract, a spring or stream of water for the use of the Penitentiary. To the Directors was also given the power of appointing the Warden, the latter to appoint his own assistants

The first Directors appointed were John S. David and John Claypole. They made their first report to the Legislative Council November 9, 1839. The citizens of the town of Fort Madison had executed a deed conveying ten acres of land for the building site. Amos Ladd was appointed Superintendent of the building June 5, 1839. The building was designed of sufficient capacity to contain one hundred and thirty-eight convicts, and estimated to cost $55,933 90. It was begun on the 9th of July, 1839; the main building and Warden's house were completed in the Fall of 1841. Other additions were made from time to time till the building and arrangements were all complete according to the plan of the Directors. It has answered the purpose of the State as a Penitentiary for more than thirty years, and during that period many items of practical experience in prison management have been gained.

It has long been a problem how to conduct prisons, and deal with what are called the criminal classes generally, so as to secure their best good and best subserve the interests of the State. Both objects must be taken into consideration in any humanitarian view of the subject. This problem is not yet solved, but Iowa has adopted the progressive and enlightened policy of humane treatment of prisoners and the utilization of their labor for their own support. The labor of the convicts in the Iowa Penitentiary, as in most others in the United States, is let out to contractors, who pay the State a certain stipulated amount therefor, the State furnishing the shops, tools and machinery, as well as the supervision necessary to preserve order and discipline in the prison

While this is an improvement upon the old solitary confinement system, it still falls short of an enlightened reformatory system that in the future will treat the criminal for mental disease and endeavor to restore him to usefulness in the community. The objections urged against the contract system of disposing of the labor of prisoners, that it brings the labor of honest citizens into competition with convict labor at reduced prices, and is disadvantageous to the State, are not without force, and the system will have no place in the prisons of the future

It is right that the convict should labor   He should not be allowed to live in idleness at public expense.   Honest men labor ; why should not they? Honest men are entitled to the fruits of their toil, why should not the convict as well?   The convict is sent to the Penitentiary to secure public safety   The State deprives him of his liberty to accomplish this purpose and to punish him for violations of law, but, having done this, the State wrongs both itself and the criminal by confiscating his earnings, because it deprives his family of what justly belongs to them, and an enlightened civilization will ere long demand that the prisoner in the penitentiary, after paying a fair price for his board, is as justly entitled to his net earnings as the good citizen outside its walls, and his family, if he has one, should be entitled to draw his earnings or stated portion of them at stated periods   If he has no family, then if his net earnings should be set aside to his credit and paid over to him at the expiration of his term of imprisonment, he would not be turned out upon the cold charities of a somewhat pharisaical world, penniless, with the brand of the convict upon his brow, with no resource save to sink still deeper in crime   Let Iowa, ' The Beautiful Land," be first to recognize the rights of its convicts to the fruits of their labor , keep their children from the alms-house, and place a powerful incentive before them to become good citizens when they return to the busy world again.

ADDITIONAL PENITENTIARY.

Located at Anamosa, Jones County.

By an act of the Fourteenth General Assembly, approved April 23, 1872, William Ure, Foster L Downing and Martin Heisey were constituted Commissioners to locate and provide for the erection and control of an additional Penitentiary for the State of Iowa.   These Commissioners met on the 4th of the following June, at Anamosa, Jones County, and selected a site donated by the citizens, within the limits of the city.   L W. Foster & Co , architects, of Des Moines, furnished the plan, drawings and specifications, and work was commenced on the building on the 28th day of September, 1872   May 13, 1873, twenty convicts were transferred to Anamosa from the Fort Madison Penitentiary.   The entire enclosure includes fifteen acres, with a frontage of 663 feet.

IOWA HOSPITAL FOR THE INSANE

Mount Pleasant, Henry County

By an act of the General Assembly of Iowa, approved January 24, 1855, $4,425 were appropriated for the purchase of a site, and $50,000 for building an Insane Hospital. and the Governor (Grimes), Edward Johnston, of Lee County, and Charles S Blake, of Henry County, were appointed to locate the institution and superintend the erection of the building   These Commissioners located the institution at Mt. Pleasant, Henry County   A plan for a building designed to accommodate 300 patients, drawn by Dr. Bell, of Massachusetts, was accepted, and in October work was commenced under the superintendence of Mr Henry Winslow   Up to February 25, 1858, and including an appropriation made on that date the Legislature had appropriated $258,555.67 to this institution but the bu____ ___ ___ __ fin_h_d ___ __ _____upancy by patients until March 1, 18_1   __ __rus_es were M__ __ __ ___ __h__, President, Farmersburg; Samuel McFarland _ecretary M_ __leasant D. L.

McGugin, Keokuk; G W Kincaid, Muscatine; J. D. Elbert, Keosauqua John B. Lash and Harpin Riggs, Mt Pleasant. Richard J. Patterson, M D, of Ohio, was elected Superintendent; Dwight C Dewey, M D, Assistant Physician; Henry Winslow, Steward, Mrs Catharine Winslow, Matron The Hospital was formally opened March 6, 1861, and one hundred patients were admitted within three months About 1865 Dr Mark Ranney became Superintendent. April 18, 1876, a portion of the hospital building was destroyed by fire. From the opening of the Hospital to the close of October, 1877, 3,584 patients had been admitted Of these, 1,141 were discharged recovered, 505 discharged improved, 589 discharged unimproved, and 1 died; total discharged, 2,976, leaving 608 inmates During this period, there were 1,384 females admitted, whose occupation was registered "domestic duties;" 122, no occupation, 25, female teachers, 11, seamstresses, and 25 servants. Among the males were 916 farmers, 394 laborers, 205 without occupation, 39 cabinet makers, 23 brewers, 31 clerks, 26 merchants, 12 preachers, 18 shoe-makers, 13 students, 11 tailors, 13 teachers, 14 agents, 17 masons, 7 lawyers, 7 physicians, 4 saloon keepers, 3 salesmen, 2 artists, and 1 editor. The products of the farm and garden, in 1876 amounted to $13 721 26

Trustees, 1877:—T. Whiting, President, Mt. Pleasant, Mrs E M Elliott, Secretary, Mt Pleasant; William C Evans, West Liberty, L. E Fellows, Lansing, and Samuel Klein, Keokuk; Treasurer, M. Edwards, Mt. Pleasant.

Resident Officers:—Mark Ranney, M. D., Medical Superintendent; H M. Bassett, M D. First Assistant Physician; M Riordan, M D, Second Assistant Physician; Jennie McCowen, M D, Third Assistant Physician, J. W Henderson, Steward; Mrs. Martha W. Ranney, Matron, Rev. Milton Sutton, Chaplain.

HOSPITAL FOR THE INSANE
Independence, Buchanan County.

In the Winter of 1867–8, a bill providing for an additional Hospital for the Insane was passed by the Legislature, and an appropriation of $125,000 was made for that purpose. Maturin L. Fisher, of Clayton County, E G. Morgan, of Webster County, and Albert Clark, of Buchanan County, were appointed Commissioners to locate and supervise the erection of the Building Mr Clark died about a year after his appointment, and Hon. G. W Bemis, of Independence, was appointed to fill the vacancy

The Commissioners met and commenced their labors on the 8th day of June, 1868, at Independence The act under which they were appointed required them to select the most eligible and desirable location, of not less than 320 acres, within two miles of the city of Independence, that might be offered by the citizens free of charge to the State. Several such tracts were offered, but the Commissioners finally selected the south half of southwest quarter of Section 5; the north half of northeast quarter of Section 7; the north half of northwest quarter of Section 8, and the north half of northeast quarter of Section 8, all in Township 88 north, Range 9 west of the Fifth Principal Meridian. This location is on the west side of the Wapsipinicon River, and about a mile from its banks, and about the same distance from Independence

Col S V Shipman of Madison Wis was employed to prepare plans, specifi   ed, were sub- mitted   unt Pleasant, who s   the building was awarded to Mr David Armstrong, of Dubuque, for $88,114. The contract was signed November 7, 1868, and Mr Armstrong at once commenced work Mr George Josselyn was appointed to superintend the work. The main buildings were constructed of dressed limestone, from the quarries at Anamosa and Farley. The basements are of the local granite worked from the immense boulders found in large quantities in this portion of the State

In 1872, the building was so far completed that the Commissioners called the first meeting of the Trustees, on the 10th day of July of that year These Trustees were Maturin L Fisher, Mrs. P A Appleman, T. W. Fawcett, C C Parker, E G. Morgan, George W Bemis and John M. Boggs This board was organized, on the day above mentioned, by the election of Hon M L Fisher, President, Rev. J. G. Boggs, Secretary, and George W Bemis, Treasurer, and, after adopting preliminary measures for organizing the local government of the hospital, adjourned to the first Wednesday of the following September A few days before this meeting, Mr Boggs died of malignant fever, and Dr. John G. House was appointed to fill the vacancy Dr House was elected Secretary At this meeting, Albert Reynolds, M. D, was elected Superintendent: George Josselyn, Steward, and Mrs. Anna B Josselyn, Matron September 4, 1873, Dr Willis Butterfield was elected Assistant Physician The building was ready for occupancy April 21, 1873

In the Spring of 1876, a contract was made with Messrs Mackay & Lundy, of Independence, for furnishing materials for building the outside walls of the two first sections of the south wing, next to the center building, for $6,250 The carpenter work on the fourth and fifth stories of the center building was completed during the same year, and the wards were furnished and occupied by patients in the Fall

In 1877, the south wing was built, but it will not be completed ready for occupancy until next Spring or Summer (1878)

October 1, 1877, the Superintendent reported 322 patients in this hospital, and it is now overcrowded.

The Board of Trustees at present (1878) are as follows· Maturin L. Fisher, President, Farmersburg; John G. House. M D, Secretary, Independence; Wm G Donnan, Treasurer, Independence, Erastus G Morgan, Fort Dodge, Mrs Prudence A Appleman, Clermont; and Stephen E. Robinson, M D, West Union.

RESIDENT OFFICERS

Albert Reynolds, M. D, Superintendent G H Hill, M D, Assistant Physician; Noyes Appleman, Steward, Mrs Lucy M Gray, Matron.

IOWA COLLEGE FOR THE BLIND.

Vinton, Benton County.

In August, 1852, Prof Samuel Bacon, himself blind, established an Institution for the Instruction of the Blind of Iowa, at Keokuk.

By act of the General Assembly, entitled " An act to establish an Asylum for the Blind," approved January 18, 1853, the institution was adopted by the State, removed to Iowa City, February 3d and opened for the reception of pupils April 4, 1853, free to all the blind in the State.

The first Board of Commissioners . . . . . orge W McClary, Secretary; John B C . . . . . . Stephen Hempstead, Mor . . . . . . ed Prof.

Samuel Bacon, Principal; T J McGittigen, Teacher of Music, and Mrs Sarah K. Bacon, Matron   Twenty-three pupils were admitted during the first term

In his first report, made in 1854, Prof Bacon suggested that the name should be changed from "Asylum for the Blind," to that of "Institution for the Instruction of the Blind."   This was done in 1855, when the General Assembly made an annual appropriation for the College of $55 per quarter for each pupil   This was subsequently changed to $3,000 per annum, and a charge of $25 as an admission fee for each pupil, which sum, with the amounts realized from the sale of articles manufactured by the blind pupils, proved sufficient for the expenses of the institution during Mr Bacon's administration.   Although Mr. Bacon was blind, he was a fine scholar and an economical manager, and had founded the Blind Asylum at Jacksonville, Illinois.   As a mathematician he had few superiors.

On the 8th of May, 1858, the Trustees met at Vinton, and made arrangements for securing the donation of $5,000 made by the citizens of that town

In June of that year, a quarter section of land was donated for the College, by John W. O. Webb and others, and the Trustees adopted a plan for the erection of a suitable building   In 1860, the plan was modified, and the contract for enclosing let to Messrs Finkbine & Lovelace, for $10,420.

In August, 1862, the building was so far completed that the goods and furniture of the institution were removed from Iowa City to Vinton, and early in October, the school was opened there with twenty-four pupils.   At this time, Rev. Orlando Clark was Principal.

In August, 1864, a new Board of Trustees were appointed by the Legislature, consisting of James McQuin, President; Reed Wilkinson, Secretary, Jas Chapin, Treasurer: Robert Gilchrist, Elijah Sells and Joseph Dysart, organized and made important changes   Rev. Reed Wilkinson succeeded Mr Clark as Principal   Mrs. L. S B. Wilkinson and Miss Amelia Butler were appointed Assistant Teachers, Mrs N A Morton, Matron

Mr. Wilkinson resigned in June, 1867, and Gen James L Geddes was appointed in his place   In September, 1869, Mr. Geddes retired, and was succeeded by Prof S. A Knapp   Mrs S C. Lawton was appointed Matron, and was succeeded by Mrs. M A Knapp.   Prof Knapp resigned July 1, 1875, and Prof Orlando Clark was elected Principal, who died April 2, 1876, and was succeeded by John B Parmalee, who retired in July, 1877, when the present incumbent, Rev Robert Carothers, was elected

Trustees, 1877–8—Jeremiah L. Gay, President, S H Watson, Treasurer, H C Piatt, Jacob Springer, C L Flint and P F Sturgis.

Faculty—Principal, Rev. Robert Carothers, A. M ; Matron, Mrs. Emeline E Carothers; Teachers, Thomas F. McCune, A. B, Miss Grace A. Hill, Mrs C A. Spencer, Miss Mary Baker, Miss C R Miller, Miss Lorana Mattice, Miss A M McCutcheon, Musical Director, S. O. Spencer

The Legislative Committee who visited this institution in 1878 expressed their astonishment at the vast expenditure of money in proportion to the needs of the State   The structure is well built, and the money properly expended; yet it was enormously beyond the necessities of the State, and shows an utter disregard of the fitness of things.   The Committee could not understand why $282,000 should have been expended for a massive building covering about two and a half acres for the accommodation of 130 people, costing over eight thousand do‥‥‥ ‥ ‥ to ‥ ‥ ‥ t ‥ ‥‥ ng the State about five hundred dollars a year ‥ ‥ ‥h ‥pil

INSTITUTION FOR THE DEAF AND DUMB.

Council Bluffs, Pottawattomie County.

The Iowa Institution for the Deaf and Dumb was established at Iowa City by an act of the General Assembly, approved January 24, 1855   The number of deaf mutes then in the State was 301; the number attending the Institution, 50   The first Board of Trustees were: Hon. Samuel J. Kirkwood, Hon. E. Sells, W. Penn Clarke, J P. Wood, H D. Downey, William Crum, W E Ijams, Principal   On the resignation of Mr Ijams, in 1862, the Board appointed in his stead Mr Benjamin Talbot, for nine years a teacher in the Ohio Institution for the Deaf and Dumb.   Mr. Talbot was ardently devoted to the interests of the institution and a faithful worker for the unfortunate class under his charge

A strong effort was made, in 1866, to remove this important institution to Des Moines, but it was located permanently at Council Bluffs, and a building rented for its use.   In 1868, Commissioners were appointed to locate a site for, and to superintend the erection of, a new building, for which the Legislature appropriated $125,000 to commence the work of construction   The Commissioners selected ninety acres of land about two miles south of the city of Council Bluffs.   The main building and one wing were completed October 1. 1870, and immediately occupied by the Institution.   February 25, 1877, the main building and east wing were destroyed by fire; and August 6 following, the roof of the new west wing was blown off and the walls partially demolished by a tornado.   At the time of the fire, about one hundred and fifty pupils were in attendance   After the fire, half the classes were dismissed and the number of scholars reduced to about seventy, and in a week or two the school was in running order

The Legislative Committee which visited this Institution in the Winter of 1857–8 was not well pleased with the condition of affairs, and reported that the building (west wing) was a disgrace to the State and a monument of unskillful workmanship, and intimated rather strongly that some reforms in management were very essential

Trustees, 1877–8.—Thomas Officer. President; N. P. Dodge, Treasurer. Paul Lange, William Orr, J W Cattell

Superintendent, Benjamin Talbot, M. A   Teachers, Edwin Southwick, Conrad S Zorbaugh, John A Gillespie, John A Kennedy, Ellen J. Israel, Ella J Brown, Mrs H R Gillespie, Physician, H W Hart, M. D.; Steward, N. A. Taylor, Matron, Mary B Swan.

SOLDIERS' ORPHANS' HOMES.

Davenport, Cedar Falls, Glenwood.

The movement which culminated in the establishment of this beneficent institution was originated by Mrs Annie Wittenmeyer, during the civil war of 1861–65.   This noble and patriotic lady called a convention at Muscatine, on the 7th of October 1863, for the purpose of devising measures for the support and education of the orphan children of the brave sons of Iowa, who had fallen in defense of national honor and integrity.   So great was the public interest in the movement the there was a large representation from all parts of the State on the day named and an association was organized called the Iowa State Orphan Asylum

The first officers were President, William M Stone Vice Presidents, Mrs G G. Wright, Mrs R L Cadle, Mrs J T Hancock, John R Needham, J W Cattell, Mrs. Mary M Bagg, Recording Secretary. Miss Mary Kibben, Corresponding Secretary, Miss M E. Shelton, Treasurer, N H Brainerd; Board of Trustees, Mrs Annie Wittenmeyer, Mrs C B Darwin, Mrs D T Newcomb Mrs. L B Stephens, O Fayville, E H Williams, T. S. Parvin, Mrs Shields Caleb Baldwin, C C Cole, Isaac Pendleton, H C Henderson

The first meeting of the Trustees was held February 14, 1864, in the Representative Hall, at Des Moines Committees from both branches of the General Assembly were present and were invited to participate in their deliberations Gov Kirkwood suggested that a home for disabled soldiers should be connected with the Asylum Arrangements were made for raising funds

At the next meeting, in Davenport, in March, 1864 the Trustees decided to commence operations at once, and a committee, of which Mr Howell of Keokuk, was Chairman, was appointed to lease a suitable building, solicit donations, and procure suitable furniture This committee secured a large brick building in Lawrence, Van Buren County, and engaged Mr Fuller, of Mt Pleasant, as Steward

At the annual meeting, in Des Moines, in June, 1864, Mrs C B. Baldwin, Mrs. G G. Wright, Mrs Dr. Horton, Miss Mary E Shelton and Mr George Sherman were appointed a committee to furnish the building and take all necessary steps for opening the 'Home,' and notice was given that at the next meeting of the Association, a motion would be made to change the name of the Institution to Iowa Orphans' Home

The work of preparation was conducted so vigorously that on the 13th day of July following, the Executive Committee announced that they were ready to receive the children In three weeks twenty-one were admitted, and the number constantly increased, so that, in a little more than six months from the time of opening, there were seventy children admitted, and twenty more applications, which the Committee had not acted upon—all orphans of soldiers

Miss M Elliott, of Washington, was appointed Matron She resigned, in February, 1865, and was succeeded by Mrs E G Platt, of Fremont County

The "Home" was sustained by the voluntary contributions of the people, until 1866, when it was assumed by the State In that year, the General Assembly provided for the location of several such 'Homes' in the different counties, and which were established at Davenport, Scott County, Cedar Falls, Black Hawk County, and at Glenwood, Mills County

The Board of Trustees elected by the General Assembly had the oversight and management of the Soldiers' Orphans Homes of the State, and consisted of one person from each county in which such Home was located, and one for the State at large, who held their office two years, or until their successors were elected and qualified An appropriation of $10 per month for each orphan actually supported was made by the General Assembly

The Home in Cedar Falls was organized in 1865, and an old hotel building was fitted up for it Rufus C, Mary L and Emma L. Bauer were the first children received, in October, and by January, 1866, there were ninety-six inmates

October 12, 1869, the Home was removed to a large brick building, about two mile   of C l   E ll   f   years, but in 1870   u   l at Cedar Falls an   l l l   l l ll

By "An act to provide for the organization and support of an asylum at Glenwood, in Mills County for feeble minded children," approved March 17, 1876, the buildings and grounds used by the Soldiers' Orphans' Home at that place were appropriated for this purpose. By another act, approved March 15, 1876 the soldiers' orphans, then at the Homes at Glenwood and Cedar Falls, were to be removed to the Home at Davenport within ninety days thereafter, and the Board of Trustees of the Home were authorized to receive other indigent children into that institution, and provide for their education in industrial pursuits.

STATE NORMAL SCHOOL
Cedar Falls, Black Hawk County

Chapter 129 of the laws of the Sixteenth General Assembly, in 1876, established a State Normal School at Cedar Falls, Black Hawk County, and required the Trustees of the Soldiers' Orphans' Home to turn over the property in their charge to the Directors of the new institution.

The Board of Directors met at Cedar Falls June 7, 1876, and duly organized by the election of H. C. Hemenway, President, J. J. Toleston, Secretary, and E. Townsend, Treasurer. The Board of Trustees of the Soldiers' Orphans' Home met at the same time for the purpose of turning over to the Directors the property of that institution, which was satisfactorily done and properly receipted for as required by law. At this meeting, Prof. J. C. Gilchrist was elected Principal of the School.

On the 12th of July, 1876, the Board again met, when executive and teachers' committees were appointed and their duties assigned. A Steward and a Matron were elected, and their respective duties defined.

The buildings and grounds were repaired and fitted up as well as the appropriation would admit, and the first term of the school opened September 6, 1876, commencing with twenty-seven and closing with eighty-seven students. The second term closed with eighty-six, and one hundred and six attended during the third term.

The following are the Board of Directors Board of Officers and Faculty.

Board of Directors.—H. C. Hemenway, Cedar Falls, President, term expires 1882; L. D. Lewelling, Salem, Henry County, 1878; W. A. Stow, Hamburg, Fremont County, 1878; S. G. Smith, Newton, Jasper County, 1880; E. H. Thayer, Clinton, Clinton County, 1880; G. S. Robinson, Storm Lake, Buena Vista County, 1882.

Board of Officers.—J. J. Toleston, Secretary; E. Townsend, Treasurer. William Pattes, Steward; Mrs. P. A. Schermerhorn, Matron—all of Cedar Falls.

Faculty.—J. C. Gilchrist, A. M., Principal, Professor of Mental and Moral Philosophy and Didactics; M. W. Bartlett, A. M., Professor of Languages and Natural Science; D. S. Wright, A. M., Professor of Mathematics; Miss Frances L. Webster, Teacher of Geography and History; E. W. Burnham, Professor of Music.

ASYLUM FOR FEEBLE MINDED CHILDREN.
Glenwood, Mills County

Chapter 1__ of the laws of the Sixteenth General Assembly, approved March 17, 1876, provided for the establishment of an asylum for feeble minded children at Glenwood, Mills County, and the buildings and grounds of the

Soldiers' Orphans' Home at that place were to be used for that purpose. The asylum was placed under the management of three Trustees, one at least of whom should be a resident of Mills County   Children between the ages of 7 and 18 years are admitted.   Ten dollars per month for each child actually supported by the State was appropriated by the act, and $2,000 for salaries of officers and teachers for two years.

Hon J. W. Cattell, of Polk County ; A. J. Russell, of Mills County, and W. S Robertson, were appointed Trustees, who held their first meeting at Glenwood. April 26, 1876   Mr. Robertson was elected President, Mr Russell, Treasurer, and Mr. Cattell, Secretary   The Trustees found the house and farm which had been turned over to them in a shamefully dilapidated condition. The fences were broken down and the lumber destroyed or carried away, the windows broken, doors off their hinges, floors broken and filthy in the extreme, cellars reeking with offensive odors from decayed vegetables, and every conceivable variety of filth and garbage. drains obstructed, cisterns broken, pump demoralized wind-mill broken, roof leaky, and the whole property in the worst possible condition.   It was the first work of the Trustees to make the house tenable.   This was done under the direction of Mr. Russell   At the request of the Trustees, Dr Charles T Wilbur, Superintendent of the Illinois Asylum, visited Glenwood, and made many valuable suggestions, and gave them much assistance

O. W. Archibald, M. D., of Glenwood. was appointed Superintendent, and soon after was appointed Secretary of the Board, vice Cattell, resigned. Mrs S. A Archibald was appointed Matron, and Miss Maud M. Archibald, Teacher

The Institution was opened September 1, 1876 , the first pupil admitted September 4, and the school was organized September 10, with only five pupils, which number had, in November, 1877, increased to eighty-seven.   December 1, 1876, Miss Jennie Van Dorin, of Fairfield, was employed as a teacher and in the Spring of 1877, Miss Sabina J Archibald was also employed

THE REFORM SCHOOL.

Eldora, Hardin County.

By "An act to establish and organize a State Reform School for Juvenile Offenders." approved March 31, 1868, the General Assembly established a State Reform School at Salem, Lee (Henry) County, provided for a Board of Trustees, to consist of one person from each Congressional District.   For the purpose of immediately opening the school, the Trustees were directed to accept the proposition of the Trustees of White's Iowa Manual Labor Institute, at Salem, and lease, for not more than ten years, the lands, buildings, etc.. of the Institute, and at once proceed to prepare for and open a reform school as a temporary establishment

The contract for fitting up the buildings was let to Clark & Haddock, September 21, 1868, and on the 7th of October following, the first inmate was received from Jasper County   The law provided for the admission of children of both sexes under 18 years of age   In 1876 this was amended, so that they are now received at ages over 7 and under 16 years.

April 19, 1872, the Trustees were directed to make a permanent location for the school and $17,000 was appropriated for the erection of the necessary buildings   The Trustees were further directed, as soon as practicable, to organize a school for girls in the buildings where the boys were then kept.

The Trustees located the school at Eldora, Hardin County and in the Code of 1873, it is permanently located there by law.

The institution is managed by five Trustees, who are paid mileage, but no compensation for their services.

The object is the reformation of the children of both sexes, under the age of 16 years and over 7 years of age, and the law requires that the Trustees shall require the boys and girls under their charge to be instructed in piety and morality, and in such branches of useful knowledge as are adapted to their age and capacity, and in some regular course of labor, either mechanical, manufacturing or agricultural, as is best suited to their age, strength, disposition and capacity, and as may seem best adapted to secure the reformation and future benefit of the boys and girls.

A boy or girl committed to the State Reform School is there kept, disciplined, instructed, employed and governed, under the direction of the Trustees, until he or she arrives at the age of majority, or is bound out, reformed or legally discharged. The binding out or discharge of a boy or girl as reformed, or having arrived at the age of majority, *is a complete release* from all penalties incurred by conviction of the offense for which he or she was committed.

This is one step in the right direction. In the future, however, still further advances will be made, and the right of every individual to the fruits of their labor, even while restrained for the public good, will be recognized.

FISH HATCHING ESTABLISHMENT.

Near Anamosa, Jones County.

The Fifteenth General Assembly, in 1874, passed "An act to provide for the appointment of a Board of Fish Commissioners for the construction of Fishways for the protection and propagation of Fish," also "An act to provide for furnishing the rivers and lakes with fish and fish spawn." This act appropriated $3,000 for the purpose. In accordance with the provisions of the first act above mentioned, on the 9th of April, 1874, S. B. Evans of Ottumwa, Wapello County, B. F. Shaw of Jones County, and Charles A. Haines, of Black Hawk County, were appointed to be Fish Commissioners by the Governor. These Commissioners met at Des Moines, May 10, 1874, and organized by the election of Mr. Evans, President, Mr. Shaw, Secretary and Superintendent, and Mr. Haines, Treasurer.

The State was partitioned into three districts or divisions to enable the Commissioners to better superintend the construction of fishways as required by law. That part of the State lying south of the Chicago, Rock Island & Pacific Railroad was placed under the especial supervision of Mr. Evans; that part between that railroad and the Iowa Division of the Illinois Central Railroad, Mr. Shaw, and all north of the Illinois Central Railroad, Mr. Haines. At this meeting, the Superintendent was authorized to build a State Hatching House, to procure the spawn of valuable fish adapted to the waters of Iowa; hatch and prepare the young fish for distribution, and assist in putting them into the waters of the State.

In compliance with these instructions, Mr. Shaw at once commenced work, and in the Summer of 1874, erected a "State Hatching House" near Anamosa, 20x40 feet, two stories; the second story being designed for a tenement; the first story being the "hatching room." The hatching troughs are supplied with water from a magnificent spring four feet deep and ten feet in diameter, affording an abundant and unfailing supply of pure running water. During the first year, from May 10, 1874, to May 10, 1875, the Commissioners distributed within the State 100,000 Shad, 300,000 California Salmon, 10,000 Bass, 80,000 Penobscot (Maine) Salmon, 5,000 land-locked Salmon, 20,000 of other species

By act approved March 10, 1876, the law was amended so that there should be but one instead of three Fish Commissioners, and B F Shaw was appointed, and the Commissioner was authorized to purchase twenty acres of land, on which the State Hatching House was located near Anamosa.

In the Fall of 1876, Commissioner Shaw gathered from the sloughs of the Mississippi, where they would have been destroyed, over a million and a half of small fish, which were distributed in the various rivers of the State and turned into the Mississippi.

In 1875-6, 533,000 California Salmon, and in 1877, 303,500 Lake Trout were distributed in various rivers and lakes in the State. The experiment of stocking the small streams with brook trout is being tried, and 81,000 of the speckled beauties were distributed in 1877 In 1876, 100,000 young eels were distributed These came from New York and they are increasing rapidly

At the close of 1877 there were at least a dozen private fish farms in successful operation in various parts of the State. Commissioner Shaw is enthusiastically devoted to the duties of his office and has performed an important service for the people of the State by his intelligent and successful operations

The Sixteenth General Assembly passed an act in 1878, prohibiting the catching of any kind of fish except Brook Trout from March until June of each year. Some varieties are fit for food only during this period.

THE PUBLIC LANDS.

The grants of public lands made in the State of Iowa, for various purposes, are as follows

1   The 500,000 Acre Grant
2   The 16th Section Grant
3   The Mortgage School Lands
4   The University Grant
5   The Saline Grant
6   The Des Moines River Grant
7   The Des Moines River School Lands
8   The Swamp Land Grant
9   The Railroad Grant
10   The Agricultural College Grant

I.   THE FIVE HUNDRED THOUSAND ACRE GRANT

When the State was admitted into the Union, she became entitled to 500,000 acres of land by virtue of an act of Congress, approved September 4, 1841, which granted to each State therein specified 500,000 acres of public land for internal improvements; to each State admitted subsequently to the passage of the act, an amount of land which, with the amount that might have been granted to her as a Territory, would amount to 500,000 acres. All these lands were required to be selected within the limits of the State to which they were granted.

The Constitution of Iowa declares that the proceeds of this grant, together with all . . . . e benefit of schools, ... throughout the Stat . . . . established a board of School Fund Commissioners, and to that board was confided the selection, care and sale of these lands for the benefit of the School Fund. Until 1855, these Commissioners were subordinate to the Superintendent of Public Instruction, but on the 15th of January of that year, they were clothed with exclusive authority in the management and sale of school lands. The office of School Fund Commissioner was abolished March 23, 1858, and that officer in each county was required to transfer all papers to and make full settlement with the County Judge. By this act, County Judges and Township Trustees were made the agents of the State to control and sell the sixteenth sections; but no further provision was made for the sale of the 500,000 acre grant until April 3d, 1860, when the entire management of the school lands was committed to the Boards of Supervisors of the several counties.

II. THE SIXTEENTH SECTIONS

By the provisions of the act of Congress admitting Iowa to the Union, there was granted to the new State the sixteenth section in every township, or where that section had been sold, other lands of like amount for the use of schools. The Constitution of the State provides that the proceeds arising from the sale of these sections shall constitute a part of the permanent School Fund. The control and sale of these lands were vested in the School Fund Commissioners of the several counties until March 23, 1858, when they were transferred to the County Judges and Township Trustees, and were finally placed under the supervision of the County Boards of Supervisors in January, 1861.

III. THE MORTGAGE SCHOOL LANDS

These do not belong to any of the grants of land proper. They are lands that have been mortgaged to the school fund, and became school lands when bid off by the State by virtue of a law passed in 1862. Under the provisions of the law regulating the management and investment of the permanent school fund, persons desiring loans from that fund are required to secure the payment thereof with interest at ten per cent per annum, by promissory notes endorsed by two good sureties and by mortgage on unincumbered real estate, which must be situated in the county where the loan is made, and which must be valued by three appraisers. Making these loans and taking the required securities was made the duty of the County Auditor, who was required to report to the Board of Supervisors at each meeting thereof, all notes, mortgages and abstracts of title connected with the school fund, for examination.

When default was made of payment of money so secured by mortgage, and no arrangement made for extension of time as the law provides, the Board of Supervisors were authorized to bring suit and prosecute it with diligence to secure said fund, and in action in favor of the county for the use of the school fund, an injunction may issue without bonds, and in any such action, when service is made by publication, default and judgment may be entered and enforced without bonds. In case of sale of land on execution founded on any such mortgage, the attorney of the board, or other person duly authorized, shall, on behalf of the State or county for the use of said fund, bid such sum as the interests of said fund may require, and if struck off to the State the land shall be held and ⟨illegible⟩ lands are known ⟨illegible⟩ cluding description a ⟨illegible⟩

IV   UNIVERSITY LANDS

By act of Congress, July 20, 1840, a quantity of land not exceeding two entire townships was reserved in the Territory of Iowa for the use and support of a university within said Territory when it should become a State   This land was to be located in tracts of not less than an entire section, and could be used for no other purpose than that designated in the grant   In an act supplemental to that for the admission of Iowa, March 3, 1845, the grant was renewed, and it was provided that the lands should be used "solely for the purpose of such university, in such manner as the Legislature may prescribe "

Under this grant there were set apart and approved by the Secretary of the Treasury, for the use of the State, the following lands :

		ACRES
In the Iowa City Land District, Feb 26, 1849 ...	.	20,150 49
In the Fairfield Land District, Oct 17, 1849	..	9,685 20
In the Iowa City Land District, Jan 28, 1850	....	2,571 81
In the Fairfield Land District, Sept 10, 1850	..	3,198 20
In the Dubuque Land District, May 19, 1852 ..	.....	10,552 24
Total	....	45,057 94

These lands were certified to the State November 19, 1859.   The University lands are placed by law under the control and management of the Board of Trustees of the Iowa State University   Prior to 1865, there had been selected and located under 282 patents, 22,892 acres in sixteen counties, and 23,036 acres unpatented, making a total of 45,928 acres

V.—SALINE LANDS.

By act of Congress, approved March 3, 1845, the State of Iowa was granted the use of the salt springs within her limits, not exceeding twelve. By a subsequent act, approved May 27, 1852, Congress granted the springs to the State in fee simple, together with six sections of land contiguous to each, to be disposed of as the Legislature might direct   In 1861, the proceeds of these lands then to be sold were constituted a fund for founding and supporting a lunatic asylum, but no sales were made   In 1856, the proceeds of the saline lands were appropriated to the Insane Asylum, repealed in 1858.   In 1860, the saline lands and funds were made a part of the permanent fund of the State University   These lands were located in Appanoose, Davis, Decatur, Lucas, Monroe, Van Buren and Wayne Counties

VI —THE DES MOINES RIVER GRANT.

By act of Congress, approved August 8, 1846, a grant of land was made for the improvement of the navigation of Des Moines River, as follows :

Be it enacted by the Senate and House of Representatives of the United States of America in Congress assembled, That there be, and hereby is, granted to said Territory of Iowa, for the purpose of aiding said Territory to improve the navigation of the Des Moines River from its mouth to the Raccoon Fork (so called) in said Territory, one equal moiety, in alternate sections, of the public lands (remaining unsold and not otherwise disposed of, incumbered or appropriated), in a strip five miles in width on each side of said river, to be selected within said Territory by an agent or agents to be appointed by the Governor thereof, subject to the approval of the Secretary of the Treasury of the United States

Sec 2   *And be it further enacted,* That the lands hereby granted shall not be conveyed or disposed of by said Territory nor by any State to be formed out of the same, except as said improvement shall progress that is, the said Territory or State may sell so much of said lands as shall produce the sum ___ ___ ___, and then the ___ shall cease until the Governor of ___ ___ ___ ___ the fact to the President of the United States that one-half of said ___ ___ expended upon ___ improvements, when the said Territory or

State may sell and convey a quantity of the residue of said lands sufficient to replace the amount expended, and thus the sales shall progress as the proceeds thereof shall be expended, and the fact of such expenditure shall be certified as aforesaid

Sec 3. *And be it further enacted*, That the said River Des Moines shall be and forever remain a public highway for the use of the Government of the United States, free from any toll or other charge whatever, for any property of the United States or persons in their service passing through or along the same *Provided always*, That it shall not be competent for the said Territory or future State of Iowa to dispose of said lands, or any of them, at a price lower than, for the time being, shall be the minimum price of other public lands

Sec 4 *And be it further enacted*, That whenever the Territory of Iowa shall be admitted into the Union as a State, the lands hereby granted for the above purpose shall be and become the property of said State for the purpose contemplated in this act, and for no other *Provided* the Legislature of the State of Iowa shall accept the said grant for the said purpose " Approved Aug 8, 1846

By joint resolution of the General Assembly of Iowa, approved January 9, 1847, the grant was accepted for the purpose specified By another act, approved February 24, 1847, entitled "An act creating the Board of Public Works, and providing for the improvement of the Des Moines River," the Legislature provided for a Board consisting of a President, Secretary and Treasurer, to be elected by the people. This Board was elected August 2, 1847, and was organized on the 22d of September following The same act defined the nature of the improvement to be made, and provided that the work should be paid for from the funds to be derived from the sale of lands to be sold by the Board.

Agents appointed by the Governor selected the sections designated by "odd numbers' throughout the whole extent of the grant, and this selection was approved by the Secretary of the Treasury But there was a conflict of opinion as to the extent of the grant It was held by some that it extended from the mouth of the Des Moines only to the Raccoon Forks; others held, as the agents to make selection evidently did, that it extended from the mouth to the head waters of the river. Richard M Young, Commissioner of the General Land Office, on the 23d of February, 1848, construed the grant to mean that "the State is entitled to the alternate sections within five miles of the Des Moines River, throughout the whole extent of that river within the limits of Iowa" Under this construction, the alternate sections above the Raccoon Forks would, of course, belong to the State: but on the 19th of June, 1848, some of these lands were, by proclamation, thrown into market On the 18th of September, the Board of Public Works filed a remonstrance with the Commissioner of the General Land Office. The Board also sent in a protest to the State Land Office, at which the sale was ordered to take place On the 8th of January, 1849, the Senators and Representatives in Congress from Iowa also protested against the sale, in a communication to Hon Robert J. Walker, Secretary of the Treasury, to which the Secretary replied, concurring in the opinion that the grant extended the whole length of the Des Moines River in Iowa

On the 1st of June, 1849, the Commissioner of the General Land Office directed the Register and Receiver of the Land Office at Iowa City " to withhold from sale all lands situated in the odd numbered sections within five miles on each side of the Des Moines River above the Raccoon Forks " March 13, 1850, the Commissioner of the General Land Office submitted to the Secretary of the Interior a list "showing the tracts falling within the limits of the Des Moines River grant, above the Raccoon Forks, etc , under the decision of the Secretary of the Treasury Mai ch 2, 1 49, and in il of April following, Mr Ewing, the secretary of the Interior on d the decision of Secretary Walker, but ordered the lands to be withheld until Con-

gress could have an opportunity to pass an explanatory act   The Iowa authorities appealed from this decision to the President (Taylor), who referred the
matter to the Attorney General (Mr. Johnson)   On the 19th of July, Mr.
Johnson submitted as his opinion, that by the terms of the grant itself, it extended to the very source of the Des Moines, but before his opinion was published President Taylor died   When Mr. Tyler's cabinet was formed, the
question was submitted to the new Attorney General (Mr. Crittenden), who, on
the 30th of June, 1851, reported that in his opinion the grant did not extend
above the Raccoon Forks.   Mr. Stewart, Secretary of the Interior, concurred
with Mr. Crittenden at first, but subsequently consented to lay the whole subject before the President and Cabinet, who decided in favor of the State.

October 29, 1851, Mr. Stewart directed the Commissioner of the General
Land Office to "submit for his approval such lists as had been prepared, and to
proceed to report for like approval lists of the alternate sections claimed by the
State of Iowa above the Raccoon Forks, as far as the surveys have progressed,
or may hereafter be completed and returned"   And on the following day, three
lists of these lands were prepared in the General Land Office

The lands approved and certified to the State of Iowa under this grant, and
all lying above the Raccoon Forks, are as follows.

By Secretary Stewart, Oct. 30, 1851.	81,707 93 acres
March 10, 1852	143,908 37 "
By Secretary McLellan, Dec 17, 1853.	33,142 43 "
Dec 30, 1853 . . .	12,813 51 "
Total	271,572 24 acres.

The Commissioners and Register of the Des Moines River Improvement, in
their report to the Governor, November 30, 1852, estimates the total amount of
lands then available for the work, including those in possession of the State and
those to be surveyed and approved, at nearly a million acres   The indebtedness
then standing against the fund was about $108,000, and the Commissioners
estimated the work to be done would cost about $1,200,000.

January 19, 1853, the Legislature authorized the Commissioners to sell
"any or all the lands which have or may hereafter be granted, for not less than
$1,300,000.'

On the 24th of January, 1853, the General Assembly provided for the election of a Commissioner by the people, and appointed two Assistant Commissioners, with authority to make a contract, selling the lands of the Improvement
for $1,300,000   This new Board made a contract, June 9, 1855, with the Des
Moines Navigation & Railroad Company, agreeing to sell *all* the lands donated
to the State by Act of Congress of August 8, 1846, which the State had not
sold prior to December 23 1853, for $1,300,000, to be expended on the im-
provement of the river, and in paying the indebtedness then due   This contract was duly reported to the Governor and General Assembly

By an act approved January 25, 1855, the Commissioner and Register of
the Des Moines River Improvement were authorized to negotiate with the Des
Moines Navigation & Railroad Company for the purchase of lands in Webster
County which had been sold by the School Fund Commissioner as school lands,
but which had been certified to the State as Des Moines River lands, and had,
therefore, become the property of the Company, under the provisions of its
contract with the

M. . . . . s again raised
and the . . . . it was limited to

the Raccoon Fork   Appeal was made to the Secretary of the Interior, and by him the matter was referred to the Attorney General, who decided that the grant extended to the northern boundary of the State, the State relinquished its claim to lands lying along the river in Minnesota, and the vexed question was supposed to be finally settled

The land which had been certified, as well as those extending to the northern boundary within the limits of the grant, were reserved from pre-emption and sale by the General Land Commissioner, to satisfy the grant of August 8, 1846, and they were treated as having passed to the State, which from time to time sold portions of them prior to their final transfer to the Des Moines Navigation & Railroad Company, applying the proceeds thereof to the improvement of the river in compliance with the terms of the grant. Prior to the final sale to the Company, June 9, 1854, the State had sold about 327,000 acres, of which amount 58,830 acres were located above the Raccoon Fork. The last certificate of the General Land Office bears date December 30, 1853.

After June 9th, 1854 the Des Moines Navigation & Railroad Company carried on the work under its contract with the State   As the improvement progressed, the State, from time to time, by its authorized officers, issued to the Company, in payment for said work, certificates for lands   But the General Land Office ceased to certify lands under the grant of 1846   The State had made no other provision for paying for the improvements, and disagreements and misunderstanding arose between the State authorities and the Company.

March 22, 1858, a joint resolution was passed by the Legislature submitting a proposition for final settlement to the Company, which was accepted.   The Company paid to the State $20,000 in cash, and released and conveyed the dredge boat and materials named in the resolution, and the State, on the 3d of May, 1858, executed to the Des Moines Navigation & Railroad Company fourteen deeds or patents to the lands, amounting to 256,703 64 acres   These deeds were intended to convey all the lands of this grant certified to the State by the General Government not previously sold, but, as if for the purpose of covering any tract or parcel that might have been omitted, the State made another deed of conveyance on the 18th day of May, 1858   These fifteen deeds, it is claimed, by the Company, convey 266,108 acres, of which about 53,367 are below the Raccoon Fork, and the balance, 212,741 acres, are above that point

Besides the lands deeded to the Company, the State had deeded to individual purchasers 58,830 acres above the Raccoon Fork, making an aggregate of 271,-571 acres, deeded above the Fork, all of which had been certified to the State by the Federal Government

By act approved March 28, 1858, the Legislature donated the remainder of the grant to the Keokuk, Fort Des Moines & Minnesota Railroad Company upon condition that said Company assumed all liabilities resulting from the Des Moines River improvement operations, reserving 50,000 acres of the land in security for the payment thereof, and for the completion of the locks and dams at Bentonsport, Croton, Keosauqua and Plymouth   For every three thousand dollars worth of work done on the locks and dams and for every three thousand dollars paid by the Company of the liabilities above mentioned, the Register of the State Land Office was instructed to certify to the Company 1,000 acres of the 50,000 acres reserved for these purposes.   Up to 1865, there had been presented by the ~ . . . . allowed, claims amounting . . . . ich had been settled

After the passage of the Act above noticed, the question of the extent of the original grant was again mooted, and at the December Term of the Supreme Court of the United States, in 1859–60, a decision was rendered declaring that the grant did *not* extend above Raccoon Fork, and that all certificates of land *above* the Fork had been issued without authority of law and were, therefore, void (see 23 How., 66).

The State of Iowa had disposed of a large amount of land without authority according to this decision, and appeal was made to Congress for relief, which was granted on the 3d day of March, 1861, in a joint resolution relinquishing to the State all the title which the United States then still retained in the tracts of land along the Des Moines River above Raccoon Fork, that had been improperly certified to the State by the Department of the Interior, and which is now held by *bona fide* purchasers under the State of Iowa.

In confirmation of this relinquishment, by act approved July 12, 1862, Congress enacted:

That the grant of lands to the then Territory of Iowa for the improvement of the Des Moines River, made by the act of August 8, 1846, is hereby extended so as to include the alternate sections (designated by odd numbers) lying within five miles of said river, between the Raccoon Fork and the northern boundary of said State, such lands are to be held and applied in accordance with the provisions of the original grant, except that the consent of Congress is hereby given to the application of a portion thereof to aid in the construction of the Keokuk, Fort Des Moines & Minnesota Railroad, in accordance with the provisions of the act of the General Assembly of the State of Iowa, approved March 22, 1858 And if any of the said lands shall have been sold or otherwise disposed of by the United States before the passage of this act, except those released by the United States to the grantees of the State of Iowa, under joint resolution of March 3, 1861, the Secretary of the Interior is hereby directed to set apart an equal amount of lands within said State to be certified in lieu thereof, *Provided*, that if the State shall have sold and conveyed any portion of the lands lying within the limits of the grant the title of which has proved invalid, any lands which shall be certified to said State in lieu thereof by virtue of the provisions of this act, shall inure to and be held as a trust fund for the benefit of the person or persons, respectively, whose titles shall have failed as aforesaid

The grant of lands by the above act of Congress was accepted by a joint resolution of the General Assembly, September 11, 1862, in extra session. On the same day, the Governor was authorized to appoint one or more Commissioners to select the lands in accordance with the grant   These Commissioners were instructed to report their selections to the Registrar of the State Land Office.   The lands so selected were to be held for the purposes of the grant, and were not to be disposed of until further legislation should be had.   D. W. Kilburne, of Lee County, was appointed Commissioner, and, on the 25th day of April, 1864, the General Land Office authorized the selection of 300,000 acres from the vacant public lands as a part of the grant of July 12, 1862, and the selections were made in the Fort Dodge and Sioux City Land Districts.

Many difficulties, controversies and conflicts, in relation to claims and titles, grew out of this grant, and these difficulties were enhanced by the uncertainty of its limits until the act of Congress of July, 1862   But the General Assembly sought, by wise and appropriate legislation, to protect the integrity of titles derived from the State.   Especially was the determination to protect the actual settlers, who had paid their money and made improvements prior to the final settlement of the limits of the grant by Congress.

VII —THE DES MOINES RIVER SCHOOL LANDS

These lands constituted a part of the 500,000 acre grant made by Congress in 1841, including the lands in Webster County selected by the Agent of the State under the act and approved by the Commissioner of the General Land Office February 20, 1851   They were ordered into the market June 6,

1853, by the Superintendent of Public Instruction, who authorized John Tolman, School Fund Commissioner for Webster County, to sell them as school
lands   Subsequently, when the act of 1846 was construed to extend the Des
Moines River grant above Raccoon Fork, it was held that the odd numbered
sections of these lands within five miles of the river were appropriated by that
act, and on the 30th day of December, 1853, 12,813 51 acres were set apart
and approved to the State by the Secretary of the Interior, as a part of the
Des Moines River grant.   January 6, 1854, the Commissioner of the General
Land Office transmitted to the Superintendent of Public Instruction a certified
copy of the lists of these lands, indorsed by the Secretary of the Interior
Prior to this action of the Department, however, Mr Tolman had sold to individual purchasers 3,194 28 acres as school lands, and their titles were, of course,
killed.   For their relief, an act, approved April 2, 1860, provided that, upon
application and proper showing, these purchasers should be entitled to draw
from the State Treasury the amount they had paid, with 10 per cent interest,
on the contract to purchase made with Mr Tolman   Under this act, five applications were made prior to 1864, and the applicants received, in the aggregate,
$949 53.

By an act approved April 7, 1862, the Governor was forbidden to issue to
the Dubuque & Sioux City Railroad Company any certificate of the completion
of any part of said road, or any conveyance of lands, until the company should
execute and file, in the State Land Office, a release of its claim—first, to certain swamp lands; second, to the Des Moines River Lands sold by Tolman;
third, to certain other river lands   That act provided that "the said company
shall transfer their interest in those tracts of land in Webster and Hamilton
Counties heretofore sold by John Tolman, School Fund Commissioner, to the
Register of the State Land Office in trust, to enable said Register to carry out
and perform said contracts in all cases when he is called upon by the parties
interested to do so, before the 1st day of January, A D 1864.

The company filed its release to the Tolman lands, in the Land Office, February 27, 1864, at the same time entered its protest that it had no claim upon
them, never had pretended to have, and had never sought to claim them.   The
Register of the State Land Office, under the advice of the Attorney General,
decided that patents would be issued to the Tolman purchasers in all cases
where contracts had been made prior to December 23, 1853, and remaining
uncanceled under the act of 1860.   But before any were issued, on the 27th of
August, 1864, the Des Moines Navigation & Railroad Company commenced a
suit in chancery, in the District Court of Polk County, to enjoin the issue of
such patents.   On the 30th of August, an ex parte injunction was issued   In
January, 1868, Mr. J A. Harvey, Register of the Land Office, filed in the
court an elaborate answer to plaintiffs' petition, denying that the company had
any right to or title in the lands.   Mr. Harvey's successor, Mr. C. C. Carpenter, filed a still more exhaustive answer February 10, 1868.   August 3, 1868,
the District Court dissolved the injunction.   The company appealed to the
Supreme Court, where the decision of the lower court was affirmed in December,
1869

VIII.—SWAMP LAND GRANT.

By an act of Congress, approved March 28, 1850, to enable Arkansas and
other States to reclaim swampy lands within their limits granted all the swamp
and overflowed lands remaining unsold within their respective limits to the
several States   Although the total amount claimed by Iowa under this act

does not exceed 4,000,000 acres, it has, like the Des Moines River and some of the land grants, cost the State considerable trouble and expense, and required a deal of legislation.   The State expended large sums of money in making the selections, securing proofs, etc, but the General Government appeared to be laboring under the impression that Iowa was not acting in good faith, that she had selected a large amount of lands under the swamp land grant, transferred her interest to counties, and counties to private speculators, and the General Land Office permitted contests as to the character of the lands already selected by the Agents of the State as "swamp lands"   Congress, by joint resolution Dec. 18, 1856, and by act March 3, 1857, saved the State from the fatal result of this ruinous policy   Many of these lands were selected in 1854 and 1855, immediately after several remarkably wet seasons, and it was but natural that some portions of the selections would not appear swampy after a few dry seasons   Some time after these first selections were made, persons desired to enter parcels of the so-called swamp lands and offering to prove them to be dry   In such cases the General Land Office ordered hearing before the local land officers, and if they decided the land to be dry, it was permitted to be entered and the claim of the State rejected   Speculators took advantage of this   Affidavits were bought of irresponsible and reckless men, who, for a few dollars, would confidently testify to the character of lands they never saw   These applications multiplied until they covered 3,000,000 acres   It was necessary that Congress should confirm all these selections to the State, that this gigantic scheme of fraud and plunder might be stopped   The act of Congress of March 3, 1857, was designed to accomplish this purpose   But the Commissioner of the General Land Office held that it was only a qualified confirmation, and under this construction sought to sustain the action of the Department in rejecting the claim of the State, and certifying them under act of May 15, 1856, under which the railroad companies claimed all swamp land in odd numbered sections within the limits of their respective roads   This action led to serious complications.   When the railroad grant was made, it was not intended nor was it understood that it included any of the swamp lands   These were already disposed of by previous grant   Nor did the companies expect to receive any of them, but under the decisions of the Department adverse to the State the way was opened, and they were not slow to enter their claims   March 4, 1862, the Attorney General of the State submitted to the General Assembly an opinion that the railroad companies were not entitled even to contest the right of the State to these lands, under the swamp land grant   A letter from the Acting Commissioner of the General Land Office expressed the same opinion, and the General Assembly by joint resolution, approved April 7, 1862, expressly repudiated the acts of the railroad companies, and disclaimed any intention to claim these lands under any other than the act of Congress of Sept. 28, 1850.   A great deal of legislation has been found necessary in relation to these swamp lands

IX — THE RAILROAD GRANT.

One of the most important grants of public lands to Iowa for purposes of internal improvement was that known as the "Railroad Grant." by act of Congress approved May 15, 1856.   This act granted to the State of Iowa, for the purpose of aiding in the construction of railroads from Burlington, on the Mississippi River, to a point on the Missouri River, near the mouth of Platte River   from the city of Davenport, via Iowa City and Fort Des Moines to

Council Bluffs, from Lyons City northwesterly to a point of intersection with the main line of the Iowa Central Air Line Railroad, near Maquoketa, thence on said main line, running as near as practicable to the Forty-second Parallel, across the said State of Iowa to the Missouri River, from the city of Dubuque to a point on the Missouri River, near Sioux City, with a branch from the mouth of the Tete des Morts, to the nearest point on said road, to be completed as soon as the main road is completed to that point, every alternate section of land, designated by odd numbers, for six sections in width on each side of said roads. It was also provided that if it should appear, when the lines of those roads were definitely fixed, that the United States had sold or right of preemption had attached to any portion of said land, the State was authorized to select a quantity equal thereto, in alternate sections, or parts of sections, within fifteen miles of the lines so located. The lands remaining to the United States within six miles on each side of said roads were not to be sold for less than the double minimum price of the public lands when sold, nor were any of said lands to become subject to private entry until they had been first offered at public sale at the increased price.

Section 4 of the act provided that the lands granted to said State shall be disposed of by said State only in the manner following, that is to say · that a quantity of land not exceeding one hundred and twenty sections for each of said roads, and included within a continuous length of twenty miles of each of said roads, may be sold, and when the Governor of said State shall certify to the Secretary of the Interior that any twenty continuous miles of any of said roads is completed, then another quantity of land hereby granted, not to exceed one hundred and twenty sections for each of said roads having twenty continuous miles completed as aforesaid, and included within a continuous length of twenty miles of each of such roads, may be sold: and so from time to time until said roads are completed, and if any of said roads are not completed within ten years, no further sale shall be made, and the lands unsold shall revert to the United States."

At a special session of the General Assembly of Iowa, by act approved July 14, 1856, the grant was accepted and the lands were granted by the State to the several railroad companies named, provided that the lines of their respective roads should be definitely fixed and located before April 1, 1857; and provided further, that if either of said companies should fail to have seventy-five miles of road completed and equipped by the 1st day of December, 1859, and its entire road completed by December 1, 1865, it should be competent for the State of Iowa to resume all rights to lands remaining undisposed of by the company so failing

The railroad companies, with the single exception of the Iowa Central Air Line, accepted the several grants in accordance with the provisions of the above act, located their respective roads and selected their lands. The grant to the Iowa Central was again granted to the Cedar Rapids & Missouri River Railroad Company which accepted them

By act, approved April 7, 1862, the Dubuque & Sioux City Railroad Company was required to execute a release to the State of certain swamp and school lands, included within the limits of its grant, in compensation for an extension of the time fixed for the completion of its road

A careful examination of the act of Congress does not reveal any special reference to railroad *companies* The lands were granted to the *State*, and the act evidently contemplate the sale of them *by the* State, and the appropriation of the proceeds to aid in the construction of certain lines of railroad within its limits   Section 4 of the act clearly defines the authority of the State in disposing of the lands

Lists of all the lands embraced by the grant were made, and certified to the State by the proper authorities.   Under an act of Congress approved August 3, 1854, entitled *"An act to vest in the several States and Territories the title in fee of the lands which have been or may be certified to them,"* these certified lists, the originals of which are filed in the General Land Office, conveyed to the State "the fee simple title to all the lands embraced in such lists that are of the character contemplated" by the terms of the act making the grant, and "intended to be granted thereby; but where lands embraced in such lists are not of the character embraced by such act of Congress, and were not intended to be granted thereby, said lists, so far as these lands are concerned, shall be perfectly null and void; and no right, title, claim or interest shall be conveyed thereby" Those certified lists made under the act of May 15, 1856, were forty-three in number, viz   For the Burlington & Missouri River Railroad, nine; for the Mississippi & Missouri Railroad, 11; for the Iowa Central Air Line, thirteen: and for the Dubuque & Sioux City Railroad, ten   The lands thus approved to the State were as follows

Burlington & Missouri River R R ..	287,095 34 acres
Mississippi & Missouri River R R. .	774,674 86 "
Cedar Rapids & Missouri River R R.	775,451 19 "
Dubuque & Sioux City R R . .	1,226,558 82 "

A portion of these had been selected as swamp lands by the State, under the act of September 28, 1850, and these, by the terms of the act of August 3, 1854, could not be turned over to the railroads unless the claim of the State to them as swamp was first rejected   It was not possible to determine from the records of the State Land Office the extent of the conflicting claims arising under the two grants, as copies of the swamp land selections in some of the counties were not filed of record.   The Commissioner of the General Land Office, however, prepared lists of the lands claimed by the State as swamp under act of September 28, 1850, and also claimed by the railroad companies under act of May 15, 1856, amounting to 553,293 33 acres, the claim to which as swamp had been rejected by the Department   These were consequently certified to the State as railroad lands   There was no mode other than the act of July, 1856, prescribed for transferring the title to these lands from the State to the companies   The courts had decided that, for the purposes of the grant, the lands belonged to the State, and to her the companies should look for their titles.   It was generally accepted that the act of the Legislature of July, 1856, was all that was necessary to complete the transfer of title   It was assumed that all the rights and powers conferred upon the State by the act of Congress of May 14, 1856, were by the act of the General Assembly transferred to the companies, in other words, that it was designed to put the companies in the place of the State as the grantees from Congress—and, therefore, that which perfected the title thereto to the State perfected the title to the companies by virtue of the act of July, 1856.   One of the companies, however, the Burlington & Missouri River Railroad Company, was not entirely satisfied with this construction.   Its managers thought that some further and specific action of the State authorities in addition to the act of the Legislature was necessary to complete their title   This induced Gov. Lowe to attach to the certified lists his official certificate, under the broad seal of the State.   On the 9th of November, 1859 the Governor thus certified to them (commencing at the Missouri River) No. 207.44 acres and December 27th, 4,775.70 acres   in aggregate of 251,073.14 acres   These were the only lands under the grant that were certified by the State authorities with any design of perfecting the title already vested in the company by the act of July, 1856. The lists which were afterward furnished to the company were simply certified by the Governor as being correct copies of the lists received by the State from the United States General Land Office. These subsequent lists embraced lands that had been claimed by the State under the Swamp Land Grant.

It was urged against the claim of the Companies that the effect of the act of the Legislature was simply to substitute them for the State as parties to the grant. 1st. That the lands were granted to the State to be held in trust for the accomplishment of a specific purpose, and therefore the State could not part with the title until that purpose should have been accomplished. 2d. That it was not the intention of the act of July 14, 1856, to deprive the State of the control of the lands, but on the contrary that she should retain supervision of them and the right to withdraw all rights and powers and resume the title conditionally conferred by that act upon the companies in the event of their failure to complete their part of the contract. 3d. That the certified lists from the General Land Office vested the title in the State only by virtue of the act of Congress approved August 3, 1854. The State Land Office held that the proper construction of the act of July 14, 1856, when accepted by the companies, was that it became a *conditional contract* that might ripen into a positive sale of the lands as from time to time the work should progress, and as the State thereby became authorized by the express terms of the grant to sell them.

This appears to have been the correct construction of the act, but by a subsequent act of Congress, approved June 2, 1864, amending the act of 1856, the terms of the grant were changed, and numerous controversies arose between the companies and the State.

The ostensible purpose of this additional act was to allow the Davenport & Council Bluffs Railroad "to modify or change the location of the uncompleted portion of its line," to run through the town of Newton, Jasper County, or as nearly as practicable to that point. The original grant had been made to the State to aid in the construction of railroads within its limits and not to the companies, but Congress, in 1864, appears to have been utterly ignorant of what had been done under the act of 1856, or, if not, to have utterly disregarded it. The State had accepted the original grant. The Secretary of the Interior had already certified to the State all the lands intended to be included in the grant within fifteen miles of the lines of the several railroads. It will be remembered that Section 4, of the act of May 15, 1856, specifies the manner of sale of these lands from time to time as work on the railroads should progress, and also provided that "if any of said roads are not completed within ten years, no *further* sale shall be made, and the lands *unsold shall revert to the United States.*" Having vested the title to these lands in trust, in the State of Iowa, it is plain that until the expiration of the ten years there could be no reversion, and the State, not the United States, must control them until the grant should expire by limitation. The United States authorities could not rightfully require the Secretary of the Interior to certify directly to the companies any portion of the lands already certified to the State. And yet Congress, by its act of June 2, 1864, provided that whenever the Davenport & Council Bluffs Railroad Company should file in the General Land Office at Washington a map definitely showing such new location, the Secretary of the Interior should cause to be certified and conveyed to said Company, from time to time, as the road progressed, out of any of the lands belonging to the United States, not sold, reserved, or

otherwise disposed of, or to which a pre-emption claim or right of homestead had
not attached, and on which a *bona fide* settlement and improvement had not
been made under color of title derived from the United States or from the State
of Iowa, within six miles of such newly located line, an amount of land per
mile equal to that originally authorized to be granted to aid in the construction
of said road by the act to which this was an amendment

The term "out of any lands *belonging to the United States,* not sold, reserved or otherwise disposed of, etc," would seem to indicate that Congress did
intend to grant lands already granted, but when it declared that the Company
should have an amount per mile *equal* to that originally *authorized to be granted,*
it is plain that the framers of the bill were ignorant of the real terms of the
original grant, or that they designed that the United States should *resume* the
title it had already parted with two years before the lands could revert to the
United States under the original act, which was not repealed

A similar change was made in relation to the Cedar Rapids & Missouri
Railroad, and dictated the conveyance of lands in a similar manner.

Like provision was made for the Dubuque & Sioux City Railroad, and the
Company was permitted to change the location of its line between Fort Dodge
and Sioux City, so as to secure the best route between those points, but this
change of location was not to impair the right to the land granted in the original act, nor did it change the location of those lands

By the same act, the Mississippi & Missouri Railroad Company was authorized to transfer and assign all or any part of the grant to any other company or
person, "if, in the opinion of said Company, the construction of said railroad
across the State of Iowa would be thereby sooner and more satisfactorily completed, but such assignee should not in any case be released from the liabilities
and conditions accompanying this grant, nor acquire perfect title in any other
manner than the same would have been acquired by the original grantee "

Still further, the Burlington & Missouri River Railroad was not forgotten,
and was, by the same act, empowered to receive an amount of land per mile
equal to that mentioned in the original act, and if that could not be found within
the limits of six miles from the line of said road, then such selection might
be made along such line within twenty miles thereof out of any public lands
belonging to the United States, not sold, reserved or otherwise disposed of, or
to which a pre-emption claim or right of homestead had not attached

Those acts of Congress which evidently originated in the "lobby," occasioned much controversy and trouble. The Department of the Interior, however recognizing the fact that when the Secretary had certified the lands to the
State under the act of 1856, that act divested the United States of title, under
the vesting act of August, 1854, refused to review its action, and also refused
to order any and all investigations for establishing adverse claims (except in
pre-emption cases), on the ground that the United States had parted with the
title, and, therefore, could exercise no control over the land

May 12, 1864, before the passage of the amendatory act above described,
Congress granted to the State of Iowa, to aid in the construction of a railroad
from McGregor to Sioux City, and for the benefit of the McGregor Western
Railroad Company, every alternate section of land, designated by odd numbers,
for ten sections in width on each side of the proposed road, reserving the right
to substitute other lands whenever it was found that the grant infringed upon
pre-empt [illegible] reserved, disposed of or any other
purpose [illegible] to select, in
lieu, lan [illegible] limits specified

X —AGRICULTURAL COLLEGE AND FARM LANDS

An Agricultural College and Model Farm was established by act of the General Assembly, approved March 22, 1858 By the eleventh section of the act, the proceeds of the five-section grant made for the purpose of aiding in the erection of public buildings was appropriated, subject to the approval of Congress, together with all lands that Congress might thereafter grant to the State for the purpose, for the benefit of the institution. On the 23d of March, by joint resolution, the Legislature asked the consent of Congress to the proposed transfer. By act approved July 11, 1862, Congress removed the restrictions imposed in the "five-section grant," and authorized the General Assembly to make such disposition of the lands as should be deemed best for the interests of the State By these several acts the five sections of land in Jasper County certified to the State to aid in the erection of public buildings under the act of March 3 1845, entitled "An act supplemental to the act for the admission of the States of Iowa and Florida into the Union," were fully appropriated for the benefit of the Iowa Agricultural College and Farm. The institution is located in Story County Seven hundred and twenty-one acres in that and two hundred in Boone County were donated to it by individuals interested in the success of the enterprise

By act of Congress approved July 2, 1862, an appropriation was made to each State and Territory of 30,000 acres for each Senator and Representative in Congress, to which, by the apportionment under the census of 1860, they were respectively entitled This grant was made for the purpose of endowing colleges of agriculture and mechanic arts

Iowa accepted this grant by an act passed at an extra session of its Legislature, approved September 11, 1862, entitled "An act to accept of the grant, and carry into execution the trust conferred upon the State of Iowa by an act of Congress entitled 'An act granting public lands to the several States and Territories which may provide colleges for the benefit of agriculture and the mechanic arts,' approved July 2, 1862" This act made it the duty of the Governor to appoint an agent to select and locate the lands, and provided that none should be selected that were claimed by any county as swamp lands The agent was required to make report of his doings to the Governor, who was instructed to submit the list of selections to the Board of Trustees of the Agricultural College for their approval One thousand dollars were appropriated to carry the law into effect. The State, having two Senators and six Representatives in Congress, was entitled to 240,000 acres of land under this grant, for the purpose of establishing and maintaining an Agricultural College Peter Melendy Esq.. of Black Hawk County. was appointed to make the selections, and during August. September and December, 1863 located them in the Fort Dodge, Des Moines and Sioux City Land Districts December 8, 1864, these selections were certified by the Commissioner of the General Land Office. and were approved to the State by the Secretary of the Interior December 13, 1864 The title to these lands was vested in the State in fee simple, and conflicted with no other claims under other grants

The agricultural lands were approved to the State as 240 000.96 acres, but as 35,691 66 acres were located within railroad limits, which were computed at the rate of two acres for one, the actual amount of land approved to the State under this grant was only 204 309.30 acres. located as follows:

In Des Moines Land District   acres
In Sioux City Land District   ..
In Fort Dodge Land District

By act of the General Assembly, approved March 29, 1864, entitled, " An act authorizing the Trustees of the Iowa State Agricultural College and Farm to sell all lands acquired, granted, donated or appropriated for the benefit of said college, and to make an investment of the proceeds thereof," all these lands were granted to the Agricultural College and Farm, and the Trustees were authorized to take possession, and sell or lease them.   They were then, under the control of the Trustees, lands as follows :

Under the act of July 2, 1852.	. .	204,309 30 acres
Of the five-section grant. .	.. . . .	3,200 00 "
Lands donated in Story County .	.	721 00 "
Lands donated in Boone County .	.. .	200.00 "
Total .	....	208,430 30 acres

The Trustees opened an office at Fort Dodge, and appointed Hon G W. Bassett their agent for the sale of these lands.

THE PUBLIC SCHOOLS.

The germ of the free public school system of Iowa, which now ranks second to none in the United States, was planted by the first settlers   They had migrated to the " The Beautiful Land " from other and older States, where the common school system had been tested by many years' experience, bringing with them some knowledge of its advantages, which they determined should be enjoyed by the children of the land of their adoption   The system thus planted was expanded and improved in the broad fields of the West, until now it is justly considered one of the most complete, comprehensive and liberal in the country.

Nor is this to be wondered at when it is remembered humble log school houses were built almost as soon as the log cabin of the earliest settlers were occupied by their brave builders   In the lead mining regions of the State, the first to be occupied by the white race, the hardy pioneers provided the means for the education of their children even before they had comfortable dwellings for their families   School teachers were among the first immigrants to Iowa   Wherever a little settlement was made, the school house was the first united public act of the settlers, and the rude primitive structures of the early time only disappeared when the communities had increased in population and wealth, and were able to replace them with more commodious and comfortable buildings   Perhaps in no single instance has the magnificent progress of the State of Iowa been more marked and rapid than in her common school system and in her school houses, which, long since, superseded the log cabins of the first settlers   To-day, the school houses which everywhere dot the broad and fertile prairies of Iowa are unsurpassed by those of any other State in the great Union   More especially is this true in all her cities and villages, where liberal and lavish appropriations have been voted, by a generous people, for the erection of large, commodious and elegant buildings, furnished with all the modern improvements, and costing from $10,000 to $60,000 each   The people of the State have expended more than $10,000,000 for the erection of public school buildings.

The first house erected in Iowa was a log cabin at Dubuque, built by James L. Langworthy and a few other miners, in the Autumn of 1833.   When it was completed, George Cabbage was employed as teacher during the Winter of 1833–4, and thirty-five pupils attended his school   Barrett Whittemore taught the second term with twenty-five pupils in attendance   Mrs Caroline Dexter commenced teaching in Dubuque in March, 1836. She was the first female teacher there, and probably the first in Iowa. In 1839, Thomas H. Benton, Jr., afterward for ten years Superintendent of Public Instruction, opened an English and classical school in Dubuque. The first tax for the support of schools at Dubuque was levied in 1840.

Among the first buildings erected at Burlington was a commodious log school house in 1834, in which Mr. Johnson Pierson taught the first school in the Winter of 1834-5.

The first school in Muscatine County was taught by George Bumgardner, in the Spring of 1837, and in 1839, a log school house was erected in Muscatine, which served for a long time for school house, church and public hall. The first school in Davenport was taught in 1838. In Fairfield, Miss Clarissa Sawyer, James F. Chambers and Mrs. Reed taught school in 1839.

When the site of Iowa City was selected as the capital of the Territory of Iowa, in May, 1839, it was a perfect wilderness. The first sale of lots took place August 18, 1839, and before January 1, 1840, about twenty families had settled within the limits of the town, and during the same year, Mr. Jesse Berry opened a school in a small frame building he had erected, on what is now College street.

The first settlement in Monroe County was made in 1843, by Mr. John R. Gray, about two miles from the present site of Eddyville, and in the Summer of 1844, a log school house was built by Gray, William V. Beedle, C. Renfro, Joseph McMullen and Willoughby Randolph, and the first school was opened by Miss Urania Adams. The building was occupied for school purposes for nearly ten years. About a year after the first cabin was built at Oskaloosa, a log school house was built, in which school was opened by Samuel W. Caldwell in 1844.

At Fort Des Moines, now the capital of the State, the first school was taught by Lewis Whitten, Clerk of the District Court in the Winter of 1846-7, in one of the rooms on "Coon Row," built for barracks.

The first school in Pottawattomie County was opened by George Green, a Mormon, at Council Point, prior to 1849; and until about 1854, nearly, if not quite, all the teachers in that vicinity were Mormons.

The first school in Decorah was taught in 1853, by T. W. Burdick, then a young man of seventeen. In Osceola, the first school was opened by Mr. D. W. Scoville. The first school at Fort Dodge was taught in 1855, by Cyrus C. Carpenter, since Governor of the State. In Crawford County, the first school house was built in Mason's Grove, in 1856, and Morris McHenry first occupied it as teacher.

During the first twenty years of the history of Iowa, the log school house prevailed, and in 1861, there were 893 of these primitive structures in use for school purposes in the State. Since that time they have been gradually disappearing. In 1865, there were 796; in 1870, 336; and in 1875, 121.

Iowa Territory was created July 3, 1838. January 1, 1839, the Territorial Legislature passed an act providing that " there shall be established a common school, or schools in each of the counties in this Territory, which shall be open and free for every class of white citizens between the ages of five and twenty-one years." The second section of the act provided that " the County Board shall, from time to time, form such districts in their respective counties whenever a petition may be presented for the purpose by a majority of the voters resident within such contemplated district." These districts were governed by boards of trustees, usually of three persons; each board was required to maintain school at least three months in every year, and later, laws were enacted providing for county school taxes for the payment of teachers, and that whatever additional sum might be required should be assessed upon the parents sending, in proportion to the length of time sent

When Iowa Territory became a State, in 1846, with a population of 100,-000, and with 20,000 scholars within its limits, about four hundred school districts had been organized. In 1850, there were 1,200, and in 1857, the number had increased to 3,265

In March, 1858, upon the recommendation of Hon. M. L. Fisher, then Superintendent of Public Instruction, the Seventh General Assembly enacted that "each civil township is declared a school district," and provided that these should be divided into sub-districts. This law went into force March 20, 1858, and reduced the number of school districts from about 3,500 to less than 900

This change of school organization resulted in a very material reduction of the expenditures for the compensation of District Secretaries and Treasurers. An effort was made for several years, from 1867 to 1872, to abolish the sub-district system. Mr. Kissll, Superintendent, recommended, in his report of January 1, 1872, and Governor Merrill forcibly endorsed his views in his annual message. But the Legislature of that year provided for the formation of independent districts from the sub-districts of district townships

The system of graded schools was inaugurated in 1849; and new schools, in which more than one teacher is employed are universally graded

The first official mention of Teachers' Institutes in the educational records of Iowa occurs in the annual report of Hon. Thomas H. Benton, Jr., made December 2, 1850, who said, "An institution of this character was organized a few years ago, composed of the teachers of the mineral regions of Illinois, Wisconsin and Iowa. An association of teachers has, also, been formed in the county of Henry, and an effort was made in October last to organize a regular institute in the county of Jones." At that time—although the beneficial influence of these institutes was admitted, it was urged that the expenses of attending them was greater than teachers with limited compensation were able to bear. To obviate this objection, Mr. Benton recommended that ' the sum of $150 should be appropriated annually for three years, to be drawn in installments of $50 each by the Superintendent of Public Instruction, and expended for these institutions." He proposed that three institutes should be held annually at points to be designated by the Superintendent

No legislation in this direction, however, was had until March, 1858, when an act was passed authorizing the holding of teachers' institutes for periods not less than six working days, whenever not less than thirty teachers should desire. The Superintendent was authorized to expend not exceeding $100 for any one institute, to be paid out by the County Superintendent as the institute might direct for teachers and lecturers, and one thousand dollars was appropriated to defray the expenses of these institutes.

December 6, 1858, Mr. Fisher reported to the Board of Education that institutes had been appointed in twenty counties within the preceding six months, and more would have been but the appropriation had been exhausted

The Board of Education at its first session, commencing December 6, 1858, enacted a code of school laws which retained the existing provisions for teachers' institutes

In March, 1858, the General Assembly amended the act of the Board by appropriating a sum not exceeding fifty dollars annually, for one such institute, held as provided by law in each county

In 1865, Mr Faville reported that "the provision made by the State for the benefit of teachers' institutes has never been so fully appreciated, both by the people and the teachers, as during the last two years"

By act approved March 19, 1874, Normal Institutes were established in each county to be held annually by the County Superintendent This was regarded as a very decided step in advance by Mr Abernethy, and in 1876 the Sixteenth General Assembly established the first permanent State Normal School at Cedar Falls, Black Hawk County, appropriating the building and property of the Soldiers' Orphans Home at that place for that purpose. This school is now " in the full tide of successful experiment "

The public school system of Iowa is admirably organized, and if the various officers who are entrusted with the educational interests of the commonwealth are faithful and competent, should and will constantly improve

" The public schools are supported by funds arising from several sources The sixteenth section of every Congressional Township was set apart by the General Government for school purposes being one-thirty-sixth part of all the lands of the State. The minimum price of these lands was fixed at one dollar and twenty-five cents per acre Congress also made an additional donation to the State of five hundred thousand acres, and an appropriation of five per cent. on all the sales of public lands to the school fund The State gives to this fund the proceeds of the sales of all lands which escheat to it. the proceeds of all fines for the violation of the liquor and criminal laws. The money derived from these sources constitutes the permanent school fund of the State, which cannot be diverted to any other purpose. The penalties collected by the courts for fines and forfeitures go to the school fund in the counties where collected The proceeds of the sale of lands and the five per cent. fund go into the State Treasury, and the State distributes these proceeds to the several counties according to their request, and the counties loan the money to individuals for long terms at eight per cent interest, on security of land valued at three times the amount of the loan, exclusive of all buildings and improvements thereon. The interest on these loans is paid into the State Treasury, and becomes the available school fund of the State The counties are responsible to the State for all money so loaned, and the State is likewise responsible to the school fund for all moneys transferred to the counties The interest on these loans is apportioned by the State Auditor semi-annually to the several counties of the State, in proportion to the number of persons between the ages of five and twenty-one years The counties also levy an annual tax for school purposes, which is apportioned to the several district townships in the same way A district tax is also levied for the same purpose The money arising from these several sources constitutes the support of the public schools, and is sufficient to enable every sub-district in the State to afford from six to nine months' school each year "

The taxes levied for the support of schools are self-imposed Under the admirable school laws of the State, no taxes can be legally assessed or collected for the erection of school houses until they have been ordered by the election of the district at a school meeting legally called The school houses of Iowa are the pride of the State and an honor to the people If they have been sometimes built at a prodigal expense, the tax payers have no one to blame but themselves The teachers and contingent funds are determined by the Board of Directors and [illegible] annually, except in the [illegible] hanged every three y [illegible] support of schools is the county school tax, which is determined by the County Board of Supervisors. The tax is from one to three mills on the dollar, usually, however, but one. Mr. Abernethy, who was Superintendent of Public Instruction from 1872 to 1877, said in one of his reports:

There is but little opposition to the levy of taxes for the support of schools, and there would be still less if the funds were always properly guarded and judiciously expended. However much our people disagree upon other subjects, they are practically united upon this. The opposition of wealth has long since ceased to exist, and our wealthy men are usually the most liberal in their views and the most active friends of popular education. They are often found upon our school boards, and usually make the best of school officers. It is not uncommon for Boards of Directors, especially in the larger towns and cities, to be composed wholly of men who represent the enterprise, wealth and business of their cities.

At the close of 1877, there were 1,086 township districts, 3,138 independent districts and 7,015 sub-districts. There were 9,948 ungraded and 470 graded schools, with an average annual session of seven months and five days. There were 7,348 male teachers employed, whose average compensation was $34 88 per month, and 12,518 female teachers, with an average compensation of $28 69 per month.

The number of persons between the ages 5 and 21 years, in 1877, was 567,859; number enrolled in public schools, 421,163, total average attendance, 251,372; average cost of tuition per month, $1.62. There are 9,279 frame, 671 brick, 257 stone and 89 log school houses, making a grand total of 10,296, valued at $9,044,973. The public school libraries number 17,329 volumes. Ninety-nine teachers' institutes were held during 1877. Teachers' salaries amounted to $2,953,645. There was expended for school houses, grounds, libraries and apparatus, $1,106,788, and for fuel and other contingencies, $1,136,995, making the grand total of $5,197,428 expended by the generous people of Iowa for the support of their magnificent public schools in a single year. The amount of the permanent school fund, at the close of 1877, was $3,462,000. Annual interest, $276,960.

In 1857, there were 3,265 independent districts, 2,708 ungraded schools, and 1,572 male and 1,424 female teachers. Teachers' salaries amounted to $198,142, and the total expenditures for schools was only $364,515. Six hundred and twenty-three volumes were the extent of the public school libraries twenty years ago, and there were only 1,686 school houses, valued at $571,064.

In twenty years, teachers' salaries have increased from $198,142, in 1857, to $2,953,645 in 1877. Total school expenditures, from $364,515 to $5,197,428.

The significance of such facts as these is unmistakable. Such lavish expenditures can only be accounted for by the liberality and public spirit of the people, all of whom manifest their love of popular education and their faith in the public schools by the annual dedication to their support of more than one per cent of their entire taxable property; this, too, uninterruptedly through a series of years, commencing in the midst of a war which taxed their energies and resources to the extreme, and continuing through years of general depression in business—years of moderate yield of produce, of discouragingly low prices, and even amid the scanty surroundings and privations of pioneer life. Few human enterprises have a grander significance or give evidence of a more noble purpose than the generous contributions from the scanty resources of the pioneer for the purposes of public education.

POLITICAL RECORD
TERRITORIAL OFFICERS

Governors—Robert Lucas, 1838–41; John Chambers, 1841–45; James Clarke, 1845.

Secretaries—William B Conway, 1838, died 1839, James Clarke, 1839, O. H. W. Stull, 1841, Samuel J Burr, 1843; Jesse Williams, 1845.

Auditors—Jesse Williams, 1840, Wm L. Gilbert, 1843 · Robert M Secrest, 1845

Treasurers—Thornton Bayliss, 1839, Morgan Reno, 1840

Judges—Charles Mason, Chief Justice, 1838, Joseph Williams, 1838: Thomas S. Wilson, 1838.

Presidents of Council—Jesse B Browne, 1838–9; Stephen Hempstead, 1839–40; M. Bainridge, 1840–1; Jonathan W Parker, 1841–2, John D Elbert, 1842–3, Thomas Cox, 1843–4: S Clinton Hastings, 1845; Stephen Hempstead, 1845–6.

Speakers of the House—William H Wallace, 1838–9; Edward Johnston, 1839–40, Thomas Cox, 1840–1, Warner Lewis, 1841–2, James M Morgan, 1842–3; James P Carleton, 1843–4, James M. Morgan, 1845, George W McCleary, 1845–6.

First Constitutional Convention, 1844—Shepherd Leffler, President, Geo S. Hampton, Secretary

Second Constitutional Convention, 1846—Enos Lowe, President; William Thompson, Secretary.

OFFICERS OF THE STATE GOVERNMENT.

Governors—Ansel Briggs, 1846 to 1850; Stephen Hempstead, 1850 to 1854; James W. Grimes, 1854 to 1858; Ralph P Lowe, 1858 to 1860, Samuel J Kirkwood, 1860 to 1864; William M Stone, 1864 to 1868, Samuel Morrill, 1868 to 1872, Cyrus C. Carpenter, 1872 to 1876; Samuel J. Kirkwood, 1876 to 1877, Joshua G. Newbold, Acting, 1877 to 1878, John H Gear, 1878 to ——.

Lieutenant Governor—Office created by the new Constitution September 3, 1857—Oran Faville, 1858–9; Nicholas J. Rusch, 1860–1, John R Needham, 1862–3; Enoch W. Eastman, 1864–5; Benjamin F Gue, 1866–7; John Scott, 1868–9, M M Walden, 1870–1; H C. Bulis, 1872–3; Joseph Dysart, 1874–5; Joshua G. Newbold, 1876–7, Frank T. Campbell, 1878–9

Secretaries of State—Elisha Cutler, Jr., Dec. 5, 1846, to Dec 4, 1848: Josiah H. Bonney, Dec. 4, 1848, to Dec 2, 1850; George W McCleary, Dec 2, 1850, to Dec 1, 1856, Elijah Sells, Dec 1, 1856, to Jan 5, 1863; James Wright, Jan 5, 1863, to Jan 7, 1867, Ed Wright, Jan. 7, 1867, to Jan. 6, 1873; Josiah T Young, Jan 6, 1873, to ——

Auditors of State—Joseph T Fales, Dec 5, 1846, to Dec. 2, 1850, William Pattee, Dec 2, 1850, to Dec 4, 1854, Andrew J. Stevens, Dec 4, 1854, resigned in 1855; John Pattee, Sept 22, 1855, to Jan. 3, 1859; Jonathan W Cattell, 1859 to 1865; John A Elliot, 1865 to 1871, John Russell, 1871 to 1875, Buren R. Sherman, 1875 to ——

Treasurers of State—Morgan Reno, Dec 18, 1846, to Dec. 2, 1850: Israel Kister, Dec 2, 1850, to Dec 4, 1852: Martin L Morris, Dec 4, 1852, to Jan 2, 1859; John W. Jones, 1859 to 1863, William H Holmes, 1863 to

1867, Samuel E Rankin, 1867 to 1873, William Christy, 1873 to 1877; George W Bemis, 1877 to ——

Superintendents of Public Instruction—Office created in 1847—James Harlan, June 5, 1845 (Supreme Court decided election void), Thomas H Benton, Jr., May 23, 1844, to June 7, 1854, James D Eads, 1854-7; Joseph C Stone, March to June, 1857; Maturin L Fisher, 1857 to Dec, 1858, when the office was abolished and the duties of the office devolved upon the Secretary of the Board of Education

Secretaries of Board of Education—Thomas H Benton, Jr., 1859-1863; Oran Faville, Jan. 1, 1864. Board abolished March 23, 1864

Superintendents of Public Instruction—Office re-created March 23, 1864—Oran Faville, March 28, 1864, resigned March 1, 1867, D. Franklin Wells, March 4, 1867, to Jan, 1870; A S Kissell, 1870 to 1872, Alonzo Abernethy, 1872 to 1877, Carl W Von Coelln, 1877 to ——

State Binders—Office created February 21 1855—William M Coles, May 1, 1855, to May 1, 1859, Frank M. Mills, 1859 to 1867, James S Carter, 1867 to 1870; J J Smart, 1870 to 1874; H A Perkins, 1874 to 1875; James J Smart, 1875 to 1876, H A Perkins, 1876 to ——.

Registers of the State Land Office—Anson Hart, May 5, 1855, to May 13, 1857; Theodore S Parvin, May 13, 1857, to Jan 3, 1859; Amos B. Miller, Jan. 3, 1859, to October, 1862; Edwin Mitchell Oct 31, 1862, to Jan 5, 1863; Josiah A Harvey, Jan 5, 1863, to Jan. 7, 1867; Cyrus C Carpenter, Jan 7, 1867, to January, 1871, Aaron Brown, January, 1871, to to January, 1875: David Secor, January, 1875, to ——

State Printers—Office created Jan. 3, 1840—Garrett D Palmer and George Paul, 1849; William H. Merritt, 1851 to 1853; William A. Hornish, 1853 (resigned May 16, 1853): Mahoney & Dorr, 1853 to 1855. Peter Moriarty, 1855 to 1857, John Teesdale, 1857 to 1861; Francis W Palmer, 1861 to 1869; Frank M Mills, 1869 to 1870; G W. Edwards, 1870 to 1872: R. P Clarkson, 1872 to ——

Adjutants General—Daniel S Lee, 1851-5, Geo. W McCleary, 1855-7; Elijah Sells, 1857; Jesse Bowen, 1857-61; Nathaniel Baker, 1861 to 1877; John H Looby, 1877 to ——

Attorneys General—David C. Cloud, 1853-56 · Samuel A Rice, 1856-60, Charles C. Nourse, 1861-4, Isaac L Allen, 1865 (resigned January, 1866), Frederick E Bissell, 1866 (died June 12, 1867), Henry O'Connor, 1867-72; Marsena E Cutts, 1872-6, John F McJunkin, 1877

Presidents of the Senate—Thomas Baker, 1846-7, Thomas Hughes, 1848; John J Selman, 1848-9; Enos Lowe, 1850-1, William E. Leffingwell, 1852-3; Maturin L Fisher, 1854-5, William W Hamilton, 1856-7. Under the new Constitution, the Lieutenant Governor is President of the Senate

Speakers of the House—Jesse B Brown, 1847-8, Smiley H Bonham, 1849-50; George Temple, 1851-2; James Grant, 1853-4; Reuben Noble, 1855-6; Samuel McFarland, 1856-7: Stephen B Sheledy, 1858-9, John Edwards, 1860-1, Rush Clark, 1862-3, Jacob Butler, 1864-5, Ed Wright, 1866-7, John Russell, 1868-9, Avlett R Cotton, 1870-1; James Wilson, 1872-3 John H Gear 1874-7 John Y Stone 1878

New Constitutional Convention 1879—Francis Springer, President, Thos. J. Saunders, Secretary

STATE OFFICERS, 1878

John H. Gear, Governor; Frank T Campbell, Lieutenant Governor: Josiah T Young, Secretary of State; Buren R. Sherman, Auditor of State; George W Bemis, Treasurer of State: David Secor, Register of State Land Office; John H Looby, Adjutant General; John F. McJunken, Attorney General; Mrs Ada North, State Librarian. Edward J Holmes, Clerk Supreme Court, John S Runnells, Reporter Supreme Court, Carl W Von Coelln, Superintendent Public Instruction, Richard P Clarkson, State Printer, Henry A Perkins, State Binder; Prof Nathan R Leonard, Superintendent of Weights and Measures, William H. Fleming, Governor's Private Secretary, Fletcher W. Young, Deputy Secretary of State; John C. Parish, Deputy Auditor of State; Erastus G. Morgan, Deputy Treasurer of State· John M. Davis, Deputy Register Land Office, Ira C. Kling, Deputy Superintendent Public Instruction

THE JUDICIARY.

SUPREME COURT OF IOWA

Chief Justices—Charles Mason, resigned in June, 1847; Joseph Williams, Jan., 1847, to Jan., 1848; S. Clinton Hastings, Jan., 1848, to Jan., 1849; Joseph Williams, Jan, 1849, to Jan 11, 1855, Geo. G Wright, Jan. 11, 1855, to Jan., 1860, Ralph P. Lowe, Jan, 1860, to Jan 1, 1862. Caleb Baldwin, Jan, 1862, to Jan., 1864; Geo G. Wright, Jan, 1864, to Jan., 1866; Ralph P. Lowe, Jan, 1866, to Jan, 1868; John F Dillon, Jan, 1868, to Jan., 1870, Chester C Cole, Jan. 1, 1870, to Jan 1, 1871, James G. Day, Jan. 1, 1871, to Jan. 1, 1872, Joseph M. Beck, Jan 1, 1872, to Jan 1, 1874, W E Miller, Jan 1, 1874, to Jan. 1, 1876, Chester C. Cole, Jan 1 1876, to Jan 1, 1877; James G. Day, Jan 1, 1877, to Jan 1, 1878; James H Rothrock. Jan. 1, 1878

Associate Judges.—Joseph Williams, Thomas S. Wilson, resigned Oct, 1847, John F Kinney, June 12, 1847, resigned Feb 15, 1854, George Greene, Nov. 1, 1847, to Jan. 9, 1855; Jonathan C Hall, Feb. 15, 1854, to succeed Kinney, resigned, to Jan., 1855, William G Woodward, Jan 9, 1855; Norman W Isbell, Jan 16, 1855, resigned 1856, Lacen D. Stockton, June 3, 1856, to succeed Isbell, resigned, died June 9, 1860, Caleb Baldwin, Jan. 11, 1860, to 1864, Ralph P Lowe, Jan 12, 1860, George G Wright, June 26, 1860, to succeed Stockton, deceased, elected U S Senator. 1870, John F Dillon, Jan 1, 1864, to succeed Baldwin, resigned, 1870; Chester C Cole. March 1, 1864, to 1877; Joseph M. Beck, Jan. 1, 1868, W E. Miller, October 11, 1864, to succeed Dillon, resigned, James G. Day, Jan. 1, 1871, to succeed Wright.

SUPREME COURT, 1878

James H. Rothrock, Cedar County, Chief Justice: Joseph M Beck, Lee County, Associate Justice, Austin Adams, Dubuque County, Associate Justice, William H Seevers, Oskaloosa County, Associate Justice; James G. Day, Fremont County, Associate Justice

CONGRESSIONAL REPRESENTATION.

UNITED STATES SENATORS

(The first General Assembly failed to elect Senators.)

George W Jones, Dubuque, Dec 7, 1848–1858; Augustus C. Dodge, Burlington, Dec 7 1848–1855, James Harlan, Mt. Pleasant, Jan 6, 1855–1865; James W. Grimes, Burlington, Jan 26, 1858–died 1870: Samuel J. Kirkwood, Iowa City, elected Jan 13, 1866, to fill vacancy caused by resignation of James

Harlan ; James Harlan, Mt Pleasant, March 4, 1866–1872 ; James B. Howell, Keokuk, elected Jan. 20, 1870, to fill vacancy caused by the death of J. W. Grimes—term expired March 3d, George G. Wright, Des Moines, March 4, 1871–1877 ; William B. Allison, Dubuque, March 4, 1872, Samuel J. Kirkwood, March 4, 1877.

MEMBERS OF HOUSE OF REPRESENTATIVES

Twenty-ninth Congress—1846 to 1847—S Clinton Hastings ; Shepherd Leffler

Thirtieth Congress—1847 to 1849—First District, William Thompson : Second District, Shepherd Leffler

Thirty-first Congress—1849 to 1851.—First District, First Session, Wm. Thompson, unseated by the House of Representatives on a contest, and election remanded to the people First District, Second Session, Daniel F. Miller. Second District, Shepherd Leffler

Thirty-second Congress—1851 to 1853—First District, Bernhart Henn Second District, Lincoln Clark.

Thirty-third Congress—1853 to 1855.—First District, Bernhart Henn. Second District, John P. Cook.

Thirty-fourth Congress—1855 to 1857—First District, Augustus Hall Second District, James Thorington.

Thirty-fifth Congress—1857 to 1859.—First District, Samuel R Curtis. Second District, Timothy Davis

Thirty-sixth Congress—1859 to 1861—First District, Samuel R Curtis Second District, William Vandever

Thirty-seventh Congress—1861 to 1863—First District, First Session, Samuel R Curtis * First District, Second and Third Sessions, James F. Wilson.   Second District, William Vandever

Thirty-eighth Congress—1863 to 1865.—First District, James F. Wilson. Second District, Hiram Price   Third District, William B Allison   Fourth District, Josiah B Grinnell.   Fifth District, John A Kasson   Sixth District, Asahel W Hubbard

Thirty-ninth Congress—1865 to 1867—First District, James F. Wilson ; Second District. Hiram Price ; Third District, William B Allison ; Fourth District, Josiah B. Grinnell, Fifth District, John A. Kasson ; Sixth District, Asahel W Hubbard

Fortieth Congress—1867 to 1869.—First District, James F Wilson ; Second District, Hiram Price, Third District, William B. Allison, Fourth District, William Loughridge ; Fifth District, Grenville M. Dodge, Sixth District, Asahel W. Hubbard.

Forty-first Congress—1869 to 1871.—First District, George W McCrary ; Second District, William Smyth ; Third District, William B. Allison, Fourth District, William Loughridge, Fifth District, Frank W Palmer, Sixth District, Charles Pomeroy

Forty-second Congress—1871 to 1873—First District, George W. McCrary ; Second District, Aylett R. Cotton ; Third District, W. G Donnan Fourth District, Madison M Waldon ; Fifth District, Frank W. Palmer ; Sixth District, Jackson Orr

Forty-third Congress—1873 to 1875.—First District, George W. McCrary ; Second District, Aylett R Cotton Third District William Y Donnan, Fourth District H O O   District, James Wilson ; Sixth District,

Vacant   James Wilson and J F Wilson his successor

William Loughridge; Seventh District, John A. Kasson; Eighth District, James W. McDill; Ninth District, Jackson Orr.

Forty-fourth Congress—1875 to 1877.—First District, George W. McCrary; Second District, John Q. Tufts; Third District, L. L. Ainsworth, Fourth District, Henry O. Pratt; Fifth District, James Wilson; Sixth District, Ezekiel S. Sampson; Seventh District, John A. Kasson; Eighth District, James W. McDill; Fifth District, Addison Oliver.

Forty-fifth Congress—1877 to 1879.—First District, J. C. Stone; Second District, Hiram Price; Third District, T. W. Burdick; Fourth District, H. C. Deering; Fifth District, Rush Clark; Sixth District, E. S. Sampson; Seventh District, H. J. B. Cummings; Eighth District, W. F. Sapp; Ninth District, Addison Oliver.

WAR RECORD.

The State of Iowa may well be proud of her record during the War of the Rebellion, from 1861 to 1865. The following brief but comprehensive sketch of the history she made during that trying period is largely from the pen of Col. A. P. Wood, of Dubuque, the author of "The History of Iowa and the War," one of the best works of the kind yet written.

"Whether in the promptitude of her responses to the calls made on her by the General Government, in the courage and constancy of her soldiery in the field, or in the wisdom and efficiency with which her civil administration was conducted during the trying period covered by the War of the Rebellion, Iowa proved herself the peer of any loyal State. The proclamation of her Governor, responsive to that of the President, calling for volunteers to compose her First Regiment, was issued on the fourth day after the fall of Sumter. At the end of only a single week, men enough were reported to be in quarters (mostly in the vicinity of their own homes) to fill the regiment. These, however, were hardly more than a tithe of the number who had been offered by company commanders for acceptance under the President's call. So urgent were these offers that the Governor requested (on the 24th of April) permission to organize an additional regiment. While awaiting an answer to this request, he conditionally accepted a sufficient number of companies to compose two additional regiments. In a short time, he was notified that both of these would be accepted. Soon after the completion of the Second and Third Regiments (which was near the close of May), the Adjutant General of the State reported that upward of one hundred and seventy companies had been tendered to the Governor to serve against the enemies of the Union.

"Much difficulty and considerable delay occured in fitting these regiments for the field. For the First Infantry a complete outfit (not uniform) of clothing was extemporized—principally by the volunteered labor of loyal women in the different towns—from material of various colors and qualities, obtained within the limits of the State. The same was done in part for the Second Infantry. Meantime, an extra session of the General Assembly had been called by the Governor, to convene on the 15th of May. With but little delay, that body authorized a loan of $800,000, to meet the extraordinary expenses incurred, and to be incurred, by the Executive Department, in consequence of the new emergency. A wealthy merchant of the State (Ex-Governor Merrill, then a resident of McGregor) immediately took from the Governor a contract to supply a complete outfit of clothing for one of the regiments organized, agreeing to receive, should the Governor so elect, his pay therefor in State bonds, at par; his con-

tract he executed to the letter, and a portion of the clothing (which was manufactured in Boston, to his order) was delivered at Keokuk the place at which
the troops had rendezvoused, in exactly one month from the day on which the
contract had been entered into.   The remainder arrived only a few days later.
This clothing was delivered to the regiment, but was subsequently condemned
by the Government, for the reason that its color was gray, and blue had been
adopted as the color to be worn by the national troops."

Other States also clothed their troops sent forward under the first call of
President Lincoln, with gray uniforms, but it was soon found that the confederate forces were also clothed in gray, and that color was at once abandoned
by the Union troops   If both armies were clothed alike annoying if not fatal
mistakes were liable to be made.

But while engaged in these efforts to discharge her whole duty in common with
all the other Union-loving States in the great emergency. Iowa was compelled
to make immediate and ample provision for the protection of her own borders,
from threatened invasion on the south by the Secessionists of Missouri, and
from danger of incursions from the west and northwest by bands of hostile
Indians, who were freed from the usual restraint imposed upon them by the
presence of regular troops stationed at the frontier posts.   These troops were
withdrawn to meet the greater and more pressing danger threatening the life of
the nation at its very heart.

To provide for the adequate defense of her borders from the ravages of both
rebels in arms against the Government and of the more irresistible foes from
the Western plains, the Governor of the State was authorized to raise and equip
two regiments of infantry a squadron of cavalry (not less than five companies)
and a battalion of artillery (not less than three companies.)   Only cavalry were
enlisted for home defense, however, · but ' says Col Wood, "in times of special
danger or when calls were made by the Unionists of Northern Missouri for
assistance against their disloyal enemies, large numbers of militia on foot often
turned out, and remained in the field until the necessity for their services had
passed.

"The first order for the Iowa volunteers to move to the field was received
on the 13th of June.   It was issued by Gen Lyon, then commanding the
United States forces in Missouri   The First and Second Infantry immediately
embarked in steamboats, and moved to Hannibal.   Some two weeks later the
Third Infantry was ordered to the same point.   These three, together with
many other of the earlier organized Iowa regiments, rendered their first field
service in Missouri   The First Infantry formed a part of the little army with
which Gen. Lyon moved on Springfield, and fought the bloody battle of Wilson's
Creek   It received unqualified praise for its gallant bearing on the field.   In
the following month (September) the Third Iowa, with but very slight support,
fought with honor the sanguinary engagement of Blue Mills Landing; and in
November, the Seventh Iowa, as a part of a force commanded by Gen Grant
greatly distinguished itself in the battle of Belmont where it poured out its
blood like water—losing more than half of the men it took into action

· The initial operations in which the battles referred to took place were followed by the more important movements led by Gen Grant, Gen. Curtis of
this State, and other commanders which resulted in defeating the armies
defending the chief strategic lines held by the Confederates in Kentucky, Tenn-
nessee.   on much of
the terri   e and other
moveme   ksburg was

captured and the Confederacy permanently severed on the line of the Mississippi River, Iowa troops took part in steadily increasing numbers. In the investment and siege of Vicksburg, the State was represented by thirty regiments and two batteries, in addition to which, eight regiments and one battery were employed on the outposts of the besieging army. The brilliancy of their exploits on the many fields where they served won for them the highest meed of praise, both in military and civil circles. Multiplied were the terms in which expression was given to this sentiment, but these words of one of the journals of a neighboring State, 'The Iowa troops have been heroes among heroes.' embody the spirit of all

' In the veteran re-enlistments that distinguished the closing months of 1863 above all other periods in the history of re-enlistments for the national armies, the Iowa three years' men (who were relatively more numerous than those of any other State) were prompt to set the example of volunteering for another term of equal length, thereby adding many thousands to the great army of those who gave this renewed and practical assurance that the cause of the Union should not be left without defenders.

"In all the important movements of 1864-65, by which the Confederacy was penetrated in every quarter, and its military power finally overthrown, the Iowa troops took part. Their drum-beat was heard on the banks of every great river of the South, from the Potomac to the Rio Grande, and everywhere they rendered the same faithful and devoted service, maintaining on all occasions their wonted reputation for valor in the field and endurance on the march.

"Two Iowa three-year cavalry regiments were employed during their whole term of service in the operations that were in progress from 1863 to 1866 against the hostile Indians of the western plains. A portion of these men were among the last of the volunteer troops to be mustered out of service. The State also supplied a considerable number of men to the navy who took part in most of the naval operations prosecuted against the Confederate power on the Atlantic and Gulf coasts, and the rivers of the West.

' The people of Iowa were early and constant workers in the sanitary field, and by their liberal gifts and personal efforts for the benefit of the soldiery, placed their State in the front rank of those who became distinguished for their exhibitions of patriotic benevolence during the period covered by the war. Agents appointed by the Governor were stationed at points convenient for rendering assistance to the sick and needy soldiers of the State, while others were employed in visiting, from time to time, hospitals, camps and armies in the field, and doing whatever the circumstances rendered possible for the health and comfort of such of the Iowa soldiery as might be found there.

"Some of the benevolent people of the State early conceived the idea of establishing a Home for such of the children of deceased soldiers as might be left in destitute circumstances. This idea first took form in 1863, and in the following year a Home was opened at Farmington, Van Buren County, in a building leased for that purpose, and which soon became filled to its utmost capacity. The institution received liberal donations from the general public, and also from the soldiers in the field. In 1865, it became necessary to provide increased accommodations for the large number of children who were seeking the benefits of its care. This was done by establishing a branch at Cedar Falls in Black Hawk County, and by securing during the same year, for the use of ___ ___ ___ ___ ___ ___ ___ City of Davenport. ___ ___ ___ ___ ___ ___ ___ ___ ___ tion, by act of Cong___

" In 1866, in pursuance of a law enacted for that purpose, the Soldiers' Orphans' Home (which then contained about four hundred and fifty inmates) became a State institution, and thereafter the sums necessary for its support were appropriated from the State treasury. A second branch was established at Glenwood Mills County. Convenient tracts were secured, and valuable improvements made at all the different points Schools were also established, and employments provided for such of the children as were of suitable age In all ways the provision made for these wards of the State has been such as to challenge the approval of every benevolent mind. The number of children who have been inmates of the Home from its foundation to the present time is considerably more than two thousand

" At the beginning of the war, the population of Iowa included about one hundred and fifty thousand men presumably liable to render military service The State raised, for general service, thirty-nine regiments of infantry, nine regiments of cavalry, and four companies of artillery, composed of three years' men ; one regiment of infantry, composed of three months' men : and four regiments and one battalion of infantry, composed of one hundred days' men. The original enlistments in these various organizations, including seventeen hundred and twenty-seven men raised by draft, numbered a little more than sixty-nine thousand The re-enlistments, including upward of seven thousand veterans, numbered very nearly eight thousand. The enlistments in the regular army and navy, and organizations of other States, will, if added, raise the total to upward of eighty thousand The number of men who, under special enlistments, and as militia, took part at different times in the operations on the exposed borders of the State, was probably as many as five thousand

" Iowa paid no bounty on account of the men she placed in the field. In some instances, toward the close of the war, bounty to a comparatively small amount was paid by cities and towns On only one occasion—that of the call of July 18, 1864—was a draft made in Iowa This did not occur on account of her proper liability, as established by previous rulings of the War Department to supply men under that call, but grew out of the great necessity that there existed for raising men The Government insisted on temporarily setting aside in part, the former rule of settlements, and enforcing a draft in all cases where subdistricts in any of the States should be found deficient in their supply of men In no instance was Iowa, as a whole, found to be indebted to the General Government for men, on a settlement of her quota accounts "

It is to be said to the honor and credit of Iowa that while many of the loyal States, older and larger in population and wealth, incurred heavy State debts for the purpose of fulfilling their obligations to the General Government, Iowa, while she was foremost in duty, while she promptly discharged all her obligations to her sister States and the Union, found herself at the close of the war without any material addition to her pecuniary liabilities incurred before the war commenced. Upon final settlement after the restoration of peace, her claims upon the Federal Government were found to be fully equal to the amount of her bonds issued and sold during the war to provide the means for raising and equipping her troops sent into the field, and to meet the inevitable demands upon her treasury in consequence of the war.

INFANTRY.

THE FIRST INFANTRY

was organized under the President's first proclamation for volunteers for three months, with John Francis Bates, of Dubuque, as Colonel, William II. Merritt, of Cedar Rapids, as Lieutenant Colonel, and A. B. Porter, of Mt. Pleasant, as Major. Companies A and C were from Muscatine County, Company B, from Johnson County, Companies D and E, from Des Moines County; Company F, from Henry County; Company G, from Davenport, Companies H and I, from Dubuque, and Company K, from Linn County, and were mustered into United States service May 14, 1861, at Keokuk. The above companies were independent military organizations before the war, and tendered their services before breaking-out of hostilities. The First was engaged at the battle of Wilson's Creek, under Gen. Lyon where it lost ten killed and fifty wounded. Was mustered out at St. Louis Aug. 25, 1861.

THE SECOND INFANTRY

was organized, with Samuel R. Curtis, of Keokuk, as Colonel; Jas. M. Tuttle, of Keosauqua, as Lieutenant Colonel, and M. M. Crocker, of Des Moines as Major, and was mustered into the United States service at Keokuk in May, 1861. Company A was from Keokuk; Company B, from Scott County, Company C, from Scott County, Company D, from Des Moines, Company E, from Fairfield, Jefferson Co., Company F, from Van Buren County; Company G, from Davis County, Company H, from Washington County, Company I from Clinton County, and Company K, from Wapello County. It participated in the following engagements: Fort Donelson, Shiloh, advance on Corinth, Corinth, Little Bear Creek, Ala.; Tunnel Creek, Ala.; Resaca, Ga., Rome Cross Roads, Dallas, Kenesaw Mountain, Nick-a-Jack Creek, in front of Atlanta, January 22, 1864; siege of Atlanta, Jonesboro, Eden Station, Little Ogeechee, Savannah, Columbia. S. C., Lynch's Creek, and Bentonsville. Was on Sherman's march to the sea, and through the Carolinas home. The Second Regiment of Iowa Infantry Veteran Volunteers was formed by the consolidation of the battalions of the Second and Third Veteran Infantry, and was mustered out at Louisville, Ky., July 12, 1865.

THE THIRD INFANTRY

was organized with N. G. Williams, of Dubuque County, as Colonel; John Scott, of Story County, Lieutenant Colonel, Wm. N. Stone, of Marion County, Major, and was mustered into the United States service in May, 1861, at Keokuk. Company A was from Dubuque County, Company B, from Marion County; Company C, from Clayton County, Company D, from Winneshiek County; Company E, from Boone, Story, Marshall and Jasper Counties, Company F, from Fayette County, Company G, from Warren County, Company H, from Mahaska County; Company I, from Floyd, Butler Black Hawk and Mitchell Counties, and Company K from Cedar Falls. It was engaged at Blue Mills, Mo.; Shiloh, Tenn., Hatchie River, Matamoras, Vicksburg, Johnson, Miss., Meridian expedition, and Atlanta, Atlanta campaign and Sherman's march to Savannah, and through the Carolinas to Richmond and Washington. The veterans of the Third Iowa Infantry were consolidated with the Second, and mustered out at Louisville, Ky., July 12, 1864.

THE FOURTH INFANTRY

was organized with G. M. Dodge, of Council Bluffs, as Colonel, John Galligan, of Davenport, as Lieutenant Colonel, Wm R English, Glenwood, as Major   Company A, from Mills County, was mustered in at Jefferson Barracks, Missouri, August 15, 1861, Company B, Pottawattamie County, was mustered in at Council Bluffs, August 8, 1861, Company C, Guthrie County, mustered in at Jefferson Barracks, Mo, May 3, 1861. Company D, Decatur County, at St. Louis, August 16th; Company E, Polk County, at Council Bluffs, August 8th, Company F, Madison County, Jefferson Barracks, August 15th, Company G, Ringgold County, at Jefferson Barracks, August 15th, Company H, Adams County Jefferson Barracks, August 15th, Company I, Wayne County, at St Louis, August 31st; Company K, Taylor and Page Counties at St Louis, August 31st. Was engaged at Pea Ridge, Chickasaw Bayou, Arkansas Post, Vicksburg. Jackson, Lookout Mountain, Missionary Ridge, Ringgold, Resaca, Taylor's Ridge; came home on veteran furlough February 26, 1864.   Returned in April, and was in the campaign against Atlanta, and Sherman's march to the sea and thence through the Carolinas to Washington and home.   Was mustered out at Louisville, Kentucky, July 24, 1865

THE FIFTH INFANTRY

was organized with Wm. H. Worthington, of Keokuk, as Colonel, C Z Matthias, of Burlington, as Lieutenant Colonel, W S. Robertson, of Columbus City, as Major, and was mustered into the United States service at Burlington. July 15, 1861   Company A was from Cedar County, Company B, from Jasper County; Company C, from Louisa County, Company D, from Marshall County, Company E, from Buchanan County; Company F, from Keokuk County; Company G, from Benton County. Company H, from Van Buren County. Company I from Jackson County; Company K, from Allamakee County, was engaged at New Madrid. siege of Corinth, Iuka, Corinth, Champion Hills, siege of Vicksburg, Chickamauga, went home on veteran furlough, April, 1864   The non-veterans went home July. 1864, leaving 180 veterans who were transferred to the Fifth Iowa Cavalry   The Fifth Cavalry was mustered out at Nashville, Tennessee, Aug 11, 1865.

THE SIXTH INFANTRY.

was mustered into the service July 6, 1861, at Burlington, with John A. McDowell. of Keokuk, as Colonel, Markoe Cummins, of Muscatine, Lieutenant Colonel, John M Corse, of Burlington, Major   Company A was from Linn County, Company B, from Lucas and Clarke Counties, Company C from Hardin County, Company D, from Appanoose County. Company E. from Monroe County, Company F, from Clarke County; Company G, from Johnson County, Company H, from Lee County; Company I, from Des Moines County, Company K, from Henry County   It was engaged at Shiloh Mission Ridge, Resaca, Dallas, Big Shanty, Kenesaw Mountain, Jackson, Black River Bridge, Jones' Ford, etc, etc   The Sixth lost 7 officers killed in action, 18 wounded; of enlisted men 102 were killed in action, 30 died of wounds, 124 of disease, 211 were discharged for disability and 301 were wounded in action, which was the largest battle casualties of both officers and men of any regiment from Iowa   Was mustered out at Louisville, Kentucky, July 21, 1865

THE SEVENTH INFANTRY

was mustered into the United States service at Burlington, July 24, 1861, with J G. Lauman of Burlington, as Colonel , Augustus Wentz, of Davenport, as Lieutenant Colonel, and E. W. Rice, of Oskaloosa, as Major Company A was from Muscatine County , Company B, from Chickasaw and Floyd Counties ; Company C, from Mahaska County ; Companies D and E, from Lee County , Company F, from Wapello County , Company G, from Iowa County ; Company H, from Washington County : Company I, from Wapello County ; Company K, from Keokuk Was engaged at the battles of Belmont (in which it lost in killed, wounded and missing 237 men), Fort Henry, Fort Donelson, Shiloh siege of Corinth, Corinth, Rome Cross Roads, Dallas, New Hope Church, Big Shanty, Kenesaw Mountain, Nick-a-Jack Creek, siege of Atlanta, battle on 22d of July in front of Atlanta Sherman's campaign to the ocean, through the Carolinas to Richmond, and thence to Louisville Was mustered out at Louisville, Kentucky, July 12, 1865

THE EIGHTH INFANTRY

was mustered into the United States service Sept. 12 1861, at Davenport, Iowa, with Frederick Steele, of the regular army, as Colonel , James L. Geddes. of Vinton, as Lieutenant Colonel, and J C. Ferguson, of Knoxville, as Major Company A was from Clinton County ; Company B, from Scott County ; Company C, from Washington County ; Company D, from Benton and Linn Counties: Company E, from Marion County , Company F, from Keokuk County ; Company G, from Iowa and Johnson Counties ; Company H. from Mahaska County ; Company I, from Monroe County ; Company K, from Louisa County Was engaged at the following battles : Shiloh (where most of the regiment were taken prisoners of war), Corinth, Vicksburg, Jackson and Spanish Fort. Was mustered out of the United States service at Selma, Alabama, April 20, 1866

THE NINTH INFANTRY

was mustered into the United States service September 24, 1861, at Dubuque, with Wm. Vandever, of Dubuque, Colonel . Frank G Herron. of Dubuque, Lieutenant Colonel. Wm H Coyle, of Decorah, Major. Company A was from Jackson County , Company B, from Jones County ; Company C, from Buchanan County , Company D, from Jones County : Company E, from Clayton County ; Company F. from Fayette County , Company G from Black Hawk County ; Company H. from Winneshiek County , Company I, from Howard County and Company K from Linn County. Was in the following engagements : Pea Ridge, Chickasaw Bayou, Arkansas Post, siege of Vicksburg, Ringgold, Dallas, Lookout Mountain, Atlanta campaign, Sherman's march to the sea, and through North and South Carolina to Richmond Was mustered out at Louisville, July 18, 1865.

THE TENTH INFANTRY

was mustered into the United States service at Iowa City September 6, 1861, with Nicholas Perczel, of Davenport, as Colonel ; W E. Small, of Iowa City, as Lieutenant Colonel , and John C Bennett, of Polk County, as Major Company A was from Polk County : Company B. from Warren County , Company C, from Tama County , Company D. from Boone County : Company E, from Washington County ; Company F from Poweshiek County , Company G, from

Warren County; Company H, from Greene County, Company I, from Jasper County, Company K, from Polk and Madison Counties. Participated in the following engagements: Siege of Corinth, Iuka, Corinth, Port Gibson, Raymond, Jackson, Champion Hills, Vicksburg and Mission Ridge. In September, 1864, the non-veterans being mustered out, the veterans were transferred to the Fifth Iowa Cavalry, where will be found their future operations.

THE ELEVENTH INFANTRY

was mustered into the United States service at Davenport, Iowa, in September and October, 1861, with A. M. Hare, of Muscatine, as Colonel; Jno. C. Abercrombie, as Lieutenant Colonel; Wm. Hall, of Davenport, as Major. Company A was from Muscatine; Company B, from Marshall and Hardin Counties, Company C, from Louisa County; Company D, from Muscatine County; Company E, from Cedar County; Company F, from Washington County; Company G, from Henry County; Company H, from Muscatine County; Company I from Muscatine County, Company K, from Linn County. Was engaged in the battle of Shiloh, siege of Corinth, battles of Corinth, Vicksburg, Atlanta campaign, battle of Atlanta, July 22, 1864. Was mustered out at Louisville, Ky., July 15, 1865.

THE TWELFTH INFANTRY

was mustered into the United States service November 25, 1861, at Dubuque, with J. J. Wood, of Maquoketa, as Colonel, John P. Coulter, of Cedar Rapids, Lieutenant Colonel; Samuel D. Brodtbeck, of Dubuque, as Major. Company A was from Hardin County, Company B, from Allamakee County. Company C, from Fayette County; Company D, from Linn County, Company E, from Black Hawk County; Company F, from Delaware County; Company G, from Winneshiek County; Company H, from Dubuque and Delaware Counties, Company I, from Dubuque and Jackson Counties. Company K, from Delaware County. It was engaged at Fort Donelson, Shiloh, where most of the regiment was captured, and those not captured were organized in what was called the Union Brigade, and were in the battle of Corinth; the prisoners were exchanged November 10, 1862, and the regiment re-organized, and then participating in the siege of Vicksburg, battle of Tupelo, Miss., White River, Nashville and Spanish Fort. The regiment was mustered out at Memphis, January 20, 1866.

THE THIRTEENTH INFANTRY

was mustered in November 1, 1861, at Davenport, with M. M. Crocker, of Des Moines, as Colonel; M. M. Price, of Davenport, Lieutenant Colonel; John Shane, Vinton, Major. Company A was from Mt. Vernon, Company B, from Jasper County; Company C, from Lucas County; Company D, from Keokuk County. Company E, from Scott County; Company F, from Scott and Linn Counties; Company G, from Benton County; Company H, from Marshall County; Company I, from Washington County, Company K, from Washington County. It participated in the following engagements: Shiloh, siege of Corinth, Corinth, Kenesaw Mountain, siege of Vicksburg, Campaign against Atlanta. Was on Sherman's march to the sea, and through North and South Carolina. Was mustered out at Louisville July 21, 1865.

THE FOURTEENTH INFANTRY

was mustered in the United States service October 1861 at Davenport, with Wm. T. Shaw, of Anamosa, Colonel; Edward W. Lucas, of Iowa City, as

Lieutenant Colonel; Hiram Leonard, of Des Moines County, as Major Company A was from Scott County; Company B, from Bremer County; Company D from Henry and Van Buren Counties; Company E, from Jasper County; Company F, from Van Buren and Henry Counties; Company G, from Tama and Scott Counties; Company H, from Linn County; Company I, from Henry County, Company K, from Des Moines County Participated in the following engagements: Ft Donelson, Shiloh, Corinth (where most of the regiment were taken prisoners of war), Pleasant Hill, Meridian, Ft. De Russey, Tupelo, Town Creek, Tallahatchie, Pilot Knob, Old Town, Yellow Bayou, etc, etc, and was mustered out, except veterans and recruits, at Davenport, Iowa, November 16, 1864

THE FIFTEENTH INFANTRY

was mustered into the United States service March 19, 1862, at Keokuk, with Hugh T Reid, of Keokuk, as Colonel, Wm Dewey, of Fremont County, as Lieutenant Colonel; W W Belknap, of Keokuk, as Major. Company A was from Linn County, Company B, from Polk County. Company C, from Mahaska County; Company D, from Wapello County; Company E, from Van Buren County; Company F, from Fremont and Mills Counties; Company G, from Marion and Warren Counties, Company H, from Pottawattamie and Harrison Counties; Company I, from Lee, Van Buren and Clark Counties; Company K, from Wapello, Van Buren and Warren Counties Participated in the battle of Shiloh, siege of Corinth, battles of Corinth, Vicksburg, campaign against Atlanta, battle in front of Atlanta, July 22, 1864, and was under fire during the siege of Atlanta eighty-one days; was on Sherman's march to the sea, and through the Carolinas to Richmond, Washington and Louisville, where it was mustered out, August 1, 1864.

THE SIXTEENTH INFANTRY

was mustered into the United States service at Davenport, Iowa, December 10, 1861, with Alexander Chambers, of the regular army, as Colonel; A. H Sanders, of Davenport, Lieutenant Colonel, Wm Purcell, of Muscatine, Major. Company A was from Clinton County; Company B, from Scott County; Company C, from Muscatine County; Company D, from Boone County, Company E, from Muscatine County; Company F, from Muscatine, Clinton and Scott Counties, Company G, from Dubuque County; Company H, from Dubuque and Clayton Counties, Company I, from Black Hawk and Linn Counties; Company K, from Lee and Muscatine Counties Was in the battles of Shiloh, siege of Corinth, Iuka, Corinth, Kenesaw Mountain, Nick-a-Jack Creek, battles around Atlanta, was in Sherman's campaigns, and the Carolina campaigns Was mustered out at Louisville, Ky, July 19, 1865.

THE SEVENTEENTH INFANTRY

was mustered into the United States service at Keokuk, in March and April, 1862, with Jno. W Rankin, of Keokuk, Colonel, D. B Hillis, of Keokuk, as Lieutenant Colonel, Samuel M. Wise, of Mt Pleasant, Major Company A was from Decatur County, Company B, from Lee County; Company C, from Van Buren, Wapello and Lee Counties, Company D, from Des Moines, Van Buren and Jefferson Counties, Company E, from Wapello County, Company F, from Appanoose County, Company G, from Marion County Company H, from Marion and Pottawattamie Counties, Company I, from Jefferson and Lee Counties, Company K, from Lee and Polk Counties They were in the following engagements Siege of Corinth, Iuka, Corinth, Jackson, Champion IHills, Fort Hill, siege of Vicksburg, Mission Ridge, and at Tilton, Ga., Oct. 13, 1864, most of the regiment were taken prisoners of war Was mustered out at Louisville, Ky., July 25 1865.

THE EIGHTEENTH INFANTRY

was mustered into the United States service August 5, 6 and 7, 1862, at Clinton, with John Edwards, of Chariton, Colonel , T. Z Cook, of Cedar Rapids, Lieutenant Colonel , Hugh J Campbell, of Muscatine, as Major. Company A, was from Linn and various other counties ; Company B, from Clark County; Company C, from Lucas County, Company D, from Keokuk and Wapello Counties , Company E, from Muscatine County; Company F, from Appanoose County , Company G, from Marion and Warren Counties ; Company H, from Fayette and Benton Counties , Company I, from Washington County, Company K, from Wapello, Muscatine and Henry Counties, and was engaged in the battles of Springfield, Moscow, Poison Spring, Ark , and was mustered out at Little Rock, Ark , July 20, 1865

THE NINETEENTH INFANTRY

was mustered into the United States service August 17, 1862, at Keokuk, with Benjamin Crabb, of Washington, as Colonel , Samuel McFarland, of Mt Pleasant, Lieutenant Colonel, and Daniel Kent, of Ohio, Major. Company A was from Lee and Van Buren Counties; Company B, from Jefferson County; Company C, from Washington County; Company D, from Jefferson County; Company E, from Lee County, Company F, from Louisa County, Company G, from Louisa County, Company H, from Van Buren County; Company I, from Van Buren County· Company K, from Henry County Was engaged a Prairie Grove, Vicksburg, Yazoo River expedition. Sterling Farm, September 29, 1863, at which place they surrendered , three officers and eight enlisted men were killed, sixteen enlisted men were wounded, and eleven officers and two hundred and three enlisted men taken prisoners out of five hundred engaged, they were exchanged July 22d, and joined their regiment August 7th, at New Orleans. Was engaged at Spanish Fort. Was mustered out at Mobile, Ala., July 10, 1865

THE TWENTIETH INFANTRY

was mustered into the United States service August 25, 1862 at Clinton, with Wm. McE Dye, of Marion, Linn Co , as Colonel . J. B. Leek, of Davenport, as Lieutenant Colonel, and Wm. G. Thompson, of Marion, Linn Co , as Major Companies A, B, F, H and I were from Linn County ; Companies C, D, E, G and K, from Scott County, and was engaged in the following battles· Prairie Grove, and assault on Fort Blakely. Was mustered out at Mobile, Ala , July 8, 1865.

THE TWENTY-FIRST INFANTRY

was mustered into the service at Clinton in June and August 1862, with Samuel Merrill (late Governor of Iowa) as Colonel , Charles W. Dunlap, of Mitchell, as Lieutenant Colonel , S. G. VanAnda, of Delhi, as Major Company A was from Mitchell and Black Hawk Counties , Company B, from Clayton County; Company C from Dubuque County , Company D, from Clayton County· Company E, from Dubuque County. Company F, from Dubuque County Company G from Clayton County Company H, from Delaware County, Company I, from Dubuque County; Company K, from Delaware County, and was in the following engagements· Hartsville, Mo., Black River Bridge, Fort Beauregard, was at the siege of Vicksburg, Mobile, Fort Blakely, and was mustered out at Baton Rouge, La., July 15, 1865

THE TWENTY-SECOND INFANTRY

was mustered into the United States service Sept 10, 1862, at Iowa City, with Wm M Stone, of Knoxville (since Governor of Iowa), as Colonel, Jno A. Garrett, of Newton, Lieutenant Colonel, and Harvey Graham, of Iowa City, as Major Company A was from Johnson County; Company B, Johnson County; Company C, Jasper County, Company D, Monroe County, Company E, Wapello County; Company F, Johnson County, Company G, Johnson County; Company H, Johnson County; Company I, Johnson County, Company K, Johnson County. Was engaged at Vicksburg Thompson's Hill, Champion Hills, Sherman's campaign to Jackson, at Winchester, in Shenandoah Valley, losing 109 men, Fisher's Hill and Cedar Creek Mustered out at Savannah, Ga July 25, 1865

THE TWENTY-THIRD INFANTRY

was mustered into United States service at Des Moines, Sept. 19, 1862, with William Dewey, of Sidney, as Colonel, W H. Kinsman, of Council Bluffs, as Lieutenant Colonel, and S L Glasgow, of Corydon, as Major. Companies A, B and C, were from Polk County. Company D, from Wayne County, Company E, from Pottawattamie County, Company F, from Montgomery County, Company G from Jasper County, Company H, from Madison County; Company I, from Cass County, and Company K, from Marshall County. Was in Vicksburg, and engaged at Port Gibson, Black River, Champion Hills, Vicksburg, Jackson, Milliken's Bend, Fort Blakely, and was mustered out at Harrisburg, Texas, July 26, 1865

THE TWENTY-FOURTH

was mustered into United States service at Muscatine, September 18, 1862, with Eber C. Byam, of Mount Vernon, as Colonel; John Q Wilds, of Mount Vernon, as Lieutenant Colonel, and Ed Wright, of Springdale, as Major. Company A was from Jackson and Clinton Counties; Companies B and C, from Cedar County, Company D, from Washington, Johnson and Cedar Counties; Company E, from Tama County; Companies F, G and H, from Linn County, Company I, from Jackson County, and Company K, from Jones County. Was engaged at Port Gibson, Champion Hills, Gen. Banks' Red River expedition, Winchester and Cedar Creek Was mustered out at Savannah, Ga, July 17, 1865

THE TWENTY-FIFTH INFANTRY

was organized with George A. Stone, of Mount Pleasant, as Colonel; Fabian Brydolf as Lieutenant Colonel, and Calom Taylor, of Bloomfield, as Major, and was mustered into United States service at Mount Pleasant, September 27, 1862 Companies A and I were from Washington County; Companies B and H, from Henry County, Company C, from Henry and Lee Counties, Companies D, E and G, from Des Moines County, Company F, from Louisa County, and Company K, from Des Moines and Lee Counties Was engaged at Arkansas Post, Vicksburg, Walnut Bluff, Chattanooga Campaign Ringgold, Ga., Resaca, Dallas, Kenesaw Mountain, battles around Atlanta, Lovejoy Station, Jonesboro, Ship's Gap, Bentonville, and on Sherman's march through Georgia and the Carolinas, to Richmond and Washington. Was mustered out at Washington, D C., June 6, 1865.

THE TWENTY-SIXTH

was organized and mustered in at Clinton, in August, 1862, with Milo Smith, of Clinton, as Colonel; S. G. Magill, of Lyons, as Lieutenant Colonel, and Samuel Clark, of De Witt, as Major. Company A was from Clinton and Jackson Counties, Company B, from Jackson County; Companies C, D, E, F, G, H, I and K, from Clinton County. Was engaged at Arkansas Post, Vicksburg, Snake Creek Gap, Ga, Resaca, Dallas, Kenesaw Mountain, Decatur, siege of Atlanta, Ezra Church, Jonesboro, Lovejoy Station, Ship's Gap, Sherman's campaign to Savannah, went through the Carolinas, and was mustered out of service at Washington, D C, June 6, 1865

THE TWENTY-SEVENTH

was mustered into United States service at Dubuque, Oct. 3, 1862, with James I. Gilbert, of Lansing, as Colonel; Jed Lake, of Independence, as Lieutenant Colonel; and G. W. Howard, of Bradford, as Major. Companies A, B and I were from Allamakee County; Companies C and H, from Buchanan County, Companies D and E, from Clayton County, Company F, from Delaware County; Company G, from Floyd and Chickasaw Counties, and Company K, from Mitchell County. Engaged at Little Rock. Ark., was on Red River expedition, Fort De Russey, Pleasant Hill, Yellow Bayou, Tupelo, Old Town Creek and Fort Blakely. Was mustered out at Clinton, Iowa, Aug 8, 1865

THE TWENTY-EIGHTH

was organized at Iowa City, and mustered in Nov. 10, 1862, with William E. Miller, of Iowa City, as Colonel, John Connell, of Toledo, as Lieutenant Colonel, and H. B. Lynch, of Millersburg, as Major. Companies A and D were from Benton County; Companies B and G, from Iowa County, Companies C. H and I, from Poweshiek County, Company E, from Johnson County; Company F, from Tama County, and Company K, from Jasper County. Was engaged at Port Gibson, Jackson and siege of Vicksburg; was on Banks' Red River expedition, and engaged at Sabine Cross Roads; was engaged in Shenandoah Valley, Va, and engaged at Winchester, Fisher's Hill and Cedar Creek. Was mustered out of service at Savannah, Ga, July 31, 1865.

THE TWENTY-NINTH

was organized at Council Bluffs, and mustered into the United States service December 1, 1862, with Thomas H. Benton, Jr, of Council Bluffs, as Colonel; R F Patterson, of Keokuk, as Lieutenant Colonel, and Charles B Shoemaker, of Clarinda, as Major. Company A was from Pottawattamie County; Company B, from Pottawattamie and Mills Counties; Company C, from Harrison County; Company D, from Adair and Adams Counties, Company E, from Fremont County, Company F from Taylor County, Company G, from Ringgold County. Was engaged at Helena Arkansas and Spanish Fort. Was mustered out at New Orleans August 15, 1865.

THE THIRTIETH INFANTRY

was organized at Keokuk, and mustered into the United States service September 23, 1862, with Charles B Abbott, of Louisa County, as Colonel, Wm M G. Torrence, of Keokuk, as Lieutenant Colonel, and Lauren Dewey, of Mt Pleasant, as Major. Companies A and I were from Lee County; Company B, from Davis County, Company C, from Des Moines County; Company D, from Van Buren County, Companies E and K from Washington County, Company F, from Davis County; and Companies G and H, from Jefferson County. Was engaged at Arkansas Post, Yazoo City, Vicksburg, Cherokee, Ala., Ringgold, Resaca, Kenesaw Mountain, Atlanta, Lovejoy Station, Jonesboro, Taylor's Ridge, was in Sherman's campaigns to Savannah and through the Carolinas to Richmond, was in the grand review at Washington, D C, where it was mustered out June 5, 1865.

THE THIRTY-FIRST INFANTRY

was mustered into the service at Davenport October 13, 1862, with William Smyth, of Marion, as Colonel, J W Jenkins, of Maquoketa, as Lieutenant Colonel; and Ezekiel Cutler, of Anamosa as Major. Company A was from Linn County, Companies B, C and D, from Black Hawk County, Companies E, G and H, from Jones County; Companies F, I and K, from Jackson County. Was engaged at Chickasaw Bayou, Arkansas Post, Raymond, Jackson, Black River, Vicksburg, Cherokee Lookout Mountain, Mission Ridge, Ringgold, Taylor's Hills, Snake Creek Gap, Resaca, Dallas, New Hope Church, Big Shanty, Kenesaw Mountain, Atlanta, Jonesboro, was in Sherman's campaign through Georgia and the Carolinas, and was mustered out at Louisville, Kentucky, June 27, 1865

THE THIRTY-SECOND INFANTRY

was organized at Dubuque, with John Scott, of Nevada, as Colonel, E H Mix, of Shell Rock, as Lieutenant Colonel, and G. A Eberhart, of Waterloo, as Major. Company A was from Hamilton, Hardin and Wright Counties, Company B, from Cerro Gordo County, Company C, from Black Hawk County; Company D, from Boone County, Company E, from Butler County, Company F, from Hardin County, Company G, from Butler and Floyd Counties, Company H, from Franklin County, Company I, from Webster County, and Company K, from Marshall and Polk Counties, and was mustered into the United States service October 5, 1862. Was engaged at Fort De Russey, Pleasant Hill, Tupelo, Old Town Creek, Nashville, etc., and was mustered out of the United States service at Clinton, Iowa, Aug. 24, 1865.

THE THIRTY-THIRD INFANTRY

was organized at Oskaloosa, with Samuel A Rice, of Oskaloosa, as Colonel; Cyrus H Maskey, of Sigourney, as Lieutenant Colonel, and Hiram D Gibson, of Knoxville, as Major. Companies A and I were from Marion County, Companies B, F and H, from Keokuk County, Companies C, D, E and K, from Makaska County, and Company G, from Marion, Makaska and Polk Counties and mustered in October 1, 1862. Was engaged at Little R... Helena, Saline River, Spanish Fort and Yazoo Pass. Was mustered out New Orleans, July 17, 1865

THE THIRTY-FOURTH INFANTRY

was organized with George W. Clark, of Indianola, as Colonel, W S Dungan, of Chariton, as Lieutenant Colonel, and R D Kellogg, of Decatur County, as Major, and mustered in at Burlington, October 15, 1862.   Companies A and I were from Decatur County, Companies B, C and D, from Warren County, Company E, from Lucas County; Company F, from Wayne County, Company G, from Lucas and Clark Counties, Company H, from Madison and Warren Counties, and Company K, from Lucas County   Was engaged at Arkansas Post, Ft Gaines etc, etc   Was consolidated with the Thirty-eighth Infantry. January 1, 1865, and mustered out at Houston, Texas, August 15, 1865

THE THIRTY-FIFTH INFANTRY

was organized at Muscatine, and mustered in the United States service September 18, 1862, with S G Hill, of Muscatine, as Colonel, James H Rothrock, as Lieutenant Colonel, and Henry O'Conner, of Muscatine, as Major. Companies A B, C, D and E, were from Muscatine County   Company F, from Muscatine and Louisa Counties, Companies G, H and I, from Muscatine and Cedar Counties, and Company K, from Cedar County   Participated in the battles of Jackson, siege of Vicksburg, Bayou Rapids, Bayou de Glaze, Pleasant Hill, Old River Lake, Tupelo, Nashville, etc   Was mustered out at Davenport, August 10, 1865.

THE THIRTY-SIXTH INFANTRY

was organized at Keokuk, with Charles W Kittredge, of Ottumwa, as Colonel; F M Drake of Unionville, Appanoose County, as Lieutenant Colonel, and T C Woodward, of Ottumwa, as Major, and mustered in October 4, 1862: Company A was from Monroe County, Companies B, D, E, H and K, from Wapello County, and Companies C, F G and I, from Appanoose County Was engaged in the following battles· Mark's Mills, Ark.; Elkins' Ford, Camden, Helena Jenkins' Ferry, etc   At Mark's Mills, April 25, 1864, out of 500 engaged, lost 200 killed and wounded, the balance being taken prisoners of war, was exchanged October 6, 1864.   Was mustered out at Duvall's Bluff, Ark, August 24, 1865

THE THIRTY-SEVENTH INFANTRY (OR GRAY BEARDS)

was organized with Geo W Kincaid, of Muscatine, as Colonel, Geo. R. West, of Dubuque, as Lieutenant Colonel, and Lyman Allen, of Iowa City, as Major, and was mustered into United States service at Muscatine December 15, 1862. Company A was from Black Hawk and Linn Counties, Company B, from Muscatine County; Company C, from Van Buren and Lee Counties, Company D from Johnson and Iowa Counties, Company E, from Wapello and Mahaska Counties; Company F, from Dubuque County, Company G, from Appanoose, Des Moines, Henry and Washington Counties   Company H, from Henry and Jefferson Counties, Company I, from Jasper. Linn and other counties, and Company K, from Scott and Fayette Counties   The object of the Thirty-seventh was to go into the field and let the young men go to the front   It was mustered out at Davenport in expiration of three years service

THE THIRTY-EIGHTH INFANTRY

was organized at Dubuque, and mustered in November 4, 1862, with D H Hughes, of Decorah, as Colonel, J. O Hudnutt, of Waverly, as Lieutenan Colonel, and Charles Chadwick, of West Union, as Major   Companies A, Ft G and H were from Fayette County, Company B, from Bremer County; Company C, from Chickasaw County, Companies D, E and K, from Winneshiek County, and Company I, from Howard County.   Participated in the siege of Vicksburg, Banks' Red River expedition, and on December 12, 1864, was consolidated with the Thirty-fourth Infantry.   Mustered out at Houston, Texas. August 15, 1865.

THE THIRTY-NINTH INFANTRY

was organized with H J. B Cummings, of Winterset, as Colonel, James Redfield, of Redfield, Dallas County, as Lieutenant Colonel; and J M Griffiths, of Des Moines, as Major   Companies A and F were from Madison County Companies B and I, from Polk County; Companies C and H, from Dallas County; Company D, from Clark County; Company E, from Greene County; Company G, from Des Moines and Henry Counties, and Company K, from Clark and Decatur Counties   Was engaged at Parker's Cross Roads, Tenn, Corinth, Allatoona. Ga; Resaca, Kenesaw Mountain, Atlanta, Sherman's march to Savannah and through the Carolinas to Richmond, and was mustered out at Washington June 5, 1865

THE FORTIETH INFANTRY

was organized at Iowa City November 15, 1862, with John A Garrett, of Newton, as Colonel, S. F Cooper, of Grinnell, as Lieutenant Colonel; and S. G. Smith, of Newton, as Major   Companies A and H were from Marion County; Company B, from Poweshiek County, Company C, from Mahaska County. Companies D and E, from Jasper County, Company F, from Mahaska and Marion Counties; Company G, from Marion County; Company I, from Keokuk County; and Company K, from Benton and other counties   Participated in the siege of Vicksburg, Steele's expedition, Banks' Red River expedition. Jenkins' Ferry, etc.   Was mustered out at Port Gibson August 2, 1866.

THE FORTY-FIRST INFANTRY,

formerly Companies A, B and C of the Fourteenth Infantry, became Companies K, L and M of the Seventh Cavalry, under authority of the War Department.   Its infantry organization was under command of John Pattee, of Iowa City.   Company A was from Black Hawk, Johnson and other counties, Company B, from Johnson County; and Company C, from Des Moines and various counties

THE FORTY-FOURTH INFANTRY (100 DAYS)

was organized at Davenport, and mustered in June 1, 1864.   Company A was from Dubuque County, Company B, Muscatine County; Company C. Jones, Linn and Dubuque Counties; Company D, Johnson and Linn Counties. Company E, Bremer and Butler Counties; Company F, Clinton and Jackson Counties; Company G, Marshall and Hardin Counties, Company H, Boone and Polk Counties. Companies I and K, Scott County   The Forty-fourth did garrison duty at Memphis and La Grange, Tenn   Mustered out at Davenport, September 17, 1864.

THE FORTY-FIFTH INFANTRY (100 DAYS)

was mustered in at Keokuk, May 25, 1864, with A. H Bereman, of Mount Pleasant, as Colonel; S A. Moore, of Bloomfield, as Lieutenant Colonel, and J. B. Hope, of Washington, as Major. The companies were from the following counties: A, Henry; B, Washington C, Lee; D, Davis; E Henry and Lee· F, Des Moines, G, Des Moines and Henry; H, Henry, I, Jefferson, and K, Van Buren. Was mustered out at Keokuk, September 16, 1864

THE FORTY-SIXTH INFANTRY (100 DAYS)

was organized with D B Henderson, of Clermont, as Colonel; L D. Durbin, of Tipton, as Lieutenant Colonel, and G. L. Tarbet, as Major, and was mustered in at Dubuque, June 10, 1864   Company A was from Dubuque, Company B, from Poweshiek; C, from Dallas and Guthrie, D, from Taylor and Fayette, E, from Ringgold and Linn; F, from Winneshiek and Delaware, G, from Appanoose and Delaware H, from Wayne; I, from Cedar, and K, from Lucas. Was mustered out at Davenport, September 23, 1864.

THE FORTY-SEVENTH INFANTRY (100 DAYS)

was mustered into United States service at Davenport, June 4, 1864, with James P Sanford, of Oskaloosa, as Colonel; John Williams, of Iowa City. as Lieutenant Colonel, and G J. Wright, of Des Moines, as Major. Company A was from Marion and Clayton Counties, Company B, from Appanoose County, Company C, from Wapello and Benton Counties, Company B, from Buchanan and Linn Counties, Company E, from Madison County; Company F. from Polk County, Company G, from Johnson County, Company H, from Keokuk County. Company I, from Mahaska County, and Company K, from Wapello.

THE FORTY-EIGHTH INFANTRY—BATTALION—(100 DAYS)

was organized at Davenport, and mustered in July 13, 1864, with O H. P Scott, of Farmington, as Lieutenant Colonel. Company A was from Warren County, Company B, from Jasper County, Company C, from Decatur County, and Company D, from Des Moines and Lee Counties, and was mustered out at Rock Island Barracks Oct. 21, 1864.

CAVALRY.

THE FIRST CAVALRY

was organized at Burlington, and mustered into the United States service May 3, 1861, with Fitz Henry Warren, of Burlington as Colonel; Chas E Moss, of Keokuk, as Lieutenant Colonel, and E W. Chamberlain, of Burlington, James O. Gower, of Iowa City. and W M G Torrence, of Keokuk, as Majors Company A was from Lee, Van Buren and Wapello Counties; Company B, from Clinton County; Company C, from Des Moines and Lee Counties; Company D, from Madison and Warren Counties, Company E, from Henry County; Company F, from Johnson and Linn Counties, Company G, from Dubuque and Black H. County · Company H from Lucas and Morrison Count   Company I Wapello and Des Moines Counties Company K, from Appanoose and Clarke Counties   Company L, from Dubuque and other counties; Company M, from Clinton County. It was engaged at Pleasant Hill, Mo.; Rolla, New Lexington, Elkins' Ford, Little Rock, Bayou Metoe, Warrensburg, Big Creek Bluffs, Antwineville, Clear Creek, etc. Was mustered out at Austin, Texas, February 15, 1866.

THE SECOND CAVALRY

was organized with W L Elliott, of the regular army, as Colonel; Edward Hatch, of Muscatine, as Lieutenant Colonel, and N P. Hepburn, of Marshalltown, D E Coon, of Mason City, and H W Love, of Iowa City, as Majors, and was mustered into the United States service at Davenport September 1, 1861 Company A was from Muscatine County; Company B, from Marshall County; Company C, from Scott County, Company D, from Polk County; Company E, from Scott County; Company F, from Hamilton and Franklin Counties; Company G, from Muscatine County; Company H, from Johnson County; Company I, from Cerro Gordo, Delaware and other counties; Company K, from Des Moines County, Company L, from Jackson County, and Company M, from Jackson County The Second Cavalry participated in the following military movements · Siege of Corinth, battles of Farmington, Booneville, Rienzi, Iuka, Corinth, Coffeeville, Palo Alto, Birmingham, Jackson, Grenada, Collierville, Moscow, Pontotoc, Tupelo, Old Town, Oxford, and engagements against Hood's march on Nashville, battle of Nashville, etc. Was mustered out at Selma, Ala., September 19, 1865

THE THIRD CAVALRY

was organized and mustered into the United States service at Keokuk, in August and September, 1861, with Cyrus Bussey, of Bloomfield, as Colonel; H H Bussey, of Bloomfield, as Lieutenant Colonel, and C H Perry, H. C. Caldwell and W C Drake, of Corydon, as Majors Companies A and E were from Davis County, Company B, from Van Buren and Lee Counties, Company C. from Lee and Keokuk Counties, Company D, from Davis and Van Buren Counties, Company F, from Jefferson County; Company G, from Van Buren County; Company H, from Van Buren and Jefferson Counties; Company I, from Appanoose County; Company K, from Wapello and Marion Counties; Company L, from Decatur County, and Company M, from Appanoose and Decatur Counties. It was engaged in the following battles and skirmishes · Pea Ridge, La Grange, Sycamore, near Little Rock, Columbus, Pope's Farm, Big Blue, Ripley, Coldwater, Osage, Tallahatchie, Moore's Mill, near Montevallo, near Independence, Pine Bluff, Botts' Farm, Gun Town, White's Station, Tupelo, Village Creek Was mustered out of United States service at Atlanta, Ga . August 9, 1865

THE FOURTH CAVALRY

was organized with Asbury B Porter, of Mount Pleasant, as Colonel, Thomas Drummond, of Vinton, as Lieutenant Colonel; S. D Swan, of Mount Pleasant, J E Jewett, of Des Moines, and G A Stone, of Mount Pleasant, as Majors, and mustered into United States service at Mount Pleasant November 21, 1861. Company A was from Delaware County; Company C from Jefferson and H   u.   ·· ··· ·I ι ι.   , ιy E from Jasper and Poweshiek Counties, Company F, from Wapello County; Company G from Lee and Henry Counties; Company H, from Chickasaw County, Company I, from Madison County. Company K, from Henry County; Company L, from Des Moines and other counties; and Company M, from Jefferson County. The Fourth Cavalry lost men in the following engagements. Guntown, Miss ; Helena, Ark ; near Bear Creek, Miss , near Memphis, Tenn , Town Creek, Miss , Columbus, Ga : Mechanicsburg, Miss ; Little Blue River, Ark., Brownsville, Miss ; Ripley, Miss.; Black River Bridge, Miss , Grenada, Miss , Little Red River, Ark ; Tupelo, Miss , Yazoo River, Miss , White River, Ark ; Osage, Kan., Lick Creek Ark . Okalona, Miss.; St. Francis River, Ark. Was mustered out at Atlanta, Ga , August 10, 1865

THE FIFTH CAVALRY

was organized at Omaha with Wm W. Lowe, of the regular army, as Colonel ; M. T Patrick, of Omaha, as Lieutenant Colonel; and C. S. Beinstein, of Dubuque, as Major, and mustered in September 21, 1861   Companies A, B, C and D were mostly from Nebraska; Company E, from Dubuque County ; Company F, from Des Moines. Dubuque and Lee Counties, Company G, from Minnesota, Company H, from Jackson and other counties; Companies I and K were from Minnesota, Company L, from Minnesota and Missouri; Company M, from Missouri, Companies G, I and K were transferred to Minnesota Volunteers Feb. 25, 1864   The new Company G was organized from veterans and recruits and Companies C, E, F and I of Fifth Iowa Infantry, and transferred to Fifth Cavalry August 8, 1864.   The second Company I was organized from veterans and recruits and Companies A, B, D, G, H and K of the Fifth Iowa Infantry, and transferred to Fifth Iowa Cavalry August 18, 1864 Was engaged at second battle of Fort Donelson, Wartrace, Duck River Bridge, Sugar Creek, Newnan, Camp Creek, Cumberland Works, Tenn , Jonesboro, Ebenezer Church, Lockbridge's Mills, Pulaski, Cheraw, and mustered out at Nashville, Tenn , August 11, 1865.

THE SIXTH CAVALRY

was organized with D. S. Wilson, of Dubuque, as Colonel; S. M. Pollock, of Dubuque, as Lieutenant Colonel; T. H Shephard, of Iowa City, E P Ten-Broeck, of Clinton, and A E House, of Delhi, as Majors, and was mustered in at Davenport, January 31, 1863.   Company A was from Scott and other counties, Company B, from Dubuque and other counties, Company C, from Fayette County, Company D, from Winneshiek County; Company E from Southwest counties of the State; Company F, from Allamakee and other counties, Company G, from Delaware and Buchanan Counties; Company H, from Linn County, Company I, from Johnson and other counties, Company K, from Linn County; Company L, from Clayton County; Company M, from Johnson and Dubuque Counties.   The Sixth Cavalry operated on the frontier against the Indians   Was mustered out at Sioux City, October 17, 1865.

THE SEVENTH CAVALRY

was organized at Davenport and mustered into the United States service April 27, 186 ;, with S. W. Summers. of Ottumwa, as Colonel ; John Pattee, of Iowa City, as Lieutenant Colonel, H H Heath and G M O Brien, of Dubuque, and John S Wood, of Ottumwa, as Majors. Companies A, B, C and D, were from Wapello and other counties in immediate vicinity, Companies E, F, G and H, were from all parts of the State, Company I, from Sioux City and known as Sioux City Cavalry; Company K was originally Company A of the Fourteenth Infantry and afterward Company A of the Forty-first Infantry, was from Johnson and other counties, Company L was originally Company B, of the Forty-first Infantry and afterward Company B of the Forty———, and was from Johnson County, Company M was originally Company C, of the Fourteenth Infantry, and afterward Company C, of the Forty-first and from Des Moines and other counties The Seventh Cavalry operated against the Indians. Excepting the Lieutenant Colonel and Companies K, L and M, the regiment was mustered out at Leavenworth, Kansas, May 17, 1866. Companies K, L, and M were mustered out at Sioux City, June 22, 1866.

THE EIGHTH CAVALRY

was organized with J. B. Dorr, of Dubuque, as Colonel; H. G. Barner, of Sidney, as Lieutenant Colonel: John J. Bowen, of Hopkinton, J D Thompson, of Eldora, and A J Price, of Guttenburg, as Majors, and were mustered in at Davenport September 30, 1863 The companies were mostly from the following counties: Company A, Page; B, Wapello; C, Van Buren; D, Ringgold; E, Henry; F, Appanoose, G, Clayton; H, Appanoose; I, Marshall; K, Muscatine, L, Wapello; M, Polk The Eighth did a large amount of duty guarding Sherman's communications, in which it had many small engagements. It was in the battles of Lost Mountain, Lovejoy's Station, Newnan, Nashville, etc. Was on Stoneman s cavalry raid around Atlanta, and Wilson's raid through Alabama. Was mustered out at Macon, Ga, August 13, 1865.

THE NINTH CAVALRY

was mustered in at Davenport, November 30, 1863, with M M Trumbull, of Cedar Falls, as Colonel; J. P. Knight, of Mitchell, as Lieutenant Colonel, E. T Ensign, of Des Moines. Willis Drummond, of McGregor, and William Haddock, of Waterloo, as Majors. Company A was from Muscatine County: Company B, Linn County; Company C, Wapello and Decatur Counties, Company D, Washington County; Company E, Fayette County: Company F, Clayton County; Companies G and H, various counties; Company I, Wapello and Jefferson Counties; Company K, Keokuk County; Company L, Jasper and Marion Counties; Company M, Wapello and Lee Counties. Was mustered out at Little Rock. Ark., February 28, 1866

ARTILLERY
THE FIRST BATTERY OF LIGHT ARTILLERY

was enrolled in the counties of Wapello, Des Moines, Dubuque, Jefferson, Black Hawk, etc., and was mustered in at Burlington, Aug 17, 1861, with C H. Fletcher, of Burlington, as Captain Was engaged at Pea Ridge Port Gibson, in Atlanta campaign, Chickasaw Bayou Lookout Mountain, etc Was mustered out at Davenport July 5, 1865.

THE SECOND BATTERY OF LIGHT ARTILLERY

was enrolled in the counties of Dallas, Polk, Harrison, Fremont and Pottawattamie, and mustered into United States service at Council Bluffs and St Louis, Mo , Aug. 8 and 31, 1861, with Nelson T. Spear, of Council Bluffs, as Captain   Was engaged at Farmington, Corinth, etc.   Was mustered out at Davenport, Aug. 7, 1865.

THE THIRD BATTERY OF LIGHT ARTILLERY

was enrolled in the counties of Dubuque, Black Hawk, Butler and Floyd, and mustered into United States service at Dubuque, September, 1861, with M. M Hayden, of Dubuque, as Captain.   Was at battle of Pea Ridge, etc., etc. Was mustered out at Davenport, Oct. 23, 1865.

THE FOURTH BATTERY OF LIGHT ARTILLERY

was enrolled in Mahaska, Henry, Mills and Fremont Counties, and was mustered in at Davenport, Nov. 23, 1863, with P H Goode, of Glenwood, Captain.   Was mustered out at Davenport, July 14, 1865.

MISCELLANEOUS.

THE FOURTH BATTALION

Company A, from Fremont County, W. Hoyt, Captain; Company B, from Taylor County, John Flick, Captain; Company C, from Page County, J. Whitcomb, Captain.

THE NORTHERN BORDER BRIGADE

was organized by the State of Iowa to protect the Northwestern frontier, James A. Sawyer, of Sioux City, was elected Colonel   It had Companies A, B, C, D and E, all enlisted from the Northwestern counties

THE SOUTHERN BORDER BRIGADE

was organized by the State for the purpose of protecting the Southern border of the State, and was organized in counties on the border of Missouri.   Company A, First Battalion, was from Lee County, Wm. Sole, Captain, Company B, First Battalion, Joseph Dickey, Captain, from Van Buren County; Company A, Second Battalion, from Davis County, Capt H B Horn, Company B, Second Battalion from Appanoose County, E B Skinner, Captain; Company A, Third Battalion, from Decatur County, J H. Simmons, Captain, Company B, Third Battalion, from Wayne County, E F Estel, Captain; Company C, Third Battalion, from Ringgold County, N Miller, Captain.

THE FIRST INFANTRY—AFRICAN DESCENT—(SIXTIETH U S)

was organized with John G Hudson, Captain Company B, Thirty-third Missouri, as Colonel; M F Collins, of Keokuk, as Lieutenant Colonel, and J L Murphy   mustered in at various   of the State and son

During the war, the following promotions were made by the United States Government from Iowa regiments·*

MAJOR GENERALS

Samuel R Curtis, Brigadier General, from March 21, 1862
Frederick Steele, Brigadier General, from November 29, 1862
Frank J Herron, Brigadier General, from November 29, 1862
Grenville M Dodge, Brigadier General, from June 7, 1864

BRIGADIER GENERALS.

Samuel R Curtis, Colonel 2d Infantry, from May 17, 1861
Frederick Steele. Colonel 8th Infantry, from February 6, 1862
Jacob G Lauman, Colonel 7th Infantry, from March 21 1862
Grenville M. Dodge, Colonel 4th Infantry, from March 31, 1862
James M Tuttle, Colonel 2d Infantry, from June 9, 1862
Washington L Elliott, Colonel 2d Cavalry, from June 11, 1862
Fitz Henry Warren, Colonel 1st Cavalry, from July 6, 1862
Frank J Herron, Lieutenant Colonel 9th Infantry, from July 30, 1862
Charles L Matthies, Colonel 5th Infantry, from November 29 1862
William Vandever, Colonel 9th Infantry, from November 29 1862
Marcellus M Crocker, Colonel 13th Infantry, from Nov 29, 1862   (Since died)
Hugh T Reid, Colonel 15th Infantry from March 13, 1863
Samuel A Rice, Colonel 33d Infantry, from August 4, 1863.
John M Corse, Colonel 6th Infantry, from August 11, 1863
Cyrus Bussey, Colonel 3d Cavalry, from January 5, 1864
Edward Hatch, Colonel 2d Cavalry, from April 27, 1864
Elliott W Rice, Colonel 7th Infantry, from June 20, 1864
Wm W. Belknap, Colonel 15th Infantry, from July 30, 1864
John Edwards, Colonel 18th Infantry, from September 26, 1864
James A Williamson, Colonel 4th Infantry, from January 13, 1864
James I Gilbert, Colonel 27th Infantry, from February 9, 1865

BREVET MAJOR GENERALS

John M Corse, Brigadier General from October 5, 1864.
Edward Hatch, Brigadier General, from December 15, 1864
Wm W Belknap, Brigadier General, from March 13, 1865.
W L Elliott, Brigadier General, from March 13, 1865
Wm Vandever, Brigadier General, from June 7, 1865

BREVET BRIGADIER GENERALS.

Wm T Clark, A A. G , late of 13th Infantry, from July 22, 1864.
Edward F. Winslow, Colonel 4th Cavalry, from December 12, 1864
S G Hill, Colonel 35th Infantry, from December 15, 1864   (Since died)
Thos H Benton, Colonel 29th Infantry, from December 15, 1864
Samuel L Glasgow, Colonel 23d Infantry, from December 19, 1864
Clark R Wever, Colonel 17th Infantry, from February 9, 1865
Francis M Drake, Lieutenant Colonel 36th Infantry, from February 22, 1865
George A Stone, Colonel 25th Infantry, from March 13, 1865
Datus E Coon, Colonel 2d Cavalry, from March 8, 1865
George W Clark, Colonel 34th Infantry, from March 13, 1865
Herman H Heath, Colonel 7th Cavalry, from March 13, 1865
J M Hedrick, Colonel 15th Infantry, from March 13 1865
W W. Lowe, Colonel 5th Cavalry, from March 13, 1865

*Thomas J McKean was appointed Paymaster in U S A from Iowa and subsequently promoted Brigadier General, to date from Nov 21, 1861

NUMBER OF CASUALTIES AMONG OFFICERS OF IOWA REGIMENTS DURING THE WAR.

REGIMENT OR BATTERY.	KILLED In action.	KILLED Accidentally.	KILLED Total.	DIED Of wounds.	DIED Of disease.	DIED By drowning.	DIED Total.	DISCHARGED For disability.	DISCHARGED Cause unknown.	DISCHARGED Total.	WOUNDED In action.	WOUNDED Accidentally.	WOUNDED Total.	Resigned.	Dismissed.	Total casualties.	Captured.	TRANSFERRED To Vet. Res. Corps.	TRANSFERRED By appointment.	TRANSFERRED Total.
First Cavalry	1		1	1	2		3	1		1	4		4	34	3	46	1		3	3
Second Cavalry	1		1		2		2		2	2	12		12	35	3	45	1		5	5
Third Cavalry	3		3	2	4		6	3		3	9		9	49	4	63	5		3	3
Fourth Cavalry	3		3		4		4				8		8	31	2	55	4		3	3
Fifth Cavalry	5		5		2		2	1		1	6		6	35		51	8		2	2
Sixth Cavalry											1		1	15	2	21				
Seventh Cavalry	1		1						2	2				13	6	23			1	1
Eighth Cavalry	6		6		2		2				10		10	23	1	41	22		2	2
Ninth Cavalry	2		2		1		1							25		30				
Artillery, First Battery														6		10	No casualt's rep.			
Artillery, Second Battery											2		2							
Artillery, Third Battery														4		8				
Artillery, Fourth Battery	1		1					2		2	1		1		1	5	1	1		1
First Infantry	6		6		2		2				4		4	25		51				
Second Infantry	2		2	4			6				23		23	8		9			8	9
Second Veteran Infantry		1	1				1				3		3	3		6	8	1	1	1
Second and Third Infantry (consolidated)											1	1				6				2
Third Infantry				4			4				34		35	40	1	81			2	2
Third Veteran Infantry																				
Fourth Infantry	2		2	3	2		5	1	4	6	16		16	34	1	59	7		5	5
Fifth Infantry	2		2		2		4	1	4	5	17		17	28	2	63	21		8	8
Sixth Infantry	5		5		7		6	2		2	18		18	37	3	67	6		1	1
Seventh Infantry	7		7	1	4		5				22	1	23	32	2	73	12		7	7
Eighth Infantry	4		4	3	1		3	2	2	4	14		14	30		57	9		3	3
Ninth Infantry	6		6	1	2		6	1	4	5	26		26	32		72	1		6	6
Tenth Infantry	6		6		3		3		9	9	16		16	32	2	58	4		1	1
Eleventh Infantry	3		3		1		5				8		8	25		47	4		5	5
Twelfth Infantry	3		3	2	1		4	2		2	18	2	18	19	3	45	22	1	5	5
Thirteenth Infantry	2		2	4	3		7	1		1	19		19	36	1	65	4	1	4	4

Fourteenth Infantry

Fourteenth Residuary Battalion

Fifteenth Infantry

Sixteenth Infantry

Seventeenth Infantry

Eighteenth Infantry

Nineteenth Infantry

Twentieth Infantry

Twenty-first Infantry

Twenty-second Infantry

Twenty-third Infantry

Twenty-fourth Infantry

Twenty-fifth Infantry

Twenty-sixth Infantry

Twenty-seventh Infantry

Twenty-eighth Infantry

Twenty-ninth Infantry

Thirtieth Infantry

Thirty-first Infantry

Thirty-second Infantry

Thirty-third Infantry

Thirty-fourth Infantry

Thirty-fourth [34th and 38th] consolidated

Thirty-fifth Infantry

Thirty-sixth Infantry

Thirty-seventh Infantry

Thirty-eighth Infantry

Thirty-ninth Infantry

Fortieth Infantry

Forty-fourth Infantry

Forty-fifth Infantry

Forty-sixth Infantry

Forty-seventh Infantry

Forty-eighth Infantry (battalion)

First Colored Regiment of Iowa (60th U. S.)

Total

NUMBER OF CASUALTIES AMONG ENLISTED MEN OF IOWA REGIMENTS DURING THE WAR.

REGIMENT OR BATTERY.	KILLED. In Action.	KILLED. Accidentally.	KILLED. Total.	DIED. Of Wounds.	DIED. Of Disease.	DIED. By Suicide.	DIED. By Drowning.	DIED. Total.	DISCHARGED. For Disability.	DISCHARGED. Cause Unknown.	DISCHARGED. Total.	WOUNDED. In Action.	WOUNDED. Accidentally.	WOUNDED. Total.	Missing.	Total Casualties.	Captured.	TRANSFERRED. To V.R. Corps.	TRANSFERRED. By Appointment.	TRANSFERRED. Total.
First Cavalry	12	8	42	26	184	1	4	212	187	19	206	68	13	81	9	546	21	14	21	35
Second Cavalry	55	3	46	25	191		3	222	140	29	169	158	3	161	10	602	73	26	11	37
Third Cavalry		4	62	19	224	2	3	245	220	85	305	155	2	157	1	770	141	24	7	31
Fourth Cavalry	52	6	47	11	126		4	201	151	82	233	108	4	112	3	590	90	23	8	33
Fifth Cavalry	11	3	42	7	69		4	137	172	51	223	47	3	50		452	204	14	6	17
Sixth Cavalry	57	8	10	6	60		1	70	70	16	246	15	3	18	2	198		1	3	6
Seventh Cavalry	59	8	45	2	92		4	161	228	18	246	75	2	77		402		20	5	8
Eighth Cavalry	24	1	27	9	91			104	44	18	62	13	2	15	2	274	257	10	6	20
Ninth Cavalry		2		3	102			172	49	15	64	28	1	25		256	257	3	3	11
Artillery, 1st Battery			1	1	51			64	25	9	33	14	1	15		124		3	3	6
Artillery, 2d Battery		1		1	20			30	16		16	28		25		62				
Artillery, 3d Battery		2	3	1	35			34	16	11	26	14	1	16		79				
Artillery, 4th Battery					5			6	11	7	11	13		13		17				
*Independent Company Sioux City Cavalry																				
Company A, 11th Pennsylvania Cavalry	1				4		4									3				
Dodge's Brigade Band																				
First Infantry	125		12		107		4	13	137	191	325	187	1	137	3	165	13	9	6	16
Second Infantry	55	2	58	17	11		5	128	14	191	3	244	1	245		758		1	1	8
Second Veteran Infantry	11	4	11	1	27			14	74	11		41		41		69	18	6	4	8
Second and Third Consolidated Infantry	4		1		50			27	14	67	250	6		6		67	88	18	2	17
Third Infantry	52	1	55	28	237		1	125	163		250	335	1	335	10	749	22	9	4	27
Third Veteran Infantry	11		17		90		2	10			1									
Fourth Infantry	57	7	58	51	237		5	250	132	146	298	319	4	322		975	23	30	22	62
Fifth Infantry	59	1	60	61	90		5	126	222	95	287	278	4	282		699	44	45	4	47
Sixth Infantry	102		92	20	124		2	154	211	47	258	331	4	335		855	96	15	7	7
Seventh Infantry	94	1	102	35	131			172	180	108	288	210	4	381		884	64	21	22	22
Eighth Infantry	49	1	94	44	137		1	182	245	26	269	354	6	214		761	72	21	18	34
Ninth Infantry	76	2	78	55	208		2	206	243		260	356	4	356	8	973	882		13	24
Tenth Infantry	56		65	26	164		1	170	137	115	252	257	4	261	1	739	16	41	5	48

Regiment																					
Eleventh Infantry	54	1	55	25	148		174	1	121	30	151	220	6	220	4	610	59	26	11	37	
Twelfth Infantry	30		30	32	243		276	1	124	133	257	208	1	209		768	382	19	3	22	
Thirteenth Infantry	65	1	66	34	182		217	1	192	77	269	290	4	294		852	84	15	15	30	
Fourteenth Infantry	27	1	28	23	122		145	1	137	53	190	162		162	1	526	249	13	10	23	
Fourteenth Residuary Battalion									7		11					11		1	1	2	
Fifteenth Infantry	52		52	78	194		274	2	270	32	302	394	2	392		1029	78	13	14	27	
Sixteenth Infantry	57		57	82	217		249		160	49	209	290	1	289		819	242	21	6	27	
Seventeenth Infantry	43		43	18	97		116	1	222	98	221	225	1	225		611	261	23	3	26	
Eighteenth Infantry	26	2	28	7	109		119	3	183	6	228	71	1	190		419	63	5	6	10	
Nineteenth Infantry	53		53	33	91		130	6	157	5	188	191	1			562	204	27	13	40	
Twentieth Infantry	8		8	4	180		142	7	189	6	163	46				359	10	36	5	38	
Twenty-first Infantry	37		38	29	157		188	2	157	14	153	150	3	147		531	20	49	2	54	
Twenty-second Infantry	53	1	64	52	126		180	2	150		158	215		215		634	79	40	1	42	
Twenty-third Infantry	39		39	30	196		228	2	171	8	177	126	3	153		570	3	41	6	42	
Twenty-fourth Infantry	58		58	53	197		253	3	200	6	204	243	3	240		761	72	48	8	54	
Twenty-fifth Infantry	39		39	22	199		219		120	4	138	164	3	162		564	17	69		69	
Twenty-sixth Infantry	40	2	42	25	201		236	3	140	18	141	143	3	140		562	24	69	6	69	
Twenty-seventh Infantry	7		7	14	162		180	4	134	1	202	183	3	132		530	32	40	5	45	
Twenty-eighth Infantry	52		52	24	180		206	1	166	68	182	216	3	242		696	89	83	10	43	
Twenty-ninth Infantry	19	2	21	17	248		266	1	117	16	121	99	4	97		511	53	31		37	
Thirtieth Infantry	39	1	40	24	233		257		129	16	112	205	6	202		646	19	46	1	47	
Thirty-first Infantry	11		11	16	261		277		137	13	175	77	3	77		540	18	72		72	
Thirty-second Infantry	56		56	33	203		237		156	38	164	183	1	132		589	93	27	6	33	
Thirty-third Infantry	25		26	37	160		236	1	109	10	143	168	2	166		580	73	18	10	28	
Thirty-fourth Infantry	1		1	2	228	1	231	3	286	34	313	13		13		561	3	22		22	
Thirty-fourth consolidated Battalion Infantry										27						6					
Thirty-fourth [34th and 38th] Infantry consolidated	3	1	4	2	10		12	1	3												
Thirty-fifth Infantry	23	2	25	19	182	1	201	1	29	7	36	11	2	12		66	15	51	14	66	
Thirty-sixth Infantry	85		35	24	226		251	1	172	17	189	98		93		510		17	6	23	
Thirty-seventh Infantry					141		142	1	187	4	191	142		142		619	437			2	
Thirty-eighth Infantry	3		3	3	310		311	1	326	30	356	2	2			503		2	4	12	
Thirty-ninth Infantry	1				119		108	1	108	9	117	2				131		8		15	
Fortieth Infantry	33		84	21	119		141	5	89	34	123	108	3	103		406	203	12	4	15	
*Forty-first Infantry (battalion)	5		5	10	179		194		117	4	121	41		41		361	2	20	3	26	
Forty-fourth Infantry					2		14		15		15					17		1	6		
Forty-fifth Infantry	1	1	1	1	11		19									15					
Forty-sixth Infantry	2	2	2		17		24						1			22					
Forty-seventh Infantry	2	2	2	1	23		46						1			28	3				
Forty-eighth Infantry					45							21				47					
First African Infantry [60th U S]	4	1	5	1	331	5	337		40		40	1		1		383		1		1	
Total	1940	78	2017	1199	8695	8	10011	82	8005		9987	8282	112	8180	115	30891	4189	1264	231	1545	

* Before transferred to 7th Iowa Cavalry   ) Partial returns

NUMBER OF TROOPS FURNISHED BY THE STATE OF IOWA DURING THE WAR OF THE REBELLION, TO JANUARY 1, 1865

No. Regiment	No. of men	No Regiment	No of men
1st Iowa Infantry	959	39th Iowa Infantry . . .	933
2d " "	1,247	40th " "	900
3d " "	1,074	41st Battalion Iowa Infantry .	294
4th " "	1,184	44th Infantry (100-days men) .	867
5th " "	1,037	45th " " " .	912
6th " "	1,013	46th " " " .	892
7th " " ...	1,138	47th " " " .	884
8th " " ..	1,027	48th Battalion ' "	346
9th " "	1,090	1st Iowa Cavalry	1,478
10th " " . .	1,027	2d " " . . .	1,394
11th " "	1,022	3d " "	1,360
12th " "	981	4th " "	1,227
13th " " . .	989	5th " "	1,245
14th " " . .	840	6th " "	1,125
15th " "	1,196	7th " "	562
16th " " ...	919	8th " "	1,234
17th " " . .	956	9th " "	1,178
18th " "	875	Sioux City Cavalry* .	93
19th " "	985	Co A, 11th Penn Cavalry	87
20th " "	925	1st Battery Artillery....................	149
21st " " . ..	980	2d " "	123
22d " "	1,008	3d " "	142
23d " "	961	4th ' "	152
24th " " .. .	979	1st Iowa African Infantry, 60th U S†	903
25th " " . . .	995	Dodge's Brigade Band	14
26th " " . . .	919	Band of 2d Iowa Infantry . .	10
27th " "	940	Enlistments as far as reported to Jan 1,	
28th " "	956	1864, for the older Iowa regiments	2,765
29th " "	1,005	Enlistments of Iowa men in regiments	
30th " "	978	of other States, over	2,500
31st " "	977		
32d " "	925	Total	61,653
33d " " ..	985	Re-enlisted Veterans for different Regi-	
34th " " .	953	ments .	7,202
35th " "	984	Additional enlistments .	6,664
36th " " . .	986		
37th " "	914	Grand total as far as reported up to Jan	
38th " "	910	1, 1865 . .	75,519

This does not include those Iowa men who veteranized in the regiments of other States, nor the names of men who enlisted during 1861, in regiments of other States

* Afterward consolidated with Seventh Cavalry

† Only a portion of this regiment was credited to the State

POPULATION OF IOWA,

By Counties.

COUNTIES	AGGREGATE					
	1875.	1870.	1860.	1850.	1840.	Voters.
Adair...	7045	3982	981		.	1616
Adams . . .	7832	4614	1533	.		1727
Aliamakee.	19158	17868	12237	777	.	3653
Appanoose	17405	16456	11931	3131	.	3679
Audubon	2370	1212	451			527
Benton .. .	28807	22154	8496	672	. .	4778
Black Hawk .	22913	21706	8244	135	.	4877
Boone . .	17251	14584	4282	735	.	3515
Bremer .	13220	12528	4915	.		2656
Buchanan .	17315	17034	7906	517	.	3890
Buena Vista . .	3561	1585	57	.	.	817
Buncombe*		... ..				
Butler	11734	9951	3724	.		2598
Calhoun	3185	1602	147	.	. .	681
Carroll	5760	2451	281	.	....	1197
Cass	10552	5464	1612	.	. ...	2122
Cedar	17879	19731	12949	3941	1258	3934
Cerro Gordo	6685	4722	940	....		1526
Cherokee	4249	1967	58	.	.	1001
Chickasaw	11400	10180	4336	.	.	2392
Clarke . .	10118	8735	5427	79	.	2213
Clay. . .	3559	1523	52	. .		868
Clayton . . .	27184	27771	20728	3873	1101	5272
Clinton . .	34295	35357	18938	2822	821	5569
Crawford .	6039	2530	383		.	1244
Dallas .	14386	12019	5244	854	.	3170
Davis	15757	15565	13764	7264	.	3448
Decatur . . .	13249	12018	8677	965	. .	2882
Delaware . .	16893	17482	11024	1759	168	3662
Des Moines	35415	27256	19611	12988	5577	6654
Dickinson	1748	1389	180	. ....		394
Dubuque	43845	38969	31164	10841	3059	8759
Emmett	1436	1392	105	...	.. ..	299
Fayette	20515	16973	12073	825	. .	4687
Floyd	13100	10768	3744	.	. ..	2884
Franklin . . .	6558	4738	1309	.	..	1374
Fremont	13719	11173	5074	1244	.	2998
Greene	7028	4627	1374	....	. ... ..	1622
Grundy . . .	8134	6399	793	.		1525
Guthrie . . .	9638	7061	3058	....		2389
Hamilton	7701	6053	1699	.	.	1455
Hancock	1482	999	179	. ..		303
Hardin	15029	13681	5440	... ..	..	3215
Harrison . .	11818	8931	3621	...	.	2658
Henry	21694	21163	18701	8707	3772	4641
Howard	7875	6282	3168	....	. .	1712
Humboldt . .	3455	2596	332	. ..	.	695
Ida	794	226	43	. . .	.	172
Iowa . . .	17456	16644	8029	822	. .	3576
Jackson . .	23061	22619	18493	7210	1411	4901
Jasper . . .	24128	22116	9883	1280	..	3239
Jefferson . .	17127	17839	15038	9904	2773	3721
Johnson	24551	24568	17573	4472	1491	5225
Jones	19148	19731	13306	3007	471	4180

* In 1862, name changed to Lyon

POPULATION OF IOWA—Concluded

COUNTIES.	AGGREGATE					
	1875.	1870.	1860.	1850.	1840.	Voters.
Keokuk	20488	19434	13271	4822	.	4202
Kossuth	3765	3351	416	...	...	773
Lee	33913	33210	29232	18861	6093	7274
Linn	31815	28852	18947	5444	1373	7509
Louisa	12499	12877	10370	4939	1927	2899
Lucas	11725	10388	5766	471	..	2464
Lyon*	1139	221	..			287
Madison	16030	13884	7339	1179	.	3632
Mahaska	23718	22508	14816	5989	.	5287
Marion	24094	24436	16813	5482	.	4988
Marshall	19629	17576	6015	338	...	4445
Mills	10555	8718	4481	..	.. '.	2365
Mitchell	11523	9582	3409	..	.	2338
Monona	2267	3654	832	.	.	1292
Monroe	12811	12724	8612	2884	.	2743
Montgomery	10389	5934	1256		.	2485
Muscatine	21623	21688	16444	5731	1942	6588
O'Brien	2349	715	8	..		595
Osceola	1778	...	..	. ..		498
Page	14274	9975	4419	551	.	3222
Palo Alto	2728	1336	132	.	..	556
Plymouth	5282	2199	148	.	...	1136
Pocahontas	2249	1446	103		.. ...	464
Polk	31558	27857	11625	4513	... ...	6842
Pottawattomie	21665	16893	4968	7828	. .	4392
Poweshiek	16482	15581	5668	615	.	3634
Ringgold	7546	5691	2923	.	. ...	1496
Sac	2873	1411	246	.	...	657
Scott	39763	38599	25959	5986	2140	7109
Shelby	5664	2540	818	.	.	1084
Sioux	3120	576	10	..	.	637
Story	13111	11651	4051	... .	.	2574
Tama	18771	16131	5285	8	. .	3911
Taylor	10418	6989	3590	204	.	2282
Union	8827	6986	2012	.	.	1924
Van Buren	16980	17672	17081	12270	6146	3893
Wapello	23865	22346	14518	8171	. .	5346
Warren	18541	17980	10281	961	.	4168
Washington	19269	18952	11235	4957	1594	4168
Wayne	13978	11287	6409	340	.	2947
Webster	13114	10484	2504	..		2747
Winnebago	2986	1562	168		...	406
Winneshiek	24233	23570	13942	546	. .	4117
Woodbury	8568	6172	1119	... .	.	1776
Worth	4908	2892	756		.	763
Wright	3244	2392	653			694
Total	1353118	1191792	674913	192214	43112	284557

* Formerly Buncombe

ILLINOIS.

Length, 380 miles, mean width about 156 miles. Area, 55,410 square miles, or 35,462,400 acres. Illinois, as regards its surface, constitutes a table-land at a varying elevation ranging between 350 and 800 feet above the sea level, composed of extensive and highly fertile prairies and plains. Much of the south division of the State, especially the river-bottoms, are thickly wooded. The prairies, too, have oasis-like clumps of trees scattered here and there at intervals. The chief rivers irrigating the State are the Mississippi—dividing it from Iowa and Missouri—the Ohio (forming its south barrier), the Illinois, Wabash, Kaskaskia, and Sangamon, with their numerous affluents. The total extent of navigable streams is calculated at 4,000 miles. Small lakes are scattered over various parts of the State. Illinois is extremely prolific in minerals, chiefly coal, iron, copper, and zinc ores, sulphur and limestone. The coal-field alone is estimated to absorb a full third of the entire coal-deposit of North America. Climate tolerably equable and healthy; the mean temperature standing at about 51° Fahrenheit As an agricultural region, Illinois takes a competitive rank with neighboring States, the cereals, fruits, and root-crops yielding plentiful returns; in fact, as a grain-growing State, Illinois may be deemed, in proportion to her size, to possess a greater area of lands suitable for its production than any other State in the Union. Stock-raising is also largely carried on, while her manufacturing interests in regard of woolen fabrics, etc, are on a very extensive and yearly expanding scale. The lines of railroad in the State are among the most extensive of the Union. Inland water-carriage is facilitated by a canal connecting the Illinois River with Lake Michigan, and thence with the St. Lawrence and Atlantic. Illinois is divided into 102 counties; the chief towns being Chicago, Springfield (capital), Alton, Quincy, Peoria, Galena, Bloomington, Rock Island, Vandalia, etc By the new Constitution, established in 1870, the State Legislature consists of 51 Senators, elected for four years, and 153 Representatives, for two years; which numbers were to be decennially increased thereafter to the number of six per every additional half-million of inhabitants. Religious and educational institutions are largely diffused throughout, and are in a very flourishing condition. Illinois has a State Lunatic and a Deaf and Dumb Asylum at Jacksonville, a State Penitentiary at Joliet; and a Home for

Soldiers' Orphans at Normal.   On November 30, 1870, the public debt of
the State was returned at $4,870,937, with a balance of $1,808,833
unprovided for.   At the same period the value of assessed and equalized
property presented the following totals: assessed, $840,031,703; equal-
ized $480,664,058.   The name of Illinois, through nearly th whole of
the eighteenth century, embraced most of the known regions north and
west of Ohio.   French colonists established themselves in 1673, at
Cahokia and Kaskaskia, and the territory of which these settlements
formed the nucleus was, in 1763, ceded to Great Britain in conjunction
with Canada, and ultimately resigned to the United States in 1787.
Illinois entered the Union as a State, December 3, 1818; and now sends
19 Representatives to Congress.   Population, 2,539,891, in 1870.

INDIANA.

The profile of Indiana forms a nearly exact parallelogram, occupying one of the most fertile portions of the great Mississippi Valley. The greater extent of the surface embraced within its limits consists of gentle undulations rising into hilly tracts toward the Ohio bottom. The chief rivers of the State are the Ohio and Wabash, with their numerous affluents. The soil is highly productive of the cereals and grasses—most particularly so in the valleys of the Ohio, Wabash, Whitewater, and White Rivers. The northeast and central portions are well timbered with virgin forests, and the west section is notably rich in coal, constituting an offshoot of the great Illinois carboniferous field. Iron, copper, marble, slate, gypsum, and various clays are also abundant. From an agricultural point of view, the staple products are maize and wheat, with the other cereals in lesser yields ; and besides these, flax, hemp, sorghum, hops, etc., are extensively raised. Indiana is divided into 92 counties, and counts among her principal cities and towns, those of Indianapolis (the capital), Fort Wayne, Evansville, Terre Haute, Madison, Jeffersonville, Columbus, Vincennes, South Bend, etc. The public institutions of the State are many and various, and on a scale of magnitude and efficiency commensurate with her important political and industrial status. Upward of two thousand miles of railroads permeate the State in all directions, and greatly conduce to the development of her expanding manufacturing interests. Statistics for the fiscal year terminating October 31, 1870, exhibited a total of receipts, $3,896,541 as against disbursements, $3,532,406, leaving a balance, $364,135 in favor of the State Treasury. The entire public debt, January 5, 1871, $3,971,000. This State was first settled by Canadian voyageurs in 1702, who erected a fort at Vincennes ; in 1763 it passed into the hands of the English, and was by the latter ceded to the United States in 1783. From 1788 till 1791, an Indian warefare prevailed. In 1800, all the region west and north of Ohio (then formed into a distinct territory) became merged in Indiana. In 1809, the present limits of the State were defined, Michigan and Illinois having previously been withdrawn. In 1811, Indiana was the theater of the Indian War of Tecumseh, ending with the decisive battle of Tippecanoe. In 1816 (December 11), Indiana became enrolled among the States of the American Union. In 1834, the State passed through a monetary crisis owing to its having become mixed up with railroad, canal, and other speculations on a gigantic scale, which ended, for the time being, in a general collapse of public credit, and consequent bankruptcy. Since that time, however, the greater number of the public

works which had brought about that imbroglio — especially the great
Wabash and Erie Canal — have been completed, to the great benefit of
the State, whose subsequent progress has year by year been marked by
rapid strides in the paths of wealth, commerce, and general social and
political prosperity. The constitution now in force was adopted in 1851.
Population, 1,680,637.

I O W A .

In shape, Iowa presents an almost perfect parallelogram, has a
length, north to south. of about 300 miles, by a pretty even width of 208
miles, and embraces an area of 55,045 square miles, or 35,228,800 acres
The surface of the State is generally undulating, rising toward the
middle into an elevated plateau which forms the "divide" of the
Missouri and Mississippi basins. Rolling prairies, especially in the south
section, constitute a regnant feature, and the river bottoms, belted with
woodlands, present a soil of the richest alluvion. Iowa is well watered;
the principal rivers being the Mississippi and Missouri, which form
respectively its east and west limits, and the Cedar, Iowa, and Des
Moines, affluents of the first named. Mineralogically, Iowa is important
as occupying a section of the great Northwest coal field, to the extent of
an area estimated at 25,000 square miles. Lead, copper, zinc, and iron,
are also mined in considerable quantities. The soil is well adapted to
the production of wheat, maize, and the other cereals; fruits, vegetables,
and esculent roots; maize, wheat, and oats forming the chief staples.
Wine, tobacco, hops, and wax, are other noticeable items of the agricultural yield. Cattle-raising, too, is a branch of rural industry largely
engaged in. The climate is healthy, although liable to extremes of heat
and cold. The annual gross product of the various manufactures carried
on in this State approximate, in round numbers, a sum of $20,000,000.
Iowa has an immense railroad system, besides over 500 miles of water-
communication by means of its navigable rivers. The State is politically
divided into 99 counties, with the following centers of population: Des
Moines (capital), Iowa City (former capital), Dubuque, Davenport, Burlington, Council Bluffs, Keokuk, Muscatine, and Cedar Rapids. The
State institutions of Iowa—religious, scholastic, and philanthropic — are
on a par, as regards number and perfection of organization and operation,
with those of her Northwest sister States, and education is especially
well cared for, and largely diffused. Iowa formed a portion of the
American territorial acquisitions from France, by the so-called Louisiana
purch   till 1812,

when it merged into the Missouri Territory; in 1834 it came under the Michigan organization, and, in 1836, under that of Wisconsin Finally, after being constituted an independent Territory, it became a State of the Union, December 28, 1846 Population in 1860, 674,913; in 1870, 1,191,792, and in 1875, 1,353,118.

MICHIGAN.

United area, 56,243 square miles, or 35,995,520 acres Extent of the Upper and smaller Peninsula — length, 316 miles; breadth, fluctuating between 36 and 120 miles. The south division is 416 miles long, by from 50 to 300 miles wide. Aggregate lake-shore line, 1,400 miles. The Upper, or North, Peninsula consists chiefly of an elevated plateau, expanding into the Porcupine mountain-system, attaining a maximum height of some 2,000 feet Its shores along Lake Superior are eminently bold and picturesque, and its area is rich in minerals, its product of copper constituting an important source of industry. Both divisions are heavily wooded, and the South one, in addition, boasts of a deep, rich, loamy soil, throwing up excellent crops of cereals and other agricultural produce. The climate is generally mild and humid, though the Winter colds are severe The chief staples of farm husbandry include the cereals, grasses, maple sugar, sorghum, tobacco, fruits, and dairy-stuffs. In 1870, the acres of land in farms were: improved, 5,096,939, unimproved woodland, 4,080,146, other unimproved land, 842,057. The cash value of land was $398,240,578, of farming implements and machinery, $13,711,979. In 1869, there were shipped from the Lake Superior ports, 874,582 tons of iron ore, and 45,762 of smelted pig, along with 14,188 tons of copper (ore and ingot). Coal is another article largely mined. Inland communication is provided for by an admirably organized railroad system, and by the St. Mary's Ship Canal, connecting Lakes Huron and Superior Michigan is politically divided into 78 counties; its chief urban centers are Detroit, Lansing (capital), Ann Arbor, Marquette, Bay City, Niles, Ypsilanti, Grand Haven, etc. The Governor of the State is elected biennially. On November 30 1870, the aggregate bonded debt of Michigan amounted to $2,385,028, and the assessed valuation of land to $266,929,278, representing an estimated cash value of $800,000,000. Education is largely diffused and most excellently conducted and provided for The State University at Ann Arbor, the colleges of Detroit and Kalamazoo, the Albion Female College, the State Normal School at Ypsilanti, and the State Agricultural College at Lansing, are chief among the academic institutions Michigan (Census of City)   in, and signifying "Great Lake), was discovered and first settled by French Canadians, who, in 1670, founded Detroit, the pioneer of a series of trading-posts on the Indian frontier. During the "Conspiracy of Pontiac, following the French loss of Canada, Michigan became the scene of a sanguinary struggle between the whites and aborigines In 1796, it became annexed to the United States, which incorporated this region with the Northwest Territory, and then with Indiana Territory, till 1803, when it became territorially independent Michigan was the theater of warlike operations during the war of 1812 with Great Britain, and in 1819 was authorized to be represented by one delegate in Congress, in 1837 she was admitted into the Union as a State, and in 1869 ratified the 15th Amendment to the Federal Constitution. Population, 1,184,059.

WISCONSIN.

It has a mean length of 260 miles, and a maximum breadth of 215. Land area, 53,924 square miles, or 34.511,360 acres. Wisconsin lies at a considerable altitude above sea-level, and consists for the most part of an upland plateau, the surface of which is undulating and very generally diversified Numerous local eminences called mounds are interspersed over the State, and the Lake Michigan coast-line is in many parts characterized by lofty escarped cliffs, even as on the west side the banks of the Mississippi form a series of high and picturesque bluffs. A group of islands known as The Apostles lie off the extreme north point of the State in Lake Superior, and the great estuary of Green Bay, running far inland, gives formation to a long, narrow peninsula between its waters and those of Lake Michigan The river-system of Wisconsin has three outlets — those of Lake Superior, Green Bay, and the Mississippi, which latter stream forms the entire southwest frontier, widening at one point into the large watery expanse called Lake Pepin Lake Superior receives the St. Louis, Burnt Wood, and Montreal Rivers; Green Bay, the Menomonee, Peshtigo, Oconto, and Fox; while into the Mississippi empty the St Croix, Chippewa, Black, Wisconsin, and Rock Rivers The chief interior lakes are those of Winnebago, Horicon, and Court Oreilles, and smaller sheets of water stud a great part of the surface The climate is healthful, with cold Winters and brief but very warm Summers Mean annual rainfall 31 inches. The geological system represented by the State, embraces those rocks included between the primary and the Devonian series, the former containing extensive deposits of copper and iron ore. Besides these minerals, lead and zinc are found in great quantity together with kaolin, plumbago, gypsum, and various clays Mining, consequently, forms a prominent industry, and one of yearly increasing dimensions. The soil of Wisconsin is of varying quality, but fertile on the whole, and in the north parts of the State heavily timbered The agricultural yield comprises the cereals, together with flax, hemp, tobacco, pulse, sorgum, and all kinds of vegetables, and of the hardier fruits In 1870, the State had a total number of 102,904 farms, occupying 11,715,321 acres, of which 5,899,343 consisted of improved land, and 3,437,442 were timbered. Cash value of farms, $300,414,064 , of farm implements and machinery, $14,239,364. Total estimated value of all farm products, including betterments and additions to stock, $78,027,032 of orchard and dairy stuffs, $1,045,933 ; of lumber, $1,327,618; of home manufactures, $338,423 , of all live-stock, $45,310,882. Number of manufacturing establishments, 7,136, employing 39,055 hands, and turning out productions valued at $85,624,966. The political divisions of the State form 61 counties, and the chief places of wealth, trade, and population, are Madison (the capital), Milwaukee, Fond du Lac, Oshkosh, Prairie du Chien, Janesville, Portage City, Racine, Kenosha, and La Crosse. In 1870, the total assessed valuation reached $333,209,838, as against a true valuation of both real and personal estate aggregating $602,207,329. Treasury receipts during 1870, $886,-696; disbursements, $906,329. Value of church property, $4,749,983. Education is amply provided for Independently of the State University at Madison, and those of Galesville and of Lawrence at Appleton, and the colleges of Beloit, Racine, and Milton, there are Normal Schools at Platteville and Whitewater. The State is divided into 4,802 common school districts, maintained at a cost, in 1870, of $2,094,160. The charitable institutions of Wisconsin include a Deaf and Dumb Asylum, an Institute for the Education of the Blind, and a Soldiers' Orphans' School. In January, 1870, the railroad system ramified throughout the State totalized 2,779 miles of track, including several lines far advanced toward completion. Immigration is successfully encouraged by the State authorities, the larger number of yearly new-comers being of Scandinavian and German origin. The territory now occupied within the limits of the State of Wisconsin was explored by French missionaries and traders in 1639, and it remained under French jurisdiction until 1703, when it became annexed to the British North American possessions In 1796, it reverted to the United States, the government of which latter admitted it within the limits of the Northwest Territory, and in 1809, attached it to that of Illinois, and to Michigan in 1818 Wisconsin became independently territorially organized in 1836, and became a State of the Union, March 3, 1847 Population in 1870, 1,064,985, of which 2,113 were of the colored race, and 11,521 Indians 1,206 of the latter being out of tribal relations.

MINNESOTA.

Its length, north to south, embraces an extent of 380 miles; its breadth one of 250 miles at a maximum. Area, 84,000 square miles, or 54,760,000 acres. The surface of Minnesota, generally speaking, consists of a succession of gently undulating plains and prairies, drained by an admirable water-system, and with here and there heavily-timbered bottoms and belts of virgin forest. The soil, corresponding with such a superficies, is exceptionally rich, consisting for the most part of a dark, calcareous sandy drift intermixed with loam. A distinguishing physical feature of this State is its riverine ramifications, expanding in nearly every part of it into almost innumerable lakes—the whole presenting an aggregate of water-power having hardly a rival in the Union. Besides the Mississippi — which here has its rise, and drains a basin of 800 miles of country — the principal streams are the Minnesota (334 miles long), the Red River of the North, the St. Croix, St. Louis, and many others of lesser importance; the chief lakes are those called Red, Cass, Leech, Mille Lacs, Vermillion, and Winibigosh. Quite a concatenation of sheets of water fringe the frontier line where Minnesota joins British America, culminating in the Lake of the Woods. It has been estimated, that of an area of 1,200,000 acres of surface between the St. Croix and Mississippi Rivers, not less than 73,000 acres are of lacustrine formation. In point of minerals, the resources of Minnesota have as yet been very imperfectly developed, iron, copper, coal, lead — all these are known to exist in considerable deposits; together with salt, limestone, and potter's clay. The agricultural outlook of the State is in a high degree satisfactory, wheat constitutes the leading cereal in cultivation, with Indian corn and oats in next order. Fruits and vegetables are grown in great plenty and of excellent quality. The lumber resources of Minnesota are important, the pine forests in the north region alone occupying an area of some 21,000 square miles, which in 1870 produced a return of scaled logs amounting to 313,116,416 feet. The natural industrial advantages possessed by Minnesota are largely improved upon by a railroad system. The political divisions of this State number 78 counties; of which the chief cities and towns are: St. Paul (the capital), Stillwater, Red Wing, St. Anthony, Fort Snelling, Minneapolis, and Mankato. Minnesota has already assumed an attitude of high importance as a manufacturing State; this is mainly due to the wonderful command of water-power she possesses, as before spoken of. Besides her timber-trade, the milling of flour, the distillation of whisky, and the tanning of leather, are prominent interests, which in 1860, gave a combined product of $14,831,043.

Education is notably provided for on a broad and catholic scale, the entire amount expended scholastically during the year 1870 being $857,816; while on November 30 of the preceding year the permanent school fund stood at $2,476,222. Besides a University and Agricultural College, Normal and Reform Schools flourish, and with these may be mentioned such various philanthropic and religious institutions as befit the needs of an intelligent and prosperous community. The finances of the State for the fiscal year terminating December 1, 1870, exhibited a balance on the right side to the amount of $136,164, being a gain of $44,000 over the previous year's figures. The earliest exploration of Minnesota by the whites was made in 1680 by a French Franciscan, Father Hennepin. who gave the name of St. Antony to the Great Falls on the Upper Mississippi. In 1763, the Treaty of Versailles ceded this region to England. Twenty years later, Minnesota formed part of the Northwest Territory transferred to the United States, and became herself territorialized independently in 1849. Indian cessions in 1851 enlarged her boundaries, and, May 11, 1857, Minnesota became a unit of the great American federation of States. Population, 439,706.

NEBRASKA.

Maximum length. 412 miles; extreme breadth, 208 miles. Area, 75,905 square miles, or 48,636,800 acres. The surface of this State is almost entirely undulating prairie, and forms part of the west slope of the great central basin of the North American Continent. In its west division, near the base of the Rocky Mountains, is a sandy belt of country, irregularly defined. In this part. too, are the ' dunes," resembling a wavy sea of sandy billows. as well as the Mauvaises Terres a tract of singular formation, produced by eccentric disintegrations and denudations of the land. The chief rivers are the Missouri. constituting its entire east line of demarcation; the Nebraska or Platte, the Niobrara, the Republican Fork of the Kansas, the Elkhorn, and the Loup Fork of the Platte. The soil is very various, but consisting chiefly of rich, bottomy loam, admirably adapted to the raising of heavy crops of cereals. All the vegetables and fruits of the temperate zone are produced in great size and plenty. For grazing purposes Nebraska is a State exceptionally well fitted, a region of not less than 23,000,000 acres being adaptable to this branch of husbandry. It is believed that the, as yet, comparatively infertile tracts of land found in various parts of the State are susceptible of productivity by means of a properly conducted system of irrigation. Few minerals of moment have so far been found within the limits of

Nebraska, if we may except important saline deposits at the head of Salt Creek in its southeast section. The State is divided into 57 counties, independent of the Pawnee and Winnebago Indians, and of unorganized territory in the northwest part. The principal towns are Omaha, Lincoln (State capital), Nebraska City, Columbus, Grand Island, etc. In 1870, the total assessed value of property amounted to $53,000,000, being an increase of $11,000,000 over the previous year's returns. The total amount received from the school-fund during the year 1869-70 was $77,999. Education is making great onward strides, the State University and an Agricultural College being far advanced toward completion. In the matter of railroad communication, Nebraska bids fair to soon place herself on a par with her neighbors to the east. Besides being intersected by the Union Pacific line, with its off-shoot, the Fremont and Blair, other tracks are in course of rapid construction. Organized by Congressional Act into a Territory, May 30, 1854, Nebraska entered the Union as a full State, March 1, 1867. Population, 122,993.

HUNTING PRAIRIE WOLVES IN AN EARLY DAY.

CONSTITUTION OF THE UNITED STATES OF AMERICA AND ITS AMENDMENTS.

We, the people of the United States, in order to form a more perfect union, establish justice, insure domestic tranquillity, provide for the common defense, promote the general welfare, and secure the blessings of liberty to ourselves and our posterity, do ordain and establish this Constitution for the United States of America.

ARTICLE I

SECTION 1   All legislative powers herein granted shall be vested in a Congress of the United States, which shall consist of a Senate and House of Representatives.

SEC. 2.   The House of Representatives shall be composed of members chosen every second year by the people of the several states, and the lectors in each state shall have the qualifications requisite for electors of the most numerous branch of the State Legislature.

No person shall be a representative who shall not have attained to the age of twenty-five years, and been seven years a citizen of the United States, and who shall not, when elected, be an inhabitant of that state in which he shall be chosen.

Representatives and direct taxes shall be apportioned among the several states which may be included within this Union, according to their respective numbers, which shall be determined by adding to the whole number of free persons, including those bound to service for a term of years, and excluding Indians not taxed, three-fifths of all other persons. The actual enumeration shall be made within three years after the first meeting of the Congress of the United States, and within every subsequent term of ten years, in such manner as they shall by law direct.   The number of Representatives shall not exceed one for every thirty thousand, but each state shall have at least one Representative, and until such enumeration shall be made the State of New Hampshire shall be entitled to choose three, Massachusetts eight, Rhode Island and Providence Plantations one. Connecticut five, New York six, New Jersey four, Pennsylvania eight, Delaware one, Maryland six, Virginia ten, North Carolina five, and Georgia three.

When vacancies happen in the representation from any state, the Executive authority thereof shall issue writs of election to fill such vacancies.

The House of Representatives shall choose their Speaker and other officers, and shall have the sole power of impeachment.

SEC. 3.   The Senate of the United States shall be composed of two Senators from each state, chosen by the Legislature thereof for six years; and each Senator shall have one vote.

Immediately after they shall be assembled in consequence of the first election, they shall be divided as equally as may be into three classes. The seats of the Senators of the first class shall be vacated at the expiration of the second year, of the second class at the expiration of the fourth year, and of the third class at the expiration of the sixth year, so that one-third may be chosen every second year; and if vacancies happen by resignation or otherwise, during the recess of the Legislature of any state, the Executive thereof may make temporary appointments until the next meeting of the Legislature, which shall then fill such vacancies.

No person shall be a Senator who shall not have attained to the age of thirty years and been nine years a citizen of the United States, and who shall not, when elected, be an inhabitant of that state for which he shall be chosen.

The Vice-President of the United States shall be President of th Senate, but shall have no vote unless they be equally divided.

The Senate shall choose their other officers, and also a President *pro tempore*, in the absence of the Vice-President, or when he shall exercise the office of President of the United States.

The Senate shall have the sole power to try all impeachments. When sitting for that purpose they shall be on oath or affirmation. When the President of the United States is tried the Chief Justice shall preside. And no person shall be convicted without the concurrence of two-thirds of the members present.

Judgment, in cases of impeachment, shall not extend further than to removal from office, and disqualification to hold and enjoy any office of honor, trust, or profit under the United States; but the party convicted shall nevertheless be liable and subject to indictment, trial, judgment, and punishment according to law

, SEC. 4. The times, places and manner of holding elections for Senators and Representatives shall be prescribed in each state by the Legislature thereof; but the Congress may at any time by law make or alter such regulations, except as to the places of choosing Senators.

The Congress shall assemble at least once in every year, and such meeting shall be on the first Monday in December, unless they shall by law appoint a different day.

SEC. 5. Each house shall be the judge of the election, returns, and qualifications of its own members, and a majority of each shall constitute a quorum to do business; but a smaller number may adjourn from day to day, and may be authorized to compel the attendance of absent members in such manner and under such penalties as each house may provide

Each house may determine the rules of its proceedings, punish its members for disorderly behavior, and, with the concurrence of two-thirds, expel a member.

Each house shall keep a journal of its proceedings, and from time to time publish the same, excepting such parts as may, in their judgment, require secrecy; and the yeas and nays of the members of either house on any question shall, at the desire of one-fifth of those present, be entered on the journal

Neither house, during the session of Congress, shall, without the consent of the other, adjourn for more than three days, nor to any other place than that in which the two houses shall be sitting

SEC. 6. The Senators and Representatives shall receive a compensation for their s   e t   as   ntained by law, and paid out of the treasury of the United t   shall in all c   , except treason, felony, and breach of the peace, be privileged from arrest during their attendance at the session of their respective houses, and in going to and returning from the same; and for any speech or debate in either house they shall not be questioned in any other place

No Senator or Representative shall, during the time for which he was elected, be appointed to any civil office under the authority of the United States, which shall have been created, or the emoluments whereof shall have been increased during such time; and no person holding any office under the United States, shall be a member of either house during his continuance in office.

SEC. 7.   All bills for raising revenue shall originate in the House of Representatives; but the Senate may propose or concur with amendments as on other bills.

Every bill which shall have passed the House of Representatives and the Senate, shall, before it becomes a law, be presented to the President the United States, if he approve he shall sign it, but if not he shall return it, with his objections, to that house in which it shall have originated, who shall enter the objections at large on their journal, and proceed to reconsider it.   If, after such reconsideration two-thirds of that house shall agree to pass the bill, it shall be sent, together with the objections, to the other house, by which it shall likewise be reconsidered and if approved by two-thirds of that house, it shall become a law.   But in all such cases the votes of both houses shall be determined by yeas and nays, and the names of the persons voting for and against the bill shall be entered on the journal of each house respectively.   If any bill shall not be returned by the President within ten days (Sundays excepted), after it shall have been presented to him, the same shall be a law, in like manner as if he had signed it, unless the Congress, by their adjournment, prevent its return, in which case it shall not be a law.

Every order, resolution, or vote to which the concurrence of the Senate and House of Representatives may be necessary (except on a question of adjournment), shall be presented to the President of the United States, and before the same shall take effect shall be approved by him, or, being disapproved by him, shall be re-passed by two-thirds of the Senate and House of Representatives, according to the rules and limitations prescribed in the case of a bill.

SEC 8.   The Congress shall have power—

To lay and collect taxes, duties, imposts and excises, to pay the debts, and provide for the common defense and general welfare of the United States; but all duties, imposts, and excises shall be uniform throughout the United States;

To borrow money on the credit of the United States;

To regulate commerce with foreign nations, and among the several States, and with the Indian tribes;

To establish a uniform rule of naturalization, and uniform laws on the subject of bankruptcies throughout the United States;

To coin money, regulate the value thereof, and of foreign coin, and fix the standard of weights and measures;

To provide for the punishment of counterfeiting the securities and current coin of the United States;

To establish post offices and post roads;

To promote the progress of sciences and useful arts, by securing, for limited times, to authors and inventors, the exclusive right to their respective writings and discoveries;

To constitute tribunals inferior to the Supreme Court.

To define and punish piracies and felonies committed on the high seas, and offenses against the law of nations;

To declare war, grant letters of marque and reprisal, and make rules concerning captures on land and water;

To raise and support armies, but no appropriation of money to that use shall be for a longer term than two years;

To provide and maintain a navy;

To make rules for the government and regulation of the land and naval forces;

To provide for calling forth the militia to execute the laws of the Union, suppress insurrections, and repel invasions;

To provide for organizing, arming and disciplining the militia, and for governing such part of them as may be employed in the service of the United States, reserving to the states respectively the appointment of the officers, and the authority of training the militia according to the discipline prescribed by Congress;

To exercise legislation in all cases whatsoever over such district (not exceeding ten miles square) as may, by cession of particular states, and the acceptance of Congress, become the seat of the government of the United States, and to exercise like authority over all places purchased by the consent of the Legislature of the state in which the same shall be, for the erection of forts, magazines, arsenals, dock yards, and other needful buildings; and

To make all laws which shall be necessary and proper for carrying into execution the foregoing powers, and all other powers vested by this Constitution in the government of the United States, or in any department or officer thereof.

SEC 9. The migration or importation of such persons as any of the states now existing shall think proper to admit, shall not be prohibited by the Congress prior to the year one thousand eight hundred and eight, but a tax or duty may be imposed on such importation, not exceeding ten dollars for each person.

The privilege of the writ of habeas corpus shall not be suspended, unless when in cases of rebellion or invasion the public safety may require it.

No bill of attainder or *ex post facto* law shall be passed.

No capitation or other direct tax shall be laid, unless in proportion to the census or enumeration hereinbefore directed to be taken.

No tax or duty shall be laid on articles exported from any state.

No preference shall be given by any regulation of commerce or revenue to the ports of one state over those of another; nor shall vessels bound to or from one state be obliged to enter, clear, or pay duties in another.

No money shall be drawn from the Treasury, but in consequence of appropriations made by law, and a regular statement and account of the receipts and expenditures of all public money shall be published from time to time.

No title of nobility shall be granted by the United States · and no person holding any office of profit or trust under them, shall, without the consent of the Congress, accept of any present, emolument, office, or title of any kind whatever, from any king, prince, or foreign state.

SEC. 10.   No state shall enter into any treaty, alliance, or confederation, grant letters of marque and reprisal; coin money; emit bills of credit; make anything but gold and silver coin a tender in payment of debts; pass any bill of attainder, *ex post facto* law, or law impairing the obligation of contracts, or grant any title of nobility.

No state shall, without the consent of the Congress, lay any imposts or duties on imports or exports, except what may be absolutely necessary for executing its inspection laws, and the net produce of all duties and imposts laid by any state on imports or exports, shall be for the use of the Treasury of the United States; and all such laws shall be subject to the revision and control of the Congress

No state shall, without the consent of Congress, lay any duty on tonnage, keep troops or ships of war in time of peace, enter into any agreement or compact with another state, or with a foreign power, or engage in war, unless actually invaded, or in such imminent danger as will not admit of delay.

ARTICLE II.

SECTION 1.   The Executive power shall be vested in a President of the United States of America   He shall hold his office during the term of four years, and, together with the Vice-President chosen for the same term, be elected as follows.

Each state shall appoint, in such manner as the Legislature thereof may direct, a number of Electors, equal to the whole number of Senators and Representatives to which the state may be entitled in the Congress; but no Senator or Representative, or person holding an office of trust or profit under the United States, shall be appointed an Elector.

[* The Electors shall meet in their respective states, and vote by ballot for two persons, of whom one at least shall not be an inhabitant of the same state with themselves.   And they shall make a list of all the persons voted for, and of the number of votes for each; which list they shall sign and certify, and transmit, sealed, to the seat of the government of the United States, directed to the President of the Senate.   The President of the Senate shall, in the presence of the Senate and House of Representatives, open all the certificates, and the votes shall then be counted. The person having the greatest number of votes shall be the President, if such number be a majority of the whole number of Electors appointed; and if there be more than one who have such majority, and have an equal number of votes, then the House of Representatives shall immediately choose by ballot one of them for President and if no person have a majority, then from the five highest on the list the said House shall in like manner choose the President.   But in choosing the President, the vote shall be taken by states, the representation from each state having one vote , a quorum for this purpose shall consist of a member or members from two-thirds of the states, and a majority of all the states shall be necessary to a choice.   In every case, after the choice of the President,

* This clause has been superseded and annulled by the Twelfth amendment

the person having the greatest number of votes of the Electors shall be the Vice-President. But if there should remain two or more who have equal votes, the Senate shall choose from them by ballot the Vice-President]

The Congress may determine the time of choosing the Electors, and the day on which they shall give their votes; which day shall be the same throughout the United States.

No person except a natural born citizen, or a citizen of the United States at the time of the adoption of this Constitution, shall be eligible to the office of President, neither shall any person be eligible to that office who shall not have attained the age of thirty-five years, and been fourteen years a resident within the United States

In case of the removal of the President from office, or of his death, resignation, or inability to discharge the powers and duties of the said office, the same shall devolve on the Vice-President, and the Congress may by law provide for the case of removal, death, resignation, or inability, both of the President and Vice-President, declaring what officer shall then act as President, and such officer shall act accordingly, until the disability be removed, or a President shall be elected.

The President shall, at stated times, receive for his services a compensation which shall neither be increased nor diminished during the period for which he shall have been elected, and he shall not receive within that period any other emolument from the United States or any of them.

Before he enters on the execution of his office, he shall take the following oath or affirmation:

"I do solemnly swear (or affirm) that I will faithfully execute the office of President of the United States, and will, to the best of my ability, preserve, protect, and defend the Constitution of the United States."

SEC. 2. The President shall be commander in chief of the army and navy of the United States, and of the militia of the several states, when called into the actual service of the United States; he may require the opinion, in writing, of the principal officer in each of the executive departments, upon any subject relating to the duties of their respective offices, and he shall have power to grant reprieves and pardon for offenses against the United States, except in cases of impeachment.

He shall have power, by and with the advice and consent of the Senate, to make treaties, provided two-thirds of the Senators present concur; and he shall nominate, and by and with the advice of the Senate, shall appoint ambassadors, other public ministers and consuls, judges of the Supreme Court, and all other officers of the United States whose appointments are not herein otherwise provided for, and which shall be established by law; but the Congress may by law vest the appointment of such inferior officers as they think proper in the President alone, in the courts of law, or in the heads of departments.

The President shall have power to fill up all vacancies that may happen during the recess of the Senate, by granting commissions which shall expire at the end of their next session.

SEC 3. He shall from time to time give to the Congress information of the state of the Union, and recommend to their consideration such measures as he shall judge necessary and expedient; he may on extraordinary occasions convene both houses, or either of them. and in case of disagreement between them, with respect to the time of adjournment, he may adjourn them to such time as he shall think proper; he shall receive ambassadors and other public ministers; he shall take care that the laws be faithfully executed. and shall commission all the officers of the United States.

SEC. 4. The President, Vice-President, and all civil officers of the United States, shall be removed from office on impeachment for, and conviction of, treason, bribery, or other high crimes and misdemeanors.

ARTICLE III

SECTION I The judicial power of the United States shall be vested in one Supreme Court, and such inferior courts as the Congress may from time to time ordain and establish. The Judges, both of the Supreme and inferior courts, shall hold their offices during good behavior, and shall, at stated times, receive for their services a compensation, which shall not be diminished during their continuance in office.

SEC. 2. The judicial power shall extend to all cases, in law and equity, arising under this Constitution, the laws of the United States, and treaties made, or which shall be made, under their authority; to all cases affecting ambassadors, other public ministers, and consuls; to all cases of admiralty and maritime jurisdiction; to controversies to which the United States shall be a party, to controversies between two or more states, between a state and citizens of another state, between citizens of different states, between citizens of the same state claiming lands under grants of different states, and between a state or the citizens thereof, and foreign states, citizens, or subjects

In all cases affecting ambassadors, other public ministers, and consuls, and those in which a state shall be a party, the Supreme Court shall have original jurisdiction

In all the other cases before mentioned, the Supreme Court shall have appellate jurisdiction, both as to law and fact, with such exceptions and under such regulations as the Congress shall make.

The trial of all crimes, except in cases of impeachment, shall be by jury, and such trial shall be held in the state where the said crimes shall have been committed; but when not committed within any state, the trial shall be at such place or places as the Congress may by law have directed

SEC. 3. Treason against the United States shall consist only in levying war against them, or in adhering to their enemies, giving them aid and comfort No person shall be convicted of treason unless on the testimony of two witnesses to the same overt act, or on confession in open court.

The Congress shall have power to declare the punishment of treason but no attainder of treason shall work corruption of blood, or forfeiture except during the life of the person attainted.

ARTICLE IV.

SECTION 1. Full faith and credit shall be given in each state to the public acts, records and proceedings of every other state. And the Congress may, by general laws, prescribe the manner in which such acts, records, and proceedings shall be proved, and the effect thereof.

SEC. 2. The citizens of each state shall be entitled to all privileges and immunities of citizens in the several states.

A person charged in any state with treason, felony, or other crime, who shall flee from justice and be found in another state, shall, on demand of the executive authority of the state from which he fled, be delivered up, to be removed to the state having jurisdiction of the crime.

No person held to service or labor in one state, under the laws thereof escaping into another, shall, in consequence of any law or regulation therein, be discharged from such service or labor, but shall be delivered up on the claim of the party to whom such service or labor may be due.

SEC. 3. New states may be admitted by the Congress into this Union; but no new state shall be formed or erected within the jurisdiction of any other state; nor any state be formed by the junction of two or more states, or parts of states, without the consent of the Legislatures of the states concerned, as well as of the Congress.

The Congress shall have power to dispose of and make all needful rules and regulations respecting the territory or other property belonging to the United States; and nothing in this Constitution shall be so construed as to prejudice any claims of the United States or of any particular state.

SEC. 4. The United States shall guarantee to every state in this Union a republican form of government, and shall protect each of them against invasion, and on application of the Legislature, or of the Executive (when the Legislature can not be convened), against domestic violence.

ARTICLE V.

The Congress, whenever two-thirds of both houses shall deem it necessary, shall propose amendments to this Constitution, or, on the application of the Legislatures of two-thirds of the several states, shall call a convention for proposing amendments, which, in either case, shall be valid to all intents and purposes as part of this Constitution, when ratified by the Legislatures of three fourths of the several states, or by conventions in three-fourths thereof, as the one or the other mode of ratification may be proposed by the Congress. Provided that no amendment which may be made prior to the year one thousand eight hundred and eight shall in any manner affect the first and fourth clauses in the ninth section of the first article; and that no state, without its consent, shall be deprived of its equal suffrage in the Senate.

ARTICLE VI.

All debts contracted and engagements entered into before the adoption of this Constitution shall be as valid against the United States under this Constitution as under the Confederation.

This Constitution, and the laws of the United States which shall be made in pursuance thereof, and all treaties made, or which shall be made, under the authority of the United States, shall be the supreme law of the land; and the Judges in every state shall be bound thereby, anything in the Constitution or laws of any state to the contrary notwithstanding

The Senators and Representatives before mentioned, and the members of the several state Legislatures, and all executive and judicial officers, both of the United States and of the several states, shall be bound by oath or affirmation to support this Constitution; but no religious test shall ever be required as a qualification to any office or public trust under the United States.

ARTICLE VII.

The ratification of the Conventions of nine states shall be sufficient for the establishment of this Constitution between the states so ratifying the same

Done in convention by the unanimous consent of the states present, the seventeenth day of September, in the year of our Lord one thousand seven hundred and eighty-seven, and of the independence of the United States of America the twelfth. In witness whereof we have hereunto subscribed our names.

GEO. WASHINGTON,
President and Deputy from Virginia.

New Hampshire.
JOHN LANGDON,
NICHOLAS GILMAN.

Massachusetts
NATHANIEL GORHAM.
RUFUS KING.

Connecticut.
WM. SAM'L JOHNSON,
ROGER SHERMAN.

New York.
ALEXANDER HAMILTON.

New Jersey.
WIL. LIVINGSTON,
WM. PATERSON,
DAVID BREARLEY.
JONA. DAYTON.

Pennsylvania.
B. FRANKLIN,
ROBT. MORRIS,
THOS FITZSIMONS,
JAMES WILSON,
THOS MIFFLIN,
GEO. CLYMER,
JARED INGERSOLL,
GOUV. MORRIS.

Delaware
GEO. READ,
JOHN DICKINSON,
JACO BROOM,
GUNNING BEDFORD, JR.,
RICHARD BASSETT.

Maryland.
JAMES M'HENRY,
DANL CARROLL,
DAN. OF ST. THOS. JENIFER.

Virginia.
JOHN BLAIR,
JAMES MADISON, JR.

North Carolina.
WM BLOUNT,
HU. WILLIAMSON,
RICH'D DOBBS SPAIGHT.

South Carolina
J. RUTLEDGE,
CHARLES PINCKNEY.
CHAS. COTESWORTH PINCKNEY.
PIERCE BUTLER.

Georgia.
WILLIAM FEW,
ABR BALDWIN.

WILLIAM JACKSON, *Secretary.*

ARTICLES IN ADDITION TO AND AMENDATORY OF THE CONSTITUTION OF THE UNITED STATES OF AMERICA.

Proposed by Congress and ratified by the Legislatures of the several states, pursuant to the fifth article of the original Constitution.

ARTICLE I.

Congress shall make no law respecting an establishment of religion, or prohibiting the free exercise thereof; or abridging the freedom of speech, or of the press; or the right of the people peaceably to assemble, and to petition the Government for a redress of grievances.

ARTICLE II.

A well regulated militia being necessary to the security of a free state, the right of the people to keep and bear arms shall not be infringed.

ARTICLE III.

No soldier shall, in time of peace, be quartered in any house without the consent of the owner, nor in time of war but in a manner to be prescribed by law.

ARTICLE IV.

The right of the people to be secure in their persons, houses, papers, and effects against unreasonable searches and seizures, shall not be violated, and no warrants shall issue but upon probable cause, supported by oath or affirmation, and particularly describing the place to be searched and the persons or things to be seized.

ARTICLE V.

No person shall be held to answer for a capital or otherwise infamous crime, unless on a presentment or indictment of a Grand Jury, except in cases arising in the land or naval forces, or in the militia when in actual service in time of war or public danger, nor shall any person be subject for the same offense to be twice put in jeopardy of life or limb; nor shall be compelled in any criminal case to be a witness against himself, nor be deprived of life, liberty, or property, without due process of law; nor shall private property be taken for public use, without just compensation.

ARTICLE VI.

In all criminal prosecutions, the accused shall enjoy the right to a speedy and public trial, by an impartial jury of the state and district wherein the crime shall have been committed, which district shall have been previously ascertained by law, and to be informed of the nature and cause of the accusation; to be confronted with the witnesses against him, to have compulsory process for obtaining witnesses in his favor; and to have the assistance of counsel for his defense.

ARTICLE VII.

In suits at common law where the value in controversy shall exceed twenty dollars, the right of trial by jury shall be preserved, and no fact

tried by a jury shall be otherwise re-examined in any court of the United States than according to the rules of the common law.

ARTICLE VIII.

Excessive bail shall not be required, nor excessive fines imposed, nor cruel and unusual punishments inflicted.

ARTICLE IX.

The enumeration, in the Constitution, of certain rights, shall not be construed to deny or disparage others retained by the people.

ARTICLE X.

The powers not delegated to the United States by the Constitution, nor prohibited by it to the states, are reserved to the states respectively, or to the people.

ARTICLE XI.

The judicial power of the United States shall not be construed to extend to any suit in law or equity commenced or prosecuted against one of the United States by citizens of another state, or by citizens or subjects of any foreign state.

ARTICLE XII.

The Electors shall meet in their respective states and vote by ballot for President and Vice-President, one of whom, at least, shall not be an inhabitant of the same state with themselves; they shall name in their ballots the person to be voted for as president, and in distinct ballots the person voted for as Vice-President, and they shall make distinct lists of all persons voted for as President, and of all persons voted for as Vice-President, and of the number of votes for each, which list they shall sign and certify, and transmit sealed to the seat of the government of the United States, directed to the President of the Senate The President of the Senate shall, in presence of the Senate and House of Representatives, open all the certificates, and the votes shall then be counted. The person having the greatest number of votes for President shall be the President, if such number be a majority of the whole number of Electors appointed; and if no person have such majority, then from the persons having the highest number not exceeding three on the list of those voted for as President, the House of Representatives shall choose immediately, by ballot, the President. But in choosing the President, the votes shall be taken by States, the representation from each state having one vote; a quorum for this purpose shall consist of a member or members from two-thirds of the states, and a majority of all the states shall be necessary to a choice. And if the House of Representatives shall not choose a President whenever the right of choice shall devolve upon them, before the fourth day of March next following, then the Vice-President shall act as President, as in the case of the death or other constitutional disability of the President. The person having the greatest number of votes as Vice-President, shall be the Vice-President, if such number be the majority of the whole number of electors appointed, and if no person have a majoriity, then from the two highest numbers on the list, the Senate shall choose the Vice-President, a quorum for the purpose shall consist of two-thirds of the whole number of Senators, and a majority of the whole number shall be necessary to a choice. But no person constitutionally ineligible to the office of President shall be eligible to that of Vice-President of the United States.

ARTICLE XIII.

SECTION 1. Neither slavery nor involuntary servitude, except as a punishment for crime, whereof the party shall have been duly convicted, shall exist within the United States, or any place subject to their jurisdiction.

SEC. 2. Congress shall have power to enforce this article by appropriate legislation.

ARTICLE XIV.

SECTION 1. All persons born or naturalized in the United States and subject to the jurisdiction thereof, are citizens of the United States, and of the state wherein they reside. No state shall make or enforce any law which shall abridge the privileges or immunities of citizens of the United States, nor shall any state deprive any person of life, liberty, or property, without due process of law, nor deny to any person within its jurisdiction the equal protection of the laws.

SEC. 2. Representatives shall be appointed among the several states according to their respective numbers, counting the whole number of persons in each state, excluding Indians not taxed; but when the right to vote at any election for the choice of Electors for President and Vice-President of the United States, Representatives in Congress, the executive and judicial officers of a state, or the members of the Legislature thereof, is denied to any of the male inhabitants of such state, being twenty-one years of age and citizens of the United States, or in any way abridged except for participation in rebellion or other crimes, the basis of representation therein shall be reduced in the proportion which the number of such male citizens shall bear to the whole number of male citizens twenty-one years of age in such state

SEC. 3. No person shall be a Senator or Representative in Congress, or Elector of President and Vice-President, or hold any office, civil or military, under the United States, or under any state, who, having previously taken an oath as a Member of Congress, or as an officer of the United States, or as a member of any state Legislature, or as an executive or judicial officer of any state to support the Constitution of the United States, shall have engaged in insurrection or rebellion against the same, or given aid or comfort to the enemies thereof. But Congress may by a vote of two-thirds of each house, remove such disability.

SEC. 4. The validity of the public debt of the United States authorized by law, including debts incurred for payment of pensions and bounties for services in suppressing insurrection or rebellion, shall not be questioned. But neither the United States nor any state shall pay any debt or obligation incurred in the aid of insurrection or rebellion against the United States, or any loss or emancipation of any slave, but such debts, obligations, and claims shall be held illegal and void.

ARTICLE XV

SECTION 1 The right of citizens of the United States to vote shall not be denied or abridged by the United States, or by any State, on account of race, color, or previous condition of servitude

VOTE FOR GOVERNOR, 1877, AND PRESIDENT, 1876

COUNTIES.	1877 Governor				1876 President		COUNTIES	1877 Governor				1876 President	
	Rep	Dem	Gr	Pro	Rep	Dem		Rep	Dem	Gr	Pro	Rep	Dem
Adair	982	161	581	15	1344	593	Johnson	1584	2345	18	273	2345	3563
Adams	876	397	455	38	1376	626	Jones	1865	1218	14	68	2591	1763
Allamakee	1547	1540	69	36	1709	1646	Keokuk	1772	1526	322	105	2364	1862
Appanoose	1165	1019	729	32	1711	1419	Kossuth	463	236	13	89	638	227
Audubon	410	352	26		427	352	Lee	2157	2863	350	293	3163	3632
Benton	1432	712	567	419	2001	1354	Linn	2524	2316	75	583	4331	2917
Black Hawk	1780	1111	95	244	2979	1592	Louisa	1328	817	89	108	1920	1008
Boone	1612	981	466	10	2018	1305	Lucas	1203	804	103	12	1478	1044
Bremer	1180	582	196	1	1737	757	Lyon	261	17	9	11	262	46
Buchanan	1290	769	725	223	2227	1416	Madison	1792	1077	616	56	2246	1538
Buena Vista	747	192	161	20	770	200	Mahaska	1824	1086	1011	596	3221	1701
Butler	1453	758	19	95	1828	780	Marion	1976	1866	760	95	2736	2344
Calhoun	418	75	171	74	622	196	Marshall	1448	837	329	501	3056	1189
Carroll	633	744	141	11	799	771	Mills	1435	1162	98	28	1452	1165
Cass	1592	839	116	30	1876	979	Mitchell	1396	459	35	36	1663	671
Cedar	1315	1093	206	416	2328	1413	Monona	580	119	432	9	713	304
Cerro Gordo	903	315	72	40	1271	418	Monroe	1084	928	217	26	1418	1246
Cherokee	662	74	383	86	861	175	Montgomery	1122	411	512	47	1749	759
Chickasaw	1279	1107	37	94	1574	1090	Muscatine	1753	1775	171	387	2523	2075
Clark	1054	267	813	19	1405	816	O'Brien	306	21	264	14	463	116
Clay	517	16	20	67	567	94	Osceola	295	40	13	31	329	59
Clayton	1873	1770	66	167	2662	2621	Page	1166	564	348	293	2243	861
Clinton	2111	2327	286	66	3654	3398	Palo Alto	311	357		3	343	333
Crawford	898	651	19	111	1943	638	Plymouth	779	457	77	39	835	502
Dallas	1541	215	1241	80	2136	752	Pocahontas	370	94	44	36	374	141
Davis	993	1231	803	12	1586	1631	Polk	3171	1885	1273	94	4321	2382
Decatur	1269	961	310	19	1617	1292	Pottawattamie	2253	1559	125	121	2665	2414
Delaware	1226	1143	32	525	2233	1446	Poweshiek	1496	882	420	346	2609	1083
Des Moines	2315	1384	767	6	3325	2917	Ringgold	964	71	671	47	1216	422
Dickinson	197	8		12	259	48	Sac	666	125	177	13	661	166
Dubuque	1587	3415	406	53	2798	4777	Scott	3031	1963	309	37	3819	2853
Emmett	213	28			246	36	Shelby	288	639	3	16	897	611
Fayette	1933	1067	889	27	3029	1709	Sioux	436	132	49		439	220
Floyd	1233	208	162	30	2042	751	Story	1260	344	644	187	1813	579
Franklin	1311	336	16	10	1178	379	Tama	1426	833	196	133	2137	1317
Fremont	1250	1331	334		1658	1652	Taylor	1226	293	868		1727	676
Greene	1031	215	551	27	1310	510	Union	899	516	830	63	1238	795
Grundy	909	504		8	1099	417	Van Buren	1490	1205	301	130	2113	1661
Guthrie	1160	496	364	21	1434	629	Wapello	1740	1629	165	296	2982	2412
Hamilton	842	263	422	57	1187	425	Warren	1726	944	742	101	2139	1315
Hancock	340	95	29	2	281	89	Washington	1487	1221	203	112	2447	1805
Hardin	1092	661	238	151	2152	980	Wayne	1146	832	404	3	1692	1341
Harrison	1348	864	523	19	1557	1386	Webster	850	127	1121	47	1290	987
Henry	1770	124	1041	140	2809	1453	Winnebago	544	40			438	89
Howard	551	647	201	519	1194	600	Winneshiek	2074	1009	279	238	2491	1617
Humboldt	382	149	115	64	523	183	Woodbury	1119	867	226	9	1034	997
Ida	321	54	104		212	57	Worth	625	132	8	11	70	119
Iowa	1132	1120	642	225	1870	1343	Wright	531	166	117	95	571	184
Jackson	1019	1966	224	15	2126	2185							
Jasper	1977	1154	1018	205	3375	1804	Totals	121546	79553	34229	10639	171133	142127
Jefferson	1396	753	576	166	2166	1449	Minorities	41.9				29211	

Total vote, 1877, 245,766; 1876 (including 919 Greenback), 292,943

VOTE FOR CONGRESSMEN, 1876

District	Rep	Dem	R Maj	Total	Maj '74	District	Rep	Dem	R Maj	Total	Maj 74
I	17188	14814	2374	32002	D 1863	VII	19496	11688	7808	31184	R 2300
II	16439	14683	1756	31122	R 657	VIII	19458	15236	4122	34594	R 2147
III	17423	16100	1323	33523	D 63	IX	19563	10583	8980	30146	R 5849
IV	20770	9379	11391	30149	R 3824						
V	19274	11154	8120	30428	R 5243						
VI							168259	118350	49914	290409	

Total vote, 1874,

PRACTICAL RULES FOR EVERY DAY USE.

How to find the gain or loss per cent. when the cost and selling price are given

RULE.—Find the difference between the cost and selling price, which will be the gain or loss.

Annex two ciphers to the gain or loss, and divide it by the cost price; the result will be the gain or loss per cent

How to change gold into currency.

RULE.—Multiply the given sum of gold by the price of gold.

How to change currency into gold.

Divide the amount in currency by the price of gold.

How to find each partner's share of the gain or loss in a copartnership business.

RULE.—Divide the whole gain or loss by the entire stock, the quotient will be the gain or loss per cent

Multiply each partner's stock by this per cent., the result will be each one's share of the gain or loss.

How to find gross and net weight and price of hogs.

A short and simple method for finding the net weight, or price of hogs, when the gross weight or price is given, and vice versa

NOTE—It is generally assumed that the gross weight of hogs diminished by 1-5 or 20 per cent. of itself gives the net weight, and the net weight increased by ¼ or 25 per cent of itself equals the gross weight

To find the net weight or gross price.

Multiply the given number by 8 (tenths)

To find the gross weight or net price

Divide the given number by .8 (tenths)

How to find the capacity of a granary, bin, or wagon-bed.

RULE.—Multiply (by short method) the number of cubic feet by 6308, and point off ONE decimal place—the result will be the correct answer in bushels and tenths of a bushel

For only an approximate answer, multiply the cubic feet by 8, and point off one decimal place

How to find the contents of a corn-crib.

RULE.—Multiply the number of cubic feet by 54, short method, or by 4½ ordinary method, and point off ONE decimal place—the result will be the answer in bushels

NOTE—In estimating corn in the ear, the quality and the time it has been cribbed must be taken into consideration, since corn will shrink considerably during the Winter and Spring This rule generally holds good for corn measured at the time it is cribbed, provided it is sound and clean.

How to find the contents of a cistern or tank.

RULE.—Multiply the square of the mean diameter by the depth (all in feet) and this product by 5681 (short method), and point off ONE decimal place—the result will be the contents in barrels of 31½ gallons

How to find the contents of a barrel or cask.

RULE.—Under the square of the mean diameter, write the length (all in inches) in REVERSED order, so that its UNITS will fall under the TENS; multiply by short method, and this product again by 430; point off one decimal place, and the result will be the answer in wine gallons.

How to measure boards.

RULE.—Multiply the length (in feet) by the width (in inches) and divide the product by 12—the result will be the contents in square feet.

How to measure scantlings, joists, planks, sills, etc.

RULE —Multiply the width, the thickness, and the length together (the width and thickness in inches, and the length in feet), and divide the product by 12—the result will be square feet.

How to find the number of acres in a body of land.

RULE —Multiply the length by the width (in rods), and divide the product by 160 (carrying the division to 2 decimal places if there is a remainder); the result will be the answer in acres and hundredths.

When the opposite sides of a piece of land are of unequal length, add them together and take one-half for the mean length or width.

How to find the number of square yards in a floor or wall

RULE.—Multiply the length by the width or height (in feet), and divide the product by 9, the result will be square yards.

How to find the number of bricks required in a building.

RULE —Multiply the number of cubic feet by 22½.

The number of cubic feet is found by multiplying the length, height nd thickness (in feet) together

Bricks are usually made 8 inches long, 4 inches wide, and two inches thick; hence, it requires 27 bricks to make a cubic foot without mortar, but it is generally assumed that the mortar fills 1-6 of the space

How to find the number of shingles required in a roof

RULE.—Multiply the number of square feet in the roof by 8, if the shingles are exposed 4½ inches, or by 7 1-5 if exposed 5 inches

To find the number of square feet, multiply the length of the roof by twice the length of the rafters.

To find the length of the rafters, at ONE–FOURTH pitch, multiply the width of the building by .56 (hundredths); at ONE–THIRD pitch, by 6 (tenths); at TWO–FIFTHS pitch, by .64 (hundredths); at ONE–HALF pitch by 71 (hundredths). This gives the length of the rafters from the apex to the end of the wall, and whatever they are to project must be taken into consideration.

NOTE—By ¼ or ⅓ pitch is meant that the apex or comb of the roof is to be ¼ or ⅓ the width of the building higher than the walls or base of the rafters

How to reckon the cost of hay.

RULE —Multiply the number of pounds by half the price per ton, and remove the decimal point three places to the left.

How to measure grain.

RULE —Level the grain, ascertain the space it occupies in cubic feet; multiply the number of cubic feet by 8, and point off one place to the left.

NOTE—Exactness requires the addition to every three hundred bushels of one extra bushel

The foregoing rule may be used for finding the number of gallons, by multiplying the number of bushels by 8.

If the corn in the box is in the ear, divide the answer by 2, to find the number of bushels of shelled corn, because it requires 2 bushels of ear corn to make 1 of shelled corn

Rapid rules for measuring land without instruments.

In measuring land, the first thing to ascertain is the contents of any given plot in square yards, then, given the number of yards, find out the number of rods and acres

The most ancient and simplest measure of distance is a step. Now, an ordinary-sized man can train himself to cover one yard at a stride, on the average, with sufficient accuracy for ordinary purposes.

To make use of this means of measuring distances, it is essential to walk in a straight line; to do this, fix the eye on two objects in a line straight ahead, one comparatively near, the other remote, and, in walking, keep these objects constantly in line

Farmers and others by adopting the following simple and ingenious contrivance, may always carry with them the scale to construct a correct yard measure.

Take a foot rule, and commencing at the base of the little finger of the left hand, mark the quarters of the foot on the outer borders of the left arm, pricking in the marks with indelible ink.

To find how many rods in length will make an acre, the width being given.

RULE —Divide 160 by the width, and the quotient will be the answer.

How to find the number of acres in any plot of land, the number of rods being given.

RULE.—Divide the number of rods by 8, multiply the quotient by 5, and remove the decimal point two places to the left.

The diameter being given, to find the circumference.

RULE —Multiply the diameter by 3 1-7.

How to find the diameter, when the circumference is given.

RULE.—Divide the circumference by 3 1-7

To find how many solid feet a round stick of timber of the same thickness throughout will contain when squared.

RULE —Square half the diameter in inches, multiply by 2, multiply by the length in feet, and divide the product by 144.

General rule for measuring timber, to find the solid contents in feet

RULE.—Multiply the depth in inches by the breadth in inches, and then multiply by the length in feet, and divide by 144.

To find the number of feet of timber in trees with the bark on

RULE —Multiply the square of one-fifth of the circumference in inches, by twice the length, in feet, and divide by 144. Deduct 1-10 to 1-15 according to the thickness of the bark.

Howard's new rule for computing interest.

RULE —The reciprocal of the rate is the time for which the interest on any sum of money will be shown by simply removing the decimal point two places to the left, for ten times that time, remove the point one place to the left; for 1-10 of the same time, remove the point three places to the left.

Increase or diminish the results to suit the time given.

NOTE—The reciprocal of the rate is found by inverting the rate, thus 3 per cent per month, inverted becomes ⅓ of a month or 10 days

When the rate is expressed by one figure, always write it thus: 3-1, three ones.

Rule for converting English into American currency.

Multiply the pounds, with the shillings and pence stated in decimals, by 400 plus the premium in fourths, and divide the product by 90.

U. S. GOVERNMENT LAND MEASURE.

A township—36 sections each a mile square.

A section—640 acres.

A quarter section, half a mile square—160 acres.

An eighth section, half a mile long, north and south, and a quarter of a mile wide—80 acres.

A sixteenth section, a quarter of a mile square—40 acres.

The sections are all numbered 1 to 36, commencing at the north-east corner

The sections are divided into quarters, which are named by the cardinal points. The quarters are divided in the same way. The description of a forty acre lot would read · The south half of the west half of the south-west quarter of section 1 in township 24, north of range 7 west, or as the case might be; and sometimes will fall short and sometimes overrun the number of acres it is supposed to contain.

The nautical mile is 795 4-5 feet longer than the common mile

SURVEYORS' MEASURE.

7 92-100 inches	. .	make 1 link.
25 links	. "	1 rod.
4 rods . .	. "	1 chain.
80 chains	. . . '	1 mile.

NOTE.—A chain is 100 links, equal to 4 rods or 66 feet.

Shoemakers formerly used a subdivision of the inch called a barleycorn; three of which made an inch

Horses are measured directly over the fore feet, and the standard of measure is four inches—called a hand.

In Biblical and other old measurements, the term span is sometimes used, which is a length of nine inches

The sacred cubit of the Jews was 24 024 inches in length.

The common cubit of the Jews was 21.704 inches in length.

A pace is equal to a yard or 36 inches.

A fathom is equal to 6 feet.

A league is three miles, but its length is variable, for it is strictly speaking a nautical term. and should be three geographical miles, equal to 3.45 statute miles, but when used on land, three statute miles are said to be a league.

In cloth measure an aune is equal to $1\frac{1}{4}$ yards, or 45 inches.

An Amsterdam ell is equal to 26 796 inches.

A Trieste ell is equal to 25 284 inches.

A Brabant ell is equal to 27.116 inches.

HOW TO KEEP ACCOUNTS.

Every farmer and mechanic, whether he does much or little business, should keep a record of his transactions in a clear and systematic manner. For the benefit of those who have not had the opportunity of acquiring a primary knowledge of the principles of book-keeping, we here present a simple form of keeping accounts which is easily comprehended, and well adapted to record the business transactions of farmers, mechanics and la....

1875.	A. H. JACKSON.		Dr.		Cr.	
Jan.	10	To 7 bushels Wheat at $1.25	$8	75		
"	17	By shoeing span of Horses			$2	50
Feb.	4	To 14 bushels Oats at $.45	6	30		
"	4	To 5 lbs. Butter at .25	1	25		
March	8	By new Harrow			18	00
"	8	By sharpening 2 Plows				40
"	13	By new Double-Tree			2	25
"	27	To Cow and Calf	48	00		
April	9	To half ton of Hay	6	25		
"	9	By Cash			25	00
May	6	By repairing Corn-Planter			4	75
"	24	To one Sow with Pigs	17	50		
July	4	By Cash, to balance account			35	15
			$88	05	$88	05

1875.	CASSA MASON.		Dr.		Cr.	
March	21	By 3 days' labor at $1.25			$3	75
"	21	To 2 Shoats at 3.00	$6	00		
"	23	To 18 bushels Corn at .45	8	10		
May	1	By 1 month's Labor			25	00
"	1	To Cash	10	00		
June	19	By 8 days' Mowing at $1.50			12	00
"	26	To 50 lbs. Flour	2	75		
July	10	To 27 lbs. Meat at $.10	2	70		
"	29	By 9 days' Harvesting at 2.00			18	00
Aug.	12	By 6 days' Labor at 1.50			9	00
"	12	To Cash	20	00		
Sept.	1	To Cash to balance account	18	20		
			$67	75	$67	75

INTEREST TABLE.

A SIMPLE RULE FOR ACCURATELY COMPUTING INTEREST AT ANY GIVEN PER CENT. FOR ANY LENGTH OF TIME.

Multiply the *principal* (amount of money at interest) by the *time reduced to days*; then divide this *product* by the *quotient* obtained by dividing 360 (the number of days in the interest year) by the *per cent.* of interest, and *the quotient thus obtained* will be the required interest.

ILLUSTRATION. Solution.

Require the interest of $462.50 for one month and eighteen days at 6 per cent. An interest month is 30 days; one month and eighteen days equal 48 days. $462.50 multiplied by .48 gives $222.0000; 360 divided by 6 (the per cent. of interest) gives 60, and $222.0000 divided by 60 will give you the exact interest, which is $3.70. If the rate of interest in the above example were 12 per cent., we would divide the $222.0000 by 30 (because 360 divided by 12 gives 30); if 4 per cent., we would divide by 90; if 8 per cent., by 45; and in like manner for any other per cent.

$462.50
.48
370000
185000
60) $222.0000 ($3.70
180
420
420
00

MISCELLANEOUS TABLE.

12 units, or things, 1 Dozen. | 196 pounds, 1 Barrel of Flour. | 24 sheets of paper, 1 Quire.
12 dozen, 1 Gross. | 200 pounds, 1 Barrel of Pork. | 20 quires paper 1 Ream.
20 things, 1 Score. | 56 pounds, 1 ... | ...

NAMES OF THE STATES OF THE UNION, AND THEIR SIGNIFICATIONS.

Virginia.—The oldest of the States, was so called in honor of Queen Elizabeth, the "Virgin Queen," in whose reign Sir Walter Raleigh made his first attempt to colonize that region.

Florida.—Ponce de Leon landed on the coast of Florida on Easter Sunday, and called the country in commemoration of the day, which was the Pasqua Florida of the Spaniards, or "Feast of Flowers."

Louisiana was called after Louis the Fourteenth, who at one time owned that section of the country.

Alabama was so named by the Indians, and signifies "Here we Rest."

Mississippi is likewise an Indian name, meaning "Long River."

Arkansas, from Kansas, the Indian word for "smoky water." Its prefix was really *arc*, the French word for "bow."

The *Carolinas* were originally one tract, and were called "Carolana," after Charles the Ninth of France.

Georgia owes its name to George the Second of England, who first established a colony there in 1732.

Tennessee is the Indian name for the "River of the Bend," *i e*, the Mississippi which forms its western boundary.

Kentucky is the Indian name for "at the head of the river."

Ohio means "beautiful," *Iowa*, "drowsy ones," *Minnesota*, "cloudy water," and *Wisconsin*, "wild-rushing channel."

Illinois is derived from the Indian word *illini*, men, and the French suffix *ois*, together signifying "tribe of men."

Michigan was called by the name given the lake, *fish-weir*, which was so styled from its fancied resemblance to a fish trap.

Missouri is from the Indian word "muddy," which more properly applies to the river that flows through it.

Oregon owes its Indian name also to its principal river.

Cortes named *California.*

Massachusetts is the Indian for "The country around the great hills."

Connecticut, from the Indian Quon-ch-ta-Cut, signifying "Long River."

Maryland, after Henrietta Maria, Queen of Charles the First, of England.

New York was named by the Duke of York.

Pennsylvania means "Penn's woods," and was so called after William Penn, its original owner.

Delaware after Lord De La Ware

New Jersey, so called in honor of Sir George Carteret, who was Governor of the Island of Jersey, in the British Channel

Maine was called after the province of Maine in France, in compliment of Queen Henrietta of England, who owned that province

Vermont, from the French word *Vert Mont*, signifying Green Mountain.

New Hampshire, from Hampshire county in England. It was formerly called Laconia.

The little State of *Rhode Island* owes its name to the Island of Rhodes in the Mediterranean, which domain it is said to greatly resemble

Texas is the American word for the Mexican name by which all that section of the country was called before it was ceded to the United States.

POPULATION OF THE UNITED STATES.

STATES AND TERRITORIES	Total Population
Alabama	996 992
Arkansas	484 471
California	560,247
Connecticut	537 454
Delaware	125,015
Florida	187,748
Georgia	1 184,109
Illinois	2,539,891
Indiana	1,680 637
Iowa	1,191 792
Kansas	364,399
Kentucky	1 321,011
Louisiana	726 915
Maine	626 915
Maryland	780 894
Massachusetts	1,457 351
Michigan	1,184 059
Minnesota	439 706
Mississippi	827,922
Missouri	1,721 295
Nebraska	122 993
Nevada	42 491
New Hampshire	318 300
New Jersey	906 096
New York	4 382 759
North Carolina	1 071,361
Ohio	2,665,260
Oregon	90,923
Pennsylvania	3,521,791
Rhode Island	217 353
South Carolina	705 606
Tennessee	1,275,520
Texas	818 579
Vermont	330,551
Virginia	1 225 163
West Virginia	442,014
Wisconsin	1,054,670
Total States	**38 113,253**
Arizona	9,658
Colorado	39 864
Dakota	14 181
District of Columbia	131 700
Idaho	14 999
Montana	20,595
New Mexico	91,874
Utah	86 786
Washington	23,955
Wyoming	9,118
Total Territories	**412 730**
Total United States	**38 555,983**

POPULATION OF FIFTY PRINCIPAL CITIES.

CITIES	Aggregate Population
New York N Y	942 292
Philadelphia, Pa	674,022
Brooklyn, N Y	396,099
St Louis, Mo	310 864
Chicago, Ill	298,977
Baltimore, Md	267,354
Boston, Mass	250 526
Cincinnati, Ohio	216 239
New Orleans, La	191,418
San Francisco, Cal	149 473
Buffalo N Y	117 714
Washington D C	109,199
Newark N J	105 059
Louisville, Ky	100 753
Cleveland, Ohio	92 829
Pittsburg Pa	86 076
Jersey City, N J	82 546
Detroit, Mich	79,577
Milwaukee, Wis	71,440
Albany, N Y	69 422
Providence, R I	68 904
Rochester, N Y	62 386
Allegheny, Pa	53 180
Richmond, Va	51 038
New Haven, Conn	50 840
Charleston S C	48 956
Indianapolis, Ind	48 244
Troy, N Y	46 465
Syracuse, N Y	43 051
Worcester, Mass	41 105
Lowell Mass	40 928
Memphis, Tenn	40 226
Cambridge, Mass	39 634
Hartford, Conn	37,180
Scranton, Pa	35 092
Reading, Pa	33,930
Paterson, N J	33 579
Kansas City, Mo	32,260
Mobile, Ala	32 034
Toledo, Ohio	31,584
Portland, Me	31,413
Columbus Ohio	31,274
Wilmington Del	30 811
Dayton Ohio	30,473
Lawrence Mass	28,921
Utica, N Y	28,804
Charlestown, Mass	28,323
Savannah, Ga	28,235
Lynn Mass	28,233
Fall River, Mass	26,766

POPULATION OF THE UNITED STATES.

STATES AND TERRITORIES.	Area in square Miles.	POPULATION. 1870.	1875.	Miles R. R. 1872.	STATES AND TERRITORIES.	Area in square Miles.	POPULATION. 1870.	1875.	Miles R. R. 1872.
States.					*States.*				
Alabama	50,722	996,992	....	1,671	Pennsylvania	46,000	3,521,791	....	5,113
Arkansas	52,198	484,471	....	25	Rhode Island	1,306	217,353	258,226	136
California	188,981	560,247	....	1,013	South Carolina	29,385	705,606	925,145	1,201
Connecticut	4,674	537,454	....	820	Tennessee	45,600	1,258,520	....	1,520
Delaware	2,120	125,015	....	227	Texas	237,504	818,579	....	865
Florida	59,268	187,748	....	466	Vermont	10,212	330,551	....	675
Georgia	58,000	1,184,109	....	2,108	Virginia	40,904	1,225,163	....	1,490
Illinois	55,410	2,539,891	....	5,904	West Virginia	23,000	442,014	....	485
Indiana	33,809	1,680,637	....	3,529	Wisconsin	53,924	1,054,670	1,236,729	1,725
Iowa	55,045	1,191,792	1,350,544	3,160					
Kansas	81,318	364,399	528,349	1,760	*Total States*	1,950,171	38,113,253	....	59,587
Kentucky	37,680	1,321,011	....	1,123					
Louisiana	41,346	726,915	857,039	539	*Territories.*				
Maine	31,776	626,915	....	871	Arizona	113,916	9,658	....	....
Maryland	11,184	780,894	....	820	Colorado	104,500	39,864	....	392
Massachusetts	7,800	1,457,351	1,651,912	1,606	Dakota	147,490	14,181	....	*
Michigan*	56,451	1,184,059	1,334,031	2,235	Dist. of Columbia	60	131,700	....	*
Minnesota	83,531	439,706	598,429	1,612	Idaho	90,932	11,999	....	
Mississippi	47,156	827,922	....	990	Montana	143,776	20,595	....	
Missouri	65,350	1,721,295	....	2,580	New Mexico	121,201	91,874	....	
Nebraska	75,995	123,993	246,280	828	Utah	80,056	86,786	....	375
Nevada	112,090	42,491	52,540	593	Washington	69,944	23,955	....	
New Hampshire	9,280	318,300	....	790	Wyoming	93,107	9,118	....	498
New Jersey	8,320	906,096	1,026,502	1,265					
New York	47,000	4,382,759	4,705,208	4,470	*Total Territories.*	965,032	442,730	....	1,265
North Carolina	50,704	1,071,361	....	1,190					
Ohio	39,964	2,665,260	....	3,740					
Oregon	95,244	90,923	....	159	Aggregate of U. S.	2,915,203	38,555,983	....	60,852

* Last Census of Michigan taken in 1874. * Included in the Railroad Mileage of Maryland.

PRINCIPAL COUNTRIES OF THE WORLD;

POPULATION AND AREA.

COUNTRIES.	Population.	Date of Census.	Area in Square Miles.	Inhabitants to Square Mile.	CAPITALS.	Population.
China	446,500,000	1871	3,741,846	119.3	Pekin	1,648,800
British Empire	226,817,108	1871	4,677,432	48.6	London	3,251,800
Russia	81,925,490	1871	8,002,778	10.2	St. Petersburg	667,000
United States with Alaska	38,925,600	1870	2,603,884	7.78	Washington	109,199
France	36,469,800	1866	204,091	178.7	Paris	1,825,300
Austria and Hungary	35,904,400	1869	240,348	149.4	Vienna	833,900
Japan	34,785,300	1869	149,399	232.8	Yeddo	1,554,900
Great Britain and Ireland	31,817,100	1871	121,315	262.3	London	3,251,800
German Empire	29,906,092	1871	160,207	187.	Berlin	825,400
Italy	27,439,921	1871	118,847	230.9	Rome	244,484
Spain	16,642,000	1867	195,775	85.	Madrid	332,000
Brazil	10,004,000		3,253,029	3.07	Rio Janeiro	420,000
Turkey	16,463,000		672,621	24.4	Constantinople	1,075,000
Mexico	9,174,000	1869	761,526		Mexico	210,300
Sweden and Norway	5,941,500	1870	292,871	20.	Stockholm	136,900
Persia	5,000,000	1870	635,964	7.8	Teheran	120,000
Belgium	5,021,300	1869	11,373	441.5	Brussels	314,100
Bavaria	4,861,400	1871	29,292	165.9	Munich	169,500
Portugal	3,995,200	1868	34,494	115.8	Lisbon	224,063
Holland	3,688,300	1870	12,680	290.9	Hague	90,100
New Grenada	3,000,000	1870	357,157	8.4	Bogota	45,000
Chili	2,000,000	1869	132,616	15.1	Santiago	115,400
Switzerland	2,669,106	1870	15,992	166.9	Berne	36,000
Peru	2,500,000	1871	471,838	5.3	Lima	160,100
Bolivia	2,000,000		497,321	4.	Chuquisaca	25,000
Argentine Republic	1,812,000	1869	871,848	2.1	Buenos Ayres	177,800
Wurtemburg	1,818,500	1871	7,533	241.4	Stuttgart	91,600
Denmark	1,784,700	1870	14,753	120.9	Copenhagen	162,042
Venezuela	1,500,000		368,298	4.2	Caraccas	47,000
Baden	1,461,400	1871	5,912	247.	Carlsruhe	36,600
Greece	1,457,900	1870	19,353	75.3	Athens	43,400
Guatemala	1,180,000	1871	40,879	28.9	Guatemala	40,000
Ecuador	1,300,000		218,928	5.9	Quito	70,000
Paraguay	1,000,000	1871	63,787	15.6	Asuncion	48,000
Hesse	823,138		2,969	277.	Darmstadt	30,000
Liberia	718,000	1871	9,576	74.9	Monrovia	3,000
San Salvador	600,000	1871	7,335	81.5	Sal Salvador	15,000
Hayti	572,000		10,205	56.	Port au Prince	20,000
Nicaragua	350,000	1871	58,171	6.	Managua	10,000
Uruguay	300,000	1871	66,722	6.5	Monte Video	44,500
Honduras	350,000	1871	47,092		Comayagua	12,000
San Domingo			17,887		San Domingo	20,000
Costa Rie			21,495		San Jose	2,000
Hawaii			7,634		Honolulu	7,634

ABSTRACT OF IOWA STATE LAWS.

BILLS OF EXCHANGE AND PROMISSORY NOTES.

Upon negotiable bills, and notes payable in this State, grace shall be allowed according to the law merchant. All the above mentioned paper falling due on Sunday. New Year's Day, the Fourth of July, Christmas, or any day appointed or recommended by the President of the United States or the Governor of the State, as a day of fast or thanksgiving. shall be deemed as due on the day previous. No defense can be made against a negotiable instrument (assigned before due) in the hands of the assignee without notice, except fraud was used in obtaining the same. To hold an indorser, due diligence must be used by suit against the maker or his representative. Notes payable to person named or to order, in order to absolutely transfer title, must be indorsed by the payee. Notes payable to bearer may be transferred by delivery, and when so payable. every indorser thereon is held as a guarantor of payment, unless otherwise expressed

In computing interest or discount on negotiable instruments, a month shall be considered a calendar month or twelfth of a year, and for less than a month. a day shall be figured a thirtieth part of a month. Notes only bear interest when so expressed, but after due, they draw the legal interest, even if not stated

INTEREST

The legal rate of interest is six per cent. Parties may agree, in writing. on a rate not exceeding ten per cent. If a rate of interest greater than ten per cent is contracted for, it works a forfeiture of ten per cent. to the school fund, and only the principal sum can be recovered

DESCENT

The personal property of the deceased (except (1) that necessary for payment of debts and expenses of administration. (2) property set apart to widow, as exempt from execution, (3) allowance by court, if necessary, of twelve months' support to widow, and to children under fifteen years of age), including life insurance, descends as does real estate

One-third in value (absolutely) of all estates in real property, possessed by husband at any time during marriage, which have not been sold on execution or other judicial sale and to which the wife has made no relinquishment of her right, shall be set apart as her property in fee simple, if she survive him.

2\`\`)

The same share shall be set apart to the surviving husband of a deceased wife

The widow's share cannot be affected by any will of her husband's, unless she consents, in writing thereto, within six months after notice to her of provisions of the will.

The provisions of the statutes of descent apply alike to surviving husband or surviving wife.

Subject to the above, the remaining estate of which the decedent died siezed, shall in absence of other arrangements by will, descend

First. To his or her children and their descendants in equal parts, the descendants of the deceased child or grandchild taking the share of their deceased parents in equal shares among them

Second. Where there is no child, nor descendant of such child, and no widow or surviving husband, then to the parents of the deceased in equal parts; the surviving parent, if either be dead, taking the whole, and if there is no parent living, then to the brothers and sisters of the intestate and their descendants

Third When there is a widow or surviving husband, and no child or children, or descendants of the same, then one-half of the estate shall descend to such widow or surviving husband, absolutely, and the other half of the estate shall descend as in other cases where there is no widow or surviving husband, or child or children, or descendants of the same

Fourth If there is no child, parent, brother or sister, or descendants of either of them, then to wife of intestate, or to her heirs, if dead, according to like rules

Fifth If any intestate leaves no child parent, brother or sister, or descendants of either of them, and no widow or surviving husband and no child, parent, brother or sister (or descendant of either of them) of such widow or surviving husband, it shall escheat to the State.

WILLS AND ESTATES OF DECEASED PERSONS

No exact form of words are necessary in order to make a will good at law. Every male person of the age of twenty-one years, and every female of the age of eighteen years, of sound mind and memory, can make a valid will, it must be in writing, signed by the testator, or by some one in his or her presence, and by his or her express direction, and attested by two or more competent witnesses   Care should be taken that the witnesses are not interested in the will Inventory to be made by executor or administrator within fifteen days from date of letters testamentary or of administration.   Executors' and administrators' compensation on amount of personal estate distributed, and for proceeds of sale of real estate, five per cent for first one thousand dollars, two and one-half per cent on overplus up to five thousand dollars, and one per cent on overplus above five thousand dollars, with such additional allowance as shall be reasonable for extra services

Within *ten days* after the receipt of letters of administration, the executor or administrator shall give such *notice of appointment* as the court or clerk shall direct

Claims (other than preferred) must be filed *within one year* thereafter, are forever barred unless the case is pending in the District or Supreme Court, or unless peculiar circumstances entitle the claimant to equitable relief

Claims are *classed* and *payable* in the following order:
1. Expenses of administration
2 Expenses of last sickness and funeral.
3 Allowance to widow and children, if made by the court.
4. Debts preferred under laws of the United States.
5 Public rates and taxes
6. Claims filed within six months after the *first publication* of the notice given by the executors of their appointment.
7 All other debts.
8 Legacies.

The *award*, or property which must be *set apart to the widow, in her own right*, by the executor, includes all personal property which, in the hands of the deceased, as head of a family, would have been *exempt from execution*.

TAXES

The owners of personal property, on the first day of January of each year, and the owners of real property on the first day of November of each year, *are liable* for the taxes thereon.

The following property is exempt from taxation, viz:

1. The property of the United States and of this State, including university, agricultural, college and school lands and all property leased to the State; property of a county, township, city, incorporated town or school district when devoted entirely to the public use and not held for pecuniary profit, public grounds, including all places for the burial of the dead; fire engines and all implements for extinguishing fires, with the grounds used exclusively for their buildings and for the meetings of the fire companies, all public libraries, grounds and buildings of literary, scientific, benevolent, agricultural and religious institutions, and societies devoted solely to the appropriate objects of these institutions, not exceeding 640 acres in extent, and not leased or otherwise used with a view of pecuniary profit; and all property leased to agricultural, charitable institutions and benevolent societies, and so devoted during the term of such lease, *provided*, that all deeds, by which such property is held, shall be duly filed for record before the property therein described shall be omitted from the assessment

2 The books, papers and apparatus belonging to the above institutions; used solely for the purposes above contemplated, and the like property of students in any such institution, used for their education

3. Money and credits belonging exclusively to such institutions and devoted solely to sustaining them, but not exceeding in amount or income the sum prescribed by their charter

4. Animals not hereafter specified, the wool shorn from sheep, belonging to the person giving the list, his farm produce harvested within one year previous to the listing, private libraries not exceeding three hundred dollars in value; family pictures, kitchen furniture, beds and bedding requisite for each family, all wearing apparel in actual use and all food provided for the family; but no person from whom a compensation for board or lodging is received or expected, is to be considered a member of the family within the intent of this clause.

5 The polls or estates or both of persons who, by reason of infirmity, may, in the opinion of the Assessor, be unable to contribute to the public

revenue; such opinion and the fact upon which it is based being in all cases reported to the Board of Equalization by the Assessor or any other person, and subject to reversal by them

6. The farming utensils of any person who makes his livelihood by farming, and the tools of any mechanic, not in either case to exceed three hundred dollars in value

7. Government lands entered or located or lands purchased from this State, should not be taxed for the year in which the entry, location or purchase is made

There is also a suitable exemption, in amount, for planting fruit trees or forest trees or hedges

Where buildings are destroyed by fire, tornado or other unavoidable casualty, after being assessed for the year, the Board of Supervisors may rebate taxes for that year on the property destroyed, *if same has not been sold for taxes, and if said taxes have not been delinquent for thirty days* at the time of destruction of the property, and the rebate shall be allowed for such loss only as is not covered by insurance

All other property is subject to taxation   Every inhabitant of full age and sound mind shall assist the Assessor in listing all taxable property of which he is the owner, or which he controls or manages, either as agent, guardian, father, husband, trustee, executor, accounting officer, partner, mortgagor or lessor, mortgagee or lessee

Road beds of railway corporations shall not be assessed to owners of adjacent property, but shall be considered the property of the companies for purposes of taxation, nor shall real estate used as a public highway be assessed and taxed as part of adjacent lands whence the same was taken for such public purpose.

The property of railway, telegraph and express companies shall be listed and assessed for taxation as the property of an individual would be listed and assessed for taxation.   Collection of taxes made as in the case of an individual.

The Township Board of Equalization shall meet first Monday in April of each year   Appeal lies to the Circuit Court.

The County Board of Equalization (the Board of Supervisors) meet at their regular session in June of each year   Appeal lies to the Circuit Court

Taxes become delinquent February 1st of each year, payable, without interest or penalty, at any time before March 1st of each year

Tax sale is held on first Monday in October of each year

Redemption may be made at any time within three years after date of sale, by paying to the County Auditor the *amount* of sale, and *twenty per centum* of such amount immediately added as *penalty, with ten per cent interest per annum* on the whole amount thus made from the day of sale, and also all subsequent taxes, interest and costs paid by purchaser after March 1st of each year, and a similar *penalty* of twenty per centum added as before, with ten per cent *interest* as before

If *notice* has been given, by purchaser of the date at which the redemption is limited, the cost of same is added to the redemption money.   Ninety days' notice is required, by the statute, to be published by the purchaser or holder of certificate, to terminate right of redemption

JURISDICTION OF COURTS
DISTRICT COURTS

have jurisdiction, general and original, both civil and criminal, except in such cases where Circuit Courts have exclusive jurisdiction. District Courts have *exclusive supervision* over courts of Justices of the Peace and Magistrates, in criminal matters, on appeal and writs of error.

CIRCUIT COURTS

have jurisdiction, general and original, with the District Courts, in all civil actions and special proceedings, and *exclusive jurisdiction* in all appeals and writs of error from inferior courts, in civil matters. And *exclusive jurisdiction* in matters of estates and general probate business

JUSTICES OF THE PEACE

have jurisdiction in civil matters where $100 or less is involved   By consent of parties, the jurisdiction may be extended to an amount not exceeding $300. They have jurisdiction to try and determine all public offense less than felony, committed within their respective counties, in which *the fine*, by law, does not exceed *$100* or *the imprisonment thirty days*

LIMITATION OF ACTIONS

Action for injuries to the person or reputation, for a statute penalty, and to enforce a mechanics' lien, must be brought in two (2) years

Those against a public officer within three (3) years.

Those founded on unwritten contracts; for injuries to property, for relief on the ground of fraud, and all other actions not otherwise provided for, within five (5) years.

Those founded on written contracts, on judgments of any court (except those provided for in next section), and for the recovery of real property, within ten (10) years

Those founded on judgment of any court of record in the United States, within twenty (20) years.

All above limits, except those for penalties and forfeitures, are extended in favor of minors and insane persons, until one year after the disability is removed —time during which defendant is a non-resident of the State shall not be included in computing any of the above periods

Actions for the recovery of real property, sold for non-payment of taxes, must be brought within five years after the Treasurer's Deed is executed and recorded, except where a minor or convict or insane person is the owner, and they shall be allowed five years after disability is removed, in which to bring action

JURORS

All qualified electors of the State, of good moral character, sound judgment, and in full possession of the senses of hearing and seeing, are competent jurors in their respective counties.

United States officers, practicing attorneys, physicians and clergymen, acting professors or teachers in institutions of learning, and persons enrolled by bodily infirmity or over sixty-five years of age, are exempt from liability to act as jurors.

Any person may be excused from serving on a jury when his own interests or the public's will be materially injured by his attendance, or when the state of his health or the death, or sickness of his family requires his absence

CAPITAL PUNISHMENT

was restored by the Seventeenth General Assembly, making it optional with the jury to inflict it or not.

A MARRIED WOMAN

may convey or incumber real estate, or interest therein, belonging to her; may control the same or contract with reference thereto, as other persons may convey, encumber, control or contract.

She may own, acquire, hold, convey and devise property, as her husband may.

Her husband is not liable for civil injuries committed by her.

She may convey property to her husband, and he may convey to her.

She may constitute her husband her attorney in fact.

EXEMPTIONS FROM EXECUTION

A resident of the State and head of a family may hold the following property exempt from execution: All wearing apparel of himself and family kept for actual use and suitable to the condition, and the trunks or other receptacles necessary to contain the same; one musket or rifle and shot-gun, all private libraries, family Bibles, portraits, pictures, musical instruments, and paintings not kept for the purpose of sale; a seat or pew occupied by the debtor or his family in any house of public worship; an interest in a public or private burying ground not exceeding one acre: two cows and a calf; one horse. unless a horse is exempt as hereinafter provided; fifty sheep and the wool therefrom, and the materials manufactured from said wool; six stands of bees, five hogs and all pigs under six months; the necessary food for exempted animals for six months; all flax raised from one acre of ground, and manufactures therefrom, one bedstead and necessary bedding for every two in the family; all cloth manufactured by the defendant not exceeding one hundred yards, household and kitchen furniture not exceeding two hundred dollars in value, all spinning wheels and looms; one sewing machine and other instruments of domestic labor kept for actual use, the necessary provisions and fuel for the use of the family for six months; the proper tools. instruments, or books of the debtor, if a farmer, mechanic, surveyor, clergyman, lawyer, physician, teacher or professor; the horse or the team, consisting of not more than two horses or mules, or two yokes of cattle, and the wagon or other vehicle, with the proper harness or tackle, by the use of which the debtor, if a physician, public officer, farmer, teamster or other laborer, habitually earns his living, and to the debtor, if a printer, there shall also be exempt a printing press and the types, furniture and material necessary for the use of such printing press and a newspaper office to the value of twelve hundred dollars, the earnings of such debtor, or those of his family, at any time within ninety days next preceding the levy

Persons unmarried and not the head of a family and non-residents, have exempt their own ordinary wearing apparel and trunks to contain the same

There is also exempt, to a head of a family, a homestead, not exceeding forty acres, or, if inside city limits, one-half acre with improvements, value not limited. The homestead is liable for all debts contracted prior to its acquisition as such, and is subject to mechanics' liens for work or material furnished for the same

An article, otherwise exempt, is liable, on execution, for the purchase money thereof

Where a debtor, if a head of a family, has started to leave the State, he shall have exempt only the ordinary wearing apparel of himself and family, and other property in addition, as he may select, in all not exceeding seventy-five dollars in value.

A policy of life insurance shall inure to the separate use of the husband or wife and children, entirely independent of his or her creditors.

ESTRAYS.

An unbroken animal shall not be taken up as an estray between May 1st and November 1st, of each year, unless the same be found within the lawful enclosure of a householder, who alone can take up such animal, unless some other person gives him notice of the fact of such animal coming on his place, and if he fails, within five days thereafter, to take up such estray any other householder of the township may take up such estray and proceed with it as if taken on his own premises, provided he shall prove to the Justice of the Peace such notice, and shall make affidavit where such estray was taken up.

Any swine, sheep, goat, horse, neat cattle or other animal distrained (for damage done to one's enclosure), when the owner is not known, shall be treated as an estray.

Within five days after taking up an estray, notice, containing a full description thereof, shall be posted up in three of the most public places in the township; and in ten days, the person taking up such estray shall go before a Justice of the Peace in the township and make oath as to where such estray was taken up and that the marks or brands have not been altered, to his knowledge. The estray shall then be appraised, by order of the Justice, and the appraisement, description of the size, age, color, sex, marks and brands of the estray shall be entered by the Justice in a book kept for that purpose and he shall, within ten days thereafter, send a certified copy thereof to the County Auditor.

When the appraised value of an estray does not exceed five dollars, the Justice need not proceed further than to enter the description of the estray on his book, and if no owner appears within six months, the property shall vest in the finder, if he has complied with the law and paid all costs

Where appraised value of estray exceeds five and is less than ten dollars, if no owner appears in nine months, the finder has the property if he has complied with the law and paid costs.

An estray, legally taken up, may be used or worked with care and moderation

If any person unlawfully take up an estray, or take up an estray and fail to comply with the law regarding estrays, or use or work it contrary to above, or work it before having it appraised, or keep such estray out of the county more than five days at one time, before acquiring ownership, such offender shall forfeit to the county twenty dollars, and the owner may recover double damages with costs.

If the owner of any estray fail to claim and prove his title for one year after the taking u   te title vests in the fi

But if the owner appear within eighteen months from the taking up, prove his ownership and pay all costs and expenses, the finder shall pay him the appraised value of such estray, or may, at his option, deliver up the estray.

WOLF SCALPS

A bounty of one dollar is paid for wolf scalps.

MARKS AND BRANDS

Any person may adopt his own mark or brand for his domestic animals, and have a description thereof recorded by the Township Clerk

No person shall adopt the recorded mark or brand of any other person residing in his township

DAMAGES FROM TRESPASS

When any person's lands are enclosed by a *lawful* fence, the owner of any domestic animal injuring said lands is liable for the damages, and the damages may be recovered by suit against the owner, or may be made by distraining the animals doing the damage, and if the party injured elects to recover by action against the owner, no appraisement need be made by the Trustees, as in case of distraint

When trespassing animals are distrained within twenty-four hours, Sunday not included, the party injured shall notify the owner of said animals, if known; and if the owner fails to satisfy the party within twenty-four hours thereafter, the party shall have the township Trustees assess the damage, and notice shall be posted up in three conspicuous places in the township, that the stock or part thereof shall, on *the tenth day after posting the notice*, between the hours of 1 and 3 P. M , be sold to the highest bidder, to satisfy said damages, with costs

Appeal lies, within twenty days, from the action of the Trustees to the Circuit Court

Where stock is restrained, by police regulation or by law, from running at large, any person injured in his improved or cultivated lands by any domestic animal, may, by action against the owner of such animal, or by distraining such animal, recover his damages, whether the lands whereon the injury was done were inclosed by a lawful fence or not.

FENCES

A lawful fence is fifty-four inches high, made of rails, wire or boards, with posts not more than ten feet apart where rails are used, and eight feet where boards are used, substantially built and kept in good repair , or any other fence which, in the opinion of the Fence Viewers, shall be declared a lawful fence—provided the lower rail, wire or board be not more that twenty nor less than sixteen inches from the ground.

The respective owners of lands enclosed with fences shall maintain partition fences between their own and next adjoining enclosure so long as they improve them in equal shares, unless otherwise agreed between them.

If any party neglect to maintain such partition fence as he should maintain, the Fence Viewers the township Trustees, upon complaint of aggrieved party, may, upon due notice to both parties examine the fence and if found insufficient, notify the delinquent party, *in writing*, to repair or re-build the same within such time as they judge reasonable.

If the fence be not repaired or rebuilt accordingly, the complainant may do so, and the same being adjudged sufficient by the Fence Viewers, and the value thereof, with their fees, being ascertained and certified under their hands, the complainant may demand of the delinquent the sum so ascertained, and if the same be not paid in one month after demand, may recover it with one per cent a month interest, by action

In case of disputes, the Fence Viewers may decide as to who shall erect or maintain partition fences, and in what time the same shall be done ; and in case any party neglect to maintain or erect such part as may be assigned to him, the aggrieved party may erect and maintain the same, and recover double damages.

No person, not wishing his land inclosed, and not using it otherwise than in common, shall be compelled to maintain any partition fence, but when he uses or incloses his land otherwise than in common, he shall contribute to the partition fences

Where parties have had their lands inclosed in common, and one of the owners desires to occupy his separate and apart from the other, and the other refuses to divide the line or build a sufficient fence on the line when divided the Fence Viewers may divide and assign, and upon neglect of the other to build as ordered by the Viewers, the one may build the other's part and recover as above

And when one incloses land which has lain uninclosed, he must pay for one-half of each partition fence between himself and his neighbors

Where one desires to lay not less than twenty feet of his lands, adjoining his neighbor, out to the public to be used in common, he must give his neighbor six months' notice thereof

Where a fence has been built on the land of another through mistake, the owner may enter upon such premises and remove his fence and material within six months after the division line has been ascertained   Where the material to build such a fence has been taken from the land on which it was built, then, before it can be removed, the person claiming must first pay for such material to the owner of the land from which it was taken, nor shall such a fence be removed at a time when the removal will throw open or expose the crops of the other party, a reasonable time must be given beyond the six months to remove crops

MECHANICS' LIENS

Every mechanic, or other person who shall do any labor upon, or furnish any materials, machinery or fixtures for any building, erection or other improvement upon land, including those engaged in the construction or repair of any work of internal improvement, by virtue of any contract with the owner his agent trustee, contractor, or sub-contractor, shall have a lien, on complying with the forms of law, upon the building or other improvement for his labor done or materials furnished

It would take too large a space to detail the manner in which a sub-contractor secures his lien. He should file, within thirty days after the last of the labor was performed or the last of the material shall have been furnished with the Clerk of the District Court a true account of the amount of the claim, after allowing all credits setting forth the time when such material was furnished or labor performed, and when completed and containing a correct description of the property sought to be charged with the lien, and the whole verified by affidavit

A principal contractor must file such an affidavit within ninety days, as above

Ordinarily, there are so many points to be examined in order to secure a mechanics' lien, that it is much better, unless one is accustomed to managing such liens, to consult at once with an attorney

Remember that the proper time to file the claim is ninety days for a principal contractor, thirty days for a sub-contractor, as above, and that actions to enforce these liens must be commenced within two years, and the rest can much better be done with an attorney

ROADS AND BRIDGES.

Persons meeting each other on the public highways, shall give one half of the same by turning to the right.   All persons failing to observe this rule shall be liable to pay all damages resulting therefrom, together with a fine, not exceeding five dollars.

The prosecution must be instituted on the complaint of the person wronged

Any person guilty of racing horses, or driving upon the public highway, in a manner likely to endanger the persons or the lives of others, shall, on conviction, be fined not exceeding one hundred dollars or imprisoned not exceeding thirty days.

It is a misdemeanor, without authority from the proper Road Supervisor, to break upon, plow or dig within the boundary lines of any public highway.

The money tax levied upon the property in each road district in each township (except the general Township Fund, set apart for purchasing tools, machinery and guide boards), whether collected by the Road Supervisor or County Treasurer, shall be expended for highway purposes in that district, and no part thereof shall be paid out or expended for the benefit of another district.

The Road Supervisor of each district, is bound to keep the roads and bridges therein, in as good condition as the funds at his disposal will permit, to put guide boards at cross roads and forks of highways in his district, and when notified in writing that any portion of the public highway, or any bridge is unsafe, must in a reasonable time repair the same, and for this purpose may call out any or all the able bodied men in the district, but not more than two days at one time, without their consent.

Also, when notified in writing, of the growth of any Canada thistles upon vacant or non-resident lands or lots, within his district, the owner, lessee or agent thereof being unknown, shall cause the same to be destroyed

Bridges when erected or maintained by the public, are parts of the highway, and must not be less than sixteen feet wide

A penalty is imposed upon any one who rides or drives faster than a walk across any such bridge

The manner of establishing, vacating or altering roads, etc., is so well known to all township officers, that it is sufficient here to say that the first step is by petition, filed in the Auditor's office, addressed in substance as follows:

The Board of Supervisors of ——— County   The undersigned asks that a highway, commencing at ——— and running thence ——— and terminating at ——— be established, vacated or altered (as the case may be.)

When the petition is filed, all necessary and succeeding steps will be shown and explained to the petitioners by the Auditor

ADOPTION OF CHILDREN.

Any person competent to make a will can adopt as his own the minor child of another   The consent of both parents, if living and not divorced or separated, and if divorced or separated, or if unmarried, the consent of the parent lawfully having the custody of the child ; or if either parent is dead, then the consent of the survivor, or if both parents be dead, or the child have been and remain abandoned by them, then the consent of the Mayor of the city where the child is living, or if not in the city, then of the Clerk of the Circuit Court of the county shall be given to such adoption by an instrument in writing, signed by party or parties consenting, and stating the names of the parties, if known. the name of the child, if known, the name of the person adopting such child, and the residence of all, if known, and declaring the name by which the child is thereafter to be called and known, and stating, also, that such child is given to the person adopting, for the purpose of adoption as his own child

The person adopting shall also sign said instrument, and all the parties shall acknowledge the same in the manner that deeds conveying lands shall be acknowledged

The instrument shall be recorded in the office of the County Recorder.

SURVEYORS AND SURVEYS.

There is in every county elected a Surveyor known as County Surveyor, who has power to appoint deputies, for whose official acts he is responsible   It is the duty of the County Surveyor, either by himself or his Deputy, to make all surveys that he may be called upon to make within his county as soon as may be after application is made.   The necessary chainmen and other assistance must be employed by the person requiring the same to be done, and to be by him paid, unless otherwise agreed , but the chainmen must be disinterested persons and approved by the Surveyor and sworn by him to measure justly and impartially   Previous to any survey, he shall furnish himself with a copy of the field notes of the original survey of the same land, if there be any in the office of the County Auditor, and his survey shall be made in accordance therewith

Their fees are three dollars per day.   For certified copies of field notes, twenty-five cents

SUPPORT OF POOR

The father, mother and children of any poor person who has applied for aid, and who is unable to maintain himself by work, shall jointly or severally, maintain such poor person in such manner as may be approved by the Township Trustees

In the absence or inability of nearer relatives, the same liability shall extend to the grandparents, if of ability without personal labor, and to the male grandchildren who are of ability, by personal labor or otherwise

The Township Trustees may, upon the failure of such relatives to maintain a poor person, who has made application for relief, apply to the Circuit Court for an order to compel the same

Upon ten days' notice, in writing, to the parties sought to be charged, a hearing may be had, and an order made for entire or partial support of the poor person

Appeal may be taken from such judgment as from other judgments of the Circuit Court

When any person, having any estate, abandons either children, wife or husband, leaving them chargeable, or likely to become chargeable, upon the public for support, upon proof of above fact, an order may be had from the Clerk of the Circuit Court, or Judge, authorizing the Trustees or the Sheriff to take into possession such estate.

The Court may direct such personal estate to be sold, to be applied, as well as the rents and profits of the real estate, if any, to the support of children, wife or husband

If the party against whom the order is issued return and support the person abandoned, or give security for the same, the order shall be discharged, and the property taken returned.

The mode of relief for the poor, through the action of the Township Trustees, or the action of the Board of Supervisors, is so well known to every township officer, and the circumstances attending applications for relief are so varied, that it need now only be said that it is the duty of each county to provide for its poor, no matter at what place they may be

LANDLORD AND TENANT.

A tenant giving notice to quit demised premises at a time named, and afterward holding over, and a tenant or his assignee willfully holding over the premises after the term, and after notice to quit, shall pay double rent

Any person in possession of real property, with the assent of the owner, is presumed to be a tenant at will until the contrary is shown.

Thirty days' notice, in writing, is necessary to be given by either party before he can terminate a tenancy at will; but when, in any case, a rent is reserved payable at intervals of less than thirty days, the length of notice need not be greater than such interval between the days of payment. In case of tenants occupying and cultivating farms, the notice must fix the termination of the tenancy to take place on the 1st day of March, except in cases of field tenants or croppers, whose leases shall be held to expire when the crop is harvested, provided, that in case of a crop of corn, it shall not be later than the 1st day of December, unless otherwise agreed upon But when an express agreement is made, whether the same has been reduced to writing or not, the tenancy shall cease at the time agreed upon without notice.

But where an express agreement is made, whether reduced to writing or not, the tenancy shall cease at the time agreed upon, without notice.

If such tenant cannot be found in the county, the notices above required may be given to any sub-tenant or other person in possession of the premises; or, if the premises be vacant, by affixing the notice to the principal door of the building or in some conspicuous position on the land, if there be no building.

The landlord shall have a lien for his rent upon all the crops grown on the premises, and upon any other personal property of the tenant used on the premises during the term, and not exempt from execution, for the period of one year after a year's rent or the rent of a shorter period claimed falls due; but such lien shall not continue more than six months after the expiration of the term

The lien may be enforced by the commencement of an action, within the period above prescribed for the rent above, and the landlord is entitled to a writ of attachment, upon filing an affidavit that the action is commenced to reover rent accrued within one year previous thereto upon the premises described in the affidavit.

WEIGHTS AND MEASURES

Whenever any of the following articles shall be contracted for, or sold or delivered, and no special contract or agreement shall be made to the contrary, the weight per bushel shall be as follows, to-wit:

Apples, Peaches or Quinces,......	48	Sand	130
Cherries, Grapes, Currants or Gooseberries,	40	Sorghum Seed	30
Strawberries, Raspberries or Blackberries,	32	Broom Corn Seed	30
Osage Orange Seed ...	32	Buckwheat ..	52
Millet Seed .	45	Salt.	50
Stone Coal	80	Barley	48
Lime	80	Corn Meal..	48
Corn in the ear	70	Castor Beans.	46
Wheat	60	Timothy Seed	45
Potatoes.	60	Hemp Seed	44
Beans	60	Dried Peaches	33
Clover Seed	60	Oats .	33
Onions	57	Dried Apples	24
Shelled Corn	56	Bran	20
Rye	56	Blue Grass Seed	14
Flax Seed	56	Hungarian Grass Seed	45
Sweet Potatoes	46		

Penalty for giving less than the above standard is treble damages and costs and five dollars addition thereto as a fine.

DEFINITION OF COMMERCIAL TERMS.

$—— means dollars, being a contraction of U S , which was formerly placed before any denomination of money, and meant, as it means now, United States Currency

£—— means *pounds*, English money

@ stands for *at* or *to*; ℔ for *pounds*, and bbl for *barrels ;* ℔ for *per* or *by the.* Thus, Butter sells at 20@30c ℔ ℔, and Flour at $8@$12 ℔ bbl.

% for *per cent* , and # for *number*

May 1 Wheat sells at $1 20@$1.25, " seller June ' *Seller June* means that the person who sells the wheat has the privilege of delivering it at any time during the month of June.

Selling *short*, is contracting to deliver a certain amount of grain or stock, at a fixed price, within a certain length of time, when the seller has not the stock on hand It is for the interest of the person selling " short" to depress the market as much as possible, in order that he may buy and fill his contract at a profit. Hence the " shorts " are termed " bears."

Buying *long*, is to contract to purchase a certain amount of grain or shares of stock at a fixed price, deliverable within a stipulated time, expecting to make a profit by the rise in prices The " longs " are termed " bulls," as it is for their interest to ' operate " so as to " toss " the prices upward as much as possible

NOTES

Form of note is legal, worded in the simplest way, so that the amount and time of payment are mentioned

$100.   CHICAGO, Ill., Sept 15, 1876

Sixty days from date I promise to pay to E. F. Brown or order, one hundred dollars for value received   L D LOWRY.

A note to be payable in anything else than money needs only the facts substituted for money in the above form.

ORDERS

Orders should be worded simply, thus:

Mr. F. H COATS   CHICAGO, Sept. 15, 1876.
    Please pay to H. Budsall twenty-five dollars, and charge to
                                            F. D SILVA.

RECEIPTS

Receipts should always state when received and what for, thus:

$100   CHICAGO, Sept 15, 1876.
            Received of J. W Davis, one hundred dollars, for services rendered in grading his lot in Fort Madison, on account.
                                            THOMAS BRADY.

If receipt is in full, it should be so stated.

BILLS OF PURCHASE

W. N. MASON,   SALEM, Illinois, Sept. 18, 1876
                    Bought of A A. GRAHAM

4 Bushels of Seed Wheat, at $1 50 .. ..$6 00
2 Seamless Sacks   "   30   60
                                            ————
            Received payment, $6 60
                                    A A. GRAHAM.

CONFESSION OF JUDGMENT

$———   ———, Iowa, ———, 18—
        ——— after date — promises to pay to the order of ———, —— dollars, at ———, for value received, with interest at ten per cent. per annum after —— until paid Interest payable ——, and on interest not paid when due, interest at same rate and conditions

A failure to pay said interest, or any part thereof, within 20 days after due, shall cause the whole note to become due and collectable at once

If this note is sued, or judgment is confessed hereon, $—— shall be allowed as attorney fees

No —.   P O ———,   ———.

CONFESSION OF JUDGMENT

— vs. —. In —— Court of ——— County, Iowa, ———, of ——— County, Iowa. do hereby confess that —— justly indebted to ———, in the sum of —— dollars, and the further sum of $—— as attorney fees, with interest thereon at ten per cent. from ——, and — hereby confess judgment against —— as defendant in favor of said ——. for said sum of $——, and $—— as attorney fees, hereby authorizing the Clerk of the —— Court of said county to enter up judgment for said sum against —— with costs, and interest at 10 per cent. from ——, the interest to be paid ——

Said debt and judgment being for ——

It is especially agreed, however, That if this judgment is paid within twenty days after due, no attorney fees need be paid. And —— hereby sell, convey and release all right of homestead we now occupy in favor of said —— so far as this judgment is concerned, and agree that it shall be liable on execution for this judgment.

Dated ——, 18—   —— ——.
                                                   —— ——.

THE STATE OF IOWA, ⎱
—— County   ⎰

—— being duly sworn according to law, depose and say that the foregoing statement and Confession of Judgment was read over to ——, and that — understood the contents thereof, and that the statements contained therein are true, and that the sums therein mentioned are justly to become due said —— as aforesaid

                                                   —— ——

Sworn to and subscribed before me and in my presence by the said —— this —— day of ——, 18—.   —— ——, Notary Public.

ARTICLES OF AGREEMENT

An agreement is where one party promises to another to do a certain thing in a certain time for a stipulated sum. Good business men always reduce an agreement to writing, which nearly always saves misunderstandings and trouble. No particular form is necessary, but the facts must be clearly and explicitly stated, and there must, to make it valid, be a reasonable consideration.

GENERAL FORM OF AGREEMENT

THIS AGREEMENT, made the Second day of June, 1878, between John Jones, of Keokuk, County of Lee, State of Iowa, of the first part, and Thomas Whiteside, of the same place, of the second part—

WITNESSETH, that the said John Jones, in consideration of the agreement of the party of the second part, hereinafter contained, contracts and agrees to and with the said Thomas Whiteside, that he will deliver in good and marketable condition, at the Village of Melrose, Iowa, during the month of November, of this year, One Hundred Tons of Prairie Hay, in the following lots, and at the following specified times, namely, twenty-five tons by the seventh of November, twenty-five tons additional by the fourteenth of the month, twenty-five tons more by the twenty-first, and the entire one hundred tons to be all delivered by the thirtieth of November.

And the said Thomas Whiteside, in consideration of the prompt fulfillment of this contract on the part of the party of the first part, contracts and agrees with the said John Jones, to pay for said hay five dollars per ton for each ton as soon as delivered.

In case of failure of agreement by either of the parties hereto, it is hereby stipulated and agreed that the party so failing shall pay to the other, One Hundred dollars, as fixed and settled damages

In witness whereof, we have hereunto set our hands the day and year first above written
                                               JOHN JONES,
                                               THOMAS WHITESIDE

AGREEMENT WITH CLERK FOR SERVICES.

THIS AGREEMENT, made the first day of May, one thousand eight hundred and seventy-eight, between Reuben Stone, of Dubuque, County of Dubuque, State of Iowa, party of the first part, and George Barclay, of McGregor, County of Clayton, State of Iowa, party of the second part—

WITNESSETH, that said George Barclay agrees faithfully and diligently to work as clerk and salesman for the said Reuben Stone, for and during the space of one year from the date hereof, should both live such length of time, without absenting himself from his occupation; during which time he, the said Barclay, in the store of said Stone, of Dubuque, will carefully and honestly attend, doing and performing all duties as clerk and salesman aforesaid in accordance and in all respects as directed and desired by the said Stone

In consideration of which services, so to be rendered by the said Barclay, the said Stone agrees to pay to said Barclay the annual sum of one thousand dollars, payable in twelve equal monthly payments, each upon the last day of each month; provided that all dues for days of absence from business by said Barclay, shall be deducted from the sum otherwise by the agreement due and payable by the said Stone to the said Barclay

Witness our hands.   REUBEN STONE
                                               GEORGE BARCLAY

BILLS OF SALE.

A bill of sale is a written agreement to another party, for a consideration to convey his right and interest in the personal property   *The purchaser must take actual possession of the property, or the bill of sale must be acknowledged and recorded.*

COMMON FORM OF BILL OF SALE

KNOW ALL MEN by this instrument, that I, Louis Clay, of Burlington, Iowa, of the first part, for and in consideration of Five Hundred and Ten Dollars, to me paid by John Floyd, of the same place, of the second part, the receipt whereof is hereby acknowledged, have sold, and by this instrument do convey unto the said Floyd, party of the second part, his executors, administrators and assigns, my undivided half of ten acres of corn, now growing on the arm of Thomas Tyrell, in the town above mentioned, one pair of horses, sixteen sheep, and five cows, belonging to me and in my possession at the farm aforesaid, to have and to hold the same unto the party of the second part, his executors and assigns forever. And I do, for myself and legal representatives, agree with the said party of the second part, and his legal representatives, to warrant and defend the sale of the afore-mentioned property and chattels unto the said party of the second part, and his legal representatives, against all and every person whatsoever

In witness whereof I have hereunto affixed my hand this tenth day of October, one thousand eight hundred and seventy-six

                                               LOUIS CLAY.

NOTICE TO QUIT.

To John Wontpay.

You are hereby notified to quit the possession of the premises you now occupy to wit:

[*Insert Description*]

on or before thirty days from the date of this notice

Dated January 1, 1878   Landlord.

[*Reverse for Notice to Landlord.*]

GENERAL FORM OF WILL FOR REAL AND PERSONAL PROPERTY

I, Charles Mansfield, of the Town of Bellevue, County of Jackson, State of Iowa, being aware of the uncertainty of life, and in failing health, but of sound mind and memory, do make and declare this to be my last will and testament, in manner following, to-wit:

First I give, devise and bequeath unto my eldest son, Sidney H. Mansfield, the sum of Two Thousand Dollars, of bank stock, now in the Third National Bank, of Cincinnati, Ohio, and the farm owned by myself, in the Township of Iowa, consisting of one hundred and sixty acres, with all the houses, tenements and improvements thereunto belonging, to have and to hold unto my said son, his heirs and assigns, forever

Second I give, devise and bequeath to each of my two daughters, Anna Louise Mansfield and Ida Clara Mansfield, each Two Thousand Dollars in bank stock in the Third National Bank of Cincinnati, Ohio and also, each one quarter section of land, owned by myself, situated in the Township of Fairfield, and recorded in my name in the Recorder's office, in the county where such land is located The north one hundred and sixty acres of said half section is devised to my eldest daughter, Anna Louise

Third I give, devise and bequeath to my son, Frank Alfred Mansfield, five shares of railroad stock in the Baltimore & Ohio Railroad, and my one hundred and sixty acres of land, and saw-mill thereon, situated in Manistee, Michigan, with all the improvements and appurtenances thereunto belonging, which said real estate is recorded in my name, in the county where situated

Fourth I give to my wife, Victoria Elizabeth Mansfield, all my household furniture, goods, chattels and personal property, about my home, not hitherto disposed of, including Eight Thousand Dollars of bank stock in the Third National Bank of Cincinnati, Ohio, fifteen shares in the Baltimore & Ohio Railroad, and the free and unrestricted use, possession and benefit of the home farm so long as she may live, in lieu of dower, to which she is entitled by law —said farm being my present place of residence

Fifth. I bequeath to my invalid father, Elijah H. Mansfield, the income from rents of my store building at 145 Jackson street, Chicago, Illinois, during the term of his natural life Said building and land therewith to revert to my said sons and daughters in equal proportion, upon the demise of my said father

Sixth It is also my will and desire that at the death of my wife Victoria Elizabeth Mansfield or at any time when she may arrange to relinquish her life interest in the above mentioned homestead, the same may revert to my above named children, or to the lawful heirs of each

And lastly I nominate and appoint as the executors of this, my last will and testament, my wife, Victoria Elizabeth Mansfield, and my eldest son, Sidney H. Mansfield.

I further direct that my debts and necessary funeral expenses shall be paid from moneys now on deposit in the Savings Bank of Bellevue, the residue of such moneys to revert to my wife, Victoria Elizabeth Mansfield, for her use forever

In witness whereof, I Charles Mansfield, to this my last will and testament, have hereunto set my hand and seal, this fourth day of April, eighteen hundred and seventy-two.

CHARLES MANSFIELD

Signed, and declared by Charles Mansfield, as and for his last will and testment, in the presence of us, who, at his request, and in his presence, and in the presence of each other, have subscribed our names hereunto as witnesses thereof

PETER A SCHENCK, Dubuque, Iowa,
FRANK E. DENT, Bellevue, Iowa.

CODICIL

Whereas I, Charles Mansfield, did, on the fourth day of April, one thousand eight hundred and seventy-two, make my last will and testament, I do now, by this writing, add this codicil to my said will, to be taken as a part thereof.

Whereas, by the dispensation of Providence, my daughter, Anna Louise, has deceased, November fifth, eighteen hundred and seventy-three, and whereas, a son has been born to me, which son is now christened Richard Albert Mansfield, I give and bequeath unto him my gold watch, and all right interest and title in lands and bank stock and chattels bequeathed to my deceased daughter, Anna Louise, in the body of this will

In witness whereof, I hereunto place my hand and seal, this tenth day of March, eighteen hundred and seventy five   CHARLES MANSFIELD

Signed, sealed, published and declared to us by the testator, Charles Mansfield, as and for a codicil to be annexed to his last will and testament. And we, at his request, and in his presence, and in the presence of each other, have subscribed our names as witnesses thereto, at the date hereof.

FRANK E DENT, Bellevue. Iowa,
JOHN C SHAY, Bellevue, Iowa.

(Form No 1)

SATISFACTION OF MORTGAGE.

STATE OF IOWA, }
  —— County, } ss

I, ——, of the County of ——, State of Iowa, do hereby acknowledge that a certain Indenture of ——, bearing date the —— day of ——, A. D 18—, made and executed by —— and ——, his wife, to said —— on the following described Real Estate in the County of —— and State of Iowa, to-wit: (here insert description) and filed for record in the office of the Recorder of the County of —— and State of Iowa on the —— day of ——,

A. D 18—, at —— o'clock   M.; and recorded in Book —— of Mortgage Records, on page ——, is redeemed, paid off, satisfied and discharged in full ——. [SEAL.]

STATE OF IOWA, ⎫
—— County,   ⎬ ss.
                     ⎭

Be it Remembered, That on this —— day of ——, A D. 18—, before me the undersigned, a —— in and for said county, personally appeared ——, to me personally known to be the identical person who executed the above (satisfaction of mortgage) as grantor, and acknowledged —— signature thereto to be —— voluntary act and deed.

Witness my hand and ———— seal, the day and year last above written.   ————

ONE FORM OF REAL ESTATE MORTGAGE.

KNOW ALL MEN BY THESE PRESENTS: That ——, of —— County, and State of ——, in consideration of ———— dollars, in hand paid by ———— of —— County, and State of ——, do hereby sell and convey unto the said —— the following described premises, situated in the County ————, and State of ——, to wit (here insert description,) and —— do hereby covenant with the said ———— that —— lawfully seized of said premises, that they are free from incumbrance, that —— have good right and lawful authority to sell and convey the same, and —— do hereby covenant to warrant and defend the same against the lawful claims of all persons whomsoever   To be void upon condition that the said ———— shall pay the full amount of principal and interest at the time therein specified, of —— certain promissory note for the sum of —— dollars.

One note for $——, due ————, 18—, with interest annually at —— per cent.
One note for $——, due ————, 18—, with interest annually at —— per cent.
One note for $——, due ————, 18—, with interest annually at —— per cent.
One note for $——, due ————, 18—, with interest annually at —— per cent

And the said Mortgagor agrees to pay all taxes that may be levied upon the above described premises   It is also agreed by the Mortgagor that if it becomes necessary to foreclose this mortgage, a reasonable amount shall be allowed as an attorney's fee for foreclosing.   And the said ———— hereby relinquishes all her right of dower and homestead in and to the above described premises.

Signed to —— day of ——, A. D. 18—

                                                    ———— ————

                                                    ———— ————.

[Acknowledge as in Form No. 1.]

SECOND FORM OF REAL ESTATE MORTGAGE.

THIS INDENTURE, made and executed —— by and between ———— of the county of —— and State of ——, part of the first part, and ———— of the county of —— and State of —— party of the second part, *Witnesseth*, that the said part of the first part, for and in consideration of the sum of —— dollars, paid by the said party of the second part, the receipt of which is hereby acknowledged, have granted and sold and do by these presents, grant, bargain, sell convey and confirm unto the said party of the second part —— heirs and assigns forever the certain tract or parcel of real estate situated in the county of —— and State of ——, described as follows, to-wit

(Here insert description)

The said part of the first part represent to and covenant with the part of the second part that he have good right to sell and convey said premises, that they are free from encumbrance and that he will warrant and defend them against the lawful claims of all persons whomsoever, and do expressly hereby release all rights of dower in and to said premises, and relinquish and convey all rights of homestead therein

This Instrument is made, executed and delivered upon the following conditions, to-wit :

First Said first part agree to pay said —— or order ——————

Second Said first part further agree as is stipulated in said note, that if he shall fail to pay any of said interest when due it shall bear interest at the rate of ten per cent. per annum, from the time the same becomes due, and this mortgage shall stand as security for the same.

Third Said first part further agree that he will pay all taxes and assessments levied upon said real estate before the same become delinquent, and if not paid the holder of this mortgage may declare the whole sum of money herein secured due and collectable at once, or he may elect to pay such taxes or assessments, and be entitled to interest on the same at the rate of ten per cent. per annum, and this mortgage shall stand as security for the amount so paid

Fourth Said first part further agree that if he fail to pay any of said money either principal or interest, within —— days after the same becomes due, or fail to conform or comply with any of the foregoing conditions or agreements, the whole sum herein secured shall become due and payable at once, and this mortgage may thereupon be foreclosed immediately for the whole of said money, interest and costs.

Fifth Said part further agree that in the event of the non-payment of either principal, interest or taxes when due, and upon the filing of a bill of foreclosure of this mortgage, an attorney's fee of —— dollars shall become due and payable, and shall be by the court taxed, and this mortgage shall stand as security therefor, and the same shall be included in the decree of foreclosure and shall be made by the Sheriff on general or special execution with the other money, interest and costs, and the contract embodied in this mortgage and the note described herein, shall in all respects be governed, constructed and adjudged by the laws of ——, where the same is made The foregoing conditions being performed, this conveyance to be void, otherwise of full force and virtue

————— —————,

————— —————.

[Acknowledge as in form No. 1.]

FORM OF LEASE

THIS ARTICLE OF AGREEMENT, Made and entered into on this —— day of ——, A D 187– ... between ———— . of the county of ——, and State of Iowa of ... and ———— of the county of ——, and Second party, witnesseth that the said party of the first part has this day leased unto the party of the second part the following described premises, to wit ·

[Here insert description]

for the term of ——— from and after the — day of ———, A. D. 187–, at the ——— rent of ——— dollars, to be paid as follows, to wit :

[Here insert Terms]

And it is further agreed that if any rent shall be due and unpaid, or if default be made in any of the covenants herein contained, it shall then be lawful for the said party of the first part to re-enter the said premises, or to destrain for such rent, or he may recover possession thereof, by action of forcible entry and detainer, notwithstanding the provision of Section 3,612 of the Code of 1873; or he may use any or all of said remedies.

And the said party of the second part agrees to pay to the party of the first part the rent as above stated, except when said premises are untenantable by reason of fire, or from any other cause than the carelessness of the party of the second part, or persons ——— family, or in ——— employ, or by superior force and inevitable necessity And the said party of the second part covenants that ——— will use the said premises as a ———, and for no other purposes whatever; and that ——— especially will not use said premises, or permit the same to be used, for any unlawful business or purpose whatever, that ——— will not sell, assign, underlet or relinquish said premises without the written consent of the lessor, under penalty of a forfeiture of all ——— rights under this lease, at the election of the party of the first part; and that ——— will use all due care and diligence in guarding said property, with the buildings, gates, fences, trees, vines, shrubbery, etc., from damage by fire, and the depredations of animals, that ——— will keep buildings, gates, fences, etc , in as good repair as they now are, or may at any time be placed by the lessor, damages by superior force, inevitable necessity, or fire from any other cause than from the carelessness of the lessee, or persons of ——— family, or in ——— employ, excepted , and that at the expiration of this lease, or upon a breach by said lessee of any of the said covenants herein contained, ——— will, without further notice of any kind, quit and surrender the possession and occupancy of said premises in as good condition as reasonable use, natural wear and decay thereof will permit, damages by fire as aforesaid, superior force, or inevitable necessity, only excepted.

In witness whereof, the said parties have subscribed their names on the date first above written

In presence of

——— ———   ——— ———

FORM OF NOTE

$———   ——— —, 18—

On or before the — day of ———, 18— for value received, I promise to pay ——— ——— or order, ——— dollars, with interest from date until paid, at ten per cent per annum, payable annually, at ——— Unpaid interest shall bear interest at ten per cent per annum On failure to pay interest within ——— days after due, the w——— ——— principal and in——— ——— shall become due at once.

——— ——— ———

CHATTEL MORTGAGE

KNOW ALL MEN BY THESE PRESENTS· That —— of —— County, and State of—— in consideration of —— dollars, in hand paid by ——, of —— County and State of —— do hereby sell and convey unto the said —— the following described personal property, now in the possession of —— in the county —— and State of —— to wit .

[Here insert Description]

And —— do hereby warrant the title of said property and that it is free from any incumbrance or lien   The only right or interest retained by grantor in and to said property being the right of redemption as herein provided   This conveyance to be void upon condition that the said grantor shall pay to said grantee, or his assigns, the full amount of principal and interest at the time therein specified, of —— certain promissory notes of even date herewith, for the sum of —— dollars,

One note for $——, due——, 18—, with interest annually at —— per cent.
One note for $——, due——, 18—, with interest annually at —— per cent.
One note for $——, due——, 18—, with interest annually at —— per cent
One note for $——, due——, 18—, with interest annually at —— per cent.

The grantor to pay all taxes on said property, and if at any time any part or portion of said notes should be due and unpaid, said grantee may proceed by sale or foreclosure to collect and pay himself the unpaid balance of said notes, whether due or not, the grantor to pay all necessary expense of such foreclosure, including $—— Attorney's fees, and whatever remains after paying off said notes and expenses, to be paid over to said grantor.

Signed the —— day of ——, 18—.   ——— ———

[Acknowledged as in form No. 1.]   ——— ———.

WARRANTY DEED

KNOW ALL MEN BY THESE PRESENTS : That —— of —— County and State of ——, in consideration of the sum of —— Dollars, in hand paid by —— of ——, County and State of ——, do hereby sell and convey unto the said —— and to —— heirs and assigns, the following described premises, situated in the County of ——, State of Iowa, to-wit:

[Here insert description]

And I do hereby covenant with the said —— that — lawfully seized in fee simple, of said premises, that they are free from incumbrance , that — ha   good right and lawful authority to sell the same, and — do hereby covenant to warrant and defend the said premises and appurtenances thereto belonging. against the lawful claims of all persons whomsoever , and the said —— hereby relinquishes all her right of dower and of homestead in and to the above described premises

Signed the —— day of ——, A. D. 18—.

IN PRESENCE OF

——— ———
——— ——   ——— ———
——— ——   ——— ———

and .   [Acknowledged as in Form No. 1]

QUIT-CLAIM DEED.

KNOW ALL MEN BY THESE PRESENTS That ———, of —— County, State of ——, in consideration of the sum of ——— dollars, to — in hand paid by ———, of —— County, State of ——, the receipt whereof — do hereby acknowledge, have bargained, sold and quit-claimed, and by these presents do bargain, sell and quit-claim unto the said ——— and to — heirs and assigns forever, all — right, title, interest, estate, claim and demand, both at law and in equity, and as well in possession as in expectancy, of, in and to the following described premises, to wit: [here insert description] with all and singular the hereditaments and appurtenances thereto belonging.

Signed this —— day of ———, A D. 18—.

SIGNED IN PRESENCE OF

——— ———   ——— ———

——— ———   ——— ———

——— ———   [Acknowledged as in form No 1]

BOND FOR DEED.

KNOW ALL MEN BY THESE PRESENTS: That ——— of —— County, and State of —— am held and firmly bound unto ——— of —— County, and State of ——, in the sum of ——— Dollars, to be paid to the said ———. his executors or assigns, for which payment well and truly to be made, I bind myself firmly by these presents. Signed the —— day of ——— A. D 18 —.

The condition of this obligation is such, that if the said obligee shall pay to said obligor, or his assigns, the full amount of principal and interest at the time therein specified, of — certain promissory note of even date herewith, for the sum of ——— Dollars.

One note for $———. due ———, 18 —, with interest annually at — per cent.
One note for $———, due ———, 18 —, with interest annually at — per cent.
One note for $———. due ——— 18 —, with interest annually at — per cent.

and pay all taxes accruing upon the lands herein described, then said obligor shall convey to the said obligee, or his assigns, that certain tract or parcel of real estate, situated in the County of —— and State of Iowa, described as follows, to wit. [here insert description,] by a Warranty Deed with the usual covenants, duly executed and acknowledged

If said obligee should fail to make the payments as above stipulated, or any part thereof, as the same becomes due, said obligor may at his option, by notice to the obligee terminate his liability under the bond and resume the possession and absolute control of said premises, time being the essence of this agreement

On the fulfillment of the above conditions this obligation to become void, otherwise to remain in full force and virtue, unless terminated by the obligor as above stipulated.

[Acknowledgments as in form No 1]

CHARITABLE, SCIENTIFIC AND RELIGIOUS ASSOCIATIONS.

Any three or more persons of full age, citizens of the United States, a majority of whom shall be citizens of this State, who desire to associate themselves for benevolent, charitable scientific, religious or missionary purposes, may make, sign and acknowledge, before any officer authorized to take the acknowledgments of deeds in this State, and have recorded in the office of the Recorder of the county in which the business of such society is to be conducted, a certificate in writing, in which shall be stated the name or title by which such society shall be known, the particular business and objects of such society, the number of Trustees, Directors or Managers to conduct the same, and the names of the Trustees, Directors or Managers of such society for the first year of its existence.

Upon filing for record the certificate, as aforesaid, the persons who shall have signed and acknowledged such certificate, and their associates and successors, shall, by virtue hereof, be a body politic and corporate by the name stated in such certificate, and by that they and their successors shall and may have succession, and shall be persons capable of suing and being sued, and may have and use a common seal, which they may alter or change at pleasure, and they and their successors, by their corporate name, shall be capable of taking, receiving, purchasing and holding real and personal estate, and of making by-laws for the management of its affairs, not inconsistent with law.

The society so incorporated may, annually or oftener, elect from its members its Trustees, Directors or Managers at such time and place, and in such manner as may be specified in its by-laws, who shall have the control and management of the affairs and funds of the society, a majority of whom shall be a quorum for the transaction of business, and whenever any vacancy shall happen among such Trustees, Directors or Managers, by death, resignation or neglect to serve, such vacancy shall be filled in such manner as shall be provided by the by-laws of such society. When the body corporate consists of the Trustees, Directors or Managers of any benevolent, charitable, literary scientific, religious or missionary institution, which is or may be established in the State, and which is or may be under the patronage, control, direction or supervision of any synod, conference, association or other ecclesiastical body in such State, established agreeably to the laws thereof, such ecclesiastical body may nominate and appoint such Trustees, Directors or Managers, according to usages of the appointing body, and may fill any vacancy which may occur among such Trustees, Directors or Managers, and when any such institution may be under the patronage, control, direction or supervision of two or more of such synods, conferences, associations or other ecclesiastical bodies, such bodies may severally nominate and appoint such proportion of such Trustees, Directors or Managers as shall be agreed upon by those bodies immediately concerned. And any vacancy occurring among such appointees last named, shall be filled by the synod, conference, association or body having appointed the last incumbent.

In case any election of Trustees, Directors or Managers shall not be made on the day designated by the by-laws, said society for that cause shall not be dissolved, but such election may take place on any other day directed by such by-laws.

Any corporation formed under this chapter shall be capable of taking, holding or receiving any property by virtue of any devise or bequest contained in any last will and testament of any person whatever, but no person leaving a wife, child or parent, shall devise or bequeath to such institution or corporation more than one-fourth of his estate after the payment of his debts, and such device or bequest shall be valid only to the extent of such one-fourth

Any corporation in this State of an academical character, the memberships of which shall consist of lay members and pastors of churches, delegates to any synod, conference or council holding its annual meetings alternately in this and one or more adjoining States, may hold its annual meetings for the election of officers and the transaction of business in any adjoining State to this, at such place therein as the said synod, conference or council shall hold its annual meetings, and the elections so held and business so transacted shall be as legal and binding as if held and transacted at the place of business of the corporation in this State.

The provisions of this chapter shall not extend or apply to any association or individual who shall in the certificate filed with the Recorder, use or specify a name or style the same as that of any previously existing incorporated society in the county.

The Trustees, Directors or stockholders of any existing benevolent, charitable, scientific, missionary or religious corporation, may, by conforming to the requirements of Section 1095 of this chapter, re-incorporate themselves or continue their existing corporate powers, and all the property and effects of such existing corporation shall vest in and belong to the corporation so re-incorporated or continued

INTOXICATING LIQUORS

No intoxicating liquors (alcohol, spirituous and vinous liquors), except wine manufactured from grapes, currants or other fruit grown in the State, shall be manufactured or sold, except for mechanical, medicinal, culinary or sacramental purposes; and even such sale is limited as follows:

Any citizen of the State, except hotel keepers, keepers of saloons, eating houses, grocery keepers and confectioners, is permitted to buy and sell, within the county of his residence, such liquors for such mechanical, etc, purposes only, provided he shall obtain the consent of the Board of Supervisors. In order to get that consent, he must get a certificate from a majority of the electors of the town or township or ward in which he desires to sell, that he is of good moral character, and a proper person to sell such liquors

If the Board of Supervisors grant him permission to sell such liquors, he must give bonds, and shall not sell such liquors at a greater profit than thirty-three per cent on the cost of the same. Any person having a permit to sell, shall make on the last Saturday of every month, a return in writing to the Auditor of the county, showing the kind and quantity of the liquors purchased by him since the date of his last report, the price paid, and the amount of freights paid on the same, also the kind and quantity of liquors sold by him since the date of his last report; to whom sold, for what purpose and at what price, also the kind and quantity of liquors on hand; which report shall be sworn to by the person having the permit, and shall be kept by the Auditor, subject at all times to the inspection of the public

No person shall sell or give away any intoxicating liquors, including wine or beer, to any minor, for any purpose whatever, except upon written order of parent, guardian or family physician, or sell the same to an intoxicated person or a person in the habit of becoming intoxicated

Any person who shall mix any intoxicating liquor with any beer, wine or cider, by him sold and shall sell or keep for sale, as a beverage, such mixture, shall be punished as for sale of intoxicating liquor.

But nothing in the chapter containing the laws governing the sale or prohibiting the sale of intoxicating liquors, shall be construed to forbid the sale by the importer thereof of foreign intoxicating liquor, imported under the authority of the laws of the United States, regarding the importation of such liquors, and in accordance with such laws, provided that such liquor, at the time of the sale by the importer, remains in the original casks or packages in which it was by him imported, and in quantities not less than the quantities in which the laws of the United States require such liquors to be imported, and is sold by him in such original casks or packages, and in said quantities only.

All payment or compensation for intoxicating liquor sold in violation of the laws of this State, whether such payments or compensation be in money, goods, lands, labor, or anything else whatsoever, shall be held to have been received in violation of law and equity and good conscience, and to have been received upon a valid promise and agreement of the receiver, in consideration of the receipt thereof, to pay on demand, to the person furnishing such consideration, the amount of the money on the just value of the goods or other things.

All sales, transfers, conveyances, mortgages, liens, attachments, pledges and securities of every kind, which, either in whole or in part, shall have been made on account of intoxicating liquors sold contrary to law, shall be utterly null and void

Negotiable paper in the hands of holders thereof, in good faith, for valuable consideration, without notice of any illegality in its inception or transfer, however, shall not be affected by the above provisions   Neither shall the holder of land or other property who may have taken the same in good faith, without notice of any defect in the title of the person from whom the same was taken, growing out of a violation of the liquor law, be affected by the above provision

Every wife, child, parent, guardian, employer, or other person, who shall be injured in person or property or means of support, by an intoxicated person, or in consequence of the intoxication, has a right of action against any person who shall, by selling intoxicating liquors, cause the intoxication of such person, for all damages actually sustained as well as exemplary damages.

For any damages recovered, the personal and real property (except homestead, as now provided) of the person against whom the damages are recovered, as well as the premises or property, personal or real, occupied and used by him, with consent and knowledge of owner, either for manufacturing or selling intoxicating liquors contrary to law, shall be liable

The only other exemption, besides the homestead, from this sweeping liability, is that the defendant may have enough for the support of his family for six months, to be determined by the Township Trustee.

No ale, wine, beer or other malt or vinous liquors shall be sold within two miles of the corporate limits of any municipal corporation, except at wholesale, for the purpose of shipment to places outside of such corporation and such two-mile limits.   The power of the corporation to prohibit or license sale of liquors not prohibited by law is extended over the two miles.

No ale, wine, beer or other malt or vinous liquors shall be sold on the day on which any election is held under the laws of this State, within two miles of the place where said election is held, except only that any person holding a permit may sell upon the prescription of a practicing physician.

SUGGESTIONS TO THOSE PURCHASING BOOKS BY SUBSCRIPTION.

The business of *publishing books by subscription*, having so often been brought into disrepute by agents making representations and declarations *not authorized by the publisher*, in order to prevent that as much as possible, and that there may be more general knowledge of the relation such agents bear to their principal, and the law governing such cases, the following statement is made:

A subscription is in the *nature of a contract* of mutual promises, by which the subscriber agrees to *pay a certain sum* for the work described; the *consideration is concurrent* that the publisher shall *publish the book named,* and deliver the same, for which the subscriber is to pay the price named. *The nature and character of the work is described by the prospectus and sample shown.* These should be *carefully examined before subscribing*, as they are the basis and consideration of the promise to pay, and not the too *often exaggerated statements of the agent*, who is *merely employed* to *solicit subscriptions*, for which he is usually *paid a commission* for each subscriber, and has *no authority to change or alter* the conditions upon which the subscriptions are authorized to be made by the publisher. Should the *agent assume* to agree to make the subscription conditional or *modify or change the agreement of the publisher*, as set out by the prospectus and sample, in order to *bind the principal*, the *subscriber* should see that such condition or changes are stated *over or in connection with his signature*, so that the publisher may have notice of the same.

All persons making contracts in reference to matters of this kind, or any other business, should remember *that the law as written is*, that they can *not be altered, varied or rescinded verbally, but if done at all, must be done in writing.* It is therefore *important* that all *persons contemplating subscribing should distinctly understand that all talk before or after the subscription is made, is not admissible as evidence, and is no part of the contract.*

Persons employed to solicit subscriptions are known to the trade as canvassers. They are agents *appointed to do a particular business in a prescribed mode,* and *have no authority* to do it any other way to the prejudice of their principal, nor can they bind their principal in any other matter. They *can not collect money,* or agree that payment may be made in *anything else but money.* They *can not extend* the time of payment *beyond the time of delivery,* nor *bind their principal* for the *payment of expenses* incurred in their business.

It would save a great deal of trouble, and often serious loss, if persons, *before signing* their names to any subscription book, or any written instrument, would *examine carefully what it is;* if they can not read themselves call on some one disinterested who can.

STATISTICS OF AGRICULTURE OF IOWA (CENSUS OF 1875.)

COUNTIES	No of Acres of Improved Land	No of Acres Unimproved Land	No of Acres under Cultivation in 1874	Spring Wheat No of Acres	Spring Wheat No of Bushels Harv't'd	Winter Wheat No of Acres	Winter Wheat No of Bushels Harv't'd	Indian Corn No of Acres	Indian Corn No of Bushels Harv't'd	Oats No of Acres	Oats No of Bushels Harv't'd	Value of Products of Farm in Dollars
Appanoose	161039	161083	125188	9606	77789	1049	10828	64871	2385248	13756	3873	1611937
Alamakee	134167	156821	109388	61880	98.639	181	1964	24325	905920	12776	442829	145769
Audubon	21116	28819	15986	6876	89235	10	97	9225	394635	788	33233	184153
Adams	65139	43735	51353	17917	281376	7	174	25174	969777	3951	14,493	6953.8
Adair	83182	35680	66265	27350	435011	70	3500	30800	1102428	1175	159739	825171
Buena Vista	33118	37034	27010	13514	163737			7888	228231	2791	61069	201825
Benton	297318	53911	289408	99106	13.31666	7	250	85241	3328321	35190	446070	2664995
Boone	156637	71810	106643	32505	449257	11	84	46151	1595752	10101	404620	1015453
Butler	143198	58918	124877	57907	779167	20	700	38685	1270878	13527	421719	1209755
Bremer	145361	45001	104810	48875	644795			28751	1026611	11259	518571	1144620
Black Hawk	214035	156081	181256	88961	1108021			56692	1939890	16801	853496	1898424
Buchanan	19636	71418	157210	64291	812314			43831	1311250	17431	536209	261,3949
Clay	37059	39919	33373	17181	153159			8797	180190	4136	98766	133343
Cherokee	51688	28914	45412	31693	401507			9139	315315	3513	113595	38040
Cass	110861	45301	92735	40123	676209			40582	1901062	9079	178291	1284699
Crawford	58059	283414	15262	24003	321894			17957	648658	2902	99158	493357
Cedar	243869	41417	166187	10167	610511	26	295	78221	2315921	20218	675837	2606119
Cerro Gordo	52950	309995	48618	28199	415163			9512	265113	7199	228607	691617
Clayton	212291	151908	173622	86883	1305125	1347	21030	37948	1471263	20021	609895	2081793
Clinton	294835	57337		68683	1010315	12	428	89297	3061338	23701	702059	8049049
Chickasaw	96301	91772	71501	40162	613519	8	63	16821	511179	11711	446300	891686
Carroll	58065	309744	39159	26736	349161	8	20	16014	550011	3238	107577	451365
Clarke	9569.	50487	78803	17968	217090	7	55	39066	1580260	12337	305613	7054987
Calhoun	26096		26618	11040	109681	10	150	10656	351120	2993	73182	221613
Davis	150438	116003	131597	5378	80993	5379	56405	62127	2115569	13613	315707	1600090
Decatur	115751	87112	93275	5211	71469	817	13239	40184	1763110	10555	31155	10218 11
Dubuque	137631	95561	140211	49230	634135	84	1720	67118	1702491	25115	613322	1636132
Des Moines	143665	58105	94618	10615	113896	8688	117310	102924	2301938	9212	257392	1772992
Delaware	43020	63805	161357	60401	71728	5	50	56750	1690585	20577	633113	1693314
Dickinson	13770	29830	11961	5701	25822			3183	41835	2103	37252	15331
Dallas	187135	57765	114625	28256	415818	7	186	51652	2484698	6987	335124	1502047
Emmet	9989	23596	8887	3911	1510			2197	14273	1519	3921	13244
Floyd	147095	32130	110708	62067	911439			26162	612418	15161	477729	1362372
Fayette	193501	98156	183758	60779	864670	46	968	37091	1296180	20770	701107	1908127
Franklin	60859	43146	65590	31096	455009			24066	759883	9532	329679	777106
Fremont	115997	199532	103089	13229	206901	841	16625	78515	1709985	5419	179615	1046686
Grundy	116039	47326	135108	67381	976607			10175	1482582	11736	401948	1593977
Green	59840	49838	52823	19391	257160	2	44	78087	789027	4227	120948	620905
Guthrie	81259	47420	76892	27489	395574	22	210	38002	1669131	4145	158505	792461
Hardin	123431	39930	97765	88464	497251			41304	1879961	10982	356915	1066627
Humboldt	29114	36306	27013	12016	20092			9908	297381	3971	90944	200001
Howard	113823	171018	61871	36115	55 5973			9916	307012	10210	340268	734409
Harrison	94818	337451	72287	23948	145701	61	1200	14720	1620192	3462	69140	786677
Hancock	10462	341615	9005	4889	700.6			2067	57899	1958	48516	89405
Hamilton	65966	39935	52030	20676	291682			20411	670131	5108	168262	52762
Henry	182080	59219	110831	15026	180220	9041	113203	62672	2115670	13393	838221	1765670
Ida	7292	9494	6514	3109	48315			2301	108165	435	14060	7482211
Iowa	191011	63857	153188	48110	670217	96	1080	62518	2713899	11776	319071	2005049
Jackson	193290	113301	113307	43515	580000	491	7942	58962	1665318	23632	521156	1730091
Johnson	241621	71251	199019	45906	661159	100	1274	74444	3189118	17540	524197	2447875
Jasper	278831	119552	216919	79926	1107160			100377	4525983	15367	832289	2916838
Jones	208907	63298	140684	86090	462478	81	409	65423	1905524	18040	464824	1620416
Jefferson	164389	66019	125390	16287	164904	6192	66759	85601	1695510	14065	416138	1580140
Keokuk	205125	98090	149672	33278	368528	148	1363	75697	3327282	15582	447608	1997728
Kossuth	31550	49793	29333	10793	19199	140		9781	119777	5143	27857	105306
Lee	188832	58692	133380	10551	72624	15100	200107	59863	2190306	11817	279069	1681518
Lucas	109053	69557	88857	18051	153587	31	929	47022	1902930	12065	84216	1080554
Lyon	15872	319511	12766	8132	76142		54	2645	10396	3177	18789	82651
Linn	281108	67649	177635	52178	850597	12	140	91773	3139923	22650	585618	2590052
Louisa	131097	52922	104066	19704	189639	1388	162847	49612	2181655	6792	177753	1685739
Mitchell	126881	70176	91133	63534	1088811			11274	411961	14078	513762	1591878
Mahaska	232898	122190	150.68	31162	395332	205	2697	83775	3764209	16646	496248	2195785
Marion	198169	84779	153214	43196	549633	189	2212	84630	3835063	10957	335746	2181846
Mills	111512	58601	90987	24385	312961	32	513	59513	1538970	6528	282839	1003809
Madison	161998	188709	137079	37338	628314	25	484	69194	2993630	8713	285103	1700030
Monroe	102215	78206	91730	11638	101435	263	5584	45545	1738916	11512	240081	988362
Marshall	223735	47552	117979	63905	1123982	21	290	67609	2803829	15611	463245	2208278
Monona	52212	56373	39911	15791	188811			21577	815338	2304	66475	447663
Muscatine	176915	48432	128609	32575	416451	63	629	51760	1719973	13287	403562	1715906
Montgomery	104333	50607	86026	1381	551569	8	166	39241	1411461	5382	200188	1072127
O'Brien	33626	33070	26131	11901	151746			6579	104082	3107	53831	191512
Osceola	18190	31106	11651	8769	71757			2510	17279	1890	26826	69681
Polk	207689	56841	110150	31680	563369	21	341	77197	3272010	12188	431841	2100633
Pochahontas	21025	33572	19119	7411	80774			6981	229369	2541	40191	112866
Pottawattomie	126630	419189	906.9	38369	549071	43	475	47239	1750085	5278	168681	1253639
Poweshiek	208089	96097	171585	57312	762836			88718	3571105	11416	833565	2398022
Page	156783	175171	115184	22639	355792	1230	20235	71986	2289013	9758	316507	1293163
Plymouth	58273	51912	41379	33628	442736	10	140	10097	175778	4161	120437	431423
Palo Alto	18517	37225	19679	8608	23208	325		6611	144957	2979	40859	96616
Ringgold	19600	58529	50548	10038	78851	125	1762	35613	1145937	9118	215007	1115782
Scott	235515	19128	181712	47098	762815	40	618	59071	2226319	15915	528808	3011873
Story	146619	49974	91487	26155	330897	8	20	51273	1783477	11273	318265	1083743
Shelby	51180	35376	47233	22129	317941			17674	680556	2254	71070	573026
Sioux	80921	367394	35315	22096	251286			6790	82084	4591	450960	160980
Sac	31836	47200	24179	11036	110034		10	8662	279716	3035	6399	238880
Taylor	104861	233515	79112	15116	206813	211	3068	18260	1419690	8719	209657	902176
Tama	255782	90232	211941	90.03	1437907			73151	284285	13571	341169	2316405
Union	55005	33316	45526	10536	141188	55	960	21063	1130930	6147	18.718	642420
Van Buren	153671	90528	114363	7135	58808	10928	121854	50111	1829562	12570	353698	1439989
Wayne	147766	66791	118089	10375	78310	113	1256	65625	2105181	13212	367396	1361519
Warren	191265	16717	158737	42177	63619	61	910	80949	3561365	8991	281510	2208952
Winneshiek	216110	131670	239169	11217	1813163			27045	973316	21007	821630	22.5232
Woodbury	44179	57097	30003	15218	2.3875			11617	490371	3072	91617	298209
Worth											161557	896506
Washina											475320	2055261
Webster											207193	733312
Winneb											95103	140219
Wright											139376	288685
Wapello											293906	1456319
Totals	1562800	8710435	935+9051	56907411	136697511	6958	15921.1	4500176	136284524	983904	23144852	131596717

Edwin Manning

KEOSAUQUA

HISTORY OF VAN BUREN COUNTY.

GEOLOGY.

The universal desire to know the causes of manifest effects, and to ascertain the origin of all things, is as marked to-day as it was in those far-off times when the earth was deemed a flat disc resting upon the back of an elephant, the elephant upon a tortoise, the tortoise upon a serpent, and the serpent upon an undiscovered something. Each age regards its store of knowledge as almost infinite, yet each succeeding generation finds some new fund to draw from and expand the sum of wisdom. Science has opened many pages in the great book of nature, and has supplied the key to the mysteries therein recorded. Future research may modify the theories at first advanced by the patient investigators of the absorbing work: but so firmly established are many of the ideas promulgated in the school of modern science that they must be accepted as fixed facts. In no division of study has greater or more certain progress been made than in that of geology. The finest intellects of the century have been engrossed in the labor of determining the origin of the earth and the gradations by which it has reached its present habitable conditions. As a part of the history of this particular section of the globe, the formation of the rocks and soil is certainly a topic worthy of considerable space in this record of events. We have, therefore, compiled a geologic sketch of the lower valley of the Des Moines, with the belief that it will be an acceptable paper.

In the general history of the State which is given in this volume, will be found a somewhat elaborate description of the geology of Iowa, from a scientific standpoint. It remains for us to limit the circuit of our work in connection herewith to the actual boundaries of the Des Moines Valley. We shall attempt to popularize a most interesting but not generally studied theme, and endeavor to explain, in simple form, what is too often rendered obscure to the uninitiated in scientific methods by technical terms and expressions. Since those who wish to do so can turn to the general chapter and learn of the geologic structure of the State, let us now bring to a focus the more practical ideas relative to the subject of the recent or superficial formations of this region. This is designed to be only a short popular treatise, so as to interest every man and woman of good observation who shall peruse it, and to call their attention, at least, to the surface formation of the earth, so that in a few years there may be hundreds of observers of interesting geological facts where there is but one at the present time.

That geology commends itself to us as a truthful science will be very readily elucidated by a simple statement of a fact within the comprehension of all.

To illustrate: A certain kind of rocks are called Archæan, Laurentian. These are the most ancient rocks known to geologists: at the time they were

A

supposed to be destitute of fossils In all the systems of rocks, they occupy the lowest, and consequently the oldest, position ; but in whatever part of the earth found, they are always recognizable by the geologist. So the Devonian rocks are distinguished by certain fossil fishes that are found in them, and in them alone   The Carboniferous rocks are known by certain fossil mollusks ; the Cretaceous, by certain reptiles that occur in no other formation ; and so every geological period has its characteristic fossils, by means of which the formation and its comparative age may always be accurately determined

The geologist will always know the coal-bearing rocks from any other class , and this knowledge ought to be possessed by every one interested in explorations for coal.

The geologic history of Iowa is but a page in the general history of the continent of North America. This continent has been demonstrated to be the oldest portion of the earth, notwithstanding the misnomer, "New World." It is new only in civilization. The geologist reads is the rocks evidences of age that are far more reliable than those which are placed on perishable scrolls by the pen of man. The oldest groups of rocks are not found in Iowa, but are visible in the Canadas. The first system, underlying all others, in this State, is the Azoic, seen only in a small section of the northeast portion of Iowa Next come the Lower and Upper Silurian, the Devonian, the Carboniferous and the Cretaceous systems. Of the earlier formations we shall say nothing, as allusion to them necessitates a far more extended article than we desire to prepare.

The scope of this paper extends back only to the Carboniferous system, at the period known as the Subcarboniferous group. In plainer terms, this refers to the limestone which underlies the coal formations, and brings the subject at once to the visible formations in the valley   This section is rich in coal deposits, and a glance at the method of creation will be both interesting and instructive.

FORMATION OF LIME BEDS.

Limestones have mainly been formed in the bottom of the ocean ; the older and purer kinds in the deep, still sea ; the more recent and less pure in a shallow and disturbed sea   When the great limestone deposits were made in the Mississippi Valley, a deep salt ocean extended from the Alleghany to the Rocky Mountains, from the Gulf of Mexico to the Arctic Ocean This was the age of mollusks (shell fish), and the sea bottom swarmed with them. Many of the rocks seem to have been wholly made up of conglomerate shells In this age of the world there was no creature living with a spinal column or a brain ; but corals, a low order of radiates, as crinoidea, several varieties of mollusks, crustaceans called trilobites (somewhat corresponding to the river crawfish), and some lowly *worms !* These were the highest development of animal life when the earlier limestone rocks were being slowly formed

This Silurian age was succeeded by the Devonian, characterized as the age of fishes, during which were deposited the Hamilton and Carboniferous limestones   Then came the Subcarboniferous period, during which were deposited the limestone beds   These were formed in a comparatively shallow sea, a fact. proven by numerous ripple marks in the rocks, also by their sandy composition in some layers, and farther, by an occasional thin layer of clay intervening between the strata of rocks   These were uneasy times on the earth's crust, when it was given to upheavings and down-sinkings over large areas   Then it was that the whole northeastern and eastern part of the State was upraised

THE GREAT COAL BASIN

was formed west and south throughout Iowa, reaching into Missouri and Kansas, and perhaps into the Indian Territory and Texas. Over this vast area there stretched *a vast, dismal swamp.*

On this vast marshy plain grew the rank vegetation that was in the future to be pressed into coal. It was a wilderness of moss and ferns and reeds, such as can be found nowhere on earth at the present time. Prof. Gunning, in speaking of it, says: "To the land forest of coniferas and cycads, and the marsh forest of scale trees and seal trees and reed trees and fern trees, add an undergrowth of low herbaceous ferns, and you have the picture of a primeval landscape. Blot from the face of nature every flowering weed and flowering tree, every grass, every fruit, every growth useful to man or beast; go, then to the Sunda Islands for the largest club moss, to the East Indies for the largest tree fern, to the damp glades of Caracas for the tallest reeds, to the Moluccas for their cycad, and to Australia for its pine, to the ponds and sluggish streams of America for their quillwort, and place them all side by side over a vast marsh and its sandy borders, and you will faintly realize your picture of a primeval landscape. Dwarf the cycad and the pine, lift still higher the tapering column of the tree fern, multiply by two the bulk of the reed and by three the club moss, lift the quillwort from the water, and to its long, linear leaves add a fluted stem eighty feet high, and you would fully realize a carboniferous landscape—realize it in all but its vast solitudes. Not a bird ever perched on spiky leaf or spreading fern of a coal forest. No flower had opened yet to spread fragrance on the air, and no throat had warbled a note of music. Such poor animal life as the carboniferous world then possessed left its imprint on wave-washed shore and in the hollow stems of fallen trees."

This was the beginning of the age of amphibians. Then lived the progenitors of the loathsome alligator and lizard. La Conte says: "The climate of the coal period was characterized by greater *warmth, humidity,* uniformity and a more highly *carbonated condition* of the atmosphere than now obtains." We may, therefore, picture to ourselves the climate of this period as *warm, moist, uniform, stagnant and stifling* from the abundance of carbonic-acid gas.

Such conditions were extremely favorable to vegetable life, but not to the higher forms of animal life. Neither man nor monkey nor milk-giving animal of any kind, lived for many cycles of time after the Subcarboniferous period, but that vegetation grew rank, scientific facts corroborate; thus, Prof. Gunning says: "It takes between five and eight feet of vegetable debris to form one foot of coal. A Pittsburgh seam is ten feet thick, while one in Nova Scotia is thirty-five feet in depth. The Pittsburgh seam represents a vegetable deposit of from fifty to a hundred feet in depth, and the one in Nova Scotia between a hundred and seventy-five and three hundred and fifty feet in thickness. A four-foot seam in Wapello County would represent from twenty to forty feet of vegetable debris.

During the growth and decay of this vegetable matter, the surface of the earth did not sink; but this quiescent period was *followed* by one of submergence. "The surface, loaded with the growth of quiet centuries, was carried down beneath the sea, where it was swept by waves and overspread by sands and mud." It was in nature's great hydraulic press, where it remained until another upheaval again threw it to the surface, and another long era of verdure succeeded the one of submergence.

Thus, emergence and submergence succeeded each other as many times as the coal-seams and the shale, slate or sandstone alternate—in some parts of Iowa, three times, in Nova Scotia about forty times! Who can compute the centuries here recorded?

The coal-fields of Iowa are extensive. A line drawn on the map of the State as follows will about define them. Commencing at the southeast corner of Van Buren County, running to the northeast corner of Jefferson, by a waving line slightly eastward through Lee and Henry Counties; thence a few miles northward from Jefferson and northwestward, keeping six or eight miles north of Skunk River, until the southern boundary of Marshall County is reached a little west of the center; thence three or four miles northeast from Eldora, in Hardin County; thence westward to a point a little north of Webster City, in Hamilton County, and thence westward to a point a little north of Fort Dodge, in Webster County.

The coal-field in Iowa belongs to the true carboniferous system, and is, moreover, the outfield of the vast coal-basin which partly covers this State, Illinois, Indiana, Ohio and Pennsylvania. It is only in the Alleghanies that subterranean action has converted any part of the coal into anthracite. Everywhere else in the immense basin it is strictly bituminous, varying, however, from the article as first prepared by the economic forces of Nature from the block coal of Indiana to the cannel coal found in certain parts of Iowa.

It appears from the researches of Laebig and other eminent chemists, that when wood and other vegetable matter are buried in the earth, exposed to moisture and partially or entirely excluded from air, they decompose slowly and evolve carbonic acid gas, thus parting with a portion of their original oxygen. By this means they become gradually converted into lignite, or wood coal, which contains a larger proportion of hydrogen than wood does. A continuance of decomposition changes this lignite into common or bituminous coal, chiefly by the discharge of carbureted hydrogen, or the gas by which we illuminate our streets and houses. According to Bischoff, the inflammable gases which are always escaping from mineral coal, and are so often the cause of fatal accidents in mines always contain carbonic acid, carbureted hydrogen, nitrogen and olefiant gas. The disengagement of all these gradually transforms ordinary or bituminous coal into anthracite, to which the various names of glance coal, cota, hard coal, culm and many others have been given.

In explaining the cause of the freedom of coal from impurities of almost every description, Sir Charles Lyell gives a paragraph which is interesting in this connection. He says, "The purity of coal itself, or the absence in it of earthy particles and sand, throughout areas of vast extent, is a fact which appears to be very difficult to explain when we attribute each coal-seam to a vegetable growth in swamps. It has been asked how, during river inundations capable of sweeping away the leaves of ferns and the stems and roots of trees, could the waters fail to transport some fine mud into swamps? One generation of tall trees after another grew in mud, and their leaves and prostrate trunks formed layers of vegetable matter which afterward covered with mud and turned to shale; but the coal itself, or altered vegetable matter, remained all the while unsoiled with earthy matter. This enigma, however perplexing at first sight, may, I think, be solved by attending to what is now taking place in deltas. The dense growth of reeds and herbage which encompasses the margin of forest-covered swamps .... of the Mississippi, is such that the fluviatile .... are filtered .... clear themselves .... vegetable matter may accumulate for centuries, forming coal, if the climate be favorable. There is no possibility of the least intermixture of earthy matter in such cases. Thus, in the large submerged track called 'Sunk Country,' near New Madrid, forming part of the western side of the valley of the Mississippi, erect trees have been standing ever since the year 1811-12, killed by the great earthquake of that date; lacustrine and swamp plants have been growing there in the shallows, and several rivers have annually inundated the whole space, and yet have been unable to carry in any sediment within the outer boundaries of the morass so dense is the marginal belt of reeds and brushwood. It may be affirmed that generally, in the cypress swamps of the Mississippi, no sediment mingles with the vegetable matter accumulated there from the decay of trees and semi-aquatic plants. As a singular proof of this fact, I may mention that whenever any part of the swamps in Louisiana is dried up, during an unusually hot season, and the wood is set on fire, pits are burned into the ground many feet deep, or as far down as the fire can descend without meeting with water, and it is then found that scarcely any residuum or earthy matter is left. At the bottom of these cypress swamps a bed of clay is found, with roots of the tall cypress, just as the under clays of the coal are filled with *stigmaria*."

CRETACEOUS

The next formation above the coal was the cretaceous, or chalk. This formation is not seen in this region, being encountered only in the west and northwest portions of the State. If any ever existed here, it was carried away during the glacial period, which is hereafter explained. The absence of chalk brings us to speak next of the

GLACIAL PERIOD

That the surface of Iowa, and, in fact the whole of North America north of the thirty-eighth parallel, is covered by a material known as drift, has become a popular opinion. Strewed all over the country, on the hills and in the valleys and on the level prairies, covering up the native rocks to a depth of from twenty to three hundred feet, is found this peculiar deposit. The well-diggers and the colliers, in their excavations, encounter it, and the quarryman has to *strip* it from the surface of this rock bed. It is not all alike; first there are a few feet of surface soil, created by recent vegetable deposits; then a variable depth of clay, or clay and sand intimately blended; then water-worn gravel and sand, and then *blue clay*, resting upon the country rock.

Scattered over the continent are frequently seen "lost rocks," or boulders, of various sizes and of different varieties, some of granite, others of gneiss or trap, and occasionally some of limestone. These boulders are also frequently found in excavating the earth.

The blue clay which lies upon the country rocks, or the original formation, is the oldest of the drift deposits. It consists of a heterogeneous mixture of dark blue clay, sand, gravel, pebbles and irregular-shaped stones and boulders, of various kinds and sizes, unassorted and unstratified, and therefore could not have been deposited in water. Sometimes an occasional piece of stone-coal and fragments of wood are found in it. This blue clay is *boulder* or glacier clay. From whence it came and how formed is one of the most interesting subjects that scientific minds have investigated. The history of glacial phenomena is the history of the deposition of the blue clay formation.

Too much credit cannot be given to the late lamented Prof. Agassiz and Principal Forbes for their discovery of the laws regulating glacier action. These eminent *savants* built a hut on a living glacier, in Switzerland, and studied it in all its relations to the past history of the globe

Prof Gunning says: "The area of Greenland is nearly eight hundred thousand square miles, and all this, save the narrow strip which faces an ice-choked sea, on the west, is a lifeless solitude of snow and ice   The snow over-tops the hills and levels up all the valleys so that, as far as the eye can reach, there is nothing but one vast, dreary, level expanse of white   Over all broods the silence of death   Life, there is none.   Motion, there *seems* to be none—none save of the wind, which sweeps now and then, in the wrath of a polar storm, from the sea over the 'ice-sea,' and rolls its cap of snow into great billows, and dashes it up into clouds of spray   But *motion there is*, activities we shall see there are. on a scale of grandeur commensurate with the vast desolation itself."

Let the mind go back in the history of our earth, one hundred thousand years, when. Prof. Croll, from mathematical deductions, infers the existence of a snow cap, covering the whole of North America and Europe, from the thirty-eighth parallel to the north pole, then, in imagination, see the larger portion of North America, as you see Greenland now, covered with an "ice-mantle" 3,000 to 6,000 feet thick   A glacier is a *frozen river*, having motion as a stream of water has, but bound in gigantic bands by the cold atmosphere Conceive, if you please, a moving block of iron, thousands of tons in weight dragged over a plowed field   The track of this monster is marked by a *level bed* of compressed, pulverized earth.   Transfer your imagination to a mass of ice covering the entire northern hemisphere, or at least to the thirty-eighth parallel (at which point the equatorial heat began to assert itself on the ice-walls, and decompose them, carrying the debris of the glacier, in solution, southward), moving half a foot or more a day because of the hydraulic pressure from behind and within—the streams which flowed into it—and you can then have some faint idea of the incalculable force of a glacier, and the action of the ice-mass on the plastic earth

The dynamic power of such a continental mass of ice is inconceivable.   It is fit to be called one of the giant mills of the gods, which are represented " to grind slowly, but exceeding fine."   It was a monstrous ice-plane, shaving off the rugged crags of mountains, leveling up valleys and filling up ancient river-beds.   Its under surface was thickly set with rock-bowlders, which, with its ponderous weight ground the underlying rocks to powder.   This pulverized rock was washed from beneath the glacier by the overflowing waters which con-stantly gushed forth, and settled on far-off plains as alluvial sand and clay The motion of the glacier was slow, perhaps six inches in twenty-four hours This was the giant mill that ground out the *blue clay*—the glacier clay—that overlies the native formations of the entire country.   It doubtless owes its dark blue color to the Laurentian and trap rocks of Canada   Well-diggers are familiar with it and it is nearly always the same in color and composition Geologists are now unanimous in the opinion that during the glacial epoch the whole northern portion of the continent was elevated one thousand to two thousand feet above the present level. Le Conte says   "The polar ice-cap had advanced southward to 40° latitude, with still further southward projections, favored by local conditions. and an Arctic rigor of climate prevailed over the United States even to the shores of the Gulf   At the end of this epoch an opposite   downward   land-surface over the   region commenced and co   continued   by   hundred or one thousand feet below the pre   bed was

Le Conte says "This ice sheet moved, with slow, glacier motion, south-eastward, southward and southwestward, over New England, New York, Ohio Illinois, Iowa, etc., regardless of smaller valleys, glaciating the whole surface, and gouging out lakes in its course Northward, the ice-sheet probably extended to the pole, it was an extension of the polar *ice-cap*."

It is not within the province of this sketch to go into details and give the problematic causes of this glacier period The causes were mainly astronomical Mr. Croll has calculated the form of the earth's orbit a million years back and a million years forward The probable time of the last glacial period was 100,000 years back, then the eccentricity of the earth's orbit was very great, and the earth in aphelion (or when most distant from the sun, being about thirteen millions of miles further than in summer) in midwinter, then the winters were about thirty days longer than now. In summer, the earth would be correspondingly nearer the sun, and would receive an excess of heat, thus giving the earth in the northern hemisphere *short, hot summers and long, cold winters*

The subsidence referred to above forms the beginning of

THE DRIFT PERIOD.

Now let us see how the drift was deposited on the bowlder clay. When the continental depression took place, a large portion of the Mississippi Valley was submerged Le Conte says ' It was a time of inland seas * * * Another result, or at least a concomitant, was a moderation of the climate, a melting of the glaciers, and a retreat of the margin of the ice-cap northward. If was, therefore, a time of flooded lakes and rivers. Lastly, over these inland seas and great lakes, loosened masses of ice floated in the form of icebergs It was, therefore, a time of iceberg action "

For a time the ideas upon the subject of glacial and iceberg action were confused, until Prof Agassiz practically demonstrated the difference,' on the glacier in Switzerland. The iceberg period followed that of the glacier The depression of the continent, from 1,000 to 2.000 feet, created a sea-bed. This was filled by the melting of the glacier Meanwhile, the water supply on the glacier continued, but the moderated climate prevented the formation of the ice-cap. As a result, the hydraulic pressure from behind forced the glacier, or frozen stream, into the sea The buoyancy of the water counteracted on the specific gravity of the glacier, and, when the ice had projected beyond a point at which it could resist the upward pressure of the sea-water, great masses of it were broken off These masses floated away and are known as *icebergs*

The glacier was frozen to the bottom of its river-bed, congealing in its embrace rocks, gravel, sand and whatever substances lay thereon These substances were held firmly during the progress of the iceberg, after its liberation from the parent glacier, until it had floated into warmer waters Then began a gradual dripping of the freight of the berg, until finally the ice itself disappeared in the mild waters of a tropic ocean

The opinion prevails among geologists that the glacier motion was from the east of north, but that the Champlain flow was from the northwest. Corroborating this hypothesis is the marked difference in color of the bowlder clay and the Upper Drift deposit. If the glacier motion was from the north, or east of north, it did not produce the beds of our present rivers Glaciation on the process of leveling the earth's surface by the pressure of moving glaciers, only wore off and smoothed down the surface of the country leaving it a vast undu-

lating plain of dark blue mud, a heterogeneous mass of clay, sand, gravel and
bowlders.   The old river courses and valleys were completely obliterated
That the great beds of alluvium which cover up the blue clay were deposited
in water, is clearly proven by its stratification, which can be observed in almost
any excavation where a hill or bluff has been cut through in constructing railroads or mills, or where brick clay has been procured

But let us see how the Champlain or Drift period was produced

A continental subsidence came on and large inland lakes were formed   The
climate became modified , the glaciers melted more rapidly ; vast icebergs broke
loose from the mountain-like glaciers and floated over the land, carrying rocks
and clay and debris with them, and as they melted, strewed them over the surface, sometimes grounding and excavating basins for future lakes and ponds.
Thus, year after year and age after age, did the muddy waters and freighted icebergs flow over the country the former depositing our present alluvial drift, the
latter dropping here and there the bowlders and debris that we now find scattered over the country   No erosion or wearing away, save from a stranded iceberg, occurred at that time, but it was a period of filling in, a period of distribution over the submerged land, of powdered rocks, sand and clay, and an
occasional bowlder   But when the continent emerged from the abyss, and the
waters flowed off, and the higher undulations of the land appeared, then the
erosive action of winds and waves and storms and currents took place   The
waters, as they flowed toward the sea and Gulf, produced their inevitable
channels.

There was much of the drift carried into the streams and borne away in the
floods to the sea   Then was the stranded bowlder, by wind and wave, stripped
of its soft, alluvial bed, left high and dry on the surface of the hereafter prairie.
Then were the gravelly knolls that are found in some parts of the State robbed
of every fine sediment, and the gravel and stones left to tell the story of the
floods   Then were the great valleys washed out ; then did the annual wash-
outs all along the water-courses—rapidly at first, but more slowly in after
ages—eat away the drift accumulations and form *the hills*.   The hilly districts
generally lie contiguous to the streams   Back from these water courses, the
land is usually undulating prairie, showing but little erosion

The country contiguous to the Des Moines River and its tributaries bears, in
many localities, unmistakable evidences of the action of the retiring waters of the
Champlain period   As geology has written its history in the rocks, so the latest
action of the waters has left its legible records in the drifts—*it made tracks*.
and by its tracks we can see where it was and what it did

When two currents of water flow together, charged with sediment, where
the currents meet there will occur an eddy, the eddy-water will throw down its
load of floating mud and build up a bar   In the valley of every creek in this
locality, may be found many of those silted-up banks and promontories, the
deposits of the waters during the later Champlain period

If our readers will but notice the action of any swollen creek, they will at
once perceive how the prairie streams have silted or thrown up the hillocks so
frequently met with.   Notice the little brook that meets the larger creek yon-
der   At the mouth of the brook is a *firmer bit of ground* in the slough, upon
which the horseman at an early day, safely crossed the miry ford.   That firm
ground was formed by the heavy sediment of the brook.   The two streams produced an eddy on meeting   the waters were delayed an instant   Some of
the sand brought down the brook during this pause, and a hillock in embryo
was made

Years from this time, the course of that stream will be changed because of an impeding elevation of land, and that elevated land will be cultivated, with rich returns. So the surface of the prairies was formed into irregular hills and dales

BOWLDERS

are frequently found scattered over the surface of the country, and very commonly in ravines or sloughs. because. when denudation was taking place by the agency of the subsiding waters, they invariably moved down hill when the earth was washed from under them This readily accounts for their being usually found in ravines

ORIGIN OF THE PRAIRIES

Prof. Hall, in his Geological Report of Iowa, says

The subject of the origin of the prairies, or the cause of the absence of trees over so extensive a region, is one which has often been discussed, and in regard to which diametrically opposite opinions are entertained

The idea is very extensively entertained throughout the West, that the prairies were once covered with timber, but that it has been deen destroyed by the fires which the Indians have been in the habit of starting in the dry grass, and which swept a vast extent of surface every Autumn A few considerations will show that the theory is entirely untenable

In the first place, the prairies have been in existence at least as far back as we have any knowledge of the country, since the first explorers of the West describe them just as they now are There may be limited areas once covered with woods and now bare, but, in general, the prairie region occupies the same surface which it did when first visited by the white man

But, again, prairies are limited to a peculiar region—one marked by certain characteristic topographical and geological features, and they are, by no means distributed around wherever the Indians have roamed and used fire Had frequent occurrence of fires in the woods been the means of removing the timber and covering the soil with a dense growth of grass, there is no reason why prairies should not exist in the Eastern and Middle States, as well as in the Western The whole northern portion of the United States was once inhabited by tribes differing but little from each other in their manner of living

Again, were the prairies formerly covered by forest trees, we should probably now find some remains of them buried beneath the soil, or other indications of their having existed Such is not the case, for the occurrence of fragments of wood beneath the prairie surface is quite rare And when they are found, it is in such position as to show that they had been removed to some distance from the place of their growth

It has been maintained by some that the want of sufficient moisture in the air or soil was the cause of the absence of forests in the Northwest and it is indeed true that the prairie region does continue westward, and become merged in the arid plains which extend along the base of the Rocky Mountains, where the extreme dryness is undoubtedly the principal obstacle to the growth of anything but a few shrubs peculiarly adapted to the conditions of climate and soil which prevail in that region This, however cannot be the case in the region of the Mississippi and near Lake Michigan, where the prairies occupy so large a surface, since the results of meteorological observations show no lack of moisture in that district, the annual precipitation being fully equal to what it is in the well-wooded country farther east in the same latitude Besides, the growth of forest trees is rich and abundant all through the prairie region under certain conditions of soil and position showing that their range is not limited by any general climatological cause

Taking into consideration all the circumstances under which the peculiar vegetation of the prairie occurs, we are disposed to consider the nature of the soil as the prime cause of the absence of forests, and the predominance of grasses over the widely-extended region And although chemical composition may not be without influence in bringing about this result, which is a subject for further investigation, and one worthy of careful examination, yet we conceive that the extreme fineness of the particles of which the prairie soil is composed is probably the principal reason why it is better adapted to the growth of its peculiar vegetation than to the development of forests

It cannot fail to strike the careful observer that where the prairies occupy the surface, the soil and superficial material have been so finely comminuted as to be almost in a state of an impalpable powder This is due, partially, to the peculiar nature of the underlying rocks and the facility with which they undergo composition and also to the chemical causes which have acted during and since the accumulation of these materials and from the prairie soil

If we go to the thickly-wooded regions, like those of the northern peninsula of Michigan, and examine those portions of the surface which have not been invaded by the forest, we shall observe that the beds of ancient lakes which have been filled up by the slowest possible accumulation of detrital matter and are now perfectly dry, remain as natural prairies and are not trespassed upon by the surrounding woods   We can conceive of no other reason for this than the extreme fineness of the soil which occupies these basins, and which is the natural result of the slow and quiet mode in which they have been filled up.   The sides of these depressions, which were lakes, slope very gradually upward, and being covered with a thick growth of vegetation, the material brought into them must have been thus caused   Consequently, when the former lake has become entirely filled up and raised above the level of overflow, we find it covered with a most luxuriant crop of grass, forming the natural meadows from which the first settlers are supplied with their first stock of fodder

Applying these facts to the case of the prairies of larger dimensions farther south, we infer, on what seems to be reasonable grounds, that the whole region now occupied by the prairies of the Northwest was once an immense lake, in whose basin sediment of almost impalpable fineness gradually accumulated   that this basin was drained by the elevation of the whole region   but, at first, so slowly that the finer particles of the deposit were not washed away, but allowed to remain where they were originally deposited

After the more elevated portions of the former basin had been laid bare, the drainage becoming concentrated into comparatively narrow channels, the current thus produced, aided, perhaps, by a more rapid rise of the region, acquired sufficient velocity to wear down through the finer material on the surface, wash away a portion of it altogether, and mix the rest so effectually with the underlying drift materials, or with abraded fragments of the rocks in places as to give rise to a different character of soil in the valleys from that of the elevated land   The valley soil being much less homogeneous in composition and containing a larger proportion of course materials than that of the uplands, seems to have been adapted to the growth of forest vegetation, and in consequence of this we find such localities covered with an abundant growth of timber

Wherever there has been a variation from the usual conditions of soil, on the prairie or in the river bottom, there is a corresponding change in the character of the vegetation   Thus on the prairie we sometimes meet with ridges of coarse material   apparently deposits of drift, on which, from some local cause   there never has been an accumulation of fine sediment   In such localities we invariably find a growth of timber   This is the origin of the groves scattered over the prairies, for whose isolated position and peculiar circumstances of growth we are unable to account in any other way

The condition of things in the river valleys themselves seems to add to the plausibility of this theory   In the district which we have more particularly examined, we have found that where rivers have worn deep and comparatively narrow valleys, bordered by precipitous bluffs, there is almost always a growth of forest, but where the valley widens out, the bluffs become less conspicuous, indicating a less rapid erosion and currents of diminished strength, there decomposition takes place under circumstances favorable to the accumulation of prairie soil, and the result has been the formation of the bottom prairie, which becomes so important a feature of the valleys of the Mississippi and Missouri below the limits of Iowa   Where these bottom prairies have become, by any change in the course of the river currents, covered with coarser materials, a growth of forest trees may be observed springing up, and indicating by their rapid development a congenial soil

This theory is noticeably substantiated by the formation and condition of the valley of the lower Des Moines.

DESCRIPTIVE GEOGRAPHY

Van Buren County is bounded on the east by Lee and Henry Counties, on the north by Jefferson County, on the west by Davis County, and on the south by the Missouri line.   It embraces a fraction over thirteen townships, or about four hundred and eighty square miles of surface, and is one of the best timbered counties in this part of the State.   The Des Moines River runs diagonally through the county from northwest to southeast, affording a considerable belt of timber and an abundant supply of stock-water in ordinary seasons.   The country lying north of the river is marked with Crooked. Lick, Coates, Reed and Cedar Creeks   each skirted with timber from their source to their outlet

The prairies are generally small, with a rolling surface and a soil fully equal to the average prairie soil of the West   The upland timber consists of black and white oak   hickory   elm   linden and cherry   while upon the Des Moines bottom may be found black and white walnut, sugar and white maple, ash, hack-berry, cottonwood, sycamore, honey-locust and mulberry.

At least three-fourths of the superficial area of this county is underlaid by deposits belonging to the coal formation, but it is not probable that a workable coal-seam will be found to extend over more than one-half or two-thirds of the territory so underlaid

At least two workable coal-seams outcrop in the county, varying in thick-ness from two to five feet The upper one is exposed in the vicinity of Iowa-ville, on the south side of the Des Moines and at Business Corners and vicin-ity, on the north side of the river. The lower seam, where it occurs of suffi-cient thickness to afford a profitable bed, seems to have been deposited in basins or depressions in the limestone The coal at Farmington, both at Williams and Johnson's bank, occurs in a basin of this kind and is about two miles in width from east to west, and extends south a half mile beyond the Des Moines River, varies from two to three feet in thickness

On the prairies, good wells of living waters are obtained from twenty to thirty feet below the surface But along the river-bluffs and on the timbered lands generally, considerable difficulty is experienced in procuring good water, and cisterns are in general use

Quarries of the best building material abound in the bluffs of almost every stream On Chequest Creek is a fine-grained, compact limestone of a light gray or dove color, and susceptible of a fine polish The rock seems well adapted to many purposes for which an ornamental stone is required, and has acquired some reputation as Chequest marble Tin copper and iron have been discov-ered, and, excepting the mineral productions of Dubuque and Jackson Coun-ties, Van Buren County contains more variety in its geological features than any other in the State.

For beauty of scenery, extent of cultivation and fertility of soil, the county stands unrivaled

So much for generalizing. Now for a more definite dwelling upon the min-eral products.

The full thickness of the coal-bearing strata in this county is not accurately known Some of the oldest mines in the State are located here. The strata, however, probably nowhere exceeds one hundred and fifty feet, and is known to be usually much less. The number of different beds of coal has not been fully made out, but there are probably three, only one of which is usually of suffi-cient thickness for purposes of working. This bed, if it be always the same one in which the mines are opened, is of very considerable importance and from it large quantities of coal have been, and very much more may yet be obtained A mine has for a long time been opened in a three-and-one-half-foot bed of coal, a little below the town of Independent, in the extreme northwest corner of the county About two and a half miles eastward from the same town, a mine has been opened in a four-foot bed About half a mile up the same creek valley in which the latter is located, another opening has been made in a four-foot bed, which appears to be a separate bed from the others, being quite above it Half a mile south of Burnes' Corners, is one of the oldest mines in the county, situated in a half-foot bed A little south of this, near Doud's Station, some mines were formerly successfully operated and they may, doubtless, be re-opened At and in the vicinity of Keosauqua, several openings have been made in a bed of coal of the feet thick and have for many years been worked to supply local demand. A thin of bed and has also been opened in the same township

At Farmington, large quantities of coal were formerly mined These mines were successfully worked. In the northeastern corner of the county some mines have been profitably worked for many years, to supply a local demand There have been also other openings made in coal-beds in this county

The clay associated with the coal-bearing strata of this county has been extensively used at Vernon for the manufacture of stone pottery

An artesian well 705 feet deep has been bored at Farmington, and a full flow of water was the result The water, as analyzed by Prof Emery, is proved to contain, per liter, 1.12 grains of ferruginous sediment, and 8 18 grains of solid matter in solution, making a total of 9 3 grains of solid matter per liter. Its principal constituent is ferric sulphate. It also contains considerable gypsum, sodium and hydrochloric acid. A portion of the sulphuric acid is free ; the amount, per liter, contained in the water being 3 306 grains. The matter also contains 1 58 grains of ferric oxide and 0.403 grains of calcium oxide, per liter.

The following is a list of timber found within the county White-maple. sugar-maple, buckeye, water-birch, hickory, pignut-hickory, pecan, hackberry, black wild-cherry, white-ash. honey-locust, Kentucky coffee-bean, butternut, white-walnut, black-walnut, box-elder, button, sycamore, cotton-wood, aspen. white-oak. burr-oak, black oak, linden bass-wood, common elm and slippery-elm.

THE UNKNOWN RACE

The cession of the lands once owned by the Indians, opened up this region to the whites, and brought the county of Van Buren within the limits of settlement. In 1836, the last traces of resistance to a superior power disappeared from the Indian bands, and impetus was given to progression Piece by piece the lands of Iowa had been wrested from the aborigines, until a t last there remained but one step between them and utter rout The time was fast approaching when the voice of authority should cry " depart," and the vanguard of the pale-faced invaders on the hunting-grounds and homes of the natives was fretting in the invisible chain which held it back

The legends of this fated people are rich with unwritten poetry and romance The spectacle of fallen greatness is sad in any case, and invests the victims of adverse fate with a halo, perhaps inconsistent with reality, but nevertheless worthy of a passing thought

But, before we reach the era of Indian occupancy, there is encountered that which gives pause to the prosecution of research in that direction, and opens up a fruitful field for speculation The history of Van Buren County is so much older than the period embraced even by Indian legends, that we stand in grave silence before the evidences of those who have gone before The red man alone is not the only denizen of these groves, these hills and vales Long before the war-whoop of the Indian awoke echoes in the silent watches of the night. or the plaintive song of Indian lover aroused the dusky maiden to the thought of love, there lived a race of men with passions, ambitions and desires perhaps akin to those we know The march of time destroyed these primitive dwellers of the earth, leaving but vague traces of their existence for us to ponder over A broken flint, an arrow-head, a bit of crudest pottery—what are these? Traces of a lost people, of whom even legends have become extinct forever.

Such sights as these suggest the thought that Nature too reproduces her grandest works in eras marked by æons of ages

Those who struck the first blows, in the name of Improvement, upon the banks of the Des Moines, have beheld a ruined nation depart, never to return   May it not be that our race, too, must some day stand before a superior power, and watch its noblest efforts grow pale before the light of other minds?

In the womb of centuries may there not be those who will repeople what are to become the vast solitudes of these broad acres, now so busy with teeming millions, and read with curious eyes the evidences of ourselves—a forgotten race?   Perhaps beneath the sea there slumbers now a continent that will some day grow rank with life, and send forth pioneers to seek new worlds   The record of the rocks tells us that these things have been, and what was once performed may be again accomplished.   The mold of centuries may rise above our streets   The wash of waves may erode our noblest monuments   Ruin and decay give birth to youth and grandeur   A language strange to ears in being now, may portray the marvels of a land in which primeval forests thrive, where stores of virgin wealth lie deep within the bowels of the earth, where fertile plains wave with luxuriant vegetation; where the ax was never heard, and where the ground was never trodden by human foot   Then will the husbandman's implement reveal the broken columns which centuries have concealed beneath their accumulation of waste, and the archæologist wax wise over the fragments of our vaunted might

As these things may be, let us, while now we can, pay to those who have preceded us the passing tribute of a sigh.

That these broad lands were once the home of a people now no longer numbered among the living, there can be no doubt   Evidences of their existence are at the very doors of those who dwell in the fertile valley of the Des Moines

The Mound-Builders, as modern tongue is pleased to term them from lack of a better name, have left traces of their presence here which admit of no dispute.   Who they were and from whence they came, the wisest archæologists are puzzling their brains to determine   The secret of their lives has perished with their mortal frames, leaving naught but food for speculation behind   Some future generation, it is true, may chance upon a hidden tablet or a source of light which will illumine the darkness of the present respecting the prehistoric race   Even here, where such lavish manifestations of their sojourn exist, there may be stored the key to the vast mystery.   Some day the truth may be made clear, but now we can only record the facts made patent to us, and hope for the dawn of that eventful morn when the cabalistic signs on table and on rock shall become like opened books before our eyes

Among the numerous gentlemen resident in Ottumwa, or in the Des Moines Valley, who have given intelligent thought to the investigation of this absorbing topic, we first name Mr Samuel B Evans, of the Ottumwa *Democrat*, as an authority upon the subject of the local mounds   Mr Evans has acquired a reputation as a patient worker in this broad field, and has prepared many articles for the press, pertaining to the mounds in Wapello and Van Buren Counties   A paper was requested of him by the Smithsonian Institution, elaborating the location and character of the ancient works in this section of the State, and, through the kindness of Mr Evans, we are permitted to illustrate this brief chapter with copies of diagrams prepared by him for the paper referred to   These outline cuts will convey to the reader a better idea of the position

of the mounds, and, what is even more important, they will preserve a record
of their topography in the event of their destruction by the rapid encroachments of modern improvements.

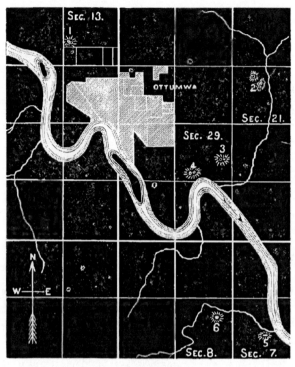

DIAGRAM A.

Mounds near Ottumwa, Wapello Co., on the Des Moines River and adjacent thereto.

REFERENCE.

No. 1 Mound, on Section 13, Township 72, Range 14, is known as the "Caldwell Mound."
On the highest lands in Wapello County, about a quarter of a mile south of the Caldwell Mounds, are the Hed-
rick Mounds, not shown on diagram. These latter are doubtless mounds of observation.
No. 2, on Section 21, Township 72, Range 13, are known as the "Sugar Creek Mounds."
Nos. 3 and 4, on Section 29, Township 72, Range 13, are known as the "Trowell" and the "Stiles" Mounds, re-
spectively.
Nos. 5 and 6, on Sections 7 and 8, Township 71, Range 13, are known as the "Village Creek Mounds," from the
stream which flows by them.
Scale of diagram, five-eighths of an inch to the mile.

It is the purpose of this article to deal solely with facts; to confine the
range of topic exclusively to a description of the location, character and contents of the mounds in the counties of Wapello and Van Buren, so far as
research has furnished data for the perfection of this design. We leave to our
readers the interesting work of solving the origin of the *tumuli*, the habits of
the strange people who constructed them, and the fate of the race which now
excites our profoundest curiosity. If this imperfect sketch serves to stimulate
latent forces to action in the direction of study, its purpose will be fully
accomplished.

The diagram herewith given, and marked "A," exhibits all the mounds in
the vicinity of Ottumwa which have been explored and may be said to embrace
all that are known to exist. Future investigation may reveal mounds at present unknown, but that is scarcely probable. The examination of all the mounds

herein referred to has been conducted by Mr Evans, in company with the several gentlemen named, in the following order:

Sugar Creek—Capt W. H Kitteiman, S. H. Burton and D. T. Miller

The Stiles, by Hon. E. H Stiles. The Trowell has not been opened, so far as can be ascertained.

Village Creek, by Mr. Richard Williams and Mr A. T Holly

Keosauqua, or Ely Ford Group (shown here in diagram "B"), by Judge Robert Sloan, Mr. J. J. Kinnersly. Mr. D. C Beaman, Messrs Robert N and Charles L Dahlberg and Ben Johnson, Esq

The names of these gentlemen are ample guaranty of the thoroughness and intelligence of the search made. Capt. Kitteiman, Mr. Williams, Mr. Holly and Judge Sloan are especially qualified to prosecute so important an undertaking

The Sugar Creek Mounds (Sec. 21. T. 72, R. 13) are simple *tumuli*. The first one opened stands upon a high elevation, and may be termed a mound of observation From it, those lying to the southwest, the Trowell Mounds, are visible, although a mile and a half distant From this post, a series of communication might be maintained with a person stationed on the Trowell hillock, if the intervening growth of young trees was removed. From this mound, nothing of value was obtained save bits of charcoal and decomposed ashes This fact goes to confirm the theory that it was designed as a station of survey. The second of the Sugar Creek group contained a few decayed bones, but no estimate of their character was possible

From the Trowell Mound the Stiles *tumuli* are plainly seen. These mounds lie in the suburbs of Ottumwa. When they were opened in the spring of 1878, no traces of human burial were found There were but few, and those unsatisfactory, evidences of cremation In one of the largest, a small hatchet was obtained, which was made of green stone, highly finished. The character of this hatchet led the explorers to believe that its deposit was accidental. No other implements in entire form were discovered, but several bits of broken arrow-heads and a few chips or cherts of obsidian were taken This flint is exceedingly rare. If the valley and intervening ridges were denuded of the growing young timber, one group of the Village Creek mounds could be seen from this mound, although the Creek groups are more than three miles distant.

In the fall of 1877, three of the Village Creek mounds were carefully examined A reference to diagram "A" will show that there are two groups, each composed of seven or eight individual mounds, lying in line The groups are about one mile apart Those which were opened contained evidences of cremation. Successive layers of ashes and charcoal intermingled with calcined bones No implements of any kind were discovered in a complete state, and but few broken arrow-heads

From this record it will be seen that the mounds removed from the river—the Sugar Creeks—are in line of direct communication with those on the stream, by means of signals. This fact is mentioned merely as an incidental one, perhaps worthy of consideration Recent examination of the Caldwell and Hedrick Mounds resulted in nothing important They contained no remains, human or otherwise, but were doubtless mounds of observation solely Still, subsequent research may reveal relics, and it is to be hoped that the investigation will be carefully made at an early day.

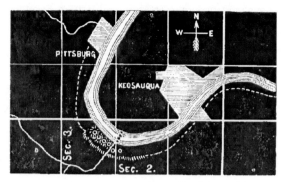

DIAGRAM B.

Mounds near Keosauqua and Pittsburg, Van Buren County.

REFERENCES.

A bluff extends over Sections 2 and 3, Township 68, Range 10.
Mounds on Section 3 are known as "Ely Ford Mounds," because of creek and old ford.
The square on right of creek, near mouth, is the Shell Heap, referred to herein.
The stream running through Pittsburg is Chequest Creek.
The dotted line around the southern shore indicates where the chain of mounds exists.
Scale, five-eighths inch to the mile.

In July, 1878, the Ely Ford Mounds in Van Buren County were opened. The location of these *tumuli* is as follows : Counting from the left bank of the creek northwestward, No. 1 is 20 rods north, 55° west from mouth of creek ; 20 feet above river-bed ; 40 feet from water's edge. There is no timber. In this were found fresh-water muscle-shells in large quantity, and pieces of pottery, arrow-heads, bones (probably animals'), part of a human jaw with teeth, and foot and leg bones of a human skeleton in fair state of preservation. There was a surface deposit of about two feet over these remains.

No. 2 was 10 rods north, 60° west from No. 1, on Bluff Point, 100 feet above river-bed, 200 feet from water's edge. On this mound were the decayed remains of a large white-oak tree, which was two feet in diameter ; also young oak growing. In the mound was found

A HUMAN SKULL

entire, except the lower jaw. A portion of the upper jaw was decomposed, but one tooth remained. The leg-bones were also discovered. The position of the skeleton was two feet beneath the surface, with head southeast, horizontal. The same pottery as in No. 1. The dimensions of this skull are as follows : horizontal circumference, 20 inches ; longitudinal arc, from nasal depression, along middle line of skull to occipital protuberance, 13 inches ; transverse measurement, 5 inches ; vertical height, 3 75-100 inches ; longitudinal measurement, 8 inches. This skull approaches very nearly to the famous Neanderthal, or Cave skull, of Prussia.

No. 3 is half-moon shaped, 15 rods north, 550 west from No. 2, on same bluff, 120 feet above the river-bed, and 200 feet from water's edge. In it were found thigh-bones.

No. 4 was 15 rods north, 45° west from No. 3, but contained nothing valuable, and may be modern.

No. 5 was a large mound, 50 feet in diameter and 5 feet in height ; located 30 rods south, 15 east from mouth of Ely's Creek, on high bluff point, 100 feet above river-bed, and 20 rods from water's edge. Upon it was a decayed white oak tree, 24 inches in diameter, located 12 feet north, 10° west from the center of the mound, and another stump of similar character 16 inches in diameter, 4 feet north from center. In this mound were discovered human thigh-bones under the south side of the large stump, five feet from the surface, and subsequent investigation revealed

TWO SKELETONS

in excellent state of preservation   The wood of the oak crumbled in the hand because of its exceedingly rotten condition.   There were fragments of the arm-bone, and the position of the body must have been horizontal, with head toward the west and leg doubled under   Quantities of shells were found, as in No 1. Later research revealed the best preserved skull ever found in this country   It is now in the possession of Mr Evans, of Ottumwa, and is a proper object of elaborate study and comparison   The region about Keosauqua is evidently rich in evidences of ancient sepulture.

The river-bank is thickly covered with these mounds   The diagram does not show the twentieth part of the *tumuli* in Van Buren County.   Nearly fifty have been discovered in the immediate vicinity of Keosauqua.   We aim to locate only those which have been explored by Mr. Evans, or some one skilled in the detection of relics.

Judge Sloan has devoted a considerable portion of the leisure which his arduous professional duties grudgingly gave him to the contemplation of this subject   From him we learn that he is aware of the existence of some forty-five mounds, besides many "pockets," or places of deposit in the bluffs, where shells, bits of bone—probably of animals that served as food—and fragments of pottery are placed, and slightly covered with earth

The most valuable discovery yet made in the Des Moines Valley is the skull which we have described   It is the remains of a race the like of which does not exist on earth at the present time.   The doubts created as to the antiquity of the stone implements found are natural and reasonable   Any race of stone-workers might have produced them; but the irrefutable evidence of the skull silences comment and arouses profound conjecture.   The modern Indian possesses no characteristics like those which must have been the portion of this man, whose gaping sockets mock us as we gaze into them   Could the tongue which once formed syllables of command beneath that moldering jaw be re-invested with the power to speak, what tales it could unfold !

The race of which this is a type was easily led, low in intellect, and not far different from the patient toiler on the Pyramids of Egypt

Messrs. Robert N and Charles L Dahlberg, explored the region of the mouth of Chequest Creek, at Pittsburg, Van Buren County, with satisfactory results, on the 31st of July, 1878   Ancient pottery was discovered   A description of the ware prepared by the gentlemen who unearthed it, is herewith appended .

The pieces of pottery found are composed of clay and sand, mixed with small pebbles, forming a cement which appears to be baked rather than burned   The most of the pieces found show that the heat applied in their construction was not sufficient to melt the sand or pebbles, or in any way to affect their original condition   No glazing appears on the pottery, and yet it is of a hard, firm, durable substance which is impervious to water   One piece of pottery is about four inches square, but of an irregular shape   At one point it is shown to be a part of the top of a wide-mouthed vessel, evidently about two inches less in diameter at the neck than at the top Judging by the arc described by the piece in question, the neck of the piece must have been at least 18 inches in diameter

This piece also ... attempts at ... having horizontal ... beads, about an inch and ... from ... these have the ... having been made by punctures ... on the inside of ... essel, and are about half ... or seven-eighths from center ... uter

There are also parallel lines running about it horizontally, about half an inch apart, which were evidently made by some blunt instrument about one-eighth of an inch square, pressed into the clay, leaving little ridges between each impression of the instrument that would average about one-sixteenth of an inch thick. There are a number of small pieces one showing distinctly that the neck and rim of the vessel above it were quite flaring, though this rim does not show entire. The rim is ornamented by diamond shaped figures made by lines crossing each other, which lines are formed very much like the parallel lines in the larger piece.

Another piece shows parallel lines. One small piece is corrugated as the Ely Ford pottery, and shows distinctly the application of heat sufficient to fuse the silex in the composition of the pottery, making it a very hard and firm substance, this piece is thinner than the baked pieces. Another piece shows bead-work distinctly about an inch from the top of the vessel, the body of the vessel is ornamented with parallel lines running at right angles with the top of the vessel, made as in the first piece described, and the top ornamented very much as our mothers used to ornament the edge of a pie.

Several other pieces show the application of heat sufficient to fuse the silex in their composition. Several, including the larger piece described above, show on the edges and upon both surfaces glittering particles, which appear to be small pieces of isinglass. This pottery was nearly all found upon the surface of the ground, having been washed out by the action of the water, some were found on the creek-bank, and some on the river-bank near the edge of the water, but all at the mouth of Chequest, which empties into the river at Pittsburg. In the river-bank in front of the village is also a bed of ashes and charcoal, about three inches in depth, and about two feet from the surface of the ground.

Mr. Evans recently contributed to the Chicago *Times* a series of letters descriptive of the mounds in this locality, and speculative as to their origin. We quote so much of the contributions as treats of the appearance of the *tumuli:*

The mounds which I have examined on Village Creek presented the following conditions, They are found on natural elevations, the highest in the vicinity. They are regular in shape and regular in the arrangement of the materials which compose them. The second stratum of earth composing them, immediately beneath the natural soil, accumulated by the decay of vegetation, is very often foreign to the surroundings. Then succeed strata of ashes, charcoal and earth, averaging about five inches in thickness. Human remains are found in these mounds, but not always, which indicates that they were not originally made for burial places, and give color to the idea that they were utilized by succeeding populations for uses foreign to the design of the builders. But in Iowa they are not numerous enough to encourage the supposition that they were merely sites of dwelling-places, because of the labor to build them. It is not reasonable to believe that any people, whether civilized or barbarous, would build a mound which would require the labor of ten men for fifty days, on the top of which a wooden building could be constructed less than twenty feet in circumference.

In Wapello County we have a range of mounds about two miles from the river, on a ridge running parallel with the Des Moines, on the southern side which overlooks the plateau or bottom land of the stream, and is in plain view of a corresponding range of mounds situated on a high hill north of the river. These mounds are similar in shape, and having examined many of them on each side of the river, I find their interior composition to be very much alike. The layers of ashes, charcoal and earth are the same, and in some of them human remains were found. In a few of them I have discovered flint implements. I must confess, however, that after all my examinations I cannot settle down on any well-grounded opinion as to the objects for which these mounds were created, except to disagree with all the theories so far advanced. The ashes and charcoal and human remains showing the action of fire, have at times induced me to believe that the Mound-Builders practiced cremation, and that after the rites were performed the remains were covered with earth, each succeeding funeral pyre adding to the height of the mound. Yet, while this theory has in my mind more proofs than any other yet advanced, I am not prepared to accept it without additional evidence.

Archæologists have determined that the mounds of America may be properly classed under three general heads, viz: Mounds of Observation, Mounds of Sacrifice and Mounds of Burial. The first were doubtless used as posts of communication between distant bands. They are always found on elevated lands, from which wide areas of territory may be seen, if modern timber or edifices do not intervene. From one to another a signal fire or flag might have conveyed intelligence of invasion, of joy or of distress. This class of work is found in W____ _____ in ___ excellent ___ of preservation. The large _____ __ __ _ _____ __ having been erected for such purposes, rather than _____ _ __ _ _ _ __ for the disposal of the dead; although some of the *tumuli*, undoubtedly, were devoted separately to each of the three purposes

In Van Buren County, the dwelling-places of the Mound-Builders are more distinctly marked While observation hills are found there, also. the larger number of mounds bear striking testimony of other uses The unearthing of the skeletons from Mounds Nos. 2 and 5, are events worthy of the consideration of scientists the world over. The fragments of pottery, the stone implements and the heaps of shells and animal bones, furnish food for deepest thought The ground is rich in remains of every character, and should be thoroughly investigated.

From far above Pittsburg to a point several miles below Keosauqua, a continuous chain of works is to be seen The diagram of the great bend in the river, near Keosauqua, shows but a faint outline of the place where future archæologists will delve with satisfactory results.

It is not within the province of this chapter to enter into an elaborate discussion of the subject, but, as has already been intimated, merely to suggest where the labor should be undertaken. Van Buren County should be made the theater of exhaustive research, and if this paper prepares the way for such enterprises, its mission will be fully accomplished.

HISTORY OF THE ABORIGINES

From the contemplation of this primordial race—a people which must be termed the originals, so far as our imperfect knowledge extends, but which may, after all, have been but the last fragments of a nation greater even than our own—let us pass to the consideration of those tribes which are not mythical

Human improvement, rushing through civilization, crushes in its march all who cannot grapple to its car This law is as inexorable as Fate "You colonize the lands of the savage with the Anglo-Saxon," says Stephen Montague, "you civilize that portion of the earth : but is the savage civilized? He is exterminated' You accumulate machinery, you increase the total of wealth ; but what becomes of the labor you displace? One generation is sacrificed to the next You diffuse knowledge, and the world seems to grow brighter, but Discontent at Poverty replaces Ignorance happy with its crust. Every Improvement, every advancement in civilization, injures some to benefit others, and either cherishes the want of to-day or prepares the revolution of to-morrow "

It is, as it were, but yesterday since the hills and valleys of the Des Moines re-echoed the mournful dirge of the departing red man. The years are few in number since the sorrowful *cortege* passed slowly toward the setting sun, leaving behind the noble dead. sleeping in the cold embrace of the grim monarch, by the side of their beloved white father; leaving the homes they had been taught to claim as their own , leaving all, even hope, behind There still live many persons who beheld the strange sight of a remnant of a race departing forever from the scenes of their early life, and such will, doubtless, be disposed to sneer at the pen which finds a source of sadness in the contemplation of this event But worthy hands have written lines of living power upon the theme, nor can the harsh character of fact denude the subject of a glamour which poetry and rom... have cast ... the dusky subject and ' ' ... There is a grandeur in the record of the ... which the stern force ... with is powerless to dispel

Those men who were compelled to meet the groveling band which had survived the first shock of defeat, saw only the ruin which the strong had wrought upon the weak   The native power had fled; a subjugated race was subsisting in its helplessness upon the bounty of its conquerors   There was no spot on earth left for them   Foot by foot their mighty possessions were taken from them, not in the din and whirl of battle, but by the humiliating processes of peace   Here, at last, they stood, with bowed heads, meekly awaiting the decree which should compel them to resume their endless march   Behind them was the tradition of their strength; before them, annihilation of their clans.   Even their warlike instincts were dwarfed in the presence of their masters   Had they disputed titles with the whites, the memories clustering about them now would be far different.   But that resort to arms, that defiant struggle to the end, that disappearance in dramatic furor—all was denied them   Had they been other in nature than they were, this placid surrender to fate would seem less pitiful   Once fierce and bloody, then subdued, their stolid acceptance of destiny carried with it a mournful air that will be breathed through history's pages while our race shall live

The Indian is the embodiment of the dramatic, and when the curtain is rung down upon a scene so spiritless and tame as this of which we write, the admiration which is his due is turned to pity.   The actual spectators of the drama find it impossible to forget the sordid character of the players, it is true; but at even so short a remove of time as this which has already elapsed since this county was the theater of the play, a shade of romance is imparted and the events become absorbing in their interest

KEOKUK, THE ORATOR CHIEFTAIN

The soil of Van Buren County has been trodden by two of the greatest red men of recent times.   Keokuk, the Chief, and Black Hawk, the Brave, both found thereon a resting-place, while within the limits of the region were enacted many of the most important scenes of their eventful lives

Keokuk, the grand sachem, was a man of tall, commanding presence, straight as an arrow, and, when aroused, could make an eloquent speech to his tribe   He was selected by the United States Government to distribute the annuities to the Sacs and Foxes—not only for his energies when opposed to the nation in battle, but for his influence among the red men everywhere   But he was avaricious and intemperate, putting any amount of whisky under his royal toga, and stealing from his red brothers the hard silver so kindly given them by the Great Father at Washington   He had a chronic quarrel with Hardfish's band, that lived in Kishkekosh, near Eddyville, and receiving a severe wound from one of this tribe, he died soon after reaching Kansas, in 1845

From a sketch of Keokuk, published in the 'Annals of Iowa,'' 1865, by Uriah Biggs, one of the pioneers of Van Buren, the following interesting extracts are made:

"Keokuk is deserving of a prominent page in the history of the country, and a truthful history of his life would be read and cherished as a memento of one of nature's noblemen.   As an orator, he was entitled to rank with the most gifted of his race   In person, he was tall and of portly bearing, and in his public speeches he displayed a commanding attitude and graceful gestures   He spoke rapidly, but his enunciation was clear and distinct and very forcible, culling his figures from the stores of nature, and basing his arguments in skillful logic   He maintained in good faith the stipulations of treaties with the United States and with the neighboring tribes   He loved peace and the social amenities of life, and was fond of displaying those agreeable traits of character in ceremonious visits to neighboring chiefs, in which he observed the most punctilious etiquette and dignified decorum. He possessed a ready insight into the motives of others, and was not easily misled by sophistry or beguiled by flattery, and in the field of wit, he was no mean champion It is not my purpose to write a history of his life, but I will give one anecdote in illustration of these traits of his character

"While residing near Ottumwah-noc, he received a message from the Mormon Prophet, Joe Smith, inviting Keokuk, as King of the Sacs and Foxes, to a royal conference at his palace at Nauvoo, on matters of the highest importance to their respective people The invitation was readily accepted, and a train of ponies was soon wending its way to the Mormon city, bearing Keokuk and his suite in stately procession and savage pomp

"Notice had circulated through the country of this diplomatic interview, and a number of spectators attended to witness the *denouement* The audience was given publicly in the Mormon temple and the respective chiefs were attended by their suites, the Prophet by the dignitaries of the Mormon Church, and the Indian potentate by the high civil and military functionaries of his tribe, and the gentiles were comfortably seated as auditors

'The prophet opened the conference in a set speech of considerable length, giving Keokuk a brief history of the children of Israel, as detailed in the Bible, and dwelt forcibly upon the story of the lost tribes, and of the direct revelation he had received from a divine source, that the North American Indians were these identical lost tribes, and that he, the prophet of God, held a divine commission to gather them together and to lead them to a land 'flowing with milk and honey.' After the prophet closed this harangue, Keokuk 'waited for the words of his pale-faced brother to sink deep into his mind,' and, in making his reply, assumed the gravest attitude and most dignified demeanor. He would not controvert anything his brother had said about the lost and scattered condition of his race and people, and if his brother was commissioned by the Great Spirit to collect them together and lead them to a new country, it was his duty to do so But he wished to inquire about some particulars his brother had not named, that were of the highest importance to him and his people. The red men were not much used to milk, and he thought they would prefer streams of water, and in the country where they now were there was a good supply of honey. The points that they wished to inquire into were whether the new government would pay large annuities, and whether there was plenty of whisky. Joe Smith saw at once that he had met his match, and that Keokuk was not the proper material with which to increase his army of dupes, and closed the conference in as amiable a manner as possible.

"He was gifted by nature with the elements of an orator in an eminent degree, and as such is entitled to rank with Logan, Red Jacket and Tecumseh, but unfortunately for his fame among the white people and with posterity, he was never able to obtain an interpreter who could claim even a slight acquaintance with philosophy. With one exception only, his interpreters were unacquainted even with the elements of their mother-tongue Of this serious hindrance to his fame, Keokuk was well aware, and retained Frank Labashure, who had received a rudimental education in the French and English languages, until the latter broke down by dissipation and died But during the meridian of his career among the white people he was compelled to submit his speeches for translation to uneducated men whose range of thought fell below the flights of a gifted mind, and the fine imagery drawn from nature was beyond their

powers of reproduction.   He had sufficient knowledge of the English tongue to
make him sensible of this bad rendering of his thought, and often a feeling of
mortification at the bungling efforts was depicted upon his countenance while
he was speaking   The proper place to form a due estimate of his ability as an
orator was in the Indian council, where he addressed himself exclusively to
those who understood his language, and where the electric effects of his eloquence could be plainly noted upon his audience.   It was credibly asserted that
by the force of his logic he had changed the vote of a council against the
strongly predetermined opinions of its members.   A striking instance of the
influence of his eloquence is related as occurring while the forces under Black
Hawk were invading Illinois, in 1832.

"Keokuk knew from the first that this reckless war would result in great
disaster to the tribe, and used all diligence to dissuade warriors from following
Black Hawk, and succeeded in retaining a majority with him at his town on the
Iowa River.   But, after Stillman's defeat, the war-spirit raged with such ardor
that a war-dance was held, and Keokuk took part in it. seeming to be moved
with the current of the rising storm. and when the dance was over, he called a
council to prepare for war   In his address he admitted the justice of his
complaints against the white man, and to seek redress was a noble aspiration of
their natures.   The blood of their brethren had been shed by the white man,
and the spirits of their braves slain in battle called loudly for vengeance   'I
am your chief,' he said, 'and it is my duty to lead you to battle, if, after fully
considering the matter you are determined to go   But, before you take this
important step, it is wise to inquire into the chances for success'   He then
represented to them the great power of the United States, against whom they
would have to contend—that their chances of success were utterly hopeless.
'But if you now determine to go upon the war-path, I will agree to lead
you upon one condition—that before we go we kill all our old men and our
wives and children to save them from a lingering death by starvation, and that
every one of us determine to leave his bones on the other side of the Mississippi.'

' This was a strong and truthful picture of the project before them, and was
presented in such a forcible light as to cool their ardor and to cause them to
abandon their rash undertaking   Many other incidents are related of his eloquence and tact in allaying a rising storm, fraught with war and bloodshed, not
only in his own tribe, but also among neighboring tribes, where his people had
been the aggressors   Some of these incidents have been preserved by writers
on Indian research, but many will be lost to history   He delivered a eulogy
upon Gen Harrison at the Sac and Fox Agency, which was interpreted by Mr.
Antoine Le Claire, and considered by many who heard its delivery, as one of
his best efforts   This speech, however. was not written down and is lost to history, but enough of the incidents of his career as an orator have been saved
from the wreck of time to stamp his reputation for natural abilities of the highest order, and furnish another positive refutation of Buffon's theory on the
deterioration of men and animals on the American Continent

"We have thus far portrayed the bright side of Keokuk's character, but
like most, if not all great intellects, there is a dark background which the
truth of history demands shall be brought to view.   His traits of character
thus far sketched, may not inaptly be compared to the great Grecian orator:
but here the similitude ends   The great blot on Keokuk's life was his inordi-
nate lov   and   to be   a   inebriate   His
withering   a pure stroke
of wit,

"A bitter and incurable feud existed in the tribe during their time of residence on the Des Moines River, between what was denominated 'Keokuk's band' and 'Black Hawk's band,' the latter recognizing Hardfish as their leader This distrust and, indeed, hatred were smothered in their common intercourse when sober, but when their blood was fired with whisky, it sometimes assumed a tragic feature amongst the leaders of the respective bands An instance of this character occurred on the lower part of the Des Moines on a return of a party making a visit to the 'half-breeds' at the town of Keokuk, on the Mississippi In a quarrel, excited by whisky Keokuk received a dangerous stab in the breast from a son of Black Hawk The writer of the present sketch saw him conveyed by his friends homeward, lying in a canoe, unable to rise

"Hardfish and his coadjutors lost no occasion to find fault with Keokuk's administration. The payments were made in silver coin, put in boxes, containing $500 each, and passed into Keokuk's hands for distribution. The several traders received each his quota, according to their several demands against the tribes admitted by Keokuk, which invariably consumed the far greater portion of the amount received The remainder was turned over to the chiefs, and distributed among their respective bands Great complaints were made of these allowances to the traders, on the ground of exorbitant prices charged on the goods actually furnished and it was alleged that some of these accounts were spurious In confirmation of this last charge, over and above the character of the items exhibited in these accounts, an affidavit was filed with Gov Lucas by an individual, to which the Governor gave credence. setting forth that Keokuk had proposed to the maker of the affidavit to prefer a purely fictitious account against the tribe for the sum of $10,000, and he would admit its correctness. and when paid, the money should be divided among themselves, share and share alike To swell the traders' bills, items were introduced of a character that showed fraud upon their face, such as a large number of 'blanket coats,' articles which the Indians never wore, and 'telescopes,' of the use of which they had no knowledge This shows the reckless manner in which these bills were swollen to the exorbitant amounts complained of, in which Keokuk was openly charged with being in league with the traders to defraud Hardfish's band At this time, the nation numbered about two thousand three hundred souls, and only about one-third of the whole number belonged to Keokuk's party. Gov Lucas warmly espoused the popular side in the controversy that arose in relation to the mode and manner of making the annual payment, and the matter was referred to the Indian Bureau, and the mode was changed, so that payments were made to the heads of families, approximating a per-capita distribution This method of making the payments met the unqualified disapprobation of the traders. and after one year's trial, fell back into the old channel Keokuk led his tribe west to the Kansas country, in 1845. and, according to reports, died some years after of delirium tremens."

Mr James Jordan relates the following anecdote of Keokuk "In 1837, the chief's son was prostrated with fever. Keokuk was absent at the time, but there chanced to be in the camp an old squaw, who was alleged to be invested with supernatural powers When Keokuk returned, his valiant heir informed him that the witch had cast an evil spirit into the settlement, which had increased the fever and rendered it impossible to overcome disease while she lived Thereupon Keokuk took the old woman without the settlement and deliberately cut off her head with a hatchet This slaughter was witnessed by Mrs Phelps wife of Billy Phelps one of the original settlers of that sec-

346   HISTORY OF VAN BUREN COUNTY

tion." The scene of this sacrifice was near Independent, adjacent to Jordan's farm

Keokuk's son is at the head of the Sac and Fox Nation, in the Indian Territory

BLACK HAWK, THE BRAVE

The most conspicuous figure in the list of noted Indians of the Northwest is Black Hawk. This remarkable man was more like a white man in his domestic tastes and instincts than any of his cotemporaries; but was, withal, a warrior of the true savage type During his sojourn in Van Buren County, probably no one was more intimately acquainted with Black Hawk than James Jordan was Mr Jordan's opportunities for knowing the Indian, and also for acquiring a thorough knowledge of the language in which he spoke, were unusual. For years, the two families lived side by side, and maintained a degree of intimacy peculiar and incidental to the isolated life then led A feeling of friendliness sprang up between the native and the pioneer resident, which was but little removed from that of brotherhood Hence it is that the statements of Mr. Jordan relative to Black Hawk and his life are accepted without reservation by all who hear them.

In personal appearance, Black Hawk was distinguished. He was five feet and eleven inches tall; weighed about one hundred and forty to one hundred and fifty pounds, and had an eye black and piercing as a wild beast

Many errors have crept into history concerning Black Hawk. The most important one is that which fixes his birth in 1767 It will be observed in the State history, which precedes this sketch, that he was born in the Sac village, about three miles from the junction of Rock River with the Mississippi, in Illinois, in 1767. Mr Jordan pronounces the date an error. From Black Hawk's own lips he learned that the time of his birth was 1775, but the day is not given.

As to the Indian orthography of the name, Mr. Jordan gives Mu-ca-tah-mich-a-ka-kah, and this is confirmed by several other well-posted persons. Maj. Beach, in his admirable papers on the Indian Agency in Wapello County, a subject he was well fitted to write about, because of his having been Agent after Gen Street's death in 1840, gives a slightly different spelling; but only such as might naturally arise from an attempt to spell an Indian word by sound The Major spelled the name Muck-a-ta-mish-e-ki-ak-ki-ak, and the reader will observe the general similarity in the two methods. Probably Mr Jordan's way is the correct one The literal translation of the name into English is *a black hawk*

Another error exists concerning the official position of the man He was not a chief, either by inheritance or election His father was a leading spirit, perhaps a prophet or a man of commanding influence in the councils of the Sacs At an early age, Black Hawk was allowed to don the war-paint, because of his having slain an enemy of his tribe This rather traditionary statement comes unsupported, but is given for what it is worth The story runs that the youth was but sixteen years old when he hung his first scalp upon his wigwam.

In character the Indian h   as brave, cautious and ambitious. He aspired to rank and sought the g   ion of his passion for power by stealthy means. He possessed marvelous   torical abilities, in that gift equaling the great speaker Keokuk. As a warrior, he was dependent more upon strategy than upon the qualities which white men deem essential o military prowess, but Black Hawk was not a cruel or blood thirsty man wh kw merely for the sake of slaughter He was peculiar in some characteristics and the report given by Mr. Jordan, of his latter days, contradicts the generally believed accounts of his early methods of self-promotion. However, one can accept the statements of his friend without too great a tax on one's credulity, when it is remembered that the last years, and not the first, were spent in this vicinity. Black Hawk the youth was very different from Black Hawk the old and defeated man.

History teaches that Black Hawk's efforts at generalship were failures, when military method was required. His power lay in sudden and fierce attacks, with dramatic strategy and rush of mounted braves. It was by such means, and the employment of his great eloquence in council, that he gained his eminence as a leader. He assumed the place of authority over Keokuk, his ranking officer, and maintained his hold upon his men without ever claiming to be a chieftain. He called himself a Brave, and delighted in the title.

The Sacs and Foxes, according to their traditions, once dwelt upon the shores of the great lakes. Gradually they were pushed westward, until in time they came to occupy a large portion of Northern Illinois. In spite of the pressure of the whites, this band occupied a site on the east shore of the Mississippi, near Rock River. Here Black Hawk was, in 1832, the controlling spirit. "He was never a chief, either by inheritance or election," declares Major Beach, "and his influence was shared by a wily old savage, of part Winnebago blood, called the Prophet, who could do with Black Hawk pretty much as he pleased; and also by a Sac named Na-pope, the English of which is Soup, and whom the writer found to be a very friendly and manageable old native, as was also Black Hawk."

As relevant to the history of the Indian occupation of Van Buren County, we quote from a paper prepared by Uriah Biggs, and published in the "Annals of Iowa," the following authentic account of Black Hawk's first battle. The battle-field was on the present site of Iowaville, which was long ago the principal seat of the Iowa nation of Indians, and was where Black Hawk afterward died. At the time of the massacre, Black Hawk was a young man, and the graphic account of his first steps toward leadership, as related by Mr. Biggs, is made up of the details given by the Indians who participated in the battle.

"Contrary to long established custom of Indian attack, this battle was brought on in daytime, the attending circumstances justifying this departure from the well-settled usages of Indian warfare. The battle-field is a level river-bottom prairie, of about four miles in length and two miles wide, near the middle, narrowing down to points at either end. The main area of the bottom rises perhaps twenty feet above the river, leaving a narrow strip of low bottom along the river, covered with trees that belted the prairie on the river-side with a thick forest, and the river-bank was fringed with a dense growth of willows. Near the lower end of the prairie, and near the river-bank, was situated the Iowa village, and about two miles above the town and near the middle of the prairie, is situated a small natural mound, covered at that time with a tuft of small trees and brush growing on its summit.

"In the rear of this mound lay a belt of wet prairie, which, at the time here spoken of, was covered with a dense crop of rank coarse grass; bordering this wet prairie on the north, the country rises abruptly into elevated and broken river-bluffs, covered with a heavy forest for many miles in extent, portions of it thickly clustered with undergrowth, affording a convenient shelter for the stealthy approach of the cat-like foe. Through this forest the Sac and Fox war-party made their way in the night-time and concealed themselves in the tall grass spoken of above, intending to remain in ambush through the day, and make such observations as this near proximity to their intended victims might afford, to aid them in the contemplated attack on the town during the following night From this situation their spies could take a full survey of the situation of the village, and watch every movement of the inhabitants, by which means they were soon convinced the Iowas had no suspicion of their presence

"At the foot of the mound above noticed, the Iowas had their race-course, where they diverted themselves with the excitements of the horse, and skilled their young warriors in cavalry evolutions. In these exercises, mock battles are fought, and the Indian tactics of attack and defense, of victory and defeat, are carefully inculcated, by which means a skill in horsemanship is acquired which is rarely excelled Unfortunately for them, this day was selected for these equestrian sports, and, wholly unconscious of the proximity of their foes, the warriors repaired to the race-ground, leaving the most of their arms in the village, and their old men and women and children unprotected.

"Pashapaho, who was chief in command of the enemy's forces, perceived at once the advantage this state of things afforded for a complete surprise of his now doomed victims, and ordered Black Hawk to file off with his young warriors through the tall grass, and gain the cover of the timber along the river-bank, and, with the utmost speed reach the village and commence the battle, while he remained with his division in the ambush, to make a simultaneous assault on the unarmed men, whose attention was engrossed with the excitement of the races. The plan was skillfully laid and most dexterously prosecuted Black Hawk, with his forces, reached the village undiscovered and made a furious onslaught upon its defenseless inhabitants, by firing one general volley into their midst, and completing the slaughter with the tomahawk and scalping-knife, aided by the devouring flames with which they engulfed the village as soon as the fire-brand could be spread from lodge to lodge.

"On the instant of the report of fire-arms at the village, the forces under Pashapaho leaped from their couchant position in the grass, and sprang tiger-like upon the astonished and unarmed Iowas in the midst of their racing sports. The first impulse of the latter naturally led them to make the utmost speed to reach their arms in the village, and protect, if possible, their wives and children from the attacks of the merciless assailants

"The distance from the place of the attack on the prairie was two miles, and a great number fell in the flight by the bullets and tomahawks of their adversaries, who pressed them closely with a running fire the whole way, and they only reached their town in time to witness the horrors of its destruction Their whole village was in flames, and the dearest objects of their lives lay in slaughtered heaps amidst the devouring element, and the agonizing groans of the dying mingled with the exulting shouts of a victorious foe, filled their hearts with a maddening despair. Their wives and children who had been spared the general massacre were prisoners, and, together with their arms, were in possession of the victors, and all that could now be done was to draw off their shattered and defenseless forces and save as many lives as possible by a retreat across the Des Moines River, which they effected in the best possible manner, and took a position among the Soap Creek hills

"The complete success attending a battle does not always imply brave action, for, as in the present instance bravery does not belong to a wanton attack on unarmed foes and defenseless women and children Yet praise is due to Pashapaho, the commander of the expedition, for his full share, for his quick perception of the advantages which were within his reach, and for his sagacity in at once changing the programme of attack to meet occurring events, and the courage and intrepidity to seize these events and insure his success. The want of these essential qualities in a commander has occasioned the loss of many a battle in what is courteously termed civilized warfare.

"The Iowas, cut off from all hope of retrieving their loss, sent a flag of truce to Pashapaho, submitting their fate to the will of their conqueror, and a parley ensued which resulted in the Iowas becoming an integral part of the Sac and Fox nation; but experiencing the ill-usage that is the common fate of a conquered people, they besought the United States authorities to purchase their undivided interest in the country and thus allow them to escape from the tyranny of their oppressors. The purchase was accordingly made in 1825, and they removed to the Missouri River, and have so wasted in numbers as to scarcely preserve their existence as an independent tribe. The sole cause of this war was the insatiable ambition of the Sac and Fox Indians, as this was their first acquaintance with the Iowa nation or tribe."

Mr. Biggs differs from other writers concerning some points in Black Hawk's character. We give the following description from his pen:

"My first and only interview with Black Hawk was at Rock Island, at the time of the treaty for the Iowa Reserve, in 1836, about one year before his death. I was introduced to him by his intimate acquaintance and apologist, the late Jeremiah Smith, of Burlington. He asked where I resided, and being told on the Wabash River, in Indiana, he traced on the sand the principal Western rivers, showing their courses and connections, and exhibiting a general knowledge of the prominent features of the topography of the Western States.

"The interview occurred after his first visit to Washington, where he was taken by way of the Ohio River to Pittsburgh, and returned by Philadelphia, Baltimore, Albany, Buffalo and Detroit, affording him a good opportunity to form a salutary impression of the military resources of the United States, and also to acquire a general knowledge of its geography. Its great military strength seemed to arouse his keenest observation, and furnished the main topic of his remarks upon the country as he passed through, as well as on his return to his tribe. The colloquy at this interview afforded an occasion to express his bitter reflections upon this painful theme. Mr. Smith, unfortunately for the repose of Black Hawk's feelings, and unconscious of its effect, mentioned the writer of this sketch as a surveyor of public lands, a character always unwelcome among the Indians. This remark I much regretted, as Black Hawk's countenance was instantly covered with gloom, and he rather petulantly said: 'The Shomokoman was strong, and would force the Indians to give up all their lands.'

"The colloquy here ended, as this barbed arrow, inadvertently thrown by Mr. Smith, had occasioned a tumult in Black Hawk's mind that rendered further conversation on his part disagreeable. The impressions of the writer in regard to Black Hawk's personal appearance were those of disappointment. He was attired in a coarse cloth coat, without any semblance of fit or proportion, with his feet thrust into a pair of new stoga shoes that were without strings, and a coarse wool hat awkwardly placed on his nearly bald pate, and presenting a very uncouth and rather ludicrous personal bearing.

"This toggery perhaps, had its share in lowering my previously-estimated claims of Black Hawk to distinction among the celebrated men of his race. 'The fine head, Roman style of face, and massive ____ ___ features ____ that so favorably impr___ ___ the us ____ ____ ____ ____ iting him while a pr___ ____ d Person ____ ____ ____ ____ ____ dull comprehension.

"It would, indeed, be difficult to find a name in history that attained so great a notoriety, associated with such limited mental endowment and true military skill. Every prominent act of his life gave evidence of the lack of sound discretion and prudent forethought We find him as early as 1804 visiting the Spanish Governor at St Louis, at the time the United States' agents called to accept the transfer of the authority of the country Black Hawk being informed of the purpose of their visit, refused to meet these agents of the new government, he passing out of one door as they entered at the other, and embarking with his suite in their canoes and hastening away to Rock Island, saying he liked his Spanish father best. This was a mere whim, as he had, as yet. no acquaintance with the Government and people of the United States. He, however, at once determined on hostility to both; and this ill-advised and hasty determination was his ruling passion while he lived

"Lieutenant Pike, on behalf of the Government, made him a friendly visit to Rock Island, the following year, and, as a token of friendship, presented Black Hawk with an American flag, which he refused to accept He embraced the first opportunity that offered to form an alliance with the British authorities in Canada, and eagerly attached himself and 500 warriors of his tribe to the British standard, at the commencement of the war of 1812. Here, his lack of capacity to command an army, where true courage and enduring fortitude were requisite to success, was fully demonstrated His warlike talents had hitherto been only tested in stealthy and sudden onslaughts on unprepared and defenseless foes; and, if successful, a few scalps were the laurels he coveted, and he retired, exulting in the plunder of a village and these savage trophies His campaigns against the Osages and other neighboring tribes, lasted only long enough to make one effort, and afforded no evidence of the fortitude and patient skill of the able military leader His conduct under the British flag as 'General Black Hawk' showed him entirely wanting in the capacity to deserve that title. He followed the English army to Fort Stephenson, in expectation of an easy slaughter and pillage . but the signal repulse the combined forces still met by the gallant Col Croghan, completely disheartened him, and he slipped away with about twenty of his followers to his village on Rock River, leaving his army to take care of themselves

"He entertained no just conception of the obligations of treaties made between our Government and his tribe, and even the separate treaty by himself and his 'British Band,' in 1816, was no check on his caprice and stolid self-will. and its open violation brought on the war of 1832, which resulted in his complete overthrow, and ended forever his career as a warrior.

"The history of his tour through the United States as a prisoner, is a severe reflection upon the intelligence of the people of our Eastern cities, in regard to the respect due to a savage leader who had spent a long life in butchering his own race. and the frontier inhabitants of their own race and country His journey was, everywhere throughout the East, an ovation, falling but little short of the respect and high consideration shown to the nation's great benefactor, La Fayette, whose triumphal tour through the United States happened near the same period But as an offset to this ridiculous adulation in the East, when the escort reached Detroit, where his proper estimate was understood, Black Hawk and his suite were contemptuously burned in effigy But due allowance should be made for the ignorance concerning true Indian character, among the Eastern people as their conceptions are formed from the fanciful creations of the Coopers and Longfellows immeasurably above the sphere of the blood-thirsty War Eagles and the filthy paint bedaubed Hiawathas of real savage life.

Black Hawk died in the fall of 1838, near Iowaville, the scene of his triumph, under Pashapaho, over the Iowas in the early part of his warlike career. He was buried in a sitting posture, in a frail tomb made of wooden slabs set upon the ground in the form of an inverted V. His war-club, a staved post four or five feet high, was placed in the front of his rude tomb, upon which a great number of black stripes was painted, corresponding with the number of scalps he had taken during life. Openings were left in his tomb so that his friends and curious visitors could witness the progress of decay. Some-time after the removal of his friends higher up the river, and after the flesh had wasted away, a Dr. Turner of Van Buren County, removed his skeleton to Alton, Ill., and had the bones handsomely polished and varnished, preparatory to connecting them by wires in the skeleton form. When Black Hawk's wife heard of the exhumation, she affected great and incontrollable grief, and poured out the burden of her sorrows to Robert Lucas, Governor of the Territory, and ex officio Superintendent of Indian Affairs, who promptly recovered the bones and placed them in a box in his office at Burlington, and dispatched a message to the bereaved family, then staying on the Des Moines, some ninety miles dis-tant. A cavalcade was soon in motion, bearing the disconsolate widow and a retinue of her friends to Burlington. On the evening of their arrival, the Gov-ernor was notified of their readiness to wait upon him, who fixed the audience for 10 A. M. the next day. Several visitors were in attendance. The box containing the august remains opened with a lid, and when the parties were all assembled and ready for the awful development, the lid was lifted by the Gov-ernor, fully exposing the sacred relics of the renowned chief to the gaze of his sorrowing friends and the very respectable auditors who had assembled to wit-ness the impressive scene.

"The Governor then addressed the widow, through John Goodell, the inter-preter of the Hardfish band, giving all the details of the transfer of the bones from the grave to Quincy and back to Burlington, and assured her that they were the veritable bones of her deceased husband, that he had sympathized deeply with her in her great affliction, and that he now hoped she would be consoled and comforted by the return of the precious relics to her care, under a strong confidence that they would not again be disturbed where she might choose to entomb them. The widow then advanced to the lid of the box, and, without the least seeming emotion, picked up in her fingers bone after bone, and examined each with the seeming curiosity of a child, and, replacing each one in its proper place, turned to the interpreter, and replied that she fully believed they were Black Hawk's bones, and that she knew the Governor was a good old man, or he would not have taken the great pains he had manifested to oblige her, and, in consideration of his great benevolence and disinterested friendship, she would leave the bones under his care and protection. The con-ference then closed, and the distinguished visitors took leave of the Governor and the assembled auditors. This scene was detailed by the Governor to the present writer while standing at the side of the famous box soon after its occurrence.

"On the accession of Gen. Harrison to the Presidency, Gov. Lucas was removed from the gubernatorial office of the Territory, and removed his private office into the same room with Dr. Enos Lowe, now of Omaha City, Nebraska. An historical society was organized in Burlington about this time, and an effort was made to get these relics into their cabinet and under the control of their society. This arrangement was never formally effected, but in the course of events, they happened to be in the same building with the society's collection and the whole were consumed in the burning of the building, which occurred later '

On page 74 of this volume is given the generally accepted version of the causes which led to the Black Hawk war of 1832, but that story is vague and unsatisfactory. On page 157 another, and in the main a correct, account is given. From Mr. Jordan we learn facts of more than local interest in this disputed case, and give them here

Somewhere about 1828–29, a man named Watts, while driving cattle through this region about where Iowaville now is was beset by Indians Watts had with him a man whose name is not remembered now. This man was killed by a savage The murder was committed on Indian territory, and a demand was made on Black Hawk for the criminal. He was delivered up to the United States authorities and taken to St Louis, where he was tried and condemned. Some of the tribe went to St Louis to intercede for their companion, but did not accomplish their purpose. The Indian was hanged However, while the Indians were in St Louis they fell victims of sharpers, who obtained a professed title to Black Hawk's village on the Rock River by presents of less value than the Government price of the land When the embassy returned with their ill-gotten trinkets, Black Hawk was wroth, and denounced the fraud Subsequently, probably the next spring, on the opening of the season of 1830, the men who had obtained such title to the land came on, and drove the Indian women and children from the village, during the temporary absence of the braves. Black Hawk made issue with the fraudulent possessors of his home, and offered to stake thirty of his braves against thirty white soldiers to test the question of title by a fight This offer was declined by the military, but the whites said they would pit the United States army against the Indians of his tribe Black Hawk took up the gauntlet, and hence the famous, but disastrous, Black Hawk war

This version, it will be seen, substantially corroborates the story obtained by research in Illinois

Of the Black Hawk war it is not within the province of this sketch to speak : it belongs to the history of Illinois, and has been repeatedly written up. After the defeat of Black Hawk in 1832, he was captured and taken to Prairie du Chien. After an imprisonment in Jefferson Barracks, and, subsequently, in Fortress Monroe, whither he was taken, he was returned at the intercession of Keokuk to this region In his old age, Black Hawk sought the company of the garrison, his band was broken up, and the once great man was left alone in his declining years. Maj. Beach relates the following incident derived from personal observation.

"Black Hawk's lodge was always the perfection of cleanliness, a quite unusual thing for an Indian The writer has seen the old woman busily at work with her broom, by time of sunrise, sweeping down the little ant-hills in the yard that had been thrown up during the night. As the chiefs of the nation seemed to pay him but little attention in the waning years of his life, Gen. Street, the Agent, looked out for his comfort more carefully than otherwise he would have thought it needful to do, and, among other things, gave him a cow —an appendage to an Indian's domestic establishment hitherto unheard of The old squaw and daughter were instructed in the art of milking her, and she was held among them in almost as great reverence as the sacred ox Apis was held among the ancient Egyptians

"This was in the summer of 1838, when the Agency was in process of erection and Black Hawk had established his lodge on the banks of the Des

Moines, about three miles below Eldon. Close by was the trading-house of Wharton McPherson, with whom the writer stayed one night in August of said year (1838), and, as he rode past the lodge, Mme Black Hawk was complacently sitting upon a log by the side of her cow, under a heavily-branched tree, industriously brushing the flies and mosquitoes from the bovine with a rag tied to the end of a stick. Mr. McPherson said this was her daily occupation in fly-time, often following the animal around as it grazed at a distance. This was the last occasion that ever the writer had for an interview with Black Hawk, as he died within two months of that time (September 15, 1838), and was even then so infirm that he could barely move about his wigwam "

Still another mooted question is that concerning the death, burial and resurrection of Black Hawk, for the old brave was not permitted to rest in his tomb after his fitful life-fever was over The best authority on this subject is Mr Jordan From him the following statement was obtained ·

On the 1st day of September, 1838, Mu-ca-tah-mich-a-ka-kah sickened with fever The old brave requested Mr. Jordan to send to Fort Edward (now Warsaw) for Dr. Peel A letter was duly dispatched, in which the doctor was promised the sum of $300 if he would attend the summons The message was slow in going, and before a response could be made the soul of the brave old Indian had passed to the happy hunting-ground.

Black Hawk died September 15, 1838, in the sixty-third year of his life Before he died, he requested Mr Jordan to observe certain ceremonies in his burial. His body was to be clothed in full uniform, a suit of military clothes presented him by Gen Jackson, upon which was a pair of epaulets valued at $500 Three medals, which had been given him by the British, the French and the American Governments, respectively, and valued in the aggregate at $1,200, were to be placed upon his breast He was to be buried in a sitting posture, and a mound of earth erected above him in such a manner as to leave an unobstructed view of the interior, through orifices left for the purpose The locality was designated by Black Hawk himself, as the site of his last friendly council with the Iowa Indians This point was upon Mr Jordan's farm, on Section 2, Township 70 north, Range 12 west.

The injunction was faithfully carried out The body was dressed as the brave had directed, and blankets and gloves were added Some time later, Mrs Black Hawk came to Mr. Jordan with the alarming story that her husband's head had been stolen. Upon investigating the sepulcher it was found that the head had dropped over from its own weight. Mr Jordan replaced the member and repaired the tomb

The alarm thus given was not entirely groundless, however, for on the 3d of July, 1839, Dr Turner stole the head and made off with it. In February, 1840, the act of desecration was completed, when the entire body was removed. It was taken to Alton, Ill., and there the bones were cleaned and wired by a professional anatomist Mrs. Black Hawk and her sons made a disturbance over the affair, and the matter was taken up by Gov Lucas The widow painted her face with black, in spots, and passed two days without food, in mourning, walking up and down the river-bank When at last the bones were discovered, the family was notified and visited Burlington They saw that the skeleton "was in a good, dry place," and concluded to let it remain there Maj Beach said that he notified the widow of the willingness of the authorities to surrender the bones, but that she seemed indifferent to the matter At all events, nothing was done by the family to secure a re-interment of the remains Subsequently, the State building in which the remains were placed,

at Burlington, was consumed by fire   One report says that the skeleton was
destroyed therein   but another story is that some physician had borrowed the
bones to exhibit them before a class in anatomy, and that they were not in the
building when it burned   The latter report is wholly improbable, for if it was
true some one would know of the fact, and publicly acknowledge the existence
of the skeleton   It is also said that the skull is in the Smithsonian Institution,
at Washington, but that is more unreasonable than any of the wild inventions
The truth is, probably, that Black Hawk found a final earthly resting-place
amid the ashes of the ruined structure, and that the last act of his eventful
career was not less dramatic than the first public appearance of the brave
Literally and truthfully may we say, dust to dust, ashes to ashes, and may
they rest in peace

Black Hawk's wife and sons are dead   A daughter is living with the Sac
and Fox nation, near Fort Sill   An incident or two will not be out of place
here   It is asserted that, during the troubles of 1812, the British Government
offered Black Hawk a medal and $5,000 worth of blankets to fight for them.
He accepted the offer, for he never liked the United States Government over-
well, and signified his readiness to move his men   He then found that the
British commander insisted upon his giving up his authority over his own braves
and intrusting it to an English officer   This arrangement he scorned, and giving the order of stampede to his men, they dashed away like shot from a cannon's mouth   This scene is located at Malden, near Detroit.

Black Hawk used to boast that he never killed a prisoner. He had captured many, but had treated them magnanimously. This, we infer, relates to
white prisoners.

ADVENT OF THE WHITE MAN

Having traced the existence of the two preliminary races—the Mound-
Builders and the Indians—which dwelt within the region of the Des Moines,
we introduce, in regular order, the pale-faced intruder on the domain of the
savage. The first settlement in Southern Iowa was made in the vicinity of
Burlington, and through that gate entered the vast army that has worked such
wonders in the way of improvement   A brief description of who began the
labor of developing Iowa, and how it was performed, is necessary to perfect the
thread of this narrative of fact. From the pen of Dr. William R Ross is
gathered the following interesting record:

"It may not be uninteresting,' observes the Doctor, "to give some of the
names of those who first explored Southern Iowa, in 1832 prior to making
a permanent settlement in 1833. First, among others, were Maj Joseph B. Teas
and Joseph Morgan, afterward citizens of Albia, Col William Morgan, William
Stewart, John Ward, Isaac Canterberg, Lewis Watters, Isaac Cranshaw, Benjamin Tucker, Ezekiel Smith and sons Paris and Lineas, John Bullard
Richard Sand, Thomas Doyrell, David Tethro, S S White M. M. McCarver,
Berryman Jenkins, William Wright, John Harris and Charles Teas, with others
that were in Iowa when I came in July, 1833   Mrs Sarah Hilleary, wife of
Alexander Hilleary, near Burlington, came with her father, Col William Morgan, in February, 1832, to do the domestic work, while her father was improving his claim and built a house preparatory to moving his family, and was
one of the families driven to the big island just below Burlington, by soldiers
from Rock Island as the Indian title had not been extinguished

"The title remained in the Indians until June, 1833   At this time, Richard Chaney resided at Fort Madison, and Dr Garland and Mr Campbell, and, perhaps, a few others on the half-breed tract   After June 1, 1833, the country was settled very rapidly; as every one then had the liberty of taking to themselves a claim of half a section of land, one-quarter of timber and one of prairie, and the right to purchase as many claims as he had the money for   This rule occasioned much disturbance by new immigrants coming into the country and finding one man holding more than one claim   It drove them back into the new region against their will   In the winter of 1833–34, we were attached to Michigan Territory for judicial purposes, and the laws, with instructions, were sent me by the Legislature of Michigan to organize Des Moines County, by appointing special elections to be held to elect officers to discharge the duties of an organized county   Col William Morgan was elected Superior Judge, and Henry Walker and Young L. Hughes, Assistants, of Circuit Court, which was the highest court we had in Iowa at that time   Col W. H. Chapman was Prosecuting Attorney; W R Ross, Clerk, Solomon Perkins, Sheriff, John Barker, Justice of the Peace; W. R. Ross, Treasurer and Recorder, and, at the time, acting Postmaster in the only post office in the Territory. He was the only practicing physician in that part of the Territory, meanwhile carrying on a dry goods and drug store   In addition to this, Mr. Ross inclosed, in 1834, 160 acres of prairie land with a stake-and-rider fence, grew eighty acres of corn, on another claim, and improved still another forty acres back of Burlington   He also improved some twenty acres, and erected buildings for a private residence

There was a settlement from near the mouth of Long Creek, northeast of Augusta, made by six or seven families from Indiana, in July, 1833, eight miles west of Burlington

"In regard to public improvements, in the fall of 1833, Mr. Ross built the first schoolhouse, on his claim just back of the public square, at his own expense, and, in the spring of 1834, Z C Ingraham was employed to teach. Mr Ross boarded him free of cost   This was the first English school taught in Iowa   In 1834, Mr. Ross organized the first Sunday school in Iowa, furnishing a library from Cincinnati, at a cost of $12 50, and taught the school himself   As the population increased, a new library was needed, the old one was donated to Mt Pleasant, where a school had been organized, and a new lot of books, costing $25, was put in   Of those denominations who joined in the work of maintaining the school, Mr Ross remembers Mr and Mrs J Edwards, W H Stair (then a lawyer, of the Congregational faith), George Partridge (who became a wholesale merchant of St Louis), of the Unitarian faith, David Rover, of the Presbyterian faith, John B Gray, of the Baptist faith   Mr Newhall and Dr John Campbell are warmly spoken of in this connection, also

"The day school was taught by Mrs Shelton and Mrs Mayfield; and after the old Zion M E Church was built, Rev. E M Scott, the tallest man in the neighborhood, lived in the basement of the church and taught school therein   Afterward a man named Townsend taught

Dr Crawford, from Brooke County, Va, settled in Burlington in 1833 he practiced during the winter and then moved to Texas   In the spring of 1834, Drs Shuff, of Kentucky, and Center of Indiana, located in Burlington, and formed a ___ ___ ___ ___ ___ ___ ___ to Kentucky ___ ___ ___ ___ ___ ___ ___ York, located there ___ ___ ___ ___ ___ ___   Dr ___ ___, of

Vermont. settled there about the same date. Dr E Lowe, of Indian. came in 1836; he afterward removed to Omaha

"The first court ever held in Southern Iowa, convened at the house of Mr. Ross, on the block immediately east of the public square, in the spring of 1835. Judges presiding: William Morgan, Henry Walker and Young R. Hughes. Resident lawyers· W W Chapman, Robert Williams, Isaac Leffler, Joseph B Teas Visiting lawyers Mr Little, of Carthage. Ill. and James W Woods, usually called 'Old Timber." Mr. Ross owned the only law library then in Burlington, and that was a small one. In the spring of 1836, David Rover began the practice of law: in 1836–37, M D Browning and J. W Grimes, also. In 1836–37, Joseph B Teas and Jeremiah Smith, Jr, represented Des Moines at the Legislature which organized the Territory of Iowa. In the spring of 1838, Charles Mason moved to Burlington and began the practice of law There was an exodus of lawyers from that place about then. J C. Hall William Thompson, J B. and G. W. Teas and Van Allen located at Mt Pleasant; Thomas and Springer, at Wapello, Louisa County: Daniel Miller and Rich, at Ft Madison

"In 1837–38, the Territory was established. and Burlington made the capital The first session was held in the old Zion Church

"In March, 1834, Barton H Cartright preached in Burlington. Asa McMurtry preached for two weeks, shortly after W. D R. Trotter followed. In May, 1834, Peter Cartright held two days' camp-meeting near the public square In the winter of 1834–35, Seamen B Stateter, of the Missouri Conference, formed the Burlington Circuit. and appointed John H. Ruble preacher in charge. This Circuit included all the territory south of Rock Island to the southern boundary, and west to the Missouri River In 1835–36. Andrew Monroe held quarterly meeting In May, Mr. Ruble died and Peter Brown, of Quincy, Ill, preached his funeral sermon Wilson Pitner supplied the place for a short time. Nicholas S Barton next preached, and in 1837, Moses McMurtry had charge In 1839. Asa West followed, and, in 1840, J Arvington, as preachers on the Circuit Isaac S Stewart was located preacher in charge of the Burlington Church."

In 1838, Gen Joseph Street was transferred from the Agency of the Winnebagoes at Prairie du Chien, Wis, to Iowa, for the purpose of establishing a military outpost for the protection of the general interests of the Government. He made a barrack at Agency City. in Wapello County, and may be esteemed the first white man to open the onward march of the pale-faces toward Monroe County

In a dense wilderness he built up for himself a home of as comfortable a character as the times and circumstances would permit He improved a farm and availed himself of such opportunities as lay within his reach. Joseph Smart, the interpreter, and a man named Baker, who was a blacksmith by trade, were the only white persons, beside the garrison, in the settlement. A trading-post was soon established by Messrs Ewings & Phelps, near the Agency

In 1841, J. P. Eddy, from St. Louis, opened a trading-post where Eddyville now stands, near the northeast corner of Monroe County. He at once secured the friendship of the Indians

W. .... Sacs and Foxes built his village on the right bank ... . Indians grew corrupt .... growing out of the Black Hawk treaty of peace they would not hunt or fish, and subsisted on their grants from the Great Father The Indians became so demoralized by the freedom from labor thus secured that the mortality of the tribe was greatly increased The prophet told them that the cause of all their woes arose from the relinquishment of their lands to the Government There is something sad in the spectacle of a once powerful race of men thus driven to the extremity of extinction In 1845, the Indians were removed entirely from the State, to reservations in Kansas

John Goodell, the interpreter of Hardfish's band, was the next to move toward Monroe County He improved a farm not far from the line between Wapello and Monroe, known as the Ogden place, located some four miles below Eddy's post

"In 1843," says Dr Ross, "I visited the country as far up as where Eddyville now stands, at that time an Indian village called Hardfisher J. P Eddy was located there as a trader with the Indians I found a few old friends, who had made claims on both sides of the river, among them John B. Gray, who had located about three miles west, on Gray's Creek, in Kishkekosh County"

THE PIONEERS OF VAN BUREN COUNTY

The first appearance of white men in Van Buren County occurred long before local boundaries or a name marked the geographical existence of the county. As is shown by the preceding chapters relative to the trading-posts on the Des Moines and as will be, further on, confirmed by extracts from Judge Wright's address before the Pioneer Association of Van Buren County, the first white men came into this region in 1832 There were Capt. William Phelps. Peter Avery, and possibly one or two others (but that point is not clear, and the names of those men alone are positively correct) in the trading movement. It is believed that they arrived at their destination in November, 1832 Avery spent the winter of 1832–33, opposite the site of Kilbourne, at the mouth of Lick Creek

The first settlements for purposes of actual improvement were made near the site of Farmington. The first man, it is claimed, to locate in the county, however, was Abel Galland, who made a claim near the site of Farmington, some time in 1833; but the date is not definitely given

We here give. in the way of general credit, the authorities upon which these and subsequent statements are made ; for the purpose of this work is to weave into consecutive order all information relative to the early life of this county. First, we shall hereafter quote freely, and in many places literally, from Judge George G Wright's address, delivered August 28, 1872. before the Pioneer Association, at Keosauqua ; from the speech of A H McCrary from the speech of Edwin Manning. from the speech of Charles Baldwin, and from other sources obtained from Mr Ed Goddard, Secretary of the Pioneer Association Where such quotations are made we shall omit special credit or quotation marks ; for this is not claimed as an original composition, but merely as a compilation of reliable data. With this explanation, let us proceed·

Abel Galland and William Jordon in the spring of 1833. settled at Farmington ; and William Avery (brother of Peter) and James Jordon. the same spring. established a small trading-post at the mouth of the stream before named (Lick Creek); and James Lamb (who afterward, it will be remembered was among the first of those who made the overland trip to Oregon). in 1835, settled just al—   —— ———   — —— —   — about this time, Jan— · —— —— — ——— — —— ———   —— n that vicinity, in addition — those ab—— —— — John Fi— — Jonas — Denny,

Zeke McCarty, John Maxwell and Samuel Maxwell   Soon thereafter, we find
the Swazeys, Houghtons, Crows. Henry Bateman, John Newport, H. G. Stuart,
Tilford Reed, William Brattain, and above there, on the river, Dr R N Cresap
and Samuel C Reed

THE FIRST BIRTH

There are, naturally, several claimants to the distinction of being the first-
born in Van Buren County   February 14, 1836, John M Whitaker located
in Union Township   His son, Samuel V., was born May 9, 1837   By some,
this is regarded as the first birth, but it is manifestly not so, since Jacob
Alfrey was born, near Farmington, January 17. 1834.   Charles Johnson, son
of Abington Johnson, was born February, 1836   Humphrey Brittain, son of
William Brattain, Sr , was born June 8, 1836   Mrs Lorenzo Dow Borden,
daughter of John Newort, was born, near Farmington. July 31, 1835   From
these dates of the several claimants, there is no alternative but to place Jacob
Alfrey as the first boy and Mrs. Borden as the first girl born in the county.
If this conclusion is wrong, then the source from which the information is
obtained is alone responsible.   The only person who has seriously disputed this
statement is Mr A. W. Harlan, who gives a son of Jonas F Denny the preced-
ence, but does not furnish the necessary date.   This Denny was quite a
character   He went to California. at an early day, and there became the subject of a novel.   Mark Twain also wrote of him in "Innocents Abroad," as
Denny was of that famous party

THE FIRST DEATH

The first death in the county occurred near Farmington, but the exact date
is not obtainable   It was, probably, as early as 1833   A man named
Williams, a stranger, whose Christian name is unknown, was traveling through
on horseback.   He was prostrated with fever and died   He was buried in a
rough puncheon box

THE FIRST MARRIAGE

The first marriage license recorded, and the first that was celebrated in the
county, so far as any reliable data shows, was that of Norris Steier and Lethe
M. Reed, married June 15, 1837, by Samuel C Reed, Justice of the Peace

ANECDOTES OF THE TRADING-POSTS

As incidental to the settlement of the region, we quote from Maj Beach's
history of the Agency such portions as refer to well-known settlers in Van Buren and the Indian territory immediately adjacent thereto:

"On the Des Moines, a mile or so below the County Farm, where the bluff
approaches nearest to the bank, was the trading-post of P Chouteau, Sr., &
Co, but later more familiarly known as the 'Old Garrison.'   This was usually
superintended by Capt William Phelps.   And just above the mouth of Sugar
Creek, on the creek-bank, at the old road crossing, lived the miller, Jeremiah
Smith, Jr , with his family.   This embraced all the whites lawfully living in the
country at the time.

"Through some unfortunate misunderstanding in regard to the boundary
line, several persons had intruded upon the Indian land upon the Iowaville
bottoi   as   the south le of the river,
and a   no alternative
but to   and was a very
unwe.   the intruders were per-

sons who would not willingly have violated any law   Among them was that
fine old specimen of West Virginia hospitality, Van Caldwell, but by reason of
his location, and his readiness by any reasonable arrangement to escape the
terrors of fire and sword, the writer obtained permission from the Department
that he should remain, upon the condition of his maintaining a ferry for access
to Soap Creek Mills during high water.

"For some years previously to the writer's appointment as Agent, Messrs.
P Chouteau Jr. & Co of St Louis, had been the only traders among the Sacs
and Foxes, and the magnitude of their interests was enough to excite any
rivalry   Col George Davenport, of Rock Island, had been admitted as partner
to their trade with that particular tribe, and he was looked to to reside among
them and to carry it on   S S Phelps, Esq, of Oquawka, in connection with
his brother, Capt. William Phelps, of jovial memory had been gaining a foothold on trade for two, three, or perhaps, four years before the treaties of 1836
and 1837, and, after the removal of the Agency from the island, and its consequent effect of rendering a change in the location of the chief trading-post
inevitable, Col. Davenport, who had already acquired a comfortable fortune,
concluded to withdraw   Mr. S S Phelps fell into the position thus made
vacant in the company, although he relied upon his brother to reside in the Indian country and maintain personal oversight of the company's affairs   A new
trader now appeared in the field, with at least means enough to prevent the old
company from being its monopolists   Of course, rivalry of feeling and interest
would now spring up and every occasion be employed by each rival to gain and
secure what advantage he could   The writer is not intimating any idea of his
own that any unfair or dishonorable appliances would be used by the gentlemen
heads respectively of the rival establishments; but their employes, or others
hoping advantage to themselves in the success of either party might be less
scrupulous

"It was probably through some such strategy that Gov Lucas became impressed with the most sincere conviction that the Chouteau Company supplied
whisky, with their other merchandise, to the Indians, and a conviction once
fixed with the Governor was pretty apt to stay   So persuaded was he of the
truth of his belief, that he was never disposed to the least reticence upon the
subject; and it was generally believed in Burlington that if the Trading Company could be caught, *flagrante delicto*, it would prove a pretty good haul for
the catcher—certainly not less than the transfer to his own pocket of the half
value of a large stock of goods

"As the writer soon saw that any effort of his own, however reasonable, to
lead the Governor to a different opinion was opening the way to suspicions
against himself of some personal interest in the company's affairs, prudence
naturally admonished him to desist.   One morning Mr. S. S Phelps, to whom
the Governor's belief—and propensity to express it—was no secret, being in
Burlington, stepped into a place where the Governor happened at the moment
to be engaged in his favorite pastime of denouncing Mr Chouteau's establishment, etc, and the Governor, totally unacquainted with Mr Phelps, still kept
up in his presence his conversation on the subject.

"Now, if there was anything Capt Billy Phelps loved better than another,
it was to play off a trick; or if anything he knew better than another, it was
how to plan and play it   The company had on its license a man named Simpson Vassar, who was better known at the Agency and its various dependencies
under the *sobriquet* of 'Suggs'   When any deviltry lurked in Capt Billy's
mind, 'Capt Suggs' was his most reliable assistant in getting rid of it   So a

scheme was planned   Suggs was sent over on pretext of some message to
Phelps, at Oquawka, with instructions not to leave Burlington until he had executed his part of the programme

"A person, who was either the City Marshal or attached to his official revenue, soon heard of Suggs in Burlington, and became so ambitious of his
acquaintance as to introduce himself without delay.   He learned from Suggs
that the latter lived out in the Agency neighborhood, that he knew the Trading
Company, in fact, sometimes worked for them when an extra force was needed
—clever people good paymasters, with the cash always in hand, knew nothing of their dealing in whisky, had never seen them supply it to the Indians;
and, even if he had as he had heard they were accused of it, a dollar, when
needed, was not so easily made out there that a man could afford to make enemies out of good-paying employers!   After several interviews, Suggs embarked
upon the ferry-boat.   But his newly-made friend was not long in joining him,
and during the crossing Suggs yielded to the potent arguments and promises
that had already shaken his sense of personal honor and interest.   He admitted that he had seen a large lot of kegs, and these not empty, landed by night
at the trading-house from a boat, not long before, and immediately buried upon
the bank, where most of them were, and if he could be guaranteed against
suspicion as the informer, and terms arranged to suit—as he expected to
remain about the place some time after his return—he would put his friend
upon the right track   The boat having landed them, and all details being adjusted, each party went on his way rejoicing—Suggs' way being to Oquawka,
and at once back to the trading-house to report to Capt Phelps

"Not many days later, an hour or so before dinner time Col Jesse Williams—later of Henn, Williams & Co, of Fairfield, but then Private Secretary
to Gov Lucas—rode up to the Agency.   Being doubtless himself disposed (as
indeed the Agency hospitality would suggest) to consider that an expedition
which would demand a three-mile ride and several hours of time, could be more
satisfactorily completed as a post-prandial duty, he made no mention of his
business   But as soon as the meal was over, he handed to the Agent a pack-
age from the Governor, containing a deposition in full form, taken before Judge
Mason, of the Territorial Supreme Court, by Suggs' Burlington friend, to the
effect that so many kegs of whisky, etc, etc, and were then secreted, etc,
etc, in violation of the statute, etc by the said P. Chouteau Jr.'s Company.
traders, etc, as aforesaid.   And there was also a line to the Agent, that, in the
execution of so delicate a duty, which must involve judicial process, he had
deemed it best to send out Col Williams to *assist* the Agent   Whatever the
motive may have been, it is certain that until both were in their saddles, Col
Williams proved himself able to *watch* the Agent with untiring eye.

"Reaching the trading-house, the person who took the deposition and a
companion were found there waiting, they having 'forked off' by another trail
so as not to be seen   Suggs was on hand, having taken the opportunity to post
the Burlingtonians about the locality   And also Capt Billy Phelps, called by
the Indians Che-che-pe-qua or the 'Winking Eyes,' was there, those visuals
fairly gleaming with joy over the anticipated fun.

"The Agent proceeded at once to business, expressing to Capt Phelps his
regret that so unpleasant a duty should have devolved upon him, his hope that
it would prove that so serious a complaint had originated in some error, but sug-
gesting   e contraband
article   lenency than
efforts   m the impeach-

ment, stating that it would require a much wiser man than himself to discover where such an article then was, or ever had been kept upon their premises The complainant was now appealed to, who led the party a short distance to a spot where, with a triumphant air, he pointed to an X that the edge of Suggs' boot-sole had made in the sandy bank

"They began digging and soon reached some matting that was removed, and thus uncovered a lot of lard kegs, too greasy to suggest a thought of any other article being contained within them The immediate 'sold, by thunder !' of one of the moiety gentlemen and in accents too lugubrious to be listened to without exciting a sense of sadness Suggs, meanwhile, had come up missing, and the 'Winking Eyes' walked off with a most disdainful air, leaving the Agent and his party on the spot whence they soon returned to the Agency, where the Agent made his report that the informer had pointed out a place, where, by digging, a large quantity of lard in kegs was found that had been buried to avoid loss by heat, and in the night to conceal the fact from vagabond whites and Indians The disappointed informer and his companion hastened homeward, but Col Williams remained until next morning and then returned, bearing the Agent's report.

"But the unkindest cut of all was six months later, when, about the last of February, Capt Phelps addressed a letter to Gov. Lucas in the most respectful and official form, saying, that having heard he had declared his determination not to continue in office under such an old Tory as Gen Harrison, and fearful that whoever his successor would be, he might not feel so friendly toward the company as he had proved in the matter of exhuming their lard, and as they would soon be much in need of some, and the ground was then very hard frozen, the company would be under great obligations if he would at once send some one out to dig up the rest of it

"Previous to the treaty of 1842 some few changes were made in their location, both by the Indians and among the whites The house at the Old Garrison ' was broken up, and one established in its stead up in the Red Rock region, near the mouth of White Breast and Keokuk, also, moved his village into the same neighborhood "

ORGANIZATION OF THE COUNTY.

The successive steps of organization which led to the independent division of Van Buren as a county may be summarized thus · Originally, this vast area was included in the Louisiana Purchase, approved by Congress in 1803 In 1807, Iowa was included in the Territory of Illinois ; in 1812, in the Territory of Missouri in 1834, the Black Hawk Purchase having been made, all of the territory west of the Mississippi and north of the northern boundary of Missouri was made a part of the Territory of Michigan. In September, 1834, the Legislature of Michigan established two precincts, or counties, in Iowa, as it is now called These counties were Dubuque, including all territory north of a line drawn westward from the foot of Rock Island, and Des Moines, including all territory south of that dividing line. The Territory of Wisconsin was organized in 1836, and Iowa was a part of that political division The third act of the first Legislature of the Territory of Wisconsin, which met in October, 1836, at P̶ ̶ ̶ ̶ ̶ ̶ ̶ ̶ ̶ ̶ ̶ ̶ ̶ ̶ B̶ ̶M̶ ̶ ̶ ̶ ̶ ̶ ̶ ̶e, Van Buren, Des ̶nts of Van Buren, ̶st, but extended, as was the custom, to the farthest boundary of the territory possessed by the United States   Henry, Louisa and Muscatine Counties were each thus unbounded within lines drawn from their northern and southern extremities.

Farmington was fixed upon as the county seat of Van Buren County. The Representatives from Southern Iowa at this Legislature were · Council, Jeremiah Smith, Joseph B. Teas and Arthur B Ingram , House, Isaac Leffler, Thomas Bean, Warner L Jenkins, John Box, George W Teas, Eli Reynolds and Daniel R. Chance.

THE FIRST COURT.

The first court was held at Farmington, beginning April 10, 1837, with Hon David Irvin on the Bench   Henry G. Stewart was appointed Clerk, but was succeeded by Fry B Hazletine and he, in turn, by Elisha Cutter, Jr There was a grand jury, but no petit jury   The former was composed of the following men : Isham Keith, Foreman, Alexander Keith, Samuel Clayton, Elijah Purdon, Sr , John Whittaker, Joseph Hill, Charles H. Price, James Smart, Abington Johnson, Jonas F. Denny, William Jordon, Obediah Cook, William Judd, Thomas Summerlin, John Moffatt, A. V. Syhawk, J. G. Mc-Cutchen, William Brattain, Sr., Abel Galland, John Crow, Lewis Crow, Joseph A Swazey and John Patchett. This grand jury found an indictment against one Doose, for exercising the office of Constable within our territory under the laws of Missouri , and in this it is believed we have the first judicial assertion of jurisdiction over a territory afterward the theater of a most bloodless war, and yet fraught with the very greatest results and importance to this and every part of the State

Isaac J Nowell, who was among the first, if not the first, settler on Indian Creek, was the officer who, as Sheriff, first opened our courts and arrested those violating the law   Isaac carried no sword or other insignia of office, but he had a well-tanned and closely-fitting suit of buckskin, which was quite as much a terror to all evil-doers and those not having the fear of the law before their eyes as the heaviest baton or loudest or most formal proclamation of " God save the Court "   He was succeeded by Henry Heffleman, and he by that acknowledged prince of good men, Capt J H. Bonney—who still lives, believing in acting as he has through life, upon the elevating maxim that " it is more blessed to give than receive "

The second term was held at the same place, commencing April 14, 1838, and a petit jury impaneled to try a member of the first grand jury, who, at the first term, was indicted for *house breaking*   The members of this jury were Thomas L Pickett, William Minear, Thomas Keith, B. F Anderson, James Sanders, Leonard Whitcomb, William Williams, John Newport, Henry Hampton, Charles Graves, H D Swazey and Robert Ewing

The member of the legal profession who first settled in the county was H. H Buckland   He was from New England—settled in Bentonsport, and, after remaining a year or more, returned to his former home   Isaac N. Lewis, subsequently a member of the Third Territorial Legislature (he was also a member of the Fifth), was the second.   He was the first attorney admitted to practice (November 12, 1838) in the county.   Following him and very soon were S W. Summers, Richard Humphreys and Oliver Weld, who died in October, 1843 He was Judge Wright's partner at the time of his death.   He was an honest man, and in his death the State lost a citizen of rare ability, the profession a sound lawyer, and society one of big heart, and if eccentric, as able as eccentric

The record of the court held at Farmington shows that, in April, 1837, Samuel McBrice was granted a license to keep a ferry across the Des Moines, at that place, for one year.

The first case of record was that of Simeon Rider (or Ryder) and Charles L Frost, of Alton, Ill, doing business as merchants, under the firm name of S. Rider & Co. vs Achemiah Barber Action for debt Judgment for plaintiff for the sum of $2,232 50

There were four assault and battery, two gaming, one house-breaking, three debt and one attachment suits on the docket, and also a petition for prohibition There were eight indictments and five suits commenced.

The first petit jury was impaneled at the April term of court, 1838, and was composed of Henry King, John Maxwell, W Job, Robert Kent, Lucius Lee, Uriel Neal, John Kennedy, Hiram Brown, William Matthews, John Browning, Martin A Britton, Noah Franklin, William Welch, R. N. Cresap, H. D Swazey, V F Jones, A. Mahnrou, R Jordan, A Galland and Jacob Crow.

John Crow was naturalized at this term, the first foreigner to assume such relations in the county. He was a subject of Great Britain

FIRST MILITIA.

By referring to the records of the Secretary of State, I find that on the 9th of January, 1830, Gen E. A. M Swazey was appointed Brigadier General of the First Brigade, First Division of the Territorial Militia Many of you remember the times and scenes when, on the Utica Prairie, the General, with Col Giles Wells, Maj Henry King, Capt Finess Killebrew, and other officers marshaled their forces, and had those remarkable and most imposing regimental trainings

On the 18th of the same month, the Governor appointed the following Justices of the Peace for the county: Wilson Stanley, Sewall Kenney, John Cochran, Thomas J Cox, David Tade, James Robb, Silas Stone, James Moffett, James E Rickey, John Whittaker, John Groom, Robert Gardner, Benjamin B Throop, Martin A Britton, William Kendrick, Samuel C. Reed, George Reynolds, William Miller, Jesse Sutton, Alexander Woods, Joel Knight, David Casebar, John Marshall, Bushrod W Cravens and John Taylor.

FIRST RECORDS.

The first Recorder was William Welch, and the first instrument of record in that office is a "quitclaim" deed, from William Clift, dated February 23, 1837, to Joseph A Swazey and Vincent M Jones, the consideration $350—premises on Des Moines River, between the claims of E A M and H D Swazey and T A. Martin, as is inferred from subsequent knowledge of the parties, near Farmington, but there is nothing in the deed to indicate definitely either the location or the size of the premises. This deed was filed for record March 20, 1837, and witnessed by E. A M Swazey and H. King The oldest instrument in date of record, however, is a bond from J. T Holmes and Henry Bateman to John Crow, dated August 25, 1836 and filed for record November 6, 1837, for Lot 5, Block 3, Farmington This was before the land sales; for Farmington, it is proper to say, like many of the towns of the West, was laid out, lots sold, and improvements made long before the Government title was obtained With faith in the Government full of enterprise and "goah datriveness," with a spirit adventure and pluck, fortunes were made and lost on mere promises and hope; and thus the pioneers of this rich valley and the West generally invited emigrants, and rapidly developed its resources. It will be found that the first warranty deed of record is for lots in Pittsburg, from Abiathar Buck, Williams and wife, and John Groom and wife, to Lemuel Mussetter, while the oldest deed of the kind is from David Taylor to Edward Nance, for twenty acres, in Section 32, Township 69, Range 8 (Harrisburg), dated November 22, 1838. Abram Foster made the first entry of land, his entry being October 2, 1838 (ninety-seven acres, in Section 6, Township 69, Range 10—Van Buren), and he was followed on the 5th of October, 1838, by Robert J. Sturdivant, of 160 acres, in Section 35, Township 69, Range 8—Harrisburg.

During the same month (October, 1838), James F Westcott entered the quarter section adjoining Keosauqua, which to this day is known as the Westcott quarter. James Bell made his entry of his farm in Washington Township the same month. When he crossed the Des Moines River at Keosauqua, a few months before with his family, he borrowed money from Capt James Hall to pay his ferriage, and he thus reached his claim without a cent in money, but with pluck and courage that carried him through. James N McCutchen, Thomas Anson, Peter Gillis and Thomas Beer bought their lands in this township the same month.

In Cedar Township, Samuel Huddleston; in Union, John M Whittaker, in Farmington, Richard Cave, William Williams, James Rhodes, John Newport, in Vernon, Alexander Davis (whose wife hauled the rails with one horse to fence the improvement, while he split them), Nahum Sargent, in Des Moines, Delaney Dillingham; in Jackson, William and Jonathan McClure, William Brooks, Martin Tate, George Reynolds and John Cantrel, in Village, Riley Gilbert and John D. Walker, in Lick Creek, William S Whittaker and Hiram Hill, in Chequest, Stiles S Carpenter, Sylvester Riley and Asheel Lane, made among the first entries

OFFICIAL ROSTER OF THE COUNTY.

Appended is a roster of the officers who have held places of trust under the State and county, from Van Buren County :

Representatives in United States Congress —1855–57—Augustus Hall, Keosauqua . George W McCrary, formerly of Van Buren

United States Senator —George G Wright, from 1871 to 1877

Chief Justice Supreme Court of Iowa —George G Wright

Representatives in Third Constitutional Convention —1857, Squire Ayers, Timothy Day.

Representatives in the Legislature —Senate—1846–48, John M Whitaker, John F. Sanford, 1848–49, John F Sanford, George G Wright: 1850–51, George G Wright, John B Spees, 1852–53, John B Spees, George Schramm, 1854–56, George Schramm, A. H. McCrary ; 1856–57, David T Brigham, A H McCrary; 1858, David T Brigham, Gideon S. Bailey ; 1860–61, Gideon S. Bailey, 1862–64, A H. McCrary, 1866, Eliab Doud; 1868, Jacob G. Vale, 1873, James B Pease. *House*—1846–48, George Montague, Anderson McPherrin, Dudley Hardy, R. B Willoughby ; 1848–49, John Alexander, J. W. McManaman, A. H McCrary. Willard Elmer ; 1850–51, A H McCrary, George C. Allender C G. Dibble, 1852–53, Anderson McPherrin. Lewis Fordyce, Jacob Ream, Robert Russell ; 1854–56, George N Rosser, Joseph Barker, Robert Meek, Henry Weatherington; 1856– . . . . 1858, Squire Ayers . . . . Caldwell; 1862, ... nett, J W

Latham, 1866, Joel Brown, Jonathan Thatcher, 1868, Joel Brown, Seth Craig, 1870, Joel Brown, George N Rosser ; 1872, Samuel Whitten, John R. Wright, 1874, Joseph Work, 1876, Thomas Christy, 1878 Oliver Hazard, Perry Scott

District Judges —The first appointment of District Judge was under the Territorial law Hon David Irvin was the first to serve, in 1838. He appointed Henry G Stewart as Clerk.

Charles Mason succeeded Judge Irvin and served until 1847 Stewart acted as Clerk until the appointment of Frye B Hazeltine Elisha Cutler, Jr also acted as Clerk This ended the Territorial District Judgeship, and in the spring of 1847, Cyrus Olney was elected He resigned in the spring of 1851, and Judge Joseph C. Knapp was appointed to fill the vacancy, which he did until the election of William H. Seevers in 1852 In the fall of 1856, Seevers resigned and Caleb Baldwin was appointed to fill the vacancy In the spring of 1856 H. B. Hendershott was elected, and owing to a change in the limits of the district his term expired in the winter of 1859, when John S Townsend became Judge of this district

The following, therefore, would be the roster from the beginning down to the present 1838, David Irvin, 1839, Charles Mason 1847, Cyrus Olney, 1851, Joseph C Knapp, 1852, William H. Seevers 1856, Caleb Baldwin, 1856, H. B Hendershott, 1859, John S. Townsend, 1863, Henry H Trimble, 1867, Harvey Tannehill, 1871, Morris J Williams; 1875, Joseph C. Knapp, 1879 E. L. Burton

Circuit Court Judge —In 1868, the Circuit Court was established, and Hon Robert Sloan was chosen to the Bench He has been re-elected twice since then, and is still filling the office

District Clerks —1838, Henry G Stewart; 1840, Frye B Hazeltine; 1841, Elisha Cutler, Jr ; 1846, D. C. Bonney, 1848–50, Seth Millington, 1852, Charles Baldwin, 1854–56, Alexander Burns; 1857, William J. Johnson; 1858–60, L D. Morris, 1861–66 John A Miller, 1868–70 J W Latham, 1872–74, Russell Johnston 1876, W A Gebhardt; 1878, James Gillespie

Prosecuting Attorneys —1846, George G Wright, 1848, Henry M Shelby, 1850, Henry M. Shelby 1852, Charles C Nourse; 1854, Samuel M Mills, 1856, H C. Caldwell

The office of District Attorney was instituted in 1856–57, which took the place of the Prosecuting Attorney The list ran ·

District Attorneys.—1858, Amos Harris, 1862, Amos Harris, 1866, James B Weaver; 1870, Maston H. Jones, 1874, Thomas M Fee; 1878, R. B Townsend.

County Judges —1851–55, Emanuel Mayne. 1857, Thomas Rankin ; 1859, Joshua S Sloan 1861–65, H Strickling, 1867, Alexander Brown.

The County Judge system was superseded by the election of Auditor.

Auditors —1868–73, Alexander Brown 1875–77, Bernard F Rehkoph

Assessors —1839, Obediah Selby, 1840 S S Carpenter ; 1857, Cranston Allen

Sheriffs —The first Sheriff of Van Buren County was a Mr Knowles He was appointed by the Governor of Wisconsin The year is not certain, but he served until   d from 1838 to 18   red M Lyon was in   ess, the office of Sheriff became an elective one   The list of names from that time until the present was as follows .

1844–46, J. H Bonney. 1846–48, James Johnston ; 1848–50. Seth St. James , 1850–52, Benjamin B Marlow , 1852–54. Thomas Christy , 1854–56, James M Tuttle ; 1856–58 Joseph Barker , 1858–60. Robert B. Rutledge ; 1860–62, Robert B Rutledge ; 1862–63, John T Stuart , 1863–65, John T. Stuart , 1865–67 J. C. McCrary ; 1867–69, George W Sommerville ; 1869–71, John W Shane ; 1871–73. John W Shane ; 1873–75, John W Shane , 1875–77 John W Shane , 1877–79, Francis Johnston.

Recorders.—1839, Jacob Lane, 1841, Jacob Lane, 1850 Edwin R Cutter, 1851, George Parker , 1853–55, Thomas Rankin . 1857–59. James M Tuttle, 1861–63, Joshua S Sloan , 1864, Edwin Goddard , 1868–70, Russell Johnston , 1872–78, D K Kittle

Surveyors—1841, Ira Claflin , 1851, Nathaniel Myer , 1852, William Munroe ; 1853, Ira Claflin , 1854–55. Isaac Connelly ; 1857, Seth Millington , 1858 Erastus Hoskins , 1859, George R Graves , 1861. W C Blackstone ; 1862–67, Ira Claflin . 1869–71. E B Kirkendall ; 1873, George R Graves , 1875–77, Ira Claflin.

County Treasurers —1857 Roger N Cresap ; 1838–41 James H. Jenkins ; 1842, Edward R. Tyler ; 1843, Philip Hartzell ; 1844–48, Gideon B. Alexander , 1849–50. Edwin R. Cutter , 1851, George Parker , 1853–55, Thomas Rankin . 1857–59, James M Tuttle , 1861–69, Joshua S Sloan ; 1871–77, Robert L. Clark.

Coroners.—1851, John W. Gale ; 1852. L. H Riley , 1853, George C. Allender ; 1855. Cranston Allen , 1857–59. George C. Allender ; 1861, John Barnes , 1863–67, L W Thornburg, 1869. Silas Tolman , 1871, George Stidger ; 1873, Robert Hunter , 1875, W P. L. Mun ; 1877, Dr. D. W Stutsman.

School Fund Commissioners.—1847 Samuel Clayton ; 1852, Henry Whelen ; 1854, Henry Whelen : 1856. Lorenzo Dow Morris.

Superintendents of Schools —1858, Anderson McPherrin , 1859, M. H. Cooley ; 1861–65, D. G Perkins , 1866–69, George B Walker ; 1871, Francis Miller ; 1873, Archie McDonald ; 1875–77 John W. Rowley.

Road Supervisors.—1851, George Whitall , 1852. Madison Dagger

Supervisors —The following is a complete list of the names of County Supervisors since the organization of the Board in 1837, then termed Board of Commissioners

1837—John Bending, Isham Keith, Enoch P. Blackburn.

1838—Isham Keith, John Whitaker, Enoch P Blackburn

1839—John Carnes, Charles Davis, John Sailor (or Maryland Jones, the record contains both names).

1840—John Whitaker, James McCrary. Joseph Miles

1841—William Whitaker, David Ferguson, Frye B Hazeltine.

1842—David Ferguson, W. S. Whitaker, Jesse Wright

1843—David Ferguson, W S Whitaker, Jesse Wright

1844—Robert Meek, John Alexander, David Ferguson.

1845—John Alexander, Rezin B. Willoughby. Robert Meek.

1846—John Alexander, Ira Claflin, Robert Meek.

1847—John Alexander, Obadiah S Freeman Ira Claflin.

1848—John D Woodworth Obadiah S Freeman Ira Claflin.

1849—Ira Claflin Obadiah S Freeman Robert Green

1850—Ira Claflin, Joel Knight, Robert Green

In 1851, the "Judge system" was made to prevail over that of County Commissioners. This system ran until 1861. The last meeting of the Board of Commissioners was held July 29, 1851. The last official act was to assign each member $5 for fees. An adjournment was then taken sine die. The first Judge elected was E. Mayne. His first official act was to approve the bond of B. B. Marlow, as Sheriff. This, August 18, 1851. Judge Mayne served until 1857, and on August 12 of that year, Judge Thomas Rankin succeeded him. His time expired the latter part of 1859, and on January 3, 1860, Judge Joshua S. Sloan took his seat. He served until 1861, when a new twist of the law threw the county again under the control of a Board of Supervisors, one from each township. The appended list is official.

1861—John D. Baker, Matthew Creswell, Lorenzo Ellis, Seth Fordyce, Erastus Hoskin, J. A. Hughes, L. J. Mason, E. Mayne, J. G. Newbold, John Perry, Joseph Rabb, Harvey Robb, Jacob Silvers.

1862—George C. Allender, W. H. Alexander, J. D. Baker, C. L. Bonney, J. D. Elbert, Lorenzo Ellis, William Huber, Onias Hale, Joseph Kean, L. J. Mason, S. M. Morris, John Perry. William J. Parker.

1863—George C. Allender, William H. Alexander, C. L. Bonney, John D. Elbert, L. Ellis, William Huber, Onias Hale, J. A. Kean, L. J. Mason, A. McCullough, W. J. Parker, E. B. Sample, W. H. Turton.

1864—W. H. Alexander, C. L. Bonney, Lorenzo Ellis, Onias Hale, L. J. Mason, A. McCullough, R. N. McLeland, B. F. Miller, Uriel Neal, W. J. Parker, E. B. Sample, W. H. Turton, Joseph Warren.

1865—W. H. Alexander, C. L. Bonney, Milton Chalfaut, Lorenzo Ellis, Onias Hale, R. N. McLeland, A. McCullough, B. F. Miller, Alexander Newbold, Uriel Neal, Joseph Warren, Jacob Wagner.

1866—W. H. Alexander, C. L. Bonney, Milton Chalfaut, Jonathan Ferris, William Huber, Onias Hale, L. J. Mason, Andrew McCullough, R. N. McLeland, Uriel Neal, Ralph Peterson, Jacob Wagner.

1867—W. H. Alexander, Milton Chalfaut, Jonathan Ferris, William Huber, Onias Hale, L. J. Mason, R. N. McLeland, W. S. Mayne, J. H. McVeigh, Uriel Neal, Isaac Nelson, Ralph Peterson, Jacob Wagner.

1868—O. B. Brown, John Brooks, James Elerick, Thomas H. Hopkins, S. S. Henry, Edmund Hilles, Onias Hale, James H. McVeigh, B. F. Miller, W. S. Mayne, Isaac Nelson, John T. Stewart, Jacob Wagner.

1869—John Brooks, James Elerick, James Green, Onias Hale, S. S. Henry, Thomas H. Hopkins, Edmund Hilles, J. H. McVeigh, B. F. Miller, John A. Miller, John T. Stewart, John Perry, Samuel Whitten.

1870—John Brooks, W. W. Byers, Harrison Blackledge, Matthew Creswell, James Green, Onias Hale, S. S. Henry, Thomas H. Hopkins, J. H. McVeigh, J. S. Miller, John A. Miller, John Perry, Samuel Whitten, W. P. L. Muir.

Again, in 1871, was the law changed, and the "legislative system" driven out to give place to the Board of three members. The latter system prevails at present. Those who have served may be found after:

1871—Onias Hale, Isaiah Meek, Erastus Pitkin
1872—Onias Hale, Isaiah Meek, Erastus Pitkin
1873—Onias Hale, Thomas Christy, Erastus Pitkin
1874—Samuel Nixon, Benjamin Wagner, Erastus Pitkin.

"Prior to 1840 but little attention was paid to the political preferences of candidates," observes Judge Wright as witness the honor of L. A. Keith and Gen Swazey to the first Council, both Whigs, while Bailey and Barker, in the House, were both Democrats, and their colleague, Hall, a Whig It was in 1840 that our Democratic friends in the county were called upon to rally by that man of irrepressible and versatile genius, John Carnes, known then and somewhat since as 'Pious John;' and rally they did   An organization was effected, and soon those figuring lived to enjoy the fruits; and others, I remember, as, for instance, the so-called 'Union Year' of 1842, when Bailey and Whittaker were defeated for the Council by Elbert and Jenkins : Bonney by Lyon, for Sheriff, to say nothing of others, who were occasionally led to realize that a dominant party is not always successful under the most vigorous party drill.   That year of 1842, by the way, was about my first active recollection of a political contest   It was peculiar, it will be remembered by the voters, some of whom I see here to-day, as having a so-called *religious element* in it.   Dr. Bailey, Capt. Bonney, Ezra M Jones, and their colleagues on the Democratic ticket, we hungry Whigs styled *the infidel party*   Many amusing incidents might be related.   I remember one in connection with A. J Davis, who was known as a most indefatigable worker in politics, as in everything else.   While talking with John Workman, a Democrat and a Methodist, who lived on the place where 'Uncle' Isaac Barker lived so long, Davis warned Barker of the danger to the cause of holiness if such infidels were elected, and finally concluded by saying that '*he'd be damned* if our holy religion was not in danger if the Democrats succeeded '"

REMINISCENCES

From the speech of Mr. A. H. McCrary, we quote the following description of the days of 1836 :

When I first stood on the bank of the Des Moines River, in the fall of 1836, the spot where we are now assembled was covered with the foliage of forest-trees and down on the bank of the river, very near to where Mr Manning's store is now situated, there were two or three small buildings being erected Immediately above the then projected town was Father Purdom's cabin, and a few acres of ground cleared   Father Purdom's was a kind of headquarters and boarding-house for all who came along The next cabin above was David Ely's, whose name that ford still bears With Mr Ely lived a brother-in-law, John Goodin John was a fine, jovial young man large and handsomely formed, and Father Purdom had some very excellent daughters John was then very much like the young men are now, and while Father P was very much opposed to young gentlemen decoying his daughters away from his humble cottage, John, not always having the fear of that good old gentleman before his eyes, wooed and gained the hand of Miss Purdom, and marriage-pledges were doubtless exchanged But Father P , not having all the confidence in John that was necessary to give his consent, therefore most positively refused, waxing wrathy   At this, John's ambition became somewhat aroused, and so began to plot treason against the old gentleman's rights, and, in order to carry out his treasonable purpose, he hired Aaron W Harlan, the hero of the Des Moines, to assist him   Aaron was an Aaron of old Mighty in words, and still more powerful in deeds, he procured an Indian canoe, and just as the moon was showing her broad face in the east, it was quietly landed at a suitable landing, and, while the unsuspecting father was quietly reposing, naughty John and crafty Aaron were stealthily assisting Miss P to get her necessary apparel and herself safely conveyed to the landing All safely on board, Aaron loosed the cable, and, there being no dams in the river (and the old gentleman being too pious to use any of the other kind), they glided smoothly down to the town of Sweet Home, in Missouri, where Esq Beedle officiated, making the late Miss Purdom Mrs Goodin Subsequently, other young gentlemen, being encouraged by John's success, made raids upon the old gentleman's household, until he was compelled to succumb and submit to an inglorious defeat This old gentleman's cabin was one of the most public places in the county at that time Besides its being the home of his family, it was used as public boarding-house, church, and I am not sure but it was sometimes used as a Court House While old Father Purdom may have had traits in his character peculiar to himself, he was one of God's noblemen . . . .
In . . . . the hardest times we ever . . . . during the . . . . many were in very uncomf . . . . but there were no

mills in the country nearer than Waterloo, Mo., to grind it, and a very severe winter upon us. For weeks, many of us subsisted on boiled corn or beat meal bread. That beating process could be endured for the sake of a change, but very soon we would fall back to hominy again. Those mortars, in which we would beat the corn into meal, were worked by hand and were called "Armstrong's mill." In some localities, horse-mills were erected. That class of machinery was only temporary, and I consider a description of them more tedious than profitable; and yet they afforded a temporary relief, and were regarded an improvement on the beating or hominy process. About the year 1837, William Duncan commenced the erection of a mill on the Des Moines River, just where Kinnersly's mill now stands, and, about the same time, William Meek & Sons commenced building a mill at Bonaparte. Duncan threw out a wing-dam about half-way across the river, and constructed a singular kind of wheel, which was called a screw wheel. The rushing of the water through the wheel gave it motion, to which the machinery was attached. While its likeness was never seen before or since, yet, by wallowing in water, we were able to get our corn ground, and we were so highly elated that I believe some of us tried to send Mr. Duncan to the Legislature. But I believe we failed.

From the speech of Mr. Edwin Manning we quote the following concise and admirable record of his experiences from 1837:

In the winter of 1837, I was sojourning in Missouri, and fell in with Capt. Hall Fairman and Carnes, all looking for homes in the West. The Captain and myself engineered a jumper-ride on the Des Moines River from St. Francisville to the rapids, in January, 1837 (now Mr. Kinnersly's famous water-power). How we were delighted, first with our ride up the river on the smooth ice, blanketed with pure snow, and next with the little water-fall that we imagined was an embryo fortune for some ingenious Yankee to develop into hydraulic powers. Hence the location of the county town here. But this was not all of our sight-seeing. Mr. Fairman and I made a trip across the half-breed tract to Fort Madison, and on our way we visited old Black Hawk in his camp, then located on Devil Creek, just below Fort Madison. I shall never forget the peculiar look and air of the old fallen chief. He received us kindly, but was extremely reticent, and would not encourage conversation to much extent. The country, at this time, was nearly all vacant, the settlements being confined to the streams. Claims had been made along and up the "Demoin" for nearly one hundred miles, or as far west as the first purchase reached. My first trade in Iowa was for a "half-breed" claim. This consisted of several hundred acres of land and some twenty-five town lots in Keokuk, costing me some $500. I then left the country, and returned in 1838, and attended the first land sale held in Burlington, in November, 1838. In the spring of 1839, I opened out the best stock of goods in the valley. I continued my business prosperously, and, in 1841, I contracted to supply the Government fort at the Raccoon Forks with provisions. This I did by chartering a steamboat at St. Louis and delivering my goods by steam. The upper country in and about Raccoon Forks was then peopled wholly by the red men. In honor of my bringing a boat from St. Louis, and giving the officers and Indian chiefs a free ride upon the river, Capt. Allen sent his couriers to the head men of the nation to come and pay their respects to us and give us a war-dance. This was done on a magnificent scale. Not less than three hundred of the best braves, Sacs and Foxes, assembled and gave one of their best performances, with all their paraphernalia, bells, feathers and paint. Altogether, it was the greatest feat I had ever witnessed in my Western life, thus far. Soon after this, the fort was moved further west, and the Indians went to their new home south of the Missouri. In 1843 the country was opened up for white settlement on the new purchase, and great and rapid emigration commenced from all parts of the Western States, and many from the East.

The navigation of the river was obstructed by occasional mill-dams, and the steamboat men of those days were too timid to risk their fortunes on the Des Moines to fight mill-dams. The next great era in enterprise in the valley was flatboating, and in this particular vocation, perhaps your speaker was one of the most successful men in advancing and practically demonstrating the Des Moines River to be a natural channel for commerce.

Other operators in the valley followed in quick pursuit, and soon the river navigation was fully appreciated. My peculiar forte was to build but few, but those were good and seaworthy crafts. In this I was successful, but nevertheless my fate was to sink one boat two times—first, at Bentonsport dam, and next at Croton—and finally got it into market and realized more money for it than it could have brought if it had reached the market without delay. The moral of this act teaches "help yourselves, and good surely follows." Such was the experience of your speaker. Now to give you another page of this history, transpiring at the same time, illustrates more fully the subject in question. My neighbor embarked in the same enterprise. He built cheap and frail boats, and hired men to run them, and out of a dozen or more started for market but one single craft lived through the voyage, and that was lost in damages. Thus, you see, what I . . . . all flat-boating on the b . . . . . . 7. At this period, the . . . . in. It was not forgotten . . . . ce why not again? This was the cry, "Out with the dams." This was the alarm sounded through the valley. Your speaker was not hard to understand what was most needed in the carrying-on of trade in the valley. Accordingly, he canvassed the matter with due consideration, and ventured upon another commercial enterprise. I proceeded to St. Louis, contracted with Capt. Allen at once to load the "Jennie Lind" and barge for Keosauqua and Eddyville. Arriving at Keokuk in due time, and having favorable water, my ambition was up to fever heat. But, to my utter astonishment, the Captain had learned through the skillful boatmen at Keokuk that they could not navigate the beautiful Des Moines. This brought dismay and trouble for a short time, but my perseverance and indomitable will-power to make the effort a success, if possible, overcame the embarrassment. The Captain was an old and good waterman. He became convinced that my heart was in the enterprise, and the more we argued the case the better he liked my logic. We became familiar boating companions for the trip, and finally we cast off the lines and set our face for the 'Diamond Navigation.' Arriving at Farmington in a few hours, our steam and whistle made the village alive, and in a few minutes the whole town was on the bank of the river admiring the beautiful "Jennie Lind." All was sunshine and glory to everybody except the mill-owners. Here again came the tug of war. It was fight or die. It would never do to stop here. The gates were closed, and apparently there was no entrance possible, being too old and weak to open, hence the trouble.

Finally, says I to Capt. Allen: "I brought you here to do my work; my order is that you at once remove these gates, at my risk and expense, and go ahead." No sooner said than all hands laid hold and demolished the gates and sent them floating down stream. This brave act of Capt. Allen at an opportune time opened up commerce throughout the valley, and it was never closed until superseded by rail. In this little enterprise, I was more than compensated in my own limited business, and what it did for me it did for the whole valley. I did not stop to calculate its importance, nor did I realize it fully till its development almost overwhelmed us, of such value was commerce brought to our doors by this great natural channel.

Our next great hope was the Des Moines improvement. In this we all expected to be enriched and made happy for the rest of our days. The great river grant was procured through Gen. Dodge, a veteran pioneer and popular politician in the State in those palmy days of Bourbon Democracy. With this munificent land grant for a great and good special object, the State accepted, but finally limited, and failed to aid and foster the enterprise. The magnitude of the work contemplated State indorsement; failing to obtain this, the work languished, and was finally abandoned as being behind the age and progress of the times at that period. In approximating its final adjustment with contracting parties, your speaker occupied a responsible position, having been appointed by Gov. Grimes, and subsequently elected, Commissioner of the Improvement. I was let into the secret of rat internal improvement contracts. It was not unfashionable in those days to carry a good supply of old Bourbon, and when the wheels got slow to use a little for propelling power. It so happened, in one of my sittings, criticising the accounts of Improvement expenditures, we all become very jolly, but it was a habit of mine not to sign papers without understanding their full import. This kind of sharp practice had been indulged in of occasionally asking a Commissioner to certify lands before they were fully paid for, and it was considered quite courteous to obtain an accommodation of this kind, but I was always so slow to understand such things that they did not get my name as often as they wanted it to such papers.

But in one grand levee we held over a settlement, the Company limbered up with Bourbon, and gave me the snug little sum of $75,000 discount on their regularly-entered charges against the State improvement. This was an eye-opener to all the people. The State at once proceeded to make a final settlement with the New York company. Subsequently, the remaining lands of the grant were negotiated for by the Valley Railroad. Thus ended the great farce of the first land grant to the Des Moines Valley.

From the speech of Mr. Charles Baldwin, we quote:

In coming to this new country, we came poor, most of us. We came to better our condition, to make homes which we were too poor to do in the older States. In making these homes, we had to struggle with the hardships of a new country, as well as with poverty. With good luck, it took eight or ten days to get a load of provisions. The great river could only be crossed by row-boat. If the river or wind was high, the poor settler had to wait often for days before he could cross. In the mean time, the good wife and the little ones were alone, nestled in the little cabin behind some far-off point of timber, hourly, hungrily scanning the wide prairie as far as the eye could reach, anxiously looking for husband and father with something to eat. Brave wives, noble mothers! right well have you earned your homes. May you long live to enjoy them.

Mark the contrast of to-day. Over the same routes we then traveled, we now send food for thousands upon thousands of hungry people. And we can go to Illinois and back in as many h   r   bridges that defy wind a   b   ch the banks of the M   the Atlantic Ocean on the one ha   M   now, on the other

(DECEASED)

In those days, too, we had a weekly mail, if the season and the roads were good, bringing us newspapers and letters from our friends. Perhaps they had been weeks on the way, but they were always fresh. For the coveted letters we had to pay 25 cents postage, and it was freely given. Now for 1 cent we send our letters to Maine or Georgia, or the far-off States of the Pacific, and we are not satisfied unless we have mail twice a day. If impatient of this delay, we can, by the magic wire, talk with our friends thousands of miles away, almost as if we were face to face.

Then it took two bushels and a half of corn to pay postage on one letter. Now for one bushel we can pay postage on fifty letters.

Then it took six dozen of eggs to get a letter from mother or sister. Now we can get from ten to twenty for one dozen of eggs.

When we remember that the usual time for our letters and papers to reach us was ten to thirty days, we can hardly realize the fact that the full proceedings of this meeting of Iowa Pioneers, to-day can be printed and read by the people of San Francisco, 2,000 miles away before the sun goes down.

My friends, your thoughts go back to-day to your old log cabins, claim-pens, as they were sometimes called. But little and mean as they looked, they held all that was dearest and brightest to you—your wives and little ones—while the bright halo of hope shed its rays around them gilding, with its glory, the horizon of all your future. And I appeal to you, venerable pioneers, if in those little log cabins you did not spend the happiest days of your lives, the brightest hours of your existence.

As I have before stated, immigration flowed into this county rapidly from 1836 to 1843. In 1838 the population of the county was about 3,000. In 1840, it was 6,140. In 1840, the New Purchase was opened to settlement, and many who had stopped in this border county only until they could get a chance to "go West," moved on into the new country.

The first assessment of property for taxation in the county, that I can find on record, was in 1839, on about $152,336 of property, and the tax collected was $873.83. In 1840, there were sixteen towns recorded in the county, and the town property was assessed at $59,550.50. Their names were Rising Sun, Rochester, Philadelphia, Birmingham, Harrisburg, Des Moines City, Watertown, Keosauqua, South Keosauqua, Hedvolant, Winchester, Farmington, New Lexington, Columbus, North Bentonsport and South Bentonsport, each town looking grandly on paper, and in the estimation of their founders, the embryo of great cities—all blowing their trumpets and making a great noise in the world on an average capital of $3,722.22 each.

The annual assessment of property shows our progress in wealth, while the National census shows our increase in population. But time will not permit a statement of the assessment of each year. I will therefore take periods that sufficiently illustrate our advancement in wealth and population.

In 1850, our population was 12,270, an increase of 100 per cent in ten years, 10 per cent per annum. Our property was assessed that year at $1,358,671. In 1860, our population was 17,081, an increase of about 40 per cent in ten years, or 4 per cent per annum. The assessment that year was of farms, $2,811,859, of personal property $984,661 of town property, $386,070, total, $3,662,590, showing an increase in ten years, of about 170 per cent, or 17 per cent per annum. In 1870, our population was 17,672, an increase in ten years of only 591, about ⅓ of 1 per cent only, in that time. The assessment for that year was farms, $3,264,862, personal property, $1,623,387, towns, $552,304, total, $5,440,553, showing that, while from 1860 to 1870, our population increased only about ⅓ of 1 per cent, our property increased in the same period about 50 per cent, or at the rate of 5 per cent per annum.

For this year, 1875, the assessment is farms, $3,827,543, personal property, $1,501,402, towns, $530,730, railroads, $261,890, total, $5,621,565. There are 65 miles of railway in the county. They were not assessed in 1870 nor at any time before that year. Showing that the assessed value of our property has increased in five years only $181,012 about 3½ per cent in five years. Deduct the railroad property, and our other property has gone back in valuation since 1870, $90,878.

To form a just idea of the progress we have made, we will take a view of the revenues of the county from time to time. As I have said, the taxes collected in 1839 were $873.83, in 1850, the levy was $10,581.70, in 1860, $26,996.32, in 1870, $78,717.

About 1850 is, perhaps, the period when the increase of our population and the development of our county settled into something like a normal condition. It will be observed that the value of the property of the county has increased about ten times as fast as our population. This increase is almost entirely the result of the labor of its citizens. It will also be observed that the annual increase in the value of property has not kept pace with the rate of interest upon money. And it will be further observed that the increase in direct taxes is about twice as great as the rate of property increase.

ALVAH CLAYTON'S ADDRESS

From an address delivered by Mr. Alvah Clayton, of St. Louis, before the Pioneers' Association in 1875, we take the following extract:

The incidents of which I propose to speak are necessarily of a private nature, and I must ask you to excuse the seeming egotism of incidental observations. My visit will be immediate to

D

the younger portion of this audience the trials, privations and self-sacrificing labors of the early settlers of this county, and to give them an insight into the state of society as it then existed. The experiences of our own family were no doubt very similar to those of the other pioneers. My father, leaving his family in the State of Ohio, came into this valley in the spring of 1836, and laid his claim, as I have before said, at the mouth of the Chequest Creek, just above the present village of Pittsburg. His claim embraced a frontage of half a mile on the river, and extended up the creek about a mile, and included what he regarded at the time as an excellent site for a water-mill, and there he subsequently erected one of the first mills ever erected in this county. Alone and unaided, he built him a cabin on the bank of the river, and cleared off the timber and brush from five acres of the ground, preparatory to planting a crop of corn and other vegetables. By this time the season was well advanced. He had no team, except a poor old ox, which he had purchased of Mr. Peter Gillis, who had already settled a short distance below the site of the city, on the opposite side of the river. For this ox he made a single yoke, with ropes attached for traces. But, unfortunately, he had no agricultural implements—no plow, no harrow, nor even a hoe. The nearest point where such articles could be secured was the then village of Quincy, Ill. Thither he determined he would go, late as was the season. Taking his Indian canoe, which was his only means of transportation, he paddled his way to the mouth of the river, where he was fortunate enough to meet a steamboat, on which he took passage to Quincy. Procuring the irons for a plow, and other implements which he needed, he returned by steamer to the mouth of the Des Moines River, whose rapid current he ascended in his canoe, by the toilsome process of paddling, poling and towing. Finally, after a wearisome voyage of many days, he reached home—hastily constructed a stock for his plow, hunted up his old ox, which had by this time become fat and strong from feeding upon the luxuriant grass of the rich bottom land, and was ready to commence plowing. But the middle of June had now arrived, the grass and weeds had grown up nearly as high as the back of his ox, and all he had time to do was to run single furrows in which to plant his corn. He afterward plowed out the intervening spaces, and thus, by dint of hard work and perseverance, succeeded in raising a fine crop of corn. Meanwhile, he had written back to my brother, who was in charge of the family in Ohio (the brother who has been a resident in your midst during the last forty-two years), to bring the family on as soon as possible. This he hastened to do, making the long and tedious journey overland through the black swamps of Indiana and the seemingly boundless prairies of Illinois. Crossing the Mississippi at what is now the city of Nauvoo, we made our way through the trackless prairies without seeing any signs of a white settlement until we arrived on the bank of the Des Moines, opposite my father's cabin, in the month of November, 1836, after a toilsome journey of five weeks. Then commenced our long and laborious struggle for a subsistence in this wild but fertile valley. The obstacles and discouragements were met and overcome, not without the sorest trials, both mental and physical. Of the luxuries of life, which you now enjoy so abundantly, we were wholly deprived. For a time, it was with the utmost difficulty that we could obtain even those things which now seem absolutely necessary.

It is true, we never suffered for the want of food and clothing, though what we had was necessarily of the plainest and coarsest kind. At first the rifle supplied our table with meat, and for bread we were limited to corn and buckwheat. But even these we had no means of grinding. Forty miles away in Missouri was the nearest mill, and thither, occasionally, would my father and brother go with a wagon-load of corn to be ground into meal. When it was inconvenient to make this long journey, we had to resort to the expedients of the tin "grater," the wooden mortar and the coffee-mill. With the manner of using these implements many of you are doubtless familiar.

At first the Indians were our most numerous neighbors. They were constantly passing up and down the river, sometimes on foot, but generally in canoes. They seldom passed our door without stopping to beg or steal—and you can readily imagine that their visits were not cordially welcomed. A few white people soon settled around us, and we hailed their coming with joy. To show you how gladly we welcomed new comers, I will mention an incident which occurred in the spring of 1837—the spring following our own arrival. In April, there arrived on the bank of the river opposite our residence, two large families from Illinois, both well provided with teams, wagons and stock cattle. They were to be our neighbors, and we rejoiced to see them. We assisted them in getting their teams and effects across the river by lashing two canoes together and placing planks across to form a platform. On this rudely and hastily constructed boat, all were safely ferried over.

If I mistake not, each family consisted of ten persons, making twenty in all. They had come without any previous preparations for houses in which to dwell. Although our cabin contained but one room, sixteen feet square, yet we took them all in, and sheltered them as best we could for about two weeks, until they had erected cabins for themselves, on claims they had previously selected not far from our own homestead. Just how we succeeded in accommodating so many people in so very small a space, I am utterly unable to tell you. I remember, however, that at night . . . . in the low attic overhead. Even . . . . numbered . . . . . . to sleep in the wagons out of . . . . could not be accommodated at the first table had to wait for th . . . . though way of entertaining visitors, but it was the best we could do under the circumstances, and it is but just that I should say that our guests accepted the rude hospitality we had to offer with thankful hearts And now, it would hardly be proper for me to close this narrative without saying that these two families bore the honored names of Duffield and Swearingen The heads of these families, with the exception of the aged Mrs Duffield, have long since been called to their last reward, but they have left behind them a numerous progeny, many of whom are now respected and influential citizens among you

I might detain you a long time by the recital of interesting incidents connected with early times in this county, but, lest I weary you, I will ask your attention only a few minutes longer.

At the early date at which my father arrived here, this territory was nominally under civil jurisdiction of the Territory of Michigan, but no courts had been established, or officers appointed to execute the laws Practically, we had no laws except such rules as the settlers found it necessary to establish for their own protection. Every man was, to a limited extent, a law unto himself, and was not molested in the exercise of his own free will, unless he infringed upon the rights of his neighbors Hence, many things were done which would hardly be considered proper in the present advanced state of society To illustrate, I will mention one incident, and then I will close

There lived in our neighborhood a man having a wife and two children —a boy and a girl There was another lady, somewhat advanced in years, who had been a member of his family for some considerable length of time He also had in his employment an unmarried man, on the shady side of thirty It happened that the husband and wife did not dwell together as harmoniously as husband and wife ought to Just what was the cause of the trouble I never knew, but in order to settle the difficulty, a mutual agreement was entered into of the following nature The husband transferred his wife to his hired man, and himself took the other woman for a wife As the arrangement was agreeable to the ladies, all parties were satisfied The mother took the daughter and the father retained the son There was also some agreement as to the division of property, and to give the whole transaction a show of legality, some neighbors were called in to witness the contract

JUDGE WRIGHT'S PERORATION

The address referred to in the foregoing pages, delivered by Judge Wright, was concluded with the following personal mention, which is too valuable to be omitted :

I have purposely omitted any reference to Keosauqua and its settlement for the reason that I told what I knew on that subject in an address before its Library Association, March 4, 1856, and as the collection and preservation of facts connected with the early settlement of the county is one object of the Association, that being published can be used, and I have hence for the most part devoted my attention to other localities To other towns and neighborhoods and individuals I should with pleasure have referred, if I had been successful in gathering the material, or if time permitted Indeed, I feel that I am not to be excused for passing over many others Thus I would like to refer at length to my early and warm friend, Isaac N Lewis, who had so much to do with laying the foundations, who struggled with the rest of us amid the trials of a frontier life, and who, to use his own energetic method of profanity, "by gum!" could do anything else but drink whisky with the best of us And he that, with the rest of us, Isaac was accustomed to call his competitor, now Col Summers who it were hard to tell whether he loved *congenial company, a fine horse* or a *big fee best* And to Uncle Jonny Seaman* (I wonder if he rides a "blue buck" yet?) And to Uncle Tommy Beer, honest, quaint and ever inoffensive And that other Uncle Tommy (Hearn), loving Maryland first and Iowa last and best And Uncle Ira Claflin, from the Land of Steady Habits, and whose habits are always steady, with his good wife with her good black eyes, and once again to Capt Josiah Bonney, with his big heart, and by his side Orpha, whom he found at Rochester when he and I were young—once more afflicting Father Stannard with a Democratic son-in-law, and George W Games, and Eliza, too, who were the life of the social circle years long gone, but now, alas! the "weight of years," just a little, is upon them, and John, of the tribe of Goodall—good old Kentucky stock—among our best and truest citizens—most of them "across the River" now, the Great River—but those remaining as were those gone, worthy and respected by all, and that enthusiastic friend and Whig his brother in-law, Isaac W McManaman, who did nothing by halves, and whether at home or in a political convention, or the Legislature, by his very earnestness and whole-souled manner, won the esteem and respect of all, and up the Des Moines, just below Iowaville, that man of positive character and Baptist proclivities. Benjamin Saylor, and his long line of boys, John, Conrad, Hiram, Jehu, and perhaps a dozen others, who made big farms in this and Polk County, and who, by his force of character commanded attention in all circles

And again, the long line from near Posey County, Ind —they of the tribe of McCrary—James and Abner and John with their relatives and children—for have th[...] [...]uires, and Senators, and [...] intimate and [...] and M[...] tilling t[...] [...] ality? and Andrew (he of [...]—Meredith who with his industrious wife [...] [...] ife with

*Died August 5, 1[...]

the best home of the early days, which I shall never forget, for at their table more than once I have been cared for when tired and hungry, and that woman of marked character, the wife of Obed, who was the son of William Stannard, for she and her husband truly made their impress upon the country, and all remember them to praise, and Russo (of the royal family of Kings), who made our mills, built our houses, and at the same time builded, as he deserved, well for himself and family, and Roger N. Cresap, with that wife who has accomplished more and with more life and good-humor than any one that lives—he I should not forget, for whether in Louisiana or Texas, wherever thrown by fate or fortune, he still turned to the same beautiful and rich land where he now lives as the brightest and most pleasant spot on earth and then, there is Harvey —of the long tribe of Alexanders—irrepressible in his politics, endless in his story-telling, never exaggerating in the least, whether on the block or off and is still *going, going, going*, and will be till he's *gone*, and my old friend Robert Forbes, who never had but a "mere whang of apples," which meant more than all his neighbors, and who never let any poor Whig or Radical rest if he could get a chance to punch him in the ribs, and those pioneers of large personal, political and social influence, Capts Hancock and Sanford, and that blessed good man, Sheriff Johnson, with his son-in-law, McPherrin—twice a member of the General Assembly—and of whom to say that he is as good and honest as the father-in-law, is but simple truth and no faint praise, and that fine specimen of manhood and old fashioned Methodism Uncle Johnny Spencer and his good and solid neighbors, Groom and Warren and that jolly Democrat from Delaware, Billy Holland, and his equally jolly neighbor, Onias Hale, and scores of others in the same vicinity, from the land of Rush, in the much-noused State of Indiana, and then, too, he that was among our earliest and truest men, Mark C Thatcher, of Quaker stock, and that quiet wife of his, and their boys almost numberless, Jonathan, Isaac Thomas, Aaron, Amos, Ezekiel, and how many more I cannot tell, and his old neighbors, whose influence was fully equal to any others in their vicinity, Lippincott, and Muir, and Burns, and Ralph, of the house of Peterson, than whom no county ever had truer men, and of course Dr Nathan Shepherd, always fighting for the right and peddling pills, while James, of the same name, dealt in politics, and Benjamin F Pearson, also, who kept public house in Pittsburg at the time of the Young Mormon war there, in the winter of 1840-41, and which I shall never forget, and who did build our houses, fought for his country, and esteems Republicanism next to Methodism, and Ashahel, who went home within the last few years, who owned those rich acres just down the river from where we now are, a good citizen, and his children do follow him, and Benjamin of the numerous tribe of Barkers, and that other Barker (Esq Joseph) who started in the woods, but woods no longer, and who has more children to love than any man in the county, for he beats Dr Sturdivant, having, as I am told, eighteen, the Doctor only fourteen, and Joel and Wesley Walker, from the land of Penn, who have had as much to do with Keosauqua and its growth as most others, perhaps any, unless it be one I should not forget, Edwin Manning, of the strong frame and marked face, rather slow of speech and movement, and yet never idle, and who holds the largest purse and more lands than any other, save his friendly rival, Seth of the land of Bentonsport, both of them still New Englanders somewhat in manners and habits notwithstanding their many days in the West, and the neighbor of Seth, Dr Cowles, recognized among the best physicians of the early days, and, perhaps still so, and Timothy, whose other name is Day, that never tires, with energy and good sense enough to govern a nation, and who has added more to the (stock) wealth of the county than all others and Harvey Robb, who goes (or did) to New York, Albany, Chicago and Philadelphia, with more cattle and hogs than any man in the county, and who, if not the handsomest man, is as good and energetic as many claiming better looks (He and 'Squire Neal can settle the question of good looks, and if it should be a tie they might divide honors with Billy Holland, or with John R Wright, who I know belongs to a good-looking family), and that most devoted of all Methodists, Father Thomas Miller, and I must not forget him or them, James J (the White Pigeon) and Margaret, his wife, for they were the friends of everybody, good to the sick, always well and happy, and John Lyon, the man of inventive genius, and whose shop and name are known all over this and adjoining counties, and that stern old Presbyterian, James A Brown, of Bear Creek first, then of Bentonsport, could I forget him and his true friendship I should be indeed most ungrateful, and I must not pass by Samuel of the red bar—Robinson, John of Irish Bend—Parks, who has "awful" nice apples, an "awful" good farm, is an "awful" good man, and has an "awfuller" good wife, and then, too, his old neighbors, the Johns, Steeves, Baggs and McKibben, and Miner, in name merely, always old enough to take care of himself since I knew him, Lashing, of the brick house in Harrison, and perhaps the first in the township, and the sons-in-law of Jacob Ream, Mussetter and Smith and their neighbor and friend, Lorenzo Ellis and Brad Ellis, too, and his late neighbor Langford as good men as we have, and the taller boys, and Benson and Thomas, of Farmington, John Besecker, Billy Johnson and George Huffman, of Bonaparte, and the Rutledges and Penetts—I hope they will live forever, and Esq William Hickney, bless him, how he and that other good soul, Sam Merritt, used to work for old-fashioned Whiggery, and Miles McSurley, who, when last I met him, was as jolly ... I cannot, that personal ... han Nelson, and his equally ... the Walkers, who always ... hospitable pioneer,

Jordan, and Father Brewster and his well-brought-up family, and Henry Anson, now gone, but his boys still among you of good habits and growing prosperity, and Isaac W McCarty, the politician of the first years, still of Appanoose County, able to use more tobacco than any man in his neighborhood, and Dudley Hardy, twice a member of the General Assembly and Charles Jackson, who kept the big hotel at Utica, where we had those big musters, and Father Dibble whose name I mention with reverence, a member of the Second Constitutional Convention, and a man of as clear a head and honest a heart as ever lived in this or any county and that decided genius of irrepressible Whig faith, Samuel Holcomb, near Portland, and the large family of that name, and those pioneer preachers, Samuel Clark and Milton Jameson, possessing an unction, eloquence and power seldom found now or at any time in the State or elsewhere, and he of commanding presence big heart, great energy and fine ability in his profession, Dr J D Elbert and those men of prowess, Amos Strickland, Theodorus Davis, John and Josephus Medley, Charles Davis, Jehiel Smith, the Billups, who knew no fear, and many of them preferring a square fight to a square meal and those men who have performed so important a part in the well-being and good name of their respective neighborhoods Barger, the Watsons and Morrises, of Cedar, Fordyces of Union, Wells and Cassady and McIntire of Jackson, Moore and Vanfleet of Chequest, and Henry, Dodson, Ellis and Thompsons of Vernon, and I should be thought most remiss if I should pass Chandler E. Yeager, whom I met at Father Purdom's, as I remember, the first meeting I ever attended in this place November 15, 1840, who still lives to love his Church and to be respected by all, and those physicians of quick movement and great practical sense in their profession Ober and Barton, and the brother of the latter, William H Barton and his long-tried friend and associate, William B Willes, who, like all of us, is getting old, but who believes, as we should, in driving dull care away and that pioneer Abolitionist, Charles Gardner, at Business Corner, who was as fearless in the defense of his principles as he was straightforward in his business habits, and his near neighbor Riley, who has gone to the old brick structure (Mt Moriah) regularly each Sabbath for these many years, who throttles vice wherever he sees it, and has given to his honest father-in-law, Malachi Vinson, over on Indian Prairie, a bevy of grandchildren of which we know neither of them are ashamed, and then again, James H, the son of Samuel Clayton, before named and his unequaled helpmeet, and where the young people always love to go, and whose invitations to their good cheer and happy home we seniors always accept with pleasure, and, too, the widow of James, who passed to his rest years long gone, known to us all as Mother Daughrity,* the godmother or grandmother of all the children hereabouts, who delights in the offices of administering to the woes and sufferings of others, and not less in expressing her mind most freely if necessity demands it, and Titus Moss, the father, whose benevolent face made you love humanity, and his son, Lloyd, the stillest and quietest, and yet busiest, man in your county, and away over by the long-known "Brattain's Grove," Joseph, of the *Children of Israel*, and, a little further away, Alexander of the *Christian* tribe, who though they take radically different routes politically, agree in friendly competition as to which shall have the tallest corn, the most wheat, and the best farms, and Father John Goddard, whose name was the synonym for honest and blunt frankness, whose children bless the name of father, and to one of whom (Edwin Goddard Esq), I most cheerfully acknowledge my great obligation for many of the facts herewith presented I say, to these and scores of others whose names faces and deeds come trooping into my mind, I should like so much to refer· but you know and I know I cannot, for I must hasten on to that conclusion which I am sure you think I should have reached long since And with a few more words you shall have it

I have been frequently asked, as you have, doubtless, why Van Buren County has not increased more rapidly in population I will give you one or two reasons It is certainly not because the location is undesirable, nor yet because the soil is not fertile But, in the first place, there is no large town or city in the county It is emphatically an agricultural county And, in the next place, it is a noticeable fact that it filled up very rapidly at its first settlement Thus, in 1838, it was the second county in population having 3,174, Des Moines being first, and Van Buren being in advance of Lee or Dubuque In 1840 it had the largest population, 6 166, Lee being next and Des Moines third In 1844, it was third, having then over 9 000 Other counties just as large did not fill up so rapidly at first, and hence the subsequent years show a greater relative increase This county, it will also be remembered, was the seat of empire—the capital, so to speak, for several years, of the far-famed Des Moines Valley or Republic Until the new settlements west of us opened up it was the place sought for by those coming into the Territories Then most emigrants wanted to get as far south as possible, and this was the "Eldorado" In course of time we had a country west and north the notions of people as to climate changed, and this county did not, therefore, get the same proportion as at first of emigrants, nor could it retain, of course, all those here, and while the growth has been healthy, and the advance in wealth very satisfactory, there was no room or chance for that marked increase as in other counties where the settlements were at first sparse And yet, if you leave out the large cities in the old counties such as Keokuk, Burlington, Davenport and Dubuque you will find that this county bears comparison with most others

However this may be it is a matter of congratulation that few counties, if any, have been better managed in their finances, or by better officers While it may not be within miles of

* Died at her residence in Keosauqua, May 6, 1873

railway, or endeavored by township taxation and county bonds to build railroads, neither has it as many *outstanding bonds* nor as many *masters* as some others   It may not have as expensive public buildings, nor manifest as much so called public spirit in its improvements , yet it is a matter of pride that it had the first organized County Agricultural Society dating back to 1841 , that the county is surpassed by few in the natural advantages of coal, stone, water and rich lands, and has never been afflicted with defaulting public officers, never been compelled to hawk its securities in the market to raise revenue, seldom have its warrants been below par, and as far as I know, never a dollar lost by an officer's dishonesty   Its schools and churches have constantly increased in number, and I doubt whether any county responded more promptly or nobly to the call of the country for the defense of the flag, or was more generous or liberal in caring for the soldier's family and children while he was in the field or after he fell in maintaining the nation s honor and unity   It has performed no small part in the history of the State

THE DISTINGUISHED MEN OF VAN BUREN.

No county in the State has sent out a greater number of noted men than has Van Buren.   Appended is a list of those who now come to mind ·

George G Wright, State Senator, Judge and Chief Justice of the Supreme Court, and United States Senator

Dr J D Bailey United States Marshal four years

Dr J D Elbert, President of the Territorial Council two sessions

Samuel Elbert (son), Territorial Secretary of Colorado and Acting Governor for a time—since then appointed Governor and elected Supreme Judge of the State

Elisha Cutler Jr , Secretary of State two years

Josiah H Bonney, Secretary of State two years, and Commissioner of Des Moines River Improvement for some time

Paul Brattain, Treasurer of Des Moines River Improvement

Samuel Parker, President of Oregon Territorial Council

Edwin Manning, Commissioner of Des Moines River Improvement for over two years, and first successful navigator of the river to Des Moines City

Dr Brainard, Member of the first Board of Education from Harrison County in the Fourth Judicial District

J C Knapp, United States District Attorney and District Judge

Augustus Hall Member of Congress, and United States District Judge of Nebraska

C C Nourse, Chief Clerk House of Representative, Secretary of Senate, Attorney General of the State, and District Judge

J B Howell, United States Senator, and Member of Claims Committee

H C Caldwell, Colonel Third Cavalry, and United States District Judge in Arkansas

B F Elbert, Member of House of Representative from Monroe County, Thirteenth General Assembly

S W Summers, Colonel of Eighth Iowa Cavalry

P. M Cassady, Recorder of Public Moneys, and Judge of State District Court, and Member of State Senate, Polk County

Madison Dagget, Major and Civil Engineer, connected with Des Moines Improvement Company

George F Wright, State Senator from Council Bluffs

Aaron W Harlan, in the United States Secret Service during the Rebellion

Paul C Jefferies, Register Des Moines Improvement Company, and a leading man in Wapello County at an early day

J G Newbold, Speaker of House of Representatives, Lieutenant Governor, and at one time Acting Governor of Iowa

F K Valentine, Judge in Nebraska , elected, in 1878, to Congress from there

J S Porter, Lieutenant Colonel Fifteenth Iowa Infantry, County Judge of Wapello County, and Mayor of Ottumwa

Hugh Brown, Brevet Lieutenant Colonel of Volunteers, and now in regular army on Gen Ord's Staff

J M Tuttle, Colonel Second Iowa Infantry, Brigadier General United States Volunteers, and Member of Legislature Fourteenth General Assembly

Henry Ford District Attorney and Judge of District Court, Fourth Judicial District, for ten years

Robert Sloan, Judge Circuit Court, now (1878) serving his third term—elected without opposition

Wareham G Clark, Member of Second Constitutional Convention from Monroe County

James H Weaver Colonel Second Iowa Infantry Brevet Brigadier United States Volunteers, United States A   District Attorney of Iowa Member of Congress

Set   W Walden of Penitentiary and Member of Assembly

R   Hodge, Provost Marshal

N B Preston and John Clark, Members of the General Assembly from Monroe County

Henry Stewart and Timothy Day, Members of State Agricultural College Board, and long most prominently connected with State Agricultural Society

John W Jones, County Judge of Hardin County, and State Treasurer for four years

George W Jones, Member of Thirteenth General Assembly from Polk County

Josiah Clifton, Member of First State General Assembly from Lee County

George W McCrary, Member of House and Senate of the State, three times elected to Congress from this District, and Secretary of War under President Hayes

Edwin O Stannard, Lieutenant Governor of Missouri, and most prominently connected with the trade and commerce of St Louis

R T Dibble, Member of the Missouri Legislature two terms

Delazon Smith, a prominent politician in Oregon and United States Senator from that State

H W Sample, Commissioner Des Moines River Improvement, and a leader wherever he went

John F Dillon, Judge of State District and Supreme Courts, and Judge of United States Circuit Court

John F Sanford, a celebrated surgeon

Stiles S Carpenter, Prosecuting Attorney and District Clerk of Davis County

Uriah Biggs United States Surveyor

Alexander Henry, Sheriff of Dale County, Mo

Lieut O W Claflin, graduate of West Point, in regular army

Capt L S Cutter graduate of West Point, officer in regular army

S M Clark, editor *Gate City*, Keokuk

J H Gear, Speaker House of Representatives, wholesale merchant in Burlington, and Governor of the State of Iowa

Abner Kneeland one of the scholars and thinkers of his day

S T Caldwell, a member of the Twelfth and Fourteenth General Assemblies from Wapello County

J B Miller, County Judge and County Auditor of Polk County

David Ferguson, Member House of Representative, Ninth General Assembly from Davis County

Andrew Leach, Member of House of Representatives First General Assembly, from Davis County

Israel Kister, State Treasurer in 1850 and 1852

John J Selman, Member of Second Constitutional Convention, Senator and President of the First and Senator of the Second General Assembly

So far as known, the State never lost a cent by the fraud, dishonesty, or mismanagement of any of these officers, nor the world made worse by their acts or omissions   There is here an honest population and they have sent out, as a rule if not always, honest representatives to fill places of trust.

In addition to the above list there are seventeen editors, nine ministers, five lawyers, and an endless number of active leading men in various parts of the country claiming birth or residence at one time in Van Buren County

HOW PIONEERS LIVED

In choosing his home the pioneer usually had an eye mainly to its location, and for that reason settlers were oftener than not very solitary creatures, without neighbors and remote from even the common conveniences of life.   A desirable region was sure to have plenty of inhabitants in time, but it was the advance guard that suffered the privation of isolation   People within a score of miles of each other were neighbors, and the natural social tendencies of mankind asserted themselves even in the wilderness by efforts to keep up communication with even these remote families

' The first business of a settler on reaching the place where he intended to fix his residence, was to select his claim and mark it off as nearly as he could without a compass   This was done by stepping and staking or blazing the lines as he went   The absence of section lines rendered it necessary to take the sun at noon and at evening as a guide by which to run these claim so many steps each way counted three hundred and twenty acres more or less, the then legal area of a claim   It may be readily supposed that these lines were far from correct, but they answered all necessary claim purposes, for it was understood among the settlers that when the lands came to be surveyed and entered, all inequalities should be righted. Thus, if a surveyed line should happen to run between adjoining claims, cutting off more or less of the other, the fraction was to be added to whichever lot required equalizing, yet without robbing the one from which it was taken, for an equal amount would be added to it in another place.

The next important business was to build a house. Until this was done, some had to camp on the ground or live in their wagons, perhaps the only shelter they had known for weeks. So the prospect for a house, which was also to be home, was one that gave courage to the rough toil, and added a zest to the heavy labors. The style of the home entered very little into their thoughts—it was shelter they wanted, and protection from stress of weather and wearing exposures. The poor settler had neither the money nor the mechanical appliances for building himself a house. He was content, in most instances, to have a mere cabin or hut. Some of the most primitive constructions of this kind were half-faced, or as they were sometimes called "cat-faced" sheds or "wike-ups," the Indian term for house or tent. It is true, a claim cabin was a little more in the shape of a human habitation, made, as it was, of round logs light enough for two or three men to lay up, about fourteen feet square—perhaps a little larger or smaller—roofed with bark or clapboards, and sometimes with the sods of the prairie; and floored with puncheons (logs split once in two, and the flat sides laid up), or with earth. For a fire-place, a wall of stone and earth—frequently the latter only, when stone was not convenient—was made in the best practicable shape for the purpose, in an opening in one end of the building, extending outward, and planked on the outside by bolts of wood notched together to stay it. Frequently a fire-place of this kind was made so capacious as to occupy nearly the whole width of the house. In cold weather, when a great deal of fuel was needed to keep the atmosphere above freezing point—for this wide-mouthed fire-place was a huge ventilator—large logs were piled into this yawning space. To protect the crumbling back wall against the effects of fire, two back logs were placed against it, one upon the other. Sometimes these back logs were so large that they could not be got in in any other way than to hitch a horse to them, drive him in at one door, unfasten the log before the fire place, from whence it was put in proper position, and then drive him out at the other door. For a chimney, any contrivance that would conduct the smoke up the chimney would do. Some were made of sods, plastered upon the inside with clay; others—the more common, perhaps—were of the kind we occasionally see in use now, clay and sticks, or "cat in clay," as they were sometimes called. Imagine of a winter's night, when the storm was having its own wild way over this almost uninhabited land, and when the wind was roaring like a cataract of cold over the broad wilderness, and the settler had to do his best to keep warm, what a royal fire this double-back-logged and well-filled fire-place would hold! It must have been a cozy place to smoke, provided the settler had any tobacco, or for the wife to sit knitting before, provided she had needles and yarn. At any rate it must have given something of cheer to the conversation, which very likely was upon the home and friends they had left behind when they started out on this bold venture of seeking fortunes in a new land.

For doors and windows, the most simple contrivances that would serve the purposes were brought into requisition. The door was not always immediately provided with a shutter, and a blanket often did duty in guarding the entrance. But as soon as convenient some boards were split and put together, hung upon wooden hinges, and held shut by a wooden pin inserted in an auger hole. As substitute for window glass, greased paper, pasted over sticks crossed in the shape of a sash was sometimes used This admitted the light and excluded the air, but of course lacked transparency.

In regard to the furniture of such a cabin, of course it varied in proportion to the ingenuity of its occupants, unless it was where settlers brought with them their old household supply, which, owing to the distance most of them had come, was very seldom. It was easy enough to improvise tables and chairs; the former could be made of split logs—and there were instances where the door would be taken from its hinges and used at meals, after which it would be rehung—and the latter were designed after the three-legged stool pattern, or benches served their purpose. A bedstead was a very important item in the domestic comfort of the family, and this was the fashion of improvising them: A forked stake was driven into the ground diagonally from the corner of the room, and at a proper distance, upon which poles reaching from each wall were laid. The wall ends of the poles either rested in the openings between the logs or were driven into auger holes. Barks or boards were used as a substitute for cords. Upon this the tidy housewife spread her straw tick, and if she had a home-made feather bed, she piled it up into a luxurious mound and covered it with her whitest drapery. Some sheets hung behind it, for tapestry, added to the coziness of the resting-place. This was generally called a "prairie bedstead," and by some the "prairie rascal." In design it is surely quite equal to the famous Eastlake models, being about as primitive and severe, in an artistic sense, as one could wish.

The house thus far along, it was left to the deft devices of the wife to complete its comforts, and the father of the family was free to superintend out-of-door affairs. If it was in season, his first important duty was to prepare some ground for planting, and to plant what he could. This was generally done in the edge of the timber, where most of the very earliest settlers located. Here the sod was easily broken, not requiring the heavy teams and plows needed to break the prairie sod. Moreover, the nearness to timber offered greater conveniences for fuel and building. And still another reason for this was, that the groves afforded protection from the terrible conflagrations that occasionally swept across the prairies. Though they passed through the patches of timber, yet it was not with the same destructive force with which they rushed over the prairies. Yet by these fires much of the young timber was killed from time to time, and the forests kept thin and shrubless.

The first year's farming consisted mainly of a "truck patch," planted in corn, potatoes, turnips, etc. Generally, the first year's crop fell far short of supplying even the most rigid economy of food. Many of the settlers brought with them small stores of such things as seemed indispensable to frugal living, such as flour, bacon, coffee and tea. But these supplies were not inexhaustible, and once used, were not easily replaced. A long winter must come and go before another crop could be raised. If game was plentiful, it helped to eke out their limited supplies.

But even when corn was plentiful, the preparation of it was the next difficulty in the way. The mills for grinding it were at such long distances that every other device was resorted to for reducing it to meal. Some grated it on an implement made by punching small holes through a piece of tin or sheet iron, and fastening it upon a board in concave shape, with the rough side out. Upon this the corn was rubbed to produce the meal. But grating could not be done when the corn became so dry as to shell off when rubbed. Some used a coffee-mill for grinding it. And a very common substitute for bread was hominy, a palatable and wholesome diet, made by boiling corn in weak lye till the hull or bran peels off, after which it was well washed, to cleanse it of the lye. It was then boiled again to soften it, when it was ready for use as occasion required, by frying and seasoning it to the taste. Another mode of preparing hominy was by pestling

A mortar was made by burning a bowl-shaped cavity in the even end of an upright block of wood. After thoroughly clearing it of the charcoal, the corn could be put in, hot water turned upon it, when it was subjected to a severe pestling by a club of sufficient length and thickness, in the large end of which was inserted an iron wedge, banded to keep it there. The hot water would soften the corn and loosen the hull, while the pestle would crush it

When breadstuffs were needed, they had to be obtained from long distances. Owing to the lack of proper means for threshing and cleaning wheat, it was more or less mixed with foreign substances, such as smut, dirt and oats. And as the time may come when the settlers' methods of threshing and cleaning may be forgotten, it may be well to preserve a brief account of them here. The plan was to clean off a space of ground of sufficient size, and if the earth was dry, to dampen it and beat it so as to render it somewhat compact. Then the sheaves were unbound and spread in a circle, so that the heads would be uppermost, leaving room in the center for the person whose business it was to stir and turn the straw in the process of threshing. Then as many horses or oxen were brought as could conveniently swing round the circle, and these were kept moving until the wheat was well trodden out. After several "floorings" or layers were threshed the straw was carefully raked off, and the wheat shoveled into a heap to be cleaned. This cleaning was sometimes done by waving a sheet up and down to fan out the chaff as the grain was dropped before it, but this trouble was frequently obviated when the strong winds of autumn were all that was needed to blow out the chaff from the grain

This mode of preparing the grain for flouring was so imperfect that it is not to be wondered at that a considerable amount of black soil got mixed with it, and unavoidably got into the bread. This, with the addition of smut, often rendered it so dark as to have less the appearance of bread than of mud; yet upon such diet, the people were compelled to subsist for want of a better.

Not the least among the pioneers' tribulations, during the first few years of settlement, was the going to mill. The slow mode of travel by ox-teams was made still slower by the almost total absence of roads and bridges, while such a thing as a ferry was hardly even dreamed of. The distance to be traversed was often as far as sixty or ninety miles. In dry weather, common sloughs and creeks offered little impediment to the teamsters; but during floods, and the breaking-up of winter, they proved exceedingly troublesome and dangerous. To get stuck in a slough, and thus be delayed for many hours, was no uncommon occurrence, and that, too, when time was an item of grave import to the comfort and sometimes even to the lives of the settlers' families. Often, a swollen stream would blockade the way, seeming to threaten destruction to whoever should attempt to ford it

With regard to roads, there was nothing of the kind worthy of the name. Indian trails were common, but they were unfit to travel on with vehicles. They are described as mere paths about two feet wide; all that was required to accommodate the single file manner of Indian traveling

An interesting theory respecting the origin of the routes now pursued by many of our public highways is given in a speech by Thomas Benton many years ago He says the buffaloes were the first road engineers, and the paths trodden by them were, as a matter of convenience, followed by the Indians, and lastly by the whites, with such improvements and changes as were found necessary for civilized modes of travel It is but reasonable to suppose that the buffaloes would instinctively choose the most practicable routes and fords in their migrations from one pasture to another. Then, the Indians following, possessed of about the same instinct as the buffaloes, strove to make no improvements, and were finally driven from the track by those who would.

When the early settlers were compelled to make those long and difficult trips to mill, if the country was prairie over which they passed, they found it comparatively easy to do in summer, when grass was plentiful By traveling until night, and then camping out to feed the teams, they got along without much difficulty But in winter, such a journey was attended with no little danger. The utmost economy of time was, of course, necessary When the goal was reached, after a week or more of toilsome travel, with many exposures and risks, and the poor man was impatient to immediately return with the desired staff of life, he was often shocked and disheartened with the information that his turn would come in a week Then he must look about for some means to pay expenses, and he was lucky who could find some employment by the day or job Then, when his turn came, he had to be on hand to bolt his own flour, as in those days, the bolting machine was not an attached part of the other mill machinery This done, the anxious soul was ready to endure the trials of a return trip, his heart more or less concerned about the affairs of home

These milling trips often occupied from three weeks to more than a month each, and were attended with an expense, in one way or another, that rendered the cost of breadstuffs extremely high If made in the winter, when more or less grain feed was required for the team, the load would be found to be so considerably reduced on reaching home that the cost of what was left, adding other expenses, would make their grain reach the high cost figure of from three to five dollars per bushel And these trips could not always be made at the most favorable season for traveling In spring and summer, so much time could hardly be spared from other essential labor yet, for a large family it was almost impossible to avoid making three or four trips during the year

Among other things calculated to annoy and distress the pioneer, was the prevalence of wild beasts of prey, the most numerous and troublesome of which was the wolf While it was true in a figurative sense that it required the utmost care and exertion to "keep the wolf from the door," it was almost as true in a literal sense.

There were two species of these animals—the large, black timber wolf, and the smaller gray wolf, that usually inhabited the prairie At first, it was next to impossible for a settler to keep small stock of any kind that would serve as a prey to these ravenous beasts Sheep were not deemed safe property until years after, when their enemies were supposed to be nearly exterminated Large numbers of wolves were destroyed during the early years of settlement —as many as fifty in a day in a regular wolf-hunt. When they were hungry, which was not uncommon, particularly during the winter, they were too indiscreet for their own safety, and would often approach within easy shot of the settlers' dwellings. At certain seasons their wild plaintive yelp or bark could be heard in all directions at all hours of the night, creating intense excitement among the dogs, whose howling would add to the dismal melody.

It has been found, by experiment, that but one of the canine species, the hound, has both the fleetness and courage to cope with his savage cousin, the wolf. Attempts were often made to capture him with the common cur, but this animal, as a rule, proved himself wholly unreliable for such a service. So long as the wolf would run, the cur would follow, but the wolf, being apparently acquainted with the character of his pursuer, would either turn and place himself in a combative attitude, or else act upon the principle that " discretion is the better part of valor," and throw himself upon his back, in token of surrender   This strategic performance would make instant peace between these two scions of the same house, and not infrequently, dogs and wolves have been seen playing together like puppies.   But the hound was never known to recognize a flag of truce, his baying seemed to signify " no quarter," or at least so the terrified wolf understood it

Smaller animals, such as panthers, lynxes, wildcats, catamounts and polecats, were also sufficiently numerous to be troublesome   And an exceeding source of annyoance were the swarms of mosquitoes which aggravated the trials of the settlers in the most exasperating degree   Persons have been driven from the labors of the field by their unmerciful assaults

THE COUNTY SEAT QUESTION.

Farmington had numerous rivals for the honor of being the county seat. For two years, or thereabouts, the archives were retained where placed by the original act, but soon an effort was made in behalf of Rochester, Keosauqua and other points.   The Legislature did pass a bill selecting Rochester as the future seat, but the Governor refused to approve of the act   Finally, the contest was ended by the adoption and approval of the following bill, in January, 1839.

An Act *to relocate the County Seat of Van Buren County, and for other purposes*

SECTION 1   *Be it enacted by the Council and House of Representatives of the Territory of Iowa,* That Benjamin F Chastain, of Jefferson County, Michael H Walker, of Lee County, and Stephen Gearheart, of Des Moines County, be and they are hereby appointed Commissioners to relocate the county seat of Van Buren County, whose duty it shall be to meet (or a majority of them) at the town of Keosauqua, in said county, on the first Monday of May next, and proceed forthwith to locate a suitable place for the seat of justice of said county, having reference to the geographical center, convenience and welfare of said county

SEC 2   The Commissioners, or a majority of them, shall, within ten days after their meeting at the aforesaid place, make out and certify to the Clerk of the County Commissioners of Van Buren, under their hands and seals, a certificate containing a particular description of the situation of the location selected for the aforesaid county seat, together with the deed or deeds of any grant of land or lands, or bond or bonds for the payment of money, that may have been made by any individual or individuals for the benefit of the county

SEC 3   The Commissioners aforesaid shall, before they enter upon their duties, severally take and subscribe an oath before some person legally authorized to administer the same, viz. " I, A B , do solemnly swear [or affirm] that I am not, either directly or indirectly interested in the location of the seat of justice of Van Buren County nor do I own any property in lands or claims within the said county of Van Buren   So help me God'

SEC 4   If it shall be shown at any time within one year that the said Commissioners, or any of them, received any present, gratuity, fee or reward, in any form other than that allowed by law, or, before the expiration of six months from the time said location was made, becomes interested in said town, or in any lands in its immediate vicinity, the Commissioner or Commissioners shall, upon conviction thereof, by indictment in the District Court of the county in which he or they may reside, be guilty of a high misdemeanor, and be forever after disqualified to vote at any election, or of holding any office of profit or trust within this Territory

SEC 5   It shall be the duty of the Commissioners aforesaid to receive, in the name of the Board of County Commissioners for the county of Van Buren, for the use of the county any bond for the payment of money, or deed of land that may be made by any individual or individuals for the purpose of building public buildings at the said seat of justice   And they shall receive the sum of $ 00 a day each for their services during the time they may be necessarily employed in making said location and also the sum of $ 00 for every twenty miles, going from and returning to their respective homes.

HISTORY OF VAN BUREN COUNTY 385

SEC 6 The District Court of the county of Van Buren shall be held, for the first term after the passage of this act at the town of Keosauqua, but forever thereafter at the place selected as the seat of justice for said county by the provisions of this act

SEC 7 The Commissioners created by this act shall receive pay for their services upon a presentation of a certificate to the County Commissioners of their services, signed by said Commissioners, out of any money in the County Treasury not otherwise appropriated

SEC 8 *Be it further enacted*, That the proprietors of the town of Keosauqua shall, on or before the 1st day of April next, enter into good and sufficient bonds, with security to be approved of by the County Commissioners, to the County Treasurer, for the benefit of the said county, for the sum of $5,000, payable in town lots in the said town of Keosauqua, or other real estate, at a fair cash value or cash, or such other materials as the County Commissioners may deem proper to receive, for the purpose of carrying on or completing the public buildings in said county

SEC 9 The payments to be divided into three equal parts, and paid annually in one, two and three years

SEC 10 *Be it further enacted*, That if the said proprietors shall enter into bonds, as provided for in the eighth section of this act, then this act to be null and void, otherwise to remain in full force and value

Approved January 25, 1839

The terms of the bill were complied with, and Keosauqua became and has ever since remained the seat of justice Substantial county buildings were erected in 1839–40, as is shown by the abstract of the proceedings of the Board of Commissioners given elsewhere

The apparent conflict of dates between the approval of the bill locating the seat at Keosauqua and the records of the Board, is explainable on the ground that the Board knew of the nature of the bill, and acted rather in anticipation of its approval by the Governor. It is a well-known fact that all bills are not signed immediately, through a pressure of business, but sometimes lie for days awaiting executive action of which they are certain The vote of the people had decided the question of location in 1838, and the passage of the bill was but a formality Hence, when we read that the Board met at Keosauqua January 7, 1839, while the bill was not approved until the 25th of that month, the inference is that the Board acted advisedly in anticipation of the Governor's approval

THE COUNTY COMMISSIONERS.

The first Board of Commissioners met in Farmington It was composed of the following members · John Bending, Isham Keith and Enoch P. Blackburn

The first session was held May 4, 1837 The first work done was to elect the following officers Recorder, William Welch ; Clerk, Enoch P. Blackburn , Collector, Isaac J. Nowell , Coroner, Roger N Cresap, Assessors, Giles O Sullivan, William Nelson, William Judd ; Road Commissioners, Sanford Burlingham, James Hall, Truelove Sparks , Overseers of the Poor, Asbil Van Sivauk Robert McElhany ; Fence Viewers John Newport, Charles Davis, William Duncan ; Poundmaster, Robert W Magruder

On June 17. 1838, the Board allowed " Lewis Alfrey $6 for guarding Isaac Hendershott while a prisoner," for the alleged murder of Nathaniel Knapp

Among the records of the Supervisors is the following quaint piece of work bearing date of entry April, 1838. The ill-spelling and capitalization are as per copy ·

KENTUCKY. CHRISTAIN County

At the Solem Call of the Baptist Church of Christ Sinking Fork of Little River we have set apart and ordained our Beloved Brother William Bradley By the imposition of hand to Preach the Gospel and to administer the ordinancis agreeable to the Word of God Wherever his Lot is Cast

Oct 22, 1801

Another is dedicated to " Micajah B Rowland, May 25, 1801," and signed
at " Kentucky, Caulwell Co   Fielding Woolf James Rucker, Presbitry "

The first election ordered by the Board was August 7, 1838, for September 10,
1838, when one delegate to Congress, members of the Council and House of
Representatives of the Legislature of Iowa Territory, one Coroner, one Treasurer, three County Commissioners, one County Assessor. one Recorder and
Constables of the county were to be chosen.

Meanwhile, a contest had arisen over the location of the county seat   Bentonsport, Pittsburg, Rochester, Keosauqua and perhaps. other points labored
for the prize   The question became a political one

The election referred to was held at Farmington. " agreeable to provisions
of the Council and House of Representatives of the Territory of Wisconsin,
passed June 22, 1838 , the two places contending for the seat of justice of the
county of Van Buren or what was then the Territory of Wisconsin (now Iowa)
being Bentonsport and Keosauqua (this being the name given to the towns of
Van Buren and Des Moines City united), and at that election Keosauqua received
a majority of the whole number of votes given by the people of said county as
the seat of justice (county seat) thereof '   The election returns were certified
to by the Board January 9   It is claimed that Pittsburg also contended for the
county seat at that time (Mr Goddard thinks so)   Bentonsport recently clam-
ored for it.

On October 12, 1838, Maryland Jones, one of the Board, was empowered
to take measures toward " securing to this county the quarter-section on which
the seat of justice for said county is located, agreeable to an act of Congress,
granting the right of pre-emption on said quarter to said county "

An adjournment was then taken until Monday, January 7, 1839, when the
Board met at Keosauqua

On Thursday, June 13, 1839 the Board authorized that lots be laid off on
the county quarter and sold at auction, the proceeds of the sale to be applied
toward the erection of public buildings , the terms of the sale to be one-fourth
cash, one-fourth in six months, one-fourth in twelve months and one-fourth in
eighteen months

Prior to this, a square building of hewed logs had served as the Jail, the
Sheriff's portion being of frame, over which was located the District Court room.

The building, what remains of it, is now used as a wagon-shop

The superintendency of the new Jail was given to William Stanley on August
7, 1839, and Henry King was the builder.

The contract for building the Court House was given to John Fairman and
James Hall, with the understanding that it should be finished for $6,000, and
within two years from June 1 1840

An auspicious event was that which was ushered in August 10, 1840, but
the beginning of the end of which was not until 1846

On the first date mentioned, the Board ordered that a vote be taken to ascertain whether a convention was desired by the people to discuss the question of
admitting the Territory of Iowa into the Union as an independent State.   The
convention was called according to the necessary form of procedure, and delegates were sent to consult with the Members of Congress ; but the scheme fell
through on account of the non-acceptance by Congress of the proposition made
with regard to the boundary lines

In ???? ?? ?? ? ????? (??? Des Moines) Lick Creek Van Buren,
Jackson Farmington ???? ? Washington Chequest and Village Townships
were cr   ????

The first reward offered for wolves' scalps was made in January, 1841. This law was rescinded February 11, 1841   Notwithstanding the latter action, Isaac Sutherland, as late as April 6, 1841, "was allowed $2 for two wolves' scalps, killed by him on or about the 20th of February, 1841," ten days after the repeal of the law.

An action of the Board, Wednesday, January 6, 1847, altered the boundary line of Lick Creek Township   The change affected the line so as to make it "extend from the east boundary south to the southeast corner of Section 1, in Van Buren Township, thence west along the line between Sections 1 and 12, until the said line intersected the left bank of the Des Moines River, thence up the left bank of the said river to the point where the present southern boundary of Lick Creek Township intersected the said river.   And further, that the portion of Van Buren Township included within the boundaries as above altered be taken from said Van Buren Township and attached and made a part of Lick Creek Township"

The first record made of an inquest was May 14, 1856, when the body of an unknown child was found.   The verdict of the jury was that the child came to its death through felonious means, a string having been tied about its neck. The jury was composed of John Douds, Daniel McCoy and Simeon Martin Ambrose Fitzgerald was the Justice before whom the inquest was held

EARLY CRIMINAL EVENTS.

The criminal record of Van Buren County is not burdened, either of early or late years—in fact, there is little to make a record from   There have been but few high crimes   The first arrest made to compensate for the shedding of innocent blood, was that of Luthelus Gillespie, who was arraigned before the Court, the first of the April term, 1837, on the charge of manslaughter.   The result of a trial was "we, the jury, find the prisoner not guilty."   This was case No 42 on the calendar

Then came a case that caused a great deal of trouble, and finally wound up in smoke   In April, 1838, Isaac Hendershott was taken into custody on the charge of alleged murder   Read the summing-up of the grand jurors' report. "Isaac Hendershott, not having the fear of God before his eyes, but being moved and seduced by the instigation of the devil on the 11th day of July, in the year of our Lord one thousand eight hundred and thirty-seven, at Columbus, upon one Nathaniel Knapp, feloniously, willfully, and of his malice aforethought, did make an assault on the said Nathaniel Knapp (with a certain drawn sword made of iron and steel, of the value of 50 cents, which he the said Isaac Hendershott, in both his hands then and there had and held), in and upon the left side of the body between the ribs of him, the said Nathaniel Knapp ; and then and there feloniously, willfully and of his malice aforethought did strike and thrust, giving the said Nathaniel Knapp, then and there, with the sword aforesaid, in and upon the aforesaid Nathaniel Knapp, one mortal wound of the breadth of one inch and of the depth of six inches, of which mortal wound the said Nathaniel Knapp then and there instantly died "

The cause of the affray is said to have been a dispute which arose between the two men as to their sleeping apartments   Knapp made a sarcastic remark to which Hendershott took exceptions and the finale was as related.   It is claimed, however, that the "sword" in question was a cane-sword, or piece of steel used in the head of a cane

Hendershott escaped from prison and fled toward Mt City but when twenty-three miles west of Lexington Mo report says he was taken sick and died

There was also tried a man named John G McCutchen, during November, 1838, term of the Court, the charge being that he was criminally guilty of destroying written instruments He was adjudged guilty, and compelled to pay a fine of $30

The first indictment found for larceny was against John G. McCutchen, John Burton and Stephen Baldwin, in April, 1839 The verdict of the Court was as per entry on the docket, "Prosecution severed"

The first case of kidnapping was in 1839, when indictments for the alleged crime were found against Shapely P Ross, Shapely Walkfork, Benjamin B Throop and Giles O Sullivan

A number of indictments were found in those "by-gone" days against parties for selling liquor to the Indians

Probably the most notable happening in the annals of Washington and Van Buren County crime, was in 1845; so, because the hissing ball that robbed a man of his blooming life came but a hair's-breadth of nipping the bud that the father held in his arms; so, because in that instance the law would not allow outsiders to insult its dignity, and the consummation of the chilling crime came quickly by trial, judgment, sentence, the rope And, inasmuch as this was the only execution ever effected in this county, the fact rightly claims a few lines in history

The summer of 1845 was the date of the deed, the date in which a young man named William McColly, shot and instantly killed Mr. Don Ferdanand Coffman who, with his wife, and carrying a child in his arms, was passing a cornfield. The crime was committed in Washington County, but a change of venue was taken and the case came up for a hearing in the Van Buren County Court, then being held at Keosauqua. The prisoner's plea of "not guilty" was, at his request, withdrawn, and he pleaded "guilty" Upon which the Court sentenced him to be hanged, which was done on Tuesday, the 13th day of May, 1845, in the jail-yard

The difficulty grew out of domestic troubles. Coffman's wife and McColly had eloped together. Coffman had induced her to return, at which McColly became offended

LEGISLATIVE ENACTMENTS

From the session laws of 1840–47, the following abstract of enactments is made, showing all of the essential bills passed which affected Van Buren County, or all of those not given in proper form in other portions of this volume.

January 17, 1840, a bill was approved by the Governor of the Territory of Iowa, providing for the settlement of the claim that Des Moines County had upon the counties of Lee, Van Buren, Henry, Slaughter (Washington), Louisa and Muscatine, in accordance with an act of the Legislature of Wisconsin Territory held at Belmont in 1836. The sentiment was based upon the assessment of property in the several newly-created counties.

The old Territorial road from Black Hawk, Louisa County, to the Missouri line, through Van Buren County, was relocated, or so much of it as lay between Bentonsport and the residence of James Robbs in Van Buren County. Sylvester Henry, John B. Smith and James A Brown, Commissioners Approved January 15, 1841

An act approved January 15, 1841, changed the name of Rising Sun to Pittsburg The town was surveyed by Uriah Biggs By a special act, approved February 17 1842 that part of the plat "down the mouth of Chequest Creek, known as [illegible] Addition was also changed in name to agree with the main pl

A Territorial road was relocated in July, 1841, from Keosauqua via Rising Sun (Pittsburg) and Philadelphia, to Fairfield, Jefferson County, or so much as passed through the estate of James F Westcott   William D. McBride, Elijah Purdom, Sr , and Sewall Kenney, Commissioners

An act, approved January 28, 1842, reads .

Be it enacted, etc , That the County Commissioners of Van Buren County be, and they are hereby authorized and directed, to grant a license to Jesse Wright and Henry Bateman, of said county, for the term of five years, to keep a ferry across the Des Moines River, opposite Watertown , *provided*, said Wright and Bateman shall, in all cases, be subject to the laws regulating ferries in this Territory

The bill expressly provided that this act should not interfere with L P. Harris' right to obtain a similar license at any time

February 2, 1842, a Territorial road from Keosauqua to the southern boundary of the Territory, via Hale's bridge, on Fox River, and a quarter of a mile north of William Wooden's, on the Wyaconda, was established.   John Cantrel, William Cassady and William Brooks, of Van Buren County, Commissioners.

The road from the southeast corner of Section 7, Town 27, Range 8 west, to Keosauqua, ordered July, 1841, was authorized by special act, January 3, 1843, to be established by the County Commissioners of Van Buren County.

February 6, 1843, the Judge of Probate of Van Buren County was authorized to have the records of his office retranscribed, or so much of them as were written prior to August, 1841

A Territorial road was established from the north boundary of Missouri, at the southwest corner of Section 9, Town 67 north, Range 8 west; thence west to southeast corner of Section 36, Town 68, Range 9, thence west eighty rods. thence to James Burns' smith-shop; thence the shortest and best route to Keosauqua   Charles Dailey and Thomas Cox, Commissioners   Samuel Gilland. Surveyor

February 13, 1843, a Territorial road was established from Birmingham, via the Colony in Jefferson County, to Indian Agency   William Shepherd, Robert Ruthdge and John F Mudget, Commissioners

In 1843, that part of the road from Fort Madison, Lee County, to Iowaville, between Hiram Holmes' and the latter place, was resurveyed by E. A. Boyer, John Saylor and William Meacham

The Farmington Insurance Company was incorporated February 17, 1842, with a capital of not less than $50,000, nor more than $500,000, on the stock plan.   Jonas Houghton, Isaac A Le Fever, Jesse Wright, Lawrence Scott and Solomon Beckley were designated Commissioners to open the stock subscription-books   The Company was empowered to write all varieties of risks, on sea or land, loan money at not more than 10 per cent interest, and re-insure their risks, as is customary.   The business was placed under the management of a Board of Directors, consisting of five   In short, the Company was a regularly organized and full-fledged concern.

By an act approved February 17, 1842, all that tract of land recorded by James Hall & Co as the town of Keosauqua, and described as the northwest quarter of Section 36, Town 69, Range 10, was duly incorporated as the "City of Keosauqua."   It was the usual incorporating act, defining the powers of the Mayor and Councilmen.

By an act approved December 19 1843, John Godard and Jesse Wright, of Van Buren County, and Van Caldwell, of Wapello County, were appointed Commissioners to locate a Territorial road from Farmington via Hartford,

Green's mill and Wood's mill to "Autumwa" (the old way of spelling the name). The Commissioners were ordered to meet at Farmington on the first Tuesday in April, of that year, and were duly cautioned as to observing the best interests of the settlers in the two counties

A special act, approved January 25, 1844, ordered the County Commissioners of Van Buren to allow Thomas Summerlin, Collector for said county, "such time as they may deem reasonable for said Collector to make return of the tax-list of said county, placed in his hands for collection, for the year 1843, provided that the time did not extend beyond January 1, 1845." The Board was authorized to postpone the sale of lands or lots in the county, for delinquent taxes of 1843, not to extend beyond the first Monday in December, 1844. The act also provided for the Board's fixing the date of the tax sales for that year.

February 5, 1844, Robert Merchant and Levin N. English, of Davis County, and James Jordan, of Van Buren County, were appointed Commissioners to locate a Territorial road from Iowaville, on the Des Moines River, "to a point on the line of the State of Missouri, where the Mormon trace crosses said line." The Commissioners met at Iowaville on the first Monday in May, 1844. The road was ordered to be laid out "via the residences of William Wooden and L. N. English."

February 7, 1844, James Hall, of Van Buren, William Ingersoll, of Jefferson, and Jacob Marshall, of Wapello, were appointed Commissioners to lay out a Territorial road from Iowaville to Autumwa. They were ordered to meet on the first Monday in May, of that year.

February 13, 1844, John Godden, Samuel Clark, John Groom, Archibald McDonald and P. M Janney were given two years additional time in which to construct a dam and lock at Pittsburg across the Des Moines River

February 14, 1844, Samuel Morton, St Clair Griffin and John Arrowsmith, of Van Buren County, were appointed Commissioners to locate a Territorial road from Keosauqua to the county seat of Davis County; thence to the county seat of Appanoose County, or as near the center of that county as practicable; thence to the west line of that county The Commissioners were ordered to meet at the house of Solomon Richardson on the first Monday in June, and begin the road at his place. The road already established out of Keosauqua, via Ely's Ford, on the Des Moines River, between Keosauqua and Richardson's, was to form that portion of the new road

The old road from Fort Madison, in Lee County, to Iowaville, was ordered reviewed and established in August, 1844. Benjamin Saylor and Joel Avery were appointed Commissioners

February 15, 1844, the name of Hartford was changed to that of Fleming

A joint resolution was passed by the Legislature February 14, 1844, requesting the establishment of numerous weekly mail-routes in the State Among them one from Fox Post Office, Van Buren County, to Davis Court House, thence to center of Appanoose County.

Uriah Biggs, of Van Buren, was appointed, by the Legislature, Subagent for that county of the University lands.

In 1845, a Territorial road was established by Samuel Swearingen and Israel Kister, of Davis County, and John B Wilson, of Van Buren, from the Sullivan line of Missouri, where the road from Keosauqua to Churchville crossed, thence on the divide between Fox River and Indian Creek via Fox Post Office, thence to center of Appanoose County along the divide between Fox River and Indian Creek to the western line of Davis County. The Commissioners were ordered to meet on the first Monday in July.

January 15, 1846, Elisha Center, Jr., Clerk of the District Court for Van Buren County, was authorized to refile, transcribe and arrange all papers, books and documents in his office.

In 1847, a State road was laid out from West Point, in Lee County, to Bonaparte Jacob Henkle, Sr., and Jacob Grewell, of Lee County, and Giles Wells, of Van Buren, Commissioners Ordered to meet the second Monday in April

A State road was established, in 1847, from Wood's Mills, in Van Buren County, to Bloomfield, in Davis County John Hale, of Van Buren, James Hawkins and Reason Wilkerson, of Davis County, Commissioners Ordered to meet the first Monday in May

A State road was laid out between Iowaville to Lancaster, Keokuk Co, by way of Creaseville, in 1847. Michael Peibler and Jacob L Sears, of Jefferson County, and Joel Skinner, of Keokuk County Commissioners. Met in April

A State road was laid out, in 1847, from Portland to Bloomfield Banks Winton and Adam Row, of Davis, and James S. Parks, of Van Buren, Commissioners

David Ferguson was appointed agent to select two townships of land for the State University, and was allowed $2 per day for his actual time thus employed.

The city of Farmington was incorporated, by act of the State Legislature, approved February 22, 1847

INCIDENT IN THE LIFE OF WAREHAM G. CLARK

The sketch here given serves to illustrate the dangers and hardships attending the settlement of this region, even as late as 1842.

In the year 1840, William W. Rankin emigrated from La Fayette, Ind., and located on a temporary or small claim near the extreme western line of the then defined Government lands The treaty of 1837 opened up to claimants a large area of lands which had been, prior to that date, the stamping-grounds of the Indians It is necessary to merely allude to this limit here, as the subject is properly treated in another portion of the work.

When Van Buren County was geographically defined, the western boundary extended to a point within the ceded territory A strip of land was still left west of the county about a mile and a half in width. This strip lay in what afterward became subsequent to the Indian treaty of 1842, the county of Davis. The strip was attached to Van Buren County for all judicial and official purposes, but at the period of which we write was without distinctive title.

The year 1840, was a comparatively late one in the settlement of Van Buren, but the attached wild lands had not received much benefit from the civilizing influences of the influx of pioneers in the eastern and central part of Van Buren West of the county line all was a wilderness

It will be remembered by the early settlers that the general laws of the country forbade encroachments on the Indian lands by white men Location of claims could not be made except at the hazard of loss of property, if not at the peril of life Timber could not be cut, nor could game be pursued by whites without risking severe punishment It is folly to assert that the laws defensive of the rights of the red man were fully observed, for it is a known fact that timber was stripped from the eastern boundary, and that many a venturesome hunter added to the zest of his sport by combining the excitement of the chase with a vigorous watchfulness for the stealthy red man Had an Indian detected a poacher on his domain the latter would have been summarily disposed of. This fact is corroborated by the stories told of hair-breadth escapes of hunters under such circumstances.

Nor were hunters the only violators of the law of trespass. Some men, foreseeing the advantages of early possession, were reckless enough to make settlers' claim to some of the best locations, just across the boundary, and erect thereon log cabins The class which carried matters to such an extreme, encountered more than the hostility of outraged Indians, for at that time the Government made a show of protecting poor Lo in his rights. A system of espionage was maintained after a fashion commensurate with the importance of the case and the crudity of the times. It is not to be supposed that the most thorough watchfulness was observed, for that would be attributing to the Government a higher degree of paternal feeling than it has ever manifested ; but the appearance of authority was kept up by the appointment of agents and the occasional visitation of suspected localities by those properly empowered representatives of the Great Father at Washington

The men who actually made claims on the Indian territory were, very naturally, persons of the most heedless disposition The pleasure of making locations there consisted fully as much in the consciousness of law violated, as it did in the sense of semi-proprietorship It is likely that some of these men were connected with the organized gangs of horse-thieves and counterfeiters which infested the West at that time, and found more freedom there for the prosecution of the latter part of their nefarious trades, as well as a greater immunity from the law of the better settled counties of the Territory The cabins of such "claimants" may have been places of refuge for dangerous men, when pursued by the officers of the law. A sort of friendship may have existed between some of the white renegades and the Indians, which served as a protection to them At all events, whether these conjectures be reasonable or not, it is certain that the squatters on Indian lands dreaded the white men more than the Indians, and were always ready to defend their wilderness homes from the agents of the Government

When Mr. Rankin located in the narrow strip of land adjacent to Van Buren County, he did so with the intention of seeking a better site as soon as it was possible to do so with safety He was residing on his claim, which was three miles of the present village of Drakeville, in the year 1842.

In 1840, W G Clark, who figured so largely in the early history of Monroe County, gave up the idea of spending his life in New York City, where he had resided for some ten years, and concluded to seek his fortune in the West. The Territory of Iowa was regarded by the young New Yorker as the furthermost limit of the desirable country, or, at all events, far enough away from the whirl of the metropolis to be an available prospecting-ground He prepared to shake Eastern dust from his feet and join the great army of emigrants which was then moving westward Among the supplies purchased by him, as a necessary preliminary to fortune-hunting, was a pair of very fine bay horses The team was not only a particularly good one, but it was also a decidedly noticeable pair, because of size and marks They stood eighteen hands high, were very speedy travelers, and, more remarkable than all else, had been treated to the "docking process" Their tails were cut short after the fashion of that time. In the West, the few teams met with were allowed their normal quantity of caudal appendage and the introduction of a pair of big "bob-tailed" bays caused considerable comment among the pioneers of the new country

Mr Clark came on to Iowa, and entered the southern portion of the Territory He was in no special haste to locate permanently, and devoted his time to going about from settlement to settlement.   Wherever he went, his fine team excited remark, and he was soon known throughout Van Buren County   His horses were also known in the entire region.

During the course of his investigation of the country, Mr Clark went into the attached portion of Van Buren County, and there formed the acquaintance of Mr Rankin, wife and daughter   The year 1842 found Mr Clark not only a friend of the Rankins, but a still more particular guest at their house, for he had become engaged to the daughter.   The marriage day was not decided upon at once as it was deemed essential to first select a site for a home.   Thus the spring of 1842 beheld Mr. Clark more eager than ever for a speedy termination of his protracted search for a claim.   The Indian treaty of 1842 was pending, but no locations could then be made on the beautiful lands contained in the reserve   The sight of the rolling prairies and beautiful groves was too tempting to be withstood and Mr. Clark determined to make a tour of examination in anticipation of the time when he could legally lay claim to a farm site thereon.

One day in the late spring, Mr Clark persuaded the Rankins to join him in a short excursion over the Indian lands, with the view of aiding him in his ultimate choice of a home   The famous team was hitched to a comfortable spring-wagon, and the two ladies, Mrs. and Miss Rankin, were snugly seated for a genuine camping-out trip   The party was provided with necessaries in the way of blankets, etc , but only a limited amount of provisions were taken, as it was not intended to remain out more than two or three days.

The first day's journey was a delightful one   The party had driven about sixteen or seventeen miles through a region in a perfect state of nature, and at one of the most charming seasons of the year   Night overtook them just as they came in sight of a deserted log cabin   The discovery of such a building, where reason and law taught them to suppose no building stood was a surprise indeed.   The men made a careful inspection of the premises, and concluded that some' squatter had ventured on the reserve, but had become tired of his claim and had forsaken it   Mr. Rankin made the most of their apparent good-fortune, and proceeded to arrange a snug sleeping-place in the cabin for the women   He and Clark fitted up a bed in the wagon for themselves.   The horses were tied in a clump of trees some twenty rods from the wagon, and there left in supposed security for the night.

The weary travelers were soon fast asleep.   Mr. Clark says that he has no idea just how long he slept, but he was awakened in the night by the restlessness of his horses   He thought nothing of the disturbance, however, and proceeded to compose himself for another nap   Later in the night he was again aroused, but this time by hearing one of his horses break his halter and dash off over the prairie at high speed.   Even then his suspicions of evil were not aroused, because he was firm in his belief that no human beings, save themselves, were within miles of his team   Again he laid his head down, but could not sleep soundly   For a short time all was quiet, when suddenly the remaining horse broke loose and scudded away to join its mate   The night was so dark that search was impossible then, and Mr. Clark concluded that he would wait until daylight before beginning his tramp   He thought his horses had gone but a short distance out on the prairie, where they would soon eat their fill and remain quietly until he could capture them.   He noticed that neither Mr. Rankin nor the women had been awakened by the disturbance, and that confirmed him in his determination to await until he could reasonably call upon Mr R. for assistance.

Mr Clark did not sleep again that night, and as soon as it was daybreak he silently arose, without awakening Mr Rankin, and went over to where his team had stood. The high grass was trampled down in one direction, and thither he went until he could obtain a commanding view of the surrounding country.

He could see that the horses had gone eastward, and the first idea that occurred to him was that they had started back toward the settlement from whence they had come. Mr Clark felt that every moment was precious, and that he could scarcely afford the time required to return to camp and arouse his friends. If he kept on at once, he might soon overtake the team and get back before the camp was awake. He had taken no food with him, however, and a long tramp was imprudent; but he would go a short way further and then, if he saw no traces of his horses he would go back to camp and prepare for a thorough search. So on he pushed, through the wet, harsh prairie grass for some distance. The heavy tread of the horses had left a deep impress in the sod and the rank vegetation was bent and twisted by their rapid movements. Along this trail Mr Clark hurried, expecting every moment to reach some point from which he could discover more encouraging prospects. Suddenly he came upon a blind track over the prairie. The newly-made trail of his horses ceased, but along the older path he saw the hoof-marks of his team. But that was not all. Side by side with his own horses, another animal had ran from this point on. From the size of the track, Mr. Clark concluded that it must have been an Indian pony.

The discovery of this alarming evidence of the cause of the stampede did not create any unpleasant feelings in Mr. Clark's mind. A more experienced Westerner would have retraced his steps at once and aroused the camp; but Mr. Clark was new to the ways and dangers of the West. He had come from a region where crime was guarded, regulated and spied upon by professionals: where it was not incumbent upon every citizen to play many parts in turn. He did not understand woodcraft or know that detective work was a part of a pioneer's duty. He was not a Leatherstocking, or to the wilderness born. Hence, when the third hoof-print was discovered, he merely surmised that some Indian had gone that way the day before. He did not associate the contiguity of tracks as cause and effect.

By this time, Mr Clark had gone so far that returning without his team seemed impossible. So, on he went. On and on he pushed, now losing the trail and anon finding it, until it became broad day. High noon found him still rambling on, hungry and footsore, but determined to work out the salvation of his favorite animals.

When the meridian of day was passed, and the sunlight fell from the westward, stray patches of cloud occasionally obscured the rays. These shadows were grateful to the weary man, who did not then realize the awful danger of becoming hopelessly lost on the trackless prairie or in the wild growth of trees that bordered some stream.

As night settled down, the clouds increased in density and concealed the sun entirely. The inexperienced young man, deprived of the only sure director, was left in total ignorance of his whereabouts. His long fast of nearly twenty-four hours began to tell upon his unaccustomed muscles. A man bred in city ways cannot endure the privations of wild life like those who are inured to such hardships   The comparative inactivity of mercantile life had made Mr Clark, who was not thirty years of age at the time of which we write, little fitted for a protracted tramp through the woods   He naturally could not husband his strength, nor could he practice any of the many physical economies known to hunters.

In this pitiable plight, night found the wanderer   He had long before that given up search for the trail of his horses, for he had learned that self-preservation was Nature's first law   At last, exhausted and half-despairing, he set down upon an old log and turned his coat collar about his neck   Compressing himself into as small a compass as possible, he tried to pass the night   Imagine the scene!   A young man, who but a day before saw life stretching out pleasantly in anticipation before him, sound in mind and body, and with every reasonable expectation of prosperity, now lost in the wilderness, without the slightest ray of hope, alone in the darkness and the rain, with the prairie winds whistling and groaning around him as though to aggravate his sense of terror at his situation, and chilling him to the marrow as it drove the gusts of rain upon his unprotected head.   Think of that long, dreary night, which seemed interminable to him   Added to all the imaginary dangers, were the ever-present pangs of hunger, gnawing at his vitals and weakening him minute by minute

If ever the daylight was welcomed by mortal in distress, surely that which told the hero of this sketch the east from the west was   The long hours which succeeded the rising of the sun behind a gray and crimson bank of clouds were but repetitions of those of the preceding day.   Early in the morning, the rain began to fall, and continued ceaselessly day and night   The tall prairie grass, which cut like knife-blades, soon wore away the fine cloth pants which Clark then wore, leaving the flesh naked to their cruel teeth.   In self-protection, he bound leaves about his legs, and plodded on, not knowing whither   More than once, a bird, startled by the strange apparition of an unknown being, flew from her nest, revealing the brood of unfledged young within.   The instinct to devour those little birds was strong; but the force of civilized habits overcame, for the time, the savage nature of man   Now and then, an elm-tree was found, and from the inner bark of it the famished man ate greedily.   Wild strawberry leaves, and such vegetation as was known to be edible, formed the staple of his unsatisfactory diet.

Again night shut down upon him, and despair hovered over the almost desperate man.   In the darkness he heard the weird cry of nocturnal birds.   His ears were keen to detect unnatural sounds   Above his hard resting-place rang out the terrifying shriek of a panther, and in the distance the barking of wolves could be distinctly heard.   In the darkness he arose and moved about, impressed with a sense of greater security if in motion.

Day succeeded night.   Another weary march, another fruitless search for traces of human habitation   Again the sun sank and shut out the monotonous landscape.   The wanderer gathered boughs and made a rude shelter from the piercing wind.   Sleep forsook him, and a long watch for light began.

Three days had passed since he had eaten Christian food   The fearful thought that he had gone from his friends without acquainting them of his purpose intensified his agony of mind and body   The horses gone and he himself missing must have aroused the strangest thoughts among his friends   The morning came at last, but it found him in nearly an exhausted frame

Fortune at last smiled upon the persistent efforts made by Mr. Clark   Had the last day of his experiences in the wilderness ended like those which preceded, this story would have been far different in character.   A tale of secret disappearance, a few bleached human bones, discovered by some settler on the spot, and an unraveled mystery, would have been the leading points   As it proved, the search made for a habitation led to the discovery of a cabin on the plains.   A fierce dog bounded out to attack the poor, tattered man, as he staggered up to the door and called for aid   The settler came to his rescue, and soon supplied him with food   His life was saved

Mr Clark remained a short time at the cabin, and then pushed on toward where he learned the campers must be   The settler aided in the work of re-uniting the separated friends   As good luck would have it Mr Rankin was soon seen coming toward them, and the story of Mr. Clark's bewilderment and escape was speedily told.

It was afterward ascertained that Mr. C traveled some twenty miles or more from the camp, and that at least three times that distance must have been traversed by him in his wanderings.

The sequel to this story is fully as interesting as the account here given of the experiences of Mr C.   The pony-track seen in the grass on the first day satisfied the settlers that Mr. Clark's horses had been stolen.   The amateur detectives took up the clue from the known occupants of the cabin where the party camped, the fact of the absence of the men, etc, and followed the trail south, into Missouri.   The peculiar docking of the horses' tails, the large size and fine appearance made it an easy task to trace the animals out.   Near Lancaster, Mo., the team was recovered, and a man named Shaffer was arrested by the posse, charged with the crime.   A fellow named Wooden was suspected of complicity in the matter, but he was not proved guilty.

Shaffer was taken by force and brought into Van Buren County.   As the posse had no warrant to take him in Missouri, he was allowed to go free on Van Buren soil, and then immediately arrested on a legal process.   The crime for which he was taken having been committed on Indian territory, which was not within the jurisdiction of the Van Buren District Court, necessitated his trial at Fort Madison, in the United States District Court   Shaffer was confined at Keosauqua pending the required preliminary proceedings, and thence taken to Fort Madison   There the trial resulted in a verdict of guilty.   The law did not provide incarceration for such offenses, but it did not allow a total relinquishment of a prisoner proven guilty   The verdict, in compliance with the general statute, was the infliction of twenty-odd lashes upon the bare back   Accordingly, the proper officer proceeded to carry out the finding of the Court   Shaffer was stripped, and the lash was heartily laid on his quivering flesh   This was probably the last public whipping ever administered in the Territory under orders of a lawful court   Judge Lynch often ruled such punishment, but the more civilized officers of the regular judiciary adopted a less summary method of punishment   The whipping was done in 1843

The place where Mr. Clark was lost is now known as Hacklebarney, in Davis County

POEM.

ritten for and read before the Old Settlers of Van Buren County, at their Annual Meeting, at Keosauqua, Iowa
August 19, 1874

BY KATE HARRINGTON

Kind friends, 'twas something new for me to say
I'd meet the dear Old Settlers here to-day
Tis passing strange I should consent to come,
To leave the privacy of hearth and home,
And thus present a paradox to you—
A maiden effort at full forty-two
Yet 'tis appropriate—I mean the age—
For veteran soldier, not yet gray-haired sage,
E'er looks for fresh young spring to re-appear
When autumn strews the ground with leaflets sere.

Life's soft October with its golden glow,
Brings back to us the vanished long ago
The eyes that followed us, the hands we prest,
The smile that thrilled us and the voice that blessed
From countless homes, Old Settlers, have there passed
Lives all too beautiful and bright to last,
The dear ones cherished in our bosom's core
Who wait for us till life's brief dream is o'er

This ground is hallowed Though our mortal sight
May not behold the ladder from yon height
Let softly down, that shining ones may stream
Along its path, as in the patriarch's dream,
Still do they come, their white robes gleaming there
The sunlight shimmering through their golden hair,
All silently they join your waiting throng,
And, hushed and solemn, list to prayer and song

Go with me first to quiet Farmington
From my old home my flight shall be begun,
And ere my fancy takes its circling round
Kneel with her there on consecrated ground
With the low murmur of the near Des Moines,
In solemn requiem let our voices join,
Our footfalls, too, must take a softer tread
Above the sacred sods that hold our dead.
Tis most like home—that city on the hill,
Whose inmates sleep so peacefully and still
'Tis there the oldest settler calmly rests,
With still hands folded on his pulseless breast
Upon the marble, gleaming pure and white,
We read the names of Alfrey, Dickey, Wright,
Swazey and Kelley, Bolter Good and Shreeves,
From slumbers roused not by the whispering leaves
All undisturbed by the green boughs that moan
Their ceaseless miserere o'er each stone

Oh ! stout the hearts beyond the ocean's waves,
Who left, on England's shores, their fathers' graves,
Who came, Columbia's wilderness to tread
Without the sacred ashes of their dead ,
Who felt that nevermore might lips be pressed
To flowers that bloomed above a mother's breast
Who left behind, mid throes of anguish wild,
The consecrated mound that held a child
'Twould matter little where my steps might rove
Did not this magnet draw—*the graves I love.*

In Farmington, a score of years ago,
When times were easy—locomotion slow—
We used to be so quietly content
We wondered what life's hurried action meant
'Twas Smith and Barton through that peaceful calm,
But when the action came 'twas Smith and Schramm,
For, with the railroad came a change of work,
And pills and powders must give way to pork
There s many a sturdy farmer here to-day
Who took his porkers there with loud display,
And, home returning with his merchandise,
Displayed to wife's and daughter's wondering eyes
The lovely dresses, they had oft been told
Would surely come the day the pork was sold

Republicans ! if any man you seek
To prove your doctrine, take old Dr Meek !
I heard him at the opening of the war,
When every word he uttered left a scar
You see, just then, we didn t quite agree,
And so he made his opening charge on me
Am I disloyal ? Wait, and hear me through,
And then pass sentence, ye who donned the blue

The upward growth of Farmington was planned
When Charley Gleckler left the Fatherland ,
For her it were indeed a sad affair
Had he not settled permanently there,
And with him all such men as Tuttle, Bower,
Perry and Whitlock, Anderson and Tower,
Cooley and French, with Campbell, Browning, Rice,
Stoddard and Miller, Thompson, Ringer, Price,
Manning and Bateman, Church and Kings the twain,
Goodin and Davidson, Flood, Willis, Hayne,
And dear old Deacon Smith, whose blindness here
Will make Heaven's cloudless radiance dawn more clear

If Henry Benson ever moves away,
'Twill be for Farmington a sorry day
This much I prophesy , and, more than that,
'To " Blow to every Democrat
the price too would feel a heavy shock
We be compelled to lose the old man Bro

George Whitfall would be apt to miss him most,
But, crowded with the duties of a host,
He might not grieve as men of leisure do,
But, rushed with business, *work* his sorrow through

Hail to inventor—Dibble is the man
With hand to fashion and with brain to plan,
Like old Goliath, tallest of the braves,
Van Buren cries, " Comest thou to me with staves ? '
And Dibble answers, with triumphant shout,
"I come just see how fast I turn them out
My last improvement you have not yet seen
It crowns mine as the Model Stave Machine '

A passing glance is all my space allows
Of Jimmy Thomas, driving home his cows
And dear old Aunty, weak and pale to-day,
Straining the milk, and bearing it away
To cellar cool, where cream would shortly rise
As golden as our glorious sunset skies

And Frederick Rueckmeyer's kindly hand appears ,
I've watched it oft, through bitter, blinding tears,
For when, each time, the coffin's sable lid
Closed o er, and a white face in darkness hid,
That sympathizing hand would tremble so
I knew one pitying heart could feel my woe

If upon Seth Craig you wish to call,
You ll have to venture near a prison-wall
Ah ' Good Samaritan, your kind heart grieves,
Perchance, for him who fell among the thieves
Yet, spare your sympathy, or else divide
With Pharisee, who seeks the other side
He s only Warden of the thieving clan—
An honest, upright, generous-hearted man
Who puts their deeds of infamy to shame
By pointing to his own untarnished name

Come, Harvey Adams, make the closing prayer,
And then dismiss the group assembled there
The Reaper has not passed his golden grain
Some ripened shocks, though scattered, yet remain ,
They, with the aged Sower, waiting stand
For their ingathering to the better land

Never be Lawrence by the brave forgot,
While she can claim as hers O H P Scott '
Like ancient kinsman, when the pibroch rung,
With sword in belt, carbine from shoulder flung,
Calling young Strawn—the eldest of his clan,

He went as Captain—every inch a man '
He fought as heroes fight while near him stood
The son whose veins showed his father's blood
He rose to Colonel's rank, nor asked release,
Furlough nor rest until the dawn of peace

But, ah! I know who suffered most! 'Twas she,
The wife and mother, who so silently
Waited and watched in her deserted home
With bursting heart, and lips all white and dumb,
Fearing when battle's roar had died away,
To read their names coupled with "killed to-day"
I watched her through those years of dread suspense,
And when, at last, there came a recompense—
The glad return of husband and of son—
I felt her share of victory had been won,
Her faith been tried by sacrifice as grand
As heaven required at the old patriarch's hand

And hers but one of twice ten thousand hearts
Wounded and tortured by those barbed darts—
The arrows of suspense that rankled there,
The spears of doubt, the wounds of black despair
Oh, mothers, daughters, wives, your country's weal
Was purchased not alone by shot and steel!

Stand forth, ye braves! Speak out, each dauntless soul!
Answer, if present, as I call the roll!
Are Wilkins, Johnson, and brave Cutler here?
Do Cy and Tillman Langford re appear,
As, after fourteen days of travel sore,
They stood within the Union lines once more?
If he be absent, soldiers, search the prairie,
And bring old trusty Major John McCrary!
He flinched not 'neath the rain of shot and shell,
Had more engagements than a modern belle,
Fulfilled them all, yet never once was stung
By questions of his faith in Brigham Young

Captain Leroy S. Elbert answers not,
Yet never by his bravery forgot!
Entwined with laurel and embalmed with bay,
Our memories fold it tenderly away

If Hoskins and the Messrs Brown are here,
Let them arise, and brave Lieutenant Muir-
Receive your share of glory with the rest,
You, who with Sherman to Atlanta pressed!
And Thatcher, too, who joined that living wall,
Built of the bravest hearts the North could call

A little east of old Van Buren's heart,
You strike against a rib—a bony-part (Bonaparte)—
And there, Old Settlers, you may fondly dwell
Upon the memory of Van Caldwell
The Old Dominion gave his great heart birth,
Van Buren cherished his exalted worth,
And Iowa to consecrate her trust,
Unveiled her bosom to receive his dust

With reverent pleasure do we turn away
What persevering energy will do
The Meek are blessed and for their quiet worth

Says prophecy, "they shall inherit earth"
Their factory, with loom and flying-wheel,
Attests their industry, while years reveal
What patient, unremitted toil may claim
The title to an honest, upright name

Good Dr Cresap rises at my call,
His dapple gray, old saddle-bags and all
His finger on the pulse, his solemn guise,
For which you all pronounce him wondrous wise

Josiah Clifton with the brothers Scott,
The Keiths and Reeds can never be forgot
And Wrigglesworth and Singleton and Lee,
With Warner, Smith, Ray, Richardsons the three,
And Doans, Ellis, Lingford, Boston, Stotts
(To save the time, I give them thus in lots),
And Reynolds, Bower, Claflin Enerick,
Johnson and Stewart (Christian name was Dick),
And Judd and Welch, who near old Jordan stand
To test the riches of their promised land,
While Slaughter, Nelson, Cave, propose to show,
How red men fled and left their Jericho,
How valiant to the core, and brave of heart,
The "pale-face" met, and called it Bonaparte

Would see a specimen—a matchless job
Of nature's handiwork?—take Harvey Robb,
His generous nature, unassuming worth
Can scarcely claim a counterpart on earth
You'll find more wisdom, he makes no pretense
To erudition, but for common sense,
Plain go-ahead-a-tive-ness, bring your man
And prove you have excelled him—*if you can*

Benton, I stood in cool Bellefontaine's shade
And saw thy grave, before thy form was laid
Beneath the mold, and said, with tearful eye
"'Twill hold as much of greatness as could die"
Yet there I erred, 'twas but thy feeble frame
They hid that day, thy glory and thy fame
Live after thee—e'en from yon distant hill
We hear thy honored name re-echoed still

'Twas not Seth Richards (this you know, of course)
Proposed to give his kingdom for a horse
He earned it all, and knows its value well,
And therefore is not keen to trade or sell

It took some people of the queerest sort
In early days, to settle Bentonsport
The name of Green, for instance, brings to view
Actions and manners of a kindred hue.
We never deem its brains sharp or tough,
But verdant innocent, not "up to snuff."

Yet does our neighboring paper-mill proclaim
Its builders were not green, except in name,
But men, whose judgment ripe and honor rare,
Made friends throughout the country everywhere.

And then the man who boasted least was found
To be one Bragg—called so the country round,
While Brown was whiter than his neighbor Snow
Moore long enough, and Long extremely low

Sanford and Sullivan and Ross can tell
How much it cost to keep a good hotel,
In early days, when men, without pretense,
Lived by their labor and plain common sense.

Does Dr Bailey feel content. repaid,
For building such a home in Vernon's shade?
It must be satisfying thus to dwell
With friends he's known so long and proved so well

I tell you what, there's not a bit of sham
In the school founded up at Birmingham
It does the county credit and you'll see
How wonderful its future growth will be
Descendants of such men as Cameron,
Rutledge and Norris—(I mean Dr. John),
Of Miller, Plaskett, Bryant, Christy, Crumb,
Will prove by this their ancestors were "some,
A Western phrase you doubtless comprehend,
At least you do, Old Settlers of this Bend

Hill, Holcomb, Johnson, and the Tollmans, too,
Belong to Portland, where Jo Dickey grew
Into a merchant —a successful one,
And then moved down and sold at Farmington
Whitten and Walker, Moreton, Belknap, Dowd.
Remained behind at Portland with the crowd

If ever Milton's citizens feel sick,
They straightway send for Doc Gillfillin quick '
So at Mt Sterling, when they feel the need
Of counsel in their town affairs, with speed
They seek James Alcorn, who by prompt advice,
Settles disputes and discords in a trice

Mechanics you have reason to rejoice,
For, lo, a Carpenter, the people's choice
stands at your head, and right before you, here,
A Mason, whom you honor and revere
Judge Hendershott should not be far away
When to the honored we our tribute pay
And not our county only, but our State
Enrolls Charles Negus with her truly great

Though the machinery of sister States

Our Miller's strength we surely, too, should know,
Because he served in Congress years ago
You take no risks, though, for McCrary's known,
And Palmer's latent force may yet be shown.

The welcoming shouts will scarce have died away
From this fair valley where you meet to-day
Until there rises jubilant and free,
An answering chorus from the plains of Lee
Then unto you will flash, as from afar,
E'en as the golden beams of star to star,
The light of Intellect, of Genius true,
That warms, electrifies and thrills you through

You know that Lee has heroes of her own,
Old Settlers some, some ripe in wisdom grown,
Though not in years, for Craig, McCrary, Browne
Rice, Howell, Gillmore have achieved renown
And Hornish, Lomax, Anderson can claim
The foremost ranks upon the rolls of fame
Then Marshall, Gibbons, Lowry, Sprague are found
High up the ladder, on the topmost round,
While Cochran, Ballinger and Edwards stand
With Hagerman and Collier on each hand,
Each weaving in the galaxy of fame
The glorious sheen of an immortal name
At Keokuk no stranger need to wait,
If he would enter, open is her "Gait,"
Its keeper ne'er extorts an extra toll,
He even "dead-heads" those who wish to stroll,
When he discovers that his favored man
Is a stanch, out-and-out Republican
Another editor (Old Settler, too),
Asserts his health has proved this statement true,
That fearless, bold attacks on party wrong
Have made his *Weekly Constitution* strong

With the Old Settlers' early hopes and fears
Came thoughts of John F Sandford's former years,
And with these thoughts the labor he has done,
The wide-spread reputation he has won.
And wondering what experience and skill
Might yet in future, lead him to fulfill
My ear was startled when the words were said
' His work is finished—Sandford's soul has fled '
And can it be? Has Science lost so soon
The life that had not reached its brilliant noon '
Have the hands fallen, pulseless, at his side,
Whose matchless skill was tested far and wide?
Van Buren, 'tis a loss *you* may deplore,
Where will you turn since Sanford is no more '

Twas D F Miller, friends, who bade me say
· 'tet · · · · · ·   ·t ·
When list he · · · · · · · ·
· · · ·at· · t ta· · · · t |·· · ·

He linked his fate with hers, and near and far
Is justly called the Nestor of her Bar

Can I refer to David, Jesse's son,
Without a word of praise for Jonathan?
Can Damon's constancy through memory pass
Without a thought of faithful Pythias?
Miller and Viele? Death will not divide
Their friendship on the golden other side
Beyond the darksome river they will meet,
And through Eternal Day hold converse sweet

What sister State from Oregon to Maine,
Can fairer record than our own sustain?
Explore the continent! Its crowded mart
Yields not for our own Dean his counterpart
What brighter history can you wish to boast
Than Delazon has left Pacific's coast?
Look north and south with persevering ken,
And show, if you can find them, nobler men
Go back through all the years and search in vain
For minister that graced the court of Spain,
Whose native dignity and courtly mien
Entranced the eyes of an admiring Queen,
As did our own, who, with his modest ways
Would Dodge, could he escape a word of praise

Then on to Washington! (not Richmond now)
Count, when you reach it, each familiar brow,
Looming ahead, like a resplendent star,
Behold our Secretary, first, of War,
See Williams, Miller and McCrary there,
Of honors reaping an abundant share
Then back returned, perhaps within your sight
Search out the man you know is always Wright
Each thistle of your prairie he has trod,
His intellect expanded on your sod,
Be true to him, your champion and guide,
Even though politics your views divide

Many the vessels wrecked upon life's sea,
But squadron-like your own can never be
'Twill steer aloof of breakers and the shore
With matchless Baldwin for its Commodore
Was ship e'er known to sink or yet to strand
When she a Bonney Captain could command?
What dauntless courage, vigilance and skill
Are there to ward off every coming ill
When, with a Pilot's ever-watchful eye,
Goddard the far off danger can espy,
The old "Van Buren" weathering each gale,
Safe into port, at last, will proudly sail,
S.......   .. all her gallant crew
.... deck to watch the passing view
M..... ....y foremost in the ...

Marlow its captain, Brown its leading man,
While other ships hold Kinnersly and Moore,
Parker and Pittman, Millers three or four,
Morris and Christy, Ober, Barton, Gaines,
Mills and St John—both good Old Settler names,
Smith Hall and Wood with Jackson, too, appear,
And young George Wright (whose starting-point was here),
Cowles, Moss and Rankin (once a favorite beau),
The D'Orsay of this region long ago,
And last, because the eldest of the crew,
"Pap" Shepherd's kindly face is held to view
It often takes a superhuman rap
To wake a man from a continuous nap (Knapp),
But when aroused, his full expanded soul,
Longing for action, will not brook control

It is not needful that a man depart
From jurist's bench to manifest a heart
Of generous friendship and a mind of grace,
For, in his daily life, in honored place,
Judge Sloan shows both, on the broadest plan—
An upright Judge, a Christian gentleman

I had a friend, 'twas in those earlier days,
Whose giant efforts won him highest praise,
He shone in magnitude the first, a star,
Illumed with brightness Keosauqua's bar
And yet he shines, and yet his radiance gleams,
In meteor flashes, yet with purer beams,
For in one rapturous, pentecostal hour,
The Holy Spirit came with might and power
And thus renewed, he dares not pause and shrink,
But cries to all that thirst, "Ho! come, and drink"
Israel was ruled by Judges, till her call—
"A king! a king!'" (her trouble came with Saul)
And they who judged found succor ever nigh,
Because they trusted in the Lord Most High

The age repeats itself; in its advance,
Weak, timid woman clamors for a chance,
And man looks on and thinks it wondrous strange
That we should dare demand *a little change*
Yet, years ago, here, ere the "move" began
The nurse (Nourse) you called and trusted *was a man*,
And, wondrous to relate, whenever tried,
Success attended, all were satisfied

Clark, Lane and Jewett, names that we revere,
Good Shepherds, are your flocks now gathered here?
The fields beyond the blue are fresh and green,
The waters cool that gently flow between
Not long your sheep o'er earthly steeps will roam,
But to the Fold above will hasten home

Before me gathered by group here
The members of thy far-famed Bar appear,

Here thy physicians, men of judgment sound
Thy ministers to hallowed labor bound ;
Soldier or citizen whiche er you be,
Each seems alike a cherished friend to me
Were I a priestess 'neath this vaulted dome,
I'd pray that Israel's tribes be gathered home !
And, when each solemn rite was softly said
Would breathe my benediction on thy head.
Yet, after that, 'neath the shekinah's glow
I'd proceed alone, and there in whispers low
Would plead that, most of all, kind heaven would bless
For auld lang syne *the heroes of thy Press*

As some lone pilgrim, weary, faint and worn,
Musing on what may nevermore return
Sees suddenly the vanished years come back,
And finds herself returned to childhood's track,
So I, with faithful hand and heart, have come
To pay this tribute to my early home ;
To kneel, as at a sainted mother's knee,
And breathe my prayer, Keosauqua, to thee

Van Buren, one Old Settler proudly stands
Pledged unto thee with loyal heart and hands,
And by these furrowed cheeks, these locks of gray,
Through which the loyal winds now fondly play,
She feels that unto thee, through woe and weal
Are pledged, till death, ten thousand hearts of steel
Our banner, foremost in the ranks of war,
With shattered staff and many a veteran scar,
Snatched from the thickest of the deadly fray,
Is seen within our Capitol to-day
'Twas old Van Buren sent that banner out,
With many a jubilant, triumphant shout .
'Twas old Van Buren sent the young Voltaire,
Who held the colors firmly, proudly there ;
'Twas old Van Buren sent the Colonel, too,
Who led to victory the Boys in Blue

The Boys in Blue ! Oh, mothers, most of all
Be yours the praise whose heroes went—*to fall !*
Who, after weary waiting, prayers and tears,
Felt blight and desolation crown your years
But yet, remember, 'twas your country's call,
You bravely answered when you gave your all
And ask no brighter, more enduring fame
Than what, through them, still glorifies your name

Old Settlers, when the final debt is paid
Here in Van Buren's arms may you be laid
Be this our Mecca—sanctified this soil
By the sweet thought, you mounted thence to God !
And oh' if seraphs in that loftier sphere
M[...] [...] [...] the feet still lingering here,
When we return [...] the each [...] that
M[...] [...] [...] waiting, hovering here

THE STATE BOUNDARY DIFFICULTY

Hon Charles Negus is the author of the following history of the Missouri-Iowa boundary difficulty. The story as here told contains none of the personal incidents of the "war," but must be accepted as a reliable record, worth preserving and fair in every particular He says

"Soon after the organizing of the territorial government of Iowa. there arose a dispute between Missouri and Iowa about the jurisdiction of the State and Territorial authorities over a tract of country in the southern part of Iowa, which Missouri claimed as being within the boundary of that State as defined by Congress.

"The act of Congress, passed March 6, 1820, authorizing the Territory of Missouri to form a State government, provided that (if the State should ratify the boundaries) the State of Missouri 'should consist of all the territory within the following boundaries· Beginning in the middle of the Mississippi River, on the parallel of 36° north latitude : thence west. along that parallel of latitude, to the St Francis River, thence up and following the course of that river, in the middle of the main channel thereof. to the parallel of 36° 30'; thence west along the same to the point where the said parallel is intersected by a meridian line passing through the middle of the mouth of the Kansas River, where the same empties into the Missouri River; thence. from the point aforesaid, north along the west meridian line, to the intersection of the parallel of latitude which passes through *the rapids of the river Des Moines*, making said line to correspond with the Indian boundary line etc. , thence east, from the point of intersection last aforesaid, along the said parallel of latitude to the middle of the channel of the main fork of the said River Des Moines ; thence down and along the middle of the said River Des Moines. to the mouth of the same, where it empties into the Mississippi,' etc These boundaries. as defined by Congress, were adopted by Missouri through the Convention which formed the State Constitution.

"The northern boundary of the State, which was defined as ' *the parallel of latitude which passes through the rapids of the river Des Moines,*' though it might have been well understood at the time, was vague and uncertain, and subsequently gave grounds for an open dispute

" In the treaties made with the Sacs and Foxes and the Iowa Indians on the 4th of August, 1824, for the purchase of a portion of their lands, it is set forth that they sold to the United States all their lands within the limits of the State of Missouri, which are situated. lying and being between the Mississippi and Missouri Rivers, and a line running from the Missouri at the mouth of the Kansas River, north 100 miles to the northwest corner of the State of Missouri, and thence east to the Mississippi The line, as defined in this treaty, commencing at the mouth of the Kansas River, thence running 100 miles due north, and thence east until it strikes the Des Moines River, had been run in 1816. by John C Sullivan, and duly marked by blazing trees. driving stakes and erecting mounds.

'· But in a period of between twenty and thirty years, those marks had become so obliterated that they were not easily to be found, and the rapids of the river Des Moines was so uncertain a place that it was hard for those first settling the country at the   · Iowa was   ·   to designate where the northern boundary   M   was located.   several rapids in the Des Moines River and   of considerable   K   auqua, in Van Buren County (a fall in eighty rods of twenty-one inches), the Missourians claimed that the latter were the rapids referred to, in the act of Congress authorizing Missouri to form a State Constitution, as a point in defining their boundaries. And in 1837, the authorities of Missouri, without the co-operation of the United States, or of the Territory of Iowa (then Wisconsin), appointed Commissioners to run and mark the northern boundary.

"The Commissioners so appointed, instead of commencing to run the line upon the parallel of latitude which passes through the rapids of the river Des Moines in the Mississippi, proceeded to search for rapids in the Des Moines River itself, from which to commence. They finally fixed upon the ripples in the great bend in the Des Moines River, in Van Buren County, which they assumed to be the rapids of the Des Moines River named in the act of Congress of 1820, and in the Constitution of Missouri, notwithstanding those ripples had never been known as 'the rapids of the river Des Moines.' From this point, the Commissioners proceeded to run and mark a line, which the authorities of that State claimed was the northern boundary, while the early history of the West showed, and it was subsequently decided by the Supreme Court of the United States, that the rapids of the river Des Moines were in the Mississippi River.

"Gen. Pike, who first explored the Upper Mississippi, after the acquisition of the Louisiana Purchase by the United States, in his journal, kept while ascending the river in 1805, says he 'arrived at the foot of the rapids Des Moines at 7 o'clock,' and thus goes on to give an account of the difficulties he had in getting over those rapids with his boat, on his way up the Mississippi River And. after passing the rapids, in writing to Gen Wilkinson, he dates his letter, 'Head of the Rapids Des Moines' Also, in his map of the Upper Mississippi, Pike lays down the Rapids Des Moines as being in the Mississippi River, a short distance above the mouth of the Des Moines River And, before the United States acquired possession of this territory in 1779, Zenon Tendeau, acting as Lieutenant Governor of Upper Louisiana, in one of his official acts, says: 'It is permitted to Mr Lewis (Fesson) Honore to establish himself at the head of the rapids of the river Des Moines' Upon this grant, Honore made an actual settlement and improvement immediately upon the banks of the Mississippi River, at the head of the Des Moines Rapids in that River, some eighteen or twenty miles above its mouth.

"These, with other references, go to show that, at an early day, the rapids in the Mississippi opposite the southern extremity of Iowa, were known as the 'rapids of the river Des Moines,' but the authorities of Missouri claimed and contended for many years that the rapids referred to by Congress, and in their Constitution were in the Des Moines River and near Keosauqua The northern boundary of that State, as long as there were no settlements there, was a matter of little consequence to her citizens, and there was no one to dispute their claims until after the Black Hawk Purchase, which was made in 1832.

"The Territory of Wisconsin, in organizing the county of Van Buren, made her southern boundary extend to the southern line, and the same boundaries were claimed by Iowa as soon as she assumed a territorial government The territorial government of Iowa went into operation on the 4th day of July, 1838, and at that time the boundaries between Missouri and Iowa had not been settled, and there was a strip of Government land about ten miles wide which both governments claimed The county of Van Buren, as organized by the Legislature of Wisconsin. before Iowa assumed a territorial government, embraced within her boundary a portion of this disputed tract of land

"The County Court of Clark County, Mo, in levying the taxes for that county, enrolled the settlers on this disputed tract, as being citizens of that State and belonging to that county, and, having placed their names upon the tax-list, ordered Uriah S Gregory, the Sheriff of that county, to collect the taxes Accordingly, the Collector of Clark County went on the disputed tract to collect the taxes, but the tax-payers refused to pay, and the officer undertook to collect them by levying upon their property, but while endeavoring to do this, some of the citizens of Van Buren County sued out a warrant from a magistrate and placed it in the hands of Henry Heffleman, the Sheriff of Van Buren County, who arrested the Missouri officer, and there being no jail suitable for retaining prisoners nearer than Muscatine, he was taken to that county and there lodged in jail.

"This act aroused the citizens of Clark County, and an application was made to Gov. Boggs, of Missouri, for the military power of the State to aid the civil officers in maintaining their authority and to enforce the law of Missouri over the disputed tract   He accordingly dispatched Gen. Allen, with a thousand men, to the place of contention

"Gov Lucas, of Iowa, was as determined and fixed in his purpose to maintain the rights of his State as the authorities of Missouri were to exact theirs, and for this purpose ordered Maj Gen J. B. Brown to call out the militia and march with his forces to Van Buren County to protect the citizens.

"At this time, the militia of Iowa was poorly organized, but Gen. Brown gave orders to his subordinates to beat up for recruits, and the citizens were not backward in enrolling themselves by voluntary enlistment, and, in a short time, about five hundred men, with arms, were assembled in Van Buren County and others were on their way, amounting, in all, to about twelve hundred men, and the gathering of military forces had all the appearance of a fierce and bloody civil war   But before there was any collision between the two forces, Gen Brown, from his officers, selected Gen. A. C. Dodge, of Burlington, Gen. Churchman, of Dubuque, and Dr. Clark, of Ft. Madison, as an embassy to the enemy to try to negotiate a peace

"On arriving at Waterloo, the county seat of Clark County, they found that the County Court of that county had rescinded the order to the Sheriff to collect the taxes on the disputed tract, and had sent a special delegation to wait upon Gov. Lucas and the Legislature of Iowa, then assembled at Burlington, for the purpose of making some amicable adjustment of the difficulties and that Gen. Allen, with his forces, had withdrawn from the contest.   Upon receiving this information the embassy returned to their headquarters, and the Iowa forces were disbanded and permitted to return to their homes.

"Col McDaniels and Dr. Wayland, the representatives of Clark County, came to Burlington and waited upon Gov Lucas, who, not evincing much disposition to adjust matters, they then went before the Legislature, which body, after hearing their proposition, passed a set of resolutions, with a preamble, expressing their views   In the preamble, they set forth the difficulties existing between Iowa and Missouri, and that Iowa, under any circumstances, deprecated any military collision between the forces of the State of Missouri and the Territory of Iowa, and reciprocated the kind feelings evinced by the delegation from the County Court of Clark County, and *Resolved*, That the officers now on the part of Missouri be respectfully requested to suspend all further military operations on the part of said State until these resolutions can be submitted to His Excellency, Gov Boggs, that His Excellency, Gov Boggs, be requested to authorize a suspension of hostilities on the part of the State of Missouri until the 1st day of July next, with a view to having the unfortunate difficulties now existing between the State of Missouri and the Territory of Iowa adjusted by the act of Congress, that His Excellency, the Governor of Iowa, be requested to suspend all further military operations until the decisions of his Excellency, Gov. Boggs, may be obtained relative to the proposition herein contained: that the Governor be requested forthwith to forward a copy of these resolutions to the Governor of Missouri, one to the County Court of Clark County and copies to the officers in command on the disputed grounds, to be by them presented to the officers of the Missouri forces.

" These proceedings on the part of the Legislature had a tendency to quiet things for a time The Sheriff of Clark County was, however, indicted at the next term of the court in Van Buren County for his attempt to collect taxes in the disputed tract, but the Prosecuting Attorney entered a *nolle prosequi*, and he was discharged from custody

" On the 10th of November, 1841, Thomas Reynolds, Governor of Missouri, who was the successor to Gov Boggs, addressed a letter to John Chambers, who was at that time Governor of Iowa, in which he informed him that the Legislature of Missouri at their last session, passed an act directing the Governor of Missouri to bring a suit on behalf of Uriah S. Gregory, the late Collector of Clark County, against Henry Heffleman, the Sheriff of Van Buren County, for the purpose of having the question of boundary between Iowa and Missouri finally adjusted in the Supreme Court of the United States As Heffleman and others who arrested Gregory resided in Iowa, such a suit should have been commenced in Iowa Gov Reynolds wished to know if suit was thus commenced whether the authorities of Iowa would consent to make such an agreed case on the record as would insure a decision of the Supreme Court of the United States on the question of boundary.

" To this Gov Chambers replied that this question, as it appeared to him, was one over which the Territorial authorities had no control; for, ' by an express reservation in the laws organizing the Territory of Iowa, the boundary remained subject to the future control of Congress ' And Gov Chambers also expressed his doubts whether, under the Constitution of the United States, the Supreme Court, even upon an agreed case and by consent of parties, would take jurisdiction of an alleged controversy between one of the States and a Territory remaining subject to the laws of Congress. But he assured Gov Reynolds that he would lay his communication before the next Legislature of the Territory, and if that body should differ from the views he had entertained upon the subject, their decisions should immediately be made known to him But it appears that the Legislature concurred with the views of Gov Chambers, for there were no steps taken to comply with the request of Missouri as made by Gov Reynolds.

· The expenses of Iowa in calling out the militia to maintain her rights and enforce the laws on the disputed tract were upward of $13,000 Some of those expenses were borne by individuals whose circumstances were such that they could not well afford to lose the amount justly due them Congress was memorialized by the Territorial Legislature to make an appropriation to meet these expenses, and on two occasions a bill was passed through the House providing for their payment but both bills failed to pass the Senate

" Samuel C Reed, of Van Buren County, who lived near where the troops were r ·   ·   · ·   ·   · ·'·   ·   I w · ·_ ·st the intru-sion o ·   _   ·   ·   ·   ·· ·· unt of nearly $200,   ·   · ·   ·   · ···· · · · ·   ·   · · · · several years with the hope of getting something from the General Government, and not succeeding, petitioned the Territorial Legislature to allow and make an appropriation for his claim

"Reed was regarded as a patriotic and generous man, and he did all he could to sustain the rights of Iowa in her troubles with Missouri, and having met with misfortunes, and being much reduced in his circumstances, his appeal to the Legislature elicited their sympathy, and they passed a bill allowing his claims, with 6 per cent interest, and made an appropriation for paying it, but this did not meet with the approbation of Gov Clark, at that time Governor of the Territory, and he returned the bill with his veto His objections were that the Legislature should make no discrimination among those who aided the authorities in the troubles with Missouri. if the Territory undertook to pay one they should pay all, that if Iowa should assume these debts the United States, which was in duty bound to pay them. would not. that Iowa was soon to become a State, when she would have a representation and vote in both branches of Congress, and then, in all probability, would be able to get an appropriation to defray those expenses But for one cause or another, neither Reed nor any of the others who furnished means or rendered services in the war with Missouri, got pay for that which was justly their due.

"For the purpose of ascertaining and defining the southern boundary of Iowa, Congress, on the 18th of June 1838, passed an act in which it was provided that the President should cause to be surveyed, and distinctly marked, the southern boundary line of Iowa, and for that purpose he was required to appoint a Commissioner on the part of the United States, who, with the necessary surveyors, was to act in conjunction with a Commissioner to be appointed by the State of Missouri and one to be appointed by the Governor of Iowa, in 'running, marking and ascertaining' the boundary line, and it was made the duty of the Commissioner who was to be appointed by the President, to prepare three plats of this survey one of which was to be returned to the Secretary of State of the United States, one to the office of the Secretary of State of Missouri and one to the Secretary of the Territory of Iowa.

"And it was also provided that if the Commissioner on the part of Missouri, or of Iowa, should fail to attend, or if either or both the State of Missouri or the Governor of Iowa should fail to appoint, then the Commissioner of the United States by himself, or such Commissioner as did attend. should proceed to run the boundary line between Missouri and Iowa But the line so run and marked was not to be fully established until the survey should be submitted to, and the boundary thus ascertained and marked be approved of and ratified by Congress

"In pursuance of this act the President appointed Maj A M Lee as Commissioner on the part of the United States, and Dr James Davis was appointed for Iowa, but Missouri failed to make any appointment Maj Lee, in company with Dr Davis, proceeded to make the survey as required by Congress, and made their report to the Secretary of the Territory of Iowa, on the 15th of January, 1839. about the time the difficulty was taking place on the disputed tract in Van Buren County But it seems that the line surveyed by Lee and Davis was never approved of by Congress, and consequently did not become the boundary between Missouri and Iowa

"Soon after the troubles in Van Buren County, the Legislature of Iowa passed a law th⸱⸱ ⸱⸱⸱⸱⸱⸱⸱⸱ ⸱⸱⸱⸱⸱⸱⸱⸱⸱⸱ in the jurisdiction of ⸱ ⸱⸱⸱⸱⸱⸱⸱ ⸱ ⸱⸱⸱⸱⸱ ⸱ ⸱ nerein, by virtue of an ⸱⸱⸱⸱⸱⸱ ⸱⸱⸱⸱⸱ ⸱ ⸱ ⸱⸱⸱⸱ ⸱⸱⸱ ⸱ ⸱ r Government of the United States, every person so offending should be fined, not exceeding $1,000, or be imprisoned not exceeding five years. That if any person residing within the limits of the Territory should accept of any office or trust from any State or authority other than the United States or the Territory of Iowa, every person so offending should be fined not exceeding $1,000, or be imprisoned not exceeding five years.

"Soon after the organization of the county of Davis, this law was called into requisition The county of Adair, as it was then organized, embraced within its boundaries a portion of what now composes Davis County. The Sheriff of Adair County, Preston Mullinix, and his Deputy, William P. Linder, were indicted in Davis County, the Sheriff for exercising his office within the boundaries of Iowa, without legal authority and contrary to the statutes, and the Deputy for an assault and battery and kidnapping and falsely imprisoning one Frederick Acheson, a citizen of Iowa, which acts were done on the disputed tract.

"Mullinix and Linder were both arrested and held under bail to answer to the indictment at the next term of court. At that time they both appeared and Linder went to trial, which resulted in his conviction and a sentence of a fine and ten days' imprisonment in the Penitentiary. The trial of Mullinix, the Sheriff, was continued to the next term of Court, and he was required to enter into a recognizance (without security) for his appearance, which he refused to do, and the Court ordered him to be committed to prison.

"As soon as these transactions were made known to Gov Chambers, he pardoned Linder and remitted his fine, and also pardoned Mullinix for the offense for which he stood committed, and ordered him to be discharged from prison After the arrest of Mullinix and Linder, the county of Adair was divided, and the territory adjoining Davis County was embraced within the limits of Schuyler County.

"After the county of Schuyler, Mo, was organized, about the 1st of January, 1846, Samuel Riggs, the Sheriff of Davis County, Iowa, had put into his hands a writ of attachment against the property of an individual on the tract of land in dispute, and while attempting to serve the writ, he was arrested by the Sheriff of Schuyler County, on a charge of attempting to execute the functions of his office in Missouri, and was required to give security for his appearance at the next term of the Court in that county. A few days after this, another attempt was made by a large number of men from Missouri to resist the execution of a process in the hands of the Sheriff of Davis County, but without success, for the Sheriff and his posse, though inferior in numbers, executed the writ, and secured the property attached This dispute, as to who had jurisdiction over this country, had a bad influence in the community, and caused many reckless and desperate characters to rendezvous in that vicinity, with the hope that in the contest with the authorities they might escape the punishment justly due their crimes

"The arrest of the Sheriff of Davis County called forth a special message from Gov Clark. then Governor of the Territory, to the Legislature of Iowa, which was then in session, and they passed a special law authorizing the Governor to draw upon the Territorial Treasurer for the sum of $1,500, and that the sum, or any amount thereof, which he might think proper, should be placed at his discretion for the employment of counsel to manage and defend all cases growing out of this difficulty in which the Territory or any of the citizens thereof, should be party on the one side and Missouri or the authorities of that State upon the other The court of Schuyler County convened at

Lancaster, the county seat, on the 9th of May, and an indictment was found against Riggs, who immediately appeared and answered thereto in discharge of his bail

"David Rorer, of Burlington, a gentleman of high legal talents, was employed by Gov Clark on behalf of Iowa, to defend Riggs. Rorer attended this term of Court for the purpose of defending him, but from a desire on the part of both parties to defer judicial action in the case until an adjustment of the disputed boundary question could be effected, the case was continued until the next term of Court, and Riggs was discharged upon his own individual recognizance, and he was subsequently discharged entirely To compensate him for his trouble and expense, the Iowa Legislature passed a law authorizing him to file his petition in the District Court of Davis County claiming compensation for his time and expenses in defending himself against all prosecutions which had been commenced against him by the authorities of Missouri for exercising his office on the disputed territory, and they provided that the Court should hear the case and determine the amount which was justly due Riggs, and the amount so determined was directed to be paid out of the State Treasury

"On the 17th of June, 1844, Congress passed an act respecting the northern boundary of Missouri, in which it was provided that the Governor of Iowa, by and with the advice and consent of the Council of the Territory, should appoint a Commissioner to act in conjunction with a Commissioner to be appointed by the State of Missouri, and the two were to select a third person, and it was made their duty to ascertain, survey and mark out the northern boundary of Missouri, and to cause plats of their survey to be returned to the Secretary of the United States, and to the Secretary's office of Missouri and Iowa—which plats were to be accompanied with their proceedings in the premises. The Commissioners were empowered to employ surveyors and other hands necessary to accomplish the survey, and the line established and ratified by them, or any two of them, was to be final and conclusive, and to be and remain as the northern boundary line of the State. But it was provided that this act should not go into effect until it should be assented to by Missouri and Iowa Iowa was willing to accede to this proposition, and the Legislature of Missouri passed an act assenting to this mode of settling the difficulty; but the Governor of Missouri, John C Edwards, placed his veto on the bill, and it failed to become a law The Governor's objection to this mode of settling the difficulty seemed to be, that it involved legal rights, and should be adjudicated by a judicial tribunal

"After this, application was made by both contending parties to Congress to pass a law authorizing them to institute a suit in the Supreme Court of the United States and have the controversy judicially settled This application was made on the part of Missouri by an act passed by the Legislature, on the 25th of March, 1845, and on the part of Iowa by a memorial of her Council and House of Representatives, passed on the 17th of January, 1846, in which both parties asked for 'the commencement and speedy determination of such a suit as might be necessary to procure a final decision by the Supreme Court of the United States, upon the true location of the northern boundary of the State' Congress respected these requests and passed the necessary law

"After the passage of the law by Congress, authorizing the settling of the dispute in the Supreme Court the Legislature of Iowa passed an act empowering the Governor to agree with Missouri for the commencement of such a suit as might be necessary to procure from the Supreme Court of the United States a final decision upon the true location of the southern boundary of the State. This act made it the duty of the Governor to cause to be procured all evidence which might be necessary to the legal and proper decision of such a suit. and to employ counsel and do whatever else might be necessary to maintain the rights of the State   Charles Mason was employed on the part of Iowa, who hunted up and prepared the testimony of the trial, and he got Thomas Ewing, of Ohio, to assist him in arguing the case before the Court   The State of Missouri filed the original bill against the State of Iowa, and Iowa filed a cross bill against Missouri.

"This case was tried at the December term of 1848, and the Supreme Court decided that the line as surveyed by Sullivan was the northern boundary of Missouri, which decision gave Iowa all the territory she claimed   The Court appointed Henry B Hendershott, of Iowa, and Joseph C Brown, of Missouri, Commissioners to run out and mark the boundary line   Brown having died before the work was commenced, Robert W Wells was appointed in his place, but he resigned the trust, and William G. Minor received the appointment on the part of Missouri

"The Commissioners, for the purpose of making the necessary arrangements for the survey, met at St Louis in March, 1850, and selected their surveyors.   William Dewey was selected on the part of Iowa, and Robert Walker for Missouri   The Commissioners made their arrangements to meet with their surveyors and other parties, at the point where Sullivan had established the northwest corner of Missouri.   They left their respective homes on the 10th of April and met on the 28th.   To aid them in their work before they started, they obtained from the office of the Surveyor General at St Louis a copy of the field-notes of Sullivan's survey; but the space of nearly thirty-four years having elapsed since this work was done, the marks of the survey being nearly all obliterated, they could not readily find the spot they sought   No precise traces of the old northwest corner remained, the witness-trees to it were on the margin of a vast prairie, and had apparently been destroyed years before, consequently its exact position could not be ascertained from anything visible near the spot.

"The point known as the old northwest corner of Missouri was the northern termination of Sullivan's line, running north and south, run by him in 1816 and was 100 miles north of the mouth of the Kansas River, and the point at which he turned east run to the Des Moines River   His field-notes showed that his miles were numbered north from the Kansas River, and cast from the northwest corner of the State, beginning anew at that corner   Finding no conclusive evidence of the exact site or the required corner, they undertook to trace those lines for the purpose of finding some evidence of the old survey.

"Near the supposed spot of the location of the ninety-ninth mile-corner, on the north line, they found a decayed tree and stump, which corresponded in course, distance and description with the witness-trees to that corner, and cutting into the tree they saw what they supposed to be the remains of an old blaze, upon which was preserved a part, apparently, of the letter M   This supposition was verified by then measuring two miles further south to a point which they found to be Sullivan's ninety-seventh mile-corner, from one witness-tree, which was perfectly sound, the marks upon it two or three inches beneath the bark were plain and legible.   On the east line they found the witness-tree to the third mile-corner, the wood upon which the marks had been inscribed was decayed, but their reversed impression repeated upon the new growth which covered the old blaze, and was cut out in a solid block   Prolonging these lines three miles from the points thus determined, their intersection was assumed as the required corner, and at that point was planted a monument designating the northwest corner of Missouri as the boundary existed before acquiring that tract of land known as the 'Plat Purchase,' lying between the old west line of that State and the Missouri River, which point was found to be in the northeast quarter of Section 35, in Township 67 north, Range 33 west, in latitude 40°, 34′, 40″ north. and in longitude about 94° 30′ west from Greenwich.

"At this point they planted a large cast-iron pillar, weighing between fifteen and sixteen hundred pounds, four feet six inches long, twelve inches square at the base and eight inches at the top. This pillar was legibly marked with the words 'Missouri' on the south side, 'Iowa' on the north side. and 'State Line' on the east. From this corner they ran one west, keeping on the same parallel of latitude on which the pillar was erected, till they reached the Missouri River They commenced the survey on the 24th of May, and reached the river, a distance of sixty miles and sixty-one chains, on the 12th of July. At the terminus of the sixtieth mile, as near the bank of the Missouri River as the perishable nature of the soil would permit, they planted a monument similar to the one erected at the old northwest corner of Missouri, the words 'State Line' facing the east

"The Commissioners then returned to the old northwest corner, and commenced to run the line east, and, by close examination, they were enabled to discover abundant blazes and many witness-trees of the old survey, by which they easily found and re-marked the line run by Sullivan in 1816 The surveying of the eastern portion of the line was commenced on the 13th of August, and terminated on the 18th of September, it being a distance of one hundred and fifty miles forty-one chains and eight links, which, with the sixty miles and sixty-one chains first surveyed, makes the southern boundary of the State between the Missouri and Des Moines Rivers two hundred and eleven miles, thirty-two chains and eight links

Near the west bank of the Des Moines River, where the boundary terminates, on the line was planted a cast-iron pillar similar to the other two, with the words "State Line' fronting the west The line was also designated by cast-iron pillars four feet long, eight inches square at the base and five inches at the top, placed at intervals of thirty miles apart, and one four feet long, seven inches square at the base and four at the top, at intermediate spaces of ten miles apart. all of which pillars mark in iron monument every ten miles the whole length of the boundary line

"Sullivan's line was found in some places to deviate from a true east and west line, which was corrected by the surveyors The iron pillars were planted in Sullivan's line as found at the particular points; but as the line was bending in the ten-mile spaces between the pillars, it was found necessary to erect wooden posts at the termination of each mile in order to mark the line with more accuracy. In the prairies the mile-posts were marked with the letters 'B. L' facing the east, the letter 'I' facing the north, and the letter 'M.' facing the south, and the number of miles on the west face of the post. Where timber exists, the number of the mile is marked on witness-trees, or pointers, with letters appropriate to each stake, there being one tree marked on each side of the line wherever it was possible to do so The front of each witness-tree is marked with the letters 'B L.' In all cases where the posts are set in mounds, the post is invariably nine links west to designate it firm other survey This line, as surveyed and designated under the direction of the Commissioners Hendershott and Minor was adjudged and decreed by the Supreme Court to be the true and proper boundary line between Missouri and Iowa   And thus closed a long and vexed dispute between the two authorities about the extent of their jurisdiction   To defray the expenses of establishing and running this line, the State of Iowa and the State of Missouri each placed at the disposal of the Commissioners the sum of $2,000   But this was not sufficient to meet their expenses, for they were engaged at the work 180 days, and the Supreme Court allowed the Commissioners each the sum of $10 per day for their services, and $2 per day for their expenses, and each of the surveyors $8 per day   These allowances, with other expenses, cost over $10,000, which left over $3,000 apiece for each of the States to pay   The Legislatures of either State made up the deficiencies, and that was an end to the boundary war "

THE DES MOINES IMPROVEMENT SCHEMES

Mr. Charles Negus, an authority in matters pertaining to the history of Iowa, published the following interesting account of the various improvement schemes connected with the Des Moines River, in the "Annals of Iowa"   We give the entire article.

"The river Des Moines has connected with its history many things of interest   It is purposed at this time to notice some of the historical events connected with this river since the land through which it passes was purchased by the Government from the Indians.

"On the first settlement of Iowa, the building of railroads had just commenced, and but very few in the West knew anything about this mode of conveyance for travel and commerce   At that time, steamboats for these purposes were the great absorbing idea.   This river, in high stages of water, was thought to be susceptible of steamboat navigation far into the interior of the State, and those who first settled in the vicinity of this river eagerly looked forward to the day when steamboats would move up and down these waters in large numbers, and when from long distances from its banks, travel and commerce would seek a conveyance through this channel   And these expectations were apparently well-founded.   In 1836, the Sacs and Foxes, having disposed of their reservation on the Iowa River, where they had villages, moved West, and settled in the valley of the river Des Moines, in what is now Wapello County, and, as a natural consequence, trading-posts were established in this vicinity, which had to be supplied with goods; and in the fall of 1837, the few settlers along the banks of this river were, for the first time, gladdened with the sound of the shrill whistle of a steamboat, making its way up the river with supplies for these trading-posts

"This boat was the S. B. Science, commanded by Capt. Clark, which, by forcing its way against the swift current, passing safely over the concealed sand-bars and hidden rocks, demonstrated that the waters of this river, at high stages, was navigable, much to the joy and satisfaction of those who lived in the vicinity, and afforded a theme for pleasant conversation for days and months

"By the treaty of 1842, by which the Sacs and Foxes sold all their lands in Iowa, they were permitted to retain possession of that portion which lay west of Red Rock for three years, and the Indians moved up the river and located themselves near the Raccoon Fork, and the Government thought proper to locate a body of troops at that point   and for the conveyance of soldiers and their equipage to that place the little steamer Ione was employed and laden with stores, and a detachment of troops landed on the site where is now the city of Des Moines, on the 9th of May, 1843 This is the first steamboat that ever ventured to disturb the waters of this river so far from its mouth The Ione, having made a successful trip, added greatly to the expectation of the estimated importance and value of this thoroughfare, which was brought to the attention of Congress, and on the 8th of August, 1846, a law was enacted giving to Iowa, for the purpose of aiding to improve the navigation of the river Des Moines from its mouth to the Raccoon Fork, an equal moiety in alternate sections of the public lands remaining unsold, in a strip five miles wide on each side of the river, to be selected within the territory of Iowa by an agent, or agents, who should be appointed by the Governor of the Territory, subject to the approval of the U S Treasury

"When this grant was first made, it was not supposed by any one that it extended above Raccoon Fork, and Gov. Clark, in communicating the intelligence to the Legislature, estimated the grant to amount to about three hundred thousand acres. This part of the Governor's message was referred to a select committee, for them to take into consideration whether it was advisable for the State to accept the grant, and if so, to devise the method of disposing of the lands and the mode of improving the river

' The committee, after having the matter under consideration several weeks, through their Chairman, Dr. James Davis, of Wapello County, made a very lengthy report, in which they took the ground that the grant was not limited to lands below the Raccoon Fork, but extended to every alternate section for five miles on each side of the river to the northwestern boundary of the State, if not to the source of the river They estimated the grant to contain 400,-000 acres below the Raccoon Fork, and 560,000 above, making 960,000 acres of land. The report of the committee at first was looked upon as visionary, and but very little calculation was made on getting any land above the fork of the river; but a matter of so much importance was not passed over without examination and full discussion.

"From this time on, for several years, the improvement of the river Des Moines entered largely into the politics of the State Politicians became interested in it, the construction put upon the grant by the committee was the popular side, and found many advocates, and scarcely any one opposed it. The committee reported in favor of receiving the grant, with provisos, and a bill for creating a Board of Public Works. On this report the Legislature passed an act accepting the grant, with a proviso that it was not to form a part of the 500,000 acres which the State was entitled to by an act of Congress of 1841, giving to each new State that amount of land for internal improvements This was conceded by the General Government, and it also permitted the State to divert 500,000 acres from works of internal improvement to the purpose of education The Legislature, on the 5th of February, 1847, also passed an act creating a Board of Public Works, and providing for the improvement of the river. The Board consisted of a President, Secretary and Treasurer, who were to be elected by the qualified electors of the State, on the first Monday of the following August The President was to be the active agent of the work, and was required to make monthly reports of his doings and of the progress of his work to the Board; the Secretary was to record the proceedings of the Board and to sell the lands, the Treasurer was to receive and disburse the moneys The officers were required to commence the work on the Mississippi, near Keokuk, at the mouth of Dead Slough, or of the Nassau Slough, and then up the slough to the river. And subsequently the work was commenced by undertaking to dig a canal from the mouth of the Nassau Slough to St Francisville, the first place on the river where it was thought practicable to build a dam

" About $150,000 was expended in the effort, but the attempt proved to be an impracticable undertaking and after expending this large amount of money, the work of digging a canal was abandoned.   At the August election, Hugh W. Sample, of Jefferson County. was elected President , Charles Corckery, of Dubuque County, Secretary, and Paul Braton, of Van Buren County, Treasurer   The officers elected were qualified, and at first opened their offices at Fairfield   Samuel Curtis. from Ohio, was selected by the Board as Chief Engineer ; but there was very little done this season toward improving the river, further than making surveys   The necessary surveys having been completed, early in the spring of 1848, the work was commenced.   The canal and three dams were put under contract, and about five hundred hands were put at work   On the 21st of August, the building of ten more dams was contracted for, and there seemed to be a fair prospect for the speedy completion of the entire improvement.

" There was at this time but very little known of the resources of the upper valley of the river Des Moines   This year, by authority of the United States, provisions were made for a geological survey in Iowa, and a party was sent up the river, which explored it to its source   The report made by this party was very flattering   They reported that coal was found for two hundred miles on the Des Moines. and from indications, heavy deposits of iron were believed to exist : that gypsum in abundance, forming cliffs for miles, was encountered ; and that limestone, that makes a superior hydraulic lime, existed in abundance ; limestone suitable for lime, clay suitable for brick, rock suitable for polishing. for grindstones, whetstones and for building purposes, some of superior quality, were found in abundance along the Des Moines   And Col Curtis, in speculating upon the future, in his report to the Legislature, led the people to anticipate great results from this improvement.   He said . ' No country can afford like accommodations to manufacturers ; no country can produce more agricultural wealth than that within sixty miles on either side of this river '   And further . ' That, taking all things into consideration, the matter is mathematically certain (except in times of high water in the Missouri), the trade of Council Bluffs will incline to follow down the improvement   But it is not this point alone that is reached , we enter the great valley of Nebraska, and the upper branches of the Missouri. and offer the commerce of these valleys the cheapest and most expeditious route for their products   A country of a thousand miles extent, capable of furnishing vast and unknown agricultural and mineral products may, by wise and discreet energy in the prosecution of this work. become tributary to the improvement now in progress on the Des Moines.'

" These glowing reports of the country and the advantages to be derived from the improvement of the river excited the public mind to the highest expectations, and the people became very anxious to secure as much of the public lands as possible. that this great undertaking might be speedily completed ; and to ascertain the construction put upon the grant by the General Government, application was made to the Land Department for a decision. Richard M. Young, the Commissioner of the General Land Office on the 23d day of February, 1848, in a letter addressed to the Board of Public Works. gave it as his opinion that the State was entitled to the alternate sections within five miles of the Des Moines River, through the whole extent of Iowa. This decision gave assurances that the amount of land claimed would be received   The Board of Improvement made great preparation for rapidly pushing on the work, and the public mind was exhilarated with the greatest hopes of speedily realizing the great advantages represented to be derived from this undertaking

"But, as it is the lot of man to meet with disappointments, such seems to have been the result in this case, for it was found that the lands could not be sold fast enough to meet the expenses of so extensive a work as had been undertaken To remedy this difficulty, the Board of Public Works recommended to the Legislature 'that bonds, bearing the sanction of the supreme power of the State, should be issued by the Board, and pledging the proceeds of the sales of the lands, as well as the tolls of the improvement, for their redemption But this policy did not meet with the sanction of some of the leading Democrats of the State, who regarded such a measure as not being in accordance with Democratic principles, among whom were Ver Plank Van Antwerp. Van Antwerp, having held the office of Receiver in the first land office established in the Southern Iowa, and then holding the same office at Fairfield, and also, for awhile, editor of a paper, was extensively known, and at that time exerted much influence among the people, and he took a very active part against the proposition recommended by the Board He claimed that the measure was not only Antidemocratic, but impolitic, and went to Iowa City as a lobby member, and made himself very busy with the members to defeat it; and the opposition with which it met from Van Antwerp and other private individuals had its effect with the members of the Legislature, and the measure was defeated, much to the discomfiture of Sample. The interference of Van Antwerp with the recommendations of the Board created a coolness between Sample and Van Antwerp which caused some singular results in the future political matters of the State

"During the summer of 1848, a portion of the land above the Raccoon Fork was brought into the market and offered for sale at the land office at Iowa City, and some of the lands which it was supposed were embraced within the river grant were sold by the General Government The failure of the Board to get the Legislature to authorize them to issue bonds, and the selling of these lands by the General Government, greatly frustrated the plans of the Board and put a damper upon the public expectation For the purpose of securing the full amount of land claimed, the Legislature passed a memorial asking Congress to enact an explanatory law confirming to the State the quantity of land claimed But Congress did not feel disposed to do this, and the extent of the grant was a disputed question for several years.

"At the August election, in 1849, the officers of the Board of Public Works were to be again elected, and the old officers were desirous of holding on to their offices, and Sample made great efforts to have the old officers renominated by the State Convention for candidates before the people Those who were in favor of issuing bonds for the speedy completion of the work were in favor of re-electing the old Board; those who were against this measure were opposed to them Among those who took an active part against the old Board was Van Antwerp, and his opposition was particularly made against Sample, which got up much ill-feeling between them Van Antwerp, to accomplish his ends before the convening of the Convention, prepared a stricture on Sample's political acts. which 'showed him up' in no very enviable light. Van Antwerp went to Iowa City, where the Convention was to be held a short time before it convened, and had his strictures printed in handbill form, and on the morning of the Convention circulated copies all over the city, so that a copy found its way into the hands of every delegate. This had the effect to beat Sample and the other

officers of the Board, and William Patterson, of Lee County, was nominated for
President; Jesse Williams, of Johnston, for Secretary ; and George Gillaspy,
of Wapello, for Treasurer

"These individuals were all elected, entered upon the duties of their trust,
and with energy undertook to complete all the work which had been put under
contract   But they soon found that they could not sell lands fast enough to
meet their expenditures, and had to suspend a portion of the work.   But they
did not do this until they had contracted a large amount of debts, which they
had not the means to pay   The new board, on making settlements with the
contractors, not having the money to pay them, issued bonds or certificates of
indebtedness, pledging the lands for their payment, and binding the Board to
redeem them as soon as they had the means to do it   So the new Board, without the sanction of law, did what the old Board had tried to get the Legislature
to authorize them to do by law, and for which policy they were turned out of
office and others put in their place   Those contractors who were stopped from
going on with their work claimed damages, legal proceedings were had and
some of them recovered large amounts

"The course pursued by the new Board met with much censure from the
public and the newspapers, particularly the Whig press was very severe in its
strictures   The course which had been pursued by the Board of Public Works
made the improvement of the river Des Moines a prominent matter before the
Legislature, which convened in December, 1850   The issuing of bonds did not
meet with the approval of that body, and a law was passed abolishing the offices
of President, Secretary and Treasurer, and the offices of 'Commissioner and
Register of the Des Moines River Improvement' were created, which, instead
of being elected by the people, were appointed by the Governor, by and with
the consent of the Senate

"As soon as the law abolishing the Board of Public Works went into effect,
the Governor appointed Ver Planck Van Antwerp Commissioner, and George
Gillaspy Register of the Improvement, who, on the 9th of June, 1851, entered
into a contract with Bangs Brothers & Co., of New York, in which they stipulated to complete the whole work, from the mouth of the river to the Raccoon
Fork, in four years from the time when for the improvement of the river a
confirmation should be secured of the extension of the grant of land above that
point   When the contract was closed, Bangs Brothers & Co and the officers of
the Improvement went to work and succeeded in getting the Land Department
of the General Government to reconsider the decision in which it had been held
that the grant of land only extended to the Raccoon Fork, and obtained a
decision that it extended to the northern boundary of the State, which gave
hopes that the river would soon be made navigable.   On the first reception of
the news, there was much rejoicing, but when the details of the contract with
Bangs, Brothers & Co were made public, it was found that the contract provided that the lands below the Raccoon Fork were not to be sold for less than
$2 00 per acre, and those above for not less than $5 00

"This gave great dissatisfaction, for a great portion of these lands was
occupied by claimants who expected to buy their claims at $1 25 per acre, as
others had done who had settled upon Government lands.   This provision
stirred up much ill-feeling among the settlers; public meetings were held, and
this part of the contract was condemned in the strongest terms; and such were
the feelings that there were apprehensions of serious difficulties if this part of
the contract should be enforced   But when these excitements were at their
highest news came that Bangs Brothers & Co had failed, and probably their

R. N. Aesop M.D.

BONAPARTE

contract would be annulled. and this allayed the public feeling. Bangs Brothers & Co did not comply with their contract in furnishing means, and the work on the river did not go on, and the public expectation of a speedy completion of the proposed improvement vanished.

" The officers of the Improvement were appointed for only two years, and at the expiration of their term of office, Van Antwerp was re-appointed Commissioner, and Paul C Jeffries was appointed Register. But these last appointed officers held their trust but a short time, for during the past two years the work on the river had progressed very slowly; the contract with Bangs Brothers & Co had been declared forfeited, and it was understood that other sources were to be looked to for going on with the work. The officers appointed by the Governor not being successful in their undertaking. the Legislature, on the 1st of January, 1853, repealed the law authorizing the Governor to appoint, and made these officers again to be elected by the people, and on the first Monday in the following April, Josiah Bonney, of Van Buren County, was elected Commissioner and George Gillaspy, Register And, for the purpose of aiding the Commissioners in conducting and concluding any contract on the subject of improving the river. the Legislature appointed George G Wright, of Van Buren County, and Uriah Biggs, of Wapello, his assistants, ' with equal powers of the Commissioner in making and determining such contract.'

" From past experience, it was not deemed advisable to parcel out the work to many individuals, and consequently these officers were required by the Legislature not to make any contract, unless such contract stipulated for ' at least $1,300,000 to be faithfully expended in the payment of the debts and liabilities of the Improvement, and its completion to the greatest extent possible.' And to this end, if it was necessary, they were authorized ' to sell and dispose of all and any lands which had been or might hereafter be granted by Congress for the improvement of the river, and, if it was necessary to effect a contract, they were authorized to convey the right to tolls and water rents arising from the Improvement, for the length of time and upon such terms as they might deem expedient. But in disposing of the lands, they were not to contract them for less than $1.25 per acre,' and if no contract of this character should be made before the 1st of September, 1853, then the pay of all the officers connected with the work, except the Register and one engineer, was to cease, and all operations connected with the work, except such parts as were under contract, were to be suspended until further action by the Legislature. The Register was required to put all unfinished work then under contract in such a condition as to prevent it from injury, and to see that all property of the State connected with the work was carefully preserved If the Register, at any time subsequent, should receive propositions which he deemed sufficient for consideration. he was to submit the same to the Commissioner, and should a contract be made on the terms required by the Legislature, then the pay of the officers should commence and the work go on as though it had not been suspended

" The new Commissioner, being conscientious about the expending of money, immediately after taking charge of the work, dismissed all the engineers, except Guy Wells, the chief engineer, and employed no officer or other persons, except when the necessity of the work imperatively demanded it There were in several places of the river snags and bowlders, which much obstructed the navigation, and had become a source of much inconvenience and complaint; but during the official term of Bonney the river was 'cleared of snags bowlders and other obstructions to such an extent as to make the navigation of the river, at proper stages of the water, safe.

"The Commissioner and his associates, after assuming the duties of their trust, entered into correspondence with such persons and companies as they thought likely to embark in such an enterprise And by this means they succeeded in eliciting the attention of capitalists to such an extent that a number of persons came to the State for the purpose of investigation These persons, by an examination of the valley of the Des Moines personally, and making themselves acquainted with the resources of the country, on their return East, imparted to others the undeveloped wealth and advantages of the valley, which was the means of bringing many good and enterprising citizens to the State Among others who visited Iowa for the purpose of investigation was Henry O'Rielly, a man who had acquired some considerable notoriety as a contractor in putting up telegraph wires, and he proposed to undertake the work Such was the known reputation of O'Rielly as a contractor that the Commissioner and his associates commenced the negotiating of a contract And 'on the 17th of December, 1853, Henry O'Rielly, Esq of New York, entered into a contract with the Commissioners, in which, for the consideration of the unsold lands belonging to the Improvement, and tolls and water rents and other profits arising from the work, for the term of forty years, agreed to complete the entire work within a period of four years from the 1st day of July, 1854, according to the original surveys and specifications made by the engineers.'

"Immediately upon entering upon this contract, O'Rielly returned East and organized a company, under the laws of Iowa, called the 'Des Moines Navigation & Railroad Company,' to which O'Rielly assigned his contract, himself being one of the officers of the Company. On the 9th of June, 1854, by the consent and request of O'Rielly, and with the approbation of the officers of the River Improvement, the contract with O'Rielly was canceled, and another contract was made with the Des Moines Navigation & Railroad Company. In this contract, the Company agreed to pay all outstanding debts against the Improvement within ninety days from the date of said contract, to settle and pay all damages against the State of Iowa on account of the prosecution of said work, to mill-owners, or others who have, or might thereafter, sustain damages on account of the same; to pay the salaries and expenses of the officers and engineers in charge of the work, to complete the Improvement from the mouth of the Des Moines River to Fort Des Moines, in accordance with the original plans and specifications of the State Engineer, by the 1st day of July, 1858, and to construct the whole work in such a manner as to assure the navigation of the same for the longest period each year practicable, and to complete at least one-fourth of the work each and every year, commencing on the 1st day of July, 1854

"In consideration of this understanding, the Commissioner agreed to convey to the Company all the unsold lands belonging to the Improvement, the use of the work, the tolls and water rents for the term of forty-one years And afterward, in consideration of the Company enlarging the works and making some other improvements in the navigation of the river, and also on account of there not being as large a quantity of land undisposed of below Fort Dodge as was understood to be by the Commissioners and the Company at the time of making the contract, a majority of the Commissioners, Bonney and Biggs, entered into an article of agreement with the Company, in which they promised to extend the time of the Company's use and control of the work to seventy-five years

"Under his contract, it could be expected that the work would be immediately commenced by the new contractors and speedily completed The great expectations which at first had been raised by the contractors, under the name of the 'Des Moines Navigation & Railroad Company,' soon after they undertook the work began to diminish; for there soon arose disagreements and misunderstandings among themselves. The Company had been organized under the general incorporation laws of Iowa, and, consequently, was subject to the laws of the State. At the called session of the Legislature, in 1856, Donald Mann, a stockholder of the Company, memorialized the Legislature to correct the 'manifold abuses' of which he charged the Directors of the Company to have been guilty. In this memorial, he charged that the managers of the Company had, in various ways, 'corruptly, and for corrupt purposes,' violated the laws of the State, 'greatly to the injury of the people thereof, and to the great loss and damage of the stockholders,' and showed in detail wherein they had acted corruptly and violated the laws under which the Company was incorporated. Among other things, he stated that, 'for the purpose of deceiving the people and individuals in relation to their means,' they had represented to the public and to individuals that there had been paid into the treasury 'enormous sums of money, on account of stock sold, for much larger amounts than had been received.' And, the better to accomplish and maintain such deceptions, the Managers (or a majority of them) caused to be issued certificates of stock to the amount of, nominally, $630,000, or six thousand three hundred shares of $100, for cash, of which shares they had represented to the public and individuals that the holder had paid the sum of $100, amounting to $630,000, when, as a matter of fact, there was only 5 per cent paid on each share, by which means the public and many individuals were deceived.'

"Henry O Rielly, the individual with whom the contract had first been made, a stockholder and one of the Directors, also memorialized the Legislature for an investigation of the affairs of the Company, in which he re-asserted the charges made by Mann, and stated that he held himself ready, if the Legislature would order an investigation of the doings of the Company, to prove, from the records of the Company and from other evidence, 'that there was scarcely an important provision in the code of Iowa (applicable to corporations), scarcely an important point in the Des Moines Improvement laws, scarcely an important provision in the contract which the Company agreed to fulfill, scarcely an essential provision in its by-laws, or even in the charter which gave it legal existence, which had not been violated and violated with a recklessness that will form a memorable feature in the history of Iowa.'

"A joint committee was appointed from both branches of the Legislature, at the called session to investigate the alleged abuses; but, owing to the short time in which they had to act, it was impossible for them to make the necessary investigation. An attempt was made to create a committee for this purpose to act after the Legislature adjourned; but this failed, so that the alleged abuses passed by without examination at that time. These memorials to the Legislature and the discussion of these matters by the newspapers greatly prejudiced the public mind against the Company; and while these discussions were going on, W. C. Johnson, the President of the Company, requested the Governor to examine into its affairs, in person or by committee, and proposed to pay the expenses of such an examination. The Governor did not feel disposed to comply with the request, but referred the matter to the Legislature, which convened the following December, and recommended that a committee should be appointed with power to administer oaths and to send for persons and papers with instructions to inquire into all the transactions of the former Commissioners and Registers of the Improvement.

" This part of the Governor's message was referred to a committee of twelve, consisting of members of both branches of the Legislature, who immediately proceeded to the discharge of their duties. After a careful and thorough examination, this committee reported that they did not consider the contract made by the Commissioners with the Company a valid contract on behalf of the State, for the law which authorized the Commissioner and Register to make contracts required that any contract made by them, to be valid, must be approved by the Governor, and that the subsequent law, which created two Assistant Commissioners, did not do away with the provision requiring the Governor to approve of such contracts And, as the contract made with the Company had never been approved by the Governor, they did not regard it as binding on the State. The Committee also reported that the Company had acted in bad faith, and violated their charter in many ways ; and, among other things, they found that over $1,000,000 of full-paid stock had been issued by the Company, upon which had been received but $167,000, leaving a deficit of $833,000, for which certificates of full-paid stock had been issued, for which not a farthing had been received by the Company, which had been sold to innocent purchasers for a valuable consideration who had purchased, believing its full value had been paid into the treasury of the Company The Company had come far short of completing the amount of work which they were required to do under their contract, and their acts gave strong indications that their object was to expend money enough to get possession of all the available lands, and then abandon the work , for more than one-half of the time which was given for completing the entire contract had expired, and on a work which was estimated to cost about $2,000,000 they had expended about $185 957 44 for an actual construction of the work, while the Company claimed that they had expended $104,180 74 for incidental expenses, the most part of which did not, in any manner, benefit the Improvement Yet the Company claimed that they were entitled to land at $1.25 per acre in payment for the whole amount

" On the 2d of April, 1855. William McKay, of Polk County, was elected Commissioner, and John C Lockwood, of Louisa County, Register ; but in November 1856, McKay resigned, and Edwin Manning, of Van Buren County, was appointed by the Governor to fill his place Manning bore the name of a good business man and a close financier, and he was not willing to audit the claims for incidental expenses, as one for which the Company were entitled to receive land . and this became a matter of dispute between the Company and Commissioner, and, in order to have the matter adjusted, the President proposed to make an abatement of $72,000 , but Manning did not feel disposed to settle the matter himself. and referred the whole claim to the Legislature

" Manning, in his report to the Legislature, showed that there had been sold by the State, through the Board of Public Works, during the six years that the State prosecuted the work, about $75,000 worth of land , and for this sum only ' three stone-masonry locks' and two dams had been completed; and there had been certified to the Des Moines Navigation & Railroad Company, by Bonney and Gillaspy, 88,853 19-100 acres of land, and by McKay and Lockwood, 116,636 4-100 acres, at $1.25 per acre, making $256,861.53 worth of land, which had been disposed of to the present Company. a part of which amount was for old debts which they had paid

" The report of the Committee and Commissioner having been made to the Legislature, that body, acting upon the premises that the contract which had been made by the Commissioners with the Company was not binding upon the

State, on the 29th of January, 1857, passed an act by which there was to be a Commissioner appointed by the Governor, who, with the regular Commissioner, was authorized to contract for the speedy prosecution of the work, and it was made their duty to ascertain and pay off all just claims against the Improvement, and they were authorized to contract with any company for the sale of all lands, tolls and water rents who would give satisfactory evidence and security for the completion of the Improvement. But they were not to bind the State by any contract further than the appropriation of the land and the income of the Improvement; and no contract made by the Commissioners was to be valid until approved by the Governor. And by this act, the offices of Register and Assistant Commissioner were abolished, and the Register was required to deliver over to the State Land Office all books and papers in his office; and the Register of the State Land Office was required to perform all the duties which the Register of the Improvement had done. And by thus doing, the Legislature gave the Des Moines Navigation & Railroad Company to understand that they did not regard the contract made by them with the Commissioners as binding upon the State, though by this act they made arrangements for auditing their claims and paying them their just dues.

About this time. the question was brought up in the Land Department at Washington as to the extent of this grant of land and the opinion was made public that the original intention of Congress was to only give to the State the lands below the Raccoon Fork; but a disposition was manifested to compromise by the department recognizing as being in the grant all lands adjacent to the river within the State. But assumptions had heretofore met with success, and now those interested in the land-grant claimed and contended that this grant embraced all the lands to the source of the river. This difficulty about the extent of the land-grant, together with the action of the Legislature, nearly suspended all operations on the river, and much was said by the Company about enforcing their claims by law.

"The Commissioners appointed to audit and pay the claims against the Improvement did not succeed in adjusting the claims of the Company, and the matter was again referred to the Legislature; and. on the 22d of March, 1858, there was a joint resolution passed by the Legislature, defining the basis upon which the State would settle, and the Des Moines Navigation & Railroad Company was given sixty days to consider whether they would accept of and ratify this proposition. and if they did not, within that time, then it was made the duty of the Governor to enjoin them from further proceeding with the work of the Improvement. Also, on the same day of adopting this resolution, there was an act passed giving all the lands which remained after settling with this Company, 'and also all the stone. timber and other materials turned over to the State by the Company, to the Keokuk, Fort Des Moines & Minnesota Railroad Company, for the purpose of constructing a railroad from Keokuk up the Des Moines Valley, to the northern line of the State. except the material which it might be necessary to use for the completion of the locks and dams at Croton, Plymouth, Bentonsport and Keosauqua, which the Railroad Company were to complete, and also, all debts which grew out of the Improvement. which at that time remained unsatisfied, or were, in some manner, provided for. But in this grant there was a provision made that it should not, in any manner, conflict with the lands which had previous to that time, been given to the State by Congress for railroad purposes which. on the 15th of July 1856 had been given by the Legislature to the companies formed to build the four roads designated by the grant. But it was understood that these lands, having been donated by Congress for the improvement of the navigation of the river Des Moines, could not be diverted to the building of a railroad without the consent of Congress, and measures were immediately taken to get Congress to sanction the diversion, but this attempt failed, so that the action of the Iowa Legislature did not avail the Railroad Company anything that session. The Railroad Company determined to make another effort at the next session of Congress; but before the time for this effort, another difficulty arose in the way of obtaining the lands for the Keokuk, Fort Des Moines & Minnesota Railroad Company.

" In setting up the claims that the grants for improving the river Des Moines extended above the Raccoon Fork, the citizens of Iowa were united until after the grant of lands by Congress for railroad purposes was made After this, the railroad companies became interested in the lands claimed for the River Improvement, and claimed that the grant did *not* embrace any lands above the Raccoon Fork, on which the citizens of Iowa were now divided, and both sides of the question were represented Upon this phase of the case, the officer of the Land Department at Washington had but very little hesitation in deciding against the claims of the River Improvement. After this decision was made, the legal tribunals were resorted to, and a case was taken to the Supreme Court of the United States, where the same decision was given as in the Land Office

On the 3d of March, 1860, there was an act passed abolishing the office of Commissioner of the Des Moines River Improvement, and George G Wright, Edward Johnson and Christian W. Slagle were appointed a Board of Commissioners for the purpose of ascertaining all the liabilities against the Des Moines River Improvement, and against the State of Iowa, growing out of the Improvement They were required to meet at Keosauqua, and were clothed with power similar to the District Court, to hear and determine all claims growing out of the Improvement, and were authorized to sell all the interests of the State, and all dams and improvements, and the lands appertaining thereto. These Commissioners proceeded with their duties, and with their labors closed all official acts, as far as the State was concerned, in applying the proceeds of this land grant toward the improvement of the navigation of the river Des Moines

" This was a most magnificent grant, embracing some of the best lands in the State, and if the proceeds had been judiciously and properly expended, would have made a great thoroughfare for steamboats, besides affording an immense water-power for driving machinery But, through the incompetency of managing the means, and the intrigues of designing men, the whole of the lands below the Raccoon Fork, and a large quantity above, were disposed of, and very little practical good accomplished toward the navigation of the river "

ORIGIN OF THE NAME DES MOINES

In Nicollet's " Report of the Upper Mississippi River," made to Congress, February 16, 1841, and published in 1843, he gives the following account of the origin of the name of the Des Moines River :

" The Des Moines is one of the most beautiful and important tributaries of the Mississippi north of the Missouri, and the metamorphosis which its name has undergone from its original appellation is curious enough to be recorded

" We are informed that Father Marquette and M. Joliet, during their voyage in search of the Mississippi, having reached the distance of sixty leagues below the mouth of the Wisconsin, observed the footprints of men on the right side of the great river, which served as a guide to those two celebrated explorers to the discovery of an Indian trail, or path, leading to an extensive prairie, and which they determined to follow Having proceeded about two leagues, they first saw one village on the bank of the river, and then two others upon the slope, half a league from the first. The travelers, having halted within hailing distance, were met by the Indians, who offered them their hospitalities, and represented themselves as belonging to the Illinois nation.

" The name which they gave their settlement was *Moningouinas* (or *Moingona*, as laid down in the ancient maps of the country), and is a corruption of the Algonquin word, *Mikouang*, signifying *at the road*, by their customary elliptical manner of designating localities, alluding, in this instance, to the well-known road in this section of the country which they used to follow as a communication between the head of the lower rapids and their settlement on the river which empties itself into the Mississippi, to avoid the rapids, and this is still the practice of the present inhabitants of the country

" Now, after the French had established themselves on the Mississippi, they adopted this name, but with their custom (to this day also that of the Creoles) of only pronouncing the first syllable, and applying it to the river as well as to the Indians who dwelt upon it—so they would say, '*la riviere des Moines*' (*the river of the Moines*). '*allez chez les Moines*' (to go to the Moines people). But in latter times the inhabitants associated this name with that of the Trappist Monks (*Moines de la Trappe*), who resided with the Indians of the American Bottom

" It was then concluded that the true reading of the *riviere des Moines* was the '*riviere des Moines*,' or river of Monks, by which name it is designated on all the modern maps. The Sioux, or *Ndakotah* Indians, call the Des Moines *Inyan-sha-sha-watpa*, or Redstone River, from *inyan*, stone, *sha-sha*, reduplication of *sha*, red, and *watpa*, river They call the upper east fork *Inyan-sha-sha-watpa-sunkaku*, the Brother of the Redstone River "

WAR RECORD

If there is any one thing more than another of which the people of the Northern States have reason to be proud, it is of the record they made during the dark and bloody days when red-handed rebellion raised its hideous head and threatened the life of the nation. When the war was forced upon the country, the people were quietly pursuing the even tenor of their ways, doing whatever their hands found to do—working the mines, making farms or cultivating those already made, erecting houses, founding cities and towns, building shops and manufactories—in short, the country was alive with industry and hopes for the future The people were just recovering from the depression and losses incident to the financial panic of 1857. The future looked bright and promising, and the industrious and patriotic sons and daughters of the Free States were buoyant with hope, looking forward to the perfecting of new plans for the insurement of comfort and competence in their declining years; they little heeded the mutterings and threatenings of treason rife in the Slave States of the South. True sons and descendants of the heroes of the times that tried men's souls'—the struggle for American Independence—they never

dreamed that there was even one so base as to dare attempt the destruction of
the Union of their fathers—a government baptized with the best blood the
world ever knew   While immediately surrounded with peace and tranquillity,
they paid but little attention to the rumored plots and plans of those who lived
and grew rich from the sweat and toil, blood and flesh, of others—aye, even
trafficking in the offspring of their own loins   Nevertheless, the war came,
with all its attendant horrors

April 12, 1861, Fort Sumter, at Charleston, South Carolina, Maj. Anderson, U S A , Commandant, was fired on by rebels in arms   Although basest
treason, this first act in the bloody reality that followed was looked upon as the
mere bravado of a few hot-heads—the act of a few fire-eaters whose sectional
bias and hatred was crazed by the excessive indulgence in intoxicating pota-
tions   When, a day later the news was borne along the telegraph wires that
Maj Anderson had been forced to surrender to what had first been regarded as
a drunken mob, the patriotic people of the North were startled from their dreams
of the future, from undertakings half completed, and made to realize that
behind that mob there was a dark, deep and well-organized purpose to destroy
the Government, rend the Union in twain, and out of its ruins erect a slave
oligarchy, wherein no one should dare to question their right to hold in bondage
the sons and daughters of men whose skins were black, or who, perchance,
through practices of lustful natures, were half or quarter removed from the
color that God, for His own purposes, had given them   But they "reckoned
without their host "   Their dreams of the future, their plans for the establishment of an independent confederacy, were doomed from their inception to sad
and bitter disappointment

When the Southern rebels fired upon Fort Sumter, it found this vast North
unarmed, untrained in the art of war, and in a state of such profound peace as
to warrant the belief that hostilities could not be begun by those who had,
since the foundation of this Union, boasted loudly of their loyalty to the Constitution of the United States.   The rumors of disaffection that had alarmed
the more watchful had aroused but trifling fears in the breasts of the great mass
of Northern citizens   War between the States had, prior to that time, been
deemed an impossibility   The sentiments of fraternal unity were so deep-
abiding in the hearts of the North, that treason was regarded as an improbable
crime, and overt acts of antagonism to the Government too base in their
intent to be worthy of serious consideration

But the hand of the aged Ruffin, as he laid the blazing torch upon the gun
within Stevens' battery lighted a flame which spread throughout the land with
electric rapidity, and illumined the nation with a glare that revealed the truth
of rebel threats   The boom of that first gun awakened the passive people to
the dread reality of their position.   From Maine to Oregon, from Superior to
the Ohio, the country arose, as with a single impulse, to respond to the demands
of the hour.   There was no need of prompting them, no need of canvassing
for strength, no hesitating as to measures, no thought of compromise.   But one
course could be pursued, and that the people comprehended as though inspired
by some higher mentor   The Union must be preserved   Each individual
member of society felt the urgent necessity of prompt and concerted action
Towns did not wait to hear tidings from sister towns, each heard in the roar
of brave old Sumter's guns a summons direct, imperative and irresistible, for
aid in . . . . R . . . . nd in politics
grasp . . . . l . . . . . . l . . . . no longer, save
in the . . . . f . izen-soldiery.

Almost simultaneous with the news of the attack upon Sumter, came the call from President Lincoln for troops. In the remote towns and rural localities, where telegraphic communication had not then penetrated the appeal and the response were recorded at the same time.

On the 15th of April, the President issued his call for 75,000 ninety-days troops. The State of Iowa was particularly fortunate in having as its Chief Executive Samuel J. Kirkwood, whose loyalty and unceasing devotion to the cause of the Union have embalmed his name forever in the annals of the State. Within thirty days after the President's demand was made public, Iowa had a regiment in the field.

If it was within the province of this work to relate the story of Van Buren's loyalty, the limits of this volume would be extended far beyond those anticipated by the publishers. Some future historian, we have no doubt will find a fruitful topic in this record of war, and lay before the people of this county a narrative of unsurpassed interest. Surely the opportunity exists and awaits the patient labors of a competent writer.

The county lay so near the line of the Slave States that party feeling ran high throughout all the war. Local agitations were frequent over rumored invasions. The loyalty of the county was all the more marked because of the hazard of entertaining such sentiments.

The long list of brave men who formed the volunteer companies from Van Buren is here appended.

VOLUNTEER ROSTER.

TAKEN PRINCIPALLY FROM ADJUTANT GENERAL'S REPORTS

ABBREVIATIONS.

Adjt.	Adjutant	inf	infantry
Art	Artillery	I V I	Iowa Volunteer Infantry
Bat	Battle or Battalion	kld	killed
Col.	Colonel	Lieut	Lieutenant
Capt	Captain	Maj	Major
Corp	Corporal	m o	mustered out
Comsy	Commissary	prmtd	promoted
com	commissioned	prisr	prisoner
cav	cavalry	Regt	Regiment
captd	captured	re-e	re-enlisted
desrtd	deserted	res	resigned
disab	disabled	Sergt	Sergeant
disd.	discharged	trans	transferred
e.	enlisted	vet	veteran
excd	exchanged	V R C	Veteran Reserve Corps
hon disd	honorably discharged	wd.	wounded
inv	invalid		

SECOND INFANTRY

[Note.—The non-veterans of this regiment were mustered out in April, May and June, 1864. The veterans and recruits were consolidated into the Second Veteran Infantry, which was made a full regiment November 8, 1864, by consolidating with the Third Veteran Infantry. Was mustered out at Louisville July 12, 1865.]

Col. Jas. M. Tuttle, com lieut col May 31, 1861, prmtd col Sept 6 1861 wd Ft Donelson, brig gen U. S. Vols June 22, 1862

Q. M. John T. Stewart, com 2d lieut Co F June 1, 1861, prmtd June 6 1861, resd Aug 7, 1861

Company F

Capt Allen T. Brooks, com June 1, 1861, resd Nov 1, 1861

First Lieut Chas C. Parker, e as sergt May 1, 1861, prmtd 1st lieut May 14 1862 wd Corinth

Second Lieut Wm C Harper, e as sergt May 1 1861, prmtd 2d lieut Aug 21, 1861 kld Ft Donelson

Second Lieut Wm Browner e as sergt prmtd sergt maj, prmtd 2d lieut Feb 17, 62, wd Shiloh died Savannah, Tenn

Second Lieut V P. Twombly e as corp May 1, 1861, wd Ft Donelson, prmtd 2d lieut Aug 1, 1862 wd Corinth

Sergt James Ferry, e May 1, 1861

Sergt John H Hall e May 1 1861 died April 6, 1862

Sergt Wm M M

Sergt Wm Sawyer May 1 1861, died April 1

Sergt Geo J Bonney e May 1 1861

Sergt Geo W Morse, e May 1, 1861, kld battle Ft Donelson

Sergt Peter Watts, e May 1, 1861

Sergt Cyrus Bartow, e Nov 5. 1861, vet. Dec 28, 1863, from 1st lieut. Aug 18, 1864, kld in action Aug. 30

Corp Saml Huffman. e May 1, 1861, died wds March 23, 1862

Corp Benj Wilson, e May 1, 1861 died at Keokuk Oct 23, 1862.

Corp Jas Schrawger. e May 1 1861, wd Ft Donelson

Corp M A Lane e May 1 1861, disd Aug 25 1861

Corp Jas. Carr, e May 1 1861 wd. Fort Donelson

Corp John F Bateman, e May 1, 1861, disd Feb 7, 1862

Corp Wm C Dicus, e May 1, 1861 disd March, 1863

Corp Wm Van Fleet, e May 1, 1861, died Feb 24, 1862

Drummer J N Tutewiler, e May 1 1861, disd Dec 2 1862

Wagoner Jas Pickett e Aug 1, 1861, wd died Keokuk

Armstrong, T M, e May 1, 1861, disd July 21, 1862.

Allinsworth, James, e May 1, 1861, disd Sept 6, 1862

Brownfield Zadoc, e. May 1, 1861, disd April 2 1862 disab

Bakeman, Henry, e May 1, 1861

Bradford, A, e May 1, 1861, wd Ft Donelson

Buddle, Wm A e May 1, 1861

Botkin, Oscar, e May 1, 1861, disd Oct 9, 1861

Boehm, Solomon e May 1, 1861

Brewington C e May 1, 1861

Belott, L W, e May 1, 1861, disd Jan 16, 1862

Bint H e May 1, 1861, disd Nov 15 '61, disab

Banst, Wm, e May 1, 1861, died July 24, 1862

Brewington, L F, disd June 13, 1862

Crane Wm M, e May 1, 1861

Crooks, W S, e May 1, 1861, kld bat Ft Donelson

Caruthers, C, e May 1, 1861 died May 16 1862

Coger, C L, e May 1, 1861, disd July 22, 1862, wds

Cummings, A W, e May 1, 1861 died Oct 20 1861

Dunlap, John A, e May 1, 1861, died at Memphis

Dahlburg, John P e May 1, 1861, died Sept 28, 1861

Duffield, H e May 1, 1861, wd Ft Donelson, disd Oct 12, 1862

Duffield, J H, e May 1 1861, disd Sept 14, 1862

Dannels D P, May 1, '61

Elrod I H, May 1 '61, wd Corinth Inf

Feathers, S G, e May 1, 1861, wd Corinth

Goddard, C., e May 1, 1861, disd wds Sept 13, 1862

Hirt, Saml F, e May 1, 1861

Hornbacker, David, e May 1 1861, disd Dec. 6, 1861, disab

Hilliard, Aaron e May 1, 1861, disd Sept 19, 1861 disab

Hoak, H C, e May 1, 1861 kld Ft Donelson

Hoon, Wm J, e May 1, 1861

Henry, John B, e May 1 1861

Henry T P e. May 1, 1861, wd Corinth

Hall, Jas S e May 1 1861

Hearn, Saml, e May 1, 1861, wd Corinth

Krause, Henry, e May 1, 1861

Loring L H, e May 1, 1861

McClelland, Benj A, e May 1, 1861

May, Chas e May 1, 1861

Mitchell, H D, e May 1, 1861 died Aug 20, 1861

Marriott, John S e May 1 1861, wd Ft Donelson

Meltz, F G, e May 1 1861 kld. Ft Donelson

Mayne, Leroy, e May 1, 1861 trans to 3d Cavalry, Co G

Mowrie, A W, e May 1, 1861, disd April 2, 1862, disab

Morrow, John, e May 1, 1861, died June 22 1862

Nixon, Geo W, e May 1, 1861, died Jan, 1862

Perry, Jesse e May 1, '61, disd Jan 29, '63

Parker, J M, e May 1, 1861, wd Corinth, disd Jan 29 1863

Row, Jacob, e May 1, 1861

Robinson, J W, e May 1, 1861, died May 5, 1862

Skems, T H, e May 1 1861

Sagers, Jas H, e May 1, 1861, deserted at Keokuk June 1, 1861

Spenser, E, e May 1, 1861, disd Oct 14, 1861, disab

Sullivan, John M, e May 1, 1861

Smith, Geo e May 1, 1861, wd Ft Donelson and Corinth

Sherod, M C, e May 1, 1861, disd Nov 21, 1861, disab

Shiver A J, e May 1, 1861, died, date unknown

Smith, Thos, e May 1, 1861 died July 26, 1862

Steele, Geo K, e May 1, 1861, disd Sept 19, 1861.

Shriver, G B, e May 1, 1861, kld bat Ft Donelson

Stewart, H, e May 1, 1861, disd April 2, 1862

Shepard, Jas W, e May 1, 1861, disd Oct 10 1861

Town, Edwin, e May 1, 1861

Town, S J, e May 1, 1861, died Nov. 14, 1861

Tower, D W, e May 1, 1861, disd Dec 14, 1861

Vincent W W, e May 1, 1861, kld Ft Donelson

Vandoren, John S, e May 1, 1861, kld Ft
Donelson
Wilson F B, e May 1, 1861, disd Nov
20, 1862, wd
Ware, E W, e May 1, 1861
Reed, John, e May 1, 1861.
Riggin R A, e May 1, 1861
Robbinson, R R, e. May 1 1861 disd
July 31, 1862

Company C.

Proctor, David, e May 6 1861, captd Corinth

COMPANY UNKNOWN

Fowler, Jas A, e Jan 4, 1864
Robinson, Richard, e Jan 4, 1864
Stephens, Henry e Jan 4, 1864
Potter H C, e March 30, 1864
Potter, Edwin M, e Feb 29, 1864

SECOND VETERAN INFANTRY

Adjt Voltare P Twombly com June
25 1864, wd Aug 31, 1864

Company B

Davidson, Sailes, e Nov 23, 1861, vet Dec.
23 1863

Company C.

Leach, K N e April 24, 1861, vet Dec
18, 1863

Company E.

First Lieut Cyrus Bartow, com Aug 18,
1864, kld Jonesboro, Ga

Company H.

Fowler, James A, e Jan. 4, 1864.
Stevens, H S, e Jan 4, 1864

Company K.

Sergt Thos P Henry, e May 1, 1861, vet.
Dec 28, 1863
Corp A C Pickett, e May 1, 1861, vet
Dec 28, 1863
Corp. Edwin Towne, e May 1, 1861, vet
Dec 28, 1863
Corp John S Marriott, e May 1, 1861, vet
Dec. 28, 1863
Brewington, Chas, e May 1, 1861, vet Dec
28, 1863
Brooks Allen F, e March 21, 1864,
Feathers Sam'l G e May 1, 1861, vet
Dec 28, 1863
Henry, John B. e May 1, 1861, vet Dec
28, 1863
Klause Henry, e May 1 1861, vet Dec
28, 1863
May, Chas, e May 1 1861, vet Dec 28 '63
McAnnulty, Jas, e May 1, 1861, vet Dec
28, 1863
Pickett, Jas M, e Jan 16, 1864
Robbinson, R Richard, e Jan 4, 1864
Rowe, Jacob, e May 1, 1861 vet Dec 28,
1863
Work, Benj, e March 21, 1864
Ware, Elias M, e May 1 1861, vet Dec
28, 1863

SECOND CONSOLIDATED VET-
ERAN INFANTRY

Company K.

Capt. Voltaire P Twombly, com adjt
June 25, 1864, prmtd capt Nov 10, 1864

FIFTH INFANTRY

[NOTE—This regiment was mustered out August, 1864,
Veterans and recruits were transferred to Fifth Cavalry]

Chaplain Jas C Sharon, com April 12,
1862, resd Sept 3, 1862

Company C.

Hensley, Jas, e July 1, 1861, disd Dec 10,
1861 disab)
Jenkins, G, e July 1, 1861, wd Iuka, trans
to Inv Corps
Jones, Chas, e July 1, 1861, reported kld

Company H.

Capt John M Shaw, com July 15, 1861,
resd Oct 6, 1861
Capt Joel Brown, com 1st lieut July 15,
1861, prmtd capt Oct 6, 1861 wd Iuka
resd March 8, 1863
Capt Sam'l B Lindsay, e as sergt June
24, 1861, prmtd 1st lieut Nov 1, 1861,
prmtd capt March 9, 1863, kld battle
Champion Hills while 1st lieut
Capt Wm C Huber, e as sergt June 24,
1861, prmtd 2d lieut Jan 20 1862, prmtd
1st lieut March 9, 1863, prmtd capt
March 17, 1863, m o Aug 1, 1864, term
expired
First Lieut John W Huffman e as sergt
June 24, 1861, prmtd 2d lieut March 9,
1863, prmtd 1st lieut March 17, 1863,
captd Nov 25, 1863, disd March 24, '65
Second Lieut Bowen P Hurt com 1861
resd Jan 19, 1862
Second Lieut Jas A Woodson, e as corp
June 24, 1861 prmtd 2d lieut March 17,
1863, m. o July 31 1864, term expired
Sergt Wm S Hackney, e June 24, 1861,
disd July 12, 1861, disab)
Sergt H J Foster, e June 24, 1861
Sergt John Walker, e June 24, 1861, wd
Vicksburg
Sergt. Geo W Overturf, e June 24, 1861,
captd Missionary Ridge
Sergt R B Hughes, e June 24, 1861, kld
at Iuka
Sergt Robt Cunningham, e June 24, '61,
kld Champion Hills
Corp S B Culbertson, e June 24, 1861
Corp Chas Herriman, e June 24 1861
Corp Geo W Allender, e June 24, 1861,
wd Champion Hills, trans Inv Corps
Corp Porter Pleasants e June 24, 1861,
disd Dec 6, 1862, disab
Corp John H Fenning, e June 24, 1861
Corp R Speiry e June 24, 1861, disd
Sept 10 1862 disab
Corp. John Whitter e June 24, 1861,
captd Missionary Ridge

Corp R J H Huffman, e June 24 1861, captd Missionary Ridge

Corp Jacob T Overturf e June 24, 1861, wd Iuka disd Jan 19, 1863

Corp Wm Sutton, e June 24, 1861, wd Champion Hills, died there June 20, 1863

Corp Benj Watson, e June 24 1861, trans to Inv Corps Feb 15, 1864

Musician Wm W Miller, e June 24, 1861

Musician Enoch Augustine. e June 24, 1861, disd Sept 2, 1862

Armentrout, Geo W e July 21, 1861, kld. at Iuka

Arrington, M J, e June 24 1861, wd at Iuka

Allender, Wm, e Aug 25, 1862, wd at Champion Hills

Brown, Benj e June 24, 1861, disd Sept 25, 1862

Barker, E E, e Aug 15, 1862

Baldwin, Geo W, e June 24, 1861 wd at Iuka, trans to Inv Corps Feb 15, 1864

Coombs Jas e Aug 15, 1862

Campbell, Jas, e June 24, 1861 disd Oct 11 1862, disab

Cole, C S, e Aug 20 1862

Cole, Jno E, e June 24, 1861

Church, M H, e June 24, 1861 disd Oct 15, 1862

Carson, Samuel S e June 24 1861

Drake, H L e Nov. 17, 1861 died March 30, 1862

Elliott, R G, e June 24, 1861

Ebbert, Wm H, e Aug 26, 1862, wd at Champion Hills

Elmer, Edwin e June 24 1861 disd Oct 24, 1862, disab

Elmer, Adelbert, e June 24, 1861, disd Sept 10, 1862, disab

Elmer, Oliver e June 24, 1861, disd Oct 24, 1862, disab

Estal Thos P, e June 24, 1861, wd Iuka disd Feb 23, 1863, disab

Ester, M E e. June 24 1861, died Aug 24 1862

Ebbert, A C, e June 24, 61, kld at Iuka

Farrer, L P, e Aug 11, 1862

Fenning, C W, e June 24, 1861

Farrar Jno F, e June 24, 1861

Flickner Jno, e June 24, 1861, wd at Champion Hills

Fenning, Jas M e June 24, 1861

Grague, Alfred, e Sept 13 1861, disd April 13, 1862, disab

Garlinghouse, L e June 24 1861, captd at Chattanooga

Grommer, Wm., e Sept. 17, 1862, disd Aug 9, 1863, disab

Gilberts, C P, e June 24, 1861.

Hall, Benj, e Aug 14 1862, captd at Chattanooga

Huffman Fred'k, e June 24, 1861

Hackney, A S, e June 24 1861, disd July 26, 1862, sick

Hall, L M, e Aug 14 1862

Harris, C M, e June 24, 61

Hand, A S, e June 24, 1861

Hendricks Wm T e June 24, 1861, disd Oct 14, 1861, sick

Hughes Wm T, e June 24, 1861, wd at Iuka

Hill, Wm H e June 24, 1861

Johnson, Aug e Jan 1, 1862.

Jackson, C R, e June 24, 1861

Johnson Henry, e Aug 30, 1862

Jolley, Jno, e June 24, 1861, died Dec. 1, 1862

Jolley, Alex, e June 24, 1861

Johnson, H, e Aug. 15, 1862

Knapp, P. J e June 24, 1861, captd at Chattanooga

Knapp, Jos W e June 24, 1861, wd at Iuka and Champion Hills

Latimore, J B, e June 24, 1861, disd May 12, 1862

Lewis, J W e Aug 15, 1862, died at Memphis

Loynes, L K, e June 24, 1861, wd at Vicksburg

Malvin, J, e Aug 13 1862

McCall, Jno W, e June 24, 1861, wd at Champion Hills

McAllister Jas e Aug 19, 1862

Miller, Wm C, e June 24, 1861, disd. Dec. 14, 1862 disab

Miller, F M, e June 24, 1861, captd at Chattanooga

Miller, D E, e Aug 31, 1862

Murphy, Wm, e. June 24, 1861, disd Sept. 12, 1862

McCall Robt e June 24, 1861

McWilliams T D, e Aug 2, 1862, wd at Champion Hills

Morris, H F, e June 24, 1861, disd Oct. 2 1862

Motley Wm H H, e June 24, 1861, disd April 3, 1862, disab

McClellan, Jas A, e June 24, 1861

Nutt, Thomas I, e. June 24, 1861, kld Iuka

Nelson, Wm W e June 24 1861, disd April 3, 1863, disab

Pratt, D, e Dec 13, 1863

Penn, Benj, e June 24 1861, wd Iuka, disd Nov 6 1862, disab

Penn, Wm R, e Nov 26, 1861, died at Memphis

Pinkerton, W H. H, e June 24 1861

Pleasants, C H, e Aug 14, 1862.

Pierse Jno A, e June 24, 1861, wd Iuka, disd Nov 8, 1863, disab

Ratcliff, Jacob e Nov 26, 1861, disd Oct 12, 1862, disab

Rodgers Hamilton, e June 24, 1861, kld Iuka

Roberts Elijah, e June 24, 1861, wd Iuka and Champion Hills

Russell M, e Aug 31, 1862

Stookey, Jno H, e June 24, 1861 died Syracuse Mo

Sutton, S e Aug 31, 1862, captd at Chattanooga

South N J, e June 24 1861, disd Jan. 19, 186 disd

Stull Jno Aug 31, 1862

Stout, Chas, e June 24, 1861, died Oct 13, 1862
Sutton, J, e Aug 31, 1862
Sheppard J W e. Sept 1 1862, died at Huntsville, Ala
Sutton, W e June 24 1861 disd Sept. 2, 1862
Shebby H E Sept 1, 1862
Smith, F J, e June 24, 1861, disd Sept 14, 1862
Shaw, M. W, e June 24, 1861, wd Iuka captd Chattanooga
Sutton, A., e June 24, 1861, wd Iuka
Troette, Jno A, e June 24, 1861, wd Iuka, disd April 3, 1863
Umphenour, Jas, e Aug 1, 1862
Walden, Benj, e June 24 1861, disd April 3, 1863
Winchell, Wm R, e Aug 31, 1862, kld Champion Hills
Winscott, S K e June 24, 1861, wd Iuka, disd Oct 12, 1862, disab
Winchell, Jesse, e June 24, 1861
Widger, J K, e June 24, 1861
Walker, Geo M, e June 24, 1861
Whittea, e Nov 26, 1861
Whitten, J A e Aug 30, 1862, wd Iuka, Champion Hills captd Chattanooga
Waybill A A, e Aug 31, 1862

Company I.

Nevell, Morgan, e June 24, 1861, died Feb 1, 1862

FOURTEENTH INFANTRY

[NOTE—This regiment, except veterans and recruits, was mustered out at Davenport, Nov 16, 1864 The veterans and recruits were consolidated into two companies, called Residuary Battalion Fourteenth Infantry, which was mustered out Aug 8, 1865]

Lieut Col Joseph H Newbold, com. capt Co F Nov 4, 1861, captd at Shiloh, prmtd lieut col March 13, 1863, kld at battle Pleasant Hill

Company A.

Zink, George, e Oct 2, 1861, wd at Pleasant Hill, La
Zink, William, e Jan 28, 1863

Company D.

Sergt William E Ayers, e Sept 28, 1861, captd at Shiloh trans to V R C. April 29, 1864
Corp Alfred M Wilson, e Sept 28, 1861
Bucher, Abram, e Sept 28, 1861, died at Corinth
Cleason, W H, e Sept 28, 1861, kld at Shiloh
Campbell, W H, e Sept 28 1861.
Campbell, M B, e Sept 28, 1861
Henry, N B, e Oct 14 1861, died Jan 19, 1862
Lootborous, J S, e Sept 28, 1861
Nixon, W H, e Sept 28 1861

Company F.

First Lieut Wm H Dodds, e as sergt Oct 14, 1861, prmtd 2d lieut March 29, 1862, prmtd 1st lieut March 14, 1863
Second Lieut Cyrus Bitner, com Nov 4, 1861, resd March 28, 1862
Sergt Robert Hayes, e Oct 14, 1861, kld at Tupelo
Corp David Harlan, e Oct 14. 1861, deserted Aug 10, 1862
Burns, James, e Oct 2, 1861, captd at Shiloh, disd Jan 8, 1863
Crist, Jacob, e Oct 14, 1861
Con, T
Coro, Wm, e. Oct 14, 1861
Detwiler, Hugh, e Oct. 14, 1861
Detwiler, J W, e Oct 14, 1861, wd at Pleasant Hills, disd Oct 25, 1862
Hill, James, e Oct 14, 1861, disd April 24, 1862
Jones, O F, e Oct 14, 1861, disd April 27, 1862, disab
Jackson W F, e Oct 14, 1861, captd at Shiloh
Meller, Z, e Oct 14, 1861
Miller, Chauncey, e Oct 14, 1861.
Pierce, Douglass, e Oct 14, 1861, died at St Louis
Speers, William, e Oct 14, 1861, captd at Shiloh
Speers, Irwin, e Oct 14, 1861
Slegh Joseph e Oct 11, 1861
Sade, William, e Oct 14, 1861
Zink, George, e Oct 2, 1861

RESIDUARY BATTALION FOURTEENTH INFANTRY

Company B.

Corr, Thomas, e March 3, 1863
Douthart, H F, e Aug 21, 1863
Gauther, J W, e Dec 1, 1863
Isaman, La Fayette, e Aug 23, 1863
Kines, Royal, e Dec 14, 1863
Wheatley, R W, e Aug 23, 1863
White, Elza, e Aug 23, 1863
Walker, J E, e Aug 23, 1863

FIFTEENTH INFANTRY

[NOTE—This regiment was mustered out at Louisville, July 24 1865]

Assistant Surgeon Wm W Nelson, com Aug 19 1862
Adjutant W C Stidger, e as sergt Oct 14, 1861, wd at Shiloh, prmtd 2d lieut Co E, June 15, 1864, prmtd adjutant Oct 26, 1864
Sergt Maj Alexander Brown e. Oct. 20, 1861, wd at Shiloh and Corinth, disd Feb 12, 1863

Company E.

Capt John P Cragg, com 1st lieut. Dec. 1, 1861, prmtd capt July 9 1863, resd Dec 24, 1862.

First Lieut Hugh G Brown, com 2d lieut Dec 1, 1861, pmtd 1st lieut July 9 1862, capt and A D C, U S V, Aug 28, 1863, brevet maj U S V Dec 29, 1864, brevet lieut col March 31, 65

First Lieut Wm P L Mun, e as seigt Oct 14 1861, wd at Corinth, pmtd 2d lieut Feb 2, 1863, pmtd 1st lieut Nov 9, 1863, missing in action at Atlanta

Seigt C W Woodrow, e Oct 20, 1861 trans to 17th Regt

Seigt A D Thatcher, e Oct 14, 1861

Corp Wm M McCrary, e Oct. 14, 1861, disd Oct 30 1862

Corp James W Henry, e Oct 14, 1861 wd. at Corinth, vet March 31, 1864, pmtd seigt maj July 1 1864, missing in action July 22, 1864

Corp Wm W Glanville, e Oct 14, 1861, disd. May 29, 1862, disab

Corp Wm H Sellers, vet March 15, 1864 wd near Atlanta

Corp George Harbaugh, e Nov 1, 1861, vet Jan 1, 1864, wd near Atlanta

Corp Morris A Lane, e Oct 14, 1861

Corp George De Hart, e Dec 2, 1861, vet Jan. 1, 1864

Corp Geo W Toole, e Nov 27, 1861

Corp E G Black, e Oct 14 1861, wd at Corinth died date unknown

Drummer Melville Davis, vet Dec 6, 63, wd at Kenesaw Mountain and Nick-a-Jack, Ga., disd May 19, 1865

Anthony, D M, e Oct 14 1861, disd Dec 16 1862

Anhart, John, e Jan 10, 1862

Buckmaster, F, e Nov 20, 1861, trans to Co K

Beers, John e Aug 30, 1862, died at Memphis

Burton, J W, e Aug 30, 1862.

Cheney, J W e March 17, 1864, wd at Atlanta, disd May 6 1865

Cuthburth, Benjamin, e Dec. 20, 1861

Doty, Joseph, e Nov. 18, 1861, trans to Co. K

Gephart, W A, e Oct. 18, 1861

Hopkins, Merritt, e Oct 18, 1861, vet Jan 1, 1864, died at Vicksburg

Hornbaker, D R, e March 6, 1862 vet March 7, 1864

Helwick Charles, e Oct 14, 1861, vet Dec 6 1863

Huff, Z M, e Jan 2, 1864

Hearn, Benjamin, e Oct 14, 1861 died Aug 6, 1862, at Bolivar, Tenn

Hopkins, M, e Feb 6, 1864, died at Keosauqua

Hilliard, A, e March 31, 1864

Harryman, W. H, e Oct 14, 1861, wd at Shiloh, vet Jan 1 1864.

Hopkins, M, Aug 22, 1862

Johnston, Benjamin, e Oct 14, 1861, vet Dec 6, 1863, disd to accept promotion as 1st lieut in 3d Mo A D.

Jamison, C W, e March 22 1864

Jones, J M, e Oct 26, 1861 vet Jan 1, 1864

Jones, J P, e Oct 26, 1861 disd Jan 16, 1863, disab

Jameson, Josiah, e Oct 1, 1861, disd Jan. 22, 1862, disab

Lock, J F, e. Oct 14, 1861, vet Jan 1, '64 wd near Atlanta

Minnick, S, e Aug 30, 1862

Moore, Henry e. Oct 14, 1861, disd Feb. 23, 1863 disab

Miller, John e Nov 4, 1861 wd at Shiloh, disd Aug 21, 1862, wds.

McArthur, William, e Oct 14 1861, trans to Co K

McArthur H C, e Oct 14, 1861, trans to Co. K as seigt

Marriott, Samuel, e March 30, 1864, wd at Kenesaw Mountain

Moore, Henry, e Jan. 2, 1861, wd near Atlanta, disd July 10, 1865

Mun, T I, e Aug 30, 1862

Orm, Robert, e Jan 18 1861 wd near Atlanta

Orm Oliver, e Jan 18, 1861, wd at Kenesaw Mountain

Orm, J F e Jan 18 1861, wd near Atlanta

Platt, Edward, e March 23, 1861

Phillips, Perry, e Oct 14, 1861, died at Keosauqua, March 9 1862

Peyton, George, e Nov 4 1861 kld in battle of Shiloh

Paquin Oliver, e Nov 4, 1861, vet Jan. 1, 1864, died June 17, 1864

Richmond, J M, e Nov 14 1861 vet Dec 6 1863, wd July 5 1864

Rhaney W H e March 31 1864, captd near Atlanta

Roberts W M, e Aug 31, 1862, wd Oct 5, 1864, disd April 4, 1865, disab

Shriver C E, e March 26, 1864

Smith, James, e March 31, 1864

Scott, William, e Aug 30, 1862

Smith, J W, e Oct 14, 1861, died July 23, 1862

St John J F, e Oct 18, 1861

Shriver Thomas, e Oct 14, 1861, vet Jan 1, 1864

Thomas, J M, e Jan. 2, 1864

Thomas, Benjamin, e Dec 22, 1863

Thatcher, J B, e Oct 14, 1861, wd at Shiloh and Corinth disd March 21 1863, disab

Thatcher, I, e Aug 30, 1862.

Vantruse, J S, e Oct 14, 1861, wd at Corinth and Atlanta

Watson, Otis, vet Jan 1, 1864

Warren, C, e Oct 14, 1861, wd near Atlanta

Westcott C, e Oct 14, 1861

Zachari, N e Dec 11, 1861, disd June 27 1862, wds recd near Shiloh

Company H.

First Lieut Henry C McArthur, e as seigt Co K Oct 14 1861 wd at Shiloh, pmtd 1st lieut April 16 1863, wd at Atlanta

Julien, Ed S, e Feb 13, 1864, kld Atlanta
Wilson, Thos H, e Oct 10, 1861

Company I.

Sergt Thos B Coffman, e Feb 8 1862, disd June 30 1862.
Corp Benj F Keck e Oct 1, 1861, disd Aug 15, 1862, wd Shiloh
Gould, Theo e Oct 26, 1861, disd Jan 1, 1863, disab
Halthill Luke e Dec 27 1861 vet Dec 27 1863, wd Kenesaw Mountain, trans V. R C
McCanna Francis, e Dec 27, 1861 vet Dec 27 1863
Mahan, Thos, e Oct 10, 1861
Mahan, Jos W e Nov 10, 1861
Nelson Jas F, e March 31, 1864, wd at Ezra Church Ga
Smallwood, Elijah, e Dec 19, 1861, died June 12 1862

Company K.

First Lieut Jas G Shipley, e as private Aug 21, 1862, prmtd 1st lieut, Feb 9 1865
Sergt Wm A Gephart e, Oct. 18, 1861 vet Jan 1, 1864
Sergt Wm. McArthur, e Oct 14, 1861 disd, Jan 6, 1863, disab
Corp John I St. John, e Oct 18, 1861, vet Jan 1, 1864, wd June 27, 1864.
Airhart John, e Jan 10 1862, died near Vicksburg
Buckmaster F, e Nov 12, 1861, vet Jan 1 1864, wd and captd near Atlanta, died at Andersonville
Bixber, Wm W e Feb 1, '62, wd Shiloh
Doty, Joseph, e Nov 18, 1861, disd Aug 1, 1862 disab
Griffith Ezekiel, e Feb 10, 1862 disd March 1, 1862, disab
Hunt Geo L, e Feb 17 1862, wd Shiloh
Parker, Wm, e Feb 17, 1862, died June 26, 1862
Steele, Geo K, e Feb 6, 1862
Sappenfield Jacob, e Feb 6, 1862
Sewell, Elias, e Feb 17, 1862
Sappenfield, A, e Feb 26, 1862
Wescott, C L, e Oct 24 1861 disd June 6 1862, disab

COMPANY UNKNOWN

Bean, A. A, e Jan 4, 1864
Bish, Wm G e. Dec 22 1863
Burnhart, Geo e Jan 4, 1864
Huff, Z M, e Jan 2, 1864
Moore, Henry, e Jan 2, 1864
Thomas, Benj T, e Dec 22, 1863
Thomas John M, e Jan 2, 1864
Wyley, John, e March 31, 1864

SEVENTEENTH INFANTRY.

[NOTE—This Regiment was mustered out at Louisville, Ky, July 25, 1865]

Surg Christopher C Biser comd ass sng Nov 5 1862 prmtd surg June 17, 1865

Com Sergt M A Lane, e Oct 14, 1862, trans for promotion in 11th La Vols

Company A.

Carr, Wm W, e March 20, 1862

Company B.

Musician Geo Jewett, e March 18 1862, disd Sept 11 1862, disab
Jackson John T, e March 26 1862, vet March 27, 1864

Company C.

Sergt Geo W Tool, e Nov 29, 1861
Walker, James e March 18, 1862
Jackson, Wm W e March 10, 1862, vet. March 12, 1864

Company D.

Corp J N Henry, e Feb 25, 1862, disd Oct 4 1862, disab
Corp. Danl L Rowe e March 12 1862, vet March 26, 1864
Corp J D Nesbett, e March 4, 1862, captd. Tilton, Ga
Adams J D, e March 8, 1862 disd Dec 16, 1862
Boyster, H C, e March 8 1862 wd Inka
Brown, Robt D, e March 13, 1862, vet March 25, 1864
Belknap, F, e March 25, 1862, captd
Carter Samuel P, e Feb 25, 1862, vet March 30, 1864
Carter Joab, e March 7, 1862 disd Dec. 9, 1862, captd Tilton, Ga
Fisher, John e March 21 1862 disd Nov. 12, 1862, disab
Martin, Josiah, e March 18, 1862
Miller James H, e March 23 1862
Morgan Wm H, e March 24, 1862
Noell, M, e March 17, 1862 wd and died at Champion Hills
Nelson, Wm P e March 18, 1862, vet March 26, 1864
Sanders John L, e March 1, 1862, captd Tilton, Ga
Sailor, F M e March 3, 1862
Tolbert, F M e March 10, 1862

Company I.

Capt Alphonso A Rice, e as sergt April 1, 1862, prmtd 1st lieut June 27, 1862, prmtd capt Nov 20, 1862 resd Feb 28, 1863
Sergt Edward Fasnacht e March 7, 1862 died Nov 18, 1872
Corp John Bartow, e March 27 1862 kld. Jackson, Miss
Campbell, A W, e March 18, 1862
Daughter Samuel, e Feb 19, 1862
McCarty, John, e March 24 1862, disd Nov 18, 1863
Maxson, G N e March 28 1862, died Aug 20, 1862
Price Moses A, e March 21 1862, disd Sep 25 1862
Scats John e March 18 resd March 6, 1863

Company K.

Cresswell, Isaac, e Feb 17, 1862, dlsd Oct 13, 1862
French, Samuel R , e March 10, 1862, disd Sept 28, 1862

NINETEENTH INFANTRY

[NOTE —*This regiment was mustered out at Mobile, Ala , July 10, 1865*]

Lieut. Col Daniel Kent com maj Aug 2. 1862, prmtd lieut col Dec 8, 1862, res March 9, 1864
Chaplain J D Sands, com March 22, '64
F Maj James Payne, e Aug 9, 1862, captd Atchafalaya, La

Company A.

Seigt H L Ethridge, e Aug 9, 1862 disd March 20, 1863, disab
Sergt Thos Deal, e. Aug 9, 1862
Amoss Barney, e Aug 9, 1862, captd Atchafalaya, La
Brown, F M , e. Aug 13, 1862
Cross Jno T , e Aug 9, 1862. wd , place unknown
Chilton. Jos , e Aug 12, 1862, disd Feb 22, 1863
Goodwin, Benj F , e Aug 13, 1862, captd Atchafalaya
George Wm , e Aug 13, 1862
Johnson, Henry. e Aug 9, 1862
Lyon, Jno W., e. Aug 13, 1862, disd April 28, 1863, disab
Marks, Geo A. e Aug 9, 1862, captd Atchafalaya
Pence, Jos C , e. Aug 9, 1862
Paine, Wm . e Aug 22, 1862 disd Feb 27, 1863, disab
West, Wm H , e Aug 14, 1862
Walker, A R e Aug 9 1862

Company B.

Ethridge, Henry, e. Aug 5, 1862
Rushton, Elam, e April 29, 1863.

Company H.

Capt Theo W Richmond, com Aug 21, 1862, captd and paroled battle Prairie Grove, res Aug 2 1863
Capt Silas Kent, com 1st lieut Aug. 21, 1862 prmtd capt Aug 3 1863, kld. (while 1st. lieut) Sterling Farm La
Capt Geo W Sommerville, e as sergt Aug 4, 1862, prmtd 2d lieut Feb 27 1863, prmtd 1st. lieut Aug 3, 1863, prmtd capt Sept 30, 1863
First Lieut Wm. W Buyers, e as corp Aug 14, 1862, captd Atchafalaya. La, prmtd 1st lieut. Sept 30, 1863.
Second Lieut Amos A Wood. e as priv Aug 14 1862, prmtd 2d lieut July 1, 1865. n o as 1st sergt
Sergt Samuel Bonner e Au , 2 1862, kld in battle Prairie Grove

Sergt Samuel Baker, e Aug 7, 1862
Sergt Jas A. Russell, e. Aug. 5, 1862, disd March 27, 1863, disab
Sergt A J Smith, e Aug 4, 1862, wd Prairie Grove, captd Atchafalaya, La
Sergt Christopher Mort, e Aug. 14, 1862, captd Atchafalaya, La
Sergt Geo A Paxton, e Aug 8 1862
Corp Robt A Alcorn, e Aug 5, 1862
Corp Wm R Tock, Aug 14, 1862, kld battle Prairie Grove
Corp Jas F. King, e. Aug 8, 1862, captd Atchafalava, La
Corp Wm W Phillips, e Aug 9, 1862, disd Feb 25, 1863, disab
Corp Jno F Daugherty, e Aug 2, 1862, captd Atchafalaya, La
Corp Wm. H. Smith, e. Aug 14, 1862 captd Atchatalaya, La.
Musician Alfred Morris, e Aug 9, 1862, died Pittsburg
Akers, Jas C, e Aug 14, 1862, captd Atchafalaya, La
Byers, Marshall e Aug 5, 1862, kld Prairie Grove
Bennett, Jas H e Aug 5, 1862
Boyd, Geo e Aug 14, 1862
Cochran, Albt. e Aug 2, 1862, wd Prairie Grove, disd March 16, 1863.
Cravens. L P, e Aug 5, 1862, disd May 12, 1863, disab
Crail, Geo P e Aug 5 1862, disd Dec 9 1862
Cook, F M , e Aug 5, 1862. wd Prairie Grove, disd March 8, 1863, disab
Cretcher, J M W , Aug 14, 1862, wd. Prairie Grove disd March 28, 1863
Carter, D J, e. Aug 2, 1862
Cochran, Alfred, e. Aug 14, '62 disd. March 2, 1863, disab
Clark, Wm , e Aug 5, 1862, disd July 5, 1864, disab
Dean, Z C, e Aug 5, 1862, captd Atchafalaya, La
Drew, Wm P., e Aug. 14, 1862
Drummond, J A , e. Aug 14, 1862
Duley Jas, e. Aug 14, 1862, disd April 4, 1864
Eaton. Wm S , e Aug 5, 1862, died Springfield, Mo
Eaton, Robt B , e Feb 22, 1863, died New Orleans
Evans, I D , e Aug 5, 1862, captd Atchafalaya, La
Fisher, C W , e Aug 5, 1862, kld Prairie Grove
Foster, Robt D , e Aug 14, 1862, wd Prairie Grove
Groom, M , e Aug 14, 1862, wd. Prairie Grove and died there Dec 9, 1862
Groom, T J , e Aug 5, 1862
Godom, T J , e Aug 5, 1862
Green, Alfred, e Aug 14, 1862
Green, Henry, e Aug 14, 1862, wd Prairie Grove, disd March 14, 1863
Gurison, N e Aug 14 1862
Gideon Theo, e Aug 14, 1862, died Springfield Mo

Greene, J , e Aug. 14, 1862, died Dec 4 1862

Hartson, Wm M , e Aug 5, 1862

Hearne, Thos E , e Aug 5, 1862, died Ozark, Mo

Hunter, Hugh, e Aug 14, 1862

Hartson, P. M , e Aug 4, 1862

Hoskins, Omar, e Aug 14 1862 captd at Atchafalaya, La

Holmes Wm C , e Aug 14, 1862, captd at Atchafalaya, La

Jones, H C , e Aug 9, 1862 captd at Atchafalaya, La

Jones A W , e Aug 9, 1862, captd at Atchafalaya, La

Jones, E H , e Aug 9, 1862

Keller, L , e Aug. 14, 62, kld Prairie Grove

Langford, S , e Aug 9, 1862, wd Prairie Grove, captd at Atchafalaya, wd at Spanish Fort

Langford, Fillman, e Aug 9, 1862 wd. at Prairie Grove

Luning, T B , e Aug 14, 1862, kld Prairie Grove

Lanum, Jos H , e Aug 14, 1862, wd Prairie Grove, captd Atchafalaya La

Murphy, Daniel e Aug 2, 1862

Morrison, Wm , e Aug 2, 1862, died Port Hudson, La

Mort Jos , e Aug 9, 1862, captd at Atchafalaya, La, wd Spanish Fort

McIntosh, Jno G , e Aug 9 1862, captd Atchafalaya, La, drowned at Barrancas, Fla

McCray, Sam'l R e Aug 14 1862, disd March 14, 1863, disab

Nixon, J , e Aug 5, 1862 captd at Atchafalaya, La

Nagle, Jacob, e Aug 2, 1862, disd April 22, 1864, disab

Phillips, J T., e Aug 2, 1862, kld Prairie Grove

Prosser, H. L . e Aug 13, 1862, died at Vicksburg

Parsons, R. H , e Aug 9, 1862, wd at Prairie Grove, captd Atchafalaya, La

Parsons, L , e Aug 9, 1862

Robinson, R F , e Aug 2, 1862, wd at Prairie Grove, disd March 25, 1863

Reed, F W , e Aug 14, 1862, trans to Inv Corps Feb 15, 1864

Strang, Jno , Jr , e Aug 14, 1862, died at Rolla, Mo

Stone, Jno H , e Aug 14, 1862

Steves, Jno C , e Aug 14, 1862

Stewart, Jno H , e Aug. 14, 1862, disd Feb 25, 1863, disab

Smith, David, e Aug 14, 1862, captd at Atchafalaya, La

Taylor, E P , e Aug 9, 1862, captd at Atchafalaya, La, wd Spanish Ft , Ala

Teeter, Wm , e Aug 9, 1862, drowned at Round Island, Miss

Tackaberry, Jno. S , e Aug 14, 1862

Taylor, L W , e Aug 14, 1862, kld at Prairie Grove

Umphrey, Thos , e Aug 9, 1862 captd at Atchafalaya, La

Utt, N. J , e Aug 14, 1862, disd Feb 9, 1863, disab

Veilher, Francis, e Aug 8, 1862

Vail, E E , e Aug 8, 1862, died Natchez.

Woods, Jos , e Aug 8, 1862

Wilber, C P , e Aug 2, 1862, captd at Atchafalaya, La

Woods A A , e Aug 14, 1862

Work, Samuel, e Aug 14 1862, trans to Inv Corps

Williams, W H H e Aug 14, 1862 disd March 4, 1863 disd

Company I.

Capt Saml E Paine, com Aug. 21 1862, wd bat Prairie Grove disd April 1, '63

Capt Alonzo H Parker, e as sergt Aug 6, 1862, prmtd 2d lieut Dec 1, 1862, prmtd 1st lieut Dec 8, 1862 prmtd capt Oct 1, 1863

First Lieut. Andrew C Payne, com Aug 21, 1862, resd Nov. 18, 1862

First Lieut Thos Johnson, com 2d lieut Dec 1, 1862, prmtd 1st lieut Nov. 19, 1862, kld (while 2d lieut) at battle of Prairie Grove

First Lieut John S Ragsdale, e as sergt Aug 6, 1862, captd at Atchafalaya, La , prmtd 1st lieut Oct 1, 1863

Second Lieut Francis Johnson, e as priv Aug 9, 1862, prmtd 2d lieut July 1, 1865, m o as 1st sergt

Sergt H H Martin, e Aug 6, 1862

Sergt D. D Prosser, e Aug 14, 1862, wd Prairie Grove captd. Atchafalaya, La

Sergt James Lawrence, e Aug 14, 1862

Sergt Geo P. Linaweaver, e Aug 14, '62, disd July 9, 1863, disab

Sergt. Wm A Strong, e Aug 12, 1862, wd Prairie Grove, died Fayetteville, Ark

Sergt Thos E Doan, e Aug 6, 1862, disd Feb 6, 1863, disab

Sergt Jacob Nixon, e. Aug. 6, 1862, wd at Prairie Grove, disd. Feb 25, 1863

Corp Alex Fix, e Aug. 14, 1862, wd at Prairie Grove, disd March 28, '63, disab

Corp John Douglass, e Aug 13, 1862, kld at Prairie Grove.

Corp S. Whittlesey, e Aug 14, 1862, disd March 8, 1863, disab

Corp. Wm. I Bragg, e Aug 6, 1862, captd at Atchafalaya, La

Corp Geo W Merideth, e Aug. 14, 1862, captd at Atchafalaya, La

Corp Wm N Holiday, e Aug 9, 1862, captd at Atchafalaya, La , kld. Spanish Fort

Corp Aug C Rehkoft, e Aug 6, 1862, kld at Prairie Grove

Corp Wm P Dunham, Aug 14, 1862, disd Feb 24, 1863, disab

Musician Jas M Miller, e Aug 6, 1862, captd. at Atchafalaya, La

Musician Jas Payne e Aug 9 1862

Musician Mark Godown e Aug 9, 1862, disd. Jan 16, 1863, disab

Wagoner John A Downard e Aug 9, '62

H

Wagoner Jesse Merideth, e Aug 14, 1862, captd at Atchafalaya, La.

Barker, John T , e Aug. 6, 1862, captd at Atchafalaya, La

Barker, David, e. Aug. 9, 1862, captd at Atchafalava, La

Barker, Joseph A , e. Aug 6, 1862, died at Lebanon, Mo.

Batchelder, Geo , e Aug 14, 1862, disd Feb 23, 1863, disab

Brooks, L A , e Aug 6, 1862, wd Prairie Grove, trans to Inv Corps Jan 15, 1864

Bowles Wm R , e Aug 14, 1862, disd March 27, 1863, disab

Campbell, John C , e Aug 14, 1862

Cupp, Geo D , e Aug 9 1862.

Calhoun, D K , e Aug 19, 1862, captd at Atchafalava, La

Crawley H W , e. Aug 13, 1862, disd Feb 3, 1863, disab)

Collins, R. E. e. Aug 13, 1862, captd at Atchafalava, La , kld Pierce's Pt , Fla

Chana, E . e. Aug. 21, 1862

Douglass, A e. Aug 9, 1862, trans to Inv Corps Aug 4, 1863

Doan, Malon, e Aug 6, 1862

Eastling, H L , e Aug. 14, 1862

Edmondson, H. B , e Aug. 6, 1862, wd at Prairie Grove

Forbus, Robert, e Aug 9, 1862

Fry, Jas L , e Aug 21, 1862, wd Prairie Grove, disd June 21 1863, disab

Gaddis, A V , e Aug 6, 1862, kld battle Prairie Grove

Gillaspie, J , e Aug 6, 1862

Gaddis, I R , e Aug 9, 1862, disd Feb 5, 1863 disab

Gilbert, Harvey, e Aug 9 1862 disd March 20, 1863, disab

Homblin, J H , e Aug 6 1862

Humbert, G. W , e Aug 6, 1862, trans for promotion to hosp steward 4th La Engineers Oct 22, 1863

Hughs, J W , e Aug 13, 1862, disd Feb. 21, 1863, disab

Houts, W R , e. Aug 14, 1862

Heinboker, M , e Aug 14, 1862, wd at Prairie Grove trans to Inv Corps April 10, 1864

John, R H e Aug 6, 1862

Jameson, F , e Aug 9, 1862

Johnson, Russell, e Aug 14, 1862 wd at Prairie Grove, disd March 14, 1863, disab

Johnson, Oliver, e Aug 6, 1862, captd at Atchafalava, La

Johnson, J H , e Aug 13, 1862, disd Feb 25, 1863

Klise, Geo , e Aug 6, 1862, captd at Atchafalava, La

Kelley, John, e Aug 9, 1862

Lennon, F M , e Aug 13, 1862

Lennon, George, e Aug 13, 1862, disd Feb 11 1863

Lee J J , e Aug 9 186 , e at Prairie Grove Ark

Long, Jerome e Aug 14 1862

Lorton, John, e Aug. 12 1862 disd Feb 25, 1863 disab.

McKinney, Wm , e Aug 13, 1862, kld at Prairie Grove.

McGinniss, L , e. Aug. 14, 1862, died at Keokuk

Martin, Joseph, e Aug 13, 1862

Moody, David, e Jan 29, 1863

Merritt, Isaac. e. Aug 14, 1862

Murphy, Edward, e May 7 1863

Newton, John, e Aug 6, 1862, captd at Atchafalaya, La

Orr, Wm e Aug 13, 1862

O'Hara, H , e Aug 6, 1862, wd at Prairie Grove, died at Fayetteville, Ark.

Price, S D , e Aug. 14, 1862, died at Vicksburg

Price, W J , e. Aug. 13, 1862, disd Feb 23, 1863, disab

Pender, Thomas, e Aug 6, 1862

Patterson, James, e Aug 14, 1862, kld at Prairie Grove.

Patterson H , e Aug 4, 1862 disd Feb 6, 1863, disab

Roth, J R e Aug 6, 1862, captd Atchafalaya, La.

Robb, James, e Aug 12, 1862, wd Prairie Grove.

Row, Israel, e Aug 6, 1862, captd at Atchafalaya, La

Robinson, R S , e Aug 9, 1862, disd. Feb 23, 1863, disab

Smith, T J , e Aug 9, 1862

Stewart, H , e Aug 9 1862

Short, John, e Aug. 13, 1862

Spraker, George, e Aug 13, 1862

Spraker, W T , e. Aug. 21, 1862, captd at Atchafalaya, La

Sherrod Amos, e Aug 6, 1862, died at St Louis

Swartz, J W , e Aug 6, 1862, wd and died at Springfield, Mo

Stewart, C , e Aug 9, 1862

Stevens, G P , e Aug 21, 1862, captd at Atchafalaya, La

Teal, F , e Aug 9 1862, wd at Prairie Grove, died on steamer 'City of Memphis"

White, John, e Aug 12, 1862

Weber, J. H , e Aug 13, 1862, wd Prairie Grove, captd. at Atchafalaya, La

Ward, H S., e Aug. 21, 1862.

THIRTIETH INFANTRY

[Note.—This regiment was mustered out at Washington, D C., June 5, 1865]

Company D.

Capt Wm H Randall, com 2d lieut Sept 23, 1862, prmtd capt March 12, 1863, died of wds at Cherokee Sta , Ala.

Capt Geo W Elench, e as corp Aug 2, 1862 prmtd 1st lieut March 12 1863, prmtd capt Oct 18 1864

First Lieut David Leach com Sept 23, 1862, resd March 2 1863

First Lieut Henson H Cross, e as priv Aug. 15, 1862, pimtd. 2d lieut June 6, 1864, wd at Atlanta, pimtd 1st lieut. Oct 18, 1864

Seigt Marion C Martin, e Aug 15, 1862.

Sergt Jno R Rogers, e Aug 8, 1862, wd. and died at Vicksburg

Seigt Bowen P Hurt, e Aug 2, 1862, died at Marietta, Ga

Seigt T W Detwiler, e Aug 19 1862, wd. at Arkansas Post, died on steamer D A January.

Corp D P Todd, e Aug 15, 1862, wd Ringgold, Ga, disd May 11, 1865 disab

Corp Goldson Prewitt, e August 15, 1862.

Corp Albt Herbert e Aug 19, 1862 died Oct. 27, 1862

Corp Jno Cross, e Aug 15, 1862, died Jan. 5, 1865

Corp Jas Fowler, e Aug 19, 1862

Corp Jas Gianque e Aug 15, 1862

Corp C M Baber, e Aug 15, 1862

Corp Geo R Plaskett, e. Aug. 15, 1862

Musician Jas Prewitt, e Aug. 15, 1862

Musician Wm E Huff, e Aug. 15 1862, trans to Inv Corps April 10, 1864

Archer, C E, e Aug 15 1862, wd Arkansas Post

Anderson, Benj, e Aug 15 1862, died on steamer Von Phul

Anderson Levi, e Aug 15 1862

Bennett, Isaac, e Aug 4, 1862

Beale, Jno W, e Jan, 25, 1864

Beedle, Andrew, e Aug 14, 1862, kld. at Vicksburg

Birch, Jas, e Aug 15, 1862, disd May 21, 1863, disab

Bethers, Samuel, e Aug 15, 1862

Binder, Henry, e Aug 15, 1862, died Nov 25, 1862

Bonnett, Jno M, e Aug 15, 1862, died Marietta, Ga

Bradford L, e Aug 19, 1862, died Dec 5, 1862

Bickford, Jno, e Aug 19, 1862

Coulter, Wm, e Aug 19, 1862, disd May 7, 1863, disab

Coulter, Robt W, e Aug 19, 1862

Corwin, Wm E, e Aug 19, 1862

Cottman Thos B, e Aug 19, 1862 kld at Manchester Va

Clark, David, e Aug 2, 1862, disd April 12, 1865, disab

Coleman, T M, e Feb. 6, 1864

Canada Isaac, e Aug 8, 1862, trans to Inv. Corps Dec 27, 1863

Crum Jos T, Jan 5, 1864

Crum, Wm F, e Aug 15, 1862

Crum, S L, e Aug 15, 1862

Clark, Jno W, e Aug 15, 1862, died at Young's Pt., La.

Casner, Jno C, e Aug 15, 1862

Camblin, Asbury, e Aug 15, 1862

Doty, Wm, e Aug 7 1862

Dehart, Wm., e Aug 18, 1862 trans to Miss Marine Brig Dec 31, 1862

Fox, Geo W, e Aug 14, 1862

Gaddis, H C, e Aug. 19, 1862, died on steamer Decatur

Goodell, J G, e Aug. 14, 1862

Giles, Jno T. e Aug 9 1862, wd, disd May 19, 1865, wds

Hite, H. C, e Aug 19, 1862

Humbert, E. B, e. Aug 19, 1862, wd at Arkansas Post, disd Oct 26, 1863, disab

Harness, J B, e. Aug 15, 1862, died at Keokuk

Henderson, T M e Aug 15, 1862.

Holcomb, Jno M e Aug 15, 1862, disd. Oct 31 1862

Herrman, J D C, e Aug 15 1862

Hollen, Robt E, e Aug 19, 1862.

Hix, Robt C, e Aug. 19. 1862, died at Memphis

Hix, Wm W, e Aug 15, 1862, died at Vicksburg

Harden Saml e Aug 19, 1862

Latimer, Jas H, e Jan 5, 1864

Lichty, Cyrus e Aug 13, 1862, disd Oct. 31, 1862, disab

Mallett, Jno, e Aug 19, 1862 disd March 14, 1864, disab

Murphy, A J, e Aug. 11, 1862, wd at Atlanta

Murphy, S Z, e Aug 28 1862, wd at Resaca, Ga

McCrory, A e Aug 15, 1862, died at Black River Bridge

Martin, T J, e Aug 15, 1862, trans to Inv Corps Sept 29, 1863

Newman, A G, e Aug 19, 1862

Nutt, Owen, e Aug. 15, 1862

Ogilbee, H W, e Feb 8, 1864

Prewitt, Z, e Aug 15, 1862 died at Birmingham.

Park, Wm P, e Aug 15, 1862

Ruark, Jas, e. Aug 8, 1862, wd at Champion Hills

Robison, Wm, e Aug. 15, 1862, disd Oct 31 1862

Robison, Wm H. e Aug 15, 1862

Robertson Wm H, e Aug 15, 1862, wd. at Vicksburg, died at Memphis.

Sherman, U H, e Aug 14, 1862.

Sadler, Jacob, e Aug 15, 1862, kld at Missionary Ridge

Swasey, H. M, e Aug 14, 1862

Smith, Wm T, e Aug 15, 1862, disd Feb 20, 1864, disab

Snyder, Geo W, e Aug 15 1862 wd. at Vicksburg, disd Dec 16, 1863.

Sadler, Geo, e Aug 15, 1862

Salter Robt A, e Aug 19, 1862, wd at Atlanta

Tolman, Jas R, e Aug 13, 1862, trans to Inv Corps May 1, 1864

Vanausdellen, J L, e Aug 15, 1862

Williamson, Jno W, e Aug 2, 1862, died at Young's Pt, La

Wne, Wm, e Aug 11, 1862.

Walker, Jes, e Aug 6 '62 died Oct 27, 62

Weekly T M e Aug 14 1862, kld Vicksburg

Wolmer Jno H, e Aug 15, 1862, wd at Resaca

Company F.

Brumley, A, e Aug 13, 1862 kld Vicksburg

Conaway R W e Aug 13, 1862 wd at Arkansas Post, died at St Louis

Company G.

Freeman, John H, e Aug 12, 1862, wd at Atlanta

Howard, Wm H, e Aug 7, 1862, died at Memphis

James Samuel E, e Aug 15, 1862 wd at Cherokee, Ala, disd Feb 25, 1864

Vincent, Wm, e Aug 12, 1862

Company H.

Brady, Wm R e Aug 15, 1862, wd at Resaca

Ellsworth, Wm W, e Aug 15, 1862, disd Nov 22, 1862, disab)

Garrison, Robert M, e Aug 22, 1862, died at Milliken's Bend, La

Marsh, A A, e Aug 15, 1862

Winsell, A T, e Aug 13, 1862

Company I.

Reuben Sperry, e Aug 22, 1862.

Ruark, James, e Aug 20, 1862

Company K.

Bartholomew, L, e Aug. 16, 1862, kld at Ringgold, Ga

Brown, James, e Aug 16, 1862, wd at Vicksburg

THIRTY-SEVENTH INFANTRY

[NOTE —*This Regiment was mustered out at Davenport, Iowa Date not given in Adjutant General's Reports*]

Company C.

Capt. Ezekiel A M Swasey, com Dec 15, 1862 died at Farmington Jan 3, 1863

Sergt Alex Holladay, e Oct 3, 1862 died at St Louis

Corp David Garrett, e Oct 3, 1862

Corp T C Ware, e Oct. 8, 1862

Corp Edward Sleigh, e Oct 8, 1862

Corp. J. Oliver, e Oct 8, 1862, disd Sept 26, 1864

Alexander, J L, e Oct 19, 1862, disd Sept 26, 1864.

Bateman, W., e. Oct 8, 1862

Brown, W, e Oct 3, 1862

Carr, J, e Oct 24, 1862, disd Oct 23, '63

Davis. Jas, e. Sept. 24, 1862

Fuller, John, e Oct 9, 1862, disd March 6, 1863

Geabel, John, e Oct 8, 1862

Myers, Samuel, e Sept 30, 1862, died at Alton, Ill

Newsome, Stephen, e, Oct 1, 1862, disd March 6, 1863, disab)

Sivil, John, e Oct 9, 1862, died Memphis

Walker, Jesse e Oct 8, 1862

Company E.

Bean, Wm W, e Sept 19, 1862, disd May 18, 1864, disab

Holcomb Wm H, e Oct 1, 1862

Talbert, E, e Oct 1, 1862

Veasey, John H., e Sept 19, 1862

Company H.

Murphy, Edw, e Oct 10, 1862, disd April 12, 1863, disab)

FORTY-FIFTH INFANTRY

[One hundred days]

[NOTE.—*This Regiment was mustered out at Keokuk, Sept. 16, 1864*]

Chaplain Anson Skinner, com May 25, '64

Surg Saml H Stutsman, e May 25, 1864

Company A.

Gableman, F, e May 7, 1864

Gableman, Chas, e May 9, 1864

Company C

Armstrong, O H P, May 10, 1864

Green, F M, May 10, 1864

Company E.

Wallam, Jacob e May 6, 1864

Company H.

Endersby, Jas H, e May 3, 1864

Taylor, Calvin, e May, 15, 1864

Wheatley, Job, e May 15, 1864

Company I.

Sergt Henry Moss, e May 9, 1864

Corp Benj. Widner, e May 9 1864

Crum, C C, e May 9, 1864

Carr, T J, e May 18, 1864

Faith, W S, e May 9, 1864

Green, D H e May 9 1864

Gurwell, Ezra, e May 9, 1864

Hughes, J G, e May 9, 1864

Hornby, John D, e May 9, 1864.

Hurt W S, e May 9, 1864

Harness Taylor, e May 9, 1864

Kelley, Samuel, e May 9, 1864

Knox, Nelson, e May 9, 1864

Low, Nathaniel H, e May 14, 1864

Latimer, J B, e May 9, 1864

Levacy, Taylor, e May 9, 1864

Maddix, J C, e May 16, 1864

Moore, D H, e May 9, 1864

McCausland, J, e May 9, 1864

Moss, Edgar, e May 17, 1864

Oglebee, John W, e May 7, 1864

Stansbery, R R, e May 9, 1864

Torrence Wm C., e May 16, 1862

Company K.

Capt Isaac B Thatcher, com May 25, '64

First Lieut. Andrew C Paine, com May 25, 1864

Second Lieut Clement Wood, com May 25, 1864

First Sergt Jas N McCrary, e May 1, 1864
Sergt Jas M McLane, e May 7, 1864
Sergt Wm V Schuyler, e May 7, 1864
Sergt Ed Dibble, e May 9, 1864
Sergt Henry Freed, e May 7, 1864.
Corp Jas L Michael, e May 7, 1864
Corp Edw R Mason, e May 9 1864
Corp Oliver O Stokes, e May 7, 1864
Corp R B Curtis, e May 11, 1864
Corp Andrew Hoffman, e May 9, 1864
Corp Silas A Jameson, e May 13, 1864
Corp Perry Sutton, e May 7, 1864
Corp Silas Lichty, e May 10, 1864
Musician Jno W Gilbert, e May 7, 1864
Cook Abraham Ford, e. May 25, 1864
Antill, John, e May 16, 1864
Alexander, Andrew, e. May 9, 1864
Bell, Hugh, e May 14, 1864
Benson, Wm H, e May 11, 1864
Brown, Ira, e May 9, 1864
Bond, Jno P, e. May 9, 1864
Bostock, Jno W, e May 11, 1864
Colton, Erastus, e May 9, 1864
Cleveland, Cyrus, e May 12, 1864
Cassiday, Frank, e May 12, 1864
Coolidge, H L, e May 12, 1864
Clark, Irus, e May 16, 1864
Carnes, A, e May 3, 1864
Cochrell, James e May 18, 1864
Delker, Geo, e May 13, 1864
Duer, Jas H, e May 19, 1864
Elliott, Simon, e May 16, 1864
Everts, A, e May 7, 1864
Frazee, Samuel J, e May 18, 1864
Fulton, O C, e May 9, 1864
Franklin, Geo W, e May 7, 1864
Fichey, Jas, e May 18, 1864
Fry, Wm F, e May 19, 1864
Gardner, Robt, e May 7, 1864
Gardner, Jno, e May 7, 1864
Garreson, McKinza, e May 7 '64, drowned at Moscow, Tenn, while bathing
Goble, Henry, e May 7, 1864
Goddard, T R, e May 3, 1864
Gilbert, Jno W, e May 7, 1864
Houghton, O L, e May 7, 1864
Jack, Jno F, e. May 23, 1864.
Kimbel, Francis, e May 7, 1864
Kendall, Wm, e May 7, 1864
Lucas, Samuel, e May 18, 1864
Lidolph, Ernst, e May 12, 1864
Miller, T C, e May 16, 1864
Morrill, Benj F, e May 3, 1864
Michael, Jos F, e May 7, 1864
McCan, Wm, e May 16, 1864
McElfresh, Wm H, e May 16, 1864
McKenny, E W, e May 16, 1864
Meek Samuel G, e May 7, 1864
Mitchell, Jos E, e May 9, 1864
Miller, Jos W, e May 12, 1864
Park, Samuel C, e. May 7, 1864
Phillips, E S., e May 7, 1864
Ricketts, J J, e May 14, 1864
Ramsey, R P, e May 7, 1864
Rogers, Jos, e May 7, 1864
Roberts, A W, e May 14, 1864
Root, E. D, e May 6, 1864

Richardson, W H, e May 11 1864
Sprague, Solomon, e May 21, 1864
Stewart, J F, e May 9, 1864
Santord, S S, e May 9 1864
Stine, Arnold, e May 16 1864
Smith, W E, e May 12, 1864
Sheppard, H M, e May 17, 1864
Sawyer, A W, e May 9, 1864
Tregloan, John, e May 9, 1864
Trembath Wm, e May 7, 1864
Turton, H A, e May 14 1864
Taylor, J F, e May 14, 1864
Thompson, Hiram, e May 3, 1864
Walker, J R, e May 7, 1864
Ward D W, e May 9, 1864
Walker, W M, e May 12, 1864
Wagers, W M, e May 11, 1864
Wheeler, C F, e May 3, 1864
White, Robert, e May 3, 1864

THIRD CAVALRY

[Note.—This regiment was mustered out at Atlanta, Aug 9, 1865]

Col Henry C Caldwell, com maj, Aug 26, 1861, prmtd lieut col Sept. 5, 1862, prmtd, col May 1, 1864, appointed U S District Judge Arkansas August 23 1864
Maj Oliver H P Scott, com capt, Co B Aug 30, 1861, prmtd maj Oct 25, 1862, resd Aug 3, 1863
Maj John McCrary, com 1st lieut Co G Aug. 30, 1861 prmtd capt Aug 7, 1862, prmtd maj May 23, 1864, resd Jan 4 1865.
Maj Peter H Walker, e as corp Co H Aug 28, 1861, prmtd sergt, then capt Nov 20, 1862, prmtd maj Sept 16, 64
Asst Surg Samuel Whitten, com March 30, 1864
Q M Thomas S Wright, com Nov 3, 1864, not mustered, captd Dec 4, 1864, m o as private Co G
Bat Adjt Rufus L Miller, com Aug 26, 1861.
Chaplain Jas W Latham, com Oct 1, 64
B Q M S Wm A Grayum, e Aug 30, 1861

Company A.

Hoskins, Clark, e Jan 2, 1864
Haylen, Wm, e Dec. 29 1863
Holt, Randolph, e Dec 26, 1863
Isaac, Griffith, vet Jan 1, 1864
Murray, James, e Jan 21, 1864
Park, A B, e. Dec 30, 1863
Richards, Wm, e Dec 23, 1863.
Stephenson, J M, e Jan 4, 1864.
Toler, J L, e Jan 16, 1864, kld Atlanta
Vandyke, Wilbur, e Feb 10 1864.

Company B.

Capt Samuel J McKee, com 2d lieut. Aug. 30, 1861, prmtd 1st lieut Nov 13, 1862 prmtd capt Sept 27, 1864, res March 31 or June 19 1865.

First Lieut Wm E Forker, e as bugler
Aug 23, 1861, prmtd 2d lieut Sept 27,
1861 prmtd 1st lieut July 20, 1865, m
o as 2d lieut
Sergt C. M. Ware, e Aug 23, 1861
Corp Jno A Perry e Aug 23, 1861, disd.
Jan 6, 1862, disab
Corp C Westcott, e Aug 23, 1861
Corp C Hatrick, e Aug 23, 1861
Corp W H Spears, e Aug 23, 1861, vet.
Jan 1, 1864
Corp G A A Dean, e Aug 23, 1861
Corp H Enbody, e Aug 23, 1861, vet Jan
1 1864, disd Dec 23, 1864
Farrier G Nasker, e. Aug 23, 1861
Wagoner Elias D Carpenter, e Aug 23,
1861, vet Jan. 1, 1864
Amos, I , e Jan 2, 1864
Alexander, Wm , e Aug 23, 1861, died at
Memphis
Bailey, D. A., e. Feb 9, 1864
Beeson Jno M., e Aug 23, 1861
Bremer, A , e. Aug 23, 1861.
Clefford S. K , e. Dec 31, 1864
Carr, Jno. e Aug. 23, 1861, disd Nov.
20, 1862
Carpenter E E , e Aug 23, 1861
De Witt, Nelson, e Dec 1, 1863, died at
Memphis
Dunn, Jno T , e Aug. 23, 1861, died at
St. Louis
Fox, H W , e Jan. 1, 1864, disd Jan 11,
1865, disab
French, D A., e Aug 23, 1861, vet Jan
1 1864
Fenechole, Chas , e. Feb 29, 1864
Glasser, Jacob, e Aug 23, 1861, died at
Keokuk
Hill, Geo W , e Aug. 23, 1861, disd Dec
26, 1861, disab
Harlen, Elihu, e Feb 29, 1864
Harper, Geo A , e Feb 16, 1864
Johnson, Jno , e March 14, 1864, died at
Memphis
McComb, Hugh, e Feb 27, 1864
McCoy, H. J., e. Dec. 28, 1863
Leaser, Robt. e Aug 23, 1861, vet Jan
1, 1864.
King, Miles, vet Jan 1, 1864, wd at Osage,
Mo , died at Columbus, Ga
Lundy Nathan, e Aug 23, 1861, vet Jan
1, 1864
McCoy, Anderson, e Aug 23, 1861, disd
March 5, 1863
Mattox, Wm M , e Aug 23, 1861 disd
Dec 27, 1861
Pool, Jos P , e Aug 23, 1861, vet Jan 1,
1864, wd at Osage, Mo
Proper, Wm , e Dec 30, 1863
Parker, Wm N e Dec 25, 1863
Penson, James, e. Jan 2, 1863, wd at Big
Blue, Mo
Risner, Chas , e Jan 2, 1864
Rhoads, Geo W , e Feb 10, 1864, killed
near Ripley, Miss
Schneider Wm e Aug 23 1861
Scott, S I , e Aug 23 1861 e disd July
3, 1862

Smith, Isaac F , e Aug 23, 1861, vet Jan
1, 1864
Wilson, Samuel e Aug 23, 1861, vet Jan
1, 1864
Wright, Noah, e Dec 30, 1863
Wilcoxson, H C., e. Aug 23, 1861 died
Oct 26, 1861

Company C.

Ellis, Edw , e Jan 4, 1864
Gamble, Harvey, e Dec 23, 1863
Miller, Nathan, e Feb 9, 1864
Palmer, Wm F , e Jan 4, 1864
Pratt, E , e Jan 4, 1864
Pennell, Garrett, e Feb 13, 1864, killed at
Osage, Mo
Palmer, H W , e Jan 1, 1864
Pratt, C C , e Jan 4, 1864

Company D.

Second Lieut. Francis M. Ross, e as sergt
Aug 24, 1861, prmtd 2d lieut Jan 1,
1862, resd Feb 14, 1863
Corp Edward Nelson, e Aug 24, 1861
Benning, H S , e Sept 13, 1861, captd at
La Grange, Ark. vet. Jan 1, 1864,
prmtd corp , kld at Ripley, Miss
Bell, D S , e Sept 26, 1861, captd at La
Grange, Ark
Crawford, Wm , e Sept 17, 1861, vet Jan
1, 1864
Edwards, W H , captd at Oakland, Miss ,
vet Jan 1, 1864
Mercer, Jas F , e Sept 17, 1861, kld bat-
tle Pea Ridge and scalped by Indians
Mercer, Elijah, e Sept 17, 1861, disd
June 5, 1862, disab
Moore, Levi J , e Sept 17, 1861, trans to
Inv Corps
Paxton, Jas W , vet Jan 1, 1864
Salter, Wm F , e Aug 24, 1861, vet Jan
1, 1864
Salter, G W , e Feb 22 1864, deserted
June 22, 1864

Company E.

Armstrong, B S , e Nov 12, 1863
Phelps, A H , e Oct 26, 1863

Company F.

Granfield, L , e Aug 26, 1861

Company G.

Capt Emanuel Mayne, com. Aug 30,
1861, kld at Kirkville, Mo , Aug 6, '62
Capt. Jno S Stidger, com 2d lieut Aug
30, 1861, prmtd 1st lieut Aug 7, 1862,
prmtd capt Aug 10, 1864
First Lieut Jas H. Watts, e as sergt
Aug 26, 1861, prmtd 2d lieut Aug 7,
1862, prmtd 1st lieut. Aug 10, 1864, wd
Independence, Mo , died Leavenworth,
Kan
First Lieut Chas B Leach, e as sergt
Aug 26 1861 prmtd 2d lieut Aug 10,
1861 prmtd 1st lieut Nov 5, 1864

Second Lieut Jno F Watkins, e as corp Aug 26, 1861, pintd com sergt. then 2d lieut Nov. 5, 1864

Q M Sergt Franklin Miller, e Aug 26, 1861, vet Jan 1, 1864, wd and captd June 11, 1864, died Cahaba, at Ala

Sergt F. A Moxley, e Aug 26, 1861. disd April 2, 1862

Sergt C B Leach, e Aug 26, 1861, vet Jan. 1, 1864

Sergt O H Graham, e Aug 26, 1861, vet Jan 1, 1864

Sergt David B Smith, e Aug 26, 1861, disd. date unknown died

Sergt H W Hutton, e Aug 26, 1861 vet Jan 1, 1864, disd Dec 11, 1864

Sergt James E Miller, e Aug 26, 1861, disd Nov. 9, 1862, disab.

Sergt Jas A Dunnan, e Aug 26, 1861, vet. Jan 1, 1864.

Sergt R R Watts, e Aug 26, 1861, vet Jan 1, 1864

Corp T. B Hutzell, e Aug. 26, 1861, vet Jan 1, 1864.

Corp David Miller, e Aug 26, 1861, vet Jan. 1, 1864, kld at Guntown,, Miss

Corp Solomon F Baker, e Aug 26, 1861, disd April 22 1864, disab

Corp J L Brown, e Aug 26, 1861, vet Jan 1, 1864

Corp Jas N McCrary e Aug 26, 1861, disd Jan 29, 1862, disab

Corp Albert Baker, e. Aug 26, 1861

Corp Robert R. Watts, e Aug 26, 1861

Corp Geo W Tuttle, e Aug 26, 1861, vet Jan 1, 1864

Bugler Jesse Cubberly, e Aug 26, 1861, disd July 1 1862, sick

Bugler A. Van Brink, e Aug 26, 1861, died at St Louis

Bugler Geo L Kutzner, e Aug 26, 1861, disd April 25, 1863, to accept prom

Farrier Geo M Cox, e Aug 26, 1861, disd June 26, 1862, disab

Farrier A H Botkin. e Aug 26, 1861, disd Jan 26 1862

Farrier Jos Bonnegar, e Aug 26, 1861, vet Jan 1, 1864

Saddler Wm H Miller, e Aug 26, 1861

Saddler M J Burns, e March 11, 1862

Wagoner D B. Smith, e Aug 26, 1861, disd. July 4, 1864, disab

Wagoner Wm. L Thompson, e Aug 26, 1861, vet Jan 1, 1864

Teamster Jos. Wagner, e Aug 26 1861

Teamster Daniel R Shaw, e Aug 26 1861

Aylon, Wm , e. Aug 26, 1861, died at Little Rock, Ark

Bockman. J A , e Aug. 26, 1861. disd Jan 6-7, 1863, disab.

Brooks, John, e Aug 26, 1861, disd at Keokuk, 1861

Burns, J W , e Aug 26, 1861, vet Jan 1, 1864

Burton, Ira, e Aug 26, 1861, disd Oct. 1861, vet. Jan 1 1864

Barker, A S. e. Aug 26, 1861

Bishop, Richard e Aug 26, 1861

Bailey, David, e Feb 18, 1864, wd.

Boston, A. R , e Feb 27, 1864

Botkin, O F , e Feb 26, 1864

Baker, C A, e Nov 5, 1861, died at Little Rock

Burns, M S, e Feb 25, 1864, died May 11, 1864

Bingaman, W. H , e Dec 25, 1863

Barker, J H , e Dec 25, 1863

Cocherell, Alpheus, e Feb 29, 1864

Carter, James, e Feb 16, 1862

Crandall, J N , e Feb 20, 1864

Cochrun, T H , e Aug 26, 1861, died Dec. 24, 1861

Clark, W W , e Aug 26, 1861, vet Jan 1, 1864

Carter, M D, e. Aug 26, 1861, vet Jan 1, 1864

Carter, James, e Aug 26, 1861

Dunlapp R E , e Aug. 26, 1866, vet Jan. 1, 1864

Edmonston, J G , e Aug 26, 1861, vet Jan 1, 1864.

Fray, George, e. Aug 26, 1861, vet Jan 1 1864

Fletcher, H N , e Aug 26, 1861, vet Jan 1, 1864

Gnash, T , e Dec 31, 1863

Goughnout, J , e Aug. 26 1861, vet. Jan 1 1864

Gillett, N H , Feb 17, 1864

Graynum, W A , e Aug 30, 1861, pintd bat Q M sergt Sept 10, 1861, disd Oct. 3, 1862

Hamlin, H C, e Aug 26, 1861, disd April 7, 1862, disab

Hamilton, W B, e Aug 28, 1862

Hunter, E , e Aug 26, 1861 vet Jan 1, '64

Hathaway, S , e Aug 26, 1861, vet Jan 1, 1864

Henry, Volney. e Aug 26, 1861, vet Jan 1, 1864, disd June 29, 1865

Hollingsworth, W J , e Dec. 31, 1863

Hollingshead, G S , e. Jan 4, 1864

Hamilton, W M B , vet. Jan 1, 1864

Hines, John, e Feb 29, 1864

Hardin, J M , e Dec 26, 1863

Jones, I. A , e Jan 4, 1864

Jewitt, Orin, e Aug 26, 1861, vet Jan 1, 1864

Jones, Isaac, e Aug. 26, 1861, vet Jan 1, 1864

Jewett, F D, e Aug 26, 1861, vet Jan 1, 1864

Kutzner, George L , e Sept 6, 1861

Kimball, S C , e Aug 26 1861

Kerwin, Thomas, e Aug 26, 1861, trans to gunboat service Feb 17, 1862

Kent, E. e Feb 16, 1862

Knox, James M , e Aug 26, 1861, died at Rolla, Mo

Knox, Xerxes, e Aug 26, 1861, captd May 1, 1864

Lane, A H , e Nov 11, 1863

Loring, L H , e. Aug 26, 61, vet Jan 1 '64

Linn, Isaac, e Aug 26 1861

Livingston, H K , e Aug 26, 1861, vet Jan 1, 1864

Leeper, James e Aug 26, 1861, vet Jan 1, 1864, trans V R. C Nov 22, 1861
Lowe, John E, e Dec 29, 1863
Long, George, e Feb 29, 1864
Lane Alden, e Feb 29, 1864
Murray, James, e Feb 16, 1862
Matheson, James L, Jan 4, 1864
Miller, John, e Aug 22, 1862
Miller, J J, e Feb 22 1864
McCrary, A N, e Feb 20, 1864
Mayne, Leroy, e May 1 1861 trans for pmtn 2d heut Marine Brigade March 30, 1863
Miller, Rufus L, e Aug 26, 1861
Miller Benjamin e Aug 26, 1861, disd Sept 27, 1862, disab
Miller, J S, e Aug 26, 1861, disd Feb 25, 1862, disab
Miller, W H, e Aug 26, 1861
McCue, B, e March 11, 1862
McSurley, Benjamin, e Aug 26, 1861, died Aug 26, 1862
Madtkin, W H, e Aug 26, 1861, missing in action at Harrisburg, Miss, died at Louisville, Ky
Mast, I W, e Aug 26, 1861, vet Jan 1, '64
Norris, John, e Aug 26, 1861, disd March 23, 1863, disab
Nagle, Volney, e Dec 1, 1863
Owings, D C, e Aug 26, 1861
Owings, John W, e Aug 26, 1861, disd Feb 25, 1862
Pace, James W, e Aug 26, 1861, vet Jan 1, 1864
Parker, Robert M, e Aug 26, 1861, kld battle Moore's Mills, July 28, 1862
Peterson, Jacob R, e. Dec. 11, 1863
Paine, Thomas, e Aug. 26, 1861, disd April 16, 1862
Pratt, Isaiah, e Jan 2, 1864
Palmer, J W, e Aug 26, 1861, vet Jan 1, 1864
Peterson, W H, e Dec 7, 1863
Pierce, W W, e Aug 26, 1861, vet Jan 1, 1864, disd July 10, 1865
Row, John, e Aug 26, 1861
Ricketts, James M, e Aug 26, 1861
Reed, Andrew, e Aug 26, 1861
Smith, H H, e Aug 26, 1861, vet Jan 1 1864
Shane, John W, e Aug 26 1861 vet. Jan 1, 1864
Sadler, Samuel, e Aug 26, 1864
Shuey, A J, e Aug 26, 1861, vet Jan. 1, 1864
Simmons, Thomas, e Aug 26, 1861, vet Jan 1, 1864
Stull, F e Aug 26, 1861, vet Jan 1 1864
Smith, John E, e Aug 26, 1861, disd March 20, 1862
Snyder, James T, e. Jan 4, 1864
Stock, James A, e Dec 23, 1863
Stiger, George A, e. Feb 22, 1864
Stone, James Y, e Feb 24, 1864
Sullivan William J, e Sept 30, 1864 vet Jan 1 1864
Shephard C W, e Aug 26, 1861 vet Jan 1 1864, disd to accept promotion

Thurber, William H, e Aug 22, 1864
Thompson J G, e Aug 26 1861, vet. Jan 1, 1864
Tuttle, George W, e Aug 29, 1861
Tackerberry, John e Aug 26, 1861, disd. Feb 25, 1862 disab
Vandyke, W, e Aug 26, 1861, disd Jan. 25, 1863, disab
Wilson James, e Aug 26 1861, vet Jan 1, 1864
Wilson, Omer, e Jan 4 1864
Wright, John W, e Feb 23 1864
Wright, T S, e March 13, 1864, pmtd adjt Nov 3, 1864, captd Memphis
Whitelsey, L H, e May 9 1863, died at Memphis

Company H.

Capt Jas Hughes, com Sept 10 1861, resd Nov 18, 1862
Capt Jas R. Gronsbeck, e as priv Aug 28, 1861, pmtd 2d heut March 8, 1863, captd near Fulton, Mo pmtd 1st heut, April 23, 1864, pmtd capt Jan. 22, 1865
First Lieut Hiram Barnes, com Sept 10, 1861 resd March 7 1863
First Lieut Geo W Newell, com 2d heut Sept 10, 1861, bat Q M Sept 20, 1861, returned to Co, pmtd 1st heut. March 8, 1863, m o April 22, 1864
First Lieut Samuel A Young, e as priv Aug 28, 1861, pmtd 2d heut April 23, 1864 pmtd, 1st heut Jan 22, 1865
Second Lieut Mitchell I Buch, e as sergt Aug 28, 1861, pmtd 2d heut Dec 10, 1861 resd July 24, 1862, erroneously apptd
Second Lieut. Wm Wycoff, e as corp. Aug. 28, '61, pmtd 2d heut Jan 22, '65
Q M Sergt John D Gibson, e Aug 28, 1861, disd Dec 25, 1862
Com Sergt Newton L Calhoun, e Aug 28, 1861
Sergt Wm Buch, e Aug 28, 1861, disd. May 27 1863, disab
Sergt Hiram Coffman, e Aug 28, 1861, disd July 8 1865
Sergt I C Gillett Aug 28, 1861
Sergt Wm Wycoff, e Aug 28 1861, vet Jan 1 1864
Sergt Miles N Newman, e Aug 28, 1861, vet Jan 1, 1864
Corp N J. Moore, e Aug 28, 1861, vet Jan 1 1864
Corp M V B Sigler, e Aug 28, 1861.
Corp Jas P. Beale, e Sept 9, 1861 captd at Whitewater, Mo, vet Jan 1, 1864
Corp James A Barnes, e Aug 28, 1861, disd April 30, 1862, disab
Corp Thos Lonnon, e Aug 28, 1861, died Dec 28, 1861
Corp John D Maddix e Sept 2, 1861, vet Jan 1, 1864
Corp Marion Bechtel, e Aug 20, 1862, died at Winchester
Corp Chas A Skinner, Sept 7, 1861 vet Jan 1, 1864

Corp Bazwell Gurwell, e Sept 11, 1861 vet Jan 1, 1864

Bugler Jacob C Boon e Aug 28, 1861, captd at Whitewater Mo kld at Carondelet, Miss

Farrier M B Stewart, e. Aug 28, 1861

Farrier H A Standish e. Aug 28, 1861.

Farrier John L Kirkhart, e Oct 16 1861, disd. Nov 18, 1862 disab

Teamster Wm Robertson, e Sept 7 '61, vet Jan 1 1864

Anderson J e. Feb 15, 1864

Saddler Wm F James, e Aug 28 1861, wd at Whitewater, Mo

Allen Daniel, e Feb 1, 1864

Brown Geo W, e Aug 28 1861

Butler Wm, e Sept 2, 1862, vet Jan 1, 1864, disd May 17, 1865, disab

Butterfield E, e Sept 9 1861, captd at Whitewater and Camden, Ark

Balback, Andrew, e Sept 11, 1861, captd at Whitewater, and again Nov 11, 63

Barker Arnold C, e Sept 10, 1862, wd at Moore's Mills, Mo, vet Jan 1, 1864

Boon, Robert L, e Feb 1, 1864

Borden, Harmon, e Dec 26 1863

Culbertson, John R e Feb 1 1864

Calhoun, Saml, e. Feb 1, 1864 died May 1, 1864

Clark, W M Feb 15, 1864, died May 23, 1864, at Memphis

Curtis, Anson, e Dec 29 1863

Campbell, F W, e Aug 28 1861, wd at Moore's Mills captd at Whitewater

Chapman, Wm, e Aug 28, 1861, captd at Camden, Ark

Dcahl, Wm R, e Aug 28, 1861, disd July 26, 1863

Ealer, C e Sept 18, 1861

Estle, Geo e Sept 18, 1861 disd March 13, 1862, disab

Freshwater, A, e Feb. 1, 1864

Faler, S A, e Aug 2, 1862, vet Jan 1, 1864

Freshwater, Daniel, e Feb 1, 1864

Gleason, C W, e Sept. 18 1861, wd at Moore's Mills, Mo, disd Oct 17, 1862

Groesbeck, D L e. Feb 15, 1864

Gibson, John D, e Jan 4, 1864

Hope, Wm H, e Feb 15 1864

Haney, Samuel J, e. Dec 4, 1864

Haney, Jas, e Dec 25 1864 captd near White's Station, Tenn

Harker, Clayton, e Feb 3, 1863 captd near White Station, Tenn

Hurlbut, D S, e Dec 19, 1863

Hesket, E, e Sept 18 1861, disd Nov 18 1862, disab

Howard John F, e Sept 18 1861, vet Jan 1, 1864

Hurlbut E C, Sept 9, 61, vet Jan 1 '64

Johnston David e Feb. 1 1864

Johnston, Russell, e. Feb 27, 1864

Kirkhart S D, e Sept 9, '61, vet Jan 1 '64

Light, Jas A, e Sept 9, 1861

Lane, Saml E, e Sept. 9 1861 vet Jan 1, 1864

Masterson John F, e Aug 28 '61 died Oct 25, 1861.

McGuire, John A, e Sept 2 1861, kld at Mexico, Mo, by Bushwhackers

Moss, Martin, e Feb 29, 1864.

Miller, John W, e Dec 29, 1863

Maddox, Jos

McLanahan, Thos, e Feb 12, 1864

Moore, Orrin P, e. Nov 20, 1863

Newell, Wm, e. Feb 1 1864, captd at White's Station, Tenn

Norris, Samuel C, e Feb 15 1864, captd at White's Station, Tenn

Newell, Leonidas e Dec 30, 1863

Norton, N O, e Sept 2, 1861, disd March 13 1862

Patterson John F, e Aug 28, 1861 disd March 13, 1862

Piatt O A, e Aug 28, '61, vet Jan 1, '64.

Piatt, Robert, e Aug 28, 1861, disd Sept. 12, 1863

Pettit Daniel C, e March 15, 1861, vet Jan 1, 1864

Parker, O B, e Feb 22, 1864

Rand Jas. M, e Feb 15 1864.

Ready, Chas G, e Feb 15, 1864.

Swartz, D H, e Feb 22, 1864

Simon, F, e Feb 25, 1864.

Stump David J, e. Dec 29, 1863, captd at White's Station, Tenn

Stump, Jas W, e Jan. 4, 1864

Sperry, Walter I, e Feb 6, 1864

Shaw, J R, e Aug 28, 1861, vet Jan 1, 1864

Sutton J, vet Jan 1 1864

Simmons, T A, e Aug 28, 1861, vet Jan 1 1864

Saddler, Josiah e Aug 2, 1861, vet Jan 1 1864

Smith, W R, e Sept 7, 1861, disd May 20, 1863, disab

Sanders Z W, e Aug 28, 1861, vet Jan 1, 1864

Trotter, C D e Aug 28, 1861

Vansickle S, e Aug 28 1861, captd at Whitewater, Mo

Vansickle Harrison, e Aug 28, 1861, captd. at Whitewater, Mo wd Tupelo

Walters, M W, e Aug 28, 1861, disd Jan 13, 1862

Work Wm e Aug. 28, 1861, captd at Camden

Whitaker, F G, e Aug 28, 1861, disd. April 30, 1862 disab

Wycoff Jos, e Aug. 20, 1862, vet Jan 1 1864

Company I.

Linn, Isaac, e, Aug. 26, 1861

Standish, H A, e Aug 28, 1861 disd

Company K.

Homer, Johnson e Sept 3, 1861

Company M.

Lane, F M, e Feb 24 1864

COMPANY UNKNOWN

Abbott, J H, e Dec 7, '63

Amos, Isaac, e Jan 1 '64

Brooks, E M , e. Feb 23, 1864
Borden, H , e Dec 26, 1863
Brooks, E C., e Feb 29, 1864
Bingman, W H , e. Dec 25, 1863
Barker, J H , e Dec 25, 1863
Clifford, S K , e Dec 31, 1863
Cowen, G H , e Feb 8, 1864
Curtls, A L , e Dec 29 1863
Crandall, J N , e Feb 20, 1864
Calhoun, Hugh, e Jan 4 1863
Dewight, Nelson, e Dec 1, 1863
Ellis, Edward, e Jan 4, 1863
Fox, H W , e Jan. 1, 1863
Gibson, J D , e Jan 4, 1863
Gamble, Harvey, e Dec 23, 1863
Gnash, Allen, e Dec 31, 1863
Gnash, Thomas, e Dec 31, 1863
Hagler, Wm , e Dec 29, 1863.
Hannan, G T , e Dec 1, 1863
Hawk, R T , e Jan 28, 1864
Hollingshead, G S , e Jan 4, 1863
Hollingsworth, W J , e Dec 21, 1863
Haskins, Clark, e Jan 2, 1863
Hardin, J M e Dec 26, 1863
Holt, Randolph, e Dec 26, 1863
Hurlbert, D S , e Dec 19, 1863
Jones, J A , e Jan 4, 1863
Lowe, J E , e Dec 29, 1863
Moore, O P. e Nov 20, 1853
Mattocks J L , e Dec 29, 1863
McCoy, H J , e Dec 28, 1863
Miller, J W , e Dec 29, 1863
Mathieson, J L , e Jan 4, 1863
Mercer, Elijah, e Jan 4, 1863
Nagle, Volney, e Dec 1, 1863
Newell, Leonidas, e Dec 30, 1863
Norton, N D , e Dec 29, 1863
Ormsby A W , e Nov 10, 1863
Palmer, W F , e Jan 4, 1864
Prall, C C , e Jan 4, 1864
Phillips, H F e. Feb 15, 1864.
Prall, E , e Jan 4, 1864
Palmer, H W , e Jan 4, 1864
Platt, Isaiah, e Jan 2, 1864
Park, A B , e Dec 30, 1863
Peterson, J R , e Dec 11, 1863
Peterson, W H e Dec 7, 1863
Pierson, James, e Dec 25, 1863
Parker, W N , e Dec 30, 1863
Rull, J A , e Nov 9, 1863
Richards, Wm , e Dec 23, 1863
Risner, Charles, e Jan 2, 1864
Roberts, I J , e Jan 4, 1864
Robinson, W J , e Dec. 11, 1863
Rigsby, Benjamin, e Dec. 1, 1863
Seells, W H , e Dec 10, 1863
Smith, J E , e Dec 21, 1863
Stephenson, J M , e Jan. 4, 1864
Stump, J W , e Jan 4 1864
Stuck, J A , e Dec 23, 1864
Scott, S F , e Jan 4, 1864
Wilson, Omer, e Jan 4, 1864
White, O J , e Dec 25, 1864
Wright Noah, e Dec. 30, 1864
Wedge, Austin, e Dec 1, 1864
White J H e. Dec. 27 1864
White, I D , e Dec 2 1864
Walters, Joseph, e Dec 2 1864

SEVENTH CAVALRY

Company A.

[NOTE—This regiment was mustered out at Leavenworth, Kan , May 17, 1866, and June 22, 1866]

Corp Wm H. Boyd e Nov 18, 1862
Corp David Huddleston e Nov. 18, 1862
Campbell, E , e Nov. 18, 1862
Gardner, J , e Nov 7, 1862, drowned at Ponca, N T
Harrell, Peter, e Nov 18, 1862
Lewis, Dempster, e Feb 12, 1862
Lemmon, Jno A , e Oct 17, 1862
Powell, Ancil, e Nov 18, 1862
Robison, James, e Nov 18, 1862

Company C.

Corp J J. Nelson, e Jan 20, 1863
Saddler Jas M Knapp, e March 2, 1863
Wagoner S A Brown, e Feb 1, 1863
Abenathy, Wm T , e Dec 27, 1862
Brown, Smith A , Jr , e Feb 1, 1863
Bean Wm. W , e March 2, 1863
Canterbery, Q A , e March 7, 1863
Cackley, C. J , e. March 7, 1863
Spurbeck, W E e March 31, 1864
Ryan, Chas , e March 31, 1864
Smith, Jno T , e March 31, 1864
Climie, Robt , e March 19, 1862
Coon, Jas W , March 28, 1864
Coon, John, e Jan 1 1863
Hix, Robt M. e Dec. 15, 1862
Miller, Hiram, e Dec 10, 1862
Penrod, E , e March 28, 1864
Riffle, Lemuel, e March 12, 1863
Torrence, Robt , e Jan 1, 1863
Tompkins, Jas H., e March 18, 1863
Tutwiler, Jos N , e March 16, 1863

Company D.

Corp Wm Bryan, e April 1, 1863
Corp Reuben Sperry, e March 20, 1863
Atkins, Benj , e April 20, 1863
Brown, Wm N , e April 1, 1863, died at Davenport
Colson, Wm , e March 13, 1863
Daniels, J E O A , e Feb 22, 1863
Lewis, Samuel, e April 1, 1863
Mercer, Jacob N , e April 18, 1863
Morrison, Wm H , e April 1, 1863
Trout, Jno W e March 20, 1863

Company E.

Conn, Jas , e May 20, 1863
Frazer, Jno J , e May 11, 1863
Rice, Philip, e May 20, 1863

Company H.

Bonner, Crawford, e June 18, 1863
Elmer, Adelbert, e June 17, 1863

Company L.

Russell, Jno E , e Feb 22, 1864

COMPANY UNKNOWN

Moore Samuel March 31 1864
Salter, Ezra April 4 1864

EIGHTH CAVALRY

Note.—This regiment was mustered out at Macon, Ga August 13, 1865.]

Maj Jas. W Moore, com 1st lieut Co C Sept. 30, 1863, prmtd. capt April 8, 1864, captd at Newnan, Ga , prmtd maj. May 22, 1865

Company C.

Capt Edgar Pickett, com Sept. 30, 1863, resd April 7, 1864

Capt Geo W Detwiler, e prmtd 2d lieut March 12, 1864, prmtd 1st lieut April 18, 1864, prmtd capt June 24, '65

Q M Sergt H. A Hamlin, e July 23, '63

Sergt Jno B Loomis, e. July 29 1863

Sergt Geo A Junk e July 30, 1863, wd and captd near Palmetto, Ga , died at Andersonville

Sergt M Lyon e July 29, 1863, captd at Newnan, Ga.

Corp H C Miller, e July 29, 1863

Corp Jno P Campbell, e. July 21, 1863

Corp Jno I Fulton, e July 29, 1863

Corp Albert Raney, e July 29, 1863, killed near Tilton, Ga

Corp A R Smith, e Aug 3, 1863

Trumpeter H R Hayden, e July 30, 1863

Farrier E Longley, e June 16, 1863

Farrier A Dunn, e. July 25 1863

Wagoner Wm. A Sherod, e July 28, 1863, died at Evansville, La

Arrington. Albert, e July 29, 1863

Belknap Aug J, e. Aug 15, 1863

Benning, C , e Aug 15, 1863

Corns, Rufus. e July 23, 1863

Coughnoui. B P. e July 29, 1863

Day, Geo S , e July 31 1863

Findlay, Hugh e July 29, 1863, captd at Newnan, Ga

Graham Jos , e July 25, 1863

Green, Rufus, e July 29, 1863

Gilbert, Harvey, e July 29, 1863

Gleeson, Wm H , e July 29, 1863

Hoverstock, Geo H , e July 28, 1863

Henry Benj F e July 24, 1863, captd near Pleasant Ridge, Ga., killed at Kingston Ga by bushwhackers

Hunter, Cyrus E , e July 29, 1863

Hudson Lemuel e July 20, 1863

Lee. John, e Aug. 15, 1863, disd June 15, 1864 disab

Miller, Eli, e July 20 1863

Medaugh, John, e July 20 1863

Miller, Jacob, e July 23 1863, captd near Pleasant Ridge. Ga

Moore, John, e July 29, 1863

McClurg D S e Aug. 3, 1863, disd June 12, 1865, disab

McMillen, David, e Aug 5, 1863

Marshall. Chas , e. Aug 3, 1863

Nixon, Jos , e. July 20, 1863 killed at Franklin, Tenn

Pace, Jos C , e July 29, 1863, died Oct 10, 1863

Park, P. H , e Aug 28 1863, died at Newnan, Ga

Ratchff, A L , e Aug 4 1863

Rodabaugh, C , e July 29 1863

Robertson Jno C , e July 27, 1863

Rutledge, Wm B , e July 29, 1863, disd Dec. 12 1863, to ree prom in pro mar dep

Sample, Alex , e July 28, 1863, captd at Newnan, Ga

Stansburg, Jno S , e July 18, 1863, trans to V R C Jan 15 1865

Smith, D C , e July 13, 1863, captd at Pleasant Ridge

Stevens, H R , e July 28, 1863

Smith. D M., e July 30, 1863, captd at Newnan, Ga

Sadler, Simon, e Aug 1, 1863

Sears, Jas W., e Aug 15, 1863

Skinner, Jno B , e. July 28, 1863

Thompson, Harvey, e July 29, 1863

Company E.

Bradford, Leander, e July 11, 1863

Batchelor, Geo. H., e. July 15, 1863 captd at Newnan, Ga , died at Baltimore. Md

Dewit, Elisha, e Aug 10, 1863

Ehrman, Henry, e Aug 10, 1863

Grimsley, H M , e July 3, 1863

Hart Wm H , e July 15, 1863, captd at Newnan, Ga

Hillard, Samuel A , e. July 3, 1863, captd at Newnan, Ga

Jennison John, e June 25, 1863

Leonard, A L , e July 30, 1863

McCoy, Laben, e July 18, 1863

Turton, E J , e July 20, 1863

FIRST INFANTRY (A D)

(60 U S V., A D)

[Note.—This regiment was mustered out at Duvall's Bluff Oct 16, 1865]

Lieut Col G A A Deane, com capt Co B from Bugler Co D, Third Cavalry, prmtd lieut col

Company A.

Patton, Hayden, Aug 19, 1863

Company B.

Capt G A A. Deane, Aug 23, 1861, from musician Co B, Third Cavalry

Bivans, Enoch, Aug 23, 1863, died Helena, Ark

Biggs, Jackson, e Aug 23, 1863

Caldwell, Daniel, e Aug 23, 1863, died Dec 22, 1863

Green, Geo W , e Aug 19, 1863

Matson Henry, e. Aug 23, 1863, died Dec 16, 1863

McCracken, Merit, e Aug 19 1863

Morgan, Albt , e. Aug 23. 1863, died at Helena, Ark.

Nichols, Samuel, e Aug. 23, 1863

Orrison, Jas , e Aug 20, 1863, disd June 23, 1865, disab

Templeton. Robt , e Aug 29, 1863

Sales Wm , e Aug 23 1863 died at Helena, Ark

Sanders, Jas , e Aug 22, 1863.
White, Robt , e Aug. 19, 1863

Company H.

Williams, Robt , e Sept 25, 1863

SOUTHERN BORDER BRIGADE, FIRST BATTALION

[NOTE—Adjutant General's Report gives no date of m o f this regiment]

Company B.

Capt Jos Dickey, com Oct 11 1862
Lieut Silas S Boner com Oct 11, 1862
O Sergt. C A. Manning, e Oct. 11, 1862
Bugler Adam Burkheiser, e Oct. 11, 1862.
Armstrong, C A e Oct 11. 1862
Bell, Elias, e Oct 11, 1862
Blackledge, H , e Oct 11, 1862
Blackledge, E , e Oct 11, 1862
Bateman, M W., e Oct 11, 1862
Bailey, Geo W , e. Oct 11, 1862
Cook, L C , e Oct 11, 1862
Curtis, Adolphus, e Oct 11, 1862
Curtis, R B , e Oct 11, 1862.
Camblin, Jno L , e Oct 11, 1862
Dodson, T C e Oct. 11. 1862
Dickey, John, e Oct 11, 1862
Dickey, A L e Oct 11, 1862
Gleckler, Chas , e 11 1862
Goodin, Asa , e Oct 11 1862
Good, Geo W , e Oct 11, 1862
Gwinnus John, e Oct 11 1862
Harness, M , e Oct 11 1862
Jenkins, Geo W , e Oct 11, 1862.
King, Geo e Oct 11, 1862
Morse, M. H , e Oct 11, 1862
McHenry, M , e Oct 11, 1862
Pettit, Isaiah, e Oct 11, 1862
Ross, Abram, e Oct 11, 1862
Roberts, Wm , e Oct 11 1862
Rhodes Geo , e Oct 11, 1862
Stoddard, A , e Oct. 11, 1862
Sorge, Oscar, e Oct 11, 1862
Steinmyer, F , e Oct 11, 1862
Simmons, D , e Oct 11, 1862
Spencer, John e Oct 11, 1862
Shrewe, Samuel K , e Oct 11, 1862
Schmidt, Jno P , e Oct 11, 1862
Templeton, H , e Oct 11 1862
Van Anken, H , e Oct 11, 1862.
Willbaum, Benj , e Oct 11, 1862
Woolen, Josiah, e Oct 11, 1862.
Walker, Addison, e Oct. 11, 1862
Williamson, John, e Oct 11, 1862
White, Robt , e Oct 11 1862
Wagoner, Gustavus, e Oct 11, 1862.
Wolf, Geo , e Oct 11, 1862
Winlock, H , e Oct 11, 1862

SEVENTH MISSOURI CAVALRY.

Company A.

Q M Sergt G W Alphin e Aug 9 1861, disd Feb 10, 1863
Sergt C N H ... e Aug ...

Sergt S H Crowder, e Aug 9 1861, deserted Sept. 16 1862
Corp A S Wells e Aug 9, 1861
Corp George W Hagler, e Aug 9, 1861 went into ranks
Corp Jefferson Sevier e Aug 9 1861, went into ranks
Bugler Samuel J Backus, e Aug 9, 1861
Allender, A T , e Sept 25 1861, deserted Feb 18, 1862
Brown George, e Aug 9, 1861, wd
Brown, David J e Sept 24, 1861
Brown, H C , e Sept 12 1861
Bailey, George W , e Oct 18, 1861
Barnett, A S , e Sept 9, 1861, kld at battle Lone Jack
Collins, James, e Oct 19, 1861
Christian, John L , e Sept 19, 1861
Christian, Samuel, e Oct 12, 1861
Eakis, D B , e Nov 1, 1861
Fisher, John T., e Aug. 9 1861, wd at Lone Jack
Fisher, Robert F , e Aug 9, 1861
Franklin, Thomas T , e Aug. 9, 1861.
Gruber, T C , e. Aug 9. 1861, pmtd. Q M sergt
Hart J W , e Sept 10, 1861, deserted Oct 10, 1861, from corp
Holder, George W , e Aug 9, 1861
Huddleston, C , e Aug 9, 1861
Hancock, Paul, e Sept 25, 1861
Harrington, Simeon, e. Dec 16, 1861.
Jamison, Henry, e Sept 9, 1861
Jones, Thomas, e Aug 9, 1861
Lagle, James A , e Aug 9, 1861
McCrary James C , e Aug 9, 1861
Murray, Wm , e. Feb 16, 1861
Montgomery, James, e Aug 9, 1861, disd
O'Hara, Samuel, e Aug 9, 1861
Shuster, Isaac, e. Sept 9, 1861
Woodruff, D G , e Aug 9, 1861
Woodruff, Mark, e Sept 9, 1861
Wortman, W G , e Aug 9, 1861

Company C.

Gallop, DeW Clinton, e Feb 5, 1862

Company D.

Polack, L O died at Hudson City, April 19, 1862
Walker, Thomas, e Aug 13, 1862, m o by special order, Aug 27, 1862

TWENTY-FIRST MISSOURI IN-FANTRY

Company F.

Musician Joseph May, e Nov 15 1861

Company G.

Williford, Martin, e Sept 24, 1861

Company H.

Corp Franklin Blackledge, e Oct 1, 1861
Corp C M Bryant, e June 17 1861, deserted

Bryant, Thomas, e June 17 1861, disd
Sept 4, 1862, disab
Elican, Israel, e Nov 6, 1861
Fuqua James W, e Dec 26 1861, disd
Feb 28, 1862, disab
Glasgow, W H, e June 17, 1861
Kinton, F B, e Oct 14 1861
Pollock, William C e Nov 14, 1862
Postlethwait, Chas, e Aug 20, 1861
Wilson, George, e Oct 14, 1861, captd at
Shiloh

Company I.

Thorington, Oscar, e Sept 28, 1861

MISCELLANEOUS

Fourth Infantry.

Simmons, Cornelius, e. July 10, 1861, m o
July 24 1865

Sixth Infantry.

Cleveland, E A, e Aug 15, 1861, m o
July 21, 1865
Ware Isaiah, e July 12, 1861, vet. Jan 1,
1864, m o July 21, 1865
Carter, J, e Aug 8, 1861, pmntd to sergt,
wd and trans. to V R C
Wentworth, A, e July 12, 61, wd Shiloh
Yates, Jacob e July 12, 1861, disd Jan
12, 1862
Quillen, Thomas, e Aug 6, 1861, m o
July 21, 1865
Cassday, Jos, e March 31, 1864, m o
July 21, 1865

Seventh Infantry.

Corp David Thomas, disd Dec 2, 1862

Eighth Infantry.

Frenk, Cyrus, e Aug 15, 1861, disd April
26, 1862, disab

Ninth Infantry.

Huffine, John, e Nov. 15, 1864, m o July
18, 1865
Jolly, Beaden B, e Nov 10, 1864, m o
July 18, 1865
Newman, James H, e Oct 25, 1864, m o
July 18, 1865

Eleventh Infantry.

Corp Rawley Shaw, e Sept 17, 1861, disd
June 18, 1862, disab
Alvey, James M, e Sept 23, 1861, disd
Oct 31, 1862, wds
Black, Wm, e Sept 14, 1861, kld April
6, 1862, at Shiloh
Crooks, Lawson e Sept 28, 1861, trans to
Miss Marine Brigade
Merralt, David, e. Sept. 28, 1861 m o
July 15, 1865
Newman, A G, e Sept 26, 1861, disd
Feb 11, 1862, disab
Kenedy, Daniel, e Sept. 4, 1861, vet Jan.
1, 1864, m o July 15, 1865
Richardson, James e Sept 4, 1861 wd at
Atlanta

Shipley, S H, m o July 15 1865
Shaw, Wm, e Nov 7, 1861, m o July
15, 1865
Stults, G F, e March 16 1864 wd at
Atlanta
Wgly, George, e Sept 16 1861, m o July
15, 1865

Thirteenth Infantry.

Note —This Regiment was mustered out July 21, 1865]

Amos, John, e Oct 25, 1864
Ayler, Geo H, e Oct 25, 1864
Abbott, N R, e Oct 25, 1864
Abernathy, Jas T, e Oct 25, 1864
Alden, Geo W, e Nov 10, 1864
Brown, Jas H e Oct 25, 1864
Bickle, Jacob, e Oct 25, 1864
Bennett, Daniel, e Oct 6, 1864
Bennett, Wm J, e Nov 14 1864
Casey, John, e Oct 25 1864
Curry, W L, e Oct 25, 1864
Clark, John A, e Oct 25, 1864
Campbell, E B, e Oct 25, 1864
Corsen Lewis, e Nov 10 1864
Drew, Wm, e Oct 25 1864
Douthart, I W, e Nov 10, 1864
Fulton, Henry, e Oct 25, 1864
French, Samuel T, e Oct 25, 1864
Harbin, John C, e Nov 4, 1864
Heddleston, Willis, Oct 25, 1864
Hosmor, L, e Oct 25, 1864
Knowles, George, e Oct 25, 1864
Lane, Wm, e. Oct 25, 1864
Marshall, Jas, e Oct 24, 1864
Nicholas, Jos E, e Oct 25, 1864
Seetz, George, e Oct 25, 1864
Sphon, Henry, e Nov 3, 1864
Sage, James, e Oct 25 1864
Smith, Simon, e Oct 25, 1864
Stark, John, e Oct 25, 1864
Speers James W, e Nov 10, 1864
Sympkins, James D, e Nov 10, 1864
Triggs, John F, e Oct 25, 1864
Unwin John, e Oct 25, 1864
Welsh, Lawrence, e Oct 25 1864
Winney, John J, e Oct 25, 1864

Sixteenth Infantry.

Pickett, J C, e Dec 10, 1861, died Jan
28, 1862

Eighteenth Infantry.

Gregg, John, e July 7, 1862, died Nov
5, 1862

Twenty-third Infantry.

Powers, M S, e Aug 11, 1862, m o July
26, 1865

Thirty-fifth Infantry.

Assistant Surgeon Charles Fitch, comd
Oct 26, 1863, com canceled Jan 14, '64

Thirty-sixth Infantry.

Custer, John W, e Aug 11, 1862, m o
Aug 24, 1865
Custer, W N, e Aug 11, 1862, m o Aug
24, 1865

Custer, B O, e Aug 11, 1862, kld at
 Mark's Mills
Barker, Peter N, e Aug 9 1862, m o
 Aug 24, 1865
Henderson, James e Aug 9, 1862, m o
 Aug 24, 1865
Pearson, P A, e Feb 24, 1864, m o Aug
 24, 1865

Forty-fourth Infantry.

Baldwin, W W, e May 4, 1864, m o
 Sept 15 1864
Calhoun, Ross, e May 13, 1864, m o Sept
 15, 1864

Forty-eighth Infantry.

Lieut Col Oliver H P Scott, comd June
 7 1864, m o Oct 21. 1864

First Cavalry.

Adjt Henry L Morrill e as corp, prmtd
 sergt maj, prmtd adjt Dec. 1, 1864,
 brevet capt and maj U S Vols, m o
 Feb 15, 1866
Chaplain James W Latham, comd Aug
 20, 1862, resd Feb 5, 1863
Sergt H L, Morrell, vet Jan 1 1864, m
 o Feb 15, 1866
Farrier F Torrence, m o Feb 15, 1866
Farrier Aaron A Thatcher, m o. Feb
 15. 1866
Carter, Alex, e July 18 1861, m o Feb
 15, 1866
Carter, William, e July 18, 1861, m o Feb
 15, 1866
Lyon John C, e Feb 23, 1864, m o Feb
 15, 1866
Lyons, C H, vet Jan 1, 1864, m. o. Feb.
 1866.
Morrell, Charles L, e March 21, 1864, died
 Sept 13, 1864
Williams, O G, e Aug 20, 1862, kld Sept.
 27, 1864, murdered by guerrillas
McBroom, A J, e March 14, 1864, died
 Sept 20, 1864
Cooke, Tracy W, e March 15, 1864, m o
 Feb 15. 1866

Fourth Cavalry.

Asst Surg Charles Fitch, comd July 6,
 1863, not mustered, m o Aug 10, 1865
First Lieut John S Keck, e as private
 Oct 6, 1861, prmtd 1st lieut June 25,
 1863, m o Aug 10, 1865
Second Lieut Peter R Keck, e as private
 Oct 6, 1861, prmtd 2d lieut Dec 5,
 1864, m o Aug 10 1865
Kelly, John L, vet Dec 11, 1863, m o
 Aug 10, 1865

Fifth Veteran Cavalry.

Jolley, Alexander, e June 24, 1861, vet
 Feb. 8, 1864, m o Aug 11, 1865
Pratt, Daniel, e Dec 30 1863 m o Aug
 11, 1865
Widger, T D, e June 24 1861 vet Jan.
 5, 1864, m o Aug 1, 1865

Whitten, J A, e Aug 30, 1862, captd.
 Nov 25, 1863 m o Aug 11, 1865.
Sergt Thomas L Bennett, e Sept 1, 1861,
 m o Aug 11, 1865
Corp John L Eager, kld in battle July
 30, 1864

Ninth Cavalry.

Trumpeter John C Harriman, e Oct 8
 1863, m o March 15, 1866
Hagler, T L, e Oct 26, 1863, disd Aug.
 19, 1864, disab.
Walters, Matthew, e Sept 30, 1863, died
 at St Louis
Buckner, Calvin, e. Dec 9. 1864

First Battery Light Artillery.

Sergt Levi Amoss, m. o July 5 1865

Second Battery Light Artillery.

Baxter, Samuel B e Jan 2, 1864, m o.
 Aug 7 1865
Brown, James D, e Dec 22, 1863, m o
 Aug 7, 1865
Brown, C H, e Dec 29, 1863 m o Aug.
 7, 1865
Crown, William H, e Dec 29 1863, m o.
 Aug 7, 1865
Lewis, Abner, e Nov 28, 1863, died Feb.
 12, 1863, at Memphis
Rhoades John H, e Jan 5, 1864, m o.
 Aug 7, 1865
Ratecliff, Jaco, W, e Feb 6, 1864, m o.
 Aug 7, 1865

Fourth Battery Light Artillery.

First Lieut Jr Francis W McClellan,
 comd Nov, 23, 1863, m o July 14, 1865
Boon, George D e Oct 3, 1863, m o July
 14, 1865
Christie, I D, e, Aug. 7, 1863, m o July
 14, 1865
Harlan, Elihu, e Aug 25, 1863, m o. July
 14, 1865
Harlan, H A, e Nov 2 1863, m o July
 14, 1865
Robison, William, e Oct 9 1863, m o July
 14, 1865
Smith, J H, e Aug 17, 1863, m o July
 14, 1865

Second Cavalry Missouri State Militia.

Gilbert, Joseph S, e March 10, 1862
Ambrose Martin, e March 5, 1862, disd.
 Sept 19, 1862

Sixteenth Illinois Infantry.

Arrington, Wm, e May 24, 1861

Thirty-third Illinois Infantry.
(Veterans)

Lee Jefferson, e Jan 1 1864

Fiftieth Illinois Infantry.

Lawson, James F., e Oct 8, 1861

Sixty-first Illinois Infantry.

Phillips, Theo e March 28, 1862, vet
April 30, 1864

U. S. Infantry (Colored).

Foutz, S J, e Oct. 31, 1864
Jackson, Wyatt, e Nov 2, 1864
Washington James, enlisted November 2,
1864

IN MEMORIAM.

An elaborate monument was erected in 1868 dedicated July 4, in memory of those soldiers whose enlistment carried them down to death and crowned their names with a wreath of honor, although the men lived not to herald the announcement of the nation's victory. Among the active citizens who managed the enterprise, an association was formed, with J. C McCrary, President; Joshua J. Sloan, Treasurer and John A Miller, Secretary The dedicatorial address was delivered by Rev Isaac P Teter

The monumental list of names follows.

Second Iowa Infantry. —Company A, George Reisner; Company E, Oliver H. Miller, Cyrus Bartow, Samuel Hoffman, Stillman J Town James F Johnson, William Browner, John Dunlap, William Baust, William C Harper, George W. Nixon, Franklin G Metz, John P Dahlberg, Henry Houk, Benjamin F Wilson, John Morrow, Cornelius Caruthers, John Van Dorn, Levi Mitchell, George W. Moise, John W Robinson, Wilson Crooks, A W Cummings, Edwin M Potter, Henry C Potter, Andrew J. Shriver, George B Shriver, William Van Fleet, Wesley W. Vinson, Augustus Mitchell; Company G. Solomon W. Bunner, Joel Lichty.

Fifth Infantry. —Company H, John Jolley, Alvin Ebert, Milton Shaw, Reason B. Hughes, Hamilton Rogers, Robert Cunningham, Samuel Lindsey, John Stookey, Milton Easter, R. J. H Huffman, Thomas P. Nutt, Charles Stout, G W Armentrout, George W. Overturff, Henry L. Drake, Hannibal Johnson, Francis M Miller, William R Penn, William H Pinkerton, John W Shepherd, Josiah A Whitten

Sixth Infantry. —Company D, George Black, Company K. George H Martin

Seventh Infantry —Company E, Socrates Pyle, Henry McDougal. Company I, Joseph R. Moore

Eleventh Infantry. —Company G, William Black

Twelfth Infantry —Company G, Strawder Ballard, Company K, Benjamin Cackley, James Cackley James W. Miller

Thirteenth Infantry. —Company A. Henry Spohn; Company F. William T Stanley, James D Simpkins, John C Harbin, Murray Jackson, James Spear

Fourteenth Infantry. —Company D, Joseph H Newbold, Abram Bucher, William H. Creason, Napoleon B. Henry, Edward Endersby; Company F, Samuel J Lane, William A Sunitz, David H. Grim, Henry J Chapman, James Hill, William S. Percival, Robert Hays

Fifteenth Infantry —Company C, John W Smith, George Peyton, Benjamin Hearn, John Beers, John Miller, Albert Bean, Merritt Hopkins, Milton Hopkins, Milan Hopkins, Eldridge Black, Perry Phillips; Company H, E. S Julien; Co. K, John Airhart, Fred A. Buckmaster.

Seventeenth Infantry —Company A, C. C. Biser, William A. Carr; Company I, John R... Edward F su...

Nineteenth Infantry —Company D, Alden Stump, Company H Jefferson Green, Theodore Gideon, Charles W Fisher, William Ke... Thomas E Hearn, Samuel Benney, Silas Kent, Alfred Morris, H. L Prosser, Moses Groom.

William Morrison, Francis M Cook, William Peter, Levi W Taylor, Levi Keller, Samuel M Byres, Joshua T. Phillips, Eli Vale, William R. Lock, John G McIntosh, Robert B Eaton, William S Eaton, Thomas B Lining, John Strong, Jr , Volney R Bunner, Company I, William Short, Amos Sherrod, Furguson Peal, George Lemon, John W Swartz, William A. Strong, Stephen Price, James Patterson, Jonathan J. Lee, William N Holliday, John Douglas, Lawrence McGinnis, Harrison O'Harra, Henry V Gaddis, Augustus B Rehkoph, Thomas Johnston, William McKinney, Rufus Collins Joseph A. Barker

Twenty-Fifth Infantry.—Company C, Hadley Fry, Robert Shields, Harry Cade, Stephen D Alton, William Simons, Andrew J. Standley, George W Standley, Henry Boley

*Thirtieth Infantry —*Company B, Henry H Haney John Henderson ; Company D, Henry Binder, John R Rogers, Albert Herbert, Isaac W Detwiler, Thomas Smith, Andrew Beadle, Thomas B Coffman, Jesse Walker, Jr , Francis M Weekly, W H. Randall, John M Bonnett, Benjamin Anderson, William M Robertson, Bowen P. Hurt, John Work, J. W. Williamson, Howard C Gaddis, George Saddler, Jacob Saddler, John B Harness, Zachariah Prewett, Thomas Martin, James Birch, John W. Clark, Robert C. Hix, William H. Robison, Andrew McCrary, Company F, Lester Bradford , Company G, William H Howard , Company H, Samuel S Culbertson   Co K, Ezra Bartholomew, Fernando C Robertson.

*Thirty-Fifth Infantry —*Company D, Ewalt Pool

*Thirty-Seventh Infantry —*Company C, E A M. Swasey, Samuel Myers, James Davis.

*Forty-Fifth Infantry —*Company K, McKinsey Garrison

*Fifteenth U. S Infantry.—*Company H, James B. F Adams

*Engineer Corps.—*Thomas D. Simpkins.

*M M. Brigade —*Lee Roy Mayne, G P Holder

*Second Iowa Battery —*Abner Lewis

*United States Navy —*Charles S. Wells

*First Cavalry.—*Company A, Charles L Morrill

*Third Cavalry.—*Company A, William W Hagler, John Toler , Company B, Miles King, Jacob Grasser, John Carr, George Rhoads, Noah Wright, Hiram W Fox, William Alexander, Wesley Love, John Brown, Frederick Lundy , Company C, Pennel Garrett , Company D, James F. Mercer, Henry S. Benning; Company G, David Thompson, William C Tedlock, James M Knox, L L H Whittlesey, Joseph Walters, Allen Gnash, E Blanchard, George H. Cowan, Emanuel Mayne, Albert Baker, Charles Baker, Franklin Miller, David Miller, William Matkin, Robert M Parker, Douglas C Owings. James H Watts, S. M Burns, Thomas Cochran, Andrew Van Brink, Benjamin McSurely, Hiram Dehart, F J. Roberts, Thomas Coleman, William Aylor, Company H, Nathan Norton, Widdons M Clark, John H Masterson, Marion Bechtel, Samuel Calhoun, Franklin Whitaker, Thomas Lemon, John A McGuire, Perry A. Newell, Jacob C. Boon, William Deal, William Chapman, Robert Cronsbeck, James Cronsbeck , Company I, James M Monroe, John Hines.

*Seventh Cavalry —*Company A, David Huddleston, William Gallahar, Calvin Gallahar, Company C, John Coon, Thomas C Torrence, Henry F. Tannahill, William N. Brown.

*Eighth Cavalry —*Company C, George Junks, Joseph Nixon, David I. McClurg, William A Short, David M Smith, Albert Raney Company E, Franc A Chapman, Leonard W Bennett, George Batchelor.

*Ninth Cavalry —*Company I, M Jay Walters

Eighteenth Missouri Infantry—Company C, David M Aylor

Twenty-First Missouri Infantry—Company H, Israel Elnean, Gustave Burner; Company I, Revel A Park, George W Drew

Second Missouri Cavalry—Company C, John Wire

Seventh Missouri Cavalry—Company A, Joseph Harridge, James R Seiver, Lafayette Bunner, George N Holder, Lathon O Pollock, George Brown, Thomas P. Franklin Paul Hancock, Henry C Brown, Amos S Barnett, Samuel Christian, Robert Fisher, Samuel O'Harra, Company E, Ernst Hagelstange

Tenth Missouri Infantry—Company D, Stephen Holcomb

Eleventh Illinois Infantry.—Company E, James J. Edwards.

One Hundred and Seventeenth Illinois Infantry—Company D, Benjamin Brown

One Hundred and Forty-Eighth Illinois Infantry—Company G, John A Smith.

Third Illinois Cavalry.—Company B, Simeon D. Yates

Twelfth Kansas Infantry—Company C, John M. Byers

Second Colored Cavalry—Company K, James W Shepherd

First Pennsylvania Cavalry.—Samuel Holsworth.

Not Assigned—Nathan Abbott.

The monument grounds are beautifully arranged

The monument and grounds are under charge of Edwin Goddard, such charge having been bestowed by action of the Board of Supervisors of Van Buren County

POPULATION AND GENERAL STATISTICS

The Census of 1875, the last one taken in the State, shows Van Buren County to have been populated, at that time, as follows

TOWNS AND TOWNSHIPS	Males	Females	Total
Bentonsport, town of	159	175	234
Birmingham, town of	296	291	587
Bonaparte	668	671	1339
Cantral, town of	94	93	187
Cedar	490	427	917
Chequest	516	480	996
Des Moines	561	502	1063
Farmington	425	413	838
Farmington, town of	345	331	676
Harrisburg	482	473	955
Henry	310	329	639
Jackson, except Cantral	845	787	1632
Keosauqua	341	374	715
Lick Creek	503	450	953
Union, except Birmingham	459	423	882
Van Buren, except Keosauqua	726	702	1428
Vernon	432	390	822
Village	734	705	1439
Washington, except Bentonsport	242	214	456
Total	8688	8290	16858
Colored	0		122
Total of Cour			16980

The first assessment of property in the county was made in 1839. The total value was estimated at $152,336, and the total tax levied was $837 83½

The population under the several census enumerations was as follows · 1838, 3,174 · 1840, 6,166 , 1844, 9,019; 1846, 9,870 , 1847, 10,203 ; 1849, 11,-577 , 1850, 12,269 , 1851, 13,000; 1854, 13,843 ; 1856, 15,921; 1860, 17,-081; in 1863, the war made a perceptible decrease, the population being reduced to 15,862; 1870, 17,672 ; 1875, 16 980

The church statistics for 1876 showed 8 pastoral charges , 1,296 members : 24 church-buildings ; 5 Sunday schools and 1,400 scholars : and $41,800 worth of property.

EDUCATIONAL

While the question of how to get a living was the foremost one in the minds of the pioneers, the less direct though none the less important one of how to educate their children was not overlooked   Almost cotemporaneous with their own dwellings, they began the building of such schoolhouses as they could, crude and primitive in the extreme, for such only would their appliances admit, and put together without regard to externals.

These same pioneer schoolhouses will, in the future, be a theme for the artist—quite equal in every way to those supplied by the peasantry in the old world—with their quaint, simple fashions and unperverted lives.   The eye of the connoisseur delights in those realistic representations of still life—the white-haired old grandfather, whose toil of years has only brought him his cottage and bit of land ; the still hard-working "gude wife," with bent body and withered but cheerful old face , the next generation just in the prime of labor, rough, uncouth, and content to have for recreation a pipe and a mug of ale ; and the children, with rosy cheeks and stout limbs dressed in veritable costumes their grandmothers wore before them.   And no wonder such a picture pleases and charms the jaded senses of the worn-out worldling   But even that is not more fresh and unaccustomed than this log shanty, with its one small room, a window of but few panes of glass, and possibly a dirt floor ; and with rough-hewn benches ranged round the walls for seats, over which the pupil made a fine gymnastic flourish whenever he felt it necessary to reach his teacher, with his forefinger firmly planted on the knotty word or sum that puzzled him

These are the picturesque features for the artist's pencil   And what " learn-ing " there was, must have been a " dangerous thing " for it was certainly " little , " the grading was far from exact , the system was a kind of hit-or-miss affair , but, nevertheless, it was " school,' and from the first there was a deeply-rooted prejudice among the Iowa settlers in favor of schools.   School for week-days and a meeting-house for Sunday ' this same little pen of a house served two purposes   And could anything except the groves themselves—" God's first temples "—be nearer to nature as a tabernacle than was this, where some chance circuit preacher would have for his congregation every man, woman and child in the entire settlement?   None of those hypercritical listeners there, you may be sure, who gauge the preacher by his " intellectuality," his " magnetism " or his " culture "   It was the Word preached—welcome, pure and life-giving always—and not the preacher, which these listeners crowded to hear.   If he but had the good Methodist zeal then he was sure of devout hearers.   He did not need to urge   the prairie , nor did he find necessary   the pulpit in the interests of politics—if he knew his Bible he was qualified and his flock feel called upon to put their hands into their pockets and contribute toward sending their Pastor on a summer vacation to the sea-side or to Europe. All these improvements have come in with better churches and more advanced ways of thinking. That was the old way, and a direct contrast to the new.

Now, nothing which the architect's taste can devise is too good for school-house or for church. Look at the plenitude of tidy, commodious buildings in every county, and not designed for double service, either, but dedicated solely to the use of the schoolma'am, who hereabouts is thoroughly skilled in her profession. She has had, aside from such education as her means have enabled her to obtain, good, practical drill in the normal institutes. She not only knows her text-books, but she knows how to *teach.* And then, the ingeniously-devised school-books, in which every point of information is adjusted to such a nicety that they are rather works of art and books of entertainment than but the dull means to a desired end.

The little flocks of children who run along the country roads in their bare feet and sun-bonnets, and chip hats, do not have to squirm and twist their uneasy legs all day over a page in the English reader which they cannot understand. They begin their morning's work with a chorus, which puts them all in good humor to start with. Then they come to timed classes, at the tinkle of the bell; they are entertained and diverted as well as instructed at every step. Before there is any possibility of restlessness, they go through a five-minutes round of calisthenics, which puts a wholesome quietus upon their muscles and their mischief. Wise play is so mixed with teaching that they never really discover which is which until they find themselves ready to teach school themselves in turn.

This is the ease of the present compared with the labor of the past. And in this way is the generality of education secured. The ways are smoothed, the tediousness beguiled and the deprivation supplanted by an affluence of aids.

In 1854, Gov. Grimes, in his inaugural message, said: "The safety and perpetuity of our Republican institutions depend upon the diffusion of intelligence among the masses of the people. The statistics of the penitentiaries and alms-houses throughout the country show that education is the best preventive of crime. They show, also, that the prevention of these evils is much less expensive than the punishment of the one and the relief of the other."

So, with all our new-fangled methods, our ornamental, well-ventilated and well-furnished schoolhouses, our accomplished instructors with modern notions, we are not extravagant. We are simply taking from the expenses of crime and pauperism and putting it into enduring and beautiful shape. We are helping to sustain the Government by rearing up in every town and in every country neighborhood a generation of enlightened and intelligent people, cosmopolitan in the sense of schools, if not in that wider cosmopolitanism which comes alone from actual contact with the great world.

The following statement is compiled from the last annual report of the County Superintendent of Schools, J. W. Rowley:

Number of district townships	8
Number of subdistricts	65
Number of independent districts	45
Total number of school districts	118
Number of ungraded schools	104
Number of graded schools	
Average number of months taught	
Number of male teachers	
Number of female teachers	

Average compensation per month to male teachers $36 73
Average compensation per month, to female teachers 29 11
Number of male pupils between 5 and 21 years of age   .   3,431
Number of female pupils between 5 and 21 years of age.   3,173
Number of pupils enrolled   5,377
Total average attendance   3,113
Average cost of tuition for each pupil, per month $1 42
Number of frame schoolhouses   89
Number of brick schoolhouses   17
Number of stone schoolhouses   3
Number of log schoolhouses   1
Total value of school-buildings   .. . $116,030
Total value of apparatus   178

SCHOOLHOUSE FUND

Total receipts during the year   .   . $14,313 08
Paid for schoolhouses and school sites   ..   4,770 92
Paid on bonds and interest 4,944 62
Paid for libraries and apparatus 1,139 57
Amount on hand 3,457 97

CONTINGENT FUND

Total receipts during the year   .   ... .. ~ . $ 8,787 93
Paid for repairing schoolhouses   . ..   935 53
Paid for fuel   .   .   1,638 03
Paid secretaries   .   .   .   364 97
Paid treasurers 218 25
Paid for records and apparatus 63 65
Paid for various purposes 2,003 51
Amount on hand 3,563 99

TEACHERS' FUND

Total receipts $43,651 97
Paid teachers 25,226 74
Amount on hand 18,425 23

THE MILLER–THOMPSON CONTESTED ELECTION

The most interesting contest over an election which has ever transpired in this region is that of the Miller-Thompson case. The peculiar character of the circumstances attending the affair, which can never be reproduced in this State, and the closeness of the vote, as well as the bitterness of party feeling at the time, conspire to render this case an exceedingly entertaining topic for introduction here. It is not the purpose of this sketch to indulge in strictures upon the methods employed by either faction, but it is designed to give as impartial a statement of the matter as careful research enables us to do. The heat of the contest has long since passed away, and we have no doubt that the survivors of the fight will read this chapter with a feeling of enjoyment, as it revives recollections of the days gone by. The authorities from which these facts are gathered are perfectly reliable, being the official documents of Monroe County (examined expressly for the purpose), numerous files of the leading journals of the time, among which are the *Des Moines Courier* and the Burlington *Hawk-Eye*, and personal interviews with some of the most prominent men connected with the affair.

The contest arose over the alleged election of William Thompson to a seat in the Thirty-first Congress. In 1848 the candidates for the honor of representing the southern half of the First District of Iowa, were William Thompson (Democrat), of Mt. Pleasant, and Daniel F. Miller (Whig), of Fort Madison. The election was held on August 7.

In 1848, the Democratic managers were greatly agitated over the apparent growth of Whig sentiments in this district The eastern counties were fast becoming uncertain territory and some expedient was essential to the life and prosperity of the party The leading spirits among the Democrats were men of fertile resources, thoroughly posted in the ways of politics, and full of shrewd energy A plan presented itself to their inventive minds, nor were they slow to avail themselves of it The machinery of the party was set to work at once to secure the needed strength so opportunely, but accidentally, proffered them as they sincerely believed

It is necessary to revert to historic events of an earlier date, and in other localities, to explain the proceedings recorded hereafter. The Mormons, who figure conspicuously in this chapter, had suffered overthrow in their stronghold at Nauvoo, Ill, in 1846. The misdeeds of the leader, Joseph Smith, had resulted in the violent death of that head of the sect, and the ascension to power of Brigham Young. The latter saint and ruler had decreed that the society should separate into numerous bands and travel westward in search of freedom. The exodus of the Latter-day Saints began in the year 1846. Iowa was the scene of unwonted activity occasioned by the flight of the refugees from the law Some bands moved through the State on the line of the forty-second parallel, some went through the southern tier of counties, and some passed over the territory now composing the range in which Monroe is located. The ultimate destination of all these parties was Kanesville, or what is now known as Council Bluffs Many of the Mormons did not reach the river in 1846, nor even in 1847 Hundreds camped in Marshall County during that year, and scores of the poor wretches died from actual starvation Women were confined in the open country during the long, cold season, and filled unmarked graves The suffering of those people in camp, during the winter of 1846–47, will never be described by human agency, and can be but faintly realized by the comfortably sheltered readers of this brief sketch

This chapter, however, has to deal with but one division of the Mormon party Those who passed through this tier of counties reached Lucas County in the winter of 1846–47, and located a few miles southeast of the present town of Chariton There rude huts were erected, and the party sojourned for several months. Subsequently, they passed on to the Missouri River, where they also tarried for a time. They were the first white "settlers" in Lucas County

A portion of the band of Mormons did not remain in Lucas that year, but pushed westward in hopes of gaining the place of rendezvous designated by Young Their hopes were blighted, however, for the weather was so inclement that they could not proceed. They did not reach a point beyond Clarke County Three men, John Conyer, James and John Longley, became separated from the party and lost their way They concluded to encamp for the winter (of 1846–47) where they were, and constructed a log hut In this they lived, and attached to it the name of "Lost Camp," a title by which the locality is still known and pointed out In the spring, these men found other Mormons but a few miles from them, in the same county The village of Kanesville became the headquarters of the faithful to the creed of the Golden Book, and was the resting-place of the weary bands There they recruited their wasted forces, and prepared to encounter fresh cares in the slow journeys across the plains to Salt Lake City

It was thus that the year 1848 found a settlement of white men in the territory supposed to be attached to Monroe County for election and judicial purposes, and it was by virtue of their forced residence in Iowa that the Mormons became, under the general statutes, legal voters in the State. Had it not been for the expulsion of the saints from Nauvoo and the unusually early winter which followed their exodus, or, had it not been for the accident of circumstances, this somewhat singular history could not now be written.

At the time of the occurrence of the events written above, the county of Monroe was composed of all the territory from the west line of Wapello County to the Missouri River. The unorganized counties of Lucas and Clarke were at that time defined in a manner preliminary to permanent establishment, the latter, however, being entirely unsettled by white men. The former contained not more than eight or ten families.

The August election, 1848, was an important one to the people of Southern Iowa, as has already been observed. The office of Representative in Congress was to be filled, and the two parties in contest Democrats and Whigs, were violent in their determination to win the prize. The Whigs were gaining strength, and it was all-essential that the county of Monroe then a Democratic region, should give a large majority to overcome the Eastern vote.

The investigation of old records impresses one with the fact that politicians of the old school, in the early days, were intensely shrewd, possibly no more so than those of to-day, but the methods of working were very different then, and it may be that the apparent boldness was the result of a lack of means to 'cover up the tracks.' At all events, it seems to one who carefully looks at the matter that more summary ways and means were then in vogue than could be successfully employed now.

The opposing factions in 1848 were exceedingly jealous of one another. Every possible opportunity was improved to win the day. Because of this vigilance, perhaps, the Argus-eyed Democracy discovered a grand chance to effect the defeat of their hated rival. The Mormon vote was not only desirable, but was available! Happy thought! Golden possibility!

Who first conceived the plan of wheeling the Mormons into line is not clearly established. Judge Mason, J. C. Hall, and possibly a well-known jurist, who still lives in Wapello County, might have been the authors of the shrewd scheme, but that is immaterial.

In 1847, the region lying upon the Missouri River, in a line supposed to be due west of Wapello County, was thickly inhabited, for so westerly a point, thanks to the Mormon colony, and naturally asserted its right of independence. A party of representative men came east and waited upon influential men at Iowa City, when the scheme was discussed. Gen. Dodge became much interested in the matter, foreseeing the possible strength such an organization might bring them. Nothing was then done, however, to effect the formation of the county, but the Democrats did not lose sight of the tide of Mormons moving westward, and halting for breath on the shores of the river. In Nauvoo, the Mormon vote had been a powerful ally to the Democrats at general elections, and a continuance of their support was both desirable and reasonable, according to the logic of Gen. Dodge.

The organization of the new county rested with Judge Carleton, of the then Fourth Judicial District, and there is evidence which warrants the belief that the Judge counseled with the General in this matter.

A ... 1847. Whigs claimed to know as certainty that the Mormons ... ... political affinities, and the young party was not backward ... ... change of belief in its own favor. Elder Orson Hyde was in command of the refugees, and his will was practically a law unto them

Col. Warren, in a speech delivered in Burlington, in September, 1848, after the election had been held made what the *Hawk-Eye* termed a full explanation of the affair, and from that address is gathered a portion of the data relative to this part of our sketch

The time elapsed by which it was necessary to create a new county at the river, prior to the election of 1848, but there still remained an opportunity to form a polling precinct there and thus secure the vote. The only question to be decided was that of the political complexion of the district. If the Democrats could be assured of support, the necessary formalities would be proceeded with at once.

Now ensued a sharp encounter of wits. Gen Dodge felt that he held the key to the situation. since through him alone could the desired organization be compassed. The Whigs, on the other hand, apprised themselves of the fact that the Mormons were becoming anxious to show their ill-will toward the Democratic party. as a means of avenging themselves for their expulsion from Nauvoo

Messengers were dispatched from both camps to feel the pulse of the people in the West, and each faction returned bearing metaphorical bunches of huge grapes, while their reports were that the land flowed with oil and honey for their respective candidates In all this bartering there was evidently an understanding between the Whigs and the Mormons , for a flat refusal on the part of the latter to vote the Democratic ticket would certainly have prevented their voting at all The powers that were had to be mollified, and a go-between was found to represent to the Democrats the solidity of the Pottawattamie precinct

When the character of the vote was satisfactorily determined, there still remained the question of its legality. If the territory lay west of the last organized county. which was then Monroe, that county had the power to create a precinct. If it did not, then there was an opportunity to contest the validity of returns from the river precinct. The Democrats believed that Kanesville, as the Mormon settlement was called, did lie within the legal territory of Monroe, but a survey was deemed necessary to settle the point. In accordance with that idea, a party was engaged to ascertain the geographical whereabouts of the village and a random line was run. Subsequent surveys have shown that the line was, indeed a random one but that point did not come up in the contest which followed For all practical purposes, the place lay west of Monroe In the decision of this question, the Whigs wisely submitted to the Democrats, and the work of establishing the locality was performed by such means as the Democrats could, under no circumstances, thereafter dispute It was highly important for the Democrats to locate Kanesville in Monroe territory, because Monroe was then Democratic, and they feared'that the Whigs would oppose the organization of so strong a precinct, if they had it in their power so to do

The Whigs, meanwhile, confident of the victory they were to win, offered no objections to the formation of the precinct, but seemed quiescent in the matter. On the 3d of July, 1848, the Monroe County Commissioners issued the following order

Ordered, by said Board, that that portion of country called Pottawattamie County, which lies directly west of Monroe Co be organized into a township and that Kanesville be a precinct for election purposes in said township and that the election held at the Council House in said village and that Charles Bird Henry Miller and William Huntington be appointed Judges of said election and that the boundaries of said township extend east as far as the East Nish na-bot-na

This public announcement of the plan warned the Whigs to work   Greek met Greek.   It was known that the Board, then consisting of Andrew Elswick, William McBride and George R. Holliday, and Dudley C. Barber as Clerk, was Democratic   The latter officer made out the poll-books and sent them to the new precinct   Both parties sought the field of battle, and, for a time, the Mormon element became the favorites of the politicians, since they held the balance of power.   The Mormons at home in Nauvoo were Democratic in sentiment, it was argued, and the Democrats were confident of their co-operation in the time of need.

The election took place on the 7th day of August.   To the consternation of the Democrats and the joy of the Whigs, the vote of the new precinct was cast almost solidly for Daniel F. Miller, the Whig candidate, and the Democratic candidate, William Thompson, was left out in the cold

No sooner was the result of the election made known, than the Democratic leaders took counsel, one with another, what to do   J C Hall went to Albia from Mt Pleasant, and it is asserted that he and others advised the rejection of the poll-books.   The messenger with the returns arrived in Albia, and the canvass of the votes was held on the 14th day of August   Dudley C. Barber, as Clerk of the Board, had a deciding voice in the matter.   The canvass was made at his log cabin, one of the three or four buildings then standing on the town plat

Among the prominent men at Albia at that time, was Dr Flint, who subsequently removed to Wapello County, and there became County Judge, and also State Senator from that county.   He was brother-in-law to Barber, the Clerk who made out the poll-books, and who was authorized to pass upon their acceptance for canvass   Dr. Flint exercised a strong influence over Barber, and was an intense partisan   He urged the arbitrary rejection of the books. The little cabin was filled with excited men, and the canvass could not proceed Among the Democrats were Mr Hall and Israel Kister, of Davis County, who subsequently was elected State Treasurer on that ticket.

The Whigs were determined to see the Pottawattamie vote counted, since they had beaten the Democrats at what they considered their own game Among those men was Mr. Mark, who was Postmaster at Albia at a later date He stood directly behind Barber when the latter decided to reject the books. Mr Mark inquired

"Do you really intend to reject the returns made out on poll-books prepared by yourself, and in legal form, Mr Barber ? "

"Yes, sir, I do ' " responded the Clerk.

At this juncture, further examination of the books was to be made, when the disputed volumes could not be found   Search was instituted and vigorously prosecuted, but to no effect   The books were gone from the table where they had lain but a moment before   It was announced that the books had been stolen, and could not, therefore, be used as returns.

It is reported by an eye-witness of the scene that pistols were drawn and a general riot seemed imminent ; but no serious outbreak followed the *coup d'etat* of the Democrats   Of course it was clear that the Whigs had not stolen the books, since it was for their interest to retain them.   It rested, consequently, with the opposing faction to explain the mysterious disappearance of the documents

The canvass of the Board consisted of two Justices and, it is said, with locked doors in consideration of the vote of Monroe throwing out the vote from Pottawattamie county   This action of the western vote secured the election of Thompson, and he accordingly took his seat in the first session of the Thirty-first Congress

If we may be allowed to parody a classic quotation, uneasy sits the Congressman who is not soundly elected ! No sooner was he there than the Whigs made an effort to oust him The case was laid before a proper committee, and voluminous discussion ensued Finally, the case was remanded to the District Court at Keokuk. Before a decision could be reached, an election took place in the State for State officers and member of the Thirty-second Congress The campaign was a ' hot one During the stump-speech season, and just prior to the election in August, a meeting was held at Albia, at which A. C Dodge, Mr Baker, et al , addressed the Democracy At this meeting cheers were proposed for Mr Barber, on the grounds that he had defeated the election of Miller

It may be here incidentally remarked that the August election resulted in the seating of Bernhart Henn, of Fairfield, in the Thirty-second Congress from this district, his term beginning in 1851

There still remained one session of the Thirty-first Congress, and after the August election referred to, the Miller–Thompson fight was renewed During the controversy, Mr. Miller, or one of his friends, desired certain papers of Judge Mason, who was a strong counsel on the Democratic side By mistake, the missing poll-books were handed to the Whig, who immediately announced the fact with an appropriate demonstration.

This startling *denouement* completely upset the Democratic case, and a new election was ordered to" fill vacancy " in the First District The election took place September 24 1850, and resulted in the choice of Mr. Miller, who filled the seat in Congress one session

The question reverts to the cause of the Mormon change of front in 1848. All manner of rumors were afloat at the time, some of them even charging that the Democrats had offered but $1,000, while the Whigs had paid $1,200 for the vote On the authority of one who admits that he was a party to the barter, we state as fact that the only gift presented to Elder Hyde by the Whigs was a printing office and some ten reams of printing-paper and a keg of ink. Hyde wanted an office, and the Whigs were willing to give him one. The materials for the office were shipped to him by the Whigs prior to the casting of the vote. Hyde had a grudge against the Democrats, which he desired to pay, and therefore refused to listen to overtures of a financial character from them It was a case of diamond cut diamond, in which the Whigs proved the hardest.

As to the missing books : it is a matter of evidence that Israel Kister placed them in Mr. Hall s saddle-bags, during the heated discussion, probably with no real intention to steal them at the time, but supposing that they would be discovered before Hall left. They were not detected, and the lawyer rode away with them. It was then too late to acknowledge the error, and so the case stood until accident brought them to light

The Whig papers made furious onslaught against the Democrats over the affair, and there is but little doubt that it caused a decidedly good political war-cry during those days Dr Flint was openly charged with having burned the books, and Barber was figuratively drawn and quartered continuously The vigorous attacks upon Barber finally undermined his health and he died, a victim of mistaken sense of duty Dr Flint's career in the county of Wapello was one of considerable importance until he was guilty of eloping it is alleged, with a lady of his acquaintance, although he was an old man at the time. It is believed that he died, some years since, in Canada

THE KNEELAND MOVEMENT.

In January, 1834, Abner Kneeland, a former Orthodox minister, who had become an unbeliever, established himself at the head of a society in Boston called the "Free Inquirers." The organ of this society was called the *Investigator.* Of course, this departure from the good old ways aroused popular resentment, and Kneeland was indicted December 20, 1833, on the grounds of publishing   1. A scurrilous extract from Voltaire ridiculing the miraculous generation of Jesus   2 An article declaring the practice of addressing prayers to God to be absurd   3. A letter to the editor of the *Tempest* in which he says "Universalists believe in a god (sic) which I do not, but believe that their god (sic), with all his moral attributes (aside from nature itself), is nothing more than a chimera of their own imagination '

On this indictment Kneeland was tried, found guilty and sentenced to three months' imprisonment   From this he appealed, but he was finally sentenced for two months   A petition for his release was drawn up and signed by William Ellery Channing and 167 others , but this was rejected.

In 1837–38, a scheme was set on foot by the *Investigator* to found a colony at Salubria, about two miles south of Farmington, in this county.   A levy of $10 was made upon each member of the society, to further this scheme, and among the first commissioners sent out were Abner Kneeland, E Cutler, S Smith, James W Rice and Mr. Tower.   But disagreements arose in the society, and the scheme fell through, the colony in the mean time going to ruin   During its existence, however, it had some political influence, but now it has few survivors   The town of Salubria was a regular lithographed town, and was laid out by Mr Kneeland, in Boston, and was mostly owned there   Its site is now only the common open country

Mr. Kneeland died August 27, 1844, aged seventy years, and is buried on his own soil, with his wife beside him.   She was the mother of James W Rice, one of the same band who came out originally from Boston   Mr Kneeland was a man of more than usual ability, a radical and individual thinker, and one whose strong opinions amounted to positive convictions.   At that period, there was less latitude in religious matters than at the present day, and a liberalist, by an open avowal of his lack of belief, placed a wider chasm between himself and the people at large than it would be possible to do in modern times   But Mr Kneeland's sincerity, which is conceded has gone far toward softening the severity of judgment which at one time, set in heavily against him, and what was sterling in his character is respected in his memory

THE VAN BUREN COUNTY PRESS.

The first paper ever published in Van Buren County was at Keosauqua. It was called the *Iowa Democrat and Des Moines River Intelligencer*

In July, 1843, James Shepherd started from Springfield, Ill , for the West, and on his way to Iowa was met by Cyrus Walker, who recommended Keosauqua as a good point to start a newspaper   Mr Shepherd arriving at this place, a meeting was called, and the prospectus left with William Steele, a merchant, old c ... and To ... f Keosauqua to procure subscribers   It was the intention of Mr Shepherd to issue a paper advocating the Democratic principles of th t ... t and under the name of the *D ... tic Times*

On his return to Springfield, he sent the material and printing press West by means of an ox-team and wagon. in care of his son. Jesse M Shepherd, and J L T. Mitchell, a young man who was to receive one-half the profits of the concern to compensate for his labor. Mr. Shepherd instructed his son not to allow any person the control of dictation whatever over the policy of the paper This, Mr Steele did not like, and threw the prospectus into the fire

Mitchell being a Whig and young Shepherd a Democrat, they, upon the action of Steele, agreed to balance their political opinions and run the paper as a neutral sheet

A copy of the paper was sent to Springfield, and this was the first notice that Mr. Shepherd had received of the neutral policy

In the spring of 1844, he came out again, and immediately made arrangements to purchase Mitchell's share, for which he (Shepherd) was to pay $25, and Mitchell to step out at the end of one year This sum was given, and a horse in the bargain

There was a valedictory written by Mitchell and published in the last number of the paper of which he was partner that is worth preserving. It ran as follows "We (Shepherd, Jr , & Mitchell) both knew, by observation, that there was a certain set who would take the lead in acting for the people, and, when opportunity offered, cut from the loaf the largest slice for themselves To these we gave our decided opposition. no matter what their faith or belief Herein, then, consists our neutrality—determined opposition to demagogues , a set that may be found in every community and in every party and who deserve the contempt of every honorable and high-minded man."

Upon Mitchell's withdrawal from the *Intelligencer*, he established a Whig paper, known as the *Border Pioneer* It was run but a short time

At the expiration of one year, party spirit began to manifest itself among the people, and party lines were drawn at the approaching Presidential canvass between Henry Clay and James Polk Besides this, what was denominated the American system bank tariff and other measures were put into issue before the people, and they began to choose sides. The *Intelligencer* was then changed to a political paper, advocating Democratic principles James and Jesse M Shepherd assumed the editorship They continued it until 1850, when they sold to Ezra M. Jones. James Shepherd says upon this subject:

' During the next ten years. the office of the *Democrat* changed owners several times. the proprietors being the father of S M Mills, Seth Millington, Daniel Morris (who changed it to a Whig paper), J. M. Estes (who changed it back to the Democratic side); then Oliver J Taylor run it into the *Des Moines News*, and in 1860. James and Jesse M. Shepherd purchased it and continued the publication under the name of the *Des Moines News*, on the same press and fixtures. It was Democratic in politics up to 1865, when they sold to G. S Bailey, and he moved the press and fixtures to Albia, Monroe Co , Iowa, and published a paper there. In 1843. when the publication of the *Democrat* was commenced, it was the sixth in the Territory of Iowa I recollect very well the notice given of its advent by J. Russell. who published a paper at Bloomington (now Muscatine), Iowa It was as follows · 'Two more candidates for the Poorhouse ' "

In 1845–46, the *Des Moines Valley Whig* was published at Keosauqua, by Howell & Cowles No files exist from which to gain any correct information concerning this paper, and from the fact that it had passed out of mind, until revived through the research of the writer it is safe to say that it did not long survive the shocks of adversity

Beginning with the year 1850, the newspapers of the county have appeared as follows.

Keosauqua *Jeffersonian* April 29, 1850, by Arlando E. Jones, to May 26, 1851.

Western American by L. D. and H. Morris, July 5, 1851, to July 3, 1852. Motto, "Distinct, like the billows—one, like the sea." Introductory. "Our watchword is Union now and forever, one and inseparable."

Democratic Union (purchased of H. and L. D. Morris), H. and S. M. Mills. Issued July 17, 1852, run to January 15, 1853. Motto "A jealous care of the rights of the people. Absolute acquiescence in the decision of the majority."

Seth Millington, editor, and Rufus Summerlin, publisher, came into possession of the *Union*, January 29, 1853. Their first issue was No. 27 of Vol. I.

Democratic Union, Vol. III, No. 1, R. Summerlin editor and proprietor, was the next step. This continued until August 5, 1854.

November 25, 1854, James Shepherd became editor of the *Union* and Summerlin, publisher. This until Vol. III, No. 17.

The *Democratic Mirror* was named by John M. Estes, editor and proprietor. Jesse M. Shepherd, publisher, December 6, 1855. The paper was purchased from Millington. The motto was "See Ahead."

Oliver O. Taylor, editor and proprietor of the *Des Moines News*, published the next paper in this line under the motto, "Constitutional Liberty," the change in names being made with No. 18 of Vol. I on May 7, 1858. His salutatory was "The harmonious blending of freedom and restraint, upon which the whole fabric of our Republic rests, and upon which it must continue to flourish, or perish." He continued it until March 31, 1860, when James Shepherd became editor and Jesse M. Shepherd publisher. The first issue was Saturday, April 7, 1860.

The *Shady Side* was the title of another paper published at Keosauqua. It was Republican in politics. Vol. I, No. 1, was published Friday morning October 27, 1871, by Joel Mayne, editor and proprietor. With No. 16 of Vol. I, Mayne withdrew and D. H. Burton became possessed of it. He issued No. 17 on Friday morning, March 8, 1872, and continued until No. 27, the last number being published July 26, 1872.

The Keosauqua *Republican* was established September 12, 1854, by W. C. Worden and by him sold to L. D. Morris in 1855, the latter transferring to John S. Stidger in 1856. Stidger sold to L. D. Morris in 1858, and Morris sold to Joel Mayne in 1859. In 1868, he sold to George E. Henry, who, on February 12, 1877, sold one-half interest to W. H. Bleakmore and, on August 30, 1877, the other half to J. M. Strong. Mr. Strong transferred his interest December 27, 1877, to Judge Joshua S. Sloan. The firm is now known as Sloan & Bleakmore.

The *Democrat* was established at Bonaparte, January 19, 1870, by George F. Smith and R. I. Holcomb. After three months, Holcomb retired. Smith continued the publication until December 1, 1876, when he removed the paper to Keosauqua, where it is still published.

Vernon cradled one of the first papers in the county. It was known as the *Democratic Mirror*, John M. Estes, being the editor and proprietor and J. S. Shepherd publisher. The motto of the paper was "Submission to the will of majorities when constitutionally expressed." The first number was published Friday December 7, 18—. The paper was continued until No. 42 of Vol I. Then it was removed to K——. On October 17, 1856, No. 43 was issued. The paper was continued until December 1857, Vol II No. —— and took the name of the *Valley Weekly News*, and the motto, ' Devoted to general intelligence, the best interest of Southern Iowa, the Des Moines Valley, and of Van Buren County. John M. Estes continued as editor and proprietor. The first issue under the new name was January 1, 1858. The publication continued until April 30, 1858

The Bonaparte *Signal* was the first newspaper published at Bonaparte. A C Bailey was editor and proprietor. The date of the beginning was January 31, 1866. Wednesday was the publication day, but it was subsequently changed to Thursday. The paper was Democratic in politics. The motto was ' The affections of the people the only solid cement of union." The last number was issued Thursday, July 30, 1868, No 27 of Vol III.

The *Des Moines Valley Reporter*, Republican in politics, was established January 18, 1872, by H. C. Ashbough. The paper bade the word good-by with Vol. I, No. 27, July 18, 1872

On April 5, 1877, J W and John H Sherman, started the Bonaparte *Journal*, a weekly publication, independent in politics. The firm is known as Sherman Brothers. They are the youngest editors in the county

The Birmingham *Enterprise* was established in October, 1869, by W. J Moore. He continued in charge one and one-half years, and sold to J A T Hull, who continued as proprietor eighteen months and then transferred the paper to J S Ragsdale. This arrangement continued one year and a half, when W. R Parker came into possession of it. He had charge of it six months, when he sold one-half of his interest to C. L. Sheward. The firm is now known as Sheward & Parker. The politics of the paper is Republican

The history of the press of Farmington, dates back only to the month of February, 1874, when M L. Mooers started the *Gazette*. The paper was published under that management until February 18, 1876, Vol III, No I, Mr Mooers then being succeeded by A Ditson, who published No 2 of Vol III, on February 25, 1876. J. M. Elliott came in possession of the *Gazette* soon after that, but the exact date is not known. He published the paper until the summer of 1878, when it was discontinued

George W Baer established the *Record*, in 1878, the first number being published November 8. Its tone is neutral

The Milton *Headlight* was established in October, 1876, by Allen Ditson. He run it three months and sold it to Marsan & Baxter. They continued until October, 1877, when Marsan became sole owner. He run it until March, 1878, and then suspended

The Milton *Herald* was started in April, 1878, and is now run by McNeill & Baxter.

KEOSAUQUA.

Some Frenchmen, in an early day, inhabited the bend of the river Des Moines, in the pocket of which lies the village of Keosauqua. Around the bend dwelt a number of monks. The Indians, discovering these places of habitation, named the section where now lies the city, Keosauqua, the meaning of which is in Indian parlance, " The river of monks."

Keosauqua was laid off in April, 1839, by John Carnes, James Hall, James and Edwin Manning, John J. Fairman and Robert Taylor, these composing the " Van Buren Company."

Two triangular pieces of ground, or, more properly, fractions, first composed the town, the south fraction or triangle being known as Van Buren and the

north triangle as Des Moines. Later, a diamond-shaped piece of land was
entered (one-fourth section lying obliquely been the triangles) and together
with the Van Buren triangle assumed the name Keosauqua. Des Moines
refused to come under the yoke or in any way affiliate with its neighbor   Both
began contending for the county seat   In time, the settlers assembled (it was
one Sunday night) and talked over a name under which both the triangles and
diamond might be known.   John Carnes suggested Port Oro (a Spanish name,
meaning "Port" or "Land of Gold")   There was some objection to this, as
being a too high-sounding title for the place.   Finally, Judge Irvin asked how
they would like to have their three towns known under the name of Keosauqua.
All agreed to it, and the matter was settled then and there

Down to the year 1846, the town had been growing steadily, and the country
around, having become thickly settled, afforded the advantages of a large trade.
This will be shown by the accompanying directory of Keosauqua, giving the
places of business, etc, that the place then counted as its own:

Dry Goods, Groceries, Hardware, etc—Manning & Wasky, B. P. Marlow & Co, John Carnes, A. J. Davis, William Steel

Druggists—Henry Whelin, Benjamin Barker

Physicians.—F. W. Taylor, C H Ober, H H. Barker, John D. Elbert,
D Peck, J Tarbell

Lawyers—James B Howell, H M. Shelby, George G Wright, J C.
Knapp, S E Seargent, Richard Humphreys, Augustus C Hall, S W Summers, J. D Devine.

Carpenters—Jamison & Gilchrist, Walker & Hartzell, —— & Jamison.
Dugen & Service.

Cabinet-Makers—Ruple & Thornburg, Green B. Morton, Russo King.

Coopers.—E. F. Burton, —— Anderson

Tailoring Establishments.—J J Kinersly, Robert Orr

Shoemakers—William Hoker, A B Moore.

Jewelry.—E. J. Harper

Blacksmiths—Hinkle & McCrary, Richard Benjaman

Saddle and Harness Makers—George W. Games, Joseph Barker.

Wagon-Makers—Benson Hinkle, Philip Hartzell.

Brickmasons.—Jesse Winn, B. F Pearson

Bakery—E. F Burton.

Tanneries.—C Baldwin & Co, G W. Games, —— Anson.

Groceries and Coffee-Houses.—Julian & Billops, Griffiths & Livingston,
David & Pease

Mills.—Steam flouring and saw mill, G W Games, ditto, Hugh Brown;
ditto, D Maguire

Printing Offices—*Des Moines Valley Whig*, published by Howell & Cowles,
editors and proprietors, *Iowa Democrat*, published every Friday by J & J. M.
Shepherd, editors and proprietors

Lodges—Keosauqua Lodge, No. 10, Free and Accepted Masons, Keosauqua Lodge, No 3, Independent Order of Odd Fellows, Keosauqua Lodge, No.
1, Iowa Hunters

Hotels.—Keosauqua Hotel, J Bruyet, Des Moines House, —— Clymer.

Churches—Methodist, Congregational, and several other denominations

Compared with 1878, the 1846 directory was small   There are now five
dry goods and groceries, one groceries and hardware, one furniture, one
drug, three groceries, one saad, a military company, one bank, two gunsmiths,
two jewelers, two harness shops, two boots and shoes, two hotels, two tailors,

one musical instruments, one market, three millinery, one tinware, one artist, one marble-shop, opera-house, one baker, one lumber-yard, two livery, three wagon-makers and blacksmiths, seven attorneys, four physicians, one dentist, two barbers, two agencies, two printing offices, two mills, six builders, one cooper, three painters, county buildings, churches and school

Keosauqua was incorporated as a city under a general act of the Legislature, February 17, 1842. This act not being sufficient to cover the ground, a special act was passed in 1846. It was as follows:

An Act to amend an act entitled " An act to incorporate the city of Keosauqua "

Section 1. Be it enacted by the Council and House of Representatives of the Territory of Iowa, That in case it shall become necessary to sell real estate in said city, for the payment of taxes, the same shall be sold in the manner, and under such regulations, as the Mayor and Aldermen may have ordained, and at the time and place when and where the Mayor and Aldermen may order and direct, Provided, four weeks' notice shall be given of such sale by advertisement in any newspaper published in said city, and by posting on the Court House door of said city a written notice of such sale, for the space of four weeks.

Sec. 2. Such real estate shall be sold to the bidder who will pay the taxes, costs and expenses of such sale, for the lowest quantity of such real estate, to be taken off of such part of such real estate as the Mayor and Aldermen may direct.

Sec. 3. Such real estate may be redeemed from such sale at any time within two years from the time of such sale, by the owner paying to the purchaser, or Recorder of said city, for the use of such purchaser, the amount for which such real estate shall have been sold, and costs, with fifty per centum per annum until paid.

Sec. 4. The Mayor and Aldermen shall, at the expiration of two years from such sale, execute, in their corporate capacity, a deed for any real estate so sold and not redeemed to the purchaser or his assigns, which deed shall be sufficient to convey the estate in fee to such purchaser, and shall be prima-facie evidence of the regularity of the proceedings; and no person shall ever question the title under such deed, either in a court of law or equity until such person shall have paid to or tendered to the purchaser the amount for which such real estate may have been sold, and fifty per centum per annum and the costs of sale.

Approved January 19, 1846

The first meeting was held January 7, 1843, with James Hall, Mayor; William Kemp, Recorder; James B. Howell, Deputy Recorder.

Nothing was done, however, until the meeting of May 13, 1844, for which the people had elected a City Council composed of Elisha Cutler, Jr., Mayor; Edward R. Tyler, Recorder; and James J. Kinersly, Henry M. Shelby, Richard Humpheries, Benson Henkle and Stephen Livingston, Aldermen. With this meeting the work of the city fathers commenced.

The present city government is cared for by William Moore, Mayor; Solon Nourse, James Shepherd, William Ford, Edwin Walker, W. H. Monroe and Samuel Fasnacht, Aldermen.

The first marriage solemnized at Keosauqua was between Lewis Le Plont and Nancy Hill, on January 27, 1839, the ceremony having been performed by William Stanley, Justice of the Peace.

The first claimant or squatter on the site of the present town was John Silvers, who built, in the winter of 1835 and 1836, a small claim-pen of round logs, on the bank of the river, near where the Keosauqua Hotel now stands. This pen was perhaps eight or ten feet square. At that time, or soon after, E. Purdom Sr., had taken the claim immediately above town.

Mrs. Sigler is believed to be the first white woman who ever made her home no the site now occupied by Keosauqua.

In the fall of 1836, Silvers was bought out by Mesonhack Sigler for $300, who came here at that time with his father-in-law and brother-in-law Eph. and William D. McBride. The elder McBride and Sigler came to Indiana the same fall.

The first house (after the Silvers claim-pen) was built in 1837 by the Van Buren Company In this Messrs Carnes & Fairman kept the first store About this time, Fairman was appointed the first Postmaster of the place—the name of the office being Port Oro

In the year 1839 the first brick house was erected by Edward R Tylee The same year, Elias Elder erected a part of what is now known as Alexander's brick or barracks

T Lane opened the first tailor-shop, in the upper room of the building now occupied by Burton & Minich During the next year. he formed a partnership with J J Kinersly

The first physician was Cyrus H. Ober followed soon after by the late H H. Barker.

The first attorney was Isaac N Lewis, now of Missouri, who soon after had a competitor (as he often facetiously expressed it), in Samuel W Summers, now of Ottumwa.

. A Myon and George W Games located here in 1839, and started the first tan-yard. at the point below town. It was later on owned by the junior partner of the firm who successfully run it until within a few years past, when it was closed.

The first tavern was kept by Elisha Puett, in a one-story log house, on or near the ground now occupied by the tin-shop of Mr. Grayum. He is said to have been a rough specimen of border life. and to have kept a house characteristic of the man He also, it is believed, kept the first grocery in the place

The first blacksmith was David Smith He put up a frame shop

The first political convention of the county was held by the Democratic party, in the spring of 1840, in the District Court room

Of the first alleged " duel," Judge George G. Wright speaks as follows ·

" About this time (1836 or 1837), two of our citizens appealed to the code of honor for the settlement of their grievances The parties were Aaron W Harlan and one Bushnell Their seconds were Russo King and M Sigler— the place of meeting near where the Odd Fellows' Hall now stands. They had pistols without the coffee, and I am happy to state, that their friends reconciled the belligerents without the shooting In the settlement, blows ensued, however Harlan came off victor, and thus ended the first, and it is hoped the last appeal to the bloody code in our law-abiding and peaceable community "

Wilson Stanley and Sewall Kenney were the first Justices in the place They were appointed by the Governor

Alfred Veatrees is believed to have been the first Constable.

The first white child born in the place was a daughter to William Billups.

William Billups was the first ferryman

The District Court was first held in this place in April, 1839—the Hon Charles Mason (afterward Commissioner of Patents) presiding Mr Duncan. before named, was Foreman of the grand jury, and the first trial by jury was that of the United States vs Blankenship and Helms, for riot.

Judge Wright, in an address speaks of Van Buren Company. and in one place, of a member, he says ·

" John Carnes might be called appropriately the talking, bragging member of the firm It was his peculiar province to dwell on the advantages of the place and its high destiny in the future. He originated the flaming handbills, and m'.. fi l l ii 'h   the privileges connected with our location at the Des Moine R 1 I- A l ... p i- n a--dis me that t. the-e handbills, and Carne ... gge ate·l statements as t) the amount of water-fall and character of

Joshua S Sloan

KEOSAUQUA

the Rapids at this point, may be traced the idea in the minds of the Missourians that these Rapids were those meant in their State Constitution

In 1850, a private bank grew out of the savings of a number of citizens, among them J. H Bonney, G G Wright, J. J Kinersly, Joel Walker and George W Games, each of whom deposited $1 originally, and afterward twenty-five cents per week, with the condition that it was not to be drawn excepting for loans and purchases of notes. At the length of four or five years the amount deposited had grown to $5,000, and was divided among the depositors.

EARLY AND LATE EDUCATORS.

The pioneers of Van Buren County commenced their work by preparing themselves and their successors for the work before them, by the institution of a good system of popular education   But, as their means were limited, their first seminaries were like their dwellings—of logs; the seats were benches made by splitting small logs, mostly of basswood, with very little polish and that little done with an ax, their desks were made by boring into the wall with a large auger, and inserting strong pins, inclining to the front, on which was fastened a plank, if any was to be had   if not what was called a "puncheon," hewed on one side   The windows, instead of being perpendicular were horizontal   And to these rude cabin-schools do Hon G W McCrary, Hon H C Caldwell and many other men of prominence owe their primary education.

As the above mention applies to Van Buren County at large, it may, with propriety, be localized so as to apply to Keosauqua

Tom Wilkinson kept the first school at the (now) county seat in 1839   He taught in a log cabin standing in a lot now owned by Judge Sloan.   Wilkinson left in 1842, and married a half-breed of the Cherokee nation

Caroline McBride taught at Keosauqua about 1840.

Necessity brought into vogue the private subscription schools, and these continued from fifteen to twenty years   Mr Lane taught one of these schools in 1851, in the Odd Fellows' rooms   The system of private schools was continued as late as 1866, during which time a small brick schoolhouse was put up The independent school system was introduced about the year 1866

Keosauqua now has one of the finest graded school buildings in the county. There are five departments.   The Principal of the school is Mr John R Landes   The teachers are, Miss Mary E Brown, First Primary, Second Primary, Miss Ada Redd, Intermediate, Clara Hartson; Grammar School, Emma Layton

The report for November, 1878 showed the names of two hundred and seventy-nine scholars on the roll

The schoolhouse was erected in 1866, at a cost of $18,000.

In 1839, a literary lyceum was established, the following being the act of incorporation

AN ACT *to incorporate the Keosauqua Lyceum*

SECTION 1   *Be it enacted by the Council and House of Representatives of Territory of Iowa,* That James Hall, John Fairman, S W Summers, S. N Lewis, Elisha Puell, John Carnes, Richard Billups, Simon Drouillard, Jacob Lane John Goodwin, John Purdon, Sewell Kinney, C Stevenson, John Stevenson, M Sigler, John Sigler, Cyrus H Ober Wilson Stanley, Russell King, Thomas Wilkinson, Alfred Vesters and such other persons as shall from time to time, become members of said corporation, shall be and are hereby ordained, constituted and declared to be one body corporate and politic, in deed, fact and name, by the name and style of "The Keosauqua Lyceum," and by that name they and their successors shall have succession and shall be persons in law capable of suing and being sued pleading and being impleaded to answering and being answered, defending and being defended in all suits and complaints, matters and cases whatsoever   and that they and their successors by the same name shall be persons in law capable to

ʜ

purchase, take, receive, hold and enjoy, to them and their successors, any real estate in fee-simple, or for term of life or lives, or otherwise, and any goods, chattels, or any personal estate, for the purpose of enabling them the better to carry into execution, encourage and promote such measures as may tend to the advancement of science and literature, and also to whatever else that may tend to the promotion of education, the advancement of knowledge, and the development of truth in the sciences *Provided*, the clear yearly value of such real and personal estate shall not exceed the sum of $5,000 And that they and their successors shall have full power and authority to give, grant, sell lease, devise and dispose of the said real and personal estate, or any part thereof, at their will and pleasure, and that they and their successors, shall have power from time to time to make constitute, ordain and establish such by-laws, ordinances and regulations as they shall judge proper, for the election of their officers, for the election and admission of new members of said corporation, and the terms and manner of such admission for the better government of their officers and members, or fixing the time and place of the meetings of said corporation, and for regulating all the affairs of said corporation, *Provided* such by-laws and regulations shall not be repugnant to the Constitution or laws of the United States or of this Territory

Sec 2   And for the better carrying on the affairs of said corporation, there shall be a President, Vice President, Treasurer and Secretary of the corporation, who shall hold their offices from the time of their appointment, or election, until the first Monday of March then next or until others shall have been chosen in their places And that the said J N Lewis is hereby appointed President, the said Wilson Stanly, Treasurer, and the said John Carnes, Secretary, until the first Monday of March next, and that said officers shall on the first Monday of March next, and always thereafter, be chosen by the members of the said corporation in such manner, and afterward at such time and places, as shall be directed by the by-laws of said corporation to be made for that purpose, and that the President or Vice President, and any seven members of said corporation, shall be sufficient to constitute a legal meeting for the transaction of business

Sec 3   This act shall be subject to amendment by any future Legislature

Approved, January 24 1839,

There was, during a period encircling the year 1851, an academy at this place   It ran a successful race with other schools of learning.

In 1842, a lyceum was started under the management of Hon George G. Wright, Hon J B. Howell, J J Kinersly, C. Baldwin, J. H. Bonney, Elisha Cutler, James Hall, Samuel Summers and others.   It was carried on with spirit for about two years, when it was discontinued.

THE CHURCHES

Father Purdom's was where the minister first found a home and a place to preach   The house was a double log cabin, with an entry between, and stood on the bank of the river, about three hundred yards above the town   Preaching was heard but seldom. and as late as 1840 the Methodist minister preached once a month   Even then, one of these rooms would scarcely be filled   Bryant, Hawk, Summers, Arrington, Shinn, of the Methodist, Bell and the two Rankins (the uncle and nephew), of the Presbyterian, and Post, of the Baptist Church, if not the first, were among those who first taught the way of life to those attending upon their ministry at this place.   They preached at the house in the winter, and frequently in the grove in the summer   The congregations were not large, but uniformly attentive, manifesting an appreciation of the moral lessons inculcated   Father Purdom was a Kentucky Methodist.   His house was always open, however, to the traveling ministry of all denominations   While he had strong prejudices and great quaintness of character, he was a warm friend and as warm an enemy.   He had a very strong attachment for his church, his home and his family   In 1848 he departed this life, much respected and lamented— and sleeps in the grave-yard—a tract which he gave from his premises for the town burying-ground   He left a large family. all of whom left and settled in Western Missouri

The first church organization was by the Methodists under the leadership of Leonard B Stacker, son-in-law of Elijah Purdom, who was appointed Class-Leader.

Mr. Hadden built the first church at Keosauqua, in 1840. It was used by all denominations.

The Rev. Daniel Lane has furnished the following descriptive article of the history of the Congregational Church:

The first Congregational ministers who made a settlement with the people of Van Buren County were myself and Rev. Harvey Adams, the latter settling at Farmington, and myself at Keosauqua. This occurred in November, 1843. We were from Andover Theological Seminary, graduates of the same year of our arrival. There were seven other Congregational ministers, young men who came to the then Territory of Iowa, with us, and two more followed us the next year, making in all a company of eleven young men, all of whom were from the Seminary at Andover, Mass., and all belonging to the same theological class—all classmates.

One of the two who joined us in 1844, Rev. Erastus Ripley took for his ministerial fields Bentonsport and its surroundings.

At this early period, Van Buren County was considered one of the most important counties in the Territory, made so by both the number of its inhabitants and by the fact that it was the home of Abner Kneeland, and his infidel colony. Mr. Keeland often lectured in Farmington, Bonaparte, Bentonsport and Keosauqua in the interest of his peculiar views, and, of course, in opposition to Christianity. He had many converts—so many that in 1841 or 1842, an attempt was made to carry the county, politically, by an *infidel* ticket. The effort, however, was a failure.

In entering upon my ministerial work in Keosauqua, however, I very soon made up my mind that the fundamental truths of the Gospel, and their practical bearing and influence in society, were what the people needed more than any discussion upon infidelity. This decision I saw no reason for reversing during my ten years of ministerial labor in the town.

The Congregational Church was organized in a little more than one year after my arrival in Keosauqua. The membership consisted only of five persons—two males and three females. Two of the five lived four miles from town. Only Mrs. Lane, my wife, lived in town, and the other two at a distance of two miles out. There was no church edifice in the place finished and dedicated until December, 1847, at which time the brick church in which the Congregationalists now worship, was completed and occupied.

The effort in building that church edifice, and the sources whence came the funds for the payment of the bills were somewhat peculiar. Being satisfied that a church edifice had become an actual necessity, in order to secure efficiency to my labors as Pastor of the Congregational Church, I called a meeting of those interested in such an enterprise, and laid before them my views of the whole matter. All present felt the importance of having a house of worship, but whence the money to secure it? This was the practical question. In those early days in the county, there was but little money in anybody's pocket.

Estimates were made of the cost of the house in question. About $140 must be raised at once, in payment for the brick. To raise this in cash, and to do it immediately, was an obstacle which seemed to those present insurmountable. The deliberations were closed with the conviction that the erection of a "meeting-house" must be deferred until another year.

I went home from that small gathering of six or seven persons with feelings in close proximity to discouragement. I had already labored some three years in Keosauqua, and only about one-half of that time had our Church been favored with any place for regular preaching each Sabbath. To continue this was contrary to all my ideas of ministerial usefulness. My salary, at this time, was $400, the greater part paid in cash by the American Missionary Society, of New York. On reaching home I unburdened my mind to my wife, and a long conversation ensued. I finally asked her if she thought we could possibly get along with family expenses if I should make myself responsible for the payment for the brick which would be required for the house in contemplation. To take $140 out of $400, when we had no other pecuniary resource whatever, seemed, at first, like opening the door to financial helplessness. After a long talk, we came to the conclusion that our friends in Keosauqua would not allow us to die of starvation in any event which might result from the diminished salary. And so, under the quieting thought, wife says: "Yes, we will try to do without the $140, if, by so doing, we can have a house of worship of our own." This answer given my plan was at once determined upon, and I was at rest. I slept soundly that night, and the next morning, was ready for further action.

There was a brickmason then living in Keosauqua, of the name of Jesse Winn. He had always promised me that when we were ready to build a church, if we would put one up of brick and give him the job, he would do a good thing for us. The first thing to be done was to see him. I found him finishing the cornice of a small brick building. Ascending the ladder to where he was standing, in the familiar language of Iowa's infancy, I said to him: "Jesse, if I will furnish the brick from my own purse for a church edifice, will you lay them up free of charge?"

He looked at me as if I was in earnest. That question settled, he sat down upon the bricks, straightened himself up with folded arms, and said: "I don't know, Mr. Lane, that is a temptation." A moment intervened and then he added: "I give Jesse Ridder $50 on an *election bet*   I lost the bet and gave him my note for $50   If you will go to him and get him to give me that note on condition that I do the brick work of the church, I will do it '

I was at the bottom of the ladder   I had descended in quicker time than I went up , and my next man was Jesse Elder and I said to him   " Jesse, if I will furnish the brick for a church of 30x40 feet, and 14-foot post and Jesse Winn will lay them up on condition that you will surrender to him that election-bet note which you hold against him, will you do it? '   He replied without a moment's reflection   " Tell Jesse Winn if he will do that, there will be no trouble about his $50 note "

The house of worship, in my enthusiasm for the moment, was built   That was one of the best mornings of my life   He who makes "the wrath of man praise Him " was now extolled by an election bet'   This was something that no theologian, however learned had thought of

But there was something else to be done   Another meeting was called of the six or seven who had met the previous night and decided adversely   Now, at their second deliberation, the whole face of the enterprise was so changed that all were encouraged to rise up and build   A subscription—including the gift of a lot for the site of the church—was raised, of $600, the Pastor, however, subscribing only $100, instead of $140   Against his paying the latter sum, there was such an earnest protest from those present that, instead of carrying out his first decision, he diminished the sum by $40   Afterward, however before the building was finished, he paid $20 more

But the brick, the brick work and the subscription, including the church lot, being secured, the next thing was provision for the foundation of the house   There was a stone-quarry near, and from its owner I gained permission to get all the necessary stone free of charge   Then, mounting my horse, I rode to the two members of my Church living four miles from town   They were husband and wife, the husband was a stone-mason   Telling him my errand, he immediately agreed to do the foundation work for his share in the enterprise   But both the stone and the brick must be transferred to the church lot before either the stone or the brick-masons could enter upon their work

There were living then two friendly families the one six and the other seven miles from town   Both had good double teams, with accompanying wagons   To think of those friends was equivalent to immediate action   Again I was on my horse, bound for their prairie homes   Finding the men and telling my errand, they agreed at once to see the stone and brick in their proper place on the church lot , and all this free of charge

Triumphant moment that, under responses so favorable!   Again, in imagination, the house was built   Perhaps it was ministerial which prevented a victorious "hurrah'" with the usual swinging of the hat   Be this as it may there was at that moment, as I hope, some gratitude to the Author of sanctuary worship for this preliminary success

And now, strange to say, it took us about one year and a half to complete the building, notwithstanding our auspicious beginning   The times were hard, lumber was dear, carpenter work was costly funds came in slowly, and many were the obstacles causing delay of the work   Finally it was done, except a few last things, the cost of which would be some $30—a small amount , but how to raise it at first was not very apparent for it seemed to me the members of the church had given the last cent they could spare   The building had now cost us about $1,000

At length, a happy thought, as it afterward proved, occurred to me, and I went into my study—which was originally a smoke-house, but now finished for a theological sanctum—caught up a slip of paper and wrote upon it the name of every man in town outside of our Church membership who, I thought, would be willing to give me $1 toward the $30 needed   I then sallied forth to try success in this new direction   It is enough here to say that, with only one exception, I secured the dollar of every man whose name I had written upon that paper

All was now ready for the final finish of the building, which was soon done, and the house, with thankful hearts, was then dedicated, free of debt and with no solicited aid from abroad, to the God of sanctuaries and sanctuary worship

The church in which the Methodist denomination now worship was built in 1851   Rev Henry Clay Dean was the Pastor at that time.   The membership is, perhaps. two hundred.   Rev. S. S. Murphy is Pastor.   The church was remodeled in 1874

The colored people have two churches here.   The Baptists use the building on the hill formerly occupied as a schoolhouse, while the Methodists worship in the little brick church near the river-bank.

THE AGRICULTURAL SOCIETY

In conformity with an act of the Territorial Legislature of Iowa, approved December 19 1838 a meeting of the citizens of Van Buren County was held in the town of Keosauqua on Saturday September 11, 1841, for the purpose of organizing a county agricultural society

Obed Stannard was elected President, George Wright, Secretary, and J H. Bonney, Treasurer. There were seven Directors chosen.

The first fair held was in the fall of 1842. Col. Stiles S. Carpenter delivered the address It was the first agricultural address in the county, and probably the first ever delivered in the State of Iowa. A W. Harlan, James H King, William Hadden, W S Wright and William Duncan took part in the first meeting.

There were one or two fairs held, after which the interest seems to have lagged, until September 27, 1851, when a meeting was held "for the purpose of forming an agricultural society" Dr. J B Elbert was appointed Chairman and L. D. Morris, Secretary

A committee of seven were appointed to draft Articles of Incorporation. Those seven were Capt. J E Miller, A H McCrary I W McManaman, Seth Millington, H C Caldwell and L D Morris

A vote was then taken for officers and Directors of the Society. The result was Dr. J. D. Elbert, President; Robert Meeks and Capt J E. Miller, Vice Presidents; H C. Caldwell, Recording Secretary L D. Morris, Corresponding Secretary; Seth Millington, Treasurer, I. W. McManaman, A H. McCrary, James Burns, John M. Whitaker, C H Bonner, A Phillips, Nathanal Myer, E. Mayne and Seth Fordyce, Directors

The first fair was held Tuesday, October 28, 1851

The Society has held successful meetings each fall since

There was a historical society formed at Keosauqua in 1838, which had a successful and protracted life. The society is now defunct

PIONEER ASSOCIATION.

' One of the institutions at Keosauqua (belonging equally to all sections of the county) is the Pioneer Association.

The call for a meeting of the citizens was made in June, 1871. The call was signed by Edwin Manning, Charles Baldwin, J. J. Kinersly, Thomas Rankin, James Bell, Bertrand R. Jones, Joel Walker, Russo King, George W Games and James Shepherd

The first meeting was held Saturday, July 22, 1871. On motion of Charles Baldwin, Dr. N Shepherd was called to the chair, and Bertrand R Jones was appointed Secretary. The Chairman stated the object of the meeting

The following resolutions were adopted : •

"*Resolved*, That this meeting do now adjourn to meet again the 5th day of August, and that a committee of five be appointed by the Chair, whose duty it shall be to give notice of the adjourned meeting in the county papers, and to invite all the old settlers of Van Buren County to attend said adjourned meeting, for the purpose of organizing an Old Settlers' Association"

The Chair appointed as such committee, Charles Baldwin, James Shepherd, Dr R N Cresap, Capt F Hancock and Maj J. C McCrary.

In accordance with the resolution of the previous meeting, the Association met August 5, 1871, Dr. N. Shepherd in the chair

It was resolved that all persons who had resided in Van Buren County thirty years be invited to become members of the Association.

The first permanent members were Abner H McCrary, President Capt. Frederick Hancock Vice President. B. R. Jones Secretary and Jonathan Thatcher, Treasurer

Successive meetings were held, and to-day the Association is in a prosperous condition

The present officers are as follows   Capt. Frederick Hancock, President; Charles Baldwin, Vice President, Edwin Goddard, Secretary, Harvey Duffield, Treasurer; Jonathan Thatcher, Marshal   Board of Control—Cedar Township, William C. Morris, Union Township, George Parker; Lick Creek Township. Charles Porter; Village Township, Jonathan Nelson, Chequest Township, Ira Claflin; Van Buren Township, Stephen Fellows, Washington Township, Mrs Marguerite Sanford, Harrisburg Township, Robert Sturdivant; Farmington Township, Robert Gray, Bonaparte Township, Isiah Meek, Vernon Township, Aaron H Thatcher, Henry Township, Sylvester S Henry. Des Moines Township, Hyram Baird, Jackson Township, John C Holland.

The members of the Association number about five hundred.

KEOSAUQUA INCIDENTS.

A bridge across the river at Keosauqua was commenced in 1850, but never completed. It fell down when partly erected. in 1851   The ferry was then used until the new bridge was built   The bridge enterprise cost the citizens about $6,000. for which they received nothing in return

The first, and probably only, flatboat from Keosauqua direct to New Orleans was built by Samuel Morton, two miles below town, in the spring of 1841. It was loaded with pork by Manning & Steeles   A. W Harlan, was the commander and pilot.   It reached the port in May

William Duncan commenced erecting a mill in the fall of 1837, below town

Mr. Kinersly tells that, in 1838, there were but three or four women here, and, in 1842, the number of old bachelors had increased to thirty-five   Edwin Manning was the first to leave the ranks of single blessedness.

Kinersly was the only man who had a stove in those days.   Quail were worth $1 apiece; and, although an expensive luxury, the rush to get a meal of quail cooked over Kinersly's stove was great

In 1845 and 1846, there were but three families out of the seven hundred people who were not ill   Bilious and intermittent fevers raged, and there was a heavy mortality list in consequence.

A story is told of Lorenzo Ellis.   He went to Des Moines in an early day to purchase a grindstone   He bound it to his back and started home   He wandered around until lost, and did not find his way home for ten days.

In " Tyler's time,' the Rev. Delazon Smith was sent to Ecuador as Commercial Agent, at a salary of $8 per day and expenses.   He was called home several times, but could never be induced to come until the Government stopped his salary   This circumstance earned him the nom de plume of " Lost Smith," or " Tyler's Lost Minister."

As an interesting incident, it may be well to mention that Keosauqua has paid in hard cash $25,000 for railroad schemes. the consummation of which was never known

MILLING INTERESTS

It has been mentioned elsewhere that in 1837 Duncan, Weatherly & King built a saw-mill   Previous to this the people had been obliged to go thirty-five miles to get their milling done   In 1838 the company in question added a small grist   and destroyed their mill in the great freshet   In 1842 or 1843, a flour-mill was erected by William Hadden Beesucker & McGune.   The mill finally run into the hands of McGuire, and he sold it to J J Kinersly and Elisha Cutler in February, 1849   Cutler died in July of that year, and Kinersly became sole proprietor.   He improved it in 1850, and. in 1852, put up an additional building at a cost of $5,000, the improvement embracing a saw-mill, carding machine, turning-lathes, and circular saws.   In 1854, the State commenced making improvements along the river   A lock and part of a dam were built   In February, 1857, the ice-gorge knocked the mills from their foundations, and they floated down the stream   The State improvement was abandoned in 1858, and, in 1860, Mr. Kinersly began the erection of his present mill, which was completed in February, 1862

Mr. Kinersly has now in process of building a new twelve-foot dam   The water-power at this point is highly valuable, there being a fall of twelve feet in the river, commencing above Pittsburg

There was a steam saw-mill put up in 1845 by Johnson & Brown.   The former died, and, in 1854, the structure was torn down

There was a pottery established here in 1846.   It was run five or six years and closed out   Dr Strickland started one in 1871, which, after two or three years, shared the fate of its former sister-pottery.

McNeal & St John had a plow-factory here in 1865, and they operated it until 1870, when it was closed.

THE BRIDGE

Keosauqua has a bridge.   It was commenced in February, 1873 and completed by October 1, 1873, at a cost of $45,000.

The bridge has 4 spans of 153 feet each, making the total length of the superstructure 612 feet.   There are 3 piers and 2 abutments   The distance from low-water mark to the floor of the bridge is 32 feet   The arches are 17 feet high.   The bridge is built to accommodate 2,000 pounds to the lineal foot, using one-fourth the entire capacity.

THE LODGES

Keosauqua Lodge, No 3, I O O F, was organized July 22, 1845.   It was the first Lodge in the county and third in the State   The organizers were W. H. Mauro, N. G.; David Roroer. V. G., Richard Mansly, William Garrett.   Petitioners—Frank Bridgeman, J. Johnson. B P. Marlow. J. J Kinersly, George Montague

The Degree of Rebekah was introduced into the Lodge in the summer of 1852

The present officers of the Lodge are Lee R Merideth N G., J. C McCrary, B T.; M. O. Ketchum, Sec , J H Duffield. F S ; Solon Nourse, Treas

There is a benevolent feature of the Lodge worth mentioning   During thirty years, there has been paid in $10.000 and the contributions for relief have been generous

In 1845. a literary organization was started and the effort supplied the Lodge with a library   The movers in this direction were George A Chittenden, Judge Wright, J P Howell, Judge Knapp, J. H Bonney, Charles Baldwin, H M Shelby and J. J. Kinersly

The Lodge now numbers eighty members, and has property valued at $2,500.

There is a lodge in the town of Van Buren with a branch granges There is a membership of [...]   The society was organized in 1872.

The date of [...] the Keosauqua Lodge [...] A M.,

The charter officers were: James Shepherd W M.. Isaac Reed S. W: Frederick Hancock. J. W.: John Carnes. Tiler and Treasurer Moses Bigford. Noble Barron James H Boon. Master Masons.

This Lodge was second in the county until the charter of the Farmington Lodge. No. 9. was surrendered. which places Keosauqua Lodge first on the roll.

The Lodge possesses the charred remains of Black Hawk's sword. The lodge-building was burned November 24. 1871. and the charter was destroyed A new charter was granted the following year.

The present officers of the Lodge are. Stephen D. Fellows. W M: James Shepherd. S W: Robert Dolburg. J. W. H G Miller. Secretary. Joshua S. Sloan. Treasurer. John Varner. S D. Abe Wilkin. J. D.: J. J. Kinersly Tiler.

Knights Templar Lodge. Eli Chanau. No 28. was chartered in October. 1875. It was constituted February 4. 1876 The grand officers were: O P Waters. G C.. Robert F. Bower T. G. John C. Parish D G C The first appointed officers were. Robert L. Clark. E C.: George C. Gebhardt. Gen. The present officers are I D Pergrin. C G · R Lea. S. W.: Abe Wilkin. J W. O. B. Brown P.· L L. Therme. Treasurer: C. A Gleckler. Recorder.

A dispensation was originally issued for Moore Chapter. No. 23 at Farmington. July 18 1857. but. before the charter was granted. the Order was moved to Keosauqua. and a charter granted September 8. 1859 The charter officers were: George C Gebhardt. H. P.. James Shepherd. King. Henry King. S The present officers are· Benjamin Johnston. H P: James S Shepherd. King: D. C Beaman S The membership of the Lodge is forty-three.

SOUTH KEOSAUQUA

was laid out February 19. 1840 by James Hall. proprietor. Nothing ever came of the town. except a few dwelling-houses

PLEASANT HILL.

Just across the bridge from Keosauqua. lies the hamlet of Pleasant Hill with perhaps one hundred dwellers. It was laid out March 20. 1850. by John Purdom. There is a hotel and blacksmith-shop there Also. the Christian Church. erected in 1866. and one small schoolhouse. There was once a store in the town.

FARMINGTON.

Farmington was laid out in 1839 by Henry Bateman At this village. the county seat was first located. and two sessions of court were held.

At that time. the "Jail" for the holding of prisoners was a stump to which prisoners were chained. Finally. an 8x10 pine Jail was put up. The story goes that. once upon a time. a man was incarcerated here who worked a peculiar escape. He lifted the Jail on his shoulders by getting under the rafters and carrying it to a trench or hollow. over which he set the building. and then crawled out by way of the hollow.

The .... W.... I.. D.... T. J Wright. Col.
Davidso   wett. James
Alirey.   graen. Able
Garland

James Burns was here in that early day and kept the first hotel, and James F Death had the first mill here and in the county as well

Jacob Alfrey, a son of James and Maggie Alfrey, was the first child born at Farmington

A Mr Williams, a stranger in the county was the first one to die at Farmington At that time, there were no coffins in this part of the county and the death of Mr Williams compelled the pioneers to make a rude coffin of linn puncheons

William Brattin and Miss Croxwell were the first couple married at Farmington.

Dr Miles was the first physician

The first Justice of the Peace was Henry Bateman

Dr. R. D. Barton was the first Postmaster. and for a time kept the office in his hat

CITY GOVERNMENT

The population of Farmington is about one thousand inhabitants. It is an incorporated city, having become so during the General Assembly of the Iowa Legislature in 1846–47 The first election of officers was held on the second Saturday of March 1847 Henry Benson was elected Mayor The Aldermen were Festus Dunning H D Swasey Jehu Stewart and James Craig.

The present city government consists of A. J. Shaw Mayor; John Whitten, Register, William Goodin Treasurer George Miller. Marshal and J. T Cross, William Bank. Busiel Boyer and James Carr, Aldermen Henry Benson and A J Shaw are Justices of the Peace

Farmington to-day supports one printing office. four dry goods stores two drug stores, three grocery stores. three millinery establishments three hotels, one livery stable. three commission and two agricultural houses. two agencies, three hardware stores one harness-shop three wagon-shops two blacksmith-shops. one cigar manufactory two shoe-shops two furniture houses one gristmill and one saw-mill. The place supports three lawyers. five physicians and two Justices of the Peace

THE MANUFACTURES

The noticable branch of manufacturing done here is the Farmington Wagon and Carriage Works, owned by Lewis Burg Mr Burg learned his trade and then worked seven years during which time he saved $1,400 With that he erected a shop 20x40 and started with three hands That was in 1865 and in the following fall. he built a new shop. and the year after that he added to it and employed seven hands. His business has grown until his works cover one-quarter of a block He employs sixteen to eighteen hands. and makes 250 wagons and 40 buggies each year

The Burlington & Southwestern Railroad Company have a portion of their shops here, and employ from ten to twelve hands

In the spring of 1844 James F Death put up the first steam flour-mill in the place That was soon closed and. in the year of 1852, Week & Stoddard built a new mill This was run until 1866 when the ice-gorge carried it down the stream. Joseph Dickey then built one and operated it until 1875 when S M Hurd & Son bought it and built the Diamond Mill. They run it until April, 1878. when C A Gleckler purchased it The capacity of this mill is 200 bushels

The first   place.
was in the G____ _____ ___ ____ __ _____ ___ _____ __ granted

January 8, 1846, and the Order called Farmington Lodge, No. 9   The charter members were J. W. Creal, Lewis Teuischer, C. G. Dibble, T. Heaight.   The officers under the charter were J. W. Baker, W. M., T. S. Crooks, S. W.; M. A. Britton, J. W., Ira Babcock Treas.; R. D. Barton, Sec., Silas Salsbury, S. D.; Alfred Forbes, J. D., A. Collingswood Steward, and O. Tower, Tiler.

The charter was surrendered on Wednesday, June 4, 1851.   Since that time, No. 9 has remained blank.

On the same day as surrendered, the Grand Lodge granted a charter for Mt. Moriah Lodge, No 27, to be located at Farmington.   The following were officers under the new charter   Lewis Teuischer, W. M.; R. D. Barton, S. W., Samuel Schreve, J. W., H. H. Slaughter, Treas.; C. F. Schramm, Sec., George W. Ringler, S. D.; William R. Osmond, J. D., Hiram Bolton, Tiler. George Schramm and George Johnston were Master Masons.   The present officers are G. W. Good, W. M., John Whitten, S. W.; James Moreland, J. W., J. A. Campbell, Sec.; William Gooden, Treas., George Beason, S. D., John Mackleroy, J. D., J. C. Martin, Tiler.

Wildey Lodge, No 17, I. O. O. F. was organized by R. W. G. M. Garner.   The charter was granted August 8, 1858.   The charter officers were A. W. Sweet, N. G.; R. H. Wyman, V. G., J. C. Elbert, Secretary, J. H. Bell, Treasurer.   It is at present officered by Linden H. Cooley, N. G., J. A. Campbell, V. G.; Bunyan Turton, Secretary, and Daniel Texter, Treasurer.

The Encampment —On July 8, 1852, Farmington Encampment, No 8, I. O. O. F. was instituted at this place by J. M. Tuttle, M. H. Cooley, C. H. King, George Green, James Myers, R. D. Barton, Joseph A. Smith, O. H. Brewer and John Folz.   The charter officers were   J. M. Tuttle, C. P.; J. A. Smith, S. W.; M. H. Cooley, H. P.; R. D. Barton, J. W., C. H. King, G. J.; J. Folz, S.; O. H. Folz, Scribe, J. Myers, Treasurer.

September 1, 1875, the Order was re-instituted, and, on October 20, of the same year, a new charter was granted, with the following officers: Herman Black, G. P., William Ganes, G. S.   The charter members were C. A. Gleckler, J. A. Campbell, George Whittally, B. F. Hill, D. E. Millard, E. H. Wickersham and M. H. Cooley.   On December 18, 1877, proceedings for the removal of the Encampment to Bonaparte were commenced, and, on February 5, 1878, the object was consummated, and the Encampment taken to Bonaparte, Lodge, No 22, I. O. O. F.   W. W. Entler and Samuel Spurgeon were the committee on removal.

Farmington has a small lodge of Good Templars, that was organized in June, 1876.

THE CHURCHES

The first minister who preached at Farmington was Richard Jones.   He had a house on the island, where he held forth for a considerable time.   He belonged to the Christian order.

There are now five denominations at Farmington, the first formed being the Congregational.   An extract from the record of the Church, says·

"On Sunday, June 14, A. D. 1840, several individuals convened at the house of M. A. Britton, Esq., who were desirous of forming themselves into a church in Farmington.   Present, Rev. Asa Turner, of Denmark, and the Rev. Clark, of Fort Madison   Rev. W. F. Barnes was chosen clerk, pro tem. Where a . . . . gave in their names favorable to the object of the . . . . John Conwell and Ellen his wife, from the Presbyterian Church in Catholic Ohio   W. F. Barns from the Congregational Church at Warsaw, Ill., and Maria M., his wife, from the Presbyterian Church at Maysville, Ky., A J Houghton, of the Congregational Church at Berlin, Mass ; John C White, from the Congregational Church Mission Institute, near Quincy, Ill ; Edward T Colton, and Mary, his wife. from the Congregational Church at Quincy, Ill. , Eli Millard, and Phœbe, his wife, from the Congregational Church at Manchester, Conn., and Marcia Colton.''

The denomination built their church in 1848 Rev Harvey Adams served as their Pastor from 1843 to November 11 1866. The society have 181 members. They are without a minister now.

The Baptist society of Farmington was organized Saturday, August 28, 1841. at 2 o'clock P. M., by Elder Daniel Jewett The society struggled along. meeting at the houses of the Church members until 1851 and 1852, when they erected a church, the Pastor of which was Rev W H. Turton The present Pastor is Rev William Young, assisted by Rev Mr Turton.

The German Methodist society of this place was organized in 1853, by Rev H Ellback, and a church was erected, and dedicated the last Sunday in May, 1855 The Rev William Cuppen is present Pastor.

In 1862, the German Lutherans, under the leadership of Rev. Oswald Meibitz, organized a society and built a church. The society is still in a prosperous condition

The Catholic Church of Farmington was built in 1863-64. Rev Father Hayes was first Pastor, and has been succeeded by three or four clergymen, until Father O'Brien was assigned to the charge. He continues at Farmington at present

In 1875, the society of the Latter Day-Saints was formed by Rev. James McKiernan and has continued since that time.

The Methodist society of Farmington was formed as early as 1840 In 1845, a church was erected, which has served the worshipers since

THE SCHOOL

Prior to the building of the public schoolhouse, in 1870, the city of Farmington educated her children in rented houses and other places of convenience. There is no record of who the first teacher was, or where the school was kept In 1866. the district became independent. The schoolhouse cost $10,000 and is used as a graded institution The first teacher in the house was L M. Moores

Among the early legislative records is found the following bill, incorporating the first high school or academy ever instituted in the county. The appearance of this document will doubtless serve to refresh the memories of some of the early settlers of Farmington, and may serve to stimulate research for school records among the members of the Pioneer Association

AN ACT to incorporate the Farmington Academy and High School

SECTION 1 Be it enacted by the Council and House of Representatives of the Territory of Iowa' That there shall be established in the town of Farmington in Van Buren County, an institution of learning to be known and designated as the " Farmington Academy and High School,' and by that name may sue and be sued, contract and be contracted with, use a common seal, purchase, receive by gift or devise, hold control, enjoy, sell and convey, any property, real, personal or mixed, for the use and benefit of said institution

SEC 2 The design of the institution hereby created is declared to be for the instruction of youth in the arts and sciences, and to advance learning and sound morals, by the establishment of good schools, procuring competent teachers, a library, scientific instruments and apparatus and the colle...

SEC 3 ... Banning ... Smith ... Houghton, O Tu... H ... Stewart are constituted Trustees of said Academy and High School a majority ... shall be a quorum, open books and receive subscriptions to the stock of said institution ... professors and make and ordain all needful by-laws rules and regulations

484 HISTORY OF VAN BUREN COUNTY

Sec 4   The Trustees may divide the capital stock into as many shares as they deem fit, setting out the ownership of each share upon the books of Trustees and stockholders, each share being $5

Sec 5   All books, maps medals, scientific apparatus cabinets of minerals, plants and curiosities belonging to said corporation shall be forever free and exempt from taxation by the laws of this Territory

Sec 6   That any future Legislature may amend, alter or repeal this act

Sec 7   This act to take effect and be in force from and after its passage

Approved January 27, 1844

INCIDENTAL AND ACCIDENTAL

There was an ice freshet at this point in 1832, when the water stood four feet over the territory now occupied by the village of Farmington. The overflow extended as far north as Bonaparte.

The high water of 1851 did not seriously affect this village

In the winter of 1866, Farmington was bothered with an ice-gorge, which commenced at Athens and extended up the river five miles. The flow of the tide did considerable damage. Meek & Stoddard's flour-mill was washed away, and also a number of small houses between Front street and the river.

About ten years ago, occurred the only murder that ever happened at Farmington A prisoner named Cockley shot and killed Constable Feustemaker, while the latter was in the performance of his duty transferring the prisoner to the Jail for a thieving offense. Cockley made his escape and was never found

In the autumn of 1874, occurred the only fire of note ever happening at Farmington The flames licked up the stores of L L Therme & Son, drugs; Charles Doeling, cigar manufacturer, Charles Kessler, dry goods, George Perry, hardware, Will Gooden, groceries. The Masonic lodge-room, in the third story of Therme's building, was also destroyed The loss caused was $20,000, on which there was a partial insurance. The fire is supposed to have originated from a lamp explosion

BONAPARTE

The village of Bonaparte was commenced in the year 1837, by Messrs. Meek & Sons and Dr R. N. Cresap, whose initiatory step embraced the building of a dam across the Des Moines River. The early settlers, whose presence was marked by the year in question, were P. R. Rice, Joseph Rabb, Erwin Wilson, David Sewell, Lewis Christian and William Welch A few cabins were built about the wild country, and from the rude hut-town the place has grown until the din of machinery and clang of the mills is heard by 1,200 people, who constitute the present population of the place

This population support four dry goods stores, two drug stores, four grocery stores, one harness-shop, one jewelry house, two boot and shoe stores, one clothing house, one general store, three millinery establishments, two furniture stores, three tailor-shops, two commission houses, two agricultural marts, two butcher-shops, two hotels, and a photograph establishment; while the following branches of manufacturing also thrive: a woolen-mill, wagon-factory, brick-yard, pottery, blacksmith shop, flouring-mill, saw-mill and stove-factory. There is one printing office in the place three churches one schoolhouse Masonic and Odd Fellows' Halls and a livery barn There are four physicians and two Justices of the Peace in the place

The following legislative enactment will be read with interest by the people who first settled near Bonaparte.

An Act to authorize William Meek & Sons to erect a dam across the Des Moines River

SECTION 1   *Be it enacted by the Council and House of Representatives of the Territory of Iowa,* That William Meek & Sons be, and they are hereby authorized to construct a dam across the Des Moines River, in Van Buren County, in said Territory, between Sections 8 and 17, in Township 68 North, Range 8 west of the fifth principal meridian, which said dam shall not exceed three feet in height above common low-water mark, and shall contain a convenient lock, not less than one hundred and thirty feet in length and thirty-five feet in width, for the passage of steam, keel and flat boats, rafts and other water-craft, provided said water-craft will bear two tons burthen

SEC 2   It shall be the duty of the persons authorized in the preceding section of this act to build said dam, at all times to keep the lock in the same in good repair, and they shall, at all reasonable times, pass any water-craft above-mentioned, through, free from toll without any unnecessary delay   And any person who shall be unnecessarily detained, shall be entitled to recover of said owners double the amount of damages they shall prove to have sustained by reason of such detention

SEC 3   Any person who shall destroy or in anywise injure either said dam or lock, shall be deemed to have committed a trespass, and shall be liable accordingly   And any person who shall willfully or maliciously destroy or injure said lock or dam shall be deemed guilty of misdemeanor and, on conviction thereof, shall be fined treble the amount of damages the owners may have sustained, or be imprisoned, at the discretion of the court

SEC 4   Nothing herein contained in this act shall authorize the individuals named in this act, their heirs or assigns, to enter upon and flow the lands of any person, without the consent of such person, and they shall remove all such nuisances as may be occasioned by the erection of said dam, which may endanger the health of the vicinity

SEC 5   The Legislature of this Territory (or State) may at any time alter or amend this act so as to provide for the navigation of said river

SEC 6   The dam and lock specified in the first section of this act shall be completed within three years from the 1st day of May next

SEC 7   The right of constructing and continuing the aforesaid dam and lock across the Des Moines River shall be vested in the said William Meek & Sons for the term of fifty years from the 1st day of May next

SEC 8   This act to take effect from and after its passage
Approved January 17, 1839

John Bundy and William Meek, Sr, are both credited with having kept the first store in the village   Dr. R N. Cresap kept the first hotel   The first blacksmith was R B Willoughby, and Hamilton Kearns was the first wagon-maker.

Jackson Myers is said to have started the first flouring-mill, although William Meek & Sons put up one in 1844, which served until the fall of 1878, when Robert Meek & Brothers erected a new one, at a cost of $15,000.   The structure is of brick, size 40x50 and four stories in height   The mill has six runs of buhrs

Meek & Brothers also erected a saw-mill in 1860, which has run since that time.

The manufacturing interests of this place are nearly all centered in the woolen-mill, and manufacturing has received a healthy start, and the life instilled into this branch of industry at the beginning, instead of growing less, has been fanned into a noticeable flame, which spreads with the tread of time

One of the most extensive and successful woolen-factories of the State is situated at Bonaparte   It was built in the summer of 1853, by William Meek & Sons, who run it at a paying rate until 1863, when it was burned down, causing the firm a loss of $20,000.

Robert F. Meek & Brothers immediately commenced rebuilding, and at a cost of $50,000, made of brick a structure 50x85, and four stories high.   The machinery is propelled by water-power   The firm employs seventy-five hands.   The capacity of the mill is a matter worthy of mention   There are 1 640 spindles in use six sets of carding machines and two shearing machines.   The mill hands turn out 22,000 yards of cloth every four weeks and from 1,600 to 1,800 pounds of stocking-yarn

A pottery was started in 1866 by Parker & Handback This firm continued in business five years, when Mr Wilson succeeded Mr Parker and became known as the junior partner The firm are now known as Handback & Wilson. In November, 1876, the pottery building was burned, at a loss of $1,200 It was rebuilt at once, the outlay being $1,300 The firm now employ ten hands and make 75,000 gallons of pottery per year A new feature has been added recently It is a tile-factory, with a capacity for turning out 6,000 feet of tile per day. The machinery throughout is run by steam-power

THE BONAPARTE BRIDGE.

There are two bridges in the county of Van Buren over the Des Moines River, for the accommodation of the general public—that is, foot-travelers and teams The larger of the two is at Bonaparte, it having 5 piers, 6 spans of 150 feet each, 23-foot truss and an 18-foot roadway

This structure was commenced November 25, 1877. On Tuesday, January 29 1878, the bridge was tested and formally accepted

Word was sent to the farmers in the neighborhood that teams and men would be required to fix the approaches and test the strength of the bridge The test consisted of twenty-two heavily-loaded wagons, averaging fifty hundred weight. besides horses, mules and men. The aggregate burden on each span was recorded at seventy-five tons, and in but one place did the settle exceed one-eight of an inch The superstructure is 900 feet long Each span weighs 60 tons. The bridge stands 35 feet above low-water mark and from the bed of the river to the top of the truss the distance is 60 feet The capacity of the bridge is 11,440 pounds per lineal foot. The approaches of the bridge are protected by a wing-wall and two abutments The piers are 10 feet by 30 at their base. The cost of the superstructure was $35,000.

The following gentlemen composed the executive committee at the date of acceptance· Isaiah Meek, Thomas Christy. Uriel Neal, A Whitlock, T. W. Boyer and Dennis Haney.

THE CHURCHES.

The date of church organizations at Bonaparte does not run back far The earliest move made in the direction of establishing churches was in 1853, when the Baptists, under the pastorate of Rev. William Sutton, began building a church, which was finished in the year 1857. Prior to that, however—1851— the same society had been organized at Mt Zion. where they worshiped until 1853, when they removed to Bonaparte The second Pastor was Rev. William Eggleston. the third. Rev. Mr Burkholder ; the fourth, Rev Mr Inskeep: the fifth was Rev William Johnson the sixth, Rev. Mr. Trevitt and the seventh, Rev. W C Pratt. At present the society are without a Pastor They have one hundred and twenty-five members and a house of worship that cost $2,800.

The date at which the Methodist society of this place was organized is not known, neither are there any records of early work For a time, however, the Methodists used the schoolhouse, where they worshiped until that building was burned down, when they rented the Baptist Church which served them down to the year 1862. when they built a new church at a cost of $700. The society numbers about fifty members Who organized it is not known Rev Mr. Johnson preached to a term—the first in the new church. but who led the flock in the olden day memory does not reveal. The Rev. Charles W. Shepherd is the present Pastor.

In 1869, the Presbyterian society was organized, and, in 1871, they built a $2,800 church, of which Rev. H. R. Lewis was the first Pastor. Next came Rev. H. K. Heighney, followed by Rev James Welch, who is the present one. There are fifty members belonging to the Church.

THE SCHOOLS

Bonaparte has quite a school history. The first district schoolhouse was put up in 1844. Thomas Charlton was the first teacher in the village. The house stood until 1859, when it was burned down. However, in the mean time, schools were kept in the buildings at present occupied by Mr Cair as a shop, and in what is now Mr King's house. After the old schoolhouse burned, the district rented schoolroom until the Directors purchased the academy in 1871.

The academy in question was erected in 1865, 1866 and 1867, by the Bonaparte Academy Association, at a cost of $20,000. The Association used it as an academy from 1867 to May 26, 1871, when they sold it as above stated for the sum of $12,000. The Association was an incorporated body. The following lines are extracted from the beginning of the articles of agreement or incorporation : "We, Isaiah Meek, Thomas Christy, Joseph A. Keen, J. G. Vale Benjamin Wagner, John T Stewart, George W. Sturdevant and A. H Leach, do hereby incorporate ourselves, and all other persons who may become members of the corporation hereby created, into a body corporate and politic, by the name and style of the 'Bonaparte Academy Association' "

The purpose of this institution was "the promotion of literature, science and art." The articles of agreement further provided that the capital stock must not run below $10,000.

The first Principal of the Academy was E P Howe

One year prior to the purchase of the Academy, the Bonaparte district became independent. The October, 1878, report showed that the total enrollment in all the departments of the school was 168, and the average daily attendance about 126. The school is divided into four departments. Annie E Packer is the present Principal.

CITY GOVERNMENT

Bonaparte is not an incorporated town. The officers embrace two Justices of the Peace and a Constable. The first Justice was Samuel Reed, who lived two and a half miles from town ; but the first in the village proper was R B Willoughby. A J Myers was the first Constable. The present Justices are W W. Entler and Joseph Perkins. Samuel Spurgeon is Constable

The village Postmaster is J. P Davis. When the place was introduced to a mail-route, Thomas Charlton had the honor of being the first Postmaster. R. Moffit was the first Postmaster at Lexington, just above town.

The first physician in the village was Dr. R N. Cresap.

William Willoughby, son of R B Willoughby, was the first child born at Bonaparte. The first death was in the person of Mrs Angeline, wife of Dr Cresap

The first marriage that took place was April 8, 1841, when James A Kearn and Elizabeth Williamson were joined in the holy bonds of wedlock

SECRET ORDERS

Of the Orders akin to secrecy in the village of Bonaparte, the Bona paite Lodge of Independent Oider of Odd Fellows, No 22, is the most ancient, its chaiter having been granted November 8, 1849. The charter members weie R H Wyman, L. R Beckley, John H Bell, W. E Kurtz and W Cassiday. The charter officeis were R H. Wyman, N G ; J H Bell, V. G , L R Beckley, Seci etary , and J B. Cave, Tieasurei. The Lodge now numbeis fifty members. They have a libiaiy consisting of 200 volumes

The piesent officers are Joseph G Whitely, N G., Jacob Muellei, V. G : W. A. George. Secretaiy ; and Joseph A King, Treasuiei.

In connection with this lodge-room is the society known as the Farmington Encampment, No S, I O O F This Order was instituted at Farmington, July 8, 1852, by J. M. Tuttle, M. H. Cooley, C. H. King, George Green, James Myers. R D Barton, Joseph A Smith, O H Biewer and John Folz.

The chartei officers weie J M Tuttle, C P ; J A Smith, S W ; M H Cooley H P ; R D Barton, J W.; C H King. G : J Folz, S , O H Brewei, Sciibe , J. Myers. Tieasurer.

At Farmington, September 1, 1875, the Ordei was re-instituted, and, on October 20 of that year, a new charter was granted, with Herman Block, G. P., and William Ganes, G S. The following weie chaitei members : C. A. Gleckler, J. A Campbell, George Whittally, B F Hill, D. E. Millard, E H Wickersham and M H Cooley

Proceedings for the iemoval of the Encampment from Farmington to Bonaparte, were commenced Decembei 18, 1877, and on Febiuary 5, 1878, the Encampment was moved to the hall of Bonaparte Lodge, No. 22, I O O F The committee on removal weie W W Entlei and Samuel Spurgeon.

The present officeis of the Encampment are these. Samuel Spurgeon, C. P.; Jacob Muellei, H. P.; C. W. Wilson S W ; C Hasslei. J W ; W. W. Entler, Scribe ; A W Steadman, Treasurei

The Masonic fraternity of this place number about seventy-one The charter foi Bonaparte Lodge, No 73, F & A M was gianted June 2, 1856. The charter officers were : Oliver George, W M , John H. Bell, S. W., S F Bradley, J W

At present, the officers are as follows. Di. D. W. Stutsman, W M.; Hugh Bell, S. W , William Sivil, J. W ; R. F. Meek, Treasurer, Robert Wilson, Seci etary , James Humphrey, S D , William Wilson. J. D , E W. Corwin. Tilei , Joseph A Keen, S. S ; J. W Whitely, J. S The Lodge has a libiaiy of 300 volumes.

There is also identified at this Lodge. the Lafayette Chapter, No 61 The first meeting under the dispensation was held November 10, 1870. The dispensation officers weie Geoige Beason. H. P., Benjamin Walker, King , and II F Greef, Scribe

On Novembei 2 1871, the Chapter was chaitered with these officers· George Beason. H. P.; H. F. Gieef, King; Thomas H Hopkins, S. , J. W. Whitely, Tieasuier, and R D Ryland, Secretaiy

The Chapter now numbeis thirty-four membeis, with the following officers. I. D. Poigrm, H P.; William Sivil. King. Geoige W Jack. Scnbe, Julius Greef Treasurer, Dr D W. Stutsman. Secietaiy

BENTONSPORT.

In the year of 1839, John Bending, as President of the Company, and Charles O. Sanford and H. P. Graves as associates, laid out the town of Bentonsport

This town had a healthy start, and the little neighborhood of people who had come to settle there were loyal, too, and did not forget or turn their backs upon the good old-fashioned way of celebrating Independence Day. In the same year the town was laid out, the hearts of the stalwart pioneers and their families, clubbed together and prepared for a grand Fourth of July celebration.

In connection with the other preparations, a barbecue had been determined upon, and when word to that effect went out, "everybody in the county and miles and miles outside" (to use the language of Mrs. John D Sanford) began to fix up for the event, and when the time came, all were in attendance Capt James Hall was the orator of the day.

H. P Graves and Alva White were keeping a store at this time—the first at Bentonsport

John Burton and his mother kept the first hotel in the village.

The first shoemaker is said to have been A. W. Harlan, Sylvester S. Henry also claims to be first.

Moses Springston was the pioneer blacksmith.

McHenry & Slagle kept the first harness-shop.

The first wagons made here were by John and Marshall Cottle

Seth Richards was the first Postmaster.

The first minister was a Cumberland Presbyterian named Williams.

A Mr Conner was the earliest Constable.

The first Justice of the Peace was David Tade.

William Sample kept the first school

Dr. C. W. Cowles was the pioneer physician.

H H Bucklin was the first lawyer.

The first child born in Bentonsport was Henry Sullivan

The first death recorded was of a colored woman with a slave name, "Aunt Mournin." She was brought here as a slave by Shapley Ross

Greef & Company were the first bankers, having conducted this business on a private plan for about six years past.

Bentonsport now has a population of 600 inhabitants. The place affords three general stores, one millinery establishment, one shoemaker, one blacksmith, one wagon-shop, one tailor-shop, one stove and tinware and one butchershop, and four insurance agencies

The first paper-mill built in the State of Iowa was at Bentonsport, by Green Brothers, in 1852. The concern was run until 1874. when it was closed up, and the machinery taken to Blue Rapids, Kan

In 1843 Hitchcock & Noble built a flouring-mill and a saw-mill on the bank of the river. A new flouring-mill was built in 1854 by James A Brown, which serves the community at present The building is of brick, four stories in height. It has three runs of buhrs. The saw-mill was run until 1866, when it was stopped.

An oil-mill was put up in 1865 by James A. Brown, which served until 1867. This was the first linseed-oil mill built in Southern Iowa It did a prosperous trade down to the year mentioned when it was converted into a

L

woolen-mill by Brown & Moore They continued the manufacture of cloth until 1876, since which time the mill has stood idle.

The first flatboat loaded with produce that ever went out of the Des Moines River started from Bentonsport. The boat was owned by Hugh W. Sample.

THE SCHOOLS.

The school district of Bentonsport is an independent one. It is not within the memory of man where the first school was taught—other than that it was in a log cabin—neither the date in which teaching began The district struggled along, however, using a building here and there, until 1870, when the Directors purchased the academy for school purposes, for which it is still used

This academy was an individual enterprise, and erected in 1851, by John D. Sanford, H. F. Greef, James A Brown, Seth Richards and Dr. C. W Cowles It cost them $3,000, and they sold it for $1,000 The district had used it before the date of purchase The first Principal of the academy was John W. Allen.

The number of scholars enrolled in this district is ninety-one, there being thirty-five in the first department and fifty-six in the second. This, as shown by the November, 1878, report.

CITY GOVERNMENT

Bentonsport is an incorporated city, having become so under the Iowa code of 1851 The first Mayor of the city was George Green The Councilmen were James A Brown, M. O Cresswell, C E Newlon, G. W Marley and W. N. Bragg The first meeting of which the records tell, was held January 21, 1854

The present city officers are William Gregson, Mayor, and Joseph Montgomery, A. C. Rehkoph, Alexander C Harlan and John F Stewart, Aldermen

SECRET ORDERS

Bentonsport Lodge, No. 47, A , F. & A M. met under dispensation, June 9, 1854, and on June 5, 1855, the charter was granted.

The charter officers were: William Quaintance, W. M , W N Bragg, S. W., Benjamin Walker, J. W., H. A. Rehkoph, Tiler, F. Hancock, Secretary James Johnson and B F Sims were members

The Lodge numbers fifty-five members. The names of the officers follow: I. D. Pergnm, W M.; J F Stewart, S. W.; R. Walters, J. W , Julius Greet, Treasurer; N G Brown, Secretary; G. W Jack, S D , H Hait, J. D., W. H. Carter, Tiler.

Des Moines Valley Lodge, No 258, I O O F. was instituted May 18, 1872, and charter granted October 20, 1873 The charter members were: Stephen Newson, Frank Eberhardt and John Drake The officers under the charter were: C Heinz, P G , Jacob Leffler, V G , and James Leffler, Secretary

The present officers are: J. M Tracy, N G , John Grinsley, V G.; Joe Montgomery, Treasurer, and William Gregson, Secretary.

THE CHURCHES

The people of Bentonsport began to incline religiously as early as 1841, when meetings were held out in the houses Mrs. Sanford says: "The first people who knocked at the door when they came to church were around in 1844.'

The first church organization was in 1843, when the Congregational society was cemented under the leadership of the Rev Harvey Adams.   Their first regular Pastor was Rev Erastus Ripley   The denomination erected their church in 1856

This society had the first church-bell, and conducted the first Sabbath school in the place   It was a union school, yet under Congregational leadership

The society have no regular Pastor now.

The date of organization of the Methodist society is not known, beyond the fact that, in the early days, Bentonsport, like all other places, was visited by various itinerant ministers and it is not at all unlikely the seed was planted as far back as 1840.

The society built their first church in 1857   The flock of the fold which is quite numerous, is watched over by the Rev Charles W Shepherd

The first Pastor of the Presbyterian Church was Rev William Harsha The society was organized in 1853 two years after the Church erected an edifice in 1851.   There is no Pastor now

There was a Universalist society formed at Bentonsport in about 1858, and a church-building was erected   The prime movers in this cause were Henry Clay Clinton. H F. Greef and William Quaintance   The pioneer Pastor was Rev Mr Ballinger   The society was continued but a few years when it disbanded.

The Universalist Church is now occupied by the Seventh-Day Adventists who established a society in the summer of 1878   Rev Mr McCoy. a missionary, is the Pastor

VERNON

By crossing the ferry from Bentonsport, one is landed on the levee of the little village of Vernon   This town was laid off June 12, 1837, by Henry Smith John Smith S C Reed and Isaac Reed   It was for a time called South Bentonsport

John Allender had the first store at Vernon, and Henry Smith kept the first hotel

The first Postmaster was John M. Estes.

John Allender was the first miller

Andrew Ewings had the first blacksmith-shop

The first Justice of the Peace was James Rabb

Dr G S Bailey was the first physician

The first teacher in the place was John M. Estes

Samuel Clark was the pioneer minister.

A daughter of Dr Bailey has the honor of being the first child born at Vernon.

The first marriage was between Dortha Smith and a Mr. Les Prouse

John Smith was the first to die within the precincts of Vernon

The village now has three dry goods stores. one general store, one drug store. one hotel. one shoe-shop, one harness-shop, two blacksmith-shops, and supports two lawyers and a physician

There is a flouring-mill at Vernon that owns quite a scrap of history   The mill was pu   1   k   l   It was used as a gr   w r   through and left the   l   e shore It was repaired, and, in 1857, George C. Allender started it as a woolen-mill.

It was successfully used for a few years and then allowed to stand idle until the fall of 1878, when a Mr Gillett secured a contract to manufacture woolen for the Government, and began putting the old mill into condition to manufacture.

George C Allender and Freeman, in 1858, built a flour-mill which has served until the present time, with some changes in ownership Freeman transferred his share to John D Sanford in 1861, and Allender & Sanford was the style of the firm until 1870, when Allender sold to Benjamin Kyes The latter sold to William Moore in 1875, and Sanford went out in the same year, transferring to B O. Nelson The latter sold to Doudy, who, in the fall of 1878, released his hold and Whiting took it. The mill firm is now Whiting & Moore

Vernon had a pottery as early as 1848, James Clark coming to the place and starting a log kiln and mud oven In April, 1852, R M Dixon and J Calmbourn came and put up a new shop and the next summer a new oven In November of 1852, Calmbourn was drowned in the river. Dixon run the pottery alone until 1868, when he took as a partner J C Grimsley. This pottery was the first in the county It has been a very successful enterprise The capacity of the factory is 240,000 gallons per year.

<h3>THE SCHOOL</h3>

The first school at the village of Bentonsport was taught in John M Estes' house in 1852 In a few months, a brick schoolhouse was erected which stood until 1869, when a new one was built It has served until the present The school district is independent

<h3>RELIGIOUS.</h3>

The structure used for the Methodist Episcopal Church of Vernon—the only church here—was erected, in 1852, for a dwelling-house by Able Choate, and was converted into a church in 1856 The Rev. I P. Teeters was the first Pastor

Years before that, however, the faithful had worshiped in the houses of citizens who kindly donated space for that worthy object, and the members of the society increased until the Church in question was prepared to accommodate the congregation The present Pastor is Rev. Charles W. Shepherd.

BIRMINGHAM.

John Harrison, the proprietor of Birmingham, laid the place out in June, 1839. The place has grown to contain perhaps seven hundred inhabitants, and, although a railroad never belted this town with any other, there is a deal of business done here. There are three stores here, each doing a general line of business. The place is an incorporated city The first charter was dated June 1 1856 The first meeting was held June 3 The first officers were: President, Joseph Talbott. Councilmen—J. B Spears, J. N. Norris, E Pitkin Recorder, Robert Porter Treasurer, George Parker A second charter was granted June 1, 1869, with H Clay Clinton, Mayor; Robert Porter, Recorder Joseph Graham, S A Bogle, C C Pleasant, F. B Huffman and J N Smith, Councilmen The present officers are: Samuel Wilson, Mayor, Robert P... Rec... Jos... Gra... Tr... George Deahl, Marshal, F. Eich... H Ba... D M M... George Chakesbeard and Newton Calhoon ...

A man named Berry was the first settler in the town although Dr. I. N Norris passed over the land where the city now stands when that plat was all grass-grown. That was in 1839   James Steel kept the first hotel here   The man Berry referred to was the first blacksmith

The first physician was William Miller, and H. C. Clinton was the first lawyer.

A daughter of Dr. Norris was first to be born, while the first death was of a child of Titus Moss.

Jacob Lawton was the first Postmaster, and carried the mail to Winchester.

THE SCHOOLS.

The school district of Birmingham has been independent since 1860.   Dr. Norris taught the first school here, in 1838–39   The term was worried through in a log hut, which soon gave way to a frame schoolhouse   In 1872, a public schoolhouse was erected, and the district is now a prosperous one, employing four teachers

There is a public academy here, too.   It was built in 1857, and styled the " Birmingham Collegiate Institute "   The enterprise was started by the Rev. Mr McArthur, a United Presbyterian   He raised a stock company.   This company at length sold the building, Rev G. P Bergen taking it in the interest of the Presbyterians, who later sold it to Prof. J W Wolf, the present owner   The institution is a very successful one, having half a hundred scholars on an average throughout the year

THE CHURCHES.

There are four churches at Birmingham   The Presbyterians and Methodists came in 1839.   Rev. Joel Arrington was the first minister who came here He was a Methodist, and in the service of the Missionary Society.   He preached in the old log schoolhouse first in 1838   He was an eloquent man, and won a wide reputation in those early days   The society of Methodists was formed in 1839.   They worshiped in the log house until 1847 or 1848, when they built a frame church   That served until 1857 or 1858, when it was vacated and a larger church built

The Rev. Solomon Coles organized the Presbyterian society in 1839, the first meeting being in a barn   A church was built in 1850, and, in 1854, a new one was erected to take the place of the first one, that had been sold for a barn   The building is still standing.

The United Presbyterians, at first called the " Seekers," established their society in 1839   They built a church in 1848.   Rev. Mr Vincent was the first Pastor.

The Free Methodist society was organized in 1874, by the Rev Mr. Douty. The church was built in the same year.

Next to the village of Bonaparte, Birmingham is probably the most important town in the county of Van Buren for extensive manufacturing

The plow and wagon factory of Shott & Hope is situated here.   The works were established in 1866, under the name of Shott & Brown, after which the firm became known as Moss, Shott & Brown.   Then Moss went out.   Finally, Brown sold his interest, and the firm became Shott & Hope.

In 1856, D. C Cramer & Co (Cramer, Moss & Cramer) built a woolen-factory.   It was not put into operation, however, until about 1861.   The factory was run successfully until 1870.

The saw and grist mill of Gwinn & Bott was erected in 1850 It was burned in the spring of 1854, and soon rebuilt This, by the way, with the burning of John Barnes' house, was the only fire that ever occurred at Birmingham

There was a cheese-factory put up in 1871, by C. L Moss This is still in successful operation

Birmingham had a tannery in 1868, under the management of James Glanden, Joseph Porter, "Tanner" Ross and John Park. The tannery run one year, when Benjamin Smith took the building and converted it into a pork-packing house. He run it two seasons and then moved his business to Keokuk

The only sensation ever occurring at this place was the suicide of William Winny in 1858. He was walking with his sisters one day, in the country, and, when near a clump of hazel bushes, he stepped behind them and shot himself. There was no cause assigned for the deed.

THE LODGES.

Birmingham Lodge, No. 36, I O O. F., was chartered October 27, 1852, W H Tuthill, G. M., and Joseph Bridgman, G. S. The charter members were Samuel Fasnacht, G A. Chittenden, Samuel Taylor, Zion Rains and Jonathan W. Sage The membership of the Lodge is about sixty. The present officers are John W. Ferrell, N. G.; J S Skinner, V. G.; William Hope, R, S · D. C Petit, P. S.

Birmingham Lodge, No. 56, F & A. M, was organized June 6, 1855, Simon Graham, W. M.; H Huffman, Secretary. The charter members were Moses Bigford, J A. Archer, J L Gwinn

There is a membership of forty belonging to this Lodge

The present officers are Simon Graham, W M: S B Shott, S. W, C L. Sheward, J W.; J. S. Miller, Treasurer, H. Huffman, Secretary.

IOWAVILLE.

The village of Iowaville was laid out by a company in 1838. The Sac and Fox Indians had sold 1,250,000 acres of land in this vicinity, and reserved two years' time on the land after which, James Jordan, William Phelps and John Tolman bought the Indians' time for $3,000 The sale of time was made in the fall of 1837, and in 1838, the Indians vacated, and the spring of that year, the place now known as Iowaville was laid off Black Hawk and a few Indians remained Phelps and Jordan were the earliest settlers, they having come in the fall of 1837. Jordan had the first trading-post.

The next settlers to arrive were Joel T. Avery, John Newport, Job Carter and Crittenden Forquraen and their families, and Peter Avery, William Avery and William McMullen, bachelors

William Avery was the first Postmaster, the mail being brought in on horseback

Lauson Smith, who came later, was the first physician

The first blacksmith was Robert Rathburn.

The first boat up the river as far as this point was the "Pavilion," belonging to the American Fur Company. This boat was poled up in the year 1838 Traders' keelboats were in town about this time

The denouse of Daniel McMullen was the first in the place.

Minerva Forquraen was the first child born

Tom Gardner and Cerilda Moody were the first couple to submit to the darts of Cupid to that extent which ended in matrimony.

William Avery was the first Justice and Bill Kirkham the first Constable

All now remaining of the once brisk village of Iowaville is a few houses and one or two stores

An effort was made in 1841 to build a church here, but the object was never consummated The first preaching was by a missionary, in 1834. He came, and promised an interpreter named Frank Lavish $50 to aid him He preached three sermons, after which the Brave of the tribe ordered him to stop; and he did Rev. Mr Rowlander, a Methodist, was one of the earliest ministers who came here The village to-day has no church

The educational plans of the neighborhood were first unfolded in 1843, the teacher being a Mr Clark, who held forth in a log schoolhouse put up in the year mentioned In 1857, the district became independent, and a new schoolhouse was built, which has served until the present

INCIDENTAL.

James Jordon tells of a rain of seventy-two consecutive days and nights in 1831, when nearly all the soldiers and a great many Indians died of cholera.

He tells of the "roll-call" of 1846, when, every morning, the "grand round' was made to ascertain if any of the settlers had been kidnapped, or deserted He says the roll always began with 'Robert Rathbun," and the " R's ' were rolled out like the long beat of the snare drum

There were no mills in those days, and for a year the settlers ground their buckwheat in a coffee-mill This continued for a year or more, when the inconvenience was relieved by the putting-up of a corn-cracker and the flouring-mill by Samuel Clayton, near the mouth of Chequest Creek, and Foster's mill on Lick Creek.

THE LODGES

On the 18th day of August, 1850, at the town of Black Hawk, on the Des Moines River, opposite Iowaville, in Van Buren County, Pulaski Lodge, No 28, was instituted, with twelve charter members

The location remained here until October 27, 1852, when it was removed to Iowaville and the name changed to Iowaville Lodge, No. 28.

It remained in active operation here until September 27, 1863, when it suspended work and remained in this condition until May 26, 1872 Then thirteen members—W H. Cross, J. F. Alverson, B T. Welch, T. M. Taylor, T P. Kelley, T Barnes, T B. Allen, J. Beatty, E. T. Roland, D Yeoder, J C. Nelson, J. W. Nicholas and W. H. Nicholas—of Magnolia Lodge, No 24. located at Agency City, on petition, were granted the privilege of removing the Lodge to Eldon and changing the name to Eldon Lodge, No. 28.

The charter, in accordance with the above, was granted on the 17th of October, 1872 ; and, on the 27th of December, 1872, the Lodge was removed to Eldon, where it occupied a rented hall until 1876, when it built a hall, which, with the fixtures, is valued at $1,400.

Since the removal of the Lodge to Eldon, members have withdrawn to start Floris Lodge, No 272, and Van Buren Lodge, No 350.

The Lodge now has a membership of ninety-five, all in good standing; and has paid out in benefits $1,580 65, and has buried three of its members.

On the 19th of October, 1876, Rebecca Lodge was organized with a membership of eleven, and now numbers thirty-one members

PITTSBURG.

The village now known as Pittsburg was formerly called Rising Sun   This place was laid off in March, 1839, by Ephraim Warner, A. B Williams and John Groom   In the vicinity at that time, lived John Spencer, James Duffield, Elisha Morris and Samuel Clayton

John Purdham had made the first claim in this region, and sold to Peter S Wood, John Goodwin and D. A. Ely

A B. Williams kept the first store and Cyrus Gibson was Postmaster.

The first blacksmith was Frank Mauk

John Groom was the first Justice, and Gain Robinson the earliest physician.

James Hanshaw made the first wagons in the place.

The first death was Mrs. Goodwin, daughter of Elisha Purdham.   David Deffenbaugh and the widow Judd were the first couple married.   The husband was a farm hand of Samuel Clayton; the lady was a Mormon   After the marriage, the couple went West and joined the Mormons.

The first child born in this town was Ed. Janney, who is still living there

There have been several efforts made to force manufacturing interests into the throat of Pittsburg, but without success   The only business now done in the place is by one flour-mill and one store

Samuel Clayton built the first flour-mill ever put up in this vicinity, in 1836 and 1837, near the mouth of Chequest Creek.   A steam mill, by William Funk, followed in 1854.   In 1860, a saw-mill was added to the enterprise, and in 1875, Mr Funk rebuilt the mill throughout.

In 1861, William Funk erected a distillery, which run three or four years, and was then closed

The following bill will serve to revive old memories :

An Act to allow John Godden, Samuel Clark, John Groom, Archibald McDonald and P M Janney, of Van Buren County, further time to construct a dam and lock across the Des Moines River, at Pittsburg, in the above-named county

SECTION 1   *Be it enacted by the Council and House of Representatives of the Territory of Iowa,* That John Godden, Samuel Clark, John Groom Archibald McDonald and P M Janney be and are hereby allowed two years' additional time to complete a dam and lock as above specified, and a required in the sixth section of an act entitled " An act to authorize John Godden, his heirs and assigns, to build a dam across the river Des Moines "

SEC 2   That the eighth section of the above named act, to which this act is amendatory, is hereby amended so as to constitute the said John Godden, Samuel Clark, John Groom, Archibald McDonald and P M Janney tenants in common, and vest in the said tenants in common, their heirs and assigns, an equal undivided interest in said dam, and the privilege thereto appertaining

SEC 3   This act to take effect and be in force from and after its passage

Approved 13th of February, 1844

The earliest school taught at Pittsburg Sub-district No 2, was in 1842, by George N. Rosser   The place was a round log cabin, and after one term a brick schoolhouse was put up, which served until 1854, when the present frame building was erected.

The first minister in this vicinity was Rev. Newton Smith, a Methodist missionary.   Rev. Mr. Summers was the first Presiding Elder of this circuit There is but one society here—Methodist.   It was formed in 1838.   The schoolhouse was used as a house of worship until 1871, when the church was built, the Pastor at that time being Rev Mr. Thomas   The present Pastor is Rev Jesse Craig.

There are no secret orders at this village   A Good Templar lodge was organized in 1857 but after three years, it became defunct

MT. STERLING.

Mt. Sterling, with its 300 people, keeps alive four dry goods and general stores, one harness-shop, one hotel, one shoemaker, two blacksmiths, one wagon-shop, a lumber-yard and a hoop manufactory.

The village is universally known as Dogtown, and the inhabitants relate how it gained its name They say that shortly before 1840, the first arrivals in the (now) village were Horace and George Wood, who saw in the distance the rapid growth of a town, and they therefore built a saw-mill and corn-cracker near by, and awaited the result. Horace had three hounds that would devour the meal as it came from the buhrs Nearly every man who came to mill brought two or three dogs with him, and the result was a row At the height of a dog rumpus one day, before the town had been named, a stranger rode in. "What do you call this place?" he asked "It has no name," was the reply. "I think it is dog town," came the self-answer. And by that name it has gone ever since, although an attempt was once made to name it " Wood's Mill," then " Union Corners," and later, " Mt Sterling "

A steam saw and flour mill was put up in 1855 by Hayes, Kuhn & Kuk. The mill run until 1861, when it was torn down and the works taken to Keokuk

Henry Lockhart built a distillery and saw-mill in 1851, and, after operating four years, tore the building down

A barrel-hoop manufactory was started at Mt Sterling two years ago by J. Holingshead, and has prospered since that time

The first store at this place was kept by a man whom customs had nick-named "Yankee" Andrews; and, although the last name was correct, the man's first name was never known.

George Wood, and Mary, his sister, were keepers of the first inn.

George Wood was also first Postmaster.   The present one is H E Bradford. The first blacksmith was Reuben Pfoutz

M C. Thatcher was first Justice.   James A. Alcorn is the present one Parnic George was the first wagon-maker.

The first child born in the town was in the family of Dr. Joel Knight

And this same Joel Knight was the first physician who came to town   He put up in a bark tent down in what is now Thatcher's pasture.   He had a " specialty ' with him which he advertised as the panacea for all diseases.   The medicine in question he labeled " Dr. Joel Knight's celebrated Screw Auger Pills, one hundred in a box, one dollar per box "

I B Thatcher had the first lumber-yard in the place

THE SCHOOL.

Mt. Sterling began to educate its young in 1841, when Freeman Spaulding taught the first school in Carnes' log cabin, in (now) Sample's field The next school was in a log cabin one mile southeast of town.   The next was in a private cabin in town.   Then one was taught on (now) James Cavitt's place, one and a quarter mile northeast of the place The next step was the building of a log schoolhouse in 1850, Harry Hill being teacher.   This house was burned in the winter of 1855—the fire said to have resulted from an over-heated stove, while "the boys ' were playing poker.   School was afterward kept in private houses until 1861, when the house now standing was built. Carlos S Baker was the first teacher in this house.

THE CHURCH.

There is but one church-building at Mt Sterling   This was erected jointly by the Methodists and United Presbyterians in 1870   There had been preaching long before this   Rev. Newton Smith and Rev Daniel Lane, the former a Methodist, the latter a Congregationalist, both preached at an early day, but there is no record of the date of society organization, and it is supposed these were the pioneer representatives of their respective denominations.   Sermons were preached in the private house, since a hotel, but now used as a blacksmith-shop   The Rev Mr Smith was the first Methodist Pastor in the new church. Rev. Father Amos Yeager is the present Pastor

The United Presbyterian society was organized in 1861. Rev. James Boyce being first Pastor   The Church has no Pastor now

GOOD TEMPLARS

The largest lodge of Good Templars in the State of Iowa is located at Mt Sterling   There are 550 members on the roll   The society was organized December 19. 1873 the originators being John A Alcoin. John Gwinnup. Isaiah Pedat A H Thatcher. D W. Fergeson   The first President was Mr. Pedat. Ferguson. Vice President. and Alcorn. Secretary.

The officers now are· Elisus Bee President. James A Alcorn Vice President. and Mattie Gwinnup Secretary

INCIDENTAL

Horace Wood has the credit of being a peculiarly liberal man   He would refuse to supply a man with meal, who offered or had money to pay for it, but a poor man, who had none would receive all the meal he wanted, for the mere asking

ONE MURDER

There was but one murder ever committed at Mt Sterling. That was in 1873 the winter of which Morgan Rupe was killed during a drunken row. James Algire was arrested for the crime but fled before the trial came off Thus the crime was never avenged.

TRADING WIVES

"Peter Wood was a peculiar man," remarked a citizen of the Mount, one day. while conversing over old-time matters   "In the year of 1840." he continued. ' Peter Wood and John Scalf traded wives. or rather Wood got rid of one of his. Wood had brought with him another man s wife from Illinois (a Mrs Annie Tyrrell). and. after the first two. came Wood's first wife Scalf was a single man. and for the consideration of $200 in lands. Wood induced Scalf to take Malinda his (Wood's) first wife. off his hands.

MILTON.

This place was settled by Dr Logan Wallace in 1847   The town was laid off in 1851   For years the place consisted of a post office dry goods store. blacks   hat the town took   Southwestern Railr

There was a Fourth of July celebration at Milton in 1854. Judge Hoskins and Dr. Elbert were the orators. The music consisted of a drum and violin

C Wandel and Levi Hayes are both claimants for the honor of having kept the first store at Milton

H. D. Wallace was the first Postmaster.

Logan Wallace was the first physician, and Thomas Hollinsworth was the first Justice

The first marriage contract was performed between Richard Abernathey and Ann Cassaday

Milton has now two drug stores, five dry goods stores, three hotels, one grocery store, one hardware store, one cabinet-shop, one harness-shop, one shoe-shop, three wagon and three blacksmith shops

C. Wandel was the first cabinet-maker here

C Feath established a successful wagon and carriage factory at this city in 1872 The capacity is about one hundred vehicles per year.

CITY GOVERNMENT.

Milton is an incorporated city, and has been since the summer of 1878 The first Council are now serving their term of office The Mayor is Freeman Bell; the Recorder is R. M McNeal The Council is composed of five Trustees—A. W. Carr, J C Hegler, H M. Dysart E Campbell, Z Cannon and H D Wallace

THE CHURCHES

Rev Mr Post, the Baptist itinerant missionary, was the first to preach at Milton. But the Methodist society was the first organized, in 1840 The name of the first minister is uncertain, although Rev Mr Bryant was among the earliest who came The Methodists built a church in 1867, at which time Rev Mr Coddington was Pastor The present minister is Rev William Patterson

The Baptists organized their society in 1841, Rev Mr Post officiating Their first regular Pastor was Rev Calvin Daughters They built a church in 1866 and have worshiped there ever since, although they have no Pastor now

The Protestant Methodist society was organized in 1870, by Rev J S Johnson They use the Baptist Church to hold service in Their Pastor is Rev A W. Williams

THE SCHOOL.

The first school taught at Milton was in a log cabin owned by L Wallace The teacher was Miss Susie Chittenden A schoolhouse was built in 1849, and, in 1867, the house was moved back and a larger building put up The district became independent in 1867.

There is a flour-mill at Milton, in connection with a saw-mill C Miller is the proprietor. He came in 1852, and erected a corn-cracker and saw-mill, and, in 1873, he built a large flour-mill with three runs of buhrs

The only notable crime ever committed here was the shooting of Charles Brewer by Garrett Thompson, in November, 1856 or 1857 The affray grew out of a debt Thompson had dunned Brewer, and the latter, becoming incensed, followed him and Thompson shot him, claiming self-defense He was sentenced to a term of years in the State Prison, and afterward was pardoned by the Governor. He was enlarged and now lives in Monroe County, for he ....

THE LODGES.

There are five secret Orders at Milton. The oldest Order is that of the Masons. The Lodge was organized at Mt Sterling, and was known as Mt Sterling Lodge, No. 50. The charter was granted June 6. 1855. Henry King was W. M., W. J. Clark, S. W., J. W. Kirk, J. W.

On October 3, 1857, the order was moved to Niles

February 16. 1867, the Lodge was again moved, this time to Milton, where it has since remained. The charter officers were James McCance W. M., A Holder, S. W., H. T. Patten, J. W.; J. Cassada, Treas.; Ed. Hilhs, Sec.

The present officers are as follows. J. C. Holland, W. M., J. Q. Hargrove, S. W.; S. L. McClean, J. W., J. W. Carr, Treas., R. A. McNeal, Sec., C. Bauch, Tiler

There is a Good Templars' Lodge at this place. It was organized September 20, 1872.

Jackson Lodge, No. 28, K. of P., was instituted in March, 1875. The charter was granted February 8, 1876. The charter officers were Z. Cannon, P. C. and D. D. G. C.; William Gnash, C. C. S. L. McClean, V. C., J. D. Wallace, P., Conrad Feath, M. of Ex., William Murry, M. of F., W. B. Flemming, K. of R. S., R. A. Gibson, M. at A., V. Wescott, I. G.; William Crockett, O. G.

The present officers are Z. Cannon, D. D. S. C., L. F. Lummen, P. C., R. A. Gibson, C. C.; V. Wescott, V. C., S. L. McClean, P., George Pennington, M. of Ex., W. B. Flemming, M. of F., Z. Cannon, K. of R. S., S. W. Cooper, M. at A.; C. Feath, I. G., L. F. Summers, O. G.

The members of the Lodge number about forty

Milton Lodge, No. 155, I. O. O. F., was chartered October 17, 1867

The charter members were A. E. McNeal, N. G., William Matthews, Jacob Miller, Joshua Marsan and William Gnash

The officers at present are A. Smith, N. G., G. R. Graves, V. G., N. Henthane, Sec.; G. A. Pittman, P. S.; T. Bell, Treas.

The Order of the Daughters of Rebekah was organized here on October 27, 1874. The Order are occupying the I. O. O. F. Hall.

CANTRIL

is one of the most sprightly towns in Van Buren County. Its appearance is bright and speaks of life and vigorous push. It was laid out partially in November, 1871, and finished in the spring of 1872, L. W. Cantril being the proprietor

It is the smallest incorporated city in the county, numbering but 210 inhabitants, yet having been under city legislation four years. It is the oldest new town in Southern Iowa

L. W. Cantril kept the first store here, the first bill of goods ever sold in the place being January 31, 1872. L. W. Cantril was also the first Postmaster.

D. D. Wilburn was the first and R. D. Wilburn is the present Justice.

A child of William Drew was the first born, and also the first to die. Iola Nagle and Andrew Reed were the first couple married

C. L. Crooks was the first physician. His child was the one-hundredth born in the city.

W. J. Price was the first Constable

The place now contains three dry goods stores, one grocery store three drug stores, two millinery establishments, one harness, one shoe, two wagon, one tin and two blacksmith shops, one hardware store, one butcher-shop, two hotels, one restaurant, three agencies, one barrel-hoop factory and one lumber-yard.

The first blacksmith in the city was Joseph Bover

Cantril has one graded school.   The first schoolhouse was built in 1873, with Oscar Cooley as teacher.   But the district began to grow and the demand for more room had to be supplied   Hence, in 1878, a commodious house was erected at an outlay of $1,700.   The district has 100 scholars   The present teachers are Mr McLane and Ella Stonebreaker

THE CHURCHES.

The first sermon preached was by John Sexsmith, a Protestant Methodist

However the Methodist Episcopal Church society was organized first of all, in 1872, and a church built   Rev. John Orr was the first Pastor of the Church Rev. Mr. Patterson is the present.

The Protestant Methodist society has disbanded, but while they lasted used the Methodist Episcopal Church.

The Presbyterians organized a society in 1875, under the Rev. Mr. Van Ammond.   They have no church, although preparations are being made to build one   The present Pastor is the Rev. Mr Young.

A corn-grinder and saw-mill combined is the only form of milling done at Cantril.   This was built in 1873, by E E Cantril.

CITY GOVERNMENT

Cantril was incorporated April 16, 1874, and the first election was held May 20, of the same year   For the years since the incorporation the official roster has run as follows.

1874—Mayor, E. E Cantril: Recorder, Dr. C L. Crooks; Marshal, F M Lanam   Trustees—L. W Cantril, A F. Holder, C Isenhour, N. Pritchet, C L Crooks

1875—Mayor, E E Cantril· Recorder, W M Robertson; Marshal, F M. Lanam   Trustees—A. F. Holder, W J Price, L. T. Holder, J. H Williams, L. W. Cantril.

1876—Mayor M R Hosick, Recorder, W O Brooks: Marshal, J. H. Beuchler   Trustees—A F. Holder, E E Cantril, J. Beuchler, L T. Holder, C. K Hall.

1877—Mayor, F. L. Frazey, Recorder, John D Swartz: Marshal, M. A. Miller.   Trustees—N. Pritchet, W. J Price A J Smith, J E Johnson, R L Wilbourn.

1878—Mayor, E. E. Cantril, Recorder, J R Stevens: Marshal, M A. Miller   Trustees—C. M Gray, G. L. Norris, A Cassada, William Price, J. M Linn

Prairie Gem Lodge, No 288 I. O. O F, was organized and the charter granted August 21, 1874   The charter members were D. H Kettle, W J Price, J R Gray, J. M Hosick, F M Lanam, J Holland and C K. Hall

The charter officers were C K Hall N G W J Price V G . J. R. Gray, Secretary· F M Lanam Treasurer.

The present officers are R L Wilbourn N G: A Cassada V G. W. H. Creath, Secretary, E F Cheadle, P. S. E E Cantril, Treasurer

INDEPENDENT

is commonly known as Stumptown   This from the fact that George Stump was proprietor of the place   It was laid out in the fall of 1851

The old settlers were Capt. Miller, John Sommerlot, John Saylor, William McHue, Jerre Black, John Black and Samuel Black.

George Stump kept the first store in the place.

The first blacksmith was Alex. Nedhow

Ely, a son of Adam Young, was the first child born, George Stump, a son of Frederick, was first to die, and the first marriage contract was between Robert Gardner and Rachel Kempson

George Stump was the first Surveyor and the first Postmaster.

Jerry Black was the first Justice, and Capt. Henry Miller the earliest Constable

Subdistrict No. 2 Independent Village, built its first schoolhouse of logs in 1852   William Monroe was the pioneer teacher   In 1865 a new frame house was put up in place of the log

There are three church societies at Independent, and two churches   Rev. John Walker was the pioneer minister, and after him, in 1869, the Rev. Mr. Condit was assigned here and he organized the Methodist Episcopal Church society, which built the church.   Rev. L. Carl is the present Pastor.

The Protestant Methodist Church society was organized in 1872   They have no church-building, using that of the Methodist Episcopal   The Pastor is Rev. Mr. Tolbert

There was a small body of Presbyterians, who organized a society in 1873 and built a church.   But the project was not very prosperous, and, in 1874, the church was leased by the Moravians, a few of whom came to the surface, and have continued until the present, by the aid of itinerant ministers

ODD FELLOWS

Van Buren Lodge, I. O. O. F., No. 350, was organized July 16, 1876, and chartered July 9, 1876   The original officers were G. B. Walker, N. G. ; Rankin Smith, V. G   George Earheart, Sec   William M. Walker, P. S. ; C. T. Gardner, Treas   The present officers are W. M. Walker, N. G. , David Stump, V. G. ; W. M. Davidson, Sec. , Isaac N. Davis, P. S   R. Ritz, Treas.

Sutton & Mix are owners of the steam saw-mill that was put up in 1867 by John M. Walker

There is a steam grist-mill at Independent, that was built in 1868, by G. W. Elerick & Co.   In 1872, the property changed hands, coming into the possession of S. H. Huckleberry the present owner   The property is known as the Van Buren Mills.

The village of Independent has for its officers Jonathan Nelson, Justice of the Peace, and Perry Gilbert, Constable

PORTLAND .

Portland was a small town for which great things were predicted, but nothing ever came of it   The place was laid out in 1844 by Samuel Holcomb, Robert Leggett, David Maggard and others, and in 1847 the plat was entered by John Alexander, L. Collins and O. S. Freeman, County Commissioners.

James Pork was the first Postmaster of the town

The first physician was David Trunt.

James Adams was the first blacksmith and Jesse Sutton kept the first store

There is a schoolhouse here (Subdistrict No. 9) The original house was of logs, built prior to 1850. A new frame was built in 1850, and, in 1873, a third one was built. Caroline Lewis taught the first school here

There was a saw and grist mill put up in 1854 It was blown up in 1875, the accident causing the death of a Mr Yarnel and the serious injury of Robert Green, who was severely burned

Portland has had one sensation A man named Tom Way was unceremoniously taken from that place in an early day for the crime of horse-stealing, and sent to the Territory of Wisconsin, where the prison authorities dealt with him according to the law.

WINCHESTER

John Reynolds and Jefferson Cox were the proprietors and laid out the town of Winchester, on February 29, 1840

A man named Barnes kept the first store. There are now two stores here and a blacksmith-shop

A graded school was built in 1873, prior to which the district had used the old log schoolhouse, put up about 1840, and which had served until about 1850, when a frame house was built and lasted until the new house was built

The Methodist society, formed during the early settlement of Winchester, did not build a church until 1860 The building still serves.

The Presbyterians organized a society in 1851, but disbanded in 1856 They had a church-building, but sold it to Steven Bextle, who tore it down and built a house with the brick

The Lutherans had a church and society in 1854, but soon disbanded. A Mr Belnap bought the church and moved it away for use

A Masonic Lodge was established here in 1850, with Moses Bigford, W. M. A Gregory, N Davis, George Cupp and Jacob Archie were charter members.

The present officers are Richard Workman, W M., William Whittaker S. W., John Arnold, J. W, Will Hastings, Secretary, and Christopher Carr, Treasurer.

SUMMIT.

"Mt Zion" is the more modern term for the station known as Summit. This place was laid out in March, 1860, by John and Alexander Taylor

Seth Richards kept the first store here The first hotel-keeper was A J. Perviance

All that now remains of the town is a few dwellings, a hotel, store, church and depot

The original location of the railroad, after leaving the depot, ran from one-fourth to one-half mile south of the present location It was laid over six lengths of trestle-work, from ninety to one hundred feet high and seventy-five to two hundred yards long This continued to but Bone accident ever happened here and that was near Summit A train of cattle-cars was passing along, when two were capsized one falling the distance of ninety

feet and killing all the stock excepting one steer, and he got out of the car and
ran to Keosauqua   The other car was whirled across the track.

There is a Methodist Episcopal Church here.   The society was organized
in 1870, and the church built two years later

The village chool children patronize the district school, one mile north of
town.

There is a well at this place one hundred and seventeen feet deep, the digging of which disclosed something of interest.   At a depth of one hundred
feet, solid timbers were struck, and the further investigation brought up grape
vines and leaves in a perfect state of preservation.   Seventeen feet further
down, a vein of water was struck, and the stream burst forth three feet above
the surface.

Summit has had a blood-curdling sensation   It occurred January 23, 1860,
when an Irishman named Mike Welch nearly chopped off the head of Malachy
Curry, another man with whom he had been working on the railroad.   The
trouble arose over whisky—or, more properly, out of a drunken row.   Welch
was tried, and in September, 1860, Judge Townsend sentenced him to a term
of imprisonment for twenty-five years.   Welch served until about 1865, when
he became insane.   He was sent to the Asylum, where he died about 1870.

DOUD'S STATION.

David and Eliab Doud laid out what is now the village of Doud, in the
year 1866   The settlers at that time we Samuel Holcomb, Nathan Tolman,
David, Doud, Jr , Eliab Doud, Jack Walker, Dr Peter Walker, John Walker,
David Shelby, William Young, David Drake, William Schuyler, Moses Starr,
John D. Baker, John Hill, William C. Adams, James Johnson, Eliott Baker
and Dr. Boyer.

W S Parker kept the first store

The first blacksmith was M Martin

Eliab Doud was the first Justice, and Archable Freshwater was the first
Constable

Mary A. Doud was the first Postmistress

The first physician was James Crawford and Eliab Doud was the earliest
lawyer

Andrew Fink's child was the first one to die in the place   David Doud was
the first person born, and the first marriage performed between Thomas Doud
and Mary Sherer.

The village government of Doud is controled by a Justice of the Peace—
Eliab Doud—and a Constable—William Crawford.

There is no form of manufactory at this place   There was a saw-mill and
corn-cracker put up in 1863, by Fred Benning & Brother   The mills never
did a prosperous business and were closed in 1866.

The village supports one church-building, put up in 1869, by the Baptist
denomination   The church was opened in 1870, Rev Mr Wilson being the
first Pastor.   Subsequently, the Methodist denomination joined with the Baptists, and since that time the church has served both societies.

A log cabin owned by Eliab Doud, was pressed into service as the first
schoolhouse at Doud's   and Mary A Doud was the first teacher.   A
new schoolhouse was put up   fall of 1869 and during 1870.   The building still stands   The district is known as Subdistrict No 10

A lodge of Odd Fellows was organized July 17, 1878, with A. Bott, N. J., W. L. Reiter, V. G.; O. O. Stokes, R. S.; G. B. Walker, P. S., C. T. Gardner. Treasurer, and, in addition to those gentlemen, were the following charter members: James Crawford, D. Wiesenberger, A. L. Ratchff, W. H. Morrison, W. H. Bott, J. C. Beale, A. Benning, E. Sawvel, John Pearson, F. M. Tannehill. The Lodge is named Custer Lodge, No. 381.

PLYMOUTH.

Had the expectations of an ambitious company been realized, Plymouth might to-day have been one of the most prominent places in the county. Edward and John Colton laid the place off on April 26, 1842. Further on, an effort was made to build a dam across the river at this point, the State taking the improvement in hand. Thousands of dollars were expended on the enterprise, but it fell through. The site was just north of Farmington.

A company, with O. H. P. Scott at the head, built a fine brick hotel and a half-dozen tenement houses, at a cost of $15,000, but no one came to inhabit them, and together with the few stones that were put in to start the dam, the improvements crumbled, until to-day the entire enterprise is a tottering wreck.

BLACK HAWK CITY

Across the river from Iowaville, in the year 1848, H. A. Davis laid off the now wreck of a town known as Black Hawk City or New Market. He put up a merchant flouring-mill, carding-mill, a distillery, store, cooper-shop and blacksmith-shop. The place remained above-board until 1861, when all the buildings were torn down.

This village had its sensations, though even to a greater extent than did some of its larger sister-towns.

In the spring of 1851, during the high water, Job Carter was drowned while swimming from his house to the distillery.

In the winter of 1854, Mary Washington, the wife of George, cut her throat. No reason was assigned for the suicide.

COLUMBUS

This was another attempt upon the part of capitalists to build up a mighty city, but the effort failed. John B. Thompson and John R. Sparks were the proprietors of the town.

ROCHESTER

This village might have become notorious, had not a little incident occurred to render it otherwise. The place was laid off in 1837, by M. D. Strong, J. S. Wells and William W. Corull. On March 21, 1837, a competition began by the citizens of the place for the county seat. By the passage of an act by the Wisconsin Legislature and through the influence of certain men, Rochester was declared the county seat. Only one night was the state of affairs allowed to

M

exist   Keosauqua put in an oar, and, through the influence of Gov Henry
Dodge, the right was wrested from Rochester.

The town is now defunct

BUSINESS CORNERS

Ami Adams laid out the nucleus of this business stand in 1846   There set-
tled around the corners at that early day Silas Gorbingham, Walter Whitten,
Reuben Sperry Wesley H. Van Osdel, Charles T Gardner, Henry Drake,
Julius Clark, Nero Herington, John Clark and William Boggs.

P Allison was the pioneer store-keeper.

The first Postmaster was Charles T. Gardner.

The first physician was Dr Crawford.

William Schuyler was the first Justice of the Peace

Silas Garlinghouse was the first blacksmith

The first death was that of a child-girl of David Drake, Peter Walker and
Christy Schuyler were the first couple married, and a little girl of David Drake
was the first child born.

There is but one church here—Union Church   This was built in 1874
Rev. Mr Ridenhour was the pioneer minister, having taken charge of the
church when put up

The first schoolhouse erected was in 1869, but, prior to the building, a school
was taught in Clark's wagon-shop.   The district is known as Subdistrict No 2.

OAKLAND.

This town was laid out September 9, 1857, and joined Bentonsport on the
south   Samuel E and Mercy C Payne were the proprietors.   The place
never grew

UPTON.

On April 14, 1852, John Upton laid out this place, on the line dividing
Iowa and Missouri.   The only sign of a town now is a store and blacksmith-
shop   The place is a sort of trading corner

UTICA

John Whetsel laid out Utica June 9, 1857   From that time until the present one store and a blacksmith-shop are the only advance the place has made
toward a town

KILBOURNE.

A place formerly called Philadelphia, and afterward named Kilbourne, was
laid off in July, 1839, by John Patchett   Nothing ever became of the place
outside of a "paper" town—that is, a drawing of the shape and dimensions of
the lots on paper.

PIERCEVILLE

was laid out August 25, 1856, by Roswell F Dibble and Horace Dibble   Like
others examined the town, but is now abandoned

WATERTOWN.

Watertown was the name of a locality laid off May 26, 1837, by John Crow, Surveyor. There is nothing left of the place.

WILLETS.

Willet's Station, on the Burlington & Southwestern Railroad, is the name of a stopping-place in the county. The spot was never platted.

OAK POINT,

in Van Buren County, is but a post-office junction at a farm-house. It was never platted.

LEBANON.

This place, although containing a post office, two churches, a school, store and blacksmith-shop, was never platted. It is but " four corners," laid out on the farm of William Brooks and others.

SALUBRIA

has gained a history, owing to the " Kneeland Settlement " which occupied the plat. And although now in this county, it was not at the time the survey was made. All that remains of the once famous Salubria is a half-dozen farm-houses, browned by the blight of years.

BIOGRAPHICAL DIRECTORY.

VAN BUREN TOWNSHIP.

ANSON, FLORACE, far., S. 31, P O Keosauqua

Anson, G , far., S 31, P O Keosauqua

BAIRD, NATHAN, far , S 18, P O Pittsburg

BAKER, M. L., merchant tailor, Keosauqua, born Sept 27, 1825, in Fleming Co , Ky , parents moved to Monroe Co , Ind , in 1827, and he came from there to Bloomfield, Davis Co , Iowa, in 1855, followed his trade there till May, 1851, when he enlisted in his country's service in Co A, of the 3d Iowa Cav , was elected as first Lieutenant of his Company and was promoted to Captain June 24, 1862, resigned Aug 10, 1863, was a participant in the battle of Pea Ridge, Ark , and many skirmishes Returned to Keosauqua, having had his family removed to this place after he had entered the service has followed his present business principally ever since He was married to Isabella Hardesty Oct 22, 1852 in Indiana, she was born Sept. 3, 1834, in Indiana, have seven children— Charles A , Willie E , Frank, Mark M , George D , Samuel H and Mary Members of Christian Church , Democratic

Baker, S T , sal ... N . ..qu.

Baldwin, Charl- ....l ... . K.-sauqua

BARKER, A. C., far , S 17 ; P. O Mt Zion, owns 207 acres of land, valued at $25 per acre, was born March 18, 1842, in this county where he spent his boyhood days, and at his country's call enlisted in Co H 3d Iowa Cav Sept 8 1861, participated in the battle of Moore's Mill, Mo , where he was wounded by a ball passing through the side of the jaw and under the jugular vein, and lodging in the back of the neck from which he recovered and afterward participated in the battles of Little Rock, Ark , Tupelo and Guntown, Miss , was also with Gen Wilson, in his raid through Alabama and Georgia, was discharged Aug 25, 1865 Returned home and was married to Miss Martha M. Van Emmons of this county, she was born in Missouri in October, 1853, have 5 children—George V., John H , Maud, Nellie and William R Moved on his farm in 1871 Is a member of the Presbyterian Church , Republican.

Barker, B J & Eli, fars , Sec 35 , P O Keosauqua

BARKER, BENTON H., far , S 35, P O Keosauqua, born Sept 13, 1837, in Decatur Co Ind , came with his ... B J E. ... .unty in ... 1840 .... b. present farm of 320 ac... .... K. ... qua, in this county, with his brother, Eli

Barker, an unmarried brother, who makes his home with him, their father, B J Barker, was born Oct 20 1803, in Monongalia Co, W Va, and was married to Margaret McCoy in Indiana, June 12, 1834; she was born Nov. 25, 1817, in Ohio, they have eight children—Lovina L, Benton H., Mary L, Augustus D, Jennet, Dolly E., Julia and Eli Benton H went to Montana in 1869, and subsequently to Idaho Oregon, California and Nevada; returned home in 1876 is now stopping with his father, has no family

BARKER, WILLIAM A., far, Sec 1, P O Mt Zion Owns 685 acres of land, valued at $30 per acre, born July 3, 1833, in Carroll Co, Ohio, came with his parents to this county in the fall of 1839, since which time it has been his home, with the exception of being in California from 1854 till the fall of 1859, when he returned, and was married to Rebecca True, of this county, in September, 1860, she was born in 1844, in Carroll Co, Ohio, have seven children living—Zora E, Ætna L, Della G, Lelia O, Bessie L, Wilda A, and an infant son, lost two— Frank and Geary Mr Barker is one of the leading farmers of his township Members of the Presbyterian Church; Republican

BEAMAN, DAVID CRICHTON; born in Burlington, Lawrence Co, Ohio, Nov 22, 1838, his parents were Rev Gamaliel C and Emelia C. Beaman, is a lineal descendant of Admirable Crichton, through his mother, whose family name is Crichton, removed to Montrose, Lee Co, Iowa, in 1846 and resided there during the Mormon troubles there, and the destruction of the Mormon temple at Nauvoo just across the river, moved to Croton, on the Des Moines River in the same county, in 1852, was educated at Denmark, Iowa, and Oberlin, Ohio, went to work at Croton as a railroad station agent in 1859 Was married Dec 31, 1860, at Athens, Mo, to Miss Luella A Smith, daughter of Dabzell and Mary Smith, of St Louis his wife was born in Aug.....
meml.....
which.....

companies, participated in the battle of Athens, Mo, on the 5th of August, 1861, being one of the first battles of the rebellion Removed to Independent, Van Buren Co, in January, 1862, still being in the employ of the railroad company, continued in railroad employment at that place until 1866, went into general merchandising at the same place in 1867 and continued about two years, began the study of law in 1866, at home and in connection with other business, but under the tutorship of Hon Robert Sloan, admitted to the bar at Keosauqua, in September, 1869, and at once commenced practice in Independent, going into the courts of Van Buren, Davis Jefferson and Wapello Counties, has been practicing ever since, removed to Keosauqua in October, 1874, and formed a law partnership with Rutledge Lea, under the firm name of Lea & Beaman, in the office formerly occupied by J C Knapp, who was that year elected to the District Judgeship Was Republican candidate for the Legislature in 1875. but was defeated by a small majority They have four children— James L, born March 23, 1862 George C, born July 5, 1863, Alice M, born May 5, 1865, Arthur D, born May 11, 1871 Father, Rev G C Beaman, was one of the pioneer Presbyterian ministers of Iowa, having been a minister over forty years

Beer. James Madison, far., Sec 30, P O Keosauqua

Beer, Jas Monroe, teamster, Keosauqua

BELL. ELI D., farmer Sec 19, P O Mt Zion, he is a son of James and Barbara Bell, his father being a native of Virginia, and his mother of Kentucky, was born June 11, 1835, in Campbell Co, Ky, parents moved to Hancock Co, Ill, in 1836, and to this county in the spring of 1837, and settled in this township, where he spent his boyhood days Was married to Miss S. A Matthews Feb 12, 1857, she was born Nov 10, 1832, in Ohio In 1858, moved to Oregon Tp, Washington Co Iowa and in the spring of 1860, went..... and turned the follow..... Dutch Creek Tp, and..... 1865, came on his present farm , have two children living —James W and Edna L , lost two— Catherine C and Elizabeth D His father died in this county April 16, 1872, and his mother died Oct 8, 1862 Member Presbyterian Church , Democrat.

BELL, JOHN R., farmer, Sec 19 , P O Mt Zion , is a son of James and Barbara Bell , owns 115½ acres of land, valued at $40 per acre, it being the old homestead of his parents, born Nov 14, 1836, in Hancock Co , Ill , and, in the spring of 1837, his parents moved to this county, which has been his home ever since He was married to Sarah A Bridell March 17, 1859; she was born March 17, 1840, in Indiana, and died July 11, 1871, was again married to Almira Bell, maiden name Kimmel, January 24, 1872, she was born Sept 28, 1847, in Iowa, and died Sept 16, 1876, was again married to Mary C Miller Oct. 3, 1877; she was born Aug 24, 1842, in Indiana, have three children by first wife—Marietta, Harriet F and Addie B , and one by second wife—Don S Member of M E Church , Democratic

Bennett, Benjamin, far , Sec 35 , P O Keosauqua

Bennett, W S , far , S 35 , P O Keosauqua

Black, John, laborer, Keosauqua

Bleakmore J B , druggist, Keosauqua

BLEAKMORE, WYLIE H., publisher of the Keosauqua *Republican*, Keosauqua, with J S Sloan born July 17, 1847, in Marshall Co , W Va , came from there to Jefferson Co in the spring of 1857, in 1860, went into the office of the Fairfield *Ledger*, to learn the printer's trade , and, in 1862, went into the office of the Burlington *Gazette*, in 1863, went to Denver, Col , and worked in the Denver *News* office till the latter part of 1864, he returned to Jefferson Co , and went into the Fairfield *Democrat* office, where he remained till he came to Keosauqua in February, 1877, and went into his present office He was married to Mary E Goddard of Jefferson Co , Iowa, in September, 1868, she was born in ◌ 17 in St ◌ ◌ M have two ◌◌◌ —W◌◌◌ M ◌◌ John B ◌ ◌◌◌◌ ◌◌

Bonner, A , far , Sec 28 , P O Pittsburg

Bonner, G , far , Sec 28 , P O Pittsburg

Bonney, A L , retired, Keosauqua

BONNEY, J. H., retired merchant and farmer, Keosauqua ; born Feb 14, 1817, in Steuben Co , N Y , his father died the following summer , soon after, his mother moved to Tioga Co N Y , at the age of 14, he went to Elmira where he clerked in the dry goods business about four years, in the fall of 1838, he emigrated West, stopped in Cass Co , Ill , till the spring of 1839, when he came into this county and settled about three miles below Keosauqua at a place called Rochester, engaged in the mercantile business In August, 1840, he was elected Sheriff of the county, being the first elected by the people , he then came to Keosauqua after his term of office expired, he clerked in a general store about a year At the August election in 1843 he was elected a member of the Legislature , was again elected Sheriff of the county in 1844, and, in 1846, was elected County Clerk, which was the first elected by the people In fall of 1848, was elected Secretary of State In 1851, he again commenced the mercantile business, which he continued about five years In 1853, he was elected as one of the Commissioners for the improvement of the Des Moines River , was also one of the contractors for the improvement in Keosauqua He opened an exchange business in 1855, which he continued till 1860 ; since that time he followed clerking, farming, etc , till February, 1871, he was appointed Steward of the Poor-Farm of this county, which he held till February, 1878 He was married to Orpha F Stannard, in this county, May 20, 1841, she was born Sept. 16, 1822, in Newport, N H , have six children living—Mary J , Anna A , Arma F , Orpha Estella R C Hinman , lost two —Sarah J , Laura C Democrat

Brill, D O , far ; P O Pittsburg

Brooks, W , far , Sec 8 , P O Pittsburg

BROWN, ALEXANDER, attorney, Keosauqua , son of Hugh and Mary Brown , born May 3, 1837, in ◌◌◌◌ C ◌ P ◌ ◌◌◌◌ came to ◌◌ ◌◌ ◌ ◌ 1842 commenced th ◌ ◌dy ◌ law ◌◌ ◌ d J ◌ Wright in 1858, and was admitted to the bar in September, 1859 ; he then went to Magnolia, Harrison Co , Iowa, and practiced law till in the year 1861   He returned to this county and enlisted in Co L, of the 15th I V I , Oct 20, 1861 ; was promoted as Sergeant Major of the regiment, March 1, 1862 , participated in battle of Pittsburg Landing, where he was wounded, and afterward, at the battle of Corinth from the effects of which wound he was discharged Feb. 12, 1863   Returned home, and was clerk in Provost Marshal's office at Burlington till fall of 1865 ; then, returned to Keosauqua and was elected County Judge the fall of 1865, which office was changed to Auditor after first year, and he was elected Auditor three successive terms , after which, he commenced the practice of law with his present partner —W A. Work.   He was married to Mary Rankin, of Keosauqua, June 9, 1870 , she was born June 16, 1848, in this county, have one son—Ord born Feb 22, 1876   Republican

Brown, John G , banker, Keosauqua

BROWNE, JOHN, farmer, Sec 10, P O Kilbourne, son of Wm and Elizabeth Browne (nee Alexander), was born May 4, 1833, in West Meath, Ireland . father came to this county in 1847, and settled on the farm where John Browne now lives, his mother having died in Ireland Jan. 1, 1827, and his father here Nov 12, 1851   Was married to Eliza Craig Feb 22, 1860, in this county , she was born in Ireland in 1831 , have six children—James R , born Dec 13, 1860 , Eliza, born Dec 23, 1862 , Mary J , born Sept 11, 1865 , Sarah, born March 28, 1868 , Hester, born Oct 10, 1870   William, born May 26, 1873   Mr Browne, owns the homestead farm of 135 acres, valued at $25 per acre   Politics, Republican

BURTON. E. F., Keosauqua proprietor of restaurant and dealer in groceries , born Sept 1 1812, in Fredericksburg Va , in 1833 came to Greene Co , Ohio, worked at millwright business and coopering till he came to this county in August 1841 settled in Keosauqua and has followed his present business most of the time   He was married to Elizabeth McDill of Virginia

March 1, 1838 , she was born in Pennsylvania in 1807, have six children living—Julia, Elizabeth, Margaret A , John, Daniel H , Edward F., lost three —Mary A , William and Ira   Republican

CAHILL, TIMOTHY, retired physician, Mt Zion

CAHILL, JOHN, proprietor of a saloon, and dealer in groceries, notions, etc , born June 24, 1832, Mt Zion, in County Kerry, Ireland , came to the United States in the fall of 1851 , followed railroading in New Hampshire and Massachusetts till the spring of 1857 , came to Jefferson Co , Iowa, and, the following fall, came to Van Buren Co , which has been his home since, with the exception of some traveling through Missouri and elsewhere   He was married to Mary Breen April 8, 1856, in New Hampshire , she was born in County Kerry, Ireland, in 1830 , have three children—Mary, born Jan 3, 1859 , James, born Dec 2, 1864 , Catharine, born May 16 1867 , lost two—Julia and Margaret   Member of the Catholic Church , Democratic

CAMPBELL, BETHEL, farmer, Sec 8, P O Mt Zion , owns 200 acres of land, valued at $30 per acre ; born March 24, 1833, in Brooke Co , W Va , came with his parents to this county in 1840, and settled on the farm where he now lives went to Idaho in the spring of 1862, and returned in the fall of 1866   Married Mary E Johnston Nov 28, 1867 , she was born in Ohio July 27, 1843, have three children—Thos E , Charles A and Myrtes , lost Ira W   Democratic

Carruthers, J far , S 17 , P O Pittsburg

Cheney, E. J , carpenter, Keosauqua.

CLARKE, ROBT. L., County Treasurer, Keosauqua, born April 2, 1838, in Portage Co , Ohio, parents moved to White Co , Tenn , in 1854, and came from there to this county in the spring of 1856 and settled in Vernon Tp , the second year after arriving here, he moved into the village of Vernon in Henry Tp and taught school there one season b fore coming to this state Mr Clarke had spent three years at the Western Reserve College at Hudson, Ohio, during the winter of 1859, he moved into Bentonsport and engaged in the drug business for about three years, then went into the office of the K. & D. M. R. R. Co, as Station Agent, which he filled for nine years. In the fall of 1871, he was elected as County Treasurer, which he has filled up to the present time. Mr Clarke organized the A, F & A M Chapter in Keosauqua, and has held the position of High Priest for five years. He was married to Miss Jennie M. Yeager, of this county Nov 30, 1858, she was born in Pennsylvania in 1840, have five children—Carrie A, Ellen B, Kate G, Libbie B and Leora B. Member of the Congregational Church, Republican.

CLAYTON, JAMES H., far., S. 27, P O Pittsburg, owns 110 acres of land, valued at $35 per acre, son of Samuel Clayton, was born Sept 30, 1816, in Perry Co, Ohio, parents moved to Washington Co in 1832, in the winter of 1836, his father came to this county and made his claim at the mouth of Chequest Creek, he being the first settler in the township west of the Des Moines River, the following fall, James H came out and stopped with his parents, his mother died in 1848, father died August 27, 1872. Was married to Mary A Bowers (maiden name Saunders) Sept 28, 1843, she was born Oct 22, 1813, in Ohio, died July 17, 1878, leaving her husband alone in the world, they having no children. Mr Clayton is a member of the M E Church and a Republican.

Clark, W, far., S 29, P O Pittsburg
Clemmens, J, far, P O Pittsburg
Clemens, S O, far, S 28; P. O. Pittsburg
Cocherell, Alpheus, lab, Mt. Zion
Cocherell, Henson far, P O Keosauqua
Cocherel, W H, lab, P O Keosauqua
Cook, J D, far, S 14, P O Pittsburg
Cowan, A H far, S 32, P O Pittsburg
Craig, A, far See 15 P O Pittsburg
CRAIG, WILLIAM, Keosauqua born July 29, 1817, in Westmoreland Co, Penn, parents moved to Indiana Co in 1824, and, in 1833, he went into Jefferson Co and to Clarion Co in 1837, and commen... study ... under Dr Jno ... during the ...

Geneva, N Y; in 1845, he went into Somerset Co., and commenced the practice of medicine, and subsequently attended the Cleveland Medical College, Ohio, where he graduated in 1850, and, in the fall of 1851, came to Keosauqua, of this county, where he has practiced medicine more or less ever since, and in connection therewith has carried on the the drug business some ten or twelve years, owns a farm of 115 acres near town. He was married to Miss Anna Brown, of this place, Nov 24, 1858, she was born in Pennsylvania, have five children—Jean, Hugh B, Colin S, Wm G, and James A, lost one—Mary Member of Congregational Church, Republican.

Craig, Wm, far, S 11, P O. Pittsburg
Creasy, Jacob, far, S 17, P O Pittsburg
Cresap, J T B, engineer, P O Pittsburg
CUBBERLEY, JESSE, farmer and blacksmith, Keosauqua, born Jan 15, 1820, in Licking Co, Ohio, learned the blacksmith's trade in early life, came to Keosauqua in the spring of 1849, where he has made his home ever since. In August, 1861, he enlisted in the service of his country in the 3d I V C, Co G, and was honorably discharged July 1, 1862, for disability, his service was in detached service, skirmishing, etc, in Missouri. He was married to Miss Lydia W Lewis, of Washington Co., Ohio, Sept 24, 1846, she was born in same State Nov 6, 1818, have four children—Mary, born July 31, 1847, in Ohio, James, born Dec 6, 1849, in Iowa, Edward H, born Sept 1, 1852, in Iowa, and John M, born March 4, 1855, in Iowa. Member of the Congregational Church, Republican.

DOUGHERTY, JOHN F merchant Keosauqua
Dougherty & Shane, mer, Keosauqua
Davis, H far, S 30, P. O Pittsburg
Davis, A F, clerk, Keosauqua
Dawson, N R tailor, Keosauqua
De Gallyer, James, laborer, Keosauqua
Denning Jonathan, far, P O Portland
Dewey, J C, far, S 22, P O Pittsburg
Disbrow, H H, artist Keosauqua
Downing John far P O Portland
DUFFIELD, GEO. C., farmer and stock-raiser P O Pittsburg, owns about 500 acres of land ... at $25

per acre, son of James and Margaretta (Bierly) Duffield, his father was a native of Maryland, and his mother of Pennsylvania, they were married in Franklin Co, Penn, in 1815; moved to Jefferson Co, the same year, he was born in that county May 13, 1824, in the fall of 1834, moved to Fulton Co, Ill, his father and brother John, in December, 1836, made claims of land in Van Buren Tp, the following spring, moved on the claim, their wagon-track was the first west of the Des Moines River in this township, when young, Mr Duffield spent some time in Louisiana, in St Paul, Minn, then a small trading-post, in 1849, assisted in unloading the first printing press brought to that place, in 1849, went to California, in the spring of 1853 returned, has been engaged in the stock business extensively, went to Texas, purchased 1,500 head of cattle, and drove them to market, has been Superintendent of the stock, hog and sheep department for the State Agricultural Society for twelve years, and one of the Directors the last three years. Served as a scout for the 3d Iowa Cavalry, about one year Married Zervia Stannard April 17, 1856, she died March 4, 1857, was married again to Addie Stidger, March 18, 1867, she was born Jan 4, 1843, in this county, have three children living —Glenn S, Mary C and Ada E, lost one—Howe H Mr Duffield's father died Jan 20, 1875, his mother is living at his brother James', she is in her 84th year Republican

Duffield, H P, retired merchant, Keosauqua

DUFFIELD, JOHN, far, S 21, P. O Pittsburg, owns 144 acres of land, valued at $35 per acre, he is a son of James Duffield, Sr, born Sept 1, 1820 in Jefferson Co, Ohio, his father moved to Fulton Co, Ill, in the fall of 1833, and, in the fall of 1836, he, in company with his father, came to this county and located the land upon which he now lives, and returned to Illinois, the following spring of 1837, the family came the ... driving the ... wagon over ... the Des Moines River in ... three ... county which was then

a wild, uninhabited region, except by the red men of the forest, wild animals, game, etc He was married to Jane H McKibben, of this county, April 27, 1848, she was born January 2, 1829, have five children—Margaretta J, George W, Zervie A, Orion J and Henry—two of whom are married, George W and Margaretta Mr Duffield holds the position of Elder in the Presbyterian Church, Democrat

Duffield, J, far, S. 21; P O. Pittsburg

DUFFIELD, J. H., Postmaster, Pittsburg; dealer in dry goods and general merchandise, born Jan 27, 1835, in Fulton Co, Ill, his parents moved to this county in the fall of 1837, settled west of the Des Moines River in what is now known as Van Buren Tp, of this county, he attended the Iowa Wesleyan University at Mt Pleasant from 1859 to 1861 He then enlisted in his country's service in Co F, 2d Iowa Inf; participated in the battle of Ft Donelson, where he was wounded by a minie-ball striking him in the neck and passing under the jugular vein and through the shoulder-blade, which wound disabled him so that after his recovery he was discharged, and came home in the spring of 1865 In the spring of 1866, he came to Pittsburg, where he continued four years, then returned to Keosauqua, and was in partnership with a Mr Harrison two years, and with J S Sloan, four years, bought out Mr Sloan's interest in the fall of 1877, and removed to Pittsburg He was married to Melissa M. Stannard April 18, 1875, she was born in March, 1842, in this county, they have three children living—Mary E, Ida M and James E, lost one, Charles S Members of the Presbyterian Church, Republican

ENO, N G, physician, Keosauqua

Entler Bros, hardware, Keosauqua

FASNACHT, LEWIS E, artist, Keosauqua.

Fasnacht, S, butcher, Keosauqua

Fellows, E, far, S 20, P. O Pittsburg

Fellows, W M V B, far, Sec 4, P O Pittsburg

FELLOWS, STEPHEN D., farmer Sec 4, P O Keosauqua, born

. Oct 3, 1833, in Luzerne Co, Penn, his parents emigrated West in 1836, stopped in Michigan till spring of 1837, then came on to Van Buren Co, and settled on the farm upon which he now lives, his father, Asahel Fellows, died here March 19, 1869, his mother is still living and makes her home with her children Mr Fellows married Ann Bowen, of this county, in 1862; she was born in Wales, in 1842, have six children—Asahel G, Allen D, Sherman G, Thomas H., Chloe and Stephen L Member of the Christian Church, is also member of A, F & A M, and I O O F Democrat

FELLOWS, WHITING A., farmer, Sec 8, P O Pittsburg; son of Asahel and Susanna (Harrison) Fellows, born May 22, 1828, in Luzerne Co, Penn, his parents moved to Kalamazoo Co, Mich, in the spring of 1836, and, in the fall of the same year, he came to this county, and located his claim just below Keosauqua and the following spring of 1837, moved his family, where he lived till March 19, 1869, when he departed this life for that country from whose bourn no traveler returns Mr Fellows pre-empted his present farm of 180 acres, from the Government, and came on to it in 1858 He was married to Miss Susan E Dodson, in Luzerne Co, Penn, March 12, 1862, she was born in this county, February 27, 1843, her parents having moved to this county in 1837, her father died in 1847, and her mother returned to Pennsylvania in 1848, but is now living with her daughter Susan Mr and Mrs Fellows have but one son, Harry D, born Jan 16, 1863 Democrat

Forbes, A, far, Sec 13, P O Pittsburg
Forbes, B, far, Sec 9, P O Pittsburg
Forbes, R, Sr, far, S 18, P O Mt Zion
Forbes, R, Jr, far, S 14, P O Pittsburg
Forbes, T, far, S 5, P O Mt Zion
Ford, Wm H, mechanic, Keosauqua
Forman, Daniel, lab, Keosauqua
Frazee, S C, far, S 12, P O Kilbourn

FRY, ISAAC, far S 24, P O Keosauqua, owns 233 acres of land, valued at $4 . . . . 1813, in W . . . . ents moved . . . . Co Oh . . in

1828, were there a few years, then went to Union Vale and Little York, where he was engaged in the manufacture of threshing machines for about nine years; afterward, went to Cincinnati, Ohio, where he was engaged in a planing and saw mill about ten years, came to this county in 1854, and settled near Winchester, moved to Missouri in the spring of 1864, and returned and purchased his present farm in 1872 He was married to Margaret Allen March 13, 1832, in Ohio, she died in 1842, was again married to Charlotte Roach March 23, 1843, she was born Jan 8, 1822, in Jefferson Co, Ohio, have three children living by first wife—Abiah, Josephus and Caroline, lost one—Angeline, and by second wife eight—Thomas A, Johnson F, William H, Sarah A, Margaret L Cassius M C, John C F and Abraham L, lost two—James L and Harry H His son, William H, was admitted to the bar as attorney at the August term of the District Court, 1878 Republican

Funk, Wm, mill-owner, Keosauqua

GAYLORD EDWARD, teamster, Mt. Zion

Gebhardt, G C, retired, Keosauqua

GEBHARDT. W. A., County Clerk, Keosauqua, born Dec 10 1840, in Pickaway Co, Ohio, came to this county in 1856 Enlisted April 16, 1861, in the 11th Indiana Zonaves for ninety days, after which he returned to Iowa and enlisted in Co K, of the 15th Iowa Inf, and re-enlisted as a veteran in 1864, was discharged in October, 1864, and promoted to First Lieutenant of the 70th U S C. Inf, was mustered out of the service March 4, 1866, he participated in the battles of Shiloh, siege of Corinth, Iuka, siege of Vicksburg, was also with Sherman in his march to the sea At the close of the war, returned to Keosauqua and went into the County Treasurer's office, and subsequently into the County Judge's office and County Clerk s office, in which last he acted as deputy eight years and was elected to the office in the fall of 1876, by the largest majority ever given . . . . . Repu . . . . in the pro . . h . . . . . d th udy of . . . . wh . . . to the

bar in August, 1874 he has recently
been commissioned as Lieut Colonel
and Aide-de-camp on Gov Gear's
staff He married Harriet E Silver in
Ohio April 16, 1869, she was born
Nov. 8, 1841, in Ohio; have four children—Bessie L, Fred L, George C.
and an infant daughter. Republican

GODDARD, EDWIN, abstract
office and Notary Public, Keosauqua,
born June 12, 1821 in Champaign Co,
Ohio, came to this county in the fall of
1840, settled in Chequest Tp, in 1849,
came to Pittsburg, the following January in company with Geo Duffield and
Jesse Elder, started for California, followed mining there most of the time
near Sonora, returned to this county
in May of 1853, and remained at Pittsburg most of the time till 1859, then
bought a farm about three miles south
of Keosauqua and commenced improving it At his country's call, he enlisted
in Co F, 2d I V C, in May, 1861,
was wounded at Ft Donelson, which
disabled him for further duty, and was
finally discharged at St Louis Sept 13,
1862 He then returned home, in the
fall of 1864, he was elected County
Recorder, and re-elected in 1866, he
was elected Secretary of the Old
Pioneer Society, at their second annual
meeting, in August, 1872, which position he has filled up to the present time
with credit to himself and the satisfaction
of the Society Mr Goddard has taken
great pains in preserving reminiscences
of the early history of Van Buren Co
Republican

Groon, W S, far, P O Lebanon

HANEY, MOSES, farmer Sec 34,
P. O Pittsburg

Harrington, John, R R employe, P O
Mt Zion

Harrison, Wm, agent, Keosauqua

HEARN, JOHN W., farmer, Sec.
9, P O Douds Station, owns a farm of
173 acres, valued at $20 per acre, is a
son of Thomas Hearn, deceased, born in
this county July 8, 1849, his father
died Sept 4, 1877 Was married to
Anna Jamison, daughter of D S Jam-
son Sept 21 1876, and is on to his
present on the farm, all is
born June 4 52 in and in they
one son Thomas M born July

31, 1877 Member of the M E Church.
Republican

HEARN, PERRY, farmer, Sec 23,
P. O Keosauqua son of Thomas and
Nancy Hearn, was born in this county
May 13, 1857; his father was born in
Maryland March 11, 1805, and mother
Aug 30, 1812, in same State, and were
married Dec 30, 1833, and emigrated
to this county in 1836, and settled on
the farm where they are still living, his
father died Sept 4, 1877, there are four
other children in the family—Martha,
Samuel, John W, and Rachel, Perry
being the youngest, who is living with
his mother on the homestead

Hearn, Samuel, far, S 9, P O Pittsburg
Hearn, William, farmer
Hellyer, M, far, S 7, P O Portland.
Holbert, Wilham, brickmason, Keosauqua

HOOTMAN, HENRY, far., Sec.
5, P O. Mt. Zion born May 1, 1827,
in Harrison Co, Ohio, came with his
parents to this county in the fall of
1839 He was married to Miss Mary
Barker of this county, Oct 17, 1850,
she was born in Carroll Co, Ohio, Jan.
25, 1830, have ten children—Martha
L, Mary C, Anna M, Jacob G, Maria
C, Ezra J, Ada D, Joseph T, Henry
H and Orpha O He owns 320 acres
of land, valued at $40 per acre Is
a member of the Presbyterian Church,
Democrat

Horn, W H, far, S 6, P O Pittsburg
Hortman, Augustus, carpenter, Mt Zion

HOUK, JACOB, far, Sec 18, P
O Mt Zion, owns 125 acres of land,
valued at $30 per acre, born April 8,
1810, in Tuscarawas Co, Ohio,
came from there to this county in
the spring of 1839, and settled in
Washington Tp, and came on to his
present farm in 1858 Married Nancy
Campbell in Ohio, in October, 1829,
she was born in 1811, and died
in May, 1840, was again married to
Lucinda Barker April 5, 1843, she was
born in Ohio in 1822, have two children by first wife, living—David and
Mary, lost two—Clarissa, and Harry,
who was killed at the battle of Fort
Donelson by second wife has six
children Adolphus T, Alice,
Catharine William A Melissa J and
Ann S who was the

wife of William Price   Members of the Presbyterian Church, Republican House, Thomas, far , P O Portland

HOWARD, SAMUEL, dealer in dry goods and general merchandise, Mt Zion, born Jan 13, 1836, in Montgomery Co , Mo , parents moved to Taney Co in 1845, left there in 1848 and came to Decatur Co , Iowa, where he made his home mostly till 1866, during that time, however, he spent a couple of years in Oregon, Idaho and Montana, also spent three summers in Kansas, came to this county in 1866, and commenced his present business in 1873 Married Miss Margaret J Kishing Jan 6, 1859, she was born in 1839 in Indiana, have six children—George F, Florence M , William C , Adolphus, Leonard and an infant   Independent in politics

HUNTER, JOSEPH, farmer, Sec 24, P O Mt. Zion, owns 120 acres of land, valued at $40 per acre, born May 2, 1833, in Perry Co Penn, came from there to this county in the spring of 1844, he went to California in the spring of 1855, by overland route, and returned home in 1858, via New York Was married to Mary Trebilcock May 4 1859 , she was born in December, 1835, in Ohio, and died March 23, 1873, was again married to Mrs Sarah Massey March 26, 1874, her maiden name was Price, she was born July 21, 1848, in Iowa, has five children by first wife—Francis M , Ann, Joseph W , Ella and Eva M , by second wife—James E and Virginia; lost two, Theodore and Udora   Member of the Presbyterian Church

Hunter, R , clerk, Keosauqua

IRISH, J. D , farmer and merchant Keosauqua

JACKSON, J retired far , Keosauqua

JACKSON, JONATHAN, farmer, Sec 23, P O Keosauqua, owns 113 acres of land, on the banks of the Des Moines River, which is very pleasantly located, being above high water, his father, Jeremiah Jackson, came from Maryland to this county in 1837, he bein...   ... the ...   tlers of th... unt... the ... this sketch was born May 29 1845 in

this county and lives on the old homestead farm   He was married May 5, 1875, to Minnie M Short, daughter of Benjamin and Rhoda Short, of Lick Creek Tp , of this county , have one son—Benjamin, born Dec 11, 1876 Member of the M. E Church   Democrat

JACKSON, T. C., station agent on K & D M R R , Mt Zion, son of William Jackson who came from Belmont Co , Ohio, to this county in 1850, and settled in Village Tp , near Doud's Station, where he still lives , the subject of this sketch was born July 2, 1851, in this county, where he spent his boyhood days , at the age of 15, he commenced to learn railroading in the Des Moines office of this company and after one year's service was appointed agent at Doud's Station, where he continued about five years, then went into the County Treasurer's office at Keosauqua a short time, was then appointed agent at the station where he now is   He was married to Miss Sadie E Arnold, of Lee Co , Iowa June 3 1873 , she was born in September, 1851, in Ohio , have one daughter—Orpha L , born April 9 1876   Republican

JAMISON, DANIEL S., far , S 29, P O Keosauqua, owns ninety-three acres of land, valued at $35 per acre , born Aug 25, 1822, in Westmoreland Co , Penn , came from there to this county in the spring of 1844, and settled in Keosauqua, followed his trade of carpenter and joiner work till he came on to his present farm in the spring of 1853 Was married to Martha E Alexander, of this county, Nov 13, 1845 , she was born Oct 14, 1825, in Missouri, and died Jan 19, 1858; was again married to Louisa Broadwell Feb 21, 1861, she was born Aug 27, 1836, in Sangamon Co , Ill , have three children by first wife—Marian, Florence L and Ann A , and by second wife five—Charles E , Cora M , Hugh S , Bob S and Ralph L   Mr Jamison has been Assessor for Van Buren Tp for ten years   Republican

Jameson, Wm , lab , Keosauqua

J... Dani... C K...

J... David ... M... Zi...n

Johns...n John ... ...

Johnson,Richard, lab., Keosauqua

JOHNSON, W. R., proprietor of portable steam saw-mill and millwright, Keosauqua, born July 13, 1831, in Newark, Ohio, parents moved to Richmond, Ind, in 1841, while there he was apprenticed to a millwright and learned the trade, and from there he came to Northern Missouri in 1859, where he followed building mills principally In the spring of 1861 enlisted in the Home Guards, and subsequently, in Co G of the 2d Mo V C, worked mostly with construction train, was with Gen Banks in the Red River expedition, was discharged in 1863, for disability Returned home and engaged at his trade, contracting, building, etc, putting up thirty-two mills west of the Mississippi River, in 1869, he came to Keosauqua and put up sixty-three buildings the first year He was married to Laura M. Marine Oct. 31, 1850, in Indiana, she was born Dec 10, 1832; have three children—Martha C, James H and Christopher C Republican

JOHNSTON, BENJAMIN, attorney, Keosauqua, born March 9, 1845, in Keosauqua, his parents came from Luzerne Co, Penn, in 1842 At his country's call, he enlisted in Co E, of the 15th Iowa V. I, Oct 13, 1861, and re-enlisted as veteran, in December, 1863, and, the following March was promoted as 1st Lieutenant of Co G, in the 67th U S C Regiment, he was mustered out at Baton Rouge, La, Aug 14, 1865, returned to Keosauqua and engaged in the drug business, which he continued till 1869, and the following two years he traveled for a Burlington book and stationery house, in 1872, engaged in the dry goods business and continued for one year, he then assumed the charge of the engineer corps for the St L, K & St P R R, after which he traveled through Kansas, returned and clerked for Mr Ed Manning one winter, in 1875, again commenced the drug business, sold out in 1877, and commenced reading law with Judge Robert Sloan,and was admitted to the bar in April, 1878 he was recently commissioned as Captain of the military company of Keosauqua is also member of the A F &

A M Order, is Generalissimo in the commandery Was married to Miss Anna Purviance Nov 7, 1867, she was born in August, 1845, in Jefferson Co, Ohio, have four children—Margaret, James A, Mary B, and Ella C Member of the Episcopal Church, Republican

Johnston Francis, Sheriff, Keosauqua
Jones, Leander, far, P O Keosauqua
Jones, Wm, far, S. 30, P. O Keosauqua.
Jones, J, far, Sec 30, P O Keosauqua

KELLER, A, farmer, Sec 19; P O Pittsburg
Keller, J, far, Sec 19, P O Pittsburg.
Kerr, S, far, Sec 10, P O Pittsburg

KITTLE, D. K., County Recorder and proprietor of the Shepherd House, Keosauqua, son of Phineas W and Margaret (Luke) Kettle; born Aug 2, 1826, in Hamilton Co, Ohio, his parents moved to Dearborn Co, Ind, in 1829, went to Knox Co, in 1839, in the spring of 1841, his father returned to Dearborn Co, and died there In the summer of 1841, D. K. was attacked with a white swelling, with which he has been afflicted ever since In the spring of 1842, he returned to Dearborn Co, on his uncle's invitation, to live with him and go to school, which he did some three years, supposing it was through his uncle's generosity, but learned a few years ago that it was his brother John who paid the expense, commenced teaching school in 1845, in the spring of 1854, he came to Iowaville, of this county, and followed teaching until 1872, filled several official positions in his township—Justice of the Peace, Township Clerk Assessor, etc., in the fall of 1872, was elected County Recorder, and for four successive terms Married Lovina McCullough, of this county, Nov 26, 1854 she was born Oct 30 1837, in Indiana, have four children living—Dora, Della, Roger and George; lost three, Edgar, Ida and Carrie. Member of the M E Church; Republican
Kettle, S, far, P O Portland

KINERSLY, J. J., proprietor of Orion Mills P O Keosauqua, born in Staffordshire, England, May 4, 1813, he learned the tailor's trade there, and emigrated to the United States in 1835, stopped at Manayunk, Pa., where he remained till the summer of 1837, then went to Martinsburg, in Belmont Co., Ohio, and remained about a year, from there he went to Princeton, in Butler Co., Ohio, and in the spring of 1839, started for Iowa, and came to this county, and stopped about a month at a place on the Des Moines River, in Farmington Tp., called Salubria, a paper town, he then came to Keosauqua, followed tailoring till 1845, when he commenced the business of selling dry goods and general merchandise, which he continued till 1862 He purchased the mills built by Maj King and others, in 1849, which were destroyed by the ice in 1857; he commenced building his present mill in 1860, which was completed in 1861 He was married to Mrs M D Pratt, of this place, whose maiden name was Kendall, on the 15th of June, 1843, she was born Dec 11, 1812, in Boston, Mass, she had two children by her first husband, and eight by Mr Kinersly, four of whom are living—Charlotte A, Edwin R, Lucy A and Orion, those dead are Volney, Robert, Ruthbin and Ainsworth Mr Kinersly can say what but few persons can that he was never sick a day in his life, with the exception of a little ague in 1839, and his wife about the same He was brought up a Catholic, but after coming to this country, changed his views He has made it a point to live uprightly in his dealings with all mankind, but has never been identified with any church Democrat

KING, RUSSO, farmer, formerly millwright, P O. Keosauqua, owns a farm of 200 acres adjoining the town of Keosauqua, born June 11, 1811, in Luzerne Co Penn, in the spring of 1834 emigrated to Kalamazoo, Mich., and, in the spring of 1837, to Van Buren Co, and settled on his present farm, Keosauqua was then in its infancy, there being but few families here and plenty of native Americans in the vicinity, he followed his trade, that of millwright, for several years, he, in company with others, put up the first grist and saw mill here, just below where the present mill stands He was married to Miss

Elizabeth McGuire, of this place in 1842, she died within one year thereafter, was again married to Margaret J Nixon in August, 1845, she was born July 11, 1815, in Belmont Co., Ohio, have three children living—Stephen, Virginia and Adelia, lost two—Elizabeth and Franklin Democrat

Kirkendall, E B far, S 6, P O Doud's Station

Knapp, J C, Hon, Judge District Court, Keosauqua

LEACH, MATTHEW, far, Sec 11, P O Pittsburg

LEA, RUTLEDGE, attorney, Keosauqua, born Nov 4, 1843, in Adams Co, Ohio, parents moved to Fairfield, Jefferson Co, Iowa, in the spring of 1855, and to Keosauqua, of this county, in April, 1856, commenced the study of law in 1860, in the office of Judge Knapp & Wright, and was admitted to the bar Sept 5, 1864. Was married to Victoria Henry, of Keosauqua, April 9, 1868, she was born July 2, 1851, in Johnstown, Penn, have three children—Iola, born Nov 9, 1872, Henrietta, born May 11, 1875, Mamie, born Jan 20, 1877 Mr Lea was appointed as one of the United States Circuit Court Commissioners in May, 1871, which office he resigned in 1876, and was elected as one of the Republican Presidential Electors for that year

Leach, Wm, far, S 11, P O Pittsburg

Lenager, R far, S 29, P O Pittsburg.

Lewis George W, far, P O Pittsburg

Long, George, carpenter, Keosauqua

Lowe, C, far, Sec 30, P O Pittsburg

Lowe, J. E, far, P O Pittsburg

McCARTY, JOHN, R R employe, P O Mt Zion

McCRARY, A. H., retired farmer, P O Keosauqua, born July 23 1814, in Vanderburgh Co, Ind, emigrated West in 1835 stopped in McDonough Co, Ill, till fall of 1836, then, in company with his brother J C McCrary and A W Mangum came to Van Buren Co, and made their claims just below Keosauqua on the south side of Des Moines River, returned and moved their families out in the spring of 1837 The following July Iowa was organized as a Territory Mr McCrary was elected Justice of the Peace of his township

(Vernon) in 1841, which office he filled
till 1848, when he was elected to represent his county in the House of Representatives of Iowa, and was re elected
in 1850, and, in 1852, was elected as
State Senator, and again in 1860, at
the expiration of this term he retired
to private life upon his farm, in 1876,
left his farm and moved into Keosauqua
on south side of the River, where he
now lives He was married to Miss
Nercissa Mangum of Gibson Co, Ind,
Feb 6, 1834, she was born April 1,
1816, in Indiana, have six children—
William M., Marietta, James N, Alvin
J, Curtis R and Ira C Members of
Christian Church Republican

McPherrin, A, far, Sec 29, P O Keosauqua

Maltbie, M B, wagon-maker, Keosauqua

MANGUM, A. W., retired farmer,
P O. Keosauqua, born Feb. 5, 1813,
in Gibson Co, Ind, came to McDonough Co, Ill, in fall of 1836, stopped
a short time there, came on to this
county in company with A H and J
C. McCrary, and selected their claims
on the south side of Des Moines River,
below Keosauqua, returned to McDonough Co, and brought their families
out in the spring of 1837, Mr Mangum followed teaching some before coming here, and continued for a time after
coming to this county He was married to Miss Minerva McCrary, Dec
19, 1836, in Illinois: she was born in
1811, in Indiana, and died in this county March 25, 1849, was again married,
to Jane Irvine, Dec 29, 1850, she
died March 2, 1862, was again married,
to Mary E Taylor Nov 13, 1864, she
was born Nov 31, 1837, in Ohio, Mr
Mangum has had eighteen children—
six by each wife, two by first wife are
living—Ruth E. and Rebecca J, lost
four—Silas M, Leander F, Finis C, and
an infant, by second wife, three living—
Samantha C, Mileta E. and Clara, lost
three—Lysander F, Alice J. and Mary
O, by third wife, five living—Edwin
C, Charles A, Alcephas F, Patience I
and Lena, lost one—Willie Members
of Christian Church, Republican

MANNING, EDWIN, banker and
dealer in general merchandise and real
estate Keosauqua, has branch stores at

Vernon, Doud's Station, Portland and
Indedendent, of this county, also, half-
owner of bank at Chariton and is President of the same, Mr Manning is one
of the leading business men of Southern
Iowa, and estimated to be worth over
$1,000,000, which he has accumulated
by his own industry and far-seeing business qualifications, he is of English
descent and son of Calvin and Desire
(Gurley) Manning, and was born in
South Coventry, Tolland Co., Conn., Feb
8, 1810, was raised on a farm and educated in the common schools until he was
16 years old, he then started out in
the world for himself, went to New
York and caught his first glimpse of the
great metropolis, after which he went to
Bethany, Penn, and entered his uncle
James Manning's store as clerk, at a
salary of $10 per month, after four
years he was taken in as a partner, with
a one-third interest in the business, in
the summer of 1831, he took his uncle's
family horse and made a tour through
the northern counties of Pennsylvania,
and finally located at Canton Corners,
in Bradford Co, where he commenced
mercantile business with a Mr J C
Rose under the firm name of Manning
& Rose, which was carried on successfully till the autumn of 1836, he sold
out his interest and in accordance
with a subsequent suggestion made by
Horace Greeley, concluded to go West,
accordingly he came to St Louis, Mo;
and was advised by Col Benton that,
there was the place to make a start t
but he concluded that his purse was not
heavy enough for that place, he went
on West as far as Lexington, Mo,
where he made some purchases of land,
but not liking the system of slavery, he,
with others, came on up the Mississippi
and Des Moines Rivers to St Francisville, Lee Co, which was in December,
1836, made some investments in half-
breed tracts, went on up to Fort Mad
ison and visited the wigwam of the noted
chief Black Hawk, who appeared rather
reticent, though friendly, seeming to fully
realize his lost power, in January, 1837,
Mr Manning, with James Hall and
others made the claim of the land and
laid out the town of Keosauqua, that
being the Indian name of the river,

after which he returned to Pennsylvania, and, in 1838, returned to Iowa and attended the first land sale at Burlington, and purchased several small tracts for himself, with quite a large amount for others, in 1839, he purchased in New York the first stock of merchandise ever brought to Keosauqua, and shipped them via ocean and Mississippi and Des Moines Rivers to Keosauqua, they were seven weeks on the way, he also built the first flatboat that ever passed out of the Des Moines River, in 1851, he ran a loaded steamer from St Louis to Des Moines, he was also Commissioner of the Des Moines River Improvement from 1856 to 1859, during the late civil war, he was a firm supporter of the Government, having unbounded faith in its perpetuity, taking $10,000 of the first 5-20 bonds and subsequently many thousands more, he is at present owner of about 8,000 acres of land in this and adjoining counties, also a fine farm and residence in his native State. He was married to Sarah J Sample, of Lee Co, March 8, 1842, she was born in Pennsylvania July 21, 1816, and died June 1, 1857, was again married, to Nannie Bryant, an adopted daughter of the late Joseph A Wright, Nov 3, 1859, she was born Feb 3, 1832, in Indiana, has three children by first wife living—Hannah G, Calvin and William S, lost two—Mary and Edwin, by second wife, five children—Edward B, Albert W, Kate W, Stanley W and Craig I. Is a liberal supporter of the churches, Republican

MARLOW, B. P., clerk in the dry goods store of Edwin Manning, Keosauqua, born Aug 2, 1819, in Ohio Co, Ky, came to Vermilion Co, Ind, in the fall of 1829, and to Burlington, Iowa, in the spring of 1836, and to Keosauqua in 1845, has been engaged in the dry goods business most of the time since, was in the wholesale house of M. Seaton & Sons, in Keokuk, from 1855 to 1857, was Deputy Sheriff of this county under Robert Rutledge, during 1858-59, after which he engaged in the mercantile business till 1867, spent one season since in a wholesale boot and shoe house of St Louis, he has

been in the employ of Edwin Manning since 1871. Was married to Miss Hannah W Hinkle in Burlington Nov 21, 1844, she was born in 1819, in Pennsylvania, have two children living—Hinda W and Isabell, lost three—Alice, Virginia and Milton H. Republican

Martin, Abner, far, Sec 17, P O Mt Zion

Mathias, J J, far, S 7, P O Pittsburg
Mathias, T farmer, P O Pittsburg
May, M, far, Sec 34, P O Pittsburg
McGrath, H M, farmer, P O Pittsburg

MERIDETH, LEE ROY, farmer, P. O Keosauqua, owns 260 acres of land, valued at $25 per acre, born Dec 31, 1833, in Washington Co, Ind, came with his parents to Mercer Co, Ill, in 1836, and, in the fall of 1837, came to Van Buren Co and settled in Bentonsport, came from there to Keosauqua in 1840, and has lived in this vicinity ever since. Married Miss Susannah Mullen, of St Clair Co, Ill, March 21, 1858, she was born Aug 21, 1828, in West Virginia, have four children living—Harvey E, Abbie L, Anna B and Lizze V, lost two—Henry A and David W. Members of the M. E Church, Republican

Miller, Daniel, farmer, P O Pittsburg
Miller, Geo W, Postmaster, Mt Zion

MILLER, HENRY, far, Sec 18, P O Mt. Zion, owns 194 acres of land, valued at $35 per acre, born Oct 30, 1831, in Columbiana Co, Ohio, his parents moved to Perry Co when he was a small boy, and came from there to this county in 1839, and settled on the farm he now owns, in 1850, he went to California by overland route in 1853, and returned home in 1856. Married Lucinda Hunter May 21, 1857, she was born Feb 14, 1841, in Pennsylvania, have four children living—Isadora, Curtis M, Mary E and Craig, lost three—William F, John S and Ella T. Members of the M E Church, Republican

Miller, Jacob, farmer, P O Pittsburg

MILLER, JOHN A., Deputy Auditor, Keosauqua, born Dec 12, 1831, in Perry Co, Ohio, came to this county in the spring of 1847 and settled in Keosauqua in 1853, engaged in the drug business with Dr Craig, which he continued till 1859 when he was appointed Deputy County Clerk, which he held for two years, in 1869, he was again appointed County Clerk, and was elected to the office for three successive terms, since which time he has acted as Deputy Auditor He was married to Amanda J Hartzell, of Keosauqua Oct 23, 1856, she was born Oct 23, 1837, in Indiana, have six children—Mary George Craig Maud Paul and Ed Republican

MILLER, J. J., far , Sec 17, P. O Doud's Station, owns 160 acres of land, valued at $30 per acre , is a son of Daniel and Margaret (Jackson) Miller , was born Oct 15, 1833, in Perry Co , Ohio , came with parents to this county in the fall of 1841 and settled on the farm where he yet lives He enlisted in the service of his country in February, 1863, in Co G of the 3d Iowa V C , participated in the battle of Guntown Miss , was also with Gen Wilson in his raid through Alabama and Georgia at the capture of Selma and Columbus , was discharged at Atlanta in August 1865 He was married to Sarah E Tolman, of this county, May 1, 1856 , she was born in Ohio April 1, 1835 , have seven children—Clifton T Edwin, Charles Alpha Mary I Nettie and Frederick , lost one—Fannie T Member M E Church, Republican

Miller, T , retired farmer Keosauqua
Minnich S , carpenter Keosauqua
Moore, H far , S 30 , P O Pittsburg
MOORE, HENRY H., Postmaster, Keosauqua, born March 22 1835, in Bedford Co , Penn , came with parents to Perry Co , Ohio, in 1838, and to this county in the spring of 1840, and settled in Keosauqua , he served as Deputy Postmaster during President Polk's administration , was appointed Postmaster in October 1862, which office he has filled since, with the exception of ten months in 1870 and 1871 He was married to Adeline M Walker Dec 23, 1858, in Keosauqua, she was born in June 1837, in York Co , Penn , have four children—Frank, Effie Lida and Edna Mr Moore owns a farm of 124 acres
lican

Moon, Samuel, teamster, Keosauqua
Mott C , far , S 15 , P O Pittsburg
Mott, J , far , Sec 28 , P O Pittsburg
Morton, John N , merchant, Keosauqua
Moore. Wm , attorney and mayor, Keosauqua
Mullen, Amandus painter, Keosauqua
Murphy, Daniel merchant, Keosauqua
Murty, J , far , S 32 , P O Pittsburg
Myers M M , farmer Keosauqua
NIXON JONATHAN, lime burner, P O Keosauqua
Norris, Samuel, far , P O Keosauqua
NOURSE. SOLON, professor of music, Keosauqua, owns a farm of 85 acres valued at $25 per acre, was born June 8, 1817 in Sullivan Co N H , came to Cincinnati in 1844, where he followed his profession till 1859 , then came to Van Buren Co. and settled in Keosauqua, where he still follows his profession He was married to Amanda A Hodgman, of Stillwater N Y in July, 1852, she was born in 1817 and died at Fort Edward, N Y , May 19, 1854 , was again married, to Mrs Cardine E McBride, whose maiden name was Abbott Dec 14, 1859, she was born June 20, 1827, in Athens Co, Ohio , have had one daughter, by second wife—Carrie B who is dead , his wife has one son by first husband—Wm E McBride Member of Presbyterian Church Independent

ORTH, WM H , butcher, Keosauqua
Overman James, Keosauqua
PACE THOMAS, farmer , P O Keosauqua.
Parker, Alfred, far , P O Pittsburg.
Parker, Calvin S , far , P O Pittsburg
Parks, John far , S 15 P O Pittsburg
Payne, Jordan, laborer, Keosauqua
Peacock, James, far , Sec 30 , P O Pittsburg
Pearson, F A , Keosauqua
Pfoutz, Reuben, blacksmith, Keosauqua
Phillips J W , wagon-maker, Keosauqua
RICKETTS, JOSHUA, farmer , P O Doud's Station
RANKIN. THOMAS, retired merchant, Keosauqua, born January 16, 1821, in Licking Co , Ohio , came to this county in 1842 commenced the   Keosauqua in   ed till 1853,

when he was elected County Treasurer, which office he filled for two terms, in 1857, he was elected County Judge, and, in 1859, commenced the mercantile business, which he continued till 1875, since that time has been interested in the business at Davis City, Decatur Co, with his sons, J C and A. T. He was married to Amanda Bonner, of this county, Oct 8, 1845, she was born in July, 1821, in Greene Co, Ohio, they have four children living—James C, Mary E, Archie T and George A, lost two—Martha and Samuel Members of the M E Church, Democrat

Ream, B, far, Sec 20, P O Pittsburg

REHKOPF, B. F., County Auditor, Keosauqua, born July 20, 1846, in Galveston, Texas, came with his parents to St Louis, Mo, in 1849, and, in the spring of 1852, came to Bentonsport, of this county, he succeeded his father in the harness business there in 1867, which he followed till 1877, he was elected to the office of County Auditor in 1865, and re-elected in 1877. He married Aralda J. Cheney, of this county, Feb 12, 1874, she was born Feb 8, 1850, in this county, have two children—Laura R and Ned B Member of the Congregational Church, Republican

Ricketts, James, far, P O Pittsburg

Roberts, A W far, P O Keosauqua

ROBERTS, WYATT, far, Sec 6, P O Keosauqua, son of Isaiah Roberts, born July 16 1849, in Highland Co Ohio, came with his parents to this county in 1859, and settled on the farm upon which he now lives, his father having died Jan 6, 1870, was born Feb 16 1805, in Ohio, his mother is still living with him on the homestead, she was born March 20 1809, in Ohio Mr Roberts was married to Carrie Gustin Oct 15, 1874, she was born in 1851, in Ohio, have two children—Albert and Roy Member of the Christian Church Republican

ROBERTSON, D. W. M., physician and surgeon, Keosauqua, born Feb 23, 1844 in Muskingum Co, Ohio, his parents moved into Holmes Co ___ 1852 ___ this county ___ western pa ___

menced the study of medicine under Dr Whitton, of Doud's Station in 1867, and subsequently attended lectures at the medical college of Keokuk, where he graduated Feb 2, 1870, commenced practicing at Newbern, Marion Co Iowa, in the spring of 1870, returned to Cantril in 1872, and went to El Paso Colo in 1874, where he remained till June, 1877, and then came to Keosauqua Mr Robertson at his country's call, enlisted in Co H, of the 3d Iowa V C, was at the battles of Mooresville and Kirksville Mo, Little Rock Ark, Guntown and Tupelo, Miss, Pea Ridge, Ark, Selma, Ala, was discharged in the fall of 1865 Was married to Mary A Park, of this county Oct. 11, 1870, she was born Feb 26, 1846, in Guernsey Co Ohio, have two children living—Hugh L and an infant, lost one, Clarence A Member of the United Presbyterian Church, Republican

Robinson, J, blacksmith Keosauqua

Robinson, S, Sr, far, Sec 5, P O Pittsburg

Root, A R, gunsmith, Keosauqua

Roush A, far, Sec 8, P O Pittsburg

RUSSELL, ALLEN, farmer, carpenter and joiner, Sec 32, P O Lebanon, owns 95 acres of land, valued at $25 per acre, born June 2, 1829, in Venango Co, Penn, moved from there to Erie Co, in 1848, and to Livingston Co, Mo in 1855, and to Davis Co, Iowa, in 1861, and to this county in 1862, and in 1864 returned to Erie Co, Penn, and from there to Venango Co, in 1865, and, in the fall of 1866, returned to Van Buren Co He was married to Louisa Perry, in Pennsylvania, July 4 1853, she was born in New York Dec 15, 1834, and died April 2, 1859, was again married to Nancy E Brent, June 26, 1859, she was born Dec 5, 1834, in Kentucky, has two children by his first wife—Perry and Wilson A; by his second wife, five—Elizabeth, Sarah L, Aaron, Simon G and Allen Member of the M E Church

SANDERSON, H, far, Sec 7, P. O M Z ___ ___ ___ O Mt ___

Schreckengast, J , far , Sec 25 , P O Keosauqua

Schreckengast, W , far , Sec 25 , P O Keosauqua

Scott. Wm , laborer, Keosauqua.

Seaman, R , far , P O Keosauqua

Seawright, D J, harness-maker, Keosauqua

SHEPHERD, JAMES, Justice of the Peace, Keosauqua , born March 15, 1800, in Alleghany Co , Md , his parents moved to Fayette Co , Penn , in 1801, and to Cincinnati, Ohio, in 1804 He subsequently lived in Warren and Clinton Counties, till 1827, he then moved to Sangamon Co , Ill , and in the spring of 1843, came to Keosauqua and issued the first newspaper, called the *Iowa Democrat*, July 1, 1843 , in 1844, he brought his family, he continued the publication of said paper in the county, with his son, J M Shepherd, till 1850 , he also commenced running the Keosauqua House, in 1847, which he run for several years In 1860, he bought the *Iowa Democrat*, and run it till 1865 , he then engaged in the hotel business up to 1874, since which time he has rented his hotel Mr Shepherd was elected Colonel of the 31st Ill Regt , in 1830 , he was also the first Master of Keosauqua Lodge, No 10, A , F & A M , which was organized in 1845, and for several years thereafter , he is one of the honored and respected members of the Order, he is also a member of the M E Church, and has been a licensed minister for five years Mr Shepherd was married to Jane Sherman, of Clinton Co , Ohio, March 7 1821 , she was born Feb 20, 1806, in North Carolina, and died Sept 20, 1870 , have six children living— Jesse M , Elizabeth, James S , Charles W , Lewis C and Stephen H , lost five— Mary, Rebecca, Jane, Elvira and Helen C His sons, Jesse M and Stephen H , are publishing a paper in Baker Co , Oregon, and Charles W , a Methodist minister, is now at Bentonsport, of this county

SHEPHERD, J. S., fire and life insurance agent, Keosauqua, born Dec 4, 1834 in Sangamon Co Ill , came with his father James Shepherd, to this county in 1844 commenced work in the office of the *Iowa Democrat*, published by his father and brother, which office he continued to work in till 1855 , was Postmaster in Keosauqua office from 1856 to 1861 ; then commenced to work on the *Des Moines News*, published by himself and father, till 1865, when he sold out, and worked in the *Republican* office a short time, and then worked in the office of the *Des Moines Register*, a short time , since 1868, has been engaged in the insurance business He was married to Mary Moore Jan 9, 1862 , she was born Aug 25, 1838, in Ohio , have four children—Minnie E., Little J , Alva C and George S Member of A., F. & A M., and of the M E Church , Democrat

SIGLER, ANDREW, proprietor of livery and express, with William M Stewart , P O Keosauqua , born Feb 14, 1846, in Putnam Co., Ind In the fall of 1855, his parents immigrated to this country, and the following spring went to Wayne County Enlisted in the Government service as wagoner, Aug 12, 1861, in Co. B, of the 6th Kansas Cavalry, with rank as Sergeant, was mustered out Oct 17, 1864 Returned to Wayne County and came to Keosauqua in 1866, and followed butchering one year, then farmed till 1874, when he went into the hardware business, in Milton, till the spring of 1877, then engaged in the lumber business till the November following, then came to Keosauqua and bought out Mr F Johnson's interest in the livery and express business Married Emma C Orth April 10, 1865 , she was born in this county in 1844 , have three children —Iola, Luella and Alva W. Greenbacker

SLOAN, J. S., publisher of Keosauqua *Republican*, with W H Bleakmore, Keosauqua born Jan 29, 1822, in Chester Co , Penn , his parents moved to Columbiana Co , Ohio, in 1823, where his early years were spent; by his own perseverance he gained a thorough knowledge of the common branches from the common schools, and followed teaching in Ohio, about twelve years, in the spring of 1853, came to Iowa, and stopped at Lowaville, of this county, his father,

Robert Sloan, settling near there, in Davis Co, he remained there but a short time, and then went into Davis Co, was there only a few months, he then went to Agency City and taught school there one year, and then returned to Village Tp, of this county, served as Justice of the Peace there two years, in 1859, was elected County Judge of this county, which office he filled till 1861, he was then elected County Treasurer, and for four successive terms thereafter, at the close of which he was appointed County Clerk for one year, to fill the vacancy caused by the death of the County Clerk In 1873, he engaged in the mercantile business, in which he continued till the fall of 1877, he then came in as a partner in the *Republican* office, with Mr. Bleakmore, and the same fall was elected as County Supervisor, and at the first meeting of the Board, was elected Chairman He married Sarah A Sinclair April 14, 1853, in Ohio, she was born Nov 12, 1827, in Allegheny Co, Penn. have five children living—Fanny, Maggie E, George S, Rutledge and Hattie C, lost two, Ida B. and Robert Member of the Congregational Church, Republican

SLOAN, ROBERT, Keosauqua, Circuit Judge for Second District, son of Robert and Elizabeth (Steapleton) Sloan, born Oct 21, 1835, in Columbiana Co, Ohio; the Sloans are of Scotch-Irish descent, his great-grandfather, Robert Sloan, was an officer under Gen Braddock, and subsequently a Captain in the Revolutionary war Judge Sloan was employed on a farm till 17 years of age, received a common-school education, with one year's attendance at New Lisbon, Ohio, came with his parents to Davis Co in the spring of 1853, and settled near Iowaville, he followed teaching principally, from that time till in 1860 he commenced the study of law in the office of Hon Judge George G. Wright of Keosauqua, was admitted to the bar in March, 1861, soon after commenced the practice of law in partnership with Mr William W ⸺ ⸺ ⸺ ⸺ elected Judg ⸺ ⸺ ⸺ ⸺ ⸺ the Second Ju⸺ ⸺ ⸺ ⸺ ⸺

close of the term, was elected Judge of the Second Judicial District, which he has filled since, his present term expires in December, 1880. Married Mary Brown, of this county, July 15, 1863, she was born Jan 11, 1838 in Ireland, have seven children—Stella B, Hugh B, Lizzie Mary E, Della, Io G and Robert E Members of the Congregational Church, Republican

SMITH, GEORGE F., publisher of the *Van Buren Democrat*, born April 27, 1847, in Jefferson Co, N Y · in 1850, his parents moved into St Lawrence Co, and, in 1854, came to La Salle Co. Ill, to Grundy Co in 1855, in 1863, he went into the Mt. Morris *Herald* office to learn the printer's trade, remained about a year, then went into the Chicago *Tribune* office about a year, and, subsequently into the *Times* office six months, he commenced attending the Jennings Seminary at Aurora, Ill, in 1866, subsequently attended Lombard University, at Galesburg, three years, three months of which time he published a paper called *College Items*, came to Bonaparte, this county, in January, 1870, and issued the first number of the *Van Buren Democrat* the 19th of that month, in company with R I Holcomb, whose interest he purchased the following spring, in December 1876, he came to Keosauqua with his paper Married Carrie J Johnson of Bonaparte, Feb 22, 1871, she was born January 11 1849, in this county have two children—Pussie E and M Irene Democrat

SMITH, JAMES, far, Sec. 32, P O Lebanon, owns 170 acres of land, valued at $30 per acre, born May 4, 1805, in Albemarle Co, Va, moved to Logan Co, Ohio in 1833, and from there to Washington Co, Tenn, in 1837, and to Greene Co in the spring of 1838, the same fall, returned to Washington Co, from there he came to this county in the fall of 1853 Married Elizabeth Garber Sept 27, 1827, she was born Oct 9, 1809. in Augusta Co. Va. have ten children living— G ⸺ ⸺ ⸺ ⸺ ⸺ ⸺ ⸺ as J, G ⸺ ⸺ ⸺ ⸺ ⸺ ⸺ m H, John C ⸺ ⸺ ⸺ M ⸺ C and

Elizabeth J Members of the M E Church

SMITH, JOSEPH F., attorney at law, Keosauqua; born April 26, 1823, in Selby, Yorkshire, England, came to Springfield, Ohio, in 1841, entered Kenyon College at Gambier, Knox Co, the next year, continued till 1846, then went to Columbus, and commenced the study of law in the office of Judge Swan, was admitted to the bar at the sitting of the Supreme Court in 1849, followed his profession at Columbus till 1854, then moved to Ottumwa, Iowa, in 1855, came to Keosauqua, continued law practice until four years ago, when an inflammation of the eyes produced blindness, within the last few months has been recovering his sight Married Miss Frances A Mills, of Licking Co, Ohio, April 30, 1850 she was born Feb 20, 1828, in Jefferson Co, N Y, have four children living—Carrie H, Fanny H, Josephine and Samuel M; lost three—Mary H, George C. and Helen F Members of the Protestant Episcopal Church, Republican.

Smith, W D, jeweler, Keosauqua

Snead Egbert, laborer, Keosauqua

Snider, Jacob, far, P O Keosauqua

Spencer, Elburt, far, P O Pittsburg

Spencer, Thos, far, P O Lebanon

STANNARD, O., MRS., Keosauqua, widow of Obed Stannard, born May 2, 1808, in Sullivan Co N H and was married to Mr Obed Stannard June 18, 1828, in same county ; he emigrated to Beardstown, Ill, in the fall of 1836, and, in the spring of 1837, went to Rushville, of same county, and, Feb 20, 1838, arrived in Van Buren Co, settled about three miles below Keosauqua, on the Des Moines River, moved into a log cabin, and over the places for windows were pasted greased paper to let the light shine through, there were but few white neighbors, but plenty of the native Americans, came into the town of Keosauqua in 1849 Mr Stannard was Deputy Sheriff of this county for several years, he died in Keosauqua Sept 28, 1869, leaving his wife and three children to mourn his loss—Alfonso W born — 24 1829 and Edwin born Jan — — in New Hampshire and Me — n N — — — — — his

county, lost three—Zeriah A, William H and Sarah E Her son Edwin went to Missouri several years ago, has served the State as Lieutenant Governor, Member of Congress and is at present President of the St Louis Board of Trade Mrs Stannard is a member of the Free-Will Baptist Church

Starr, R H, attorney, Keosauqua

Steves, Morris, far, P O Pittsburg

Stewart, G W, retired liveryman, Keosauqua

STEWART, W. M., Keosauqua, proprietor of livery and express, with A Sigler, born Dec 17, 1852, in Keosauqua, he, in company with his brother-in-law, Frank Johnson, succeeded his father, J W Stewart, in the livery and express business in 1875, and in November, 1877, Mr Johnson sold his interest to A Sigler He was married to Delia King, daughter of Russo King, of this place, April 19, 1877, have one infant daughter.

Steves, J, far, S 15, P O Pittsburg

Stidger, Geo, physician, Keosauqua

STIDGER, T. F., dentist, Keosauqua, son of Dr. George Stidger, of this place, born Sept 20, 1854, in Marshall Co, W Va, came with his father to this county in 1858, commenced the study of dentistry at Washington, Iowa, in 1873, under a Dr Rowk, where he continued until 1875, when he returned to Keosauqua and commenced the practice of dentistry Republican

STRAIT, SAMUEL, far., S 18, P O. Doud's Station, owns 678 acres of land and his wife 156 acres, valued at $25 per acre, he was born Aug 5, 1820, in Perry Co, Ohio, where he lived till he came to this county in the spring of 1877 He was married to Miss Cordelia Hitchcock, of same county, March 4, 1847, she was born Nov 14, 1820, have five children living—Mary J, Leonidas H, Israel H, Warren B and William C., lost three—Clarissa F, Thomas E and Charles. Member M E Church

STRICKLING, HENRY, physician and surgeon Keosauqua, born — 27 1 21 in Frederick Co, Va, — with — parents to Belmont Co, Ohio in 1 — — commenced the study of .

medicine in 1844 with a Dr Walker, of St Clairville, of said county, in 1848, commenced practicing medicine; removed to Guernsey Co, Ohio, in 1850, came to Iowa in the fall of 1854, stopped in Henry Co till the spring of 1855, then came to Winchester, of this county, and to Corydon, Wayne Co, in 1857, returned to Winchester in 1858, in the fall of 1861, was elected County Judge, he then came to Keosauqua, was elected two successive terms, while he was acting as Judge, he commenced the study of law, and was admitted to the bar in 1867, engaged in the grocery business in 1868, and, shortly after, in the boot and shoe business, and, still later, in the pottery business, which did not prove very successful, he resumed the practice of medicine in 1873 He was married to Sarah A Kinkead, of Guernsey Co, Ohio, she was born Dec 1, 1830, in Ohio, and died March 11, 1877, have five children living—Beatrice, Joseph C, William J, Lydia and Evalina, lost three—Maria E, Henry and Harley Member of M E Church, Republican

Strickling, Joseph C, clerk, Keosauqua

Stout, Moses, far, Sec 6, P O Pittsburg.

Stull, Francis, farmer, Keosauqua

Sniers, John, farmer, Sec 19 P O Pittsburg

Sniers, Wm, farmer, Sec 5, P O Pittsburg

TREBELCOCK, JOHN, farmer, Sec 30, P O Keosauqua

TAYLOR, PATIENCE; P O Keosauqua, owns one-third interest in the farm of 230 acres, the estate of her deceased husband, maiden name, Frybarger, born Dec 12, 1816, in Warren Co, Ohio, married to Samuel Taylor Oct 6, 1836, of same county, he was born May 22, 1817, came to this county September, 1863 settled on the farm upon which she now lives, he died Sept 26, 1875, leaving herself and nine children to mourn his loss—Mary E, John E, Catharine E, Henry J, Jacob F, Caleb W, William G, Samuel A and Harriet L, her son Jacob F served in the 100-days service, in Co K, 45th I V I, under Capt I B Thatcher Mrs Taylor is a member of the Christian Church

THATCHER, JONATHAN, farmer and nurseryman, Sec 1, P O Keosauqua, owns forty-three acres, valued at $25 per acre, born April 8, 1824, in Berkeley Co, W Va; in 1826, came with parents to Wayne Co, Ohio, and in 1827, removed to Clinton Co, Ohio, and from there to this county in the spring of 1839, and settled near Mt Sterling Was married to Miss Malinda Sayre, of Scotland Co, Mo., Jan 30, 1847, she was born in West Virginia, the same year of his marriage, came to Keosauqua, followed millwright work, also carpenter and joiner business, he also followed running a stationary engine for several years, upon the breaking-out of the rebellion, he enlisted Aug 26, 1862, in Co E 15th I V I, the following January, was detailed as engineer on the tugboat Rollins, in the Mississippi River, near Vicksburg, till June, 1863, when he was transferred to the Pioneer Corps under Capt Davis, participated at the siege of Vicksburg, was also with Sherman's army in its march to the sea He was discharged Aug 3, 1865, returned home, and the following fall was elected Representative of the Eleventh Assembly, and was appointed Postmaster of the Twelfth Assembly, since that time has been engaged in nursery and fruit-growing business He has five children living—Florence, Hannah, Tamzin, Isaac A, Stella lost one—Mary F. Republican

THOMPSON, J. G., far, Sec 1, P O Keosauqua, owns 159 acres of land, valued at $30 per acre, born Nov 13, 1841, in Clermont Co, Ohio, his parents moved to Highland Co the following year—1842, came from there to this county in the spring of 1857, and settled on his present farm in the fall of 1875. Enlisted in the service of his country in July, 1861, in Co G, of the 3d Iowa Cav participated in the battles of Tupelo, Miss, Memphis, Tenn, and Little Rock, Ark, also many skirmishes with bushwhackers; at the close of the war, was mustered out June 26, 1865, returned home, and the following year, June 8, 1866, was married to Miss P A Hann of this county she was born March 1, 1844, in New Jersey came to this county—

Isaac N , Bessie M , Lavina and Phœbe M   Members of the Christian Church , Republican

TRIMBLE, D. P., manufacturer and dealer in harness, saddles, etc , Keosauqua, born April 12, 1837, in Preston Co Va ; his parents came to Burlington, this State, in the spring of 1842 , the following fall, moved into Henderson Co , Ill , learned the harness-maker's trade while there , was also engaged in carrying the mail between Oquawka and Rock Island Enlisted at St Louis in a New Mexico brigade in November, 1861 , the following winter, was transferred into Co K , of the 8th Kansas Infantry, was promoted from a private to all the intermediate offices up to First Lieutenant and Sergeant Major, participated in the battles of Mission Ridge, Chickamauga, Perrysville, Ga , and Nashville was mustered out Jan 12, 1866   The following spring, engaged in the mercantile business at Sagetown, Ill , up to 1869, and at his trade at Oquawka till 1870 , then came to Keosauqua and commenced his present business   Married Eliza Cail, of Illinois, Dec 18, 1867 , she was born in 1848, in Bangor, Me , have three children living—Hannah E , Virginia E and Gertrude I , lost one—May A   Democrat

Trites, G L , far , S 30 , P O Keosauqua

TWOMBLY, V. P., dealer in dry goods and general merchandise Keosauqua , born Feb 21, 1842, in Farmington Tp , this county , his father died the following summer, and his mother moved to Keosauqua in 1844, and married Dr H H Barker the same year, who has since died   In May, 1861, he enlisted in Co F, of the 2d Iowa Inf , was chosen one of the color bearers in the first charge on the rebel works at Fort Donelson, and the only one that escaped , he also participated in the battle of Shiloh, siege of Corinth, battle of Corinth, and with Sherman in his march to the sea, in August 1862, he was promoted as Second Lieutenant, and as First Lieutenant, in the early part of 1864, and the following fall, as Cap   . . . .
July . . . .
He . . . .

commercial college at Burlington , after which he went to Ottumwa and engaged in the grain, flour and grocery business, for two years , then came to Pittsburg, this county, and followed milling about nine years , then came to Keosauqua , and commenced his present business   Married Miss Chloe A Funk, of this place, May 1, 1866 , she was born Feb 9, 1845, in Ohio, have one son—Willie T , born Feb 16, 1871, lost three —Cora, Gracie and Henry   Members of the Congregational Church , Republican

VALENTINE, L , furniture dealer Keosauqua

Varner, J , shoemaker, Keosauqua

WALKER, C L , telegraph operator. Keosauqua

Walker, E H , far , P O Keosauqua

Walker, J , ret far   P O Keosauqua

Walker, Josiah, far , P O Keosauqua

WALKER, WESLEY, farmer, Sec 1 , P O Keosauqua, owns 120 acres of land in this county, valued at $40 per acre, and 100 acres in Missouri, born June 11 1820, in York Co , Penn , came to Keosauqua in the spring of 1839; followed house-building and carpenter work for several years, went to California in 1849 via Panama and a sail vessel, which, after about three months, landed at Monterey, Cal , and nearly starved to death; followed mining till he returned home in December, 1850, bought his present farm in 1851 and moved on it in 1868   Married Rosa A Robbins June 17, 1846 , she was born Dec 19, 1828, in Lebanon Co , Penn , and died Aug 27, 1873 Have five children living—Mary, William, Flora, Emma and Morris, lost one—Alice   Is a member of the Christian Church , Democrat

WALLS, P. B., dealer in lumber, lath, shingles etc , Keosauqua , born March 12, 1808, in Danville, Ky , in fall of 1831, came to St Louis, Mo , where he followed dealing in stock, running hotel and farming till the fall of 1846, came to Keosauqua, from which time he followed the dry goods business most of the time till 1871, since which . . . he has . . . . in his present . . . . He was married to Frances . . . . . of Kentucky Aug 28, 1828 she was born in 1808, and died Dec 20, 1842, in St Louis, was again married to Mrs E. J. Collins (whose maiden name was Kinkead) Jan 2, 1868, she was born in Ohio, have but one child living—Priscilla J lost three—John A, Mary A. and B. F. P. Republican

Whitney, Mark, proprietor marble works, Keosauqua

Whorton, J W, minister, Pittsburg

Wiley, J C, far, P O Pittsburg

WILKIN, ABE, CAPT., farmer, P O Keosauqua, born Nov. 20, 1837, in Greene Co, Ohio, moved to Edgar Co, Ill in 1852, and to Stearns Co, Minn, in 1855, and to Burlington, Iowa, in 1856, and came to this county in 1859 Enlisted in the service of his country in April, 1861, in Co F, 2d Iowa V I, and was elected as Second Lieutenant by the company, and, the following October, was promoted as Captain of the company, participated in the battles of Fort Donelson and Shiloh, at which latter place he was wounded, recovered so as to be with Sherman in his march to the sea; was mustered out in February, 1865 After returning home, spent four years in the mercantile business in Keosauqua, and for a few years has followed farming or carrying on his farm of 160 acres He was married to Jennie Roberts Feb 4, 1864, in this county, she was born April 12, 1843, in Highland Co, Ohio, have two children living—Carrie A and Minnie M, lost two—Vinnie and Neal Member Christian Church, Republican

WILLIAMSON, THOMAS A., proprietor Russell House, Keosauqua, born Oct 11, 1826, in Harrison Co, W Va, came from there to this county in 1854, stopped at Winchester a short time, then purchased a farm lying on the county line, being in Jefferson and this county, on which he lived about one year, then sold, and purchased a farm near Winchester remained there and at Birmingham till 1862, he went to California, Montana and Oregon, returned home in 1865, and, in 1868, moved into Birmingham until 1870 came to Summit in July 1871 and to Keosauqua and purchased the Rus-

sell House, which he is still running He was married to Miss Harriet Kinnard, of Taylor Co, W. Va, June 28, 1848, she died in this county in 1853 He was again married to Barbara Walter Feb 3, 1857 she was born March 24, 1833, in Randolph Co, W Va, have two children living by first wife—Mary J and James K, and three by second wife—Hattie, A, Thomas R and George M, his oldest son, William H, died at Birmingham, had previously been admitted to the bar as an attorney Democrat

Wilmot, H H, far, P O Pittsburg

WILSON, BENJAMIN, Keosauqua born Nov. 23, 1804, in Cheshire Co, N H, parents emigrated to Guernsey Co, Ohio in 1815, and from there to Morgan Co in 1817, where he remained until 1822, he then left home and went into Washington Co, Ohio, followed boating on the river to New Orleans, and, latterly, in the dry goods business till the spring of 1845, he then came to Keosauqua, followed farming till 1850, then engaged in the dry goods and general merchandise business, which he continued till the fall of 1870 He was married to Miss Elizabeth Abbott, of Athens Co, Ohio Dec 8, 1836, she was born Nov 4, 1813, in Ohio, have four children living—Boyleston S, Alice M, Flora A and Lizzie L; lost three—Frances J, Caroline E and Solon N Members of the Congregational Church, Republican

WILSON, E. G., farmer and proprietor steam thresher; P O Kilbourn, owns 123 acres of land, valued at $30 per acre, son of Adam B and Sarah M (Dean) Wilson, was born Nov 8, 1826, in Highland Co, Ohio, his father was a native of North Carolina, and mother of Ohio Mr E G Wilson followed the business of buying and driving stock to the New York, Philadelphia and Baltimore from 1840 to 1850 came to this county in the spring of 1855 and settled on his present farm in 1857 Married Mary A Lea Nov 3, 1852, in Ohio, she was born Sept 26, 1830, have six children living—Herbert L, Joseph M, Adam C, Amy L, Lora and Nellie C, lost three—James D and two babies Members of the Presbyterian Church; Republican.

WORDEN, HENRY J., farmer, Sec. 21; P. O. Pittsburg; owns 130 acres of land, valued at $25 per acre; he was born May 19, 1846, in Lorain Co., Ohio; parents moved to Kelly's Island, in Lake Erie, in 1856; they were engaged in the grape culture, his father working at carpenter and joiner work during winters, in which he also engaged. He enlisted in Co. K, 130th O. V. I., in May, 1864, and was discharged in the fall of 1864; was employed principally in and about fortifications near Richmond and Petersburg, Va. Married Mary Ward, of Kelly's Island, Aug. 10, 1868; she was born Jan. 19, 1849; in the fall of 1872, came to this county, and settled where he now lives; have four children—Harry, Albertie, Grace and Edna. Members of the Presbyterian Church; Republican.

WORK, WILLIAM A., attorney, Keosauqua; born Dec. 25, 1844, in Jefferson Co., Iowa; parents moved into Union Tp., in 1845, and settled on a farm adjoining Birmingham, part of which was platted in the town. Served his country in the United States navy, on board the gunboat Benton, in the lower Mississippi, from 1863 to 1864. He had previously attended the Iowa Wesleyan University at Mt. Pleasant one year, and on returning from the navy he again entered the university and graduated in 1867; then came to Keosauqua and commenced the study of law under Judge Robert Sloan, and was admitted to the bar in January, 1869; he was Principal of the Keosauqua school nine months. Married Hinda H. Marlow, of this place, Oct. 9, 1869; she was born April 28, 1849; have three children—Craig M., Benjamin M. and Emmett A. Member of the M. E. Church; Republican.

Workman, John, farmer; P. O. Mt. Zion.

Wright, William, far.; P. O. Pittsburg.

YEAGER, C. E., retired farmer; P. O. Keosauqua; born March 5, 1814, in Columbia Co., Penn.; learned the carpenter and joiner trade in Pennsylvania, and, in 1831 went to Lockport, N. Y., and worked at his trade there; from there he went to St. Joseph Co., Mich., in 1833, and from there to this county in 1837; there were then but a few log cabins in Keosauqua, a Mr. Harlan and one other man had small stores; there were also plenty of the native Americans in the vicinity; Mr. Yeager worked at his trade principally for twenty-five years after coming here, since which time he has followed farming most of the time. He was married to Minerva Dodson, of this county, May 31, 1840; she was born in 1819, in Pennsylvania, and died Aug. 31, 1875. Was again married to Mrs. Sarah Cook, whose maiden name was King, Dec. 21, 1876; had two children by first wife—William and Eliza A., both of whom are dead; his second wife has three children—Jesse, Mary and Maggie. Mr. Yeager is a member of the M. E. Church; Republican.

ZACHAN, NICHOLAS, furniture dealer, Keosauqua.

VILLAGE TOWNSHIP.

ADAMS, DAVID, far, S 24, P O Doud's Station

ADAMS, F. G., Postmaster at Independent, P O Hickory, born in Bowling Green, Wood Co, Ohio, in 1835, moved to Holmes Co, Ohio, with his parents, in October, 1846, moved to Union Tp, Van Buren Co, Iowa, in March following, they moved to Business Corner, he was engaged in farming until 1865, when he moved to Independent and engaged in mercantile pursuits with his brother, S A Adams, until 1876 In September, 1874, was appointed Postmaster, which position he now holds He married Elizabeth Reniker Aug 28, 1859, she was born in Harrison Co, Ohio, Aug 25, 1841, they have three children—Leanah, Rosetta and Allen B Adams

Adamson, S, far, S 32, P O Hickory

ARMENTROUT, MICHAEL, far, S 16, P O Hickory, born Sept 30, 1807, in Rockingham Co, Va, in 1836, moved to Butler Co, Ohio, in in 1840, moved to Van Buren Co, farming has been his business, but has given some of his time to the public, having held several township offices He married Diana Potram Sept 25, 1828, she was a native of Rockingham Co Va, and died in April, 1832 they had one child which died in infancy, on Nov 30, 1832, he married Mary A Detamore she was born June 20, 1814, in Rockingham Co, Va they have had eleven children, two are dead, one died in infancy and the other named George, was killed at the battle of Iuka, the living are Henry, Diana, David, Amanda D, Lydia A, Thomas J, Christy A, Peter and Lucinda Mr and Mrs Armentrout are members of the Christian Church. He has 160 acres of land, valued at $5,000

AVERY, JOEL T., far, Sec 16, P. O. Hickory, born Sept 9, 1808, in Blount Co, Tenn, moved to Spencer's Hill, Tenn, in 1812, in 1814, to Jackson Co, Tenn, two years after, to White Co, Tenn, September, 1830, moved to Sangamon Co Ill in 1832, Jackson Co, Ill, and worked at bricklaying

about two years, being also interested in trade, followed mercantile pursuits exclusively two years, Mr Avery came to Van Buren Co prospecting in fall of 1838, and remained one month, returned to Illinois, in April, 1839, moved to Village Tp in this county, where he has followed farming since, went to Texas in winter of 1860, returned in July, 1865, spent the winter of 1875–76, in Oregon Was Justice of the Peace in Village Tp, from 1843 to 1847 Married Sarah Campbell Feb 22, 1838, in Jackson Co, Ill., she was born in Mercer Co, Tenn, died March 4, 1843, had three daughters, all of whom are dead He has 440 acres of land, valued at $12 500

BACON, T, far S 27, P O Doud's Station

Baker, G A, physician, Hickory

Baldwin, E T, far, S. 2, P O. Doud s Station

Bean, Wm W, Iowaville, P O Hickory

Beitle, Joseph E, far, Sec 21, P O Hickory

Berger, A, far, S 29, P O Hickory.

BICKFORD, G. W., merchant, Independent P O Hickory, born in Hamilton Co, Ohio, March 10, 1828, went to Sangamon Co, Ill, in 1830 eight years later, to Lee Co, Iowa, remained one year, then to Van Buren Co, when 18 years old, went to Mt Vernon, Posey Co., Ind, remained five years and returned to Van Buren Co, a year after, went to Appanoose Co and remained one year, moved to Prairie City, Decatur Co, and engaged in agricultural and mercantile pursuits for eight years, then moved to Columbia, Marion Co, and engaged in mercantile pursuits for five years, came to Independent, his present home, in January, 1870 In 1849, he married Mary Ann Way, she was a native of Indiana, they had two children, a boy and a girl, both dead, his wife died March 25, 1853, July 4, 1854, he married Tacey A Sherrow, she was born in Harrison Co, Ohio, died April 20 1863, had six children two living—D R and James M, Jan 3 1864 married Sarah M

Gardner, she was born Oct 6, 1836, in Charlotte Co, Maine, had five children, two living—Amzy, aged 12, and Harvey A, aged 6 Members of the Methodist Church Owns eighty acres of land, valued at $1,800

Birch, Wm, far, Sec 2, P O Doud's Station

Bishop, B J, far, S 4, P O Hickory

Bishop, Paton, far, S 4, P O Hickory

Black, M E, far, S 18, P O Hickory

Black, S, far, Iowaville, P O Hickory

Breckenridge, Newt., far, Sec 31, P O Hickory

Brewster, Norman, far, Sec 14, P O Doud's Station

Brewster & Ritz, merchants, Portland, P O Doud s Station

Brown, G, far, Portland, P O. Doud's Station

Brown, Lloyd, far, S. 28, P O Doud's Station

Bryan, A, far, Sec 22, P. O Doud s Station

Bryant, M, Business Corner, P O Doud s Station

CAMPBELL, J P, far S 29, P O Hickory.

CAMPBELL, ARCHIBALD, farmer, S 26, P O Doud's Station, born May 11, 1806, in Brooke Co, Va in 1842, he moved to Summit, Van Buren Co, in 1867, he moved to his present home in Village Tp, farming has been his occupation Married Catherine Houk June 17, 1830, she was born in Tuscarawas (now Carroll) Co, Ohio, April 15, 1813, have had twelve children, two are dead, one in infancy and the other (John C) from disease contracted in the army March 13, 1875, ten living—Alexander, Bethyel, Henry, James, Margaret J Martha E, Mary A, Nancy C, A Pierce and Alice J two were in the army He owns 100 acres of land, valued at $3,000

Campbell, W, far, S 19, P O Hickory

Camblin, A S, Notary Public, Independent, Hickory

CAMBLIN, CEPHAS D.. farmer, Sec 15, P O Hickory, born March 3, 1809, in Washington Co Penn, in 1811, . . W . . . . 1828, . . . M . . . . in 18 . . . . Buren . . . . .

farming has been his occupation He married Delilah Ball Oct 25, 1832, she was born Sept 12, 1811, and died Feb 23, 1837, they had two children, both are dead On Dec 5, 1840 he married Hannah Briney she was born Dec. 7, 1821, in Warren Co, Ohio, they have had eleven children, two are dead, the living are Sarah C, Asbury, Mary, Jane, Martha, Delilah, George, John and Alice M Members of the M E Church He has 320 acres of land, valued at $10,000

Carr, S, laborer, Independent, P O. Hickory

Casner, B. far, S 15, P O Hickory

Clifford, J, far, S 34, P O Doud's Station

Colton, G, laborer, Independent, P O Hickory.

Crandall, C, far, S 27, P O Doud's Station

CRAWFORD, JAMES, physician, Doud's Station, born Dec 28, 1828, in Perry Co, Ohio, in 1844, he moved to Washington Co, Iowa, he attended the Washington Seminary two years, then began the study of medicine under Dr William McClellan, went to California in the spring of 1849; two years after, returned to his home and began the practice of medicine with Dr Robert McCall in Crawfordsville, in the fall of 1851, he moved to Business Corners and entered practice alone, in 1868, he moved to Doud s Station He married Candace Whitten Nov. 18, 1852, she was born Feb 5, 1831, in Lawrence Co. Ohio, they have three children — Walter D, Ella R and James G.

Crandall Robert, far, Sec 32, P O Doud's Station

Crawford, William B, hotel, Doud's Station

Creek, Samuel, far S 13, P O Doud's Station

Countryman, J, far, S 11, P O Doud's Station

Culbertson, William. far, S 1, P O Doud's Station

DOUD, S M., farmer, S 35, P O D. . . . . .

DOUD, DAVID, . Sec 26 P O D . . . Station . . n Oct 15, ... Luzerne n w Bradford) Co,

Penn , moved to Hamilton Co , Ohio , in 1818, moved to Clark Co in 1820 , in 1823, he moved to Licking Co. he was there engaged in farming and collecting , he bought his claim in Van Buren Co in 1841, and moved his family in 1844 , his principal business has been farming , he acted as Justice of the Peace seven years , he was elected to the State Legislature in 1856, for two years, but on account of the changing of the State Constitution at that time, he only served one year He married Nancy B Blood April 10, 1832, in Licking Co. Ohio, she was born August 9, 1810 in Massachusetts; she died March 23, 1834 , they had one child—Nancy B On Oct 14, 1840, he married Ann M Schuyler, she was born Oct 8, 1821, in Montgomery Co , N Y , they have had four children, one dead—Upton A J., and three living—Thomas P , Lewis K and Seymour McC He has 410 acres of land, valued at $12,500

DOUD, ELIAB. far , P O Doud's Station, born Oct. 16, 1812, in Luzerne (now Bradford) Co , Penn , moved to Hamilton Co , Ohio in 1818, moved to Clark Co , Ohio, in 1820 , in about three years, moved to Licking Co , Ohio. He was educated at Granville College, in 1837, he went to Bourbon Co , Ky , and engaged in teaching; in 1843, came to Van Buren Co He has devoted much of his time to the public service , he has acted as Justice of the Peace ten years, re-elected in 1878 for two years more , has held other township offices, in 1865, he was elected State Senator for four years, and prides himself as being able to assist by his vote the passage of the bill indorsing the national bill forbidding slavery in the United States He was, also, the author of the "Doud Amendment" to the bill empowering the State to regulate railroad tariffs. He married Mary J Whitten Jan 2, 1847, she was born in Lawrence Co , Ohio, Jan. 19 1829, they have had eleven children, ten living—Mary A , Winfield S , Fletcher W Harriet I , Eliab E , A Lincoln, Candace R , Elizabeth O Melissa M and Walter D Mrs. Doud is a member of the Baptist Church He

owns 400 acres of land, valued at $12,000

Doud, Stanford, far , S 21 , P O Doud's Station

Doud, Thomas P , far , Sec 28 , P O Doud's Station

Dooley, Wm , far , S 19 , P O Hickory

Drake, Francisco, far , Sec. 13 , P O Doud's Station

Drake, Henry far , Sec 13; P O. Doud's Station

Dyer, W G , far , S 32 , P O Doud's Station

ELERICK, G W , physician, Portland, P O Doud's Station

ELERICK, JAMES, CAPT., shipper of grain and stock, Doud's Station , born April 6, 1838, in Belmont Co , Ohio, came to Van Buren Co first in 1849, returned to Ohio that year , in 1854, returned to Iowa and settled permanently In 1856, in company with Benjamin Casner, he purchased a saw-mill, which they operated until 1861 On the 15th of June, he enlisted in Co A, 59th Ill V I , as a private , served in that regiment nearly five years, he was engaged in the battles at Pea Ridge, Prairieville, Ky , Stone River, Chickamauga, Lookout Mountain, Mission Ridge, Dalton, Resaca, Burnt Hickory, Kenesaw Mountain, Atlanta, Jonesboro and Nashville , he was appointed 1st Sergeant in the fall of 1861, 1st Lieutenant in November, 1862, and Captain in December, 1863 He married Margaret Short Jan 1, 1873, she was born March 23, 1849, in Van Buren Co , Iowa, they have had three children—two are dead, Weltha M remains Mrs Elerick is a member of the M E. Church He owns 305 acres of land, valued at $6,000

FELMLEE, DORCAS W , farmer, Sec 14 , P O Doud's Station

Felmlee, Peter, far , Sec 14; P O Doud's Station

FERRIS, JONATHAN N., ferryman Portland, P O Doud's Station, born in Richland Co , Ohio, April 18, 1843 , in 1848, moved to Chequest Tp , Van Buren Co and engaged in farming with his father spring of 1862 went to U T , a year after went to M T where he remained nine years, while there he was mining and farming, in the fall of 1872, he returned to his home in Iowa, farmed two years, in 1875 bought a half-interest in the ferry crossing the river between Portland and Doud's Station, and began operating it, in 1877, he bought the other half-interest, and now has full control. Married Mary A Doud, April 23, 1876, she was born Oct 14, 1847, in Village Tp, they have one child—Mary F His wife is a member of the M E Church He owns eighty acres of land, valued at $1,200

FINDLAY, ALEXANDER, farmer and coal operator, Sec 24 Business Corners, P O Doud's Station, born December 28, 1828, in Ayrshire, Scotland, when quite young, his parents left the farm and moved into the town of Catherine, in about two years, he moved to Kilmarnock, where he went into a confectionery manufactory, and remained two and a half years, he then commenced mining, which he has followed principally through life. In the spring of 1837, he was engaged by a coal company, and went to Pictou, Nova Scotia, remained there six months, and then went to Bathurst, Bay de Chaleur, N B, remained there about six months, and went to Pottsville, Penn, where he remained four weeks, and went to Alleghany Co, Md, in 1855 he moved to Jefferson Co, Iowa, in 1856, moved to Van Buren Co Married Margaret Whitfield April 22, 1841, at Mount Savage, Md, she was born in Ayrshire, Scotland, April 23, 1824, have had twelve children, nine living—Margaret, Hugh, Mary, Janet, Agnes, Helen, Alexander Sarah N and George W Mr and Mrs Findlay are members of the M E Church He has 80 acres of land, valued at $2,500

Fulton, J, far, Sec 5, P O Hickory

GARDNER, J, far Sec 28, P O Doud's Station

GARDNER, CHARLES T., farmer, Sec 13, Business Corners, P O Doud's Station, born May 4, 1815, in Rutland, Meigs Co, Ohio, there he learned the tanner's trade finishing in 1836 traveled as a journeyman workman about two years, when he went to Albany Athens Co Ohio and entered

into business for himself; in 1846, he moved to Business Corners, and engaged in the mercantile business, in 1852, sold his stock and went to Ohio, where he remained a year, returned and entered business again, in 1868, he sold his stock and began farming, which he has followed since Married Margaret M Schuyler Nov 10, 1853, she was born in Licking Co, Ohio, Jan 19, 1834, have had nine children, seven living—Amanda E, Charles S, Ada M., May, Oscar S, Perry S and Otis A Mr and Mrs Gardner are members of the Universalist Church He has 245 acres of land, valued at $6,500

Gardner, R, far, Sec 9, P O Hickory

Gilbert, C P, painter, Independent, P O Hickory

Gilbert, D, far, Sec 20, P O Hickory

Gilbert, P, far, Sec 10, P O Hickory

Gilbert, Riley, farmer, Sec 14, P O Doud's Station

Gilbert, Wm A, farmer, Sec 28, P O. Doud's Station

Green, Henry, farmer, Sec 36, P. O Doud's Station.

Green, Robert, farmer, Sec 36, P O Doud's Station

Green, William, farmer, Portland, P O Doud's Station

Grimsley, W F, farmer, Sec 35, P O. Doud's Station

HANEY G W, far, Sec 31, P O Hickory

Haney, James H, far, Sec 12, P O. Doud's Station

Haney, James, Jr, far., Sec. 12, P O Doud's Station.

Haney, Robert, farmer, Sec 28, P O Doud's Station

Haney, T, far, Sec 31, P O Hickory

Hamm, H, far, Sec 30, P O Hickory.

Harlan, G W, station agent, independent, P O Hickory

Harlan, J B, station agent, Independent P O Hickory

Harrington, D, far, S 31, P O Hickory.

Hein, F, Jr, far, Sec 30, P O Hickory.

Hein, J, far, Sec 30, P O Hickory

Hewitt, P C, far, Sec 28, P O Doud's Station

HINKLE, ABRAM, CAPT., farmer and stock-breeder, Sec 17; P O Hickory, born in Pendleton Co, Va July 1, 1835, raised on a farm, at the age of 19, left Virginia and took a tour of two years through the Western States, returned to Virginia, and, in the fall of 1859, went to Pike's Peak, in the spring of 1861, again returned to Virginia, found all his friends and relatives in the Southern army, offered his services to Gen Rosecrans immediately after the battle of Rich Mountain, August 1861, was assigned duty under Gen Milroy, he continued in the service until the close of the war, then engaged in mercantile pursuits in Mt Freedom, W Va, until 1871 During that time, was a member of the Board of Supervisors, served one term in the State Legislature in 1871, moved to Van Buren Co, on his present farm, and engaged in farming and breeding fine stock Married Sarah F Jordon Dec 25, 1866, she was born Feb 8, 1844, in Van Buren Co, have had six children, five living—Lora, Arthur E, Harry Nellie and May Has 700 acres of land, valued at $2,500 and 80 acres in Kansas, valued at $1,000

Hix, Alva far, Sec 29, P O Hickory
Hix, J L, Sr, far, S 30, P O Hickory
Hix, R M., far, Sec 32, P O. Hickory
Huckleberry, S H., miller, Independent, P O Hickory
Hollen, G W, far, S 20, P O Hickory
Hull, A N, far, Independent, P O Hickory
Hunt, J H, harness-maker, Iowaville, P O Hickory

JACKSON, JOHN T, far, Sec 16, P O Hickory
Judd, H W, far, Sec 34, P. O Dond's Station

KIMBALL, F W, laborer, Iowaville, P O Hickory.
Kimball, J P, laborer, Iowaville, P O Hickory
Kindall, W, Iowaville, P O Hickory
Kingman, G far, Sec 29, P O Hickory

LEFEVER JACOB, far, Sec 17; P O Hickory
Lefever, Ellis, far, Sec 20, P. O. Hickory
Lefever, Eli, far, Sec 20; P. O Hickory
Lewis, S, far, Sec 22, P. O Doud's Station.
Lewis, W A E, far, Sec 11, P O. Doud's Station.
Liming, L C miller, Portland, P O Doud's Station

Loar, L, physician, Portland, P.O Doud's Station
Loomis. G, blacksmith, Portland; P O Doud's Station

McCOLLOM, JOHN, far, Sec 31 P. O Doud's Station
McClure, T G physician, P O Doud's Station
McCormack, G J, far, Sec 29, P O Hickory.
McCullough, A, far, Sec 23, P O Doud's Station

McGREW. FINLEY L., REV., far, S 24, P O Doud s Station, born in Allegheny Co, Penn April 7, 1843, in 1851, moved to Wapello Co, Iowa, in 1863, he went to Oskaloosa to attend college, graduated in 1867, then taught in the high school there and followed teaching several years, in 1868 moved to Van Buren Co and engaged in farming, during the years 1872-73, acted as an itinerant minister, is now a local minister Married Sarah E Brewer Dec 25, 1867, she was born in Van Buren Co Feb 24, 1845, have five children—Harry L, George E, James E, Wilham R and Helen B Members of the M E Church He has 192 acres of land, valued at $5,800. He is now Township Clerk and was elected Assessor Oct 8 1878

McGill, J, far Sec 12, P O Doud's Station
McGill, S, far, Sec 12, P O Doud s Station
McKeown, A J, far, S 2, P. O Doud s Station

MALCOMSON, JOHN, far, S 36, P O Doud's Station, born in County Down. Ireland, in April, 1810, farming was his occupation, in 1840, he moved to Peterboro, Upper Canada, thence to Cincinnati, Ohio, in 1849 he moved to his present home in Van Buren Co, and has been engaged in farming since Married Mrs Helen Waterfall (nee Thomson) in October, 1847, she was born in February, 1806, in Glasgow, Scotland, and died Sept 25, 1878, they had no children, Mrs Malcomson had five children by former marriage, one living—Margaret He has 109 acres of land v 1 t 5,500

Manning, E merchant Portland.
Manning, E merchant Independent

Manning, E, mer, Doud's Station

Martindale, W, far, S 32, P O Doud's Station

Marshall, J, far, Sec 18, P O Hickory

Martin, J, far, Sec 18, P O Hickory

Meek Jacob, grocer, Doud's Station

Meeks, William far, S 27, P O Doud's Station

Meek, William far, S 27, P O Doud's Station

Michael, J H, far, S 7, P O Hickory

Miller, George, far, Sec 36, P O Doud's Station

MILLER, JOHN, far, Sec 25, P O Doud's Station, born March 14, 1840, in Van Buren Tp, Van Buren Co, lived on a farm until 1862 when he enlisted in Co G, 3d Iowa V C, for three years at the end of eighteen months his regiment was furloughed and re-enlisted for the war, discharged Sept 19, 1865, was in the battle of White River, Little Rock, Harrison Station and various smaller battles, was wounded at Harrison Station The spring after his discharge, moved on his present farm in Village Tp, and engaged in farming Married C. Rodgers May 11, 1869, she was born in Washington Co., Ohio, Dec 25, 1850, and died March 7 1871, Oct 1, 1874, he married Rettie G McCullough, she was born in Village Tp, Dec. 16, 1855, by his first marriage he had one child—Theodore E, by second marriage two children—Nellie F and Ethel L He has 230 acres of land, valued at $7,000

Miller, William, laborer, Independent, P O Hickory

Moore, James R, far S 33, P O Doud's Station

Morrison, William H, far, Sec 4, P O Hickory

Morrison, W. H. H, harness-maker, Portland, P. O Doud's Station

MORROW, RICHARD, farmer, Sec 21, P O Hickory, born Dec 3, 1826, in Belmont Co, Ohio, lived on a farm, learned the carpenter's trade, which he followed several years before coming to Iowa in 1851, when he settled in Village Tp, Van Buren Co, was a carpenter twelve years in this county, then began farming Married Elizabeth A Schuyler Nov 23 1853 she was

born in Kentucky Sept 30, 1827, and died Feb 11, 1873, they had one child, which died in infancy he married Sarah J Parson Nov 22, 1873, she was born in Athens Co, Ohio, Nov 27, 1837, died June 11, 1877, have two children, one living—Edward, born March 29, 1876 Mr Morrow and his first wife were members of the M E Church, his second wife was a member of the Lutheran Church He has 123 acres of land, valued at $3,700

NEDROW, ALEX, blacksmith, Sec 5, P O Hickory

Nellis, Rev, Business Corners; P O Doud's Station

Nelson A, far, Sec 33, P O. Doud's Station

Nelson, I, far, Sec 6, P O Hickory

Nelson, J, far, Sec 6, P O Hickory

Newell, D C, carpenter, Portland, P O Doud's Station

Nicklin, W V, far, S 19, P O Hickory

Nutt, O, farmer. Sec 13, P O Doud's Station

OVERTURFF, ALEN, farmer, Sec 10, P O. Hickory

OVERTURFF, J. T., ferryman. Independent, P O Hickory, born in Brownsville, Fayette Co, Penn, Sept 13, 1835, moved to Van Buren Co, in 1850, and settled in Village Tp, engaged in farming two years, went to Kansas, a year, after returned to this county, in 1857, went to California overland, in 1860, went to New Orleans, in April, 1861, came up the Mississippi to his home in Van Buren Co, the last boat allowed to pass without seizure June, 1861, enlisted in Co H, 5th Iowa V I was engaged in the battles at Island No. 10, New Madrid, Iuka and various smaller battles, at Iuka received wound in right thigh, from which he is crippled, discharged in 1863 In 1865, engaged in the grocery business with D C Beaman, and remained in business about two years, when he engaged in buying and shipping stock; left that business in February, 1876, when he bought the ferry at Independent, which he now controls Fall of 1866, he married Miss S. J Walker, she was born in Village Tp Sept 6, 1844, they have five children—George E, Amaretta L, Ola R Clyde D and Ditta N Mrs

Overturff is a member of the Methodist Church

PARSONS, ANDREW

PARK, STEPHEN, far , Sec 20 , P O Doud's Station, born in Licking Co , Ohio, Aug 12, 1823 ; in 1844, he moved to Van Buren Co , he went to California in 1849, and remained there twelve years , went to Nevada and remained seven years, then returned to his home in Van Buren Co While on the coast, was engaged in farming, mining and teaming He married Mrs Matilda Garrison, nee Jackson, March 25, 1869 ; she was born Sept 17, 1843 in Jefferson Co , Iowa, they have four children— Martha M , Lucien F , Samuel W and Homer O Parks Mrs Parks had one child by former marriage—Ida L Garrison Mr and Mrs Parks are members of the M E Church , he has 220 acres of land, valued at $6,000

Parsons, Miller, far , S 33 , P O Doud's Station

Patum, William chairmaker, Portland, P O Doud's Station

Pearson, Sampson, farmer, Sec 11 , P O Doud's Station

Pearson, Young S , far , Sec 3 , P O Hickory

Perry, Daniel, far , S 30 , P O Hickory

Perry, William, far., S. 31 ; P. O. Hickory

Penn, Joseph, Sr , farmer, S 12 , P O Doud's Station

Pettet, Samuel, wagon-maker, Portland , P O Doud's Station

Plowman, Jasper, farmer, Sec 36 , P O Doud's Station

Puryear, Thomas W , far , Sec 2 , P O Hickory

ROSSER, GEORGE, far , Sec 30 ; P O Hickory

Ratchff, Aaron, far , S 27 , P. O. Doud s Station.

Ratchff, Jesse, far., Sec 23 , P O Doud's Station

Ratchff, S Z T , far , Sec 29 , P O. Hickory

Reiter, W L , station agent, Doud's Station

Ritz, J U , shoemaker, Portland , P O Doud's Station

RITZ, REINHART, of the firm of Ritz & Earhart, merchants Independent , P O Hickory , born Sept 14

1844, in Switzerland , moved to Greene Co , Ohio, in 1851 , to Bloomfield, Davis Co , Iowa, in 1854 , then to Chequest Tp , Van Buren Co., in 1856 , to Portland in 1872 , up to that time he was farming, then engaged in mercantile pursuits , in December, 1876, h sold his stock , was farming until the fall of 1877 , then moved to Independent and engaged in mercantile pursuits Oct 24, 1867, he married Margaret McIntosh , is a native of Van Buren Co , had four children, three living— Clarence Ira and Henry. He owns 160 acres of land, valued at $4,000

Robinson, Joseph, far , S 1 , P O Doud's Station

Ryan, Jacob, far , Sec 27 , P O Doud's Station

SALTERS, ASA blacksmith and farmer, Sec 27 , P O Doud's Station

Schiveley, T C , carpenter, Independent , P O Hickory

Schuyler, Phillip, hotel, Doud s Station

SCHUYLER, WILLIAM (deceased), born in New Jersey July 5, 1795, and died Sept 18, 1875 , when about 8 years old, he moved to Essex Co , N Y , and settled near Elizabethtown , when about 25 years old he went to Kentucky, and engaged in land speculation and contracting , eleven years after, he moved to Licking Co , Ohio, and followed farming and contracting , in 1841, moved to Van Buren Co, where he died Married Elizabeth Sharpensteen in New York, June 11, 1818 , she was born in New Jersey Nov 21, 1794, and died June 15, 1859. They had seven children, two living—William V and Margaret M. April 28 1861, he married Mrs Mary Featherson (nee Siddorn), she had four children by former marriage, two living—Sarah and Elizabeth , she was born in Cheshire, England, Sept. 11, 1819 Mr. Schuyler and both wives were members of the M E Church William V Schuyler was born Dec 16, 1839, in Licking Co , Ohio, and came to Iowa with his father in 1841. May 28, 1864, enlisted in Co K, 45th I V I , for 100 days, discharged at the end of his term , farming has been his occupation. He married Sarah Featherson Sept 24 1870 she was born Feb 24 1848 in Cheshire England

2

Shearer, J V, farmer, Portland, P O Doud's Station

Shearer, M., far, S 35, P O Doud's Station

Shelby, D, far, S 3, P O Hickory

Spinbeck, W far, S 28, P O Doud's Station

Snelling, G, far, S 32, P O Doud's Station

Stamm J W far, S 12, P O Doud's Station

STOKES, JOSE N., far, S 1, P O Doud's Station, born July 23, 1822 in Logan Co, Ohio, in the fall of 1843, he moved to Village Tp, Van Buren Co, where he now resides, farming has been his occupation through life On July 25, 1844, he married Mary D Walker, she was born May 6, 1822 in Fairfield Co, Ohio, they have had six children, four living—Oliver O., born Aug 27, 1845, John W., born June 5, 1847, Mary A born June 14, 1849 and George N, born April 7, 1856 Mrs Stokes is a member of the M E Church He has 200 acres of land, valued at $6 000

Stokes, J W, far, S 1, P O Doud's Station.

Stokes, O O, far, S 1; P O Doud's Station

STOOPS, JESSE T., farmer, P O Hickory, born March 6 1820, in Hamilton Co, Ohio, in 1823, moved to Switzerland Co, Ind, at the age of 17, he went to the village of Harrison, remained about five years, moved to Van Buren Co in the fall of 1849, the following spring, he went to California, returned in the spring of 1853, and located in Village Tp, where he now resides Married Elmira McCullough in Switzerland Co, Ind, Feb 10, 1846, she was born in that county May 17, 1821, had seven children, six living—Eugene T, Obid F, Ida A, Mary M, Albia I and George M. Mrs. Stoops is a member of the M E Church He has 197 acres of land, valued at $8,000.

Strang, John, Sec 26, P O Doud's Station

TANNAHILL, W, far, S 21, P O Doud's Station

TOOL, GEORGE W, CAPT., manager of stores for Mr J Manning at Doud's Station, Portland and Inde-

pendent, born in Posey Co, Ind, Sept. 6, 1838, moved to Keosauqua in 1851, in 1858-61 clerked in a grocery store. Nov. 27, 1861, enlisted as private, Co C, 17th I. V. I, for three years, was gradually promoted to Orderly Sergeant, July 18, 1863, was discharged for promotion and transferred to the 50th U S C I with the rank of Captain of Co. C, which he organized, while in the Iowa regiment, he was in the first and second battles of Corinth, and at Jacinto, Iuka, Jackson, Champion Hills and the seige of Vicksburg; afterward, in the battles at Port Gibson, Grand Gulf, Mobile and various smaller engagements, mustered out of service March 12, 1865. Came home and was in the grocery business about two years, and then sold his stock. June 20, 1868, he entered the store of Manning & Parker at Doud's Station, as clerk, in 1870, Mr Manning became sole proprietor and appointed Capt Tool manager, in 1875, another store was started at Portland, and in 1877, one at Independent, both of which Capt Tool has the management Married Fanny J Scott Dec 12, 1865 she was born in Indiana, they have four children—Flora S, George S, Mary M. and Hattie S Members of the M E. Church He has forty acres of land, valued at $500

Tatum, W A, far and chairmaker, S 21, P O Doud's Station

Taylor, I, lab, Doud's Station

Trout, John, Sr, far, S 1, P O Doud's Station

UTTER, A, far, S 4, P O Hickory

VAN SEGGEN, T W, blacksmith, Doud's Station

Van Antwerp, H, far, Sec. 27, P O Doud's Station

WAINSCOTT, M, far, S 34, P O Doud's Station

Walker, G B, far, S 14, P O. Doud's Station

WALKER, JOHN M., far, S 4, P O Hickory, born Dec 4, 1837, in Champaign Co, Ohio, in 1841, moved to Van Buren Co., he was raised on a farm, and farming has been his principal business from 1861 to 1868 he was engaged in operating a saw-mill in partnership with his father, Zachariah Walker, the mill was first a mile below Doud's Station, afterward, moved to Independent Married Elizabeth W Camblin Dec 17, 1863, she was born Feb 10, 1842, in Montgomery Co, Ohio, have had seven children, five living—Anna L, John A, Mary V, Charles R and George Members of the M E Church He owns 209 acres of land, valued at $5,300.

WALKER, PETER. REV., M. D. (deceased), born April 21, 1814, in Ross Co, Ohio, moved to Champaign Co, Ohio, in 1823, about the year 1834, began the study of medicine in West Middlebury, in 1843, moved to Village Tp, Van Buren Co, and engaged in farming and practicing medicine, also acted as local preacher, in the fall of 1854, moved to Libertyville, Jefferson Co, where he continued practicing. In October, 1861, he was elected Representative for Jefferson Co for two years, at an extra session in September, 1862, he was commissioned by Governor Kirkwood as First Assistant Surgeon in the 30th Iowa V I, resigned his seat in the Legislature, rejoined his regiment at Keokuk, and was mustered in Sept 12, on account of sickness, he was obliged to resign his commission, which he did Dec 26, 1862 and returned to his home in Libertyville, where he died Jan 13, 1863 He married Sarah G Stokes March 29, 1838, she was born Nov 15, 1818, in Logan Co, Ohio, and died Jan 3, 1850, they had six children, two living—Moses B and John R On May 23, 1850, he married Christiann Schuyler, she was born Nov 25, 1830, in Licking Co, Ohio, and died April 6, 1859, they had four children, three living — William M, Peter E and Francis E On Jan 6, 1860, he married Mrs Mary Drake (nee Brewer), she was born Jan 18, 1818 in New York Mr Walker was a prominent member of the Masonic and Odd Fellows fraternities, he was Master Mason, Royal Arch Master, and Knight Templar.

WALKER, ZACHARIAH, deceased, born July 15, 1811, in Pickaway Co Ohio, and died March 4, 1875, moved to Champaign Co., Ohio, in 1823 There married Lydia A Thomas June 12, 1834 He came to Van Buren Co in 1839, made three claims for himself and brothers, returned to Ohio and moved his family to Iowa in 1840, in 1850, he went to California, returned in 1851, he was chosen Captain of the company taking the trip, they suffered considerably from cholera during the trip, from which many of the party died were, also, attacked by Indians, on Humboldt River, but no live lost, a bullet tore a lock of hair from Mr Walker's head, but he was not otherwise injured, farming was his occupation through life He served as Justice of the Peace about twelve successive years Mrs Walker was born Jan 6, 1815, in Champaign Co, Ohio, they had ten children, eight living—Harriet E, John M, Mary E, Sarah J, Moses P, George A, Joseph E and Francis R G Mr Walker was and his wife is a member of the M E Church The farm contains 200 acres of land, valued at $5,500

Wear, John T, far See 26, P O Doud's Station

Whetsel, Emory, grain dealer, Independent, P, O Hickory

Wiley, Clark, far, Sec 33, P O Doud's Station

Williams, Henry, farmer, Sec 31, P O Hickory

Williams, Joshua, far..Sec 1, P O Doud's Station

Willis, John S, merchant, Doud s Station

Willis, John A, farmer, Sec 35; P O Doud's Station

Wirt, David B, farmer and molder, Sec 21, P O Doud's Station

Weissenburger, David, laborer, P O Doud's Station

YOUNG, J T, far, Sec 3, P O Hickory.

Young, William, farmer, Sec 3, P. O Hickory.

WASHINGTON TOWNSHIP.

BAKER, HIRAM, shoemaker, Bentonsport.

BAILEY, JAMES F., far, Sec 26, P O Bentonsport, owns 252 acres of land, valued at $40 per acre Born Aug 23, 1825, in Belmont Co, Ohio, parents moved to Morgan Co in 1835, from there to this county in the spring of 1850, lived in Bonaparte till the fall of 1851, then went to California via New Orleans, from there to the Isthmus by steamer, from there to San Francisco in a sailing-vessel, came near perishing for want of food and water, being out seventy-seven days, while there, was engaged in mining, and on the public works; returned in 1855, and married Celestine Davidson July 25, 1855, she was born April 10, 1835, in Illinois, came on to his present farm in January, 1855, have one daughter—Ella, married to H T Shepherd Nov 12, 1872 Mr Bailey served in the Mexican war in Co H, 3d Ohio Inf, was in the service about one year Member of the M E Church, Republican

Barber, Alonzo, painter, Bentonsport

BARKER, JAMES C., farmer, Sec 9, P O Mt. Zion, owns 157 acres of land, valued at $30 per acre, son of John and Elizabeth Barker, born in this county July 12, 1844, his father died the following October, his mother subsequently married a man of the name of Robinson, and died Jan 29, 1874 Mr Barker married Miss Jane Agnew May 7, 1873; she was born March 17, 1848, in county of Antrim, Ireland, have three children— Elizabeth J., Robert J and Mary A Members of the Presbyterian Church, Republican

Barker, J, far., Sec 4, P O Mt Zion
Bart, Jas, railroad engineer, Bentonsport.
Boenstler, Daniel, farmer, Sec. 12, P. O. Pierceville
Bragg, W N, paper-maker, Bentonsport
Brooks, L A carpenter, Bentonsport

BROWN, NOAH G., station agent on the K & D M R R P O Bentonsport, son of James A and Rachel Brown, was born Jan 1 1836, in Westmoreland Co, Penn., came with parents to this county in April, 1840, stopped on a farm two miles south of Vernon, after two years, came to Bentonsport, where his father commenced building the Bentonsport Mills, worked in the mills till 1859, then went to California via overland route with an ox-team, followed the milling business at Ione City in Amador Co till 1865, when he returned to this county, followed the milling business here and two years at Oskaloosa, took charge of the railroad office in 1870 Married Lutitia Freeman Feb 5, 1857, she was born June 7, 1832, in Ohio, have three children—Cora, Harriet and Elbert, lost one—James A His father died Nov 21, 1865. Members of the Presbyterian Church, Republican

Burton, J. W, far, S 34, P O Bentonsport

CARTER, C A, butcher, Bentonsport
Carter, Heziah, Bentonsport
Carter, R. S, dealer in rags, Bentonsport.
Carter, R F, coal-miner, Bentonsport.
Cochenour, H, farmer, P O Bentonsport
Colton, E, farmer and cloth-dresser, S 36, P O Bentonsport
Corns, Ira M, millwright and farmer, P O Bentonsport

COWLES, C. W., M. D., retired physician, Bentonsport, was born March 10, 1808, in Hampshire Co., Mass, at the age of 17, he started out for himself, came to Lexington, Ky, where he taught school about one year, taught two years at Elizabethtown, then returned to Massachusetts and finished his studies at Amherst College, graduated in August, 1831; he afterward entered Berkshire Medical College, graduated in the winter of 1835 and 1836, the following spring, came to Crawfordsville, Ind., practiced medicine there till he came to Bentonsport, in this county, in the spring of 1838, he being the first physician so far west Dr Cowles has followed his profession ever since till within the last three years also dealt some in real estate, and was a partner with a Mr Seth

Richards about six years, owned a store at Chariton, Lucas Co, several years Married Miss Martha Howe in July, 1846· she was born Feb 26, 1825, in Massachusetts, have three children living—George H Hester W. and Sarah I, lost one—And George H is engaged in the banking business at Osceola Clark Co, Iowa Members of the Congregational Church, Republican

DINGS, C, far, P. O Bentonsport.

Drumm, C, painter, Bentonsport
Dunn, A, far and minister, Bentonsport

EATON W, laborer, Bentonsport

Edmondson, H B, far, Sec 26, P O Bentonsport

FULTON, A, teamster, Bentonsport

Fulton, H, railroad engineer, Bentonsport
Fulton, W S., railroad section-hand, Bentonsport

GADDIS, W, far, Sec 12, P O Pierceville

Gast, J D, retir'd far, P O Pierceville
Greyson, W, carpenter, Bentonsport
Greef, C E, ferryman, Bentonsport
Greet, J, merchant. Bentonsport

HART, W, blacksmith, Bentonsport

HANCOCK, FREDERICK,
P O Bentonsport, Justice of the Peace and Notary Public; born Dec 13, 1815 in Luzerne Co, Penn at the age of 12, he went to Philadelphia, came to Van Buren County in the fall of 1838, took his claim about four miles north of Bentonsport, commenced the mercantile business in Bentonsport in 1848, and continued till the spring of 1864 Was appointed Captain and Quartermaster in the Military Department of the Southwest, received his discharge in 1866, returned home and engaged in the lumber business until 1875 Was married to Ann P Collins, of Delaware, in September, 1837, she died in January, 1864, was again married to Martha Brown, May 1, 1873 she was born Sept 23, 1840, in Pennsylvania, have four children living—Fanny, mai'[?] [illegible] lives at W[illegible] ried to E [illegible]

Boston, Mass, Mary, married to J S Keck, of this county, and Frederick, who is in Kansas, lost two, his son, Paul, enlisted in Co II, of the 7th Missouri Cavalry, was discharged in October, 1864, and died on the cars, at Keokuk, while on his way home, and Mattie died Oct 4, 1878, at her sister's in California Mr Hancock represented his county in the Legislature, in 1844-45 Member of the Congregational Church Republican

Harwood T, far, Sec 3, P O Utica
Heinz, C, tailor, Bentonsport
Hooper, Chas, far, S 12, P O Pierceville
Hooper, S, far Sec 12, P O Pierceville

JOHNSTON, S B, far, Sec 1, P O Utica

JACK, GEORGE W., dealer in general merchandise, drugs, etc., Bentonsport, born Nov 2, 1834, in Morgan Co, Ohio, came to this county in 1856, and settled in Vernon, where he engaged in stone-cutting and selling paper for the mills, came to Bentonsport in the spring of 1861, in 1867, he opened his present business Married Elizabeth Hart Feb 24, 1859, she was born July 31, 1838, near Dayton, Ohio, have seven children—Delbert A, John W, Edward George L, Clara, Chester C and Albert, lost one—Ella L Has held the offices of Mayor and City Treasurer, and member of the School Board Member of the M E Church, Republican

KECK, P R, far, Sec 34, P O Bentonsport.

Kisling, S, far, S. 3, P. O Mt. Zion

McCRACKEN, I, stone-mason and farmer, Bentonsport

McCUNE, ALEXANDER S., farmer and stock-raiser, P O Pierceville, owns about 1,000 acres, valued at $50 per acre, born Oct 6, 1817, in Cumberland Co, Penn, came to Van Buren Co, in April, 1857, and settled in Harrisburg Tp, engaged in mercantile business in Pierceville in 1866, but did not move his family till 1869, continued in the business till 1873, is, at pr[illegible] [illegible] in office whi[illegible] ve years M[illegible] M[illegible] [illegible] ughter of

Benjamin Walker, Nov 25, 1857, she was born Oct 25, 1829, in Cincinnati Ohio, have three children—Eleanor S, Hester F and Minnie B Demo-Greenback

McCutcheon, Robert, far, Sec 15, P O Bentonsport

McSurley James H, far, Sec 9, P O Mt Zion

McSURELY, MILES, far, Sec. 9, P O Mt Zion, owns 180 acres of land, valued at $30 per acre born Feb 1, 1809, in Mason Co, Ky His father, James McSurely, moved to Adams Co, Ohio, fall of 1809, where he died in 1840, his mother, Maria, died in 1833, he went to Scioto Co in 1830 was married there to Catharine McCan Jan 24, 1833, she was born in same county, Nov 28 1816, moved to Fulton Co, Ill, fall of 1836, the following spring to Van Buren Co, made his claim about three miles west of his present farm, moved his family out in the spring of 1838, he is among the early settlers of this county, and, by his own industry and economy, has acquired a handsome property Has seven children living—Mary J, William, Anderson, Hannah, James, Kate and John M., lost two—Benjamin and Margaret Anderson and Benjamin were in Co G of 3d Iowa Cavalry, while there Benjamin died Aug 26, 1862, his son James yet single, remains at home, and owns 120 acres of land, his other three sons are in California Republican

McVity, John, shoemaker, Bentonsport

McVity, Thomas, shoemaker, Bentonsport

MASON, GEORGE H., Bentonsport, proprietor of Ashland House, son of Lewis J and Nancy Mason (nee Winslow) of Chenango Co., N Y, he was born in Cattaraugus Co Feb 18, 1842, came with his friends to this county in 1857, his father bought au hotel, and the following year traded for the one now occupied by George H, his father died in September, 1868, and mother in May, 1875 Married Rebecca Williamson May 1, 1861, she was l.. .. l' 18 1'.. .. O f, 1 C. Main W..... l........ ..
the F.. .. '.. ... mor... .. ..
and 1.. .. ..   l'

port, and, in 1876, moved to Des Moines, where he was foreman in Mason & Co's wholesale tinware manufactory, returned and took charge of the Ashland House Have four children—Harry C, Mary F, Nellie and Wm E, has five brothers and two sisters living, six dead—Frank and Edward R, attorneys, are of the firm of Mason Bros Des Moines, Edward being Clerk of the U. S Court, and Wm E. is practicing law in Chicago, Linn W. is in Pennsylvania, and James L is in Memphis, Tenn

MOORE, GEORGE L.; P. O Bentonsport, dealer in dry goods and general merchandise, son of Robert and Elizabeth Moore, born April 4, 1826, in Dearborn Co Ind, came with his parents to this county in the spring of 1837, and settled in Harrisburg Tp, went to California in the spring of 1850, followed mining and dealing in stock, returned in the spring of 1854, the same year, engaged in the mercantile business at Leon, Decatur Co, which he continued till 1857, when he returned to Bentonsport and engaged in his present business He owns a farm of 107 acres adjoining the town is one of the leading business men of Bentonsport Married Hannah A Brown, Aug 29, 1854, of Bentonsport, has seven children living—Georgia A., Seth R, Mary L, Rachel E, Sarah C, Robert P and James B, lost three—Johnson, Benjamin and James A Georgia A was married to O S Hurd, Sept 13, 1877, is living at Atchison, Kan Father died in 1861, and mother in 1859 Member of Presbyterian Church

MORRIS, SAMUEL M., farmer, Sec 24, P O Bentonsport, owns 352 acres of land, valued at $25 per acre; son of Henry and Jane Morris, born Jan 14, 1827, in Harlan Co, Ky, came with parents to this county in June, 1838, settled in Cedar Tp, where his father died Feb 18, 1871, and mother the 24th of same month Mr Morris was married to Charlotte A. Robbins May 21, 1854, she was born April 7, 18.. in Ch....... p.. C N Y Have .. l.. .. .... Edmund, John ... L.. .. .... William W, lost .. (.. .. R p dbl.. ..

MONTGOMERY, JOS., proprietor of Bentonsport Mills, Bentonsport, born Nov 14, 1826, in Washington, Co, Penn, came with parents to this county in 1842, settled in Washington Tp, commenced to learn the trade of miller in Pennsylvania, worked in the mill at Bentonsport several years prior to 1852, then went to California, was there several years engaged in farming, brickmaking, house-building and teaming, returned in 1859, and went to work in the mill again, of which he is now half-owner with Joseph Scott, having recently purchased it Married Mary A Miles Jan 4, 1849, she was born in Kentucky in 1832, have one son—John C, born Feb 19, 1851 Members of Presbyterian Church, Republican

Montgomery & Scott, millers, Bentonsport

Morrill, B F, retired far, Bentonsport

NEWLON, C E, carp, Bentonsport

NELSON, JOHN W., far, S 4, P O Mt Zion owns 500 acres of land, valued at $35 per acre, son of William and Elizabeth Nelson, born Sept 25, 1832, in Wayne Co, Ohio, parents moved into Richland Co, in 1836, to this county in the fall of 1845, his mother died Oct 17, 1857, and father Sept 24, 1860; Mr Nelson has two brothers and one sister living, five have died He was married to Eliza Boner, of this county, Jan 12, 1860, she was born Nov 27, 1838, in Sangamon Co, Ill, have six children living—Minnie, Marietta Ethel N, Nellie M, Edna M and John E Republican

Nichols, Seba, P O Pierceville

PARKER, MARLOW, coal-digger, Bentonsport

Patten, B M, far, P O Bentonsport

Payne, B, far, S 10, P O Mt Zion

Pender, Henry, far, P O Mt Zion

Perkins, A, far, S 1, P O Mt Zion

QUAINTANCE, WM, plasterer Bentonsport

RALSTON, J H, physician, Bentonsport

Rehkopf, A C, cabinet-maker Bentonsport

Row, O, far, S 12, P O Pierceville

SANFORD, I N O, Bentonsport

Schriever, L

SCOTT, JOS. W., proprietor, with Joseph Montgomery, of Bentonsport Mills, Bentonsport, born Oct 1, 1840, in Columbiana Co, Ohio, came with his parents to Lee Co, Iowa, in 1846, in 1847, to this county, settled in Vernon and commenced learning the trade of miller, in 1850, in the Vernon Mills Enlisted, Aug 7, 1861, in Co A, of the Black Hawk Cavalry, was transferred to 7th Mo Cav, was in the battles of Lone Jack, Prairie Grove, Van Buren, Duvall's Bluffs, Little Rock, Pine Bluffs and Saline, discharged in October, 1864 Returned, and again engaged in the milling business in 1869, went to Knoxville, Marion Co, Iowa, in 1877, to Creston, Union Co, returning to Vernon in 1878, and, in September, purchased, with his partner, the Bentonsport Mills Married Amelia G Barnett Feb 28, 1865, she was born Sept 14, 1846, in Ohio, have four children living—Cynthie C, Grant C, Cora and Roy, lost one—Amos S H Republican

Shepherd, F O, far, Sec 22, P O Bentonsport

Shepherd, Henry T, far, Sec 27, P O Bentonsport

Shepherd, N, far, Sec 27, P O Bentonsport

SMART, JAMES, far, Sec 2, P O Utica, owns 174 acres of land, valued at $30 per acre, born Dec 7, 1803, at Barren Co., Ky., parents moved into Robinson Co, Tenn in 1805, to Morgan Co, Ill, in 1823, He was married there to Tabitha Carter March 17, 1825, she was born March 13, 1807, in Nelson Co, Ky Came to this county in October, 1835, made his claim at the mouth of Copperas Creek, cleared off nine acres the following spring put it in corn, the next fall sold his claim and moved on his present farm, Mr Smart is one of the oldest pioneers of Van Buren Co, having been here forty-five years, and will soon pass to that "undiscovered country from whose bourn no traveler returns" He has seven children living—Jackson Greenberry, William, Jabanon, Mary Martha and Me- . . . . . . d James . . . . Church,

Stevens A N , retired far Bentonsport
Stewart J F , farmer, Bentonsport
Stewart, R , miller Bentonsport
Strunk, H C , farmer, Bentonsport
Syfert, Benjamin far , Sec 16 P O Mt Zion
TUSSEY M L , Bentonsport

VANCE A , far S 1 P O Utica

WALSH L , lab , Bentonsport
WALKER, BENJAMIN. far , Sec 24 , P O Bentonsport , owns 320 acres of land, valued at $30 per acre , born Nov 4, 1802, in Butler Co , Ohio, served an apprenticeship at bricklaying and followed the business at Cincinnati, Ohio, about thirteen years returned

to Butler Co , in 1833 , engaged in farming till the fall of 1850, when he came to this county and settled on his present farm. Married Hester A Reese Jan 1, 1829, she was born April 9, 1808, in Virginia , died March 7, 1834, has two children—Mary A , married to Alexander S McClune Nov 25, 1857, and Frances E , married to Allen W Stevens Oct 20, 1858, the latter resides with Mr Walker. Democrat
Ward W W far , Sec 36 , P O Bentonsport
Warner, H , far., S 13 , P O Pierceville
Warner, S , far , S 13 , P O Pierceville
Weaver, Geo., far , S 36 , P O Bentonsport
Wood, C , mail-carrier, Bentonsport
Work, J far S 4 , P O Mt. Zion.

VERNON TOWNSHIP.

ALCORN, JAMES A merchant, Mt Sterling
Aldred, Stephen, far , P O Vernon
Aldridge, S G , far , P O Vernon
Algue, G W , far , P O Willits
Anderson, A , far , Sec. 12 , P O Willits
Anderson, L , far , P O Willits
BELL, ELIAS far , Sec 7 , P O Mt Sterling
Blackledge, F , far , P O Mt Sterling
Blackledge S far , Sec 10 , P O Mt Sterling
Bradford, H E , merchant and Postmaster, Mt Sterling
Bradford, L , far , P O Vernon
Brewster, H , far , Sec 20 , P O Keosauqua
Brown, Daniel, far , P O Keosauqua
Burns, J W far , Sec. 24 , P O Vernon
Butler, N , far , Sec 5 , P O Vernon
CACKLEY, W C C , far , Sec 23 , P O Vernon
Calahan, H J , merchant, Mt Sterling
Carlston, A S , far , P O Mt Sterling
Cavitt, J H far , Sec 9 , P O Mt Sterling
Clark, J , physician, Mt Sterling
Cox, A , far , Sec 17 , P O Keosauqua
COX, RANDOLPH - 17 P O uqua land, v

7, 1821, in Jefferson Co , Ind In 1827 parents moved to Sangamon Co , Ill , he went into Menard Co in 1838 , while there learned the trade of stone and brick mason Enlisted during the Mexican war in Co F, 4th Illinois Volunteers, in May, 1846 , was under Brigadier Gen Shields, in Taylor's army , while below Matamoras was taken sick, finally discharged and returned home via New Orleans and the Mississippi River June, 1847, came to this county Married Sarah McIntosh April 22, 1849 , she was born Feb 10, 1826, in Tazewell Co W Va , her parents came to this county in 1838 , have nine children —Juliette, Alonzo, Harvey R , Agnes, Clarinda, Florence, Eudora, Carrie and Alice Mr Cox settled on his present frame in 1849 Member M E Church, Independent
Cresswell, R., Jr , far Sec 25 , P O Vernon
Currier, Sargent, far , P O Vernon
DAVIS, EXTINE, far , Sec. 22 , P O Vernon
DeHart, G , far , S 29 , P O Mt Sterling.
ENGLEBRIGHT, A , far , Sec 36 ;
ELLIS, GEORGE, farmer, Sec. 22 P O Vernon son of Jeremiah

and Rebecca (Miller) Ellis, born March 26 1825, in Sullivan Co., N Y, his father and mother were born in New York, his mother died in this county Oct 15, 1853, his father is living in Keosauqua, with a widowed daughter, Eleanor Anderson Mr Ellis' parents moved into Tompkins Co., N Y., in 1827, to Hamilton Co Ohio, in the fall of 1837, to this county in the spring of 1839, settled near Keosauqua, where his early days were spent, he moved on the farm now owned by D Rockafellow, in 1855, he sold that and came on to his present farm in 1869 Was married to Ruth A. Gale, March 31, 1850, a daughter of John W and Rebecca G (McCrary) Gale, she was born Jan 18, 1830, in Gibson Co, Ind, have no family, his wife's father died Feb 1, 1854, aged 48 years, his mother died April 12, 1869, aged 62 years Her grandfather, John McCrary, was an able and zealous minister of the Christian Church, died at the residence of his son, Maj J C McCrary, Sept 19, 1857, at the age of 86, and his wife, Ruth, died Dec 12, 1859, at the same place, aged 84 years Mr Ellis owns a farm of 241 acres, valued at $35 per acre   Republican

Evans, A , far ; P O. Vernon

FITZGERALD, J., far., Sec. 26, P O Vernon

FOWLER, JAMES A., farmer and Township Assessor Sec. 9, P O Mt Sterling, son of Henry and Mary Fowler, born June 14, 1842, in Indiana, his parents came to this county in the spring of 1843, and settled in Bentonsport, his father was drowned in the Des Moines River the same spring, his mother died in February, 1855, from that time till 1862, he lived with the Meek Brothers, of Bonaparte. In August, 1862, he enlisted in Co D, of the 30th Iowa V I, was at the siege of Vicksburg, Resaca, Dallas, Lookout Mountain, Mission Ridge, Atlanta, Macon, Ga , and with Sherman in his march to the sea, mustered out in June, 1865 Married Amanda Perkins, of this county, Feb 12, 1867 ; she was born in this county in 1848, have three children—William H , Anna M and an infant daughter

Came on to his present farm of 105 acres, in 1874   Republican

Fowler, L far . S 29 , P O Mt Sterling

GASTON, J W , far , Sec 5, P O Sterling

GWINNUP, JOHN, farmer, P O Mt Sterling, owns about 700 acres of land adjoining Mt Sterling , the eastern addition to the town was laid out by him, born Feb 13, 1823, in Clermont Co , Ohio, came to Iowa in 1849, purchased part of his present farm and returned to Ohio Was married to Isabel Jones Feb 13, 1850, she was born March 28, 1829, in the spring of 1850, moved to his present farm, since which time farming and stock-raising have been his business , has seven children — Martha J , Francis M., Alice C , Mary E , Juliette E., John L. and Temperance B   Democrat

HALES, JOHN, far , Sec 29 , P O Vernon

Hales, Thomas, Sr , far , Sec 21 , P O Mt Sterling

Hanna, S., far , P. O. Mt. Sterling

Hardin, Geo L , far., P O Mt. Sterling.

Harvey, Norman B , far , Sec 6 , P O Mt Sterling

Heminger, Valentine, far . S 17 , P O Keosauqua

Hunter, Wm , far , P O Vernon

Huston, John R , far , Sec 6 ; P O Mt Sterling

JOHNSON, JOHN F , far , S. 12 P. O Mt Sterling

LANAM, JACOB, farmer, P O Vernon

Lanam Joseph farmer , P O Vernon

Lineweaver, Geo P , far , Sec 26 , P O Vernon

Lineweaver, John, Sr , far , Sec. 22 , P. O Vernon

Lippincott, Wm P , far , Sec 27 ; P O. Vernon

Long, Henry, far , Sec. 34 , P. O Willits

Long, Titus, far , P O Mt Sterling

Lundberg Frederick, far , P O Willits

McELROY, A J , farmer, P O Mt Sterling

McINTOSH, THOS. B., far , S. 17, P O Keosauqua, owns 280 acres of land, valued at $25 per acre , son of [illegible] born Sept 12 1847 [illegible] Co., W Va came about [illegible] this county in the fall of 1839, and settled on the farm part of which he now owns, his father died Nov 26 1863, mother died Sept 9 1865 Was married to Rebecca E Fitzgerald June 13, 1852, she was born May 4, 1831, in Kalamazoo Co, Mich; her parents came to this county in July, 1837, and settled near Keosauqua, have eight children—James M, George S, John W, Mary L, Thomas A, Jane E, Catharine I. and Rosa M Members of the M E Church, Independent

McManaman, Isaiah W far, P O Wilhts

Madden, Thomas, far., P O Mt Sterling

Matlock, David, far, Sec 23, P O. Bonaparte

Miller, David, far, P O Mt Sterling

Miller, Samuel, retired farmer, P O Mt Sterling

Muir, W P L, far, P O Vernon

NELSON, JOHN E, far, Sec 12, P O Wilhts

OWING, J W, farmer, P O Wilhts

PETTIT, GILES, far, S 9, P O Mt Sterling

PETERSON, RALPH, far, S 19, Keosauqua, owns 250 acres of land, valued at $30 per acre, born Sept 29, 1808, in Adams Co, Ohio Married there to Mary Grove, March 2, 1830, she was born Jan 28, 1811, moved to Fountain Co, Ind, in the fall of 1834 and from there to this county in October, 1839 Mr Peterson has served his Township as Trustee, and his county as Supervisor, for the years 1866 and 1867 Have eight children living—John G, Jacob R, William H, Mary E, Martha E, Ralph B George A and Edwin O, lost three—Thomas R, Matilda A and Henry C Members of the Christian Church, Republican His son Edwin was born June 25, 1856, is running the home farm, was married to Flora J Walker, daughter of Wesley Walker, of Pleasant Hill, Oct 10, 1877, she was born Dec 1, 1856, in this county, have one daughter—Mary E

REITH, JOHN, far, Sec 32 P O M

Rogers, ...

Ross, Abraham, far, Sec 10, P O Mt Sterling

SAMPLE, JEREMIAH, far., Sec 6, P O Mt Sterling

Skriver, William, far, Sec 5, P O Mt Sterling

Simmons, D, far, Sec 26, P O Vernon

Simmons, J, far, S 26, P. O Vernon

Simmons, M, far, S 36, P O Vernon

Simmons, R., far., S 32; P O Vernon

Simmons, T, far, P O Vernon

Snare, G, far, S 31, P O Mt Sterling

Snare, Robert, far, P O Mt Sterling

Snare, Wm M far, P O Mt Sterling

Spencer, John, far, P O Vernon

Stewart, S M, merchant, Mt Sterling

Stone, Crawford, laborer, Mt Sterling

Story, J, far, Sec 25, P O Vernon

Swanson, G, far, Sec 12, P O Wilhts

Swanson, G E, far, S 12, P O Wilhts

Sutton, S S, far, S 8, P O Mt Sterling

TAYLOR, FREDERICK, farmer and physician, S 19, P O Keosauqua

Thatcher, A H, blacksmith, Mt. Sterling

THATCHER, I. B., dealer in grain, lumber, etc, Mt Sterling, son of Mark C and Hannah P Thatcher, born Nov 2, 1836, in Clinton Co, Ohio, came with his parents to this county in the spring of 1839, settled in this township Enlisted in Co E, of the 15th Iowa Inf Oct 5, 1861, in the battle of Pittsburg Landing was wounded in the right arm, was also in battles of Iuka and Corinth, Miss, at the latter place, was wounded in the right hand, taken to the St Louis Hospital, came home was discharged for disability in March, 1863, in the fall of 1864 assisted in recruiting Co K, of the 45th Iowa Inf, was elected Captain of the company, was out about four months, having enlisted in the 100-days service Married Mary W S Morse March 12, 1868, she was born April 17, 1844, in Essex Co, Mass, have three children—Charlie E, Frank H and Harry M Followed farming after the war, till the railroad was built through Mt Sterling, since which time, he has been engaged in his present business, is also proprietor of the grain ... own Republican

Thatcher, M ... P O Mt Sterling

Thompson Hiram, far , Sec 25 ; P O Bonaparte

Thompson, Otis, farmer, Sec 25 , P O Bonaparte

VANAUKEN, M P , far., Sec 3 , P O Mt Sterling

WALTER, JAMES F , far . P O Willits

Ward, Alfred, far , P O Vernon

Ward, Calvin, far , P O Vernon

Warren Christopher, far., Sec 30 , P O Mt Sterling

WARREN, JOSEPH, retired farmer, Sec 30 , P. O Keosauqua , is of English descent , was born July 12, 1814, in the county of Wexford, Ireland , came to this county in the spring of 1854 served the county as one of the Board of Supervisors, in 1863–64, and his township as Justice of the Peace, one term, and at present makes a specialty of administering upon estates, etc. He was married to Ann Pierce Oct 17, 1840, in Ireland , she was born May 8, 1817 , have four children living—Christopher, Ellen, Sarah and Jane , lost three, Susan and Maggie dying on the way from Ireland here, the first on the ocean, and the second in St Louis, Mo , and Maggie No 2, since , his youngest daughter, Jane, was married to a distant relative of the name of Samuel Warren, Sept 12, 1876, he was born July 31, 1840, in the same county, Ireland and came to the United States in 1848, stopped at Sandusky, Ohio till 1854, and then went to Dunleith, Ill , and from there to Kansas, in 1857, where he still has a farm Mr Joseph Warren has given the homestead farm of 310 acres, to his wife Jane, the parents living with them. Mr Warren is a member of the M E Church , Republican

Warren, S H far , Sec 30 , P O Mt Sterling

White, David, far , P O Mt Sterling

WILLITS, ALBERT S.. Postmaster of Willits P O , and farmer , brother of E W Willits born Dec 11, 1840, in Wayne Co , Ind , came with his parents to this county in fall of 1842 Married Jane Beck Dec 19, 1861, she was born ... ... Perry Co, ... this county ... ...

on to his present farm in the spring of 1863 , have four children—John B , Robert E , George L and Sarah M , lost two, Mary S and an infant Democrat

WILLITS, E. W., farmer, Sec 1 , P O Willits, son of Robert and Sarah (Beard) Willits, born Oct 17, 1838, in Wayne Co , Ind , his father was a native of Pennsylvania, his mother of South Carolina, his parents came to this county in the fall of 1842 , and settled on Sec 28, of this township, where his father died Sept 27, 1869 He purchased his present farm of 280 acres, in 1862, since which time the B & S W R R , running through it, has made Willits' Station He was married to Nancy Craig, of this county, Sept 13 1870 , she was born Aug 8, 1850, in Clarion Co , Penn , have one daughter—Della B Democrat

WILLITS, I. N., far , S 28 P O Vernon , son of Robert and Sarah Willits (nee Beard), born Oct 26, 1836, in Wayne Co , Ind , parents came to this county in 1842, and settled upon the farm on which he now lives in April, 1843 He was married to Nancy Beck Nov 27, 1856, she was born Jan 8, 1838, in Perry Co , Ohio, have seven children living—Frank L , Hiram S , Austin J , James, George B , Charley L and Ella, lost one—Norine In 1864, Mr Willits moved to Story Co , Nevada , fall of 1865, went to Mendocino Co , Cal , his father died Sept 27, 1869, and at the solicitation of his mother, he returned to the old homestead in the fall of 1872

Wilson, Christ, far , P O Mt Sterling

Wilson, John, far , P O Mt Sterling

Wolf, Alfred, far. , P O Vernon

Wolf, David M , far , Sec 27 , P O Mt Sterling

Wolf, Jacob, far , S 21 , P O Vernon

Wolf, James M , far , Sec 34 , P O Mt Sterling

Wollam, Henry, far , Sec 9 , P O Mt Sterling

Wollam, John G , far , Sec 4 , P O Mt Sterling

Wollam, John, far , Sec 11 , P O Mt Sterling

W... ... ... Bonaparte

LICK CREEK TOWNSHIP.

ARBAUGH. J , far , Sec 19 , P O Doud's Station

Arbaugh, A far Sec 19 , P O Douds Station

Anson, H , Sr , far., Sec. 3 , P O Kilbourn

Arbaugh J far . Sec 7 , P O Doud s Station

Anderson, L , far , S 34 , P O. Kilbourn

BALDWIN J , far , Sec 3 , P O Birmingham

Barthelow, J M , far , Sec 5 , P O Doud's Station

Beale. J W , far Sec 6 P O Doud s Station

Beale P , far., S 6 , P O. Doud's Station

BENNETT. JOHN, farmer, Sec 10 , P O Birmingham , born in Bradford Co. Penn , Jan. 21, 1798 , in 1836, he moved to Franklin Co , Ohio, a year after to Van Buren Co. which has since been his home , farming has always been his occupation Married Sarah Bagley Nov 11, 1821, she was born in Bradford Co , Penn , Dec 4, 1804 , had fourteen children, thirteen now living—Harriet A , R Durinda, William J , M Orris, Celinda O , A Matilda, L Thomas, Sarah A., Esther A , Nancy A , Emily M and Eliza J (twins), and Edwin M Mrs Bennett is a member of the Baptist Church Their son, William J was born in Bradford Co , Penn , March 14, 1829 ; in the spring of 1850, he went to California and engaged in mining , returned in August. 1852 , in 1853, he moved to Davis County, and engaged in farming , in 1857, he traded his farm for goods, and entered the mercantile business with M Shively a year , dissolved partnership, and Mr Bennett continued in business one year , then traded his stock for a farm in Schuyler Co , Mo In 1861, he enlisted in Co B, Missouri State Militia, for 100 days, in 1862, he traded his farm for land in Van Buren Co., and moved on it On Nov 14, 1864, he enlisted in Co B, 13th Iowa V I , discharged July 21, 1865, was in the battle of Nashville, ... since .... riet ....

was born in Mercer Co K) , May 27, 1833, and died Aug 12, 1876 · had eight children—Thomas, Mary E , Lawrence, Spencer, James, Orlando, Minnie and George A , married Mrs. Lucy Yarnall (nee Mattox), June 28. 1877 , they have one child from this marriage, Eva M Mrs Bennett had seven children from her former marriage—Leora G , Mary O , Emma J , John F , Charles L , Eli E and Debby L He owns 210 acres of land, valued at $7 000

Birch, W , far , S 1 , P O Birmingham.

Bonnett, G W , far , S 34 , P O Kilbourn

Bott, A . far , S 32 ; P O Doud's Station

Bott, W. H., far , Sec 33 , P O Doud s Station

Boyd, S , far , S 22 , P O. Birmingham

BRYAN, WILLIAM, farmer, Sec 28 , P O Doud's Station, born June 8, 1815, in Randolph Co , Va , moved to Van Buren Co , in 1838, and settled in Lick Creek Tp , farming has always been his occupation He married Nancy Christie Sept 12, 1844 , she was born in Harrison Co , Ohio, Aug 21, 1818 , died May 2, 1873 had eight children, five living—James, Mary J , Thomas N., John L. and Milton He married Milly Price (nee Farrell) March 24, 1878 , she was born in Athens Co , Ohio, June 6, 1833 , she had four children by former marriage one living— Ettie J. Members of M E Church. He owns eighty acres of land, valued at $1,500

Buckey, C S 13 , P O Birmingham

Buckmaster, J., far , S 35 , P O Kilbourn

CARL, H G , farmer Sec 8 , P O Birmingham

Carr, A., far , S. 8 . P O Doud's Station

Carson, W G , far , S 9 , P O Birmingham

Catcott, S V . far , S 36 , P O Kilbourn

Chalfant. M , far , S 19 , P O Doud's Station

CHANNELL. GEORGE, farmer Sec 31 , P O Doud's Station, born in Harrison Co Ohio April 30, 1819 , in 1820, moved with his parents to Carroll Co, Ohio, in 1845, moved to Van Buren Co, and settled on his present farm Held several township offices, now serving second term as Trustee Married Rachel Hendricks Jan 17 1844, she was born in Carroll Co, Ohio, Sept 24, 1824, have had ten children, nine living—Edward, William, Mary M, John W, George W, Jeremiah, Samuel R, Andrew J and Margaret E He owns 164 acres of land, valued at $4,000

Christy, M. A far Sec 29, P O Doud's Station

Clinkinbeard, Mace, far, Sec 10, P.O. Birmingham

Coleman, Joseph, far Sec 10, P O Birmingham

Caude, Samuel, far, Sec 2; P O Birmingham

Cook, Moses B, far, Sec 19, P O Doud's Station

Countryman, Noah, far, Sec 18, P O Doud's Station

Countryman, M L, far, Sec 17, P O Doud's Station

Cox, J, far, Sec 27; P O Kilbourn

Crane, S, far, Sec 3; P O Kilbourn

Crumine, William, far, S. 23, P O. Doud's Station

Crum, I, far, S 3, P O Birmingham

Crum, William F, far, Sec. 9, P O Birmingham

DEAHLE, S, far, Sec. 11, P O Birmingham

ELERICK, L C, far, Sec 22, P O Birmingham

Elliott, W, far, S 1, P O Birmingham

Enlow, William H, far, Sec 1, P. O Birmingham

FERRELL, JAMES, far., Sec 8, P O Birmingham

Fleming, W J. B, far., S 30, P O. Doud's Station

GILBERT, JAMES, blacksmith, Kilbourn

Gilchrist, J, far, Sec 16, P O. Birmingham

Gire G, far S 16, P O Birmingham

Glotfelty, N far., Sec 1, P O Birmingham

Goodall, J, far, S 1, P O Birmingham

Goodall, L E, far, S 1, P O Birmingham

Graham, J, Jr., merchant, Birmingham

Graham, S., far, S 12, P O Birmingham

Green, C L, far, S 5, P O Birmingham

Greenfield, J, far., S 6. P. O Doud's Station

HANSHAW, S, far S 20, P O Doud's Station

Harness, H, far, S 11, P O Birmingham

Harness, S, far, S 2, P O Birmingham

Hendricks, E, far, S 17, P O Doud's Station

Herriman, J C, blacksmith, Kilbourn

HOOTMAN, CHRISTOPHER, farmer, Sec. 1, T. 69, R 10, P O Mt Zion, born in Harrison Co., O, Oct 19, 1813, fall of 1839, moved to Van Buren Co and settled on his present farm During the earlier settlement of the county, his mechanical genius brought him in general demand for all kinds of repairing; served his township one year as Trustee Married Elmira Dyer in September, 1839, she was born in New York March 17, 1819, died Nov 8, 1856, they had eight children, six living—Joseph M, Mary C, Jacob, David C, Eliza J and Hannah A; he married Jane Ager Sept 19, 1859, she was born Aug 11, 1825, in Montgomery Co., Ohio, have had three children, Oscar A is still living Mr Hootman is a believer in the Lutheran faith He has 165½ acres of land, valued at $4,500

Hootman, D C, far, Sec 36, P O Birmingham

Hootman, Jacob, far, Sec 29, P O Doud's Station.

Hootman, James H, far Sec 34, P O Kilbourn

Horton, John, far, Sec 36, P O Kilbourn.

Huffman, Fred B, far, Sec 13, P O Birmingham.

Hull, Daniel L, far, Sec 31, P O Doud's Station

JOHNSON, ZACHARIAH, farmer, Sec 8, P O Birmingham.

Jones, James L, far, S 7, P O Doud's Station

Jones, Jasper, far Sec 35, P O. Kilbourn

KENNEDY, AMBROSE, farmer, Sec 12 P O Birmingham

Kimmel, Henry, far Sec 25, P O Kilbourn

Knox, David, far, S 10, P O Birmingham

Knox, Nelson, far Sec 17, P O Birmingham

Kimmel, Jacob, far, S 26, P O Birmingham

LAUGHLIN WILLIAM G, farmer, Sec 30 P O Doud's Station

McCAUSLAND, HENRY, farmer, S 10; P O Birmingham

McCausland, Jonathan, far, S 11, P O Birmingham

McGraff, M, far, Sec 35, P O Kilbourn

Martin, John. far, S 8, P O Birmingham

Mathias Simon P., far., Sec. 17, P O Birmingham

Maxwell, R, far, S 34, P O Kilbourn

Mercer, J, far, S 28, P O Kilbourn

Mescher, W A, far, S 20 P O Doud's Station

Minear, George W, far, Sec 2, P O Kilbourn

Monahan, H, far, S 1, P O Kilbourn

Moore, W, far, S 14, P O Birmingham.

Morrow, A, far, S 19, P O Doud's Station

Morrow, E, farmer and carpenter, Sec. 6, P O Doud's Station.

MORROW, GEORGE B., farmer, S 32, P O Doud's Station, born in Belmont Co, Ohio Oct 15, 1817, in 1858, he moved to Van Buren Co, and settled in Village Tp, in 1876, moved to his present farm in Lick Creek Tp, farming has been his business, from 1838 to 1840 followed butchering in Wheeling, W Va Married Elizabeth Guthrie Dec 27, 1839, she was born in Harrison Co, Ohio, June 16, 1818, have had six children, one died in infancy, living—Sylvester, Samuel Thomas D, Jane, Richard and George W Mrs Morrow is a member of the Presbyterian Church He owns 603 acres of land, valued at $15,000

Moyer, T G, far, S 16, P O Doud's Station

NELSON, W. W., farmer and physician, S 13, P O Birmingham

NEDROW, GEORGE, far, S 20, P O Doud's Station, born Sept 24, 1807 in Somerset Co, Penn, in 1832 moved to Tuscarawas Co, Ohio

in 1844, to Van Buren Co, while in Pennsylvania, he followed milling, afterward farming, which has been his occupation since Married Mary Nedrow in June, 1832, she was born in Somerset Co, Penn, in March 1812, and died Oct 17, 1856, had ten children, three living—Margaret, Simon P and Sarah A. Members of the Lutheran Church He owns 120 acres of land, valued at $3,500 His son Simon P was born on their present farm Sept 5, 1848, and is now working the farm He married Rosannah J Arbaugh Sept 19, 1872, she was born in Van Buren Co, Sept 9, 1854, had two children, one living—Irvin L Members of the Lutheran Church

NEDROW, MICHAEL (deceased), born in Somerset Co, Penn, Sept 10, 1802, and died Oct 25 1875, in 1832 moved to Tuscarawas Co, Ohio, while in Pennsylvania was engaged in farming and milling, since then, in farming, alone, while in Ohio, filled the office of Justice of the Peace six years, came to Iowa in 1844 and settled in Lick Creek Tp Married Sarah Nedrow, May 13, 1827, she was born in Somerset Co, Penn, Oct 15, 1805, had nine children, seven living—Adaline, George, Michael, Sarah A., Mary, Aaron and David Members of the Lutheran Church The farm contains 200 acres, valued at $6,000

PLATT, EDWARD H, wagon maker, Kilbourn

PERRINE, SAMUEL, far, Sec 15, P O Birmingham, born in Washington Co, Penn, Nov 15, 1820, when about 2 years old, moved with his parents, to Wayne Co, Ohio, in 1845, moved to Van Buren Co, and settled in Lick Creek Tp, his present home; went to California in the spring of 1850, returned in June 1853, while there, he was mining and gardening on the Sacramento River, also kept a wood yard, has been Justice of the Peace three years, Trustee one year Married Phidelia E Shankland Sept. 25, 1845, she was born in Wayne Co, Ohio Aug 25, 1823 and died June 2 1874, had five children—Selucia A, Millard W, Samuel W, Harriet E and Emma A Married Minerva A Cole man, Oct 3, 1874, she was born in Van Buren Co Sept 29, 1838, have two children—Lilly M and John M He owns 265 acres of land, valued at $7,500

Pool, B, far, Sec 33; P O Kilbourn

Pool, E, far, S 28, P. O Doud's Station

Porter, C, far, P. O Kilbourn •

Prewitt, T, far, S 2, P.O Birmingham

RAIL, ADAM, farmer Sec 25 P O Birmingham

RAIL, JOSEPH, farmer, Sec. 24, P O Birmingham, born in Dauphin Co, Penn, Nov 12, 1817, when 5 years old, moved with his parents to Seneca Co, N Y, in 1826, moved to Yates Co, N Y, September, 1838, to Fort Madison, Iowa, the following spring, to Van Buren Co, and settled in Lick Tp, farming has been his principal occupation, worked six months in 1841 as a tanner in Keosauqua, moved to Birmingham, followed that business alone about four years Married Sarah Hootman Nov 23, 1843; she was born in Harrison Co, Ohio, Feb 10, 1824, have had twelve children, eight living— George H, Mary S, Jay, Sarah C, Margaret A, John B Adam G and Martha E Members of M E Church He has 160 acres of land, valued at $5 000

Remker, D, far, S 33, P. O Kilbourn

Remker, E, far, S 8, P O Birmingham.

Remker, Jacob, far, S 33, P O Kilbourn

Remker, J, far, S 33, P O Kilbourn

Robertson, M, far, S 4, P O. Birmingham

ROBISON, JAMES, farmer, Sec 25 P O Birmingham, born in Wayne Co, Ohio, April 5, 1818, in 1834, moved to Harrison Co Ohio; in 1839, to Van Buren Co, and settled on his present farm He served his township one year as Trustee Married Sarah A. Wilbur April 18, 1844, she was born in Campbell Co, Ky, July 21, 1825, have had eleven children, eight living— George W, Isaiah W., Lorena E, Lemira S, James T, Mary A, Sarah B and William R Members of the Presbyterian Church He has 425 acres of land valued at $8,500

Rutledge, John M far, Sec 2 P O Birmingham

SADLER, JACOB, farmer, Sec 7; P O Doud's Station

SADLER, GEORGE (deceased); born in Harrison Co, Ohio, March 2, 1828, moved to Tuscarawas Co, Ohio, in 1847, to Van Buren Co, where he engaged in farming In August, 1862, enlisted in Co D, 30th Iowa Vol Inf, died of lung fever in the hospital at Charleston, Tenn, Jan 20, 1865 Married Adaline Nedrow Jan 17, 1849, she was born in Somerset Co, Penn, April 21, 1828, they had eight children, seven living—Martin L, Francis M, Michael N, Mary A, Jacob S, Henry C and St Valentine Mrs Sadler is a member of the Lutheran Church The farm contains 125 acres, valued at $2,500

Sanford, B, far, S 21, P O Birmingham

Scott D, far, S 27, P O Kilbourn

Scott, J P, far, S 23, P O Birmingham.

SHAEFFER, GEORGE (deceased), born April 14, 1791, in Bedford Co, Penn, died May 18, 1875, in early manhood, moved to Harrison Co, Ohio, in 1845, to Van Buren Co, up to that time, his business was that of carpenter, afterward farmer Married Margaret Saulsgiver in the year 1823, she was a native of Adams Co, Penn, had ten children, nine living—Mary, Hiram Q, Henry I, John A, Sarah Jane, Jacob L, S. Peter, Elizabeth and Matilda Were members of the Lutheran Church, later in life, he joined the U P Church His son Hiram Q was born in Harrison Co, Ohio, March 21, 1826, and moved to Van Buren Co with his parents in 1845; farming has been his occupation, followed threshing about ten years Married Nancy J Johnson May 5, 1853, she was born in Westmoreland Co, Penn, March 16, 1833 Are members of the Lutheran Church. Have one child (adopted)— Stephen A Owns 263 acres of land, valued at $6,000

Short, B, far., S 3, P. O Kilbourn

Short, C R, far S 34, P O Kilbourn

Siemon, F, far, S 27 P O Birmingham

Skinner C A far, S 25, P O Birmingham

Smith, R., far., S. 15; P. O. Birmingham.

Sowvell, E., far., S. 7; P. O. Doud's Station.

Spohen, J., far., S. 7; P. O. Doud's Station.

Stagers, J., far., S. 19; P. O. Doud's Station.

Stansbury, G., far., S. 3; P. O. Birmingham.

Stansbery, R., far., S. 7; P. O. Doud's Station.

Stewart, T., far., S. 28; P. O. Birmingham.

Strong, J., merchant, Kilbourn.

TAYLOR, J., far., S. 11; P. O. Birmingham.

Taylor, S., carpenter, Kilbourn.

TOBIAS, MICHAEL B., farmer, Sec. 32; P. O. Doud's Station; born in Lebanon Co., Penn., Dec. 15, 1807; when quite young moved with his parents to Berks Co., Penn, in 1829 to Montgomery Co., Ohio; followed the cooper trade until 36 years old, the latter part of this time also engaged in farming; in 1851, moved to Van Buren Co.; farming his occupation since. Married Sarah Good Nov. 12, 1835; she was born in Montgomery Co., Ohio, Nov. 6, 1817; had two children; William V. is still living. He has 375 acres of land, valued at $12,000. His son William V. was born in Montgomery Co., Ohio, Nov. 12, 1847, and came to Van Buren Co., with his parents in 1851; when 18, he began selling lumber and machinery; continued three years, then engaged in the mercantile business about nine months; afterward purchased a saw-mill, which he has operated in connection with farming since. Married Martha E. Short Dec. 1, 1868; she was born Aug. 30, 1850, in Van Buren Co. Have three children—Charles R., Guy O. and William O.

Tobias, M. B., far., S. 32; P. O. Doud's Station.

Torrence, H., far., S. 11; P. O. Birmingham.

Tower, J. H., far., S. 6; P. O. Doud's Station.

Towne, E., station agent, Kilbourn.

Towne, O., carpenter, Kilbourn.

VAN EMAN, G., farmer and preacher, Sec. 1; P. O. Kilbourn.

WELLS, J. C., far., S. 13; P. O. Birmingham.

Wiley, Hans, far., Sec. 20; P. O. Doud's Station.

Wiley, W. J., far., Sec. 15; P. O. Birmingham.

Williams, T., far., S. 26; P. O. Kilbourn.

Woodrow, A., far., Sec. 2; P. O. Birmingham.

YAST, A., far., Sec. 5; P. O. Birmingham.

CHEQUEST TOWNSHIP.

AYLOR, JOHN M , farmer, P O Lebanon

BARKER, JAMES H., farmer, Sec 25, P O Lebanon.

Benjamin, A , far , S 8 , P O Portland

BENJAMIN, JOSEPH L., farmer, Sec 11 , P O Doud's Station ; born in Vigo Co , Ind , July 20, 1820 , when about 2 years old, moved with parents to Warren Co , Ind , in 1834, moved to Du Page Co , Ill , in 1853, to Van Buren Co , and settled on his present farm. Married Calista E. Lawson Jan. 16, 1851, she was born in Pennsylvania , died Nov 26, 1854 , they had one child, which died in infancy He married Rose A Crandel Aug 27, 1856 , she was born in Caldwell Co Mo , Oct 4, 1837 , had one child who died in infancy He owns eighty acres of land, valued at $2,000

BERGER, JASPER, farmer, Sec. 36 , P O Lebanon, born in Hunterdon Co , N J., Aug 27, 1813 , in 1833, moved to Franklin Co , Ohio , in 1853, to Van Buren Co , and settled on his present farm , in early life, he followed milling, of late years, farming Married Susan A Clickinger July 3, 1849 , she was born in Hunterdon Co , N J , April 15, 1819 , had five children , Rachel A only is living, and married to W A Winn Members of the M E Church He owns eighty acres of land, valued at $4,500

Bowen, R M., far , S. 2 , P. O Portland

Brooks, G , far , P O Troy, Davis Co

Brown, D , far , S 35 , P O Lebanon

Buckls, A J , far , S 20

CAMBRIDGE, JOHN, far , S 31 , P O Milton

Carpenter, H M , far , S. 18 , P O Troy, Davis Co

Canfield, H M , far., S 33 ; P. O. Lebanon

CLAFLIN, IRA, farmer and County Surveyor, Sec 36 , P O Lebanon, born in Addison Co , Vt , March 12, 1808, in November, 1838, moved to Van Buren Co and settled in Van Buren Tp., in 1841 to Chequest Tp farming has been his principal occupation, after coming to Iowa, in 1840, he was engaged as assistant under Judge Biggs on the Government surveys , he showed such an aptitude for the business that the Judge encouraged him to fit himself for a surveyor, which he did and was elected County Surveyor, which office he has held eighteen years, was also engaged, as principal or assistant, in Government surveys for a number of years , in 1845, he was elected County Commissioner, and held the office until 1851 , he has also held several township offices Married Hannah W Richardson March 7 1833 , she was born in Windsor Co Vt , June 8, 1814 , have had eight children , one died in infancy , another, Ira W , graduated at West Point in 1857, entered the service as Second Lieutenant in the U S Mounted Rifles, and was assigned to duty in New Mexico , in 1862 was assigned to duty under Gen McClellan, as Captain in the 6th U S Cav , and served through the war ; at Gettysburg. he was wounded through the lungs, after the war he was appointed a tutor at West Point , he served as such a short time, when, with the rank of Major, was assigned to duty in Texas, where he died in November, 1867 , the remaining children are Hannah E , Mary F , George A and Julia A (twins), Emeline and Charles He owns 160 acres of land, valued at $4,000

Clark, C. C , far , S. 3 , P. O Portland

Clayton, A , far S 27 , P O Lebanon

Clayton, Geo W , far , P O Lebanon

Covault J. A , far , P O Lebanon

Cresswell, J , far , S 7 P O Troy

DAVIS, A , far , S 24 , P O Lebanon

Davis, D , Sr , far , S 24 ; P O Lebanon

Davis, R , far , S 11 , P O Portland

Denning, W P , far , S 9 , P O Portland

Downing, L , far , P O Portland.

Downing, R , far , P O Portland

EMERICK, J , far , S 35 , P O Lebanon

Emery, W , far , S 18 , P O Lebanon

Erickson, J A , far , S 9 , P O Portland

FRIBERG, O , far , P O Portland

Ferris A H far P O Troy

FERRIS, JONATHAN, farmer, Sec 17, P O Troy born in Loudoun Co, Va, Feb. 17 1804, his mother died when he was about 6 years old, and his father died a soldier in the war of 1812, during that war, Jonathan was employed in a woolen factory, which was closed at the termination of the war throwing him out of employment, being an orphan and poor, the authorities bound him as an apprentice to a wagon-maker for over six years, until about 14 years old, he ran away at 17, and went to Franklin Co, Penn, where he apprenticed himself to another wagon-maker for two and a half years he then went to Bedford Co, Penn, and engaged in the business for himself, in 1834, moved to Richland Co, Ohio, and bought a farm, in 1848, to Van Buren Co, and settled where he now lives He was County Supervisor one term, was elected Township Trustee in October, 1878 Married Mary Langham May 14, 1826, she was born in Bedford Co, Penn, and died June 6, 1836, married Charlotte Fullmer March 11, 1838, she was born in Luzerne Co., Penn, Jan 21 1812, and died March 11, 1871, had ten children, seven living—James L, John S., Jonathan N, William A, Samuel F, Alvius H and Maria S, married Elizabeth Baker, nee Parks, Sept 1, 1874, she was born in Claiborne Co, Tenn, July 29 1825, is a member of the Baptist Church Mr Ferris is a member of the M E Church He owns 384 acres of land, valued at $7 000

Fritz, Levi, farmer, P O Doud's Station

GLANVILLE, J. B, farmer, P O. Lebanon

Goff, J M, farmer, P. O Portland

Groves, Thomas M, far, Sec 22; P O Lebanon

HANEY, FRANCIS M, farmer, P O Doud's Station

HANEY, THOMAS, far, Sec 6, P O Doud's Station, born in Belmont Co, Ohio, Nov 20, 1819, in the fall of 1839, moved to Van Buren Co, and settled in Chequest Tp, moved to his present farm in December, 1865, in the spring of 1850 went to California returned in the fall of 1851 in the spring of 1853, he returned to Cali-

fornia, and remained eleven months engaged in mining Married Elizabeth Dickerson Aug 15, 1838, she was born in Morgan Co, Ohio, Feb 13, 1821, had nine children—seven living—Francis M, Thomas W, Edward R, George B, Leroy H, John W, and Laura E Mrs. Haney is a member of the Missionary Baptist Church He owns 120 acres of land valued at $2 500

Hanshaw, W, far, S 10, P O Portland.

Harmon William H far, Sec 11, P O Portland

Hurington, G W, farmer, P O Troy.

Hartley, M, far, Sec 7, P O Troy

Hastings W S, farmer, P O Lebanon

HISSEM, ABNER, farmer, Sec 5, P O Doud's Station. born in Tyler Co, W Va, Jan 8, 1830, fall of 1850, moved to Meigs Co, Ohio, spring of 1865, to Van Buren Co, and settled on his present farm, in the years 1863 and 1864, he owned and operated a saw-mill in Meigs Co, Ohio He married Serene Sayre Feb 29, 1852, a native of Ohio. died April 9 1861, had two children—Serene J, still living, he married Caroline Walker April 27, 1862, she was born in Meigs Co, Ohio, June 29, 1832, have one child—Arthur W Mr Hissem has 240 acres of land, valued at $8,000

Hissom, T, far, Sec 5, P O Portland

Holtz, H, far, P O Portland

Hootman, D, far, S 15, P O Portland.

Hull, H, far and wagon-maker, Portland.

Humphrey, G B, merchant, Lebanon

JONES, J, farmer, Doud's Station

KENNEDY, D, far, Sec 10, P O. Portland

Knight, F, far, P O Doud's Station.

LEE, J, far, Sec 6, P O Portland.

Liming, J, far, Sec 13, P O Lebanon

MARTIN, P, far, Sec 24, P O Lebanon.

Mathias, W, far., Sec 6, P O Troy, Davis Co.

Miller, Francis, far, Sec 6, P O Troy

Moore, J., far, Sec 4, P O Lebanon

MOORE, MICHAEL, farmer and stock raiser Sec 31, P O Troy, born in Lebanon Co Penn Oct 9, 1809, in 1835 moved to Franklin Co Ohio,

1848, to Van Buren Co., and settled on his present farm; he was raised on a farm, but at the age of 17, began to learn milling, which trade he followed about twelve years; since then his occupation has been farming. Married Abigail Lisle Feb. 7. 1841, she was born in Franklin Co., Ohio. Jan. 6, 1822; had ten children, nine living—Jacob, John H., Samuel H., Mary R., Angie A., Emma, Sarah C., Ettie and Michael. Members of the Lutheran Church. He owns 560 acres of land, valued at $12,000.

Morris, Thomas, far., P. O. Portland.

Morris, Wm., far., P. O. Portland.

Mussetter, H., far., S. 23; P. O. Lebanon.

NASON, JAMES, farmer, Sec. 6; P. O. Portland.

Nason, P. S., far.; P. O. Doud's Station.

Nelson, John, far.; P. O. Doud's Station.

Nicklin, F. A., far.; P. O. Pitt-burg.

PALMER, DAVID M., farmer; P. O. Portland.

Paris, M. S., far., S. 12; P. O. Portland.

Paxton, Thomas, far., S. 30; P. O. Troy.

Pickens, H. C., far., S. 11; P. O. Portland.

Plowman, F., far.; P. O. Portland.

Plowman, C. J. & G. H., fars., Sec. 4; P. O. Portland.

Poling, M., far., S. 11; P. O. Portland.

Pollock, J., far., Sec. 17; P. O. Troy.

Pugh, A. H., far., S. 22; P. O. Lebanon.

RAMBO, G. W., far., Sec. 12; P. O. Portland.

Roush, J., far., Sec. 6; P. O. Portland.

Roush, J. A., far., S. 23; P. O. Lebanon.

SAMPLE, E. B., far., Sec. 25; P. O. Lebanon.

Seitz, G., Sr., far., S. 3; P. O. Portland.

Shafer, D., far.; P. O. Portland.

Silvens, A., far.; P. O. Troy.

Slater, J. M., far., S. 24; P. O. Lebanon.

Smith, S. T., far., Sec. 13; P. O. Portland.

Stewart, J., far.; P. O. Lebanon.

Stott, J., far., Sec. 8; P. O. Lebanon.

Stott, J. A., far., Sec. 8; P. O. Lebanon.

Stover, N, far.; P. O. Hickory.

TEN EYCK, G. K., farmer, Sec. 36; P. O. Lebanon.

Thomas, B., far., P. O. Pittsburg.

Thompson, J., far.; P. O. Lebanon.

VANFLEET, A., far., Sec. 35; P. O. Lebanon.

VANFLEET, ABRAHAM, farmer and stock-raiser, Sec. 35; P. O. Lebanon; born in Hunterdon Co., N. J., March 4, 1817; in 1836, moved to Franklin Co., Ohio; in 1842, to Iowa, and settled on his present farm. Married Mattie Berger October, 1835; she was born in Hunterdon Co., N. J., Aug. 1, 1811, and died Sept. 16, 1870; had six children; one died in infancy; another, William, was a member of Co. F., 2d Iowa V. I., and died of typhoid fever in the hospital at Mound City, Ill. Feb. 24, 1862; the living are Getty M., Aaron, Mary, Julia and Thomas. He married Alvira Van Treese June 15, 1871. She was born in Franklin Co., Ind., Dec. 22, 1840; had four children; three living—George, Jerry and Clarence. He owns 180 acres of land, valued at $6,000.

Vernon, J. G., far., S. 24; P. O. Lebanon.

Vinson, C., far.; P. O. Lebanon.

Vinson, M., far., S. 36; P. O. Lebanon.

WEBSTER, S. B., far.; P. O. Troy.

Webster, W. J., far.; P. O. Lebanon.

Weyer, J. A., far., S. 31; P. O. Troy.

Wilson, E., far., Sec. 33; P. O. Lebanon.

Wilson, P., far., Sec. 34; P. O. Lebanon.

Wilson, V., far., Sec. 36; P. O. Lebanon.

Winey, G., far.; P. O. Oak Point.

HENRY TOWNSHIP.

ANSON, THOMAS, farmer, Sec 20, P O Keosauqua son of Henry and Elizabeth Anson (nee Pierly), born July 24, 1826, in Pike Co, Mo, his father, in company with a Mr Linzey, came to this county in the fall of 1835, prospecting, and the following spring his father came and located the land upon which Thomas now lives, and in December, 1836, moved his family on it, where he lived till he died, April 5, 1850, his wife having died April 10, 1847 Thomas went to California in the summer of 1850, with an ox-team, he followed mining mostly till the spring of 1853 he came home via New York City, he has four brothers and three sisters living—Henry, George, William, Flerious, Kesiah, Catherine and Eliza, the last is keeping house for him, Peter, Francis, John and Christina have died He owns 297 acres of land, individually, and one-half interest with his brother William in 880 acres Republican

ANSON, WILLIAM, farmer, Sec 8, P O Keosauqua, son of Henry and Elizabeth Anson (nee Pierly), was born Sept 8, 1828, in Pike Co, Mo., parents came to this county in the spring of 1836, his father made his claim on the side of the Des Moines River below Keosauqua, built a cabin and put in some corn, and returned and brought his family in December following; father died April 5, 1850, aged 77 years, and mother died April 10, 1847, aged 63 years Mr Anson was married to Charlotte Martin, of this county, June 15, 1862, she was born in this county April 25, 1840, have five children—Isabel, Abner O, Iowa, Curtis and Fred, lost one —Grant. He owns one half interest with his brother Thomas, in 880 acres of land, valued at $35 per acre Republican

BATCHELOR, GEORGE, farmer, S. 23, P O Vernon

BAILEY, GIDEON S., M. D., farmer, Sec 1, P O Vernon, own 320 acres of land adjoining the village of Vernon, was born June 5, 1809, near Louisville, Ky, parents moved to

Lawrence Co, Ind, he read medicine while there one and a half years, went to Shelby Co in 1832, finished reading medicine there, and went to Charleston, Coles Co, Ill, in 1834, and began the practice of medicine, which he continued till the summer of 1837, when he came to this county, and took up the farm upon which he is still living, practiced medicine about two years, he was elected to the Legislature in 1839, and again in 1841, and, in 1843, as member of the Council same as Senator now, he was appointed United States Marshal by President Polk, which position he held four years, was elected as one of the delegates to the first Constitutional Convention, and, in 1858, was elected as State Senator also, for the successive term Married Julia Jones, whose maiden name was Manwaring, she was born in Connecticut in 1797, and died Feb 16, 1865, was again married to Anna M. Sprecht, whose maiden name was Schneck, she was born Nov. 6, 1834, had two children by first wife— Augustus C and Julia, the daughter being dead, by second wife, one son— Gideon Democrat

Beashor, D, far, S 10, P O Vernon
Bennett, S M, far; P O Vernon
Blount, E C, woolen manfr, Vernon
Booth, E C, merchant, Vernon
Boyer, Isaac, farmer, P O Vernon
BOYER, JACOB, farmer, Sec. 3, P O. Vernon, owns 160 acres of land, valued at $40 per acre, born Feb 26, 1817, in Adams Co, Penn, went to Indianapolis, Ind, in 1837 where he remained till the Spring of 1842; then went in company with Robert Green and Jacob Landis with a load of liquors on a flatboat to New Orleans, and from there he came up the Mississippi River and the Des Moines to Farmington, in this county Was married there to Elvira Davidson Dec. 13, 1844, she was born Dec 9, 1826, in Lawrence Co, Ohio, her parents came to Bentonsport, in this county, in 1838, and subsequently moved to Farmington where her father died in the spring of 1840 Mr Boyer came on his present farm in 1854; have

four children living—Isabel, Clara, Albert and Charles, lost one—Joseph, who died of disease contracted while in the army, he was in Co G, 3d I V C

Bradford, Albert, merchant, Vernon

Bradford, Anthony, far , P O Vernon

CHRISTIANS, JOHN, brickmaker, Vernon

Coffman, D S , teamster Vernon

DANIELS BERNARD laborer, Vernon

Davis, Charles, far , S 4, P O Vernon

Davis, D , teamster, Vernon

DAVIS, ENOCH, farmer, Sec 2, P O Vernon, is a son of Isaac and Sarah (Baker) Davis, they are both natives of Kentucky, his father was born April 9, 1808 and his mother in February, 1814, and he was born in Madison Co, Ky, Feb 28, 1835, parents emigrated to this county in the fall of 1836 Mr Davis is not married, owns 174 acres of land adjoining his father's on the east, he has five brothers and three sisters living—Isaac, David, Henry, Joshua, Perry and Martha J, Margaret A and Mary E , lost two brothers—Peter and William Democrat

Davis, Isaac, Sr , far , S 3 , P O Vernon

Davis, P , far , S 3, P O Vernon

DE HART, EDWARD, farmer, Sec 34, P O Vernon owns eighty-five acres where he lives, and 160 acres in Vernon Tp , valued at $30 per acre, son of Eli and Hannah De Hart, was born Feb 14, 1835, in Canada West in September, 1838, his parents left there and came via the Ohio, Mississippi & Des Moines River to Bentonsport, in this county, where they arrived in April, 1839, and, in 1840, his parents moved to Hancock Co, Ill, where they remained till 1844, then returned to this county, where they still live, this county has been Mr De Hart's home, although for the benefit of his health, he took a trip to California in the fall of 1873, and returned the following spring Was married to Martha J Hanan Feb 13, 1862, she was born in this county Aug 5, 1844, have five children—Harvey L, Marion H Mary A John John E and __ _ __

De Hart, E , far _ _ P O Vernon

De Hart, Wm , _ _ _ smith _ Vernon

Dickson, Grimsley & Co , pottery, Vernon.

DICKSON, R. M., proprietor Vernon Pottery, Vernon, born March 13, 1826, in York Co , Penn , parents moved to Muskingum Co , Ohio, in 1832, where they both died a few years after , he came to Scott Co , Ill , in 1851, and was married there to Melinda J Hanback April 4, 1852, the next day started for Iowa , arrived at Vernon the 13th of April, bought an old pottery building, and commenced business the 17th, since which time he has continued the business to the present, was burned out in 1869, after which he associated himself with J C Grimsley, who is a present partner Have four children living—Mary A , Charles T., Anna V. and Blanche lost three. Robert B. was killed in the pottery in 1863, and William C died the same year John H was killed on the U P R R , near Wolcott's Station, in 1871 Mr Dickson is an Elder in the Presbyterian Church

EHRMAN, H , laborer, Vernon

Ervin, L, far , P O Vernon.

Ervin, J H laborer, Vernon

Evans, L J , attorney, Vernon

GASTON, G W , far , S 15 , P O Vernon

Gaston, W , far , S 15 , P O Vernon

Glasscock, C , laborer, Vernon

Grages, H B , far , S 8 , P O Vernon

Grimsley, J C potter, Vernon

HALLETT, A M , far , S 9 , P O Vernon

HARDY, ALMEDA; P O Vernon, she was born Dec 27, 1818, in New York her maiden name was Olney, her parents came to this county in 1838 She was married to Mr Dudley Hardy March 21, 1839, in this county, he was born Oct 5, 1803, in New Hampshire, and came to this county in 1837, and served his county as a member of the Legislature in its early days, came on to his present homestead in 1852 Mr Hardy is at present quite sick, and unable to transact business In the home farm there are 362 acres and 171 acres elsewhere. H_ _ _ _ _ _ _ _ _ _ s A , Charlotte H W _ _ _ D Nat in O, Mary F Charles M Harriet F James

F, Ettie and Stephen A D, lost one, Sarah A William D served in Co C, of the 17th Iowa V I, about three years Mr Dudley Hardy died Sept. 30, 1878

Henry, T P, far, P O Vernon

Henry, Volney, far, S 10, P O Veron

Hornbaker, M, far, S 24, P O Bonaparte

Hornbaker, R R, far, S 24, P O Bonaparte

LEWIS, GEORGE, laborer, Vernon

Lewis, John C, stone-mason, Vernon

Lewis, R M, laborer, Vernon

LIPPINCOTT, A. G., farmer and stock raiser, S 32, P O Vernon, owns 1 220 acres of land in this county, and 80 acres in Davis Co, son of Allen and Sarah Lippincott; was born March 19, 1833, in Richland Co., Ohio, his father was a native of New Jersey, and his mother, of England, they came to this county in September, 1839, and settled on the farm now occupied by A G, his father died March 4, 1864, his mother, Oct 9, 1873 He was married to Sarah A Davis Jan 29, 1857, she was born May 27, 1836, in Kentucky, her parents came to this county in 1836, have two children—May and Sarah Democrat

McCRARY, JAMES, Sr, wheelwright, Vernon

McCRARY, J. C., far, S 5, P O Keosauqua, owns 160 acres of land valued at $40 per acre, was born June 7, 1817, in Vanderburgh Co, Ind, moved to McDonough Co, Ill, in the fall of 1835, in January, 1837, came to this county and made a claim of the land he still owns, the country was then a wild waste inhabited principally by the red men of the forest and wild game On the 15th of August 1839, he was married to Kenen Leach, of this county, she was born Dec 15, 1820, in West Virginia, have five children living—Margaret A, Abner N, Amanda, Oscar and Oran, lost one—John L At his country's call, Mr McCrary enlisted in Co G, of the 3d Iowa Cav, in the summer of 1861, he recruited for the company was elect[...] Lieutenant [...] Lambert Kirk[...] M[...] Ca[...]e[...]all d

he was then promoted as Captain, and, in June, 1864, was promoted as Major, but did not assume the duties of Major till the last of July, participated in the battle of Tupelo, Miss, and Little Rock, Ark, the post was surrendered to his regiment, which was in command of Lieut Col Duffield, was mustered out Jan 28, 1865, for disability The following fall, he was elected Sheriff of the county, and re-elected in the fall of of 1867 Republican, member of the Christian Church

Mallett, N, druggist and Postmaster, Vernon

Marriott, I, far, S 2, P O Vernon

Marriott, Wm, far, S 2, P O Vernon

Meredith, G W, farmer and stock dealer, Sec 15, P O Vernon

Meredith, J, far, S 13, P O Vernon

Mohler, Levi, far, P O Vernon

NEAL, ABEL, farmer, Sec 13, P O. Vernon.

PACE, E H, miller, Vernon

Pexley, W B, merchant, Vernon

Phillips, A, far, S 7, P O Keosauqua

RIGSBY, BENJAMIN, farmer, P O Vernon

Rinebarger, H, far, S 9, P O Vernon

Rinebarger, W, far, S 6, P O Vernon

ROBB, THOMAS, farmer, P O Vernon, owns 160 acres of land, valued at $45 per acre, son of Harvey and Rachel (Christie) Robb, was born Jan 16, 1849, in this county, parents came from Jefferson Co, Ind, to this county in January, 1838, and are now living in Bonaparte Thomas Robb was married to Amanda Brewster March 31, 1870, she was born in this county Sept 25, 1849, have two children—Mary B and Bertha J Democrat.

Robinson A, far, S 10, P O Vernon

Robinson, H. J., manufacturer, Vernon

RABB, SAMUEL, farmer, Sec 14, P O Vernon, owns 405 acres of land, valued at $40 per acre, born June 7, 1818, in Warren Co, Ohio; parents moved to Fountain Co, Ind., in the fall of 1828, and came to this county in 1839, and settled near Bonaparte Married to Melinda Willetts Oct. 1, 1846, in this county, she was born Sept 20, 1826 in Wayne Co, Ind, came on to his present farm in 1847, have one son living—Monroe, lost two—Allison and Kerry. His father, Joseph Rabb, was born in Fayette Co, Penn, and mother in New Jersey, she died in September, 1848, and father in June, 1865

SARGENT, A, far, S 14, P O Vernon

Sargent, L, far, Sec 14, P O Vernon

Shepherd, J W, teamster, Vernon

Shuster, I, laborer, Vernon

Stadler, M, laborer, Vernon

STEPHENS, GEO. P., far., Sec 33, P. O. Vernon, son of Nathaniel Stephens, of Pennsylvania, was born Nov 4, 1830, in Fayette Co, Penn, parents moved into Allegheny Co in 1831, from there he came to Iowa in 1854 and stopped in Henry Co till 1856, then came to Cedar Tp of this county, where he remained till the fall of 1873, when he came into Henry Tp, where he now lives, he enlisted at his country's call in Co F, of 14th I V I. in November, 1861, was at the battles of Fort Donelson, Shiloh and Corinth,

etc, was mustered in out fall of 1865 He was married to Elizabeth Newbold, of Pennsylvania, March 30, 1853; she died Sept 10, 1854, was again married, to Susan Salmons, July 1, 1855, she died March 6, 1875, was again married, to Margaret A Cupp, Dec 20, 1875, she was born March 5, 1850, in Ohio, have eight children by second wife living— Nathaniel F, Eliza M, Margaret A, Emma G, Mary E, Flora A, John W and Ida M, by third wife two—Katie and Clyde B. Mr Stephens has charge of a farm of 286 acres, valued at $30 per acre, the title of which is in his father's name Republican

Stephenson, J Y, far, S 3, P O Vernon

WALTERS, RAWLEY, far, S 11, P O Vernon

Waterman, H, carpenter, Vernon

Wilkinson, H, attorney and Justice of the Peace, Vernon

Wright, C., far., P O Vernon

YEAGER, AMOS, farmer and minister, S 12, P O Vernon

DES MOINES TOWNSHIP.

ALLEN, A J, far, Sec 23, P O Keosauqua

Arnold, B H, far, S 4, P O Pittsburg

BAIRD, A J, far, P O. Cantril

Baird, B P, far, P O Cantril

Beatty, H, far, S 26, P O Keosauqua

Beard, J, far, Sec 28, P O Cantril

Beatty, W, far, Sec 26; P O Mt Sterling

Beer, T. J, far. P O Keosauqua

Bink, D, far, P O Lebanon

Blackledge, E C, far, Sec 10, P O Mt Sterling

Blackledge, E, far, Sec 35, P O Mt Sterling

Blackledge, H, far, Sec 35, P O Mt Sterling

Boal, J, far, P O. Mt Sterling

Boyd, J J, far, S 29, P O. Cantril

Boyd, W H, far, P O Home

Brodrick, D. S., physician, P O Cantril

Burns, R, far, S 23, P O Keosauqua

CAMPBELL, JOSEPH, far, S, P O L

Carnes, A, far, S 10, P O Mt Sterling

Channel, W J, far, S 8, P O Upton

CLARK, JAMES, far, S 7, P O Keosauqua, owns 196 acres of land, valued at about $25 per acre, born in Greene Co, Ohio, Jan 27, 1834, left that State with his parents in August, 1840, and came to this State and county the same year His wife, Eudora Wright, was born in Harrisburg Tp, in this county, Dec 2, 1841, they were married Aug 9, 1866, have four children—Samuel M, Sofa, John W and Elizabeth B, all living Republican, Methodist

COWEN, A. H., far, S 5, P O Lebanon, owns 75 acres, valued at about $35 per acre, born in Philadelphia June 12, 1810, and came to this county in 1853, he was on the first train that went through on the Baltimore & Ohio Railroad from Baltimore to Fredericktown His wife, Clarinda M Smith, was born in Washington D C, Dec 25, 1819, they were married Feb 5, 1846, John T , is their only child living, have lost Nancy M , George H and Edward B Member of the Methodist Church , Republican

Craden, M , far , S 34 , P O Home

Craney, J , far , S 28 , P O Cantril

Cummings, O H P., far., S 32, P O Cantril.

Cretcher, J , far , P O Upton

CRETCHER, MATHEW Q., farmer, Sec 11 , P. O Mt Sterling, owns a farm of 400 acres valued at about $30 per acre, also owns 300 acres in Missouri and eighty acres in Hancock Co , born in Logan Co , Ohio, April 20, 1821 , left that State in 1843, and came to this county same year His wife, Lucinda Sayre, was born in Preston Co , Va , May 3, 1827, and emigrated with her parents to Ohio in 1836 , came to this county in 1841 , were married Jan 30, 1846 , have nine children—William, Lycurgus, Anna, Daiel, Lucy Jane, Ida May, Mary F , Lucinda and Q Mr Cretcher was an old-school Democrat, but when the party left the ancient landmarks of the fathers, he became identified with the Republican party, and, in 1856 supported Fremont In religion, Liberal

Cretcher, W., far., S. 9 , P O Upton

DEFORD, JOHN H , farmer See 27 , P O Keosauqua

Dodson, T C , far , S 14 , P O Keosauqua

Downs, A B , far , S 3 , P O Mt Sterling

Dudly, E C far , P O Upton

ELLIS, WILLIAM, farmer

ELLIS, BRADFORD, farmer, Sec 9 , P O Keosauqua, owns 280 acres of land, valued at about $30 per acre , born in Bourbon Co , Ky , March 11. 1812 left Kentucky in 1815, and came with his parents to Harrison Co , Ind., left that State in 1836, and arrived in this county in April, of the same year The name of his first wife was Elizabeth Ellis, who died Dec 4 1859 On Oct 14, 1860 he married Miss Mary Sellers, who was born in Dearborn Co Ind Mar 16 1825 his family on [illegible] of [illegible] that a eighth of wh [illegible] h m Martha E

ward, Eliza J , John J , Wesley, William, Nancy and Nelson Democrat , Religion, Liberal

FATHERSON, GEORGE, farmer, Sec 34 , P O Mt Sterling

Fatherson, Thomas, far , Sec 16 , P O Keosauqua

FERGUSON, D. W., farmer, Sec. 12 , P O Mt Sterling, owns a farm of 476 acres, valued at $30 per acre , was born in Lawrence Co , Penn , Sept. 2 1835, left that State in 1856, and arrived in this county in the autumn of the same year His wife, Sarah Alcorn was born in Lawrence Co , Penn , July 28, 1834 , they were married Nov. 2, 1858 , have had three children, two of whom are living—John Adams and Lizzie Bell; Alexander P died Sept 4 1862, aged 16 months Mr Ferguson is one of the heavy and successful stock-dealers of Van Buren County Republican , United Presbyterian

Fix, Alexander, far , Sec 3 , P O Mt Sterling

GARRET, OLIVER P , farmer , P O Keosauqua

Gibson, W W , far , S 16 , P O Keosauqua

Gilfillan J F O , far , S 5 , P O Cantril

Gray, Frank, farmer , P O Lebanon

Gray, Herbert, farmer , P O Pittsburg

HANNA, ROBERT A., farmer, Sec. 25 , P O Mt. Sterling.

Helwig, H , far , Sec 19 , P O Cantril

HILLES, EDMOND, farmer, Sec 4 , P O Cantril , owns 160 acres, valued at about $25 per acre , born in Washington Co , Penn , Nov 24, 1817, left that State in 1843, and came to this county the same year Mr Hilles enjoys the confidence of his neighbors to an eminent degree, having occupied some office nearly all the time, while in the county , was elected to the office of Supervisor in 1868, and again in 1877, which office he now holds His wife, Mary J Woods, was born in Logan Co . Ohio, Nov 7 1832, came to this county in 1841 Married Sept 15, 1850 , then children are Hugh P , Martha, Frances A , Jessie and Annie Liberal, Republican

Horne J C Sec 9 P O Keosauqua

Hoskin H C Sec 16 P O Keosauqua

Haskin, W S , far , S 17 , P O Keosauqua

Hull, A , far, Sec 19 , P O Cantril

Hull, C , far , P O Cantril

Humphrey C C , far , Sec 7 , P O Lebanon

JONES, Ira, far S 15 , P O Mt Sterling

Jones, I , far , S 22 , P O Keosauqua

KILMORE, C , farmer

Knox, W , far , S 4 , P O Upton

LANGFORD CHAS , farmer, Sec 11 , P O Mt Sterling

LANGFORD, ANDERSON, farmer, Sec. 15 P. O. Keosauqua, owns 410 acres, valued at about $30 per acre , he was born in Albemarle County, Va , December 18, 1802 , left Virginia in 1814, and came with his parents to Harrison Co , Ind , while that State was yet a Territory ; came to Illinois in 1835, and landed in Burlington in this State in March 1836 , made his claim to the farm on which he now lives the same month On May 4 1822, he married Miss Nancy Boston , she was born in Harrison Co , Ind , Aug 30, 1810, and died June 11, 1870 , his family consisted of twelve children, ten of whom are now living—Thornton, Turner, Perry Harmon H , Silas, Tillman, Charles, Arraminta, Martha and Ida. In 1873, Mr. Langford married Lucy Rine , she was born in Trumbull Co , Ohio, May 13, 1825, and came to this State in December, 1850 Republican, religion, Liberal

ANGFORD, H. H., farmer, Sec 20 , P O Cantril, owns a farm of 70 acres, valued at $25 per acre, born May 1 1834, in Harrison Co , Ind , came with parents to McDonough Co , Ill., in 1838, and from there to this county in 1842, and settled in Des Moines Tp He was married to Miss Charlotte Drew, of this county March 19. 1857, she was born April 10, 1836, in Tennessee, have four children living—Albert, Thornton, George and Sherman lost one—James H Mr Langford has held several offices of trust in his township, and is at present serving his second term as grand juryman in his county

Langford Perry , far Sec 24 , P O Keosauqua

Leaverton J , far S 17 P O Keosauqua

Linn, A , Sec 28 , P O Cantril

Linn, Alonzo, far., P O , Cantril

Linn, Milton, far , S 20 , P O Cantril

Lock, Charles M , far , S 4 , P O Mt Sterling

Long, James, farmer , P O Keosauqua

McCLELAND, J , far , Sec 4 , P O Upton

McCrary Samuel, far, S 12 , P O Keosauqua

McDonald, John & Mary, farmers , P O Keosauqua

McDonald, W A , far , S 35 , P O. Mt Sterling

Mason, E far , S 10 , P O Keosauqua

Miller, John, far, S 25 , P O Mt Sterling

Miller, Samuel Jr , far., Sec 35 , P O Mt Sterling

NICHOLSON, JOSIAH, farmer , P O Cantril

OWENS, LEWIS, far , Sec 7 , P O Cantril.

PARSONS, JAMES R., far , S. 35 , P O. Mt Sterling

Pitman, S. D , P O Cantril

Poling, R , far S 36 , P O Mt Sterling

Pollock, George, Upton

Pollock, T C , far , P O Upton

Potter L , farmer and Postmaster, S 20 , P O Home

Prall, E , far., S 3 , P O Mt Sterling

PRALL, ROBERT, farmer, Sec 24 , P O Keosauqua , owns a farm of 260 acres, valued at about $30 per acre , born in Zanesville, Ohio, Aug 7, 1833 , left that State with his parents in 1843 and came to Clarke Co , Ind , where he resided until he came to this county in September, 1852 In October, 1855, he married Miss Eliza Singleton , she was born in Carroll Co , Ohio, in November, 1831 , they have four children—Asa W , Frances M , Carrie and Della Republican , Liberal

Prall, T., far , S. 14 , P. O Keosauqua

RIDER, E , far , P O Mt Sterling.

Roberts, O far , P O Home

Ruddle, A far , S 9 ; P O Keosauqua

SAAR J , far , S 6 , P O Cantril

Shipley, S., far., S. 24; P. O. Keosauqua.
Shatten, P., far., S. 32; P. O. Cantril.
Silvers, D., far., S. 18; P. O. Home.
Silver, J. M., far., S. 20; P. O. Home.
Silvers, Wm., far., S. 30; P. O. Home.
Smith. G. W., farmer and stock dealer; P. O. Cantril.
Smith, J., far., S. 8; P. O. Lebanon.
Smith, John, far., S. 19; P. O. Home.
Smith, P., far., S. 9; P. O Keosauqua.
Smith, W. M., far., S. 16; P. O. Home.
Sparks, J., far., S. 31; P. O. Cantril.
Stott, C., far., S. 22; P. O. Home.
Stott, G., far., S. 11; P. O. Keosauqua.
Stott, J., far., S. 17; P. O. Home.
Struble, A.. far., S. 28; P. O. Home.
Struble, J., far., S. 17; P. O. Home.
Struble, P., far.; P. O. Cantril.
Struble, Wm., far.; P. O. Home.

TACKABERRY, TASSEY J., far., Sec. 24; P. O. Keosauqua.
Taylor, S., far., S. 15; P. O. Keosauqua.
Teter, Adam, far., Sec. 8; P. O. Upton.
Teter, Andrew J., far.. Sec. 8; P. O. Upton.

THORP, WILLIAM M., far., Sec. 1; P. O. Mt. Sterling; owns 1,500 acres, valued at $25 per acre; born in Lewis Co., W. Va., Jan. 28, 1842; came to this State and county in 1853; he is one of the heaviest farmers in Southern Iowa. His wife, Martha M. Withem, was born in Jefferson Co., Iowa, Nov. 15, 1847; they were married Jan. 18, 1863; they have two children—John Timothy and Adda Bell. Liberal; Democrat.
Thomas, D. M., far., Sec. 4; P. O. Keosauqua.

Thomas, R., far.; P. O. Keosauqua.
Tiffey, L., far., Sec. 20; P. O. Home.
Tulley, Wm., far., Sec. 27; P. O. Home.

WILEY, JAMES, farmer, Sec. 27; P. O. Mt. Sterling.

WARNER, NICHOLAS, far., Sec. 6; P. O. Lebanon; owns 430 acres of land, valued at about $35 per acre; born in Schoharie Co., N. Y., Aug. 30, 1799; left that State and came directly to this county in 1837, making his present location in December of that year. Feb. 3, 1820, he married Miss Rebecca Warner, who was born March 28, 1801, and died Sept. 9, 1845; at that time, his family consisted of seven children, three of whom are now living —Sylvester, Isaac and John; his present wife was Miss Elisabeth Hosford; she was born in Rutland Co., Vt., April 29, 1818; they were married Oct. 30, 1848, and have had six children, five of whom are now living—Mary E., Catharine, Harriett N., Harlow H. and and George N. Democrat; religion, Liberal.
Wallam, J., far., S. 4; P. O. Upton.
Wooden, H., far., S. 16; P. O. Home.
Work, Andrew, far., S. 18; P. O. Home.
Workman, Noah J.
Warner, John, farmer, Sec. 6; P. O. Lebanon.

VALE, AMOS, farmer; P. O. Cantril.
Vale, Johns, far., Sec. 30; P. O. Cantril.
Vance, B., far., Sec. 15; P. O. Keosauqua.

YEAGER, W. L., farmer; P. O. Upton.

FARMINGTON TOWNSHIP.

ALFREY, JACOB, farmer and coal-miner, P. O Farmington
Amos, Levi, Farmington
Allen, A B , mechanic, Farmington
Anderson, Ira, blacksmith, Farmington
Anderson J , far , S 1 , P O Farmington
BANK, WILLIAM, cooper, Farmington
Bante, Louis, blacksmith, Farmington.
Barger, M. L , far , S. 25 , P O. Farmington
Barton, W H., carpenter, Farmington
Beeson, George, grocer, Farmington
Behm, Anton, retired, Farmington
Benson, H , Justice of the Peace, Farmington
Bedell, J S , merchant, Farmington
Beeson, Geo Sr , grocer, Farmington.
Benson, Henry, attorney, Farmington
Bowers, J , far , S. 36 , P O Farmington
Bowles, W , far , S 7 , P O Boyers Sta
Bowman & Boyer, dealers in agricultural implements, Farmington
Bowman, H E , merchant, Farmington
Boyer, Adam, far , Sec 5 , P O. Boyers Station
BOYER, BASIEL, farmer, Farmington, born in Muskingum Co., Ohio, June 20, 1830 , at the age of 10, came to this county, and has made this his home since, was in California for three years, gold-mining, he has followed farming the rest of his life Married Miss Margaret Overhouse, she was born in Ohio, Darke Co , May 20, 1838, has had six children, five living —Alice B , William T., Adda L , Geo B and Glenn E., aged respectively 20, 17, 13, 10 and 3 Mr Boyer is a Free Thinker and a Greenbacker , he owns 640 acres of land, valued at $25 per acre, and house and two lots in town, and raises considerable stock
Boyer, John P , farmer, Boyers Station
Bradford, Ira, farmer , P O Farmington
Brock, Fenton, propr State Line House Farmington
Buckholz, H , blacksmith Farmington
BURG, LEWIS, wagon and buggy manufacturer, Farmington , born Feb 10, 1843, in Rhinephaltz, Bavaria , came to t' U ii l St , 1853 went directly Farlm...... remained the.....................

came here and established his present business Married, Feb 14, 1867, to Miss Cordelia Behme, she was born in Prussia May 2, 1816, had five children, four living—Albert H , Lewis W , Carrie C and Oscar E , aged respectively 8, 6, 4 and 2 Is a member of the German M E Church, politics, Independent Mr. Burg is known as a live energetic business man , came here with but little capital, but, by frugality and praiseworthy enterprise, has succeeded in establishing a business of which himself and the county may well be proud
Burrier, Iowa H , far , P O Farmington
CAPPLEMAN, PETER, capitalist, Farmington
Campbell, J A , grocer
Carter, G W , far , S 4 , P O Farmington
Carr, James, coal dealer, Farmington
Carr, Peter C , far , S 11 , P O Farmington
Carter, Josiah
Chick, Jas , prop boarding-house, Farmington
Church, A T , depot agent, Farmington
Clancy, Jas , far , P O Boyers Station
Cooley, L H , dep't P M , Farmington
COOLEY, MOSES H., Postmaster, Farmington , born March 19, 1814, at Whately, Franklin Co , Mass , lived there until he was 22, moved to Brownhelm, Lorain Co , Ohio; lived there four years; went to College at Hudson, Portage Co , Ohio , was there two years, taught school in different places, both in Ohio and Mississippi, was made an Odd Fellow in 1847, has passed the chair, was Grand Master of the Grand Lodge of the State in 1862-63, Grand Patriarch in 1861-62, Representative to the Grand Lodge of the United States in 1864, and in 1865; came to Iowa in 1847, and to Farmington in 1848, was Town Superintendent in 1860-61, was Postmaster from 1864 to 1870, re-appointed in 1871, and been Postmaster since Married Aug 3, 1848, to Selene C Hammond, she died May 10, 1859, ... 21 1850 to Eliza 1 Th..... July 25, 1851, marri......to Lucy

H Ingram, she died Dec 28, 1869, married again, May 18, 1870, to Miss Nancy S McCrary, of Vernon, has two children by third wife—Lyndon H and Clara Ida, aged 22 and 20, respectively Republican   Made a Mason in 1862, and has held positions of trust in the Lodge every year but one is also a member of Chapter   United with the Congregational Church in 1836, and is still a member

Coleman, John S, far, Sec 35, P O Farmington

Coombs, John, bridge-builder on B & S W R R., Farmington

Coughlin, Daniel, trackmaster B & S W R R   P O Farmington

Coulter, Samuel, Postmaster and merchant, Boyers Station

Crooks, Henry, section boss, B & S W R R P O Farmington

Cross, John F, Dr, druggist and physician, Farmington

Cronn, John C., laborer Farmington

Cronn, W. S., laborer, Farmington

Curtis, Adolpheus, far Sec 27, P O Farmington

DAVIDSON, JOHN W, minister, Farmington

Dibble, C G, patent-right man, Farmington

Dice, Jacob, laborer, Farmington

Dibble, C G., Farmington

Deane, E. C., Gen Agt. J. I. Case & Co., Farmington

Doeling, Charles, cigar manufacturer, Farmington

Dray, H, coal-miner, P O Farmington

Dray, Obadiah, teamster, Farmington

Dray. Wm, laborer, Farmington

Duffey, James coal-miner, P O Farmington

EATON, S. D
    Ebarling, Conrad.

Ebeling, C., far, Sec 12, P O Farmington

Eddy, J. A. merchant, Farmington

FARRIS, ROBERT, Sr, Mississippi River pilot, Farmington

Fichtenmueller, P, tinware

Flood, George, far, Sec 1 P O Farmington

Flood, Stephen, far Sec 1, P O Farmington

Folker, Cyrus far P O Farmington

Folker, John far   P O Vernon

Foregraves, J laborer Farmington

Freed, Henry, far, P O Farmington

French, E, far, S 6, P O Farmington.

Flow. B, far, S 28, P O Farmington

GABLEMAN, F, lumber dealer, Farmington

Gable, John, Sr, retired Farmington

GAFFORD, SAULSBURY B., firm of Gafford & Co, grain and agricultural implement dealers, Farmington, born in Baltimore, Fairfield Co, Ohio, May 27, 1846, lived there until 1860, went to Keokuk, lived there five years, then came here, and, with the exception of two years in Centerville, Iowa, has lived here since   Married in January, 1867, to Miss Lucy A Norris, she was born in Coshocton Co, Ohio, in 1845, they have four children—Jarvis J, aged 9, Abner, 7, Jessie, 5, Mammie, 2}   Does not belong to any secret society of any kind   Politics, Democrat   Mr Gafford began business here with very little capital, but, by strict and close attention and economy, combined with enterprise, has established a large and increasing business.

Giles, S, Farmington

Gillie, John J, proprietor machine-shop

GLECKLER, CHARLES A., general merchandise and proprietor of Diamond Mills, Farmington, born in Wurtemberg, Germany, April 16, 1835 came to the United States in 1852, lived in Newark, Ohio, three years, moved to Keokuk, Iowa, was there one year, clerked for Ogden & Brownell, book publishers, then came here, and has been living here since, engaged in the bakery and confectionery business two years, and one year in the hardware business, then entered into the firm of Sims & Gleckler, general mercantile business, which continued two years, then followed the same line of business alone up to the present time   Married, in 1860, to Miss Cordelia L Sims, had two children, one living— Clara, aged 17 years   In religion, Protestant   Mr Gleckler manufactures large quantities of flour, which finds a ready market throughout the State, he was one of the principal promoters of the old State Line R. R., now B & S W   Is a member of the Masonic fraternity   Has been City and School Treasurer for twelve years   Politics Republican

Gleckler, J G , one of the proprietors of grist-mill, Farmington

Glover, J , far , S 34 , P O Farmington

Good, G W , physician, Farmington

Goodall, George, laborer, Farmington

Goodell, Jethro G , laborer, Farmington.

GOODENOUGH, C. G., minister, Farmington.

GOODIN, WILLIAM, wholesale and retail groceries, Farmington , born in November, 1838, in Perry Co , Ohio , came to this county in 1844, and has lived here since, with the exception of three or four years' residence in Lee Co , Iowa Married, in 1864, to Miss Matilda Rogers , she was born in Ohio , two children living—Inez aged 10 , William C , aged 3 In religion is a Baptist politics, Democrat Is Treasurer of the Masonic Lodge and member of the Chapter Is also City Treasurer Served three years in Co A, 1st I V C , participated in the battles of Prairie Grove and Little Rock Ark , and all the engagements in the vicinity of Little Rock and others throughout the West

Gray, R B , far , S 12 , P O Farmington

Grubb, W F , homeopathic physician, Farmington

HARBISON, WESLEY, blacksmith Hartrick, B , carpenter, Farmington

Hartrick, C , wagon mfr , Farmington

HARTRICK, HENRY, wagon manfr , Farmington, born in Hanover, Germany March 27, 1844 ; came to the United States in 1867, and came directly to Farmington, and has lived here since Married in April, 1871, to Miss Minna Hartrick , have three children—Ida, Alma and Albert aged respectively 3, 5 and 1 years Member of the M E Church , in politics, is a Republican By frugality and economy, Mr Hartrick has succeeded in gathering the means to establish the present increasing business

Hartrick, Henry, carpenter, Farmington

Hassler, J , Sr , saloon-keeper, Farmington.

Hassler, Jos , saloon-keeper, Farmington

Hassman, George, carpenter, Farmington

Huntzell, Christian

Hellwig, G V., far , S 29 , P O Boyers Station

Hommelke, F , furniture dealer , Farmington

HOSMER, JANE, s P O. Boyers Station , born in Clark Co Ky

in 1820, left there at the age of 14, and came to this county, and, with the exception of three years passed in Ohio, has lived here since , she has lived in this township for forty years She married, in 1839, to George Hosmer , he was born in Massachusetts in 1807, and died in 1846 , has three children living—George Lorenz and Amanda, aged respectively 37, 35 and 31 Mrs Hosmer owns 160 acres of land, valued at $30 per acre

HOSMER, GEORGE, far S 9 , P O Boyers Station , born March 4, 1841, lived in Ohio for three years Enlisted in Co B 13th U S Inf , participated in the battles of Chickasaw Bayou, Champion Hills, Jackson, Miss , capture of Arkansas Post and the battles and siege of Vicksburg , served three years with credit to himself and his country

House, G H , far., Sec 32 , P O Boyers Station

House, J W , far , S 30 , P O Boyers Station

HUMMELKE, FREDERICK, hardware, stoves and tinware, Farmington, born in Hanover, Germany, in 1843, came to the United States in 1855, went to Warsaw, Ill , and remained there until 1861, then went to California and was there until 1867, engaged in gold-mining, then went to Hancock Co , Ill , and lived there until 1874, engaged in farming, then came here and established this business, and has been here since Is a member of German M E Church , is Independent in politics Married Miss Henrietta C Thero Jan 29, 1868 ; she was born in Hanover, Germany, March 13, 1848 Mr Hummelke came here with little capital, but by strict and close attention he has succeeded in building up a large and growing business

JOHNSON, JOSEPH A , far , S 30 , P O. Bonaparte

KAHOE, PATRICK, far , S 1 , P O Farmington

Kellogg, Chas , retired, P O Farmington

Kelley, A C , far., Sec 35 , P O Farmington

Kelley, D , capit der , Farmington

Kelley, J L , far , S 35 , P O Farmington

King, A , wagon manufacturer, Farmington

King, G , laborer at B & S W shops, Farmington

King, L , prop hack line Farmington.

Knouff S J , boot and shoe maker, Farmington

Knott, W , far , Sec 36 , P O Farmington

LEWIS R , far , P O Farmington

Litzrodt, F , minister, Farmington

Lorton. J , far , P O Boyers Station

Lowery, T J , far , P O Boyers Station

Lyman, G , barber, Farmington

McKINZIE, J , far , Sec 27 ; P O Farmington

Manhardt, E , far , P O Farmington

Manhardt, P , far , Sec. 26 , P O Farmington

Mantz, J , far , P O Farmington

Martin, J C., ferryman Farmington

Mathias, J W , far , P O Farmington

Meek, S G , retired physician, Farmington

Michael J F , shoemaker, Farmington

Miller, E , merchant, Farmington

Miller J , merchant, Farmington

Moore, D B , saloon, Farmington

Moore, J , prop Galt House, Farmington

Moreland, J , plasterer, Farmington

Moreland, E W , carpenter, Farmington

Moreland R , plasterer, Farmington

Morse, H T , boot and shoe maker, Farmington

Moss, G , Farmington

MUELLER, GEORGE, cabinet-maker, firm of Reckmeyer & Mueller, Farmington ; born in Province Hessen-Nassau June 3, 1835, came to the United States Oct. 31, 1855, went to Lee Co , Iowa, was there a year, then came to this place, and has been here since ; followed his trade for nine years, then formed the above partnership, which has continued up to the present time , Mr Mueller has, by close application to business, secured a competency and increasing business Married in 1863 to Miss Elizabeth Schimbeno , she was born in Lee Co , Iowa, Feb 7, 1843 Belongs to the Lutheran Church Has held several responsible positions in the township for several years

Mulvihill H blacksmith, Farmington

Murphy, C far , S 9 , P O Boyer Station

Myers, J D , painter, Farmington

NASH, T J , retired, Farmington

Nelson, L D shoemaker Farmington

Newman, A , far , S 8 ; P O Farmington.

Newman, H , far. ; P O Farmington

Newman, L , far., S 8 , P O. Farmington.

Noske, G , harness-maker, Farmington

O'BRIEN, JOHN J., REV., Farmington, born in Tipperary, Ireland, Aug 14 1846, came to the United States in July, 1865 , resided in Providence, R I, two years, then went to St Charles College, Md , in the fall of 1866, began his classical studies there, owing to the climate, which was unsuitable to him, in 1867, went to Canada to St Hyacinthe College, remained there two years, then went to L'Assumption College , in 1870, graduated at this college, in 1872, was ordained at Niagara Falls at the Seminary of Our Lady of Angels, on the 23d of December, 1876, for the the Diocese of Dubuque, Iowa, under the Right Rev John Hennessy Bishop of Dubuque, entered on his first Mission on the 9th of February, 1877 at Farmington, and the Missions connected therewith

PENDLETON WILLIAM

Perry. G , tinner, stoves and tinware, Farmington

Perry, J , carpenter and joiner, Farmington

Perry, John retired, Farmington.

Peterie, A , far , P O Farmington

Poale, B , far , S 25 , P O Farmington.

Preen, C , far , S 31 , P O Willitts

RECKMEYER FREDERICK, cabinet-maker, Farmington

Reckmeyer & Mueller, dealers in furniture, etc., Farmington

Reese, H , far , Sec 25 , P O Farmington

Reesman J T , limekiln, Farmington

Reineka, C , far , S 28 , P O Boyers Station

Reisner, H , employe of R R Co , Farmington

Rhoades, J , far , S 27 , P. O. Boyers Station

Rice A A far S 36 , P. O. Farmington.

Rice, J W undertaker and dealer in furniture, Farmington

Rider, J , coal-miner ; P O Farmington

Ringer, G W , attorney, Farmington

Risser, A , cooper, Farmington

Risser, Peter, cooper, Farmington

Roberts, E H , carpenter and joiner, Farmington

Roberts, R S blacksmith Farmington

Robertson, J W , grain dealer, Farmington

Robertson, J W , livery, Farmington

Robinson, George, far , Sec 5 , P O Boyers Station.

Roush, L , machinist, Farmington

SCHAAD, CHRISTIAN, farmer, P O Boyers Station,

Schau, Michael, far , Sec 28 , P O Farmington

Scott S F , retired grocer, Farmington

SCOTT, OLIVER H. P., farmer, Sec 35 , P O Farmington, born in Washington Co , Ohio, March 3, 1815, lived there eleven years , moved to Morgan Co , Ohio, and lived there thirty years, while there was contractor of public works, canal, railroad and river improvements he then came to this county, was engaged in the improvement of the Des Moines River, at Croton, Bentonsport and at this place , owns 700 acres of land in this and Bonaparte Tp , 400 acres of this land is underlaid with coal, raises considerable stock owns the right to the water-power of the Des Moines River at this point Is a member of the Legislature to the Seventeenth General Assembly Served in the late war as Captain of Co B, 3d I V C , was soon promoted Major of the regiment, and served as such until the surrender of Vicksburg, was promoted to the colonelcy of the 48th I V I , participated in thirty-one engagements, was requested to take charge of Government works at Nashville, Tenn , employing 1,500 men , was appointed Assessor of Internal Revenue of First Iowa District Married May 16 1843, to Miss Ellen D Fay , she was born in Watertown Jefferson Co , N Y , May 16, 1822, they have three children— Straughn F , Charles H and George D , aged respectively 34, 28 and 26 Col Scott was one of the contractors for the foundations of the Illinois and Iowa State-houses.

Shaeffer, G , wagon-maker, Farmington

Shaw, A J , Mayor Farmington

Shockley, A J , stone-mason, Farmington.

Shreeves, S K , clerk, Farmington

Smith, Russell, retired, Farmington

SMITH, JESSE, born in Smithfield, near Providence, R I , Nov 9, 1797 , lived there until he was 25 years old and then went to Knox Co , Ohio, and lived there for forty-three years, followed farming during that time , then went to Clarke Co , Mo , and lived there about four years, and then came here, and has lived here since Married Feb 17, 1820, to Miss Polly Jenks , she was born in Smithfield, R I in 1800, she died in Knox Co Ohio, July 21, 1864 Married again in 1872, to Miss Elizabeth Fensteimaker , she was born in Indiana Aug 19, 1836, has six children by first wife, all living—Harriet, Rufus, Thomas, Mary, Anna and Sarah, aged 58, 53, 49, 46 42, 38 Two by second wife—Ellen and John, aged 20 and 18 Owns town property , does not belong to any church or society of any kind Politics, Republican Served in Capt Whipple's Company of Militia at Newport, R I , during the war of 1812 Mr Smith was Captain of a vessel for ten years , lost two vessels by shipwreck and was shipwrecked twice

Smith, George W , far , S 1, P O Farmington

Spurgeon, Frank, butcher, Farmington

Spurgeon, T , carpenter, Farmington

Stephens, H , far , P O Farmington

Stoddard, M , farmer and coal dealer, Sec 1 , P O Farmington

Stoddard, R , far , Sec 1 , P O Farmington

Strau, P , far , Sec 8 , P O Farmington

TEXTER, D , boot and shoe manufacturer, Farmington

Thero, C , butcher and shipper of stock, Farmington

Theime, L L , grocer, Farmington

Theurer, J , far , Sec 28 ; P O Farmington

THOMAS, JAMES ; P O Farmington , born in Huntingdon Co , Penn June 30, 1804 ; left home on the 19th of October 1838, to attend the first land sale that took place in Iowa, which occurred in November, 1838, at this point, but Mr Thomas did not get here until March — he was detained by low water in the Ohio River and ice in the Mississippi   Mr Thomas has made this his home since 1839   Married in Center Co, Penn, to Miss Hannah Bateman, on the 5th of April 1831   Mrs Thomas was born in Center Co, Penn, on the 16th of September, 1804   Mr Thomas is a Democrat   Has been Township Trustee, and served in other public positions, he has passed thirteen or fourteen years of his life in iron, coal and gold mining, both in Pennsylvania and California

THERME, JOHN L., druggist and bookseller, Farmington, born in France, Jan 11, 1853, came to the United States in 1856, came to Keokuk, and lived there twenty years, moved to this town in 1873, and has been here, engaged in business, ever since   Married here Oct 25, 1875, to Miss Lucia Meek   she was born in this town Oct 25, 1855, has one child— Edna M, aged 2 years   Member of Masonic fraternity, Republican

TOWNSEND, A E, merchant tailor, Farmington

Turton, W. H, Bap minister, Farmington

VAUSEGGEN, FREDERICK, far, Sec 33   P O Farmington

Vanzant, Kincaid, carpenter, Farmington

WAGERS, WM M., carpenter and joiner, Farmington

Wagner, J., far, S 2, P O Farmington

Ware, Isaac

Warnock, W, far, P O Farmington

Warren, C, far, S 3, P O Farmington

Warren, J, far, P O Farmington

Weekly, S G far, Sec 2, P O Farmington

Wen, F., far, S 31, P O Farmington

Wells, A, far, S. 10, P O Farmington

Wells, J, far, S. 10, P. O. Farmington.

White, James, far, S 33, P O Boyers Station

Whittall, Fred, millwright and carpenter, Farmington

WHITLOCK, FREDERICK, W. DR.; born in Pyrmont, Germany, Nov 8, 1823, came to the United States in August, 1837, came direct to this county and has lived here up to the present time, he graduated at the Homeopathic College of Missouri in 1868 and has practiced medicine since   Dr Whitlock has had a very peculiar experience as a physician   Physics came natural to him, and he practiced medicine ten years before he graduated, being urgently requested by his neighbors to do so   Married Miss Catherine Reckmeyer in St Louis in 1849, she was born in 1830 and died April 13, 1861, has had four children, three living—Edward A, Albert and Emma C, aged 24, 22 and 18   Edward and Albert are graduates of the Pulte Medical College, Cincinnati, Ohio, and follow their profession here   Dr Whitlock married again, Christina Behme, July 6, 1862   Is a member of the German M E Church, is a Republican   He is one of the first settlers of this county, owns considerable town property, and eighty-five acres adjoining the town, valued at $40 per acre

Whitall, Geo, millwright, Farmington.

Whitten, John, express agt, Farmington

Wilson, W, far, S 30, P O Bonaparte

Woltje, C, far, S 28; P O Farmington

Wood, Zachariah, far, P O Farmington

WEEKLY, STEVEN G., Farmington, born in Shenandoah Co, Va, Dec 2, 1804, lived there until 3 years old, moved to Muskingum Co, Ohio, and lived there for thirty-three years, then came to this county, and has lived in this and Clark Co, Mo, ever since, has followed farming all his life, lived in Clark Co, Mo, for nineteen years, and the same length of time in this county   Was married Feb 20, 1834, to Miss Lydia Varner; she was born in Muskingum Co, Ohio, Feb 15, 1814, has had ten children, five living—Talitha J, Emily V, James A, Ortheha A, Marietta, aged, respectively, 43, 32, 29, 27, 23   Independent in politics, and does not belong to any secret organization   Owns five acres of land in the city limits, valued at $400 per acre, and other property in this township

BONAPARTE TOWNSHIP.

ARMSTRONG, JAMES A., farmer, S 23, P. O Farmington, owns 150 acres of land, valued at $25 per acre, born Feb 22, 1801, in Bucks Co, Penn, parents moved to Pittsburgh in 1805, commenced clerking in a drug store when about 13, when about 19, commenced the business on his own account, spring of 1825, went to Clinton, Ohio Married there Miss Hattie Driskill Dec 27, 1825, she was born in Maryland June, 1806, moved to McLean Co, Ill, in 1831, to DeKalb Co Ill, in 1832, spring of 1836, came to Van Buren Co same fall, purchased the claim of land he still owns Mr Armstrong is a man of real personal worth and integrity, and of good, sound judgment, has raised a family of eleven children, all living—Charles A, Hannibal H, Lucien C, Cyrus E, William A, Gilbert M, Clara L, James H, Fridley M, Oliver H P Zachary T and Dora G, an adopted daughter Five of his sons served their country during the war, one only was wounded

Armstrong, William A, far, Sec 14, P O Bonaparte

BABER, CHARLES M. laborer, Bonaparte

Bailey, James, far; P O Bonaparte

Barber, G W, employe of Meek Bros, Bonaparte

Barr, J H., far, P O Bonaparte

Beard, William, laborer, Bonaparte

Beck, Hellen, Bonaparte

Besecker, John, clerk, Bonaparte

BOYER, D. W., farmer, Sec 16, P. O Bonaparte, owns eighty-three acres of land, valued at $25 per acre, born Feb 22, 1806, in Frederick Co, Md, came to Lee Co, Iowa, in 1854, to this county in 1865. Married Maria Francis, Nov 8, 1830, in Maryland, she was born in Loudoun Co, Va, Nov 4, 1811, have thirteen children living—Wm F, Dewitt C, Thos W, Samuel A, Timothy T, John M, Lewis M, Mary C, Alvin O, Nancy J, James F, Benjamin O. Maria I, lost three—Mariella, Levin and Reuben his son Lewis served his country during the war Member of the Baptist Church

Boyer, G F, far, S 24, P O Farmington

Boyer, John M, Farmington

BOYER, T. W., dealer in dry goods and general merchandise, Bonaparte, born July 26, 1846, in Muskingum Co, Ohio came to Lee Co, Iowa, in the fall of 1854, received his education at the public schools of Denmark, went to St Joseph Mo., in 1859, spring of 1860 came to Bonaparte and commenced the study of medicine, with a Dr Oliver George, attended lectures at the Keokuk Medical College, where he graduated in February, 1863, practiced till 1870, when he engaged in his present business Married Miss Nancy A Meek, daughter of Isaiah Meek, May 1, 1865, she was born Feb 8, 1847, in this county, have three children—Flora N, Edson I. and an infant not named Democrat

Bridge, James, employe of Meek Bros P O Bonaparte

Brooker, Wm H, marble dealer, Bonaparte

Brower, David, far, P O Bonaparte.

Brown, Suphana, P. O Bonaparte

Burnett, Thos, far, P.O. Bonaparte

Bushell, Dan, plasterer Bonaparte

CALHOUN, JAMES, farmer, P O Bonaparte

Cassady, M, far, P. O Bonaparte

Chapman, Alfred, butcher, Bonaparte

Chapman, H H, grain dealer, Bonaparte.

Chapman, Samuel, Sr, far, Sec 3, P. O Bonaparte

Christian, A L, carpenter and joiner, Bonaparte

CHRISTY, THOMAS, dealer in dry goods and general merchandise firm of Christy & Johnson, Bonaparte, born Nov 16, 1829, in Harrison Co, Ohio, came to this county spring of 1842, and settled one and a half miles above Bonaparte, then called Lexington, two years after, moved to Lick Creek Tp, fall of 1848 came to Bonaparte and engaged upon public works, spring of 1850, went to California and followed mining, the spring of 1853, returned t Bonaparte d following fall elected Sheriff t the county an moved to Keosauqua, at the expiration of his term of office, returned to Bonaparte and commenced his present business, firm of Gregory & Christy, which was changed to the present firm in 1857 Fall of 1855, was elected member of the Legislature from this county, fall of 1872, was elected a member of the Board of Supervisors Married Miss S C. Johnnson July 24, 1853; she was born June 7, 1835, in Indiana have five children living—Gertrude E, Hattie E, Jennie A, Thomas H and Dora, lost four — Mary B, Anna, Emma and Maggie, his sister Elizabeth has been a member of his family since his marriage Democrat.

Clark, W, far, Sec 6, P O Bentonsport

Collins, H, retired, P O Bonaparte

Coolidge, H, merchant, Bonaparte

Coolidge, H L, merchant, Bonaparte

Corwin, J, canvasser, Bonaparte

CRESAP, JONATHAN, dealer in agricultural implements and furniture, also proprietor of planing-mill, Bonaparte, born March 9, 1835, in Alleghany Co, Md, came to this county in the spring of 1856, and settled in Bonaparte, has been in the employ of Meek Brothers about fifteen years—two years with Joseph Meek, in the planing-mill, commenced running the business on his own account in the fall of 1877 Married Mary Washington in April, 1858, she was born in June. 1841, in Pittsburgh Penn, have five children—George, Orion, Lulu, Delia and Jeff His wife is a member of the Baptist Church ; Democrat

Cresap. J H, saloon-keeper, Bonaparte

CRESAP, ROGER N.. DR., physician, and a partner of J P Davis in the hardware business, Bonaparte, born Sept 26, 1809, in Alleghany Co, Md, went to Hampshire Co, Va., in 1826, and commenced the study of medicine there with his brother-in-law Dr John Temple, in the fall of 1829, he moved to Marysville, Tenn, and completed the study of medicine, and graduated at the Knoxville Medical College, in 1830, came to Keokuk, Iowa, in the spring of 1833, and engaged in the grocery and drug business in the fall of 1834 he and Messrs Blackburn and Coates came here and made claims in the county of

what is now the village of Bonaparte Dr Cresap's claim embraced a part of the plat of Bonaparte, which he, in company with Mr William Meek, laid out in 1837 he followed farming and practicing medicine, also kept a hotel in Bonaparte. about twenty-five years Married Angeline Thompson in October, 1830, in Tennessee, she died in the fall of 1835, leaving one son—John B, a little daughter, Mary, having gone before, he was again married to Mary S Keith, Oct 3, 1836, she was born Nov 19, 1813 in Culpeper Co, Va, have had one daughter—Angeline, who also passed away Mr. Cresap owns several hundred acres of land in the county ; has also served as Postmaster several years Republican

CRESAP, R. T., proprietor of two billiard-halls and saloons, Bonaparte, born April 9, 1837, in Alleghany Co, Md, worked on a farm and attended school till he was 15, and then went to the carpenter trade, in the spring of 1856 he came to Bonaparte, thence to Keokuk, in the fall of 1857 he went to Kansas City, Mo, in June, 1860, he returned to Maryland on a visit, came to Bonaparte in Feb, 1861, worked at his trade five years, in Meek Brothers' woolen mills three years, also in the planing-mills in 1874, he had the misfortune of having a thumb and two fingers cut off from his right hand, after which he engaged in his present business Married Mariam W Slaughter Dec 25, 1862, of this county, she was born in February, 1845, have five children—Anna L, Byron E, Charles P, Eddie F and Jessie M Member of A, F & A M, Democrat

Cresap, V, Bonaparte

Cullen, W C, far, P O Bonaparte

CUMMINGS, ALEXANDER, farmer, S 20, P O Bonaparte, owns 350 acres of land, valued at $30 per acre, born May 20, 1823, in Donegal Co Ireland, came to Chester Co, Penn in 1842; in the spring of 1851 came to Van Buren Co, Iowa, and purchased eighty acres of his present farm, following fall went to California, returned in 1853 Married Harriet Corwin July 11, 1851, she was born Jan. 31 1837, in Scioto Co, Ohio, have seven children—William, Robert, Mary, Eliza, James, Thomas and Alexander Mr Cummings has, by his own industry and economy, accumulated a handsome property Independent

Cummins Wm, far, S 21; P O Bonaparte

Custer, J L, patentee and far, Bonaparte

DAUBER, FERDINAND, farmer, P O Bonaparte.

Davidson, G W, far; P O Bonaparte

DAVIS, J. P., dealer in hardware, groceries, etc., also Postmaster of Bonaparte, born Feb 11, 1844, in Wheeling, W Va, emigrated with his parents to Burlington, Iowa the following spring, in the fall of 1858, went to Edina, Mo, was educated at the high school there, commenced reading law in 1864 with Hollister & Perry of that place, admitted to the bar in 1868, followed his profession till fall of 1870, went to Kahoka, Mo thence to Bonaparte in 1873, was Principal of the school here until he commenced his present business, July, 1877, in company with Dr R N Cresap, appointed Postmaster July, 1877 Married Alice Sullivan, of Lewis Co, Mo, April 14, 1864, she was born in same county, Feb 10, 1840, have two children—Winnie G and Lola G Mr Davis is an Elder in the Presbyterian Church Republican.

DEMPEL, MORRIS, cabinet-maker, Bonaparte, born May 3, 1819, in Bavaria, Germany; came to America in October, 1847, and settled in Harrisburg Tp, moved to Farmington in the spring of 1851, soon after to Bonaparte, worked as millwright a year, cabinet work about a year, then for Meek Bros, in 1866, commenced present business Married Mary A Rigler Nov 22, 1849, she was born Nov 8, 1825, in Germany, have five children living—Mary A, Anna, Louisa, George and Eugene, lost one son—Charles, who was murdered at Osceola, Ark, May 27, 1878. Member of the Catholic Church

Derr, Davis, teamster, Bonaparte

Derozer, William, far P O Bonaparte

Detwiler, S C, d'g'st, photographer, Bonaparte.

Dofflemeyer, Joseph, blacksmith, Bonaparte

Dutton, Frank E, far, P O Bonaparte

Duer, James H, plasterer, Bonaparte

ERVIN, THOMAS, Bonaparte

EASON, E. W. & MARY A., proprietors of Eason House, Bonaparte, Mary A. Eason, daughter of Michael S and Sarah A Cresap, was born Oct 1, 1839, in Alleghany Co, Md Parents moved to Somerset Co, Penn, in 1843, and Fayette Co in 1851 thence to Bonaparte June, 1856, was engaged in the employ of her uncle, R N Cresap, then proprietor of the hotel now known as Eason House, she married Eli W Eason March 22, 1865, he was born in 1833 in Vermont, came into this hotel in spring of 1873, have two children living—French L and Clyde M Lost two—George and an infant

ENTLER, JOHN S., dealer in stoves and tinware, Bonaparte, son of W W and Sarah E Entler, born in Harrisburg Tp, of this county, Jan 17, 1852, lived on a farm till his father moved into Bonaparte in 1867, in 1864 his brother commenced the stove and tinware business, he learned the trade with him, and bought him out, but now are partners Married Jennette R. Sherman Oct. 1 1874, she was born May, 1853, in Bonaparte, have one daughter—Myrtle Independent

ENTLER, W W., Justice of the Peace, Notary Public, insuring and real estate agent, Bonaparte, born Jan 29, 1819, in York Co, Penn Parents moved into Adams Co, in 1826, in 1831 went to Baltimore, Md, to live with an uncle, learned the carpenter and joiner's trade, in 1839, returned to Adams Co, engaged in mercantile business about four years Married Sarah E Bodenhamer Feb 2, 1841, she was born Dec 25, 1822, in Jefferson Co, Va Fall of 1844, came to Iowa, and settled in Harrisburg Tp, of this county, served as Justice of the Peace there four years, spring of 1867, moved to Bonaparte, has since worked at his trade besides attending to official business, for the last two years has devoted his time present business. Has six children living—George W

William H., Phillip J , John S , Jacob F , Catherine J , lost three—Edward J Mary A and Franklin P Member German Reformed Church , Democrat

Ethridge, Charles, laborer, Bonaparte

FLICK, ISAAC, laborer, Bonaparte

Foster, W L fur , P O Bonaparte

Frankle, Louis, clothing merchant, Bonaparte

Fridley, W H lumber dealer, Bonaparte

GABBY JAMES B . farmer, Sec 11 , P O Bonaparte

George Bros , druggists, Bonaparte

GEORGE, WILLIAM A., physician and surgeon. Bonaparte born in Bonaparte, Iowa Jan 6, 1853 educated under Profs Mowath and Howe, and at 18, commenced his medical studies with his father, the late Dr. Oliver George, of Bonaparte continued one year then placed himself under the instructions of the eminent surgeon, Lewis A. Sayre of New York City , graduated from Bellevue Medical College in the class of 1876, with distinction, being one of nine, who received honorable mention in a class of 165 , frequently contributed verbatim reports of lectures to the various medical journals, and in addition to the labors of graduation year revised, corrected and satisfactorily carried through the press for his preceptor, a 500 page 8vo surgical work, besides much other labor in the way of reports and proof-reading He had made every arrangement for publishing a medical journal in New York, having been promised the support of the ablest practitioners of that city, when his health broke down from the effects of a severe accident and overwork combined, and he was compelled to return to his home in Van Buren Co , where his widowed mother resides and where his deceased father was widely known, and his rare medical skill generally appreciated Dr Oliver George, who died April 7, 1874, was a man of great intellectual endowments, of fine social qualities, one, whose extensive information, and almost faultless memory, gave his opinions weight not only in matter . . . . current . . . . W . . . morela . . . . he

graduated after due preparation, at the Pennsylvania Medical University at Philadelphia, at that time the best medical college in the United States , he subsequently received an *ad eundem* degree from Keokuk Medical College, and upon the organization of the Iowa State Medical Association, was made Chairman of its Committee on Correspondence with other medical societies , after seven years' practice in Olney, Ill , he removed to Van Buren Co , in 1851, where he was actively engaged in his profession until his death, having devoted thirty-three years of his life to medical practice During his residence in Olney, in the summer of 1845, he married Miss N M Powers, cousin of the eminent sculptor, Hiram Powers Was a member of the Masonic fraternity for many years, he organized Bonaparte Lodge, No 73, and was for eight consecutive years its Master , was also High Priest of the Moore Chapter A Knight of Malta, Knight of the Red Cross, Knight Templar and Deputy Grand Master of the Grand Lodge of the State of Iowa, devoting some of the best years of his life to the interests of the fraternity He was a devout believer in natural religion, took an intense delight in the works of creation , was a true worshiper of the beautiful and true, not only in the physical world, but also in the kingdom of mind

Grimsley, H M , employe of Meek Bros , Bonaparte

Guess, Elisha, sawyer, Bonaparte

HALL. CHAS L., book-keeper, Bonaparte

HANBACK, THOS., proprietor of Bonaparte Pottery, in company with Robert Wilson , Bonaparte, born Aug 13, 1838, in Scott Co., Ill ; spring of 1867, came to Vernon of this county , worked in the pottery and learned the trade , in 1866, came to Bonaparte and established a pottery, in company with Mr S Parker, who sold his interest to Mr Wilson in 1873 Married Jennette Herryman Nov. 25, 1858, she was born June 17, 1843, in Posey C . . . . two children—Mary and Alice . . . . . .—Florence and Carrie Republican

HANEY, DENNIS, farmer, Sec 7, P O Bonaparte, owns about 500 acres of land, valued at $30 per acre, born in November, 1822, in County Derry, Ireland, in 1842, came to Philadelphia, Penn, in 1845, returned to Ireland and remained nearly a year, came over to Boston in the spring of 1846 Enlisted in the general service of the United States Army, went on a recruiting tour to Chesapeake, Fort McHenry, New York, where he was attached to Co. L, of the U S 3d Artillery, went to Mexico in Gen Worth's Division, was promoted to 2d Sergeant, was in the battles of Vera Cruz, National Bridge, Cerro Gordo, Molino del Rey, Chapultepec and at the capture of the City of Mexico, was detailed as guard of a chain gang from Vera Cruz to Fort Monroe and Old Point Comfort, Md, where he was discharged Went to Washington and got his land warrant, in September, 1848, came to Iowa and located his land in Monroe Co, came to Bonaparte and went to work for Meek & Son, in the summer of 1849, went to California overland, in 1852, returned to Bonaparte, and purchased the farm upon which he still lives Married Susanna McClure Feb 22 1854, she was born in 1831, in Indiana, have four children living—Elizabeth, Lulu, Robert A and William, lost two—Rachel and Mary Mr Haney was one of the first Directors of the Bonaparte Academy, afterward purchased by the district, he has served his township as Trustee several years, is the owner of several buildings in Bonaparte, including the Masonic Hall, he being a member of the Order

Henry, Levi photographer, Bonaparte

Henneigh, H K, retired Presbyterian minister Bonaparte

HOPKINS, T. H., dealer in and manufacturer of boots and shoes, Bonaparte, born Dec 24, 1822 in Sussex Co Del, his father died when he was 1½ year old and his mother, when 9 years old, lived with Mr B H Marvel till he was 17, came to Champaign Co, Ohio, in the fall of 1834 in 1839 went to ◦ ◦l shoemaker after whi

work in different cities along the seacoast, in 1847, returned to Champaign Co Ohio Married there Miss Hannah Jones Oct 28, 1848, she was born in Ohio, March 16 1824, they moved to Bonaparte in the spring of 1850, in 1851, to Mt Sterling, this county, in 1855 returned to Bonaparte and commenced his present business, have five children living—Fidelia who lives in Kansas, Josephine, in Colorado, and Ida M, Thomas H. and Charles B are yet at home, lost three—William Henrietta and an infant not named Mr H has been a member of the Masonic fraternity since 1848 Democrat

HORNBAKER, DAVID, far. Sec 18, P O Bonaparte, owns 140 acres of land valued at $40 per acre, born Nov 11, 1841, in Preble Co, Ohio, came with his parents to this county in the fall of 1845, and settled about a mile west of his present residence Enlisted May 1, 1861, in Co F, 2d Iowa Inf, discharged in January following for disability in March 1862 re-enlisted in the same company and regiment, and again, as a veteran, in March 1864 participated in the battles of Pittsburg Landing Shiloh, Iuka, siege and battle of Corinth and siege of Vicksburg, also with Sherman in his march to the sea and all the battles during that campaign, was discharged at Davenport Iowa August 1 1865 Married Mary A Bachelor of this county, March 11 1867, she was born Aug 14 1843 in London, England, parents came the same fall to New York City, and to Cincinnati, Ohio, in 1851, and to this county in 1852, have six children—Willie H Carrie B Benjamin F David R James G and John R Republican

Hornbaker Martin, far, P. O Vernon

Huffman, Geo., merchant, Bonaparte

Humphrey H, employe of Meek Bros, Bonaparte

Humphrey, J T boot and shoe dealer Bonaparte

Humphrey, W, painter Bonaparte

JOHNSON WILLIAM, J, merchant

JOHNSON, I. B. ⸳ 18 P ◦◦ B e acres of

land, valued at $35 per acre, born Aug 12, 1842, on the farm where he now lives, Bonaparte, owns ninety-five acres of land, his father, William Johnson, came from Fountain Co, Indiana, in 1838, died Sept 25, 1845, spring of 1864, Mr Johnson went to Montana, June, 1866, returned Married Miss Rebecca J Perkins, daughter of J F Perkins, Feb 18, 1873, she was born Nov 11, 1851, in this county, have two children —Hattie and Barton Democrat

KEAN, JOSEPH A, carpenter and joiner, Bonaparte

Keashng, F, farmer, P O Bonaparte

Kelley, John, far, P O Bonaparte

Kerr, W B, dealer in lumber, Bonaparte

KETCHAM, BENJAMIN, far, Sec 1; P O Bonaparte, owns 600 acres of land, valued at $30 per acre, born Nov 19, 1829, in Allegheny Co, Penn, came to Van Buren Co., Iowa, spring of 1855, purchased a part of his present farm in February, 1856, which he improved and rented out for eight years, working on it part of the time spent some time in Pennsylvania in farming Married Miss Mary Lightfoot, of Lee Co Iowa, Oct 27, 1863, she was born in Manchester, England, Oct 25, 1843, came with parents to St Louis, spring of 1845; to Lee Co., in 1847 Mr. Ketcham moved on his farm the fall he married, have six children living—Minnie B, Joel, Lizzie J, George, Frank, and one infant not named Has been Justice of Peace and Township Trustee Member of Presbyterian Church, Democrat

LANSHAW, W, far, P O Bonaparte

Leng, J, gardener, Bonaparte

Lumb, L, employe of Meek Bros, Bonaparte.

McDANIEL, J, far, P. O Bonaparte

McDaniel, M, far, P O Bonaparte

McKasson, G, far, P. O Bonaparte

Medlock, D, far, P O Bonaparte

MEEK, H. H., book-keeper for the firm of Meek Bros, Bonaparte, son of Isaiah Meek, born June 4, 1851, in this town was educated here has been coun... from... road...

assumed the management of the books of the company Married Miss Mary C Shang Nov 29, 1870, she was born in Virginia, died June 20, 1871, again married Nannie E Duncan Nov 22, 1875, she was born April 18, 1853, in Mercer Co, Mo; have no family Democrat

MEEK, ISAIAH, of the firm of Meek Bros, proprietors of the Bonaparte Grist, Saw and Woolen Mills, Bonaparte, born Jan 31, 1821, in Warren Co, Ohio, parents moved to St Joseph Co, Mich, in 1829, to Bonaparte in the spring of 1837, his father, William Meek, in company with Dr R N Cresap, laid out the town of Bonaparte the same year; in 1844, William Meek & Sons built the grist-mills, and, in 1853, the woolen-mills, the latter burned in 1863, were rebuilt by Meek Bros the same year Mr Meek married Cynthia A Ingels in December, 1844, she was born in 1827 in Ohio, have six children—Nancy A., Phœbe L, Hugh H, Mary E, Byron and Kirk Mr Meek owns, individually, 540 acres of land, valued at $25 per acre, and about 2,000 acres in company with his brother Robert, and 500 acres with Robert and Joseph The Meek Brothers are among the leading business firms of Van Buren Co, are now building a fine new grist-mill, to contain six runs of stone, at a cost of $15,000 Democrat

MEEK, JOSEPH, one of the firm of Meek Brothers, Bonaparte, born June 9, 1830, in St Joseph Co, Mich, came with parents to this county in the spring of 1837, settled in Bonaparte has been one of the firm of Meek Brothers since the death of his father Married Mary Ward, of this county, May 18, 1852, she was born Nov 19, 1832, in Indiana, died July 12, 1853, was again married, to Mary A King Nov 2, 1856, she was born June 23, 1838, in County Galway, Ireland, has seven children living, all by second wife —Eliza, Kate, Mary A, Robert, Maggie, Priscilla D and Alice, lost one— Ann E, by first wife Mr Meek owns individuated... about 140 acres of land, has... real interest with his brother in the mill res

MEEK, RALPH F., proprietor livery stable, Bonaparte, son of Robert and Nancy (Flint) Meek, born Aug 11, 1851, in Bonaparte, was educated in the public schools of his native town, served as clerk and book-keeper in the office of Meek Bros for several years, commenced his present business in the spring of 1878 Married Miss Gertrude E Christy, daughter of Thomas Christy; she was born Nov 26, 1854, in Keosauqua, have two children—Carl E and Harry C Democrat.

MEEK, ROBERT, of the firm of Meek Brothers, proprietors of Bonaparte Grist, Saw and Woolen Mills, Bonaparte, born Jan 25, 1815, in Wayne Co, Ohio, his father, William Meek, moved to St Joseph Co, Mich in 1829, to Lee Co, Iowa, in the fall of 1836; the following spring, to this county, his father purchased the claim of a Mr Moffatt, the land upon which he and Dr R N Cresap laid out the town of Bonaparte in 1837, the grist-mills were built by William Meek & Sons in 1844, the woolen-mills in 1853, the latter were burned in 1863, rebuilt by Meek Brothers the same year, the father died Aug 9, 1863 the mother Jan 25, 1855, the Meek Bros assumed control of the mills about 1850 Mr Meek married Mary A Allen, of Lee Co, Iowa, April 23, 1838, she was born April 10 1819 died Oct 3, 1845, again married, Nancy Flint Oct 10, 1847, she was born May 24, 1815, died June 1, 1853, again married, Abigail P Barber Oct 12, 1856; she was born Oct 24, 1822, have nine children living, three by each wife—first, Elizabeth A, Sarah and Alvin second Alinda P, William and Ralph F, third, Lewis C Robert E and Oscar L, lost two of second wife's children and one of third Mr. Meek owns individually about four hundred acres of land and one-half interest in about two thousand acres and one-third interest in about five hundred acres Member of the Baptist Church, Democrat The firm of Meek Brothers are among the most solid and enterprising business men of Southeastern Io

Meek & Ker

Merrick, Le

MEEK, WILLIAM, clerk and salesman in the office of Meek Brothers, Bonaparte, son of Robert and Nancy (Flint) Meek, born in Bonaparte Sept 29, 1849, educated in the schools of his native town Married Alice Sharp, of Bonaparte July 3, 1870, she died Sept 12, 1873, again married, Magie M Johnson March 5, 1874, she was born Oct 27, 1851, in Bonaparte, has four children, two by first wife and two by second wife—Alden H and Effie, and Shirley R and Carlotta C

MILLER, E. E., farmer, P O Bonaparte, son of Peter and Mary Miller, born Dec 18, 1831, in Westmoreland Co, Penn, came with parents to Van Buren Co, Iowa, in the spring of 1854, and settled in this township, in the spring of 1859, went overland to California, in the spring of 1866, went to Montana, remained till the fall of 1872, returned to Van Buren Co. and purchased his present farm of 228½ acres, valued at $35 per acre, his father died April 6, 1873 Married Miss Martha W Ryland, of this county, Dec 14. 1875, she was born Feb 1, 1853, in this township, have two children—Glen A and one infant not named Republican

Miller, John A, far, P O Bonaparte

Miller Joseph, far, P O Bonaparte

Miller, Simon, teamster, Bonaparte

Miller, Solomon far, P O Bonaparte

MITCHELL, J. P., farmer, Sec 6, P O Bonaparte, son of John and Liddich Mitchell, born July 1, 1831, in Perry Co, Penn, came with parents to this county in the spring of 1839, and settled in Bonaparte Tp in the fall of 1842; returned to Pennsylvania and remained till the spring of 1856, then returned to their old farm in Van Buren Co, where his father died July 29 1875, in the 78th year of his age, he was a native of Armagh Co, Ireland, and emigrated to the United States in 1808, Mr J P Mitchell to California in the spring of 1864, and followed mining, in the spring of 1869, returned and took charge of his father's farm of 165 acres, of which he still has charge and

eirs, his

m Mr

publican

Murphy, Samuel, coal-miner, Bonaparte

MYERS, LEWIS, far , Sec 16, P O Bonaparte , owns 120 acres of land, valued at $35 per acre, born Oct 22, 1808, in Gallipolis, Ohio parents moved into Virginia in 1811, and in 1814, into Kentucky, opposite the mouth of the Scioto River , in 1817 moved to Scioto Co, Ohio, in the spring of 1839, came to Van Buren Co Iowa, and purchased the farm upon which he lives Married Mary Milford, of this county, in November, 1847 , she was a native of Pennsylvania, she died Dec 29, 1848, leaving one child —Mary, who died when about 3 years of age again married Mary A Cackley Sept 2, 1852, she was born Oct 23, 1819, in Pocahontas Co , Va , have four children living—Clarinda, Hugh, John and Alva , lost two—George and James , his wife's mother Frances Cackley, lives in the family Mr Myers is a member of the Masonic Order, both Blue Lodge and Chapter, at Farmington

NEAL, URIEL, farmer, P O Bonaparte, owns 240 acres of land, valued at $40 per acre, born Oct 11, 1810, in Boone Co , Ky , in the fall of 1830, parents moved into Dearborn Co , Ind , in the summer of 1835, came to Illinois, twenty miles east of Burlington , in the spring of 1836, came to Van Buren Co , Iowa, and located a part of the farm upon which he lives Married in Indiana Catherine Brokaw Sept 7, 1834, she was born in Pennsylvania April 24, 1810 ; have but one daughter—Rachel, who lives at home Mr. Neal has filled the offices of Supervisor, Justice of the Peace, Assessor and Trustee for his township several years Member of the Masonic and Odd Fellows Orders Democrat

OGLE, J , far , P O Bonaparte

PAGE, W H H far , P O Bonaparte

Parker, S , potter , P O Bonaparte

Patterson, C F , far , P O Bonaparte

PERKINS, JOSEPH F., farmer, P O Bonaparte, owns 333 acres of land, ... 21, 1... ... . paren .. ..

the fall of 1833 , in 1834, went to Indiana, and stopped near Lima, in the spring of 1836 came to Iowa, and made his claim on the south side of the Des Moines River, opposite where Bonaparte now stands, his parents and the family came the same year, subsequently went on to California, except his brother William Married Eliza Maxwell in January, 1837 , she died Oct 4, 1844, leaving two children—Joseph and Mary , again married, Eliza Myers April 1, 1847, she was born in March, 1820, in Ohio, have seven children—Sarah, Robert, Wm H , Jane, James C , Ellen and Allen Mr Perkins is among the well-to-do farmers of his township, has accumulated property by his own industry and economy, filled several official positions in his township, and is present Justice of the Peace Democrat

Perkins, Robert, Franklin and George, farmers , P O Bonaparte

Perkins, M , P O Bonaparte

Perkins, W , far , P O Bonaparte

RADISTOCK, CHARLES, farmer , P O Bonaparte

Reese, Richard, wagon-maker, Bonaparte

Rigler, Frederick far , Sec 6 , P O Bonaparte

ROBB, HARVEY, retired farmer , P O Bonaparte, son of James and Isabella Robb, born Dec 10, 1819, in Clark Co , Ky , in the spring of 1820, his parents moved to Jefferson Co , Ind , in 1834, went into Fountain Co , in February, 1838, Mr Robb came to Van Buren Co , purchased several hundred acres of land in Henry Tp , of which he still owns 578 acres, valued at $40 per acre Married Rachel Christy, of this county, Aug 31, 1843, she was born Sept. 8, 1824, in Harrison Co , Ohio Has followed farming and stock-raising, also buying and shipping to some extent, in the fall of 1875, he left his farm and moved to Chicago, and engaged in the stock commission business at the Union Stock-Yards, his health failing, he returned, and located in Bonaparte in 1876 Has three children living—Mary I , now .... W .. .. Sarah J , now M W , Cackley and Thomas, who married Amanda Brewster , all are living in this county Members of the Presbyterian Church, Democrat

Robinson, Francis, far, P. O. Bonaparte

ROBISON, J. R., barber and proprietor of Robison Block, Bonaparte, son of James and Milley Robison, born in Petersburg, Va., July 5, 1853, the year 1862, his parents spent in Woodville, Miss, returned to Petersburg, Va, he going to New Orleans in company with his brother, remained a short time, then went up the Mississippi River to Cairo, Ill, where his brother remained, he came on to Duquoin, thence to Keokuk, Iowa, to Bonaparte in the fall of 1863, and engaged in the employ of Dr. R. N. Cresap, then proprietor of what is now the Eason House, remained with him about five years, then went to Mt Pleasant and attended school about six months, returned, went to Keosauqua and attended school about six months, then went to Keokuk, and with George Caves learned the barber's trade, returned to Bonaparte and engaged in his present business, by close attention to business saved his surplus earnings, and purchased the block in which he carries on his business, and rents the store-rooms for other business Republican

Ryan, A. S., miller, Bonaparte

Ryland, B. D., miller, Bonaparte

SAGE, J. R. tailor, Bonaparte

Sanders, J., far, S 16, P. O. Bonaparte

Sedgwick, D. E., jeweler, Bonaparte

Schleter, H., far, P. O. Bonaparte

SHERMAN BROTHERS, proprietors of the Bonaparte *Journal*, Bonaparte, J. W. was born Sept 8, 1852, in Washington Co., Ill., parents came to this town in 1856, he commenced learning the printer's trade in 1870 in the office of the *Van Buren Democrat*, published in the room they now occupy, went to Leon, Decatur Co, Iowa, in September, 1875, was a partner in the Leon *Reporter*, sold out the following spring and went to Newton Jasper Co, Iowa; was a partner in the *Jasper County Independent,* sold out in the spring of 1877, and returned to Bonaparte, and, in ..... with his ... started the B. .... *..... ....* ... Jennie Broc... .... 19 1-71 ....

was born in June, 1856, have one son —Joseph A. John H was born Jan 12, 1857, in Bonaparte, commenced to learn the printer's trade with his brother at Leon in 1875, was with him as a partner at Newton, Jasper Co., Iowa, and is a partner in the *Journal* office

Sherman, N. E., Bonaparte

Smith, N. H., carpenter and cooper, Bonaparte

Smith, O., stone-mason, Bonaparte

Smith, W. employe of Meek Bros, Bonaparte

Spence A., employe of Meek Bros, Bonaparte

Stark, J., far, P. O. Bonaparte

Steadman, A., stone-cutter, Bonaparte

Steadman, Jas, stone-cutter, Bonaparte

Sterling Wm, employe of Meek Bros, P. O. Bonaparte

STIRLING, JOHN, Superintendent of the Meek Bros.' Woolen-Mills, Bonaparte, born Nov 15, 1824, in Stirlingshire, Scotland, commenced working in the Cambusbarron Mills when he was about 10 years old. He was married to Jessie Reid Nov 20, 1846, she was born in March, 1825, came to Littleton, N. H., in 1857, and, in the summer of 1866, to Warren, Ill, where he remained till January, 1868; when he came to Bonaparte, and engaged in the employ of Meek Bros, in their woolen-mills, as Superintendent of the weavers' department, which position he held till 1872, since that has been Superintendent of the mills except a year spent in visiting in the old country He has nine children living—John, William, Joseph, Mary, Janet, Ellen, George, Martha and Jean, lost four— James, Alexander, Mary and Euphemia Member of the Presbyterian Church

Stienmeyer, F. A., physician, Bonaparte

STUTSMAN, D. W., DR., Homeopathic physician and surgeon, Bonaparte, born Feb 12, 1839, in Morgan Co, Ind came with his parents to Lee Co, Iowa, in 1843, where, two years later, his father died went to Chariton Co, Mo, in 1857, in 1864, came to Bentonsport, in this county, engaged in the drug business, while he .... medi- in h .... ointed .... U. S.

Colored Regiment, discharged in November, 1865 He returned home and attended lectures at the College of Physicians and Surgeons, at Keokuk, graduated in the spring of 1867, then came to Bonaparte and commenced practice Married Emma A Lewis, July 3, 1873, she was born in Illinois, Jan 24, 1850, have one daughter—Xantippe Dr Stutsman is the present W M of Bonaparte Lodge, No 73, A, F & A. M Republican.

STURDIVANT, WM. C., farmer, dealer and shipper of stock, Sec 2, P O Bonaparte, son of Dr R J. Sturdivant, owns 180 acres of land, valued at $30 per acre, born in this county Aug 6, 1848 Married Jennie Monroe, of this county, Jan 27, 1870, she was born in London, England, in January, 1848, have five children—Guy, Leslie, Audley, J, William C. and Clyde Mr Sturdivant owns the Eason House in Bonaparte Democrat

TOMPKINS, S V, P O Bonaparte

Thompson, Otis, Bonaparte

Troutman. G W, retired far Bonaparte

VAN DORN, WILLIAM grain dealer, Bonaparte

Vauseggen, Charles H, far, Sec 21 P O Bonaparte

Vauseggen, John W, far, Sec 21, P O Bonaparte

WATTS, ISAAC, far, S 19, P O Bonaparte

WAGNER, BENJAMIN, far, P O Bonaparte, owns 254 acres of land, valued at $30 per acre, born Nov 10, 1817, in Montgomery Co, Ohio Married Margaret Shrayer Jan. 12, 1843, she was born Sept 28, 1825, in same State, came to Mt Pleasant, Iowa, in 1855 spring of 1860, came to Van Buren Co, and purchased his present farm, has served his Township as Assessor several terms, has six children living—America A, William S, Mary, Charles E, Kate E and Benjamin P, lost two—Margaret E, and one infant Is a member of A, F & A M Republican

Welch, James minister Bonaparte

White, ...

WHITLEY, J. W. .... Bonaparte ....

notions, sewing machines and attachments, etc, also, Superintendent of the wool-sorting room, in the Bonaparte Woolen-Mills, born April 28, 1826, in Yorkshire, England, came to the United States via New Orleans, and went to Cheshire Co; N H, the following year to Connellsville, Penn, married there Sarah A Giles April 25, 1852, same year moved to Belmont Co, Ohio; next year, returned to Pennsylvania, fall of 1856, came to Mt Pleasant, Iowa, spring of 1857, to Bonaparte, and engaged in the employ of Meek Bros, in the woolen-mills, commenced the grocery business in 1870 His wife died Feb 20, 1872, again married Hattie A Johnson Aug 18, 1878, have six children living—Thomas C, an attorney, in Burlington; Jos G, at home, Mary R, married to W I Allender, of Pella, Iowa, Sarah E, married to Harry Mitcheler, George A, who is studying law with his brother in Burlington and Phill S, at home, lost one daughter—Emma G Independent

Whitlock A, dealer in agricultural implements, Bonaparte

Whitmore, B F, laborer, Bonaparte

Williamson, J, far, Sec 1, P O Bonaparte

Wilson, E, laborer, Bonaparte

Wilson, E A, laborer, Bonaparte

WILSON, ROBERT. proprietor of Bonaparte Pottery with Thomas Hanback, Bonaparte, born Feb 17, 1827, in Staffordshire, England In December, 1845, enlisted in H M 24th Foot, and sailed for India the following May, served through the campaign of Punjaub, in 1848–49, received a medal and two clasps of recognition for service, was under Lord Gough, Sir Cohn Campbell and Sir Charles Napier, returned to England in August, 1856, same fall came to Boston, Mass, following summer, to Peoria, Ill In April, 1861, enlisted in Co E, of the 8th Illinois Infantry for three months, was Second Sergeant, afterward elected Captain, Co I, wounded at the battle of Fort Donelson, and left for dead on the battle field over night, recovered, and .... Corinth, after which .... Farmington, engaged in the pottery business Fall of 1863, was tendered the captaincy of the 5th U S Heavy Artillery, accepted, and again went into service, was engaged principally in garrison duty, promoted to Major and Lieut.-Colonel by brevet, for gallantry at Fort Donelson, mustered out fall of 1865 Came to Peoria, Ill, and engaged in the pottery business, December, 1866, came to Farmington, in 1871, to Bonaparte and engaged with Messrs Hanback & Parker, in 1873, bought Mr Parker's interest Married Miss Sarah J Miles, of Tazewell Co, Ill, June 9, 1863, she died December, 1868, again married, Anna M Atkinson, of Illinois, Dec 9, 1869, she was born in Wicklow Co, Ireland, Nov 26, 1839, has two children by second wife—Thomas W and Fanny H, his wife had two children by former husband—Carrie M and Cora D Republican

Wilson, W C, far, Sec 16, P O Bonaparte

WOLF, MICHAEL, far, Sec 12, P O Bonaparte, owns 242 acres of land, valued at $25 per acre, born Feb 3, 1820, in Butler Co, Ohio; parents moved to Wayne Co, Ind, in 1831 Married Melvina Tilson, of Darke Co, Ohio, July 2, 1842, she was born in same county in 1827, fall of 1844, moved into Darke Co, Ohio; his wife died the same fall, leaving a daughter—Mary A, who died the fall of 1845. Went to Williamsburg, Ind, and worked at his trade of blacksmithing nine months, then went to Hollandsburg, Ohio, and married Lucinda Harlan March, 1846, she was born in April, 1830, spring of 1847, moved to Bethel, Ind., in 1849, returned to Hollandsburg, Ohio fall of 1850, came to Lee Co Iowa, then, to Oskaloosa, Iowa, and worked at his trade, in 1852, came to Harrisburg Tp., of this county, worked at his trade and farming his wife died there Dec 31, 1859, again

married, Narcissa Brown, of Lee Co, she was born March 12, 1844, in Highland Co, Ohio, moved to Bonaparte fall of 1866, worked at his trade till 1869, in the hardware business till 1871, then came to his present farm Had seven children by second wife—Amanda J, Elizabeth A, Norman H Jacob D Mary E, Rosella B and Josephine, the last five are dead, by third wife five—Sarah F, William M., David C., Effie B and Calvin M, the last three are dead Members Baptist Church, Republican

WYER, JOHN, farmer, Sec 2, P O Bonaparte, owns 110 acres of land, valued at $35 per acre, born July 22, 1830, in Warren Co, N J, parents moved to Licking Co, Ohio, thence to Van Buren Co, Iowa, in the fall of 1852, and settled on the farm where he now lives, his father died in November, 1854, and his mother March 5, 1864 Married Mary E Miller, of this county, Nov 15, 1855, she was born Oct 1, 1833, in Pennsylvania, have five children living—Mary A, Henrietta, Emma, William and Frank, lost one—Sarah E Members of the Baptist Church, Republican

Wyer, A, far, S 20, P O Bonaparte

YOUNG, B H, far, P O Bonaparte

Young, C P carpenter, Bonaparte

ZANE, LEVI, farmer, Sec 14, P O Bonaparte, owns about 300 acres of land, valued at $30 per acre, born Nov 27, 1820, in Salem Co, N J, came to Lee Co. Iowa, in the spring of 1851, to Van Buren Co in February, 1854 Married, in New Jersey, Miss Mary A Justice Feb 28, 1847, she was born June 16, 1821, have only one son living—Wilbert, born April 21, 1865, lost five children —Levi J John Justice, William and Hannah are raising an orphan child—Adaline Fox Members of the M. E Church

CEDAR TOWNSHIP.

ALVRY, J M, far, S 8, P O Wilsonville

Alvey, J M

Anderson, J, far, Sec 5, P O Wilsonville

Askew, Wm, far, S 33, P O Utica

BAILEY, JOSIAH, far, S 11, P O Wilsonville

Baley, W A, far, S 10, P O Wilsonville

Barger, D, far, P O Wilsonville

Berry, John, coal miner, Wilsonville

Boley, George, far, P O Wilsonville

Boley, J S, far, P O Wilsonville

Boley, N, far, S 31, P O Hillsboro

Bradford, O W, far, S 19, P O. Utica.

Brooks, J T, far., P O Vega

CAMPBELL, E. B, far, S 35, P O Hillsboro.

CARMEAN, CURTIS, far, S 25, P O Hillsboro, Henry Co, owns 274 acres of land, eighty acres being in Wayne Co, home farm valued at about $7,000, born Oct 5, 1806, in Sussex Co, Md, in 1814, parents moved to Ross Co, Ohio, in 1830, to Tippecanoe Co, Ind, to Fountain Co, in 1832, thence to Vermilion Co, Ill, in 1833, and to Macon Co, in 1835, in the spring of 1839, came to Henry Co, Iowa, in the spring of 1841, to Van Buren Co. Married Mary Coddington, of Tippecanoe Co, Ind, Nov 7, 1830, she was born in Gallia Co, Ohio, Nov 20, 1809, have six children living—Josiah, Mary C, Sarah C, Marm, Elvina and Henrietta; lost three—Martha, an infant and Cyrene (wife of Lieut Col Joseph H Newbold, who was killed at the battle of Pleasant Hill, La), in October, 1872, she went to St. Louis, Mo, with a sister, who left her at a private boarding-house on Thursday, she designing to remain only till the following Monday, since which time to trace of her whereabouts has been ascertained, everything indicating that she has been foully murdered. Mr Carmean has held the office of Justice of the Peace in this township two terms. Democrat

Christie

Clark,

Cochran

Caltraine, J, far and mill-owner, Sec 2, P O Vega

Caltraine, W C, far, S 1, P O Wilsonville

Cox, D, far, S 24, P O Hillsboro

Cuddy, M T, far, P O Wilsonville

Davidson, Richard, far, P O Hillsboro, Henry Co

DAVIDSON, R., far, Sec 21, P O Wilsonville

DAY, A. H., farmer and stock-raiser, Sec 32, P O Utica, owns, in company with his brother, Ira B, 1,040 acres, valued at $45 per acre, born May 14, 1838, in Hamilton Co, Ohio, came with his parents to this county in the spring of 1844. Married Anna Fox, of this county, Feb 16, 1861; she was born March 9, 1842, have five children living—Rhoda F, William R, Oliver L, Carrie E and Timothy, lost two—Ella and Nannie. His father, Timothy Day, was born Feb 23, 1803, in Hamilton Co, Ohio, married there Elizabeth Edwards March 27, 1825, she was born March 20, 1809, in the year 1839, came to Van Buren Co, and entered 3,700 acres from Government, in Union and Cedar Tps, returned and brought his family out in 1844, and located in Union Tp, was a member of the convention that framed the Constitution of 1856 for the State of Iowa, also one of the Trustees of the State Agricultural College, has also been a member of the State Agricultural Society about twelve years. Is a successful breeder of thorough-bred stock, sold his farm in Union Tp in 1877, and came to live with his son, A H. He still owns about 600 acres of land. Democrat

DAY, IRA B., farmer and stock-raiser, Sec 32, P O Utica, son of Timothy and Elizabeth Day, born Jan 22, 1842, in Hamilton Co, Ohio, came with his parents to Van Buren Co, Iowa, in the spring of 1844, and located in Union Tp. Married Miss Hollie Robinson, of Des Moines Co, Iowa, ... born in same . . . . five children . . . M . . . , Frances E,

William E and an infant not named Mr Day owns, in company with his brother, A H, 1,040 acres of land, valued at $45 per acre Democrat

Dounard, Ephraim, far , P O Utica

Dounard, J. far , Sec 31, P O Utica

Douglas, Albert J, far. and mill-owner, S 8, P O Wilsonville

Douthart, R , far S 27, P O Hillsboro

Dow, C W , farmer, P O Wilsonville

ENDERSBY, EDMOND, far , Sec 26, P O Hillsboro

Endersby, F , far , S 22, P O Hillsboro

FARMER, SAMUEL, far , Sec 10, P O Wilsonville

Fender, Jacob J., far., P O Utica

Fickle, Samuel, far , P O Hillsboro

GIAUQUE, A T , far , Sec 11; P O Hillsboro.

Graber, C , far , S 15, P O Wilsonville

Grim, J , far , Sec 36, P O Hillsboro

HARLAN, ELIHU, far , Sec 3, P O Wilsonville

Harlan, J , far , S 10, P O Wilsonville

Harlan, Levi, farmer and merchant, Sec 9, P O Wilsonville

HARLAN, NATHAN, farmer, Sec. 17, P O Wilsonville, owns 340 acres of land, valued at $30 per acre, born Jan 20, 1821, in Union Co , Ind , came to Lee Co , Iowa, in the fall of 1849 Married there to Nancy McGreer, March 18, 1852, she was born in Fayette Co , Penn , Aug 16, 1833, the same spring, came to Van Buren Co , and located on the farm upon which he still lives , have five children living —Albert, Ann M , George W , Sarah J and John B , lost two—Samantha and Ada Member of the Christian Church , Republican

Harlan S A , far , P O Wilsonville

HELTERBRAN, D. K., farmer, Sec. 27, P O Hillsboro, Henry Co , Iowa , owns 160 acres of land, valued at $40 per acre, born Nov 22, 1831, in Westmoreland Co , Penn , went into Fayette Co in 1852 Married there to Mary Farquhar Jan 10, 1856 , she was born Dec 5, 1835, in the same county, came to this county in the spring of 1856, and settled on his present farm, during the year 1863, he was in a dry goods store in Hillsboro, Henry Co , [illegible] the Peace in t[illegible]

also Assessor and Trustee, have two children—Joshua A and Aaron F Members of the Free-Will Baptist Church , Republican

Holliday, F E and C D , fars , Sec 26 , P O Hillsboro

Howard, I L V , far , Sec 16, P O Wilsonville

Huff, J P , far , P O Wilsonville

Huffman, J R , far , S 30, P O Utica

JOHNSTON, R , far. P O Utica

JACOBS, A. J., farmer, Sec 21, P O Wilsonville, owns 150 acres of land, valued at $5,000, born Feb 8, 1829, in Fayette Co , Penn , his early life was spent on a farm , in the fall of 1855, he engaged in the mercantile business , in the summer of 1856, he came to Iowa to see the country, returned home, and in the spring of 1857, came with his family and located on the farm upon which he still lives Married Anna M Jordan, of Pennsylvania, Dec 18, 1851; she was born Feb 1, 1832, died May 5, 1871, was again married, to Mrs Clarinda Junk (nee Nixon), Oct 19, 1876 , she was born in Fayette Co , Penn , Sept 27, 1841 , had seven children by first wife, living—William R , Oscar J A , Joseph B , Ida E , Edson C and Anna M , lost one—Ella H , by his second wife, has one son by former marriage—Leroy Junk Mr Jacobs has acted as Township Clerk five years, Assessor four years, and Treasurer of his School District five years Member of the Free-Will Baptist Church , Republican

Johnston, Smith, far., P O Wilsonville

KNOWLS VIRGIL, farmer, P O Wilsonville

KECK, JOS. A., farmer, stock dealer and shipper, Sec 32, P O Utica, owns 420 acres of land, valued at $40 per acre, born Dec 9, 1827, in Westmoreland Co , Penn , came with parents to this county in the spring of 1846, and settled in Harrisburg Tp , on the farm now owned by his brother Henry Keck, in the spring of 1850, went with his brother Henry, to California overland with an ox-team, engaged in mining, returned in the summer of [illegible] ke out [illegible] while

584   DIRECTORY OF VAN BUREN COUNTY:

near the West Indies, destroying them in great numbers Married Ingaba Ebeit May 5, 1853, she was born Dec. 2, 1835, in Fayette Co., Penn, have eleven children living—Mary A E, Hugh G, Catharine B. Rose E, George C, Lida N, John H, James E, Allie J, Charles R and Robert R, lost one son—Willie Settled on his present farm in 1853 Member of M E Church, Republican

LANE, F. H, farmer, Sec 16, P O Wilsonville
Lane, Wm, far., S 3, P O Wilsonville
Lazenby, R., far., Sec. 23 P O Hillsboro

LOOFBOURROW, JAS. S., farmer, Sec 21, P O Hillsboro, Henry Co; owns 252 acres of land, valued at $40 per acre, born June 22, 1837, in Fayette Co, Penn, parents moved to Jefferson Co, Ohio, in 1840, thence to this county in the spring of 1855, and located in Harrisburg Tp Enlisted in Co, D, 14th Iowa V I., September, 1861 participated in the battles of Fort Donelson, Pittsburg Landing, Shiloh, Pleasant Hill and Old Oak, La., was with Banks in his Red River expedition, and Gen A J Smith, in his raid through Mississippi, at the battle of Holly Springs and Pilot Knob, was discharged at Davenport, Iowa, Nov 5, 1864 Married Mary Syfert April 24, 1866, she was born Dec 29, 1845, in Fairfield Co, Ohio; have three children living—Irvin, John and Ella, lost one —Laura Member of F. W Baptist Church, Republican.

LEFFLER, A. J., farmer, Sec 28, P O Utica, owns 270 acres of land, valued at $35 per acre, also owns one-third interest in 160 acres of land in Harrisburg Tp, born Feb 6, 1847, in this county, was educated at the district school and at the graded school of Bonaparte Married Lydia A Vale, daughter of Jacob G Vale, deceased, Jan 1, 1878, she was born Nov 8 1853 in Lee Co, Iowa, educated at Monmouth College, Illinois, of which she is a graduate Member of Baptist Church, Democrat

Lyon, James farmer, P O Utica
McCLELLAN B A far Sec 7 P O Wilsonville

McVeigh, J. H far, S 21, P O Wilsonville
Marshall, John, far, S 33, P O Utica.
Marshall, W G, far, P O Utica
Marriott, Jas L, far, P O Wilsonville
Martin, Alexander, retired farmer, S 15, P O Wilsonville
Millikin, C & O L, farmers, P O Wilsonville

MORRIS, A. H., far, S 7, P O Wilsonville, owns 400 acres of land, valued at $35 per acre, born Nov 1, 1833, in Harlan Co, Ky, came with his parents to Van Buren Co, Iowa, in the fall of 1838, and settled in Cedar Tp, from the spring of 1863 till the fall of 1866, he lived near Monroe, in Jasper Co, Iowa, then returned to the farm upon which he now lives Married Harriet Ebert, of this county, Nov 12, 1857, she was born in Fayette Co, Penn, Nov 12, 1839, have eight children—Rebecca E, Ellen J, Belle C, Asbury D, Margaret A, Emma, Winfield L and Mary E Mr Morris has served his township as Trustee. Member of the M E Church, Republican

Morris, George F, far, S 17, P O Wilsonville

MORRIS, HENRY T., far, Sec. 17, P O Wilsonville, owns 320 acres of land, valued at $30 per acre, born March 16 1837, in Harlan Co, Ky, came with his parents to Van Buren Co, Iowa, in the fall of 1838, and settled in Cedar Tp Enlisted in July, 1861, in Co H, of the 5th Iowa Inf, was in Gen. Pope's division in Missouri, on account of disability, was discharged in October, 1862, returned home. Married Sally A Spencer Jan 28, 1864, she was born in this county April 11, 1842, have six children living—Sherman, Frank, Charles, John H, Arthur and William Settled on his present farm in 1870 Republican

MORRIS, WM. C., far, S 17, P O Wilsonville, owns 160 acres of land, valued at $35 per acre, son of Henry and Jane (Mark) Morris, was born March 9, 1825, in Harlan Co, Ky., came with parents to Lee Co, Iowa, in June, 1838, the following September, came into Van Buren Co, and settled in Cedar Tp, father died Feb. 16,

1871, and mother died Feb 24, 1871
Mr Morris entered his present farm
from the Government in 1846   Married Sarah J Evans June 25, 1848,
she was born March, 1830, in Clark
Co, Ky, died Aug 10, 1872, again
married, Esther L Culbertson May 24,
1874, she was born in this county
Aug 25, 1841, has ten children living
by first wife—Wilburn, George L.,
Amanda, Margaret M., Thomas N,
John A, William G. B, Laura B,
Mayberry L and Sarah E., lost three
—Henry C C, Joseph T and Evans,
by second wife has two—Lloyd C and
Grace E   Mr Morris has been identified with the business of his township
officially most of the time since its organization, filling most of the offices
Member of the M E Church, Republican.

Murdock, J F, far, P O Wilsonville

NEWBOLD, ALEX, far.,S. 35, P
O Hillsboro

Newbold, C, far, P O Hillsboro

NIXON, SAMUEL, farmer, stockraiser and breeder of the choicest varieties of Poland-China hogs and fancy-bred sheep, S 31, P O Utica, owns
a farm of 420 acres, valued at $40 per
acre · born June 13, 1820, in Wayne
Co, Ohio   Married there Rachel Webb
March 25, 1841, she was born in Pennsylvania April 15, 1821, he came to
Van Buren Co in the spring of 1848,
and settled upon the farm on which he
is still living, Mr Nixon ranks among
the best farmers of Van Buren Co,
has taken an active part in the County
Agricultural Society   Served as a
County Supervisor   Has nine children
living—Jacob, Emily J, Harriet A,
George, Moses, Alonzo, Ezra, Clemenza
A and Julius G, lost one daughter—
Maria, who was the wife of R S
Wherry, died Sept 24, 1878. Wife
is a member of the Baptist Church,
Republican

PHILLIPS, CLEMENT, farmer, P
O Wilsonville

PLUMER, WILLIAM F., farmer, Sec 34, P O Utica, owns 180
acres of land, valued at $7,000, born
Feb 4, 1832, in Washington Co, Ohio,
educated at Marietta College where he
learned the business of land surveying,

which he has followed to some extent,
moved to Knox Co, Mo, in 1856;
served while there in the State Militia
three years, also as County Judge six
years, came to Van Buren Co in 1870,
located on his present farm. Married
Sarah F Beswick, of Washington Co.,
Ohio, Dec 21, 1856, she was born Nov
18, 1834, have six children living—
Happy M, John J, Augusta, K, Fanny
G, William P and George G, lost one—
Jane E   Democrat

Priestly, J, far, S 26, P O Hillsboro.

ROCKEY, E & J; P O Hillsboro

Rockey, F, far, S 27, P O Hillsboro

Rowley, T B, far, S. 19, P O Utica

ROWLEY, JOHN W., County
Superintendent of Schools, P O Utica;
son of Theodore and Emiline (Watson)
Rowley, was born July 23, 1846, in
Columbiana Co, Ohio, parents came
from there to Cedar Tp, of this county,
in December, 1854   Mr Rowley was
educated at the common schools, and the
Bentonsport and Davenport (Iowa)
graded schools, and the commercial college
of Davenport   Was elected as County
Superintendent of this county in the fall
of 1865, and re-elected in 1867, which
position he still fills, is also President
of the State and County Superintendents' Association, and of the Southeastern
Iowa Educational Association, composed
of thirteen counties, also one of the Vice
Presidents of the State Teachers' Association, and one of the editors of the
Central School Journal, of Keokuk.
Was married to Melvina Thompson,
daughter of the Rev David Thompson,
of Bonaparte, Oct. 27 1868, she was
born Oct 27, 1849, in Highland Co,
Ohio, have three children—Roland B,
Frank W and Clinton C   Member of
Christian Church and Republican

Ruby, J. H, far. Sec 16, P O Wilsonville

Runyan, A, far, P O Wilsonville

Runyon, J H, far, P O Hillsboro

Runyon, J. W, far, P O Wilsonville.

SAVAGE WILLIAM, farmer. P O.
Wilsonville

Shelman, W H far, S 12, P O Hillsboro

Sinter T, far Sec 31 P O Wilsonville.

Simpkins, T J , far , See 17 , P O Wilsonville

Smutz, B R , far S 22 , P O Hillsboro

Snider, G W , far , S 18 , P O Wilsonville

SNIDER, J. M., farmer, Sec 18 , P O Wilsonville, son of William C and Elizabeth Snider , born Feb 10, 1849, in Highland Co Ohio , in the fall of 1850, his parents came to Des Moines Co , Iowa , in the spring of 1852, to Van Buren Co , his mother died May 3, 1876 , father is living with him , is in his 79th year , lives on the old homestead of 130 acres, valued at $35 per acre   Married Mary A Archibald, Feb 10, 1869 , she was born in Jefferson Co , Iowa , in May 1853 , have only one child living—Edward J , lost four —Charles W , Alta M , Benton W and an infant daughter, all of whom died in 1876, within a space of thirty-nine days, from diphtheria. Member of M E Church   Republican.

Spencer, J M., far , S 8 , P O Wilsonville

SPENCER, WILLIAM, farmer, Sec 6 , P O Birmingham ; owns 360 acres of land, valued at $30 per acre , born Oct 5 1823, in Kentucky, in 1824, parents moved to Jefferson Co , Ind , where they remained till the fall of 1841, when they came to Van Buren Co , Iowa, and settled upon the farm where he now lives, his father, Absalom Spencer died Sept 14, 1873, and his mother, Nancy Spencer, died Oct 6. 1870   Married Sarah J Walker March 18, 1865, she was born in 1835, and died March 23, 1870 , was again married, to Susan Shott Jan. 24, 1875 , she was born Nov 8, 1834 , have two children by his first wife—Martin N. and Isabella , and, by second wife one son—William H.   Democrat

Stewart, J., sawyer, Utica

Stanley W M , far , S 11 , P O Wilsonville

Syphers, J , far , Sec 14 , P O Wilsonville

TAYLOR, C G , far , P O Wilsonville

Taylor, O P , far , P O Hillsboro

Taylor, T E , far , S 15 , P O Wilsonville

Taylor, W A far , P O Wilsonville

Thomas, E A , far , S 36 , P O Hillsboro

VEACH, SAMUEL, far , Sec. 9 , P O Wilsonville

WATSON, JAMES A , far , S 25 , P O Hillsboro

Watson, James L , far , S 25 , P O Hillsboro

Watson, John H , far., S 28 ; P O Wilsonville

Watson, William, far S 27 , P O Hillsboro

Watson, W H H , far , P O Hillsboro

Westover, Oliver, far , P O Wilsonville

Wheatley, Caleb

WHEATLEY, JOB, farmer, carpenter and joiner, Sec 27 , P O Hillsboro, Henry Co , son of Caleb and Margaret Wheatley, born June 9, 1848, in Athens Co , Ohio , came with parents to Van Buren Co in the spring of 1857, and settled on the farm (comprising 150 acres) where he now resides   His mother died Dec 15, 1874; his father living with him   Though a boy, he enlisted in Co H, of the 45th Iowa Infantry, May 1864, he went to Tennessee and participated in the battle of Memphis against the rebel Gen Forrest, was in the 100-day service service , discharged at Keokuk October, 1864   Returned home and engaged with John Ayres to learn the carpenter and joiner's trade, which he followed till 1872, since which time he has farmed   Married Nancy Taylor June 29, 1873, she was born in this county April 13, 1853; have two children—John W and Eliza M   Wife member Christian Church ; Republican

Wheatley, Ross M , far., S. 16 , P O Wilsonville

Whitaker, S , far. , P O Utica

Whitlam, Tilghman, far , P O. Wilsonville

Wise, William, far , S 33 , P O Utica

JACKSON TOWNSHIP.

ABERNATHY, IRA, far , P O Milton

Abernathy, W. M , far , P. O Milton

Anderson, W T , laborer, Milton

BAUCH, C , cabinet-maker, Milton

Bauch, H E , cabinet-maker, Milton

BAXTER. CYRUS D., publisher of the Milton *Herald,* with Richard McNeal, Milton , was born Aug 27, 1853, in De Kalb Co , Ind , in 1869, he engaged in the office of the Waterloo *Press,* of that county, to learn the printer's trade , in the spring of 1874, went to Toledo Ohio, and engaged in the office of the *Daily Democrat,* the following fall, returned to Waterloo, and, in the spring of 1875, visited the Southwest , went to Texas and engaged in the office of the Dallas *Commercial* a short time and visited the different parts of the State prospecting, hunting, etc , till in the fall of 1876, came to Milton in January, 1877, and engaged with A L Morrison in publishing the *Headlight ,* sold out the following fall, and in the spring of 1878, in company with Mr McNeal, purchased the office and commenced publishing the Milton *Herald* Mr. Baxter has no family

Baxter, M D , photographer, Milton

Beard, W., Baptist minister. Milton

Beeler, Joseph, far , P O Milton

Bell, F , superintendent hoop-pole shop, Milton

Bell, R P., far., S 8 , P O Milton

Bell, T , blacksmith, Milton

Beuchler, J H , blacksmith, Cantril.

Blanchard, A S , far , Sec 29 , P O Milton

Blanchard, G B W , laborer, Milton

Blanchard, W F , far , Sec 19 , P O Milton

Boyd, Solomon, laborer, Milton

CAMPBELL A S , far , S 4 , P O Lebanon

Campbell, E , lumber and grain dealer, Milton

Campbell, William S , far , Sec 5 , P O Oak Point

Canfield A , far S 2 P O Lebanon

Cannon, Z , produce merchant Milton

Cantril, E E , saw-mill Cantril

CANTRIL, L. W., attorney and collecting agent, Cantril, owns 116 acres of land adjoining the town, beside most of the vacant lots , came with his parents to Van Buren Co , Iowa, in September 1839, and located near Lebanon, in this township , his early life was spent on a farm, and learning the carpenter and joiner's trade, which latter business he followed principally for eighteen years , commenced reading law in 1848, which he practiced some in connection with his other business , finally completed reading in the office of Work & Main, in Keosauqua, and was admitted to the bar in 1870 , commenced the mercantile business in Keosauqua in 1866, which he continued successfully about five years purchased the land upon which Cantril is now located, in 1870 , after the railroad reached the place, in 1872, laid out the town, and gave it his name , commenced the mercantile business the same year which he continued till the fall of 1877 , sold out to S. N Norris & Son, and the same fall went to Castle Rock, Col , for his health , followed mercantile business there , returned in the fall of 1878, satisfied to remain in Van Buren Co , expecting to devote his time principally to the practice of his profession Married Lydia Roberts, of this county, March 1, 1846, and she died Sept 10, of the same year, again married, Hannah Roberts April 5, 1848, and she died March 27, 1869; was again married, to Harriet E. Brooks Jan. 2, 1870 , she was born in Ohio Dec 8, 1834, have five children living, three by second wife, and two by third wife— Melissa, Newton, Charley, Elmer and May, lost five of second wife's children—Mary L , Lydia, Nelson, Clarissa and John Mr Cantril's father died at Afton, Iowa , March 27, 1869, and his mother, Oct 13, 1875 Member of the M E Church, Republican

Carmine, Allen, retired, Milton

CARR, J. W.. dealer in dry goods and general merchandise Milton , born Nov 14 1830 in Franklin Co Ohio, his parents moved to Mercer Co , Ill ,

5

in 1844 where his father died in October, 1845, his mother returned to Ohio, in the spring of 1853, he came to Van Buren Co, and located in Jackson Tp, where he followed farming summers and teaching school winters, till July 1860, commenced the mercantile business in Milton, in company with George Smith and Robert Russell, coming in as a partner in 1862, in 1864, they purchased Smith's interest, and, in 1867, he purchased Mr Russell's interest; in January, 1875, his father-in-law, Joseph Moore, came in as a partner He was married to Henrietta Moore Dec. 20, 1860, she was born July 21, 1840, in Franklin Co, Ohio, her parents emigrated to Iowa in 1842 Mr. Carr has the reputation of being a thorough and successful business man, and the leading merchant of Milton Democrat

CASADY, ALLEN. farmer and stock-raiser, Sec 23, P O Cantril, born June 10, 1823, came to this county in 1837, owns 142 acres of land, valued at $3,000, belongs to the Universalist Church Married Betty Ann Harrison, she was born in October, 1826, mother of two living children—William C and John J, emigrated direct from Indiana with his father, when he was 14 years old, and has resided on the same farm since, moved into a little double shanty of two rooms, 12 feet square, each with a dirt floor, where thirteen persons stayed through the winter, had a chimney on each end, made out of sticks and mud, used Jackson bedsteads at that time, had never seen a stove, there were only three families in the township when he first came, the oldest building standing in the county is on his place, the first winter they had to boil corn, and grated it on a grater for thirteen persons about a month

Casady, E. P, far, Sec 19, P O Milton
Casady J J, far., P O Cantril.
Casady, Wm, wagon-maker, Milton
Casady, Wm P, far, S. 20, P. O. Cantril
Clark, G P, carpenter, Milton
Cloat, Henry, farmer P O Milton
Conwell
Cooley,

Cooper, S. W., carpenter, Milton
Cowan, J T, far, S 2, P O Lebanon
Creath, J W, far, S 36, P O Cantril
Creath, M C, far, Sec 26, P O Cantril
Creath, W H, far, Sec 35, P O Cantril
DAY, JOHN, miller, Cantril
De Hart, J M, far, Sec 15, P O Cantril
Downes, J, retired, P O Milton
Duff, T, far, Sec 6, P O Oak Point
Duncan, D E, far, Sec 34, P O Cantril
Dye, T, dairyman, S 3, P.O Milton
Dysart, H M, Postmaster, Milton
ELWELL, JACOB, far.; P. O. Oak Point
Emerick, J far, P O Lebanon
Evans, L C far, S 4, P.O Oak Point
FAETH, CONRAD, wagon manufacturer, Milton
Fisher, Thos M, far, P O. Cantril
Fleming, W B, Deputy County Clerk, Keosauqua
Foster, H, far, S 10, P O Cantril.
GIBSON, R A, harness-maker, Milton
Gilfillan, G W, physician, Milton
Gnash, Wm, druggist, Milton
Grady, John W., far, P O Lebanon
Gray, C M. cabinet-maker, Cantril
Gray, T, far, S 17, P O Milton
Gray, Wm J, far, P O Lebanon
Guthrie, Wm, far, S 7, P. O. Milton
HAGLER, D B, far, Sec 28, P O. Milton
Hagler, G W, far, S 6, P O Milton
Harris, Isaiah, butcher, P O Milton
HAGLER, J. C., farmer, stock dealer and shipper, P O Milton, owns 400 acres of land in this county and 240 in Greene Co, near Rippey, and eighty acres in Woodbury Co; he was born March 19, 1814, in Stewart Co, Tenn; parents emigrated to Madison Co, Ill, in the spring of 1832, and, in the fall, to Warren Co, he then came to Iowa, made a claim near where Burlington now stands, there was then only one log cabin there, remained there till the spring of 1833, then returned to Illinois, the winter following went up to Dubuque then a small town, followed cutting wood with a team from Galena to Mineral Point Platteville and

Dubuque, in the fall of 1833, returned to Illinois Married there Rachel Baker Nov 30, 1837, she was born May 10, 1817, in St Clair Co, Ill, in the spring of 1843, he came to Jackson Tp, this county, and located on his farm near Milton, his brother, Amos Hagler, in company with two other families, were the earliest settlers in this township, they having located here in the spring of 1838; his brother died Nov 10, 1864 Mr Hagler has followed the stock and shipping business for the last twenty years Has five children living — George W, Nancy E, Fletcher, Susannah and David M, lost two —Elisha and Mary Has served as Notary Public several years, also as Trustee, member of School Board, etc Member of M E Church, Republican

HAGLER, J. M., proprietor of Milton Steam Mills with Julius Miller, Milton, born May 4, 1833, in Warren Co, Ill, in the summer of 1853, he went with an ox-team by overland route to California, followed mining there till the spring of 1860, then went to Silver City, Nevada, mined there; in the fall of 1861, came to Van Buren Co, and purchased a farm near Milton Married Sarah A Price Aug 14, 1862, she was born Feb 18, 1843, in Rush Co, Ind Followed farming till Jan 1, 1877, he purchased one-half interest in the Milton Mills. Has seven children —Emma H., Addie K, Jane C, David F, Marietta, Alvin A, Fletcher A, lost one daughter—Lois A. Member of the M E Church, Greenbacker

Hahn, E D, far, S 32, P O Milton
Hale, O, far, S 29, P O Milton
Halstead, I far, P O Milton
Harbin, S, far; P O Milton
Harbin, Wm, far, P O Cantril
Hargrove, J Q, far, S 17 P O Milton
Hargrove, W L, retired, Milton
Harman, Henry, far, P O Cantril
Harrel, D, hardware merchant, Milton
Harrel, H, merchant, Milton
Harrel, Hiram, far, S 19, P O Milton.
Harrel, J R, far, P O Milton
Harrel, S, merchant, Milton
Helsel, T, far, S. 6, P O Oak Point
Henthorn, N laborer Milton
Herring, E, far S 7 P O Milton
Hitt, D A, far S 1 P O Lebanon

Holder, A. F, stock dealer, Cantril
Holland, E, far, S 20, P O Milton
Holland, J C, far, S 5, P O Milton
HOLLAND, WILLIAM W., retired farmer, P O Milton, born in Sussex Co, Del, June 5, 1809, came to this county in 1840, bought his land, and, in 1842, moved his family, has 700 acres of land, valued at $15,000 Married Sarah Robbins, she was born in Sussex Co, Del, Oct 20, 1811, mother of seven children, four living—John C, Hannah, Elisha, Lydia, emigrated direct from Delaware to the land where he now lives, moved into a shanty 14x16 with a man of the name of Downs, there were ten persons in the two families, next season built a log shanty 18 x20, used Jackson bedsteads—one post and two poles, went to Bonaparte to mill, had to eat flour without bolting, came here in limited circumstances, could not get credit for a scythe; was not a man that wanted much credit; was trusted by a man of the name of Thomas Downs for $1 37½, demanded a note, or what was called a due bill, the only one he has ever paid for a store debt Mr H was among the earliest settlers, and is one of the wealthiest in the township, there were at the time he first came here plenty of Indians passing through the county Deer, wolves, and all kinds of game were in abundance Burnt the first brick that was burnt in the county, when he first came here, walked most of the way from Cincinnati, over 600 miles, also looking at land in Michigan, walking on foot 800 miles

Hollingsworth, W J, plasterer, Milton
Holmes, H F, farmer, Sec 14, P O. Lebanon
Holmes, W C, far, P O Lebanon
Hoskins, John, far, P O Cantril.
Huddleston, C W, far, S 6, P O Milton
Hull, Joseph A, far, P O Milton
Humbert, E. B, far, S 9, P O. Milton
Humbert, Isaiah, retired farmer P O Milton
Humbert, P, far, S 8, P O Milton
Humphrey, Isaiah, blacksmith, Lebanon
Hunter, G, far S P O Milton
ISENHOUR, CALEB far, Sec 23, P O Cantril

JONES, W A , physician, Cantril

KENNEDY, WM., far , S 6 , P O Oak Point

Kittle, John, farmer , P O Milton

Klate, A , far , Sec 18 , P O Milton

LARKIN, A B , farmer, Sec 29 , P O Milton

Leaverton, J , far , S 15 , P O Milton

Lewis, N , far., S 6 , P O Oak Point

Lightfoot, E , far , S 11 , P O Cantril

LINN, ALEXANDER, retired farmer , P O Cantril , owns a farm in Des Moines Tp , of 300 acres, valued at $40 per acre, born Feb 8, 1808, in Crawford Co Penn Married there to Sarah Cunningham Sept 13, 1836 , in the spring of 1845 emigrated to Iowa, and located in Franklin Tp , Lee Co , where he remained till the spring of 1865, then moved into Des Moines Tp , this county , left his farm and moved to Cantril in February, 1878 , has five children living—Ebenezer, Alonzo, Milton, John M and Amelia A ; lost one— Jerusha Ebenezer served his country three years, in Co E of the 19th Iowa V I , and John M is now in the mercantile business in Cantril, having commenced in 1875 , he was born Oct 23, 1849, in Lee Co , married to Emma H Morris, of this county, Dec 25, 1873 , they have one daughter—Bertha M All are members of the Presbyterian Church Republican

Lyon, Jas R , far ; P O Oak Point

Lyon, Wm N , far , P O Milton

McBRIDE, JOHN far , Sec 24 , P O Cantril

McBride, Wm , far S 13 , P. O Cantril

McGrath, J Q A , far , S 1 , P O Lebanon

McLean, A A & Son, hardware merchants, Milton

McManus, B , far , Sec 20 , P O Milton

McManus, J , prop hotel, Milton

McManus, Jasper, farmer , P O Milton

McManus, John , farmer , P O Milton

McManus, Milton, far , Sec 29 , P O Milton

McManus, Frank, farmer , P O Milton

McManus, William, farmer , P O Milton

McNeil, A E liveryman, Milton

McNEIL & BAXTER, publishers Herald Milton

McQuoid J far Sec 2 P O Lebanon

Manson, H L , farmer , P O Milton

Manson, John B , farmer , P O Milton

Manson, R carpenter Milton

Marston, A L , far , S 5 , P O Oak Point

Martin, G W , far , S 18 , P O Milton

Matthews, W , far , P O Milton.

Messer, F , butcher, Milton

Miller, C , miller, Milton

Miller, E , far , S 5 , P O Milton

Miller & Hagler, proprietors grist-mill, Milton

Moore, A , far , Sec 5 , P O Milton

Moore H L , plasterer, Milton

Mosher, C E , far , S 12 , P O Lebanon

Mown, J A , plasterer, Milton

Munsell, A H , far , S 21 , P O Milton

Munsell, J , far , P O Milton

Murray Wm , shoemaker Milton

NORRIS, S. N., farmer and merchant , P O Cantril , owns a farm of 730 acres, near Cantril, valued at $30 per acre , he was born Dec 21, 1815, near Lawrenceburg, Ohio , parents moved to Franklin Co , Ill , in 1820, and to Vigo Co , Ind , in 1824 , thence to Van Buren Co , Iowa, in September, 1842, and located near Pierceville Married there Rachel Moore Dec 28, 1844 , she was born in 1821, in Harrison Co , Ind , in the spring of 1866, he moved on to his present farm , in the fall of 1877 he, in company with his son, George L., commenced the mercantile business, succeeding Cantril & Brooks Have five children—Sarah, George L., Des Moines, Frank H and Robert M , lost two— John W and Elizabeth Member M E Church , Republican

PATTON, S , far , S 2 , P O Milton

Peterson, J G , far , S 34 , P O Cantril

Pickett, J far , P O Lebanon

Pitman, G A far P O Cantril.

Pitman, S B , far. , P O Cantril

Pennington, G , proprietor hotel, Milton

Powell, B , far , S 13 , P O Lebanon

Price, S W , far , P O Milton

Price, T J , far., S 28 , P O Milton

Price, Thomas J , far S 33 P O Milton.

RAY, SAMUEL, far , P O Lebanon

Remingham J E , merchant, Cantril

Renfro T A plasterer and farmer, P. O Milton

Rhoades, J , far , P O Milton
Riley, Mac, far , P O Milton
Rinebargar, G , teamster, Milton
Rinebargar, H , far , P O Milton
Rinebargar, J , far , P O Milton
Rinebargar, W P., far , P O Milton
Roberts, B , far , P O Cantril
Roberts, J F , far , P O Milton
Robinson, D A , far , P O Cantril
Roby, C , far , P O Milton.
Rowland, R , dry goods merchant, Milton
Rowland, S P far , S 19 , P O Milton.
Russell, J A , far , P O Milton
Russell, J C , merchant, Milton
Russell, John far ; P O Milton
Russell, R , retired, P O Milton
Russell, W D , merchant, Milton
SALYARDS, W L , retired , P O Milton
Saylor, R B , far , S 5 , P O Oak Point
Schwachheim, T , blacksmith, Cantril
Simpson, A H , far , P O Milton.
Smith, G W , far , S 1 , P O Cantril
Smith, J C , butcher, Cantril
Smith, J P far , S 8 , P O Oak Point
Smith, O , painter Milton
Smith, R , far , P O Cantril
Snider, J T , far , P O Cantril
Spencer, B , far , S 29 P O Milton
Stephens, C , far , S 3 , P O Lebanon
Stewart, M , far , S 34 , P O Cantril
Stonebreaker, A , far , S 1 , P O Cantril
Stott, C , Jr , far P O Lebanon
Stump, J. P., far., S 5 , P O Oak Grove
Summers, L F , physician, Milton
Swartz, J D , merchant, Cantril
TALLEN, M , far Sec 21 ; P O Cantril.
Tallen, T , far , Sec 23 , P O Cantril
Taylor, N J farmer , P O Milton
Thompson, W , far , S 2 ; P O Cantril
Townsend L A , far , Sec 10 , P. O Cantril.
Treblecock, J H , far , Sec 8 , P O Milton.
VANFLEET, AARON far , S 14 , P O Lebanon
VINSON, H. B., prop of Nagle House and Livery, owns a farm of 85 acres near town, valued at $35 per acre, born Oct 23, 1833, in Mercer Co , Ohio, came with his parents to this county in the fall of 1841, and located near Lebanon in Chequest Tp where his father still lives Married then

Virginia Robertson Oct. 24, 1858 , she was born Dec 8, 1835, moved into Vernon Tp in 1861, where he remained till 1863, then went to Taylor Co Iowa, in 1866, returned to this county, and, in 1868, located on his farm in Jackson Tp , rented his farm, and came into the Nagle House in Cantril, in 1876 , in February, 1877, commenced the livery business Has six children living—Emma I , who married Henry Brooks in August, 1878 , Libbie A Alice M , Nora B , Catharine M and Arthur M , lost one— Charles Member of the M E Church , Republican

WALLIS, H D , clerk, Milton

Warner David, farmer , P O Cantril
WARNER, ISAAC N., far . Sec 26 , P O Cantril, owns 320 acres of land, valued at $30 per acre son of Nicholas and Rebecca Warner; was born April 21, 1829, in Schoharie Co , N Y , came with his parents to this county in the fall of 1838, and located in Des Moines Tp , where they still reside Married Louisa A Vinson, of this county, Aug 18, 1853, she was born April 9, 1835, in Ohio, and died Sept 30, 1861, again married, Minerva Vinson, sister of first wife March 3, 1862 , she was born Jan 1, 1838 Came on his present farm in the fall of 1856 Mr Warner has served his township as County Supervisor, also some minor offices Has two children living, by his first wife—Francis and Charles , lost one daughter—Anna , by second wife has four children—May, Minerva, Addie and Bertram Republican
Warning, John, farmer , P O Cantril
Weatherington, John, far , P O Cantril
Wellborn, S , hardware merchant, Cantril
Wilson, D L , farmer , P O Milton
Wilson, George W., far , Sec. 9 , P O Milton
Wilson, Omar, farmer , P O Milton.
Wolf, Andrew S , far , P O Cantril
Worley, A H , retired farmer , P O Milton
YEAGER, W L , farmer , P O Cantril
Young, John

UNION TOWNSHIP.

ARCHER, J A., far., S 19, P O
Birmingham

ARNOLD, JOHN BALDWIN,
farmer, Sec 34, P. O Winchester, son
of George and Rachel (Wright) Arnold,
born Jan 5, 1827, in Fairfield Co,
Ohio Married Louisa Cupp Sept 10,
1848, the same fall came to Van Buren
Co, the following spring, returned to
Ohio, in the fall of 1855, came here
and purchased 160 acres, where he now
lives, by industry and economy, he has
added to it till he now has 500 acres of
land, valued at $35 per acre, which he has
well stocked His wife was born June
20, 1828, in Ohio, have six children
living—Emeline F, Mary A, John L,
Clara A, Alpha N and Ada C, lost
two—George W and Rachel L Member of A, F & A M Democrat

BARKER, MATTHEW, farmer, Sec
32, P O Winchester

BARNES, HIRAM, farmer and
livery, P O Birmingham, owns 160
acres of land, valued at $40 per acre,
born March 18, 1818, in Harrison Co,
Ohio, parents moved to Tuscarawas Co,
in 1820, in 1834, to McLean Co, and
from there to this county in the fall of
1839, and settled near Birmingham, he
learned the carpenter and joiner's trade
in early life, which he followed till he enlisted in 1861, in Co H, of the 3d Iowa
V. C, was elected Second Lieutenant,
and soon promoted to First Lieutenant,
was discharged in March, 1863, for disability, returned home, and soon after
engaged in his present business Was
married to Hannah B. Loomis of Jefferson Co Iowa Aug 26, 1846, she was
born July 3, 1822, in Chautauqua Co,
N Y, children—Louisa, William A,
Belle, Virginia, Mary and Iola, lost two
—Lester and James A Member of the
M E Church, Republican

Bechtel, A K, far, S 15, P O Winchester

Bechtel S, far, Sec 15, P O. Winchester

Belknap, E. B, far., Sec 21, P O Winchester

Beswick, ┌ ~   ·· ┤┌ ·· ┤ ·· Winchester

BESWICK, JAMES, Jr., farmer, Sec 26, P O, Winchester, owns
320 acres of land, valued at $40 per
acre, son of James and Augusta Beswick, born March 13, 1832, in Washington Co, Ohio, his father came to
that county from Cheshire, England,
in 1818, and married there Dec 10,
1826, the family came to this county
in the spring of 1850, and settled in
this township Mr. Beswick married
Mary E Whittlesey Oct 21, 1858; she
was born Aug 18, 1840, and died Sept
4, 1868, he again married Viola Racer,
Nov 25, 1869, she was born Sept 6,
1849, in Washington Co, Ohio, have
four children by first wife—Agnes V,
Alice M Wilson S and Lena R, and
one by second wife—W Lloyd Democrat

Beswick, T T, far, S 23, P O Winchester

Beswick, W S, far., P O Winchester.

Bickford, M, retired far, P O Birmingham

Birch, M. I., mechanic Birmingham

Blackford, J W.

Bogle, S A, feather renovator, Birmingham

Bonar, D. B, plasterer, Birmingham

Bonnett H, far, S 8, P O Birmingham

Bonnett L, far, S 9, P O Birmingham

Bonnett, S J, far, Sec 9, P O Birmingham

Bowers, W F, far, Sec 34; P O Winchester

Bradford, A H, far, Sec 29; P O Winchester

Beans, J F, wagon-maker, Birmingham.

Bryant, J. M., retired far, Birmingham

Byers, I, far, S. 20, P O Winchester

CALHOUN, JOHN Sr, farmer, P
O Winchester

CALHOUN, DAVID K., farmer,
Sec. 15, P O Winchester, owns 245
acres of land, valued at $30 per acre,
born March 9, 1844, in Westmoreland
Co, Penn, came with his parents to
this county in 1855, and to his present
farm in 1858 Enlisted in Co I, 19th
I V I in August 1862 participated
in the battles   Springfield, Mo,
Vicksburg, Miss Port Hudson and

Sterling Farm. La , in the latter, he , was taken prisoner, and was confined at Shreveport, La , and Tyler, Tex , for nearly ten months , was exchanged and returned to his regiment, and was at the battles of Spanish Fort and Mobile, Ala , discharged at the close of the war and returned home   Married Emma Travis, of this county, Nov 9, 1868, she was born June 12, 1849, in Pennsylvania, they have three children—Elvina B , Mary L and Johnson B Members of the Presbyterian Church , Republican

Calhoun, J , Jr far , P O Winchester
Calhoun, V S , far , S 22, P. O. Winchester

CALHOUN, NEWTON, retired farmer, P O Birmingham , owns 368 acres of land, valued at $30 per acre , born in Beaver Co , Penn , May 19, 1809 , parents moved to Holmes Co , Ohio, when he was small, he came to Van Buren Co in the spring of 1839, and settled near Birmingham, there being but few settlers in this vicinity , in the spring of 1850, he went to California, and returned in the spring of 1852 , left his farm and came into Birmingham in 1870   Was married to Matilda Sanders April 8, 1830 , she was born Oct 16, 1811, and died June 12, 1836 , married her sister, Esther Sanders Oct 18, 1836 , she was born April 5, 1815, and died Sept 17, 1878 , has two children living by first wife—George C and Thomas E , lost one—Thomas E , by first wife and six by second wife—Vernum S , Newton L Ross, James F., Nathan S and Rosetta M , lost three—Orange S Smith C and John C   His sons Newton and Ross served their country in the late rebellion   Mr Calhoun is a member of the M E Church, and a Republican

Campbell, J , far , S 11, P O Birmingham

Christler, H G , far , S 28, P O Winchester
Christler, M , far , P O Winchester
Clark, A S , far , P O Winchester
Cole, A , hotel man, Birmingham

COLE, J. W., proprietor of Birmingham Marble Works with E M Talbott, Birmingham born June 25 1826 in Norfolkshire, England, came with parents to Chautauqua Co N Y in 1832

moved to Butler Co , Penn., in 1836 , went to Pittsburgh in 1838, and worked at the marble business till 1843 , went to Brownsville, Fayette Co , Penn., in 1847 , went to Monongalia Co , W Va , came to Keokuk, Iowa, spring of 1851 , to Quincy, Illinois, in 1853 , to Village Tp , in 1854 , in 1859, moved to Davis Co , came to Birmingham in 1873 , established the Birmingham Marble Works, with Mr E M Talbott, as partner spring of 1878   Married Everella Overturf, of Brownsville Penn , April 25, 1850 · she was born Jan 10, 1831, in Pennsylvania, have three children—Malzena B. C., M Georgie, Maud D   Republican

CORRY, JAMES, Jr., far., Sec 18, P O Birmingham , son of James and Isabella Corry , born in Allegheny Co , Penn , in 1832 , his parents were natives of Ireland, came to the United States in 1818 ; settled in Allegheny Co , Penn , his father was born in 1797, and is still living , mother died in 1841, in Pennsylvania, came to Van Buren Co , spring of 1855 and stopped in Harrisburg Tp , in 1858, moved just north of Birmingham, and came to his present farm in 1868   Married Ellen M Redman of this county, Nov 4, 1858 , she was born in this county, died Aug 8, 1863   Married Laura E Hiatt, of Lee Co Iowa, Sept 23, 1875 , she was born Feb 19, 1850, in Iowa, have one son by first wife—Chester E , and one by second wife—Clyde L , owns a farm of 306 acres of land, valued at $40 per acre   Is a member of Presbyterian Church ; Republican

Countryman, G W , furniture dealer, Birmingham
Creamer, D C , prop Woolen Mills, Birmingham
Culbertson, J S , retired farmer, Birmingham
Cupp, George, retired far , Birmingham
DUNN, ADESON, far , P O Birmingham
Daniels, T , farmer , P O Winchester
Day, C V B , far , Sec 24, P O Winchester
Deahl, George, carpenter and joiner, Birmingham
Diehl, Samuel , carpenter and joiner, Birmingham

Dill, J , far., Sec 10 , P O Birmingham
Donnell, D , far , Sec 11 , P O Birmingham
EBERT, T D stock dealer Birming
ham.
Eichleberger. F ret far , Birmingham
Evans J B far , Sec 2 , P. O. Birmingham
Evans, W A , far , S 2 , P O Birmingham
Evans W C far , S 2 , P O. Birmingham
FERRELL, JOHN W , wagon-maker,
Birmingham
FAST, WILLIAM, farmer, Sec
5 , P O Birmingham son of Jesse
and Rebecca (Gans) Fast, born Sept
23, 1824. in Greene Co Penn , parents
moved to Jefferson Co., Ohio, in 1827,
where his early life was spent , was educated at the Richmond Academy in the
same county, and followed teaching and
farming for several years   Married
Mary A McCullough, of Jefferson Co ,
Oct 11, 1849 , she was born May 17,
1828 , in the spring of 1857, moved to
Clark Co , Mo same fall to Davis Co ,
Iowa, and to his present farm in spring
of 1863 , have five children living—Jno
M , Francis D , William, Abe Lincoln
and George M , lost two—Homer J and
an infant   Mr Fast's great-grandfather, Nicholas Fast, was of German descent ; grandfather was Francis Fast, of
Pennsylvania. and on the side of his
mother his great-great-grandfather was
Jacob Gans, of Holland, and great-
grandfather was George Gans, of Maryland, and grandfather, Benjamin Gans,
of Pennsylvania   Mr Fast is a member of the M E Church, republican
FICKEL, JOSIAS, far , S 36, P O
Utica , owns 390 acres of land, valued at
$30 per acre , born Dec 22, 1819, in
Perry Co , Ohio , came to this county in
fall of 1846, and settled on his present
farm   Married Julia A Warner June
16, 1841, she was born Jan 8, 1821,
in Fairfield Co , Ohio   have eight
children living—Susannah, Mary, Samuel, Darius Jeremiah, LeRoy, Julia A
and Josias   Democrat
Ford, B F , far , Sec 28 , P O Winchester
Fordyce, '   ~
Winche

FORDYCE, SETH. farmer, S 25 ;
P O Winchester, owns 390 acres of land,
valued at $40 per acre , born March 6,
1819, in Wabash Co , Ill , came to
Iowa in fall of 1837, to Van Buren
Co in February 1839, and settled on the
farm where he still lives; his father,
Jairus Fordyce, died here July 22, 1840,
his mother, Susan Fordyce, died March
12, 1855   Married Harriet J Alexan-
der, daughter of John and Elizabeth
Alexander, of this county, Jan 24,
1844 , she was born Aug 19, 1821, in
Warren Co , Tenn , have three children
living—Lewis F Laura and Martha E ,
the first two are married, lost two—
Mary J and Louisa A   The mother of
Mrs F is living with her , is upward
of 80 years old.   Members of Christian
Church , Republican
Fry, A A , merchant, Winchester
GIANQUE CHARLES, far , S 9 ,
P O Birmingham
Gould, E S , far , S 19 , P O Birmingham
Griffith, J , far S 11 , P O Birmingham
Grousbeck, P , retired farmer, P O Birmingham
Gurwell, L , carpenter and joiner Birmingham
GRAHAM, JOSEPH, dealer in
dry goods and general merchandise, Birmingham , owns eighty acres of land,
valued at $40 per acre, born April 21,
1832, in Guernsey Co , Ohio, came to
this county in the fall of 1849, located
in Village Township, in 1852, moved into
Lick Creek Tp to Birmingham in
1870, and commenced his present business   Married Margaret Walter Oct
30 1856 , she was born in September,
1835, in Barbour Co , W Va , have
three children living—George W , Elmer E and James H., lost one—Letetia
Member Free Methodist Church , Republican
HARBAUGH, JOHN, shoemaker,
Birmingham
HASTINGS, WILL, farmer, Sec
27 , P O Winchester , owns 100 acres
of land, valued at $40 per acre , son of
John C and Mary E Hastings, born
Nov 23, 1844, in Hardin Co , Ohio ,
                    the same year,
                    Van Buren Co ,
                    his father

again married Mary E Purdum, of Keosauqua, Iowa, and settled on the farm upon which his son now lives, he came to this county in 1858, and made his home with his father, who died Dec 24, 1875, he taught school during the winters and farmed in the summers for several years, taught fourteen terms in one district and three in another Was Township Clerk and Secretary of the School Board several terms, both of which he is now filling He has no family Democrat

Henderson, J, shoemaker, Birmingham

Hoagland, F L, clerk Birmingham

Holmes, J S, far S 24, P O Bonaparte

Hootman Wm, far, Sec 32, P O Mt Zion

Hootman, Wilson, far Sec 32, P O Mt Zion

Hope, Jas, retired far, Birmingham

Howard, Wm, far, P O Winchester

Huffstedler, J H ins agt, Birmingham

Huffman, H, ret mer, Birmingham

Hughes, J, far, S 1, P O Birmingham

Huff, W E, harness-maker, Birmingham

HOPE, WILL H., stock dealer and shipper, Birmingham, son of James and Margaret Hope born June 6, 1842, in Westmoreland Co, Penn, came with parents to this county in the spring of 1852, settled near Birmingham Enlisted in Co H, 3d I V. C., in February, 1864, was in the battle of Guntown, Miss, the battles of A J Smith's campaign, and with Gen Wilson in his raid to Macon, Ga, was honorably discharged Aug 21, 1865 Returned home and engaged in the agricultural implement business in Birmingham, in the summer of 1866, went into the drug business, in 1873, sold out and commenced his present business Married Frances McDonald Jan 17, 1867; she was born in Ohio in December, 1848, have four children—Dee, Dap C, Clarence and Lida Republican

JAMESON, R, far, S 21, P O Winchester

Jefferson T, laborer Birmingham

JOHNSTON, H. S., far S 36, P O Utica, owns 176 acres of land, valued at $45 per acre, born June 14, 1817, in Giles C W Va __ ___ __ Decatur C __ __ ___ __ __ -27 in October 1__ __ __ __ __ Vol

Buren Co, Iowa, and settled on his present farm Married Margaret Brownfield Oct 17, 1844 in Indiana; she was born in 1822 in Fayette Co, Penn, have six children living—Robert M, Mary E, Lucretia A, Ida B Charles W and John F, lost one—James F, who was in Co H, of the 2d I V I died at Chattanooga, Tenn, in 1863 Republican

Johnston, P R, far, S 23, P O Winchester.

Jones J, far, S 20, P O Winchester

JULIAN, JOHN, far, Sec 21, P O Winchester, owns a farm of 268 acres, valued at $30 per acre, born March 28 1814, in Cornwall, England, and came to the United States in 1842, and settled in Coshocton Co, Ohio Married there to Jane Crawford July 6, 1843, she was born July 28 1816, in County Antrim, Ireland, and came to the United States in 1818, they came from Ohio to this county in the fall of 1852, and settled in Union Tp, have had two children—Mary, born June 16, 1847, married Ross Calhoun Nov 16, 1865, died May 27, 1874 and Margaret J, born Nov 7, 1849, and died Dec 2, 1854. Members of the M E Church, Republican

KERR CHRISTOPHER, far, Sec 16, P O Winchester.

Kirkpatrick, G O, blacksmith, Birmingham

LAWRENCE, A A, farmer, P O Winchester

Lundy, N, far S 12, P O Bonaparte

McCOY, J A, ret far, P O Birmingham

Madden, J, ret far, P O Birmingham

Manning, A, far, S 17, P O Birmingham

Mercer, H far, P O Winchester

Miller, J S, far. P O Winchester

Moore, J P, carpenter, Birmingham

Moore, N J, far, P O Winchester

Moore, D, far, P O Birmingham

Moss, C L, far and proprietor cheese-factory, Birmingham

Moss, T, far, P O Birmingham

Morse, J, miller, Birmingham

Murphy, E, far, S 36, P O Utica

NELSON, H, far, S, 18, P O Birm__ __

N w J __ __ __ __ __ __ mingham.

Newell W __ __ __ __ __ __ __ __ ___

Newman, J. D., far, S 1, P O Birmingham

NELSON, W. W., M. D., physician and surgeon, Birmingham, born Nov 30, 1834, in Wayne Co, Ohio, came with his parents to this county in the fall of 1845, and settled in Washington Tp, where he was employed on his father's farm till of age, then went to Washington College two years, after, to Wooster, Ohio, and commenced reading medicine with Dr Dane Wilson, and subsequently attended lectures at the Iowa State University, Medical Department, and at Jefferson Medical College, Philadelphia, Penn, where he graduated in the spring of 1860, returned to this county, and commenced practicing at Pierceville Was commissioned as Assistant Surgeon in 1862 in the 15th Iowa V I, which position he held till the close of the war Located in Birmingham in 1865, he owns a farm of 100 acres, valued at $3,500 Married Almira Matthews March 20, 1860, in Lawrence Co Penn, she was born July 22, 1839, have five children living—Meldon W, Nellie X, Minnie A, Audley E and Mary L., lost two—Anna M and Elizabeth S Dr Nelson moved to Sonoma Co, Cal, in 1874, and returned the following year Member of the U P Church, Republican.

NORRIS, J. N., M. D., physician and surgeon, Birmingham, born June 7, 1816, in Steuben Co, N Y., went to Millersburg, Ohio, in 1836, commenced the study of medicine with his brother-in-law, Dr Wm. Miller, came with him to Iowa in the fall of 1837, and located at the crossing of two Indian trails, where he subsequently assisted John Harrison in laying out the town which he gave the name of Birmingham, continued the study and practice of medicine and attended medical lectures at the Iowa State University, medical department, of Keokuk, where he graduated in 1853, and has continued the practice, he has had eighteen students under his supervision, fifteen of whom have graduated and become successful practitioners, Mr Norris is associated at present with his son William P Norris He was mar... M .... J ... 24, 1 .. ..

1822, in Ohio, and died Sept 30, 1847. Was again married, to Barbara Miller Oct 26, 1848; she was born Dec 22, 1823, in Ohio, had two children by first wife—Hattie F and Samuel C the latter dead, have five children living by second wife—Izora M William P, Henry W B, Jay C M and Wilmot Proviso; lost John M G and Claud S. Member Presbyterian Church, Republican

OGILBEE, A W, dealer in butter and eggs, Birmingham.

PATTISON, ALEX, Rev, minister, Birmingham

PARKER, GEORGE, retired merchant and farmer, Birmingham, born in Lewis Co, W Va, Dec 22, 1814, came to Adams Co, Ill, in the fall of 1835, and from there to this county in the summer of 1836, and made his claim adjoining what is now Birmingham, spent the time improving his land and traveling in the Southern States to Memphis, Vicksburg New Orleans, etc., till 1844; engaged in the mercantile business, which he continued till 1861, sold out and engaged as clerk for Pitkin & Moss for about ten years, and for others afterward till 1874, went to California on a visit for about seven months Mr Parker was County Treasurer during 1851–52 Married Hannah C Calhoun, of this county, Dec. 23, 1847, she was born Dec 25, 1825, in Holmes Co, Ohio, have two children—William R and Jesse F Member M E Church, Republican

PARKER, W. R., publisher and editor, with C L Sheward, of the Birmingham *Enterprise*, son of George and Hannah C. Parker, born in Keosauqua Aug 12, 1852, commenced learning the printer's trade in 1873, in the *Enterprise* office, in January, 1875. became a partner in the office. Was married to Mamie Randall June 10, 1877, she was born April 5, 1858, in Illinois Republican Mr C L Sheward, partner of W R Parker, was born April 3, 1845, in Morgan Co, Ohio, came with parents to Fairfield, Jefferson Co, Iowa, in December, 1851, commenced to learn the printer's trade in the office of the ... field Z ..... in the spring of 1859, ... in Burlington and

Milwaukee, where he enlisted in Co E, 17th Wis Regt., in December 1863 participated in all the battles in Sherman's march to the sea, mustered out in July, 1865, and returned home, and worked at journey work in different offices, including eighteen months in the *Times* office at St Louis became a partner in the *Enterprise* office in July, 1875 Was married to Margaret Skinner, of Fairfield Iowa, June 30, 1870, she was born July 11, 1845, in Pennsylvania, have one daughter—Stella A Republican.

Pepper, J S, broom-maker, Birmingham
Pettit, D C, laborer, Birmingham
Pettit G R, laborer, Birmingham
Phillips, M, far, S 22, P O Winchester
Pitkin, E, merchant and banker, Birmingham.
Pitkin & Skinner, merchants
Pleasant, C C, painter, Birmingham
Porter, Robert, photographer, Birmingham

RIDDINGTON, D, P O Winchester

RAGSDALE, J. N., Postmaster and dealer in drugs and stationery, Birmingham, born May 12, 1840, in Owen Co, Ind, came with parents to this county in the spring of 1850, stopped in Harrisburg Tp. in 1852, moved to Lucas Co, where they still reside, he returned to this county in August, 1862 Enlisted in Co I, 19th I V I, went as 1st Sergeant, was at the battle of Springfield, Mo, siege of Vicksburg, Miss, and Morganza, La, where he was captured and taken to Tyler, Tex, kept there three months, taken to Shreveport, La, was there about three months, when he, with six others, made his escape, after nineteen days of fatigue and hardships, reached the Union lines, on return to his regiment, was promoted 1st Lieutenant, discharged Aug 18, 1865 Returned home, moved to Hickory Co, Mo, returned to this county in 1869, settled near Birmingham, in 1872, moved into Birmingham and took charge of the *Enterprise* office, two years after, sold out and commenced his present business Was appointed Postmaster in 1875 Married Rachel A Cupp March 6, 1861, she was born Jan 5, 1841 in Ohio, have five chil-

dren—George W, Elmer E, Olive M, Cora B and Ella I Member of M E Church, Republican

RANDALL, J. J., dealer in dry goods and general merchandise, Birmingham, born Aug 27, 1828, in Clark Co, Ill, came from there to Birmingham, this county, in October, 1846, purchased a farm near town and followed farming till 1855 when he engaged in the general merchandise business, which he has continued till the present Married Miss Adaline E Marquis, of Marshall Co, Ill, Jan 9, 1856, she was born Sept 23, 1835, in Ohio, have eight children living—William M., Harry E, Marion R, Emma J, James N, Frank W, Mabel and Herbert R, lost one—Jessie Member Presbyterian Church, Republican.

RICHEY, ISAAC P., farmer, Sec 19, P O Winchester, son of Jas E and Elizabeth (Parker) Richey, born in Van Buren Co April 28, 1846, his parents were natives of Lewis Co, W Va, came to this county in 1836 his father died March 19, 1874 Isaac P married Abagail Matthews Feb 14, 1868, moved to Scotland Co., Mo, the same spring, returned the following fall, and lives on the home farm, has four children—Ison E, Dallas N, Shannon D and an infant. Republican

SEWARD, MATTHEW, P O Winchester

Shagley, J, far, S 15, P O Winchester

SHEPPARD, J. M., dealer in stock and proprietor of meat market, P O Birmingham, born Jan 1, 1842, in Monroe Co, Ind, came with his father E D Sheppard, to Keosauqua, of this county, in the fall of 1854 In the spring of 1861, enlisted in Co F, 2d Iowa V I, and was discharged for disability in October, 1861 Returned to Keosauqua and engaged in the grocery business for one year, went to Indianapolis, and engaged in the same business, a year after, returned to Bentonsport, this county, where he kept a harness-shop for two years, then went to Quincy, Ill, and followed the same business one year, returned to Keosauqua in the spring of 1867 came to Birmingham and the manufacture of harness which he continued till January 1873 commenced the stock trade in the fall of 1877 Married Adda Arington Dec 6, 1869 -he was born in March. 1846 in New York Have one child—Mark lost two—Stella and Water Republican

Sherod. M C far. S 33 P. O. Winchester

SHEROD. WM. N., farmer Sec 33 P O Mt. Zion, owns 167 acres of land. valued at $35 per acre, son of Amos and Mary Carnes Sherod, born March 9. 1829, in Carroll Co Ohio, came with parents to this county in the spring of 1854 and settled on the farm he now owns his father died July 26. 1854 at the age of 67 he was the first white child born in Jefferson Co Ohio his mother, a native of Pennsylvania died in this county Sept 2 1863 Married Hannah Barker. of this county June 10, 1857 she was born Jan 2 1835, died March 26. 1863 he married Elizabeth Barker Jan. 19, 1865, she was born in this county Nov 18 1840, have one child by first wife living— Henry B, lost two—Joseph P and Ethelinda, and six by second wife— Zaida E, Mary R Charles O Martha E Rosanna Amos R lost one—William A Members of M E Church, Republican

Sheward & Parker, publishers of the Birmingham *Enterprise*

SHOTT. SAMUEL B., proprietor of Birmingham Wagon and Carriage Works Birmingham is now procuring a patent for a very valuable improvement in drop end-board for lumber wagons which he will use in his manufacture of wagons born in Tuscarawas Co Ohio May 4 1826, commenced learning his trade in 1846, came to Iowa in the fall of 1853 and stopped at Fairfield, Jefferson Co., till the following spring. came to Birmingham and engaged in his present business Was married to Isabella Croft, in Ohio, April 30, 1851, she was born June 4 1834, and died Sept 8 1858, was again married to Alviza Skinner, Dec 14, 1859, she was born in Iowa Aug 30 1841 have two children by first wife living two— and

Charles A Austin B Franklin William and Alviza, lost one—Maggie Mr. Shott is among the leading and enterprising men of Birmingham

Silvis. A mechanic Birmingham

SKINNER. JOHN S., farmer, Sec 19 P O Birmingham, son of Addi Skinner, was born March 20 1812, in Steuben Co N Y, same year. his parents moved to Seneca Co. he remained at home till his father died, in April, 1830 from that time till he was married followed boating on Seneca Lake and the canal Married Catharine A Rail of Yates Co. N Y Feb 22, 1836; December 1838 moved to Iowa; stopped at Fort Madison spring of 1839 came to his present farm, have five children living—Joseph V, Charles A. George N Dick and Walrade A, lost five—Peter. Samuel, Franklin and two infants not named. his son Joseph served in Co H of the 1st Colo V I, and Charles A in Co H of the 3d I V C Republican

Smith F J far Sec. 9, P O Birmingham

SMITH. HUGH, far Sec 9, P O. Birmingham, owns 470 acres of land. valued at $30 per acre; son of John Smith, born Dec. 20, 1820 in Barren Co, Ky his parents moved to Fulton Co Ill in 1834, thence to this county in the spring of 1835, and settled on the farm he now owns, his father died in October, 1871, his mother in February, 1872 Married Martha Redman Jan 14, 1842, she was born Oct 20, 1823, in Morgan Co Ill, they have four children living—Fulton J, Rolla W George L, Minnie E, lost three— Amanda L Fanny J and an infant. He is among the leading and influential farmers of his township Republican

Spees J B M D, far, Birmingham

Spidler, L S far S 5; P O Birmingham

Stansberry R R stone-mason, Birmingham

Sull, D N far, S 5, P O Birmingham

Stonebraker Samuel M far, S 2, P O Birmingham

TEAL, JOHN, far Sec 36, P O [....]

TALBOTT T P partner with gham Marble n of Joseph

and Mary J Talbott, was born Sept 6, 1856, in Birmingham, his father was a practicing physician here, and died of cholera Nov 27, 1876, Mr E M Talbott learned the marble business in Des Moines, was there about three years, commenced working with Mr Cole in January, 1878 and, in the spring, engaged as a partner in the business Is a member of the M E Church, Republican

Teal, Thomas, far, Sec 35, P O Utica.

Thompson, W H cabinet-maker, Birmingham

TOPPING, JOHN. farmer, Sec 32, P O Winchester, son of Robert and Esther (Rowen) Topping born Dec 23, 1823, in County Cavan, Ireland, came to the United States in the spring of 1847, to Fairfield Co Conn, and engaged in a wrought-iron foundry, in June, 1851, went to California, and followed mining, returned in the spring of 1855, and worked in same foundry, in the spring of 1856, came to Iowa, settled in Union Tp, Van Buren Co Married Margaret Addy, of Orange Co, N Y., Sept 1, 1855, she was born Jan 26, 1832, in Monaghan Co, Ireland, have nine children—Robert J, John W, Homer R, George S, Maggie E, Hugh A, Samuel F, Mary E and Catharine A   Owns a farm of 246 acres, valued at $35 per acre. Member of the Presbyterian Church, Republican

TORRENCE, F. G., dealer in drugs, books, stationery, etc, Birmingham, born Jan 14, 1843, in Westmoreland Co, Penn, came with parents to this county in June, 1851, and located in Birmingham, his father carrying on the cabinet business, was educated at the Birmingham Academy Enlisted June 13, 1861, in Co A, 1st I V C., was in the battles of Blackwater, Silver Creek, Mo, and Prairie Grove, Little Rock and Camden, in Arkansas, mustered out at Davenport, Iowa, Sept 19, 1864 Returned home and commenced reading medicine with Dr Joseph Talbott, practiced two years, but, on account of ill-health, engaged in his present business   Married Belle Hancock of this county Sept 6, 1866 she was born in this

county Oct 17, 1848, have three children—Samuel G, Kitty L and William C Republican

Torrance, S G, cabinet-maker, Birmingham

Trumbo, J H far, Sec 36, P O Utica

VALE, B R

Valentine, E F, blacksmith, Birmingham

Vincent, Wm, far, P O Winchester

WALKER, J, far, S 22, P O Winchester

Walker E, far, S 22, P O Winchester

Walmer J, retired far, P O Birmingham

Walters I N, far, S 21, P O Winchester

Warner F far, S 36, P O Utica

WEBBER, JOHN H., far, S 1, P O Birmingham, owns eighty acres of land, valued at $30 per acre, son of John Webber, born Jan 20, 1838, in Somersetshire, England, parents moved to Winnebago Co, Ill, in 1850, and to Van Buren Co., in October 1857, his father died in April, 1858, and mother died Oct 12, 1877 Enlisted in August, 1862, in Co I, 19th Regiment Iowa Vols, and spent three years in fighting under the stars and stripes, except over nine months in rebel prisons; in the battle of Prairie Grove, Ark was wounded in the left thigh, and had six bullet-holes in his clothing, in his next battle, Sterling Farm, La he was taken prisoner, sent to Shreveport, La and from there to Tyler, Texas, after his exchange, was at the battle of Vicksburg, Spanish Fort and Mobile, Ala Married Hannah E Newman Dec 9, 1869, she was born Jan 20, 1851, in this county, have two children living—Ella G and Alta N, lost one —Frankie B Republican

Webber, P C, far, S 2, P O Birmingham

WEBBER, WM. H., far., S. 2, P. O Birmingham, owns 144 acres of land, valued at $25 per acre, brother of John H Webber, born Oct 15, 1841, in Somersetshire, England, came with parents to Winnebago Co, Ill, in 1850, thence to this county in October, 1857, and settled here being the one he now owns Married Hannah L Mallory, of Chicago, Ill , April 1, 1872 , she was born June 28, 1852, in town of Moscow Hillsdale Co , Mich , have two children—Charles H and Susan M Member of the M E. Church , Republican

West A . far , S 21 , P O Winchester.

WHITAKER, WM. W., farmer, P O Winchester, son of John M and Jane (Phillips) Whitaker , born Sept 17, 1826, in Hamilton Co , Ohio , parents moved to La Porte Co , Ind , when he was a boy, thence to Illinois in the fall of 1835 , the following January, came to Van Buren Co and settled on the farm where he now lives , his father was one of the delegates to the Constitutional Convention which framed the first Constitution of Iowa , also represented the county in the State Legislature at Burlington several successive terms, the last in 1861 and 1862 in 1862, moved to California, where he still lives Mr Whitaker married Miss N C Newell, of this county, Dec 5, 1858 , she was born Dec 5, 1833, in Kentucky , have three children living— Carrie Charley and Walter , lost one infant Owns a farm of 200 acres valued at $35 per acre   Democrat

Whittlesey, A P , far , P O Winchester

Wilkerson, J. S , painter, Birmingham

Williams, B F , far., S. 1 , P O Birmingham

WILSON, SAMUEL, retired farmer, and Mayor, Birmingham , owns 190 acres of land, valued at $25 per acre , born May 20, 1820, in the county of Donegal, Ireland , came to the United States in the spring of 1832, and settled in Butler Co , Penn , and to this county in the spring of 1846, and purchased a farm adjoining the town of Birmingham, part of which was subsequently platted in the town, he is the present Mayor of the town, and has served the people as Justice of the Peace about ten years, also as Mayor eight years He was married to Magdalena Shults, of Keosauqua, she was born in 1834 in Westmoreland Co , Penn , have four children living—Margretta, Mary A., James L and Willard

A , lost one infant Members of the Presbyterian Church, Republican.

WOLF, J. WESLEY, proprietor and principal of the Birmingham Academy and Boarding-School , son of William C and Rhoda (Clutter) Wolf, born Oct. 4, 1842, in Washington Co , Penn , in the spring of 1851, came with parents to Lee Co. Iowa, his early life was spent on the farm in summers, and attending school in winters, commenced teaching in 1862; was a student at Howe s school, Mt Pleasant, and at the Iowa State University, of Iowa City, normal department, where he graduated in June, 1867 , taught at Charleston, Lee Co , Boyleston, Henry Co , and Birmingham and Farmington, of this county, purchased the Birmingham Academy in the fall of 1871 He was married to Miss Maggie Hiatt July 26, 1872, of Lee Co , Iowa , she was born Jan 1, 1848, in Iowa; she is acting as one of the teachers of the Academy.

Wolgamot, J B , cabinet-maker, Birmingham

Woods, Alexander H

Work, S , far , Sec 7 , P. O Birmingham

WORKMAN, RICHARD, farmer, Sec 24 , P O Winchester, owns 240 acres of land, valued at $40 per acre , born Jan 7, 1818, in County of Londonderry, Ireland , came with parents to the Western Continent in 1834 , arrived at Quebec, where his father was attacked with the cholera and died, and his mother the day following of same disease, leaving him, a brother and sister orphans , the following year, he went to Buffalo, N Y , spring of 1838, went to Hamilton Co , Ohio Was married there to Mary A Bowers Dec 12, 1841 , in 1842, came to this county and settled in Union Tp , his wife was born Sept. 26, 1822, in Pennsylvania, have one son living—Girard W , lost nine children—William B , William L , Maria A , Mary R , Oliver P , Joshua, Girard, Lizzie and Richard A   Mr Workman is among the most influential men of his township   Democrat

HARRISBURG TOWNSHIP.

ALEXANDER, W H , farmer, Sec 20 , P O Bentonsport

BARR, ROBERT, far , S. 1 , P O Hillsboro

Baiger, L , merchant, in Harrisbuig Tp

Baugher, J , far , S 26 , P O Big Mound

Bell, J H , far , S 33 P. O Bonaparte

Bennett, J , far , Sec 25 , P. O Big Mound

BLACKFORD, J. W., Bonaparte

BOON, R. L., DR., physician and surgeon , Utica , son of Samuel and Sarah (Crawford) Boon , was born Jan 1, 1850, near Birmingham in this county, where his father still lives , his mother died Aug 26, 1856 , parents emigrated to this county in July, 1845, from Wayne Co , Ohio Dr Boon was educated at the Birmingham Academy and at Monmouth College. Illinois; commenced the study of medicine in 1873, under Dr J N Norris, of Birmingham, and subsequently attended Rush Medical College, of Chicago, Ill , commenced the practice of medicine in Bonaparte in 1875, and, in 1877 came to Utica, where he is now located Republican

BROWNFIELD, E. P., M. D., farmer and physician , P O Bentonsport , owns 350 acres of land, valued at $35 per acre , son of Robert and Sarah Brownfield , born Aug 20, 1832, in Fayette Co , Penn , parents moved to Union Co , Ind , in 1834, and to Decatur Co , in 1839, to Van Buren Co , Iowa spring of 1846, and located near Utica, in Cedar Tp , where his father died Sept 10, 1857, in the 64th year of his age, having served in the war of 1812 , his mother is living on the home farm in her 83d year Mr. Brownfield married Mary A Stevens, of this county, March 24, 1853 , she was born May 12, 1834, in Ripley Co , Ind In the fall of 1853, he moved into Wapello Co , returned to this county in the spring of of 1855 , in the fall of 1858, moved to Sullivan Co , Mo , and, in February, 1860, returned to Van Buren Co and commenced the study of medicine with Dr. Allen, of Bentonsport , since he has followed the back business continuing his studies and the practice of medicine

he graduated at the College of Physicians and Surgeons, in Keokuk, Feb. 14, 1878 , purchased his present farm in 1873 , has accumulated all his property since 1860. by economy, industry and perseverance Has been Justice of the Peace about four years Has nine children living—Sarah A , Rebecca R William A , George B , Herman G , Carrie A , John F. A., Mary E and Charles P , lost two—Andrew A and Robert V Member of the Missionary Baptist Church . Democrat

Buragrufl, J., far . S 27 , P O Bonaparte.

CAMPBELL, LEWIS, far , S 10 , O P Bonaparte owns 100 acres of land, valued at $40 per acre , he was born Jan 2, 1834, in Fayette Co , Penn , came with parents to this county in the spring of 1855 Married Minerva McDow Dec 15, 1859 , she was born Sept 25, 1832, in Illinois , have five children—Albert D , born Feb 9, 1861 , Elliott B , Feb 27, 1863 , Exavera, April 28, 1866 , Julia L , Aug 30, 1872 , Hattie T , March 9, 1874 His wife is a member of the church His father died in March, 1874 mother still lives with brother in Jefferson Co , Iowa. Republican

Cass, L far , S. 18 , P O Bentonsport

Cheney, L C , far., S 33 , P O Bonaparte

CHRISTIAN, A. J., far , S. 13 , P O Bonaparte , owns 200 acres of land, valued at $50 per acre , born Nov 17, 1814, in Hawkins Co , Tenn , parents moved into McMinn Co , in 1826. He married there Sarah McKeehan Feb 12 1832 Moved into Marshall Co in 1834 , in the fall of 1838, he came to Van Buren Co., Iowa , lived near Bonaparte till 1840, when he purchased the farm now owned by Jacob Fritsinger , in the fall of 1841, had the misfortune of having his house burned with all its contents , sold and purchased the farm now owned by W C Sturdivant, remained there a few years , then sold and came on his present farm His wife died Sept 22 1864 married, to Elizabeth Call in 1865 , she was born Jan 1843 adelphia,

Penn , has seven children by first wife living—Charles W , Asbury L , Naomi E , Mary J , Sarah J , Eliza A , Martha I , lost one—William A , by second wife—Edwin E and Lottie M. Democrat

Cline, A , far , Sec. 34 , P O Bonaparte

Connor, P , far , Sec 28 , P O Bonaparte

Cresswell, Mathew, far , S 11 , P O Bonaparte

Custer, John L , Bonaparte

DODD, D J far , Sec 9 , P. O. Utica.

Dodds, J , far , S 16 , P O Pierceville

DODDS, W. H., farmer , P O Pierceville, owns 130 acres of land, valued at $35 per acre , born Sept 19, 1838, in Jefferson Co , Ill , came with parents to Iowa in the spring of 1851, and located in Lee Co , in 1854, came to Van Buren Co. , made his home at his father's till he enlisted in Co F, 14th Iowa Inf , in October, 1861 , participated in the battle of Fort Donelson , also at Pittsburg Landing, at the latter place was taken prisoner , sent to Montgomery, Ala , thence to Macon, Ga. , then to Olivia, Va , where he was paroled and exchanged, after being in prison over nine months , re-entered the service in April, 1862 , was promoted to Second Lieutenant , in the spring of 1863 to First Lieutenant; was with Gen Banks in his Red River expedition , also with A J Smith in his raid through Mississippi , mustered out in November, 1864, and returned home Married Catherine S Geddis, of this county, June 1, 1865 , she was born in 1847, died in November, 1868 , he again married, Ellen M Perry March 1, 1872 , she was born in 1854, in Ohio , had two children by first wife—Lydia W and William V , and two by second wife—John D and Homer Mr Dodds went to California in February, 1870 , returned the following fall Is a member of the Missionary Baptist Church ; Greenbacker

DRAKES, JOSEPH, far , S. 3 , P O Utica , owns eighty acres of land, valued at $45 per acre , born March 15, 1809, in Lincoln-shire, England , followed the occupation of coachman , came to New York City in April, 1830 , rem... ...three...

Boston and engaged at same business , in 1835, went to Philadelphia ; thence to Baltimore, Md , and was a driver on the Good Intent line of stages between Baltimore and Wheeling, W Va , a year after, went to Cincinnati, Ohio , drove stage on the line between there and Springfield, then engaged with a man of the name of Basey as horseman at Hamilton City , afterward in a livery-stable in Cincinnati, after which he went to Louisville, Ky , a short time, then to Vicksburg and to New Orleans , returned to Cincinnati and engaged in the livery business , went to Uniontown, Penn , and engaged in the stage-driving business again Married, while there, Jane Nixon April 1, 1841 , she was born March 12, 1819 In the fall of 1848, he immigrated to Van Buren Co , Iowa, and located on his present farm Have no children.   Republican

EASLING, H L , far , Sec 15 , P O Bonaparte

Easling, M , far S 22 , P O Bonaparte

EICH, JACOB, farmer, Sec 28 , P O Bonaparte, son of Phillip and Catherine (Swigert) Eich , was born Nov 5, 1830, in Adams Co , Penn , came with his parents to this county in the spring of 1844 ; in the spring of 1850, went to California by overland route , remained there till the spring of 1854, and then returned to Iowa Married Agnes Beck of this county, May 31, 1855 , she was born Oct 17, 1834, in Adams Co , Penn , have eight children—Anna, Phillip, Alice, Thomas, Charles, Hattie, Katie and George In 1860, moved into Bonaparte, and engaged in the employ of Meek Brothers, in the grist-mill, till 1872, and then engaged in the grain business with Mr Chapman till 1874 then in the mercantile business till 1876, when he came on his present farm of 240 acres, owned by him in company with the other heirs of Mr George Beck, his father, who died March 4, 1854, and his mother Feb 22, 1859 Mr E has served his township as Clerk and Trustee several years, also as Assessor of Bonaparte Tp. Democrat

ENDERSBY. ARTHUR, farmer S. 12 P O Hillsboro, Henry ... own ... of land, valued at

$40 per acre, born March 11, 1835, in Bedfordshire, Eng, his parents immigrated to the United States in 1841, and located near Hillsboro, Henry Co, in 1843, came into Van Buren Co, in 1857, went to California, and, in 1859, returned to Van Buren Co, his father died in 1860 Married Anna M. Smith, of Lee Co, Iowa, May 16, 1860, she was born in 1841, near Zanesville, Ohio, have nine children living—Elizabeth S, Alvadus O, Arthur E, Ulysses S., Vincent C, William, Alonzo, Robert L and Lorenzo D Greenbacker

Ely, J W, far, Sec 7, P O. Pierceville.

Engle, S, far, Sec 22, P O Bonaparte

FARNUM, FREDERICK, far, Sec 23, P O Bonaparte

Fletcher, William, far, S 25, P O Big Mound

FRITSINGER, JACOB, far, Section 34, P O Bonaparte, owns 290 acres of land, valued at $40 per acre, born March 26, 1822, in Wayne Co, Ohio Married there Catherine Ebe March 12, 1846, she was born Sept 16, 1824, in the summer of 1848, emigrated to Iowa; stopped first at Mahaska Co a short time, then went to Lee Co, near West Point, in the spring of 1849, came to his present farm Have one son—John W born Nov 9, 1839 Member of the Missionary Baptist Church, Democrat

GILBERT, H, far, S 31, P O Bentonsport

HARLAN, CYRUS, far, S 1, P O Hillsboro

Harlan, N B, far, S 2, P O Hillsboro

Harr, H W, far, S 35, P O Bonaparte.

Harris, G, far, S 29, P O Bonaparte

Heller J A, far, S 15, P O Bonaparte

Henry, T., far., S 8, P. O. Pierceville

HORN, HUGH N., farmer, Section 1, P O Hillsboro, Henry Co, Iowa, owns a farm of 300 acres, valued at $40 per acre, born Nov 17, 1830, in Washington Co, Penn In early life, he learned the carpenter and joiner's trade, came to Van Buren Co, Iowa, in 1857, and remained till the fall of 1860; returned to Pennsylvania, and, in the spring of 1861, enlisted in an independent cavalry company, from Wash-

ington Co, Penn, in which he continued two years and eight months, when he was transferred to Co B, of the 22d Penn Cavalry, participated in the battle of Winchester, Va, also many of the battles of Hunter's raid to Lynchburg, Va, part of the time under Sheridan in his raid in the Shenandoah Valley, discharged in the fall of 1864 In the fall of 1865, returned to this county and followed his trade, in 1873, bought his present farm Married Susannah Grim Nov 17, 1871, she was born in 1843, in Pennsylvania, died Aug 8, 1876 Republican

ISRAEL, J. D., farmer, Sec 4, P O Utica, owns 710 acres of land, valued at $40 per acre, born Sept 14, 1818, in Butler Co, Ohio, parents moved to Decatur Co., Ind., in 1830, in the fall of 1843, he came to Washington Co, Iowa, in the spring of 1850, went by overland route to California, returned in the spring of 1851, and located in Harrisburg Tp Married Julia Nixon, daughter of Isaac Nixon, Sept 14, 1851, have six children living—John I, Clara B, George H, Larissa, Nettie and Joseph, lost two—Mary J and Emma Mr Israel has, by his own industry and economy, accumulated a handsome property, which will enable him to pass down the decline of life in peace and comfort Members of the Missionary Baptist Church, Republican

JEWETT, A, far, S 5, P O. Utica

Jewett, O, far, S 5, P O Utica

Johnson, B, far, S 1, P O Hillsboro

Johnson, C P, far, S 2, P O Hillsboro

KING, M, far, Sec 34, P O Bonaparte

KECK, HENRY, farmer, Sec 5, P O Utica, owns 420 acres of land, valued at $40 per acre, born Dec 4, in 1823, Westmoreland Co, Penn, went to Cincinnati, Ohio, and engaged in a wholesale and retail grocery store for his uncle, in the fall of 1849, came to Van Buren Co, in the spring of 1850, went by overland route to California, returned in 1851, in 1852, again went to California, in 1855, returned and settled on the farm where he now lives He married Mary Nixon, daughter of

6

Isaac Nixon, of this county, Dec. 13, 1855, she was born May 23, 1830, in Fayette Co, Penn, have four children living—Anna B, Elmer E, Sallie C, Henry J., lost one daughter—Ella J Mr. Keck's father died here June 10, 1863, at the age of 59, and his mother died May 20, 1874, at the age of 64. Member of the M E Church, Republican

Klise, G, far, Sec 8, P O Utica

Klise, John, far, Sec 6, P O Utica

LEFFLER, M, far, Sec 17, P O Pierceville

Lyon, F M, far and blacksmith, Sec 7, P O Pierceville

Lyon, J, far, Sec 7; P O Pierceville

MAHLER, M, far, Sec 32, P O Bonaparte

Manning, A, far, S 17, P O Birmingham

Martin, A, far, S. 11, P O. Bonaparte.

Masdon, J, far, S 1, P O Hillsboro.

McCullough, D C, far, S 4, P O Utica

McGoun, T S, far, S 25, P O Big Mound

McGrear, G, far, S 2, P O Utica

McLain, R, far, S 8, P O Pierceville

Meredith, J., far, P O Bonaparte.

Miller, A, far, S 32; P O Bonaparte

Miller, A, far, S 22, P O. Bonaparte

Miller, C O, far., S. 34, P O Bonaparte

Miller, G W, far, S 26, P O Bonaparte

Miller, J A, far, S 22, P O Bonaparte

Miller, J H, far., P O. Bonaparte.

Miller, W, far, S 34, P O. Bonaparte

MILLER, SAMUEL H., far, Sec 15, P O Bonaparte, owns 240 acres of land, valued at $40 per acre, born Feb 24 1826, in Hardy Co, W Va Married there Amelia Miller October 11, 1847; she was born March 4, 1829, came to Iowa in the fall of 1852, and settled in Appanoose Co; in the fall of 1854, he moved to California, in the fall of 1858, returned to Iowa and settled upon his present farm in Harrisburg Tp. Van Buren Co, has one daughter living, who married W A Christian in February 1870, who died in May, 1877, she now lives at her father's, lost two children—Susannah and America Democrat

Moore, H, farmer, Sec 25, P O Big Mound

Moore J, far, S 13, P O Big Mound

PERCIVAL, J B, far, S 12, P. O. Hillsboro

PEASE, J. B., farmer, Sec. 24, P O Big Mound, Lee Co, Iowa, owns 215 acres of land, valued at $55 per acre, born Jan. 24, 1817, in Washington Co, Penn, in the spring of 1851, came to Iowa, and located in Marion Tp, of Lee Co, in the spring of 1865, moved into Washington Tp, same county, thence to his present farm in Harrisburg Tp in the spring of 1866 Married Elizabeth McCullough Sept 24, 1844, in Pennsylvania, she was born in November, 1820, and died Dec 25, 1856, again married, Catharine L Crawford in Pennsylvania Nov 24, 1859, she was born in 1827, and died Dec. 29, 1865, again, married Catharine C Brownlee Oct 17 1867, she was born in 1827 in Pennsylvania, had four children by first wife—Frances M, Anna M, John M and Samuel G, who died in Tennessee in the army, had four children by second wife, all of whom died in infancy Mr Pease was elected to the House of Representatives from Lee Co in the fall of 1856, and to the Senate from Van Buren Co in 1873 Is a member of the Presbyterian Church, Democrat

Piper, John, far, S 12; P O Hillsboro

Proper, L W far, S 15, P O Bonaparte

PROPER, O. C., farmer, Sec 14; P O Bonaparte, owns 805 acres of land, valued at $45 per acre, born March 7, 1825, in Tompkins Co., N Y, in the fall of 1845, went to Mason Co, Ky, in the fall of 1846, came to Van Buren Co, Iowa, thence to Tennessee, and there appointed Assistant Quartermaster in the U S. A, and went to Mexico during the Mexican war, in the fall of 1847, returned to Van Buren Co. and purchased a part of the farm which he now owns Married to Caroline C Sedgwick, of Tompkins Co N Y, May 1, 1851; she was born Jan 12, 1831; have six children living—Alice M, Hena M., Clinton L, Marcus O, Elmira and Carlton C, lost one—Charlotte Mr Proper is the owner of one of the best farms in his township Republican

ROBBINS, W C, far. S 6, P O Utica

Rodestock, F , far , S 29 , P O Bentonsport

Rounkles, J P , far , S 27 , P O Bonaparte.

Russell, S , far ,Sec 27 , P O Bonaparte

SCHMIDT, JOHN P , farmer. Sec 32 , P O Bonaparte

Schmidt, C W., far., S 32 , P O Bonaparte

Smith. M . far , P O Bonaparte.

SNYDER, ADAM, farmer , P O Bentonsport, owns 102 acres of land, valued at $35 per acre, born Aug 10, 1816 in Chester Co., Penn , worked at farming till about 30 years of age, then worked on the P C R R about ten years, till he came to Van Buren Co , Iowa, in the spring of 1859, and settled upon the farm upon which he is still living Married Anna M Tussey March 11, 1847, in Pennsylvania , she was born April 8. 1822 ; have two children—Adelaide V., born Feb 29, 1848, and William M., born April 29, 1858, son was married to Rebecca R Brownfield, May 4, 1876, daughter was married to Harris Easling, who is in Kansas Members of the M E Church Democrat

SPROTT, SAMUEL J., farmer, Sec 3 , P O Utica, owns 185 acres of land, valued at $40 per acre, son of Thomas and Elizabeth Sprott , born Dec 9, 1829, in Beaver Co , Penn , came with parents to Lee Co., Iowa, in the fall of 1845 , in 1853, came to Van Buren Co , Iowa ; his father died Aug 23, 1876. and mother March 13, 1869 He married Sarah E. Straight Sept 15, 1857, she was born March 16, 1836, in Tyler Co., W Va , and came to Iowa in 1855 , have six children living— Samuel D , Ida, Fred, John, Frank and Fanny K lost five—Joseph T , May B , Charlie, Miriam and Willie Mr Sprott has filled the offices of Trustee and Assessor of the township Democrat

Spraker, J , mer , Sec 6 , P O Utica

Sprankle, W U , far , Sec 34 , P. O. Bonaparte

Steele H , far , Sec 3 , P. O. Hillsboro

STEPHENSON, J. H., farmer, Sec 24 , P. O. Big Mound, Lee Co , owns ninety acres of land, valued at $50 per acre; born Dec 11 1820 in Wash

ington Co. Penn , came to Van Buren Co , Iowa, in the spring of 1854, and settled on the farm where he now resides , during the year 1875, he lived in Fort Madison Married Miss Sarah J Sutherland, of Jefferson Co , Ohio, July 27, 1818, she was born Jan 10, 1826, have one daughter—Rebecca L , born July 15, 1849, married John H. Kinsley, of Fort Madison Iowa, Nov 12, 1873 Members of the Presbyterian Church Democrat.

Stephenson, J H., far , S 24 , P O Big Mound

Stevens, D F , far., Sec 21 , P O Bonaparte.

Stonehouse, Richard, far , Sec 12 , P. O. Hillsboro

Sturdivant, R J , far , Sec 35 , P O Bonaparte

Sutherland, David, far , Sec 25 , P. O. Big Mound

TADE, WM A , far , Sec 4 , P O Utica

TULLY, S. M., farmer, Section 24 , P. O Big Mound, owns 143 acres of land, valued at $40 per acre, born Jan 28, 1825, in Frederick Co , Md , went with his parents to Pickaway Co , Ohio, in the spring of 1853, in 1856, went to New York City, and shipped on board a sailing-vessel for Melbourne, Australia, was eighty-one days making the trip, followed mining, carpenter and joiner work , in 1859, left for home in a sailing-vessel to Liverpool, and steamer thence to New York City, in the fall of 1859, came to Iowa , stopped at Farmington, in Harrisburg Tp , and purchased his present farm Married Margaret Baugher Dec 25, 1859 , she was born in March, 1841, in Pennsylvania, have five children living— Mary C Alice A , William H , Rebecca L and Albert M , lost four— Jane E., Thomas, Alonzo and George Member of the Christian Church , Democrat.

VALE, BENJAMIN R., farmer and stock-raiser, makes a specialty of Mambrino horses, Sec 15 , P O Bonaparte , son of Jacob G and Anne Vale born June 4, 1848, in Jefferson Co. Ohio, his parents emigrated to Iowa in the spring of 1850, and located near Primros Lee Co , in the spring of 1850 he came into Harrisburg

Tp., Van Buren Co., where his father died Feb. 17, 1875, in the 54th year of his age, leaving a wife and three children—Benjamin R., Lydia A. and Martha. Mr. Vale was a man of ability, having served as Senator, and in other official capacity; was one of the leading farmers of the county, owning, at the time of his death, nearly 2,000 acres of land, 845 acres in the home farm, of which B. R. has charge; since the death of Mr. Vale, there have been added to the estate, so that now there are 2,080 acres of land. Mr. B. R. Vale attended the Birmingham Academy, of this county; finished his education at Monmouth College, Ill.; graduated in June, 1873. Married Nancy V. J. Biddle, of Kirkwood, Ill., Feb. 12, 1874; she was born Nov. 2, 1849, in Mercer Co., Penn.; have three children—Anne R., Mary B. and an infant. Members of the Union Presbyterian Church; Republican.

WHEATLEY, T., far., S. 11; P. O. Hillsboro.

WALLINGFORD, HENRY, farmer, Sec. 36; P. O. Bonaparte; owns 160 acres of land, valued at $40 per acre; born March 5, 1855, in Warren Co., Ill.; his parents moved to Henry Co., Iowa, in January, 1866; the following fall he came to Van Buren Co. He married Elizabeth Miller, of this county, in September, 1875; she was born April 23, 1860, in Fayette Co., Penn.; have one son—Harry, born May 18, 1878. Democrat.

WALLINGFORD, JAMES M., farmer, Sec. 22; P. O. Bonaparte; owns 160 acres of land, valued at $40 per acre; born July 9, 1857, in Warren Co., Ill.; his parents moved to Henry Co., Iowa, in January, 1866; the following fall, came into Van Buren Co., and settled on the farm now owned by his brother Henry, where his parents both died June 9, 1872. Married Fanny Talbott, of Clarke Co., Mo., Sept. 19, 1878; she was born Oct. 23, 1859, in Keokuk, Iowa. Member of Baptist Church; Democrat.

Whilhelm, D., far., S. 29; P. O. Bonaparte.

White, S., far., S. 34; P. O. Bonaparte.

WOODS, A. H., farmer, Sec. 31; P. O. Bentonsport; owns 700 acres of land, valued at $40 per acre; born Aug. 11, 1808, near Wheeling, W. Va.; his parents moved to Wayne Co., Ohio, in 1816; in 1829, he went to Constantine, St. Joseph Co., Mich., and purchased land there, but engaged in milling for William Meek. Married his daughter Elizabeth Meek, in 1834; she was born April 8, 1813, in Ohio. Came to Van Buren Co., Iowa, in the spring of 1837, and settled on a part of the land he still owns, where, by careful management and economy, he has one of the best farms in his township, and well improved. Has eight children living—William, Robert, Ellen, Elizabeth, Sarah, Henrietta, Mary and Jesse; lost three—Margaret J., Mary A. and Nancy. Democrat.

LaVergne, TN USA
18 February 2011
217130LV00003B/37/P